LASKIN'S

Canadian Constitutional Law

Cases, Text and Notes on Distribution of Legislative Power

REVISED FOURTH EDITION

Albert S. Abel
Professor of Law
Faculty of Law
University of Toronto

with

John I. Laskin
of the Ontario Bar
author of Chapter XVI

THE CARSWELL COMPANY LTD.
Toronto, Canada

1975

© The Carswell Company Limited 1975

ISBN 0459 31500 5

PREFACE TO THE FOURTH EDITION

In revising the classic on Canadian constitutional jurisprudence, I have neither presumed nor wished to depart radically from the purpose or the plan of the original editor. Again, as was observed in the preface to the third edition "the book does not pretend to cover the whole field of law relating to the exercise of governmental power; it is concerned only with the distribution of authority between Parliament and provincial legislatures and with associated problems"; and, even more rigorously than in that edition "certain administrative law and civil liberties issues that others may classify as constitutional law problems are not treated because they fall outside the scope of the work as I have conceived it"—in the hope nevertheless that they may attract their own separate and appropriate treatment.

There has been the normal process of relevant judicial and legislative activity since the previous edition. Some new cases have consequently been added. Many others, and indeed all those reported up to March, 1973 which seemed to me to be significant have been cited. They have replaced and sometimes displaced a few that appeared in earlier editions. Recent decisions and statutes, resolving the problems or changing the legal structures on which discussion in the editor's notes in earlier editions was premised, have called for some revision of those notes. Not much, though. They have been retained largely intact, a mine of ideas for students of the Constitution.

Besides updating, this edition may represent a slight change of focus. Comparison with earlier editions will reveal some redistribution of material into chapters as well as a radical shrinkage of the introductory matter and hence a prompter exposure to the terms of the British North America Act. Both are intended to enhance the book's efficiency as a teaching tool, even though at some sacrifice of its value for those concerned with the historical and conceptual foundations. What will facilitate classroom use and understanding is always a question, but that has been the only purpose and must be the only excuse for the changes indicated.

I should like to express my appreciation to the University of Western Ontario Faculty for permission to reprint from (1968) 7 Western Ontario Law Review 1 the material commencing on page 193 of the casebook and to the University of Toronto Press for permission to reprint from (1969) 19 University of Toronto Law Journal 487 the material commencing on page 97 of the casebook.

Toronto,
May 1973

ALBERT S. ABEL

PREFACE TO THE REVISED FOURTH EDITION

With the continuation of the favourable reception accorded to earlier editions necessitating a reprinting, the occasion is taken for not indeed a new edition, but a revision of this fourth edition. One recent decision is added and account is taken in the editorial notes of such others as seemed to have constitutional significance. To deal now with a number of others pending or in prospect, before the Supreme Court has ruled, would be premature. The main change has been the restoration as a final chapter of materials on civil liberties, in deference to the request of those who include consideration of them in teaching the constitutional law course. Not only has most of the material found in previous editions been reinstated, but also substantial extracts from the judgments in such leading decisions as *Drybones*, *Lavell*, *Curr*, *Burnshine*, *Hogan* and *Canard*, have been included, together with a comprehensive note on the development of the Canadian Bill of Rights. This chapter was prepared by Mr. John I. Laskin, who brings to it a background of practice in the civil rights field and of teaching at the University of Windsor. I am most grateful to him for his collaboration.

ALBERT S. ABEL

Toronto
April 1975

TABLE OF CONTENTS

CHAPTER IX

CHAPTER X

CHAPTER XI

CONTENTS

CANADIAN CONSTITUTIONAL LAW

CASES, TEXT AND NOTES ON
DISTRIBUTION OF LEGISLATIVE POWER

CHAPTER I

THE GENERAL FABRIC OF THE CONSTITUTION

The study of Canadian Constitutional Law, like most fields of inquiry, has elastic limits. Choice among them may legitimately be made in the light of the purposes at hand. The judgment as to that will no doubt reflect the tastes and attitudes of the person choosing. My controlling consideration has been the functional relevance of the materials selected for examination. What do they tell about what the provinces and the federal government can do within the framework of the British North America Act?

That criterion has involved the omission of some background matters of considerable speculative interest. Such are the nature of federalism generally and of its Canadian variety and the maxims and attitudes appropriate to constitutional interpretation. Judges and others have spoken extensively and diversely on those matters. What has resulted is more a reservoir of justifications than a basis for prediction, interesting but not very serviceable.

It has dictated too the decision not to deal with matters like disallowance and Privy Council jurisdiction which have no future and a native amending process which has no past or present. Abandoned conceptions and unexplored potentials may, indeed must, be examined to understand in the most rigorously practical sense the law, whose one constant is evolution. But the history and prognosis which is of practical use relates to existing provisions of the living constitution.

This practical emphasis is the only excuse for putting aside the sometimes intellectual fascinating problems indicated in the preceding

1

paragraphs. Those curious as to them are referred to earlier editions of this casebook for valuable analyses and collections of materials.

It would be wrong to think though that a practical understanding of the constitution calls only for an item by item look at its provisions. Distinctive pervasive concepts and formulas have evolved which affect the workings of the whole constitutional scheme, for example, ancillarity, paramountcy, the status of extrinsic materials as an aid to interpretation. The casebook starts with these. It proceeds to deal with the particular provisions.

A mildly immodest interjection attempts to elaborate a coherent structure thought to be discernible in the provisions as supplemented by the general concepts and formulas. Like any model, it attracts not acceptance but scrutiny; but it is hoped it may help organize that scrutiny.

1. A Note on Delegation

The Privy Council's "watertight compartment" view of legislative power (see Lord Atkin in *A.-G. Can. v. A.-G. Ont.*, [1937] A.C. 326, at p. 354, [1937] 1 D.L.R. 673, at p. 684, [1937] 1 W.W.R. 299, at p. 312) and the difficulties of amendment so far as concerns the distribution of legislative power had, for a long time, focussed attention on delegation as a device for realizing social and economic policies which neither the Parliament of Canada nor the provincial legislatures can implement on their own.

There is nothing express in the B.N.A. Act about delegation, but ever since *Hodge v. The Queen* (1883), 9 App. Cas. 117, it has been clear that the maxim *delegatus non potest delegare* has no constitutional significance relative to the delegation of legislative power by Dominion Parliament or provincial legislature to some other subordinate agency: see *Willis,* Delegatus Non Potest Delegare, (1943) 21 Can. Bar Rev. 257. The real question has been whether there can be delegation as between Dominion Parliament and a provincial legislature; that is, can each be a subordinate agency of the other within the meaning of the *Hodge* rule. The courts have said no: see *St. Catharines Milling & Lumber Co. v. The Queen* (1887), 13 S.C.R. 577, at p. 637; *C.P.R. v. Notre Dame de Bonsecours,* [1899] A.C. 367, per Lord Watson during argument, quoted by *Lefroy,* Canada's Federal System, at p. 70; *Rex v. Zaslavsky,* [1935] 3 D.L.R. 788, [1935] 2 W.W.R. 34. Some writers have criticised this conclusion: see *Note,* (1936) 14 Can. Bar Rev. 353; *Tuck,* Delegation—A Way over the Constitutional Hurdle, (1945) 23 Can. Bar Rev. 79; *Scott,* Note, (1948) 26 Can. Bar Rev. 984. The issues raised by delegation between Dominion and provinces and the case law were the subject of a study prepared for the Royal Commission on Dominion-Provincial Relations, 1940: see *Corry,* Difficulties of Divided Jurisdiction; Appendix: The Delegation of Power by Dominion to Province or by Province to Dominion (Appendix 7 to Royal Commission Report). In its report the Royal Commission gave its approval to delegation both on a temporary and a perpetual basis: See Book II of the Report, pp. 72-73. Since then the matter has been canvassed by the Supreme Court of Canada which affirmed the stand of earlier cases that (without amendment of the B.N.A. Act) inter-delegation between Dominion Parliament and provincial legislatures as such is unconstitutional: see *A.-G. N.S. v. A.-G. Can. (Nova Scotia Inter-delegation* case), [1951] S.C.R. 31, [1950] 4 D.L.R. 369; this decision is criticised by *Ballem*, Note, (1951) 29 Can. Bar Rev. 79. Some of the considerations which justify this result under a constitution which distributes legislative power are set out in *Read*, Is Referential Legislation Worth While?, (1940) 18 Can. Bar Rev. 415, at p. 441.

Even if inter-delegation between Parliament and provincial legislatures had been permitted by judicial approbation, would it have solved the difficulties for which it has been offered as a solution? Would it, for example, be likely—or necessary—that the ten provinces delegate to the Dominion the same power at the same time, for the same period, and on the same terms? Since delegation, generally speaking, may be withdrawn could it be expected to provide stable support for any extension of authority? It may be noted that under the Australian Constitution, s. 51 (xxxvii) provides for delegation by a state Parliament to the central Parliament, but it appears that there has been little use made of the power because it is ineffective unless all six state Parliaments agree on the matter to be referred to the central authority: see *Comans*, Note, Co-Operation between Legislatures in a Federation—Delegation—The Australian Experience, (1953) 31 Can. Bar Rev. 814.

It is important however, to appreciate the limits of the doctrine affirmed by the *Nova Scotia Inter-delegation* case. Properly understood the case does not prohibit either Parliament or a provincial legislature from incorporating referentially into the valid legislation of one the future valid enactments of the other. Illustrations of this kind of anticipatory incorporation by reference may be seen in the Criminal Code, R.S.C. 1970, c. C-34, s. 554 (fixing the qualifications for jurors in criminal proceedings as those prescribed by "the laws in force for the time being in a province"); and in the Summary Convictions Act, R.S.O. 1970, c. 450, s. 3 (making applicable to provincial summary conviction proceedings certain provisions of the Cr. Code "as amended or re-enacted from time to time"). There is no unconstitutional delegation involved where there is no enlargement of the legislative authority of the referred legislature, but rather a borrowing of provisions which are within its competence and which were enacted for its own purposes, and which the referring legislature could have validly spelled out for its own purposes. This was appreciated by Judson J. in *Re Brinklow*, [1953] O.W.N. 325, 105 Can. C.C. 203 (aff'd on appeal on other grounds). However in *Regina v. Fialka*, [1953] 4 D.L.R. 440, [1953] O.W.N. 596, 106 Can. C.C. 197 (C.A.), Laidlaw J.A. reserved the question of the validity of the provincial Summary Convictions Act if it were construed to incorporate not only provisions of the Cr. Code in existence when the provincial statute was last enacted but also provisions subsequently introduced. The doubt that this view expresses seems to have been accepted by the Statutory References Act, 1955 (Ont.), c. 80, reading as follows: "A reference in an Act of the Legislature to an enactment of the Parliament of Canada that has been re-enacted, revised or consolidated shall be deemed to be a reference to such enactment as re-enacted, revised or consolidated and in force on the day this Act comes into force [being April 1, 1955]."

This is, with respect, an unnecessary as well as an unwarranted acceptance of a limitation on legislative competence, and justifiable only as a matter of legislative policy of the referring legislature: see *Laskin*, Note, (1956) 34 Can. Bar Rev. 215; but cf. *Bourne*, Note, (1956) 34 Can. Bar Rev. 500. Once it is determined that a referring legislature is legislating in relation to a matter within its competence and that the referred legislature is similarly legislating within its competence and for its own purposes, a borrowing by the one from the other of future enactments does not involve the latter in exercise of power which it does not otherwise possess. This view is amply supported by *Regina v. Glibbery*, [1963] 1 O.R. 232, 36 D.L.R. (2d) 548.

In line with the *Hodge* rule and with the foregoing appreciation of the *Nova Scotia Inter-delegation* case, there is no reason to doubt the validity of delegation (perhaps better described for this purpose as anticipatory incorporation by reference) by Parliament or by a provincial legislature to some other legislative body. The reasons underlying the *Nova Scotia Inter-delegation* case do not apply to resort to the enactments of a non-Canadian legislative body, nor it is submitted, to delegation between provincial legislatures.

[The application or administrative operation of legislation of a province, no less than of Canada, may properly be conditioned on the existence of a fact or matter which is defined under the other's legislation. For example, a province may provide for cancellation of a driver's licence consequent upon a conviction under the Cr. Code: see *Provincial Secretary of P.E.I. v. Egan*, [1941] S.C.R. 396, [1941] 3 D.L.R. 305; or may condition payment of a required bond for persons in the securities business on commission of a criminal offence: see *Lymburn v. Mayland*, [1932] A.C. 318, [1932] 2 D.L.R. 6, [1932] 1 W.W.R. 578. However, a province may not validly provide either by its legislation (see *Switzman v. Elbling and A.-G. Que.*, [1957] S.C.R. 285, 7 D.L.R. (2d) 337) or by reposing administrative discretion thereunder in a provincial functionary (see *Re Schepull and Bekeschus and the Provincial Secretary*, [1954] O.R. 67, [1954] 2 D.L.R. 5) for matters which fall within federal authority but have not been dealt with thereby. This situation, which involves distinctions on the basis of mutually exclusive legislative powers is different from the one much litigated and discussed in the United States and involving legislative regulation conditioning the conferring or extension of a benefit or privilege upon the surrender of constitutional rights: see *Note*, Unconstitutional Conditions, (1960) 73 Harv. L. Rev. 1595.]

An escape from the doctrine of the *Nova Scotia Inter-delegation* case has been found in delegation of administrative authority by Parliament or by a provincial legislature to a subordinate agency of the other. The following case examines the device.

COUGHLIN v. ONTARIO HIGHWAY TRANSPORT BOARD

In the Supreme Court of Canada, [1968] S.C.R. 569,
68 D.L.R. (2d) 384.

The judgment of Cartwright, Fauteux, Abbott, Judson and Spence
JJ. was delivered by

CARTWRIGHT J.:—This is an appeal, brought pursuant to leave
granted by this Court, from an order of the Court of Appeal for
Ontario . . . affirming an order of Gale C.J.H.C. . . . dismissing an
application of the appellant for an order prohibiting the respondent
from proceeding with a hearing to review the terms of the certificates
which led to the issue of an extra-provincial operating licence to the
appellant. The Court of Appeal gave no written reasons for its
decision but we are informed by counsel that it stated its agreement
with the reasons of Gale C.J.H.C.

There is no dispute as to any matter of fact. All of the business
of the appellant consists of inter-provincial transport of goods and
none of its operations involves transport entirely within one province
so as to be of an intra-provincial nature. In 1954 a licence was issued
to the appellant in Ontario under the *Motor Vehicle Transport Act*
(Canada); this licence permits the inter-provincial movement of certain specific types of merchandise and is number X828. The respondent
has informed the appellant of its intention to hold a hearing under
The Motor Vehicle Transport Act (Canada) to review the terms of the
certificate which led to the issue of the licence.

The application for prohibition was founded on the ground that
the respondent was without jurisdiction because the Act which confers
upon it the jurisdiction which it sought to exercise is *ultra vires* of
Parliament. That Act is *The Motor Vehicle Transport Act*, Statutes of
Canada, 2-3 Eliz. II, c. 59.

The relevant provisions of the Act are:

Section 2:

In this Act,
  (*a*) "extra-provincial transport" means the transport of passengers or
      goods by means of an extra-provincial undertaking;
  (*b*) "extra-provincial undertaking" means a work or undertaking for the
      transport of passengers or goods by motor vehicle, connecting a
      province with any other or others of the provinces, or extending
      beyond the limits of a province;
                                    *   *   *
  (*g*) "local undertaking" means a work or undertaking for the transport
      of passengers or goods by motor vehicle, not being an extra-provincial
      undertaking; and
  (*h*) "provincial transport board" means a board, commission or other
      body or person having under the law of a province authority to control
      or regulate the operation of a local undertaking.

Section 3(1):

  (1) Where in any province a licence is by the law of the province

required for the operation of a local undertaking, no person shall operate an extra-provincial undertaking in that province unless he holds a licence issued under the authority of this Act.

(2) The provincial transport board in each province may in its discretion issue a licence to a person to operate an extra-provincial undertaking into or through the province upon the like terms and conditions and in the like manner as if the extra-provincial undertaking operated in the province were a local undertaking.

Section 5:

The Governor in Council may exempt any person or the whole or any part of an extra-provincial undertaking or any extra-provincial transport from all or any of the provisions of this Act. . . .

The only ground in support of the appeal relied upon before us was that the terms of the *Motor Vehicle Transport Act*, and particularly s. 3 thereof, constitute an unlawful delegation by Parliament to the provincial legislatures of the power to legislate in relation to the subject matter of inter-provincial motor vehicle carriage which subject matter was rightly conceded to be wholly within the legislative jurisdiction of Parliament.

Counsel for each of the intervenants supported the constitutional validity of the Act.

The Motor Vehicle Transport Act was assented to on June 26, 1954; pursuant to a proclamation of the Governor in Council issued under s. 7 of the Act it came into force in Ontario on September 15, 1954. At that date the powers as to the regulation of intra-provincial carriage of goods by motor vehicle now exercised by the respondent Board were conferred upon the Ontario Municipal Board by *The Public Commercial Vehicles Act*, R.S.O. 1950, c. 304. The respondent Board was created by Statutes of Ontario, 1955, 4 Eliz. II, c. 54, by s. 25 of which the *Public Commercial Vehicles Act*, R.S.O. 1950, c. 304 was amended so that the powers as to the regulation of intra-provincial carriage of goods by motor vehicle theretofore exercised by the Ontario Municipal Board were transferred to the respondent Board.

The rules which guide the Board in the performance of its duties are now contained in the *Public Commercial Vehicles Act*, R.S.O. 1960, c. 139 and Regulations made by the Lieutenant-Governor in Council pursuant to s. 16 of that Act.

From the above brief review of the relevant legislation it will be seen that as matters stand at present the question whether a person may operate the undertaking of an inter-provincial carrier of goods by motor vehicle within the limits of the Province of Ontario is to be decided by a Board constituted by the provincial legislature and which must be guided in the making of its decision by the terms of the statutes of that legislature and the regulations passed thereunder as they may exist from time to time.

Mr. Laidlaw argues that in bringing about this result by the enactment of s. 3 of the *Motor Vehicle Transport Act* Parliament has in substance and reality abdicated its power to make laws in relation to the subject of inter-provincial motor vehicle carriage and unlawfully delegated that power to the provincial legislature.

It is made clear by the judgment of this Court in *Attorney General of Nova Scotia v. Attorney General of Canada* [*infra*, p. 10], and by the earlier decisions . . . discussed in the reasons delivered in that case, that neither Parliament nor a Provincial Legislature is capable of delegating to the other or of receiving from the other any of the powers to make laws conferred upon it by the *British North America Act*. Bill No. 136 of the Legislature of Nova Scotia which was under consideration in that case in terms provided that the Lieutenant-Governor of the Province might:

by proclamation from time to time delegate to and withdraw from the Parliament of Canada authority to make laws in relation to any matter relating to employment in any industry, work or undertaking in respect of which such matter is, by Section 92 of *The British North America Act,* 1867, exclusively within the legislative jurisdiction of this Legislature and any laws so made by the said Parliament shall, while such delegation is in force, have the same effect as if enacted by this Legislature.

The difference between such a bill and the Act which we are considering is too obvious to require emphasis.

It is well settled that Parliament may confer upon a provincially constituted board power to regulate a matter within the exclusive jurisdiction of Parliament. On this point it is sufficient to refer to the reasons delivered in the case of *P.E.I. Potato Marketing Board v. H. B. Willis Inc.,* [[1952] 2 S.C.R. 392, 4 D.L.R. 146].

In the case before us the respondent Board derives no power from the Legislature of Ontario to regulate or deal with the inter-provincial carriage of goods. Its wide powers in that regard are conferred upon it by Parliament. Parliament has seen fit to enact that in the exercise of those powers the Board shall proceed in the same manner as that prescribed from time to time by the Legislature for its dealings with intra-provincial carriage. Parliament can at any time terminate the powers of the Board in regard to inter-provincial carriage or alter the manner in which those powers are to be exercised. Should occasion for immediate action arise the Governor General in Council may act under s. 5 of the *Motor Vehicle Transport Act.*

In my opinion there is here no delegation of law-making power, but rather the adoption by Parliament, in the exercise of its exclusive power, of the legislation of another body as it may from time to time exist, a course which has been held constitutionally valid by this Court in *Attorney General for Ontario v. Scott* [1956] S.C.R. 137, 1 D.L.R. (2d) 433] and by the Court of Appeal for Ontario in *Regina v. Glibbery* [*supra*, p. 4].

As has already been stated the point dealt with above was the only one argued before us. In regard to it I am in substantial agreement with the reasons of Gale C.J.H.C. It follows that I would dismiss the appeal.

Before parting with the matter I wish to call attention to the fact that in each of the proclamations whereby the *Motor Vehicle Transport Act* was brought into force in the various provinces it is recited that this action had been requested by the Government of the Province concerned. It seems plain that the Government of Canada in co-operation with the Governments of the Provinces concerned has sought to achieve a satisfactory manner of regulating the transport of goods by motor vehicle. Our duty is simply to determine whether as a matter of law the Act of Parliament impugned by the appellant is valid; but it is satisfactory to find that there is nothing which compels us to hold that the object sought by this co-operative effort is constitutionally unattainable.

I would dismiss the appeal with costs but would make no order as to costs in regard to any of the intervenants.

The judgment of Martland and Ritchie JJ. was delivered by

RITCHIE J. (*dissenting*) :—

. . . In the *P.E.I.* case, Parliament did nothing more than to authorize the Governor-in-Council to select as an arm of the federal authority any board or agency already established under provincial law for the regulation of Agricultural Marketing within the province and for the purpose of regulating such marketing extra provincially, to grant to it "any powers like the power exercisable by such board or agency in relation to the marketing of such agricultural products locally within the province".

The *Agricultural Products Marketing Act,* and particularly s. 2 thereof and the order-in-council made by the Governor-in-Council thereunder, when read together with the provincial legislation, constitute an example of valid co-operation between federal and provincial authorities, and the whole question in the present case is whether the same thing has been achieved by the enactment of s. 3(2) and s. 5 of the *Motor Vehicle Transport Act.*

The difficulty which presents itself to Parliament and to the legislatures in such cases is exemplified in the reasons for judgment of Lord Atkin in *Attorney General for British Columbia v. Attorney General for Canada,* where he said:

> Unless and until a change is made in the respective legislative functions of Dominion and Province it may well be that satisfactory results for both can only be obtained by co-operation. *But the legislation will have to be carefully framed, and will not be achieved by either party leaving its own sphere and encroaching upon that of the other.*

The italics are my own.

In light of these observations, it is to be noted that in the case of the *Agricultural Products Marketing Act* the extent to which the provincial powers to regulate were adopted, to be exercised in the extra-provincial field, remained within the control of the Governor-in-Council and in fact the order-in-council granting such authority to the P.E.I. Potato Board was restricted by reference to a selected number of provincially authorized regulations. In my view, the important aspect of this legislation from the point of view of the present case is that the controlling authority under that statute remained at all times in federal hands, with the result that the powers exercisable by the Board in the regulation of extra-provincial marketing are such as may from time to time be authorized by the Governor-in-Council.

In the case of the *Motor Vehicle Transport Act*, direct authority has been given to the local board in each province "in its discretion to issue a licence to a person to operate an extra-provincial undertaking into or through the province", and the manner in which that discretion is to be exercised is not limited to such provincial regulations as the Governor-in-Council may designate but is to be exactly the same as if the extra-provincial undertaking were a "local undertaking". In my view the effect of this legislation is that the control of the regulation of licensing of a "connecting undertaking", is turned over to the provincial authority, and in the Province of Ontario this means that the controlling legislation is the *Ontario Highway Transport Act*, R.S.O. 1960, c. 273, and the *Public Commercial Vehicles Act*, R.S.O. 1960, c. 319.

That this is in fact the effect of the legislation is made apparent from a consideration of the Notice of Review of the appellant's operating licence which is brought in question in the present case. It was published in the Ontario Gazette and read as follows:

The Ontario Highway Transport Board Act, 1960

The Ontario Highway Transport Board pursuant to Section 16 of The Ontario Highway Transport Board Act will review the terms of the certificates which led to the issuance of extra-provincial operating licence No. X-828, and has fixed Monday, the 14th day of September, 1964, at 10 a.m. (E.D.S.T.) at its Chambers, 67 College Street, Toronto, Ontario, for that purpose.

At the hearing the applicant will be required to show cause why these certificates should not be amended or revoked by reason of operations contrary to the public interest; the operations are, more specifically—continued disregard of The Motor Vehicle Transport Act (Canada) and The Highway Traffic Act and the regulations pursuant thereto.

The Board may amend or revoke the terms of these certificates.

Although reference is made in the Notice to "continued disregard of *The Motor Vehicle Transport Act* (Canada) and *The Highway Traffic Act*" it is nevertheless clear that the *Ontario Highway Transport Board Act* was the statute pursuant to which the Notice was issued and the hearing was to be held.

There can, in my view, be no objection to Parliament enacting a statute in which existing provincial legislation is incorporated by reference so as to obviate the necessity of re-enacting it verbatim, but in providing for the granting of licences to extra-provincial undertakings in the like manner as if they were local undertaings, Parliament must, I think, be taken to have adopted the provisions of the provincial statutes in question as they may be amended from time to time. The result is that the granting of such licences is governed by the *Public Commercial Vehicles Act, supra*, pursuant to s. 16 of which the Lieutenant-Governor-in-Council may make regulations

... (q) respecting any matter necessary or advisable to carry out effectively the intent and purpose of this Act, ...

I can only read this as meaning that the licensing regulations for extra-provincial transport may be governed by decisions made from time to time by the Lieutenant-Governor-in-Council without any control by, or reference to, the federal authority. This is very different from adopting by reference the language used in a provincial statute and, in my opinion, it means that the control over the regulation of licensing in this field has been left in provincial hands.

It is, of course, true that Parliament can at any time terminate the powers of the provincial boards to licence extra-provincial undertakings, but it seems to me that this would entail repealing s. 3(2) of the *Motor Vehicle Transport Act* and it is the constitutionality of that subsection which is here impugned.

It is also suggested that the Governor-in-Council might exercise control by acting under s. 5 of the *Motor Vehicle Transport Act* which reads as follows:

The Governor-in-Council may exempt any person or the whole or any part of an extra-provincial undertaking or any extra-provincial transport from all or any of the provisions of this Act.

With the greatest respect for those who hold a different view, I do not think that this provision vests any control in the Governor-in-Council of the kind with which he was clothed by the *Agricultural Products Marketing Act*. Under the latter statute control of the regulation of extra-provincial marketing was vested in the Governor-in-Council; whereas under s. 5 of the *Motor Vehicle Transport Act* the powers of the Governor-in-Council are limited to *exempting* any extra-provincial transport from all or any of the provisions of the Act. I do not read this latter section as reserving any power to the Governor-in-Council to nullify the effect of s. 3(2) of the Act by exempting all extra-provincial transport from its provisions.

2. Exclusiveness of Legislative Powers: The "Trenching" and "Ancillary" (Necessarily Incidental) Doctrines

Note on "Exclusiveness"

It is a well-established doctrine of the courts that Dominion legislative powers are exclusive in the sense that "the abstinence of the Dominion Parliament from legislating to the full limit of its powers could not have the effect of transferring to any provincial legislature the legislative power which had been assigned to the Dominion by s. 91. . . ." (*Union Colliery Co. v. Bryden*, [1899] A.C. 580, at p. 588). The doctrine was enunciated in *A.-G. Can. v. A.-G. Ont.*, [1898] A.C. 700 (Fisheries case), but it applies equally to provincial powers. An appreciation of the "aspect" doctrine makes it clear that the Dominion can no more legislate in relation to a matter coming within a class of subject in section 92 than can the province legislate in relation to a matter coming within a class of subject in section 91.

One of the reasons given by the Supreme Court of Canada in *A.-G. N.S. v. A.-G. Can.*, [1951] S.C.R. 31, [1950] 4 D.L.R. 369, for refusing to countenance inter-delegation between the Dominion Parliament and a provincial legislature was that their respective powers were exclusive; and, having regard to the use of the terms "exclusive" and "exclusively" in sections 91 and 92 respectively, this meant mutually exclusive.

Logically, the doctrine of exclusiveness extends not only to the enumerated powers of Dominion and provinces but also to the federal general or residuary power to make laws for the peace, order and good government of Canada. Textually, this is the Dominion's only source of power under section 91; the enumerations following are merely illustrative of what is included in the general power: see O'Connor Report, Annex 1, pp. 52 ff. Early judicial decisions had placed the general power on a different and rather special footing, and while a recession from this position has become evident there has been no crystallization of another view.

Some of the cases (e.g., *Citizens Ins. Co. v. Parsons* (1881), 7 App. Cas. 96) talk about overlapping or conflicting powers. So far as sections 91 and 92 are concerned, this is inadmissible. The expression seems to be used, however, to point up the problem of assigning particular content to the heads of powers set out in those sections. There may, of course, be conflicting or similar legislation enacted by Dominion and provinces in pursuance of their separate powers but this raises the doctrines of "paramountcy" and the "occupied field" referred to *infra*. The only instances of similar powers being conferred upon Dominion and provinces are provided by ss. 94A and 95 of the B.N.A. Act dealing with old age pensions and agriculture and immigration. Necessarily in these cases (territorial limitations aside) the aspect of legislation would be the same whether the enactments be federal or provincial; and, in the words of section 95, "any law of the legislature of a province relative to agriculture or immigration shall have effect in and for the province as long and as far only as it is not repugnant to any Act of the Parliament of Canada". Section 95 appears to be consistent with section 91 in giving dominance to *any* valid Act of the Parliament of Canada.

The exposition of the doctrine of exclusiveness, while clear in meaning in the *Union Colliery* case, was associated in the early Privy Council cases with two other doctrines which, while paying lip service to it, actually subtracted from its effect. One was the so-called "trenching" doctrine, adumbrated in *Tennant v. Union Bank of Canada, infra,* and the other was the ancillary or necessarily incidental doctrine, expressed in the *Voluntary Assignments* case (*A.-G. Ont. v. A.-G. Can.*), *infra*. Both were connected with an avowed deference to the enumerations in section 91.

TENNANT v. UNION BANK OF CANADA

In the Privy Council. [1894] A.C. 31.

Appeal from a judgment of the Ontario Court of Appeal, 19 O.A.R. 1, affirming a judgment of the Chancellor who dismissed the action with costs. The action was one for damages for conversion of certain timber which was the subject of warehouse receipts made out by a firm to itself and endorsed to respondents as security for advances. The firm became insolvent and the action was in the name of the assignee of its estate.

LORD WATSON: . . . It is not matter of dispute that the timber of which the respondents took possession, after the insolvency of the firm, was included, either as saw logs or as lumber, in all the receipts which they received as security. But it does not appear to their Lordships that these receipts could be regarded as negotiable instruments carrying the property of the timber if their effect depended upon the provisions of the Mercantile Code which is contained in the Revised Statutes of Ontario, 1887.

The Mercantile Amendment Act (c. 122 of the Revised Statutes) deals with warehouse receipts and other mercantile documents which are effectual to transmit the property of goods without actual delivery. That statute not only recognizes the negotiability of warehouse receipts by custodiers who are not the owners of the goods; it extends the privilege to receipts by one who is both owner and custodier, but that only in cases where the grantor of the receipt is, from the nature of his trade or calling, a custodier for others as well as himself and therefore in a position to give receipts to third parties. The receipts in question do not comply with the requirements of the Act, because it is neither averred nor proved, that the firm, in the course of their business, had the custody of any goods except their own.

It may also be noticed that c. 125 of the Revised Statutes enacts that when goods are transferred by way of conveyance or mortgage, possession being retained by the transferor, the deed of conveyance or mortgage, if not duly registered, shall be absolutely null and void as against creditors of the grantor or mortgagor.

In these circumstances, certain provisions of the Bank Act, which was passed by the legislature of the Dominion (46 Vict., c. 120) and is specially referred to in the receipts held by the respondents, become important. Although now repealed, the Act was in force during the whole period of these transactions; and, if competently enacted, its provisions must, in so far as they are applicable, govern the rights of parties in this litigation. . . .

. . . Sect. 54, which deals specially with the case of the custodier and owner of the goods being one and the same person enacts that:—

"If any person who grants a warehouse receipt or a bill of lading is engaged in the calling, as his ostensible business, of keeper of a yard, cove, wharf or harbour, or of warehouseman, miller, saw-miller, maltster, manufacturer of timber, wharfinger, master of a vessel, or other carrier by land or by water, or by both, curer or packer of meat, tanner, dealer in wool or purchaser of agricultural produce, and is at the same time the owner of the goods, wares and merchandise mentioned in such warehouse receipt or bill of lading, every such warehouse receipt or bill of lading, and the right and title of the bank thereto and to the goods, wares and merchandise mentioned therein, shall be as valid and effectual as if such owner, and the person making such warehouse receipt or bill of lading, were different persons."

These enactments go beyond the provision of sect. 16 of the Mercantile Amendment Act. They omit the limitation of the provincial statute, which requires, in order to validate a warehouse receipt by a custodier who is also owner, that the trade or calling in which he is ostensibly engaged must be one which admits of his granting receipts on behalf of other owners whose goods are in his possession. . . .

. . . In the Courts below, the appellant pleaded that the provisions of the Bank Act with respect to warehouse receipts, in so far as they differ from the provisions of the Mercantile Amendment Act, were ultra vires of the Dominion Legislature. The plea was not discussed, because it was admittedly at variance with the decision of the Supreme Court of Canada in *Merchants' Bank of Canada v. Smith*, 8 S.C.R. 512, which was a precedent binding on provincial tribunals. The case was therefore disposed of by the Chancellor and the Appeal Court upon the footing that the provisions of the Bank Act were not open to challenge. . . .

. . . Their Lordships . . . [are of opinion] that, assuming the provisions of the Bank Act to be intra vires, the receipts in question were such as the firm could give and the respondents could lawfully receive. The obvious effect of sect. 54 is that, for the purposes of the Bank Act, a warehouse receipt by an owner of goods who carries on, as the firm did, the trade of a saw-miller, is to be as effectual as if it had been granted by his bailee, although his business may be confined to the manufacture of his own timber. That enactment plainly implies that such a receipt is to be valid, not only in the hands of the bank, but in the hands of a borrower who gives it to the bank in security of a loan. Their Lordships do not think that the provisions of sect. 53, sub-sect. 2, which are somewhat obscure, can be held to cut down the plain enactments of sect. 54, especially in a case where the grantor of the receipt himself delivers it to the bank as a security for his own debt. . . .

. . . The appellant's plea against the legislative power of the Dominion Parliament was accordingly made the subject of further argument; and, the point being one of general importance, their Lordships had the advantage of being assisted, in the hearing and consideration of it, by the Lord Chancellor and Lord MacNaghten. The question turns upon the construction of two clauses in the British North America Act, 1867. Sect. 91 gives the Parliament of Canada power to make laws in relation to all matters not coming within the classes of subjects by the Act exclusively assigned to the legislatures of the provinces, and also exclusive legislative authority in relation to certain enumerated subjects, the fifteenth of which is "Banking, Incorporation of Banks, and the Issue of Paper Money." Sect. 92 assigns to each provincial legislature the exclusive right to make laws in relation to the classes of subjects therein enumerated; and the thirteenth of the enumerated classes is "Property and Civil Rights in the Province."

Statutory regulations with respect to the form and legal effect, in Ontario, of warehouse receipts and other negotiable documents, which pass the property of goods without delivery, unquestionably relate to property and civil rights in that province; and the objection taken by the appellant to the provisions of the Bank Act would be unanswerable if it could be shewn that, by the Act of 1867, the Parliament of Canada is absolutely debarred from trenching to any extent upon the matters assigned to the provincial legislature by sect. 92. But sect. 91 expressly declares that, "notwithstanding anything in this Act," the exclusive legislative authority of the Parliament of Canada shall extend to all matters coming within the enumerated classes; which plainly indicates that the legislation of that Parliament, so long as it strictly relates to these matters, is to be of paramount authority. To refuse effect to the declaration would render nugatory some of the legislative powers specially assigned to the Canadian Parliament. For example, among the enumerated classes of subjects in sect. 91, are "Patents of Invention and Discovery," and "Copyrights." It would be practically impossible for the Dominion Parliament to legislate upon either of these subjects without affecting the property and civil rights of individuals in the provinces.

This is not the first occasion on which the legislative limits laid down by sects. 91 and 92 have been considered by this Board. In *Cushing v. Dupuy,* 5 App. Cas. 409, their Lordships had before them the very same question of statutory construction which has been raised in this appeal. An Act relating to bankruptcy, passed by the Parliament of Canada, was objected to as being *ultra vires,* in so far as it interfered with property and civil rights in the province; but, inasmuch as "bankruptcy and insolvency" form one of the classes of matters enumerated in sect. 91, their Lordships upheld the validity of the statute. In delivering the judgment of the Board, Sir Montague Smith pointed out that it would be impossible to advance a step in the construction of a scheme for the administration of insolvent estates without interfering with and modifying some of the ordinary rights of property.

The law being so far settled by precedent, it only remains for consideration whether warehouse receipts, taken in security by a bank in the course of the business of banking, are matters coming within the class of subjects described in sect. 91, sub-sect. 15, as "Banking, Incorporation of Banks, and the Issue of Paper Money." If they are, the provisions made by the Bank Act with respect to such receipts are *intra vires.* Upon that point their Lordships do not entertain any doubt. The legislative authority conferred by these words is not confined to the mere constitution of corporate bodies with the privilege of carrying on the business of bankers. It extends to the issue of paper currency, which necessarily means the creation of a species of personal property carrying with it rights and privileges which the law of the province does not, and cannot, attach to it. It also comprehends "banking," an expression which is wide enough to embrace every transaction coming within the legitimate business of a banker.

The appellant's counsel hardly ventured to dispute that the lending of money on the security of goods, or of documents representing the property of goods, was a proper banking transaction. Their chief contention was that, whilst the legislature of Canada had power to deprive its own creature, the bank, of privileges enjoyed by other lenders under the provincial law, it had no power to confer upon the bank any privilege as a lender which the provincial law does not recognise. It might enact that a security, valid in the case of another lender, should be invalid in the hands of the bank, but could not enact that a security should be available to the bank which would not have been effectual in the hands of another lender. It was said in support of the argument, that the first of these things did, and the second did not, constitute an interference with property and civil rights in the province. It is not easy to follow the distinction thus suggested. There must be two parties to a transaction of loan; and, if a security, valid according to provincial law, was made invalid in the hands of the lender by a Dominion statute, the civil rights of the borrower would be affected, because he could not avail himself of his property in his dealings with a bank.

But the argument, even if well founded, can afford no test of the legislative powers of the Parliament of Canada. These depend upon sect. 91, and the power to legislate conferred by that clause may be fully exercised, although with the effect of modifying civil rights in the province. And it appears to their Lordships that the plenary authority given to the Parliament of Canada by sect. 91, sub-sect. 15, to legislate in relation to banking transactions is sufficient to sustain the provisions of the Bank Act which the appellant impugns.

Appeal dismissed.

Note on the "Trenching" Doctrine

The term "trench" has been used in inconsistent senses by the Privy Council. It has been used, properly it is submitted, to denote an unconstitutional encroachment by a provincial legislature on federal power: see *Union Colliery Co. v. Bryden*, [1899] A.C. 580, at p. 587. It would equally be a proper use of the term if applied to denote an unconstitutional invasion of provincial power by Parliament. However, the term has also, and more generally, been used, as in the *Tennant* case, to support an assumed impingement of federal power, under one of the thirty-one classes of subjects enumerated in section 91, upon the provincial catalogue of powers in section 92. "Trenching", in this sense, is regarded as a valid encroachment on provincial power, fortifying the Privy Council's conception of the scheme of distribution which elevates the enumerations in section 91 above the federal general power. According to the propositions laid down in the *Fish Canneries* case, *A.-G. Can. v. A.-G. B.C.*, [1930] A.C. 111, [1930] 1 D.L.R. 194, [1929] 3 W.W.R. 449, in summation of earlier Privy Council decisions, Parliament cannot "trench" in the exercise of its general power to make laws for the peace, order and good government of Canada unless the matters covered by the legislation "have attained such dimensions as to affect the body politic of the Dominion". If the matters do have those dimensions, is there any need to talk of "trenching"? Indeed, "the use of the trenching doctrine to explain a privileged encroachment on provincial legislative authority is purely gratuitous because once a court is satisfied that impugned legislation carries a federal aspect no invasion of provincial legislative authority exists": see *Laskin*, Peace, Order and Good Government Re-examined, (1947) 25 Can. Bar Rev. 1054, at p. 1060. Surely the real question in connection with the exclusive powers conferred by sections 91 and 92 is (to paraphrase the Privy Council) whether a "matter" expressed in legislation is fairly included within the class of subject to which it is sought to attribute it; and if so, then the authority is exclusive: see *Reference re Alberta Bill of Rights Act*, [1947] A.C. 503, at p. 517, [1947] 4 D.L.R. 1, at p. 9, [1947] 2 W.W.R. 401, at p. 411.

On this view, the "trenching" doctrine can be no more than a verbal rationalization of the mutually exclusive scope of authority reposed in Parliament and the provincial legislatures by sections 91 and 92 respectively. Its disparate use, however, in different senses, and, also, to signify different treatment of the federal general power *vis-à-vis* the illustrative enumerations in section 91, makes it desirable to drop it even as a rationalizing formula. It carries an *à priori* assumption about the scheme of distribution which introduces unnecessary rigidity into the difficult task of interpretation. The judgment of Rand J., for the majority of the Court in *A.-G. Can. v. C.P.R. and C.N.R.*, [1958] S.C.R. 285, at p. 290, 12 D.L.R. (2d) 625, at p. 628 turns the "trenching" doctrine on its head and gives hope that it will disappear. The learned Judge spoke as follows:

"Powers in relation to matters normally within the provincial field, especially of property and civil rights, are inseparable from a number of the specific heads of s. 91 under which scarcely a step could be taken that did not involve them. In each such case the question is primarily not how far Parliament can trench on s. 92 but rather to what extent are property and civil rights within the scope of the paramount power of Parliament. *Tennant v. Union Bank*, [1894] A.C. 31 in which a provision under the *Bank Act* for taking security for loans made by a bank in disregard of provincial forms of security and registration was upheld in a characteristic example."

The doctrine has, however, re-emerged recently in *A.-G. B.C. v. Smith*, [1967] S.C.R. 702, 65 D.L.R. (2d) 82.

A.-G. ONT. v. A.-G. CAN.

In the Privy Council. [1894] A.C. 189.

Appeal from a judgment of the Ontario Court of Appeal, 20 O.A.R. 489, upon a question referred to it by the Lieutenant-Governor as to the power of the Ontario legislature to enact s. 9 of R.S.O. 1887, c. 124, entitled "An Act respecting Assignments and Preferences by Insolvent Persons". A majority of the Court held that the section was *ultra vires*.

LORD HERSCHELL L.C.: . . . It is not contested that the enactment the validity of which is in question, is within the legislative powers conferred on the provincial legislature by sect. 92 of the British North America Act, 1867, which enables that legislature to make laws in relation to property and civil rights in the province unless it is withdrawn from their legislative competency by the provisions of the 91st section of that Act which confers upon the Dominion Parliament the exclusive power of legislation with reference to bankruptcy and insolvency.

The point to be determined, therefore, is the meaning of those words in sect. 91 of the British North America Act, 1867, and whether they render the enactment impeached ultra vires of the provincial legislature. That enactment is sect. 9 of the Revised Statutes of Ontario of 1887, c. 124, entitled "An Act respecting Assignments and Preferences by Insolvent Persons." The section is as follows:—

"An assignment for the general benefit of creditors under this Act shall take precedence of all judgments and of all executions not completely executed by payment, subject to the lien, if any, of an execution creditor for his costs, where there is but one execution in the sheriff's hands, or to the lien, if any, of the creditor for his costs, who has the first execution in the sheriff's hands."

In order to understand the effect of this enactment it is necessary to have recourse to other sections of the Act to see what is meant by the words "an assignment for the general benefit of creditors under this Act." [The Lord Chancellor here referred to other provisions of the Act.] . . . Their Lordships proceed now to consider the nature of the enactment said to be ultra vires. It postpones judgments and executions not completely executed by payment to an assignment for the benefit of creditors under the Act. Now there can be no doubt that the effect to be given to judgments and executions and the manner and extent to which they may be made available for the recovery of debts are *prima facie* within the legislative powers of the provincial parliament. Executions are a part of the machinery by which debts are recovered, and are subject to regulation by that parliament. A creditor has no inherent right to have his debt satisfied by means of a levy by the sheriff, or to any priority in respect of such levy. The execution is a mere creature of the law which may determine and regulate the rights to which it gives rise. The Act of 1887 which abolished priority as amongst execution creditors provided a simple means by which every creditor might obtain a share in the distribution of moneys levied under an execution by any particular creditor. The other Act of the same year, containing the section which is impeached, goes a step further, and gives to all creditors under an assignment for their general benefit a right to a rateable share of the assets of the debtor, including those which have been seized in execution.

But it is argued that inasmuch as this assignment contemplates the insolvency of the debtor, and would only be made if he were insolvent, such a provision purports to deal with insolvency, and therefore is a matter exclusively within the jurisdiction of the Dominion Parliament. Now it is to be observed that an assignment for the general benefit of creditors has long been known to the jurisprudence of this country and also of Canada, and has its force and effect at common law quite independently of any system of bankruptcy or insolvency, or any legislation relating thereto. So far from being regarded as an essential part of the bankruptcy law, such an assignment was made an act of bankruptcy on which an adjudication might be founded, and by the law of the Province of Canada which prevailed at the time when the Dominion Act [Insolvency Act of 1869, applicable to traders only] was passed, it was one of the grounds for an adjudication of insolvency.

It is to be observed that the word "bankruptcy" was apparently not used in Canadian legislation, but the insolvency law of the Province of Canada was precisely analogous to what was known in England as the bankruptcy law.

Moreover, the operation of an assignment for the benefit of creditors was precisely the same, whether the assignor was or was not in fact insolvent. It was open to any debtor who might deem his solvency doubtful, and who desired in that case that his creditors should be equitably dealt with, to make an assignment for their benefit. The validity of the assignment and its effect would in no way depend on the insolvency of the assignor, and their Lordships think it clear that the 9th section would equally apply whether the assignor was or was not insolvent. . . .

It is not necessary in their Lordships' opinion, nor would it be expedient to attempt to define, what is covered by the words "bankruptcy" and "insolvency" in sect. 91 of the British North America Act. But it will be seen that it is a feature common to all the systems of bankruptcy and insolvency to which reference has been made, that the enactments are designed to secure that in the case of an insolvent person his assets shall be rateably distributed amongst his creditors whether he is willing that they shall be so distributed or not. Although provision may be made for a voluntary assignment as an alternative, it is only as an alternative. In reply to a question put by their Lordships the learned counsel for the respondent were unable to point to any scheme of bankruptcy or insolvency legislation which did not involve some power of compulsion by process of law to secure to the creditors the distribution amongst them of the insolvent debtor's estate.

In their Lordships' opinion these considerations must be borne in mind when interpreting the words "bankruptcy" and "insolvency" in the British North America Act. It appears to their Lordships that such provisions as are found in the enactment in question, relating as they do to assignments purely voluntary, do not infringe on the exclusive legislative power conferred upon the Dominion Parliament. They would observe that a system of bankruptcy legislation may frequently require various ancillary provisions for the purpose of preventing the scheme of the Act from being defeated. It may be necessary for this purpose to deal with the effect of executions and other matters which would otherwise be within the legislative competence of the provincial legislature. Their Lordships do not doubt that it would be open to the Dominion Parliament to deal with such matters as part of a bankruptcy law, and the provincial legislature would doubtless be then precluded from interfering with this legislation inasmuch as such interference would affect the bankruptcy law of the Dominion Parliament. But it does not follow that such subjects, as might properly be treated as ancillary to such a law and therefore within the powers of the Dominion Parliament, are excluded from the legislative authority of the provincial legislature when there is no bankruptcy or insolvency legislation of the Dominion Parliament in existence.

Their Lordships will therefore humbly advise Her Majesty that the decision of the Court of Appeal ought to be reversed, and that the question ought to be answered in the affirmative. The parties will bear their own costs of this appeal.

Appeal allowed.

[In *Cushing v. Dupuy* (1880), 5 App. Cas. 409, a case mentioned in argument in the *Voluntary Assignments* case, *supra*, but ignored in the reasons of the Privy Council, the issue was the validity of an amendment to the Insolvency Act, 1875 (Can.), c. 16, making the judgment of the Quebec Court of Queen's Bench final in insolvency matters, i.e. taking away any appeal as of right to the Privy Council. In upholding the validity of the amendment, the Privy Council said:

"It would be impossible to advance a step in the construction of a scheme for the administration of insolvent estates without interfering with and modifying some of the ordinary rights of property, and other civil rights, nor without providing some mode of special procedure for the vesting, realisation, and distribution of the estate, and the settlement of the liabilities of the insolvent. Procedure must necessarily form an essential part of any law dealing with insolvency. It is therefore to be presumed, indeed it is a necessary implication, that the Imperial statute, in assigning to the Dominion Parliament the subjects of bankruptcy and insolvency, intended to confer on it legislative power to interfere with property, civil rights, and procedure within the Provinces, so far as a general law relating to those subjects might affect them."

Is this passage consistent with the result reached in the *Voluntary Assignments* case? Is that result compatible with the later judgments in *In re Companies' Creditors Arrangement Act*, [1934] S.C.R. 659, [1934] 4 D.L.R. 75, and *A.-G. B.C. v. A.-G. Can.*, [1937] A.C. 391, [1937] 1 D.L.R. 695, [1937] 1 W.W.R. 32?

The "ancillary" doctrine was approved in the *Local Prohibition* case, *A.-G. Ont. v. A.-G. Can.*, [1896] A.C. 348 (which also approved the "trenching" doctrine) and it was applied in *G.T.R. v. A.-G. Can.*, [1907] A.C. 65 where the Privy Council, in sustaining the validity of federal legislation prohibiting railways under federal jurisdiction from contracting out of liability to their employees for personal injuries, phrased the issue as follows: ". . . the true question in the present case does not seem to turn upon the question whether this law deals with a civil right—which may be conceded—but whether this law is truly ancillary to railway legislation".

The explanation of the "ancillary" doctrine given by Newcombe J. in *Reference re Fisheries Act, 1914*, [1928] S.C.R. 457, [1928] 4 D.L.R. 190 (aff'd *sub nom. A.-G. Can. v. A.-G. B.C.*, [1930] A.C. 111, [1930] 1 D.L.R. 194, [1929] 3 W.W.R. 449) supports the view expressed earlier by *Clement*, The Canadian Constitution, at p. 506 that "in the absence of direct authority it can only be suggested that the various cases in which so-called ancillary legislation has been upheld are cases in which the enactment in controversy dealt with an aspect of the subject upon which provincial legislation would have been incompetent; in other words, the subject in the aspect dealt with fell strictly within one of the enumerated classes of section 91". However, there is another formulation of the "ancillary" doctrine, one propounded by Duff J. in *Reference re Waters and Water-Powers*, [1929] S.C.R. 200, at p. 217, [1929] 2 D.L.R. 481, at p. 488, as follows:

> "In considering the effect of the phrase "notwithstanding anything in this Act" one must not overlook the fact that it is only the "exclusive authority" of the Dominion under the enumerated heads of s. 91 which is accorded the primacy intended to be declared by those words. In themselves they have not the effect of giving pre-eminence to the incidental or ancillary powers; which are not strictly exclusive. As already observed, in recent pronouncements touching the appropriation of Provincial Crown property in professed exercise of such powers, support is given to the view that, if such appropriation be permissible in exercise of them, then the payment of compensation may be a condition of that exercise; and there appears to be, it may be added, no decision, and, except in the observations in the judgments referred to, no dictum, giving any support to the view that in virtue of an ancillary or incidental power the Dominion Parliament is entitled to authorize the permanent occupation of Provincial Crown property.
>
> "The task of reconciling the various sections of the Act is one of great difficulty. You must give full effect to the exclusive powers of the Dominion under section 91; yet in ascertaining the scope of those powers you must have regard to the other provisions of the Act. The character of the exclusive power may be such, on the true construction of section 91, as to involve the right to take, or to give to others, possession of Provincial Crown property, for the purpose of executing the power. The decisions already cited seem to show that such a conclusion must be founded on solid, not to say demonstrative, considerations; but, where the right is unmistakably involved in the authority given, then, of course, to that right effect must be given. But although the Dominion may, by legislation enacted in exercise of its exclusive powers relating to railways and canals, authorize the construction through the property of a province of a railway or canal, to which its jurisdiction extends, this does not involve the right to appropriate the whole beneficial interest of the site of the work (including the minerals, for example), for the purpose of making it available as an asset or source of revenue for the benefit of the Dominion or of the Dominion's grantees, where that site is vested in His Majesty and is, by the B.N.A. Act, subject to the administration and control of the Provincial legislature."

It may be that this too is merely a verbal rationalization of the aspect doctrine.

In *Papp v. Papp*, [1970] 1 O.R. 331 at 335, 8 D.L.R. (3d) 389 at 395, sustaining the provisions in the Divorce Act relating to the custody of children whose parents were involved in divorce proceedings, Laskin J.A. said:

In the absence of competent and conflicting federal legislation, a provincial Legislature may deal with the custody of children as it may deal with the relations of husband and wife excluding any question of divorce. The enactment by Parliament of divorce legislation alone would still leave (and this has heretofore been the case) custody, and such incidents of the matrimonial relationship as alimony, to provincial law. In embracing custody as corollary relief under the present *Divorce Act,* Parliament has acted upon principles stated in the *Voluntary Assignments* case, *A.-G. Ont. v. A.-G. Can.,* [1894] A.C. 189, and in *Tennant v. Union Bank of Canada,* [1894] A.C. 31. These principles, which have been stated in various ways over the years, sometimes with a negative emphasis (as in the two cases just mentioned) and sometimes with a positive one (as to which see Judson J., in *Nykorak v. A.-G. Can.,* [1962] S.C.R. 331 at p. 335, 33 D.L.R. (2d) 373 at pp. 377-8, 37 W.W.R. 660, and Rand J., in *A.-G. Can. v. C.P.R. and C.N.R.,* [1958] S.C.R. 285 at p. 290, 12 D.L.R. (2d) 625 at pp. 627-8, 76 C.R.T.C. 241) concern the scope of the enumerated heads of federal power under s. 91 of the Constitution in modifying or qualifying the reach of provincial authority in relation to, mainly, property and civil rights in the Province under s. 92(13).

I do not myself favour the language of "trenching" and of "necessarily incidental" or "ancillary", found in the two Privy Council cases and through which effectuation of exercises of federal legislative power have been certified. Convenient as that language may be to signal situations in which the doctrine of exclusiveness of jurisdiction does not apply but that there is rather a legislative field with gates of entry for both Dominion and Province, it is not sufficiently neutral in its acknowledgement of a common domain. The terse phraseology of the grants of legislative power does not fall to be measured by dictionary meaning alone. The Constitution is a working instrument addressed to legislative bodies, and its implementation in legislation must be seen as a social assessment by the enacting body of the scope of the power which is invoked in any particular case. Where there is admitted competence, as there is here, to legislate to a certain point, the question of limits (where that point is passed) is best answered by asking whether there is a rational, functional connection between what is admittedly good and what is challenged.

This problem is not unique to Canadian federalism, but is evident as well under the Constitutions of the United States and of Australia. In both of those cases, its solution is assisted by explicit provision; in the United States, the Congress is empowered by art. 8, cl. 18 "to make all laws which shall be necessary and proper for carrying into execution" its enumerated powers, a clause which has been called a coefficient clause; in Australia, the Commonwealth Parliament is authorized by *placitum* (XXXIX) of s. 51 to make laws with respect to "matters incidental to the execution of any power vested by this Constitution in the Parliament . . .". The absence of a comparable clause in the Canadian Constitution has never been taken as a denial of coefficient authority, especially when regard is had to the different theory of allocation of power in Canada as contrasted with the United States and with Australia, and to the *non obstante* clause in the opening words of s. 91 of the *B.N.A. Act.* Residuary and paramount authority rests in the Parliament of Canada in the exercise of legislative power; and the paramountcy doctrine also operates in this country without the aid of such explicit provision for it as found in the Constitutions of the United States and of Australia.

All of this provides a frame of reference only and in itself does not answer the question whether Parliament in legislating in relation to marriage and divorce may embrace custody, either as "necessary and proper" (to use the American formula) or as "incidental" (to use the Australian formula) to the execution of the power invoked. Assistance in providing an answer exists in examining the aspect of the legislation under review, not in the sense merely of the subject dealt with, but in the sense as well of the purpose or object in view. In this exercise (as to which reference may be made to what Duff J., said in *Gold Seal Ltd. v. Dominion Express Co. and A.-G. Alta.*, 62 S.C.R. 424 at p. 460, 62 D.L.R. 62 at p. 83, [1921] 3 W.W.R. 710) the legislation must be taken as a whole and evaluated from the standpoint of its coherency as an integrated federal scheme. I can pose the issue shortly, if not more illuminatingly, by asking whether the custody provisions of the *Divorce Act* complement rather than supplement the admittedly valid divorce portions.

In *Northwest Mortgage Co. v. Com'r. of Excise*, [1944] 3 D.L.R. 273, [1944] 2 W.W.R. 90, 81 Can. C.C. 294, aff'd on other grounds [1945] 1 D.L.R. 561, [1945] 1 W.W.R. 182, 83 Can. C.C. 161, it was held that a provision of a federal excise statute, providing for the forfeiture to the Crown of an automobile used to transport spirits in violation of the Act, was *ultra vires* in so far as it purported to authorize the forfeiture of the interest of an innocent person, even though there was an exculpation provision in favour of such a person. Such a provision, said the Court, was not necessarily incidental to the punishment of offenders against the Act. This view was, to all intents and purposes, overruled by the Supreme Court in *Industrial Acceptance Corp. v. The Queen*, [1953] 2 S.C.R. 273, [1953] 4 D.L.R. 369, 107 Can. C.C. 1, where it sustained a section of a federal opium and narcotic statute providing for forfeiture (without any exculpation opportunity to innocent persons) of a vehicle used in connection with a narcotics offence where a conviction results.

See also *Rathie v. Montreal Trust Co.*, [1952] 3 D.L.R. 61, 5 W.W.R. (N.S.) 675, aff'd [1952] 4 D.L.R. 448, 6 W.W.R. (N.S.) 652, rev'd on other grounds, [1953] 2 S.C.R. 204, [1953] 4 D.L.R. 289, upholding, as necessarily incidental legislation, s. 124 of the Companies Act, 1934 (Can.), c. 33 providing for the transfer, with compulsory effect upon minority shareholders, of the shares of one company to another where 90 per cent. of the shareholders of the offeree company agree to the purchase of its shares. Is this not merely an application of the aspect doctrine? Cf. *C.P.R. v. A.-G. B.C.*, [1948] S.C.R. 373, [1948] 3 D.L.R. 417, aff'd [1950] A.C. 122, [1950] 1 D.L.R. 721, [1950] 1 W.W.R. 220.

The "ancillary" or "necessarily incidental" doctrine was, at long last, effectively punctured by Judson J. in the Supreme Court of Canada in *A.-G. Can. v. Nykorak* (1962), 33 D.L.R. (2d) 373, 37 W.W.R. 660. In upholding the validity of federal legislation under which the Crown in right of Canada, having assumed liability for the conduct of soldiers under a statutory master-servant relationship, sought to recover from a wrongdoer expenses incurred in the care of an injured soldier, he said that "legislation of this kind comes squarely under head 7 of s. 91, notwithstanding the fact that it may incidentally affect property and civil rights within the Province. It is meaningless to support this legislation, as was done in the *Grand Trunk* case, [1907] A.C. 65, on the ground that it is 'necessarily incidental' to legislation in relation to an enumerated class of subject in s. 91."

In thus ruling out reliance on a "necessarily incidental" doctrine, the Supreme Court of Canada must not be taken to have enlarged the scope of federal power at the expense of the Provinces but merely to have emphasized that there is an independent constitutional basis for what can "rationally" be brought within federal authority, a term to be preferred to Lord Watson's use of "strictly" in the *Tennant* case, *supra*. For an illustration of a converse situation where the matter dealt with by provincial legislation was not rationally (or strictly) within federal authority see *Duplain v. Cameron*, [1961] S.C.R. 693, 30 D.L.R. (2d) 348, upholding the validity of provincial securities legislation which embraced in its regulatory scope promissory notes when used in a defined way and for a defined purpose.

Is there a relation between the "ancillary" doctrine and the principle of severability of legislation? *Cf. Cowen v. A.-G. B.C.,* [1941] S.C.R. 321, [1941] 2 D.L.R. 687; *Reference re Alberta Bill of Rights Act,* [1947] A.C. 503, [1947] 4 D.L.R. 1, [1947] 2 W.W.R. 401.

Can the reasoning on which the "ancillary" doctrine is based be applied to provincial legislative power? See *Lefroy,* Canada's Federal System, pp. 180 ff. See *Re Sheep and Swine Marketing Scheme (P.E.I.),* [1943] 3 D.L.R. 569 and *Reference re Sask. Minimum Wage Act,* [1948] S.C.R. 248, [1948] 3 D.L.R. 801.]

3. Paramountcy and the Occupied Field: Pre-emption and Preclusion in Exercise of Exclusive and Concurrent Powers

Note on the "Paramountcy" Doctrine

In *Tennant v. Union Bank of Canada, supra,* Lord Watson stated that the legislation of the Parliament of Canada, so long as it relates strictly to matters within the enumerations in section 91, is of paramount authority. In the context of the judgment, it is clear that he associated this conception with the "trenching" doctrine. There is no necessary association between them, however, if paramountcy means only that where, in the view of the courts, valid provincial legislation and valid Dominion legislation cannot stand together, the latter must prevail; or, regarded from another standpoint, provincial legislation which would otherwise be valid is precluded where the Dominion has "occupied the field". This notion was elaborated by Lord Watson in the *Local Prohibition* case, [1896] A.C. 348, at p. 366, where he said: "It has been frequently recognized by this Board, and it may now be regarded as settled law, that according to the scheme of the British North America Act the enactments of the Parliament of Canada, in so far as these are within its competency, must override provincial legislation. But the Dominion Parliament has no authority conferred upon it by the Act to repeal directly any provincial statute, whether it does or does not come within the limits of jurisdiction prescribed by s. 92. The repeal of a provincial Act by the Parliament of Canada can only be effected by repugnancy between its provisions and the enactments of the Dominion; and if the existence of such repugnancy should become matter of dispute, the controversy cannot be settled by the action either of the Dominion or of the provincial legislature, but must be submitted to the judicial tribunals of the country." This statement makes no distinction between the general power of the Dominion and the enumerations, although such a distinction is made in the same case in connection with the "trenching" doctrine. Indeed, the absence of any distinction between legislation under the federal general power and legislation under the specific enumerations, so far as paramountcy is concerned, is emphasized by Lord Haldane's judgment in *Great West Saddlery Co. v. The King,* [1921] 2 A.C. 91, at pp. 114-115, 58 D.L.R. 1, at p. 19, [1921] 1 W.W.R. 1034, at p. 1052.

It cannot escape notice that paramountcy is tied up with the "trenching" doctrine in the first of the four propositions laid down in the Fish Canneries case (*A.-G. Can. v. A.-G. B.C.*, [1930] A.C. 111, [1930] 1 D.L.R. 194, [1929] 3 W.W.R. 149). In the sense mentioned in this Note, it appears as the fourth proposition in these words: "There can be a domain in which provincial and Dominion legislation may overlap in which case neither legislation will be *ultra vires* if the field is clear, but if the field is not clear and the two legislations meet the Dominion legislation must prevail: see *G.T.R. v. A.-G. Can.*, [1907] A.C. 65."

What is the basis of the paramountcy doctrine? In *Huson v. South Norwich* (1895), 24 S.C.R. 143, at p. 149 Strong C.J. said that "although the British North America Act contains no provisions declaring that the legislation of the Dominion shall be supreme as is the case in the constitution of the United States the same principle is necessarily implied in our Constitutional Act, and is to be applied whenever, in the many cases which may arise, the federal and provincial legislatures adopt the same means to carry into effect distinct powers." In Australia, a similar doctrine exists by virtue of the express terms of section 109 of the Commonwealth of Australia Constitution Act, 1900, reading as follows: "When a law of a State is inconsistent with a law of the Commonwealth, the latter shall prevail, and the former shall, to the extent of the inconsistency, be invalid". In the United States, where the same issue is characterized as one of occupation of the field or pre-emption, the Supreme Court has treated it as arising out of the necessary supremacy of Congressional legislation in the operation of the federal system, a supremacy declared generally in article VI of the Constitution: see *Note*, "Occupation of the Field" in Commerce Clause Cases, 1936-1946; Ten Years of Federalism, (1946) 60 Harv. L. Rev. 262. In Canada, the paramountcy doctrine or the doctrine of the occupied field likewise depends on effective operation of the federal system fortified explicitly by the *non obstante* clause of section 91 and also by the concluding clause. The paramountcy principle has become so well-established that its basis is hardly ever a matter of comment but it may be observed that in line with the Privy Council's views on sections 91 and 92, it has more generally been attributed to the concluding clause of section 91 (see, for example, *In re Bozanich, A. H. Boulton Co. Ltd. v. Trusts & Guarantee Co. Ltd.*, [1942] S.C.R. 130, [1942] 2 D.L.R. 145).

The B.N.A. Act contains one explicit reference to federal paramountcy in section 95 which, in respect of the concurrent authority thereby given in relation to agriculture and immigration, stipulates that provincial legislation has effect "as long and as far only as it is not repugnant to any Act of the Parliament of Canada." Section 94A exemplifies a different dealing with its concurrent powers, being powers to make laws in relation to old age pensions and supplementary benefits. It is declared therein that no such law made by Parliament "shall affect the operation of any law present or future of a Provincial Legislature" in relation to the concurrent authority. There seems to be some opinion that this provision subordinates federal legislation to provincial enactments on the specified matters, even to the extent of being liable to be overridden by the provincial measures: see, for example, *Lederman*, Book Review (1965), 43 Can. Bar Rev. 669, at p. 671. Can this be so? Section 94A does not use the language of repugnancy, and it would be giving its words a double effect if they were construed first, to exclude federal paramountcy or supremacy and, second, to introduce provincial supremacy. Do they do anything more than sanctify concurrent operation? Section 94A is, in truth, an express exception from the norm which envisages only federal paramountcy in any contest between the operation of federal and provincial legislation. Nonetheless, its formulation does indicate the possibility of conflict, but the protection of the provincial enactment does not mean preclusion of federal legislation.

The central problem in respect of the paramountcy doctrine is to determine the scope or limits of its operation. It is safe to say that the cases have been quite inconsistent in their appreciation of paramountcy but, on the other hand, there has been a consistent line taken by a number of text writers who have dealt with it. The following may be noted:

Clement, The Canadian Constitution, at p. 465: ". . . There cannot be two statutes determining in different ways any one of the legal relations which is bound to arise from any given state of facts. If there be two statutes purporting so to do, one of them must be of no legal effect, either because repealed by the other, or by some rule of law made subordinate thereto as to the particular legal relation."

Lefroy, Canada's Federal System, at p. 126: "But the rule as to predominance of Dominion legislation it may be confidently said, can only be invoked in cases of absolutely conflicting legislation *in pari materia*, when it would be an impossibility to give effect to both the Dominion and the provincial enactments."

MacDonald, Judicial Interpretation of the Canadian Constitution, (1936) 1 Univ. of Tor. L.J. 260, at p. 275: "There must be a real conflict between the two Acts, that is, the two enactments 'must come into collision' (*A.-G. Ont. v. A.-G. Can.*, [1896] A.C. 348) or 'come into conflict . . . over a field of jurisdiction common to both' (*City of Montreal v. Montreal Street Ry.*, [1912] A.C. 333, 343) so that while dealing with similar transactions or subject matters, they yield a different result (*Royal Bank of Canada v. Larue*, [1928] A.C. 187). The doctrine of Dominion paramountcy does not operate merely because the Dominion has legislated on the same subject-matter."

The "conflict" test espoused by the foregoing text-writers seems clear enough in principle even if it raises problems in application; but at least it avoids the confusion attendant on attempts to maintain a verbal consistency despite a clear departure in principle. Here, as in the United States, the courts have applied paramountcy to cover not only conflict of legislation but also similarity or coincidence of legislation in the same field or on the same subject matter, and also foreclosure or preclusion of a field to a provincial legislature even where it has not been completely covered by federal legislation. Different attitudes are reflected in these three situations, and it does not help clarity to find courts saying, as for example, in *Re Regina v. Dickie, Re Regina v. Pomerleau,* [1955] 2 D.L.R. 757, 13 W.W.R. (N.S.) 545, 110 Can. C.C. 168, that "I cannot accede to the Crown's argument that Dominion and provincial legislation of the same general terms or effect do not 'clash' or 'conflict'. The similarity constitutes the very reason for the clash or conflict."

There has been, however, a noticeable trend in recent decisions of the Supreme Court of Canada to the strict view of paramountcy reflected in the conflict or collision test, which may be described as the test of operating incompatibility. This has been particularly the case where federal criminal legislation is relied upon to render inoperative provincial regulatory legislation. It is not too clear, however, whether the test of operating incompatibility covers strict similarity or coincidence of legislation. Certainly, where penal legislation is involved, there must be some compelling reason to subject persons to double liability and penalty if both Dominion and provincial legislation seek to meet the same social problem in the identical way, regardless of difference of object or purpose in the constitutional sense. Moreover, operating incompatibility may reasonably be taken to cover not only the obvious cases where observance of the legislation of the one authority involves breach of that of the other, but (at least in the case of penal legislation) also situations where the federal measure is more restrictive than the provincial so as rationally to preclude the province from establishing an offence at a level more liberal to an accused; for example, a flat federal prohibition would be more restrictive than a provincial one which imposed liability only if the act was done knowingly or wilfully: but see on this question, and contrast *Regina v. Wason* (1890), 17 O.A.R. 221 (especially in the light of *Regina v. Stone* (1893), 23 O.R. 46) and *Rex v. Garvin* (1908), 7 W.L.R. 783 (B.C.). A different result might be supported if the federal legislation were the more liberal, leaving it open to a province to be more restrictive, unless the paramountcy principle should be held to embrace the preclusion of severer provincial legislation by implication from the level at which the federal prohibition was pitched. See generally on this problem *Laskin,* Occupying the Field: Paramountcy in Penal Legislation, (1963) 41 Can. Bar Rev. 234.

The courts have used, in the main, two formulae as laying down the standard for determining whether federal pre-emption or preclusion will operate against provincial enactments. They have spoken in terms of "repugnancy" (see the quotation from the *Local Prohibition* case, *supra,* and see *O'Grady v. Sparling, infra*) and also have posed the test of whether "the two legislations meet" (see *G.T.R. v. A.-G. Can.,* [1907] A.C. 65 and the *Fish Canneries* case, [1930] A.C. 111, [1930] 1 D.L.R. 194, [1929] 3 W.W.R. 449). Both formulae leave room for either a strict or broad view of paramountcy so that it becomes a matter of examining case results to appreciate what they import. A useful analysis has been provided in this connection by *Lederman,* The Concurrent Operation of Federal and Provincial Laws in Canada, (1962-63) 9 McGill L.J. 185; he would look at the relation of federal and provincial legislation in a concurrent field from the standpoint of (1) conflict, (2) supplement and (3) duplication. The following is his summary of the doctrine of paramountcy as developed by the courts (at p. 199): "Provincial legislation may operate if there is no federal legislation in the field or if the provincial legislation is merely supplemental to federal legislation that is in the field. Duplicative provincial legislation may operate concurrently only when inseverably connected with supplemental provincial legislation, otherwise duplicative provincial legislation is suspended and inoperative. Repugnant provincial legislation is always suspended and inoperative."

It is instructive to note that Isaacs J. in *Clyde Engineering Co. Ltd. v. Cowburn* (1926), 37 C.L.R. 466, at p. 489 construed the "two legislations meet" formula of the *G.T.R.* case, *supra,* as being in line with the Australian view of "inconsistency" which he expressed as follows: "If a competent legislature expressly or impliedly evinces its intention to cover the whole field that is a conclusive test of inconsistency where another legislature assumes to enter to any extent upon the same field." This reading has not been borne out by the course of Canadian decisions.

It may fairly be said that the judicial attitude to paramountcy is an indicator of the courts' appreciation of Canadian federalism. The stricter view of paramountcy prevailing under the current line of decisions gives broader scope to the exercise and play of provincial legislative power and provincial legislation than the view expressed by Masten J. in *Rex v. Thorburn* (1917), 41 O.L.R. 39, 39 D.L.R. 300, 29 Can. C.C. 329, where he said that "the Court ought not to examine the field of legislation with a microscope to find out whether every particular corner of the field has been fully occupied by the Dominion statute but rather should hold that if the Dominion has legitimately entered the field, it should be deemed to have occupied it generally."

The language of the judgments has not been addressed to any theories or schemes of federalism; Canadian courts rarely talk in such terms. Instead, there has been a continuing reference to the different objects or purposes of the competing federal and provincial legislation, as if that was in some way a determinant; and it has not been too clear in the cases whether the object or purpose that was under consideration was a positivist constitutional assessment or a social policy assessment, or whether no difference was intended in these two ways of looking at the particular problem. It is necessary to be reminded at all times that no issue of paramountcy can arise unless there is in existence federal and provincial legislation which, independently considered, is in each case valid. If either piece of legislation, standing alone, is invalid there is no occasion to consider whether the field has been occupied. The issue that will have been resolved in such case would be the anterior one of the "matter" embraced by the legislation, whether of Parliament or of the provincial legislature, as the case may be. Yet there are cases which talk in terms of paramountcy or the occupied field but clearly should turn on this anterior consideration: see, for example, *Rex v. Lichtman* (1923), 54 O.L.R. 502. It confuses the issue of paramountcy to ignore the need to make a prior assessment of whether Parliament and provincial legislature have each acted within their respective mutually exclusive powers (looking at the matter as if the field was clear so far as concerns the provincial enactment).

The paramountcy doctrine does not import any constitutional prohibition against exposure to double liability for the same act or conduct, *i.e.* under both federal and provincial legislation: See *Rex v. Kissick,* [1942] 3 D.L.R. 431, [1942] 2 W.W.R. 418, 78 Can. C.C. 34, 50 Man. R. 194; *Couture v. Lauzon School Com'rs,* [1950] Que. S.C. 201, 97 Can. C.C. 218; but see *Friedland,* Double Jeopardy and The Division of Legislative Authority in Canada (1967), 17 Univ. of Tor. L.J. 66. Again, the paramountcy doctrine does not come into play merely because there is an interference with the potential revenue either of the Dominion (see *A.-G. Man. v. Man. Licence Holders Ass'n.,* [1902] A.C. 73) or of a province (see *Russell v. The Queen* (1882), 7 App. Cas. 829). The most telling illustration of this proposition is to be found in *Forbes v. A.-G. Man.,* [1937] A.C. 260, at p. 274, [1937] 1 D.L.R. 289, at p. 297, [1937] 1 W.W.R. 167, at p. 176, where the Privy Council, in considering whether federal and provincial income tax legislation could co-exist, said: "The doctrine of the 'occupied field' applies only where there is a clash between Dominion legislation and provincial legislation within an area common to both. Here there is no conflict. Both income taxes may co-exist and be enforced without clashing. The Dominion reaps part of the field of the Manitoba citizen's income. The Province reaps another part of it". Again, there has been no disposition to apply paramountcy where there is merely the potentiality of occupation of the field, as where federal conditional legislation is for the time being inoperative: see the *Local Prohibition* case, *A.-G. Ont. v. A.-G. Can.,* [1896] A.C. 348.

Neither in Australia nor in the United States has there been any theory or notion that the "occupied field" doctrine extends only to literally conflicting or clashing legislation. The Australian doctrine was laid down in *Ex parte McLean* (1930), 43 C.L.R. 472, at p. 483 by Dixon J., as follows:

"When the Parliament of the Commonwealth and the Parliament of a State each legislate upon the same subject and prescribe what the rule of conduct shall be, they make laws which are inconsistent, notwithstanding that the rule of conduct is identical which each prescribes, and sec. 109 applies. That this is so is settled, at least when the sanctions they impose are diverse (*Hume v. Palmer,* 38 C.L.R. 441). But the reason is that, by prescribing the rule to be observed, the Federal statute shows an intention to cover the subject-matter and provide what the law upon it shall be. If it appeared that the Federal law was intended to be supplementary to or cumulative upon State law, then no inconsistency would be exhibited in imposing the same duties or in inflicting different penalties. The inconsistency does not lie in the mere coexistence of two laws which are susceptible of simultaneous obedience. It depends upon the intention of the paramount Legislature to express by its enactment, completely, exhaustively, or exclusively, what shall be the law governing the particular conduct or matter to which its attention is directed. When a Federal statute discloses such an intention, it is inconsistent with it for the law of a State to govern the same conduct or matter."

This statement of principle was approved in *O'Sullivan v. Noarlunga Meat Ltd.*, [1957] A.C. 1, at p. 28, [1956] 3 All E.R. 177, at p. 183, where the Privy Council added that "in applying this principle it is important to bear in mind that the relevant field or subject is that covered by the law said to be invalid . . ."

The decisions in the United States, while recognizing an obvious occupation of the field where there is operating incompatibility between federal and state legislation, have also proceeded on the broader lines indicated in the Australian doctrine. Here, however, the results have not been uniform, principally because the search for Congressional intent or purpose to preclude state action or pre-empt a field cannot always touch members of a court in the same way in respect of different problems: see *California v. Zook* (1949), 336 U.S. 725, 69 S. Ct. 841; *Guss v. Utah Labor Relations Board* (1957), 353 U.S. 1, 77 S. Ct. 598; *International Association of Machinists v. Gonzales* (1958), 356 U.S. 617, 78 S. Ct. 923; *Pennsylvania v. Nelson* (1956), 350 U.S. 497, 76 S. Ct. 477; *Leslie Miller Inc. v. Arkansas* (1956), 352 U.S. 187, 77 S. Ct. 257. In *Hines v. Davidowitz* (1941), 312 U.S. 52, at p. 67, 61 S. Ct. 399, at p. 404, the nature of the problem was indicated in the following terms, which could be applied to Canada: "[The] Court in considering the validity of state laws in the light of . . . federal laws touching the same subject, has made use of the following expressions: conflicting; contrary to; occupying the field; repugnancy; difference; irreconcilability; inconsistency; violation; curtailment; and interference. But none of these expressions provides an infallible constitutional yardstick. In the final analysis, there can be no one crystal clear distinctly marked formula".

[The burden of proving "conflict" is on the party asserting it: see *A.-G. Que. v. Bank of Montreal and A.-G. Can.*, [1942] 1 D.L.R. 309, affirmed [1943] Que. K.B. 543, reversed on other grounds, [1947] A.C. 33, [1947] 1 D.L.R. 81, [1946] 3 W.W.R. 659.]

HOME INSURANCE CO. v. LINDAL AND BEATTIE

In the Supreme Court of Canada. [1934] S.C.R. 33, [1934] 1 D.L.R. 497.

LAMONT J. (for the majority of the Court): In 1921, however, as already stated, the Dominion Parliament passed legislation adding a section to the Criminal Code in terms almost identical with those of the provincial enactment (section 22(2)) and making it a criminal offence, in the strictest sense, to drive an automobile while in a state of intoxication. The effect of this legislation by Parliament was to supersede existing provincial legislation, which was legislation in the same field; and thereafter, as long, at all events, as the Dominion legislation should remain in force, the provincial legislation would necessarily be inoperative. The Dominion legislation has remained in force until the present day.

[Section 22(2) of the Alberta Motor Vehicle Act, referred to above, provided as follows: "No intoxicated person shall drive or operate a motor vehicle in any place." The Dominion legislation referred to, Cr. Code, s. 285(4), reads as follows: "Everyone who while intoxicated ... drives any motor vehicle or automobile ... shall be guilty of an offence ...".

The *Home Insurance Co.* case was followed in *Kennedy v. Rowell,* [1954] 4 D.L.R. 44, 11 W.W.R. (N.S.) 177.]

PROVINCIAL SECRETARY OF P.E.I. v. EGAN and A.-G. P.E.I.

In the Supreme Court of Canada. [1941] S.C.R. 396, [1941] 3 D.L.R. 305.

Appeal from the judgment of the Supreme Court of Prince Edward Island *en banc*, [1941] 1 D.L.R. 291, dismissing an appeal by the Provincial Secretary from an order to issue to Michael Egan, upon application made in the ordinary way, a licence to operate motor vehicles in the province.

DUFF C.J.. . . . The point we have to consider is whether by reason of the enactment of section 285(7) of the *Criminal Code,* the jurisdiction *prima facie* given to the Province to enact the provisions of section 84(1) (a) and (c) of the *Highway Traffic Act* of 1936 is suspended. This section of the *Criminal Code* provides that where a person is convicted of an offence under certain sub-sections of that section, the court or justice may, in addition to any other punishment provided for such offence, make an order prohibiting such person from driving a motor vehicle or automobile anywhere in Canada during any period not exceeding three years. The attack upon the provincial legislation may, perhaps, be put in this way: the effect of section 285(7) is to bring the matters with which it deals within the subject of the criminal law, which is explicitly assigned to the Dominion as one of the enumerated subjects under section 91; then it is said that the matters so legislated upon are of such a scope that they extend to and include within their ambit the matters dealt with by section 84(1) of the *Highway Traffic Act* of 1936 and that, consequently, the clause at the end of section 91 comes into play, and that these matters are excluded, so long as the Dominion legislation remains in force, from the jurisdiction of the Province.

As against this it is argued by the Attorney-General of Prince Edward Island that section 285(7) is *ultra vires*; that the legislative prohibition which is there imposed upon convicted persons against driving a motor vehicle or automobile is not within the ambit of section 91(27) [of the B.N.A. Act].

I may say at once I cannot agree with this view. I do not think anything is to be gained by discussing the point at large. It appears to me to be quite clear that such prohibitions may be imposed as punishment in exercise of the authority vested in the Dominion to legislate in relation to criminal law and procedure.

A very different question, however, is raised by the contention that the matters legislated upon by the enactment of the Provincial *Highway Traffic Act* in question have, by force of section 285(7) of the *Criminal Code,* been brought exclusively within the scope of the Dominion authority in relation to criminal law. We are here on rather delicate ground. We have to consider the effect of legislation by the Dominion creating a crime and imposing punishment for it in effecting the suspension of provincial legislative authority in relation to matters *prima facie* within the the provincial jurisdiction. I say we are on delicate ground because the subject of criminal law entrusted to the Parliament of Canada is necessarily an expanding field by reason of the authority of the Parliament to create crimes, impose punishment for such crimes, and to deal with criminal procedure. If there is a conflict between Dominion legislation and Provincial legislation, then nobody doubts that the Dominion legislation prevails. But even where there is no actual conflict, the question often arises as to the effect of Dominion legislation in excluding matters from provincial jurisdiction which would otherwise fall within it. I doubt if any test can be stated with accuracy in general terms for the resolution of such questions. It is important to remember that matters which, from one point of view and for one purpose, fall exclusively within the Dominion authority, may, nevertheless, be proper subjects for legislation by the Province from a different point of view, although this is a principle that must be "applied only with great caution." . . .

. . . The effect of the concluding part of section 91 is that the Parliament of Canada may legislate upon matters which are *prima facie* committed exclusively to the Provincial Legislature by section 92, where such legislation is necessarily incidental to the exercise of the powers conferred upon Parliament in relation to the specified subject "The Criminal Law . . . including the Procedure in Criminal Matters." To the extent, at least, to which matters *prima facie* provincial are regulated by Dominion legislation in exercise of this authority, such matters are excepted from those committed to the provincial legislatures by section 92; and, accordingly, the legislative authority of the provinces in relation to these matters is suspended. . . .

In every case where a dispute arises, the precise question must be whether or not the matter of the provincial legislation that is challenged is so related to the substance of the Dominion criminal legislation as to be brought within the scope of criminal law in the sense of section 91. If there is repugnancy between the provincial enactment and the Dominion enactment, the provincial enactment is, of course, inoperative. It would be most unwise, I think, to attempt to lay down any rules for determining repugnancy in this sense. The task of applying the general principles is not made less difficult by reason of the jurisdiction of the provincial legislatures under the fifteenth paragraph of section 92 to create penal offences which may be truly criminal in their essential character. (*The King v. Nat. Bell Liquors Ltd.*, [1922] 2 A.C. 128, and *Nadan v. The King*, [1926] A.C. 482.)

I do not find any difficulty in dealing with the present case. Primarily, responsibility for the regulation of highway traffic, including authority to prescribe the conditions and the manner of the use of motor vehicles on highways and the operation of a system of licences for the purpose of securing the observance of regulations respecting these matters in the interest of the public generally, is committed to the local legislatures.

Sections 84(1) (a) and (c) are enactments dealing with licences. The legislature has thought fit to regard convictions of the classes specified as a proper ground for suspending the licence of the convict. Such legislation, I think, is concerned with the subject of licensing, over which it is essential that the Province should primarily have control. In exercising such control it must, of course, abstain from legislating on matters within the enumerated subjects of section 91. Suspension of a driving licence does involve a prohibition against driving; but so long as the purpose of the provincial legislation and its immediate effect are exclusively to prescribe the conditions under which licences are granted, forfeited, or suspended, I do not think, speaking generally, it is necessarily impeachable as repugnant to section 285(7) of the *Criminal Code* in the sense above mentioned.

It is, of course, beyond dispute that where an offence is created by competent Dominion legislation in exercise of the authority under section 91(27), the penalty or penalties attached to that offence, as well as the offence itself, become matters within that paragraph of section 91 which are excluded from provincial jurisdiction.

There is, however, no adequate ground for the conclusion that these particular enactments (section 84(1) (a) and (c)) are in their true character attempts to prescribe penalties for the offences mentioned, rather than enactments in regulation of licences.

It remains only to add that what I have said is strictly directed to cases in which the controversy is whether or not a criminal offence has the effect of excluding a given subject matter from the legislative authority of the province.

I have only to add that I concur with my brother Rinfret.

RINFRET J. (for himself, Crocket and Kerwin JJ.) : On November 20th, 1939, the respondent was convicted by the Stipendiary Magistrate for Queens County, in the Province of Prince Edward Island, for that he "unlawfully did operate a motor vehicle on the public highway whilst intoxicated, contrary to section 285, subsection 4, paragraph (b), of the Criminal Code of Canada."

As a result of that conviction, in virtue of section 84(1) of The Highway Traffic Act of Prince Edward Island, 1936, the respondent's licence to operate a motor vehicle, otherwise valid until February 28th, 1940, was automatically cancelled for a period of twelve months.

The relevant part of section 84 reads as follows:

84. (1) The licence of a person who is convicted of driving a motor vehicle while under the influence of intoxicating liquor or drugs, shall forthwith upon, and automatically with such conviction, be suspended for a period:

(a) of twelve months for the first offence; ...

(c) The Provincial Secretary shall not issue a licence to any person during the period for which his licence has been cancelled or suspended under this section.

On May 28th, 1940, the respondent applied for an operator's licence. The application was in the statutory form and contained the following questions and answers, amongst others:—

Has your licence ever been cancelled for any cause; if so in what year? On November 20th, 1939.

And for what reason? For conviction under Criminal Code for driving motor car while intoxicated.

The Acting Deputy Provincial Secretary [notified] the respondent that his application was refused. . . . [The learned Judge then referred to the successful proceedings taken by Egan to compel the issue to him of a licence, and he then continued:]

The reasons for judgment of the Supreme Court of Prince Edward Island were delivered by Mr. Justice Arsenault. He stated that, under the provisions of the *Criminal Code,* "the Stipendiary Magistrate could have made a further order prohibiting the accused from driving a motor vehicle for a period not exceeding three years." He pointed, however, to the fact that the Magistrate had not done so, but that he certified to the Provincial Secretary that the present respondent had been convicted; that the conviction was made on November 20, 1939, and that, had the licence not been cancelled in pursuance of section 84 of The Highway Traffic Act of 1936, the respondent's operator's licence would have expired on February 28, 1940; that the respondent took no further step to have his licence restored but that, six months afterwards, to wit, on 28th May, 1940, he made application on the regular form for an operator's licence. The learned Judge then mentioned what I have already stated: that the Provincial Secretary refused to issue the licence on account of the conviction, that upon appeal to the Judge of the County Court of Queens County, the Department of the Provincial Secretary had been ordered to issue a licence to the respondent as aforesaid, and that the Provincial Secretary now appealed to the Supreme Court (*en banc*). . . .[The learned Judge then referred to a jurisdictional issue which was decided by the Supreme Court of Prince Edward Island *en banc* and to that Court's decision affirming the order to issue a licence.]

. . . But although, in view of the above decision, it was not necessary to consider "the question of the *ultra vires* of sec. 84(1) of the Highway Traffic Act," it was thought advisable to deal with it and to say that since the Criminal Code has invaded the field by enacting sec. 285, subsec. 7, amended by 3 George VI, 1939, ch. 30, sec. 6, it follows that the provisions of the Highway Traffic Act as to cancellation of a licence on a conviction for driving a motor car whilst intoxicated, have become *ultra vires*.

It is from the above judgment that the Provincial Secretary of the Province of Prince Edward Island now appeals, with the intervention of the Attorney-General of the same province, by leave of the Supreme Court (*en banc*). The Attorney-General of Canada and the Attorney-General for Ontario were granted leave to appear before this Court and to argue for or against the judgment appealed from, on the point of the constitutionality of the relevant sections of the *Criminal Code* and of the *Highway Traffic Act* of Prince Edward Island. [The learned Judge then considered the question of jurisdiction and came to the conclusion that there was no right in Egan to appeal from the Provincial Secretary's refusal of a licence.]

. . . There being no jurisdiction in the County Court Judge of Queens County to hear the appeal of the respondent and to make any order as a result of such appeal, there was no right of appeal, if any, to the Supreme Court *en banc*, except on the question of the jurisdiction of the County Court Judge.

The Supreme Court *en banc* could decide, and in this case should have decided, that the County Court Judge of Queens County was without jurisdiction and that his order was not competently made, but nothing else. . . .

. . . The reasons already stated are sufficient to dispose of the appeal; and, following a wise and well defined tradition, this Court should, no doubt, refrain from expressing an opinion upon any other point not necessary for the decision of the case.

The Supreme Court *en banc*, however, thought it advisable to deal with the question of the constitutionality of section 84(1) of the *Highway Traffic Act, 1936*, since the *Criminal Code* has enacted sec. 285, subs. 7, amended by sec. 6 of ch. 30 of the Statutes of Canada, 3 Geo. VI (1939). And that Court declared *ultra vires* the provision of the *Highway Traffic Act* "as to cancellation of a licence on a conviction for driving a motor car whilst intoxicated."

It is because of the declaration on that point that the Attorney-General of Prince Edward Island has carried his appeal to this Court and that the Attorney-General of Canada and the Attorney-General for Ontario have been allowed to intervene. It was represented to us that this declaration has an important and wide consequence and that, while only an *obiter dictum*, it might affect the jurisprudence not only in Prince Edward Island but also in other provinces. It appears desirable, therefore, that this Court should express its opinion upon the matter.

The Criminal Code Amendment Act, 1939, c. 30, s. 6, contains an amendment whereby subs. 7 of sec. 285, as enacted by sec. 16, c. 44, of the Statutes of Canada of 1938, is repealed and the following substituted therefor:

(7) Where any person is convicted of an offence under the provisions of subsections one, two, four or six of this section the court
or justice may, in addition to any other punishment provided for
such offence, make an order prohibiting such person from driving
a motor vehicle or automobile anywhere in Canada during any period
not exceeding three years. In the event of such an order being made
the court or justice shall forward a copy thereof to the registrar of
motor vehicles for the province wherein a permit or license to drive
a motor vehicle or automobile was issued to such person. Such
copy shall be certified under the seal of such court or justice or, if
there be no such seal, under the hand of a judge or presiding magistrate of such court or of such justice.

Subsection 4 of section 285, referred to in subsection 7 above
reproduced, contains the enactment of the *Criminal Code* covering
the case of driving while intoxicated.

It follows that, under subsection 7 as now amended, a person
convicted of driving while intoxicated may be prohibited "from
driving a motor vehicle or automobile anywhere in Canada during
any period not exceeding three years"; while, under section 84(1) of
the *Highway Traffic Act* of Prince Edward Island, the licence of a
person so convicted "shall forthwith upon, and automatically with
such conviction, be suspended for a period of twelve months for the
first offence" and "not less than twelve months and not exceeding
two years for the second offence"; and for the third offence he shall
be prohibited from holding a licence.

The Supreme Court *en banc* stated that the *Criminal Code* had
"invaded the field" and that section 84 of the *Highway Traffic Act*
had thereby become *ultra vires*.

In this Court, the Attorney-General of Canada submitted that
the subsection of the *Criminal Code* in question was *intra vires*, as
being an enactment in relation to the Criminal Law. He argued that
the subsection provided an additional punishment for the various
offences in connection with the driving of vehicles under the preceding subsections of section 285; that this was not legislation in relation
to civil rights, although it may be legislation affecting civil rights,
legislation for the punishment of crime being clearly legislation within
the competency of the Parliament of Canada.

The Prince Edward Island legislation, it was submitted, was enacted as a punishment measure, rather than to provide for the safety
on the highway. Section 84 bans individuals convicted of certain
offences from the highways for short periods of time; and it is
included in a group of sections under the heading: "Penalties."

It was submitted that, although the provincial provision might
otherwise have been valid, since it conflicts with the *Criminal Code*,
the latter must now prevail (See Lord Tomlin in *Attorney-General
for Canada v. Attorney-General for British Columbia*, [1930] A.C.
111, at p. 118).

The Attorney-General for Ontario contended that, even though
it be found that section 285(7) of the *Criminal Code* is *intra vires*
of the Parliament of Canada, it is not in conflict with provincial

legislation providing that, upon conviction of a person for driving a motor vehicle while under the influence of intoxicating liquors or drugs, his licence, or permit, to drive shall be suspended. He relied upon *Grand Trunk Railway Company of Canada v. Attorney-General of Canada*, [1907] A.C. 65.

He submitted that the control of the roads and highways and the regulation of the traffic thereon are matters within s. 92 of the *B.N.A. Act* assigned exclusively to the legislatures of the provinces: Head 9, ". . . and other Licences in order to the raising of a Revenue for Provincial, Local, or Municipal Purposes"; Head 13, "Property and Civil Rights in the Province"; Head 16, "Generally all matters of a merely local or private Nature in the Province." . . .

. . . The Attorney-General of Prince Edward Island also contended that both sections of the *Criminal Code* and of the *Highway Traffic Act* could validly subsist together and that section 285(7) of the *Criminal Code* had no effect whatever on the validity of the Provincial section 84.

I am respectfully of the opinion that the field of the two enactments is not co-extensive; and it is not, therefore, necessary to pronounce upon the validity of section 285(7) of the *Criminal Code.*

The Dominion legislation would prevent the offender from operating a motor vehicle throughout Canada "during any period not exceeding three years." It would not prevent him from holding a licence or accompanying a beginner, as provided for by the Prince Edward Island legislation. The Provincial legislation in question in this case is, in pith and substance, within the classes of subjects assigned to the Provincial legislatures; it is licensing legislation confined to the territory of Prince Edward Island. The *Criminal Code* provides for an order prohibiting a person from driving, irrespective of whether a licence has been issued to him or not. The automatic cancellation of the Prince Edward Island licence would not, of itself, prevent the person affected by it from obtaining a driver's licence in other provinces.

It cannot be open to contention for a moment that the imposing of such a penalty for enforcing a law of the competency of Prince Edward Island is an interference with criminal law, under section 91, subs. 27. *Regina v. Wason,* 17 O.A.R. 221, at p. 249. It is not an additional penalty imposed for a violation of the criminal law. It provides for a civil disability arising out of a conviction for a criminal offence.

The right of building highways and of operating them within a province, whether under direct authority of the Government, or by means of independent companies or municipalities, is wholly within the purview of the province (*O'Brien v. Allen,* 30 S.C.R. 340), and so is the right to provide for the safety of circulation and traffic on such highways. The aspect of that field is wholly provincial, from the point of view both of the use of the highway and of the use of the vehicles. It has to do with the civil regulation of the use of highways and personal property, the protection of the persons and property of the citizens, the prevention of nuisances and the suppression of conditions calculated to make circulation and traffic dangerous. Such is, amongst others, the provincial aspect of section 84 of the *Highway Traffic Act*. It has nothing to do with the Dominion aspect of the creation of a crime and its punishment. And it cannot be said that the Dominion, while constituting the criminal offence of driving while intoxicated and providing for certain penalties therefor, has invaded the whole field in such a way as to exclude all provincial jurisdiction. It cannot have superseded section 84, which was obviously made from the provincial aspect of defining the right to use the highways in Prince Edward Island and intended to operate in a purely provincial field.

As to the contention that the Provincial legislation imposes an additional penalty for the punishment of an offence already punished by the *Criminal Code,* the answer, it seems to me, is simply that the Provincial legislation does not do so.

The offender found guilty under the *Criminal Code,* as already pointed out, may be prohibited from driving a motor vehicle or automobile anywhere in Canada during the period mentioned in the Code. The order, if made by the convicting magistrate, will operate quite independently of any licence granted by the Provincial authority. In that sense, it would be allowed to supersede the Provincial legislation. But section 84 of *The Highway Traffic Act* of Prince Edward Island, dealing with the case of its own licensees upon the territory of its own province, provides that a person convicted of driving while intoxicated loses his provincial licence, either for a time or forever (in the case of a third offence). It does not create an offence; it does not add to or vary the punishment already declared by the *Criminal Code;* it does not change or vary the procedure to be followed in the enforcement of any provision of the *Criminal Code*. It deals purely and simply with certain civil rights in the Province of Prince Edward Island. . . .

. . . It would seem to me beyond doubt that provisions of a provincial statute for the cancellation of licences to carry on certain kinds of business, or creating a disability from holding public offices, or creating any kind of civil disabilities, as a result of a conviction under the *Criminal Code,* does not make such provisions legislation in relation to criminal law; and, hence, they are not *ultra vires* of the Provincial legislatures. It never occurred to anybody to dispute the power of the provinces to issue licences, or permits, for the right to drive motor vehicles on the highways of their respective territories. Surely the authority to issue such licences, or permits, carries with it the authority to suspend or cancel them, upon the happening of certain conditions. The provision that a person convicted of driving while intoxicated will lose his licence for a time or forever is, in a certain sense, a condition upon which the licence, or permit, is granted by the province.

I would think, for these reasons, that section 84 of *The Highway Traffic Act* of Prince Edward Island is not unconstitutional.

Appeal allowed on other grounds.

[Hudson and Taschereau JJ. gave separate reasons to the same effect. See *Note*, (1941), 19 Can. Bar Rev. 607.

In *Ross v. Registrar of Motor Vehicles for Ontario; Bell v. A.G. P.E.I.* (1973), 23 C.R.N.S. 319, 14 C.C.C. (2d) 322, 1 N.R. 9, 42 D.L.R. (3d) 68 (Can.), the court faced a point left open in the *Egan* case. Accused was convicted of impaired driving under Cr. Code, s. 234 and the magistrate, acting under Cr. Code, s. 238 as amended by 1972 (Can.) c. 13, s. 18, made an order directing as an additional penalty that he be prohibited from driving for six months except for certain working hours on weekdays. An action for a declaration that automatic total licence suspension under *The Highway Traffic Act*, R.S.O. 1970, c. 202, s. 21, subject to being relieved by the Minister, was *ultra vires* was unsuccessful.

In *Re Regina v. Dickie, Re Regina v. Pomerleau*, [1955] 2 D.L.R. 757, 13 W.W.R. (N.S.) 545, 110 Can. C.C. 168, provincial legislation made it an offence to drive a motor vehicle while, *inter alia*, one's driver's licence was under suspension. Cr. Code, s. 285(8) (now R.S.C. 1970, c. C-34, s. 238(3)) made it an offence to drive anywhere in Canada while disqualified from driving by reason of the legal suspension or cancellation in any province of one's permit or driver's licence or by reason of a prohibitory order under Cr. Code, s. 285(7) (now R.S.C. 1970, c. C-34, s. 238(1)). *Held*, the provincial legislation, enacted subsequent to the federal, was precluded and hence *ultra vires*. Do you agree? Is it not arguable that Cr. Code, s. 258(8) is (in part, at least) *ultra vires*? See, however, *Rex v. Whynacht*, [1942] 1 D.L.R. 238, 16 M.P.R. 267, and *Regina v. Munro* (1959), 22 D.L.R. (2d) 443, 30 W.W.R. 21, holding that the provision is valid.]

O'GRADY v. SPARLING

In the Supreme Court of Canada. [1960] S.C.R. 804, 25 D.L.R. (2d) 145, 33 W.W.R. 360.

Appeal from a judgment of the Court of Appeal for Manitoba, 22 D.L.R. (2d) 150, 30 W.W.R. 156, dismissing an appeal from a judgment of Williams, C.J.Q.B., 28 W.W.R. 152.

JUDSON J.:—(for Kerwin C.J.C., Taschereau, Fauteux, Abbott, Martland and Ritchie JJ. as well as for himself): The appellant, being charged under s. 55(1) of the Manitoba *Highway Traffic Act* with driving without due care and attention, moved for prohibition on the ground that the section was beyond the powers of the provincial legislature because it was legislation in relation to criminal law, and also, because the subject-matter of the section fell within the paramount jurisdiction of the Parliament of Canada, which had occupied the field by the enactment of s. 221 of the *Criminal Code*.

The motion for prohibition was dismissed by the Chief Justice of the Court of Queen's Bench, who adopted the reasoning of the majority of the Ontario Court of Appeal in *Regina v. Yolles*, [1959] O.R. 206, 19 D.L.R. (2d) 19 reversing [1958] O.R. 786. This dismissal was affirmed on appeal, Adamson C.J.M. dissenting. The appellant now appeals pursuant to special leave granted by this Court.

Section 55(1) of *The Highway Traffic Act*, R.S.M. 1954, c. 112, reads:

"Every person who drives a motor vehicle or a trolley bus on a highway without due care and attention or without reasonable consideration for other persons using the highway is guilty of an offence."

The relevant sections of the *Criminal Code* are ss. 191(1) and 221(1), as follows:

"191.   (1) Everyone is criminally negligent who

(a) in doing anything, or
(b) in omitting to do anything that it is his duty to do, shows wanton or reckless disregard for the lives or safety of other persons."

"221.   (1) Everyone who is criminally negligent in the operation of a motor vehicle is guilty of

(a) an indictable offence and is liable to imprisonment for five years,

or

(b) an offence punishable on summary conviction."

It is at once apparent that the problem is precisely the same as the one under consideration in *Regina v. Yolles*. In the first instance, in *Regina v. Yolles* the corresponding Ontario legislation was held to be *ultra vires*. The Court of Appeal, by a majority judgment, held that it was valid provincial legislation in relation to the administration and control of traffic upon highways within the province and not legislation in relation to criminal law, and further, that it was not repugnant to, nor in conflict with s. 221(1) of the *Criminal Code*.

The central point of this appeal is the appellant's submission that whenever Parliament chooses to attach penal consequences to negligence of whatever degree, then any provincial legislation relating to negligence with penal consequences attached to it must be legislation in relation to criminal law. This submission assumes a complete identity of subject-matter which in my opinion does not exist. It is also founded, in part at least, upon a theory of the existence of a "general area" or "domain" of criminal law which has been considered and rejected by this Court.

There is a fundamental difference between the subject-matter of these two pieces of legislation which the appellant's argument does not recognize. It is a difference in kind and not merely one of degree. This difference has been recognized and emphasized in the recent writings of Glanville Williams on Criminal Law, para. 28, p. 82, and by J.W.C. Turner in the 17th edition of Kenny's Outlines of Criminal Law. I adopt as part of my reasons Turner's statement of the difference to be found at p. 34 of Kenny:

"But it should now be recognized that at common law there is no *criminal* liability for harm thus caused by inadvertence. This has been laid down authoritatively for manslaughter again and again. There are only two states of mind which constitute *mens rea,* and they are intention and *recklessness.* The difference between recklessness and negligence is the difference between advertence and inadvertence; they are opposed and it is a logical fallacy to suggest that recklessness is a degree of negligence. The common habit of lawyers to qualify the word 'negligence' with some moral epithet such as 'wicked', 'gross', or 'culpable' has been most unfortunate since it has inevitably led to great confusion of thought and of principle. It is equally misleading to speak of criminal negligence since this is merely to use an expression to explain itself."

The appellant argues that negligence of any degree may form the essential element of a criminal offence. As an abstract proposition I would not question this provided the criminal offence, in a federal state, is defined by the proper legislative authority. But it does not follow that the provincial legislature, in dealing with this subject-matter in the exercise of its regulatory power over highway traffic, is enacting criminal law.

The appellant says that the history of the common law shows that inadvertent negligence was sufficient to support a charge of manslaughter and that consequently, when penal consequences are attached to inadvertent negligence under a provincial highway code, the legislation is necessarily in relation to criminal law. This is the proposition stated by McRuer C.J.H.C. in the *Yolles* case, [1958] O.R. 786, at p. 808 in these terms:

"What the provincial legislature has done is to attempt to revive the old common law offence of causing death by mere negligence by extending it to all cases of careless driving of vehicles on a highway, whether death ensues or not."

I doubt whether the existence of such a common law offence can be deduced from the dicta of early 19th century judges sitting at *nisi prius*, as found in the scanty reports of the time. The question must have been what was meant and what meaning was conveyed by the trial judge when he used an elastic word such as "negligence" in relation to the facts of the case. Most of the cases quoted by McRuer C.J.H.C. are collected in 9 Hals., 1st ed., p. 582, note (1) where they are referred to as cases of manslaughter owing to negligent driving and riding. In the second edition, 9 Hals., 2nd ed., p. 441, note (m), they are referred to as illustrations of manslaughter by reason of "gross" negligence in driving, riding or navigation, and in the third edition, as illustrations of manslaughter occasioned by "criminal" negligence (10 Hals., 3rd ed., 717, note (h)).

I think that the same doubt is expressed in *Andrews v. Director of Public Prosecutions*, [1937] A.C. 576, at p. 581. In any event, there is no such common law offence now in England and it is not to be found in the criminal law of Canada. The *Criminal Code* confines its definition of crime in ss. 191(1) and 221(1) to a certain kind of conduct. This is not the kind of conduct referred to in the provincial legislation, nor is the provincial legislation dealing with another degree of the same kind of conduct aimed at by the *Criminal Code*.

What the Parliament of Canada has done is to define "advertent negligence" as a crime under ss. 191(1) and 221(1). It has not touched "inadvertent negligence". Inadvertent negligence is dealt with under the provincial legislation in relation to the regulation of highway traffic. That is its true character and until Parliament chooses to define it in the *Criminal Code* as "crime", it is not a crime.

The power of a provincial legislature to enact legislation for the regulation of highway traffic is undoubted. (*Provincial Secretary of the Province of Prince Edward Island v. Egan,* [1941] S.C.R. 396, 3 D.L.R. 305.) The legislation under attack here is part and parcel of this regulation. Rules of conduct on highways have been established by similar legislation in every province and the careless driving section is no different in character from the specific rules of the road that are laid down.

Much of the argument addressed to us was that there was something about the subject-matter of this legislation, careless driving on highways, which made it inherently criminal law. I do not understand this argument in relation to the subject-matter of negligence on highways. What meaning can one attach to such phrases as "area of criminal law" or "domain of criminal law" in relation to such a subject-matter? A provincial enactment does not become a matter of criminal law merely because it consists of a prohibition and makes it an offence for failure to observe the prohibition; (*Quong-Wing v. The King,* 49 S.C.R. 440, 18 D.L.R. 121). On this subject-matter there can be no such area defined either by the common law or by the statutory treatment of the subject in the United Kingdom and in Canada. In mentioning statute law, I have in mind 1938, c. 44, s. 16, *Statutes of Canada,* which did introduce into the *Criminal Code* as s. 285(6) something resembling the provincial legislation in question here, but it is not now in the *Criminal Code* . . . .

My conclusion is that s. 55(1) of the Manitoba *Highway Traffic Act* has for its true object, purpose, nature or character the regulation and control of traffic on highways and that, therefore, it is valid provincial legislation.

Nor do I think that it can be said to be inoperative because it is in conflict with s. 221 of the *Criminal Code.* There is no conflict between these provisions in the sense that they are repugnant. The provisions deal with different subject-matters and are for different purposes. Section 55(1) is highway legislation dealing with regulation and control of traffic on highways, and s. 221 is criminal law dealing with negligence of the character defined in the section. Even though the circumstances of a particular case may be within the scope of both provisions (and in that sense there may be an overlapping) that does not mean that there is conflict so that the Court must conclude that the provincial enactment is suspended or inoperative; *McColl v. Canadian Pacific Railway Company,* [1923] A.C. 126, at pp. 134, 135, *per* Duff J. There is no conflict or repugnancy between s. 55(1) of the Manitoba *Highway Traffic Act* and s. 221 of the *Criminal Code.* Both provisions can live together and operate concurrently.

The problem here seems to me to be the same in principle as that raised by the side-by-side existence of provincial legislation dealing with the duty to remain at or return to the scene of an accident for certain defined purposes, and s. 221(2) of the *Criminal Code* dealing with failure to stop at the scene of an accident "with intent to escape civil or criminal liability". The supposed conflict between these two pieces of legislation has been considered in three provinces. The first decision was *R. v. Corry,* [1932] 1 W.W.R. 414, affirmed [1932] 1 W.W.R. 853, 26 Alta. L.R. 390, which held that the provincial legislation was in relation to the regulation of traffic and not the punishment of crime. In Ontario this decision appears to have been overlooked in *Regina v. Dodd*, [1957] O.R. 5, 7 D.L.R. (2d) 436, where it was held that the corresponding Ontario legislation was in conflict with and repugnant to the *Criminal Code*. The *Corry* case has, however, been followed in *R. v. Mankow* (1959), 28 W.W.R. 433, 30 C.R. 403, and in *R. v. Stephens* (1959-60), 30 W.W.R. 145, 32 C.R. 72, both Courts being of the opinion, as I am in the present case, that the two pieces of legislation differed both in legislative purpose and legal and practical effect, the provincial Act imposing a duty to serve bona fide provincial ends not otherwise secured and in no way conflicting with s. 221(2) of the *Criminal Code*.

I would dismiss the appeal. There should be no order as to costs.

CARTWRIGHT J. (LOCKE J. concurring) (dissenting):
. . . The sole question for decision is whether s. 55(1) of *The Highway Traffic Act*, R.S.M. 1954, c. 112, is *intra vires* of the legislature; it reads:

"55(1) Every person who drives a motor vehicle or a trolley bus on a highway without due care and attention or without reasonable consideration for other persons using the highway is guilty of an offence."

A penalty for the offence created by s. 55(1) is prescribed by s. 124.

The judgment of Williams C.J.Q.B. was delivered shortly after that of the Court of Appeal for Ontario in *Regina v. Yolles* in which that Court by a majority consisting of Porter C.J.O., Gibson and Lebel JJ.A. had reversed the answer given by McRuer C.J.H.C. to a question submitted in a stated case holding that s. 29(1) of *The Highway Traffic Act,* R.S.O. 1950, c. 167, as amended, was *ultra vires* of the legislature. Roach and Schroeder JJ.A., dissenting, were of opinion that the subsection was *ultra vires* and would have dismissed the appeal.

Williams C.J.Q.B., and Schultz and Tritschler JJ.A. who formed the majority in the Court of Appeal for Manitoba in brief reasons adopted and followed the reasoning of the majority of the Court of Appeal for Ontario in *Yolles'* case, except that Tritschler J.A., who wrote the reasons of the majority, noted his disagreement with the earlier judgment of the Court of Appeal for Ontario in *Regina v. Dodd*.

Adamson C.J.M. after examining a number of authorities reached the conclusion that the impugned sub-section was *ultra vires* of the legislature as being in pith and substance criminal law and further that it was *in pari materia* with and in conflict with the *Criminal Code;* he expressed his agreement with the reasoning of McRuer C.J.H.C. and of Roach and Schroeder JJ.A. in *Yolles'* case.

Section 29(1) of *The Highway Traffic Act* of Ontario which was dealt with in *Yolles'* case reads as follows:

"29(1) Every person is guilty of the offence of driving carelessly who drives a vehicle on a highway without due care and attention or without reasonable consideration for other persons using the highway and shall be liable to a penalty of not less than $10 and not more than $500 or to imprisonment for a term of not more than three months, and in addition his licence or permit may be suspended for a period of not more than one year."

I agree with Williams C.J.Q.B., and indeed it is common ground, that, so far as the question raised on this appeal is concerned, there is no difference in substance between s. 55(1) of the Manitoba Act and s. 29(1) of the Ontario Act; we cannot allow this appeal unless we are prepared to overrule the judgment of the Court of Appeal in *Yolles'* case.

I find the reasons of Adamson C.J.M. in the case at bar and those of Roach J.A. in *Yolles'* case so satisfactory and convincing that I would be content simply to adopt them, but in the view of the differences of opinion in the courts of Manitoba and of Ontario and in this Court and in deference to the full and able arguments addressed to us I propose to add some observations of my own.

I trust that this is not an over-simplification to say that the essense of the reasons of the majority in the Court of Appeal in *Yolles'* case may be summarized in the following propositions:

(i) Section 29(1) is legislation in relation to the regulation of highway traffic.

(ii) It has been decided by this Court, notably in *Provincial Secretary of P.E.I. v. Egan*, [1941] S.C.R. 396, [1941] 3 D.L.R. 305, and in *O'Brien v. Allen*, 30 S.C.R. 340, that the field of regulation of highway traffic within a province is wholly provincial.

(iii) That consequently s. 29(1) is *prima facie* within the powers of the legislature.

(iv) That s. 29(1) is not in conflict with any existing legislation of Parliament.

It will be convenient to examine first the second of these propositions. The expressions used in the reasons in *Egan's* case, wide though they are, do not assert an unlimited power in the legislatures to control all activities upon the highways. All that the case actually decided was that the legislature had power to require persons driving motor vehicles on highways in the province to obtain a provincial licence and to enact that such licence should be automatically suspended upon the holder being convicted of driving a motor vehicle while under the influence of intoxicating liquor or drugs, which was an offence under the *Criminal Code*. The reasons stress the circumstances that the impugned provincial legislation did not create an offence. . . .

The power of the legislature to make laws in relation to its roads must, of course, be derived from s. 92 of the British North America Act and cannot extend to the making of a law which is in pith and substance in relation to a matter coming within the classes of subjects enumerated in s. 91.

Turning now to the first of the propositions set out above it is necessary to consider what is the true nature and character of the impugned subsection. Is it a law in relation to the regulation of highway traffic, or is it in pith and substance a law in relation to "the criminal law" within the meaning of that phrase as used in head 27 of s. 91 of the British North America Act? . . .

In the reasons of my brother Judson, which I have had the advantage of reading, he refers with approval to passages in Glanville Williams on Criminal Law (1953) and in the 17th Edition of Kenny's Outlines of Criminal Law in which the distinction is drawn between "inadvertent negligence" and "advertent negligence". At page 82 of his work Glanville Williams says:

"Responsibility for some crimes may be incurred by the mere neglect to exercise due caution, where the mind is not actively but negatively or passively at fault. This is inadvertent negligence. Since advertent negligence has a special name (recklessness), it is convenient to use "negligence" generally to mean inadvertent negligence. If it is said that such-and-such a crime can be committed negligently, this means that the crime can be committed by inadvertent negligence; and the reader will understand that the crime can *a fortiori* be committed recklessly.

In the law of tort negligence has an objective meaning. It signifies a failure to reach the objective standard of the reasonable man, and does not involve any inquiry into the mentality of the defendant. The same rule prevails in criminal law, in those spheres where negligence is recognised at all."

In my opinion the effect of s. 55(1) is to enact that a person who in driving a vehicle on a highway fails to reach the objective standard of the reasonable man in regard to the use of due care and attention or in regard to having reasonable consideration for other persons using the highway is guilty of an offence and subject to punishment.

In determining whether such a provision falls within s. 91(27) rather than within any of the heads of s. 92 we are entitled to consider its apparent purpose and effect and in doing this we must take into account any general knowledge of which the Court would take judicial notice.

For some years the increasing frequency of accidents on highways resulting in death, personal injury and damage to property has been a matter of grave public concern, and efforts to reduce the number of such accidents have occupied the attention of Parliament and of the provincial legislatures.

By the combined effect of sections 191(1) and 221(1) of the *Criminal Code* Parliament has made it a crime to be negligent in the operation of a motor vehicle provided that, whether the negligence consists of omission or commission, the person charged shows wanton or reckless disregard for the lives or safety of other persons; it is not a necessary element of this crime that the negligence charged shall cause injury or damage. To use the terminology of Glanville Williams, Parliament has enacted that "advertent negligence" in the operation of a motor vehicle is a crime. No counsel has questioned the competency of Parliament to enact these sections; it could not be successfully questioned. The application of these sections is not limited to the operation of motor vehicles on highways but it is obvious that in the vast majority of cases in which a charge is laid thereunder it will arise out of a highway accident.

We may, I think, take judicial notice of the fact that while many highway accidents resulting in death or injury are caused by "advertent negligence", very many are caused by "inadvertent negligence". Should Parliament in its wisdom decide that to stem the rising tide of death and injury it was advisable to make inadvertent negligence in the operation of a motor vehicle a crime as well as advertent negligence in such operation it would, in my opinion, clearly be enacting criminal law within the meaning of head 27 of s. 91. I did not understand any counsel to suggest that Parliament lacked the power to enact as part of the *Criminal Code* a provision identical with s. 55(1) should it see fit to do so. I think it clear that Parliament has such power and that if it saw fit to enact the provision contained in s. 55(1) that provision would in no sense be legislation merely ancillary or necessarily incidental to the exercise of the powers conferred upon Parliament by s. 91(27); it would be an integral part of the criminal law.

In my opinion, while the types of negligence dealt with differ, the true nature and character of the legislation contained in s. 55(1) of the Manitoba Act does not differ in kind from that of the legislation contained in sections 191(1) and 221(1) of the *Criminal Code*. Each seeks to suppress in the public interest and with penal consequences negligence in the operation of vehicles, each is designed for the promotion of public safety, each seeks to prevent substantially the same public evil, each belongs to the subject of public wrongs rather than to that of civil rights, each makes negligence a crime although one deals with inadvertent negligence and the other with advertent negligence.

In my view the impugned sub-section differs generically from those provisions of *The Highway Traffic Act* prescribing detailed rules of conduct such as rates of speed, rules of the road, traffic signals, lights, equipment and so on; on this branch of the matter I have nothing to add to what has been said by Roach J.A.

If I am right in my conclusion that the provisions of the impugned sub-section if enacted by Parliament as part of the *Criminal Code* would clearly be a law in relation to the criminal law within the meaning of head 27 of s. 91, that would seem to be an end of the matter; the true nature and character of an enactment is to be discerned by a consideration of its meaning, purpose and effect, and does not depend upon whether it is enacted by Parliament or by a provincial legislature. The statement of Lord Watson in *Union Colliery Company of British Columbia v. Bryden,* [1899] A.C. 580, at p. 588, has been repeatedly followed:

"The abstinence of the Dominion Parliament from legislating to the full limit of its powers, could not have the effect of transferring to any provincial legislature the legislative power which had been assigned to the Dominion by s. 91 of the Act of 1867."

It may well be that a growing public danger makes it desirable that inadvertent negligence in driving a motor vehicle should be made a crime. I do not express any opinion on this question which is one of public policy to be decided by Parliament. I think it clear that Parliament alone has the constitutional authority to so enact.

In my opinion there is no room in this case for the view that s. 55(1) is *intra vires* because it operates in an otherwise unoccupied field, for the field which the impugned legislation seeks to enter is one reserved exclusively for Parliament by head 27 of s. 91. This is a field which the provincial legislature is forbidden to enter whether or not Parliament has occupied any part of it.

There are two further matters which I wish to mention.

In the penultimate paragraph of his reasons Tritschler J.A. expresses the view that it is now easier to declare s. 55(1) *intra vires* of the legislature than it would have been had the provision formerly contained in s. 285(6) of the old *Criminal Code* still been in force. That sub-section reads as follows:

"(6) Every one who drives a motor vehicle on a street, road, highway or other public place recklessly, or in a manner which is dangerous to the public, having regard to all the circumstances of the case, including the nature, condition, and use of the street, road, highway or place, and the amount of traffic which is actually at the time, or which might reasonably be expected to be, on such street, road, highway or place, shall be guilty of an offence. . . ."

The validity of this view depends on the "overlapping doctrine", which is accurately defined in Varcoe on The Distribution of Legislative Power in Canada, 1954, at p. 47, as follows:

"There can be a domain in which provincial and Dominion legislative powers may overlap, in which case, a statute enacted pursuant to either power will be *intra vires* if the field is clear, but if the field is not clear and the two statutes meet, the Dominion statute must prevail."

Assuming, contrary to the opinion that I have already expressed, that s. 55(1) has a provincial aspect and so would be valid until Parliament occupies the field in which it operates, it is necessary to consider whether Parliament has done so. In my opinion Parliament has fully occupied the field.

For the purpose of reducing the number of automobile accidents occurring on the highways throughout Canada, Parliament has decided to attach penal consequences to negligence in the course of a particular specified activity, i.e., the operation of a motor vehicle. The provisions of the *Criminal Code* now in force attach those consequences to advertent negligence in such operation; when s. 285(6) of the old Code was in force it was arguable that the words therein contained, "or in a manner which is dangerous to the public having regard to all the circumstances of the case" had the effect of attaching penal consequences to inadvertent negligence; be this as it may, it is clear that Parliament has the power to attach penal consequences to inadvertent negligence and to enact as a part of the *Criminal Code* the very provisions contained in s. 55(1).

In my opinion when Parliament has expressed in an Act its decision that a certain kind or degree of negligence in the operation of a motor vehicle shall be punishable as a crime against the state it follows that it has decided that no less culpable kind or degree of negligence in such operation shall be so punishable. By necessary implication the Act says not only what kinds or degrees of negligence shall be punishable but also what kinds or degrees shall not.

The matter may be tested in this way: suppose that Parliament in the new Code had enacted the provisions of s. 55(1) of *The Highway Traffic Act* as sub-section (2) of s. 221; in such circumstances the field which s. 55(1) seeks to enter would clearly be fully occupied by valid Dominion legislation; suppose then that a few years later Parliament repealed the said sub-section thereby indicating its view that the inadvertent negligence described in the repealed sub-section should cease to be punishable as an offence against the State; could it be said that upon such repeal a provincial legislature could enact the repealed sub-section as part of its *Highway Traffic Act*? In my opinion it could not, and it appears to me that the result of holding otherwise would be to defeat the intention of the framers of the *British North America Act* that power to legislate as to the criminal law should be committed exclusively to Parliament. It is not within the power of the provincial legislature to remedy what it regards as defects or to supply what it regards as unwise omissions in the criminal law as enacted by Parliament.

It appears to me to be self-evident that the exclusive legislative authority in relation to the criminal law given to Parliament by s. 91(27) must include the power to decide what conduct shall not be punishable as a crime against the state as well as to decide what conduct shall be so punishable, and this may be the reason that there is little authority precisely on the point; it has however been touched on by the Judicial Committee in the case of *Toronto Railway v. The King*, [1917] A.C. 630. . . .

The other matter to which I wish to refer is a submission in the argument of counsel for the Attorney General of Canada to the effect that had s. 55(1) read as follows:

"(1) Every person who drives a motor vehicle or a trolley bus on a highway shall do so with due care and attention and with reasonable consideration for other persons using the highway.

(2) Every person who fails to comply with subsection (1) is guilty of an offence."

there would be no question of its validity. As to this argument it is my view that the validity of an impugned enactment depends not on the precise verbal form in which it is expressed but on the meaning of the words the legislature has used and the purpose and effect of the enactment. The question is one of substance. Had the impugned subsection been enacted in the form suggested I would have been equally of opinion that it was invalid. Were it otherwise a law in relation to the crime of theft could, by careful draftsmanship, be made to read as a law dealing with the civil right to the possession of personal property and a law in relation to highway robbery could be framed as a regulation of highway traffic.

For the above reasons and for those given by Adamson C.J.M. in the case at bar and by Roach J.A. in *Yolles'* case with which I have already expressed my full agreement I am of opinion that s. 55(1) of *The Highway Traffic Act*, R.S.M. 1954, c. 112, is *ultra vires* of the Legislature of the Province of Manitoba. . . .

Appeal dismissed.

[RITCHIE J. delivered a short judgment concurring with Judson J.]

Following the foregoing judgment, Parliament by 1960-61 (Can.), c. 43, s. 3, enacted s. 221(4) of the *Criminal Code*, restoring an offence which had been included in the predecessor *Code* under s. 285(6) but which had been omitted on the enactment of the present Code. It provides that "every one who drives a motor vehicle on a street, road, highway or other public place in a manner that is dangerous to the public, having regard to all the circumstances, including the nature, condition and use of such place and the amount of traffic that at the time is or might reasonably be expected to be on such place" is guilty of an offence. The Supreme Court of Canada held in *Mann v. The Queen* (1966), 47 C.R. 400, [1966] 2 Can. C.C. 273, 56 D.L.R. (2d) 1, that this provision did not render inoperative such a provincial careless driving statute as was considered in *O'Grady v. Sparling*. In the view of the Court, Parliament's "dangerous driving" prohibition did not make inadvertent negligence a crime (to use the language of *O'Grady v. Sparling*) because to come within s. 221(4) there had to be an extra element beyond mere inadvertence; a knowledge or wilful disregard of the probable consequences or a deliberate failure to take reasonable precautions. Thin as the line was between criminally negligent driving under *Criminal Code*, ss. 191 and 221(1) and careless driving under provincial highway traffic legislation, it must be barely perceptible when the Court can find a distinction for purposes of constitutional paramountcy between dangerous driving (which must be something less than criminal negligence in the operation of a motor vehicle) and careless driving.

In *Sabourin v. Bedard*, [1949] 2 D.L.R. 446 and *Rex v. Robison*, [1950] 1 W.W.R. 1134, 97 Can. C.C. 160, 10 C.R. 75, provincial legislation making it an offence to drive in a manner which would endanger life or property was held to be inoperative as against the federal dangerous driving prohibition then in force. This could be said to be an *a fortiori* case for paramountcy unless the applicable test, carrying through the logic of *O'Grady v. Sparling,* as discussed below, is that the same conduct could be concurrently validly prohibited by both province and Dominion. Indeed, this is a necessary conclusion in the field of safe driving legislation from *Rex v. Mantle*, [1951] 4 D.L.R. 306, 2 W.W.R. (N.S.) 388, 100 Can. C.C. 60, 12 C.R. 374. Moreover, the matter is explicit in the test propounded by Martland J. in his concurring judgment in *Smith v. The Queen, infra* (in which Judson J. joined) as follows: "The fact that both [federal and provincial] provisions prohibit certain acts with penal consequences does not constitute a conflict. It may happen that some acts might be punishable under both provisions and in this sense that these provisions overlap. However, even in such cases there is no conflict in the sense that compliance with one law involves breach of the other. It would appear, therefore, that they can operate concurrently." This standard was expressly followed by Spence J. in the *Mann* case, *supra*. It does no more than make explicit the test propounded by Judson J. in *O'Grady v. Sparling* in the following terms: Can the competing federal and provincial enactments live together and operate concurrently? This makes possible plural penal liability for the same act, and it is questionable whether it is good policy in a federal system to invite it. This may happen, of course, by legislative direction in a unitary state, (see, for example, *The King v. Hogan*, [1960] 3 All E.R. 149), but that does not make it any more palatable. Section 11 of the *Canadian Criminal Code* purports to cure such a consequence at the federal level by prohibiting punishment of an act or omission under more than one statute, unless an intention to compound liability appears.

At the time *O'Grady v. Sparling* was decided, the Supreme Court also decided: (1) *Stephens v. The Queen*, [1960] S.C.R. 823, 25 D.L.R. (2d) 296, 33 W.W.R. 379 which sustained another common provision in provincial highway traffic legislation, the punishment of failure to remain at or immediately return to the scene of an accident; and this despite a valid federal prohibition punishing failure to stop at the scene of an accident with intent to escape civil or criminal liability; and (2) *Smith v. The Queen*, [1960] S.C.R. 776, 25 D.L.R. (2d) 225 which supported as part of a general provincial scheme of regulation of the securities business, a penal prohibition of the furnishing of false information in a prospectus; and this notwithstanding a federal criminal provision punishing the making or publishing of false statements in a prospectus with intent to induce persons to become shareholders of, or advance money to or enter into any security for the benefit of a company. There were dissents in both cases.

The influence of *O'Grady v. Sparling* is seen in *Regina v. Skagstead*, [1964] 2 Can. C.C. 29, 43 C.R. 376, 43 D.L.R. (2d) 315, where the Manitoba Court of Appeal affirmed a conviction under a provincial liquor control law making it an offence for any person to be disorderly (not defined) in licensed premises. It was held that the provincial enactment did not cover the same ground as ss. 158 to 164 of the *Criminal Code* and, particularly, that s. 160 of the *Criminal Code* punishing the causing of a disturbance was a different offence. The provincial Act also prescribed suspension of licence if disorderly conduct was permitted, but this more obviously valid provision was not in issue.

[Cr. Code, s. 197 provides, *inter alia*, that everyone is under a legal duty as a parent, foster parent, guardian or head of a family, to provide necessaries of life for a child under the age of sixteen years, and it is an offence to fail without lawful excuse to perform that duty if (1) the child is in destitute or necessitous circumstances or (2) the failure endangers the life of the child or causes or is likely to cause its health to be endangered permanently. The Children's Maintenance Act, R.S.O. 1950, c. 52 makes it an offence under s. 2 for a parent, without lawful excuse, to fail to provide for the maintenance and education of a child under age sixteen according to his ability and the need of the child. Is the provincial enactment valid? See *Re Gutsch*, [1959] O.W.N. 273, 19 D.L.R. (2d) 572. See also *R. v. Chief* (1963), 42 D.L.R. (2d) 712, aff'd. 44 D.L.R. (2d) 108.]

REFERENCE RE SECTION 92(4) OF THE VEHICLES ACT, 1957 (SASK.), C. 93.

In the Supreme Court of Canada. [1958] S.C.R. 608, 15 D.L.R. (2d) 255, 121 Can. C.C. 321.

Appeal and cross-appeal from a judgment of the Saskatchewan Court of Appeal, 12 D.L.R. (2d) 470, 24 W.W.R. (N.S.) 385, 120 Can. C.C. 129, 27 C.R. 369, holding valid s. 92(4) of the Vehicles Act (Sask.) but declaring that a breath test taken in pursuance of s. 92(4) is not admissible, in view of Cr. Code, s. 224(4), in criminal proceedings under Cr. Code, ss. 222 or 223.

RAND J.: The Lieutenant-Governor in Council of Saskatchewan has submitted to the Court of Appeal for that Province the following questions:

"(1) Is subsection (4) of section 92 of The Vehicles Act, 1957, Statutes of Saskatchewan, 1957, Chapter 93, *ultra vires* of the Legislative Assembly of Saskatchewan in whole or in part?

"(2) In any proceedings in Saskatchewan under section 222 or 223 of the Criminal Code of Canada is the result of a chemical analysis of a sample of breath of a person admissible in evidence on the issue whether that person was intoxicated or whether his ability to drive was impaired by alcohol

"(a) where the provisions of subsection (4) of section 92 of The Vehicles Act, 1957 were brought to the attention of the accused before he gave a sample of his breath for chemical analysis:

"(b) where the provisions of subsection (4) of section 92 of The Vehicles Act, 1957 were not brought to the attention of the accused before he gave a sample of breath for chemical analysis."

Section 92(4)(d) of the *Vehicles Act*, 1957 (Sask.), c. 93, the controlling clause, provides:

"(4) The board may suspend an operator's, chauffeur's, learner's or instructor's licence for a period not exceeding ninety days if, after an examination of the circumstances, it is satisfied:

"(d) that, when suspected of driving, or of having driven, a motor vehicle while under the influence of intoxicating liquor, he refused to comply with the request of a police officer or police constable that he submit to the taking of a specimen of his breath; and if, after a hearing of which reasonable notice has been given to the holder of the licence and after a further examination of the circumstances, the board is again so satisfied it may suspend the licence for a stated period or revoke it."

By ss. 222, 223 and 224 of the *Criminal Code*:

"222. Every one who, while intoxicated or under the influence of a narcotic drug, drives a motor vehicle or has the care or control of a motor vehicle, whether it is in motion or not, is guilty of

"(a) an indictable offence and is liable . . .

"(b) an offence punishable on summary conviction and is liable. . . .

"223. Every one who, while his ability to drive a motor vehicle is impaired by alcohol or a drug, drives a motor vehicle or has the care or control of a motor vehicle, whether it is in motion or not, is guilty of an indictable offence or an offence punishable on summary conviction and is liable. . . .

"224(3) In any proceedings under section 222 or 223, the result of a chemical analysis of a sample of the blood, urine, breath or other bodily substance of a person may be admitted in evidence on the issue whether that person was intoxicated or under the influence of a narcotic drug or whether his ability to drive was impaired by alcohol or a drug, notwithstanding that he was not, before he gave the sample, warned that he need not give the sample or that the results of the analysis of the sample might be used in evidence.

"(4) No person is required to give a sample of blood, urine, breath or other bodily substance for chemical analysis for the purposes of this section and evidence that a person refused to give such sample or that such a sample was not taken is not admissible nor shall such a refusal or the fact that a sample was not taken be the subject of comment by any person in the proceedings."

I take the rule of immunity from incriminating evidence to be confined to that which bears a testimonial character: *A.-G. Que. v. Begin*, 112 Can. C.C. 209, 21 C.R. 217, [1955] 5 D.L.R. 394, S.C.R. 593; this judgment, in my opinion, decides that matters of fact elicited from an individual not of that character do not come within it. Whether the use, therefore, under the Provincial statute here, of a refusal to give a sample of blood or other substance as evidence for Provincial purposes, not conflicting with that protective rule of criminal law, is within the competence of the Province, and its admissibility in a prosecution under s. 222 or s. 223 of the *Code,* depend upon whether or not it is within the prohibition of s. 224.

That section declares that "no person is required to give a sample" of blood or other substance, and that the fact of a refusal to give it, or that it was not taken, is inadmissible, with comment on either fact likewise forbidden; permitting the sample to be taken is to be voluntary. The controlling word is "required"; what modes of coercion are by that word contemplated which will clash with the immunity given? As the section deals with matter analogous to self-incrimination we should look to the nature of the compulsion against which that rule is a shield, and that by which disclosure is enforced where the privilege is taken away. By s. 5(1) of the *Canada Evidence Act,* R.S.C. 1952, c. 307, a witness is not excused from answering on the ground that the answer may incriminate him or subject him to civil liability; if he refuses, by what means is the obligation to answer enforced? The word "required" is to be taken as envisaging similar means, an effective compulsion such as that, for example, exerted against a recalcitrant witness, commitment as for contempt. Is the effect of a refusal to give a sample, that it may be used as evidence by the Province in deciding upon the suspension or cancellation of an automobile licence, of that nature?

The answer to this must take into account a consideration of the impact on a constantly intensifying traffic of persons and vehicles on the highways, of their use by automobiles, and its ghastly results from mere carelessness in operation alone. When to the lethal dangers inherent and multiplying under the best of ordinary circumstances we add the most potent and destructive factor, the intoxicated driver, a stage has been reached where the public interest rises to paramount importance.

The analogous rule against self-incrimination is one for the protection not of the guilty, but of the innocent; and the grounds underlying it are the dangers of compulsion not only in bringing about incrimination to the innocent but, as Professor Wigmore points out, in its inevitable abuse and the concomitant moral deterioration in methods of obtaining evidence and in the general administration of justice in criminal matters.

Under s. 92(4)(d) the danger to the innocent is virtually nonexistent; only a failure either in the analysis itself or in the honesty of the technician can be said to present a hazard; and when the only result of either an incriminating analysis, or the initial refusal to give a sample, is the use of the one or other fact as relevant to a decision on a licence, the imperious concern of the public overbears, as factors of error, those speculative possibilities. This result of a minor and only an indirect inference from a refusal to give is in extreme contrast with the commitment of a witness until his contempt is purged, drastic enough but not to be compared with the ancient practice of torture.

The consequence of refusal under s. 92(4)(d) is not, in my opinion, within the contemplation of s. 224; the disclosure, if induced, presents only a most unlikely possibility of prejudice to an innocent person, and even should he stand on his refusal arbitrarily in an exaggerated assertion of personal dignity, the worst that can happen is to be deprived of what, in his case, may be a questionable privilege.

From this it follows that the analysis of a sample of breath obtained under s. 92(4)(d) is voluntarily furnished and is admissible as evidence in prosecutions under s. 222 or s. 223 by s. 224 or any other sections of the *Code*. There is thus no evidentiary inconsistency between different offences as was suggested on the argument.

I would, therefore, answer the questions as follows:

Q. (1). Clause (d) of s-s. (4) of s. 92 is not *ultra vires* of the Legislative Assembly of Saskatchewan in whole or in part;

Q. (2) The result of a chemical analysis of the breath of a person taken under s. 92(4)(d) is admissible in prosecutions under ss. 222 and 223 of the *Criminal Code*.

CARTWRIGHT J. (dissenting in part): . . . I have reached the conclusion that the answers to the questions should be as follows:

To Q. 1: Clause (*d*) of subsection (4) of section 92 of the *Vehicles Act*, 1957 (Sask.), c. 93 is *ultra vires* of the Legislative Assembly of Saskatchewan.

To Q. 2: (a) Yes; (b) : Yes.

In my opinion, s. 224(3) and s. 224(4) of the *Criminal Code* are *intra vires* of Parliament as being legislation, under s. 91(27) of the *B.N.A. Act*, in relation to "Criminal Law . . . including the Procedure in Criminal Matters" and the subject-matter of these subsections is not merely ancillary, or necessarily incidental, to "Criminal Law" and the "Procedure in Criminal Matters" but is an integral part thereof.

For some time it has been criminal for a person to drive a motor vehicle while intoxicated or while his ability to drive is impaired by alcohol. These crimes are now set out in ss. 222 and 223 of the *Criminal Code.*

Of recent years it has been generally accepted that the result of a chemical analysis of a sample of the breath of a person is of some assistance in determining whether he was intoxicated or whether his ability to drive a motor vehicle was impaired by alcohol. There have been differences of judicial opinion as to the circumstances under which evidence of the result of a chemical analysis of the sort mentioned could be legally admitted on the trial of a criminal charge; some of the cases in which these differences arose are referred to in *A.-G. Que. v. Begin,* 112 Can. C.C. 209, 21 C.R. 217, [1955] 5 D.L.R. 394, S.C.R. 593.

In my opinion, it is unnecessary, for the decision of the first question, to consider whether in enacting s. 224(3) and (4), or their predecessors s. 285(4*d*) and (4*e*), Parliament made any change in the pre-existing law. Those subsections now declare the law, and whether or not what they enact was previously the common law, it is now the statute law of Canada.

From their terms it is obvious that s. 224(3) applies in any proceedings under s. 222 or s. 223 and that s. 224(4) comes into play when a person is suspected of having committed an offence against either of those sections. Section 224(4), then, deals with a person who is suspected of having committed an offence against s. 222 or s. 223. It is clear from the wording of the subsection that Parliament contemplates that a person in that situation may be asked to give a sample of his breath but is left free to consent or to refuse; Parliament has seen fit to declare not only that he is not required to give the sample but also that the fact of his refusal shall not be given in evidence or made the subject of comment in proceedings under the sections mentioned. It appears to me that s. 92(4) of the *Vehicles Act* of Saskatchewan deals with a person in the same situation as that dealt with by s. 224(4) of the *Criminal Code,* and that its direct effect is to require such person to give a sample of his breath under pain of being liable to be temporarily or permanently prevented from driving a motor vehicle in the Province of Saskatchewan, a penalty which in the case of some individuals might amount to a deprivation of livelihood.

For the purposes of this appeal I am prepared to assume, although

I regard it as doubtful, that s. 92(4)(d) of the *Vehicles Act* would be *intra vires* of the Legislature if, to use the words of Lord Tomlin in *A.-G. Can. v. A.-G. B.C.*, [1930] 1 D.L.R. 194 at p. 197 (*sub nom. Re Fisheries Act*, 1914), A.C. 111 at p. 118, the field was clear; but its direct effect appears to me to be to nullify throughout the Province of Saskatchewan the provision in s. 224(4) of the *Cr. Code* that a person in the circumstances mentioned above is not required to give a sample of breath. Whatever be the precise meaning given to the word "required", unless it is to be restricted to "compelled by irresistible physical force", I am of opinion that a statute declaring that a person who refuses to do an act shall be liable to suffer a serious and permanent economic disadvantage does "require" the doing of the act. With deference to those who hold a contrary view, it appears to me to be playing with words to say that a person who is made liable to a penalty (whether economic, pecuniary, corporal or, I suppose, capital) if he fails to do an act is not required to do the act because he is free to choose to suffer the penalty instead.

It was suggested in argument that the words "for the purposes of this section" contained in s. 224(4) of the *Cr. Code* confine the effect of that subsection so as to leave unoccupied a field of legislation which it is competent for the Province to enter. I am unable to see how this argument assists the case of those who seek to support the Provincial legislation, as it seems clear that s. 92(4)(d) of the *Vehicles Act* is directed solely to a person requested by a police officer to allow the taking of a specimen of his breath for the purposes of s. 224, *i.e.* to enable a chemical analysis to be made the result of which may be admitted in evidence pursuant to s. 224(3).

For these reasons I am of opinion that s. 92(4)(d) of the *Vehicles Act* of Saskatchewan invades a field occupied by valid legislation of Parliament, is in direct conflict with that legislation, and cannot stand.

In view of the answer which I think should be given to Q. 1, Q. 2 appears to become comparatively unimportant, but, in my opinion, it falls within the reasoning of this Court in *A.-G. Que. v. Begin* (*supra*). At common law the evidence, being that of the existence of an objective fact, would, if relevant, have been admitted, although illegally obtained; and I am unable to construe the wording of s. 224(4) of the *Cr. Code* as showing an intention to change the law in this regard. Clear and unambiguous words would, I think, be necessary to effect such an alteration in the law of evidence.

To prevail upon a person, suspected of an offence against s. 222 or s. 223 of the *Code*, to give a sample of breath by threatening him with loss of his permit to drive should he refuse would, in my opinion, be contrary to s. 224(4) and an illegal act; but that illegality would not render inadmissible the evidence of the result of a chemical analysis of the sample so obtained. . . .

FAUTEUX J.: . . . The primary objection against validity being that of repugnancy with the *Cr. Code*, it is necessary to consider and construe the relevant provisions of both s. 224 of the *Code* and s. 92 of the *Vehicles Act*, 1957.

The *Criminal Code*: The provisions of s. 224 are admittedly procedural in nature and purposely ancillary to those of ss. 222 and 223 which create respectively the offence of driving while intoxicated and the offence of driving while ability to drive is impaired by alcohol. . . .

Prior to the enactment of the predecessors to s. 224(3) and (4), i.e., s. 285(4d) and (4e), a minority in the judiciary had expressed certain doubts as to the evidentiary value and relevancy of the results of a chemical analysis of a bodily substance or held the view that a warning, of the nature of the one governing the admissibility of confessions, was a condition precedent to the admissibility of such evidence on the issue of intoxication or impaired ability under what is now s. 222 and s. 223. In enacting what is now in s. 224(3), Parliament disposed of this conflict in judicial opinion but did not, as indicated in the reasons for judgment of this Court in *A.-G. Que. v. Begin*, 112 Can. C.C. 209, 21 C.R. 217, [1955] 5 D.L.R. 394, S.C.R. 593, make any innovation as to the law but simply stated what it actually was. Indeed the confession rule requiring a warning, exclusively concerns *self-incriminating statements* of the accused, and aims at the exclusion of those which are untrue. As its subject-matter or purpose, the confession rule does not embrace the *incriminating conditions* of the body, features, fingerprints, clothing or behaviour of the accused, that persons, other than himself, observe or detect and ultimately report as witnesses in judicial proceedings.

Having thus settled the matter by reiterating by the provisions of s. 224(3) that there was no duty to warn a person that he need not give a sample and that the result of its analysis might be used in evidence, Parliament, by those in s. 224(4), added that "No person is required to give a sample of blood . . . . for chemical analysis for the purposes of this section" and that the refusal to do so or the non taking of a sample could not be proved or commented upon in proceedings under s. 222 or s. 223.

The first of these two additions does not derogate from the general law, according to which no one, failing a statutory requirement to the contrary, is obliged, in law, to give a sample. In saying what it said, Parliament, in my view, simply intended to forestall, *ex abundante cautela,* any suggestion that the creation of a legal obligation was intended in the provisions now found in s. 224. By these amendments to the *Code,* the choice is not taken away from the suspected person. There is nothing, either express or implied in this part or in the whole of the section, indicating that Parliament was at all concerned with the nature of the reasons which, in any particular case, might in fact have a decisive influence on the mind of a suspected person, as is the case under the confession rule. Nor can I find, in this provision, the manifestation of any intent of Parliament to trench—as it possibly might have done as a step genuinely taken in relation to criminal procedure—upon the right of a Provincial Legislature to create for genuine Provincial purposes, a legal obligation to give a sample. Effect must be given to the words "for the purposes of this section" which, qualifying the range of this part of the provision, are indicative of the true intent of Parliament.

The prohibitive enactment, in the latter part of s. 224(4), derogates from the prior law, in that it bars, in any proceedings under s. 222 or s. 223, evidence or comment as to the fact of the refusal to give a sample or as to the fact that a sample was not taken. Thus, in these proceedings, the possibility of any inference whatever being drawn from evidence or comment with respect to either one of these two facts, is definitely ruled out; and to this extent goes the derogation.

Counsel for the Attorney-General of Canada construed s. 224(4) as having the consequential effect of excluding from the evidence the result of a test taken without a consent of the suspected person. This construction is predicated on the presence, in the enactment, of the declaration that no one is required to give a sample and of the prohibition as to evidence and comment. I am unable to agree with this submission. What, in my view, is the purpose of the declaration has already been indicated. The prohibition itself is absolute. While it might be said to confer an immunity against incriminating inferences, it rules out definitely any inference—likely or not to affect the case for the prosecution or the case for the defence—which might be drawn, not only from the refusal to give a sample, but also from the fact that none was actually taken. Moreover, the submission implies the assumption, which can hardly have been that of Parliament, that in all cases where a sample would be taken notwithstanding refusal, the result of its analysis would be incriminating; fear of incrimination is assumed to be the only possible reason for either a refusal to give a sample or the fact that none was actually taken. The acceptance of this submission would lead to the exclusion from the evidence, not only of incriminating but also of such exculpating evidence as might result from the actual taking of a test notwithstanding refusal. When enacting the provisions of s. 224(4), Parliament is presumed to have had in mind (1) the rule of evidence according to which evidence, obtained unlawfully or under compulsion of law, is not for that reason alone, inadmissible: *Kuruma v. The Queen*, [1955] A.C. 197; *A.-G. Que. v. Begin (supra); Walker v. The King,* 76 Can. C.C. 305, [1939] 2 D.L.R. 353, S.C.R. 214; and (2) the rule of construction according to which a Legislature will not be presumed to have departed from the general system of the law without expressing an intention to do so with irresistible clearness. The language, here used by Parliament, is not apt to indicate an intent such as the one contended for . . . .

As a matter of construction, it is suggested that the impugned enactment [s. 92(4)] compels, in law or at least in effect, one to do what, in a similar situation, s. 224(4) of the *Cr. Code* says he is not legally obliged to and, for this reason, the former provision is held *ultra vires,* as repugnant to the latter.

With deference, I am unable to agree with this submission. In terms, the Provincial enactment creates no legal obligation. It leaves to the licence holder the faculty to comply with or ignore what is a request and not a requirement; and no one suggested that non-compliance with the request amounts to a violation of the enactment. Indeed and under the provision, the suspected licence holder has the same right and is in a position similar to that of a person who, being suspected of physical or mental affliction likely to prevent the exercise of reasonable care and ordinary control over a motor vehicle, is requested, as a condition precedent to the issuance or maintenance of a driving licence, to submit to an examination. In either case, to deprive the suspected person of a licence, because of non-compliance, might be adopting a measure prejudicial to that person but nonetheless necessary to enable the Provincial authorities to adequately discharge their duty to protect the users of the road. In either case, the difficulty and the consequences of the choice of the suspected person do not affect the nature of his rights and are, *per se*, ineffective to create a legal obligation.

Even if it can be held, as is suggested, that in effect, if not in terms, the impugned provision does create statutory compulsion, on a considered view of the true character of s. 224(4) of the *Cr. Code*, the former provision does not clash with the latter. I have already indicated that in stating "no person is required to give a sample. . . for chemical analysis *for the purposes of this section*", Parliament, in my view, simply meant to silence any suggestion that the amendments then made carried an obligation to give a sample for the purposes of these criminal proceedings. In the statement itself, there is an implication that, for the purposes other than criminal proceedings, one might be required to give a sample. This implication, consonant with the general law, negatives any intent of Parliament to invade the field in such a way as to trench upon Provincial jurisdiction to create such an obligation for genuine Provincial purposes. And it is significant that, as above indicated, Parliament did not see fit, on the occasion, to depart, as it might have done, from the general rule of evidence according to which the result of a test authorized for genuine Provincial purposes is admissible in evidence in criminal proceedings. The situation dealt with in s. 224(4) is not the one arising when a sample has been given or taken but when it has not. I cannot therefore see the alleged conflict and hold that the impugned enactment will operate to prevent the attainment of the object of s. 224 of the *Cr. Code* according to its true intent, meaning and spirit.

I am also in respectful agreement with the view that the impugned legislation is not, as contended, legislation in relation to criminal law but in relation to the administration and control of highways in the Province for the protection of the travelling public and of the automobile insurance fund created under the Provincial legislation. . . . *Provincial Secretary of P.E.I. v. Egan,* 76 Can. C.C. 227, [1941] 3 D.L.R. 305, S.C.R. 396. What, in the latter decision, was said, particularly by Sir Lyman P. Duff C.J.C. in affirmation of validity, finds its application in this case.

I would, therefore, answer the questions as follows:

Q. (1). Clause (*d*) of s-s. (4) of s. 92 is not *ultra vires* of the Legislative Assembly of Saskatchewan in whole or in part:

Q. (2) The result of a chemical analysis of the breath of a person taken under s. 92(4) (d) is admissible in prosecutions under ss. 222 and 223 of the *Criminal Code.*

Appeal allowed; cross-appeal dismissed.

[Kerwin C.J.C. did not take part in the judgment owing to illness. Taschereau, Abbott and Judson JJ. concurred with Fauteux J. Locke J. concurred with Cartwright and Martland JJ., the latter of whom delivered a separate judgment in which he agreed with the conclusions of Cartwright J. See *Note,* (1958) 36 Can. Bar Rev. 265. For an application of this decision to Alberta legislation making it an offence to refuse to submit to a breath test on penalty of suspension of one's driving licence, see *Regina v. Tenta* (1968), 67 D.L.R. (2d) 536; the legislation was sustained in a majority decision. See also *Regina v. Clements* (1967), 63 D.L.R. (2d) 513.

Because of the truncated federal trade and commerce power, the important paramountcy issues in Canada have arisen in respect of competing penal legislation and not, as in the United States, between federal and state regulatory measures. However, there are other areas in which in Canada paramountcy questions have had to be determined, and illustrations follow.

In *In re Bozanich, A. H. Boulton Co. Ltd. v. Trusts & Guarantee Co. Ltd.,* [1942] S.C.R. 130, [1942] 2 D.L.R. 145, Duff, C.J.C. held that the preference provisions of provincial voluntary assignments legislation were superseded by the preference sections of the federal bankruptcy statute; see also *Nash v. Guelph Engineering Co.* (1964), 48 W.W.R. 420. In *In re Christian* (1957), 36 C.B.R. 131 (Ont.), Smily J. held that the distribution provisions of s. 42 of the Bankruptcy Act, R.S.C. 1952, c. 14, superseded those under the Creditors Relief Act, R.S.O. 1950, c. 78 in respect of money in the hands of a Sheriff resulting from executions against a bankrupt debtor.

Section 50(6) of the Bankruptcy Act, R.S.C. 1970, c. B-3 reads as follows:

"The provisions of this Act shall not be deemed to abrogate or supersede the substantive provisions of any other law or statute relating to property and civil rights that are not in conflict with this Act, and the trustee is entitled to avail himself of all rights and remedies provided by such law or statute as supplementary to and in addition to the rights and remedies provided by this Act."

What effect does this provision have on the operation of the paramountcy doctrine? Does it state merely a rule of construction or is it open to Parliament to preclude the application of the paramountcy principle by a legislative assertion?

In *John M. M. Troup Ltd. et al. v. Royal Bank of Canada,* [1962] S.C.R. 487, 34 D.L.R. (2d) 556, the respondent bank (which succeeded on another ground) disputed the validity of s. 3 of The Mechanics' Lien Act, R.S.O. 1950, c. 227, am. 1952, c. 54, s. 1, which creates a trust in respect of, *inter alia,* holdback money owing under a building contract, and under which the bank was alleged to be a participant in a breach of trust by applying the proceeds of a cheque from the owner to the builder on the latter's overdraft. The bank relied on the federal banking and bankruptcy powers and on federal legislation in relation thereto. The Supreme Court rejected the contention, holding that the provincial measure was valid, that there was no conflict with banking legislation but only another instance of the bank having to face a trust situation, and no conflict with bankruptcy legislation even though the trust would affect the amount of property divisible among creditors.

Is the field occupied where federal legislation prohibits the sale or possession for sale of a drug so as to preclude provincial legislation prohibiting its mere possession? See the contrasting views in *Regina v. Snyder and Fletcher* (1967), 61 W.W.R. 112, 576 and *Regina v. Simpson, Mack and Lewis* (1968), 1.D.L.R. (3d) 597, 66 W.W.R. 621.

In *McKay v. The Queen*, [1965] S.C.R. 798, 53 D.L.R. (2d) 532, Cartwright J., speaking for the majority of the Court in a case involving (1) the construction of a zoning by-law prohibiting signs on private property and (2) the applicability of the by-law to federal election signs, said that although it was not necessary to come to a definite conclusion on the matter, he was inclined to agree that Parliament had occupied the field in respect of signs for federal elections by enacting s. 71 of the Canada Elections Act, 1960 (Can.), c. 39.

Prior to confederation with Canada in 1949, Newfoundland had as part of its law a "drunk driving" statute. After Confederation and at a time when the federal Criminal Code (which included "drunk driving" provisions) had not yet been brought into force in Newfoundland, the latter purported to amend its "drunk driving" legislation. Could it constitutionally do so? *See Saunders v. Hollett*, [1950] 4 D.L.R. 260, 97 Can. C.C. 276, 25 M.P.R. 85.

Pre-confederation legislation of the "provinces" was subject, after confederation, to change or repeal by the competent legislature, Dominion or provincial, as the case might be: see B.N.A. Act, s. 129; *Dobie v. Temporalities Board* (1881), 7 App. Cas. 136. Where pre-confederation legislation includes provisions which under the B.N.A. Act (after confederation) could only have been enacted in part by the province and in part by the Dominion, it is wrong to say that after confederation the legislation may not be altered by the Dominion or the province in those respects in which it falls within their respective legislative powers: see *Re Bowater's Newfoundland Pulp & Paper Mills Ltd.*, [1950] S.C.R. 608, [1950] 4 D.L.R. 65.]

4. Extrinsic Aids to Interpretation

Determining Meaning of B.N.A. Act

Constitutional cases are unique illustrations of the need for some rationalization of the use and admissibility of extrinsic aids in interpretation. While on one view a constitutional issue raises two separate problems of interpretation—first, the object or purpose, the "constitutional value", or the pith and substance of the impugned statute; and secondly, the scope or content of the heads of power in the B.N.A. Act—yet on another view, the second problem is inevitably involved in any consideration of the first.

A collection of instances in which there has been resort to extrinsic materials will be found in *MacDonald*, Constitutional Interpretation and Extrinsic Evidence, (1939) 17 Can. Bar Rev. 77; there is no attempt in this article to articulate any theory or principle upon which the use of such materials depended.

Interpretation of the B.N.A. Act, whether regarded as a constitution or as a statute, is not inhibited by any rules of evidence which govern proof of disputed issues of fact. The traditional attitude has been that the matter is a question for the Court on which the admissible materials are governed by the rules of statutory interpretation. Is this sufficient or desirable in the case of the B.N.A. Act? *Cf. J. ten Broek*, Admissibility and Use by the United States

Supreme Court of Extrinsic Aids in Constitutional Construction, (1938) 26 Calif. L. Rev. 287, 437, 664; (1939) 27 Calif. L. Rev. 157 and 399; and note the following (26 Calif. L. Rev. at p. 289):

"More serious in its consequences has been the almost universal failure to distinguish between the problem involved in statutory construction and that involved in constitutional construction. Statutes are usually specific efforts to accomplish individual or highly related ends. As such, the conditions surrounding their origin and the intent of the legislature in passing them are matters possessing an informative value. They are the instruments of relatively small bodies composed of members presumably capable of understanding and using comparatively exact and technical language. Secondly, aside from the fact that statutes aim to meet temporary and changing conditions and the fact that they are generally judicially construed before these conditions have passed away, there is the extremely important circumstance that legislative bodies meet in frequent session and hence may change the words used if their actual intention is not effectuated. But not so constitutions! They are vastly more general, and are intended to be relatively permanent. As a result of these two factors, the judicial function of moulding constitutions by construction is proportionately greater than in the case of statutes, and the court's freedom of decision is less restricted. Moreover, constitutions are framed and adopted by different bodies, and if the intent of those who gave the instrument force is to be sought, the matter of numbers alone seems preclusive, and the meaning of language must be taken from its most common, untechnical, and uniform use. Finally, if the original intent is not carried out by the courts, there is not the ready opportunity to revise and restate which exists in the case of statutes."

In *In re Prohibitory Liquor Laws* (1894), 24 S.C.R. 170, Sedgewick J., speaking of the B.N.A. Act, said (at p. 231): ". . . it must be viewed from a Canadian standpoint. Although an Imperial Act, to interpret it correctly reference may be had to the phraseology and nomenclature of pre-confederation Canadian legislation and jurisprudence, as well as to the history of the union movement and to the condition, sentiment and surroundings of the Canadian people at the time. In the British North America Act it was in a technical sense only that the Imperial Parliament spoke; it was there that in a real and substantial sense the Canadian people spoke, and it is to their language, as they understood it, that effect must be given." This call for resort to contemporary references on a Canadian level went largely unheeded; and, in any event, it was understandable not only that Canadian references might provide no answer but that the longer the lapse of time from Confederation the less useful contemporary references would be. However, Sedgewick J.'s remarks must not be construed as calling for consideration of extrinsic materials contemporary only with Confederation. The adaptability of a Constitution to changing conditions necessitates a use of contemporary references that are not limited in time or in space.

Illustrative Cases

MAHER v. TOWN OF PORTLAND

In the Privy Council. 1874.

Wheeler, Confederation Law of Canada, 362 ff.

Joseph Brown, Q.C., during argument: "When the Earl of Carnarvon introduced the B.N.A. Bill. . . ."

James L.J.: "We shall not be influenced by anything then said".

[During the argument in *Hodge v. The Queen* (1883), 9 App. Cas. 117, counsel referred to Cooley on Constitutional Limitations whereupon Lord FitzGerald remarked: "We will take the passages from Cooley as part of your argument but not as authority".]

A.-G. ONT. v. WINNER

In the Privy Council. [1954] A.C. 541, [1954] 4 D.L.R. 657, 13 W.W.R. (N.S.) 657

H. J. Wilson, Q.C. for the Attorney-General for Alberta, an appellant, during the argument:

"It is proposed next to refer to the London Resolutions which preceded the passing of the British North America Act, 1867; although their evidential value may be slight, it is submitted that the resolutions are admissible."

C. F. H. Carson, Q.C. for the respondent Winner: "The Board refused to look at a draft bill in *Attorney-General for Canada v. Hallet & Carey Ltd.,* [1952] A.C. 427, 433; [1952] 1 T.L.R. 1408."

After their Lordships had conferred among themselves, Lord Porter announced that their Lordships were persuaded that the material was not only of little evidentiary value but was not even admissible.

Any consideration of resort to external aids in construction of the B.N.A. Act must begin with some assessment of the kind of aids that are available. We do not possess any such records of our "constitution making" conferences, whether at Charlottetown, Quebec or London, as are possessed by the United States or by Australia. There is nothing in Canada comparable to The Federalist, comprising writings of Hamilton, Jay and Madison. The Confederation Debates, 1865, recording the deliberations of the members of the Legislature of the then Province of Canada on the Quebec Resolutions contain by and large merely generalized assessments of the division of legislative authority. Pope's Confederation Documents (1895) add little to our understanding of the scope and relationship of the heads of power distributed by the B.N.A. Act. There is no verbatim record of debate at either the Quebec Conference of 1864 or the London

Conference of 1866 but only the conclusions reached in the resolutions and successive drafts of the proposed confederating statute.

While there is a good deal of "history of surrounding circumstances", it could only be helpful in a broadly general way. The Courts were left largely with their tools of logic and precedent, with contemporary or past legislative comparisons, with such rules of construction as they chose to apply, with dictionaries and other works of reference and, above all, with their own particular philosophies of federalism in general and Canadian federalism in particular. Those philosophies, whatever they were, would be more telling the more there was adherence to a principle of strict construction. The influence of the few text writers on constitutional law that we have had is not measurable; and although there has been a considerable literature by scholars in the past half century there is no evidence that it carried any weight with the Privy Council. The Supreme Court of Canada, unlike that of the United States, is not given to frequent reference to periodical literature, and it is, in any event, too early to speak of any settled tradition of that Court in its role as a final court so far as concerns recourse to external aids.

[Resort to external aids being to assist in determining the ambit of the heads of power in the B.N.A. Act, there is always the question whether particular legislation (whose object or purpose has been ascertained) falls within one head or the other. Save in respect of concurrent powers under ss. 94A or 95, it must fall within federal *or* provincial competence. But there has been one instance of an opinion holding that the object may fall within the competence of both (see Cartwright J. in *Saumur v. Quebec and A.-G. Que.*, [1953] 2 S.C.R. 299, [1953] 4 D.L.R. 641) and one instance of an opinion holding that it does not fall within the competence of either (see Abbott J. in *Switzman v. Elbling and A.-G. Que.*, [1957] S.C.R. 285, 7 D.L.R. (2d) 337.]

ST. CATHARINES MILLING & LUMBER CO. v. THE QUEEN

In the Supreme Court of Canada. (1887), 13 S.C.R. 577.

Appeal from a decision of the Ontario Court of Appeal, 13 O.A.R. 148, affirming a judgment of the Chancery Division, 10 O.R. 196. restraining defendants at the suit of Her Majesty in right of Ontario from cutting timber on certain lands in Ontario. The plaintiff alleged that the lands were public lands of the province and relied on ss. 92(5), 109 and 117 of the B.N.A. Act. The defendants justified under a Dominion licence in respect of which the issue was raised whether the lands in question were subject to Dominion legislation under the enumeration in s. 91 (24) of the B.N.A. Act reading "Indians and lands reserved for the Indians". The appeal was dismissed by a Court composed of six Judges of whom two dissented.

STRONG J. (dissenting, at p. 606): The questions to be determined are therefore now restricted entirely to the construction to be placed on the words, "lands reserved for the Indians," in sub-section 24 of section 91, and we are to bear in mind that whatever are the lands subjected by this description to the exclusive legislative power of the Dominion they cannot be lands belonging to the Province, since all these last mentioned lands are expressly subjected to the exclusive legislative powers of the Provinces. In construing this enactment we are not only entitled but bound to apply that well established rule which requires us, in placing a meaning upon descriptive terms and definitions contained in statutes, to have recourse to external aids derived from the surrounding circumstances and the history of the subject-matter dealt with, and to construe the enactment by the light derived from such sources, and so to put ourselves as far as possible in the position of the legislature whose language we have to expound. If this rule were rejected and the language of the statute were considered without such assistance from extrinsic facts, it is manifest that the task of interpretation would degenerate into mere speculation and guess work.

[The judgment of the Supreme Court was affirmed by the Privy Council (1888), 14 App. Cas. 46. *Cf. Reference as to whether "Indians" in Section 91(24) of the B.N.A. Act Includes Eskimo Inhabitants of Quebec*, [1939] S.C.R. 104, [1939] 2 D.L.R. 417. The question was answered in the affirmative with resort being had to reports of missionaries, explorers, government officials, cartographers; and see Duff C.J. at p. 106 S.C.R., p. 418 D.L.R.: *"The British North America Act* is a statute dealing with British North America and, in determining the meaning of the word 'Indians' in the statute we have to consider the meaning of that term as applied to the inhabitants of British North America".

In *Edwards v. A.-G. Can.*, [1930] A.C. 124, [1930] 1 D.L.R. 98, [1929] 3 W.W.R. 479, where the question was whether s. 24 of the *B.N.A. Act* (which provides that "the Governor-General shall . . . summon qualified persons to the Senate . . .") permitted a woman to be appointed if she had the qualifications set out in s. 23, the Privy Council said through Lord Sankey L.C.: "In coming to a determination as to the meaning of a particular word in a particular Act of Parliament, it is permissible to consider two points, namely: (i) The external evidence derived from extraneous circumstances such as previous legislation and decided cases. (ii) The internal evidence derived from the Act itself. As the learned counsel on both sides have made great researches and invited their Lordships to consider the legal position of women from earliest times, in justice to their argument they propose to do so. . ." The Privy Council also agreed that while history may be called in aid to show what facts existed to bring about a statute, the inferences to be drawn therefrom are very slight. See also the following statement by Duff J. in the Supreme Court, [1928] S.C.R. 276, at p. 297, [1928] 4 D.L.R. 98, at p. 118, expressly concurred in by the Privy Council which reversed the Supreme Court on the merits: "Nor am I convinced that the reasoning based upon the 'extraneous circumstances' we are asked to consider (the disabilities of women under the common law and the law and practice of Parliament in respect of appointment to public place or office) establishes a rule of interpretation for the *British North America Act*, by which the construction of powers, legislative and executive, bestowed in general terms is controlled by a presumptive exclusion of women from participating in the working of the institutions set up by the Act."]

Construction of the B.N.A. Act poses a problem of approach beyond that involved merely in determining the type and range of external aids available to that end. The issue may be framed as follows: Should the meaning of the provisions of the Act be interpreted as of 1867? Or, as of the time when the question of meaning arises in any particular case? Or, as of the time when the question of meaning arises considered in the light of what would have been the view taken in 1867 had the question arisen at that time? See *Labour Relations Board (Sask.) v. John East Iron Works*, [1949] A.C. 134, [1948] 4 D.L.R. 673, [1948] 2 W.W.R. 1055; *A.-G. Ont. v. A.-G. Can.*, [1947] A.C. 127, [1947] 1 D.L.R. 801, [1947] 1 W.W.R. 305, [1947] 1 All E.R. 137.

There has been no consistency in this matter by the Courts, and, indeed, they have changed their position on particular heads of power. Thus, while Lord Haldane insisted on a sterile "domain of criminal jurisprudence" for the federal criminal law power (see *In re Board of Commerce Act, 1919, etc.*, [1922] 1 A.C. 191, 60 D.L.R. 513, [1922] 1 W.W.R. 20), that view was subsequently rejected (see *P.A.T.A. v. A.-G. Can.*, [1931] A.C. 310, [1931] 2 D.L.R. 1, [1931] 1 W.W.R. 52; *A.-G. B.C. v. A.-G. Can.*, [1937] A.C. 368, [1937] 1 D.L.R. 688, [1937] 1 W.W.R. 317), and it is now clear that in the criminal law power we have an "expanding field": see *Provincial Secretary of P.E.I. v. Egan and A.-G. P.E.I.*, [1941] S.C.R. 396, [1941] 3 D.L.R. 305; *Lord's Day Alliance of Canada v. A.-G. B.C.*, [1959] S.C.R. 497, 19 D.L.R. (2d) 97, 123 Can. C.C. 81. Similarly, the Courts have adopted what may be termed a progressive approach to the federal "banking" power (see *Reference re Alberta Statutes*, [1938] S.C.R. 100, [1938] 2 D.L.R. 81; *A.-G. Can. v. A.-G. Que.*, [1947] A.C. 33, [1947] 1 D.L.R. 81, [1946] 3 W.W.R. 659; *Reference re Alberta Bill of Rights Act*, [1947] A.C. 503, [1947] 4 D.L.R. 1, [1947] 2 W.W.R. 401) and to the federal power in relation to bankruptcy and insolvency (see *A.-G. B.C. v. A.-G. Can.*, [1937] A.C. 391, [1937] 1 D.L.R. 695, [1937] 1 W.W.R. 320; and cf. *A.-G. Que. and Royal Bank v. Larue and A.-G. Can.*, [1928] A.C. 187, [1928] 1 D.L.R. 945, [1928] 1 W.W.R. 534; *In re Companies' Creditors Arrangement Act*, [1934] S.C.R. 659, [1934] 4 D.L.R. 75). On the other hand, the treaty implementing power under s. 132 has been rigidly confined to an 1867 approach within the terms in which that section is expressed, and there was a corresponding refusal to find any such authority, as an independent source of legislative competence, in the federal general power (see *A.-G. Can. v. A.-G. Ont.*, [1937] A.C. 326, [1937] 1 D.L.R. 673, [1937] 1 W.W.R. 299). Similarly, the Courts have adopted a fixed definition of direct and indirect taxation for purposes of s. 92(2), based on John Stuart Mill's definition as laid down in his sixth edition of Political Economy, published in 1865 (see *Bank of Toronto v. Lambe* (1887), 12 App. Cas. 575; *Brewers and Maltsters' Assoc. of Ont. v. A.-G. Ont.*, [1897] A.C. 231). This definition has been qualified only in avoidance of its application as a test for classifying "old and well known species of taxation"; for example, "the imposition of taxes on property and income, of death duties and of municipal and local rates is, according to the common understanding of the term, direct taxation, just as the exaction of a customs or excise duty on commodities or of a percentage duty on services would ordinarily be regarded as indirect taxation": *Halifax v. Estate of Fairbanks,* [1928] A.C. 117, [1927] 4 D.L.R. 945, [1927] 3 W.W.R. 493; and see Chapter X on Taxing Powers, *infra,* for a fuller exposition of these matters.

Again, there was an early reduction of the federal trade and commerce power (see *Citizens Insurance Co. v. Parsons* (1881), 7 App. Cas. 96; *In re Board of Commerce Act, 1919, etc.,* [1922] 1 A.C. 191, 60 D.L.R. 513, [1922] 1 W.W.R. 20) from which there has only recently been recession, see Chap. IV, *infra.* Equally, the Privy Council took a strict view of the federal fisheries power based on a pre-confederation assessment of its scope (see *A.-G. Can. v. A.-G. B.C.,* [1930] A.C. 111, [1930] 1 D.L.R. 194, [1929] 3 W.W.R. 449).

For the kinds of external aids referred to in the cases see *Mac-Donald,* Constitutional Interpretation and Extrinsic Evidence, (1939) 17 Can. Bar Rev. 77; *Strayer,* Judicial Review of Legislation in Canada, pp. 155 ff.

In Determining "Character" of Impugned Legislation: Proof of Constitutional Facts

GOSSELIN v. THE KING.

In the Supreme Court of Canada.   (1903), 33 S.C.R. 255.

TASCHEREAU C.J.: . . . I deem it expedient, . . . to say a few words upon the question raised during the argument of the reference by counsel to the debates in Parliament for the purpose of construing any statute. Such a reference has always been refused by my predecessors in this court and, when counsel in this case began to read from the Canadian Hansard the remarks made in Parliament when the *Canada Evidence Act* in question was under discussion, I did not feel justified in departing from the rule so laid down, though, personally, I would not be unwilling, in cases of ambiguity in statutes, to concede that such a reference might sometimes be useful. The same rule is observed in England. Alderson B. says, *In re Gorham,* 5 Ex. 667: "We do not construe Acts of Parliament by reference to history." And, in *Barbat v. Allen,* 7 Ex. 616, Pollock C. B. says: "I must at the same time state that the history of a clause in a statute is certainly no ground for its interpretation in a court of law and I would guard myself against being considered as resorting to any such means." . . .

In the case of *The Queen v. The Bishop of Oxford,* 4 Q.B.D. 525, it is true, a reference to a speech of the Lord Chancellor in the House of Lords, relating to a certain statute, was allowed by the Court of Appeal, but the remarks of the learned judges upon that point, if I read them correctly, are far from justifying the contention raised in some quarters that they intended to alter the general rule on that point. . . .

That case is, however, no authority upon the question, for when in the House of Lords, *sub nomine, Julius v. Oxford,* 49 L.J.Q.B. 578,

> "In the course of the arguments strong disapprobation was expressed by the Lord Chancellor (Earl Cairns), and Lord Selborne of the course taken by the Court of Appeal in allowing to be cited a speech made by the Lord Chancellor in the House of Lords."

In *South-Eastern Railway Company v. The Railway Commissioners and the Mayor, etc., of Hastings,* 49 L.J.Q.B. 273, 291, Cockburn C.J. had also referred to a speech in the House of Lords, but in that same case, 50 L.J.Q.B. 203, upon counsel saying "The Act cannot be construed by reference to a debate in Parliament," Selborne, Lord Chancellor, said:

> "That is so. It has been regretted in the House of Lords that the Court of Appeal had allowed such a reference to be made in *The Queen v. The Bishop of Oxford.*"

In the United States the rule seems to be the same. . .

In Lefroy's valuable book, (The Law of Legislative Power in Canada), pages 1 and 21, are collected the judicial opinions wherein the general rule has been more or less disregarded in the construction of the British North America Act. The reports of the codifiers of the Civil Code of Lower Canada are also often referred to in Quebec and in this court, as also in the Privy Council, (*see* for instance, *Symes v. Cuvillier,* 5 App. Cas. 138), but these cannot be put upon the same footing in regard to this rule as are the debates in Parliament upon a bill. . . .

[As to the position in the United States, see *Note,* Trends in the Use of Extrinsic Aids in Statutory Interpretation, (1950) 3 Vand. L. Rev. 586; *Note,* A Re-Evaluation of the Use of Legislative History in the Federal Courts, (1952) 52 Col. L. Rev. 125. Cf, also *Note,* Social and Economic Facts— Appraisal of Suggested Techniques for Presenting Them to the Court, (1948) 61 Harv. L. Rev. 692.

For an excellent treatment, see *Kilgour,* The Rule against the Use of Legislative History: "Canon of Construction or Counsel of Caution"?, (1952) 30 Can. Bar Rev. 769; and see also *Corry,* The Use of Legislative History in the Interpretation of Statutes, (1954) 32 Can. Bar Rev. 624, at p. 637: "All that reference to legislative history can do is to help mask the Judge's law-making".

The rule stated in the *Gosselin* case was applied at trial in *Canadian Wheat Board v. Manitoba Pool Elevators,* [1949] 2 D.L.R. 726, [1948] 1 W.W.R. 945, in respect of an outline statement of government policy as well as in respect of speeches in Parliament. A different view seemed to be taken on appeal by Adamson J.A. speaking for the majority: see [1949] 2 D.L.R. 537, [1949] 1 W.W.R. 599, 57 Man. R. 1. There was no express advertence to the admissibility of extrinsic material either in the Supreme Court which affirmed the judgments appealed from (see [1951] S.C.R. 81, [1951] 1 D.L.R. 466) or in the Privy Council which reversed the judgments below (see [1952] A.C. 427, [1952] 3 D.L.R. 433, 6 W.W.R. (N.S.) 23, *sub nom. A.-G. Can. v. Nolan and Hallet & Carey Ltd.*). The matter is discussed by *Davis,* Legislative History and the Wheat Board Case, (1953) 31 Can. Bar Rev. 1.

See the following comment on English statutory construction, one as apt for Canadian statutory construction, by Frankfurter J., dissenting, in *Commissioner of Internal Revenue v. Acker* (1959), 361 U.S. 87, at p. 94, 80 S. Ct. 144, at p. 148:

"English courts would decide the case as it is being decided here. They would do so because English Courts do not recognize the relevance of legislative explanations of the meaning of a statute made in the course of its enactment. If Parliament desires to put a gloss on the meaning of ordinary language, it must incorporate it in the text of legislation. See Plucknett, A Concise History of the Common Law (2d ed.), 294-300; Amos, The Interpretation of Statutes, 5 Cam. L.J. 163; Davies, The Interpretation of Statutes, 35 Col. L. Rev. 519. Quite otherwise has been the process of statutory construction practiced by this Court over the decades in scores and scores of cases. Congress can be the glossator of the words it legislatively uses either by writing its desired meaning, however odd, into the text of its enactment, or by a contemporaneously authoritative explanation accompanying a statute. The most authoritative form of such explanation is a congressional report defining the scope and meaning of proposed legislation. The most authoritative report is a Conference Report acted upon by both Houses and therefore unequivocally representing the will of both Houses as the joint legislative body."

For reference to legislative history on the issue of constitutionality, see *P.A.T.A. v. A.-G. Can.*, [1931] A.C. 310, at p. 317, [1931] 2 D.L.R. 1, at p. 4, [1931] 1 W.W.R. 552, at p. 554, where Lord Atkin said: "Their Lordships entertain no doubt that time alone will not validate an Act which when challenged is found to be *ultra vires;* nor will a history of a gradual series of advances till this boundary is finally crossed avail to protect the ultimate encroachment. But one of the questions to be considered is always whether in substance the legislation falls within an enumerated class of subject, or whether on the contrary in the guise of an enumerated class it is an encroachment on an excluded class. On this issue the legislative history may have evidential value."

In *Toronto Electric Com'rs v. Snider*, [1925] A.C. 396, at p. 400, [1925] 2 D.L.R. 5, at p. 5, [1925] 1 W.W.R. 785, at p. 786, the Privy Council said that it will only with reluctance "come to a conclusion adverse to the constitutional validity of any Canadian statute that has been before the public for years as validly enacted". It did come to such a conclusion in that case. See also *Nadan v. The King*, [1926] A.C. 482, [1926] 2 D.L.R. 177, [1926] 1 W.W.R. 801.

Where the validity of legislation is in issue, other "relevant" legislation may be looked at, especially where it forms a scheme with the challenged legislation: *Reference re Alberta Statutes*, [1938] S.C.R. 100, [1938] 2 D.L.R. 81, aff'd [1939] A.C. 117, [1938] 4 D.L.R. 433, [1938] 3 W.W.R. 337; *I.O.F. v. Lethbridge Northern Irrigation District*, [1938] 3 D.L.R. 89, [1938] 2 W.W.R. 194, aff'd [1940] A.C. 513, [1940] 2 D.L.R. 273, [1940] 1 W.W.R. 502; *Plourde v. Roy*, [1942] 3 D.L.R. 646, [1942] 2 W.W.R. 607, rev'd on other grounds, [1943] S.C.R. 262, [1943] 3 D.L.R. 81; *Reference re Section 16 of the Special War Revenue Act*, [1942] S.C.R. 429, [1942] 4 D.L.R. 145.]

A.-G. ALTA. v. A.-G. CAN.

In the Privy Council. [1939] A.C. 117, [1938] 4 D.L.R. 433, [1938] 3 W.W.R. 337.

Appeal by special leave from a judgment of the Supreme Court of Canada, [1938] S.C.R. 100, [1938] 2 D.L.R. 81, declaring, on a reference, that three bills passed by the Alberta Legislative Assembly but as to which the Lieutenant-Governor withheld his assent, were *ultra vires*. The bills were respectively entitled: (1) An Act respecting the Taxation of Banks; (2) An Act to Amend and Consolidate the Credit of Alberta Regulation Act; and (3) An Act to Ensure the Publication of Accurate News and Information. On the hearing of the appeal it appeared that since the Supreme Court judgment the Alberta Legislature, by repealing the Social Credit Act, 1937, had abolished the agencies upon which powers had been conferred by the second and third bills referred to above; and consequently those bills could not become operative. The appeal then proceeded on the bank taxation bill alone.

The Privy Council described the bank taxation bill in these terms:

"This Bill applied to every corporation or joint stock company, other than the Bank of Canada, incorporated for the purpose of doing banking or savings bank business and transacting such business in the Province. The Bill imposed upon every such bank an annual tax, in addition to any tax payable under any other Act, of (a) ½ per cent. on the paid-up capital, and (b) 1 per cent. on the reserve fund and undivided profits. Default on payment of tax was to be visited with penalties, and payment of either tax or penalty could be enforced by distress and sale of goods and chattels, or by action for civil debt. The tax was declared to be payable to the Provincial Secretary on behalf of His Majesty for the use of the Province. It is important to note that the tax is calculated by reference to the whole of the paid-up capital and reserves made throughout Canada and abroad."

LORD MAUGHAM L.C.: . . . Bill No. 1, the "Act respecting the Taxation of Banks," . . . purports to be concerned with taxation of a direct character, differing, however, from ordinary taxing statutes in that it singles out for taxation only banks which transact business in the Province. The word "bank" is defined as meaning "a corporation or joint stock company, other than the Bank of Canada, wherever incorporated and which is incorporated for the purpose of doing banking business or the business of a savings bank and which transacts such business in the Province whether the head office is situate in the Province or elsewhere." No other body, corporation, institution or person is the subject of taxation under the Bill. It is sought to be justified by s. 92 (2) of the British North America Act, 1867, as being within the class of subjects described as "Direct taxation within the province in order to the raising of a revenue for provincial purposes." It may be stated at the outset, if indeed it is not self-evident, that the mere fact that revenue to a greater or smaller amount would be raised in the Province by a highly selective measure of this unusual character is not sufficient to justify it as coming within s. 92. Under the guise of discriminatory taxation in the Province it would be easy not only to impair, but even to render wholly nugatory, the exclusive legislative authority of the Dominion over a number of the classes of subjects specifically mentioned in s. 91 by making them valueless. Instances could be found in bills of exchange, and promissory notes, patents, and copyrights, which could be so heavily taxed as entirely to destroy their use as well as their value in the Province. A number of other illustrations could be given arising under s. 92(10). No one would suggest—and certainly counsel for the appellant in his able argument did not—that Provincial legislation of this character would be valid. Whether a Provincial Act, which indirectly interferes in some degree with one of the powers of the Dominion, is or is not *ultra vires* must be determined in each case as it arises, for no general test applicable to all cases can safely be laid down: *John Deere Plow Co., Ld. v. Wharton*, [1915] A.C. 330; *Great West Saddlery Co., Ld. v. The King*, [1921] 2 A.C. 91.

There are cases on each side of the line. For example, the decision of the Judicial Committee in *Russell v. The Queen*, 7 App. Cas. 829, is an authority on one side; the decisions in *Abbott v. City of Saint John*, 40 S.C.R. 597, *Forbes v. Attorney-General for Manitoba*, [1937] A.C. 260, and *Judges v. Attorney-General of Saskatchewan*, [1937] 2 D.L.R. 209, may be cited on the other side. In the view of their Lordships these cases in no way conflict.

Admitting that a test applicable to every case of overlapping powers specified in ss. 91 and 92 is more than elusive, yet it is often comparatively easy to determine that the particular piece of legislation is an encroachment on a forbidden territory.

Some propositions may be stated that are not in dispute. Clearly, it is necessary in dealing with such a question to consider the whole scheme for distribution of powers contained in the two sections. The "classes of subjects" enumerated, looked at singly, overlap in many respects. It is obvious, for example, that currency, paper money, patents, trade-marks and so forth are different kinds of property, and therefore as a matter of verbal definition within s. 92(13); but this occasions no logical difficulty, for, as has been repeatedly observed, the concluding paragraph of s. 91 declares that any matter coming within any of the classes of subjects enumerated in that section "shall not be deemed to come within the class of matters of a local and private nature" assigned exclusively to the Provinces. As pointed out in the judgment of Duff C.J. (concurred in by Davis J.), it is well established that if a given subject-matter falls within any class of subjects enumerated in s. 91, it cannot be treated as covered by any of those within s. 92: *Attorney-General for Ontario v. Attorney-General for the Dominion*, [1896] A.C. 348; *Great West Saddlery Co., Ltd. v. The King*, [1921] A.C. 91.

It is therefore necessary to compare the two complete lists of categories with a view to ascertaining whether the legislation in question, fairly considered, falls *prima facie* within s. 91 rather than within s. 92. The result of the comparison will not by itself be conclusive, but it will go some way to supply an answer to the problem which has to be solved.

The next step in a case of difficulty will be to examine the effect of the legislation: *Union Colliery Co. of British Columbia, Ld. v. Bryden*, [1899] A.C. 580. For that purpose the Court must take into account any public general knowledge of which the Court would take judicial notice, and may in a proper case require to be informed by evidence as to what the effect of the legislation will be. Clearly, the Acts passed by the Provincial Legislature may be considered, for it is often impossible to determine the effect of the Act under examination without taking into account any other Act operating, or intended to operate, or recently operating in the Province.

A closely similar matter may also call for consideration, namely, the object or purpose of the Act in question. The language of s. 92(2), "Direct taxation within the province *in order to the raising of a revenue* for provincial purposes" is sufficient in the present case to establish this proposition. The principle, however, has a wider application. It is not competent either for the Dominion or a Province under the guise, or the pretence, or in the form of an exercise of its own powers, to carry out an object which is beyond its powers and a trespass on the exclusive powers of the other: *Attorney-General for Ontario v. Reciprocal Insurers*, [1924] A.C. 328; *In re The Insurance Act of Canada*, [1932] A.C. 41. Here again, matters of which the Court would take judicial notice must be borne in mind, and other evidence in a case which calls for it. It must be remembered that the object or purpose of the Act, in so far as it does not plainly appear from its terms and its probable effect, is that of an incorporeal entity, namely, the Legislature, and generally speaking, the speeches of individuals would have little evidential weight.

If these principles are borne in mind, it appears to their Lordships, as it appeared to the Supreme Court, that the specific question that arises in relation to the Bill No. 1 presents no serious difficulty. In the first place, it is plain that the taxation is aimed simply at banks, including savings banks; and by s. 91(15) and (16) "banking" and "savings banks" are within the exclusive legislative authority of the Dominion. On the other hand, it is strange to find the Province singling out, "in order to the raising of a revenue for provincial purposes," banks and savings banks and no other wealthy corporation, body or persons in the Province.

Next, if the effect of the Bill is examined on the footing that it becomes operative in the Province, some remarkable facts emerge. As Kerwin J. (in a judgment concurred in by Crocket J.) observed ([1938] S.C.R. at p. 147): "Our attention has been called to the increase in the taxation of banks that would be effected by the provisions of this Bill. As provincial legislation stood prior to the First Session of the Alberta Legislature in 1937, the tax on all banks doing business in the province amounted to $72,200 per annum. By chapter 57 of that session a tax was imposed which would increase the sum realised by $140,000 per annum. The additional tax proposed by Bill 1 amounts to $2,081,295 in each year."

It does not seem to be necessary to set out the undisputed tables of figures showing the particulars of this gigantic increase in the taxation of banks within the Province. Their Lordships do not disagree with the Chief Justice and Davis J. that the facts are sufficient ([1938] S.C.R. 128) "to show that such a rate of taxation must be prohibitive in fact and must be known to the Alberta Legislature to be prohibitive." In coming to this conclusion it seems to their Lordships that the learned judges were justified in considering that the magnitude of the tax proposed for Alberta was such that, if it were applied by each of the other Provinces, it would have the effect of preventing banks from carrying on their businesses. It would be strange if each of the Provinces were successively to tax banks and the results on the question of *ultra vires* were to be that the Acts of those Provinces who were earliest in the field were valid, whilst the Acts of those who came a little later were to be held *ultra vires*. It must be remembered in this connection that the tax proposed is based on the paid-up capitals and on the reserve funds of the banks wherever situate.

It was rightly contended on behalf of the appellant that the Supreme Court and the Board have no concern with the wisdom of the Legislature whose Bill is attacked; and it was urged that it would be a dangerous precedent to allow the views of members of the Court as to the serious consequences of excessive taxation on banks to lead to a conclusion that the Bill is *ultra vires*. Their Lordships do not agree that this argument should prevail in a case where the taxation in a practical business sense is prohibitive. If, however, any doubt could be entertained on the question of fact, there is in this case a further point which seems to their Lordships to be decisive.

In their opinion, it was quite legitimate to look at the legislative history of Alberta as leading up to the measure in question, including the attempt to create a new economic era in the Province. At the time when the Bill was passing through the Legislature the most profound and far-reaching changes in the operations of commerce, trade, and finance were intended by Bills before the Provincial Legislature and by Acts already passed. It was plain that banks and savings banks operating in Alberta might greatly interfere with those proposed changes. The examination of the Province of Alberta Social Credit Act leaves little doubt that the Act was an attempt to regulate and control banks and banking in the Province. In the second 1937 session an Act called "The Credit of Alberta Regulation Act" was passed. The recitals in that Act are as follows: "Whereas the extent to which property and civil rights in the Province may be enjoyed depends upon the principles governing the monetization of credit and the means whereby such credit is made available to the Province and to the People collectively and individually of the Province; and "Whereas it is expedient that the business of banking in Alberta shall be controlled with the object of attaining for the People of Alberta the full enjoyment of property and civil rights in the Province."

In the same session an Act entitled "An Act to provide for the Restriction of the Civil Rights of Certain Persons" was passed, and it contains a similar recital. Both these latter Acts were part of the general scheme of social credit legislation in Alberta. Their Lordships agree with the opinion expressed by Kerwin J. (concurred in by Crocket J.) that there is no escape from the conclusion that, instead of being in any true sense taxation in order to the raising of a revenue for Provincial purposes, the Bill No. 1 is merely ([1938] S.C.R. 151) "part of a legislative plan to prevent the operation within the Province of those banking institutions which have been called into existence and given the necessary powers to conduct their business by the only proper authority, the Parliament of Canada." This is a sufficient ground for holding that the Bill is *ultra vires*.

There are other and narrower grounds on which the validity of Bill No. 1 has been attacked, but in view of the above conclusions it does not seem to be necessary to deal with them in any way.

Their Lordships think, however, that it may be useful to make some observations on the well-known and often cited decision of the Board in *Bank of Toronto v. Lambe,* 12 App. Cas. 575. That case seems to have occasioned a difficulty in the minds of some of the learned judges in the Supreme Court. It must, however, be borne in mind that the Quebec Act in that case was attacked on two specific grounds, first, that the tax was not "taxation within the Province", and secondly, that the tax was not a "direct tax." It was never suggested, and there seems to have been no ground for suggesting, that the Act was by its effect calculated to encroach upon the classes of matter exclusively within the Dominion powers. Nor, on the other hand, was there any contention, however faint or tentative, that the purpose of the Act was anything other than the legitimate one of raising a revenue for Provincial needs.

It is, moreover, important to note that the taxes were not directed against a particular class of business or employment, but were imposed within the Province on every bank, insurance company, incorporated company carrying on any labour, trade or business in the Province, and on a number of other specified companies. Nor was it suggested that the taxation was of such a character that it might hamper the Dominion in exercising their powers under s. 91. In these circumstances, Lord Hobhouse, in delivering the judgment, refuted a contention on behalf of the appellants (12 App. Cas. 586-7) in language which, as it seems to their Lordships, has sometimes been misunderstood. Its true meaning may be appreciated by stating in effect the argument to which it was addressed in the following form:—"A bank is an institution which comes within the words of s. 91(15). To tax a bank with sufficient severity would destroy it. Therefore the Province cannot tax a bank at all." The answer of the Judicial Committee in substance was not more than this:—"You are asking the Board to imply in s. 91 a proviso to the effect that if a power expressly given to the Provinces is capable, by a particular and unusual application, of infringing a power given to the Parliament of Canada, then no similar use of the Provincial power, however moderate, can be permitted under any circumstances. The answer is that the Legislature, in passing the British North America Act, did not assume that a misuse of the Provincial powers was likely to occur and accordingly had to be provided for. No such proviso can therefore be implied." It was never laid down by the Board that if such a use was attempted to be made of the Provincial power as materially to interfere with the Dominion power, the action of the Province would be *intra vires*. To quote the actual language of the Board, they said—"If [the Judges] find that on the due construction of the Act a legislative power falls within s. 92, it would be quite wrong of them to deny its existence because by some possibility it may be abused, or may limit the range which otherwise would be open to the Dominion parliament." This proposition is no more than what was stated in precise terms by Davies J. in *Abbott v. City of Saint John* when he observed (40 S.C.R. 606): "Time and again the Judicial Committee have declined to give effect to this anticipatory argument or to assume to refuse to declare a power existed in the Legislature of the Province simply because its improvident exercise might bring it into conflict with an existing power of the Dominion." Their Lordships are not aware of any decision of the Board which travels beyond the proposition laid down in *Lambe's* case as explained above. . . .

Appeal dismissed.

[*Quaere*, whether the steps in constitutional construction set out by Lord Maugham should not be put in a different (and, indeed, reverse) order!

In *Tolton Manufacturing Ltd. et al. v. Advisory Committee*, [1940] O.R. 301, [1940] 3 D.L.R. 383, Roach J., in dismissing an action for a declaration that the Industrial Standards Act, R.S.O. 1937, c. 191 was *ultra vires*, held that the case was not one "where the Court requires to be informed by evidence as to what the effect of the legislation will be. The whole question can be determined by examining the Act itself. The meaning of the words employed is plain and I cannot find anything within its four corners which requires to be explained by evidence." See *Note*, (1940) 18 Can. Bar Rev. 657. On appeal, the Court felt that the absence of facts in the record precluded intended argument by counsel attacking the Act; and on the Court's sugges-tion, in which counsel present acquiesced, leave was given to plaintiffs to amend the statement of claim, and a re-trial was directed at which all evidence tendered by plaintiffs was to be accepted subject to objection. At the new trial judgment was given upholding the validity of the Industrial Standards Act: see [1942] O.R. 518, [1942] 3 D.L.R. 705, aff'd [1943] O.R. 526, [1943] 3 D.L.R. 474. The judgment was further affirmed by the Supreme Court of Canada, [1944] S.C.R. 349, [1944] 4 D.L.R. 273. Leave to appeal to the Privy Council was refused.

In *Turner's Dairy Ltd. v. Lower Mainland Dairy Products Board*, [1941] 2 D.L.R. 279, [1941] 3 W.W.R. 342, 56 B.C.R. 103, O'Halloran J.A., stated that the trial Judge has a "wide judicial discretion" to determine whether the case is a proper one for the Court to be informed by evidence as to what the effect of impugned legislation will be. On appeal to the Supreme Court of Canada (*sub nom. Lower Mainland Dairy Products Board v. Turner's Dairy Ltd.*, [1941] S.C.R. 573, at p. 583, [1941] 4 D.L.R. 209, at p. 216), Taschereau J. (for himself and Rinfret and Crocket JJ.) said, *inter alia:* "The appellants have also submitted that some evidence given to show the intent and effect of the orders was improperly admitted. I agree with the majority of the Court of Appeal, that the evidence was admissible and that the objection cannot stand. In certain cases, in order to avoid confusion extraneous evidence is required to facilitate the analysis of legislative enactments, and thus disclose their aims which otherwise would remain obscure or even completely concealed. The true purposes and effect of legis-lation, when revealed to the courts, are indeed very precious elements which must be considered in order to discover its real substance. If it were held that such evidence may not be allowed and that only the form of an Act may be considered, then colourable devices could be used by legislative bodies to deal with matters beyond their powers. The Privy Council took similar views in *Attorney-General for Alberta v. Attorney-General for Canada*, [1939] A.C. 117, at p. 130. . . .

. . . I believe that this is the law that should govern this case. It applies to the interpretation of federal and provincial statutes, and I cannot see why the courts should withhold its application to orders of a board which is an emanation of a body subject to this rule." For an application of the *Turner's Dairy* case to show purpose, see *Anthony v. A.-G. Alta. and Minister of Lands & Mines*, [1942] 1 W.W.R. 833, aff'd [1942] 3 D.L.R. 421, [1942] 2 W.W.R. 554, aff'd [1943] S.C.R. 320, [1943] 3 D.L.R. 1.]

CAIRNS CONSTRUCTION LTD. v. GOVERNMENT OF SASKATCHEWAN

In the Saskatchewan Court of Appeal. (1958), 16 D.L.R. (2d) 465, 27 W.W.R. 297.

Appeal and cross-appeal from a judgment of Davis J. (1957), 9 D.L.R. (2d) 721, 22 W.W.R. 193, holding that plaintiff was entitled to recover money paid under protest for taxes levied under the Education and Hospitalization Tax Act, R.S.S. 1953, c. 61, as amended. The trial Judge concluded that the Act was inapplicable to plaintiff but on appeal this judgment was reversed, Gordon J.A. dissenting, and the Court held, moreover, that the Act was valid as imposing a direct tax within the Province. The judgments given on appeal are reproduced here only on the issue of admissibility of certain evidence.

MARTIN C.J.S.: . . . The question as to whether the Court should hear evidence as to the detailed operation of an Act in order to determine its validity was argued at the hearing of the appeal at some length. Mr. Noonan for the Government of Saskatchewan contended that the Court should confine itself to the provisions of the Act. The language of the statute itself must, of course, be the primary consideration. . . .

In recent times Courts appear to have looked outside the legislation for evidence as to its character: *Re Reciprocal Insurance Legislation, supra.* In *Re Alberta Legislation,* [1938] 2 D.L.R. 81, S.C.R. 100, members of the Supreme Court of Canada held three Alberta Statutes *ultra vires* as forming part of the general scheme of Social Credit legislation, the basis of which was another statute, the *Social Credit Act,* which was itself declared to be *ultra vires.* In considering the Alberta measure for the taxation of banks, Sir Lyman P. Duff C.J.C. stated that its true character was to be found by ascertaining the effect of the legislation in the known circumstances to which it is to be applied and noted that if the same right of taxation was applied in other Provinces, the result would be prohibitive. In the Privy Council [[1938] 4 D.L.R. 433, [1939] A.C. 117], Lord Maugham L.C. stated that in examining the effect of the legislation "the Court must take into account any public general knowledge of which the Court would take judicial notice" [p. 438 D.L.R., p. 130 A.C.], and in coming to the conclusion that the rate of taxation was prohibitive, the Judges "were justified in considering that the magnitude of the tax proposed for Alberta was such that if it were applied by each of the other Provinces, it would have the effect of preventing banks from carrying on their businesses" [p. 440 D.L.R., p. 132 A.C.]

Cases, however, where Courts have considered extrinsic matters are confined in narrow limits. I can find no case where evidence of the type given by Dr. Eric J. Hanson, Professor of Economics in the University of Alberta, has been admitted. He was called by the plaintiff and while I doubt the admissibility of his evidence I will refer to it. . . .

GORDON J.A., dissenting: . . . Some time was spent on the argument of the question of whether or not the Court could consider evidence as to the working of the Act in order to arrive at its validity. Mr. Noonan contended that the Court should confine itself to the four corners of the Act. I am clearly of the opinion that some such evidence is admissible. The only difficulty is in deciding to what extent. I do not propose citing authorities on the question as they are covered by an article written by Mr. Vincent C. MacDonald, later Mr. Justice MacDonald of the Court of Appeal of Nova Scotia, published in 17 Can. Bar Rev. 77. With every respect, I do not think that anything could be added to this statement of the legal position. Although primarily we must look at the Act itself, the Supreme Court and the Privy Council have always looked at evidence of the administration of the questioned Act when it is challenged as colourable. These authorities are more particularly set forth on pp. 88-92 of the above article. . . .

At the trial of the action the plaintiff called as its witness one Dr. Eric John Hanson, an Associate Professor of Economics at the University of Alberta, and Administrative Officer of the Department of Political Economy. This witness had made a careful analysis of the tangible personal property sold in the Province as gathered largely from the Department of Statistics at Ottawa. He divided these into durable and non-durable goods and gave the value of the various items sold in the Province in the year 1951. According to this compilation, which was filed as ex. P. 35, durable goods amounted to a total of $333,500,000; non-durable goods only $85,800,000. On the hearing of the appeal general objection was taken to the arbitrary division made by Dr. Hanson and a new table filed, materially altering these figures. With every deference I do not think it is possible for the Court to enter upon such an inquiry and it will have to be left for later decisions to decide whether any particular item is subject to the tax or not. . . .

There have been so many cases laying down the general principles to be applied that it would be futile to repeat them. All are agreed that the question whether a tax is direct or indirect is a question of law and not of fact, but there must be a definite set of facts to which the law can be applied. . . .

CULLITON J.A.: . . . It was further argued that the general incidence of the taxing Act is that it imposes a tax upon durable commodities, a subject of commercial transactions, and must, therefore,
be indirect. In support of this contention Professor Hanson, a Professor of Political Economy, was called as witness at the trial. He
gave evidence at great length concerning durable and non-durable
goods. He also expressed at length his opinions as to the economic
tendency of the tax.

In my opinion there are sound reasons why this evidence was not
admissible on the question of the validity of the legislation. It is a
well-accepted principle that in determining whether a tax is direct
or not, it must be determined, from the four corners of the taxing
statute, whether it can be said that it was the intention of the
Legislature that the person paying the tax indemnify himself. While
in some economists' point of view some taxes may, in their actual
incidence, involve a passing on to others of the impost, nevertheless
the question of whether a tax be indirect or direct at law cannot be
determined by the economists' criteria: *vide Royal Trust Co. v.
Minister of Finance of B.C.*, 61 D.L.R. 194 at pp. 198-9, [1922] 1 A.C.
87 at p. 93 *per* Viscount Cave; *Kerr v. Provincial Treasurer of
Alberta*, [1933] 4 D.L.R. 81 at p. 88, A.C. 710 at pp. 722-3; and *Re
Flavelle*, [1943] 1 D.L.R. 756 at p. 776, O.R. 167 at p. 187 *per* Rose
C.J.H.C. Too, it can be said that the definition of a direct tax as
adopted by the Privy Council and which it has consistently applied,
is now one of law and has become a permanent criterion. That being
so, the validity of a taxing statute must be determined within that
definition and not according to the theories and opinions of economists.

While there are cases in which the Courts have considered extrinsic
matters and thus have gone beyond the four corners of the statute in
determining its validity, that field is indeed restricted. Mr. Vincent
C. MacDonald, later Mr. Justice MacDonald, in his article "Constitutional Interpretation and Extrinsic Evidence", 17 Can. Bar Rev.
77 at p. 81, states the general rule as follows: "The general situation
as to the non-admissibility of extrinsic evidence has been well and
accurately put by Professor Kennedy as follows: 'The Act is to be
expounded and given effect to according to the terms set out in it,
finding the intention from its words, upholding it precisely as framed,
ascertaining its true meaning within itself and clear of any qualifications which the Imperial Parliament has not expressed in it, and
apart from any questions of expediency or of political exigency. . . .
A complete examination of all the cases in all the courts in which
have arisen problems connected with the B.N.A. Act discloses that,
in the overwhelming majority of them, the ratio decidendi depended
on reasoning entirely divorced from external sources or references,
to which we cannot allow even a secure position as persuasive
authorities'."

The Courts have only departed from this general rule in considering, in particular cases, matters of history, law and practice; circumstances leading to the passage of the Act and facts of which the
Court could and should take judicial notice. I can find no cases, since

the definition of a direct tax was adopted by the Privy Council, in which the evidence or opinions of political economists were considered by the Court.

I think I can take judicial notice of the fact that there has developed in recent years in the commercial field a widespread practice of trading in certain types of goods, for the purpose of obtaining a credit on the purchase-price of new goods. This is purely a business and economic development and clearly not a factor to be considered in the determination of the classification of a tax contemplated by the legislators who passed the *B.N.A. Act* in 1867.

Prior to the trial the respondents examined for discovery Mr. Schuck, Administrator of the Act. As part of the respondent's case at trial, counsel for the respondent read into the record numerous questions and answers from this examination. Such evidence is, in my opinion, of no value in determining the validity of the legislation. The reason for such a conclusion is obvious. It seems clear that an Act which in law is *intra vires* could not be declared *ultra vires* because of the method in which it is administered; and conversely, legislation which in law is *ultra vires* could not be declared *intra vires* because of its method of administration. Methods or instances of administration would only go to the question of the applicability of the law in particular cases and not to the validity of the legislation. For the same reason the Regulations or Rulings made under the Act are of no assistance in determining its constitutionality. . . .

Appeal allowed; cross-appeal dismissed.

[Procter and McNiven JJ.A. concurred with Culliton J.A. The judgment of the majority on the merits was affirmed by the Supreme Court of Canada: [1960] S.C.R. 619, 24 D.L.R. (2d) 1.

In *Utah Co. of the Americas and Texada Mines Ltd. v. A.-G. B.C.* (1959), 19 D.L.R. (2d) 705, 28 W.W.R. 529, reversing 17 D.L.R. (2d) 16, 26 W.W.R. 481, the trial Judge referred to press and radio statements by the Premier and the Minister of Mines, and to allegedly companion legislation, as showing the purpose of a certain statute which was challenged as imposing an indirect tax. He stated that "at the time of their publication, in common with other citizens, I became personally familiar with and interested in said statements", and he quoted a press item "which was produced at trial although not entered as an exhibit". After reviewing the case law indicating that extrinsic evidence was admissible he concluded as follows:

"It is inconceivable that any person of average intelligence, resident in British Columbia and having the slightest concern about the mining or industrial affairs of his Province could come, reasonably, to the conclusion that this legislative scheme had as its purpose the 'raising of a revenue'. Whether or not the well-known and widely publicized statements of the Premier and Minister of Mines are proper matters for consideration by the Court in its efforts to determine the 'real intention' of the Legislature, one would have to be very gullible indeed to think for a moment that such 'real intention' were other than these estimable Ministers of the Crown have stated it to be, or that the tax imposed by the *Mineral Property Taxation Act* could be described accurately as anything but 'the iron ore export tax'."

In reversing the judgment and upholding the challenged enactment, O'Halloran J.A. said on the evidence point:

"There is no legal evidence, as counsel for the appellant pointed out in argument, to support the submission that prominent Ministers of the Crown Provincial publicly made the statements attributed to them that the *Mineral Property Taxation Act,* 1957, constituted an export tax to prevent export of British Columbia iron ore to Japan or elsewhere outside the Province. But even if responsible Ministers of the Crown Provincial had publicly made such statements political statements of that type are not a legal guide to this Court in determining whether the *Mineral Property Taxation Act,* 1957, is in its pith and substance a land tax, or, as alleged was devised as an export tax upon iron ore from this Province exported to Japan or elsewhere." The judgment of the Court of Appeal was reversed on the merits by the Supreme Court of Canada: [1960] S.C.R. 713, 24 D.L.R. (2d) 81, 32 W.W.R. 37. In commenting on the evidence point, Locke J., speaking for the Court, said that the statements attributed to the provincial Ministers of the Crown had not been proved at the trial where the Judge who referred to them made it clear that he came to his conclusion without reference to them; and, further, that "had the evidence been tendered, it would no doubt, have been rejected as inadmissible." In *Attorney-General of Canada v. Reader's Digest Association (Canada) Ltd.,* [1961] S.C.R. 775, 30 D.L.R. (2d) 296, the Supreme Court approved this dictum of Locke J. as representing a correct statement of the law. In consequence, it was held that the budget speech of the Minister of Finance was not admissible in evidence to support an allegation that certain federal taxing legislation was colourable and an encroachment on provincial legislative power. Moreover, neither the then Minister nor his successor, nor a deputy minister, nor the Clerk of the House of Commons, nor a press correspondent (who had received an advance copy of the budget speech) could properly be asked questions touching the speech and its relation to the character of the impugned legislation or whether it reflected government policy which was later translated into legislation. Cartwright J. (for himself and Locke J.) reviewed the course of decision and concluded as follows:

> "In the case at bar it will be open to the parties to lead evidence to show the circumstances to which the impugned sections are to be applied but it must be evidence in a form that is legally admissible and the statement of the Minister, alleged in the plaintiff's declaration to have been made, is not in my opinion legally admissible. . . .
>
> Something was said in argument as to the necessity of ascertaining the true intention of Parliament in enacting the impugned sections. But Parliament is an entity which from its nature cannot be said to have any motive or intention other than that which is given expression in its formal acts. . . .
>
> While I have reached the conclusion that the evidence in question in this appeal is inadmissible as a matter of law under the authorities and on principle and not from a consideration of the inconvenience that would result from a contrary view, it may be pointed out that if it were held that the Minister's statement should be admitted there would appear to be no ground on which anything said in either House between the introduction of the bill and its final passing into a law could be excluded."

In the United States, explanatory statements by persons in charge of a bill are admissible on the construction of legislation relative to constitutionality: see *Wright v. Vinton Branch of Mountain Trust Bank of Roanoke* (1937), 300 U.S. 440, 57 S. Ct. 556, where Brandeis J., for the Court, said:

> "Since the language of the Act is not free from doubt . . . . we are justified in seeking enlightenment from reports of Congressional committees and explanations given on the floor of the Senate and House by those in charge of the measure."

Quaere, whether this should not be all the more so in the case of the piloting of a government bill by a Minister acting within a system of responsible government!

For the position in Australia, see Latham C.J. in *South Australia v. The Commonwealth* (1942), 65 C.L.R. 373, at p. 410: "Neither the validity nor the interpretation of a statute passed by Parliament can be allowed to depend upon what members, whether Ministers or not, choose to say in parliamentary debate. The Court takes the words of Parliament itself, formally enacted in the statute, as expressing the intention of Parliament." He said further that this intention cannot be controlled or modified in a Court by reference to extrinsic material, but the case is different if the statute refers to such material or possibly if the *bona fides* of Parliament or of the Crown in Parliament can be and is challenged.]

HOME OIL DISTRIBUTORS LTD. v. A.-G. B.C.

In the Supreme Court of Canada. [1940] S.C.R. 444, [1940] 2 D.L.R. 609.

Appeal from a judgment of the British Columbia Court of Appeal, [1939] 3 D.L.R. 397, [1939] 2 W.W.R. 418, which reversed a judgment of Manson J., [1939] 1 W.W.R. 666, declaring certain sections of The Coal and Petroleum Products Control Board Act, 1937 (B.C.), c. 8, to be *ultra vires.* Upon institution of the action, an interim injunction was obtained against enforcement of an order of the Board, the injunction being founded on facts disclosed in the report of a commissioner under the Public Inquiries Act (B.C.). The report had been laid before the legislative assembly of British Columbia before the statute in question was enacted.

In a judgment continuing the injunction ([1939] 1 W.W.R. 449) the Court of Appeal declared (McQuarrie J.A. dissenting) that the commissioner's report was admissible in evidence only in so far as it found facts relevant to the ascertainment of the alleged purpose and effect of the statute. Thereafter the Legislature amended the statute by adding section 42 which declared that the Act "was not intended to implement or carry into effect the recommendations or findings of any report" and that "in construing this Act and in ascertaining its purpose, intention, scope and effect no reference shall be made to any such reports." The amendment was stated to be retroactive.

At the trial on the merits Manson J. stated that the amendment must be ignored on the issue of constitutionality. He then proceeded to hold that the report was admissible and that certain sections of the statute were *ultra vires.* On appeal, the statute was held to be valid, and it was pointed out that in coming to this conclusion the Court gave no effect to the amendment. A majority (McQuarrie J.A. dissenting) held that the report was admissible.

KERWIN J. (for himself and Rinfret J.) after stating that the Act was valid on the authority of *Shannon v. Lower Mainland Dairy Products Board,* [1938] A.C. 708, [1938] 4 D.L.R. 81, [1938] 2 W.W.R. 604: In coming to this conclusion I have taken the report of a commissioner appointed by the Lieutenant-Governor in Council as being a recital of what was present to the mind of the legislature, in enacting the principal Act, as to what was the existing law, the evil to be abated and the suggested remedy (*Heydon's Case*, 2 Coke 18). There can, I think, be no objection in principle to the use of the report for that purpose, and Lord Halsbury's dictum in *Eastern Photographic Machine Company v. Comptroller General of Patents*, [1898] A.C. 517 at p. 575, is to the same effect. It was argued by counsel for the appellants that the statements in the report were to be taken as facts admitted or proved, but that this cannot be done is quite clear from the authorities, the most recent of which is *Assam Railways and Traders Company v. The Commissioners of Inland Revenue*, [1935] A.C. 445.

I have not considered the provisions of the amending Act which are objected to, and make no comment as to those provisions.

DAVIS J.: Sections 14 and 15 of the statute are as follows:—

14. (1) The Board may from time to time, with the approval of the Lieutenant-Governor in Council, fix the price or prices, maximum price or prices, minimum price or prices at which coal or petroleum products may be sold in the province either at wholesale or retail or otherwise for use in the province.

(2) Without limiting the generality of the powers conferred by subsection (1), the Board may:—

(a) Fix different prices for different parts of the province;
(b) Fix different prices for licensees notwithstanding that they are in the same class of occupation;
(c) Fix schedules of prices for different qualities, quantities, standards, grades and kinds of coal and petroleum products.

15. Where the Board has fixed a price for coal or for petroleum or for any petroleum product, it may, with the approval of the Lieutenant-Governor in Council, declare that any covenant or agreement for the purchase or sale within the province of coal or petroleum or a petroleum product for use in the province contained in any agreement in existence at the time of fixing such price shall be varied so that the price shall conform to the price fixed by the Board, and the agreement, subject only to the variation declared by the Board, shall in all other respects remain in full force and effect.

The appellants' case rests in substance upon the basis that the report of a commissioner appointed November 29th, 1934, by the Lieutenant-Governor in Council of the Province of British Columbia under its *Public Inquiries Act* to inquire (a) into matters respecting coal mined in or imported into the province and used for fuel purposes in the province, and (b) into matters respecting petroleum products imported into or refined or produced in the province and used or designed for use therein for fuel, lighting and motor vehicles' operation, discloses the true intent and purpose of the subsequent legislation now in question and that the report with all the evidence contained in its three volumes was open to the Court and should be accepted as *prima facie* evidence of the facts for the purpose of a proper understanding of the legislation. Mr. Farris in an unusually powerful argument attacking the legislation made it abundantly plain that his contention was based upon the industry affected by the legislation being what he called "an integrated industry, interprovincial and international" and the legislation an invasion of the Dominion's power to regulate trade and commerce. His contention was that the subject-matter of the impeached legislation was not local or provincial within the competence of the legislature.

Leaving aside any reference to the report of the commissioner and assuming for the moment that it must be excluded, the language of the statutory provisions is itself plain and unambiguous. The Board appointed under the provisions of the Act is empowered from time to time "with the approval of the Lieutenant-Governor in Council" to fix the prices at which petroleum products may be sold—and then follow the limiting words, "in the province" and "for use in the province"—and where the Board fixes a price it may, with the approval of the Lieutenant-Governor in Council, declare that any covenant or agreement for the purchase or sale — and again the limiting words, "within the province" and "for use in the province"— contained in any agreement in existence at the time of fixing such price shall be varied so that the price shall conform to the price fixed by the Board.

On the face of the legislation it appears that the legislature is dealing solely with the sale within the province for use in the province of petroleum products; legislation in relation to the petroleum industry in its local aspects within the province. There is nothing in the language of the statute which necessarily gives to its enactments an extra-territorial effect.

There is no necessity to refer at any length to the long line of authorities on the constitutional validity or invalidity under the *British North America Act* of this sort of legislation and we are not concerned with whether the legislation appears to us to be commercially fair and reasonable or not. The sole question is whether the provincial legislature had authority to enact such legislation. . . . Taking the legislation as it stands, alone, secs. 14 and 15 are within the competence of the provincial legislature.

But it is said that if we examine the commissioner's report and the evidence (a part of which only was issued and before the legislature at the time the enactment was made) we shall discover the mischief at which the legislation was aimed and that the real purpose and intent of the legislation was to control the petroleum industry at large and in the State of California particularly, and that the legislation is directed to the control of the industry in its interprovincial and international aspects. Briefly, what is said is that the legislature, with the commissioner's report before it, thought that the large California oil companies having a very limited market in California for their fuel oil, due to the warm climatic conditions there, sought a market for their fuel oil in the province of British Columbia and in order to gain that market adopted the policy of dumping their fuel oil into British Columbia for sale at very low prices, with great mischief to the coal industry in British Columbia; but of selling their gasoline, with which there was no natural resource in British Columbia to enter into competition, at exorbitant prices. Upon an examination of the evidence in the elaborate inquiry by the commissioner and of his report it is said that it plainly appears that the hand of the legislature was reaching out far beyond the limits of its own province in an effort to control an integrated industry with wide interprovincial and international activities.

Generally speaking, the Court has no right to interpret legislation by reference to such extraneous material as the evidence taken before and the report of a public inquiry under a Royal Commission. It would be a dangerous course to adopt. The principle was stated by Lord Wright in the *Assam* case, in House of Lords, where, with reference to an attempt to introduce certain recommendations from a report of a Royal Commission to show that the words of the section of a statute there in question were intended to give effect to them, he said:

"But on principle no such evidence for the purpose of showing the intention, that is the purpose or object, of an Act is admissible"; and distinguished the dictum of Lord Halsbury in the *Eastman Photographic* case. The statement of Lord Langdale in the *Gorham* case in Moore, 1852 edition, p. 462, was accepted. That statement was this:

"We must endeavour to attain for ourselves the true meaning of the language employed—in the Article and Liturgy—assisted only by the consideration of such external or historical facts as we may find necessary to enable us to understand the subject-matter to which the instruments relate, and the meaning of the words employed."

The furthest the courts have gone recently, I think, is in the case of *Ladore v. Bennett* in the Privy Council, [1939] A.C. 468, where Lord Atkin (who had agreed in the House of Lords with the opinion of Lord Wright in the *Assam* case) said:

"Their Lordships do not cite this report as evidence of the facts there found, but as indicating the materials which the Government of the Province had before them before promoting in the Legislature the statute now impugned."

That was an action raising a constitutional issue on certain Ontario statutes. There was a complicated piece of municipal legislation whereby the city of Windsor in the province of Ontario and three adjoining municipalities were, on account of their financial difficulties, put into one amalgamated whole. Not only did the parties consent before the Judicial Committee to the report being before their Lordships, but it would be useful, to readily understand the framework of the particular legislation, to have a convenient reference to the problems involved and disclosed by the report.

A rule somewhat wider than the general rule may well be necessary in considering the constitutionality of legislation under a federal system where legislative authority is divided between the central and the local legislative bodies. But even if that be so, the legislation here in question is expressly confined and limited to the sale of the products of the particular industry in, and for use in, the province and must, upon the well settled authorities, be held to be valid legislation.

I have refrained from any mention of an amendment to the statute because I think the above conclusion is inevitable without regard to the amendment. [The learned Justice then referred to the amendment and to the concession of the provincial Attorney-General who appeared in the case that "a legislature cannot support an Act attacked as being *ultra vires* by denying to a citizen access to the courts for purpose of attacking the legislation or by denying to the courts access to the evidence."]

Appeal dismissed.

[Duff C.J., Crocket and Hudson JJ. agreed that the *Shannon* case governed disposition of the appeal.

In *A.-G. B.C. v. A.-G. Can.*, [1937] A.C. 368, [1937] 1 D.L.R. 688, [1937] 1 W.W.R. 317, where the issue was whether an anti-monopoly provision of the Criminal Code (s. 498A) was valid, Lord Atkin said, *inter alia:* "Counsel . . . called the attention of the Board to the Report of the Royal Commission on Price Spreads, which is referred to in the order of reference. It probably would not be contended that the statement of the Minister in the order of reference that the section was enacted to give effect to the recommendations of the Royal Commission bound the Provinces or must necessarily be treated as conclusive by the Board. But when the suggestion is made that the legislation was not in truth criminal legislation, but was in substance merely an encroachment on the Provincial field, the existence of the report appears to be a material circumstance."

In commenting on this statement and on his judgment in the *Home Oil Distributors* case, *supra*, Kerwin C.J.C. said in *A.-G. Can. v. Reader's Digest Assoc. (Canada) Ltd.*, [1961] S.C.R. 775, at p. 782, 30 D.L.R. (2d) 296, at p. 302, speaking for the majority of the Court, that the commission reports in the aforementioned cases were considered for the purpose only of showing what was present to the mind of Parliament. Cartwright J. (for himself and Locke J.) said in the same case (at p. 791 S.C.R., p. 311 D.L.R. (2d)) that "there is no decision which requires us to hold that a Report of a Royal Commission made prior to the passing of a statute and relating to the subject matter with which the statute deals, but not referred to in the statute, is admissible in evidence in an action to impugn the validity of that statute. In my opinion, the general rule is that if objected to it should be excluded." In addition, Ritchie J. (for himself and Martland J.) said (at p. 796 S.C.R., p. 315 D.L.R. (2d)) that when Royal Commission Reports have been referred to in the Courts in cases involving the constitutional validity of a statute "they have been referred to otherwise than as direct evidence of intention." Does it make a difference if a report is referred to in the statute? See *Swait v. Board of Trustees of Maritime Transportation Unions* (1966), 61 D.L.R. (2d) 317.

In *Letang v. Cooper*, [1964] 2 All E.R. 929, at p. 933, Lord Denning M.R. referred to the use of a committee report, to construe subsequently enacted legislation, in the following terms: "It is legitimate to look at the report of such a committee so as to see what was the mischief at which the Act was directed. You can get the facts and surrounding circumstances from the report, so as to see the background against which the legislation was enacted. This is always a great help in interpreting it. But you cannot look at what the committee recommended, or at least if you do look at it you should not be unduly influenced by it. It does not help you much, for the simple reason that Parliament may, and often does, decide to do something different to cure the mischief. You must interpret the words of Parliament as they stand without too much regard to the recommendations of the committee. . . ." In the particular case what Parliament enacted was in certain respects different from the recommendations of the report. See also *Re Harpur's Will Trusts,* [1961] 3 All E.R. 588.]

REFERENCE RE VALIDITY OF WARTIME LEASEHOLD REGULATIONS

In the Supreme Court of Canada. [1950] S.C.R. 124, [1950] 2 D.L.R. 1.

RINFRET C.J.C.: The question referred by the Governor in Council to the Court is:

"Are The Wartime Leasehold Regulations *ultra vires* either in whole or in part and, if so, in what particulars or to what extent?"

After having heard arguments on behalf of the Attorney-General of Canada, the Attorney-General of Ontario, the Attorney-General of Quebec, the Tenants within Canada, the Property Owners' Association, the Dominion Command of the British Empire Service League and the Canadian Congress of Labour, I am of opinion that the question should be answered in the negative.

These References, under s. 55 of the *Supreme Court Act,* R.S.C. 1927, c. 35, merely call for the opinion of the Court on the questions of law or fact submitted by the Governor in Council and the answers given by the Court are only opinions. It has invariably been declared that they are not judgments either binding on the Government, on Parliament, on individuals, and even on the Court itself, although, of course, this should be qualified by saying that, in a contested case where the same questions would arise, they would no doubt be followed. But precisely on account of their character the opinions are supposed to be given on the material which appears in the Order of Reference and the Court is not expected to look to outside evidence. It is clear that the Court may take into consideration any fact which is of common, or public, knowledge, or of which it could ordinarily take judicial notice. Otherwise, however, excepting very exceptional cases, which it would be quite impossible to enumerate and in respect of which the present Reference is not concerned, the Court is limited to the statements of fact contained in the Order of Reference. I would venture to say that this has been the constant practice of this Court on References submitted under s. 55 of the *Supreme Court Act.*

As to the first proposition, it was pointed out by Earl Loreburn, L.C., in *A.-G. Ont. et al. v. A.-G. Can.,* [1912] A.C. 571 at p. 589, that the opinions provoked by such questions "are only advisory, and will have no more effect than the opinions of the Law Officers", to which Duff J. (as he then was) in *Re Water Powers' Reference*, [1929] S.C.R. 200 at p. 228, after having quoted the statement of Earl Loreburn, observed that "when a concrete case is presented for the practical application of the principles discussed, it may be found necessary, under the light derived from a survey of the facts, to modify the statement of such views as are herein expressed." As a matter of fact, in the *Water Powers' Reference*, following an objection raised by Mr. Tilley, K.C., representing the Attorney-General for Ontario, to certain material which had been included in the appendix of the factum of the Attorney-General for Canada, the Court ordered two hundred and forty pages stricken from the appendix and made the following observation: "It must be obvious that any statements of facts, upon which answers to the questions must be based, should form part of the Case submitted, and it would be highly inconvenient and most dangerous to receive documents such as these in question as part of the Case, unless with the full consent and concurrence of all parties."

In that case, Smith J., concurring with Duff J., but writing separately, thought that he would explain certain references made in his judgment to a situation which did not appear in the record by saying [p. 233 S.C.R.]: "We might, perhaps, take judicial notice of some of the facts, and might gather others from statutory enactments . . . I have gone beyond the record, not to obtain material as a basis for answering the questions, but merely to emphasize what my brother Duff has said to the impracticability of giving full and definite answers to all the questions that would have general application, regardless of particular circumstances capable of proof but not established or admitted in the record."

No doubt anybody attacking Parliament's legislation as colourable would have to introduce evidence of certain facts to support the contention, for it can hardly be expected that the Order of Reference would contain material of a nature to induce the Court to conclude as to the colourability of the legislation. It may be that it would be so apparent that the court could come to that conclusion without extraneous evidence, and an example of that situation might be found in *Reference Re Section 16 of The Special War Revenue Act*, [1942] S.C.R. 429 at p. 434, where Sir Lyman P. Duff C.J.C., delivering the judgment of the Court, found that the section was *ultra vires* in its entirety on the ground that under the guise of legislation affecting British and Foreign Companies and extra Canadian exchanges, the enactments were really adopted in relation to the business of insurance within the Provinces and could not be upheld as alien legislation in the proper sense.

But it would seem that the constitutionality of legislation disputed on the ground of colourability should really be brought before the Courts not on a Reference, but in an ordinary case. It is no doubt in that sense that we must understand the dictum of Lord Maugham L.C. in *Reference re Alberta Bills*, [1939] A.C. 117 at p. 130: "The next step in a case of difficulty will be to examine the effect of the legislation (*Union Colliery Co. of B.C. Ltd. v. Bryden,* [1899] A.C. 580). For that purpose the Court must take into account any public general knowledge of which the Court would take judicial notice, and may in a proper case require to be informed by evidence as to what the effect of the legislation will be. Clearly the Acts passed by the Provincial Legislature may be considered, for it is often impossible to determine the effect of the Act under examination without taking into account any other Act operating or intended to operate or recently operating in the Province."

And again at p. 131 A.C.: "Matters of which the Court would take judicial notice must be borne in mind, and other evidence in a case which calls for it."

In both quotations the words used by the noble Lord are "in a proper case" and "in a case which calls for it". He does not say "on a Reference", and I cannot see how two *obiter dicta* of that character can be invoked as meaning that outside evidence may be called on a Reference.

Fort Frances P. & P. Co. v. Man. Free Press Co., [1923] A.C. 695, was such an ordinary case between two private litigants, and in delivering the judgment of the Judicial Committee in that case Viscount Haldane at p. 706 A.C., expressed the view: "No authority other than the central government is in a position to deal with a problem which is essentially one of statesmanship. It may be that it has become clear that the crisis which arose is wholly at an end and that there is no justification for the continued exercise of an exceptional interference which becomes *ultra vires* when it is no longer called for. In such a case the law as laid down for distribution of powers in the ruling instrument would have to be invoked. But very clear evidence that the crisis had wholly passed away would be required to justify the judiciary, even when the question raised was one of *ultra vires* which it had to decide, in overruling the decision of the Government that exceptional measures were still requisite. In saying what is almost obvious, their Lordships observe themselves to be in accord with the view taken under analogous circumstances by the Supreme Court of the United States, and expressed in such decisions as that in October, 1919, in *Hamilton v. Kentucky Distilleries* (1919), 251 U.S. Rep. 146."

Some allusion was made to the same point in *Re Regulation & Control of Radio Communication,* [1931] S.C.R. 541, aff'd [1932] A.C. 304]. A mere glance at the Order in Council reproduced at that and the following pages is sufficient to show to what extent the facts in that matter were there started. It is to be noted that the opinion of Newcombe J. starts by saying [pp. 548-9 S.C.R.]: "My trouble with this case is to know the facts. Although the narrative of the order of reference and the printed statement of principles were not at the hearing seriously disputed, one is apt to suspect that the knowledge of the art of radio, which we have derived from the submissions and what was said in the course of argument, is still incomplete and, perhaps, in some particulars, not free from error;

that some accepted theories are still experimental or tentative, and that there may be possibilities of development and use, not only in the Dominion but also in a provincial field, which have not yet been fully ascertained or tested."

It is obvious that if Newcombe J., whose experience in these matters cannot be disputed, had thought that he was entitled to hear outside evidence on a Reference, he would have availed himself of the opportunity. It is true that in that Reference an article compiled by J. W. Bain, a radio engineer of the Marine Department, was printed in the case, but, as stated by Smith J. at p. 569 S.C.R. "This document is inserted for the convenience of the Court, and it is stated that its accuracy may be verified by reference to the various standard textbooks on the subject. Its general accuracy was, I think, not controverted, and I therefore resort to this document for a brief general description of how radio communication is effected."

Radio communication was, of course, of a highly technical nature and it was felt necessary that the Court should at least be informed of how it worked.

In *Re Eskimos,* [1939] S.C.R. 104, in the order fixing the date for hearing Sir Lyman P. Duff C.J.C. appointed the Registrar of the Court to hear and take all evidence, oral and documentary, which the Attorney-General of Canada or any other interested parties desired to submit, or adduce, in relation to the question referred to the Court. He ordered further that all the evidence so adduced and submitted on behalf of each of the interested parties be included *quantum valent* and subject to all just exception in the case, and printed in such groups and order as the interested parties might agree upon, subject to the approval of the Registrar. It is to be noted that all interested parties, including, of course, the Attorney-General of Canada, were given the opportunity to submit relevant evidence and particularly that such evidence was incorporated in and formed part of the case.

I must say, therefore, that, for the purpose of my answer, I am limiting myself strictly to the situation disclosed in the Order of Reference and the different declarations which appear in the successive Acts adopted by Parliament. Thus limiting my consideration of the Reference and the extent of my answer, I have very few remarks to make.

There is no doubt that under normal conditions the subject-matter of rents belongs to the provincial jurisdiction under the head of Property and Civil Rights, in s. 92 of the *B.N.A. Act*. There is equally no doubt that under abnormal conditions, such as the existence of war, Parliament may competently assume jurisdiction over rents. The fact is that, as a consequence of the last war, 1939-45, Parliament has taken over the control of rents. The *Fort Frances* case, *supra,* is authority for the proposition that, notwithstanding the cessation of hostilities, Parliament is empowered to continue the control of rents for the purpose of concluding matters then pending, and of its discontinuance in an orderly manner, as the emergency permits, of measures adopted during and by reason of the emergency. It follows from the different Orders in Council and Acts of Parliament, recited in the Order of Reference, that the exceptional conditions brought about by war, which made the *Wartime Leasehold Regulations* necessary, are still continuing, that the orderly transition from war to peace has not yet been completed, and that, in such circumstances, Parliament is entitled and empowered to maintain such control as it finds necessary to ensure the orderly transition from war to peace. The judgments of the Judicial Committee of the Privy Council in the *For Frances* case *supra,* and in *Co-operative Committee on Japanese Canadians v. A.-G. Can.,* [1947] A.C. 87, are conclusive on this point. . . .

[Kerwin, Taschereau, Rand, Kellock, Estey and Locke JJ. also gave reasons sustaining the validity of the leasehold regulations but without raising issues as to admissibility of extrinsic materials on a Reference.

Is it not odd that Rinfret C.J.C. should rely on the *Alberta Bank Taxation* case, [1939] A.C. 117, [1938] 4 D.L.R. 433, [1938] 3 W.W.R. 337, to support his view that "outside evidence" may not be adduced on a Reference when that "case" was itself a Reference? And does he mean that the assertions in an Order of Reference are binding on the Court without any right of contra-diction except by consideration of facts of which the Courts may take "judicial notice"? Would this not put too much power in the hands of those preparing the Order of Reference? See, for example, the Order in the *Margarine* case, [1949] S.C.R. 1, [1949] 1 D.L.R. 433, aff'd [1951] A.C. 179, [1950] 4 D.L.R. 689, reported *infra,* at p. 269.]

A Note on Constitutional Facts

"The question of the method of informing the Court on facts re-levant to the constitutionality of a statute is in need of special and frank consideration": so it is said in 9 *Wigmore,* Evidence, s. 2568a(n). What are facts in this connection is itself a matter of debate because the line between validity and invalidity of a statute may be drawn not according to the truth of an allegation but accord-ing to judicial acceptance or rejection of opinion that the challenged legislation embodies an object within the power of the enacting legis-lature. The scope of a legislative power, its breadth or narrowness as the case may be, has a decided bearing on the kind of material (whether called facts or extrinsic evidence or simply extrinsic aids) that may be relevant to support a statute addressed to that power. Companion or associated legislation may, in a sense, be considered a fact to be taken into account in measuring the validity of an enact-ment; see, for example, the *Texada Mines* case, [1960] S.C.R. 713, 24 D.L.R. (2d) 81, 32 W.W.R. 37. So too may the preamble or even a sub-stantive term of the enactment, when used by the legislature as the vehicle for expressing its constitutional basis. In *Citizens Insurance Co. v. Parsons* (1881), 7 App. Cas. 96, the Privy Council remarked (at pp. 115-6) that "the declarations of the dominion parliament are not, of course, conclusive upon the construction of the British North America Act; but when the proper construction of the language used in the Act to define the distribution of legislative powers is doubtful, the interpretation put upon it by the dominion parliament in its actual legislation may properly be considered".

Other legislation and preambles and the like stand apart from the questions that call for discussion here. They are traditional sources, like judicial decisions and are considered to be "legal" materials which may be freely pressed upon a Court in written brief or oral argument. Constitutional issues arise, however, when the validity of a statute is postulated on the existence of a condition or, even more narrowly, on an underlying "fact", and the postulate is challenged. On a secondary level, it may be urged that valid though the statute be in its under-lying circumstances, it does not apply to a litigant unaffected by those circumstances. Cf. *Holmes,* Evidence in Constitutional Cases, (1949) 23 Aust. L. J. 235.

What extrinsic material may be brought before the Court in such cases? And how may this be done? In the United States, the "Brandeis brief" has had great vogue, coming into prominence after being used in *Muller v. Oregon* (1908), 208 U.S. 412. The *Brandeis* technique of marshalling social and economic data in the brief presented to the Court in argument to support the constitutionality of a statute was addressed to "judicial notice". Brewer J. who spoke for the Court in that case, referring to the brief filed by Brandeis, stated that "we take judicial cognizance of all matters of general knowledge". (The brief is reproduced in part in *Lief* (ed.), The Social and Economic Views of Mr. Justice Brandeis, p. 337). See *Morgan,* Judicial Notice, (1944) 57 Harv. L. Rev. 269; *Nokes,* The Limits of Judicial Notice, (1958) 74 Law Q. Rev. 59. Corry has aptly pointed out (The Use of Legislative History in the Interpretation of Statutes, (1954) 32 Can. Bar Rev. 624, at p. 635) that the Brandeis brief is peculiarly applicable to show the reasonableness of legislative re-straints in the light of the United States Bill of Rights; and, indeed, resort to evidence of Congressional committee hearings on a bill and debates is likewise supportable as designed to show the abuses which the corrective and protective legislation is intended to combat. As has been said elsewhere, "in the constitutional fact cases [in the United States] the burden is on the party attacking a statute to show beyond a reasonable doubt that there are no social facts which would justify the passage of the statute. This burden of proof has the effect of requiring that facts be indisputable in order to make a statute invalid. Judicial notice therefore is usually adequate, thus making understandable the slowness to develop other techniques for proving constitutional facts. . .": see *Note,* Social and Economic Facts—Appraisal of Suggested Techniques for Presenting Them to the Court, (1948) 61 Harv. L. Rev. 692, at p. 696; see also *Bikle,* Judicial De-termination of Questions of Fact Affecting the Constitutional Validity of Legislative Action, (1924) 38 Harv. L. Rev. 6.

Judicial notice, as a basis for introduction of social and economic arguments and statistics, raises a more difficult problem when ad-dressed to the invalidation of a statute, but the problem is more one of the weight of the data than of its admissibility. Cf. *Cahn.* (ed.), Supreme Court and Supreme Law (1954), at pp. 47 ff. It must be such as to meet and overcome the so-called presumption of constitu-tionality which is no more than a canon of construction: see *Note.*

The Presumption of Constitutionality, (1931) 31 Col. L. Rev. 1136;
Note, The Presumption of Constitutionality Reconsidered, (1936) 36
Col. L. Rev. 283.

Some of the problems raised by the Brandeis brief are discussed
by *Freund*, On Understanding the Supreme Court (1949), pp. 86 ff.
He raises the question whether the data in the brief ought not to be
placed on the record through the testimony of expert witnesses who
would submit such data not for the truth of what is asserted but as
evidence of responsible opinion underlying the reasons for (or, the
reasons against) the legislation in issue. Being in the record, there
would be a more effective opportunity to impeach the data than
through a brief in reply. *Quaere,* whether this could be done in the
constitutional reference which has become almost the normal method
of resolving constitutional issues in Canada!

Mere marshalling of social and economic facts in a brief is, of
course, no guarantee that a Court will be influenced by them: see
Mason, Brandeis: Lawyer and Judge in the Modern State, chap. VI.
There is, however, a growing tendency in Canada of introducing such
extrinsic materials in briefs of counsel: see *MacDonald,* Constitutional
Interpretation and Extrinsic Evidence, (1939) 17 Can. Bar Rev. 77,
at p. 92. That this can be overdone is evident from *Saumur v. Quebec
and A.-G. Que.,* [1953] 2 S.C.R. 299, [1953] 4 D.L.R. 641, where the
Court deprived the successful appellant of costs for preparation of a
factum because his counsel had overwhelmed the Court with a brief
of two volumes containing 912 mimeographed pages and an appendix
of 86 such pages. Apart from this, there is a problem of constitutional
construction in Canada which, although related to, stands above the
use of extrinsic materials in connection with impugned statutes; and
that is whether the scope or content of the various heads of legislative
power is broad or ample enough to make reliance on anything more
than precedent and logic worth while in assessing the validity of
legislation. This is particularly important in respect of such apparently wide grants of legislative power as are given by the opening words
of section 91, by the terms of section 91(2) and those of section
92(13).

[The following are illustrative problems:

(1) Is it open to the Court to take evidence of the underlying "constitutional fact" that an emergency has not arisen or no longer exists (relative to
the validity of the National Emergency Transitional Powers Act, 1945 (Can.),
c. 25 and orders-in-council thereunder)? See *Canadian Wheat Board v.
Manitoba Pool Elevators* (which was a "case" not a "reference") referred to
supra, at p. 159.

(2) Where a municipal by-law prohibiting distribution of pamphlets or
handbills without a police permit is challenged as invalid or inapplicable in
respect of religious activities, is evidence of ministers of various religious
faiths admissible to show that Jehovah's Witnesses are not a religion? See
Saumur case, *supra,* and especially the judgment of Locke J.

(3) Where the validity of a regulatory statute on atomic energy is
supported or challenged as being in relation to defence, is evidence admissible
to show the special military and non-military value of atomic energy?

(4) Where a provincial marketing statute is challenged, is evidence admissible to show as an underlying fact that the principal market for the regulated products is outside the province?]

A further problem may be noticed, which arose in connection with the Canada Temperance Act, the validity of which was first sustained by the Privy Council in *Russell v. The Queen* (1882), 7 App. Cas. 829. Having regard to the explanation of that case in *Toronto Electric Commr's. v. Snider*, [1925] A.C. 396, [1925] 2 D.L.R. 5, [1925] 1 W.W.R. 785, and to the reason there given for the decision in the *Russell* case, it appeared that in changed circumstances a different decision would be given, unless an inflexible conception of *stare decisis* took hold or, indeed, unless the basis of decision in the *Snider* case was rejected. There was, of course, the possibility that a Court could be persuaded that even the controlling factors as laid down in the *Russell* case itself were no longer present. The answer of the Courts was given in *Re Canada Temperance Act*, [1939] O.R. 570, [1939] 4 D.L.R. 14, aff'd on appeal *sub nom. A.-G. Ont. v. Canada Temperance Federation*, [1946] A.C. 193, [1946] 2 D.L.R. 1, [1946] 2 W.W.R. 1. Cf. *Rottschaefer*, Handbook of America Constitutional Law, at p. 34: "It sometimes occurs that a statutory provision sustained as valid at one time is subsequently held invalid because of changed circumstances at the time of its later application, or that such change in circumstances is recognized as invalidating a provision which the court assumes could have been validly applied under the conditions existing at the time of its enactment. The correct theory is not that the changed circumstances have invalidated an originally valid enactment but rather that from the very time of its enactment it would have been invalid to have applied it under the conditions existing in the case in which it was subsequently declared unconstitutional. The changed circumstances have merely created the situations in which its application is invalid, but it would have been equally invalid to have applied it to those situations had they existed when, or immediately after, the provision was enacted. That is, as applied to them, the provision had no legal force from the very time of its enactment. The same reasoning requires the conclusion that a statutory provision is valid from the time of its enactment as applied to all the cases within its terms in which it can at any time be validly applied, and that changed conditions may create such situations even though none existed at the time, or immediately after, it was enacted. The changed conditions considered in this paragraph exclude constitutional changes that might affect the issue, including changes due to reversals of position by the courts".

A good illustration of the principles just quoted is provided by the *Margarine* case (*Canadian Federation of Agriculture v. A.-G. Que.*, [1951] A.C. 179, [1950] 4 D.L.R. 689). There, federal legislation prohibiting the manufacture and sale of margarine, originally enacted at a time when the wholesomeness of the product was suspect, was held *ultra vires* because in the meantime improvements in ingredients and manufacturing processes had removed any danger to health.

5. Limitations on Legislative Power

In *Bank of Toronto v. Lambe* (1887), 12 App. Cas. 575, 4 Cart. B.N.A. 7, the Judicial Committee said (at p. 588) that "the Federation Act exhausts the whole range of legislative power, and . . . whatever is not thereby given to the provincial legislatures rests with the parliament". Recently, Rand J. made the same point more cautiously in *Murphy v. C.P.R. and A.-G. Can.*, [1958] S.C.R. 626, 15 D.L.R. (2d) 145, as follows: "It has become a truism that the totality of effective legislative power is conferred by the Act of 1867, subject always to the express or necessarily implied limitations of the Act itself." There is, however, the contrary intimation by Lord Haldane during the argument in *Toronto Electric Commrs. v. Snider*, [1925] A.C. 396, [1925] 2 D.L.R. 5, [1925] 1 W.W.R. 785. When counsel contended that all legislative power was distributed between Dominion and provinces, he replied, "That is a popular expression, and even judges in the Judicial Committee are human; you must not strain casual expressions in connections where they are not applied. It is not true." (See O'Connor Report, Annex 1 pp. 15-16.)

What the learned law lord meant is not clear, but it is true, as Rand J. indicated, that the expression is subject to qualifications. They are, however, fewer in number since the Statute of Westminster, 1931 (Imp.), c. 4 than before. Limitations on legislative power in Canada immediately following the enactment of the British North America Act, apart from those inhering in the distribution of legislative power effected by the Act, were as follows: (1) There was no general provision in the Act respecting its amendment by effective action in Canada; and while the provinces were authorized to amend their constitutions except as regards the office of Lieutenant-Governor (the amending authority being referable to the structure and organization of organs of government), similar power in respect of the federal organs of government was withheld from Parliament until 1949. (2) The Colonial Laws Validity Act, 1865 (Imp.), c. 63 affirmed the effectiveness in Canada, as in other colonies or Dominions, of British legislation extending thereto by express words or necessary intendment. Not only were the local legislatures powerless to repeal or alter the effect of such existing British legislation but they were equally subject to future enactments so extending to them. (3) The Parliament of Canada was, apparently, precluded from legislating with extraterritorial effect, although this was not explicit in the British North America Act in its case as it was, by and large, in respect of the provincial legislatures: see *Nadan v. The King*, [1926] A.C. 482, [1926] 2 D.L.R. 177, [1926] 1 W.W.R. 801. (4) Sections 55, 56, 57 and 90 of the British North America Act provided for reservation of bills and for disallowance of legislation, both in respect of Parliament (the enactments of which were subject to reservation by the Governor-General for the signification of the Queen's pleasure and subject to disallowance by the Queen in Council) and in respect of the provincial legislatures (the enactments of which were subject to reservation by the Lieutenant-Governor for the signification of the pleasure of the Governor-General and subject to disallowance by the Governor-General in Council). (See *La Forest*, Disallowance and Reservation of Provincial Legislation (1955)). (5.) There was, of course, no power to deal with succession to the throne. (6) While the office of Governor-General was mentioned in the British North America Act (see for example, sections 24, 55, 56, 57, 105), it was not created thereby but by exercise of the prerogative, and the legal and conventional position was that its establishment and authority depended on the British rather than the Canadian executive, and, *a fortiori*, it was subject to the ultimate control of the Parliament of Great Britain.

Some of these limitations were affected by the Statute of Westminster and others by conventional understandings through the Imperial Conferences of 1926 and 1930; but one, the absence of a Canadian amending procedure, especially in respect of legislative power, has remained untouched.

The Statute of Westminster by sections 2 and 7(2) not only removed from Parliament and the provincial legislatures the disability of the Colonial Laws Validity Act, as well as any possible anterior disability to enact legislation repugnant to the law of England or to enactments of the Parliament of the United Kingdom, but expressly authorized them to repeal or amend such enactments in so far as they were part of the law of Canada or of a province. In addition, section 4 (going beyond the conventional effect of a pre-amble to the same effect) declared that no British Act should thereafter extend, expressly or by necessary intendment, to a Dominion as part of its law unless it was expressly declared therein that the Dominion requested and consented to its enactment. How far, in law, this did or could operate as anything more than a rule of construction or whether it operated as a limitation on the competence of the Parliament of the United Kingdom have been the subjects of conflicting opinions: see *British Coal Corp. v. The King*, [1935] A.C. 500, [1935] 3 D.L.R. 401, [1935] 2 W.W.R. 564; *Dixon*, The Statute of Westminster 1931, (1936) 10 Aust. L.J., Supp. 96; *Jennings*, Law and the Constitution (5th ed., 1959), pp. 163 ff; *Wheare*, The Statute of Westminster and Dominion Status (5th ed., 1953), pp. 153 ff; *Ndlwana v. Hofmeyr*, [1937] A.D. 229, at p. 237.

Section 3 of the Statute of Westminster expressly authorized Parliament to legislate with extraterritorial effect, although it may be doubted in view of *Croft v. Dunphy*, [1933] A.C. 156, [1933] 1 D.L.R. 225, [1932] 3 W.W.R. 696, whether this provision was really necessary: see *Wheare, op. cit.*, at p. 194; *O'Connell*, The Doctrine of Colonial Extra-Territorial Legislative Incompetence, (1959) 75 Law Q. Rev. 318; and see *B.C. Electric Ry. Co. v. The King*, [1946] A.C. 527, [1946] 4 D.L.R. 81, [1946] 3 W.W.R. 737; see also The Extra-territorial Act, R.S.C. 1952, c. 107.

It must be noted that such legislative authority as was given by sections 2, 3, 4, and 7(2) of the Statute of Westminster was expressly subordinated (by section 7(1)(3)) to the supremacy of the British North America Acts, 1867 to 1930, and to the distribution of power effected thereby. This protection of the British North America Act gave rise to a circular argument in *Nanaimo Community Hotel v. Board of Referees,* [1945] 3 D.L.R. 225, [1945] 2 W.W.R. 145, because of section 129 which declared, *inter alia,* that British statutes in force in Canada by express words or necessary intendment were subject to repeal only by the Parliament of Great Britain. A majority of the British Columbia Court of Appeal sustained the effect of section 2 of the Statute of Westminster as against section 129 of the British North America Act in the respect noted.

Reservation and disallowance as between Canada and the British authorities were nullified conventionally by the Imperial Conference of 1930; and while they remained untouched by the Statute of Westminster, it is fairly arguable that the Parliament of Canada may itself abolish them in law as a result of the British North America Act, No. 2, 1949 (Imp.), c. 81. This Act, being a later one, is outside of the protection of s. 7(1) of the Statute of Westminster and, indeed, modifies that statute. Unless it be construed strictly as referable only to the structure and organization of federal organs of government, it is in terms wide enough to embrace repeal of the reservation and disallowance provisions not only as they affect Canada and the United Kingdom *inter se* but also as they affect the provinces and Canada *inter se.* It is clear that as they now exist in the British North America Act, reservation and disallowance are subsisting limitations on provincial authority: see *Reference re Disallowance and Reservation of Provincial Legislation,* [1938] S.C.R. 71, [1938] 2 D.L.R. 8. And, convention apart, they are equally subsisting limitations on federal authority.

A conventional change only, based on the Imperial Conference of 1930 and on a preamble in the Statute of Westminster, was directly effected in respect of the succession to the throne and the royal style and titles. Changes in the law in those matters were to require the assent of the Parliaments of the Dominions as well as of the Parliament of the United Kingdom. In view of section 4 of the Statute of Westminster, however, there is legal reinforcement in the need for request and consent by Canada to any such changes made by the United Kingdom if they are to be effective in Canada; see in this connection, Succession to the Throne Act, 1937 (Can.), c. 16. It would seem to be open to Canada to make changes for its own purposes, subject to the conventional arrangement for assent or even, as a matter of law, despite it.

The Imperial Conferences of 1926 and 1930 established conventional rules respecting the office of Governor-General, recognizing it as in all respects subject to the dictates of responsible government and to be the concern, in respect of appointment and authority, of the Crown personally and the Canadian ministry. Section 9 of the British North America Act declares that "the executive government and authority of and over Canada is hereby declared to continue and be vested in the Queen"; and the evolution in respect of the office, appointment and authority of the Governor-General suggests, in line with section 9 and with the British North America Act, 1949, No. 2, that effective authority in that behalf now rests with the Parliament of Canada; but not so as to interfere (in view of section 55 of the Act of 1867) with the Governor-General's representative function in law-making, so long as that office exists. This again raises a nice question of the reach of the British North America Act, 1949, No. 2, in authorizing the Parliament of Canada, subject to specified exceptions, to legislate in relation to "the amendment from time to time of the Constitution of Canada".

Apart from the limitations on legislative power discussed above, the scheme of distribution of such power as between Parliament and provincial legislatures poses a number of questions as to other possible limitations despite the declared doctrine of exhaustiveness. Thus, it may be asked whether the exclusion from section 92(1) of the Act of 1867 of provincial competence "as regards the office of Lieutenant-Governor" necessarily means (in view of federal residuary authority) that the office and function of Lieutenant-Governor are subject to the legislative control of Parliament. In view of the fact that his appointment and tenure are at the disposition of the Governor-General in Council and Governor-General respectively and that his salary comes from the Parliament of Canada (see sections 58, 59 and 60 of the Act of 1867), the constitutional duty of making an appointment and paying an incumbent may indicate that whatever problem there is lies not in arbitrary legislative power but in the willingness *vel non* to carry out the duty. (See, generally, *Saywell*, The Office of Lieutenant-Governor (1957)). Similar arguments could be made in respect of the office of Governor-General, especially because its functions are associated with various kinds of appointments, such as to Lieutenant-Governorships, to the Senate and to the bench. But since he is acting representatively, may not his principal act personally in his stead?

A somewhat similar question arises in respect of provincial limitation to "direct taxation within the province in order to the raising of a revenue for provincial purposes", as prescribed by section 92(2). May Parliament then impose indirect taxation for provincial purposes? It has assumed that it may by an amendment (1957 (Can.), c. 15) to the Agricultural Products Marketing Act, R.S.C. 1952, c. 6. Yet there is ground for saying, having regard to the conventional and, indeed, constitutional position respecting revenue or taxing measures (see sections 54 and 90 of the Act of 1867) that there is no competence in Parliament to fill this gap in provincial taxing power: see *Laskin*, Provincial Marketing Levies: Indirect Taxation and Federal Power, (1959) 13 Univ. of Tor. L.J. 1, at p. 20.

Other gaps in total legislative power are also present, as, for example, inter-delegation as between Parliament and provincial legislatures (already considered), and the want of treaty implementing power by reason of the restricted interpretation of section 132 (see *infra*, Chap. III), although it may be urged that what cannot be implemented by Parliament may be implemented by provincial legislatures. There are also the explicit guarantees of section 93 and later comparable provisions respecting certain provinces, e.g. Newfoundland, with respect to denominational schools and of section 133 respecting the use of the English or French language, and there is the protected tenure of Judges under section 99, subject, however, to compulsory retirement at age 75. In *Switzman v. Elbling and A.-G. Que.*, [1957] S.C.R. 285, 7 D.L.R. (2d) 337, Abbott J. broke with the doctrine of exhaustiveness by finding an implicit limitation against federal interference with freedom of debate and discussion in addition to the express limitation against provincial interference in that respect.

It is one thing for a Court to avoid or refrain from passing on the constitutionality of legislation, but an entirely different thing for a legislature, whether Dominion or provincial, to preclude such a determination, either directly or by imposing *a priori* conditions to litigation which remain unsatisfied. The case law has, quite properly, reflected the acknowledged role of the Courts as expounders of the limits of legislative powers by denying both to Parliament and provincial legislatures the power to shield their legislation from curial review of its validity: see *Note*, (1941) 19 Can. Bar Rev. 45; *Electrical Development Co. of Ont. v. A.-G. Ont.*, [1919] A.C. 687, 47 D.L.R. 10; *Ottawa Valley Power Co. v. H.E.P.C.*, [1937] O.R. 265, [1963] 4 D.L.R. 594. A particular illustration of this role of the Courts may be found in *B.C. Power Corp. Ltd. v. B.C. Electric Co. Ltd. and A.-G. B.C.*, [1962] S.C.R. 642, 34 D.L.R. (2d) 196, at p. 274, 38 W.W.R. 701, where the Supreme Court upheld a claim for appointment of a receiver respecting assets claimed by the Crown in right of the Province when the Crown's right depended on the validity of legislation which was challenged in the action. Kerwin C.J.C., after referring to the circumstances, stated that "in a federal System . . . . the Court has the same jurisdiction to preserve assets whose title is dependent on the validity of the legislation as it has to determine the validity of the legislation itself."

A related problem is raised by the judgment of the Ontario Court of Appeal in *Beauharnois Light Heat & Power Co. v. H.E.P.C.*, [1937] O.R. 796, [1937] 3 D.L.R. 458. After a judgment in that case declaring invalid provincial legislation abrogating certain electric power contracts, the legislature passed a statute declaring the meaning and effect of an enactment forbidding suit against the Power Commission without consent of the Attorney-General. This declaratory statute came into force before the hearing of the appeal. In the judgment on appeal, Middleton J.A., for the Court, stated that "the rights of the parties had already passed into judgment and the legislation had no effect upon this action". He continued as follows:

> The intention of the Legislature is embodied in the formal Act of Parliament and can only be gathered from the words used in that enactment. The Legislature, in matters within its competence, is unquestionably supreme, but it falls to the Courts to determine the meaning of the language used. If the Courts do not determine in accordance with the true intention of the Legislature, the Legislature cannot arrogate to itself the jurisdiction of a further appellate Court and enact that the language used in its earlier enactment means something other than the

Court has determined. It can, if it so pleases, use other language expressing its meaning more clearly. It transcends its true function when it
undertakes to say that the language used has a different meaning and
effect to that given it by the Courts, and that it always has meant something other than the Courts have declared it to mean. Very plainly is this
so when, as in this case, the declaratory Act was not passed until after
the original Act had been construed, and judgment pronounced.

For these reasons the subsequent legislation has no effect upon this
case. . . .

A contrary view was taken on a similar problem in *Matthew v.
Guardian Assur. Co.* (1918), 58 S.C.R. 47, 45 D.L.R. 32, [1919] 1
W.W.R. 67, and, similarly, in *Gold Seal Ltd. v. Dominion Express Co.
and A.-G. Alta.* (1921), 62 S.C.R. 424, 62 D.L.R. 62, [1921] 3 W.W.R.
710. The matter was reviewed again, with particular reference to
and disapproval of the *Beauharnois* case, in *Western Minerals Ltd. v.
Gaumont and A.-G. Alta.*, [1953] 1 S.C.R. 345, [1953] 3 D.L.R. 245
where Cartwright J. stated that "if and in so far as the . . . *Beauharnois* case negatives the power of the Legislature to declare the
law retrospectively or otherwise, in regard to matters entirely within
the ambit of its constitutional powers, it ought not to be followed".

6.   The Logic of 91 and 92

The potential in the peculiar structure of the grants of legislative
authority in sections 91 and 92 of the British North America Act,
1867, implied for Canadian constitutional doctrine a coherence let slip
away by speech and thought patterns which have obscured and eventually ousted the orderly sequence of examination indicated by the
peculiar structure of sections 91 and 92.

What is that structure? And that sequence?

The cited sections empower parliament and the provincial legislatures alike 'to make laws in relation to [a] matters [b] coming within . . . [c] classes of subjects.' The 'matter' of the challenged law, the
proper scope of each 'class of subjects,' and deciding what class of
subjects a matter 'comes within' are the relevant factors in the scheme
the Act provides. So one must in every case (1) identify the 'matter'
to which a statute relates, (2) define the scope of each 'class of subjects' which might be thought to be relevant, (3) assign the 'matter'
as identified to the most appropriate 'class of subjects' as defined.

One may hopefully believe that this systematic approach, calling
for disclosure of what consideration was given to the whole range of
materials relevant to decision and how they were appraised by stating
and calling attention to decisional factors hitherto unarticulated or ignored, would at a minimum make the law more visible, hence more
predictable. Moreover I think it would be wiser. Informed criticism
is the best cure for, as apprehension of it is the best preventive of,
defective judgment. When the grounds for judgment are scattered
fragments, arranged in no particular order and with some pieces
missing, criticism is perforce uninformed and judgment the sufferer.

What's the "Matter"?

Each measure has its own 'matter'.

That quality has been well described as a concern with 'the pith and substance' of the statute. The working out of what the notion expresses should be the first step in resolving issues of legislative competence in the Canadian constitutional scheme. All too often recognition that this is what is involved has led immediately to a characterizing conclusion without any connecting demonstration. Good as it is for intuitive judgments to state accurately what they are being intuitive about, that they are intuitive is a basic flaw. We need to know how the conclusion about a law's pith and substance was arrived at.

In having its distinctive 'matter,' its own pith and substance, a statute is just like any other written text. True, it is distinguished among written texts as being one which is an expression of legislative will. But, for determining the 'matter,' not that specific feature but its generic character is relevant. Like any written text, its 'matter' depends on what it says read in the context in which it speaks.

Before ruling whether a trust is charitable or not with whatever consequences ensue, it is the regular practice to investigate what kind of provisions it makes for whom. The operative consequences of its particular terms are explored before determining whether a writing gives rise to a sale or a security arrangement. The tenor of its own particular claims falls to be assessed where the scope of protection under a patent is to be determined. Always the pith and substance, the 'matter' of the writing is a threshold inquiry, which precedes and should proceed independently of the content of the competing legal categories whose application flows from it. Indeed the same processes are appropriate for any writing whether with or without a legal bearing. Whether for sermons, statutes, sonnets, surety bonds, or scientific reports, epitomization, however various in purpose, is achieved the same way.

In disregard of this elementary notion, the tendency has been to speak of the 'matter' of a statute in terms of the 'classes of subjects' set forth in the BNA Act. The result is to collapse 'matter' and 'class of subjects' into a single inquiry. That technique, besides doing violence to the sequence of analysis the Act prescribes, neglects appraisal of the 'matter' in the way texts are ordinarily read. It would be best to forget all about 'classes of subjects' at this stage. Statutes of like content usually are dealing with the same matter whether they be enacted in New Brunswick, New Zealand, or New Jersey; and it is highly unlikely that lawyers abroad would think of their pith and substance in terms reflecting Canadian constitutional categories or that Canadian lawyers would so describe the gist of New Zealand or New Jersey statutes.

A topical catchword seldom if indeed ever adequately specifies the 'matter' of a statute. That exercise is inherently more complex. It amounts to an abstract of the statute's content, instancing the subjects or situations to which it applies and the ways it proposes to govern them, spelled out sufficiently to inform anyone asking, 'What's it all about?' Narrow statutes admit of sharper answers to that question; comprehensive ones demand broader and more generalized ones; but in either case there normally will be some central theme which can be appropriately paraphrased to complete the sentence, 'This Act provides . . .' 'Matter' is synonymous with the true, full, and exact summarization which does so.

The task is often not simple. Long intricate statutes may be taken as dealing with one or with several matters. The inescapable ambiguity of language will leave meaning to be derived using whatever literary or extra-literary guides are available and acceptable. Control over one set of circumstances may be mediated through dealing with another. These quandaries for the classical rhetorical trilogy: unity, coherence, and emphasis, are certain to be found as much in statutes as elsewhere. With each the courts have coped. Usually they do it by labelling, a handy economical device but one which tends to conceal the common nature of a variety of notions as all bearing on definition of the 'matter'. The labels thus have obscured the light that might have been shed on that central issue. An examination of certain of these stock concepts showing their connection with the 'pith and substance' inquiry may make them more translucent.

The typical statute is a composite, assembling many specific and detailed provisions into a single package, separating them into parts and sections, each with its own morsel of meaning. Since ordinary litigation arises out of the attempt to apply some one provision and even many references have addressed themselves especially to designated portions, one must start by settling on the pith and substance of what is relevant.

The alternatives are to view the statute as an integrated whole or to disaggregate it into components of any desired size. Is one inspecting the forest or the trees? Whether the gaze is to be fixed intently on a section banning the manufacture, selling, keeping, or offering for sale, or importing of margarine or whether the field of vision shall instead take in a great sprawling statute concerned with many phases of and operations in the processing for market and marketing of dairy products may be decisively important. No discernible general logical compulsion favours either the broad or the narrow approach. The presumption of constitutionality—more talked about in the United States than in Canada—may here find its place. In any given case choice is for the court and lies within that large realm of judicial discretion where demonstration of error is difficult. What is blameable is the very general failure to indicate the existence and nature of the alternatives with the fullest possible exposition of reasons for preferring one, a failure rather aggravated than excused by unawareness.

Even if it is decided to look at the thrust of the whole statute, the inspection of the particulars does not become irrelevant. The relevant 'matter' is then indeed not their special 'matter' and they are to be viewed not as independent measures in their own right but as functional elements in the larger scheme. The various components in that larger scheme will differ both in their own natures and in how they relate to it. If the 'matter' both of the part and of the whole, or con-

versely of neither, turns out upon definition and assignment to a
'class of subjects' to be constitutionally vulnerable, the hair usually
goes with the hide and decision gets rested upon the conclusion about
the whole statute without further elaboration. Where all parties agree
always about the statue's over-all constitutionality and the whole issue
centres on the peculiarities of the particular provision, this can be an
unsatisfactory shirking of responsibility. But ordinarily the fate of
the parts can be left to stand or fall with the whole if item-by-item
analysis of the 'matters' would wind up exactly the same as the integrated analysis.

The trouble comes when they diverge. The statute's pith and substance may be so resolved as to place it outside any class of subjects
assigned the enacting legislature but the particular provision's matter
as independently evaluated may bring it within one of them. Conversely, although the pith and substance of the whole statute be such
as to come within an available class of subjects, the separately considered matter of a particular provision might not. What governs?
Does the good redeem, perish with, or survive the bad? The principle
of redemption underlies the doctrine of ancillariness. The doctrine of
severability comes into play to determine the issue of guilt by association or salvation by dissociation. While both ancillariness and severability are familiar terms in Canadian constitutional discourse, with
neither perhaps has its significance been clearly enough recognized
as being in connection with defining the relevant 'matter'. Some attention to each is in order.

The ancillary doctrine is used when the pith and substance of the
whole statute has been defined so as to legitimate it, never to make
the 'matter' of a particular provision spill over onto its companions.
Adverted to mostly but not only in connection with federal legislation,
it applies, after a statute has been read as in pith and substance dealing with matter found to come within an allowable class of subjects,
to validate component provisions which (by hypothesis or prima
facie) looked at alone, deal with matter having a more dubious status.
In effect it polarizes the statute so that no part of it is conceived as
having an independent direction but all are seen as pointed toward the
one central matter. It has been criticized as an unnecessary and insub-
stantial complication. If it be understood as sanctioning a shifting
around of the boundaries of classes of subjects to suit occasional convenience (a reading which the context of its use at times suggests),
the criticism is apt. But if, as is my submission, its office is in connection with definition of the 'matter' of the statute, for that purpose
suppressing the special tendencies of special provisions and treating
all of them as merely elements in the common structure, it is intellectually serviceable. Under what circumstances that will be done is another question, resembling and sometimes blurred into that already
noted of whether to look to the matter of the whole statute or of the
isolated provision as the key question and, like it, leaving much room
for judgment.

Ancillariness deals with fusion, severability with fission. Each
arises where there is possibly a different orientation of a statute and

of some of its components. They are mutually exclusive in their operation. With ancillariness, the pith and substance of the whole swallows
up the matter of the part which then has no independent significance;
with severability, the difference is not only preserved but insisted on
and the question is what consequences flow from a plurality of 'matters'. If the matter of the part and that of the whole each comes within
a class, though a different class, of subjects open to the enacting legislature, their diversity is of no practical importance in the absence of
any requirement of singleness of object such as is sometimes found in
the states of the American union.

The quality of severability becomes relevant only on the premise
that one at least of the 'matters', whether that of the whole statute or
that of a part, may not come within any class of subjects within the
ambit of the enacting legislature's authority. If, in that situation, the
portion is severable, the matter of each fragment into which the statute
is decomposed is assigned to the class of subjects deemed appropriate.
Either the portion exscinded or the mass from which it is drawn may
then be sustained despite the shakiness of the other. But if, resisting
assimilation under the doctrine of ancillarity, a part of a statute deals
with some 'matter' which is alien to the pith and substance of the
whole statute and they are not severable, the illegitimacy of either's
matter affects the other and both must fall. It is severability's place
as involved in fastening on the critical 'matter' to which attention is
here directed. How to tell what is severable raises questions of another
order to which I shall not digress except to note that, while either the
bulk of the statute or a particular provision can benefit from application of the notion, usually it is the former that does because it more
often possesses the independent functional sufficiency and appeal which
are the root of the doctrine.

Besides those arising from the characteristic length and complexity
of legislation, other special problems derive from the circumstance,
happily less characteristic, of the deviousness of some statutes. For
them, too, the law has propounded a concept, that of colourable legislation.

Even under a unitary government with an omnicompetent parliament, the heart of a statute may be its secondary impact rather than
its primary command. In a federal state, where not only political but
constitutional constraints operate, this is much more so. A statute
scrupulously drawn to respect constitutional limitations may by
manipulation of what lies within them project its control over things
outside. It can be read as dealing either with the surface or with the
subsurface. If the latter, the statute is stigmatized as colourable legislation.

That is an unfortunate expression. On the one hand, it offends the
proprieties by charging the legislature with duplicity smacking of
dishonesty, contrary to the conventional canon that the courts will
not impugn the motives of the other branch. On the other, it obscures
the reality that the courts are only engaged in their own proper and
imperative duty of defining the 'matter' of the statute. Comment on
legislative guile is irrelevant, serving at most to spell out rather in-

vidiously that here, as with other written texts, form is not controlling in the determination of essential character. The principle is sound but guidance to what *is* controlling would help more than does its reiteration. The virtue of the colourability doctrine is its insistence on the real pith and substance of the statute as the primary concern. Its vices have been (a) resolving consideration of 'matter' by this self-sufficient epithet without guidance about what is to be taken into account and (b) erratic application or non-application which makes it suspect as a mere doctrine of convenience.

Ancillariness, severabiliy, colourability—these well-worn expressions are all of them only variations on a theme, the theme of identifying the statutory 'matter'. Their formalization into tagged categories may aid indexing and the consequent quick search of analogies. It ought not hide that common concern nor substitute for its explicit and reasoned formulation.

Slipshod performance of that task has been a great curse of constitutional analysis. Much of the time all that is proffered in explanation are conclusory assertions about the legislature's purpose or intention. Their artificiality is manifest in the light of the traditional distaste for letting the most direct evidences of what was in mind, such as related Royal Commission reports or statements of sponsoring ministers be shown as aids to interpretation. Supposing a majority of the individual legislators to have been fully cognizant of the terms of each proposed enactment and to have entertained a single view of the objectives to be attained, perhaps that ought ideally to govern—and all of the resources of sophisticated psychological science be employed to discover it. But why play games? In the real world the existence of any such legislative intention is probably a fiction and its content certainly an unfathomable mystery. Intention, if one is going to talk it, necessarily must be and hence it is no objection that it always is imputed, not real. Reasonable as the imputations may generally have been, this spurious explanation obfuscates discussion and could well be dropped. This is no ordinary unrewarding quibble about words but a case where imprecision in speech indulges imprecision in thinking where precision is vital.

Because ascertainment of the 'matter' is not an essentially legal exercise even though the circumstances call for it to be carried out by legal personnel, legal formulas are inherently inadequate. Relevant procedures have indeed been proposed in legal contexts—the doctrine of *Heydon's case* comes readily to mind. Moreover the grist of adjudication which calls for examining and applying all kinds of instruments in all kinds of situations is useful experience for sensing the purport of writings. But it is critically important that the own meaning of the particular text be kept constantly to the forefront as the subject of inquiry. It should not be subjected to stylized routines summoned as maxims of construction nor falsified by refusing to look at the environing circumstances of the law-making process and the social setting which animate the phonemes.

Related enactments may help place the statute in an over-all pattern. Kindred laws elsewhere may provide analogies. Such elements as preambles, titles, or purpose clauses, though rightly not treated as binding, may furnish useful clues. In these various ways, its position in the universe of statute law of which it is a part may shed light on the 'matter' of the statute at hand. Judicial pronouncements and administrative operations may be pertinent too, especially those which are contemporaneous or notorious or inhibiting. These are technical legal materials and do lend themselves to handling by standard legal techniques.

Normally they must be supplemented by others which are not and so resist disposition by purely professional rubrics. The occasional reference to the statute's consequences recognises the fact even when stultifying it in practice by making projections having no explicit and possibly *no* basis in data from the relevant disciplines. Though this strictly speaking is not recourse to extrinsic facts (for nothing in the future is a fact), one should not quibble about that. Most assertions about things past and present likewise only propound probabilities though ones rather more firmly grounded.

Viewing the statute as one element in a larger complex is what is important. That is how its 'matter' must be sought. Scrutiny of just the text or just the legal fabric does not suffice.

The interests represented by those who urged or opposed it, the *travaux préparatoires* which now are shunned, the cataloguing of what and how transactions would be different with and without the provision in operation, a sketch of the institutional setting into which it is injected—these illustrate without exhausting the range of materials useful for deciding the true matter of any written instrument, statutes included. Reliance on the wan light of 'judicial notice' to the exclusion of expert opinion evidence, wariness about informative innovations like the 'Brandeis brief'—the evidential and procedural residues of Anglo-American legal history produce a self-imposed ignorance of the facts as little excusable as is ignorance of the law.

Shut out from discovering the 'matter' by outside exploration, the courts have proceeded to invent it by inward meditation. With all its high integrity and general wisdom, the judiciary should not go on playing this kind of blindman's bluff with a matter as constitutionally important as the 'matter'. We need search, not surmise.

A Plea for 'Class' Consciousness

One cannot use for 'classes of subjects', as one must for 'matters', the case-by-case approach which looks in each instance for the pith and substance of the particular statute. The former calls not for particularizing but for generalizing, for fixing the limits of the range of activities embraced within each of an array of listed items. This business of assigning content to concept labels, of prescribing which of its potential meanings a term shall bear with legal effects is a standard legal operation for which the distinctive traditional materials and techniques of the law ought to be used. True, the meanings that emerge will be those the judges put there, not those they find there, but elaboration of authoritative meaning is not merely a proper judicial function, it is a judicial duty.

The 'classes of subjects' have been the classical arena of constitutional controversy in Canada. Strangely enough, however, the content of no one of them has been stated.

For many it has indeed been obliquely indicated. Even the bare affirmation or negation of a claim of constitutionality referring to some 'class of subjects' supplies one bit of information; whether one that will be distinguished and confined or one that will burgeon into a doctrine is anybody's guess. Broader enlightenment often takes the negative form of foreclosing reference to passably clear cut historical conceptions as criteria—there is no closed domain of criminal law; banking is not limited to what bankers did at the time of Confederation. But this only eliminates one possible definition and provides no substitute. Again, attributes of a class of subjects have been indicated by forbidding or specifying features as elements-prohibition is not regulation, trade and commerce means commerce generally and does not include a particular trade in a province, John Stuart Mill's test of shiftableness supplemented by practice at the time of Confederation separates direct from indirect taxation, 'works' are physical things and not services. Propositions of this order, whether intrinsically sound or unsound, are commendable approaches to supplying definitions, but, as with the six blind elephant viewers of Hindustan, too incomplete to describe the object adequately. Instead of a formulation of its scope, there is only this medley of miscellaneous clues and suggestions for even the most fully elaborated 'classes of subjects'. So one can only 'by indirection find direction out' with respect to a foundation element in the Canadian pattern of constitutional competence.

There is even on occasion a deliberate refusal of guidance, evidenced by declining to enter more largely into what a class of subjects includes beyond a ruling which disposes of the case at hand. It is all very well to avoid issues not up for decision. But where, as under the scheme of 91 and 92, the constitutional status of an enactment requires discovery of its 'matter' and attribution of that to the appropriate 'class of subjects', the scope of all plausibly relevant classes of subjects is necessarily up for decision and to fail to spell them out is to duck an essential issue in the case.

Yet eschewing definition of the 'classes of subjects' was a natural consequence, even a prudent precaution, once the initial misstep of not giving heed to the three-stage pattern had been taken. Two things made it so. Once 'matter', with its particularization and resulting potential for differentiation was emasculated, the elasticity and expansive capacity a constitution needs had to be built in elsewhere, in the 'classes of subjects', which had to be kept fluid. Also, with 'classes of subjects' treated as primary heads of grant through disregard of a complex structure where they fitted as one constituent factor, their taxonomy was less obviously urgent.

Relaxing the logical constraints of the 'matters coming within classes of subjects' formula meant not just that cases were left to be disposed of on policy grounds—as they would have been in any event—

but that they were disposed of *ad hoc*. It left small need for coherent integration of the member items of 91 and 92, either within or between those sections, and none was forthcoming. Instead there came a jumble of conclusory evaluations locating particular instances of federal or provincial legislation within or outside suggested 'classes of subjects', exemplified but left undefined. Plausible and even meritorious the evaluation often might be in the context of the single case, and a series of cases might even disclose a consistent bias in a particular era serviceable as a basis for prediction. But this method could not and did not map the grants of 91 and 92 in the co-ordinated way their conjoint functioning demanded and their stated formula presupposed.

The misdirection in the cases correspondingly warped comment on the cases. That naturally took the same course they did. Thus constitutional law thinking in Canada has normally been in terms of whether the federal or the provincial power over what you will—trade and commerce, criminal law, property and civil rights, for instance— does or does not sanction such and such an exercise of legislation. It is predicated on government at each level having a heap of legislative powers to be disjunctively scrutinized.

What instead is expressed for each is one compound power to make laws with relation to 'matters coming within' its own universe of 'classes of subjects'. The legislative power of each is an ensemble of designated items. This entails that, for each, one is to seek an integrating principle capable both of differentiating it from the ensemble bestowed on the other and of assigning to every designated item a proper sphere of operation special to it but harmonious with that principle. Viewed in isolation, each item is of ambiguous amplitude and the choice of a broader or narrower meaning for it almost a matter of taste, rarely demonstrably right or wrong. But that such discrete choices should add up to a system would be a happy accident, even a near miracle.

Concentration on the content of 'classes of subjects' was sound. The manner only was at fault. Examining them as themselves primary heads of power has deflected attention from their distinctive role as members of a coherent universe of lawmaking authority with which the 'matter' of a statute is to be connected. To function thus, the dimensions of each class of subjects must be specified and in such a way as to accommodate it to the coexistence of all the others so that they form a compendium of governmental power allocated between the two levels without voids and without overlaps. Divorced from that setting, pronouncements about the attributes of classes of subjects are meaningless or at least defective.

I can fairly be asked (if I am not being merely captious) to sketch in a general way how the classes of subjects might be dealt with to make them serviceable fields of reference for 'matters', their proper office as I read the Act. This I here do, fully recognising that other models can be proposed with the classes of subjects somewhat differently constituted and arranged. A model is needed. What follows may not be the right one but it looks right to me for reasons that will appear from the discussion.

One of the most obvious things about the classes of subjects is that there are lots of them. Almost equally obvious is the fact that they are of the most various sizes and complexions. How is a system to be made out of this gallimaufry?

A basic feature generally overlooked is the grand division of the residuary power between the Dominion and the provinces, with the former empowered to 'make the Laws for the Peace, Order and Good Government of Canada' and the latter for 'Generally all Matters of a merely local or private Nature in the Province'. That these are correlative and that the specifically enumerated 'classes of subjects' are specified as particular instances of things so dominantly partaking of the character of the respective general grants as by definition and in their totality to be so regarded, I have recently argued elsewhere and so I shall not repeat the demonstration. It is the first datum.

The second is the different orientation characteristic of the sets of governmental power given the one and the other level of government. For both alike, a number of 'classes of subjects' are merely institutional, confirming them in the management of their corporate affairs, and not truly governmental in setting them to rule over the affairs of the people.

Of the truly governmental, a half dozen assigned to the Dominion represent 'special situations'—defence and relations with persons outside the political community, to which a common attitude and a central direction are presuppositions of even loosely knit alliances, criminal law and procedure (and, by association, penitentiaries) which are historical residues of the Quebec Constitutional Act's introduction of English criminal law. All but one, which will be more particularly examined in due course, of section 91's other specific 'classes of subjects' of a governmental nature relate to concerns which cluster around economic activities and business enterprise. The detailed list of items may overspecify and, if they are considered separately, the listing may tend to confuse. What clearly emerges is a bestowal on the Dominion of responsibilities which have as their characterizing trait the management of the economy. The central complex of federal concerns was essentially a nineteenth-century equivalent, for the British North American community, of what the Treaty of Rome gave the European Economic Community. The different terms of the two texts naturally reflect the shifts in styles of speech and thought and the special preoccupations of their respective times. But the universe of controls envisaged is in each instance the same and the content of any given class of subjects in 91 is properly determinable only by having regard to its being a member of that universe. What seems at first glance a mere congeries of specifics turns out to be (save for the 'special situations') really a roll call of what the then current vulgar economic doctrine recognised as standard pressure points for effectuating financial and market regulation—economic planning, if you will. That in sum was what the Dominion was given. If this, like all attempts at exhaustive listing, was doomed to reveal deficiencies as situations arose, at least its recognition provides a powerful conceptual category giving body and direction to the included 'class of subjects' which without it are mere verbal blanks.

92's much shorter list of provincial 'classes of subjects', a half dozen or so all told aside from those institutional in nature, is less focussed. Too brief to shed much light, a yet greater difficulty is its relative heterogeneity reflecting the greater diffuseness of the provincial assignment. The life of the neighbourhood, its lawsuits and weddings, its local communications facilities, and its local forms of business organization were for the provinces to deal with. One can discount these as parochial or dignify them as grassroots concerns. Epithets aside, it was the patterns, values and institutions of everyday community contact that were indicated as the legitimate domain of the provinces. A sweeping directive in this sense was expressed by the famous clause 13, 'Property and Civil Rights'. They thus provide this important 'class of subjects' with a useful reference model and one, be it noted, which its more narrowly phrased companions may be seen as supplementing.

Broadly, the federal 'classes of subjects' had regard to Canada as an economy, the provincial to Canadians as members of societies. The distinction is only a beginning to assigning content to either, for the approaches cut across each other in application and both are highly abstract. But it is a good beginning in that it tells us that the limits of the federal 'classes of subjects' are to be drawn to embrace operations that are the primary concern of economists, those of the provincial, the relations that are primarily the concern of sociologists—with the 'special situations' lying outside this general organizing principle. No class of subjects should be stretched out of its genus to include matters whose dominant orientation is towards the other discipline.

'Marriage and divorce' looks like a glaring exception. Really it is consistent with the above analysis and shows the treacherous guidance the naked text gives as to the ambit of a class of subjects. The contemporary materials (which it has been held we may not look at) prove that (1) divorce, not then dealt with by laws but as an *ad hoc* exercise of legislative grace, was made federal in order to serve practical inconvenience and (2) formal solemn assurance was given that 'marriage' was federal, merely to permit Dominion enactment of a uniform conflicts rule for marriage recognition. For that purpose alone (now) section 91(26) mentioned 'marriage' which was otherwise 'amongst [the] rights' under the 'civil laws' and as such within provincial competence under the rubric 'property and civil rights'. It was not 'proposed to take away with one hand from the Local Legislature what . . . had [been] reserved to it by the other'. Shrunken from broad expression to narrow original design, the clause does not run counter to the suggested grand division of federal and provincial classes of subjects.

Examining each set of 'classes of subjects' first as itself a class, to discover what if anything characterises it, one thus finds for each a common trait. For those 'classes of subjects' stated in general, and hence potentially elastic, language, the canon of construing words in their context, *noscitur a sociis*, would seem relevant, leaving each to be interpreted as including only what significantly partakes of the relevant trait, be it economic direction or community behaviour. The words that sprawl and brawl outside their context harmonize within it. Even so, there are two complications, one, the precision of some of the clauses, the other, the need for some standard less arbitrary than personal inclination for distinguishing between the essentially economic and the essentially sociological, given their constant reciprocal feedback. The first is only an apparent difficulty. The second is real.

In the measure that they are detailed and specific, words leave little room for construction. They tend to be self-defining. True, it may be shown as well for them as for broader terms that they were not aptly chosen to express the real intention of the users in which case they may, by something akin to a process of judicial reformation, be so applied as to make them operate in the way aptly chosen words would have, a notion arguably applicable to 'marriage and divorce' in view of the peculiar origin of that clause. Failing evidence of that, words are to be taken as they stand and if, as they stand, they give no room for construction, that ends the matter.

Possibly there are no unequivocal expressions. Certainly very few used or appropriate for use in constitutional instruments are massively nuclear with almost no electronic cloud.

Perhaps 'Currency and Coinage,' 'Legal Tender,' 'The Solemnization of Marriage in the Province' are so minutely specified as to escape serious differences of opinion over what falls within or without them. Then their definition is easy—but trivial. The near consensus that makes dispute about them infrequent makes a choice between the minutely variant views inconsequential. Their definition may be one of the rare cases calling for the application of the overworked 'plain meaning' rule which should be reserved for just those cases where differences in result flowing from a choice of meaning are truly *de minimis* in number and importance.

However for most of the 'classes of subjects' enumerated the range of possible meanings is considerable. For many it is appreciably, for some vastly, larger. The grand division noted between the federal and the provincial spheres of concern calls for selecting from among them one which falls on the right side of the line. But, to do that, with economy and society interacting the way they do, it must first be settled where the line itself is to be taken as running, for purposes of applying the constitution. Some suitable standard is required to determine that. That standard to be functional must be external— external to the words themselves whose directiveness decreases as their coverage increases, external to the interpreter if the law is to be anything more respectable than an assortment of frozen whims.

The one obvious reference for an external standard is history. True, there are always unfillable gaps in the record and disagreements over its appraisal which prevent even history from providing an assured exact meaning. But one is not needed. All that is called for is a fixed external standard and a reasonable facsimile serves that end practically as well as a minutely accurate replica. It lends itself to relatively objective examination and thus reduces the risk of unconscious biases and policy preferences which bedevil interpretation.

If the bits and pieces of an intricate construction like the BNA Act are not to be displaced or distorted to their utter confusion, the whole project must be assumed to have been, in the minds of its authors, harmonious and consistent and the speech patterns of the time must be looked at to discover what was in their minds. The Fathers of Confederation, greatly prophetic though they may have been, used words in the sense they had for the men of their time. Were the 'classes of subjects' the primary heads of grant, it might indeed be impolitic to bind the future by letting the historical sense of words control. But where, as under the Act, the 'classes of subjects' are labels for pigeonholes in which to place laws on ascertained 'matters' and those which fit in none may yet be valid, the requisite constitutional elasticity is not endangered. Absent clear definition, they are a hodge-podge, not a system; and, for the reasons stated, a historically oriented definition is indicated.

A prime instance of history's help is 'property and civil rights.' That textually amorphous phrase was, as has been noted, shorthand for the array of subjects ruled by the Civil Code and by the corresponding case and statute law in the common law provinces. Its provenance and purpose are unmistakeably clear from the historical record. The relative silence of the cases on the matter, by way either of acknowledgement or of repudiation, has been in line with the general downgrading of what that record has to teach.

The record was not just neglected, it was positively abjured in the case of 'The Criminal Law,' that floodplain clause which has enabled the Dominion parliament to engulf whatever it will though more clearly defined channels of authority have been judicially dammed. The assertion from on high that 'criminal law' means 'the criminal law in its widest sense' and 'is not confined to what was criminal by the law of England or of any Province in 1867,' now enshrined as constitutional doctrine, is a fabrication at odds with all the record suggests as the sense of the Act. First appearing on the Canadian legal scene in the Quebec Act, along with 'property and civil rights,' in order to extend to the population the benefit of the English criminal law while retaining for them the use of the familiar French civil law, 'the criminal law' about which parliament was talking was the same thing about which Blackstone had just written. Perusal of Stephen confirms and nothing in the intermediate course of Canadian lawmaking casts doubt on the continuance of those ideas about the nature of the criminal law. Here was a grouping of traditional concerns, within which 'matters' could by easy reference be said to come (or not to come). The discarding of the criterion has given rise to the logically impossible, even though politically convenient, operation of determining what comes within a class of subjects that has no discernible limits.

'The regulation of Trade and Commerce' too has been falsified by the neglect of history, not indeed by making it, like 'The Criminal Law' (and the Commerce Clause of the United States Constitution), include practically everything but by letting it include virtually nothing. Despite a Canadian legal lineage less clear cut than either of the 'classes of subjects' just discussed, there is yet a respectable though loose body of materials indicative of its meaning. Mention of 'Regulation of Commerce' in the Constitutional Act, 1791, plainly looks to the meaning it then had in British legislation—legislation styled Acts of Trade—which was the latest development in a series of parliamentary enactments going back several centuries, a meaning further revealed by the functions and concerns of the recently created Board of Trade. It lay outside anything the Civil Code or the corresponding parts of the common law dealt with, and that it was not to be assimilated to the contents of the Code de Commerce is evidenced by use of 'Commercial Law' and 'Regulation of Commerce' to mean different things. In twentieth-century terms it may be paraphrased as the complex of matters we talk of as government regulation of business. That was an area ruled by imperial legislation primary or subordinate where the coming of self-government to Canada called for designation of a successor authority to take over.

It may be urged in objection to the foregoing analysis that, under the head 'Trade and Commerce' in the statutory compilations at Confederation, there appeared provisions dealing with such things as bills of exchange and promissory notes, copyright, insolvency, and banking. These will be readily recognized as themselves 'classes of subjects' in section 91. From that it might be claimed, had they not been mentioned in the BNA Act, that they were components of the class of subjects, 'the regulation of Trade and Commerce.' But they are mentioned. That demonstrative specification can hardly shrink the rest of the genus. The problem it does raise: the peaceful coexistence of 'classes of subjects' of different orders of particularity, can best be considered in examining how one decides what matters 'come within' what classes of subjects rather than at the definition stage.

To run through the catalogue of clauses of 91 and 92, showing for each that it had a contemporary content and what it was, would be relatively unrewarding. 'Banking' may deserve special mention because of the gratuitous assertion, now hardening into a commonplace, denying it a historical content. So may the similarly inspired inclusion of 'seacoast and inland fisheries,' reduced to triviality by later judicial interpretation, dealing with an activity for which regulation of enterprise was an important lever of control in the Canadian economy of 1867, given its prime importance to that economy. Here clearly are clauses where the grand division alluded to earlier confirmed contemporary usage to the effect that sectors of the economy, not the routines of fishing (and, comparably, farming) were envisaged in the specification of federal concerns.

Recourse to historical understanding need not limit the particulars of regulation to subjects or forms then current or familiar. The 'classes of subjects' were fields of competence. The fields might yield different crops at different times, in the future as in the past. Without being a closed catalogue of instances, history was, for the Fathers as for practical men of affairs in all generations, the environing premise of their thinking. They dealt in 'classes' of subjects—capable as classes are of having changing members but always members with the class characteristics. To those classes changing technology and changing institutions would predictably give new contents. They would not give new content.

In leaving an opening for legislative innovation, the courts are to be praised, not faulted. What is wrong is how they did it. To blur the three-stage pattern of constitutional inquiry, concentrating on 'classes of subjects' the burden of bearing meanings alien to the ideas of those who specified them, was to sacrifice the one reasonably objective guide to their content. It is its judicial reading that would in any event govern what elements of the historical record to select and how to generalize them in defining the attributes of a class of subjects; but, without that exercise, the 'classes of subjects' are only variable verbalisms to hide whatever policy predilections may be judicially in fashion.

The "Coming" Thing

The matter so particularized is the key, the 'classes of subjects' so generalized the lock, to the portal of constitutionality. They must fit together. The Act says that the 'matter' must be one 'coming within' an appropriate 'class of subject' for exclusive competence to be attributed to parliament or to a legislative assembly.

History's silence about the draft stage leaves it unprovable whether the 'coming within' formula was deliberate or accidental. But its sophisticated and selective use in other sections may be noted. Uniformly omitted from those whose grants of competence did not have to do with exclusive unqualified heads of authority, it was retained outside 91 and 92 only in the one which undertook to reflect for post-Confederation administrative restructuring those two sections' allocations of legislative authority. This discrimination in literary form, without quite proving that the formula was a meditated one, is a striking coincidence, which at the least fortifies the impulse not to dismiss but to respect as significant the text of 91 and 92.

The Act does contemplate that there will be matters which come within no class of subjects. For such, the residuary clauses 'Peace, Order, and good Government of Canada' and 'Generally all Matters of a Merely local or private Nature in the Province' are provided. They complete the hierarchy of the scheme of distributed powers. Also they shed light on the interplay between the 'classes of subjects' as will be shown later on. The point here is that, even if the legislative power of the two levels together equals—or at least approaches—the total authority of the British parliament, the massed 'classes of subjects' are not that comprehensive. A 'matter' exists for every statute but there is not a class of subjects to accommodate every 'matter.' This has at times had offhand recognition. But an equally fundamental presupposition of the Act has been overlooked and indeed the exact opposite routinely assumed.

Categorical classification, for the specific grants on which system 91 and 92 are framed, logically requires that every category be distinct, occupying no common ground with any other. Its vague groping for this proposition makes some sense of the otherwise indefensible statement that anything listed in 91 falls outside not only clause 92(16), so expressly the target of 91's concluding language, but also all the provisions of 92. Through distortion of 91's terminal clause, a conclusion was deduced which was not merely sound but required if the scheme of the Act was not to be distorted. No class of subjects in 92 effectively extends to anything coming within any class of subjects in 91. The converse is just as true. Furthermore, no class of subjects in either section extends to anything coming within any other class of subjects in that same section. If, instead of mauling its text, 91's final phrase had been recognized as dealing with 92(16) not as just one more class of subjects but as a residuary clause, it would have been seen to be tidying up by express extension to it the exclusiveness implicit as between 'classes of subjects.'

The corollary is that no 'matter' can, without a quantum shift to a different energy state, come within more than a single class of subjects. Yet opinions upholding and those condemning legislation have alike tended to implicate plural classes of subjects. This started early and naturally. Counsel, more concerned with client victory than with constitutional theory and with arguments advancing the 'classes of subjects' as immediate heads of legislative competence than as categories instrumental to its allocation, brought forward in the case every one having any conceivable verbal potential helpful to the client's position. The judgments, preoccupied with disposing of the litigation, fell into the trap and uncritically accepted multiple classes of subjects as appropriate. Thus arose a practice which has done much to obscure the need for precise delineation of the classes of subjects on which the Act was premised.

What made the mistake hard to avoid was that superficially some of the classes of subjects seem to merge. The federal set, close packed into the area of economics and finance as many of them are seen to have been, filled it so full as to risk treading on each other. The provincial mixed bag and, in particular, 'property and civil rights,' so spacious when looked at separately and literally, suggested a wide range of conjunctions. Could not 'Lines of steam ships between the Province and any British or Foreign Country' also be considered 'Navigation and Shipping'? By legislating on 'Weights and Measures' would not one generally be 'regulat[ing] Trade and Commerce'? Did not 'the incorporation of companies with Provincial objects' normally involve 'property' and always 'civil rights in the Province'? The answer in each instance had to be yes, if the clauses were read as naked words. But yes it could not be if they were to operate together as members of an internally consistent constitutional structure. That would not allow 'matters' to have multiple domiciles.

The classes of subjects are variously related. Paired off, some will present situations where one of the two might with dictionary warrant be regarded as something comprised within the other, in contrast with other pairs whose respective topics have no regular association. The assignment of a 'matter' between 'classes of subjects' will reflect these various relationships. 'Indians and lands reserved for the Indians' and 'Naturalization and Aliens' are mostly independent of each other. Doubtless there are extra-Canadian Indians and there may be legislation affecting their situation; but here the probe to find the 'matter' will commonly suffice to show a focus of the legislation on other 'alien'-ness or 'Indian'-ness. 'Banking [and] the incorporation of banks' cannot be dissociated from, on the one hand, 'the Regulation of Trade and Commerce' or, on the other, 'Savings Banks'; it might quite plausibly be included in the former and include the latter. The distillation of the 'matter,' however neat, cannot take legislation out of a class of subjects inclusive of another. That can only be done by not letting any one include any other and *that* can only be done by recognizing enclave classes of subjects which, though totally surrounded by, yet form no part of a more inclusive class.

That necessarily imposes an artificial meaning on the circum-ambient class. But artificial meanings are a staple of the legal system which has as one important function the generation of predictability. Not artificiality *per se* but displacement of a term to a sense wholly outside its normal range or its use without consistency or without a logical basis is objectionable. Legal nomenclature must all be somewhat artificial, a proposition under which companion classes of subjects fit as a special though extreme case.

It is no great trick to provide living space for each of them. The obvious way is to treat the 'matter' of legislation as 'coming within' the most particular of the alternative 'classes of subjects.' The broader band would first be appropriately defined as discussed above, then the narrower one similarly, and all 'matters' coming within the latter be reciprocally expelled from the former. There would be no practical effects since, once an enactment is found to come within a permitted or an unpermitted class of subjects as the case may be, a second vital or fatal ascription is redundant and not reinforcing. The effect is on the logical structure whose preservation calls for dealing with each class of subjects as a discrete, definable—and defined—entity embracing suitable 'matters.' This method of disentangling 'classes of subjects' wrests no term from its normal range. It admits of consistent application. It has bases both in interpretational tradition and in utility.

For many kinds of writings, the law when called on to apply specific or general provisions therein contained, either being capable of serving as a basis for decision, has preferred the specific to the general. The latter is effective only outside the limits of the former. Usually this is justified as being presumptively the writer's intention, which it may have been.

Besides fiction, function supports the practice in the present context. The smaller a class of subjects and the sharper its contours, the fewer and more distinctive will be the 'matters' which can come within it and the faster and fuller the agreement about which do. The more diffuse the candidate 'class of subjects,' the more difficult and debatable is the choice among the policies and values involved. Often the courts cannot escape those hard choices but they ought not squander their time or their credit in going out of the way to face them need-lessly.

A parallel may be found in legislation which comes within no class of subjects. It must be assessed as either going to 'the peace, order, and good government of Canada' or, alternatively, as being merely local or private within a province. Which it is assessed as is a question of degree. Subjective factors enter into the answer more largely than when passing on questions of kind with their definitional constraints, however loose.

Prudently anxious to avoid the strains which would obviously result from leaving personal philosophies on federalism as the routine inarticulate premises of decision, the Act elaborated its extensive list of 'classes of subjects,' thus reserving the more contentious question of degree for cases where no relevant category was found within which the 'matter' came.

Once a matter was found to come within the limits as fixed for any class of subjects in 91, it could 'not be deemed' of a local or private nature and the exclusive legislative authority of parliament extended to it whatever its particulars. Thus, it is suggested, a special charter to operate a bank in a named village could not be a local or private matter despite its limited scope. Arguably it might come within either 'Banking [and], the Incorporation of Banks . . .' or 'The Incorporation of Companies with Provincial Objects' though, on the principle of preferring the more specific to the less specific, 'Incorporation of Banks' should in this instance get the nod over the broader 'Incorporation of Companies' as the class of subjects in which it would come.

Complementarily, parliament's power to make 'Laws for the Peace, Order, and good Government of Canada' embraced no 'matters ... coming within the classes of subjects ... assigned exclusively to the ... Provinces' (to which all the classes of subjects specified in 92 were assigned).

Thus, the Act itself dictated a preliminary canvass of the 'classes of subjects' in search of one in which the 'matter' of the law could fairly be said to come, leaving, however, the Canadian or local character of its concern to carry the day when, but only when, it could not be so assigned.

It is true that for each level of government the Act only directs a search of the other's 'classes of subjects.' There is no comparable requirement that its own list be inspected. The omission is understandable. Which among the enacting government's specifics validates legislation is of little practical moment. What is of moment and not to be assumed is whether the legislation is referrable to a specific and is therefore categorically warranted or whether it is left to fall within the unspecified residuary grant and so makes necessary the balancing process. That can only be dispensed with for a matter coming within a class of subjects. If one does, that ends the inquiry; if it does not, it only continues it. So an unproductive rundown of the other list must always be accompanied by examining the enacting government's own. The cases seldom bother to do a thorough job here. More frequently perfunctory invocation of several classes of subjects has helped spawn confusion about the scope of each and, even worse, has stifled the reasoned development of the residuary clauses so central to a viable Canadian federalism.

A 'matter' for every law and every 'matter' either coming within a uniquely appropriate class of subject or falling outside all of them into the residuary grants and the balancing process—the Act's scheme was comprehensive, intelligible, and tidy. With clearly fixed, firmly maintained boundaries for the classes of subjects, all could peacefully coexist and relatively large agreement could be had on the status of most legislation. Some cases would remain where the 'matter' had affinities with two classes of subjects, more perhaps where it came within none and its national or local orientation must be resolved. Much room for judgment remained and the process of decision could never be mechanical. It could be refined and sharpened, with attention and explication centred on the critical considerations, if the structure the Act prescribed were observed.

It was not. Early on it was said that a 'sharp and definite distinction ... could not be attained,' a meek abdication of the judicial mastery over words so stoutly maintained on other occasions, and so 'it will be a wise course ... to decide each case which arises as best they can without entering more largely upon an interpretation of the statute than is necessary for the decision ...' Thus, almost at the outset, the Act's scheme was scrapped. Once the fences between the classes of subjects were down, it was anybody's guess how to brand the creatures anywhere on the range.

Collision between 'classes of subjects, which as concepts exist only in the legal order could have been and can be prevented. The possible impingement on activities, which are regulable by virtue of several classes of subjects, that may result from compliance with a statute's commands cannot be prevented. Those activities are facts of life not artifacts of law. Recognition that human behaviour cuts across legal categories is quite compatible with keeping the 'classes of subjects' pure.

The standard way of putting the matter in the simplest case is that it is no ground for objection that legislation otherwise adequately grounded 'incidentally affects' concerns and situations amenable to be, and which often are, dealt with under a class of subjects assigned to the other level. The notion is akin to ancillariness. Probably, like it, it has to do more with determining the 'matter' than with what class of subjects it 'comes within.' There is one big difference though it is little mentioned. Ancillariness is usually associated with an explicit statutory provision of a peripheral nature; talk about 'incidentally affecting' crops up in connection with the potential of a non-differentiating statute to affect indiscriminately in its application matters assertedly immune from control and others. But it seems immaterial really whether it is its words or its works which draw the flotsam within the statute's wake.

The 'aspect' doctrine bears some resemblance to those just noted but, unlike them, deals not with what the 'matter' is but with what it 'comes within.' First ambiguously uttered about 'subjects' ['matters'?

'classes of subjects'? *Non constat.*], it applies where some of the constitutive elements about whose combination the statute is concerned
(that is, they are its 'matter'), are a kind most often met with in
connection with one class of subjects and others are of a kind mostly
dealt with in connection with another. As in the case of a pocket
gadget compactly assembling knife blade, screwdriver, fishscaler, nail-
file, etc., a description of it must mention everything but in characterizing it the particular use proposed to be made of it determines
what it is.

So far as I know, the doctrine has been alluded to only where the
relevant classes of subjects are diversely federal and provincial. In
principle there is no reason why they should be. Could not a statute
penalizing the suppression or concealment of bills of exchange with
the intent of defeating proceedings to fix secondary party liability be
in relation to a matter coming in one aspect within 'The Criminal
Law,' and in another within 'Bills of Exchange and Promissory Notes'?
Both being 'classes of subjects' confided to parliament, nothing would
of course turn on it except in the most extraordinary case. That
probably explains the silence. It is likely that many of the cases where
legislation has been found to rest on plural classes of subjects all
within 91 or all within 92 in fact illustrate this aspect of the 'aspect'
doctrine, slurring it over as inconsequential.

With measures in one respect pointing to a section 91 and in
another to a section 92 class of subjects, the doctrine operates gener-
ously. Parliament's concern is taken as being with those aspects
characteristically federal, the legislative assemblies' with those characteristically provincial, and the ambivalent matter found to come within
a class of subjects open to whichever body enacted the legislation.

The residuary grants are not available. Only 'matters' that blend
elements usually regulated in the context of different 'classes of subjects' invite an alternative assignment under the 'aspect' doctrine. It
would be illegitimate to reason that a matter was in one aspect 'for
the peace, order, and good government of Canada' or 'merely local
and private within the Province' with another aspect in some 'class of
subjects.' The assertion would be directly at odds with the reciprocal
exclusiveness which the Act directs insofar as the class of subjects
was one listed in the other section and otiose insofar as it and the
residuary grant were in the same section.

Talk about 'trenching' should, as has been well said, in any event
be avoided. This spurious notion is always inept and often misleading.
Legislation either does or does not fall within a conferred competence,
specific or residual. A decision that it does not disposes of it. A
decision that it does settles that its author has not entered and ergo
has not trespassed on any other field of competence. If its reach is not
ancillary or incidental to a matter coming in any aspect within an
available class of subjects, the nature of the placement of the 'matter'
eliminates it and it is incapable of 'trenching' on anything unless
indeed it is rested on a residuary power when again there can be no
trenching; for then by hypothesis there remains no pertinent 'class of

subjects' to be trenched on and, as between the residuary powers, their either-or quality precludes the possibility of trenching.

A traffic light green in both directions would do very well at an intersection when there was no cross traffic. The same is true of the 'aspect' doctrine's green light. Where only a province or only a parliament has legislated, no trouble. If both have, there are complications. Having, as a preliminary step, found for each a matter which in a relevant 'aspect' comes within a legitimating class of subjects (otherwise it would be *ab initio* vulnerable), the very mixture of elements that occasioned the quest, for at least one of them, for viable 'aspects' implies the contingency of two independently valid commands addressed to the same conduct. The 'matter' of each—and they could be identical—normally coming within an available class of subjects, by virtue often of 'aspect,' is all right and the legislation good. The problem is how far the valid command shall be operative.

It is resolved by the paramountcy principle.

Paramountcy falls somewhat outside the subject of this article because all issues of legislative competence under 91 and 92 are out of the way by the time one gets to it. Yet the occasions for it arise so regularly in connection with what we have been considering that a brief digression may be excused as, also, it is hoped, may its inadequate treatment of a topic deserving its own full-scale examination.

Judicially created for Canada, to deal with the considerations intrinsic to federalism which led elsewhere to supremacy clauses, it operates much as they do. Provincial or state laws which, standing alone, would govern all conduct within their terms will, when the federal government has valid legislation applicable to the same or some of the conduct, have their operation suspended so far as may be needed for the federal enactment to operate fully. Those laws are not extinguished or invalid, they are only inoperative to that extent. If member and federal measures are substantial duplicates, every situation covered by the one is likewise covered by the other and there is no provincial room left, given full operation of the federal law. If they are repugnant, in the true sense that obedience to one would require violation of the other, again the provincial ordering must perish for the federal to flourish. The puzzling cases are those of measures neither identical nor repugnant which address themselves to a common range of conduct but with different prescriptions. Operative incompatibility has been suggested as the appropriate formula. The suggestion is congenial with the notion of clearing the way for full operation of the federal measure. But it is not the universal solvent. It says nothing for instance about whether inspection or licensing provisions are to operate cumulatively.

Leaving for another time the resolution of these quandaries, I pause to comment on certain correlations of operative incompatibility and the 'aspect' doctrine. Both grapple with the issues arising from the composite nature of a statute, one as regards the preclusory impact of federal law on provincial measures bearing on constituents of federally regulated conduct, the other to identify what parts of the whole making up a 'matter' bring it within a class of subjects. Conceivably, 'aspect' could shed light in paramountcy's dark corners, allowing complementary operation with respect to those features which give the 'matter' a provincial aspect but excluding it for those which give it its federal aspect. This must not be taken to imply that paramountcy problems always arise in an aspect setting, although they usually do. How far the ancillary provisions and incidental effects of provincial laws are comparably sterilized and those of federal laws comparably sterilizing have not been systematically examined. They should be. But these are ramifications of the paramountcy doctrine and it is high time to end this extended digression and return to the main theme, the scheme for distribution of legislative competence under 91 and 92.

The discussion so far has been directed to showing as the Act's standard pattern a uniquely appropriate class of subjects for each matter and to accounting for exceptional situations either where none exists or, where through combination of disparate elements, the 'matter' is a hermaphrodite. It would have been premature, without an explanation of the critical importance of seeking its answer, to raise the ultimate question of how to tell what comes within what.

There is no equation by which to distribute matters among classes of subjects. Their potential connections are infinitely variable because, though the classes of subjects are finite in number and each is flexibly finite in capacity, the 'matters' to be matched with them can be infinite in variety. As in the resolution of a statute's 'matter,' so in its assignment to a class of subjects, there is no slide rule answer. At best, guides can be suggested.

Happily much of the task will already have been accomplished once the classes of subjects are defined and the matter of the particular statute is refined. With those operations performed, most of the more than two-score classes of subjects in 91 and 92 will manifestly have no bearing. At most a handful of plausibly relevant ones will remain. Consideration can be limited to them in any actual case.

For the short list of candidates remaining, one simplifying principle already suggested would hasten and bolster judgment, the hierarchy of classes of subjects from the very particular to the very general. Its most obvious advantage is economy. A not inconsiderable mass of legislation, which it is true is the least often and the least seriously challenged, deals with matters traditionally the content of the narrower classes of subjects. The more difficult exploration of the big classes of subjects need not be undertaken if initial scrutiny of the littler ones proved fruitful. A more obscure though still more substantial advantage is enhanced credibility. The sharper focus of the smaller classes of subjects makes for more agreement, both on and off the bench, about what comes or does not come within them. In the sensitive universe of power allocation in a federal system, the big packages hold the most dynamite; they should not be tossed about needlessly or heedlessly.

The relative generality principle is cross-applicable between 91 and 92, not just within each of them. To illustrate again from section 92(11), the provinces certainly may incorporate companies to carry

on trade and commerce, though section 91(2) names the regulation
of trade and commerce among the federal classes of subjects; they
could not incorporate them to engage in banking for 91(5) deals particularly with the 'Incorporation of Banks.' Conversely, the law on
the formation and performance of contracts, a major division of the
civil law, is clearly within 92(13) but legislation about the interest
terms of contracts comes within the more specific 91(19), so that the
other more inclusive class of subjects need not and should not be considered. Reflection on these examples may suggest that a matter
which comes within a narrow class carved out of a broader one cannot
in another aspect come within the latter. Ancillary provisions and
incidental operation, which go to what the matter is not to what it
comes within, are another story.

'Aspect' comes into play where the 'matter' implicates 'classes of
subjects' which have only occasional contacts. For instance, a statute
providing what ceremonial should suffice for a valid marriage between
Indians prima facie brings to mind both 91(24) and 92(12), one providing what should be done about a salvor's claim against a cargo
owner subject to contribution in the event of the latter's insolvency
to both 91(10) and 91(21).

Where there is nothing clearly associating a properly defined matter more closely with one than another of two or more classes of
subjects of comparable specificity, opinions are bound to differ over
which it comes within. Certainly the grounds of choice ought to be
articulated. Certainly they ought, at a minimum, to say enough to
demonstrate the appropriateness of the chosen class of subject were
there no other in the picture and even enough to justify ending the
search without having to turn to a more inclusive class. But there are
no rules to dictate a preference though there are some broad principles to give direction.

One such, of great potential utility, is the venerable norm of
application *ut res magis valeat quam pereat*. The *res magis* here is
the over-arching scheme of functioning federalism which inspires the
BNA Act, more particularly indicated in the grant structure of 91 and
92. Earlier set out in discussing 'classes of subjects,' it embraces (as
was noted), for both federal and provincial governments, a purely
institutional group and another group properly governmental in character, the latter including for parliament things having to do with the
Canadian economy plus some 'special situations,' for the provinces the
life styles and social values of their people. The force of this arrangement is not spent when it has served to help define the 'classes of
subjects.' It also can help to determine 'coming within.'

If and to the extent that a 'class of subjects' proposed as its receptacle is institutional rather than governmental, it is there the 'matter'
belongs. Suppose a statute disqualifying for membership in a provincial assembly anyone convicted of a crime and that regardless of a
pardon; certainly one element smacks of 'the Criminal Law,' a governmental class of subjects, but another is linked to an institutional
one, 'the Constitution of the Province' and, it is submitted, it is within
it that a measure with this matter would come. *Ladore v. Bennett* is

a leading case decided in line with this principle though the analysis is opaque. Legislation specifying the language or languages to be used by officials in the performance of their duties in my view is to be sustained on comparable grounds.

As for legislation establishing public enterprises in the sector traditionally private, controlled by regulation and not direct operation, to determine its 'matter' one needs to know whether it confines itself to establishing a Crown enterprise and the rules for its functioning or deals also with individuals' transactions in the line of activity involved. Only in the event it is found, in pith and substance, to be non-regulatory can it rely on the claim that it be assigned to an institutional 'class of subjects.'

Similarly, for classes of subjects where the competence granted is regulatory in character the generic attributes of those in 91 and 92 respectively deserve respect. Measures with primarily economic objectives will find lodgment in one of the federal complex centring on economic institutions, those aimed at the relations between man and man will belong under a provincial head. The 'special situation' classes of subjects need to be taken into account. With those federal concerns, as well as the central economic group, it is useful to reflect on what distinguishes the realms of behaviour to which they advert—the malefactions reprobated by English law as violations of the king's peace, the involvement of non-Canadian and extra-Canadian actors or factors, the limited scope and operation contemplated for the marriage and divorce clause. For these as for the other classes of subjects, the assignment of a matter as coming within one should be responsive to the position of the policy issues resolved by the questioned legislation in the division of realms of social and political policy disclosed by the pattern of the Act in historical context.

A good example of where that principle should have been applied—but was not—is *In re the Board of Commerce Act and the Combines and Fair Prices Act 1919.* Here, it will be recalled, the validity of a federal law creating a board empowered to forbid with penal sanctions the withholding of the necessities of life as designated and to direct their sale at reasonable prices or reasonable profits was challenged, in the event successfully. Without implying agreement with anything therein said about the Dominion residuary power, one may accept its dismissal as appropriate on the basis (which was *not* that invoked), that the matter came within one of the specific classes of subjects. Three were discussed, with different evaluations in various opinions— 'The Regulation of Trade and Commerce,' 'Criminal Law,' and 'Property and Civil Rights in the Province.' All of them are fairly broad, the first and third notably so. Forestalling and regrating had certainly a long, though very obsolete, career as statutory offences in England but possibly they were thought of as mercantile rather than criminal measures. That possibility, as well as the procedural considerations which induced Anglin J. to refrain from placing primary reliance on 91(27), must be my excuse for passing on to consider the other two. The legislation bore only the remotest resemblance to anything dealt with in the Civil Code. That, rather than the glib but essentially

meaningless contrast of 'civil rights' and 'public wrongs' urged by
counsel, might well have been vouched against 92(13). Still, the legislation did clearly address itself to contracts, specifying that and on what
terms persons must in certain circumstances contract. How important
that feature was in the total statutory scheme went to the 'matter' of
the statute but, accepting it as a critical component and not merely
ancillary or incidental, the question arose, in what class of subjects
did it come? Unlike the unconscionable transactions Acts aimed at
keeping conduct while contracting within the bounds of decency, the
challenged acts involved a substantive contract term and one, the price
term, which lies at the very heart of marketing theory and practice.
Designed to tilt the workings of supply and demand, they were out-
and-out economic controls. Hence, the class of subjects they came
within was plainly 'The Regulation of Trade and Commerce' (economics) rather than 'Property and Civil Rights' (personal conduct)
unless, as Lord Haldane toyed with doing, the former was to be judicially expunged from the BNA Act.

Exhausting the narrower grants first; preferred status for the
'institutional' classes of subjects, respect for the mission orientations
indicated by the clusters of 91 and 92, each has a contribution to make
to telling within what class of subjects a matter comes. Had they been
used, the courts would have spared themselves much work and the
users of their utterances much trouble and would have created an
intellectually more respectable corpus of constitutional doctrine.

That is not to say that singly or together these indicia offer a
talisman for judgment. There remain, in applying them or after
applying them, 'matters' that they do not place. Their serviceability,
like that of any set of general propositions, is not for deciding concrete cases but for sorting out situations calling for the application
of one or another member of the set. In both the sorting and the
eventual application, the fact settings and the policy elements will
be combined and apprehended in many, many ways. It is quite conceivable, even, that a statute whose matter at one time comes within
one class of subjects may in a different era come within another.

CHAPTER II

THE GENERAL POWER OF THE PARLIAMENT OF CANADA

1. Earlier Development

RUSSELL v. THE QUEEN

In the Privy Council.   (1882), 7 App. Cas. 829.

Appeal from a judgment of the Supreme Court of New Brunswick discharging a rule *nisi* for *certiorari* to remove into the Court a conviction against the appellant for unlawfully selling, bartering and disposing of intoxicating liquors contrary to the second part of the Canada Temperance Act, 1878.

Benjamin, Q.C., and *Reginald Brown,* for the appellant, contended that the Dominion Parliament had no power to pass the Act in question: see *Citizens Insurance Company v. Parsons,* 7 App. Cas. 96, at p. 107, according to which it is not necessary to shew that the Act comes exclusively within sect. 91 of the British North America Act, 1867, for the two sections may be read together. Reference was made to sects. 91 and 92, subsects. 9, 13, 16, to sects. 94 and 121 . . . Up to the time of the passing of the Act of 1867 the Legislatures of the several provinces had always exercised the power of dealing with the sale of liquors within their provinces, and with the granting of licenses for the purposes of local revenue. They distributed the right of granting such licenses amongst the various municipalities for purely local purposes: see New Brunswick Acts, 11 Vict. c. 61, s. 59; 17 Vict. c. 15, s. 21; 22 Vict. c. 8, s. 74; 36 Vict. c. 10, s. 32. All provided fees for licenses. Under the provincial Acts prior to 1867 the municipalities had a revenue, the power of legislating with regard to which is preserved to the Provincial Legislatures by sub-section 9 of sect. 92. These licensing powers were continued in the municipalities by sect. 29 of 39 Vict. c. 105 (Consolidated Statutes of New Brunswick, 1876), and were in force up to the 1st of May, 1879. The local Legislatures had exclusive power to raise money by licenses, and the Dominion cannot interfere therewith by legislating with regard to the commodities which are the subject of licenses. The Legislature having treated this as a local matter, can the Courts say that it is not? This is a law in relation to licenses of a local nature; if a criminal law it comes under sub-sect. 15 of sect. 92. It is not a law for the peace, order, and good government of Canada, for it is a law relating to a locality. If it applied to the whole Dominion without local option it would then be within the power of the Dominion Parliament. . . .

[SIR MONTAGUE E. SMITH:—Their Lordships do not require to hear the respondent's counsel in reference to sub-sects. 9 and 13, but only in regard to sub-sect. 16.]

Maclaren, Q.C., and *Fullarton,* for the respondent:—

The words "matters of a merely local or private nature in the province" means matters the interest or effect of which does not transcend the locality or the private person. If a matter can only affect the particular locality directly or indirectly then it is left to local legislation. If, on the other hand, such private or local matter falls within any of the subjects enumerated in sect. 91, provincial legislation cannot deal with it. Drunkenness affects the whole community, its character, health, and efficiency, more than any other matter; and giving local option does not render the Act which deals with such a matter local in its nature. On the contrary, local option is usually given where the subject is of great general interest, opinion divided as to the change, and large interests threatened thereby. This is the case here. One test whether a matter is "merely" (a restrictive word) local or private is the magnitude of the interests involved, such as temperance, education, public rights, health, etc. Reference was made to the Quebec Resolutions (No. 45), which are referred to in the preamble of the Act of 1867 as the foundation of the Act. . . .

Further, the case comes within the words "regulation of trade and commerce" in sect. 91, sub-sect. 2. The Act, moreover, is a criminal statute, creating a new offence, the whole tenor being of a criminal nature: see 31 Vict. c. 1 (Interpretation Act), s. 7, sub-sect. 20 (Canada) making this offence a misdemeanour. It is therefore within sect. 91, sub-sect. 27. [SIR JAMES HANNEN:—If the subject matter be purely provincial could the Dominion Parliament take possession of it by making it criminal?]

SIR MONTAGUE E. SMITH:. . . . The Supreme Court of New Brunswick made the order now appealed from in deference to a judgment of the Supreme Court of Canada in the case of the *City of Frederickton v. The Queen.* In that case the question of the validity of the Canada Temperance Act, 1878, though in another shape, directly arose, and the Supreme Court of New Brunswick, consisting of six Judges, then decided, Mr. Justice Palmer dissenting, that the Act was beyond the competency of the Dominion Parliament. On the appeal of the City of Frederickton, this judgment was reversed by the Supreme Court of Canada, which held, Mr. Justice Henry dissenting, that the Act was valid. (The case is reported in 3rd Supreme Court of Canada Reports, p. 505.) The present appeal to Her Majesty is brought, in effect, to review the last-mentioned decision.

The preamble of the Act in question states that "it is very desirable to promote temperance in the dominion, and that there should be uniform legislation in all the provinces respecting the traffic in intoxicating liquors." The Act is divided into three parts. The first relates to "proceedings for bringing the second part of this Act into force;" the second to "prohibition of traffic in intoxicating liquors;" and the third to "penalties and prosecutions for offences against the second part."

The mode of bringing the second part of the Act into force, stating it succinctly, is as follows: On a petition to the Governor in Council, signed by not less than one fourth in number of the electors of any county or city in the Dominion qualified to vote at the election of a member of the House of Commons, praying that the second part of the Act should be in force and take effect in such county or city, and that the votes of all the electors be taken for or against the adoption of the petition, the Governor-General, after certain prescribed notices and evidence, may issue a proclamation, embodying such petition, with a view to a poll of the electors being taken for or against its adoption. When any petition has been adopted by the electors of the county or city named in it, the Governor-General in Council may, after the expiration of sixty days from the day on which the petition was adopted, by Order in Council published in the *Gazette,* declare that the second part of the Act shall be in force and take effect in such county or city, and the same is then to become of force and take effect accordingly. Such Order in Council is not to be revoked for three years, and only on like petition and procedure.

The most important of the prohibitory enactments contained in the second part of the Act is s. 99, which enacts that, "from the day on which this part of this Act comes into force and takes effect in any county or city, and for so long thereafter as the same continues in force therein, no person, unless it be for exclusively sacramental or medicinal purposes, or for bona fide use in some art, trade, or manufacture, under the regulation contained in the fourth sub-section of this section, or as hereinafter authorized by one of the four next sub-sections to this section, shall, within such county or city, by himself, his clerk, servant, or agent, expose or keep for sale, or directly or indirectly, on any pretence or upon any device, sell or barter, or in consideration of the purchase of any other property give, to any other person, any spirituous or other intoxicating liquor, or any mixed liquor, capable of being used as a beverage, and part of which is spirituous or otherwise intoxicating."

Sub-sect. 2 provides that "neither any license issued to any distiller or brewer" (and after enumerating other licenses), "nor yet any other description of license whatever, shall in any wise avail to render legal any act done in violation of this section."

Sub-sect. 3 provides for the sale of wine for sacramental purposes, and sub-sect. 4 for the sale of intoxicating liquors for medicinal and manufacturing purposes, these sales being made subject to prescribed conditions.

Other sub-sections provide that producers of cider, and distillers and brewers, may sell liquors of their own manufacture in certain quantities, which may be termed wholesale quantities, or for export, subject to prescribed conditions, and there are provisions of a like nature with respect to vine-growing companies and manufacturers of native wines.

The third part of the Act enacts (sect. 100) that whoever exposes for sale or sells intoxicating liquors in violation of the second part of the Act should be liable, on summary conviction, to a penalty of not less than fifty dollars for the first offence, and not less than one hundred dollars for the second offence, and to be imprisoned for a term not exceeding two months for the third and every subsequent offence; all intoxicating liquors in respect to which any such offence has been committed to be forfeited.

The effect of the Area when brought into force in any county or town within the Dominion is, describing it generally, to prohibit the sale of intoxicating liquors, except in wholesale quantities, or for certain specific purposes, to regulate the traffic in the excepted cases, and to make sales of liquors in violation of the prohibition and regulations contained in the Act criminal offences, punishable by fine, and for the third or subsequent offences by imprisonment. . . .

The general scheme of the British North America Act with regard to the distribution of legislative powers, and the general scope and effect of sects. 91 and 92, and their relation to each other, were fully considered and commented on by this Board in the case of the *Citizens Insurance Company v. Parsons,* 7 App. Cas. 96. According to the principle of construction there pointed out, the first question to be determined is, whether the Act now in question falls within any of the classes of subjects enumerated in sect. 92, and assigned exclusively to the Legislatures of the Provinces. If it does, then the further question would arise, viz., whether the subject of the Act does not also fall within one of the enumerated classes of subjects in sect. 91, and so does not still belong to the Dominion Parliament. But if the Act does not fall within any of the classes of subjects in sect. 92, no further question will remain, for it cannot be contended, and indeed was not contended at their Lordships' bar, that, if the Act does not come within one of the classes of subjects assigned to the Provincial Legislatures, the Parliament of Canada had not, by its general power "to make laws for the peace, order, and good government of Canada," full legislative authority to pass it.

Three classes of subjects enumerated in sect. 92 were referred to under each of which, it was contended by the appellant's counsel, the present legislation fell. These were:—

9. Shop, saloon, tavern, auctioneer, and other licenses in order to the raising of a revenue for provincial, local, or municipal purposes.

13. Property and civil rights in the province.

16. Generally all matters of a merely local or private nature in the province.

With regard to the first of these classes, No. 9, it is to be observed that the power of granting licenses is not assigned to the Provincial Legislatures for the purpose of regulating trade, but "in order to the raising of a revenue for provincial, local, or municipal purposes."

The Act in question is not a fiscal law; it is not a law for raising revenue; on the contrary, the effect of it may be to destroy or diminish revenue; indeed it was a main objection to the Act that in the City of Frederickton it did in point of fact diminish the source of municipal revenue. It is evident, therefore, that the matter of the Act is not within the class of subject No. 9, and consequently that it could not have been passed by the Provincial Legislature by virtue of any authority conferred upon it by that sub-section.

It appears that by statutes of the province of New Brunswick authority has been conferred upon the municipality of Frederickton to raise money for municipal purposes by granting licenses of the nature of those described in No. 9 of sect. 92, and that licenses granted to taverns for the sale of intoxicating liquors were a profitable source of revenue to the municipality. It was contended by the appellant's counsel, and it was their main argument on this part of the case, that the Temperance Act interfered prejudicially with the traffic from which this revenue was derived, and thus invaded a subject assigned exclusively to the Provincial Legislature. But, supposing the effect of the Act to be prejudicial to the revenue derived by the municipality from licenses, it does not follow that the Dominion Parliament might not pass it by virtue of its general authority to make laws for the peace, order and good government of Canada. Assuming that the matter of the Act does not fall within the class of subject described in No. 9, that subsection can in no way interfere with the general authority of the Parliament to deal with that matter. If the argument of the appellant that the power given to the Provincial Legislatures to raise a revenue by licenses prevents the Dominion Parliament from legislating with regard to any article or commodity which was or might be covered by such licenses were to prevail, the consequence would be that laws which might be necessary for the public good or the public safety could not be enacted at all. Suppose it were deemed to be necessary or expedient for the national safety, or for political reasons, to prohibit the sale of arms, or the carrying of arms, it could not be contended that a Provincial Legislature would have authority, by virtue of sub-sect. 9 (which alone is now under discussion), to pass any such law, nor, if the appellant's argument were to prevail, would the Dominion Parliament be competent to pass it, since such a law would interfere prejudicially with the revenue derived from licenses granted under the authority of the Provincial Legislature for the sale or the carrying of arms. Their Lordships think that the right construction of the enactments does not lead to any such inconvenient consequence. It appears to them that legislation of the kind referred to, though it might interfere with the sale or use of an article included in a license granted under sub-sect. 9, is not in itself legislation upon or within the subject of that subsection, and consequently is not by reason of it taken out of the general power of the Parliament of the Dominion. It is to be observed that the express provision of the Act in question that no licenses shall avail to render legal any act done in violation of it, is only the expression, inserted probably from abundant caution, of what would be necessarily implied from the legislation itself assuming it to be valid.

Next, their Lordships cannot think that the Temperance Act in question properly belongs to the class of subjects, "Property and Civil Rights." It has in its legal aspect an obvious and close similarity to laws which place restrictions on the sale or custody of poisonous drugs, or of dangerously explosive substances. These things, as well as intoxicating liquors, can, of course, be held as property, but a law placing restrictions on their sale, custody, or removal, on the ground that the free sale or use of them is dangerous to public safety, and making it a criminal offence punishable by fine or imprisonment to violate these restrictions, cannot properly be deemed a law in relation to property in the sense in which those words are used in the 92nd section. What Parliament is dealing with in legislation of this kind is not a matter in relation to property and its rights, but one relating to public order and safety. That is the primary matter dealt with, and though incidentally the free use of things in which men may have property is interfered with, that incidental interference does not alter the character of the law. Upon the same considerations, the Act in question cannot be regarded as legislation in relation to civil rights. In however large a sense these words are used, it could not have been intended to prevent the Parliament of Canada from declaring and enacting certain uses of property, and certain acts in relation to property, to be criminal and wrongful. Laws which make it a criminal offence for a man wilfully to set fire to his own house on the ground that such an act endangers the public safety, or to overwork his horse on the ground of cruelty to the animal, though affecting in some sense property and the right of a man to do as he pleases with his own, cannot properly be regarded as legislation in relation to property, or to civil rights. Nor could a law which prohibited or restricted the sale or exposure of cattle having a contagious disease be so regarded. Laws of this nature designed for the promotion of public order, safety, or morals, and which subject those who contravene them to criminal procedure and punishment, belong to the subject of public wrongs rather than to that of civil rights. They are of a nature which fall within the general authority of Parliament to make laws for the order and good government of Canada, and have direct relation to criminal law, which is one of the enumerated classes of subjects assigned exclusively to the Parliament of Canada. It was said in the course of the judgment of this Board in the case of the *Citizens Insurance Company of Canada v. Parsons*, that the two sections (91 and 92) must be read together, and the language of one interpreted, and, where necessary, modified by that of the other. Few, if any, laws could be made by Parliament for the peace, order, and good government of Canada which did not in some incidental way affect property and civil rights; and it could not have been intended, when assuring to the provinces exclusive legislative authority on the subjects of property and civil rights, to exclude the Parliament from the exercise of this general power whenever any such incidental interference would result from it. The true nature and character of the legislation in the particular instance under discussion must always be determined, in order to ascertain the class of subject to which it really belongs. In the present case it appears to their Lordships, for the reasons already given, that the matter of the Act in question does not properly belong to the class of subjects "Property and Civil Rights" within the meaning of sub-sect. 13.

It was argued by Mr. Benjamin that if the Act related to criminal law, it was provincial criminal law, and he referred to sub-sect. 15

of sect. 92, *viz.,* "The imposition of any punishment by fine, penalty, or imprisonment for enforcing any law of the province made in relation to any matter coming within any of the classes of subjects enumerated in this section." No doubt this argument would be well founded if the principal matter of the Act could be brought within any of these classes of subjects; but as far as they have yet gone, their Lordships fail to see that this had been done.

It was lastly contended that this Act fell within sub-sect. 16 of sect. 92,—"Generally all matters of a merely local or private nature in the province."

It was not, of course, contended for the appellant that the Legislature of New Brunswick could have passed the Act in question, which embraces in its enactments all the provinces; nor was it denied, with respect to this last contention, that the Parliament of Canada might have passed an Act of the nature of that under discussion to take effect at the same time throughout the whole Dominion. Their Lordships understand the contention to be that, at least in the absence of a general law of the Parliament of Canada, the provinces might have passed a local law of a like kind, each for its own province, and that, as the prohibitory and penal parts of the Act in question were to come into force in those counties and cities only in which it was adopted in the manner prescribed, or, as it was said, "by local option," the legislation was in effect, and on its face, upon a matter of a merely local nature. The judgment of Allen, C.J., delivered in the Supreme Court of the Province of New Brunswick in the case of *Barker v. City of Frederickton,* 3 Pugs. & Burb. Sup. Ct. New Br. Rep. 139, which was adverse to the validity of the Act in question, appears to have been founded upon this view of its enactments. The learned Chief Justice says:—"Had this Act prohibited the sale of liquor, instead of merely restricting and regulating it, I should have had no doubt about the power of the Parliament to pass such an Act; but I think an Act, which in effect authorizes the inhabitants of each town or parish to regulate the sale of liquor, and to direct for whom, for what purposes, and under what conditions spirituous liquors may be sold therein, deals with matters of a merely local nature, which, by the terms of the 16th subsection of sect. 92 of the British North America Act, are within the exclusive control of the local Legislature."

Their Lordships cannot concur in this view. The declared object of Parliament in passing the Act is that there should be uniform legislation in all the provinces respecting the traffic in intoxicating liquors, with a view to promote temperance in the Dominion. Parliament does not treat the promotion of temperance as desirable in one province more than another, but as desirable everywhere throughout the Dominion. The Act as soon as it was passed became a law for the whole Dominion, and the enactments of the first part, relating to the machinery for bringing the second part into force, took effect and might be put into motion at once and everywhere within it. It is true that the prohibitory and penal parts of the Act are only to come into force in any county or city upon the adoption of a petition to that effect by a majority of electors, but this conditional application of these parts of the Act does not convert the Act itself into legislation in relation to a merely local matter. The objects and scope of the legislation are still general, viz., to promote temperance by means of a uniform law throughout the Dominion.

The manner of bringing the prohibitions and penalties of the Act into force, which Parliament has thought fit to adopt, does not alter its general and uniform character. Parliament deals with the subject as one of general concern to the Dominion, upon which uniformity of legislation is desirable, and the Parliament alone can so deal with it. There is no ground or pretence for saying that the evil or vice struck at by the Act in question is local or exists only in one province, and that Parliament, under colour of general legislation, is dealing with a provincial matter only. It is therefore unnecessary to discuss the considerations which a state of circumstances of this kind might present. The present legislation is clearly meant to apply a remedy to an evil which is assumed to exist throughout the Dominion, and the local option, as it is called, no more localises the subject and scope of the Act than a provision in an Act for the prevention of contagious diseases in cattle that a public officer should proclaim in what districts it should come in effect, would make the statute itself a mere local law for each of these districts. In statutes of this kind the legislation is general, and the provision for the special application of it to particular places does not alter its character.

Their Lordships having come to the conclusion that the Act in question does not fall within any of the classes of subjects assigned exclusively to the Provincial Legislatures, it becomes unnecessary to discuss the further question whether its provisions also fall within any of the classes of subjects enumerated in sect. 91. In abstaining from this discussion, they must not be understood as intimating any dissent from the opinion of the Chief Justice of the Supreme Court of Canada and the other Judges, who held that the Act, as a general regulation of the traffic in intoxicating liquors throughout the Dominion, fell within the class of subject, "the regulation of trade and commerce," enumerated in that section, and was, on that ground, a valid exercise of the legislative power of the Parliament of Canada.

Appeal dismissed.

[In *Riel v. The Queen* (1885), 10 App. Cas. 675, the Privy Council considered s. 4 of the *B.N.A. Act*, 1871 (Imp.), c. 28, which gave the Dominion Parliament power to make provision for the "administration, peace, order and good government of any territory not for the time being included in any province". It stated that the terms of s. 4 were "apt to authorize the utmost discretion of enactment for the attainment of the objects pointed to". See also *A.-G. Sask. v. C.P.R.*, [1953] 3 D.L.R. 785, where Viscount Simon, speaking for the Privy Council on the power of the Dominion in creating a new province under 1871 (Imp.), c. 28, to provide "for the passing of laws for the peace, order and good government of such province" said (at p. 791): "The words 'peace, order and good government' are words of very wide import and a Legislature empowered to pass laws for such purposes had a very wide discretion".

The word "order" in the opening words of s. 91 of the *B.N.A. Act* was substituted for the word "welfare" which had been used in the Quebec and Westminster Palace Hotel (London) Resolutions. *Lefroy,* Canada's Federal System, says of this substitution (at p. 93): "It places in the hands of the federal power of the Dominion the right and responsibility of maintaining public order throughout the whole country." *Quaere,* as to the effect of the substitution on the validity of federal social legislation!

Cf. *Laskin,* "Peace, Order and Good Government" Re-examined, (1947) 25 Can. Bar Rev. 1054, at p. 1066:

"A great deal has been made, both by Sir Lyman Duff [in the *Board of Commerce* case (1920), 60 S.C.R. 456, at pp. 509, 511; and in the *Natural Products Marketing Act* reference, [1936] S.C.R. 398, at pp. 409, 411] and by Viscount Haldane [in the *Snider* case, [1925] A.C. 396 at p. 411; see also another reference in the *Dominion Insurance Act* reference, [1916] 1 A.C. 588, at p. 596, which states the result accurately], of the unreported *McCarthy Act* decision of the Judicial Committee. There the Board, without giving reasons, invalidated the *Dominion Liquor License Act,* 1883, affirming, in so doing the opinion of the Supreme Court of Canada [See schedule to 1885 (Can.), c. 74]. It is important to note that this decision followed decisions of the Judicial Committee upholding the Canada Temperance Act and the Ontario Liquor License Act. An examination of the Dominion Liquor License Act reveals it to have been a purely local licensing statute, contemplating decentralized administration through district Boards of Licence Commissioners. The whole tenor of the Act indicated that it was dealing with the liquor traffic as a purely local problem in local licence districts. It is hardly a matter of surprise that the Supreme Court in Canada should have invalidated the enactment; but even so, the majority of the court saved those parts of the enactment relating to the carrying into effect of the provisions of the Canada Temperance Act. It is difficult hence to understand why Viscount Haldane in the *Snider* case ([1925] A.C. 396) should have felt that it was hard to reconcile the *Russell* case with the *McCarthy Act* decision; or why he so artfully says, "as to this last decision it is not without significance that the strong Board which delivered it abstained from giving any reasons for their conclusions" [[1925] A.C. 396, at p. 411]. For, if the *McCarthy Act* case affirms anything, it affirms the application of the aspect doctrine already referred to in the *Hodge* case."]

A.-G. ONT. v. A.-G. CAN.

In the Privy Council.   [1896] A.C. 348.

Appeal by special leave from a judgment of the Supreme Court of Canada, 24 S.C.R. 170, on a reference to it of the following seven questions:

1.   Has a provincial legislature jurisdiction to prohibit the sale within the province of spirituous, fermented, or other intoxicating liquors?

2.   Or has the legislature such jurisdiction regarding such portions of the province as to which the Canada Temperance Act is not in operation?

3.   Has a provincial legislature jurisdiction to prohibit the manufacture of such liquors within the province?

4.   Has a provincial legislature jurisdiction to prohibit the importation of such liquors into the province?

5. If a provincial legislature has not jurisdiction to prohibit sales of such liquors, irrespective of quantity, has such legislature jurisdiction to prohibit the sale by retail, according to the definition of a sale by retail either in statutes in force in the province at the time of confederation or any other definition thereof?

6. If a provincial legislature has a limited jurisdiction only as regards the prohibition of sales, has the legislature jurisdiction to prohibit sales subject to the limits provided by the several sub-sections of the 99th section of the Canada Temperance Act, or any of them (Revised Statutes of Canada, 49 Vict. c. 106, s. 99)?

7. Has the Ontario Legislature jurisdiction to enact s. 18 of Ontario Act, 53 Vict. c. 56, intituled "An Act to improve the Liquor Licence Acts," as said section is explained by Ontario Act, 54 Vict. c. 46, intituled "An Act respecting local option in the matter of liquor selling"?

Section 18, referred to in the last questions, is as follows:—

"18. Whereas the following provision of this section was at the date of confederation in force as a part of the Consolidated Municipal Act (29th and 30th Victoria, chapter 51, section 249, sub-section 9), and was afterwards re-enacted as sub-section 7 of section 6 of 32nd Victoria, chapter 32, being the Tavern and Shop Licence Act of 1868, but was afterwards omitted in subsequent consolidations of the Municipal and the Liquor Licence Acts, similar provisions as to local prohibition being contained in the Temperance Act of 1864, 27th and 28th Victoria, chapter 18; and the said last-mentioned Act having been repealed in municipalities where not in force by the Canada Temperance Act, it is expedient that municipalities should have the powers by them formerly possessed; it is hereby enacted as follows:—

"The council of every township, city, town and incorporated village may pass by-laws for prohibiting the sale by retail of spirituous, fermented, or other manufactured liquors in any tavern, inn, or other house or place of public entertainment, and for prohibiting altogether the sale thereof in shops and places other than houses of public entertainment. Provided that the by-law before the final passing thereof has been duly approved of by the electors of the municipality in the manner provided by the sections in that behalf of the Municipal Act. Provided further that nothing in this section contained shall be construed into an exercise of jurisdiction by the Legislature of the province of Ontario beyond the revival of provisions of law which were in force at the date of the passing of the British North America Act, and which the subsequent legislation of this province purported to repeal."

Act 54 Vict. c. 46, referred to above, declares that s. 18 was not intended to affect the provisions of s. 252 of the Consolidated Municipal Act, being Canada Act, 29 & 30 Vict. c. 51.

A majority of the Supreme Court, after hearing counsel for the Dominion, the provinces of Ontario, Quebec, and Manitoba, and also for the Distillers and Brewers' Association of Ontario, answered all the questions in the negative. Strong C.J., and Fournier J., while agreeing in a negative answer to questions 3 and 4, answered the remainder in the affirmative.

LORD WATSON: Their Lordships think it expedient to deal, in the first instance, with the seventh question, because it raises a practical issue, to which the able arguments of counsel on both sides of the Bar were chiefly directed, and also because it involves considerations which have a material bearing upon the answers to be given to the other six questions submitted in this appeal. In order to appreciate the merits of the controversy, it is necessary to refer to certain laws for the restriction or suppression of the liquor traffic which were passed by the Legislature of the old province of Canada before the Union, or have since been enacted by the Parliament of the Dominion, and by the Legislature of Ontario respectively.

[His Lordship here detailed pre-confederation liquor legislation in Upper Canada and its post-confederation history, and then referred to the Canada Temperance Act. He pointed out that when the Canada Temperance Act of 1886 was framed there was no provincial law authorizing the prohibition of liquor sales in Ontario save a pre-confederation Act of 1864. The Canada Temperance Act contained an express repeal of the prohibitory clauses of the provincial Act of 1864, and of the machinery thereby provided for bringing them into operation, (1) as to every municipality within the limits of Ontario in which, at the passing of the Act of 1886, there was no municipal by-law in force, (2) as to every municipality within these limits in which a prohibitive by-law then in force shall be subsequently repealed under the provisions of either Act, and (3) as to every municipality having a municipal by-law which is included in the limits of, or has the same limits with, any county or city in which the second part of the Canada Temperance Act is brought into force before the repeal of the by-law, which by-law, in that event, is declared to be null and void.

With the view of restoring to municipalities within the province whose powers were affected by that repeal the right to make by-laws which they had possessed under the law of the old province, the Legislature of Ontario passed s. 18 of 53 Vict. c. 56, to which the seventh question in this case relates. The Legislature of Ontario subsequently passed an Act (54 Vict. c. 46) for the purpose of explaining that s. 18 was not meant to repeal by implication certain provisions of the Municipal Act (29 & 30 Vict. c. 51), which limited its application to retail dealings.]

The seventh question raises the issue, whether, in the circumstances which have just been detailed, the provincial legislature had authority to enact s. 18. In order to determine that issue, it becomes necessary to consider, in the first place, whether the Parliament of Canada had jurisdiction to enact the Canada Temperance Act; and, if so, to consider in the second place, whether after that Act became the law of each province of the Dominion, there yet remained power with the Legislature of Ontario to enact the provisions of s. 18.

The authority of the Dominion Parliament to make laws for the suppression of liquor traffic in the provinces is maintained, in the first place, upon the ground that such legislation deals with matters affecting "the peace, order, and good government of Canada," within the meaning of the introductory and general enactments of s. 91 of the British North America Act; and, in the second place, upon the ground that it concerns "the regulation of trade and commerce," being No. 2 of the enumerated classes of subjects which are placed under the exclusive jurisdiction of the Federal Parliament by that section. These sources of jurisdiction are in themselves distinct, and are to be found in different enactments. . . .

The general authority given to the Canadian Parliament by the introductory enactments of s. 91 is "to make laws for the peace, order and good government of Canada, in relation to all matters not coming within the classes of subjects by this Act assigned exclusively to the legislatures of the provinces"; and it is declared, but not so as to restrict the generality of these words, that the exclusive authority of the Canadian Parliament extends to all matters coming within the classes of subjects which are enumerated in the clause. There may, therefore, be matters not included in the enumeration, upon which the Parliament of Canada has power to legislate, because they concern the peace, order, and good government of the Dominion. But to those matters which are not specified among the enumerated subjects of legislation, the exception from s. 92, which is enacted by the concluding words of s. 91, has no application; and, in legislating with regard to such matters, the Dominion Parliament has no authority to encroach upon any class of subjects which is exclusively assigned to provincial legislatures by s. 92. These enactments appear to their Lordships to indicate that the exercise of legislative power by the Parliament of Canada, in regard to all matters not enumerated in s. 91, ought to be strictly confined to such matters as are unquestionably of Canadian interest and importance, and ought not to trench upon provincial legislation with respect to any of the classes of subjects enumerated in s. 92. To attach any other construction to the general power which, in supplement of its enumerated powers, is conferred upon the Parliament of Canada by s. 91 would, in their Lordship's opinion, not only be contrary to the intendment of the Act, but would practically destroy the autonomy of the provinces. If it were once conceded that the Parliament of Canada has authority to make laws applicable to the whole Dominion, in relation to matters which in each province are substantially of local or private interest, upon the assumption that these matters also concern the peace, order, and good government of the Dominion, there is hardly a subject enumerated in s. 92 upon which it might not legislate, to the exclusion of the provincial legislatures.

In construing the introductory enactments of s. 91, with respect to matters other than those enumerated, which concern the peace, order, and good government of Canada, it must be kept in view that s. 94, which empowers the Parliament of Canada to make provision for the uniformity of the laws relative to property and civil rights in Ontario, Nova Scotia, and New Brunswick does not extend to the province of Quebec; and also that the Dominion legislation thereby authorized is expressly declared to be of no effect unless and until it has been adopted and enacted by the provincial legislature. These enactments would be idle and abortive, if it were held that the Parliament of Canada derives jurisdiction from the introductory provisions of s. 91, to deal with any matter which is in substance local or provincial, and does not truly affect the interest of the Dominion as a whole. Their Lordships do not doubt that some matters, in their origin local and provincial, might attain such dimensions as to affect the body politic of the Dominion, and to justify the Canadian Parliament in passing laws for their regulation or abolition in the interest of the Dominion. But great caution must be observed in distinguishing between that which is local and provincial, and therefore within the jurisdiction of the provincial legislatures, and that which has ceased to be merely local or provincial, and has become matter of national concern, in such sense as to bring it within the jurisdiction of the Parliament of Canada. An Act restricting the right to carry weapons of offence, or their sale to young persons, within the province would be within the authority of the provincial legislature. But traffic in arms, or the possession of them under such circumstances as to raise a suspicion that they were to be used for seditious purposes, or against a foreign State, are matters which, their Lordships conceive, might be competently dealt with by the Parliament of the Dominion.

The judgment of this Board in *Russell v. Reg.*, 7 App. Cas. 829, has relieved their Lordships from the difficult duty of considering whether the Canada Temperance Act of 1886 relates to the peace, order, and good government of Canada, in such sense as to bring its provisions within the competency of the Canadian Parliament. In that case the controversy related to the validity of the Canada Temperance Act of 1878; and neither the Dominion nor the Provinces were represented in the argument. It arose between a private prosecutor and a person who had been convicted, at his instance, of violating the provisions of the Canadian Act within a district of New Brunswick, in which the prohibitory clauses of the Act had been adopted. But the provisions of the Act of 1878 were in all material respects the same with those which are now embodied in the Canada Temperance Act of 1886; and the reasons which were assigned for sustaining the validity of the earlier, are, in their Lordships' opinion, equally applicable to the later Act. It therefore appears to them that the decision in *Russell v. Reg.*, 7 App. Cas. 829, must be accepted as an authority to the extent to which it goes, namely, that the restrictive provisions of the Act of 1886, when they have been duly brought into operation in any provincial area within the Dominion must receive effect as valid enactments relating to the peace, order, and good government of Canada. [His Lordship then held that the Canada Temperance Act could not be sustained as an Act in relation to the regulation of trade and commerce.]

The authority of the Legislature of Ontario to enact s. 18 of 53 Vict. c. 56, was asserted by the appellant on various grounds. The first of these, which was very strongly insisted on, was to the effect that the power given to each province by No. 8 of s. 92 to create municipal institutions in the province necessarily implies the right to endow these institutions with all the administrative functions which had been ordinarily possessed and exercised by them before the time of the Union. Their Lordships can find nothing to support that contention in the language of s. 92, No. 8, which, according to its natural meaning, simply gives provincial legislatures the right to create a legal body for the management of municipal affairs. Until confederation, the Legislature of each province as then constituted could, if it chose, and did in some cases, entrust to a municipality the execution of powers which now belong exclusively to the Parliament of Canada. Since its date a provincial Legislature cannot delegate any power which it does not possess; and the extent and nature of the functions which it can commit to a municipal body of its own creation must depend upon the legislative authority which it derives from the provisions of s. 92 other than No. 8.

Their Lordships are likewise of opinion that s. 92, No. 9, does not give provincial legislatures any right to make laws for the abolition of the liquor traffic. It assigns to them "shop, saloon, tavern, auctioneer and other licences, in order to the raising of a revenue for provincial, local or municipal purposes." It was held by this Board in *Hodge v. Reg.*, 9 App. Cas. 117, to include the right to impose reasonable conditions upon the licensees which are in the nature of regulation; but it cannot, with any show of reason, be construed as authorizing the abolition of the sources from which revenue is to be raised.

The only enactments of s. 92 which appear to their Lordships to have any relation to the authority of provincial legislatures to make laws for the suppression of the liquor traffic are to be found in Nos. 13 and 16, which assign to their exclusive jurisdiction, (1) "property and civil rights in the province," and (2) "generally all matters of a merely local or private nature in the province." A law which prohibits retail transactions and restricts the consumption of liquor within the ambit of the province, and does not affect transactions in liquor between persons in the province and persons in other provinces or in foreign countries, concerns property in the province which would be the subject-matter of the transactions if they were not prohibited, and also the civil rights of persons in the province. It is not impossible that the vice of intemperance may prevail in particular localities within a province to such an extent as to constitute its cure by restricting or prohibiting the sale of liquor a matter of a merely local or private nature, and therefore falling prima facie within No. 16. In that state of matters, it is conceded that the Parliament of Canada could not imperatively enact a prohibitory law adapted and confined to the requirements of localities within the province where prohibition was urgently needed.

It is not necessary for the purposes of the present appeal to determine whether provincial legislation for the suppression of the liquor traffic, confined to matters which are provincial or local within the meaning of Nos. 13 and 16, is authorized by the one or by the other of these heads. It cannot, in their Lordships' opinion, be logically held to fall within both of them. In s. 92, No. 16 appears to them to have the same office which the general enactment with respect to matters concerning the peace, order and good government of Canada, so far as supplementary to the enumerated subjects, fulfils in s. 91. It assigns to the provincial legislature all matters in a provincial sense local or private which have been omitted from the preceding enumeration, and, although its terms are wide enough to cover, they were obviously not meant to include, provincial legislation in relation to the classes of subjects already enumerated.

In the able and elaborate argument addressed to their Lordships on behalf of the respondents it was practically conceded that a provincial legislature must have power to deal with the restriction of the liquor traffic from a local and provincial point of view, unless it be held that the whole subject of restriction or abolition is exclusively committed to the Parliament of Canada as being within the regulation of trade and commerce. In that case the subject, in so far at least as it had been regulated by Canadian legislation, would, by virtue of the concluding enactment of s. 91, be exempted from the matters committed to provincial legislatures by s. 92. Upon the assumption that s. 91(2) does not embrace the right to suppress a trade, Mr. Blake maintained that, whilst the restriction of the liquor traffic may be competently made matter of legislation in a provincial as well as a Canadian aspect, yet the Parliament of Canada has, by enacting the Temperance Act of 1886, occupied the whole possible field of legislation in either aspect, so as completely to exclude legislation by a province. That appears to their Lordships to be the real point of controversy raised by the question with which they are at present dealing. . . .

The old Temperance Act of 1864 was passed for Upper Canada, or, in other words, for the province of Ontario; and its provisions, being confined to that province only, could not have been directly enacted by the Parliament of Canada. In the present case the Parliament of Canada would have no power to pass a prohibitory law for the province of Ontario; and could therefore have no authority to repeal in express terms an Act which is limited in its operation to that province. In like manner, the express repeal, in the Canada Temperance Act of 1886, of liquor prohibitions adopted by a municipality in the province of Ontario under the sanction of provincial legislation, does not appear to their Lordships to be within the authority of the Dominion Parliament.

The question must next be considered whether the provincial enactments of s. 18 to any, and if so to what, extent come into collision with the provisions of the Canadian Act of 1886. In so far as they do, provincial must yield to Dominion legislation, and must remain in abeyance unless and until the Act of 1886 is repealed by the parliament which passed it.

The prohibitions of the Dominion Act have in some respects an effect which may extend beyond the limits of a province, and they are all of a very stringent character. They draw an arbitrary line, at eight gallons in the case of beer, and at ten gallons in the case of other intoxicating liquors, with the view of discriminating between wholesale and retail transactions. Below the limit, sales within a district which has adopted the Act are absolutely forbidden, except to the two nominees of the Lieutenant-Governor of the province, who are only allowed to dispose of their purchases in small quantities for medicinal and other specified purposes. In the case of sales above the limit the rule is different. The manufacturers of pure native wines, from grapes grown in Canada, have special favour shewn them. Manufacturers of other liquors within the district, as also merchants duly licensed, who carry on an exclus:vely wholesale business, may sell for delivery anywhere beyond the district, unless such delivery is to be made in an adjoining district where the Act is in force. If the adjoining district happened to be in a different province, it appears to their Lordships to be doubtful whether, even in the absence of Dominion legislation, a restriction of that kind could be enacted by a provincial legislature.

On the other hand, the prohibitions which s. 18 authorizes municipalities to impose within their respective limits do not appear to their Lordships to affect any transactions in liquor which have not their beginning and their end within the province of Ontario. The first branch of its prohibitory enactments strikes against sales of liquor by retail in any tavern, or other house or other place of public entertainment. The second extends to sales in shops or places other than houses of public entertainment; but the context indicates that it is only meant to apply to retail transactions; and that intention is made clear by the terms of the explanatory Act 54 Vict. c. 46, which fixes the line between wholesale and retail at one dozen of liquor in bottles, and five gallons if sold in other receptacles. The importer or manufacturer can sell any quantity above the limit; and any retail trader may do the same, provided that he sells the liquor in the original packages in which it was received by him from the importer or manufacturer.

It thus appears that, in their local application within the province of Ontario, there would be considerable difference between the two laws; but it is obvious that their provisions could not be in force within the same district or province at one and the same time. In the opinion of their Lordships the question of conflict between their provisions which arises in this case does not depend upon their identity or non-identity, but upon a feature which is common to both. Neither statute is imperative, their prohibitions being of no force or effect until they have been voluntarily adopted and applied by the vote of a majority of the electors in a district or municipality. In *Russell v. Reg.*, 7 App. Cas. at p. 841, it was observed by this Board, with reference to the Canada Temperance Act of 1878, "The Act as soon as it was passed became a law for the whole Dominion, and the enactments of the first part, relating to the machinery for bringing the second part into force, took effect and might be put in motion at once and everywhere within it." No fault can be found with the accuracy of that statement. Mutatis mutandis, it is equally true as a description of the provisions of s. 18. But in neither case can the statement mean more than this, that, on the passing of the Act, each district or municipality within the Dominion or the province as the case might be, became vested with a right to adopt and enforce certain prohibitions if it thought fit to do so. But the prohibitions of these Acts, which constitute their object and their essence, cannot with the least degree of accuracy be said to be in force anywhere until they have been locally adopted.

If the prohibitions of the Canada Temperance Act had been made imperative throughout the Dominion, their Lordships might have been constrained by previous authority to hold that the jurisdiction of the Legislature of Ontario to pass s. 18 or any similar law had been superseded. In that case no provincial prohibitions such as are sanctioned by s. 18 could have been enforced by a municipality without coming into conflict with the paramount law of Canada. For the same reason, provincial prohibitions in force within a particular district will necessarily become inoperative whenever the prohibitory clauses of the Act of 1886 have been adopted by that district. But their Lordships can discover no adequate grounds for holding that there exists repugnancy between the two laws in districts of the province of Ontario where the prohibitions of the Canadian Act are not and may never be in force. . . .

Their Lordships, for these reasons, give a general answer to the seventh question in the affirmative. They are of opinion that the Ontario Legislature had jurisdiction to enact s. 18, subject to this necessary qualification, that its provisions are or will become inoperative in any district of the province which has already adopted, or may subsequently adopt, the second part of the Canada Temperance Act of 1886.

Their Lordships will now answer briefly, in their order, the other questions submitted by the Governor-General of Canada. So far as they can ascertain from the record, these differ from the question which has already been answered in this respect, that they relate to matters which may possibly become litigious in the future, but have not as yet given rise to any real and present controversy. Their Lordships must further observe that these questions, being in their nature academic rather than judicial, are better fitted for the considerations of the officers of the Crown than of a court of law. The replies to be given to them will necessarily depend upon the circumstances in which they may arise for decision; and these circumstances are in this case left to speculation. It must, therefore, be understood that the answers which follow are not meant to have, and cannot have, the weight of a judicial determination, except in so far as their Lordships may have occasion to refer to the opinions which they have already expressed in discussing the seventh question.

Answers to questions 1 and 2—Their Lordships think it sufficient to refer to the opinions expressed by them in disposing of the seventh question.

Answer to question 3.—In the absence of conflicting legislation by the Parliament of Canada, their Lordships are of opinion that the provincial legislature would have jurisdiction to that effect if it were shewn that the manufacture was carried on under such circumstances and conditions as to make its prohibition a merely local matter in the province.

Answer to question 4.—Their Lordships answer this question in the negative. It appears to them that the exercise by the provincial legislature of such jurisdiction in the wide and general terms in which it is expressed would probably trench upon the exclusive authority of the Dominion Parliament.

Answers to questions 5 and 6.—Their Lordships consider it unnecessary to give a categorical reply to either of these questions. Their opinion upon the points which the questions involve has been sufficiently explained in their answer to the seventh question.

Appeal allowed in part.

[In the formal order of the Privy Council consequent upon its judgment above, its answer to the fourth question is completely different from the answer included in the judgment. As it appears in the formal order the answer to the fourth question is as follows: "No useful answer can be given to this question in the absence of a precise statement of the facts to which it is intended to apply. There may be some circumstances in which a provincial legislature will and others in which it will not have such jurisdiction." *Quaere,* the importance of this change of position for the Dominion power in relation to the regulation of trade and commerce. For the Privy Council's formal order, see (1923) 1 Can. Bar Rev. at p. 229. This order is also referred to in *A.-G. Man. v. Man. Licence Holders Ass'n.,* [1902] A.C. 73, at p. 79; and by Orde J. in *Smith v. A.-G. Ont.* (1923), 53 O.L.R. 572, at p. 578, [1923] 4 D.L.R. 1071, at p. 1076.]

Note on the Local Prohibition Case

(*A.-G. Ont. v. A.-G. Can.,* [1896] *A.C.* 348)

The constitutionality of s. 18 of the Ontario statute 53 Vict., c. 56, as explained and limited by 54 Vict., c. 46, s. 1, was first considered by the Supreme Court of Canada in *Huson v. South Norwich* (1895), 24 S.C.R. 145, where by a bare majority (Strong C.J. and Fournier and Taschereau JJ.) it was held (Gwynne and Sedgewick JJ. dissenting) that the enactment was valid as applicable to sale by retail. Before judgment was delivered, the Governor-General in Council made the reference to the Supreme Court which became the famous *Local Prohibition* case. The Court in the *Huson* case reserved judgment until after argument in the reference. There was one change in the composition of the Court in the reference (*In re Prohibitory Liquor Laws* (1895), 24 S.C.R. 170); King J. sat instead of Taschereau J., and he joined in the views of Gwynne and Sedge-wick JJ., with the result that a majority on the reference invalidated the same enactment which was upheld in the *Huson* case; corres-pondingly, Strong C.J. and Fournier J. dissented in part on the refer-ence. Actually, however, there was little difference between the views of the majority and minority in both cases. The paramount power of the Dominion Parliament was recognized; the difference in point of view was on the question whether there was any room for pro-vincial legislation. It is instructive to refer to the views of Strong C.J. as set out in the *Huson* case (at p. 147 ff.) :

"It is established by *Russell v. The Queen* that the Dominion, being invested with authority by section 91 to make laws for the peace, order and good government of Canada, may pass what are denominated local option laws. But, as I understand that decision, such Dominion laws must be general laws, not limited to any particu-lar province. It is not competent to parliament to draw to itself the right to legislate on any subject which, by section 92, is assigned to the provinces by legislating on that subject generally for the whole Dominion, but this is of course not done where, in the execution of a power expressly given to it by section 91, the federal legislature makes laws similar to those which a provincial legislature may make in executing other powers expressly given to the provinces by section 92. Therefore it appears to me that there are in the Dominion and the provinces respectively several and distinct powers authorizing each, within its own sphere, to enact the same legislation on this subject of prohibitory liquor laws restraining sale by retail, that is to say, the Dominion may, as has already been conclusively decided, enact a prohibitory law for the whole Dominion, whilst the provincial legislatures may also enact similar laws, restricted of course to their own jurisdictions. Such provincial legislation cannot, however, be extended so as to prohibit importation or manufacture, for the reason that these subjects belong exclusively to the Dominion under the head of trade and commerce, and also for the additional reason that the revenue of the Dominion derived from the customs and excise duties would be thereby affected. That there may be, in respect of other subjects, such concurrent powers of legislation has already been decided by the Privy Council in the case of *Attorney-General of Ontario v. Attorney-General of Canada*, [1894] A.C. 189, where this question arose with reference to insolvency legislation. I venture to think the present even a stronger case for the application of such a construction than that referred to. To neither of the legislatures is the subject of prohibitory liquor laws in terms assigned. Then what reason is there why a local legislature in execution of the police power conferred by subsection 8 of sec. 92 may not, so long as it does not come in conflict with the legislation of the Dominion, adopt any appropriate means of executing that power, merely because the same means may be adopted by the Dominion Parliament under the authority of section 91 in executing a power specifically given to it? It has been decided by the highest authority that there are no reasons against such a construction. This is indeed even a stronger case for recognizing such a concurrent power than the case of the *Attorney-General of Ontario v. Attorney-General of Canada,* [1894] A.C. 189, because bankruptcy and insolvency laws are by section 91 expressly attributed to the exclusive jurisdiction of the Dominion. In the event of legislation providing for prohibition enacted by the Dominion and by a province coming into conflict the legislation of the province would no doubt have to give way. . . .

That a general police power sufficient to include the right of legislating to the extent of the prohibition of retail traffic or local option laws, not exclusive of but concurrent with a similar power in the Dominion, is vested in the provinces by the words "Municipal Institutions in the Province" in subsection 8 of chapter 92 is, I think, a proposition which derives support from the case of *Hodge v. The Queen,* 9 App. Cas. 117. It is true that the subject of prohibition was not in question in that case, but there would seem to be no reason why prohibitory laws as well as those regulating and limiting the traffic in liquors should not be included in the police power which under the words "Municipal Institutions" it was held in *Hodge v. The Queen,* 9 App. Cas. 117, to the extent of licensing, the provinces possessed. The difference between regulating and licensing and prohibiting is one of degree only.

As regards the objection that to recognize any such right of legislation in a province not extending to the prohibition of importation and manufacture would be an infringement of the power of the Dominion to regulate trade and commerce, I am not impressed by it. The retail liquor traffic can scarcely be regarded as coming directly under the head of trade and commerce as used in the British North America Act, but as the subjects enumerated in section 92 are exceptions out of those mentioned in section 91 it follows that if a police power is included in subsection 8 of the former section, the power itself and all appropriate means of carrying it out are to be treated as uncontrolled by anything in section 91. Moreover, *Hodge v. The Queen* 9 App. Cas. 117, also applies here for, although in a lesser degree, yet to some extent, the restriction of the liquor trade by a licensing system would affect trade and commerce. On the whole I am of opinion that the provincial legislatures have power to enact prohibitory legislation to the extent I have mentioned, though this power is in no way exclusive of that of the Dominion but concurrent with it."

[In *A.-G. Man. v. Man. Licence Holders Ass'n,* [1902] A.C. 73, the Privy Council reversed a unanimous judgment of the Manitoba Court of Appeal which had declared a Manitoba liquor statute *ultra vires* (*In re Liquor Act* (1901), 13 Man. R. 239). The Manitoba Court had distinguished the *Local Prohibition* case on the ground that the legislation impugned in that case involved a police or municipal regulation whereas the Manitoba statute was directly prohibitory. In the Privy Council, Lord Macnaghten found that the legislation fell within the permissive power of the province under the *Russell* and *Local Prohibition* cases. He assigned it to s. 92(16) of the *B.N.A. Act* and said (at p. 78): "Indeed if the case is to be regarded as dealing with matters within the class of subjects enumerated in No. 13 [of s. 92], it might be questionable whether the Dominion Legislature could have authority to interfere with the exclusive jurisdiction of the province in the matter." See *Note,* (1946), 24 Can. Bar Rev. 223.]

IN RE THE BOARD OF COMMERCE ACT AND THE COMBINES AND FAIR PRICES ACT, 1919

In the Supreme Court of Canada. (1920), 60 S.C.R. 456, 54 D.L.R. 354, [1920] 3 W.W.R. 658.

Case stated by the Board of Commerce for the opinion of the Supreme Court of Canada under s. 32 of 1919 (Can.), c. 37. The substance of the case is indicated in the following excerpt from the judgment of Anglin J.: [The case] states that the Board proposes to make an order in which, after reciting that it has upon an oral investigation found that in some thirty-six shops in the city of Ottawa men's ready made and partly made suits and overcoats, purchased at a cost of $30 or under, have as a practice been sold at the same percentage of gross profit or margin to the retailers as commodities purchased by them at a greater cost and that unfair profits have been made on such sales and that the merchants concerned have not offered their stock-in-trade of such commodities for sale at prices not higher than are reasonable and just, but that extenuating circumstances render a prosecution unnecessary, and that in the opinion of the Board fair profits on such commodities may be ascertained on a basis set forth, it will proceed to order that the individuals, firms, and corporations conducting such establishments, naming them, be and each of them is, restrained and prohibited from

(a) omitting or refusing to offer for sale within the city of Ottawa said commodities in accordance with the ordinary course of business at prices not higher than are reasonable and just;

(b) offering for sale within the City of Ottawa said commodities at prices higher than are reasonable and just;

(c) making or taking upon dispositions within the city of Ottawa by way of sale of said commodities unfair profits being profits greater than those hereinbefore indicated as fair profits;

(d) instituting, continuing or repeating the practice of marking for sale by retail within the City of Ottawa either the said commodities or stocks-in-trade of clothing of which said commodities form part at prices calculated or ascertained by the addition to cost of fifty per cent. or more of cost or at prices made up of cost plus a margin or gross profit of (a) a percentage greater than by this order recognized as fair, or (b) a percentage by this order indicated as unfair, whether or not sales are intended to be actually made at lower prices and in conformity with this order, such practices being in the opinion of the Board designed or calculated to unfairly enhance the price realized upon dispositions by sale of said commodities.

At bar Mr. O'Connor, representing the Attorney General, very properly conceded that clauses (a) and (b) of the proposed order would be merely repetitions of the general statutory prohibition implied in s. 17 of the Combines and Fair Prices Act and are not in a defensible form, and he accordingly abandoned them. As to the remaining clauses (c) and (d), the stated case submits two questions:

"(1) Has the Board lawful authority to make the order?

"(2) Has the Board lawful authority to require the Registrar or other proper officer of the Supreme Court of Ontario to cause the order when issued to be made a rule of said Court?"

Sec. 18 of the Combines and Fair Prices Act purports in explicit terms to confer the authority to make such a restraining or prohibitive order, and s. 38 of the Board of Commerce Act likewise purports in explicit terms to enable the Board to require that any order made by it shall be made a rule, order or decree of the Exchequer Court or of any superior court of any province of Canada. The questions presented are, therefore, in reality whether these particular provisions are within the legislative jurisdiction of Parliament.

The opinions of Davies C.J. and of Anglin and Mignault JJ. were delivered by

ANGLIN J.: . . . Section 17 of the Combines and Fair Prices Act prohibiting the unreasonable accumulation or withholding of "necessaries of life" defined by s. 18 (recently construed by this court in the case of Price Bros. Limited (see 60 S.C.R. 265)), and requiring that any excess of necessaries of life and all stocks in trade of such necessaries shall be offered for sale at reasonable and fair prices, and s. 22, which imposes penalties, *inter alia,* for contraventions of s. 17, may, I think be held valid (the latter *pro tanto*) as criminal legislation. The provisions of s. 18 authorizing the Board to make the inquiries therein provided for and to determine what shall constitute unfair profits may possibly be supported as ancillary criminal legislation, as well as for the purposes of s. 24.

But I think it is not possible to support, as necessarily incidental to the efficient exercise of plenary legislative jurisdiction over "the criminal law," the further provision of s. 18 purporting to empower the court to restrain prospective breaches of the statute, the making or taking of unfair profits, and practices calculated unfairly to enhance costs or prices, or the provisions of s. 38 of the Board of Commerce Act for making decisions or orders of the Board rules or decrees of the Exchequer Court or of any provincial superior court . . .

. . . The regulation of the quantities of "necessaries of life" that may be accumulated and witheld from sale and the compelling of the sale and disposition of them at reasonable prices throughout Canada is regulation of trade and commerce using those words in an ordinary sense. While the making of contracts for the sale and purchase of commodities is primarily purely a matter of "property and civil rights," and legislation restricting or controlling it must necessarily affect matters ordinarily subject to provincial legislative jurisdiction, the regulation of prices of necessaries of life—and to that the legislation under consideration is restricted—may under certain circumstances well be a matter of national concern and importance—may well affect the body politic of the entire Dominion. Moreover, "necessaries of life" may be produced in one province and sold in another. In the case of manufactured goods the raw material may be grown in or obtained from one province, may be manufactured in a second province and may be sold in several other provinces.

Effective control and regulation of prices so as to meet and overcome in any one province what is generally recognized to be an evil—"profiteering"—an evil so prevalent and so insidious that in the opinion of many persons it threatens to-day the moral and social well-being of the Dominion—may thus necessitate investigation, inquiry and control in other provinces. It may be necessary to deal with the prices and the profits of the growers or other producers of raw material, the manufacturers, the middlemen and the retailers. No one provincial legislature could legislate so as to cope effectively with such a matter and concurrent legislation of all the provinces interested is fraught with so many difficulties in its enactment and in its administration and enforcement that to deal with the situation at all adequately by that means is, in my opinion, quite impracticable.

Viewed in this light it would seem that the impugned statutory provisions may be supported, without bringing them under any of the enumerative heads of s. 91, as laws made for the peace, order and good government of Canada in relation to matters not coming within any of the classes of subjects assigned exclusively to the legislatures of the provinces, since, in so far as they deal with property and civil rights, they do so in an aspect which is not "from a provincial point of view local or private" and therefore not exclusively under provincial control. . . .

. . . . I ventured in the *Insurance Act Reference,* 48 S.C.R. 260, at page 310, to state what I conceive to be the result of the authorities on this particular point in these words:

> When a matter primarily of civil rights has attained such dimensions that it affects the body politic of the Dominion and has become of national concern it has in that aspect of it, not only ceased to be "local and provincial" but has also lost its character as a matter of "civil rights in the province" and has thus so far ceased to be subject to provincial jurisdiction that Dominion legislation upon it under the "peace, order and good government" provision does not trench upon the exclusive provincial field and is, therefore, valid and paramount.

In the judgment of the Privy Council on the same Reference, [1916] 1 A.C. 588, Lord Haldane said, at page 595:

> There is only one case, outside the heads enumerated in s. 91, in which the Dominion Parliament can legislate effectively as

regards a province, and that is when the subject matter lies outside all the subject matters enumeratively entrusted to the province under sect. 92. *Russell v. The Queen,* 7 App. Cas. 829, is an instance of such a case.

It may be said that if the subject matter of the Dominion legislation here in question, when its true aspect and real purpose are considered, relates to public order, safety or morals, affects the body politic of the Dominion and is a matter of national concern, so that it can be supported under the general peace, order and good government provision of s. 91 without recourse to any of the enumerated heads, it is unnecessary and inadvisable to attempt to bring it under head No. 2. But while, as Lord Haldane said in *The Insurance Case,* [1916] 1 A.C. 588, at page 596, great caution must always be exercised in applying the well established principle that

> subjects which in one aspect and for one purpose fall within the jurisdiction of the provincial legislatures may in another aspect and for another purpose fall within Dominion legislative jurisdiction,

having regard to the warning of Lord Watson in the *Local Prohibition* case, [1896] A.C. 348, at pages 360-1, I think it is better that legislation such as that which we are now dealing, which undoubtedly affects what would ordinarily be subject matters of provincial jurisdiction, should, if possible, be ascribed to one of the enumerated heads of s. 91. I prefer, therefore, to rest my opinion upholding its constitutional validity on the power of the Dominion Parliament to legislate for "the Regulation of Trade and Commerce" as well as on its power

> to make laws for the peace, order and good government of Canada

in regard to matters which, though not referable to any of the enumerated heads of s. 91, should, having regard to the aspect in which and the purpose for which they are dealt with, properly be held not to fall within any of the enumerated heads of s. 92—to "lie outside all the subject matters" thereby "entrusted to the province." . . .

No objection can successfully be founded upon the fact that the Board must exercise its powers from time to time in a particular province. *Colonial Building Association v. Attorney General of Quebec,* 9 App. Cas. 157. The necessity of such local action and regulation is perhaps the chief justification for the delegation to a Board or Commission of the power to define what shall be unfair profits and unreasonable and unjust prices. The unfairness of profits and the unreasonableness and injustice of prices, depends so largely on local conditions which vary from day to day and from place to place that Parliament could not itself deal with them by general legislation. Effective regulation of such matters can be accomplished only by some body such as the Board of Commerce endowed with the powers bestowed upon it and ready from time to time to deal promptly with the problems involved as they arise. Yet the power of Parliament to delegate its functions to the limited extent for which the Combines and Fair Prices Act provides has been challenged. We had occasion comparatively recently to consider and overrule a similar objection in *Re Gray,* 57 S.C.R. 150, at pp. 170, 175. . . .

We are for these reasons of the opinion that the power of Parliament to confer the authority, to the existence of which the questions in the stated case are directed, has not been successfully impugned and that the right of the Board of Commerce to make the proposed order, eliminating from it clauses (a) and (b) of the operative paragraph numbered 1, may be upheld as an exercise of authority validly bestowed under the jurisdiction of Parliament to make laws for "the regulation of trade and commerce" and for "the peace, order and good government of Canada," and, in so far as the findings in its recitals are concerned, possibly also under Dominion legislative jurisdiction over "The Criminal Law," although the investigation and the findings made thereon for the purpose of determining what are reasonable and just prices and of affording a foundation for an order prohibiting the making or taking of unfair profits and practices calculated to unfairly enhance costs or prices may not form part of a criminal cause or matter. . . .

We would therefore answer both the questions of the stated case in the affirmative.

DUFF J.:— . . . The second question is whether section 18 can be sustained as an exercise of the power of the Dominion under the introductory clause of section 91 to

make laws for the peace, order and good government of Canada.

Two conditions govern the legitimate exercise of this power. First —it is essential that the matter dealt with shall be one of unquestioned Canadian interest and importance as distinguished from matters merely local in one of the provinces; and, secondly, that the legislation shall not trench upon the authority of the province in respect of the matters enumerated in section 92. . . . I have already pointed out that section 18 does profess to deal with matters which in each province are, from the provincial standpoint, rights of property and civil rights there and matters which, in each province, are comprehended within the subject matter "local undertakings."

It is true that in *Russell v. The Queen,* the Canada Temperance Act was held to be validly enacted under this general power and that in the *Local Option Reference,* and in the *Manitoba License Holders'* case, the enactment of similar legislation was held to be competent to a local legislature, the legislation being, of course, limited in its operation, to the province; but it is I think impossible to draw from these authorities on the "drink" legislation any general principle which can serve as a guide in passing upon the validity of the statute before us.

Russell's case was accepted by the Judicial Committee in 1896 as decisively determining the validity of the Canada Temperance Act and to what extent it was treated as a binding authority.

But it must be remembered that *Russell's* case was in great part an unargued case. Mr. Benjamin who appeared for the appellant—the provinces were not represented upon the argument—conceded the authority of Parliament to enact legislation containing the provisions of the Canada Temperance Act to come into force at the same time throughout the whole of Canada and this Lord Herschell said in a subsequent case, was a "very large admission." The Judicial Committee proceeded upon the view that legislation containing the provisions of the Canada Temperance Act was not, from a provincial point of view, legislation relating to "property and civil rights" within the province; it was, they said, legislation dealing rather with public wrongs, having a close relation to criminal law and on this ground they held that the subject matter of it did not fall within the exceptions to the introductory clause.

The subsequent judgment of the Judicial Committee in the *Local Option Reference* of 1896 and in the *Manitoba License Holders'* case show that consistently with the validity of the Canada Temperance Act similar legislation by the provinces limited in its operation to the province, can be supported as being from a provincial point of view legislation dealing with matters merely local. In the last mentioned case Lord Macnaghten said it might be doubtful whether if such legislation were from the provincial point of view properly classified as legislation from the subjects denoted by "property and civil rights," general legislation by the Dominion such as the Canada Temperance Act could be sustained.

There is no case of which I am aware in which a Dominion statute not referable to one of the classes of legislation included in the enumerated heads of sec. 91 and being of such a character that from a provincial point of view, it should be considered legislation dealing with "property and civil rights", has been held competent to the Dominion under the introductory clause; and the effect of decisions in the Montreal Street Railway case, [1912] A.C. 333, or the McCarthy Act Reference and in the Insurance Act Reference, *Attorney General for Canada v. Attorney General of Alberta,* [1916] 1 A.C. 588, is that legislation by the Dominion applying to the whole of Canada dealing with matters which from a provincial point of view fall within No. 9 or No. 10 of sec. 92, is not a competent exercise of this general power.

"Property and civil rights," of course, taken in the most comprehensive sense, is a phrase of very wide application and like the words "Trade and Commerce," it must be restricted by reference to the context and the other provisions of sections 91 and 92. But my view is that where a subject matter is from a provincial point of view comprehended within the class of subjects falling under "property and civil rights," properly construed (*ex hypothesi* such matter could not fall strictly within any of the classes of subjects enumerated in sec. 91) it is incompetent to the Dominion in exercise of the authority given by the introductory clause to legislate upon that matter either alone or together with subjects over which the Dominion has undoubted jurisdiction as falling neither within sec. 92 nor within the enumerated heads of sec. 91; and legislation which in effect has this operation cannot be legitimised by framing it in comprehensive terms embracing matters over which the Dominion has jurisdiction as well as matters in which the jurisdiction is committed exclusively to the province.

Nor do I think it matters in the least that the legislation is enacted with the view of providing a remedy uniformly applicable to the whole of Canada in relation to a situation of general importance to the Dominion. The ultimate social economic or political aims of the legislator cannot I think determine the category into which the matters dealt with fall in order to determine the question whether the jurisdiction to enact it is given by sec. 91 or 92. The immediate operation and effect of the legislation, or the effect the legislation is calculated immediately to produce must alone, I think, be considered. I repeat that if, tested by reference to such operation and effect, the legislation does deal with matters which from a provincial point of view are within any of the first fifteen heads of section 92, it is incompetent to the Dominion unless it can be supported as ancillary to legislation under one of the enumerated heads of section 91.

This view may be supported by contrasting the decision of the Judicial Committee in *Russell's* case, with its decision on the McCarthy Act reference. The Canada Temperance Act was an attempt on the part of the Parliament of Canada to cope with the evils arising from the sale of intoxicating liquor, and that Act as already mentioned was held to be within the power of Parliament as dealing not with civil rights and property but with public wrongs, and being legislation analogous in character to the statute restricting the sale of explosives and poisons and having a close relation to the criminal law. The McCarthy Act which was passed shortly after the decision in *Russell's* case, recited that it was expedient to regulate the traffic in intoxicating liquors by a system uniform throughout Canada for the purpose of preserving public order, and then proceeded to regulate the liquor trade by a system of licensing. This decision, as already mentioned, was a logical consequence of the preceding decision of the Board in *Hodge's* case, 9 App. Cas. 117, to the effect that from a provincial point of view such a system of licensing fell within number 9 of section 92. The combined effect of these decisions seems clearly to be that while for the purpose of dealing with a matter of interest to the whole Dominion in the sense of being a matter affecting and pertaining to the public order and good government of the whole Dominion (the evils of the liquor trade), Parliament may legislate so long as its enactments are of such a character that they do not deal with matters from a provincial point of view within the specific classes of subjects enumerated in section 92, (that is the first fifteen heads) it is not within its power under the residuary clause to enact legislation which from the provincial point of view falls within any one of such classes. It is quite true that the McCarthy Act reference principally involved a consideration of only one of the enumerated heads, No. 9, but it is difficult to find any satisfactory relevant distinction between No. 9 and No. 10 (as regards matters falling under this head, the *Montreal Railway* case, seems to be conclusive), or between No. 9 and No. 13, although as regards the last mentioned head, caution must be used in observing the limits necessarily imposed by the context in the two sections upon the scope of their application.

The argument based upon the residuary clause rests upon the principles supposed to be deducible from the decisions upon the liquor legislation. The result of the decisions of the Judicial Committee in *Russell's* case, in the *Local Option Reference* in 1896, and in the *Manitoba License Holders'* case, in 1902, is that while the restriction or prohibition of the liquor traffic in the manner effected by the Canada Temperance Act within a single province, may from a provincial point of view fall within No. 16, it may also fall within the ambit of the residuary clause as subject matter of legislation; but there is in my judgment no justification for applying the reasoning of their Lordships in their judgments in the Local Option Reference, in support of the proposition that matters falling within any of the other heads of section 92 as subject matter of legislation can be dealt with by the Dominion under a general law passed under the authority of the residuary clause, and the doubt expressed by Lord Macnaghten in the *Manitoba License Holders'* case affords very weighty argument against such an interpretation of Lord Watson's judgment in the Local Option Reference.

The consequences of this proposed view of the residuary clause, can be illustrated by the present legislation. The scarcity of necessaries of life, the high cost of them, the evils of excessive profit taking, are matters affecting nearly every individual in the community and affecting the inhabitants of every locality and every province collectively as well as the Dominion as a whole. The legislative remedy attempted by section 18 is one of many remedies which might be suggested. One could conceive, for example, a proposal that there should be a general restriction of credits, and that the business of money lending should be regulated by a commission appointed by the Dominion Government with powers conferred by Parliament. Measures to increase production might conceivably be proposed and to that end nationalization of certain industries and even compulsory allotment of labour. In truth, if this legislation can be susutained under the residuary clause, it is not easy to put a limit to the extent to which Parliament through the instrumentality of commissions (having a large discretion in assigning the limits of their own jurisdiction, see sec. 16), may from time to time in the vicissitudes of national trade, times of high prices, times of stagnation and low prices and so on, supersede the authority of the provincial legislatures. I am not convinced that it is a proper application of the reasoning to be found in the judgments on the subject of the drink legislation, to draw from it conclusions which would justify Parliament in any conceivable circumstance forcing upon a province a system of nationalization of industry. . . .

[Idington and Brodeur JJ. gave separate reasons in which they reached the same conclusion as did Duff J.]

Power of Board of Commerce
sustained on equal division

[The reasoning of Anglin J. and of Duff J. on the "regulation of trade and commerce" is excluded; see however, Chap. IV, *infra.* On appeal from the Supreme Court's opinion on equal division, the Privy Council held that the Board of Commerce legislation was *ultra vires*: [1922] 1 A.C. 191, 60 D.L.R. 513, [1922] 1 W.W.R. 20. Speaking for the Privy Council Viscount Haldane said: "The first question to be answered is whether the Dominion Parliament could validly enact such a law. Their Lordships observe that the law is not one enacted to meet special conditions in wartime. It was passed in 1919, after peace had been declared, and it is not confined to any temporary purpose, but is to continue without limit in time, and to apply throughout Canada. No doubt the initial words of s. 91 of the British North America Act confer on the Parliament of Canada power to deal with subjects which concern the Dominion generally, provided that they are not withheld from the powers of that Parliament to legislate, by any of the express heads in s. 92, untrammelled by the enumeration of special heads in s. 91. It may well be that the subjects of undue combination and hoarding are matters in which the Dominion has a great practical interest. In special circumstances, such as those of a great war, such an interest might conceivably become of such paramount and overriding importance as to amount to what lies outside the heads in s. 92, and is not covered by them. The decision in *Russell v. The Queen* (1882), 7 App. Cas. 829, appears to recognize this as constitutionally possible, even in time of peace; but it is quite another matter to say that under normal circumstances general Canadian policy can justify interference, on such a scale as the statutes in controversy involve, with the property and civil rights of the inhabitants of the Provinces. It is to the Legislatures of the Provinces that the regulation and restriction of their civil rights have in general been exclusively confined, and as to these the Provincial Legislatures possess quasi-sovereign authority. It can, therefore, be only under necessity in highly exceptional circumstances, such as cannot be assumed to exist in the present case, that the liberty of the inhabitants of the Provinces may be restricted by the Parliament of Canada, and that the Dominion can intervene in the interests of Canada as a whole in questions such as the present one. For, normally, the subject-matter to be dealt with in the case would be one falling within s. 92. Nor do the words in s. 91, the "Regulation of trade and commerce," if taken by themselves, assist the present Dominion contention. It may well be, if the Parliament of Canada had, by reason of an altogether exceptional situation, capacity to interfere, that these words would apply so as to enable that Parliament to oust the exclusive character of the Provincial powers under s. 92. . . .

As their Lordships have already indicated, the jurisdiction attempted to be conferred on the new Board of Commerce appears to them to be ultra vires for the reasons now discussed. It implies a claim of title, in the cases of non-traders as well as of traders, to make orders prohibiting the accumulation of certain articles required for every-day life, and the withholding of such articles from sale at prices to be defined by the Board, whenever they exceed the amount of the material which appears to the Board to be required for domestic purposes or for the ordinary purposes of business. The Board is also given jurisdiction to regulate profits and dealings which may give rise to profit. The power sought to be given to the Board applies to articles produced for his own use by the householder himself, as well as to articles accumulated, not for the market but for the purposes of their own processes of manufacture by manufacturers. The Board is empowered to inquire into individual cases and to deal with them individually, and not merely as the result of applying principles to be laid down as of general application. This would cover such instances as those of coal mines and of local Provincial undertakings for meeting Provincial requirements of social life.

Legislation setting up a Board of Commerce with such powers appears to their Lordships to be beyond the powers conferred by s. 91. They find confirmation of this view in s. 41 of the Board of Commerce Act, which enables the Dominion Executive to review and alter the decisions of the Board. It has already been observed that circumstances are conceivable, such as those of war or famine, when the peace, order and good Government of the Dominion might be imperilled under conditions so exceptional that they require legislation of a character in reality beyond anything provided for by the enumerated heads in either s. 92 or s. 91 itself. Such a case, if it were to arise would have to be considered closely before the conclusion could properly be reached that it was one which could not be treated as falling under any of the heads enumerated. Still, it is a conceivable case, and although great caution is required in referring to it, even in general terms, it ought not, in the view their Lordships take of the British North America Act, read as a whole, to be excluded from what is possible. For throughout the provisions of that Act there is apparent the recognition that subjects which would normally belong exclusively to a specifically assigned class of subject may, under different circumstances and in another aspect, assume a further significance. Such an aspect may conceivably become of paramount importance, and of dimensions that give rise to other aspects. This is a principle which, although recognized in earlier decisions, such as that of *Russell v. The Queen,* both here and in the Courts of Canada, has always been applied with reluctance, and its recognition as relevent can be justified only after scrutiny sufficient to render it clear that the circumstances are abnormal. In the case before them, however important it may seem to the Parliament of Canada that some such policy as that adopted in the two Acts in question should be made general throughout Canada, their Lordships do not find any evidence that the standard of necessity referred to has been reached, or that the attainment of the end sought is practicable, in view of the distribution of legislative powers enacted by the Constitution Act, without the co-operation of the Provincial Legislatures."]

FORT FRANCES PULP & POWER CO. LTD. v. MANITOBA FREE PRESS CO. LTD.

In the Privy Council.   [1923] A.C. 695, [1923] 3 D.L.R. 629.

Appeal from a judgment of the Ontario Appellate Division, 52 O.L.R. 118, [1923] 3 D.L.R. 199, affirming on other grounds a judgment of Riddell J. holding certain Dominion statutes and orders-in-council *intra vires*.

VISCOUNT HALDANE:—This appeal raises questions of some novelty and delicacy.

The appellants are manufacturers of newsprint paper in Ontario and the respondents are publishers of newspapers, carrying on business at various places in Canada. The action out of which the appeal arises was brought by the respondents against the appellants to recover sums the former had paid for paper delivered to them at controlled prices. These sums, which the respondents alleged to represent margins in excess of the prices regulated by law, they claimed to be repayable to them as the result of orders of the Paper Control Tribunal of Canada, the final order having been made on July 8, 1920. The sums represented the amounts due after an adjustment of accounts in accordance with the above-mentioned final order and previous orders which it modified. For the balance so arrived at the action was brought in the Supreme Court of Ontario. It was tried before Riddell J., who gave judgment for the plaintiffs, the respondents.

No question was raised as to figures, and the learned judge treated the question before him as being only whether the Paper Control Tribunal and the Paper Controller, from whose orders the Paper Control Tribunal was in effect a Court of Appeal, had been validly vested with power to make the orders in controversy. The judgment of Riddell J. was made the subject of an appeal to the Appellate Division of the Supreme Court, which affirmed the judgment of the trial judge. There was a counterclaim by the appellants for the amount of the market prices of the paper delivered by them to the respondents, less the sums actually paid. This was dismissed by Riddell J., the dismissal being consequential on his view that the Orders were valid. The Court of Appeal did not think it necessary to go into this question of validity for they considered that notwithstanding that pressure was put on the appellants to supply the paper at the prices fixed by the Orders, they did send out invoices and supply it, and thereby in effect entered into contracts for such supply on the terms that the prices were provisional and to be finally adjusted in terms of the Orders to be made by the Paper Control Tribunal. On that footing nothing was, in the event, due on the counterclaim. Whether the action of these tribunals was legal or not, the appellate

Court therefore held that the appellants, notwithstanding that they had acted under pressure, had bound themselves to accept the prices fixed and were liable.

Their Lordships have not been able to satisfy themselves that this view was a reliable one. . . . It is therefore necessary to consider in the first place the validity of the legislation and Orders in Council by which the controlling tribunals were set up and invested with the powers exercised.

Purporting to act under the provisions of the War Measures Act passed by the Parliament of the Dominion in August, 1914, the Governor-General made an Order in Council, dated April 16, 1917, authorizing the Minister of Customs to fix the quantity and price of newsprint paper in sheets or rolls furnished or to be furnished to those who required it for publishing. The Order was to be operative from March 1, 1917, to June 1 in the same year. By further Orders this power was extended to December 1 in that year. Acting in accordance with these Orders the Minister ordered deliveries and fixed prices, and this procedure continued until Mr. R. A. Pringle K.C. was, by Order in Council dated November 3, 1917, appointed Controller as well as Commissioner with power to fix the quantities to be delivered and the prices, such prices, however, to be approved by the Governor-General in Council.

By various Orders Mr. Pringle fixed prices for a period extending from July 1, 1918, to December 1 in that year. By Order in Council dated September 16, 1918, prices were directed no longer to be supervised by the Governor in Council, inasmuch as a new tribunal called the Paper Control Tribunal was set up, and a right of appeal to it from any Order of the Controller was given. The Paper Control Tribunal made various Orders on appeals from the Controller, and on July 8, 1920, made an Order fixing a price for a period ending on December 31, 1919, and directing the appellants to refund all sums received in excess of the prices fixed. It was the amount of the excess that was the subject of the present action. . . .

So far as the relevant legislation of the Parliament of the Dominion is concerned, this consists of two statutes. The first of these is the War Measures Act, 1914. It enacts that the provisions of s. 6 (to be presently referred to) are only to be in force during war, invasion or insurrection, real or apprehended. The issue of a Government proclamation is to be conclusive evidence that these exist and are continuing, until the issue of a subsequent proclamation declaring them to exist no longer. War is to be deemed to have existed since August 4, 1914. By s. 6 the Governor in Council is to have power to do and authorize such acts and things and to make such orders and regulations as he may, by reason of the existence of real or apprehended war, invasion or insurrection, deem necessary or advisable for the security, defence, peace, order and welfare of Canada. These powers are to extend, among other matters, to trading, exportation, importation, production, manufacture, and also to appropriation, control, forfeiture, and disposition of property and of its use.

By a later Act of the Dominion Parliament, passed on July 7, 1919, relating to paper control, after referring to certain of the Orders in Council already mentioned and to the War Measures Act of 1914, on the recital that there had been investigations and work begun by the Paper Commissioner and Controller which were not completed and with respect to which appeals would lie to the Paper Control Tribunal, and that there were then matters pending before and undetermined by that tribunal, it was enacted that the powers, jurisdiction and authority of the Commissioner and Controller of Paper were confirmed and extended so as to enable him to complete all work and investigations begun by him prior to the declaration of peace, and to determine all questions and to make all necessary Orders with respect to matters coming before him prior to the publication in the Canada Gazette of a proclamation by the Governor in Council declaring the war to no longer exist.

It was further enacted that the powers, jurisdiction and authority of the Paper Control Tribunal were so confirmed and extended as to enable it to determine finally after the declaration of peace all matters pending before and not finally determined by it at the date of such declaration, and to dispose of all appeals brought before it subsequent to such declaration from any act done by or order or decision of the Commissioner and Controller under the Act. It was also provided that, except for the purpose of finally completing all matters undertaken, and determining all matters arising prior to the declaration of peace, the powers, the authority and jurisdiction of the Commissioner and Controller of Paper and of the Paper Control Tribunal should cease upon the publication of the said proclamation.

It is not clear that any such proclamation as above defined was issued. There was an Order made by His Majesty in the Imperial Privy Council on February 9, 1920, and published in the Canada Gazette on the same date, declaring January 10, 1920, as the date of the termination of the war with Germany. But there was war with other countries to which this Order did not relate, and of a proclamation as to these no evidence has been produced.

Their Lordships do not, however, consider this to be in itself important. For it is clear that on July 8, 1920, the Paper Control Tribunal when it made the Order under which the claim in this action arose, made it on an appeal from an Order of Mr. Pringle, the Controller, dated December 24, 1919. The Order on appeal of July 8, 1920, disposed of matters down to December 31, 1919. It altered certain prices governing periods, which prices the Controller had fixed in the past, increasing some of these and diminishing others, and directed any excess thus brought out of amounts charged by the appellants to be repaid, subject to set-off.

Their Lordships think that the effect of these Orders, assuming the Dominion Government and Legislature had authority to make them, was to render the appellants liable to account for the balance of the prices received by them from time to time up to the end of 1919 in excess of what was ultimately allowed, on the footing of being money had and received to the use of the respondents. No question arises as to figures, and the Orders are in such a form that they must be taken as intended to operate retrospectively.

The question, therefore, becomes one of constitutional law, as to whether the procedure thus established had a valid base. This depends, in the first place, on whether the two statutes already quoted were *intra vires* of the Dominion Parliament.

It is clear that in normal circumstances the Dominion Parliament could not have so legislated as to set up the machinery of control over the paper manufacturers which is now in question. The recent decision of the Judicial Committee in the *Board of Commerce* case, as well as earlier decisions, show that as the Dominion Parliament cannot ordinarily legislate so as to interfere with property and civil rights in the Provinces, it could not have done what the two statutes under consideration purport to do had the situation been normal. But it does not follow that in a very different case, such as that of sudden danger to social order arising from the outbreak of a great war, the Parliament of the Dominion cannot act under other powers which may well be implied in the constitution. The reasons given in the *Board of Commerce* case recognize exceptional cases where such a power may be implied.

In the event of war, when the national life may require for its preservation the employment of very exceptional means, the provision of peace, order and good government for the country as a whole may involve effort on behalf of the whole nation, in which the interests of individuals may have to be subordinated to that of the community in a fashion which requires s. 91 to be interpreted as providing for such an emergency. The general control of property and civil rights for normal purposes remains with the Provincial Legislatures. But questions may arise by reason of the special circumstances of the national emergency which concern nothing short of the peace, order and good government of Canada as a whole.

The overriding powers enumerated in s. 91, as well as the general words at the commencement of the section, may then become applicable to new and special aspects which they cover of subjects assigned otherwise exclusively to the Provinces. It may be, for example, impossible to deal adequately with the new questions which arise without the imposition of special regulations on trade and commerce of a kind that only the situation created by the emergency places within the competency of the Dominion Parliament. It is proprietary and civil rights in new relations, which they do not present in normal times, that have to be dealt with; and these relations, which affect Canada as an entirety, fall within s. 91, because in their fullness they extend beyond what s. 92 can really cover. The kind of power adequate for dealing with them is only to be found in that part of the constitution which establishes power in the State as a whole. For it is not one that can be reliably provided for by depending on collective action of the Legislatures of the individual Provinces agreeing for that purpose. That the basic instrument on which the character of the entire constitution depends should be construed as providing for such centralised power in an emergency situation follows from the manifestation in the language of the Act of the principle that the instrument has among its purposes to provide for the State regarded as a whole, and for the expression and influence of its public opinion as such. This principle of a power so implied has received effect also in countries with a written and apparently rigid constitution such as the United States, where the strictly federal character of the national basic agreement has retained the residuary powers not expressly conferred on the Federal Government for the component States. The operation of the scheme of interpretation is all the more to be looked for in a constitution such as that established by the British North America Act, where the residuary powers are given to the Dominion Central Government, and the preamble of the statute declares the intention to be that the Dominion should have a constitution similar in principle to that of the United Kingdom.

Their Lordships, therefore, entertain no doubt that however the wording of ss. 91 and 92 may have laid down a framework under which, as a general principle, the Dominion Parliament is to be excluded from trenching on property and civil rights in the Provinces of Canada, yet in a sufficiently great emergency such as that arising out of war, there is implied the power to deal adequately with that emergency for the safety of the Dominion as a whole. The enumeration in sec. 92 is not in any way repealed in the event of such an occurrence, but a new aspect of the business of Government is recognized as emerging, an aspect which is not covered or precluded by the general words in which powers are assigned to the Legislatures of the Provinces as individual units. Where an exact line of demarcation will lie in such cases it may not be easy to lay down *a priori*, nor is it necessary. For in the solution of the problem regard must be had to the broadened field covered, in case of exceptional necessity, by the language of s. 91, in which the interests of the Dominion generally are protected. As to these interests the Dominion Government, which in its Parliament represents the people as a whole, must be deemed to be left with considerable freedom to judge.

The other point which arises is whether such exceptional necessity as must be taken to have existed when the war broke out, and almost of necessity for some period subsequent to its outbreak, continued through the whole of the time within which the questions in the present case arose.

When war has broken out it may be requisite to make special provisions to ensure the maintenance of law and order in a country, even when it is in no immediate danger of invasion. Public opinion may become excitable, and one of the causes of this may conceivably be want of uninterrupted information in newspapers. Steps may have to be taken to ensure supplies of these and to avoid shortage, and the effect of the economic and other disturbance occasioned originally by the war may thus continue for some time after it is terminated. The question of the extent to which provision for circumstances such as these may have to be maintained is one on which a Court of law is loath to enter. No authority other than the central Government is in a position to deal with a problem which is essentially one of statesmanship. It may be that it has become clear that the crisis which arose is wholly at an end and that there is no justification for the continued exercise of an exceptional interference which becomes *ultra vires* when it is no longer called for. In such a case the law as laid down for distribution of powers in the ruling instrument would have to be invoked. But very clear evidence that the crisis had wholly passed away would be required to justify the judiciary, even when the question raised was one of *ultra vires* which it had to decide, in overruling the decision of the Government that exceptional measures were still requisite. In saying what is almost obvious, their Lordships observe themselves to be in accord with the view taken under analgous circumstances by the Supreme Court of the United States, and expressed in such decisions as that in October, 1919, in *Hamilton v. Kentucky Distilleries Co.*, 251 U.S. 146.

When then, in the present instance, can it be said that the necessity altogether ceased for maintaining the exceptional measure of control over the newspaper print industry introduced while the war was at its height? At what date did the disturbed state of Canada which the war had produced so entirely pass away that the legislative measures relied on in the present case became *ultra vires?* It is enough to say that there is no clear and unmistakeable evidence that the Government was in error in thinking that the necessity was still in existence at the dates on which the action in question was taken by the Paper Control Tribunal. No doubt late in 1919 statements were made to the effect that the war itself was at an end. For example, in the Order in Council made at Ottawa on December 20, 1919, it is stated that it must "be realised that although no proclamation has been issued declaring that the war no longer exists, actual war conditions have in fact long ago ceased to exist, and consequently existence of war can no longer be urged as a reason in fact for maintaining these extraordinary regulations as necessary or advisable for the security of Canada."

The Order in Council then goes on to say that in consequence of the armistice of November, 1918, the Expeditionary Force had since been withdrawn and demobilised, and the country generally is devoting its energies to re-establishment in the ordinary avocations of peace. In these circumstances, it states, the Minister of Justice considers that the time has arrived when the emergency Government legislation should cease to operate. This was in December, 1919. The Order then goes on to declare repealed all Orders and Regulations of the Governor in Council which depend for their sanction upon s. 6 of the War Measures Act, 1914, and repeals them as from January 1, 1920. But from this repeal it expressly excepts, among other Orders and Regulations specified, those relating to paper control, which are to remain in force until the end of another session of Parliament.

It will be observed that this Order in Council deals only with the results following from the cessation of actual war conditions. It excepts from repeal certain measures concerned with consequential conditions arising out of war, which may obviously continue to produce effects remaining in operation after war itself is over.

Their Lordships find themselves unable to say that the Dominion Government had no good reason for thus temporarily continuing the paper control after actual war had ceased, but while the effects of war conditions might still be operative. They are, therefore, unable to accept the propositions submitted to them in the powerful argument for the appellants.

Appeal dismissed.

[The doctrine of the *Fort Frances* case was applied in *Co-operative Committee on Japanese Canadians v. A.-G. Can.*, [1947] A.C. 87, [1947] 1 D.L.R. 577, and in *Reference re Validity of Wartime Leasehold Regulations*, [1950] S.C.R. 124, [1950] 2 D.L.R. 1; and see also *Canadian Wheat Board v. Manitoba Pool Elevators*, [1949] 2 D.L.R. 537, [1949] 1 W.W.R. 599, 57 Man. R. 1, aff'd on other grounds, [1951] S.C.R. 81, [1951] 1 D.L.R. 466, rev'd [1952] A.C. 427, [1952] 3 D.L.R. 433, 6 W.W.R. (N.S.) 23.

Note, however, the qualification of the *Board of Commerce* case and of the *Fort Frances* case which appears in the following passage from Lord Wright's judgment in the *Japanese Canadians* case ([1947] A.C. 87, at p. 101, [1947] 1 D.L.R. 577, at p. 585): "Upon certain general matters of principle there is not since the decision in *Fort Frances P. & P. Co. v. Manitoba Free Press Co.*, [1923] A.C. 695, any room for dispute. Under the *B.N.A. Act* property and civil rights in the several Provinces are committed to the provincial Legislatures, but the Parliament of the Dominion in a sufficiently great emergency such as that arising out of war has power to deal adequately with that emergency for the safety of the Dominion as a whole. The interests of the Dominion are to be protected and it rests with the Parliament of the Dominion to protect them. What those interests are the Parliament of the Dominion must be left with considerable freedom to judge.

Again if it be clear that an emergency has not arisen or no longer exists, there can be no justification for the exercise or continued exercise of the exceptional powers. The rule of law as to the distribution of powers between the Parliament of the Dominion and the Parliaments of the Provinces comes into play. But very clear evidence that an emergency has not arisen or that the emergency no longer exists is required to justify the judiciary even though the question is one of *ultra vires*, in overruling the decision of the Parliament of the Dominion that exceptional measures were required or were still required.

To this may be added as a corollary that it is not pertinent to the judiciary to consider the wisdom or the propriety of the particular policy which is embodied in the emergency legislation. Determination of the policy to be followed is exclusively a matter for the Parliament of the Dominion and those to whom it has delegated its powers.

Lastly it should be observed that the judiciary are not concerned when considering a question of *ultra vires* with the question whether the executive will in fact be able to carry into effective operation the emergency provisions which the Parliament of the Dominion either directly or indirectly has made."]

TORONTO ELECTRIC COMMISSIONERS v. SNIDER

In the Privy Council.   [1925] A.C. 396, [1925] 2 D.L.R. 5, [1925] 1 W.W.R. 785.

Appeal by special leave from a judgment of the Appellate Division of the Supreme Court of Ontario, 55 O.L.R. 454, [1924] 2 D.L.R.

761, affirming (Hodgins J.A. dissenting) a judgment of Mowat J. holding that the Industrial Disputes Investigation Act, 1907 (Can.) c. 20 was *intra vires*. In interlocutory proceedings for an injunction until trial Orde J. was of opinion that the Act was *ultra vires*. He held that the Dominion legislation interfered with provincial rights under s. 92 in a fashion which could not be supported under any of the enumerated heads in s. 91, and therefore could not be sustained by invoking the general words with which that section commences. The decision in the *Fort Frances Pulp* case afforded no analogy on which such a contention as this last could be based.

Mowat J., before whom the action came for trial, dissented from this reasoning and referred the issues to the Appellate Division. He thought that the legislation in question was a matter of national importance, dealing with a subject which affected the body politic of the Dominion as in *Russell v. The Queen*.

In the Appellate Division, Mulock C.J., Smith J.A. and Magee J.A. concurred in the judgment delivered by Ferguson J.A. That learned judge held that the Act in question was not, "in its pith and substance," an Act relating to merely provincial matters falling within s. 92, but related to industrial disputes which might develop into disputes affecting, not only the immediate parties, but the national welfare, peace, order and safety. He cited the analogy of the Australian Constitution Act, which, by s. 51, placed such disputes within the competence of the Australian Parliament when they extended beyond the limits of any single state. He was of opinion that, even if the Dominion legislation actually interfered with Provincial powers, it might be supported if necessary as dealing with the interests of the peace, order and good government of Canada, but he thought that it was necessary to go further in point of principle than to treat *Russell v. The Queen* as showing that, where an abnormal condition in a great emergency demanded it, the Parliament of Canada might legislate for such a case without even trenching on the powers allocated to the Provinces under s. 92. He also thought that the Act was not one to control or regulate contractual or civil rights, but that its object was to authorize inquiry into conditions or disputes, and that the prevention of crimes, the protection of public safety, peace and order, and the protection of trade and commerce, were of its pith and substance and paramount purpose. The Act could also be supported as Dominion legislation under the overriding enumerated heads of s. 91, as being legislation in relation to the regulation of trade and commerce, and also to the criminal law.

Hodgins J.A. dissented. In his view, industrial strife was nothing more than the result of an undesirable use of the civil right to cease work in the operation of various businesses. The argument in support of the Act was practically an endeavour to invent a new field, which was only a department or development of one of those exclusively possessed by provincial legislatures. Nor was the matter made better by the contention that the Act, when examined in the light of the evidence adduced, dealt with a subject which transcended Provincial limits and was of Dominion importance. It was, no doubt, true that owing to the highly organized methods of modern labour, strikes might spread and extend to other businesses. This might happen, and the state of things might conceivably reach a height in which it became comparable to war, famine or rebellion, and justify Dominion action. But on the only facts proved, in the learned judge's view, this Act could not be supported as dealing with a case of (1) emergency, or (2) general Canadian interest and importance, or (3) with a power conferred under any of the enumerated heads in s. 91. No great national emergency was shown to have existed when the statute was enacted in 1907, or to have occurred since, and the statute was not framed so as to come into operation only when such emergency arose. The statute was further not framed so as to confer the drastic powers that would be necessary in such a case, but was based on the normal working of industrial relations which often required time and patience and some restraint, if dislocation was to be avoided. It was essentially a sedative measure. The special and exceptional conditions of emergency required by the judgments in the *Board of Commerce* case and the *Fort Frances Pulp* case did not appear to him to have existed in point of fact. So far as anticipations of changes in the future were concerned, Hodgins J.A. thought that the question was whether regulation of civil rights or invasion of property rights in the fashion provided by the Act, in order to bring about a uniform and desirable method of dealing with industrial disputes, admirable as its purpose might be, could be valid in view of the exercise of the powers given to the Provinces. That the Provinces had such powers, as complete as those in this Act given to the Dominion, he entertained no doubt. Several Provinces had on their statute books legislation of much the same kind. Even granting the national importance of the question, the whole success of this method of dealing with it depended on the capacity to seize on local disputes and their conditions, and to manage the exercise of civil rights in relation to them. The circumstance that the dispute might spread to other Provinces was not enough in itself to justify Dominion interference, if such interference affected property and civil rights. The Province in the present case was simply the scene of municipal action. As the result of his consideration of the principles laid down for the interpretation of the British North America Act, the learned judge was of opinion that the Act could not stand.

VISCOUNT HALDANE: It is always with reluctance that their Lordships come to a conclusion adverse to the constitutional validity of any Canadian statute that has been before the public for years as having been validly enacted, but the duty incumbent on the Judicial Committee, now as always, is simply to interpret the British North America Act and to decide whether the statute in question has been within the competence of the Dominion Parliament under the terms of s. 91 of that Act. In this case the Judicial Committee have come to the conclusion that it was not. To that conclusion they find themselves compelled, alike by the structure of s. 91 and by the interpretation of its terms that has now been established by a series of authorities. They have had the advantage not only of hearing full arguments on the question, but of having before them judgments in the Courts of Ontario, from which this appeal to the Sovereign in Council came directly. Some of these judgments are against the view which they themselves take, others are in favour of it, but all of them are of a high degree of thoroughness and ability.

The particular exercise of legislative power with which their Lordships are concerned is contained in a well-known Act, passed by the Dominion Parliament in 1907, and known as the Industrial Disputes Investigation Act. As it now stands it has been amended by subsequent Acts, but nothing turns, for the purposes of the question now raised, on any of the amendments that have been introduced.

The primary object of the Act was to [settle] industrial disputes between any employer in Canada and any one or more of his employees as to "matters or things affecting or relating to work done or to be done by him or them, or as to the privileges, rights and duties of employers or employees (not involving any such violation thereof as constitutes an indictable offence)", relating to wages or remuneration, or hours of employment; sex, age or qualifications of employees, and the mode, terms and conditions of employment; the employment of children or any person, or classes of persons; claims as to whether preference of employment should be given to members of labour or other organizations; materials supplied or damage done to work; customs or usages, either general or in particular districts; and the interpretation of agreements. Either of the parties to any such dispute was empowered by the Act to apply to the Minister of Labour for the Dominion for the appointment of a Board of Conciliation and Investigation, to which Board the dispute might be referred. The Act enabled the Governor in Council to appoint a Registrar of such Boards, with the duty of dealing with all applications for reference, bringing them to the notice of the Minister, and conducting the correspondence necessary for the constitution of the Boards. The Minister was empowered to establish a Board when he thought fit, and no question was to be raised in any Court interfering with his decision. Each Board was to consist of three members, to be appointed by the Minister, one on the recommendation of the employer, one on that of the employees, and the third, who was to be chairman, on the recommendation of the members so chosen. If any of them failed in his duty the Minister was to make the appointment. The department of the Minister of Labour was to provide the staffs required. The application for a Board was to be accompanied by a statutory declaration showing that, failing adjustment, a lock-out or strike would probably occur.

The Board so constituted was to make inquiry and to endeavour to effect a settlement. If the parties came to a settlement the Board was to embody it in a memorandum of recommendation which, if the parties had agreed to it in writing, was to have the effect of an award on a reference to arbitration or one made under the order of a Court of record. In such a case the recommendation could be constituted a rule of Court and enforced accordingly. If no such settlement was arrived at, then the Board was to make a full report and a recommendation for settlement to the Minister, who was to make it public.

The Boards set up were given powers to summon and to enforce the attendance of witnesses, to administer oaths and to call for business books and other documents, and also to order into custody or subject to fine, in case of disobedience or contempt. The Board was also empowered to enter any premises where anything was taking place which was the subject of the reference and to inspect. This power was also enforceable by penalty. The parties were to be represented before the Board, but no counsel or solicitors were to appear excepting by consent and subject to the sanction of the Board itself. The proceedings were normally to take place in public.

By s. 56 of the Act, in the event of a reference to a Board, it was made unlawful for the employer to lock-out or for the employees to strike on account of any dispute prior to or pending the reference, and any breach of this provision was made punishable by fine. By s. 57, employers and employed were both bound to give at least thirty days' notice of an intended change affecting conditions of employment with respect to wages or hours. In the event of a dispute arising over the intended change, until the dispute had been finally dealt with by a Board and a report had been made, neither employers nor employed were to alter the conditions, or lock-out or strike, or suspend employment or work, and the relationship of employer and employee was to continue uninterrupted. If, in the opinion of the Board, either party were to use this or any other provision of the Act for the purpose of unjustly maintaining a given condition of affairs through delay, and the Board were so to report to the Minister, such party was to be guilty of an offence and liable to penalties.

By s. 63(a), where a strike or lock-out had occurred or was threatened, the Minister was empowered, although neither of the parties to the dispute had applied for one, to set up a Board. He might also, under the next section, without any application, institute an inquiry.

Whatever else may be the effect of this enactment, it is clear that it is one which could have been passed, so far as any Province was concerned, by the Provincial Legislature under the powers conferred by s. 92 of the British North America Act. For its provisions were concerned directly with the civil rights of both employers and employed in the Province. It set up a Board of Inquiry which could summon them before it, administer to them oaths, call for their papers and enter their premises. It did no more than what a Provincial Legislature could have done under head 15 of s. 92, when it imposed punishment by way of penalty in order to enforce the new restrictions on civil rights. It interfered further with civil rights when, by s. 56, it suspended liberty to lock-out or strike during a reference to a Board. It does not appear that there is anything in the Dominion Act which could not have been enacted by the Legislature of Ontario, excepting one provision. The field for the operation of the Act was made the whole of Canada.

In 1914 the Legislature of the Province of Ontario passed a Trade Disputes Act which substantially covered the whole of these matters so far as Ontario was concerned, excepting in certain minor particulars. One of these was the interference in the Dominion Act with the right to lock-out or strike during an inquiry. This was not reproduced in the Ontario Act. Another difference was the necessary one that the operation of the Ontario Act was confined to that Province, instead of extending to other parts of Canada. It was, of course, open to the Legislatures of the other Provinces to enact similar provisions, and some of them appear to have done so.

Subject to variations such as these there is, in the Ontario Act, little alteration in substance of the provisions of the Dominion statute. The Lieutenant-Governor of the Province, instead of the Minister of Labour, appoints the Registrar. There are to be set up two different kinds of statutory Council, one of Conciliation, the four members of which are to be nominated by the parties, the other a Council of Arbitration, consisting of three members, two of whom are to be appointed by the Lieutenant-Governor of the Province on the recommendation of the parties, and the third, the chairman, to be nominated by the Lieutenant-Governor on failure of the parties to agree and name. The mayor of any city or town in the Province, on being notified that a strike or lock-out is impending, may inform the Registrar of the fact, and a Council of Arbitration may then be empowered to inquire and to mediate. Unless there is an agreement by one or both of the parties, in which case the award of the Council may be enforced as on an arbitration, there is no power given to suspend the right to strike or lock-out.

It is clear that this enactment was one which was competent to the Legislature of a Province under s. 92. In the present case the substance of it was possibly competent, not merely under the head of property and civil rights in the province, but also under that of municipal institutions in the Province. For the appellants are incorporated, by the Province, a Public Utility Commission within the definition in ch. 204 of the Revised Statutes of Ontario, 1914, relating to the constitution and operation of works for supplying public utilities by municipal corporation and companies, and are employers within the meaning of the Ontario Trade Disputes Act already referred to. Their function is to manage the municipal electric light, heat, and power works of the City of Toronto.

The primary respondents in this appeal are the members of a Board of Conciliation appointed by the Dominion Minister of Labour under the Act first referred to. There was a dispute in 1923 between the appellants and a number of the men whom they employed, which dispute was referred to the first respondents, who proceeded to exercise the powers given by the Dominion Act. The appellants then commenced an action in the Supreme Court of Ontario for an injunction to restrain these proceedings, on the allegation that the Dominion Act was *ultra vires*. The Attorneys-General of Canada and of Ontario were notified and made parties as intervenants. . . .

. . . The Dominion Parliament has, under the initial words of s. 91, a general power to make laws for Canada. But these laws are not to relate to the classes of subjects assigned to the Provinces by s. 92, unless their enactment falls under heads specifically assigned to the Dominion Parliament by the enumeration in s. 91. When there is a question as to which legislative authority has the power to pass an Act, the first question must therefore be whether the subject falls within s. 92. Even if it does, the further question must be answered, whether it falls also under an enumerated head in s. 91. If so, the Dominion has the paramount power of legislating in relation to it. If the subject falls within neither of the sets of enumerated heads, then the Dominion may have power to legislate under the general words at the beginning of s. 91.

Applying this principle, does the subject of the legislation in controversy fall fully within s. 92? For the reasons already given their Lordships think that it clearly does. If so, is the exclusive power *prima facie* conferred on the Province trenched on by any of the over-riding powers set out specifically in s. 91? It was, among other things, contended in the argument that the Dominion Act now challenged was authorized under head 27, "the Criminal Law, except the Constitution of Courts of Criminal Jurisdiction, but including the Procedure in Criminal Matters." It was further suggested in the argument that the power so conferred is aided by the power conferred on the Parliament of Canada to establish additional Courts for the better administration of the laws of Canada.

But their Lordships are unable to accede to these contentions. They think that they cannot now be maintained successfully, in view of a series of decisions in which this Board has laid down the interpretation of s. 91, head 27, in the British North America Act on the point. In the most recent of these cases, *Attorney-General for Ontario v. Reciprocal Insurers,* [1924] A.C. 328, at p. 342, Duff J. stated definitely the true interpretation, in delivering the judgment of the Judicial Committee. Summing up the effect of the series of previous decisions relating to the point, he said: "In accordance with the principle inherent in these decisions their Lordships think it is no longer open to dispute that the Parliament of Canada cannot, by purporting to create penal sanctions under s. 91, head 27, appropriate to itself exclusively a field of jurisdiction in which, apart from such a procedure, it could exert no legal authority, and that if, when examined as a whole, legislation in form criminal is found, in aspects and for purposes exclusively within the Provincial sphere, to deal with matters committed to the Provinces, it cannot be upheld as valid."

In the earlier *Board of Commerce* case the principle to be applied was laid down in the same way. It was pointed out that the Dominion had exclusive legislative power to create new crimes "where the subject matter is one which, by its very nature, belongs to the domain of criminal jurisprudence." But "it is quite another thing, first to attempt to interfere with a class of subject committed exclusively to the Provincial Legislature, and then to justify this by enacting ancillary provisions, designated as new phases of Dominion criminal law, which require a title to so interfere as the basis of their application."

Their Lordships are of opinion that, on authority as well as on principle, they are to-day precluded from accepting the arguments that the Dominion Act in controversy can be justified as being an exercise of the Dominion power under s. 91 in relation to criminal law. What the Industrial Disputes Investigation Act, which the Dominion Parliament passed in 1907, aimed at accomplishing was to enable the Dominion Government to appoint anywhere in Canada a Board of Conciliation and Investigation to which the dispute between an employer and his employees might be referred. The Board was to have power to enforce the attendance of witnesses and to compel the production of documents. It could under the Act enter premises, interrogate the persons there, and inspect the work. It rendered it unlawful for an employer to lock-out or for a workman to strike, on account of the dispute, prior to or during the reference, and imposed an obligation on employees and employers to give thirty days' notice of any intended change affecting wages or hours. Until the reference was concluded neither were to alter the conditions with respect to these. It is obvious that these provisions dealt with civil rights, and it was not within the power of the Dominion Parliament to make this otherwise by imposing merely ancillary penalties. The penalties for breach of the restrictions did not render the statute the less an interference with civil rights in its pith and substance. The Act is not one which aims at making striking generally a new crime. Moreover, the employer retains under the general common law a right to lock-out, only slightly interfered with by the penalty. In this connection their Lordships are therefore of opinion that the validity of the Act cannot be sustained.

The point was also put in a somewhat different form. It was said that the criminal law of Canada was in its foundation the criminal law of England as at September 17, 1792; that, according to the criminal law of England as at that date, a strike was indictable as a conspiracy; that, consequently, strikes were within the ambit of the criminal law; and that as a law either declaring strikes illegal as at common law, or making them illegal would be a proper enactment of the criminal law, so, though this is rather a non sequitur, it was only a branch of that law to enact provisions which should have the effect of preventing strikes coming into existence.

It is not necessary to investigate or determine whether a strike is per se a crime according to the law of England in 1792. A great deal has been said on the subject and contrary opinions expressed. Let it be assumed that it was. It certainly was so only on the ground of conspiracy. But there is no conspiracy involved in a lock-out; and the statute under discussion deals with lock-outs *pari ratione* as with strikes. It would be impossible, even if it were desirable, to separate the provisions as to strikes from those as to lock-outs, so as to make the one fall under the criminal law while the other remained outside it; and, therefore, in their Lordships opinion this argument also fails . . .

. . . A more difficult question arises with reference to the initial words of s. 91, which enable the Parliament of Canada to make laws for the peace, order and good government of Canada in matters falling outside the Provincial powers specifically conferred by s. 92. For *Russell v. The Queen* was a decision in which the Judicial Committee said that it was within the competency of the Dominion Parliament to establish a uniform system for prohibiting the liquor traffic throughout Canada excepting under restrictive conditions. It has been observed subsequently by this Committee that it is now clear that it was on the ground that the subject matter lay outside Provincial powers, and not on the ground that it was authorized as legislation for the regulation of trade and commerce, that the Canada Temperance Act was sustained: see *Attorney-General for Canada v. Attorney-General for Alberta,* [1916] 1 A.C. 588. But even on this footing it is not easy to reconcile the decision in *Russell v. The Queen* with the subsequent decision in *Hodge v. The Queen* that the Ontario Liquor Licence Act, with the powers of regulation which it entrusted to local authorities in the Province, was *intra vires* of the Ontario Legislature. Still more difficult is it to reconcile *Russell v. The Queen* with the decision given later by the Judicial Committee that the Dominion licensing statute, known as the McCarthy Act, which sought to establish a local licensing system for the liquor traffic throughout the Dominion, was *ultra vires* of the Dominion Parliament. As to this last decision it is not without significance that the strong Board which delivered it abstained from giving any reasons for their conclusion. They did not in terms dissent from the reasons given in *Russell v. The Queen.* They may have thought that the case was binding on them as deciding that the particular Canada Temperance Act of 1886 has been conclusively held valid, on the ground of fact that at the period of the passing of the Act the circumstances of the time required it in an emergency affecting Canada as a whole. The McCarthy Act, already referred to, which was decided to have been *ultra vires* of the Dominion Parliament, was dealt with at the end of 1885. Ten years subsequently another powerful Board decided *Attorney-General for Ontario v. Attorney-General for the Dominion,* known as the *Distillers' and Brewers' case,* [1896] A.C. 348. Lord Herschell and Lord Davey, who had been the leading counsel in the *McCarthy* case, sat on that Board, along with Lord Halsbury, who had presided at it. In delivering the judgment, Lord Watson used in the latter case significant language: "The judgment of this Board in *Russell v. The Queen,* has relieved their Lordships from the difficult duty of considering whether the Canada Temperance Act of 1886 relates to the peace, order, and good government of Canada, in such sense as to bring its provisions within the competency of the Canadian Parliament." That decision, he said, must be accepted as an authority to the extent to which it goes—namely, that "the restrictive provisions of the Act of 1886, when they have been duly brought into operation in any Provincial area within the Dominion, must receive effect as valid enactments relating to the peace, order and good government of Canada."

The Board held that, on that occasion, they could, not inconsistent-
ly with *Russell v. The Queen,* declare a statute of the Ontario Legislature establishing Provincial liquor prohibitions, to be within the competence of a Provincial Legislature, provided that the locality had not
already adopted the provisions of the Dominion Act of 1886.

It appears to their Lordships that it is not now open to them
to treat *Russell v. The Queen* as having established the general
principle that the mere fact that Dominion legislation is for the
general advantage of Canada, or is such that it will meet a mere
want which is felt throughout the Dominion, renders it competent
if it cannot be brought within the heads enumerated specifically in
s. 91. Unless this is so, if the subject matter falls within any of the
enumerated heads in s. 92, such legislation belongs exclusively to
Provincial competency. No doubt there may be cases arising out of
some extraordinary peril to the national life of Canada, as a whole,
such as the cases arising out of a war, where legislation is required of
an order that passes beyond the heads of exclusive Provincial competency. Such cases may be dealt with under the words at the
commencement of s. 91, conferring general powers in relation to
peace, order and good government, simply because such cases are not
otherwise provided for. But instances of this, as was pointed out in
the judgment in *Fort Frances Pulp and Power Co. v. Manitoba Free
Press* are highly exceptional. Their Lordships think that the decision
in *Russell v. The Queen* can only be supported to-day, not on the
footing of having laid down an interpretation, such as has sometimes been invoked of the general words at the beginning of s. 91,
but on the assumption of the Board, apparently made at the time of
deciding the case of *Russell v. The Queen,* that the evil of intemperance at that time amounted in Canada to one so great and so general
that at least for the period it was a menace to the national life of
Canada so serious and pressing that the National Parliament was
called on to intervene to protect the nation from disaster. An epidemic
of pestilence might conceivably have been regarded as analogous. It
is plain from the decision in the *Board of Commerce* case that the
evil of profiteering could not have been so invoked, for Provincial
powers, if exercised, were adequate to it. Their Lordships find it
difficult to explain the decision in *Russell v. The Queen* as more than
a decision of this order upon facts, considered to have been established
at its date rather than upon general law . . .

. . . Their Lordships have examined the evidence produced at
the trial. They concur in the view taken of it by Hodgins J.A. They
are of opinion that it does not prove any emergency putting the
national life of Canada in unanticipated peril such as the Board
which decided *Russell v. The Queen* may be considered to have had
before their minds.

As the result of consideration, their Lordships have come to the
conclusion that they ought humbly to advise the Sovereign that the
appeal should be allowed, and that judgment should be entered for
the appellants for the declaration and injunction claimed.

Appeal allowed.

[The recital of the holdings by the lower courts is taken from the judgment of Viscount Haldane.

In *The King v. Eastern Terminal Elevator Co.*, [1925] S.C.R. 434, [1925] 3 D.L.R. 1, Anglin C.J.C., dissenting, said, in reference to Viscount Haldane's explanation of the *Russell* case (at p. 438, S.C.R.; p. 3, D.L.R.): "In alluding to the Lemieux Act judgment I feel that I should respectfully take exception to the suggestion there made, that the Board which decided *Russell v. The Queen* must be considered to have had before their minds an emergency putting the national life of Canada in unanticipated peril as the occasion of the enactment by Parliament of the Canada Temperance Act, 1878 . . . I cannot find anything in the judgment delivered by Sir Montague E. Smith in the *Russell* case suggestive of such a view having been entertained by the Judicial Committee. On the contrary, the whole tenor of the judgment seems to me inconsistent with its having proceeded on that basis. I should indeed be surprised if a body so well informed as their Lordships had countenanced such an aspersion on the fair fame of Canada even though some hard driven advocate had ventured to insinuate it in argument."]

REFERENCE RE NATURAL PRODUCTS MARKETING ACT

In the Supreme Court of Canada. [1936] S.C.R. 398,
[1936] 3 D.L.R. 622.

The judgment of the Court was delivered by

DUFF C.J.: . . . Turning now to the contention that this statute is a valid exercise of the power of Parliament under the introductory clause of section 91, there is a preliminary observation to be made. This argument has been pressed upon us in support of six of the statutes which have been referred to us for consideration. These are the statutes relating to the *Minimum Wages*, to *Limitation of Hours of Work, to a Weekly Rest Day, to Employment and Social Insurance*, to *Farmers' Creditors Arrangements* and to the statute immediately under consideration, the *National Products Marketing Act*. The discussion which follows was written with special reference to the first three of these statutes; the argument upon the reference relating to them being that, apart altogether from the circumstance that the subject matters of the enactments are subjects of international agreements in respect of which international obligations have been assumed, they are dealt with in aspects which do not fall under section 92 and can only be the subject matter of legislation under the initial clause of section 91. What follows, however, in substance pertains to the argument as presented in support of all the statutes mentioned and it has been thought convenient to produce it in this place.

It is important not to lose sight of the language of the statute itself. The initial words of section 91 empower

> the Queen by and with the advice and consent of the Senate and the House of Commons to make laws for the peace, order and good government of Canada in relation to all matters not coming within the classes of subjects by this Act assigned exclusively to the legislatures of the provinces.

By section 92,

in each province the legislature may exclusively make laws in relation to matters coming within the classes of subjects enumerated.

These classes of subjects include (No. 13) Property and Civil Rights in the Province. . . .

Language could not be more plain or, indeed, more explicit to declare that the subjects, Property and Civil Rights, are not subjects assigned to the Parliament of Canada under the initial words of section 91.

We are not concerned with the enumerated subjects assigned to Parliament under the second limb of that section; or with the concluding paragraph of the section which, as the Courts have recognized, has obviously no application to the first limb of the section, which alone is now pertinent.

It is settled by the decisions of the Judicial Committee that the phrase "Property and Civil Rights" is used in the "largest sense," subject, of course, to the limitations arising expressly from the exception of the enumerated heads of section 91, and impliedly from the specification of subjects in section 92.

The legislation admittedly affects civil rights and interferes with, and controls, and regulates the exercise in every one of the provinces of the civil rights of the people in those provinces; but it is said that the real subject matter of the legislation is not these civil rights, which are controlled and regulated, but something else.

The initial clause of section 91 has been many times considered. There is no dispute now that the exception which excludes from the ambit of the general power all matters assigned to the exclusive authority of the legislatures must be given its full effect. Nevertheless it has been laid down that matters normally comprised within the subjects enumerated in section 92 may, in extraordinary circumstances, acquire aspects of such paramount significance as to take them outside the sphere of that section.

The argument is mainly supported by two sentences in the judgment of the Board in *A.G. for Ontario v. A.G. for Canada*, [1896] A.C. 348. The judgment of the Board in that case was directed to the answers to be given to certain questions submitted by the Governor General in Council to this Court, all of which questions immediately concerned the jurisdiction of a provincial legislature in respect of the prohibition of certain phases of the liquor traffic. The two sentences occur in the discussion of the seventh question which relates to the jurisdiction of the Ontario Legislature to enact a section of a statute of that Province entitled "An Act respecting local option in the matter of liquor selling." In the course of that discussion, their Lordships dealt with the general authority given to the Parliament of Canada under the first of the introductory enactments of section 91 which is quoted above, and their Lordships observed,

". . . to those matters which are not specified among the enumerated subjects of legislation, the exception from s. 92, which is enacted by the concluding words of s. 91, has no application; and, in legislating with regard to such matters, the Dominion Parliament has no authority to encroach upon any class of subjects which is exclusively assigned to provincial legislatures by s. 92. These enactments appear to their Lordships to indicate that the exercise of legislative power by the Parliament of Canada, in regard to all matters not enumerated in s. 91, ought to be strictly confined to such matters as are unquestionably of Canadian interest and importance, and ought not to trench upon provincial legislation with respect to any of the classes of subjects enumerated in s. 92. To attach any other construction to the general power which, in supplement of its enumerated powers, is conferred upon the Parliament of Canada by s. 91, would, in their Lordships' opinion, not only be contrary to the intendment of the Act, but would practically destroy the autonomy of the provinces. If it were once conceded that the Parliament of Canada has authority to make laws applicable to the whole Dominion, in relation to matters which in each province are substantially of local or private interest, upon the assumption that these matters also concern the peace, order and good government of the Dominion, there is hardly a subject enumerated in s. 92 upon which it might not legislate, to the exclusion of the provincial legislatures."

Their Lordships proceeded, in the two sentences which are now mainly relied upon,

"Their Lordships do not doubt that some matters, in their origin local and provincial, might attain such dimensions as to affect the body politic of the Dominion, and to justify the Canadian Parliament in passing laws for their regulation or abolition in the interest of the Dominion. But great caution must be observed in distinguishing between that which is local and privincial, and therefore within the jurisdiction of the provincial legislatures, and that which has ceased to be merely local or provincial, and has become matter of national concern, in such sense as to bring it within the jurisdiction of the Parliament of Canada."

It seems to us right, if these two sentences are to be properly understood, that they should be read with the preceding sentences; and experience seems to shew that there has been a disposition not to attend to the limits implied in the carefully guarded language in which the Board expressed itself. It has been assumed, apparently, that they lay down a rule of construction the effect of which is that all matters comprised in any one of the enumerated subdivisions of section 92 may attain "such dimensions as to . . . cease to be merely local or provincial" and become in some other aspect of them matters relating to the "peace, order and good government of Canada" and subject to the legislative jurisdiction of the Parliament of Canada.

The difficulty of applying such a rule to matters falling within the first subdivision, for example, of section 92, which relates to the amendment of the provincial constitutions "notwithstanding anything in this Act," must be very great. On the face of the language of the statute, the authority seems to be intended to be absolute. In other words, it seems to be clearly stated that matters comprised within the subject matter of the constitution of the province "except as regards the office of Lieutenant-Governor" are matters local and provincial, and that they are not matters which can be comprised in any of the classes of subjects of section 91.

Then the decision in the *Montreal Park & Island Railway v. City of Montreal*, [1912] A.C. 333, seems to be final upon the point that local works and undertakings, subject to the exceptions contained in subdivision no. 10 of section 92 and matters comprised within that description, are matters local and provincial within the meaning of section 92 and excepted from the general authority given by the introductory enactment of section 91.

The same might be said of the solemnization of marriage in the province. Marriage and divorce are given without qualification to the Dominion under subdivision 26 of section 91, but the effect of section 92(12), it has been held, is to exclude from the Dominion jurisdiction in relation to marriage and divorce the subject of solemnization of marriage in the province. It is very difficult to conceive the possibility of solemnization of marriage, in the face of this plain declaration by the legislature, assuming aspects which would bring it within the general authority of the Dominion in relation to peace, order and good government, in such fashion, for example, as to enable the Dominion to prohibit or to deprive of legal effect a religious ceremony of marriage. The like might be said of no. 2, Taxation within the Province; the Borrowing of Monies on the Sole Credit of the Province; Municipal Institutions in the Province; and the Administration of Justice, including the constitution of the Courts and Procedure in Civil Matters in the Courts. . . .

As we have said, Lord Watson's language is carefully guarded. He does not say that every matter which attains such dimensions as to affect the body politic of the Dominion falls thereby within the introductory matter of section 91. But he said that "some matters" may attain such dimensions as to affect the body politic of the Dominion and, as we think the sentence ought to be read having regard to the context, in such manner and degree as may "justify the Canadian Parliament in passing laws for their regulation or abolition . . ." So, in the second sentence, he is not dealing with all matters of "national concern" in the broadest sense of those words, but only those which are matter of national concern "in such sense" as to bring them within the jurisdiction of the Parliament of Canada.

The application of the principle implicit in this passage must always be a delicate and difficult task. This is shewn by reference to the history of the Canada Temperance Act. [His Lordship then discussed *Russell v. The Queen*, the *Board of Commerce* case, and the *Snider* case.]

. . . On behalf of the Dominion it is argued that the judgment in the *Aeronautics* case, [1932] A.C. 54, at p. 71, constitutes a new point of departure. The effect of that judgment, it seems to be argued, is that if, in the broadest sense of the words, the matters dealt with are matters "of national concern" matters which "affect the body politic of the Dominion," jurisdiction arises under the introductory clause. One sentence is quoted from the judgment in the

Aeronautics case which we will not reproduce because we do not think their Lordships can have intended in that sentence to promulgate a canon of construction for sections 91 and 92. We see nothing in the judgment in the *Aeronautics* case to indicate that their Lordships intended to detract from the judicial authority of the decisions in the *Combines* case and *Snider's* case.

In the *Aeronautics* case it is true, their Lordships called attention to the circumstance that, by section 132, the Dominion possesses powers to legislate in relation to matters which, in the domestic sense, would fall within section 92 when these matters have become affected by an international obligation by which Canada is bound; and in the subsequent case, reported in the same volume of the Appeal Cases, the *Radio Reference*, [1932] A.C. 304, it was held that matters affected by an obligation arising under an international arrangement, not falling within section 132, but constituted in virtue of powers acquired in course of the recent constitutional developments, would fall within the general authority of section 91 because such international obligations were not comprehended within any of the specific subjects enumerated within section 91 or section 92; and in the *Aeronautics* case, as already observed, the authority of the decision in the *Fort Frances* case is expressly recognized. The judgments in the *Combines* case, the *Fort Frances* case, *Snider's* case, obviously have no reference to legislation dealing with matters of civil right from the international point of view. We are bound, in our view, by the decisions in the *Combines* case and in *Snider's* case as well as by the decision in the *Fort Frances* case, and, consistently with those decisions, we do not see how it is possible that the argument now under discussion can receive effect.

To summarize: in effect, this statute attempts and, indeed professes, to regulate in the provinces of Canada, by the instrumentality of a commission or commissions appointed under the authority of the statute, trade in individual commodities and classes of commodities. The powers of regulation vested in the commissions extend to external trade and matters connected therewith and to trade in matters of interprovincial concern; but also to trade which is entirely local and of purely local concern . . .

The legislation, for the reasons given, is not valid as an exercise of the general authority of the Parliament of Canada under the introductory words of section 91 to make laws "for the peace, order and good government of Canada." . . .

[The judgment of Duff C.J.C. was affirmed by the Privy Council, *sub nom.* *A.-G. B.C. v. A.-G. Can.*, [1937] A.C. 377, [1937] 1 D.L.R. 691, [1937] 1 W.W.R. 328. This reference, involving the validity of the so-called Canadian "new deal" legislation was the subject of a symposium in (1937) 15 Can. Bar Rev. 393 ff.

Duff C.J.C.'s statement that the phrase "property and civil rights" is used in the "largest sense" and that this view is "settled" is based only on what was said in *Citizens Insurance Co. v. Parsons* (1881), 7 App. Cas. 96, at p. 111. For another view see Lord Haldane in *John Deere Plow Co. v. Wharton*, [1915] A.C. 330, at p. 340, 18 D.L.R. 353, at p. 360, 7 W.W.R. 706, at p. 715, where in speaking of section 91(2) he said that "this head must, like the expression 'Property and Civil Rights in the Province' receive a limited interpretation".

In *A.-G. Can. v. A.-G. Ont.*, [1937] A.C. 326, [1937] 1 D.L.R. 673, [1937] 1 W.W.R. 229 (*Labour Conventions* case), Lord Atkin spoke as follows with reference to Lord Watson's two sentences in the *Local Prohibition* case: "It is interesting to notice how often the words used by Lord Watson in *Attorney-General for Ontario v. Attorney-General for the Dominion* have unsuccessfully been used in attempts to support encroachments on the Provincial legislative powers given by s. 92. They laid down no principle of constitutional law, and were cautious words intended to safeguard possible eventualities which no one at the time had any interest or desire to define. The law of Canada on this branch of constitutional law has been stated with such force and clarity by the Chief Justice in his judgment in the reference concerning the Natural Products Marketing Act dealing with the six Acts there referred to, that their Lordships abstain from stating it afresh. The Chief Justice, naturally from his point of view, excepted legislation to fulfil treaties. On this their Lordships have expressed their opinion. But subject to this, they agree with and adopt what was there said. They consider that the law is finally settled by the current of cases cited by the Chief Justice on the principles declared by him. It is only necessary to call attention to the phrases in the various cases, "abnormal circumstances," "exceptional conditions," "standard of necessity" (*Board of Commerce* case), "some extraordinary peril to the national life of Canada," "highly exceptional," "epidemic of pestilence" (*Snider's* case), to show how far the present case is from the conditions which may override the normal distribution of powers in ss. 91 and 92. The few pages of the Chief Justice's judgment will, it is to be hoped, form the *locus classicus* of the law on this point, and preclude further disputes."]

A.-G. ONT. v. CANADA TEMPERANCE FEDERATION

In the Privy Council. [1946] A.C. 193, [1946] 2 D.L.R. 1,
[1946] 2 W.W.R. 1.

Appeal from a judgment of the Ontario Court of Appeal, [1939] O.R. 570, upholding the validity of the Canada Temperance Act, R.S.C. 1927, c. 196, on a reference to the Court by the Lieutenant-Governor in Council.

VISCOUNT SIMON: . . . The object of the appeal is to challenge the decision of this Board in the case of *Russell v. The Queen* (1882), 7 App. Cas. 829, or at any rate to deny its applicability to the Act now in question. The majority of the [Ontario] Court held that that decision governed the present case and obliged it to answer the question referred to it in the affirmative. The statute which was declared to be within the legislative competence of the Dominion Parliament in *Russell's* case was the Canada Temperance Act, 1878 (Can.), c. 16. That Act has been amended from time to time by the Dominion Parliament and has been revised and re-enacted in a consolidated form on more than one occasion under the provisions of the Acts relating to the revision of Statutes of Canada. The last revision took place in 1924 under the provisions of the Dominion Act, 1924 (14 & 15 Geo. V., c. 65) and now appears on the statute roll as the Canada Temperance Act, R.S.C. 1927, c. 196. The material provisions of the Act of 1927 are admittedly identical with those of the Act of 1878 . . .

The Act having been passed in 1878, its constitutional validity was challenged in 1882 in *Russell's* case, *supra,* which arose out of a conviction of the appellant Russell for unlawfully selling intoxicating liquor contrary to the provisions of Part II of the Act. It was argued in that case that the Act was *ultra vires* of the Dominion Parliament on the ground that the matter was one which fell within s. 92 of the *B.N.A. Act* and was therefore within the exclusive jurisdiction of the provincial Legislatures. The Board, however, held that the Act did not deal with any of the matters exclusively reserved to the Provinces and upheld the validity of the statute on the ground that it related to the peace, order and good government of Canada. This decision has stood unreversed for 63 years. More than that, it has received the express approval of the Board in subsequent cases. A notable instance is to be found in *A.-G. Ont. v. A.-G. Dom.,* [1896] A.C. 348. In that case Lord Watson, in delivering the judgment of the Board said at p. 362: "The judgment of this Board in *Russell v. Reg.* has relieved their Lordships from the difficult duty of considering whether the Canada Temperance Act of 1886 relates to the peace, order and good government of Canada, in such sense as to bring its provisions within the competency of the Canadian Parliament." After pointing out that the provisions of the Act of 1878 were in all material respects the same as those embodied in the Act of 1886, which was the statute the Board had then to consider, he continued. "The reasons which were assigned for sustaining the validity of the earlier, are, in their Lordships' opinion, equally applicable to the later Act. It therefore appears to them that the decision in *Russell v. Reg.* must be accepted as an authority to the extent to which it goes, namely that the restrictive provisions of the Act of 1886, when they have been duly brought into operation in any provincial area within the Dominion, must receive effect as valid enactments relating to the peace, order and good government of Canada". In 1883, in the earlier case of *Hodge v. The Queen,* 9 App. Cas. 117, the Judicial Committee had referred to *Russell's* case without any indication of disapproval, nor is any to be found in the judgment of Lord Macnaghten in *A.-G. Man. v. Manitoba Licence Holders' Ass'n,* [1902] A.C. 73, where the decisions of 1882 and 1896 were contrasted. In many subsequent cases the case has been cited in judgments of the Board; it will be enough to mention *A.-G. Can. v. A.-G. Alta. (The Insurance Case),* [1916] 1 A.C. 588, the *Board of Commerce Case,* [1922] 1 A.C. 191 and *King-Emperor v. Benoari Lal Sarma,* [1945] A.C. 14. It was also quoted as an authority by Lord Atkin in his speech in the House of Lords in *Gallagher v. Lynn,* [1937] A.C. 863, a case relating to the legislative powers of the Parliament of Northern Ireland.

But in 1925 *Russell's* case was commented upon in a judgment of the Judicial Committee delivered by Lord Haldane in *Toronto Electric Com'rs v. Snider,* [1925] A.C. 396, and it is upon this comment that the present appellants largely rely in support of their contention that it was wrongly decided. [Viscount Simon here quoted Viscount Haldane's explanation of the *Russell* case.] . . . .

. . . The first observation which their Lordships would make on this explanation of *Russell's* case is that the *B.N.A. Act* nowhere gives power to the Dominion Parliament to legislate in matters which are properly to be regarded as exclusively within the competence of the Provincial Legislatures, merely because of the existence of an emergency. Secondly, they can find nothing in the judgment of the Board in 1882 which suggests that it proceeded on the ground of emergency; there was certainly no evidence before that Board that one existed. The Act of 1878 was a permanent, not a temporary, Act and no objection was raised to it on that account. In their Lordships' opinion, the true test must be found in the real subject matter of the legislation: if it is such that it goes beyond local or provincial concern or interests and must from its inherent nature be the concern of the Dominion as a whole (as for example in the *Aeronautics* case [*Re Aerial Navigation, A.-G. Can. v. A.-G. Ont.*], [1932] A.C. 54, and the *Radio* case [*Re Regulation & Control of Radio Communication, A.-G. Que. v. A.-G. Can.*], [1932] A.C. 304) then it will fall within the competence of the Dominion Parliament as a matter affecting the peace, order and good government of Canada, though it may in another aspect touch upon matters specially reserved to the Provincial Legislatures. War and pestilence, no doubt, are instances; so too may be the drink or drug traffic, or the carrying of arms. In *Russell v. The Queen* Sir Montague Smith gave as an instance of valid Dominion legislation a law which prohibited or restricted the sale or exposure of cattle having a contagious disease. Nor is the validity of the legislation, when due to its inherent nature, affected because there may still be room for enactments by a Provincial Legislature dealing with an aspect of the same subject in so far as it specially affects that Province.

It is to be noticed that the Board in *Snider's* case nowhere said that *Russell v. The Queen* was wrongly decided. What it did was to put forward an explanation of what it considered was the ground of the decision, but in their Lordships' opinion the explanation is too narrowly expressed. True it is that an emergency may be the occasion which calls for the legislation, but it is the nature of the legislation itself, and not the existence of emergency, that must determine whether it is valid or not.

The appellant's first contention is that *Russell's case* was wrongly decided and ought to be overruled. Their Lordships do not doubt that in tendering humble advice to His Majesty they are not absolutely bound by previous decisions of the Board, as is the House of Lords by its own judgments. In ecclesiastical appeals, for instance, on more than one occasion, the Board has tendered advice contrary to that given in a previous case, which further historical research has shown to have been wrong. But on constitutional questions it must be seldom indeed that the Board would depart from a previous decision which it may be assumed will have been acted upon both by governments and subjects. In the present case the decision now sought to be overruled has stood for over 60 years; the Act has been put into operation for varying periods in many places in the Dominion; under its provisions business must have been closed, fines and imprisonments for breaches of the Act have been imposed and suffered. Time and again the occasion has arisen when the Board could have overruled the decision had it thought it wrong. Accordingly, in the opinion of their Lordships, the decision must be regarded as firmly embedded in the constitutional law of Canada and it is impossible now to depart from it. Their Lordships have no intention, in deciding the present appeal, of embarking on a fresh disquisition as to the relations between ss. 91 and 92 of the *B.N.A. Act*, which have been expounded in so many reported cases; so far as the *Canada Temperance Act*, 1878, is concerned the question must be considered as settled once and for all.

The second contention of the appellants was that in 1927, when the statute now in force was enacted, there were no circumstances which enabled the Parliament of the Dominion to legislate anew. The Act of 1927 is one promulgated under the provisions of the Act of 1924 for the revision of the Statutes of Canada. Its full title is "An Act respecting the traffic in Intoxicating Liquors" and its short title is the *"Canada Temperance Act"*, R.S.C. 1906, c. 152. As has already been said, it is, in all respects material for this appeal, identical in its terms with the Act of 1878, and also with the Act of 1886 [R.S.C. 1886, c. 106] which itself was a revised edition of 1878 and was the Act in force in 1896 when the case of *A.-G. Ont. v. A.-G. Dom., supra,* was heard. It was not contended that if the Act of 1878 was valid when it was enacted it would have become invalid later on by a change of circumstances, but it was submitted that as that Act and the Act of 1886 have been repealed, the Act of 1927 was new legislation and consequently circumstances must exist in 1927 to support the new Act. Then it was said (and this apparently was the opinion of Henderson J.A. who dissented from the other members of the Supreme Court of Ontario), that no circumstances could exist in 1927 to support the Act, in view of the legislation that had been passed in the Provinces, including Ontario, for the regulation of the liquor traffic. Their Lordships do not find it necessary to consider the true effect either of s. 5 or s. 8 of the Act of 1924 for the revision of the Statutes of Canada, for they cannot agree that if the Act of 1878 was constitutionally within the powers of the Dominion Parliament it could be successfully contended that the Act of 1927 which replaced it was *ultra vires*. The same ground is not covered by provincial legislation setting up a licensing system and making the sale of liquor a government monopoly. Moreover, if the subject-matter of the legislation is such that it comes within the province of the Dominion Parliament that Legislature must, as it seems to their Lordships, have power to re-enact provisions with the object of preventing a recurrence of a state of affairs which was deemed to necessitate the earlier statute. To legislate for prevention appears to be on the same basis as legislation for cure. A pestilence has been given as an example of a subject so affecting, or which might so affect, the whole Dominion that it would justify legislation by the

Parliament of Canada as a matter concerning the order and good government of the Dominion. It would seem to follow that if the Parliament could legislate when there was an actual epidemic it could do so to prevent one occurring and also to prevent it happening again. Once it has been decided that the Act of 1878 was constitutionally valid, it follows that an Act which replaces it and consolidates therewith the various amending Acts that have from time to time been enacted must be equally valid. It is to be noted that in 1896 Lord Watson's judgment appears to take it for granted that the position was in no way affected by the fact that the Act of 1878 had been repealed and replaced by the Act of 1886.

Accordingly their Lordships are not prepared to hold either that *Russell v. The Queen* was wrongly decided or that it has ceased to be binding authority by reason that the 1878 Act has been re-enacted in 1927. It is by repeal by the Dominion Legislature, and not by appeal to the Judicial Committee, that the enactment might cease to be effective. Their Lordships will humbly advise His Majesty that this appeal should be dismissed. There should be no costs awarded in respect of the appeal.

Appeal dismissed.

[In *Canadian Federation of Agriculture v. A.-G. Que., Reference re Validity of Section 5(a) of the Dairy Industry Act,* [1951] A.C. 179, [1950] 4 D.L.R. 689, the Privy Council (speaking through Lord Morton of Henryton) rejected the exposition of the federal general power set out in the *Canada Temperance Federation* case and reverted to the earlier views as finally sanctified in the *Labour Conventions* case; cf. the following passages from Lord Morton's judgment: "In support of their third argument, counsel relied principally on the case of *Russell v. The Queen* (1882), 7 App. Cas. 829 and the recent case of *A.-G. Ont. v. Canada Temperance Federation,* [1946] A.C. 193, in which *Russell's* case, not for the first time, was considered and commented upon. [Here His Lordship quoted a passage from Viscount Simon's judgment, and then continued as follows:] This passage must, however, be considered in conjunction with the words used by Lord Atkin when delivering the judgment of the Board in the *Labour Conventions* case (*A.-G. Can. v. A.-G. Ont., Reference re Weekly Rest in Industrial Undertakings Act,* etc.), [1937] A.C. 326 at pp. 352-3. . . . "Their Lordships think it sufficient to say . . . that the prohibition now under consideration relates to civil rights within each of the Provinces and that neither the facts set out in the Order of Reference, nor any other facts of which their Lordships could take judicial notice, lead to the conclusion that there exist in the present case the conditions which may override the normal distribution of powers in ss. 91 and 92."

For another illustration of reliance by the Privy Council after its decision in the *Canada Temperance Federation* case, on the earlier views which were given definite expression in the *Labour Conventions* case, see *C.P.R. v. A.-G. B.C.,* [1950] A.C. 122, [1950] 1 D.L.R. 721, [1950] 1 W.W.R. 220, upholding the application of provincial hours of work legislation to employees of a hotel operated by a railway company.

The lingering influence of the emergency aspect of the general power is seen in *Swait v. Board of Trustees of Maritime Transportation Unions* (1966), 61 D.L.R. (2d) 317.]

2. Review and Reconsideration of the General Power

JOHANNESSON v. WEST ST. PAUL

In the Supreme Court of Canada.   [1952] 1 S.C.R. 292,
[1951] 4 D.L.R. 609.

Appeal from a judgment of the Manitoba Court of Appeal, [1950] 3 D.L.R. 101, [1950] 1 W.W.R. 856, affirming a judgment of Campbell J., [1949] 3 D.L.R. 694, [1949] 2 W.W.R. 1, dismissing an application to invalidate s. 921 of the Municipal Act (Man.) and a by-law passed thereunder.

RINFRET C.J.C.:—Notwithstanding that the International Convention under consideration in the *Aeronautics* case [*Re Aerial Navigation*], [1932] 1 D.L.R. 58, A.C. 54, 39 C.R.C. 108, was denounced by the Government of Canada as of April 4th, 1947, I entertain no doubt that the decision of the Judicial Committee is in its pith and substance that the whole field of aerial transportation comes under the jurisdiction of the Dominion Parliament. In the language of their Lordships at p. 70 D.L.R., p. 121 C.R.C., p. 77 A.C. "Aerial navigation is a class of subject which has attained such dimensions as to affect the body politic of the Dominion."

In those circumstances it would not matter that Parliament may not have occupied the field. But, moreover, the Convention on International Civil Aviation, signed at Chicago on December 7, 1944, has since become effective; and no doubt what was said in the *Radio* reference by Viscount Dunedin [*Re Regulation & Control of Radio Communication*], [1932] 2 D.L.R. 81 at pp. 84-5, A.C. 304 at 313, 39 C.R.C. 49 at pp. 83-4, applies here. Although the Convention might not be looked upon as a Treaty under s. 132 of the *B.N.A. Act*, it comes to the same thing.

I fail to see how it can be argued that the Dominion Parliament has not occupied the field. The *Aeronautics Act*, R.S.C. 1927, c. 3, as amended by 1944-45, c. 29, 1945, c. 9, and 1950, c. 23, makes it the duty of the Minister "to supervise all matters connected with aeronautics . . . to prescribe aerial routes . . . to prepare such regulations as may be considered necessary for the control or operation of aeronautics in Canada . . . and for the control or operation of aircraft registered in Canada wherever such aircraft may be . . . for the licensing of navigation and the regulation of all aerodromes and airstations, etcetra."

Such Regulations have been passed under the authority of the Aeronautics Act by P.C. 2129 [[1948] S.O.R. 1348], part of which deals with the subject-matter of airports and provides for the issuing of licences by the Minister. In the circumstances, the Dominion legislation occupies the field, or at least so much of it as would eliminate any provincial legislation, and more particularly, that here in question.

I think, therefore, that the provincial legislation under discussion is *ultra vires* and the by-law adopted by the respondent, the Rural Municipality of West St. Paul, falls with it. . . .

KERWIN J.: . . . Section 921 of the *Municipal Act* appears in Division II "Public Safety and Amenity" under the subhead "Aerodromes" and reads as follows:

"921. Any municipal corporation may pass by-laws for licensing, regulating, and, within certain defined areas, preventing the erection, maintenance and continuance of aerodromes or places where aeroplanes are kept for hire or gain."

This section first appeared in 1920, being enacted by s. 18 of c. 82 of the statutes of that year as para. (*y*) of s. 612 of the *Municipal Act,* R.S.M. 1913, c. 133. That s. 612 was one of a group of sections appearing in Part IX of the Act "Legislative Powers of Councils", under the subhead "Various Trades and Occupations". It next appeared in s. 97 of the Consolidated Amendments to the Municipal Act, 1924, [c. 133] and then, in 1933, as s. 910 in Division II of the *Municipal Act,* 1933, c. 57, "Public Safety and Amenity" under the subhead "Aerodromes"—the same relevant position that the present s. 921 now occupies.

The enacting parts of by-law 292 of the Rural Municipality of West St. Paul provide:

"1. No aerodrome or place where aeroplanes are kept for hire or gain shall be erected or maintained or continued within that part of The Rural Municipality of West St. Paul, in Manitoba, bounded as follows: . . .

"2. No aerodrome or place where aeroplanes are kept for hire or gain shall be erected or maintained or continued in any other part of the said Rural Municipality of West St. Paul, unless and until a license therefor shall first have been obtained from the said Municipality.

"3. No building or installation of any machine shop for the testing and/or repairing of air-craft shall be erected or maintained or continued in that part of The Rural Municipality of West St. Paul in Manitoba described in paragraph One (1) hereof.

"4. No building or installation of any machine shop for the testing and/or repairing of air-craft shall be erected or maintained or continued in any other part of the said Municipality unless and until a license therefor shall first have been obtained from the said Municipality."

Section 921 of the *Municipal Act* does not confer powers to provide generally for zoning, or for building restrictions; the powers are specifically allotted with reference to "aerodromes or places where aeroplanes are kept for hire or gain". The by-law follows the section so that, if the latter is *ultra vires* the provincial Legislature, the former cannot be upheld.

The circumstances which give rise to the present dispute are important as showing the far-reaching effect of the provisions of the section. The appellant Johannesson had been engaged in commercial aviation since 1928 and held an air transport licence, issued by the Air Transport Board of Canada, to operate an air service at Winnipeg and Flin Flon. The charter service which he operated under this licence covers territory in central and northern Manitoba and northern

Saskatchewan, and had substantially increased in volume over the years. This service was operated with light and medium weight planes, which in the main were equipped in summer with floats and in winter with skis in order to permit landing on the numerous lakes and rivers in this territory, and these planes had to be repaired and serviced in Winnipeg, which was the only place within the territory where the necessary supplies and any facilities were available for that purpose. The use by small planes of a large airfield, such as Stevenson Airport near Winnipeg which was maintained for the use of large transcontinental airplanes, was impractical and would eventually be prohibited. No facilities existed on the Red River in Winnipeg for the repairing and servicing of planes equipped with floats, and repairs could only be made to such planes by dismantling them at some private dock and transporting them, by truck, through Winnipeg to Stevenson Airport. After a long search by Johannesson in the suburbs of Winnipeg for a site that would combine an area of level land of sufficient area and dimensions and location to comply with the Regulations of the Civil Aviation Branch of the Canadian Department of Transport relating to a licensed air-strip with access to a straight stretch of the Red River of sufficient length to be suitable for the landing of airplanes equipped with floats, he found such a location (but one only) in the Rural Municipality of West St. Paul and acquired an option to purchase it but, before the transaction was completed By-law 292 was passed. Title to the land was subsequently taken in the name of both appellants and these proceedings ensued. The Attorney-General of Canada and the Attorney-General of Manitoba were notified but only the latter was represented before the Judge of first instance and the Court of Appeal. Leave to appeal to this Court was granted by the latter.

On behalf of the appellants and the Attorney-General of Canada, reliance is placed upon the decision of the Judicial Committee in the *Aeronautics* case, [1932] 1 D.L.R. 58, A.C. 54, 39 C.R.C. 108. Irrespective of later judicial comments upon this case, in my view it is a decision based entirely upon the fact that the Dominion *Aeronautics Act* there in question had been enacted pursuant to an International Convention of 1919 to which the British Empire was a party and, therefore, within s. 132 of the *B.N.A. Act:*

"132. The Parliament and Government of Canada shall have all Powers necessary or proper for performing the Obligations of Canada or of any Province thereof, as Part of the British Empire, towards Foreign Countries, arising under Treaties between the Empire and such Foreign Countries"

However, in the subsequent decision in the *Labour Conventions* case (*Reference re Weekly Rest in Industrial Undertakings Act*), [1937] 1 D.L.R. 673, A.C. 326, Lord Atkin, who had been a member of the Board in the *Aeronautics* case, said with reference to the judgment therein [p. 681]: "The *Aeronautics* case concerned legislation to perform obligations imposed by a treaty between the Empire and foreign countries. Section 132 therefore clearly applied: and but for a remark at the end of the judgment, which in view of the stated ground of the decision was clearly *obiter,* the case could not be said to be an authority on the matter now under discussion."

The remarks of Viscount Simon L.C. in *A.-G. Ont. v. Canada Temperance Federation,* [1946] 2 D.L.R. 1, A.C. 193, 85 Can. C.C. 225, must be read when considering the words of Lord Sankey L.C. in the *Aeronautics* case in another connection. At the moment all I am concerned with emphasizing is that the *Aeronautics* case decided one thing, and one thing only, and that is that the matter there discussed fell within the ambit of s. 132 of the *B.N.A. Act.*

At this stage it is necessary to refer to a matter that was not explained to the Courts below. According to a certificate from the Under-Secretary of State for Foreign Affairs, the Convention of 1919 was denounced by Canada, which denunciation become effective in 1947. This was done because on February 13, 1947, Canada had deposited its Instrument of Ratification of the Convention on International Civil Aviation signed at Chicago December 8, 1944, and which Convention came into force on April 4, 1947. With the exception of certain amendments that are not relevant to the present discussion, the *Aeronautics Act* remains on the statute books of Canada in the same terms as those considered by the Judicial Committee in the *Aeronautics* case. Section 132 of the *B.N.A. Act* therefore ceased to have any efficacy to permit Parliament to legislate upon the subject of aeronautics.

Nevertheless the fact remains that the Convention of 1919 was a Treaty between the Empire and foreign countries and that pursuant thereto the *Aeronautics Act* was enacted. It continues as c. 3 of the Revised Statutes of Canada, 1927, as amended. Under s. 4 of that Act, as it stood when these proceedings were commenced, the Minister, with the approval of the Governor in Council, had power to regulate and control aerial navigation over Canada and the territorial waters of Canada, and in particular but not to restrict the generality of the foregoing, he might make regulations with respect to "(c) the licensing, inspection and regulation of all aerodromes and air-stations". Pursuant thereto Regulations have been promulgated dealing with many of the matters mentioned in the section, including provisions for the licensing of air ports. If, therefore, the subject of aeronautics goes beyond local or provincial concern because it has attained such dimensions as to affect the body politic of Canada, it falls under the "Peace, Order and Good Government" clause of s. 91 of the *B.N.A. Act* since aeronautics is not a subject-matter confined to the Provinces by s. 92. It does not fall within head (8), "Municipal Institutions", as that head "simply gives provincial legislatures the right to create a legal body for the management of municipal affairs. . . . The extent and nature of the functions" the provincial Legislature "can commit to a municipal body of its own creation must depend upon the legislative authority which it derives from the provisions of s. 92 other than No. 8": *A.-G. Ont. v. A.-G. Can.,* [1896] A.C. 348, at p. 364. Nor, on the authority of the same decision is it within head (9): "Shop, Saloon, Tavern, Auctioneer, and other Licences in order to the raising of a Revenue for Provincial, Local, or Municipal Purposes". Once it is held that the subject-matter transcends "Property and Civil Rights in the Province" (head (13)) or "Generally all Matters of a merely local or private Nature in the Province" (head (16)), these two heads of s. 92 have no relevancy.

Now, even at the date of the *Aeronautics* case, the Judicial Committee was influenced (*i.e.,* in the determination of the main point) by the fact that in their opinion the subject of air navigation was a matter of national interest and importance and had attained such dimensions. That that is so at the present time is shown by the terms of the Chicago Convention of 1944 and the provisions of the Dominion Aeronautics Act and the Regulations thereunder referred to above. The affidavit of the appellant Johannesson, from which the statement of facts was culled, also shows the importance that the subject of air navigation has attained in Canada. To all of which may be added those matters of everyday knowledge of which the Court must be taken to be aware.

It is with reference to this phase of the matter that Viscount Simon's remarks in *A.-G. Ont. v. Canada Temperance Federation,* [1946] 2 D.L.R. at p. 5, A.C. at p. 205, 85 Can. C.C. at pp. 229-30, must be read. What was there under consideration was the *Canada Temperance Act,* originally enacted in 1878, and Viscount Simon stated: "In their Lordships' opinion, the true test must be found in the real subject-matter of the legislation: if it is such that it goes beyond local or provincial concern or interests and must from its inherent nature be the concern of the Dominion as a whole (as for example in the *Aeronautics* case . . . and the *Radio* case . . .), then it falls within the competence of the Dominion Parliament as a matter affecting the peace, order and good government of Canada, though it may in another aspect touch upon matters specially reserved to the Provincial Legislatures." This statement is significant because, while not stating that the *Aeronautics* case was a decision on the point, it is a confirmation of the fact that the Board in the *Aeronautics* case considered that the subject of aeronautics transcended provincial legislative boundaries. . . .

KELLOCK J.: . . . It is no doubt true that legislation of the character involved in the provincial legislation regarded from the standpoint of the use of property is normally legislation as to civil rights, but use of property for the purposes of an aerodrome, or the prohibition of such use cannot, in my opinion, be divorced from the subject-matter of aeronautics or aerial navigation as a whole. If that be so, it can make no difference from the standpoint of a basis for legislative jurisdiction on the part of the Province that Parliament may not have occupied the field.

Once the decision is made that a matter is of national interest and importance, so as to fall within the peace, order and good government clause, the Provinces cease to have any legislative jurisdiction with regard thereto and the Dominion jurisdiction is exclusive. If jurisdiction can be said to exist in the Dominion with respect to any matter under such clause, that statement can only be made because of the fact that such matters no longer come within the classes of subjects assigned to the Provinces. I think, therefore, that as the matters attempted to be dealt with by the provincial legislation here in question are matters inseparable from the field of aerial navigation, the exclusive jurisdiction of Parliament extends thereto. . . .

In my opinion, just as it is impossible to separate intraprovincial flying from interprovincial flying, the location and regulation of airports cannot be identified with either or separated from aerial navigation as a whole. The provincial legislation here in question must be held, therefore, to be *ultra vires,* and the by-law falls with it. . .

ESTEY J.:— . . . The Judicial Committee having decided that legislation in relation to aeronautics is within the exclusive jurisdiction of the Dominion, it follows that the Province cannot legislate in relation thereto, whether the precise subject-matter of the provincial legslation has, or has not already been covered by the Dominion legislation.

It is then submitted that if aeronautics is within the legislative competence of the Parliament of Canada, including the power to license and regulate aerodromes, it would not include the location and continuation of aerodromes, which would be a provincial matter under Property and Civil Rights. With great respect, it would appear that such a view attributes a narrower and more technical meaning to the word "aeronautics" than that which has been attributed to it generally in law and by those interested in the subject. Indeed, the definition adopted by Dysart J.A. [[1950] 3 D.L.R. at p. 123, 66 C.R.T.C. at p. 82], as he found it in 2 Corpus Juris Secundum, pp. 900-1, "The flight and a period of flight from the time the machine clears the earth to the time it returns successfully to the earth and is resting securely upon the ground", contemplates the operation of the aeroplane from the moment it leaves the earth until it again returns thereto. This, it seems, in itself makes the aerodrome, as the place of taking off and landing, an essential part of aeronautics and aerial navigation. This view finds support in the fact that legislation in relation to aeronautics and aerial navigation, not only in Canada, but also in Great Britain and the United States, deals with aerodromes, as well as the Conventions above mentioned. Indeed, in any practical consideration it is impossible to separate the flying in the air from the taking off and landing on the ground and it is therefore, wholly impractical, particularly when considering the matter of jurisdiction to treat them as independent one from the other.

The submission that in the granting of the licence the sufficiency of the location will always be considered and might even be the controlling factor in the granting or refusing of a licence, in so far as it may be of assistance, emphasizes the importance of the location of the aerodrome and of the essential part the aerodrome plays in any scheme of aeronautics. Legislation which in pith and substance is in relation to the aerodrome is legislation in relation to the large subject of aeronautics and is, therefore, beyond the competence of the provincial Legislatures.

It is submitted that s. 921 is zoning legislation, as that term is now understood in municipal legislation. The general provisions for the enactment of zoning by-laws are contained in ss. 904, 905 and 906 of this statute. As notwithstanding this general provision such legislation may be enacted under other sections, it is necessary to determine the nature and character of the provisions of s. 921. . . . The end and purpose of zoning legislation, as the name indicates, is to authorize the municipality to pass by-laws in respect of certain areas and make those areas subject to prohibitions and restrictions designed to provide uniformity within those particular areas. The Legislature, in enacting s. 921, provided that, without regard to the nature and character or the use and purpose made of the area, the municipality may prohibit entirely, or permit only under a license issued by it, an aerodrome within certain areas. Such legislation is in pith and substance in relation to aerodromes and, therefore, in relation to aeronautics rather than to zoning. . . .

LOCKE J.: . . . If the validity of the Aeronautics Act and the Air Regulations be conceded, it appears to me that this matter must be determined contrary to the contentions of the respondent. It is, however, desirable, in my opinion, that some of the reasons for the conclusion that the field of aeronautics is one exclusively within federal jurisdiction should be stated. There has been since the First World War an immense development in the use of aircraft flying between the various Provinces of Canada and between other countries. There is a very large passenger traffic between the Provinces and to and from foreign countries, and a very considerable volume of freight traffic not only between the settled portions of the country but between those areas and the northern part of Canada, and planes are extensively used in the carriage of mails. That this traffic will increase greatly in volume and extent is undoubted. While the largest activity in the carrying of passengers and mails east and west is in the hands of a Government-controlled company, private companies carry on large operations, particularly between the settled parts of the north and mails are carried by some of these lines. The maintenance and extension of this traffic, particularly to the north, is essential to the opening up of the country and the development of the resources of the nation. It requires merely a statement of these well-recognized facts to demonstrate that the field of aeronautics is one which concerns the country as a whole. It is an activity, which to adopt the language of Viscount Simon in *A.-G. Ont. v. Canada Temperance Federation,* [1946] 2 D.L.R. at p. 5, A.C. at p. 205, 85 Can. C.C. at pp. 229-30, must from its inherent nature be a concern of the Dominion as a whole. The field of legislation is not, in my opinion, capable of division in any practical way. If, by way of illustration, it should be decided that it was in the interests of the inhabitants of some northerly part of the country to have airmail service with centres of population to the south and that for that purpose some private line, prepared to undertake such carriage should be licensed to do so and to establish the southern terminus for their route at some suitable place in the Municipality of West St. Paul where, apparently, there is an available and suitable field and area of water where planes equipped in a manner enabling them to use the facilities of such an airport might land, it would be intolerable that such a national purpose might be defeated by a rural municipality, the council of which decided that the noise attendant on the operation of airplanes was objectionable. Indeed, if the argument of the respondents be carried to its logical conclusion the rural municipalities of Manitoba through which the Red River passes between Emerson and Selkirk, and the City of Winnipeg and the Town of Selkirk might prevent the operation of any planes equipped for landing upon water by denying them the right to use the river for that purpose.

It is true that the decision in the *Aeronautics Reference,* [1932] 1 D.L.R. 58, A.C. 54, 39 C.R.C. 108, really turned upon the point that by virtue of s. 132 of the *B.N.A. Act* it was within the power of Parliament to enact s. 4 of the *Aeronautics Act,* and to authorize the adoption of the Air Regulations referred to in the questions submitted to the Court. There were, however, expressions of opinion on other aspects of the matter in the judgment delivered by Lord Sankey L.C. which are of assistance. . . .

While the statement of Lord Sankey in the *Aeronautics Reference* that aerial navigation is a class of subject which has attained such dimensions as to affect the body politic of the Dominion as a whole, and that of Viscount Simon in the *Canada Temperance* case in referring to that case and the *Radio* case, were perhaps unnecessary to the decision of those matters, they support what I consider to be the true view of this matter that the whole subject of aeronautics lies within the field assigned to Parliament as a matter affecting the peace, order and good government of Canada. Section 921 of the *Municipal Act* of Manitoba clearly trespasses upon that field and must be declared *ultra vires* the Province. As to the by-law I am unable, with respect, to agree with the contention that it is a mere zoning regulation or that, even if it were, it could be sustained. On the contrary, I consider it to be a clear attempt to prevent the carrying on of the operation of commercial aerodromes within the municipality. As the right to do this must depend upon s. 921, the by-law must also be declared *ultra vires.*

If this matter were to be considered as dealing with a legislative field where the powers of Parliament and of the provincial Legislature overlap, I think the result would necessarily be the same since for the reasons above stated it appears to me that the *Aeronautics Act,* and in particular s. 4, is legislation in this field with which s. 921 of the *Municipal Act* clearly conflicts.

Appeal allowed.

[Taschereau J. concurred with Estey J. Cartwright J. concurred with Kellock J. Does this judgment exclude application of general municipal zoning by-laws to land intended for use as an airport?

Contrast with the Supreme Court's views in the *Johannesson* case the position which it took (and see particularly the views of Rinfret J., as he then was) in the *Aeronautics* case, [1930] S.C.R. 663, [1931] 1 D.L.R. 13.

See also *Jorgenson v. Pool* (1959), 28 W.W.R. 265, 124 Can. C.C. 39 (B.C. C.A.), rejecting the argument that Parliament cannot legislate in respect

of aircraft operating solely within a Province; and for a general discussion
see *McNairn,* Aeronautics and the Constitution (1971), 49 Can. Bar Rev. 411.

Under the Aeronautics Act, R.S.C. 1970, c. A-3, the Minister is authorized
to make zoning regulations in respect of lands adjacent to or in the vicinity
of airports for purposes relating to navigation of aircraft and use and operation of airports.]

MUNRO v. NATIONAL CAPITAL COMMISSION

In the Supreme Court of Canada, [1966] S.C.R. 663, 57 D.L.R.
(2d) 753.

The judgment of the Court was delivered by

CARTWRIGHT J.:—This is an appeal from a judgment of Gibson J.
in the Exchequer Court [[1965] 2 Ex. C.R. 579] pronounced on April
28, 1965, answering in the negative the following question which, by
order of the President of the Court, had been directed to be tried
before the trial of the other questions raised in the action:

Whether, on the special case stated by the parties, the expropriation of the lands
of the defendant by the National Capital Commission therein referred to is a
nullity because the legislative authority of the Parliament of Canada under
the *British North America Act,* 1867 to 1960, does not extend to authorizing
the expropriation.

On June 25, 1959, the respondent, with the approval of the Governor in Council, expropriated a farm of 195 acres in the Township of
Gloucester in the Province of Ontario owned by the appellant. In so
doing the respondent was acting under subs. (1) of s. 13 of the
National Capital Act, Statutes of Canada 1958, 7 Elizabeth II, Chap.
37, hereinafter sometimes referred to as "the Act", which came into
force on February 6, 1959 . . .

The question which Gibson J. was called upon to decide is limited
to whether the expropriation of the appellant's land is a nullity for a
single specified reason:

because the legislative authority of the Parliament of Canada under the
British North America Act, 1867 to 1960, does not extend to authorizing the
expropriation.

The main ground relied on by counsel who support the appeal is
that the power of expropriation which the Act gives to the respondent
has been exercised, in the case of the appellant's land, for the imposition upon the use of land within the National Capital Region of controls or restrictions of the nature of zoning regulations contemplated
by the Planning Acts passed by the Provinces. It is said, more particularly, that the power has been used for the purpose of the establishment
of a "Green Belt" in the Region. It is argued that such a use of the
power of expropriation is in its nature, character and purpose a use in
relation to a matter falling within the classes of subjects assigned exclusively to the Legislatures of the Provinces by the *British North
America Act* and that, consequently, if the *National Capital Act*

purports to confer such a power upon the Commission it is, *pro tanto,* *ultra vires* of Parliament. . .

The learned trial judge has made a careful review of the legislative history of the *National Capital Act* and of the *Planning Act,* R.S.O. 1960, c. 296, and of the development of the Master Plan for the Region. I do not find it necessary to repeat this review because I propose, for the purposes of this appeal, to accept the following conclusions that counsel for the appellant and for the intervenant seek to draw, in part, from that history: (i) that the making of zoning regulations and the imposition of controls of the use of land situate in any province of the sort provided, for example, in the *Planning Act* (Ontario) are matters which, generally speaking, come within the classes of subjects assigned to the Legislatures by s. 92 of the *British North America Act*; (ii) that the legislative history of the predecessors of the *National Capital Act* indicates that Parliament, up to the time of the passing of that Act contemplated that the "zoning" of the lands comprised in the National Capital Region should be effected by co-operation between the Commission established by Parliament and the municipalities which derive their powers from the Provincial Legislatures; and (iii) that it was only after prolonged and unsuccessful efforts to achieve the desired result by such co-operation that Parliament decided to confer upon the National Capital Commission the powers necessary to enable it to carry out the zoning contemplated in the Master Plan.

It is first necessary to consider what is the matter in relation to which the *National Capital Act* was passed and this requires an examination of its terms.

Its full title is "an Act respecting the Development and Improvement of the National Capital Region".

It establishes a "National Capital Region", described in the Schedule to the Act, comprising approximately 1,800 square miles, including and surrounding the City of Ottawa, situate partly in the Province of Ontario and partly in the Province of Quebec. This region is defined as "the seat of the Government of Canada and its surrounding area". It includes the lands of the appellant in the Township of Gloucester.

By s. 3 of the Act, the respondent is created as a corporation to be called the "National Capital Commission" and by s. 27 it and the Federal District Commission are declared for all purposes to be one and the same corporation. By s. 4(1) it is declared that the Commission is for all purposes of the Act an agent of Her Majesty and that its powers under the Act may be exercised only as an agent of Her Majesty.

Section 10 defines the objects and purposes of the Commission and confers the powers to be used for the purpose of the Act. It reads as follows:

10.(1) The objects and the purposes of the Commission are to prepare plans for and assist in the development, conservation and improvement of the National Capital Region in order that the nature and character of the seat of the Government of Canada may be in accordance with its national significance.

(2) The Commission may for the purposes of this Act,

(*a*) acquire, hold, administer or develop property;

(*b*) sell, grant, convey, lease or otherwise dispose of or make available to any person any property, subject to such conditions and limitations as it considers necessary or desirable;

(*c*) construct, maintain and operate parks, squares, highways, parkways, bridges, buildings and any other works;

(*d*) maintain and improve any property of the Commission, or any other property under the control and management of a department, at the request of the authority or Minister in charge thereof;

(*e*) co-operate or engage in joint projects with, or make grants to, local municipalities or other authorities for the improvement, development or maintenance of property;

(*f*) construct, maintain and operate, or grant concessions for the operation of, places of entertainment, amusement, recreation, refreshment, or other places of public interest or accommodation upon any property of the Commission;

(*g*) administer, preserve and maintain any historic place or historic museum;

(*h*) conduct investigations and researches in connection with the planning of the National Capital Region; and

(*i*) generally, do and authorize such things as are incidental or conducive to the attainment of the objects and purposes of the Commission and the exercise of its powers.

Section 13(1) reads as follows:

13.(1) The Commission may, with the approval of the Governor in Council, take or acquire lands for the purpose of this Act without the consent of the owner, and, except as otherwise provided in this section, all the provisions of the *Expropriation Act*, with such modifications as circumstances require, are applicable to and in respect of the exercise of the powers conferred by this section and the lands so taken or acquired.

Subsection (3) of this section provides that all claims for compensation for lands taken under the section may be heard and determined in the Exchequer Court of Canada.

By section 18, it is provided that the Commission may make by-laws for the conduct and management of its activities and for carrying out the purposes and provisions of the Act.

In my view, it is clear, from a reading of the Act as a whole, that the matter in relation to which it is enacted is the establishment of a region consisting of the seat of the Government of Canada and the defined surrounding area which are formed into a unit to be known as the National Capital Region which is to be developed, conserved and improved "in order that the nature and character of the seat of the Government of Canada may be in accordance with its national significance".

The next question is whether this subject matter comes within any of the classes of subjects which, by s. 92 of the *British North America Act*, are assigned exclusively to the Legislatures of the Provinces.

The only reference to the National Capital of Canada contained in the *British North America Act* is in s. 16, which reads as follows:

16. Until the Queen otherwise directs, the Seat of Government of Canada shall be Ottawa.

The authority reserved by this section to the Queen to change the location of the Seat of Government of Canada would now be exercisable by Her Majesty in the right of Canada and, while the section contemplates executive action, the change could, doubtless, be made by Act of Parliament in which Her Majesty acts with the advice and consent of the Senate and House of Commons of Canada.

The subject matter of the *National Capital Act*, as I have sought to define it above, is not referred to in either s. 91 or s. 92 of the *British North America Act*. In *Attorney-General for Alberta v. Attorney-General for Canada*, [[1943] A.C. 356, 1 W.W.R. 378, 1 All E.R. 240, 2 D.L.R. 1], Viscount Maugham said at p. 371:

It must not be forgotten that where the subject matter of any legislation is not within any of the enumerated heads either of s. 91 or of s. 92, the sole power rests with the Dominion under the preliminary words of s. 91, relative to "laws for the peace, order, and good government of Canada".

In *In re Regulation and Control of Radio Communication in Canada*, [[1932] A.C. 304, 1 W.W.R. 563], Viscount Dunedin had made a similar observation at p. 312:

Being, therefore, not mentioned explicitly in either s. 91 or s. 92, such legislation falls within the general words at the opening of s. 91 which assign to the Government of the Dominion the power to make laws "for the peace, order and good government of Canada in relation to all matters not coming within the classes of subjects by this Act assigned exclusively to the legislatures of the Provinces".

In *Johannesson v. Rural Municipality of West St. Paul* [[1952] 1 S.C.R. 292, [1951] 4 D.L.R. 609], in which it was held that the subject of aeronautics is within the exclusive jurisdiction of Parliament, this Court (at pages 308, 311, 318 and 328) adopted as the true test, to be applied in determining whether a subject matter falls within the legislative authority of Parliament under the general words at the opening of s. 91, that formulated by Viscount Simon in the *Canada Temperance Federations* case, [[1946] A.C. 193 at 205, 2 W.W.R. 1, 85 C.C.C. 225, 1 C.R. 229, 2 D.L.R. 1] in the following words:

In their Lordships' opinion, the true test must be found in the real subject matter of the legislation: if it is such that it goes beyond local or provincial concern or interests and must from its inherent nature be the concern of the Dominion as a whole (as, for example, in the *Aeronautics* case and the *Radio* case), then it will fall within the competence of the Dominion Parliament as a matter affecting the peace, order and good government of Canada, though it may in another aspect touch on matters specially reserved to the provincial legislatures.

I find it difficult to suggest a subject matter of legislation which more clearly goes beyond local or provincial interests and is the concern of Canada as a whole than the development, conservation and improvement of the National Capital Region in accordance with a coherent plan in order that the nature and character of the seat of the Government of Canada may be in accordance with its national significance. Adopting the words of the learned trial judge, it is my view that the Act "deals with a single matter of national concern".

There is no doubt that the exercise of the powers conferred upon the Commission by the *National Capital Act* will affect the civil rights of residents in those parts of the two provinces which make up the National Capital Region. In the case at bar the rights of the appellant are affected. But once it has been determined that the matter in relation to which the Act is passed is one which falls within the power of Parliament it is no objection to its validity that its operation will affect civil rights in the provinces. As Viscount Simon, adopting what had been pointed out by Rand J., said in *Attorney-General for Saskatchewan v. Attorney-General for Canada*, [[1949] A.C. 110 at 123, 1 W.W.R. 742, 2 D.L.R. 145]:

> Consequential effects are not the same thing as legislative subject matter. It is "the true nature and character of the legislation"—not its ultimate economic results—that matters.

The passage from the judgment of Duff J., as he then was, in *Gold Seal Limited v. Dominion Express Company and Attorney-General for Alberta* [(1921), 62 S.C.R. 424 at 460, 3 W.W.R. 710, 62 D.L.R. 62], quoted by the learned trial judge, correctly states the law. It is as follows:

> The fallacy lies in failing to distinguish between legislation affecting civil rights and legislation "in relation to" civil rights. Most legislation of a repressive character does incidentally or consequentially affect civil rights. But if in its true character it is not legislation "in relation to" the subject matter of "property and civil rights" within the provinces, within the meaning of section 92 of the British North America Act, then that is no objection although it be passed in exercise of the residuary authority conferred by the introductory clause.

I have already indicated my view that the matter in relation to which the *National Capital Act* was passed does not come within any of the classes of subjects enumerated in s. 92.

It has been said repeatedly that, in dealing with questions that arise under the *British North America Act* as to the allocation of law-making powers between Parliament and the Legislatures of the Provinces, the court will be well advised to confine itself to the precise question raised in the proceeding which is before it. It is sufficient in this case to say that in my opinion it is within the powers of Parliament to authorize the Commission, for the attainment of its objects and purposes as defined in the Act, to make the expropriation of the lands of the appellant referred to in the question submitted to the Exchequer Court. It follows from this that I agree with the conclusion of the learned trial judge that the question submitted to him should be answered in the negative.

For these reasons I would dismiss the appeal with costs.

Appeal dismissed with costs.

Note on the Residuary Character of the General Power

In *In re Initiative and Referendum Act,* [1919] A.C. 935, 48 D.L.R. 18, [1919] 3 W.W.R. 1, Lord Haldane said that "the residuary power of legislation beyond those powers that are specifically distributed by the two sections [91 and 92] is conferred on the Dominion". The terms of the B.N.A. Act do not support this statement; they make it clear that the residuary power of the Dominion— its grant of legislative authority—encompasses everything beyond what is conferred on each provincial legislature. Lord Haldane's view is, of course, a follow-up of the dichotomy established in the *Local Prohibition* case between the general power and the enumerated powers in section 91. The result of this view, and of his later expositions of the general power culminating in the *Snider case,* has been to give the general power two restricted areas of operation: (1) a closely confined scope of "normal" operation; and (2) an equally closely confined scope of "abnormal" operation. Illustrative of the first mentioned area of operation are The Canada Temperance Act, the federal power to incorporate companies with Dominion objects, see *Great West Saddlery Co. v. The King,* [1921] 2 A.C. 91, 58 D.L.R. 1, [1921] 1 W.W.R. 1034, and chapter VIII, *infra,* and legislation authorizing references by the Governor General to the Supreme Court, see *Re References by the Governor General in Council,* (1910) 43 S.C.R. 536, aff'd (*sub nom. A.-G. Ont. v. A.-G. Can.*), [1912] A.C. 571, 3 D.L.R. 509; and see *R. v Moore,* [1969] 2 O.R. 677, 6 D.L.R. (3d) 465 (designation of judges as arbitrators). The second area has, in effect, been confined to war conditions; and some lower Court judgments proceeded on this basis and took literally the Haldane-oriented Privy Council view that "emergency" legislation would become invalid with the cessation of the emergency: see *Rex v. Jones,* [1937] 1 D.L.R. 193, 11 M.P.R. 240; cf. *Re Canada Temperance Act,* [1939] O.R. 570, [1939] 4 D.L.R. 14, aff'd [1946] A.C. 193, [1946] 2 D.L.R. 1, [1946] 2 W.W.R. 1; *In re McManus,* [1939] 2 W.W.R. 199. How far the "emergency" basis of federal legislation still involves, despite the *Canada Temperance Federation* case, a temporary validity has not been examined either in that or in any subsequent case.

The chief criticism of the Haldane view and of the sequential view of Sir Lyman Duff and of the *Labour Conventions* case lies in their rigid attitude to the "normal" operation of the general power. There were some lower Court cases which regarded the "emergency" side of the general power as apt to embrace economic "emergencies" unrelated to war, *e.g. Lovibond v. G.T.R.,* [1939] O.R. 305, [1939] 2 D.L.R. 562, but this view was denied as the result of the "New Deal" cases, such as the *Natural Products Marketing Act* reference, *supra* (and see the symposium on the subject in (1937) 15 Can. Bar Rev. 393-507), and shortly afterwards Duff C.J. observed in *Reference re Adoption Act, etc.,* [1938] S.C.R. 398, at p. 402, [1938] 3 D.L.R. 497, at p. 498, that while "the subject of relief . . . has become one of enormous importance, . . . primarily, responsibility for this rests upon the provinces; the direct intervention of the Dominion in such matters being exceedingly difficult by reason of constitutional restrictions".

The *Canada Temperance Federation* case so far as it recognized that "an emergency may be the occasion which calls for . . . legislation", did not indicate any limitation on the kind of emergent conditions which may prompt legislation. Its chief importance lies, however, in its re-assertion of the strength of two cases which, coming after the Haldane era had ended, showed that the general power possessed more vitality than had been previously accorded to it and that there was no more reason to limit its ambit than there was to put predetermined restrictions on the meaning of "criminal law" or on "property and civil rights in the Province". What is equally important is that in the first of the two cases, *In re Regulation and Control of Aeronautics,* [1932] A.C. 54, [1932] 1 D.L.R. 58, [1931] 3 W.W.R. 625, Lord Sankey made a contemporary adaptation of Lord Watson's formula in the *Local Prohibition* case by viewing aerial navigation as "a class of subject which has attained such dimensions as to affect the body politic of the Dominion".

In the second of the two cases, *In re Regulation and Control of Radio Communication,* [1932] A.C. 304, [1932] 2 D.L.R. 81, [1932] 1 W.W.R. 563, Lord Dunedin referred to legislation in relation to radio communication as falling within the general words at the opening of section 91, not being mentioned explicitly in either section 91 or section 92. It is only fair to say that in both these cases there were other reasons advanced for upholding federal exercise of legislative authority in relation to the classes of subjects in question: see further, chap. III, *infra.* However, in the *Labour Conventions* case, Lord Atkin restated for the Privy Council the grounds upon which the *Aeronautics and Radio* cases rested. He said ([1937] A.C. 326, at p. 351, [1937] 1 D.L.R. 673, at p. 681, [1937] 1 W.W.R. 299, at p. 309): "The *Aeronautics* case concerned legislation to perform obligations imposed by a treaty between the Empire and foreign countries. Sect. 132, therefore, clearly applied, and but for a remark at the end of the judgment, which in view of the stated ground of the decision was clearly *obiter,* the case could not be said to be an authority on the matter now under discussion. The judgment in the *Radio* case appears to present more difficulty. But when that case is examined it will be found that the true ground of the decision was that the convention in that case dealt with classes of matters which did not fall within the enumerated classes of subjects in s. 92, or even within the enumerated classes in s. 91. Part of the subject-matter of the convention, namely, broadcasting, might come under an enumerated class, but if so it was under a heading 'Interprovincial Telegraphs,' expressly excluded from s. 92." Nonetheless, in the *Canada Temperance Federation* case, Lord Simon cited the *Aeronautics* and *Radio* cases to illustrate the proposition that if legislation is such "that it goes beyond local or provincial concern or interests and must from its inherent nature be the concern of the Dominion as a whole", then it will fall within the general power of the Dominion.

[See the following additional materials on the general power: *O'Connor,* Report to the Senate of Canada on the B.N.A. Act, annex 1, p. 52; *Richard,* Peace, Order and Good Government, (1940) 18 Can. Bar Rev. 243; *Tuck,* Canada and the Judicial Committee of the Privy Council, (1941) 4 U. of T. L.J.

33; *Labrie*, Canadian Constitutional Interpretation and Legislative Review, (1950) 8 U. of T. L.J. 298.]

The subjoined discussions which attempt an analysis of the role of the general power seem to share a common concept of its function, though with semantic differences as to the word "residuary".

1. FINAL REPORT OF THE SPECIAL JOINT COMMITTEE OF THE SENATE AND THE HOUSE OF COMMONS ON THE CONSTITUTION OF CANADA, p. 46 (1972)

Recommendations

52. The "Peace, Order and good Government" power should be retained in the Constitution as an expression of the overriding Federal legislative power over matters of a national nature.

53. Since the Federal General Legislative Power is counterbalanced by a Provincial power over matters of a Provincial or local nature, there is no place for a purely residuary power.

The legislative authority of the Parliament of Canada is principally contained in section 91 of the British North America Act. The form of the grant of power has been responsible for a great deal of constitutional litigation and is therefore worth remarking.

First, the Federal legislative power is said to reside in the Queen "by and with the Advice and Consent of the Senate and House of Commons"—a style of grant which is unnecessary in the light of section 17, which has already provided that Parliament consists of the Queen, the Senate and the House of Commons. Second, using words hallowed in British colonial tradition, the power bestowed is "to make Laws for the Peace, Order, and good Government of Canada." The power conferred on Parliament by these enacting words is known as the "General Power" of Parliament. The enacting clause goes on to provide that the General Power is "in relation to all Matters not coming within the Classes of Subjects by this Act assigned exclusively to the Legislatures of the Provinces."

The declaratory clause follows, setting out 31 heads of exclusive Parliamentary power "for greater Certainty, but not so as to restrict the Generality of the foregoing Terms of this section." Within the declaratory clause it is stated that the legislative authority of Parliament extends to the enumerated classes of subjects, "notwithstanding anything in this Act." This "notwithstanding" provision is called the *non obstante* provision. After the enumeration of exclusive Federal powers there are the following concluding words, sometimes called the "deeming clause":

> And any Matter coming within any of the Classes of Subjects enumerated in this Section shall not be deemed to come within the Class of Matters of a local or private Nature comprised in the Enumeration of the Classes of Subjects by this Act assigned exclusively to the Legislatures of the Provinces.

We are not concerned here with textual analysis as such, but we would draw attention to the judicial interpretation of the Federal General Power. The apparent legislative intent of the deeming clause was to ensure that the enumerated classes of matters in section 91 took precedence over section 92(16) in the Provincial list of powers: "Generally all Matters of a local or private Nature in the Province." Both the grammar and the phrasing of the deeming clause would appear to make this point clear. However, the Judicial Committee of the Privy Council gave that clause a wider interpretation, which at the same time had the effect of weakening the General Power. The Privy Council took the view that it was the deeming clause (rather than, as the text would appear clearly to state, the *non obstante* provision in the declaratory clause) which established the superiority of the enumerated heads of section 91 over the enumerated heads of section 92, in the event of conflict. The converse of this proposition was that, since the deeming clause established a priority only for the enumerated powers in section 91, the General Power had no priority. It was, in effect, a residuary power.

For the Privy Council by the 1920s the General Power was an emergency power to be used only in abnormal conditions such as war, famine, or pestilence, or a minor power which could justify the incorporation of companies with non-provincial objects, the expulsion of aliens, or the reference of questions to the courts for advisory opinions: in other words, it could be used only where there was no possibility of conflict with section 92, since in every case of conflict the Provincial power would prevail.

We are not so naïve as to think that this interpretation came about purely as a matter of textual analysis. Clearly, the Judicial Committee of the Privy Council, and notably Lords Watson and Haldane, came to a value judgment that the apparent meaning of the British North America Act would give too much power to the Federal Parliament, and especially that a broad interpretation of the General Power could erode Provincial power entirely. We are not without sympathy for this point of view, but we believe that the solution which the Judicial Committee decided on, viz., reducing the General Power to a merely residual power, was much too extreme.

In our view there is a fundamental need for a grant of power recognizing Federal jurisdiction in matters of national interest and possessed of a genuine national character. This would be a counterpart to the Provincial jurisdiction in section 92(16) over "all Matters of a merely local or private Nature in the Province." It would give an orientation to the whole of section 91 as subsection 16 may be thought to do to all of section 92.

The Privy Council itself began a rehabilitation of the General Power in the 1930s, and this trend continued after the Supreme Court of Canada became the court of final resort. As a result, matters such as aeronautics, broadcasting, the regulation of the national capital district, and labour relations in the atomic energy field have been assigned to the Federal Government under the General Power. We expect this trend to continue. The General Power is, therefore, no longer a merely residuary power, nor is it likely to become so again.

Some witnesses before us argued that the residuary power should rest with the Provinces rather than with the Federal Government. We could accept such a change provided that it applied only to the residuary aspect of the General Power and did not touch its positive power. For, as we have stated, we are convinced of the necessity of Federal jurisdiction over matters of a national nature. However, as we envisage the Constitution there should rather be a complete division of legislative power, with matters of a national character in Federal hands and those of a local or provincial nature under Provincial control. In such a division of powers there would be no real residuary power, since all power would initially be divided according to its aspect. In this context the location of residuary powers would be meaningless.

We frankly recognize that the triad of "Peace, Order, and good Government" is conceptually too vague to be entirely satisfactory as an expression of the Federal General Power to legislate in the national interest. However, the literal wording has now been qualified by more than a century of judicial interpretation, and we are reluctant to suggest an alternative, since we regard our task as a conceptual rather than a drafting one. We therefore content ourselves with expressing the view that whatever the language employed, the General Power should indicate the Federal Parliament's guardianship over the national interest.

2. WHAT PEACE, ORDER AND GOOD GOVERNMENT?

A.S. Abel, Western Ontario Law Review (1968), Vol. 7.

Often it is said that a fundamental difference between the Canadian federal structure and that of the United States is the location of the residual powers of government — often and falsely. There the central government has only delegated powers; all others belong to the states. Here, it is suggested, the case is reversed with the provinces having only specified powers and the Dominion competent as to everything else. A very real distinction between the two schemes does exist but not that. Instead what differentiates them is that here there is no residue of powers. None whatever. Everything is distributed. If the word "of" had been read to mean "of" and not tacitly taken as being "in", confusion would have been avoided and the claims alike to federal and provincial hegemony seen as the false issues they in fact are.

Section 91 itemizes thirty-one classes of subjects for use in sorting out situations where there is exclusive legislative authority in Parliament, section 92 lists sixteen for Provincial Legislatures. In each group, some are so particular as almost to be trivial — "Beacons, Buoys, Lighthouses and Sable Island," "The Management and Sale . . . of the Timber and Wood" on the land belonging to the provinces. Others cover a lot of ground — "Criminal Law", "Property and Civil Rights in the Province". But broad or narrow, individually, or altogether they have the appearance of furnishing a catalog of potential legislative concerns from which the courts need only select the appropriate one, not without difficulty perhaps, to determine whether a law is intra vires. Constitutional adjudication becomes a matching game with the court placing the legislative specimen alongside the colour samples to make the closest identification that judicial optics permits with one of the thirty-one or of the sixteen.

The high visibility of the listed members readily explains why that approach was taken. They stand out so; there are so many of them; and some are so invitingly precise. It seems as though he who runs may read.

In fact, he who runs is almost certain to misread, not noticing as he races through the Act that the listed heads are not made the content of granted power. They are "classes of subjects". But authority is not given to legislate on classes of subjects. Parliament is not empowered to make laws on any class of subjects named in section 91 nor the provinces on any class of subjects within section 92. What matters is "matters". The provinces may make laws as to "matters" falling within classes of subjects specified in section 92, and Parliament laws for "the peace, order and good government of Canada" which laws, if they are on "matters" falling within the classes of subjects specified in 91, have a special status allocated to them.

The role of the classes of subjects is thus much subtler than appears from a quick reading. Sections 91 and 92 are not equivalent to Article I, section 8, of the United States Constitution which forthrightly provides that "The Congress shall have Power to lay and collect Taxes . . . to regulate Commerce . . . to establish a uniform Rule of Naturalization" and all the rest.

The distinction may appear unduly refined. Nevertheless it is central to the Canadian federal scheme. Every law out of necessity will be on some "matter". But human prescience is incapable of articulating a list of classes of subjects such that every possible "matter" has some place there to go and very obviously it could not be done under such drafting circumstances as those of the British North America Act of 1867, an instrument fashioned by practical politicians to cope with problems they were encountering and not a doctrinal dream child of political philosophers.

Then how does one deal with a law on a "matter" with no "class of subject" it can call home?

There are three conceivable approaches. One is to recognize some one's possession of the undefined residue of legislative power. That was how it was done in the United States, implicitly the framers felt by giving the federal government only specified powers but in any case explicitly by the Tenth Amendment. Another is to leave a legislative gap with no government authorized to make a law about a matter falling outside every named class of subjects. But we have been told

> "the powers distributed between the Dominion on the one hand and the provinces on the other hand cover the whole area of self

> government within the whole area of Canada. It would be sub-
> versive of the entire scheme and policy of the Act to assume
> that any point of internal self government was withheld from
> Canada".

The statement quite clearly excludes the second approach. There remains a third, to eliminate both residue and gap by allowing every
"matter" to find a home somewhere but by searching the principles
of placement elsewhere than in the listed classes of subjects. On my
reading of it, this is the plan of the British North America Act—no
gap, no residue, the matter of every possible law having its accommodation provided. But if not in the listed classes of subjects, where is
one to look for the classifying principle? The answer to that is in the
interplay of 91 and 92.

Section 91 is a structurally complex section. It contains four
major components—first, a primary grant—to make laws for the
"Peace, Order and Good Government of Canada"; second, a general
qualification of the primary grant, that they be "in relation to . . .
Matters not coming within the classes of Subjects . . . assigned exclusively to the . . . Provinces"; third, an illustrative specification listing thirty-one classes of subject as exemplifying "for greater Certainty
but not so as to restrict the Generality" of the scope of the "exclusive
legislative authority of the Parliament" involved in the primary grant,
and, fourthly, an admonition that no matter coming within the thirty-
one classes of subjects shall "be deemed to come within the Class of
Matters of a Local or Private Nature . . . assigned . . . the Provinces."

Section 92 is formally simpler. Basically, it is a pendant to 91, the
second limb of which anticipated that exclusive legislative power on
matters falling within some classes of subjects was to be assigned the
Provinces and thereby taken out of the primary federal grant. That
suggestion is fulfilled by Section 92's listing of sixteen such classes
of subjects as the area of provincial competence. The sixteenth, "Generally all Matters of a merely local or private Nature in the Province"
echoes the phraseology of the fourth and final limb of 91. Of the
sixteen, it alone is there singled out as a category which matters
falling within the federal list of classes of subjects should be deemed
not to come within. Why? Is there something special about it?

It is indeed very different. In certain respects it is the provincial
equivalent of the "peace, order and good government" clause; and
between them they eliminate any occasion for a residual grant in the
Canadian federal system—or one might equally say, they effect a
twin grant of residuary power, to the Dominion *and* to the provinces.

Here is the labyrinth to be threaded if we would come to an understanding of what the Act provided as to provincial and federal jurisdiction.

A reasonable starting place is the grant of the federal power. That,
to repeat, is to "make Laws for the Peace, Order and Good Government of Canada". The phrase is familiar, so much so that like many
familiar things one no longer sees it or looks at it. "Peace, order and
good government" has become a jingle eroded by time and repetition,
like "give, devise and bequeath" or "love, honour and obey". It has

had its ups and downs. Once upon a time the incapacity of a single province to establish a uniform law throughout the Dominion was felt to bring it into play, which would have meant that it covered everything, what with every province limited to governing "within the province". That reading rendered section 94's contingent authority to make uniform laws on property and civil rights in Ontario, Nova Scotia and New Brunswick with the assent of those provinces as redundant as it has in fact proved sterile. It did not survive. There followed the obscure birth and various fortunes of the emergency doctrine conveniently and naturally invoked to validate federal wartime regulations, but revealing itself as the patched-up rationalization it was when it turned out that neither the union-management struggles attending the industrialization of the country nor the marketing plight of the great national staple, wheat, in the 1920's were emergencies, whilst "the evil of intemperance" in the late nineteenth century had "amounted in Canada to an emergency, one so great and so general that at least for a period it was a menace to the national life". A doctrine of such whimsical incidence shed only a fitful light and finally just (sort of) flickered out. There has followed a decade or so of *ad hoc* ruling that specific matters—aeronautics, telecommunications, atomic energy, the national capital—are for the federal government to regulate as involving peace, order and good government. The characterizations have made little pretence to analysis, prefigured in this by the decision which, momentarily abandoning the emergency doctrine in its heyday for the older "gap" doctrine, had supported the incorporation of Dominion companies. The principal contribution of the latest series of cases has probably been the tacit burial of the emergency concept.

The inherent vice common to these approaches has been fixation on elucidating what constitutes "peace, order and good government" as though it were some sort of a package deal given in all its frightening (or appealing, as the case may be) plenitude. But that is not what section 91 says. It gives power to make Laws for the "Peace, Order and Good Government of Canada"—of Canada, mind you, not in Canada. Had the words been said over slowly, not just rattled off, had the court faced with a statute asked itself—does this involve the peace of Canada? the order of Canada? the good government of Canada? rather than does it involve "peace, order and good government" the redirected emphasis may or may not have produced different decisions but it would almost certainly have produced more useful discussion.

I do not read "of Canada" in the text of the Act as requiring that the problem dealt with be one of uniform and universal interest through the length and breadth of the land. It suffices that the peace of Canada, the order of Canada, the good government of Canada be significantly at stake, that the matter be "unquestionably of Canadian interest and importance", "the concern of the Dominion as a whole" —a test which might well be satisfied by the Toronto Stock Exchange or the Lakehead elevators, localized though they are within a single province, with no doubt a rather more substantial impact there than in Halifax or Victoria—but a significant impact nevertheless throughout the whole of Canada. If the peace, the order, the good government of Canada in that sense be involved, there is no need to find a class of subjects in the listed thirty-one for the matter legislated on. Those are specimens, "for greater Certainty but not so as to restrict the Generality" of the granted power. The provincial list does have a bearing since it constitutes a qualification of the grant. But it is important first to insist on what it is that was granted—the power to make laws neither on matters coming within listed classes of subjects nor yet for peace, order, and good government but for the peace, order and good government of Canada.

But, if not all, only some, peace, order and good government fell within the federal grant, part must have been left out. What? and what provision was made as to legislation for that part? Peace, order and good government abroad, to be sure; but no constitutional instrument professes to prescribe the government of foreign lands so we can confine our inquiry to the Canadian scene. The answer on that basis to what was excluded is tautological but very important—the peace, order, and good government not of Canada, although in Canada, or in Lord Simon's formulation that which does not "(go) beyond local or provincial concerns or interests".

That formulation brings to mind the sixteenth item in the list of provincial legislative powers—"Generally all Matters of a merely local or private nature in the Province". That balances exactly the Dominion grant. Between them they encompass the whole possible range of legislation and there really was no need to have said more or to have elaborated either a federal or a provincial list. The last clause of section 92 is the counterpart of the opening part of 91 before 91 opens up the "for greater certainty" business.

Its character as such is revealed by an expression which has been as unduly overlooked as has the "of Canada" phrase in the peace, order, and good government clause. The expression is the word "Generally". That word which introduces item 16 is not used in connection with any listed item in 91 nor elsewhere in 92. If item 16 were only on a parity with the preceding fifteen, one would be driven to the inadmissible premise that the draftsmen of the Act inserted a word having no significance. The only escape is to recognize that here we have the real general grant of legislative power to the provinces, strictly equivalent to the Dominion power to make laws for the peace, order and good government of Canada. This is the "Generality" for 92, as the peace, order and good government of Canada is for 91, a Generality which in each case the accompanying specifics do not restrict but as to which they provide "greater Certainty". The peace, order and good government of Canada is for the Parliament, matters of a local or private nature for the provinces—there is no room for a residue.

Note on the Defence Power

Section 91(7) of the B.N.A. Act gives exclusive legislative authority to Parliament in relation to "militia, military and naval service, and defence". The scope or limits of this power have never been authoritatively defined. In view of its enumeration as a projection of the federal general power, why was it necessary for the Privy Council to develop an "emergency" (in the main, a war) concept of the general power? Cf. Kellock J. in *Reference re Validity of Wartime Leasehold Regulations,* [1950] S.C.R. 124, at p. 153, [1950] 2 D.L.R. 1, at p. 29. The defence power was mentioned as a makeweight in the *Aeronautics* case, [1932] A.C. 54, [1932] 1 D.L.R. 58, [1931] 3 W.W.R. 625. More recently, it was invoked in *A.-G. Can. v. Nykorak,* (1962) 33 D.L.R. (2d) 373, 37 W.W.R. 660, where the Supreme Court of Canada relied on it to support the validity of federal legislation under which the Crown in right of Canada was put in a master-servant relationship to members of the armed forces and sought to recover from a wrongdoer expenses incurred in the care of a soldier injured by the wrongdoer's negligence. While it may justifiably be invoked to support economic regulation during war and in the immediate aftermath of war, should it be carried any further, as for example, to support "cold war" federal policies in the economic field? Or is this an area in which a reappraised general power should be invoked? The general power proved unavailing in the *Board of Commerce* case, and it is questionable whether an argument on the defence power would have carried the day even accepting the then Privy Council view that the general power was subordinate to the enumerations in s. 91. A far-reaching conception of the defence power was indicated in the Essential Materials (Defence) Act, 1950-51 (Can.), c. 6, which provided for the control and regulation of production, distribution and use of essential materials and services, defined to include such materials as are in the Government's opinion essential for defence, and such services as in its opinion are essential for the adequate production, storage or distribution of essential materials or otherwise for defence purposes. See debate on the measure in 91 House of Commons Debates, pp. 444-457, 509-528, 532-569 and 596-597. The Act was short-lived, being replaced in 1951 by the less stringent Defence Production Act, now R.S.C. 1970, c. D-2, which, however, still empowered the Government to command priority of such services and supplies (and, indeed, to control production and fix prices thereof) as it deemed necessary for Canadian defence requirements or for cooperative defence efforts of Canada and associated (e.g. Commonwealth and NATO) Governments. Both pieces of legislation were connected with the Korean war which broke out in June, 1950 and took on new proportions in April, 1951. The Defence Production Act originally contained an expiry date of July 31, 1956 but by an amendment in 1955 (Can.), c. 52 it ceased to be temporary legislation save that the drastic compulsory powers therein were to expire in 1959.

Pronto Uranium Mines Ltd. v. Ontario Labour Relations Board, [1956] O.R. 862, 5 D.L.R. (2d) 342, discussed in (1957) 35 Can. Bar Rev. 101, held that jurisdiction to certify a union of the company's employees resides in the Canada Labour Board, not the Provincial Board, by virtue of the Atomic Energy Control Act, R.S.C. 1952, Chapter 11. The Act, declaring works or undertakings for the production or processing of fissionable materials to be for the general advantage of Canada, was sustained explicitly as an exercise of the federal general power, "the control of Atomic Energy (being) a matter which from its inherent nature is of concern to the nation as a whole". McLennan J. declined to enter into whether the controls were justified as relating to declared works under ss. 91(29) and 92(10)(c) or to defence under s. 91(7) of the British North America Act, both of which had been urged to sustain it. Why such a summary dismissal?

[On the defence power, see also *Rex v. Smith,* [1942] O.W.N. 387; *Rex v. Anderson* (1930), 54 Can. C.C. 321; and note the suggestion in *Fry v. W. H. Schwartz & Sons Ltd.,* [1951] 2 D.L.R. 198 (N.S.) that the Reinstatement in Civil Employment Act, 1946 (Can.), c. 63 was valid defence legislation.]

The war power vested in the Congress of the United States (see article 1, section 8 of the Constitution) has been held adequate to support a federal rent control law enacted after actual cessation of hostilities but while the effects of war persisted: see *Woods v. Miller* (1948), 333 U.S. 138, 68 S. Ct. 421. See also *Ludecke v. Watkins* (1948), 335 U.S. 160, 68 S. Ct. 1429. However, the Supreme Court has indicated that it is open to it, on a proper inquiry into the facts, to invalidate such postwar legislation when the emergency on which it was based has ended: see *Chastleton Corp. v. Sinclair* (1924), 264 U.S. 543. The war power has supported federal legislation mobilizing economic resources in war-time: see *Lichter v. United States* (1948), 334 U.S. 742, 68 S. Ct. 1294. See *Wambaugh,* War Emergency Legislation. (1917) 30 Harv. L. Rev. 663; Note, (1944) 12 Geo. Wash. L. Rev. 414.

In Australia s. 51(vi) of the Commonwealth of Australia Constitution Act bestows power on the central Parliament to legislate with respect to the naval and military defence of the Commonwealth and the several States, and the control of the forces to execute and maintain the laws of the Commonwealth. This power (buttressed by s. 51 (xxxix)) has been held ample enough, according to circumstances, to enable Parliament to impose control measures both in anticipation of war and after actual cessation of hostilities; see *Marcus Clark & Co. Ltd. v. Commonwealth* (1952), 87 C.L.R. 177; *The King v. Foster* (1949), 79 C.L.R. 43. Cf. *Australian Communist Party v. Commonwealth* (1951), 83 C.L.R. 1 as to some of the limits of the defence power; and see *Beasley,* Australia's Communist Party Dissolution Act, (1951) 29 Can. Bar Rev. 490.

CHAPTER III

POWER TO IMPLEMENT TREATY OBLIGATIONS

IN RE EMPLOYMENT OF ALIENS

In the Supreme Court of Canada. (1922), 63 S.C.R. 293,

65 D.L.R. 577, [1922] 2 W.W.R. 429.

DUFF J. . . . I now come to section 132, which is in these terms:—

"132. The parliament and government of Canada shall have all powers necessary or proper for performing the obligations of Canada or of any province thereof, as part of the British Empire, towards foreign countries arising under treaties between the Empire and such foreign countries."

It is a condition of the jurisdiction created by this section that there shall be some obligation of Canada or of some province thereof as part of the British Empire towards some foreign country arising under a treaty between the Empire and such foreign country. A treaty is an agreement between states. It is desirable, I think, in order to clear away a certain amount of confusion which appeared to beset the argument to emphasize this point that a treaty is a compact between states and internationally or diplomatically binding upon states. The treaty making power, to use an American phrase, is one of the prerogatives of the Crown under the British constitution. That is to say, the Crown, under the British constitution, possesses authority to enter into obligations towards foreign states diplomatically binding and, indirectly, such treaties may obviously very greatly affect the rights of individuals. But it is no part of the prerogative of the Crown by treaty in time of peace to effect directly a change in the law governing the rights of private individuals, nor is it any part of the prerogative of the Crown to grant away, without the consent of parliament, the public monies or to impose a tax or to alter the laws of trade and navigation and it is at least open to the gravest doubt whether the prerogative includes power to control the exercise by a colonial government or legislature of the right of appropriation over public property given by such a statute as the B.N.A. Act. All these require legislation. As regards these matters the supreme legislative authority in the British Empire is, of course, the Parliament of the United Kingdom. Three views are perhaps conceivable as to the scope of the authority arising under s. 132. It might be supposed that it was intended to give jurisdiction only in relation to those matters which are committed to the authority of parliament by section 91 and other provisions of the B.N.A. Act. It might be supposed, on the other hand, to constitute a delegation of the entire authority of the parliament of the United Kingdom, in so far as the execution of such authority might be required for the purpose of giving effect to the treaty obligations of the Empire within

202

Canada or in relation to Canada. On the other hand it may be supposed that a less sweeping authority is conferred by this section; that is subject to some limitations arising out of co-ordinate provisions of the B.N.A. Act itself. As to the first of these views, it may, I think, be at once rejected upon the ground that otherwise the section would be quite unnecessary. As to the other two; there are certain fundamental terms of the arrangement upon which the B.N.A. Act was founded, and these it is difficult to think it was intended that parliament should have power to disregard in any circumstances. But it is unnecessary to pass upon these points. The authority given by section 132 is an authority to deal with subjects of imperial and national concern as distinguished from matters of strictly Dominion concern only; and I am satisfied it is broad enough to support the legislation in question. The treaty validated by statute of 1913 deals with subjects which are ordinary subject matters of international convention: with precisely the kind of thing which must have been in the contemplation of those who framed this section. The effect of the Act of 1913 is, in my opinion, at least this: that with respect to the right to dispose of their labour, the Japanese are to be in the same position before the law as the subjects of the most favoured nation. Equality in the eye of the law in respect of these matters is what I think the legislation establishes. Does the Act of 1921 in its true construction infringe these rights of Japanese subjects? In my opinion it does. It excludes them from employment in certain definite cases. It is not, I think, material that the province in passing the Act is engaged in administering its own corporate economic affairs. If it goes into effect, it goes into effect (as a law of the province) abrogating rights guaranteed by the treaty. It is thus not only a law passed against the good faith of the treaty but it is, in my opinion, a law repugnant to the treaty and as such I think it cannot prevail. I think, moreover, that the Act of 1921 views Japanese and Chinese as constituting a single group and since it cannot take effect according to its terms that it must be treated as inoperative *in toto*.

[This was a reference as to the constitutionality of a British Columbia statute, 1921 (B.C.), c. 49 validating certain orders-in-council which provided that in all contracts, leases or concessions entered into, issued or made by the government, there should be a stipulation that no Chinese or Japanese persons shall be employed in connection therewith. A majority of the Court (Davies C.J., Duff and Brodeur JJ.) held that the Act was invalid on the ground, *inter alia*, that it conflicted with a Dominion statute, 1913 (Can.), c. 27, which gave the force of law to a treaty of 1913 between Great Britain and Japan. The judgment was affirmed by the Privy Council, *sub nom. A.-G. B.C. v. A.-G. Can.,* [1924] A.C. 203, [1923] 4 D.L.R. 698, [1923] 3 W.W.R. 945.

In *In re Legislative Jurisdiction over Hours of Labour,* [1925] S.C.R. 505, [1925] 3 D.L.R. 1114, the Supreme Court held on a reference that (1) the obligation of Canada as a member of the International Labour Conference under the Labour Part, Part XIII, of the Treaty of Versailles and corresponding provisions of other peace treaties, was not one to enact or promote legislation in respect of draft conventions or recommendations adopted by the Conference but simply to bring any draft convention or recommendation before the competent domestic authority; (2) in respect of the 1919 draft convention limiting hours of work in industrial undertakings, the competent authority was the provincial legislature save as to those parts of Canada not included within the limits of any Province, and save as to federal government employees, and also as to employees in services, undertakings or works within federal jurisdiction if Parliament has legislated or legislates on the matters covered by the draft convention.]

Note on the Executive Aspects of Treaty-Making Power in Canada

Since the enactment of the Seals Act in 1939 (now R.S.C. 1970, c. S-6) and the promulgation of the Letters Patent of 1947 reconstituting the office of Governor General, the procedure for the making of treaties, in the strict sense, is as follows:

Full powers may be conferred and ratification effected through Canadian action alone without the intervention of British officials. In the case of intergovernmental agreements, full powers as well as the instrument of ratification may be issued by the Secretary of State for External Affairs rather than by the Governor General, depending on the importance attached to the agreement which, in any event, is not made in the name of the Crown. Cf. *Read*, International Agreements, (1948) 26 Can. Bar Rev. 520, at p. 523:

"The procedure may take the following courses:

(a) If the document is to be passed under the Great Seal of the Realm, it is necessary to invoke the cooperation of the Commonwealth Relations Office; because the Great Seal of the Realm can only be used upon the authority of a warrant under the Sign Manual and Signet, the latter being a royal seal in the keeping of one of His Majesty's Principal Secretaries of State. The warrant sets forth on its face that it is at the request of the Government of Canada. Both the warrant and full powers are prepared in London by the British governmental authorities, and, in so doing, they consider that they are acting as agents for the Government of Canada and accept no political responsibility. This procedure is no longer in common use, but theoretically, it is still available.

(b) If the document is to be issued by the King and passed under the Great Seal of Canada or other seal coming within the provisions of the Seals Act, it is prepared by the Department of External Affairs, together with a submission to His Majesty requesting him to approve the passing of the document under the seal in question. It is transmitted by the Governor-General to the Palace, and returned by the same channel, with the King's approval endorsed on the submission and the Sign Manual on the document. The document is passed under the Great Seal of Canada by the Secretary of State of Canada.

(c) Under the new Letters Patent constituting the Office of Governor-General of Canada, dated the 7th September and taking effect on the 1st October, 1947, the document may be issued by the Governor-General, in the name of and on behalf of the King, and passed under the Great Seal of Canada. The procedural steps would be greatly simplified, and confined to Ottawa."

[Included in the Letters Patent of 1947 is para. 2, reading in part, as follows: "And We do hereby authorize and empower Our Governor

General with the advice of Our Privy Council for Canada or of any members thereof or individually, as the case requires, to exercise all powers and authorities lawfully belonging to Us in respect of Canada . . ."; and para. 3 reads: "And We do hereby authorize and empower Our Governor General to keep and use Our Great Seal of Canada for sealing all things whatsoever that may be passed under Our Great Seal of Canada".

[For literature on the subject see *Gotlieb*, Canadian Treaty Making (1968); *MacKenzie*, Canada and the Treaty-Making Power, (1937) 15 Can. Bar Rev. 436; *Matas*, Treaty Making in Canada, (1947) 25 Can. Bar Rev. 458; *Szablowski*, Creation and Implementation of Treaties in Canada, (1956) 34 Can. Bar Rev. 28; and cf. *Hendry*, Treaties and Federal Constitutions (1955).]

On the domestic effects of a treaty, see *The Parlement Belge* (1879), 4 P.D. 129, *Re Arrow River & Tributaries Slide & Boom Co. Ltd.*, [1932] S.C.R. 495, [1932] 2 D.L.R. 250; *Ritcher v. The King*, [1943] Ex. C.R. 64, [1943] 3 D.L.R. 540; *Bitter v. Secretary of State*, [1944] Ex. C.R. 61, [1944] 3 D.L.R. 482; *Mastini v. Bell Telephone Co.* (1971), 18 D.L.R. (3d) 215, 1 C.P.R. (2d) 1 (Ex. Ct.); Cf. *Rex v. Stuart*, [1925] 1 D.L.R. 12, [1924] 3 W.W.R. 648, 34 Man. R. 509 and *Missouri v. Holland* (1920), 252 U.S. 416; and see *Daggett*, Treaty Legislation in Canada, (1938) 16 Can. Bar Rev. 159.

In *A.-G. Ont. v. Scott*, [1956] S.C.R. 137, 1 D.L.R. (2d) 433, a contention was made that provincial legislation, implementing a reciprocal arrangement with other Provinces and with foreign countries (e.g. Great Britain) for enforcement of maintenance orders, involved treaty legislation which was beyond provincial competence. In rejecting the argument Rand J. said:

"The arrangement is said to be, in effect, a treaty to which the Province has no authority to become a party. A treaty is an agreement between states, political in nature, even though it may contain provisions of a legislative character which may, by themselves or their subsequent enactment, pass into law. But the essential element is that it produces binding effects between the parties to it. There is nothing binding in the scheme before us. The enactments of the two Legislatures are complementary but voluntary; the application of each is dependent on that of the other; each is the condition of the other; but that condition possesses nothing binding to its continuance. The essentials of a treaty are absent; and it would be an extraordinary commentary on what has frequently been referred to as a *quasi*-sovereign legislative power that a Province should be unable within its own boundaries to aid one of its citizens to have such a duty enforced elsewhere. The alternative entrance upon such a field by Parliament needs only to be mentioned to be rejected: and that authority must lie in the one or the other to effect such an arrangement is, in my opinion, indubitable".]

A.-G. CAN. v. A.-G. ONT.

In the Privy Council. [1937] A.C. 326, [1937] 1 D.L.R. 673, [1937] 1 W.W.R. 299.

Appeal by special leave from a judgment of the Supreme Court of Canada, [1936] S.C.R. 461, [1936] 3 D.L.R. 673, on a reference to determine the validity of three Dominion statutes enacted to implement conventions adopted by the International Labour Organization and ratified by the Dominion. The statutes were the Weekly Rest in

Industrial Undertakings Act, the Minimum Wages Act and the Limitation of Hours of Work Act, all enacted in 1935. Duff C.J., Davis and Kerwin JJ. were of opinion that save as to s. 6 of the Minimum Wages Act, the statutes were valid. Rinfret, Cannon and Crocket JJ. were of opinion that the statutes were invalid. Among the reasons given for these conclusions were the following:

DUFF C.J. (for himself, Davies and Kerwin JJ.): . . . It is, at this point, important to emphasize these two things: First, that by the combined effect of the judgments in the *Aeronautics* case and the *Radio* case, the jurisdiction of the Dominion Parliament in relation to international obligations is exclusive; and, moreover, as such matters are embraced within the authority of Parliament in relation to peace, order and good government, its power is plenary.

It was at one time supposed that s. 132 was the sole source of authority for Parliament in respect of the enforcement of international obligations, as regards matters which, otherwise, would fall within s. 92, and, at the same time, would not fall within any of the enumerated heads of section 91: that, for the purpose of ascertaining the ambit of that authority, one must look to the scope of s. 132 (and the conditions under which that section operates): and that from the language employed it was a legitimate inference that the jurisdiction did not arise until there was a treaty obligation in existence within the contemplation of the section. Four of the judges of this Court who took part in the judgment in the *Aeronautics* case expressed that view.

Moreover, it was supposed that, as regards matters normally falling within s. 92, the provinces might legislate for the purpose of giving effect to an international obligation. In the *Aeronautics* case, the members of this Court were unanimously of the opinion that, as regards such matters the jurisdiction of the Parliament of Canada was not exclusive, even though paramount.

It is now plain (as a result of these two decisions of 1932) that the provinces have no jurisdiction to legislate for the performance of such obligations, whether they be obligations within s. 132 or whether they be outside that section and within the scope of the general power to make laws for the peace, order and good government of Canada. Such obligations, we repeat, it is now settled, are not matters within the subjects of s. 92 or the enumerated subjects of s. 91.

It has been contended in respect of Dominion jurisdiction in relation to international matters, under section 132, as well as under the residuary clause (as pointed out in the judgment of Duff J. on the Reference relating to the employment of aliens (Japanese Treaty), 63 S.C.R. 330) that there are certain fundamental terms of the arrangement upon which the B.N.A. Act was framed which it is difficult to suppose Parliament could in any case disregard; and that it is a necessary inference to be drawn from the B.N.A. Act as a whole as regards such terms that the Dominion cannot, without, at all events, the assistance of the Provinces, legislate in contravention of them, even in the exercise of its authority over international relations. It is not necessary to deal with this contention; it is sufficient to say that the statutes under discussion do not deal with matters excluded from Dominion jurisdiction by any such principle. . . .

. . . From two main considerations, the conclusion follows that legislative authority in respect of international agreements is, as regards Canada, vested exclusively in the Parliament of Canada.

First, by virtue of section 132 of the *British North America Act,* jurisdiction, legislative and executive, for the purpose of giving effect to any treaty obligation imposed upon Canada, or any one of the provinces of Canada, by force of a treaty between the British Empire and a foreign country, is committed to the Parliament and Government of Canada. This jurisdiction of the Dominion, the Privy Council held, in the *Aeronautics* case and in the *Radio* case is exclusive; and consequently, under the *British North America Act,* the provinces have no power and never had power to legislate for the purpose of giving effect to an international agreement: that, as a subject of legislation, is excluded from the jurisdiction envisaged by section 92.

Second, as a result of the constitutional development of the last thirty years (and more particularly of the last twenty years) Canada has acquired the status of an international unit, that is to say, she has been recognized by IIis Majesty the King, by the other nations of the British Commonwealth of Nations, and by the nations of the world, as possessing a status enabling her to enter into, on her own behalf, international arrangements, and to incur obligations under such arrangements. These arrangements may take various forms. They may take the form of treaties, in the strict sense, between heads of states, to which His Majesty the King is formally a party. They may take, *inter alia,* the form of agreements between governments, in which His Majesty does not formally appear, Canada being represented by the Governor General in Council or by a delegate or delegates authorized directly by him. Whatever the form of the agreement, it is now settled that, as regards Canada, it is the Canadian Government acting on its own responsibility to the Parliament of Canada which deals with the matter. If the international contract is in the form of a treaty between heads of states, His Majesty acts, as regards Canada on the advice of his Canadian Government.

Necessarily, in virtue of the fundamental principles of our constitution, the Canadian Government in exercising these functions is under the control of Parliament. Parliament has full power by legislation to determine the conditions under which international agreements may be entered into and to provide for giving effect to them. That this authority is exclusive would seem to follow inevitably from the circumstances that the Lieutenant-Governors of the provinces do not in any manner represent His Majesty in external affairs, and that the provincial governments are not concerned with such affairs: in all these matters the authority of Parliament is not merely paramount but exclusive.

The first of the two cardinal questions raised by the contentions of the province has two branches, and may be stated thus: Has

Parliament authority to legislate for carrying out a treaty or convention or agreement with a foreign country containing stipulations to
which effect can only be given by domestic legislation changing the
law of the provinces (a) in matters committed by the *British North
America Act* (in the absence of any such international agreement)
to the legislatures of the provinces exclusively, and (b) in relation to
such matters where they are *ex facie* of domestic concern only and
not of international concern, such, for example (as the provinces
argue), as the matters dealt with by the conventions to which effect
is given by the statutes now before us: the regulation of wages and
of hours of labour?

The claim of Parliament to authority to execute legislative changes
in the law of the provinces in such matters naturally arouses concern
and misgiving among the authorities charged with responsibility
touching the status and rights of the provinces.

The view that the exclusive authority of Parliament extends to
international treaties and agreements relating to such subjects rests
on the grounds now outlined.

(1) As touching the view advanced that the subject matters of
the stipulations in the international agreements in question are of
exclusively domestic and not at all of international concern: the language of section 132 is unqualified and that section would appear
prima facie to extend to any treaty with a foreign country in relation
to any subject matter which in contemplation of the rules of constitutional law respecting the royal prerogative concerning treaties would
be a legitimate subject matter for a treaty; and there would appear
to be no authority for the proposition that treaties in relation to
subjects, such as the subject-matter of the statutes in question, are
not within the scope of that prerogative. The question whether the
language of section 132 is, by necessary implication, subject to some
restriction in order to preserve unimpaired radical guarantees evidenced by the B.N.A. Act as a whole is mentioned in the next succeeding paragraph. Legislative authority to give effect to treaties within
section 132 remained, of course, after the B.N.A. Act, down to the
enactment of the Statute of Westminster, in the Imperial Parliament,
although by section 132, it also became and is vested in the Parliament
of Canada; but, since the Statute of Westminster, no Act of the
Imperial Parliament can have effect in Canada without the consent
of Canada. The practice of modern times and, in particular, the
provisions of the Covenant of the League of Nations embodied in the
Treaty of Versailles would appear to demonstrate that by common
consent of the nations of the world, such matters are regarded as of
highly international as well as of domestic concern and proper subjects
for treaty stipulation.

(2) As touching the view that the legislative authority committed
to the Parliament and Government of Canada by section 132 (and
by the introductory clause of section 91 in relation to international
matters) does not extend to matters which would fall exclusively
within the legislative jurisdiction of the provinces, in the absence of
any international obligation respecting them, it is to be observed:

First, section 132 relates *inter alia* to obligations imposed upon any province of Canada by any treaty between the British Empire and a foreign country. Section 132 obviously contemplates the possibility of such an obligation arising as a diplomatic obligation under such a treaty, even although legislation might be necessary in order to attach to it the force of law. In such case, the Parliament and Government of Canada appear to be endowed with the necessary legislative and executive powers. This provision with regard to the obligations of the provinces taken together with the generality of the language employed in section 132 would seem to point rather definitely to the conclusion that the view under consideration is not tenable:

Secondly, the established practice of the Parliament of Canada and the decisions of the Courts in relation to that practice do not accord with this view. Statutes giving effect to the International Waterways Treaty (1911) with the United States, and the Treaty with Japan (1913) are instances in which treaties dealing with matters of civil right within the provinces and the management of the public property of the provinces were given the force of law by Dominion statutes. The legislation concerning the Japanese Treaty was held to be valid and to nullify a statute of the Province inconsistent with it by the Judicial Committee of the Privy Council in *Attorney-General for British Columbia v. Attorney-General for Canada,* [1924] A.C. 203.

The jurisdiction of Parliament to enforce international obligations under agreements which are not strictly "treaties" within section 132 is co-ordinate with the jurisdiction under this last named section.

It is contended by the Provinces that the Dominion cannot by reason merely of the existence of an international agreement (within section 132 or within the residuary clause) possess legislative authority enabling the Parliament of Canada to legislate in derogation of certain fundamental terms which, it is said, were the basis of the Union of 1867, and are expressly or impliedly embodied in the B.N.A. Act. For the purposes of the present reference, it is unnecessary to make any observation upon this contention further than what has already been said, viz., that the exclusive authority of the Dominion to give the force of law to an international agreement is not affected by the circumstances alone that, in the absence of such an agreement, the exclusive legislative authority of the provinces would extend to the subject-matter of it.

The second of the cardinal questions requiring determination concerns the construction and effect of article 405 of the Treaty of Versailles.

The draft conventions now in question were brought before the House of Commons and the Senate, received the assent of both Houses in the form of resolutions, which resolutions approved the ratification of them, and the statutes in question were passed for the purpose of giving legislative effect to their stipulations, the operative clauses of the statute being in each case preceded by a preamble in which it is recited that the draft conventions have been ratified by Canada. The procedure followed, if we put aside the provisions of article 405, was the usual and proper procedure for engaging in and giving effect to agreements with foreign governments. The propriety of this procedure is questioned on the ground that under the special provisions of article 405, and especially those of paragraphs 5 and 7 of the article, it was an essential condition of the jurisdiction of Parliament to legislate for the enforcement of the conventions that the conventions should have been submitted to, and should have received the assent of, the provincial legislatures before the enactment of such legislation by Parliament. Paragraphs 5 and 7 are as follows:

> Each of the Members undertakes that it will, within the period of one year at most from the closing of the session of the Conference or if it is impossible owing to exceptional circumstances to do so within the period of one year, then at the earliest practicable moment and in no case later than eighteen months from the closing of the session of the Conference, bring the recommendation or draft convention before the authority or authorities within whose competence the matter lies, for the enactment of legislation or other action.
>
> In the case of a draft convention, the Member will, if it obtains the consent of the authority or authorities within whose competence the matter lies, communicate the formal ratification of the convention to the Secretary-General and will take such action as may be necessary to make effective the provisions of such convention.

These paragraphs must be read together and, reading them together, it would appear that the "competence" postulated is the "competence" to enact legislation or to take other "action" contemplated by the article.

The obligations upon consent of the competent authority or authorities to ratify and, upon like consent after ratification, "to make effective the provisions of the convention" are both treaty obligations; and the authority or authorities competent to take legislative action where legislative action may be necessary to make the provisions of the convention effective would appear plainly to be included within the authority or authorities before whom it is provided that the draft conventions shall be brought.

It follows from what has been said that this treaty obligation is an obligation within section 132 and, consequently, that the authority to make the convention effective exclusively rests in the Parliament and Government of Canada and, therefore, that the Parliament of Canada is, at least, one of the authorities before which the convention must be brought under the terms of article 405. The question whether the provincial legislatures are also competent authorities within the contemplation of paragraph 5 would appear to be necessarily determined by the consideration that we are constrained by the decisions of the Judicial Committee of the Privy Council, [1932] A.C. 54 and 304, already referred to, to hold that the authority of Parliament in this matter is exclusive and that the provincial legislatures are not competent to legislate for giving effect to the provisions of any international convention. . . . Strictly, however, important as this question of the "competence" of the provincial legislatures in the sense of article 405 is, it is unnecessary to decide it for the purposes of this reference; as will appear from what immediately follows.

The Governor General in Council is designated by the *Treaties of Peace Act, 1919* enacted under the authority of section 132, to take all such measures as may seem to him to be necessary for the purpose of carrying out the Treaties of Peace and for giving effect to the terms of such treaties. He it was, therefore, upon whom devolved the duty of performing the obligation of Canada under art. 405 to bring the draft conventions before the authority or authorities possessing "competence" under the Constitution of Canada. He it was also on whom devolved the duty to communicate to the League of Nations the ratification by Canada upon the assent of the competent authority or authorities. Moreover, the Parliament of Canada, as we have seen, possessing exclusive jurisdiction in relation to international agreements, the creation as well as the enforcement of them, declared, by the statutes now under examination, that the conventions in question were ratified by Canada. The executive authority, therefore, charged with the duty of acting for Canada in performing the treaty obligations, of submitting the conventions to the proper constitutional authorities and of communicating ratification to the League of Nations upon the assent of those authorities, and His Majesty the King in Parliament have, in effect, combined in declaring that the ratification was assented to by the proper constitutional authorities of Canada in conformity with the stipulations of article 405.

That would appear to be sufficient to constitute a diplomatic obligation binding upon Canada to observe the provisions of the conventions.

The answer to the three interrogatories addressed to this Court under this Order of Reference is, therefore, the statutes being *intra vires* in each case, in the negative.

RINFRET J.: . . . Whether treaty or convention, the questions under consideration in the *Aeronautics* and the *Radio* references were concerned with the validity of legislation enacted for the purpose of performing obligations arising as a result of international agreements already made and the validity whereof was not disputed.

In those references, the question whether the treaty or convention had been properly and competently signed, adopted or ratified was not in question, either in this Court or in the Privy Council.

Now, with deference, I make a very great distinction between the power to create an international obligation and the power to perform it when once it has been created.

We may leave aside the aeronautics and radio decisions, which were concerned merely with the validity of laws enacted for the purpose of performing foreign obligations, because in the present case what we have mainly to consider is the power to create foreign obligations. On that particular point, that is to say: on that point of where lies the power to create an international obligation, the only decision so far is the judgment of this Court on the reference in the matter of legislative jurisdiction over hours of labour, [1925] S.C.R. 505. I fail to find anything in the subsequent judgments of the Privy Council superseding what was said unanimously by this Court on that subject. The authority, in my humble opinion, is as conclusive as it can be, since that reference was concerned with one of the draft conventions on which the Attorney General of Canada now seeks to rely in support of the validity of the legislation now submitted to us, and since no substantial distinction in the pertinent sense can be made between the draft convention then under consideration and the two other conventions dealing with *The Weekly Rest* and *The Minimum Wages*. With deference, I think, the decision of 1925 is certainly binding on this Court and that, as a consequence it must follow that the obligation of Canada with respect to these draft conventions is simply to bring them before the authority within whose competence the matter lies for the enactment of legislation or other action, or, in the premises, before the legislatures of the provinces, except for the provisions of those draft conventions in relation to servants of the Dominion Government, or in relation to those parts of Canada which are not within the boundaries of a province. . . .

While it is, no doubt, perfectly true that "overwhelming convenience—under the circumstances amounting to necessity" (Anglin C.J.C. in the *Radio Reference*) [1931] S.C.R. 541, at 545, 546, dictates the answer that the performance of obligations, both federal and provincial, arising out of international agreements must be left exclusively to the jurisdiction of the Dominion Parliament, I fail to see the same necessity with regard to the power to create these foreign obligations. When once they have been undertaken, Canada is in honour bound to perform them. If the effect of the undertaking is that a subject of legislation within the exclusive jurisdiction of the province will thereby be transferred from that jurisdiction to the jurisdiction of the Dominion Parliament, I consider it to be within the clear spirit of the British North America Act that the obligation should not be created or entered into before the provinces have given their consent thereto. In the particular case that we are now considering, it is my humble view that such was the effect of the judgment of this Court in the matter of the reference of 1925. Such, it seems to me with respect, was the interpretation put by this Court upon the pertinent clause of article 405 of the Treaty of Peace.

Under the distribution of legislative powers, Property and Civil Rights in the Province were ascribed to the exclusive jurisdiction of the legislature in each province.

A civil right does not change its nature just because it becomes the subject-matter of a convention with foreign States. It continues to be the same civil right. When once the convention has been properly adopted and ratified, it is, no doubt, transferred to the federal field for the enactment of laws necessary or proper for performing the obligations arising under the convention. That is, as I understand it, the effect of the decisions of the Privy Council on the *Aeronautics* and *Radio* References. But before the international obligation has been properly and competently created, the civil right under the jurisdiction of the provinces is always the same civil right, and I cannot see where the Dominion Parliament in the *British North America Act* finds the power to appropriate it for the purpose of dealing with it internationally without having previously secured the consent of the provinces. . . .

The treaty-making power is the prerogative of the Crown. In ordinary practice, it is exercised on the recommendation of the Crown's advisers.

In Canada, the practice has grown gradually to enter into international conventions through the medium of the Governor in Council. It does appear that it would be directly against the intendment of the *British North America Act* that the King or the Governor General should enter into an international agreement dealing with matters exclusively assigned to the jurisdiction of the provinces solely upon the advice of the federal Ministers who, either by themselves or even through the instrumentality of the Dominion Parliament, are prohibited by the Constitution from assuming jurisdiction over these matters. . . .

CANNON J.: . . . Foreign powers, when dealing with Canada, must always keep in mind that neither the Governor General in Council, nor Parliament, can in any way, and specifically by an agreement with a foreign power, change the constitution of Canada or take away from the provinces their competency to deal exclusively with the enumerated subjects of section 92. Before accepting as binding any agreement under section 405 of the Treaty of Versailles, foreign powers must take notice that this country's constitution, is a federal, not a legislative union. . . .

CROCKET J.: . . . In my opinion none of the draft conventions of the International Labour Organization of the League of Nations, upon the ratification of which by the Government of Canada it has been sought to justify the enactment of all this legislation, fall within the terms of s. 132 of the B.N.A. Act. . . .

On the appeal to the Privy Council, the judgment of the Board was delivered by LORD ATKIN, who, after stating the circumstances leading up to the reference, continued as follows: . . . It will be essential to keep in mind the distinction between (1) the formation, and (2) the performance, of the obligations constituted by a treaty, using that word as comprising any agreement between two or more sovereign States. Within the British Empire there is a well-established rule that the making of a treaty is an executive act, while the performance of its obligations, if they entail alteration of the existing domestic law, requires legislative action. Unlike some other countries, the stipulations of a treaty duly ratified do not within the Empire, by virtue of the treaty alone, have the force of law. If the national executive, the government of the day, decide to incur the obligations of a treaty which involve alteration of law they have to run the risk of obtaining the assent of Parliament to the necessary statute or statutes, To make themselves as secure as possible they will often in such cases before final ratification seek to obtain from Parliament an expression of approval. But it has never been suggested, and it is not the law, that such an expression of approval operates as law, or that in law it precludes the assenting Parliament, or any subsequent Parliament, from refusing to give its sanction to any legislative proposals that may subsequently be brought before it. Parliament, no doubt, as the Chief Justice points out, has a constitutional control over the executive: but it cannot be disputed that the creation of the obligations undertaken in treaties and the assent to their form and quality are the function of the executive alone. Once they are created, while they bind the State as against the other contracting parties, Parliament may refuse to perform them and so leave the State in default. In a unitary State whose Legislature possesses unlimited powers the problem is simple. Parliament will either fulfil or not treaty obligations imposed upon the State by its executive. The nature of the obligations does not affect the complete authority of the Legislature to make them law if it so chooses. But in a State where the Legislature does not possess absolute authority, in a federal State where legislative authority is limited by a constitutional document, or is divided up between different Legislatures in accordance with the classes of subject-matter submitted for legislation, the problem is complex. The obligations imposed by treaty may have to be performed, if at all, by several Legislatures; and the executive have the task of obtaining the legislative assent not of the one Parliament to whom they may be responsible, but possibly of several Parliaments to whom they stand in no direct relation. The question is not how is the obligation formed, that is the function of the executive; but how is the obligation to be performed and that depends upon the authority of the competent Legislature or Legislatures. . .

. . . Counsel did not suggest any doubt as to the international status which Canada had now attained, involving her competence to enter into international treaties as an international juristic person. Questions were raised both generally as to how the executive power was to be exercised to bind Canada, whether it must be exercised in the name of the King, and whether the prerogative right of making treaties in respect of Canada was now vested in the Governor General in Council, or his Ministers, whether by constitutional usage or otherwise, and specifically in relation to the draft conventions as to the interpretation of the various paragraphs in art. 405 of the Treaty of Versailles, and as to the effect of the time limits expressed both in art. 405 and in the conventions themselves. Their Lordships mention these points for the purpose of making it clear that they express no opinion upon them.

The first ground upon which counsel for the Dominion sought to base the validity of the legislation was s. 132. So far as it is sought to apply this section to the conventions when ratified the answer is plain. The obligations are not obligations of Canada as part of the British Empire, but of Canada, by virtue of her new status as an international person, and do not arise under a treaty between the British Empire and foreign countries. This was clearly established by the decision in the *Radio* case, and their Lordships do not think that the proposition admits of any doubt. It is unnecessary, therefore, to dwell upon the distinction between legislative powers given to the Dominion to perform obligations imposed upon Canada as part of the Empire by an Imperial executive responsible to and controlled by the Imperial Parliament, and the legislative power of the Dominion to perform obligations created by the Dominion executive responsible to and controlled by the Dominion Parliament. While it is true, as was pointed out in the *Radio* case, that it was not contemplated in 1867 that the Dominion would possess treaty-making powers, it is impossible to strain the section so as to cover the uncontemplated event. A further attempt to apply the section was made by the suggestion that while it does not apply to the conventions, yet it clearly applies to the Treaty of Versailles itself, and the obligations to perform the conventions arise "under" that treaty because of the stipulations in Part XIII. It is impossible to accept this view. No obligation to legislate in respect of any of the matters in question arose until the Canadian executive, left with an unfettered discretion, of their own volition acceded to the conventions, a *novus actus* not determined by the treaty. For the purposes of this legislation the obligation arose under the conventions alone. It appears that all the members of the Supreme Court rejected the contention based on s. 132, and their Lordships are in full agreement with them.

If, therefore, s. 132 is out of the way, the validity of the legislation can only depend upon ss. 91 and 92. Now it had to be admitted that normally this legislation came within the classes of subjects by s. 92 assigned exclusively to the Legislatures of the Provinces, namely— property and civil rights in the Province. This was in fact expressly decided in respect of these same conventions by the Supreme Court in 1925. How, then, can the legislation be within the legislative powers given by s. 91 to the Dominion Parliament? It is not within the enumerated classes of subjects in s. 91; and it appears to be expressly excluded from the general powers given by the first words of the section. . . .

. . . It would be remarkable that while the Dominion could not initiate legislation, however desirable, which affected civil rights in the Provinces, yet its Government not responsible to the Provinces nor controlled by Provincial Parliaments need only agree with a foreign country to enact such legislation, and its Parliament would be forthwith clothed with authority to affect Provincial rights to the full extent of such agreement. Such a result would appear to undermine the constitutional safeguards of Provincial constitutional autonomy.

It follows from what has been said that no further legislative competence is obtained by the Dominion from its accession to international status, and the consequent increase in the scope of its executive functions. It is true, as pointed out in the judgment of the Chief Justice, that as the executive is now clothed with the powers of making treaties so the Parliament of Canada, to which the executive is responsible, has imposed upon it responsibilities in connection with such treaties, for if it were to disapprove of them they would either not be made or the Ministers would meet their constitutional fate. But this is true of all executive functions in their relation to Parliament. There is no existing constitutional ground for stretching the competence of the Dominion Parliament so that it becomes enlarged to keep pace with enlarged functions of the Dominion executive. If the new functions affect the classes of subjects enumerated in s. 92 legislation to support the new functions is in the competence of the Provincial Legislatures only. If they do not, the competence of the Dominion Legislature is declared by s. 91 and existed *ab origine*. In other words, the Dominion cannot, merely by making promises to foreign countries, clothe itself with legislative authority inconsistent with the constitution which gave it birth. . . .

It must not be thought that the result of this decision is that Canada is incompetent to legislate in performance of treaty obligations. In totality of legislative powers, Dominion and Provincial together, she is fully equipped. But the legislative powers remain distributed, and if in the exercise of her new functions derived from her new international status Canada incurs obligations they must, so far as legislation be concerned, when they deal with Provincial classes of subjects, be dealt with by the totality of powers, in other words by co-operation between the Dominion and the Provinces. While the ship of state now sails on larger ventures and into foreign waters she still retains the watertight compartments which are an essential part of her original structure. . . .

Acts declared ultra vires.

[See, on the foregoing case, *Jenks,* The Present Status of the Bennett Ratifications of International Labour Conventions, (1937) 15 Can. Bar Rev. 464; *Jennings,* Dominion Legislation and Treaties, (1937) 15 Can. Bar Rev. 455, where the conclusion is reached that "treaty" as used in s. 132 includes a convention. In the *Radio* case, [1932] A.C. 504, [1932] 2 D.L.R. 81, [1932] 1 W.W.R. 563, Viscount Dunedin said: "In fine, though agreeing that the Convention was not such a treaty as is defined in s. 132 their Lordships think that it comes to the same thing. . . . The result is in their Lordships' opinion clear. It is Canada as a whole which is amenable to the other powers for the proper carrying out of the convention; and to prevent individuals in Canada infringing the stipulations of the convention it is necessary that the Dominion should pass legislation which should apply to all the dwellers in Canada". *Quaere,* whether there was any warrant for the reinterpretation of the *Radio* case in the *Labour Conventions* case as having rested on the fact that radio communication as such, and apart from any convention, fell within s. 91: See Lord Wright in (1955) 33 Can. Bar Rev. 1123, at p. 1127.

It was held in *Regina v. Sikyea,* [1964] 2 C.C.C. 325, 43 C.R. 83, aff'd [1965] 2 C.C.C. 129, 44 C.R. 266 that section 132 treaty legislation enacted before the Statute of Westminster, 1931, may be validly amended thereafter so long as the treaty has not been denounced even though the treaty concerns matters within provincial legislative jurisdiction.

The Report of the Royal Commission on Dominion-Provincial Relations, 1940, did not contain any general recommendations on the treaty power but it did deal specifically with international labour conventions (see Book II, pp. 48-49) recommending that the provinces give to the Parliament of Canada power to implement such international labour conventions as the Government of Canada has ratified, or may ratify in the future. Because labour conventions were multilateral, there need be no fear that they would be used as a colourable attempt to encroach upon provincial competence. The Report went on to say that it was outside the Commission's terms of reference to deal with the general question of legislative competence to implement Canadian treaties.

It may be noted that Lord Atkin in the *Labour Convention* case expressly refrained from deciding whether the federal executive has independent authority to enter into a treaty or convention relating to a matter which apart from the treaty or convention is within provincial legislative authority; see *Scott*, The Consequences of the Privy Council Decisions, (1937) 15 Can. Bar Rev. 486.

Article 41 of the Charter of the United Nations provides that the Security Council may decide what measures not involving the use of armed forces are to be employed to give effect to its decisions, and it may call upon the members of the United Nations to apply such measures, including interruption of economic relations and of rail, sea, air, postal, telegraphic, radio and other means of communication, and severance of diplomatic relations. *The United Nations Act*, R.S.C. 1970, c. U-3 empowers the Governor in Council to make orders and regulations to implement decisions of the Security Council on measures to be employed under article 41. Fine, imprisonment and forfeiture of goods dealt with contrary to any order or regulation are the prescribed sanctions. Is there any doubt as to the validity of the Act?

For a comparative review of the United States, Australian and Canadian positions on the matters raised in this chapter see *Nettl*, The Treaty Enforcement Power in Federal Constitutions, (1950) 28 Can. Bar Rev. 1051.

Article VI, clause 2 of the Constitution of the United States stating, *inter alia*, that "this Constitution and the laws of the United States . . . made in pursuance thereof; and all treaties made . . . under the authority of the United States . . . shall be the supreme law of the land" has been given a wide effect. Thus, a treaty will prevail against state legislation on matters otherwise within state power: see *Ware v. Hylton* (1796) 3 Dall. 199; *Zschernig v. Miller* (1968), 389 U.S. 429; and the Congress may pass necessary implementing legislation which will prevail as against any reserved powers of the states: see *Missouri v. Holland* (1920), 252 U.S. 416. Moreover, executive agreements have been recognized as the law of the land with dignity similar to that of a treaty: see *U.S. v. Pink* (1942), 315 U.S. 203, 62 S. Ct. 552. Some limitations on the treaty power are, however, assumed to exist, as, for example, those arising from the Bill of Rights or other constitutional limitations on federal action: see *Cowles*, Treaties and Constitutional Law: Property Interference and Due Process of Law (1941); *Sutherland*, Restricting the Treaty Power, (1952) 65 Harv. L. Rev. 1305; and see also *Mathews*, The Constitutional Power of the President to Conclude International Agreements, (1955) 64 Yale L.J. 345. Congressional legislation in contravention of a treaty is not on that ground alone invalid: *Chae Chan Ping v. U.S.* (1889), 130 U.S. 581.

The Australian Constitution gives the Commonwealth Parliament legislative power under s. 51 (xxix) with respect to "external affairs". Apart from such questions as whether Commonwealth legislation is in conformity with any treaty or international convention which it purports to implement (and such questions could arise equally under s. 132 of the *B.N.A. Act*), the "external affairs" power is "subject to this Constitution" (as are other federal powers under s. 51), and hence is subject (it has been suggested) to limitations arising not only in respect of the scope of the term "external affairs" but to limitations of the Constitution which do not involve the relative legislative authority of federal and state Parliaments *inter se*: see *The King v. Burgess, ex parte Henry* (1936), 55 C.L.R. 608; *Sawer*, Execution of Treaties by Legislation in the Commonwealth of Australia, (1956) 2 Univ. of Q.L.J. 297. It is, of course, clear that the external affairs power is not merely a treaty implementing power: *cf. The King v. Sharkey* (1949), 79 C.L.R. 121.]

Note on Legislative Power to Implement International Obligations

Section 132 of the B.N.A. Act is a provision whose literal terms have been overtaken by events from which there is no turning back, namely, Canada's attainment of international personality independent of support from or subservience to Great Britain. It is, hence, obsolete unless its words are tortured to meet the present international position, and this is too much to expect of the Courts. The question remains, however, whether the gap that it leaves is not filled by the federal residuary power to legislate for the peace, order and good government of Canada, particularly in view of the theory of exhaustiveness that is said to characterize the distribution of legislative power. This may be said to depend on whether the implementing of international obligations, regardless of the subject matter, is a constitutional value or matter that is appropriate for assignment as such to a head of legislative power. If it is, then, certainly, under the present scheme of distribution it cannot fall within provincial competence. Former Justice Rand had no doubt on either point; for him, "the totality of treaty-making action" was "a discrete and entire subject matter," and it was not possible to eliminate treaty character from legislation accomplishing its terms; moreover, as an entire subject matter, "its only place of reception [was] in the residual power of the Dominion:" see *Rand*, Some Aspects of Canadian Constitutionalism, (1960) 38 Can. Bar Rev. 135, at pp. 142-143.

Lord Wright, who was a member of the Board in the *Labour Conventions* case, *supra*, at p. 205 expressed his dissent from it in a later extrajudicial utterance in which he asserted that one could not take a piecemeal approach to treaty implementing; and, indeed, he felt that the matter had been settled by the *Aeronautics* and *Radio* cases.

In *Francis v. The Queen,* [1956] S.C.R. 618, 3 D.L.R. (2d) 641, Kerwin C.J.C. in approving the views of Lord Atkin in the *Labour Conventions* case as to the need of implementing legislation to make a treaty (at least if not a peace treaty) effective domestically, prefaced his approval by saying that, "it may be necessary in connection with other matters to consider in the future the judgment of the Judicial Committee on the *Labour Conventions* case."

For a canvass of these and related matters, see *Laskin*, Some International Legal Aspects of Federalism; The Experience of Canada in *Currie* (ed.), Federalism and the New Nations of Africa (1964), pp. 389 ff.

Note on The Provinces and International Agreements

Claims that have been advanced in political speeches and postures, and in some scholarly writing, for provincial competence in international relations have been fed in part by the present constitutional position in Canada on treaty implementation. The Constitution of the United States is explicit in article 1, section 10, clauses 1 and 3, on the incapacity of a state thereof to enter into any compacts with foreign states; the Canadian Constitution is silent on whether a province may reach out to treat with a foreign government. No doubt, a province, as a juridical person, may deal across provincial or international boundaries with persons or private agencies, and as well with subordinate units of foreign states without raising thereby questions of international law. The *Scott* case, *supra*, at p. 205 shows that reciprocal arrangements with a purely domestic impact may be made even with a foreign state without having binding treaty character.

It is primarily a matter of internal constitutional law whether a Province may independently make agreements with a foreign state. The question arises whether the admitted disability of a Province to legislate extraterritorially carries with it a correlative disability to exercise extraterritorial executive power which is necessary in foreign relations. An affirmative answer is compelled, both by reference to the scheme of the B.N.A. Act and by reason of the constitutional evolution of Canada to international personality culminating in the Statute of Westminster, 1931. A Province may be authorized by the national government to treat with a foreign state but any international obligation that arose therefrom would, in law, be that of Canada.

A Province that purported to treat on its own in this way, albeit on matters within its domestic competence, could not claim international validity for any ensuing agreement, nor would implementing legislation be valid when enacted in pursuance of a non-existing power to accept international commitments. On the international law side, recognition of validity by the co-contracting foreign state would fly in the face of the rule of international law that a federal state has one juridical personality (subject to constitutional and international arrangements to the contrary), and would raise an issue of independence which Canada would have to meet against both the Province and the foreign state.

[See on this question, *Laskin*, the Provinces and International Agreements in Ontario Advisory Committee on Confederation: Background Papers and Reports, (1967), p. 101; *Morin*, Treaty-Making Power — Position of the Government of Quebec (1967), 45 Can. Bar Rev. 160; *Morris*, The Treaty-Making Power: A Canadian Dilemma, (1967) 45 Can. Bar Rev. 478; *Atkey*, The Role of the Provinces in International Affairs, (1970) 26 Int.J. 249.]

Note on Provincial Legislative Power Over Foreign Governments

An unexplored constitutional question in the field of foreign relations is the extent to which provincial legislatures may regulate or tax activities or property of foreign governments which have been properly admitted to Canada in consequence of mutual recognition and establishment of diplomatic relations between Canada (acting through the federal government) and such foreign governments. This is a situation not covered by the *Labour Conventions* case, and it is arguable that, apart from any applicable federal legislation, the foreign states should be in no different position than is the federal Crown vis-à-vis provincial legislatures. The issue is more than one of jurisdiction of provincial courts over a foreign state, though even here it should be clear that it is only the Dominion that may as a matter of domestic constitutional law, modify, abolish or extend the accepted common law rules of immunity: see Diplomatic Immunities (Commonwealth Countries) Act, R.S.C. 1970, c. D-4. How far the courts recognize, in domestic litigation, the principles of international law respecting immunity of foreign diplomatic representatives from local process and liability, or the immunity of property of a foreign state from local jurisdiction, does not as such touch legislative power but it necessarily presupposes (unless this be another gap in law-making authority) that there is a competent legislature able to deal with those matters; see *Reference re Exemption of U.S. Forces from Proceedings in Canadian Criminal Courts,* [1943] S.C.R. 483, [1943] 4 D.L.R. 11. The constitutional value involved is surely a matter of the peace, order and good government of Canada. It would follow, on this basis, that while it is proper to construe provincial taxing legislation as not intended to override tax immunity recognized by international law, it would in any event be incompetent to a province to legislate in derogation of such immunity. Cf. *Reference re Power to Levy Rates on Foreign Legations and High Commissioners' Residences,* [1943] S.C.R. 208, [1943] 2 D.L.R. 481; *Jennings v. Whitby Tp.,* [1943] O.W.N. 170. This would, *a fortiori,* be so where the presence of the foreign government on Canadian soil was in pursuance of joint defence arrangements made by the Canadian Government upon Parliament's authorization as an exercise of the defence power under s. 91(7) of the B.N.A. Act: see *St. John v. Fraser Brace Overseas Corp.,* [1958] S.C.R. 263, 13 D.L.R. (2d) 177.

[See *La Forest,* May the Provinces Legislate in Violation of International Law? (1961) 39 Can. Bar Rev. 78.]

CHAPTER IV

TRADE AND COMMERCE: CONTROL OF MARKET TRANSACTIONS

1. Early Development of Limitations on Trade Regulation

CITIZENS INSURANCE CO. v. PARSONS; QUEEN INSURANCE
CO. v. PARSONS

In the Privy Council. (1881), 7 App. Cas. 96.

Appeal from a judgment of the Supreme Court of Canada, 4 S.C.R. 215, affirming judgments of the Ontario Court of Appeal which affirmed judgments in favour of respondent Parsons in actions brought upon certain policies of fire insurance. The specific constitutional issue raised in these cases concerned the validity of the Fire Insurance Policy Act, R.S.O. 1877, c. 162, first enacted by 39 Vict., c. 24, which provided for statutory conditions in fire insurance policies, and its application to policies issued by a Dominion incorporated company, a British company incorporated by Imperial charter and a pre-confederation company incorporated by charter granted by the old province of Canada but amended after confederation by the Parliament of Canada. A majority of the Supreme Court (Ritchie C.J., Fournier and Henry JJ.) held that the Ontario Act was valid. Strong J. who was present during most of the argument but did not participate in the judgment stated that he agreed with the majority. Taschereau and Gwynne JJ. dissented. Among the reasons for judgment given by members of the Supreme Court were the following:

RITCHIE C.J.: . . . No one can dispute the general power of parliament to legislate as to "trade and commerce," and that where, over matters with which local legislatures have power to deal, local legislation conflicts with an Act passed by the Dominion parliament in the exercise of any of the general powers confided to it, the legislation of the local must yield to the supremacy of the Dominion parliament: in other words, that the provincial legislation in such a case must be subject to such regulations, for instance, as to trade and commerce of a commercial character, as the Dominion parliament may prescribe. I adhere to what I said in *Valin v. Langlois,* 3 S.C.R. 1, at p. 15, that the property and civil rights referred to, were not all property and all civil rights, but that the term "property and civil rights" must necessarily be read in a restricted and limited sense, because many matters involving property and civil rights are expressly reserved to the Dominion parliament, and that the power of the local legislatures was to be subject to the general and special legislative powers of the Dominion parliament, and to what I there added: "But while the legislative rights of the local legislatures are in this sense subordinate to the right of the Dominion parliament, I think

221

such latter right must be exercised, so far as may be, consistently with the right of the local legislatures; and, therefore, the Dominion parliament would only have the right to interfere with property and civil rights in so far as such interference may be necessary for the purpose of legislating generally and effectually in relation to matters confided to the parliament of Canada."

I think the power of the Dominion parliament to regulate trade and commerce ought not to be held to be necessarily inconsistent with those of the local legislatures to regulate property and civil rights in respect to all matters of a merely local and private nature, such as matters connected with the enjoyment and preservation of property in the province, or matters of contract between parties in relation to their property or dealings, although the exercise by the local legislatures of such power may be said remotely to affect matters connected with trade and commerce, unless, indeed, the laws of the provincial legislatures should conflict with those of the Dominion parliament passed for the general regulation of trade and commerce. I do not think the local legislatures are to be deprived of all power to deal with property and civil rights, because parliament, in the plenary exercise of its power to regulate trade and commerce, may possibly pass laws inconsistent with the exercise by the local legislatures of their powers—the exercise of the powers of the local legislatures being in such a case subject to such regulations as the Dominion may lawfully prescribe.

The Act now under consideration is not, in my opinion, a regulation of trade and commerce; it deals with the contract of fire insurance, as between the insurer and the insured. That contract is simply a contract of indemnity against loss or damage by fire, whereby one party, in consideration of an immediate fixed payment, undertakes to pay or make good to the other any loss or damage by fire, which may happen during a fixed period to specified property, not exceeding the sum named as the limit of insurance . . .

I do not understand that by the Act now assailed any supreme sovereign legislative power to regulate and control the business of insurance in Ontario is claimed. As I read the Act, it deals only with this contract of indemnity; it does not profess to deal with trade or commerce, or to make any regulation in reference thereto. In my opinion, this Act has no reference to trade and commerce in the sense in which these words are used in the *British North America Act*. It is simply an exercise of the power of the local legislature for the protection of property in Ontario, and the civil rights of the proprietors thereof in connection therewith, by securing a reasonable and just contract in favour of parties insuring property, real or personal, in Ontario, and deals therefore only with a matter of a local and private nature. The scope and object of the Act is to secure to parties insuring a just and reasonable contract, to prevent the exaction of unjust and unreasonable conditions, and to protect parties from being imposed upon by the insertion of conditions and stipulations in such a way as not to be brought to the immediate notice of the insured, or capable of being easily understood, or by the insertion of conditions calculated practically in many cases to deprive the parties paying the premiums of indemnity, though justly entitled to it, and, if the statutory conditions are omitted or varied, to compel the terms of the contract to be so plainly and prominently put on the contract that the attention of the assured may be called to them, and so that he may not be misled, judicial experience having proved that the rights of the insured, and legitimate indemnity in return for the money paid, demanded that the insured should be thus protected . . .

Inasmuch, then, as this Act relates to property in Ontario and the subject-matter dealt with is therefore local, and as the contract between the parties is of a strictly private nature, and as the matters thus dealt with are therefore, in the words of the *British North America Act,* "of a merely local and private nature in the province," and as contracts are matters of civil rights and breaches thereof are civil wrongs, and as the property and civil rights in the province only are dealt with by the Act, and as "property and civil rights in the provinces" are in the enumeration of the "exclusive powers of provincial legislatures," I am of opinion that the legislature of Ontario in dealing with these matters in the Act in question, did not exceed their legislative powers.

I am happy to say I can foresee, and I fear, no evil effects whatever, as has been suggested, as likely to result to the Dominion from this view of the case. On the contrary, I believe that while this decision recognizes and sustains the legislative control of the Dominion parliament over all matters confided to its legislative jurisdiction, it, at the same time, preserves to the local legislatures those rights and powers conferred on them by the *B.N.A. Act,* and which a contrary decision would, in my opinion, in effect, substantially, or to a very large extent, sweep away.

I carefully and advisedly abstain from expressing any opinion as to the validity or invalidity of any Act of the Dominion of Canada, or of the province of Ontario, save only as to the Act now immediately under consideration. It will be time enough to discuss and decide on the validity of other statutes, whether Dominion or provincial, when properly brought before us for judicial decision. To do so now or to express any opinion as to the effect of this decision on other legislation not before us, and without argument or judicial investigation and consideration, would be, in my opinion, extra-judicial.

FOURNIER J.: . . . We find, therefore, that the federal legislation [on insurance] does not anywise affect the nature of the contract of insurance, nor the conditions forming part of such contract, and that the legislation of Ontario, now under consideration, deals exclusively with that subject,—both legislations deriving their respective powers from different sources, the first from the power of regulating trade and commerce, and the other from their power of legislating over civil rights and property. Why, if the provisions of these laws are neither conflicting nor antagonistic to one another, can we not hold that both are constitutional? I must confess that I see between them no conflict, and I see no obstacle to their being carried into operation. . . .

Although it is possible to thus reconcile these legislations, is it not evident, however, that the Act passed by the legislature of Ontario relating exclusively to the proof to be made in case of loss, and to the nature of the conditions of contracts of insurance effected in the province of Ontario, is *intra vires,* for the issuing of a policy of insurance is not necessarily a commercial transaction; it is certainly not one on the part of the assured, although, by the Civil Code of the province of Quebec, it is a commercial transaction on the part of the assurer . . .

It is the same in England; insurance is a commercial transaction, although the contract of insurance itself forms part of the civil law. In our constitutional Act I cannot find anywhere that commercial law is under the jurisdiction of the Dominion; it seems to me, on the contrary, that the Act, by assigning specifically to the Dominion legislative control over a part of the commercial law, such as any law on navigation, banking, bills of exchange, promissory notes and insolvency, has left the residue to the jurisdiction of the several provinces as coming under the head "civil law." In this view of the case, the Act now under consideration would derive its authority from the power of the provinces to legislate on civil rights. It is on this principle that the case of *Paul v. Virginia* (1868), 75 U.S. 168, was decided.

HENRY J.: . . . It would be, I think, improper to conclude that the Imperial Parliament, in the use of the words "the regulation of trade and commerce", in the peculiar connection in which we find them, could have intended them to apply, not only to the *regulation* of trade and commerce, as generally understood, but to all trading and commercial contracts, so as to limit the operation of the provision giving specifically the subject of property and civil rights to the local legislatures.

If once decided that contracts for fire insurance are necessarily beyond the powers of the local legislatures, where can a line be drawn to save to them the power to legislate touching the wages and contracts connected with manufactories, mercantile transactions, or others, or in respect to liens on personal estate, in the shape of stocks of goods, or to mercantile shops or warehouses.

The words of a statute, unless the context shows otherwise, or they have a technical meaning, are to be construed according to their well understood and accustomed meaning. "Trade" means the act or business of exchanging commodities by barter, or the business of buying and selling for money—commerce—traffic—barter; it means the giving of one article for another for money or money's worth. "Commerce" is only another term for the same thing. Neither of the terms includes the rules of law by which parties engaged in trade or commerce are bound to each other, but when their *regulation* is given to a legislative body, it must be assumed the intention was that control in some respects was to be exercised, but to what extent, we must judge in this case by taking the whole Act into consideration. I have no doubt that the Dominion parliament has power to enact general regulations in regard to trade and commerce, but not to interfere with the powers of the local legislatures in the matter of local contracts, amongst which is properly included policies of insurance against loss by fire on property in the same province.

"To regulate" trade may remotely affect some of the conditions and terms under which articles are produced, but not necessarily so; and the regulation of it may consist only in rules governing the disposition or sale of goods, or may include conditions under which goods are manufactured, by which they become liable to duty. The term or expression "Regulation of trade and commerce" cannot, under the Imperial Act, be construed to extend to and include contracts for the erection, purchase, or renting of warehouses, manufactories, or shops used for trading or commercial purposes.

TASCHEREAU J. (dissenting): . . . The relative positions of the parliament of the Dominion of Canada, and the legislatures of the various provinces, are so entirely different from those of Congress and the legislatures of the several States, that all decisions from the United States Supreme Court, though certainly always entitled to great consideration, must be referred to here with great caution. There the right to regulate commerce *in* the State is given to the State, not to the Federal power. Here, as said by Mr. Justice Strong, in *Severn v. The Queen*, 2 S.C.R. 70 at p. 104: "That the regulation of trade and commerce *in the provinces,* domestic and internal, as well as foreign and external, is by the *British North America Act* conferred upon the parliament of the Dominion, calls for no demonstration, for the language of the Act is explicit." I might also remark that, whilst in the United States constitution, the word "commerce" only is used; ours has the words "trade and commerce." Some law dictionaries give the word "trade" as meaning "internal commerce," whilst the word commerce would refer to foreign intercourse. But this appears to be a fanciful distinction, not recognized either in common parlance or in legal language . . . Every word of the Act must have its due force and appropriate meaning, and the Imperial parliament, which, no doubt, whilst creating a federal union among its North American possessions, had before its eyes the constitution of the United States, must have intended by adding this word "trade" to the word "commerce" to give to our federal authority supreme power, not only over the commerce, internal as well as external, but also over the trade of the whole Dominion, internal as well as external. Of course we are not called upon to give a general definition of this word "trade" as used in the Act. In the interpretation of the constitution, general definitions are to be avoided. In this case, all that is necessary to determine is, whether the word embraces insurance companies and their contracts, and, in my opinion, it does . . .

[It is clear] that the legislative authority of the [Dominion] parliament extends to insurance. Indeed, the Dominion parliament has given no uncertain sound on the question. Within the very first year of the Confederation (31 *Vic.*, ch. 93,) it exercised the power of legislation on the subject, and it has done so ever since, in no less than twenty-five statutes passed thereon at various periods, as follows:

1868, 31 *Vic.*, ch. 93.
1869, 32 & 33 *Vic.*, ch. 67, 70.
1870, 33 *Vic.*, ch. 58.
1871, 34 "   " 53, 55, 56.
1872, 35 "   " 98, 99, 102, 104, 105.
1873, 36 "   " 99.
1874, 37 "   " 49, 86, 89, 94, 95.
1875, 38 "   " 81, 83, 84.
1876, 39 "   " 53, 54 & 55.
1879, 42 "   " 66.

To these may be added the six license acts on Insurance Companies:—31 *Vic.*, ch. 48; 34 *Vic.*, ch. 9; 37 *Vic.*, ch. 48; 38 *Vic.*, ch. 20; 38 *Vic.*, ch. 21; 40 *Vic.*, ch. 42, in which the Dominion parliament has also exercised the right to legislate on insurance and insurance companies, and to enact regulations on their trade and business, making at least (not including those of the last session) thirty-one statutes of the Federal parliament (and I have no doubt I have not counted them all), which, if the respondent's contention should prevail, would fall to the ground as unconstitutional.

The consequence of the nullity of these statutes must be amongst a great many others, that all the amendments made by the Dominion parliament to the charters of the insurance companies existing before confederation, all the charters granted to insurance companies by the said parliament, are null and void; that all their policies of insurance are so many pieces of blank paper; that their shareholders are relieved from all liability whatsoever for the unpaid portions of their shares; that all actions pending, in which any of these companies are parties, must fall to the ground. And, as to the license acts, if they are illegal, of course these companies are not obliged to submit to them; they are, moreover, not only free from the operation of these acts for the future, but the Dominion Government is obliged to refund to them all that they have paid into the treasury under the said acts, and to remit the many hundred thousands of dollars which they have deposited with the Government. Indeed, it is impossible to foresee the grave and stupendous consequence of the nullity of the Dominion legislation on these companies, and the complications which would necessarily arise therefrom.

In fact, the Citizens' Insurance Company itself, the appellant in this case, does not exist if the Federal parliament has not the power of legislating on insurance companies and creating them . . .

. . . And if the Federal parliament has the power to create insurance companies, it has the power to regulate them, that is to say to prescribe the rules under which they can carry on their trade, by which their trade is to be governed. The respondent contends, that, assuming these companies can be created by the Federal parliament, their contracts, their policies fall under provincial control, and that the provincial legislatures alone have the power to regulate these contracts and these policies. But are not these contracts, these policies, the trade and commerce of these companies? and is it not the regulation of trade and commerce itself that the *British North America Act* vests, in express terms, in the federal authority? Is this not contending against the very words of the Act, that the federal authority can create or incorporate traders, but that it cannot regulate their trade? If such was the case, the provincial legislatures would have a power totally incompatible with the supremacy which the 91st section of the *British North America Act* gives in such clear terms, to the Federal parliament, over all the matters left under its control. Either the Federal parliament has no control at all over insurance companies, or it has it supreme, entire and exclusive. If it has it, it has necessarily the power to regulate them and to impose upon their contracts all the conditions or restrictions it may think advisable; it has the power, for instance, to enact a statute imposing upon the companies it has created the very conditions contained in the Ontario Fire Insurance Policy Act. And, if it has that power, the Ontario legislature has not got it. A contrary interpretation would be giving to one Government the power to create, and to the other the power to destroy . . .

I really fail to apprehend upon what ground the respondent and the Ontario courts with him, whilst admitting the power of the Federal parliament to incorporate insurance companies, can sustain the contention that the contract of insurance itself falls under provincial control, simply because it is a *contract or a personal contract* governed by the local laws, and falling within the words "civil rights," of the 92nd section of the *British North America Act*. Certainly a personal contract is governed by the local laws; no one denies this; but the question to be determined here is, which is the local law, the law in Ontario on the subject? Is it the Dominion or the provincial law? The respondent would seem to treat the Dominion laws as foreign laws. He forgets that before the laws enacted by the federal authority within the scope of its powers, the provincial lines disappear; that for these laws we have a *quasi* legislative union; that these laws are the local laws of the whole Dominion, of each and every province thereof; that the Dominion, as to such laws, is but one country, having but one legislative power, so that a contract made under these laws in Ontario, or any one of the provinces, is to be considered, territorially or with respect to locality, as a contract in the Dominion, and, as such governed by the Dominion laws, and not as a contract locally in the province governed by the provincial laws. This is why the contracts to convey passengers and goods on the railways under Dominion control, for instance, the contract made by the sender of a message with a telegraph company, the contracts of a sale of bank stocks, are all and every one of them when made anywhere in the Dominion, regulated by the federal authority. And the power of the federal authority to so regulate them has never been doubted; yet are they not all local transactions and personal contracts? Undoubtedly so; but these railway companies, these telegraph companies, these banking companies, being under federal control, their contracts are necessarily under the same control, absolutely and exclusively. It would be impossible for them to carry on their business, if each province could impose upon them and their contracts different conditions and restrictions. A Dominion charter would be absolutely useless to them if the constitution granted to each province the right to regulate their business. . . .

GWYNNE J. (dissenting): . . . The question . . . raised is, undoubtedly, one of a very grave character, for, as became developed in the argument of the several cases now before us, wherein the point is raised, one of which, namely, the *Western Assurance Co. v. Johnston,* was argued by the Attorney-General, who is also the Premier of the province of Ontario, in support of the constitutionality of the Act, the question before us is not one merely affecting the particular Act in question, but our judgment in this case, although the. Dominion parliament is not represented, and has not been heard in the matter, will logically affect some thirty acts of the Dominion parliament, whose constitutionality has not heretofore been questioned, and which must be *ultra vires* of the parliament, if the Act now before us be *intra vires* of the provincial legislature, and, on the contrary, if this Act be *ultra vires* of the provincial legislature a number of Acts passed by the legislature of the province of Ontario must be equally so. It is clear that the subject-matter of the Act in question is not one over which jurisdiction is by the *B.N.A. Act* given concurrently to the provincial legislatures and to the parliament. If it were, no doubt the Act would be valid *"as long and so far only as it is not repugnant to any Act of the parliament of Canada."* The subject not being one over which concurrent jurisdiction is given to the provincial legislatures and to the parliament, must be placed exclusively either under the one or the other . . .

In so far as jurisdiction over "Property and Civil Rights," in every province may be deemed necessary for the perfect exercise of the exclusive jurisdiction given to the Dominion parliament over the several subjects enumerated in sec. 91, it is vested in the parliament, and what is vested in the local legislatures by item 13 of sec. 92 is only jurisdiction over so much of property and civil rights as may remain, after deducting so much of jurisdiction over those subjects as may be deemed necessary for securing to the parliament exclusive control over every one of the subjects enumerated in sec. 91, the residuum, in fact, not so absorbed by the jurisdiction conferred on the parliament.

The only question, therefore, before us substantially is: Are or are not joint stock companies, which are incorporated for the purpose of carrying on the business of fire insurance, traders? and is the business which they carried on a trade?

If this question must be answered in the affirmative, the Act under consideration must be *ultra vires* of the provincial legislature, as much as was the Act which in *Severn v. The Queen,* 2 S.C.R. 70, was pronounced so to be, and as the Act under consideration in the *City of Fredericton v. The Queen* would have been if passed by a local legislature; indeed, it seems to me to be difficult to conceive what greater assertion of jurisdiction to regulate trade and commerce there could be, than is involved in the assumption and exercise of the right to prescribe by Act of the legislature in what manner only, by what form of contract only, by what persons only, and subject to what conditions only, particular trades, or a particular trade, may be carried on, and to prohibit their being carried on otherwise than is prescribed by the Act. If this may be done in one trade, obviously it may be done in every trade, and so all trades must be subject to the will of the legislature having jurisdiction so to legislate as to whether it shall be carried on at all or not. As to the Act under consideration, if it be open to the construction put upon it by the courts below, it seems to me to be impossible to conceive any stronger instance of the assertion of supreme sovereign legislative power to regulate and control the trade of fire insurance and of fire insurance companies, if the business of those companies be a trade. Now, among all the items enumerated in sec. 92, it is observable that not one of them in terms indicates the slightest intention of conferring upon the local legislatures the power to interfere in any matter relating to trade or commerce, or in any matter which in any manner affects any commercial business of any kind, unless it be item No. 10 . . .

When we regard the magnitude of the business of fire insurance, in which alone, in 1860, a sum exceeding one thousand one hundred and thirteen millions of pounds sterling was at risk in Great Britain, the annual premiums in respect of which amounted to nearly six millions sterling, a sum five times as great as that derived from marine insurance risks; and when we observe by the report of the Superintendent of Insurance appointed by the authority of the Dominion parliament, that there were in 1869:—

5 Canadian Fire Insurance Companies having at risk in the Dominion of Canada	$ 59,340,916.00
And 12 British Companies, having at risk	115,222,003.00
And 2 American Companies, having at risk	13,796,890.00
Amounting in all to	$188,359,809.00
Which in 1877, had increased to 13 Canadian Companies, having at risk	$217,745,048.00
12 British Companies, having at risk	184,304,318.00
3 American Companies, having at risk	18,293,315.00
Amounting in all to	$420,342,681.00

And when we consider that, but for the business of fire insurance, the trade and commerce of the world could never have attained the magnitude and success and exalted position which they have attained, we may well say, in my judgment, that the trade of fire insurance is, par excellence, the trade of trades, without which all other trades would have dwindled and decayed . . .

There can, therefore, in my judgment, be no doubt that in the contemplation of the B.N.A. Act, all insurance, whether of lives, or of real or personal property, and whether against risk by fire on land or on sea, or by storm on land or sea, or by any other casualty, must all alike be under the jurisdiction of the Dominion parliament. There can, I think, be no doubt that the object of the *B.N.A. Act*, in placing *"all matters coming within"* the term *"regulation of trade and commerce,"* under the exclusive control of the Dominion parliament, was to secure a perfect uniformity in all the provinces of the Dominion, as *to all matters whatsoever* affecting all trades, as an essential condition to the prosperous carrying on of trade, and to prevent all possible interference or intermeddling with any trade, which diverse local views entertained in the different provinces of the Dominion might be disposed to attempt, if the subject was placed under local jurisdiction, whether by prescribing a particular form of contract and prohibiting any other being used, or by prescribing a particular mode of execution of the contract, or by assuming to dictate in any other manner as to the manner in which, or the terms subject to which trading companies or other persons engaged in any particular trade, should be permitted to carry on such trade. . . .

On appeal to the Privy Council, the judgment of the Board was delivered by SIR MONTAGUE SMITH: . . . The main contention on the part of the respondent was that the Ontario Act in question had relation to matters coming within the class of subjects described in No. 13 of sec. 92, viz., "Property and civil rights in the province." The Act deals with policies of insurance entered into or in force in the province of Ontario for insuring property situate therein against fire, and prescribes certain conditions which are to form part of such contracts. These contracts, and the rights arising from them, it was argued, came legitimately within the class of subject, "Property and civil rights." The appellants, on the other hand, contended that civil rights meant only such rights as flowed from the law, and gave as an instance the status of persons. Their Lordships cannot think that the latter construction is the correct one. They find no sufficient reason in the language itself, nor in the other parts of the Act, for giving so narrow an interpretation to the words "civil rights." The words are sufficiently large to embrace, in their fair and ordinary meaning, rights arising from contract, and such rights are not included in express terms in any of the enumerated classes of subjects in sec. 91.

It becomes obvious, as soon as an attempt is made to construe the general terms in which the classes of subjects in sects. 91 and 92 are described, that both sections and the other parts of the Act must be looked at to ascertain whether language of a general nature must not by necessary implication or reasonable intendment be modified and limited. In looking at sect. 91, it will be found not only that there is no class including, generally, contracts and the rights arising from them, but that one class of contracts is mentioned and enumerated, viz., "18, bills of exchange and promissory notes," which it would have been unnecessary to specify if authority over all contracts and the rights arising from them had belonged to the Dominion parliament.

The provision found in sect. 94 of the British North America Act, which is one of the sections relating to the distribution of legislative powers, was referred to by the learned counsel on both sides as throwing light upon the sense in which the words "property and civil rights" are used. By that section the parliament of Canada is empowered to make provision for the uniformity of any laws relative to "property and civil rights" in Ontario, Nova Scotia, and New Brunswick, and to the procedure of the Courts in these three provinces, if the provincial legislatures choose to adopt the provision so made. The province of Quebec is omitted from this section for the obvious reason that the law which governs property and civil rights in Quebec is in the main the French law as it existed at the time of the cession of Canada, and not the English law which prevails in the other provinces. The words "property and civil rights" are, obviously, used in the same sense in this section as in No. 13 of sect. 92, and there seems no reason for presuming that contracts and the rights arising from them were not intended to be included in this provision for uniformity. If, however, the narrow construction of the words "civil rights," contended for by the appellants were to prevail, the dominion parliament could, under its general power, legislate in regard to contracts in all and each of the provinces and as a consequence of this the province of Quebec, though now governed by its own Civil Code, founded on the French law, as regards contracts and their incidents, would be subject to have its law on that subject altered by the dominion legislature, and brought into uniformity with the English law prevailing in the other three provinces, notwithstanding that Quebec has been carefully left out of the uniformity section of the Act.

It is to be observed that the same words, "civil rights," are employed in the Act of 14 Geo. 3, c. 83, which made provision for the Government of the province of Quebec. Sec. 8 of that Act enacted that His Majesty's Canadian subjects within the province of Quebec should enjoy their property, usages, and other civil rights, as they had before done, and that in all matters of controversy relative to property and civil rights resort should be had to the laws of Canada, and "property" and "civil rights" are plainly used in their largest sense; and there is no reason for holding that in the statute under discussion they are used in a different and narrower one.

The next question for consideration is whether, assuming the Ontario Act to relate to the subject of property and civil rights, its enactments and provisions come within any of the classes of subjects enumerated in sect. 91. The only one which the appellants suggested as expressly including the subject of the Ontario Act is No. 2, "the regulation of trade and commerce."

A question was raised which led to much discussion in the Courts below and this bar, viz., whether the business of insuring buildings against fire was a trade. This business, when carried on for the sake of profit, may, no doubt, in some sense of the word, be called a trade. But contracts of indemnity made by insurers can scarcely be considered trading contracts, nor were insurers who made them held to be "traders" under the English bankruptcy laws; they have been made subject to those laws by special description. Whether the business of fire insurance properly falls within the description of a "trade" must, in their Lordships' view, depend upon the sense in which that word is used in the particular statute to be construed; but in the present case their Lordships do not find it necessary to rest their decision on the narrow ground that the business of insurance is not a trade.

The words "regulation of trade and commerce," in their unlimited sense are sufficiently wide, if uncontrolled by the context and other parts of the Act, to include every regulation of trade ranging from political arrangements in regard to trade with foreign governments, requiring the sanction of parliament, down to minute rules for regulating particular trades. But a consideration of the Act shews that the words were not used in this unlimited sense. In the first place the collocation of No. 2 with classes of subjects of national and general concern affords an indication that regulations relating to general trade and commerce were in the mind of the legislature, when conferring this power on the Dominion Parliament. If the words had been intended to have the full scope of which in their literal meaning they are susceptible, the specific mention of several of the other classes of subjects enumerated in sect. 91 would have been unnecessary; as, 15, banking; 17, weights and measures; 18, bills of exchange and promissory notes; 19, interest; and even 21, bankruptcy and insolvency.

"Regulation of trade and commerce" may have been used in some such sense as the words "regulations of trade" in the Act of Union between England and Scotland (6 Anne, c. 11), and as these words have been used in Acts of State relating to trade and commerce. Article V. of the Act of Union enacted that all subjects of the United Kingdom should have "full freedom and intercourse of trade and navigation" to and from all places in the United Kingdom and the Colonies; and Article VI. enacted that all parts of the United Kingdom from and after the Union should be under the *same* "prohibitions, restrictions, and *regulations of trade.*" Parliament has at various times since the Union passed laws affecting and regulating specific trades in one part of the United Kingdom only, without its being supposed that it thereby infringed the Articles of Union. Thus the Acts for regulating the sale of intoxicating liquors notoriously vary in the two kingdoms. So with regard to Acts relating to bankruptcy, and various other matters.

Construing therefore the words "regulation of trade and commerce" by the various aids to their interpretation above suggested, they would include political arrangements in regard to trade requiring the sanction of parliament, regulation of trade in matters of interprovincial concern, and it may be that they would include general regulation of trade affecting the whole dominion. Their Lordships abstain on the present occasion from any attempt to define the limits of the authority of the dominion parliament in this direction. It is enough for the decision of the present case to say that, in their view, its authority to legislate for the regulation of trade and commerce does not comprehend the power to regulate by legislation the contracts of a particular business or trade, such as the business of fire insurance in a single province, and therefore that its legislative authority does not in the present case conflict or compete with the power over property and civil rights assigned to the legislature of Ontario by No. 13 of sect. 92.

Having taken this view of the present case, it becomes unnecessary to consider the question how far the general power to make regulations of trade and commerce, when competently exercised by the dominion parliament, might legally modify or affect property and civil rights in the provinces, or the legislative power of the provincial legislatures in relation to those subjects; questions of this kind, it may be observed, arose and were treated of by this Board in the cases of *L'Union St. Jacques de Montréal v. Belisle,* L.R. 6 P.C. 31; *Cushing v. Dupuy,* 5 App. Cas. 409.

It was contended, in the case of the Citizens Insurance Company of Canada, that the company having been originally incorporated by the parliament of the late province of Canada, and having had its incorporation and corporate rights confirmed by the Dominion parliament, could not be affected by an Act of the Ontario legislature. But the latter Act does not assume to interfere with the constitution or status of corporations. It deals with all insurers alike, including corporations and companies, whatever may be their origin, whether incorporated by British authority, as in the case of the Queen Insurance Company, or by foreign or colonial authority, and without touching their status, requires that if they choose to make contracts of insurance in Ontario, relating to property in that province, such contracts shall be subject to certain conditions.

It was further urged that the Ontario Act was repugnant to the Act of the late province of Canada, which empowered the company to make contracts for assurance against fire "upon such conditions as might be bargained for and agreed upon between the company and the assured." But this is, in substance, no more than an expanded description of the business the company was empowered to transact, *viz.,* to make contracts of assurance against fire, and can scarcely be regarded as inconsistent with the specific legislation regarding such contracts contained in the Act in question.

It was further argued on the part of the appellants that the Ontario Act was inconsistent with the Act of the Dominion parliament 38 Vict. c. 20, which requires fire insurance companies to obtain licences from the minister of finance as a condition to their carrying on the business of insurance in the Dominion, and that it was beyond the competency of the provincial legislature to subject companies who had obtained such licences, as the appellant companies had done, to the conditions imposed by the Ontario Act. But the legislation does not really conflict or present any inconsistency. The statute of the dominion parliament enacts a general law applicable to the whole dominion, requiring all insurance companies, whether incorporated by foreign, dominion, or provincial authority to obtain a licence from the minister of finance, to be granted only upon compliance with the conditions prescribed by the Act. Assuming this Act to be within the competency of the dominion parliament as a general law applicable to foreign and domestic corporations, it in no way interferes with the authority of the legislature of the province of Ontario to legislate in relation to the contracts which corporations may enter into in that province. The Dominion Act contains the following provision, which clearly recognizes the right of the provincial legislatures to incorporate insurance companies for carrying on business within the province itself:—

"But nothing herein contained shall prevent any insurance company incorporated by or under any Act of the legislature of the late province of Canada or of any province of the dominion of Canada from carrying on any business of insurance within the limits of the late province of Canada, or of such province only according to the powers granted to such insurance company within such limits as aforesaid, without such licence as hereinafter mentioned."

This recognition is directly opposed to the construction sought to be placed by the appellant's counsel on the words "provincial objects," in No. 11 of sect. 92,—"the incorporation of companies with provincial objects," by which he sought to limit these words to "public" provincial objects, so as to exclude insurance and commercial companies.

Ritchie, C.J., refers to an equally explicit recognition of the power of the provinces to incorporate insurance companies contained in an earlier Act of the Dominion Parliament (31 Vict. c. 48), which was passed shortly after the establishment of the Dominion.

The learned Chief Justice also refers to a remarkable section contained in the Act of the Dominion Parliament consolidating certain Acts respecting insurance, 40 Vict. c. 42. Section 28 of that Act is as follows:—

"This Act shall not apply to any company within the exclusive legislative control of any of the provinces of Canada, unless such company so desires; and it shall be lawful for any such company to avail itself of the provisions of this Act, and if it do so avail itself, such company shall then have the power of transacting its business of insurance throughout Canada."

This provision contains a distinct declaration by the dominion parliament that each of the provinces had exclusive legislative control over the insurance companies incorporated by it, and therefore is an acknewledgment that such control was not deemed to be an infringement of the power of the dominion parliament as to "the regulation of trade and commerce."

The declarations of the Dominion Parliament are not, of course, conclusive upon the construction of the British North America Act; but when the proper construction of the language used in the Act to define the distribution of legislative powers is doubtful, the interpretation put upon it by the Dominion Parliament in its actual legislation may properly be considered.

The opinions of the majority of the Judges in Canada, as summed up by Ritchie, C.J., are in favour of the validity of the Ontario Act. In the present actions, the Court of Queen's Bench and the Court of

Appeal of Ontario unanimously supported its legality; and the Supreme Court of Canada, by a majority of three Judges to two, have affirmed the judgments of the provincial Courts. The opinions of the learned Judges of the Supreme Court are stated with great fullness and ability, and clearly indicate the opposite views which may be taken of the Act, and the difficulties which surround any construction that may be given to it.

Taschereau, J., in the course of his vigorous judgment, seeks to place the plaintiff in the action against the Citizens Company in a dilemma. He thinks that the assertion of the right of the province to legislate with regard to the contracts of insurance companies amounts to a denial of the right of the dominion parliament to do so, and that this is, in effect, to deny the right of that parliament to incorporate the Citizens Company, so that the plaintiff was suing a non-existent defendant. Their Lordships cannot think this dilemma is established. The learned Judge assumes that the power of the dominion parliament to incorporate companies to carry on business in the dominion is derived from one of the enumerated classes of subjects, *viz.*, "the regulation of trade and commerce," and then argues that if the authority to incorporate companies is given by this clause, the exclusive power of regulating them must also be given by it, so that the denial of one power involves the denial of the other. But, in the first place, it is not necessary to rest the authority of the dominion parliament to incorporate companies on this specific and enumerated power. The authority would belong to it by its general power over all matters not coming within the classes of subjects assigned exclusively to the legislatures of the provinces, and the only subject on this head assigned to the provincial legislature being "the incorporation of companies with provincial objects," it follows that the incorporation of companies for objects other than provincial falls within the general powers of the parliament of Canada. But it by no means follows (unless indeed the view of the learned judge is right as to the scope of the words "the regulation of trade and commerce") that because the Dominion Parliament has alone the right to create a corporation to carry on business throughout the dominion that it alone has the right to regulate its contracts in each of the provinces. Suppose the dominion parliament were to incorporate a company, with power, among other things, to purchase and hold lands throughout Canada in mortmain, it could scarcely be contended if such a company were to carry on business in a province where a law against holding land in mortmain prevailed (each province having exclusive legislative power over "property and civil rights in the province") that it could hold land in that province in contravention of the provincial legislation; and, if a company were incorporated for the sole purpose of purchasing and holding land in the dominion, it might happen that it could do no business in any part of it, by reason of all the provinces having passed Mortmain Acts, though the corporation would still exist and preserve its status as a corporate body.

On the best consideration they have been able to give to the arguments addressed to them and to the judgments of the learned judges in Canada, their Lordships have come to the conclusion that the Act in question is valid.

Appeal dismissed.

[The broad sweep given to the federal "trade and commerce" power as an exclusive power in early judgments of the Supreme Court is indicated by *Severn v. The Queen* (1878), 2 S.C.R. 70 and *Fredericton v. The Queen* (1880), 3 S.C.R. 505. The latter case was considerably attenuated by the different approach taken in *Russell v. The Queen,* and the authority of the *Severn* case was finally demolished in *Bank of Toronto v. Lambe* (1887), 12 App. Cas. 575, at p. 586. Statements in *In re Prohibitory Liquor Laws* (1894), 24 S.C.R. 170 show that the Supreme Court's views on the scope of the trade and commerce power died hard.

Cf. the following materials on the scope and meaning of "trade and commerce": *Lefroy,* Legislative Power in Canada, pp. 550-561; *Clement,* The Canadian Constitution, pp. 683 ff.; *O'Connor.* Report to the Senate on the B.N.A. Act, Annex 1, pp. 78-109.

In the *Local Prohibition* case, Lord Watson considered whether the Canada Temperance Act could be supported under s. 91(2) and he discussed the matter as follows: "The scope and effect of No. 2 of s. 91 were discussed by this Board at some length in *Citizens Insurance Co. v. Parsons,* where it was decided that, in the absence of legislation upon the subject by the Canadian Parliament, the Legislature of Ontario had authority to impose conditions, as being matters of civil right, upon the business of fire insurance, which was admitted to be a trade, so long as those conditions only affected provincial trade. Their Lordships do not find it necessary to reopen that discussion in the present case. The object of the Canada Temperance Act of 1886 is, not to regulate retail transactions between those who trade in liquor and their customers, but to abolish all such transactions within every provincial area in which its enactments have been adopted by a majority of the local electors. A power to regulate, naturally, if not necessarily, assumes, unless it is enlarged by the context, the conservation of the thing which is to be made the subject of regulation. In that view their Lordships are unable to regard the prohibitive enactments of the Canadian statute of 1886 as regulations of trade and commerce. They see no reason to modify the opinion which was recently expressed on their behalf by Lord Davey in *Municipal Corporation of the City of Toronto v. Virgo,* [1896] A.C. 98 in these terms: 'Their Lordships think there is marked distinction to be drawn between the prohibition or prevention of a trade and the regulation or governance of it, and indeed a power to regulate and govern seems to imply the continued existence of that which is to be regulated or governed'." ([1896] A.C. 348, at p. 363).

This dictum arose from the attempt to avoid discrediting the result of *Russell v. The Queen, supra* p. 122; compare with it the statement of Strong C.J. in *Huson v. South Norwich* (1895), 24 S.C.R. 145 that "the difference between regulating and licensing and prohibiting is one of degree only" and the characterization by Marshall C.J. in *Gibbons v. Ogden* (1824), 22 U.S. 1 at 196 of the power to regulate as being "to prescribe the rule by which commerce is to be governed." It should be noted that *Toronto v. Virgo* involved construction of the scope of delegation in a municipal charter, traditionally subjected to a strict construction.

In *Montreal v. Montreal Street Ry.,* [1912] A.C. 333, at p. 344, 1 D.L.R. 681, at p. 687, Lord Atkinson referred to the "regulation of trade and commerce" as *two* of the matters enumerated in s. 91 and went on as follows: "Taken in their widest sense these words would authorize legislation by the Parliament of Canada in respect of several of the matters specifically enumerated in s. 92, and would seriously encroach upon the autonomy of the province". Cf. this reasoning with that used by Lord Watson in the *Local Prohibition* case to cut down the scope of the federal general power.

In *A.-G. Can. v. A.-G. Alta.*, [1916] 1 A.C. 588, at p. 596, 26 D.L.R. 288, at p. 292, 10 W.W.R. 405, at p. 408, Lord Haldane, making no allusion to the *Parsons* case, but relying on *Hodge v. The Queen* and the *McCarthy Act* case, said that "as the result of these decisions it must now be taken that the authority to legislate for the regulation of trade and commerce does not extend to the regulation by a licensing system of a particular trade in which Canadians would otherwise be free to engage in the provinces". Note that the *Parsons* case spoke of the *contracts* of a particular business or trade.]

IN RE THE BOARD OF COMMERCE ACT AND THE COMBINES AND FAIR PRICES ACT, 1919

In the Supreme Court of Canada. (1920), 60 S.C.R. 456, 54 D.L.R. 354, [1920] 3 W.W.R. 658.

(For a statement of this case, see p. 142, *supra*.)

ANGLIN J. (for himself, Davies C.J. and Mignault J.): . . . The jurisdiction of Parliament over "The Regulation of Trade and Commerce" (s. 91(2)) has frequently been invoked—usually without success—either in supporting federal legislation alleged to invade the provincial field or in attacking the validity of provincial legislation claimed to fall under one of the enumerated heads of s. 92. In *Citizens Ins. Co. v. Parsons,* 7 App. Cas. 96, at page 112, the Judicial Committee first points out that these words are not used in an unlimited sense as is apparent from their collocation and from the specific enumeration of several subjects which in their broadest sense the words "the regulation of trade and commerce" would include. . . . In *Bank of Toronto v. Lambe,* 12 App. Cas. 575, it was held that an attempt to make the expression, "the regulation of trade and commerce" cover direct taxation of banks so as to exclude provincial power to impose such taxation would unduly strain it. What was said in the *Parsons* case, was impliedly approved in the *Local Prohibition* case, [1896] A.C. 348. In *Montreal v. Montreal Street Rly. Co.,* [1912] A.C. 333, at p. 343, Lord Atkinson, after setting out some propositions which the *Local Prohibition* case should be taken to have established with regard to the purview of the exception to the provincial legislative authority contained in s. 91 of the B.N.A. Act at its end and the restrictions which must be imposed on the legislative powers of the Dominion over unenumerated subjects exercisable under its jurisdiction "to make laws for the peace, order, and good government of Canada," says at p. 344, that "these enactments, secs. 91 and 92, indicate that the exercise of legislative power by the Parliament of Canada in regard to all matters not enumerated in s. 91 ought to be strictly confined to such matters as are unquestionably of Canadian interest and importance and ought not to trench upon provincial legislation with respect to any classes of subjects enumerated in s. 92, . . . and that if the Parliament of Canada had authority to make laws applicable to the whole Dominion in relation to matters which in each province are substantially of local or private interest upon the assumption that these matters also concern the peace, order and good government of the Dominion, there is hardly a subject upon which it might not legislate to the exclusion of provincial legislation. The same considerations appear to their Lordships to apply to two of the matters enumerated in s. 91 *viz.*, the regulation of trade and commerce."

Ex facie the last sentence would almost seem to import that legislation properly held to fall with sec. 91(2) of the B.N.A. Act must not trench upon the provincial field—that Parliament cannot in an otherwise legitimate attempt "to regulate trade and commerce" legislate so as to affect matters with which a provincial legislature might deal in some other aspect as falling within "property and civil rights." In *The Insurance Act Reference*, 48 S.C.R. 260, at page 309, I was disposed so to interpret his Lordship's language. But if that be its real meaning "the regulation of trade and commerce" would cease to be effective as an enumerated head of federal legislative jurisdiction. In the more recent decision of *John Deere Plow Co. v. Wharton*, [1915] A.C. 330, the partial interpretation put on head No. 2 of sec. 91 in *Citizens Ins. Co. v. Parsons,* 7 App. Cas. 96, was again approved and, while it was pointed out that the exclusive power to regulate trade and commerce thereby conferred must like the expression "property and civil rights in the province" in sec. 92, receive a limited construction, it was held to "enable the Parliament of Canada to prescribe to what extent the powers of companies the objects of which extend to the whole Dominion should be exercisable and what limitation should be placed on such powers. For if it be established that the Dominion Parliament can create such companies then it becomes a question of general interest throughout the Dominion in what fashion they should be permitted to trade."

The clear effect of this last decision, I take it, is that s. 91(2) retains its place and office as an enumerative head of federal legislative jurisdiction and that legislation authorized by its terms, properly construed, is not subject to the restrictions imposed on Dominion legislation that depends solely on the general "peace, order and good government" clause, but, on the contrary, is effective although it invades some field of jurisdiction conferred on the provinces by an enumerated head of s. 92.

Probably the test by which it must be determined whether a given subject matter of legislation, *prima facie* ascribable to either, properly falls under s. 91(2) or s. 92(13) is this:—Is it as primarily dealt with in its true nature and character, in its pith and substance, (in the language of Viscount Haldane's judgment just quoted) "a question of general interest throughout the Dominion" or is it (in Lord Watson's words in the *Local Prohibition* case) "from a provincial point of view of a local or private nature?" In order to be proper subjects of Dominion legislation under "the regulation of trade and commerce" it may well be that the matters dealt with must not only be such as would ordinarily fall within that description, but, if the legislation would otherwise invade the provincial field, must also be "of general interest throughout the Dominion," or, in the language used by Lord Watson in the *Local Prohibition* case (p. 361) in regard to legislation under the peace, order and good government clause upon matters not enumerated in s. 91, must be "unquestionably of Canadian interest and importance". Mr. Justice Clement suggests this view in his valuable work on the Canadian Constitution (3 ed.), at pp. 448 and 688, and it may be that that was all Lord Atkinson intended when he said that the considerations applicable to the general powers of the Dominion Parliament supplementary to its enumerated powers apply also to the power conferred on it under the head, "The Regulation of Trade and Commerce." Otherwise I find it difficult to reconcile his views with those expressed in the *Parsons* case, and in *John Deere Plow Co. v. Wharton.* [His Lordship concluded that the legislation impugned in this case was valid as legislation in relation to the regulation of trade and commerce as well as being legislation for the peace, order and good government of Canada.]

DUFF J.: . . . The scope of the authority arising under sec. 91(2) of the B.N.A. Act has been much discussed. No precise definition of that authority has of course been given or even attempted; nevertheless, it has for 40 years been a settled doctrine that the words "regulation of trade and commerce" as they appear in that item cannot be read in the sense which would be ordinarily ascribed to them if they appeared alone and unaffected by a qualifying context. To adopt the language of Lord Hobhouse in the case of *The Bank of Toronto v. Lambe,* 12 App. Cas. 575, at page 586, "it has been found absolutely necessary that the literal meaning of the words should be restricted in order to afford scope for powers which are given exclusively to the provincial legislatures," and some definite limiting rules are deducible from the decided cases.

In the *Parsons* case, 7 App. Cas. 96, it was held that this authority does not comprehend the power to regulate by legislation the contracts of a particular business or trade in a single province, the particular business or trade there under consideration being the business of fire insurance.

In *Hodge v. The Queen,* 9 App. Cas. 117, the authority given to the Provinces by item 9 of sec. 92 to make laws with respect to licenses for raising a revenue for provincial purposes was considered sufficient to enable a province to regulate within its own boundaries the manner in which a particular trade is to be carried on and in the judgment delivered upon the reference touching the validity of the Liquor License Act of 1883, commonly known as the McCarthy Act, it was held that the authority of the Dominion in relation to trade and commerce did not include authority to regulate a particular trade by a licensing system applicable to the whole Dominion. And again on the reference upon the subject of the Dominion Insurance Act in 1916, *Attorney General for Canada v. Attorney General for Alberta,* [1916] 1 A.C. 588, this decision was affirmed and it was decided that the Dominion Insurance Act professing to regulate the business of insurance by a single system of licensing governing the whole of Canada could not be supported as an exercise of the Dominion legislative power in relation to trade and commerce.

The decisions of the Judicial Committee in the two last-mentioned cases appear to have been the logical result of the decision in *Hodge's* case, 9 App. Cas. 177. . . .

In *Parson's* case, at pages 112 and 113 appears the well known elucidation of the language of No. 2 of sec. 91 by Sir Montague Smith. In the *Montreal Street Railway* case, [1912] A.C. 333, at page 344, the substance of this passage is adopted by the Judicial Committee; and again in *John Deere Plow Co. v. Wharton*, [1915] A.C. 330, at page 340, Lord Haldane speaking for the Judicial Committee said:—

Their Lordships find themselves in agreement with the interpretation put by the Judicial Committee in *Citizens Insurance Co. v. Parsons,* 7 App. Cas. 96, at pages 112 and 113, on head 2 of s. 91, which confers exclusive power on the Dominion Parliament to make laws regulating trade.

Turning then to the exposition in *Parson's* case, thus adopted in 1912 and 1915, we find (in addition to the negative proposition that the authority in question does not comprehend the power to enact minute regulations in respect of a particular trade), 1st that the context affords an indication that "regulations relating to general trade and commerce" were in the mind of the legislature, and 2nd that matters embraced by these words would include political arrangements in regard to trade requiring the sanction of Parliament; regulation of trade in matters of interprovincial concern, and possibly general regulation of trade affecting the whole Dominion. It is not easy to ascribe a precise meaning to the words "general trade and commerce" but the passage seems to imply that the words "trade and commerce" are to be read conjunctively or at all events that the word "trade" takes on a special colour and significance from its association with the word "commerce"; and whatever be the precise significance of the word "general" we are at least able to affirm in consequence of the decisions already mentioned that it excludes regulations such as those which were in question in *Hodge's* case, in the McCarthy Act reference, in *Parson's* case, and in the *Montreal Street Railway* case. To borrow a phrase used arguendo on the Liquor Licence appeal, *Attorney-General of Ontario v. Attorney-General for Canada,* "general" in this passage means "general not as including all particulars but general as distinguished from some particulars". In the *Montreal Street Railway* case, at page 344, it was laid down in effect that the authority to deal with trade and commerce ought not to be so construed and applied as to enable the Parliament of Canada to make laws applicable to the whole Dominion in relation to matters which in each province are substantially of local or private interest and in particular in relation to matters which in each province are comprehended within the subject matters assigned to the province by No. 10 of sec. 92, viz., "local works and undertakings."

In addition to these negative and limiting rules a recent decision, *Wharton's* case, affords an illuminating example of the application of the considerations mentioned in *Parson's* case. It was there held that companies incorporated under the residuary power arising under sec. 91, having the status of corporations throughout the Dominion generally, might properly be subjects of regulation under No. 2 of sec. 91 in the sense that Parliament in the exercise of the authority thereby conferred might prescribe the extent to which such companies should be entitled to trade in any of the provinces. That is entirely consistent with the proposition laid down in *Parson's* case, that the authority of Parliament under the heading mentioned is an authority to pass regulations in relation to "general" trade and commerce. For the regulation in question in *Wharton's* case, [1915] A.C. 330, was not a regulation relating to any particular kind of trade or business, but regulation touching the trading powers of all Dominion companies engaged in any kind of business and applying to all such companies alike and thus at least potentially affecting Dominion trade and commerce in general through one of its most important instrumentalities. . . .

In so far as the Act authorizes the Board of Commerce to compel persons who are not engaged in trade to dispose of their property subject to conditions fixed by the Board and persons who are traders to dispose of property in respect of which they are not engaged in trade (the coal of the railway company or of the gas company, the dairyman's herd for example), I have not a little difficulty in classifying it as an enactment relating to the matters comprised within section 91(2), upon any fair construction of the words "regulation of trade and commerce." It is legislation affecting trade and commerce no doubt, but I am unable to distinguish such an enactment from an enactment authorizing a Board established by Parliament to take over such property on terms to be fixed by the Board and to dispose of it itself. Such compulsory enactments seem to be enactments on the subject of the rights of property, 92(13) and "local undertakings," 92(10) rather than enactments in regulation of trade and commerce.

Turning now to the authority vested in the Board by section 18, in relation to profits and prices, the provisions of section 18 on this subject appear to be obnoxious to the principles laid down in the passages referred to in *Parson's* case, the *Montreal Street Railway* case, and the *Wharton* case. The authority given to the Board is an authority to prohibit the making or taking of unfair profits upon the holding or disposition of any articles to which the statute applies, and the section provides, "that an unfair profit shall be deemed to have been made, when the Board shall declare an unfair profit to be made". It is thus left to the Board to make orders affecting individual holders or traders, to fix the terms upon which they are required to dispose of articles withheld from disposition or held for disposition, and such terms the Board is not required to fix by any general regulation, but may, and in the normal course would, fix them with reference to the circumstances of a particular case. The fixing of the terms of disposition by reference to the prohibition against unfair profits might well result in great disparity between the prices charged for the same article by different traders. The creation of an authority endowed with such powers of fixing the terms of contracts in relation to specific articles appears to involve an interpretation of the words, "regulation of trade and commerce," much more comprehensive than anything contemplated by the decisions and judgments referred to above. I have indicated the principle which in my opinion is deducible from *Parson's* case, namely that section 91(2) does not authorize an enactment by the Dominion Parliament regulating in each of the provinces the terms of the contracts of a particular business or trade, for the reason (put very broadly) that such legislation involves an interposition in the transactions of individuals in the provinces, within the sphere of "property and civil rights and local undertakings" not contemplated by section 91(2). Legislation, for example, imposing upon the trade in ready-made clothing throughout Canada, the prohibitions put into force by the order out of which this reference arises would, if my view of the effect of *Parson's* case be the right view, pass beyond the scope of the authority given in 91(2); an enactment, that is to say, by the Dominion Parliament in the precise words of the order now in question could not be supported under that head. I cannot discover any principle consistent with these conclusions, upon which an enactment delegating to a commission the authority to regulate the terms of particular contracts of individual traders in a specified commodity according to the views of the Board as to what may be fair between the individual trader and the public in each transaction, can be sustained as an exercise of that power; and if such legislation could not be supported when the subject dealt with is a single commodity, or the trade in a single commodity, or a single group of commodities, how can jurisdiction be acquired so to legislate by extending the scope of the legislation and bringing a large number of specified trades or commodities within its sweep? Every consideration which can be invoked in support of the view that the authority to regulate by general regulations of uniform application the contracts of a trade in one commodity, does not fall within section 91(2), can properly be brought to bear with I think increased force in impeaching legislation of the character now in question. . . .

It may be conceded that while section 18 could in its very terms be validly enacted by a provincial legislature, the authority reposed in a Commission created by such a legislature, would not of course extend beyond the ambit of authority committed to the legislature itself and consequently such a Commission would not acquire power to deal with matters belonging to the subjects of foreign trade, interprovincial trade, and the regulating of the management of Dominion undertakings and beyond the legitimate scope of the legislative activities of the province; but it does not follow because the Dominion could alone deal with these last mentioned matters it is itself authorized to enter upon fields exclusively reserved for the provinces, in order to carry out a legislative design necessarily incomplete without legislation on matters so exclusively reserved; co-operation between the Dominion and the provinces may be necessary to attain the ends desired by the legislators and such co-operation is of course not unknown and has indeed in some cases been expressly provided for in Dominion legislation, see for example 9 & 10 Geo. V., chapter 68, section 373, sub-section 6.

Having regard then to the scope of section 18, the authority conferred upon the Board to interfere with the proprietary rights of producers, holders and consumers of any of the articles to which the Act applies, and the authority to interfere with the management of local works and undertakings, and to prescribe the conditions of contracts relating to such articles and to the manner in which the Act takes effect, I conclude that it is not an enactment in relation to trade and commerce within section 91(2). . . .

[Idington and Brodeur JJ. also gave reasons against the validity of the legislation. On appeal to the Privy Council, [1922] 1 A.C. 191, Lord Haldane said, during the argument: "Must not it be taken that since the 1896 case at all events, perhaps earlier, subs. 2 of s. 91 must be taken as containing merely ancillary powers. A power that can be exercised so as to interfere with a provincial right only if there is some paramount Dominion purpose as to which they are applicable." (quoted in 2 Cameron, the Canadian Constitution and the Judicial Committee, p. 19). In the reasons for judgment which he gave on behalf of the Privy Council, Lord Haldane stated ([1922] 1 A.C. 191, at pp. 198 ff., [1922] 1 W.W.R. 20, at pp. 24 ff., 60 D.L.R. 513 at p. 517): ". . . Nor do the words in s. 91, the 'Regulation of trade and commerce,' if taken by themselves, assist the present Dominion contention. It may well be, if the Parliament of Canada had, by reason of an altogether exceptional situation, capacity to interfere, that these words would apply so as to enable that Parliament to oust the exclusive character of the Provincial powers under s. 92.

"In the case of Dominion companies their Lordships in deciding the case of *John Deere Plow Co. v. Wharton*, expressed the opinion that the language of s. 91, head 2, could have the effect of aiding Dominion powers conferred by the general language of s. 91. But that was because the regulation of the trading of Dominion companies was sought to be invoked only in furtherance of a general power which the Dominion Parliament possessed independently of it. Where there was no such power in that Parliament, as in the case of the Dominion Insurance Act, it was held otherwise, and that the authority of the Dominion Parliament to legislate for the regulation of trade and commerce did not, by itself, enable interference with particular trades in which Canadians would, apart from any right of interference conferred by these words above, be free to engage in the Provinces. This result was the outcome of a series of well-known decisions of earlier dates, which are now so familiar that they need not be cited. . . .

". . . It may well be that it is within the power of the Dominion Parliament to call, for example, for statistical and other information which may be valuable for guidance in questions affecting Canada as a whole. Such information may be required before any power to regulate trade and commerce can be properly exercised, even where such power is construed in a fashion much narrower than that in which it was sought to interpret it in the argument at the Bar for the Attorney-General for Canada. But even this consideration affords no justification for interpreting the words of s. 91, sub-s. 2, in a fashion which would, as was said in the argument on the other side, make them confer capacity to regulate particular trades and businesses."

Finally, see Lord Haldane's summation on the "trade and commerce" power in *Toronto Electric Commissioners v. Snider*, [1925] A.C. 396, at p. 409,

[1925] 2 D.L.R. 5, at p. 13, [1925] 1 W.W.R. 785, at p. 793: "Nor does the invocation of the specific power in s. 91 to regulate trade and commerce assist the Dominion contention. In *Citizens Insurance Co. v. Parsons* it was laid down that the collocation of this head (No. 2 of s. 91), with classes of subjects enumerated of national and general concern, indicated that what was in the mind of the Imperial Legislature when this power was conferred in 1867 was regulation relating to general trade and commerce. Any other construction would, it was pointed out, have rendered unnecessary the specific mention of certain other heads dealing with banking, bills of exchange and promissory notes as to which it had been significantly deemed necessary to insert a specific mention. The contracts of a particular trade or business could not, therefore, be dealt with by Dominion legislation so as to conflict with the powers assigned to the Provinces over property and civil rights relating to the regulation of trade and commerce. The Dominion power has a really definite effect when applied in aid of what the Dominion Government are specifically enabled to do independently of the general regulation of trade and commerce, for instance, in the creation of Dominion companies with power to trade throughout the whole of Canada. This was shown in the decision in *John Deere Plow Co. v. Wharton.* The same thing is true of the exercise of an emergency power required, as on the occasion of war, in the interest of Canada as a whole, a power which may operate outside the specific enumerations in both ss. 91 and 92. And it was observed in *Attorney-General for Canada v. Attorney-General for Alberta,* in reference to attempted Dominion legislation about insurance, that it must now be taken that the authority to legislate for the regulation of trade and commerce does not extend to the regulations, for instance, by a licensing system, of a particular trade in which Canadians would otherwise be free to engage in the Provinces. It is, in their Lordships' opinion, now clear that, excepting so far as the power can be invoked in aid of capacity conferred independently under other words in s. 91, the power to regulate trade and commerce cannot be relied on as enabling the Dominion Parliament to regulate civil rights in the Provinces."]

PROPRIETARY ARTICLES TRADE ASSOCIATION v. A.-G. CAN.

In the Privy Council. [1931] A.C. 310, [1931] 2 D.L.R. 1, [1931] 1 W.W.R. 552.

LORD ATKIN: . . . The view that their Lordships have expressed makes it unnecessary to discuss the further ground upon which the legislation has been supported by reference to the power to legislate under s. 91, head 2, for "The regulation of trade and commerce." Their Lordships merely propose to disassociate themselves from the construction suggested in argument of a passage in the judgment in the *Board of Commerce* case, [1922] 1 A.C. 191, 198, under which it was contended that the power to regulate trade and commerce could be invoked only in furtherance of a general power which Parliament possessed independently of it. No such restriction is properly to be inferred from that judgment. The words of the statute must receive their proper construction where they stand as giving an independent authority to Parliament over the particular subject-matter. But following the second principle noticed in the beginning of this judgment their Lordships in the present case forbear from defining the extent of that authority. They desire, however, to guard themselves from being supposed to lay down that the present legislation could not be supported on that ground.

[In this case the Privy Council, affirming the Supreme Court of Canada. [1929] S.C.R. 409, [1929] 2 D.L.R. 802, 52 Can. C.C. 241, upheld the validity of the Combines Investigation Act, R.S.C. 1927, c. 26 and s. 498 of the Criminal Code. The legislation was sustained largely under s. 91(27) of the B.N.A. Act as being in relation to criminal law, and partly under s. 91(3) ("The raising of money by any mode or system of taxation") and s. 91(22) ("patents of invention and discovery"). The reasons for judgment include a comparative appraisal of this legislation with the enactments which were invalidated in the *Board of Commerce* case, *supra*.]

GOLD SEAL LTD. v. DOMINION EXPRESS CO. AND A.-G. ALTA.

In the Supreme Court of Canada. (1921), 62 S.C.R. 424, 62 D.L.R. 62, [1921] 3 W.W.R. 710.

Part IV of the Canada Temperance Act, added by 1919 (Can.), c. 8, when duly brought into force, prohibited the importation of intoxicating liquor into any province where its sale for beverage purposes was prohibited by provincial law. Appellant was a distributor of intoxicating liquors carrying on an inter-provincial business. It tendered certain packages of intoxicating liquor to the defendant express company in Vancouver for carriage to Calgary, Alberta, whence it would be reshipped to points outside of Alberta. Defendant refused to accept the liquor for carriage, relying on the statute aforementioned. The Alberta Appellate Division held that the defendant could properly refuse to carry the liquor: 16 Alta. L.R. 113.

SIR LOUIS DAVIES C.J. . . . I feel bound to uphold the validity of the proceedings bringing into operation the provisions of the Act of 1919, 10 Geo. V, c. 8, prohibiting the importation into the province of Alberta of intoxicating liquors. It was admittedly not competent for the local legislature to pass such an Act, and, in my judgment, the Parliament of Canada, under its general power "to make laws for the peace, order and good government of Canada," and under its enumerated powers in sect. 91(2) (B.N.A. Act) "for the regulation of trade and commerce" had such power.

DUFF J.: . . . The capacity of the Parliament of Canada to enact the amendment of 1919 is denied. With this I do not agree. And, first, I am unable to accept the contention founded upon section 121 of the B.N.A. Act; the phraseology adopted, when the context is considered in which this section is found, shews, I think, that the real object of the clause is to prohibit the establishment of customs duties affecting interprovincial trade in the products of any province of the Union.

It is not strictly necessary to express any opinion upon the point whether this statute can be supported as passed in exercise of the power given by the second enumerated head of section 91. It has been held that the literal meaning of the words "trade and commerce" must be restricted in order to give scope for the exercise of the powers committed to the provinces by section 92. The legislation of 1919, however, deals only with imports into the provinces to which it applies and it is legislation clearly, I think, beyond the authority of a province to enact. The reason mentioned therefore seems to fail of application. It has been held also that the regulation of a particular business in each of the provinces throughout the Dominion by a general system of Dominion licensing is not a "regulation of trade and commerce" within the meaning of the phrase as here employed. That rests, in part at least, upon the ground that such a construction would give to No. 2 a scope including subjects specially dealt with by other heads of section 91, e.g. banking and shipping. This is an objection which would appear to have little force as applied to legislation dealing only with foreign or interprovincial trade and it seems at least much open to question whether the general elucidation of the language of No. 2 in *Parson's* case, when properly construed, contemplates the exclusion of legislation dealing with exports or imports even of a specified commodity from the ambit of the authority arising under that head; and in the *Insurance Act Reference*, [1916] 1 A.C. 588, it was expressly held that an enactment requiring a foreign company to take out a licence before carrying on the business of insurance in Canada was an enactment within the category of "regulation of trade and commerce."

A much more serious objection, however, arises from the decision of the Lords of the Judicial Committee in *Attorney General for Ontario v. Attorney-General for the Dominion,* [1896] A.C. 348. It was there held that the authority touching the regulation of "trade and commerce" given by section 91 contemplates the passing of laws with the view to the preservation of the thing to be regulated and not with a view to its destruction and consequently that a law abolishing all retail transactions in liquor within a specified area could not be supported as a law passed in the exercise of this power.

It is undoubted that the Act of 1919 was passed in aid of provincial liquor enactments and in substance aims at the abolition of transactions in liquor within the provinces to which it applies, and that being the case there is of course much force in the suggestion that the Act of 1919 could not be sustained as valid enactment in "regulation of trade and commerce" consistently with their Lordships' decision.

In a wider view it might be well suggested that a law prohibiting the export or the importation of a specified commodity or class of commodities from or into a particular province is, when considered in its bearing upon the trade and commerce of the Dominion as a whole, a law passed in "regulation of trade and commerce;" and it may be open to doubt whether their Lordships' decision on the reference of 1896 ought to be regarded as applying to an enactment solely directed to the prohibition of such exports or imports.

On the other hand the enactments of the amending Act are not enactments dealing with a matter falling within any of the classes of matters exclusively assigned to the provinces by section 92 and they are within Dominion competence if they are enactments touching "the peace, order and good government of Canada" which seems too clear for argument. It is argued that such an enactment must be one whose operation extends to the whole of Canada—which this enactment does, conditionally at all events. But I am not prepared without further examination of the point to agree that an enactment in the terms of the Act of 1919 confined in its operation to one province could not be sustained as relating to "the peace, order and good government of Canada." I pass no opinion upon that point.

ANGLIN J.: . . . The legislation of 1919. when brought into force prohibits the importation of intoxicating liquor into those provinces where its sale for beverage purposes is forbidden by provincial law. It was enacted as Part IV (secs. 152 to 156) of the Canada "Temperance Act" (R.S.C. 1960, c. 152) and was passed in order to supplement and make more effective such provincial prohibitory laws. Its true character therefore is temperance legislation rather than legislation regulating the importation of liquor as a matter of trade and commerce. It prohibits; it does not regulate. Moreover, it deals with trade in only one class of commodities. In view of these facts Part IV itself should be regarded, as the Canada "Temperance Act" has been (*Attorney General for Ontario v. Attorney-General for the Dominion*, [1896] A.C. 348, at pp. 362-3; *Attorney-General for Canada v. Attorney-General for Alberta*, [1916] 1 A.C. 588, at p. 597) rather as an exercise of the general power of Parliament to pass laws for the "peace, order and good government of Canada," than ascribable to its powers to legislate for "the regulation of trade and commerce" (the only enumerated head invoked to support it) or authorized by any of the enumerated powers conferred by s. 91 of the B.N.A. Act.

It is common ground that the prohibition of importation is beyond the legislative jurisdiction of the province. It is not covered by any of the enumerated heads of s. 92. It lies outside of the subject matters enumeratively entrusted to the provinces under that section and upon it, therefore, the Dominion Parliament can legislate effectively as regards a Province under its general power "to make laws for the peace, order and good government of Canada": *Attorney-General for Canada v. Attorney General for Alberta*. The Canada Temperance Act itself, the validity of which was upheld in *Russell v. The Queen*, 7 App. Cas. 829, Lord Haldane assures us is an instance of such a case.

The facts that the legislation of 1919 was designed to aid provincial prohibition legislation, that it applies only to certain provinces,—those in which a local prohibition law is from time to time in force,—that it deals with the liquor evil as a matter of local importance in each province affected, and that it interferes with civil rights of the individual citizen safeguarded by the provincial law therefore do not afford arguments against its validity. The propriety of concurrent or supplementary legislation to cover a field which lies partly within the jurisdiction of the provincial legislatures and partly within that of the Dominion Parliament was indicated by Lord Atkinson in delivering the judgment of the Judicial Committee in *City of Montreal v. Montreal Street Railway,* [1912] A.C. 333. ...

Neither is the legislation under consideration in my opinion obnoxious to s. 121 of the B.N.A. Act. The purpose of that section is to ensure that articles of the growth, produce or manufacture of any province shall not be subjected to any customs duty when carried into any other province. Prohibition of import in aid of temperance legislation is not within the purview of the section.

MIGNAULT J.: . . . I take it that the validity of the "Canada Temperance Act" having been affirmed by the Judicial Committee in *Russell v. The Queen,* the amendment of 1919, 10 Geo. V., ch. 8, being legislation of the same character, cannot be assailed as transcending the powers of Parliament.

Nor do I think that any argument can be based on sec. 121 of the British North America Act which states that "all articles of the growth, produce or manufacture of any of the provinces shall, from and after the Union, be admitted free into each of the other provinces."

This section, which so far as I know has never been judicially construed, is in Part VIII of the Act, bearing the heading "Revenues, Debts, Assets, Taxation," and is followed by two sections which deal with customs and excise laws and custom duties.

In the United States constitution, to which reference may be made for purposes of comparison, there is a somewhat similar provision (art. 1, sec. 9, par. 5 and 6) the language of which, however, is much clearer than that of sec. 121. It says:—

"No tax or duty shall be laid on articles exported from any state.

"No preference shall be given, by any regulation of commerce or revenue, to the ports of one state over those of another; nor shall vessels bound to or from one state be obliged to enter, clear or pay duties to another."

I think that, like the enactment I have just quoted, the object of section 121 was not to decree that all articles of the growth, produce or manufacture of any of the provinces should be admitted into the others, but merely to secure that they should be admitted "free," that is to say without any tax or duty imposed as a condition of their admission. The essential word here is "free" and what is prohibited is the levying of customs duties or other charges of a like nature in matters of interprovincial trade. . . .

Appeal dismissed.

[Idington J. dissented on other grounds.]

Note on Requirement of Free Admission of Goods of Provincial Origin

The meaning and effect of section 121 was first considered by the Privy Council, shortly after the *Gold Seal* case was decided, in *Rex v. Nat Bell Liquors Ltd.,* [1922] 2 A.C. 128, at p. 137, 65 D.L.R. 1, at p. 8, [1922] 2 W.W.R. 30, at p. 39, where it declared that "the word 'free' applied to admission into a Province does not further mean that when admitted the article in question can be used in any way its owner chooses . . ." Subsequent judicial consideration of section 121 took its start from the *Gold Seal* case. Thus, in *Atlantic Smoke Shops Ltd. v. Conlon*, [1941] S.C.R. 670, [1941] 4 D.L.R. 129, Crocket J. referred to the *Gold Seal* case as follows: "Whether or not that decision means that the section [121] only applies to Dominion legislation, it plainly implies . . . that the Parliament of Canada may validly go as far as to expressly prohibit the admission from one province to another of any article of the growth, produce or manufacture of another province so long as the prohibition does not involve the imposition of a customs duty". As will be seen from *A.-G. B.C. v. A.-G. Can.*, [1924] A.C. 222, [1923] 4 D.L.R. 669, [1923] 3 W.W.R. 1254, *infra*, the Dominion is not constitutionally restricted in taxing foreign goods, even where they are brought in by a Province. Taschereau J. in the *Conlon* case took up the theme of the *Nat Bell* case on section 121 in saying that "when the commodity has entered into the Province, I see no valid reason why the purchaser could not be compelled to pay a tax to the provincial authorities". When the *Conlon* case reached the Privy Council, that tribunal simply approved the interpretation put upon section 121 by the *Gold Seal* case, and Viscount Simon noted that "the meaning of s. 121 cannot vary according as it is applied to Dominion or to provincial legislation": see [1943] A.C. 550, at p. 569, [1943] 4 D.L.R. 81, at p. 92, [1943] 3 W.W.R. 113, at p. 126.

It was at the hands of Rand J. in *Murphy v. C.P.R. and A.-G. Can.*, [1958] S.C.R. 626, at p. 638, 15 D.L.R. (2d) 145, at p. 150, reproduced *infra* at p. 398 that section 121 got an expanded meaning, taking it beyond a mere taxing limitation. He declared that " 'free' . . . means without impediment related to the traversing of a provincial boundary", and suggested that it might reach burdens for equalizing competition between growers in different provinces, whether those burdens be by way of imposition of a charge or by price-fixing. There is here a connection with the "free trade" provisions of section 92 of the Australian Constitution, provisions which embody a constitutional guarantee of the absolute freedom of trade, commerce and intercourse among the States. The judicial interpretation of this Australian provision has gone much farther than has that of the Canadian section 121 in the restraints that have been declared to arise therefrom against legislative prohibition or control of trade; and, of course, it is not limited to inter-State transactions in goods, as is section 121. In *James v. Commonwealth*, [1936] A.C. 578, 55 C.L.R. 1, Lord Wright said that while "free trade means in ordinary parlance freedom from tariffs", yet "free in s. 92 cannot be limited to freedom in the last mentioned sense". He went on to say in summation that "as a matter of actual language, freedom in s. 92 must be somehow limited, and the only limitation which emerges from the context and which can logically and realistically be applied is freedom at what is the crucial point in inter-State trade, that is at the State barrier". This view is not, of course, self-explanatory; and later cases have gone beyond this limited application of section 92 (for example, in invalidating a federal prohibition of private banking) in attempting to draw the line between permissible regulation by Parliament or State Legislature and unconstitutional interference, whether by pecuniary levies or otherwise, which can be something falling short of absolute prohibition: see *Commonwealth v. Bank of New South Wales*, [1950] A.C. 235, 79 C.L.R. 497; *Hughes & Vale Pty. Ltd. v. New South Wales* (1954), 93 C.L.R. 1; *Hughes & Vale Pty. Ltd. v. New South Wales (No. 2)* (1955), 93 C.L.R. 127; and see also *Lord Wright*, Section 92 —A Problem Piece, (1954) 1 Syd. L. Rev. 145; *Hart*, Some Aspects of Section 92 of the Constitution, (1957) 30 Aust. L.J. 550.

Section 121 does not bear comparison with Article 1, section 10, cl. 2 of the United States Constitution which provides, *inter alia*, that "no State shall without the consent of Congress lay any duties or imposts on imports or exports, except what may be absolutely necessary for executing its inspection laws"; and this is because the United States provision has been construed to refer only to imports from or exports to foreign countries and does not apply to interstate transactions: see *Hooven & Allison Co. v. Evatt* (1945), 324 U.S. 652, 65 S. Ct. 670. It was this constitutional provision that gave rise to the "original package" doctrine as the test for determining how long imported goods remained immune from State taxation: see *Brown v. Maryland* (1827), 12 Wheat. 419. The immunity is lost when the importer parts with the goods or breaks the packages so as to permit the conclusion that the imported goods have become mixed with or part of the mass of the general property in the State, or if the imported goods are subjected to a manufacturing process in the receiving State: see *Youngstown Sheet & Tube Co. v. Bowers* (1959), 358 U.S. 534, 79 S. Ct. 383.

The more important question, however, is whether the federal interstate commerce power is an equally effective brake on state regulatory power in respect of imports (as contrasted simply with State taxing power) and, in any event, whether State taxing power is equally inhibited in respect of interstate imports and exports. In *Bowman v. Chicago & Northwestern Railway Co.* (1888), 125 U.S. 465 and in *Leisy v. Hardin* (1890), 135 U.S. 100, the Supreme Court extended the "original package" doctrine to State regulatory power by holding that a State could not competently prohibit the shipment into a State or the sale therein of intoxicating liquor in the original packages in which it was brought into the State. Congress relieved the situation by invoking its commerce power to subject such liquor to State laws: see *Smith*, The Commerce Power in Canada and the United States (1963), pp. 311-12. The *Gold Seal* case, *supra*, is illustrative of Canadian federal cooperation to support provincial prohibitory policies. It is, however, doubtful whether one can conclude from the *Gold Seal* case that because a Province cannot prohibit imports it cannot prohibit or regulate the sale or distribution or other dealing with the imported goods, at least where the prohibition or regulation is part of a general scheme and not one directed to imported goods. Even if it is, it may be a proper local measure if related to health or sanitary considerations.

At the tax level, the original package doctrine was rejected as not precluding a non-discriminatory state tax on goods imported from another State, at least where Congress had not intervened through an exercise of its commerce power: see *Woodruff v. Parham* (1869), 8 Wall. 123; *Brown v. Houston* (1885), 114 U.S. 622. Beyond this, the doctrine has over the years lost its vitality as a restriction on State regulatory power in respect of interstate commerce: see *Whitfield v. Ohio* (1936), 297 U.S. 431. Effective restriction has come to depend not on Congressional silence but on Congressional exercise of the commerce power: see *Southern Pacific Co. v. Arizona* (1945), 325 U.S. 761, at pp. 766-767, 65 S. Ct. 1515, at pp. 1519-1520; and see also *State Board of Insurance v. Todd Shipyards Corp.* (1962), 370 U.S. 451, 82 S. Ct. 1380, where the Supreme Court said: "The power of Congress to grant protection to interstate commerce against state regulation or taxation . . . or to withhold it . . . is so complete that its ideas of policy should prevail." See *Hartman,* State Taxation of Interstate Commerce: A Survey and An Appraisal, (1960) 46 Va. L. Rev. 1051; *Note,* Federal Limitations on State Taxation of Interstate Commerce, (1962) 75 Harv. L. Rev. 953; *Rutledge,* A Declaration of Legal Faith, pp. 45-73.

The position in Canada can be put even higher on the basis of the decisions to date. Apart from section 121, and possible invalidation of provincial legislation discriminating against imported goods as such, provincial regulatory power may encompass them as may provincial taxing power. It will be seen from *Atlantic Smoke Shops Ltd. v. Conlon, supra,* that provincial direct taxation of consumers, addressed to goods purchased for consumption in the Province, may validly embrace goods brought into the Province for consumption. There has been no development in Canada of any original package or other comparable doctrine to limit provincial regulatory authority over the sale or distribution or processing of goods within the Province although brought in from a foreign country or from another Province. Indeed, there is no reason presently to doubt the power of a Province to establish at least a public monopoly in certain goods or services, or otherwise to exclude competition in intra-provincial dealing. It may be noted that the decisions under section 92 of the Australian Constitution do not absolutely exclude such a possibility in Australia despite the wide protection given to individual or private right to carry on trade and commerce.

[For reliance on the interstate commerce power to preclude a state's right to require an out-of-state mail order firm to collect a use tax, see *National Bellas Hess Inc. v. Illinois Department of Revenue* (1967), 386 U.S. 753.]

A.-G. B.C. v. A.-G. CAN.

In the Privy Council. [1924] A.C. 222, [1923] 4 D.L.R. 669, [1923] 3 W.W.R. 1249.

Appeal from a judgment of the Supreme Court of Canada, 64 S.C.R. 377, [1923] 1 D.L.R. 223, [1923] 1 W.W.R. 241, affirming a judgment of the Exchequer Court, 21 Ex. C.R. 281, 63 D.L.R. 82, denying that appellants were entitled to import goods into the province for sale therein without liability to pay certain federal taxes.

LORD BUCKMASTER: The question raised upon this appeal is whether there is power conferred upon the Dominion Parliament by the British North America Act of 1867 to impose customs duties or excise or sales tax upon goods when they enter the Dominion although they are the property of one of the Provinces. The case arises in the following way:—

The Province of British Columbia in 1921 established Government control and sale of alcoholic liquors by various statutes, enumeration of which is unnecessary. The Dominion Parliament, on the other hand, imposed customs or sales or excise duty upon, among other things, alcoholic liquors, imported into the Dominion. In July of 1921 the appellant, acting as duly authorized agent under the British Columbia Liquor Act, purchased in Great Britain in the name and on behalf of His Majesty in right of the Province one case of "Johnny Walker Black Label" whisky, which was duly shipped from Glasgow and consigned to His Majesty in the right of the Province. Upon demand for delivery of this whisky the Collector of Customs, on behalf of the Dominion Government, refused delivery until payment of the customs duty and excise or sales tax. The appellant denied his right to claim these duties, and took the proceedings out of which this appeal has arisen to test his claim. The statutes under which it was claimed the right to impose such duties arose were the following: s. 2 and item A of the Customs Tariff Act, 1907; s. 2, sub-s. 3 of the Customs Act, 1917; s. 19BBB, sub-s. 1, of the Special War Revenue Act, 1915; and s. 6, sub-s. 1, of the Special War Revenue Act, 1915.

Nothing depends upon the language of these statutes. They admittedly embrace all consignments without distinction of consignee. The question is whether there was power so to legislate.

. . . The real issue lies in determining the true meaning to be given to s. 125 of the *British North America Act,* which provides that "No lands or property belonging to Canada or any Province shall be liable to taxation." Taken alone and read without consideration of the scheme of the statute, this section undoubtedly creates a formidable argument in support of the appellant's case. It is plain, however, that the section cannot be regarded in this isolated and disjunctive way. It is only a part of the general scheme established by the statute with its different allocations of powers and authorities to the Provincial and Dominion Governments. Section 91, which assigns powers to the Dominion, provides, among other things, that it shall enjoy exclusive legislative authority over all matters enumerated in the section, included among which are the regulation of trade and commerce and raising of money by any mode or system of taxation. The imposition of customs duties upon goods imported into any country may have many objects; it may be designed to raise revenue or to regulate trade and commerce by protecting native industries, or it may have the two-fold purpose of attempting to secure both ends; in either case it is a power reserved to the Dominion. It has not indeed been denied that such a general power does exist, but it is said that a breach is created in the tariff wall, which the Dominion has the power to erect, by s. 125, which enables goods of the Province or the Dominion to pass through, unaffected by the duties. But s. 125 cannot, in their Lordships' opinion, be so regarded. It is to be found in a series of sections which, beginning with s. 102, distribute as between the Dominion and the Province certain distinct classes of property, and confer control upon the Province with regard to the part allocated to them. But this does not exclude the operation of Dominion laws made in exercise of the authority conferred by s. 91. The Dominion have the power to regulate trade and commerce throughout the Dominion, and, to the extent to which this power applies, there is no partiality in its operation. Section 125 must, therefore, be so considered as to prevent the paramount purpose thus declared from being defeated.

Appeal dismissed.

Note on Agriculture and Marketing

Among the least illumined areas of constitutional adjudication is that concerned with the scope of the concurrent power in relation to agriculture, given by s. 95 of the B.N.A. Act. There, as much as, if not more than anywhere else in the Act, was an invitation to a working federalism by which problems in the field, if not adequately serviced by provincial legislation, could be taken up or solved through national legislative policies. The possibilities represented by s. 95 have, so far, foundered on a construction of the agriculture power which has drained it of substance, both as a source of provincial legislation and of federal legislation. Neither the Privy Council nor the Supreme Court of Canada had any occasion to consider the "agriculture" power during the first half century following Confederation. Such lower Court decisions as were given on the matter during this period touched what may be reasonably termed the periphery of that class of subject. Clement, writing in the third edition of his Law of the Canadian Constitution (1916) stated that " 'agriculture' has been given a very wide interpretation"; but his extension of this proposition shows the narrow range of the problems arising thereunder. It covered "all matters connected with the farm, such as the care and improvement of stock, horsebreeding, dairying, and kindred matters. As properly falling under this head the federal Animal Contagious Diseases Act has been upheld. And a provincial Act which provided a penalty for fraud in entering horses in a wrong class at race meetings of agricultural associations was considered as competent legislation under this head, there being no federal legislation to which it was repugnant" (at p. 776). When opportunity arose for a wider assessment of agriculture as the potent force that it was and is in the Canadian economy, there was a curious refusal to square legislative power with legislative fact. None of the considerations which moved the Courts to a narrow view of both the general power and the trade and commerce power were operable in respect of s. 95. Yet the resulting construction of the "agriculture" power, juxtaposed to that of the "trade and commerce" power, created a definite hiatus in regulatory possibilities. On the one hand, the former would not support regulation of trade in natural products (although it might support control at the production stage) while the latter could not embrace production and was limited, in respect of trade regulation, to interprovincial and export aspects in their strict sense. The expansion of the trade and commerce power, of which evidence is slowly accumulating, may very well make it unnecessary to rely on revitalization of the "agriculture" power to support national marketing policies respecting products of the soil. If this happens, it will provide another instance of a rather unnecessary reduction, not to say obliteration, of an express power.

A recent judgment sustaining the Fertilizers Act, R.S.C. 1970, chapter F9, specifying the composition and labelling of fertilizer, expressly on the basis of s. 95, *R. v. Bradford Fertilizer Co.*, [1972] 1 O.R. 229, 22 D.L.R. (3d) 617, 5 C.C.C. (2d) 325, suggests some continuing scope for it where dealings in farm produce are not involved.

[In *Lower Mainland Dairy Products Sales Adjustment Committee v. Crystal Dairy Ltd.*, [1933] A.C. 168, at p. 174, [1933] 1 D.L.R. 82, at p. 85, [1932] 3 W.W.R. 639, at p. 642, Lord Thankerton rejected an argument based on the agriculture power in support of a provincial equalization scheme respecting the marketing of milk and milk products, saying that the argument was untenable because the provincial Act "does not appear in any way to interfere with the agricultural operations of the farmers, and s. 21 of the Act expressly prohibits the Committee from fixing prices at which milk or manufactured products may be sold and from directing in what quantity, to whom or when milk or manufactured products may be sold or disposed of by a dairy farmer". When the matter arose again for judicial decision under a price fixing statute, no consideration was given to the agriculture power as a possible support for the scheme: see *Lower Mainland Dairy Products Board v. Turner's Dairy Ltd.*, [1941] S.C.R. 573, [1941] 4 D.L.R. 209, aff'g [1941] 2 D.L.R. 279, [1941] 1 W.W.R. 342.]

THE KING v. EASTERN TERMINAL ELEVATOR CO.

In the Supreme Court of Canada. [1925] S.C.R. 434, [1925] 3 D.L.R. 1.

Appeal from a judgment of the Exchequer Court, [1924] Ex. C.R. 167, holding s. 95(7) of the Canada Grain Act, 1912 (Can.), c. 27, am. 1919 (1st sess.), c. 40, s. 3; 1919 (2nd sess.), c. 6, s. 1, *ultra vires*.

ANGLIN C.J.C. (dissenting) : I understand that a majority of the court has reached the conclusion that the judgment of the Exchequer Court holding s-s. 7 of s. 95 of the *Canada Grain Act* to be *ultra vires* must be affirmed. That the impugned subsection is not necessary to the project of the statute and that, taken alone, it encroaches on the provincial domain of local works and undertakings and property and civil rights (B.N.A. Act, s. 92(10)(13)), I conceive to be the basis of the judgment of the learned President of the Exchequer Court; and his view is shared by some members of this court. Another opinion condemns s.-s. 7 as an incidental provision in a statute that does not come under any of the heads of Dominion legislative jurisdiction enumerated in s. 91 and contains many essential features which impinge on the provincial field and are so interwoven with other provisions, possibly in themselves unobjectionable, as not to be readily severable from them. Such legislation, they maintain, cannot be supported under the general power vested in Parliament to legislate for the peace, order and good government of Canada.

No good purpose will be served by an elaborate exposition of the reasons which lead me respectfully to dissent from these views. I shall, therefore, merely outline them.

Assuming that the *Canada Grain Act* as a whole is *intra vires* of Parliament, s.-s. 7 of s. 95 seems to me to be defensible as an incidental enactment designed to promote the attainment of the purposes of the Act. It not only provides for the obtaining of revenue from persons and corporations instrumental and beneficially interested in the carrying out of the scheme which it sanctions, and to be applied towards the cost of working it, but it furnishes, perhaps, the best possible security that one of the main operations for which the Act provides, namely, the cleaning of the grain so that it will actually conform to the grade and quality called for by the Government certificate based on its prior inspection, will be honestly and efficiently carried out. It removes the greatest inducement to fraud or carelessness in the cleaning. Moreover any property right of the respondent in the surplus grain left in its elevator is very doubtful. The subsection would also seem to be defensible as regulatory of the licensed elevator company's remuneration. I cannot regard it as confiscatory. *Toronto v. Can. Pac. Ry. Co.*, [1908] A.C. 54. If Parliament has jurisdiction over the subject matter of the legislation as a whole, I am not prepared to condemn this ancillary provision as in excess of its powers.

The object of Parliament in enacting the *Canada Grain Act* was, in my opinion, to provide for the economical, expeditious and profitable export and marketing abroad of what is to-day the most valuable product of Canada—the most important subject of its trade and commerce—its greatest source of wealth. The scheme of the Act is the constitution and regulation of machinery to effectuate that purpose. It provides, as only the Dominion Parliament can, for the control and handling of the grain from the moment it leaves the hands of the grower—practically always in one of the Western Provinces—until its shipment in Ontario or one of the eastern provinces for the foreign market accompanied by a government certificate of its grade and quality, upon the acceptance of which in that market the Canadian shipper can depend. Main features of this scheme are the inspection of the grain in transit at Winnipeg by Dominion Government officials and the cleaning, storing and handling of it, subsequent to inspection, under such control and supervision that it can properly and safely be accompanied on shipment by the Government certificate of grade and quality which forms the basis of our Canadian foreign grain trade. No single province could legislate to cover this field. Concurrent legislation by all the provinces interested, if practicable (which I doubt), would be ineffectual to accomplish the purpose. Dominion legislation is required.

Apart from the fact that a provincial certificate would not carry
the weight and authority attaching to a certificate issued under
Dominion sanction, the necessary control over transit and handling
in different provinces and ultimate shipment could not be exercised
under provincial legislation.

I regard the subject matter of the Canada Grain Act, therefore,
as lying outside the scope of the powers entrusted to the legislatures
by the sixteen heads of provincial legislative jurisdiction contained in
s. 92. *Insurance reference,* [1916] 1 A.C. 588.

It is established that in legislation properly ascribable to the exercise of jurisdiction conferred by one of the enumerative heads of s.
91 of the B.N.A. Act, the Dominion Parliament is supreme. Such
legislation even in provisions properly ancillary, may deal with
matters that would fall under provincial jurisdiction, if they were
not appurtenant to a subject specifically assigned to the Dominion.
Viscount Haldane, in the judgment cited, attributes the like right to
Parliament "when the subject matter (of its legislation) lies outside
all the subject matters enumeratively entrusted to the province under
s. 92. . . ."

Although counsel for the appellants invoked several of the enumerated heads of Dominion legislative power—the regulation of trade
and commerce, the raising of money by any mode or system of taxation, weights and measures (s. 91, s-ss. 2, 3, and 17), inter- and extra-
provincial transportation (s. 92(10)), and agriculture (s. 95)—the
only one of them within which, in my opinion, the *Canada Grain Act*
as a whole might fall would be "the regulation of trade and commerce," unless, perhaps, inter- and extra-provincial transportation
might also be invoked. Attempts to uphold Dominion legislation
under head no. 2 of s. 91 have hitherto received little encouragement
from the Judicial Committee. . . . In *Montreal v. Montreal Street
Railway Co.,* [1912] A.C. 333, . . . the power of Parliament when
legislating under this head to make laws applicable throughout Canada
in regard to matters which in each province are substantially matters
of local or private interest was held to be subject to like restrictions
as those which apply to its general power to legislate for the peace,
order and good government of Canada in regard to subjects not
enumerated in s. 91. Such legislation, as Lord Watson pointed out in
the *Local Prohibition* case, [1896] A.C. 348, at p. 360, "ought not to
trench on provincial legislation in respect to any of the subjects
enumerated in s. 92. . . ."

. . . While it is held that the power to regulate trade and commerce, operating independently and as an enumerated head of Federal
legislative jurisdiction, does not justify such an encroachment, the
Board of Commerce case and the Lemieux Act decision are authority
for the statement that it may do so in furtherance or aid of powers
conferred by the general language of s. 91. With the utmost respect,
I fail to appreciate the reasoning on which this view is based. If
neither the power conferred by the general language of s. 91, nor the
power under the enumerative head No. 2, to regulate trade and commerce, taken independently, warrants Dominion legislation which
trenches on the provincial field, if both powers are subject in this

respect to the like restriction, [1912] A.C. 333 at p. 344, I find rather elusive and difficult to understand the foundation for the view that legislation authorized only by the former may be so helped out by the latter that invasion by it of the provincial domain may thus be justified. But the decisive authority of the judgments which have so determined cannot now be questioned in this court. I defer to it.

If the view be sound that the subject matter of the Canada Grain Act, because it has mainly to do with the export trade in grain and the inter-provincial handling of it, and because of the magnitude of that trade and its vital importance to the entire trade and commerce of Canada—to its very solvency as a nation—is not "within the class of matters of a local or private nature comprised in the enumeration of classes of subjects assigned exclusively to the legislatures of the provinces," but lies outside that field and accordingly falls within "the Dominion powers conferred by the general language of s. 91," may not "the regulation of trade and commerce," on the authority of . . . the *Wharton* case [1915] A.C. 330, the *Board of Commerce* case and the *Lemieux Act* case, be invoked as "aiding Dominion powers conferred by general language of s. 91" and "in furtherance of a general power which the Dominion Parliament possesses independently of it" to support any necessary interference by the provisions of that Dominion statute with what might otherwise be regarded as subjects of provincial legislative jurisdiction?

But for their Lordships' emphatic and reiterated allocation of "the regulation of trade and commerce" to this subordinated and wholly auxiliary function, my inclination would have been to accord to it some independent operation, such as was indicated in *Parsons'* case, and within that sphere, however, limited, to treat it as appropriating exclusively to the Dominion Parliament an enumerated subject of legislative jurisdiction with consequences similar to those which attach to the other twenty-eight enumerative heads of s. 91. It is incontrovertible and readily apprehended that the subject matter of head No. 2 must be restricted as was indicated in *Parsons'* case of which the authority has been frequently recognized in later decisions of the Judicial Committee. But that it should be denied all efficacy as an independent enumerative head of Dominion legislative jurisdiction—that it must be excluded from the operation of the concluding paragraph of s. 91, except for the subsidiary and auxilliary purposes indicated in recent decisions,—these are propositions to which I find it difficult to accede. They seem to me, with deference, to conflict with fundamental canons of construction and with the views expressed in *Parsons'* case. I am far from convinced that the regulation of Canada's export trade in grain, including all provisions properly ancillary to its efficient exercise, may not legitimately be held to come within Dominion legislative power conferred by clause No. 2 of sec. 91 operating independently as an enumerative head of federal jurisdiction. *Gold Seal, Limited v. Attorney General for Alberta*, 62 S.C.R. 424.

But apart from any assistance afforded by head No. 2 of s. 91 I would uphold the Canada Grain Act as a statute of which the "subject matter lies outside all of the subject matters enumeratively entrusted to the provinces under s. 92," in which case, said Lord Haldane in the *Insurance Reference,* "the Dominion Parliament can legislate effectively as regards a province." His Lordship cites *Russell v. The Queen* as an instance of such a case.

In my view not only is the grain trade of Canada a matter of national concern and of such dimensions as to affect the body politic of the Dominion, but the provisions of the Canada Grain Act, with some possible exceptions, deal with matters which, as envisaged by that legislation, do not "come within that class of matters of a local or private nature . . . assigned exclusively to the legislatures of the provinces." As to most of them there is, therefore, no encroachment on the provincial domain. To enable the Dominion Government to exercise legislative control over links in the inter-provincial and extra-provincial operations of handling and transporting export grain so important as terminal elevators, I cannot think it necessary that each of them should be declared by Parliament to be a work for the general advantage of Canada, or for the advantage of two or more provinces, although such declarations might, no doubt, with propriety be made. Any sections of the Canada Grain Act which may involve undue invasion of the provincial field could probably be readily identified and severed. None such has been shewn to be vital to the scheme of the Act as a whole.

So regarded the Canada Grain Act may, I think, be supported without having recourse to the existence of abnormal conditions involving some extraordinary peril to the national life of Canada, recently indicated as a justification for the invasion by Parliament of the provincial field when legislating under the general power conferred by s. 91. But if there should be in the statute provisions essential to its effective operation for the purpose aimed at which must be regarded as trenching on the provincial domain, and if it should therefore be deemed necessary to meet this test of their validity, I know of nothing more likely to create a national emergency in Canada than a judicial determination that the Dominion Parliament lacks the power to legislate for the regulation of the export grain trade of the country. It cannot be that Parliament must defer legislative action until a national emergency with attendant disaster has developed. To protect the national interest it assuredly may anticipate and ward off such an evil. There is an emergency connected with the movement of the grain crop at the end of each season incontrovertibly greater than any which can be supposed to have existed in 1878 with regard to the liquor traffic, and it is noteworthy that this emergency is specially recognized by Parliament in the provisions of the Bank Act for relaxing the restrictions upon the issue of paper money. Regarded as legislation essential to prevent such a financial crisis as would be not unlikely to ensue upon the relinquishment, voluntary or forced, of Dominion control over the grain trade, the Canada Grain Act might well withstand the test of validity suggested in the *Board of Commerce,* the *Fort Frances* and the *Lemieux Act* cases. . .

DUFF J.: The Grain Act was passed in 1912. The authors of the legislation proceeded upon the view upon which the Dominion Parliament had acted in 1910 in enacting the Insurance Act, that, in exercise of the powers given by sec. 91(2), for the regulation of trade and commerce, the Dominion Parliament could, by a system of licences and otherwise regulate individual trades, both locally and in respect of interprovincial and external trade. The Act provides for a Board, to be known as the Board of Grain Commissioners, to be appointed by the Governor in Council, and this Board is invested with very wide powers. By sec. 20, the Board is empowered, with the consent of the Governor in Council, to make rules and regulations for the government, control and licensing of terminal and other elevators. [His Lordship here set out the material licensing provisions of the Act.] . . .

The Act is an attempt to regulate, directly and through the instrumentality of Grain Commissioners, the occupations mentioned. It is also an attempt to regulate generally elevators as warehouses for grain, and the business of operating them; and it seems, *ex facie*, to come within the decision of the Judicial Committee, *Attorney-General for Canada v. Attorney General for Alberta*, condemning the Insurance Act of 1910 as *ultra vires*.

Mr. Symington, in a very able argument, attempted to support the Act on the ground that the trade in grain is largely an external trade (between seventy and eighty per cent, apparently, of the grain produced in the country is exported); and that the provisions of the Act are, on the whole, an attempt to regulate a branch of external trade, the provisions dealing with local matters being, as a rule, subsidiary and reasonably ancillary to the main purpose of the Act.

It is undeniable that one principal object of this Act is to protect the external trade in grain, and especially in wheat, by ensuring the integrity of certificates issued by the Grain Commission in respect of the quality of grain, and especially of wheat, and the beneficent effect and the value of the system provided by the legislation as a whole is not at all disputed by anybody. I do not think it is fairly disputable, either, that the Dominion possesses legislative powers, in respect of transport (by its authority over Dominion railways, over lines of ships connecting this country with foreign countries, over navigation and shipping); in respect of weights and measures; in respect of trade and commerce, interpreted as that phrase has been interpreted; which would enable it effectively, by properly framed legislation, to regulate this branch of external trade for the purpose of protecting it, by ensuring correctness in grading and freedom from adulteration, as well as providing for effective and reliable public guarantees as to quality. It does not follow that it is within the power of Parliament to accomplish this object by assuming, as this legislation does, the regulation in the provinces of particular occupations, as such, by a licensing system and otherwise, and of local works and undertakings, as such, however important and beneficial the ultimate purpose of the legislation may be. There are, no doubt, many provisions of this statute which, as they stand, can be sustained; with them we are not concerned at this moment. The particular provision which is sought to be enforced is one of a series of provisions which are designed to regulate elevators and the occupations of those who make it their business to operate elevators. The particular provision, if it stood alone, might, perhaps, be sustained as a tax, but it cannot be separated from its context; it is only one part of a scheme for the regulation of elevators. There is one way in which the Dominion may acquire authority to regulate a local work such as an elevator; and that is, by a declaration properly framed under section 92(10) of the B.N.A. Act. See *Union Colliery Co. of B.C. v. Bryden*, [1899] A.C. 580. This, of course, is not to say that there may not be elevators subject to Dominion control, as being, for example, adjuncts of the undertaking of a Dominion railway or of a company operating a line of steamships under Dominion jurisdiction; but the general regulation of all elevators is a different matter.

There are two lurking fallacies in the argument advanced on behalf of the Crown: first, that, because in large part the grain trade is an export trade, you can regulate it locally in order to give effect to your policy in relation to the regulation of that part of it which is export. Obviously that is not a principle the application of which can be ruled by percentages. If it is operative when the export trade is seventy per cent. of the whole, it must be equally operative when that percentage is only thirty; and such a principle in truth must postulate authority in the Dominion to assume the regulation of almost any trade in the country, provided it does so by setting up a scheme embracing the local, as well as the external and interprovincial trade; and regulation of trade, according to the conception of it which governs this legislation, includes the regulation in the provinces of the occupations of those engaged in the trade, and of the local establishments in which it is carried on. Precisely the same thing was attempted in the Insurance Act of 1910, unsuccessfully. The other fallacy is (the two are, perhaps, different forms of the same error), that the Dominion has such power because no single province, nor, indeed, all the provinces acting together, could put into effect such a sweeping scheme. The authority arises, it is said, under the residuary clause because of the necessary limits of the provincial authority. This is precisely the view which was advanced in the *Board of Commerce* case and, indeed, is the view which was unsuccessfully put forward in the *Montreal Street Railway* case, where it was pointed out that in a system involving a division of powers such as that set up by the British North America Act, it may often be that subsidiary legislation by the provinces or by the Dominion is required to give full effect to some beneficial and necessary scheme of legislation not entirely within the powers of either . . . .

Fortunately, however, . . . the control possessed by the Dominion over the subject-matters mentioned, and especially over transport (both land transport and water transport) and over external trade, would really appear to be amply sufficient to enable the Dominion, by appropriately framed legislation, effectively to secure the essential objects of this statute.

MIGNAULT J.: In this case, His Majesty the King, in right of the Dominion of Canada, the appellant, claims from the respondent, the Eastern Terminal Elevator Company, Limited, operating, under a license issued by the Board of Grain Commissioners a public terminal elevator at Port Arthur, Ontario, the surplus of grain in excess of one-quarter of one per cent., alleged to be 1,107,330 pounds, found in its elevator at the close of the crop year ending 31st August, 1920, or the sum of $43,431.20, value of this surplus of grain. The action is based on subsection 7 of section 95 of The Canada Grain Act . . . Subsection 7 in its present form, reads as follows:

"7. In the month of August in each year, stock shall be taken of the quantity of each grade of grain in the terminal elevators; if in any year after the crop year ending the thirty-first day of August, 1919, the total surplus of grain is found in excess of one-quarter of one per-cent. of the gross amount of the grain received in the elevator during the crop year, such excess surplus shall be sold annually by the Board of Grain Commissioners and the proceeds thereof paid to the said Board. Such proceeds shall be applied towards the cost of the administration of *The Canada Grain Act* in such manner as the Governor in Council may direct."

The respondent denies that there was any such surplus of grain in its elevator on August 31, 1920, and, in the alternative, alleges that the said subsection, as well as *The Canada Grain Act* itself, always were and are now *ultra vires* of the Parliament of the Dominion.

The first point involves the mode of calculation of the surplus of grain in excess of one-quarter of one per cent. It will however not be necessary to deal with this question if, on the second point, the conclusion be that subsection 7, or *The Canada Grain Act* of which it is a part, was not competently enacted by Parliament. The latter question therefore must be first considered.

Before doing so, however, it will be convenient to state how the grain trade of Canada is carried on under the authority of *The Canada Grain Act*, which was first enacted in 1912.

This statute divides Canada into two subdivisions for inspectional purposes, the Western division (by far the most important) comprising that part of the Dominion to the west of the cities of Port Arthur and Fort William, these two cities included, and the Eastern Division which lies to the east of Port Arthur.

The practice followed in the Western Division, from the time the grain leaves the farm until it reaches a terminal elevator and is shipped to its ultimate market, may be conveniently stated in the language of the learned trial judge.

"The producing farmer usually sells, or stores, his grain to or in what is termed a country elevator, the business of which is to store grain for a charge, or to purchase the same outright. He may store on the basis of receiving the identical grain, or grain of the same grade at a terminal elevator. He may also load his grain on a car consigned to a commission agent to sell for his account. In due course, the grain is forwarded to a terminal elevator at say Port Arthur and in transit thereto, passes through Winnipeg, where the first inspection under the Grain Act takes place. An inspection certificate issues from the office of the chief inspector of grain of the Western Division, setting forth for whose account the grain was inspected, the number of the car, the railway station shipped from, the kind of grain, the grade, and the percentage of dockage, if any, "dockage" meaning the inspectors' estimate of unmarketable grain and foreign matter in the carload, which must be removed by the terminal elevator when cleaning the same. This non-commercial grain and foreign matter when separated from the grain at the terminal elevator are called "screenings." If the grain is considered sufficiently clean by the inspector, or is estimated not to contain more than three-fourths of one per cent. of foreign or unclean matter, the carload is marked as "clean," and is stored with grain of the same kind and grade when it reaches a terminal elevator.

"The inspected car then proceeds to Fort William or Port Arthur, the inspectors' certificate reaching there at the same time or earlier, and then being in the possession of an officer of the Board. The grain is subsequently weighed into an elevator, and pursuant to the Grain Act a certificate of weight is issued. This certificate shews the number of the car, the place where weighed, the date, the kind of grain and the weight of the carload of grain. Thereupon, and in conformity with the Grain Act, the receiving elevator issues to the owner of the grain a terminal warehouse receipt to the effect that it was received and holds, subject to the order of the owner, a specified quantity of a definite kind of grain expressed in bushels of an inspected and designated grade, to be stored with grain of the same grade. The quantity is the weight of the carload, less the deduction for dockage. The grain, or grain of the same grade, is deliverable upon the return of the warehouse receipt, properly endorsed by the holder thereof, and upon payment of storage and other charges. The certificate further states that the grain will be kept stored and insured for the benefit of the person to whose order the receipt is issued or his assignee and in conformity with the provisions and conditions of the laws of Canada relating to the warehousing of grain. The evidence shews that Canadian grain is usually sold in international markets, on the certified grades established by the inspection under the Grain Act, and the certificate shewing the grades accompanies the shipment to the ultimate market. Grain exported from Australia, India or Argentina is usually purchased on the basis of fair average quality on arbitration." . . .

Coming now to the constitutional point, the scope of the Canada Grain Act must be stated as briefly as possible. A complete analysis of the statute with its 248 sections would necessarily be very lengthy; and it has therefore seemed preferable to emphasize its main features, rather than to follow their application in minute detail to such a complex problem as the Canadian grain trade.

This problem, being largely a geographical one, the Act divides the Dominion into the two inspection divisions to which I have already referred (section 21). And as the economical transportation of the grain to its market is one of the chief objects which Parliament has in view, the statute deals with terminal elevators for the storage of the grain (sections 122 et seq.), the most important of which are at the head of the great lakes, at Port Arthur and Fort William in Ontario, and with country elevators along the railways and near the farms (sections 151 et seq.) for the receipt and storage of the grain prior to its shipment en route for the seaboard. We are told that these country elevators in Manitoba, Saskatchewan and Alberta number some 4,000. We are also informed that ninety per cent. of the shipments out of the terminal elevators are made by water.

The general administration of the Grain Act is entrusted to a Board called the Board of Grain Commissioners for Canada, consisting of three commissioners (one termed the Chief Commissioner), appointed by the Governor-in-Council, who hold office during good behaviour for a period of ten years, subject to removal by the same authority for cause (sections 3 et seq.). The duties of this Board are multifarious and are explained in a large number of sections to which it is impossible to refer in detail.

Two great objects are dealt with throughout the Act, the inspection of the grain and its proper grading.

The inspection determines the grade of the grain which is specified in the certificate granted by the inspecting officer. The Act contains elaborate provisions as to the grading of the different qualities of grain (sections 105 et seq.). All grain produced in Manitoba, Saskatchewan and Alberta and in the North-west Territories (and much the larger part of Canadian grain is produced in these provinces and territories, passing through the Winnipeg district, is inspected at Winnipeg or a point within the district, and on grain so inspected the inspection is final (section 91). All grain of the same grade is kept together and stored in the terminal elevators only with a grain of a similar grade (section 94). It is binned under the direction, supervision and control of the inspecting officer, who has full control of all grain in terminal elevators, and no grain is shipped out of, transferred or removed from any terminal elevator without his supervision (section 95). The Act provides for the appointment of a grain survey board to which an appeal against the grading of grain may be brought by the owner or possessor of the grain (sections 101 et seq.). It also makes provisions for the granting of warehouse receipts for the grain stored in terminal elevators (sections 127 et seq.).

I have mentioned several times the country and terminal elevators. The latter are often called public elevators as distinguished from private elevators. These public elevators include every elevator or warehouse which receives grain for storage from the western inspection division after it has been inspected under the Act (section

2, subsection (w)). There are, the evidence shows, a large number of private elevators at terminal points. I have found nothing in the Grain Act specifically dealing with them. But the Act mentions hospital and mill elevators, the names of which are sufficiently descriptive. There are also what are known as flat warehouses (sections 180 *et seq.*). The owner of a terminal elevator cannot buy or sell grain (section 123), but this prohibition is not extended to the country elevators.

The licensing system under the Act is most elaborate, and here we find compulsory features which shew that the statute really regulates the Canadian grain trade. Section 119 states that the Board of Grain Commissioners shall "require all track buyers (these are persons who buy grain by the car load, see sections 218 *et seq.*) and owners and operators of elevators (this term is possibly wide enough to include private elevators), warehouses and mills, and all grain commission merchants and primary grain dealers to take out annual licences". The requirement of a license is again specifically mentioned in section 122 for terminal elevators, in section 124 for hospital elevators, in sections 153 and 238 for country elevators, in section 218 for track buyers, and in section 219a for primary grain dealers. Licences granted can be revoked by the Board for cause.

The Act contains several other prohibitions and imposes penalties for various offences with which it is impossible to deal in detail without unduly lengthening this statement of the main features of the statute. Enough, however, has been said to shew that the Grain Act is an elaborate scheme of regulation of the Canadian grain trade . . .

If it be conceded that Parliament can deal with the regulation of the Canadian grain trade, with the licensing of those who take part in it, with the prohibition to operate terminal or country elevators without a licence, and with the operation generally of these elevators, I confess that I would have great difficulty in following the contention that Parliament cannot also deal, as was done by sub-section 7, with the disposal of the surplus of grain, if any, which remains in a public terminal elevator after the latter has delivered all the grain for which it has issued warehouse receipts. It is rather because sub-section 7 is a part of such a statute as I have described that I think its validity cannot be supported.

I am constrained to this conclusion by successive pronouncements of the Judicial Committee. . . .

. . . In my opinion, this legislation cannot be brought under any of the heads of section 91 of the British North America Act, as they have been construed, and it would certainly, within any of the provinces, have been competent provincial legislation under section 92. This is decisive of the question at issue.

I have not overlooked the appellant's contention that the statute can be supported under section 95 of the British North America Act as being legislation concerning agriculture. It suffices to answer that the subject-matter of the Act is not agriculture but a product of agriculture considered as an article of trade. The regulation of a particular trade, and that is what this statute is in substance, cannot be attempted by the Dominion on the ground that it is a trade in natural products. What we have here is trade legislation and not a law for the encouragement or support of agriculture, however wide a meaning may be given to the latter term.

I express no opinion on the question whether the grain surplus dealt with by subsection 7 is the property of the respondent. I merely agree, for the reasons above stated, with the holding of the learned trial judge that this subsection is *ultra vires* and that the action fails.

Appeal dismissed.

[Idington J. agreed in the result. Rinfret J. concurred with Duff J.

Following the foregoing judgment, the Dominion enacted the Canada Grain Act, 1925 (Can.), c. 33, which became R.S.C. 1927, c. 86, and by s. 233 thereof "all grain elevators and warehouses . . . mentioned in this Act . . . whether heretofore constructed or hereafter to be constructed are and each of them is hereby declared to be works or a work for the general advantage of Canada; and for greater certainty but not so as to restrict the generality of the foregoing terms of this section it is hereby declared that each and every one of the grain elevators mentioned or described in the second schedule of this Act is a work for the general advantage of Canada." This Act was repealed and replaced by the Canada Grain Act, 1930 (Can.), c. 5, save as to s. 233 which was preserved by s. 171 of the new Act. However, s. 233 was repealed by s. 13 of 1950 (Can.), c. 24; and s. 10 of this last Act enacted s. 173 of the Canada Grain Act, 1930 (Can.), c. 5 which states boldly and without enumeration or schedule that "all elevators in Canada heretofore or hereafter constructed are hereby declared to be works for the general advantage of Canada." See now Canada Grain Act, R.S.C. 1970, c. G-16, s. 174. Cf. Canadian Wheat Board Act, R.S.C. 1970, c. C-12, s. 45.

Does a parliamentary declaration under s. 92(10(c) of the B.N.A. Act, in respect of grain elevators give the Dominion any power to appropriate grain in such elevators? See *Canadian Wheat Board v. Manitoba Pool Elevators,* [1948] 2 D.L.R. 726, [1948] 1 W.W.R. 945, aff'd [1949] 2 D.L.R. 537, [1949] 1 W.W.R. 599, 57 Man. R. 1, aff'd [1951] S.C.R. 81, [1951] 1 D.L.R. 466, rev'd [1952] A.C. 427, [1952] 3 D.L.R. 433, 6 W.W.R. (N.S.) 23.

A.-G. B.C. v. A.-G. CAN.

In the Privy Council.   [1937] A.C. 377, [1937] 1 D.L.R. 691, [1937] 1 W.W.R. 328.

Appeal by special leave from a judgment of the Supreme Court of Canada, [1936] S.C.R. 398, [1936] 3 D.L.R. 622, holding unanimously that the Natural Products Marketing Act, 1934 (Can.), c. 57, am. 1935, c. 64, was *ultra vires*. Section 3 of the Act empowered the Governor-General in Council to establish a Dominion Marketing Board, and s. 4(1) empowered the Board

"(a)   to regulate the time and place at which, and to designate the agency through which the regulated product shall be marketed, to determine the manner of distribution, the quantity and quality, grade or class of the regulated product that shall be marketed by any person at any time, and to prohibit the marketing of any of the regulated product of any grade, quality or class; . . .

"(f)   to require any or all persons engaged in the production or marketing of the regulated product to register their names, addresses and occupations with the Board, or to obtain a licence from the Board, and such licence shall be subject to cancellation by the Board for violation of any provision of this Act or regulation made thereunder;"

By s. 5 provision was made for marketing schemes to be administered by a local board under the supervision of the Dominion Board and it was provided that before any scheme was approved the Governor-General in Council should be satisfied that the principal market for the natural product is outside the province of production, or that some part of the product produced may be exported.

LORD ATKIN: . . . The [Natural Products Marketing] Act consists of two parts. The first provides for the establishment of a Dominion Marketing Board whose powers include powers to regulate the time and place at which, and the agency through which, natural products to which an approved scheme relates shall be marketed, and to determine the manner of distribution and the quantity, quality, grade or class of the product that shall be marketed by any person at any time, and to prohibit the marketing of any of the regulated products of any grade, quality or class.

There are other regulatory powers which need not be further specified. A scheme to regulate the marketing of a natural product is initiated by a representative number of persons engaged in the production or marketing of the natural product. It can be referred by the appropriate Minister to the Board, and if they approve the scheme as submitted or amended by them, and it is further approved by the Minister, the Governor General in Council may approve the scheme. It is essential that the Governor General in Council shall be satisfied either that the principal market for the natural product is outside the Province of production, or that some part of the product produced may be exported. The latter provision makes it clear that the regulation may apply to marketing transactions in natural products which have nothing to do with foreign, export or inter-Provincial trade. If the Minister is satisfied that trade and commerce in a natural product are injuriously affected by the absence of a scheme prepared as above he may himself propose a scheme for approval of the Governor in Council. The Governor in Council is given power by order or regulation to regulate or restrict importation into Canada of a natural product which enters Canada in competition with a regulated product: and to regulate or restrict the exportation from Canada of any natural product. Part II contains provision for the appointment by the Minister of a Committee who may be entrusted with the duty of investigating all matters connected with the production or marketing of natural or regulated products for the purpose of ascertaining the charges made in distribution of a natural or regulated product. The receipt against the interest of the public of an excessive charge is made an indictable offence, and there are provisions for the trial of such offences.

There can be no doubt that the provisions of the Act cover transactions in any natural product which are complete within the Province, and have no connection with inter-Provincial or export trade. It is therefore plain that the Act purports to affect property and civil rights in the Province, and if not brought within one of the enumerated classes of subjects in s. 91 must be beyond the competence of the Dominion Legislature. It was sought to bring the Act within the class (2) of s. 91—namely, The Regulation of Trade and Commerce. Emphasis was laid upon those parts of the Act which deal with inter-Provincial and export trade. But the regulation of trade and commerce does not permit the regulation of individual forms of trade or commerce confined to the Province . . .

. . . There was a further attempt to support the Act upon the general powers to legislate for the peace, order, and good government of Canada. Their Lordships have already dealt with this matter in their previous judgments in this series and need not repeat what is there said. The judgment of the Chief Justice in this case is conclusive against the claim for validity on this ground. In the result, therefore, there is no answer to the contention that the Act in substance invades the Provincial field and is invalid. It was, however, urged before us that portions of the Act, notably s. 9 in the first Part, and the whole of Part II, are within the competence of Parliament. Sect. 9 because it only purports to deal with inter-Provincial or export trade; and Part II because it goes no further than the similar provisions in the Combines Investigation Act, and is a genuine exercise of the Dominion legislative authority over criminal law. Reference was made to s. 26 of the Act, which is in these terms:

"If it be found that Parliament has exceeded its powers in the enactment of one or more of the provisions of this Act, none of the other or remaining provisions of the Act shall therefore be held to be inoperative or *ultra vires*, but the latter provisions shall stand as if they had been originally enacted as separate and independent enactments and as the only provisions of the Act; the intention of Parliament being to give independent effect to the extent of its powers to every enactment and provision in this Act contained."

It is said that this is a plain indication of the intention of the Legislature to pass any portion of the Act which might be valid in itself, in however truncated form the whole Act is left after rejecting the other portions. Moreover, counsel for British Columbia urged the Board to make a declaration that it was only so far as authority was conferred on the Board to deal with local matters not necessarily ancillary to the main power that the Act was *ultra vires,* and that the validity of each scheme must be determined as matters arise under it. No such declaration was asked for from the Supreme Court. British Columbia did not even appear at the hearing in Canada: and there is no claim for such a declaration in the case filed before this Board. It is of special importance in constitutional questions that this Board should, if possible, have the assistance of the opinion

of the members of the Supreme Court: and as a general rule the
Board will not be prepared in such cases to entertain claims for relief
which have never been formulated in the Dominion Court. In no
event, therefore, would they have acceded to the request for such a
declaration as mentioned above. It does appear that the question of
severability was raised in the factums of the Dominion and Ontario,
and their Lordships were told, and of course accept the statement,
that this point was mentioned to the Supreme Court. It cannot, they
think, have been emphasized, for the very careful judgment of the
Court makes no mention of it. There appear to be two answers. In
the first place, it appears to their Lordships that the whole texture
of the Act is inextricably interwoven, and that neither s. 9 nor Part
II can be contemplated as existing independently of the provisions as
to the creation of a Board and the regulation of products. There are
no separate and independent enactments to which s. 26 could give a
real existence. In the second place, both the Dominion and British
Columbia in their Cases filed on this appeal assert that the sections
now said to be severable are incidental and ancillary to the main
legislation. Their Lordships are of opinion that this is true: and that
as the main legislation is invalid as being in pith and substance an
encroachment upon the Provincial rights the sections referred to must
fall with it as being in part merely ancillary to it. This relieves them
from the task of deciding whether they would have been justified,
when dealing with constitutional issues of this importance, in giving
effect to arguments inconsistent with the reasons formally put before
the Board in the filed Cases of the respective parties.

The Board were given to understand that some of the Provinces
attach much importance to the existence of marketing schemes such
as might be set up under this legislation; and their attention was
called to the existence of Provincial legislation setting up Provincial
schemes for various Provincial products. It was said that as the
Provinces and the Dominion between them possess a totality of
complete legislative authority, it must be possible to combine Dominion and Provincial legislation so that each within its own sphere
could in co-operation with the other achieve the complete power of
regulation which is desired. Their Lordships appreciate the importance of the desired aim. Unless and until a change is made in the
respective legislative functions of Dominion and Province it may well
be that satisfactory results for both can only be obtained by co-
operation. But the legislation will have to be carefully framed and
will not be achieved by either party leaving its own sphere and
encroaching upon that of the other. In the present case their Lordships are unable to support the Dominion legislation as it stands . . .

Appeal dismissed.

[It was pointed out by the Privy Council in the *Margarine* case (*Canadian
Federation of Agriculture v. A.-G. Que.*, [1951] A.C. 179, [1950] 4 D.L.R. 689)
that neither before the Supreme Court nor before the Privy Council was
there any argument on the "agriculture" power raised in the *Natural
Products Marketing Act*, case, *supra*. In *Reference re Section 6 of the
Saskatchewan Farm Security Act*, [1947] S.C.R. 394, [1947] 3 D.L.R. 689, aff'd

sub. nom. A.-G. Sask. v. A.-G. Can., [1949] A.C. 110, [1949] 2 D.L.R. 145, [1949] 1 W.W.R. 742, reproduced in part, *infra,* at p. 600, legislation aimed at giving farmers some relief in a year of crop failure in respect of payments due under farm mortgages and instalment purchase contracts was held invalid as invading federal power in relation to interest, with only Taschereau J. dissenting. He was of opinion that "legislation to relieve the farmers of financial difficulties, to lighten the burdens resulting from the uncertainties of farming operations is legislation in relation to agriculture". Note, however, that in the *Margarine* case, Taschereau J. rejected the argument that the agriculture power would support the legislation challenged therein. Conversely, Rinfret C.J.C. joined in the majority view in the *Saskatchewan Farm Security Act* case but dissented in the *Margarine* case in reliance on the agriculture power.

The *Natural Products Marketing Act* case was applied in *Rex v. Feldman,* [1949] 2 D.L.R. 491, [1949] 1 W.W.R. 97, 93 Can. C.C. 47.

The reasons given for the invalidation of the Natural Products Marketing Act suggested that judicial approval would be given to a provincial marketing statute provided the regulated transactions were wholly within the province; and a ruling to this effect was made in *Shannon v. Lower Mainland Dairy Products Board,* [1938] A.C. 708, [1938] 4 D.L.R. 81, [1938] 2 W.W.R. 604. (It may be noted that the *Shannon* case repudiates the assertion in *Russell v. The Queen* (1882), 7 App. Cas. 829 that s. 92(9) of the B.N.A. Act does not authorize the granting of licences to regulate trade.) That a gap in effective regulatory control still remained was apparent: see *Corry,* Difficulties of Divided Jurisdiction (Royal Commission Study, Appendix 7), pp. 11 ff., for a discussion of the problems involved in marketing. Corry points out that

"Grading, packaging and marketing provisions must be enforced at the point where the producer makes contact with the dealer or processor. However, at this point, it is very often impossible to say whether the particular lots being graded will remain in provincial trade or will ultimately be drawn into inter-provincial or export trade. Yet, even if the sole purpose were to grade surpluses in order to ensure their access to export markets, there are strong reasons for grading at this point. If grading is postponed until the product reaches an export warehouse, the uncertainty as to grade must constantly hamper movement into export channels.

"The logic of the situation argues for the grading of the whole product as early as possible in the assembling process. The difficulty is that it is often impossible to say, at this stage, whether the power to inspect and assign the grades rests with the Dominion or the province. Even if it were possible, it would be a waste and a duplication to maintain two sets of inspectors. Unified administration is necessary if the function is to be performed most efficiently."

An attempt to plug the gap was made through the Agricultural Products Marketing Act, first enacted in 1949, now R.S.C. 1970, c. A-7, which provides for Dominion-provincial cooperation through delegation to provincial marketing agencies of federal authority over interprovincial and export trade.]

REFERENCE RE VALIDITY OF SECTION 5(a) OF THE DAIRY INDUSTRY ACT

In the Supreme Court of Canada. [1949] S.C.R. 1, [1949] 1 D.L.R. 433.

Reference to the Supreme Court of Canada to determine the validity of section 5(a) of the Dairy Industry Act, R.S.C. 1927, c. 45.

RINFRET C.J.C. (dissenting): . . . The Order of Reference by His Excellency the Governor General in Council, dated July 27, 1948, (P.C. 3365) first requires our attention.

The opening paragraph refers to a motion of the Senate adopted on June 10, 1948. Then it proceeds to state that according to information furnished by the Department of Agriculture the history of margarine or oleomargarine dates back to about the year 1867 when the original formula for its manufacture was worked out by a French chemist, but that while the terms margarine and oleomargarine are commonly used interchangeably, there is a distinction between these products in this respect that margarine is a straight vegetable oil compounded while oleomargarine contains in addition an animal fat, usually beef fat. The principal vegetable oils used are cocoanut, cottonseed, peanut, soya bean and sunflower seed. None of these vegetables are produced in Canada in any considerable volume. Margarine was introduced as a food product in Europe and the United States about 1867.

The Order of Reference continues by saying that, according to information furnished by the Department of Agriculture, the process of manufacture is as follows:—

The vegetable oil is refined and bleached and hydrogenated to the end that the melting point is controlled to meet seasonal requirements. The oil is then deodorized and a sterile, bland, neutral flavourless oil produced which is mixed with fresh skim milk to which has been added a lactic acid culture, to impart a butter flavour. The mixture is then emulsified and salt and Vitamin A are added. The mixture is then tempered and again emulsified and crystallized by chilling to produce a product of uniform texture. The finished product is then moulded and wrapped for use. In the case of oleomargarine, animal fat is introduced and the process carried out as outlined.

The Order of Reference goes on to say that the Department of National Health and Welfare submitted with its approval the following extract from an article contained in the Canadian Medical Association Journal of August, 1947, respecting margarine:—

"One factor absent in vegetable oils is Vitamin A, and if the lack of this could not be remedied it would seriously weaken the value of margarine. But it is quite easy to add as much Vitamin A as is needed, and so make margarine contain more of this Vitamin than the richest butter. Even butter is liable to show seasonable variations in its content of Vitamin A. Other vitamins too could be added to margarine such as Vitamin D, for example, of which butter contains very little. As a source of energy, margarine and butter are exactly equal.

"Perhaps one of the main difficulties encountered with margarine in the early days of its development was that of its taste. That has now been so completely overcome that it is difficult to distinguish between butter and margarine. Even if it was making a virtue of wartime necessity, Britain found no difficulty in learning to like as well as depend on margarine during the war period.

"A typical margarine today, as made in the United States, consists of 80% refined vegetable oils, together with 16.5% pasteurized non-fat milk for flavour, plus small amounts of glycerin derivative to prevent spattering in frying, vegetable lecithin to prevent burning and sticking to the pan, sometimes benzoate of soda as a preservative, salt and Vitamin A concentrate up to a minimum of 9,000 U.S.P. units per pound; some brands go as high as 15,000 units per pound."

According to the Order of Reference it was in 1886 that the Parliament of Canada enacted "An Act to Prohibit the Manufacture and Sale of Certain Substitutes for Butter", namely, oleomargarine, butterine or other substitute for butter, being c. 42 of 49 Vict. The preamble of this Act reads as follows:—

"Whereas the use of certain substitutes for butter heretofore manufactured and exposed for sale in Canada is injurious to health; and it is expedient to prohibit the manufacture and sale thereof: Therefore Her Majesty, by and with the advice and consent of the Senate and House of Commons of Canada, enacts as follows:"

This Act was reproduced as c. 100 of R.S.C. 1886, the preamble thereto being omitted "as is usual in the case of such a revision", so the Order of Reference states.

In 1903 the *Butter Act* was enacted, being c. 6 of 3 Ed. VII, which prohibited the manufacture, import or sale of oleomargarine or other substitutes for butter. This Act was incorporated into the *Inspection and Sale Act,* c. 85 of R.S.C. 1906, as Part VII thereof entitled "Dairy Products".

In 1914 the *Dairy Industry Act* was enacted as c. 7 of 4-5 Geo. V. This repealed Part VIII of the *Inspection and Sale Act* and prohibited the manufacture, import or sale of oleomargarine or other butter substitutes. In the R.S.C. 1927, the *Dairy Industry Act* appears in its present form as c. 45 thereof.

Section 5(a), of the *Dairy Industry Act* provides as follows:
"5. No person shall
"(a) manufacture, import into Canada, or offer, sell or have in his possession for sale, any oleomargarine, margarine, butterine or other substitute for butter, manufactured wholly or in part from any fat other than that of milk or cream."

By P.C. 3044, dated October 23, 1917, made under the *War Measures Act,* the operation of s. 5(a) of the *Dairy Industry Act* was suspended and by c. 24 of the Statutes of Canada 1919 (2nd Sess.) provision was made for the manufacture and importation of oleomargarine until August 31, 1920, and sale thereof until March 1, 1921. By annual amendments the permissions contained in the *Oleomargarine Act* were extended to August 31, 1923, in the case of manufacture and importation, and to March 1, 1924, in the case of sale.

According to information furnished by the Department of Agriculture, during the period December 1, 1917 to September 30, 1923, oleomargarine was manufactured and imported to amounts totalling almost 17,000,000 lbs. from December 1, 1917 to March 31, 1919, almost 15,000,000 lbs. for the year ending March 31, 1920, almost 11,000,000 lbs. for the year ending March 31, 1921, somewhat more than 3,240,000 lbs. in the year ending March 31, 1922, slightly more than 3,280,000 lbs. for the year ending March 31, 1923, and 2,625,693 lbs. for the six months ending September, 1923.

During the same period of time the manufacture and importation of butter appears to have been more than 193,000,000 lbs. for the year 1918, more than 205,000,000 lbs. for the year 1919, more than 215,000,000 lbs. for the year 1920, more than 232,000,000 lbs. for the year 1922, and more than 266,000,000 lbs. for the year 1923.

During the six years in question, 1918 to 1923, the importation of butter was almost negligible, amounting to only 16,000,000 lbs. 1922 was the only year in which the figures were at all worthy of consideration, the importation of butter in that year reaching 6,000,000 lbs.

The Order of Reference goes on to say that, according to information furnished by the Department of Agriculture, milk production is an essential basic part of agriculture as certain large areas of Canada, particularly in Ontario and Quebec and the Maritime Provinces, are best suited for hay and pasture crops. Consequently milk production is the branch of agriculture which is best suited to these regions of Eastern Canada. The marginal land farmer produces much of the milk in these areas that finds its way into butter. He is able to produce milk with reasonable profit only by raising hogs and poultry, which is a natural side line of the smaller farmer who keeps a few cows. Canadian dairy products have a value of approximately $400,000,000 per annum, of which the butter industry produces about $150,000,000. Approximately 50% of all the milk produced in Canada goes into butter, and at one time or another, during the production seasons, practically all dairy farmers depend on butter as an outlet for their surplus milk, and without this outlet their operations as milk producers would be seriously affected. Butter is the largest user of milk, of which there is produced annually in Canada approximately 17 billion pounds. Approximately 400,000 farmers are producing milk for butter manufacture and about 85% of the manufacturer's price is returned to the dairy farmers. In addition to the 400,000 farmers involved, there are approximately 1,200 plants engaged in the manufacture of butter with thousands of other individuals depending for their livelihood on the butter industry.

Information concerning the production, composition and consumption of butter and margarine in most of the important countries of the world in 1931 is contained in Schedule A, appended to the Order of Reference. This schedule discloses the world production of margarine plus butter production in listed countries for the year 1931. In the United States more than 354,000,000 pounds of margarine were produced, in the United Kingdom more than 423,000,000 pounds, in Germany more than 815,000,000 pounds.

The countries listed in Schedule A are as follows:—

United States	Denmark	Portugal
Canada	Finland	Sweden
United Kingdom	France	Japan
Ireland	Germany	Australia
Belgium	Netherlands	New Zealand
Czecho-Slovakia	Norway	

Canada alone, of all these important countries of the world, prohibits the importation, production and consumption of margarine.

The same Schedule sets out a comparison of the food values per 100 grams between butter and oleomargarine. These values are practically the same with respect to calories, protein grams, fat grams, carbohydrate grams, phosphorous grams and iron milligrams. As regards calcium grams the table states that with respect to butter the food value, both in winter and summer, amounts to .016 and with respect to oleomargarine, .002 and as to Vitamin A International Units it is stated that the percentage for butter in summer is 3970 and in winter 2200 and for oleomargarine it is 1980 units.

It should be noted that no mention of Vitamin D is made in Schedule A, although in the article contained in the Canadian Medical Association Journal of August, 1947, respecting margarine, which forms part of the Order of Reference and which is quoted above, it is [referred to]. . . .

It now becomes our duty to give our answer to the question referred to this Court by His Excellency the Governor General in Council.

In order to understand properly the exact purport of s. 5(a) it is essential, in my opinion, to begin by an analysis of the *Dairy Industry Act*, which, it is stated in the Order of Reference, came into force in 1914 (c. 7 of 4-5 Geo V), the constitutional validity of which (except for s. 5(a)) has not been challenged before this Court.

Part I deals with the manufacture and sale of dairy products and butter substitutes. The interpretation section defines "butter", "creamery", "creamery butter", "dairy", "dairy butter", "dairy product", "fat", "foreign substance", "homogenized milk", "illegal dairy product", "oleomargarine", "package", "renovated butter", and "whey butter". The definition of oleomargarine in this interpretation section is as follows:—

"(n) 'oleomargarine' means any food substance other than butter, of whatever origin, source or composition which has the appearance of and is prepared for the same uses as butter."

The next section deals with the regulations the Governor in Council may make as he deems necessary. The following paragraphs are pertinent:—

"(c) the seizure and confiscation of apparatus and materials used in the manufacture of any butter, cheese or other dairy product or imitations thereof in contravention of any of the provisions of this Part or of any regulation made hereunder;"

"(e) the seizure and confiscation of any illegal dairy product as defined in this Part;"

(g) the imposition upon summary conviction of penalties not exceeding fifty dollars and costs upon any person violating any regulation made under the provisions of this Part."

Section 4 deals with the quality of milk for manufacturers and reads as follows:—

"4. No person shall sell, supply or send to any cheese or butter or condensed milk or milk powder or cassein manufactory, or to a milk or cream shipping station, or to a milk bottling establishment or other premises where milk or cream is collected for sale or shipment, or to the owner or manager thereof, or to any maker of butter, cheese, condensed milk or milk powder or cassein to be manufactured:

"(a) milk diluted with water, or in any way adulterated, or milk from which any cream has been taken, or milk commonly known as skim-milk, or any milk to which cream has been added, or any milk or cream to which any foreign fat, colouring matter, preservative or other chemical substance of any kind has been added;

"(b) milk from which any portion of that part of the milk known as strippings has been retained;

"(c) any milk taken or drawn from a cow that he knows to be diseased at the time the milk is so taken or drawn from her."

Section 5 deals with "Butter" and s-s. (a) of that section forms the question referred to this Court for consideration. As it has already been quoted above it is not necessary to repeat it here. . . .

It should be noted at once that in s. 5(a) oleomargarine, margarine and butterine are placed on the same footing as any other substitute for butter and that oleomargarine and margarine are characterized as being substitutes for butter.

The only other subsection of s. 5 that need be referred to is subsection (e) which states:—

"5. No person shall

"(e) have upon premises occupied by him where any dairy produce is treated, manipulated, manufactured, or re-worked, any substance that might be used for the adulteration of any such product and the presence upon any such premises of any fat or oil capable of being used for such adulteration shall be *prima facie* proof of intent so to use it."

Section 6 prohibits the importation into Canada, or the offering, selling or having in one's possession for sale (a) any butter containing over 16% of water, or less than 80% of milk fat; or (b) any process or renovated butter. The other subsections of s. 6 deal with the character and weight of butter.

Section 7 is as follows:—

"7. No person shall manufacture, import into Canada, sell, offer, or have in possession for sale, any cheese which contains any fat or oil other than that of milk or cream."

Section 8 deals with the adulteration of cheese.

Then follow some miscellaneous provisions providing for penalties in the case of the violation of any of the provisions of ss. 4, 6 and 8 of the Act. In this respect s. 9 states:—

"9. Any person, firm or corporation who violates any of the provisions of sections four, six or eight of this Act, shall for each offence, upon summary conviction, be liable to a fine not exceeding fifty dollars and not less than ten dollars, together with the costs of prosecution, and in default of payment of such penalty and costs shall be liable to imprisonment with or without hard labour for a term not exceeding six months, unless such penalty and costs and the costs of enforcing the same are sooner paid."

Section 10, dealing with penalties in the case of violations of ss. 5 and 7, reads:—

"10. Any person who violates any provision of sections five or seven of this Act shall be guilty of an offence and upon summary conviction shall be liable

"(a) in the case of a first offence to a fine not exceeding one thousand dollars and not less than five hundred dollars;

"(b) in the case of a second offence to a fine not exceeding two thousand dollars and not less than one thousand dollars; in each case together with the costs of prosecution and in default of payment of such penalty and costs, to imprisonment for a term not exceeding six months with or without hard labour, unless the said penalty and costs, with costs of enforcing the same, are sooner paid;

"(c) in the case of a third or subsequent offence to imprisonment for a term not exceeding six months with or without hard labour."

This section 10 was repealed and re-enacted by c. 40, 1925 (Can.), in the form just quoted.

It should be noted in the case of a third or subsequent offence, imprisonment is provided for without the alternative of a fine.

Sections 11 and 12 deal with the persons liable for violating those sections of the Act relating to milk, cheese, butter or other dairy products.

There are other sections of the Act providing for penalties for obstructing persons enforcing the Act, for the appointment of inspectors and permitting them access to all places where dairy products are manufactured, or stored or dealt in, or held for transport or delivery, and for employees assisting the inspectors.

The closing sections of Part I of the Act (16 to 20 inclusive) deal with procedure, proof in deteriorated milk prosecutions, venue, evidence, establishment of guilt for violation of the Act, summary prosecution, etc. With respect to summary prosecution it is stated (s. 19(4)):—

"In all respects not provided for in this Part, the procedure under the provisions of the Criminal Code, relating to summary convictions, shall, so far as applicable, apply to all prosecutions brought under this Part."

Part II of the Act deals with the grading of dairy produce. It defines "dairy produce", "grader", "inspector", "grading store", "package" and it states that the Minister to whom the administration of that Part of the Act is entrusted is the Minister of Agriculture.

The Governor in Council is authorized to make regulations not inconsistent with the Act and *inter alia* to provide for the establishment of standards, definitions and grades for dairy produce; and it should be remembered that the definition of "dairy produce" includes butter, cheese and other food products manufactured from milk.

Section 25 provides for penalties against any person who, not being a dairy produce grader, alters, effaces, or obliterates wholly or partially, or causes to be altered, effaced or obliterated, any dairy produce grader's brands or marks on any dairy produce which has undergone grading, or on any package containing such dairy produce.

Part III deals with the testing of glassware used in connection with milk tests and prohibits the marking of such glassware that has not been tested. The sale of glassware not marked is prohibited and so is its use. Section 30, dealing with regulations, fees and penalties reads as follows:—

"30. The Governor in Council may make regulations for the operation and enforcement of this Part, and may, by such regulations, establish fees for the verification of the apparatus therein referred to and also provide for the imposition of penalties not exceeding fifty dollars for each offence against this Part or against any regulation made hereunder. . . ."

Section 1 of the Regulations made under Part I of the *Dairy Industry Act,* R.S.C. 1927, c. 45, and amendments thereto, deals with definitions. Subsection (c) defines "butter" as "meaning the food product, commonly known as butter, manufactured exclusively from milk or cream or both, with or without colouring matter, salt or other harmless preservatives". "Cheese", "creamery", "creamery butter", "dairy", "dairy butter", "dairy product", "grader", "package", "cream cheese", "process cheese", "skim-milk cheese", "whey", "whey butter", "ice cream", "sherbet" and "milk products" are all defined.

"Dairy product" or "dairy products" are defined as meaning "any milk, cream, condensed milk, evaporated milk, milk powder, butter, cheese, ice cream or any other product manufactured from milk and all imitations thereof". Again the "Minister" to whom the administration of the Act is entrusted is the Minister of Agriculture.

Section 2 deals with compulsory branding. It is stated that "all brands required by these regulations to be placed on a cheese, and on a package containing cheese or butter of a net weight of more than twenty-five pounds shall be legible and indelible. . . ." Subsection (e) (1) refers to the branding of cheese, creamery butter or whey butter and the packages for those articles.

Section 3 deals with prohibited branding and s. 4 with the sale of dairy products, which include butter, dairy butter, whey butter, skim milk, cheese, creamery butter. It also refers to the branding of packages for these dairy products and provides for penalties for the infringement of the regulations concerning the sale of those products.

Subsections (2), (3) and (4) prohibit the manufacture, import into Canada, sale, offer or having in one's possession for sale ice cream, sherbet, ice cream cakes, chocolate-coated ice cream bars, ice cream moulded into special shapes or any other ice cream specialty or novelty of which ice cream is a part, or any frozen or semi-frozen milk product, unless the product conforms with the specifications therein mentioned. There are also elaborate provisions concerning ice cream and sherbet and for the containers or cabinets used for their storage.

Section 6 of the Regulations deals with the seizure and confiscation of apparatus or materials used or intended to be used in the manufacture of any butter, cheese, or other dairy product or imitation thereof in contravention of any of the provisions of the Act or of any regulations made thereunder. It also refers to the disposal of seized products and provides for the keeping of record books and registers.

Then follow Schedule 1 and Schedule 2. The former is a form for "application for registration of a cheese factory, a creamery, a combined factory or a factory where cheese is processed or butter is re-worked", and Schedule 2 illustrates the form and size of type number on a cheese, and on packages containing cheese or butter of a net weight of more than 25 pounds.

Regulations under Part II of the Act deal with cheddar cheese and creamery butter of Canadian origin intended for export. It refers to standards for grades of cheese, these standards being divided into first, second and third grade cheese and below third grade cheese. There are also standards for grading washed curd cheese and for grades of creamery butter.

There are also regulations under Part III of the Act dealing with the duty of verifying the glassware which comes under the provisions of that Part and which is assigned to the Weights and Measures Standards Branch, Department of Trade and Commerce, Ottawa.

In my opinion, it follows, from the analysis just made of the *Dairy Industry Act,* that, in addition to being legislation under s. 95 of the *British North America Act* dealing with agriculture (so far as it relates to that subject-matter, the Act has effect, notwithstanding any law of the Legislature of a Province relating to agriculture which may be repugnant to it), it also falls within the ambit of head 27 of s. 91 of the *B.N.A. Act* extending to "The Criminal Law, except the Constitution of Courts of Criminal Jurisdiction, but including the Procedure in Criminal Matters", because it meets the definition as stated in the decision of the Judicial Committee of the Privy Council in *Proprietary Articles Trade Ass'n v. A.-G. Can.,* [1931] A.C. 310, at pp. 324 and 325. Section 5(a) of the *Dairy Industry Act* deals truly with "acts prohibited with penal consequences" and it cannot be contended that it is colourable legislation on the part of Parliament. My brother Kerwin has satisfactorily dealt with this point in his answer to the question submitted in the Order of Reference. I agree with what he has said and do not find it necessary to add anything further on that point.

But I wish to state also that, to my mind, s. 5(a) of the Act can be supported in favour of the Dominion's contention both on the grounds that it is Agriculture (s. 95 of the B.N.A. Act) and head 2 of s. 91 of the same Act, the Regulation of Trade and Commerce.

It was not contended at bar—and I think it could hardly be contended—that the *Dairy Industry Act* and regulations thereunder are not within the dominion of the Federal Parliament by force of s. 95 of our Constitution. It is a law in relation to agriculture which the Parliament of Canada from time to time is empowered to make in relation to agriculture, and it is not within the competence of the respective Provincial Legislatures to enact legislation in this regard when Parliament has already covered the field, in view of the following words of s. 95: "and any Law of the Legislature of a Province relative to Agriculture or to Immigration shall have effect in and for the Province as long and as far only as it is not repugnant to any Act of the Parliament of Canada."

That point of view cannot be discarded on the ground that oleo-margarine or margarine are supposedly articles of trade, or com-modities which are not directly the product of agriculture. In support of that suggestion a passage in the judgment of Mignault J. in *The King v. Eastern Terminal Elevator Co.,* [1925] S.C.R. 434 at p. 457 was largely relied on. . . .

It should be noted that the passage . . . was only the expression of one Judge, about which the majority of the Court said absolutely nothing. The judgment of this Court did not in any way uphold that view and it ought to be taken as a mere *obiter* which cannot stand as a judgment of this Court. To the appellant's contention that the statute could be supported under s. 95 of the *B.N.A. Act* as being legislation concerning agriculture, Mignault J. cursorily said "It suffices to answer that the subject matter of the Act is not agricul-ture but a product of agriculture considered as an article of trade." And he added: "The regulation of a particular trade, and that is what this statute is in substance, cannot be attempted by the Dominion on the ground that it is a trade in natural products. What we have here is trade legislation and not a law for the encouragement or support of agriculture, however wide a meaning may be given to the latter term." . . .

I cannot agree, therefore, with the argument that the constitu-tional validity of the *Dairy Products Act* is not supported under s. 95 of the *B.N.A. Act.* Indeed, if Parliament does not derive its authority from s. 95 to pass such an Act, I am at a loss to perceive upon what other head of s. 91 it could be held to have been compe-tently adopted. I repeat, that it was in no way challenged in the course of the argument before the Court. In these circumstances the insertion of s. 5(a) of the *Dairy Industry Act,* dealing with the "manufacture, import into Canada, or offer for sale or have in one's possession for sale, oleomargarine, margarine, butterine, or *other substitute for butter, manufactured* wholly or in part from any fat other than that of milk or cream", being an insertion in the *Dairy Industry Act* and adopted by Parliament by virtue of its power to deal with "laws in relation to agriculture in the provinces", is, in my opinion, nothing more than the direct exercise of Parliament's juris-diction over agricultural matters, or at least necessarily incidental and necessary for the effective control of agricultural matters in respect of milk and its by-products.

It should be observed that the *Dairy Industry Act,* as I have illustrated in the opening paragraph of this judgment, deals not only with milk, but also with butter, several varieties of cheese, ice cream, sherbet, etc., all coming within the special definition contained in the Act of "dairy product", or "dairy products", or "dairy produce", and, according to the definition, meaning "any milk, cream, condensed milk, evaporated milk, milk powder, butter, cheese, ice cream or any other article manufactured from milk and all imitations thereof". It seems, in my opinion, impossible to distinguish oleomargarine or margarine from any of these other articles included in the definition of dairy products, particularly when, as set out in s. 5(a), they are likened to "butterine, or other substitutes for butter".

The fact that oleomargarine and margarine do not come directly from the cows (of course they do not) and the mere contention that they are not natural products but rather manufactured articles is not sufficient to remove them from the domain of the federal government in respect of agriculture. If this argument were sound, the same thing could be said with as much force about butter, cheese, ice cream, or, in the words of the definition of "dairy product" in the Act, "any other article manufactured from milk and all imitations thereof". From that point of view oleomargarine and margarine are strictly on a par with these commodities just mentioned; and, if the manufacture of butter, cheese, ice cream, or any other commodity manufactured from milk and all imitations thereof are properly regulated and, in many cases, prohibited by force of the *Dairy Industry Act,* it does not seem possible to say that oleomargarine and margarine cannot be competently dealt with by Parliament under the provisions of that Act on the mere pretense that they are "manufactured articles". They are just as much a dairy product as butter, cheese, ice cream, or other articles "manufactured" from milk. They are, therefore, proper subject matters of an Act adopted by Parliament in virtue of its powers under s. 95 of the *B.N.A. Act* and s. 5(a) was competently inserted in the *Dairy Industry Act,* just as much as all the other sections of the Act dealing with butter, cheese, ice cream, or other commodities manufactured from milk. In fact, the definition of "dairy product", or "dairy produce" in s. 2 of Part I of the Act indicates conclusively that Parliament intended to include as a dairy product articles manufactured from milk and, if oleomargarine and margarine had not been specifically mentioned in the Act, they would come under the definition as being "any other article manufactured from milk."

For these reasons I would answer the question put to the Court in the Order of Reference by declaring that s. 5(a) of the *Dairy Industry Act,* R.S.C. 1927, c. 45, is *intra vires* the Parliament of Canada in whole on the ground that it has constitutional validity as a proper exercise of the power of Parliament by virtue of s. 95 of the *B.N.A. Act.*

But there is yet another reason for stating that the validity of s. 5(a) must be upheld. By head 2 of s. 91 of the *B.N.A. Act* the regulation of trade and commerce has been entrusted to Parliament. It has not been disputed that the legislation submitted to us deals with trade and commerce. Indeed the contention of those who pretend that s. 5(a) is invalid from a constitutional point of view, as not being within the proper domain of the federal Parliament, is that it cannot be regarded as coming with s. 95, dealing with agriculture, for the reason, they say, that oleomargarine and margarine are not products of agriculture but that they are articles of trade". Following this contention to its necessary consequences, they say that it cannot come under federal jurisdiction because then it would be regulation of a particular trade and, as a result of numerous decisions of the Judicial Committee of the Privy Council, it does not come within head 2 of s. 91 of the *B.N.A. Act,* and the decision of the Judicial Committee in *Citizens Insurance Co. of Canada v. Parsons* (1881), 7 App. Cas. 96 at p. 113 was cited. . . .

Subsequent pronouncements of the Judicial Committee on the same subject were summarized by Sir Lyman Duff, C.J.C. in *Reference re Natural Products Marketing Act,* [1936] S.C.R. at p. 410:—

"It would appear to result from these decisions that the Regulation of Trade and Commerce does not comprise, in the sense in which it is used in s. 91, the regulation of particular trades or occupations or of a particular kind of business such as the insurance business in the Provinces, or the regulation of trade in particular commodities or classes of commodities in so far as it is local in the provincial sense; while, on the other hand, it does embrace the regulation of external trade and the regulation of interprovincial trade and such ancillary legislation as may be necessarily incidental to the exercise of such powers."

It is scarcely necessary to add that Chief Justice Duff's views were commended by the Judicial Committee in the words of Lord Atkin [in *A.-G. Can. v. A.-G. Ont.,* [1937] A.C. 326 at p. 353]:

"The few pages of the Chief Justice's judgment will, it is to be hoped, form the *locus classicus* of the law on this point, and preclude further disputes."

I should like to point out, however, that the *Dairy Industry Act* does not deal with a particular trade, or with a particular commodity. We have seen that it deals with milk, cream, condensed milk, evaporated milk, milk powder, butter, cheese, ice cream or any other article manufactured from milk and all imitations thereof; and Part II of the Act deals with the grading of dairy produce, grading store, the powers of the Governor in Council to make regulations for the establishment of standards, definitions and grades for dairy produce and for the maturing, storing, packaging, handling and transporting of dairy produce. Then Part III deals with the testing of glassware used in connection with milk tests.

The regulations, which have not been attacked, define butter as "the food product, commonly known as butter, *manufactured* exclusively from milk or cream or both, with or without colouring matter, salt or other harmless preservatives". Cheese is defined as "the product made from curd obtained from milk, skim-milk, cream or any mixture of these by coagulating the casein thereof with rennet, lactic acid or any suitable enzyme or acid, and with or without further processing or the addition of other wholesome ingredients, such as fresh milk solids, ripening, ferments, special moulds, emulsifying agents, seasoning or colouring matter, and may not contain any preservative other than salt (sodium chloride)". "Dairy product" is defined as "any milk, cream, condensed milk, evaporated milk, milk powder, butter, cheese, ice cream, or any other product *manufactured* from milk and all imitations thereof". Then the regulations deal with whey, whey cream, whey butter, ice cream, sherbet and in fact all milk products.

Reference has already been made to the fact that the regulations deal with compulsory branding, prohibited branding, the sale of dairy products, and that "every person who manufactures or intends to manufacture cheese, creamery butter or whey butter, or processes, or intends to process cheese, or reworks or intends to rework butter, shall register with and obtain a certificate of registration with a registration number from the Department, Ottawa, for each such factory owned or operated by him".

Regulations under Part II as I have mentioned above, divide cheese into first, second, third and below third grade cheese and contain elaborate provisions for the scores and definitions for grades of butter.

Regulations under Part III provide for the verification of glassware and it is stated:—

"34. All test bottles and pipettes used in connection with the testing of milk or cream, except skim-milk bottles and the tubes used in connection with apparatus known as the 'Oil Test Churn' shall be forwarded, charges prepaid, to the Weights and Measures Standards Branch, Department of Trade and Commerce, Ottawa, Canada, for the purpose of verification."

Clearly such an Act is not limited to the regulation of one particular trade or of one particular commodity, nor to one, or more than one Province; it is an Act embracing the whole Dominion.

It was also argued that the power to regulate under head 2 of s. 91 does not mean the power to prohibit, that prohibition is not regulation, that, in fact, from the moment you prohibit you exclude regulation. In my opinion such a contention cannot be supported. In the process of regulating these different commodities, or the trading in these different commodities, the *Dairy Industry Act* prescribes extensive regulations, in the course of which certain prohibitions are included. It stands to reason that, if you regulate, you may prohibit things that are not in accordance with those regulations. Section 5(a) deals with "the manufacture, import into Canada, or offer, sale or having in one's possession for sale, any oleomargarine, margarine, butterine or other substitute for butter, manufactured wholly or in part from any fat other than that of milk or cream" and it does not amount to absolute prohibition. In the precise words of the section it prohibits only those commodities which are "manufactured wholly or in part from any fat other than that of milk or cream". Therefore, it is unnecessary to reiterate that the effect of the section is that no person shall "manufacture, import into Canada, or offer, sell or have in his possession for sale, any oleomargarine, margarine, butterine, or other substitute for butter, manufactured wholly or in part from any fat other than that of milk or cream". The prohibitions which flow from this s. 5(a) are enumerated in the subsections that follow, *i.e.,* (b), (c), (d) and (e). For instance, s-s. (b) provides that:—

"5. (b) No person shall mix with or incorporate with butter, by any process of heating, soaking, rechurning, reworking, or otherwise any cream, milk, skim-milk, butter-milk or water to cause such butter when so treated to contain over sixteen per centum of water or less than eighty per centum of milk fat." The particular "mixing" or "processing" is prohibited but butter itself is not prohibited.

Subsections (c), (d) and (e) of s. 5 read as follows:—

"5. No person shall

"(c) melt, clarify, refine, rechurn, or otherwise treat butter to produce 'process' or 'renovated' butter;

"(d) manufacture, import into Canada, or sell, offer, expose or have in possession for sale, any milk or cream or substitute therefor which contains any fat or oil other than that of milk;

"(e) have upon premises occupied by him where any dairy produce is treated, manipulated, manufactured, or reworked, any substance that might be used for the adulteration of any such product and the presence upon any such premises of any fat or oil capable of being used for such adulteration shall be *prima facie* proof of intent so to use it."

It can be seen very clearly that the whole of s. 5 does not prohibit the dairy product therein mentioned; it only prohibits certain methods of manufacturing it and, if one considers all the sections of the *Dairy Industry Act,* it is apparent that oleomargarine and margarine are treated exactly on a par with all the other products. To illustrate what I have said it is only necessary to refer to s-s. (2) of s. 4 of the regulations made under Part I of the Act, dealing with ice cream and sherbet. In that subsection certain kinds of ice cream and sherbet which do not come up to the standards therein prescribed are prohibited, but no one would contend that that is prohibition within the meaning of head 2 of s. 91 of the *B.N.A. Act.* It is very proper regulation prohibiting "the manufacture, import into Canada, sale, offer or having in one's possession for sale" ice cream or sherbet which do not come up to standards established by the regulations and, at the same time, allowing the manufacture, import into Canada and sale of ice cream or sherbet which come up to the established standards.

My conclusion is, therefore, that the so called prohibition in s. 5(a) is not prohibition at all, but a regulation of trade and commerce and properly within the competence of Parliament in virtue of head 2 of s. 91 of the *B.N.A. Act.* In my opinion, when that s. 5(a) is read in conjunction with the whole of the Act there is no real prohibition. It is truly a "regulation of trade and commerce"; or that s. 5(a) is only a necessary incidental part of an Act which Parliament had full power to adopt by virtue of s. 95 of the *B.N.A. Act* and, moreover, in view of the form given to it, it also comes within head 27 of s. 91 (Criminal Law).

Of course, it may be said that the whole Act is unquestionably of national interest and importance and that the legislation as originally enacted was for the purpose of safeguarding the whole of the public generally. In this regard I think it proper to quote a passage from the decision of the Judicial Committee of the Privy Council, *A.-G. Ont. v. Canada Temperance Federation,* [1946] A.C. 193 at p. 207, where Viscount Simon said:—

"It was not contended that if the Act of 1878 was valid when it was enacted it would have become invalid later on by a change of circumstances. . . . Their Lordships do not find it necessary to consider the true effect either of s. 5 or 8 of the Act of 1924 for the revision of the Statutes of Canada, for they cannot agree that if the Act of 1878 was constitutionally within the powers of the Dominion Parliament it could be successfully contended that the Act of 1927 which replaced it was *ultra vires.*"

It was stated that the purpose of the *Dairy Industry Act* was to give trade protection to the dairy industry in the production and sale of butter as against substitutes. In this connection the Order of Reference specifically stated (s. 8):—[The learned Chief Justice here referred again to. the material and data already set out on p. 272, *supra.*]

It would seem to me that the manufacture, import or sale of oleomargarine or margarine, or other substitutes for butter, manufactured wholly or in part from any other fat other than that of milk or cream, if thought injurious to the manufacture and sale of butter which concerns such a large and important section of Canada, can hardly be said not to be of national concern. That consideration, however, goes only to the motive of Parliament in dealing with this matter by legislation. It is possible that Parliament could invoke the opening part of s. 91 as a sufficient reason for dealing with this matter in the way it has been dealt with in s. 5(a) of the *Dairy Industry Act.* But, in addition, it emphasizes very clearly the fact that such a situation does come under head 2 of s. 91, the regulation of trade and commerce, and also under s. 95, agriculture.

I need hardly add that whatever may be said of the local manufacture or sale of oleomargarine and margarine, no question can be raised as to the competence of Parliament to deal with the "import into Canada". That is, of course, essentially a matter within the competence of Parliament, as also would be the interprovincial trade in those commodities. The argument of those who opposed the constitutional jurisdiction of Parliament with regard to s. 5(a) was limited to Parliament's power to deal with local manufacture or sale within each Province; and, in my opinion, even in this respect s. 5(a) was competently enacted by Parliament.

My answer to the question submitted in the Order of Reference is, therefore, that s. 5(a) of the *Dairy Industry Act,* R.S.C. 1927, c. 45, is not *ultra vires* the Parliament of Canada in whole or in part.

KERWIN J. (dissenting): . . . The power of Parliament to enact the prohibition contained in s. 5(a) of the *Dairy Industry Act* was rested by counsel for the Dominion upon several provisions of the *B.N.A. Act,* to only one of which it is necessary to refer: head 27 of s. 91, "Criminal Law". It may be granted that, although Parliament alone could deal with the importation into Canada of oleomargarine or margarine, it could not necessarily assume authority to regulate a particular trade in a Province. However, if it be found in any particular case that Parliament is not using the cloak of "Criminal Law" to cover a foray into the regulation of a particular local trade, the matter is settled by the decision of the Judicial Committee in *Proprietary Articles Trade Ass'n. v. A.-G. Can.,* [1931] A.C. 310, followed in *Reference re Section 498A of the Criminal Code,* [1936] S.C.R. 363; aff'd [1937] A.C. 368. Adopting the principle set forth in these decisions, there is no ground on which it may be held that the legislation here in question on its true construction, is not what it professes to be, that is, an enactment creating a criminal offence in exercise of the powers vested in Parliament in virtue of the 27th head of s. 91 of the *B.N.A. Act.*

It was argued that the approval by the Department of National Health and Welfare of the statement in the Canadian Medical Association Journal shows that the recital in the original Act of 1886 no longer states correctly the present position of margarine or oleomargarine. Granting this to be so and presuming that, by force of the several Acts dealing with the various revisions of the Dominion statutes, the recital is no longer in force, other reasons may have influenced Parliament in enacting the other Acts set out in the legislative history above, including the section before us. That consideration was considered sufficient in *A.-G. Ont. v. Canada Temperance Federation,* [1946] A.C. 193. The actual decision in that case is not of assistance on the particular point we are now at but once it be concluded that this is true criminal legislation, the Privy Council decision does show that the incorrectness of the recital in the original statute has no bearing.

My answer to the question is that s. 5(a) of the *Dairy Industry Act,* R.S.C. 1927, c. 45, is not *ultra vires* the Parliament of Canada either in whole or in part.

RAND J.: . . . To a proper understanding of the controversy, a statement of the history of the legislation is necessary. The first pertinent enactment is c. 37 of 1886, an amendment to the *Customs Duties Act,* which by s. 5(2) enacted: "The importation of oleomargarine, butterine, and all such substitutes for butter, is hereby prohibited, under a penalty of not less than two hundred nor more than four hundred dollars for each offence, and the forfeiture of such goods, and of all packages in which they are contained."

Although passed on June 2, 1886 it was retroactive to May 28th of that year. In the Revised Statutes of the same year the language was changed by substituting for "and all such substitutes" the words "or other similar substitutes". This latter form has been preserved to the present time with the addition in 1907 by c. 11 of the words "and process butter or renovated butter".

Next there is c. 42 of the Statutes of 1886 passed on the same day, June 2nd: "WHEREAS the use of certain substitutes for butter, heretofore manufactured and exposed for sale in Canada, is injurious to health; and it is expedient to prohibit the manufacture and sale thereof; Therefore Her Majesty, by and with the advice and consent of the Senate and House of Commons of Canada, enacts as follows:—

"1. No oleomargarine, butterine or other substitute for butter, *manufactured from any animal substance* other than milk, *shall be manufactured in Canada,* or sold therein, and every person who contravenes the provisions of this Act in any manner whatsoever shall incur a penalty not exceeding four hundred dollars and not less than two hundred dollars, and in default of payment shall be liable to imprisonment for a term not exceeding twelve months and not less than three months."

In the same year the Act was incorporated in the Revised Statutes as c. 100, and as is usual in the case of revisions, the preamble was omitted.

In 1903 the *Butter Act* was enacted as c. 6 of the statutes of that year and an important change was introduced into the provision dealing with butter substitutes by the language of s. 5: "No person shall manufacture, *import into Canada,* or offer, sell or have in his possession for sale, any oleomargarine, butterine, or other substitute for butter, manufactured wholly or in part from *any fat other than that of milk or cream."*

This Act was in the revision of 1906 incorporated as Part VIII of the *Inspection and Sale Act,* R.S.C. 1906, c. 85. In Schedule A, vol. III, R.S.C. 1906 at p. 2941, c. 100 of the Revised Statutes is repealed.

Later, in 1914, Part VIII was repealed and the present provision enacted as s. 5 of the *Dairy Industry Act,* c. 7 of the statutes of that year. This later became c. 45, R.S.C. 1927.

The question of the preamble was raised. Ordinarily a preamble indicates the purpose of the statute and it may be a guide to the meaning and scope of the language where that is doubtful or ambiguous. But when the question is the real character of the legislation for the purposes of jurisdiction between two Legislatures under a federal constitution, different considerations arise. A legislature cannot conclude the question by a declaration in a preamble: at most it is a fact to be taken into account, the weight to be given to it depending on all the circumstances; and it is significant here that the only prohibitory enactment containing a preamble did not include margarine.

But whatever might have been the case of the 1886 legislation, the situation now is that not only has the preamble disappeared, but its recital of fact is admittedly no longer true of either margarine or oleomargarine. It is conceded that both of them—the latter containing animal fat other than milk added to the ingredients, chiefly vegetable oils, of the former—are substantially as nutritious, possess as much energy value and are as free from deleterious effects as butter itself; and that I take to have been the state of things in 1914. Between December 1, 1915 and September 30, 1923 approximately

52,000,000 lbs. of oleomargarine was either manufactured in or imported into Canada under the authorization of both order in council and statute. Margarine has become a staple in Great Britain and on the European continent, and in the United States its use is widespread. When in 1903 importation was banned, "animal substance" changed to "any fat", and the prohibited substitutes thus enlarged to include those made from vegetable oils, the value of the preamble was greatly impaired; and the repeal of Part VIII together with the enactment of the *Dairy Industry Act* in the situation of 1914 removes any residue that might have survived. To ascertain then the true nature and substance of the legislation—which is the initial determination—I deal with it as free from any such indication of purpose.

The appearance of the provision in a statute dealing comprehensively with the dairy industry and the inclusion of prohibition of importation, the ordinary mode of protection of industry in its ultimate form, are, for this initial purpose, of considerable significance. On the other hand, the scope and importance of agriculture in the economy of this country, the part played by the dairy industry as an essential branch of it, and the desirability of maintaining a market demand for butter to meet the seasonal exigencies of that industry, are beyond controversy. What, then, in that whole background is the true nature of the enactment? . . .

Is the prohibition then enacted with a view to a public purpose which can support it as being in relation to criminal law? Public peace, order, security, health, morality: these are the ordinary though not exclusive ends served by that law, but they do not appear to be the object of the parliamentary action here. The object, as I must find it, is economic and the legislative purpose, to give trade protection to the dairy industry in the production and sale of butter; to benefit one group of persons as against competitors in business in which in the absence of the legislation, the latter would be free to engage in the Provinces. To forbid manufacture and sale for such an end is *prima facie* to deal directly with the civil rights of individuals in relation to particular trade within the Provinces: *Shannon v. Lower Mainland Dairy Board,* [1938] A.C. 708.

The public interest in this regulation lies obviously in the trade effects: it is annexed to the legislative subject-matter and follows the latter in its allocation to the one or other Legislature. But to use it as a support for the legislation in the aspect of criminal law would mean that the Dominion under its authority in that field, by forbidding the manufacture or sale of particular products, could, in what it considered a sound trade policy, not only interdict a substantial part of the economic life of one section of Canada but do so for the benefit of that of another. Whatever the scope of the regulation of interprovincial trade, it is hard to conceive a more insidious form of encroachment on a complementary jurisdiction.

This conclusion is not in conflict with *A.-G. B.C. v. A.-G. Can. (Reference re Section 498A of the Criminal Code)*, [1937] A.C. 368. There, the essential nature of the legislation was not the equalization of civil rights between competitors or promoting the interest of one trade as against another; it was the safeguarding of the public against the evil consequences of certain fetters upon free and equal competition. There is no like purpose here; there is nothing of a general or injurious nature to be abolished or removed: it is a matter of preferring certain local trade to others.

Is the legislation then within the regulation of trade and commerce? As early as *Citizens Insurance v. Parsons* (1881), 7 App. Cas. 96, it was laid down that the reconciliation of the powers granted by the constitutional act required a restriction of the "full scope of which in their literal meaning they ('the regulation of trade and commerce') are susceptible"; and it was so necessary "in order to preserve from serious curtailment, if not from virtual extinction, the degree of autonomy, which as appears from the scheme of the Act as a whole, the Provinces were intended to enjoy": (*Lawson v. Interior Tree, Fruit & Vegetable Committee*, [1931] S.C.R. 357 at p. 366.) That and subsequent pronouncements of the Judicial Committee were summarized by Duff, C.J.C. in the *Natural Products Reference*, [1936] S.C.R. 398 at p. 410. . . .

Now, if the regulation of local trade in particular commodities is excluded, *a fortiori* the control of the manufacture of those commodities for that trade would be so. The logical conclusion of the contention is . . . that *The King v. Eastern Elevator Co.*, [1925] S.C.R. 434, was wrongly decided. But so far from that, the decision was expressly approved by the Judicial Committee in the *Natural Products Reference*, [1937] A.C. at p. 387.

Finally, it was said the legislation related to agriculture. Its object I agree, is to benefit the trade in a product of agriculture; but that is a mere consequential effect and does not of itself relate the legislation to agriculture. *The Natural Products Reference, supra,* by ruling out of the scope of Dominion power the regulation of local trade in the products of agriculture has done so likewise in respect of the manufacture of substitute products. Then undoubtedly the dairy industry has an aspect of concern to this country as a whole, but as it was said in *A.-G. Ont. v. A.-G. Can.*, [1896] A.C. 348 at p. 361, if the fact of such an interest or that the matter touched the peace, order and good government of Canada was sufficient to attach the jurisdiction of Parliament, "there is hardly a subject enumerated in s. 92 upon which it might not legislate, to the exclusion of the provincial legislatures". There is nothing before us from which it can be inferred that the industry has attained a national interest, as distinguished from the aggregate of local interests, of such character as gives it a new and pre-eminent aspect within the rule of the *Russell* case, 7 App Cas. 829, as interpreted in *A.-G. v. Canada Temperance Federation*, [1946] A.C. 193. Until that state of things appears, the constitutional structure of powers leaves the regulation of the civil rights affected to the legislative judgment of the Province.

There is next the prohibition of importation of these substances. It has been observed that the power of regulation assumes, unless enlarged by the context, the conservation of the thing to be regulated; Lord Watson in *A.-G. Ont. v. A.-G. Can., supra,* at p. 363. The matter being examined by Lord Watson was the power of Parliament to enact the *Temperance Act* of 1886 as being for the "regulation of trade and commerce"; the object of the statute was "to abolish all such transactions (in liquor)" within the area adopting it; and their lordships were unable to regard such prohibitions as regulation of trade. Although under the enactment certain transactions in liquor escaped the ban, it was not in their interest that other transactions were forbidden; and I do not take the judgment to mean that the prohibition of trade in a commodity for a strictly trade purpose, which was not the purpose there, can never be trade regulation. The matter of regulation here is not margarine in isolation; it is butter and its substitutes as a group of commodities in competition; and the legislation fashions their relations *inter se* in the aspect of foreign trade, clearly an exclusive Dominion field. Under the regulation of that trade, one commodity might be admitted free of duty, and others at different rates; *A.-G. B.C. v. A.-G. Can.*, [1924] A.C. 222 at p. 225; and the extension to prohibition would not change the essential nature of the restriction. To the historical references already made on this subject, there can be added that of s. 43 of the *Act of Union* (1840) which after reciting that the Imperial Parliament would not thereafter impose any taxation on the North American Provinces "except only such duties as it might be deemed expedient to impose for the regulation of commerce" proceeded to enact that nothing should prevent the exemption of any law made "for establishing regulations and *prohibitions*" in relation to commerce. As this was a reservation from provincial autonomy, the apparent disjunction of powers is not material to the language of the constitutional instrument of the Dominion; but the terms disclose the modes of trade control then practised. Such scope of action is clearly necessary to the nation's jurisdiction over trade with other states. Only Parliament can deal with foreign commerce; provincial powers cannot in any mode, aspect or degree govern it: and it would be anomalous that the jurisdiction to which regulation is committed, which alone can act, and which in this segment of trade is in substance sovereign, should be powerless to employ such an ordinary measure of control.

The remaining question is whether manufacture, sale, etc. and importation can be taken as severable. Having regard to the purpose of the legislation, the restrictions are undoubtedly intended to be cumulative. They are in no sense dependent upon or involved with each other, though no doubt both are necessary to the complete benefit envisaged. But distinct in operation and effect, they are to be taken as enacted distributively and not with the intention that either all or none should come into force.

My answers to the questions, therefore, are:—

1.   The prohibition of importation of the goods mentioned in the section is *intra vires* of Parliament.

2.   The prohibition of manufacture, possession and sale is *ultra vires* of Parliament.

ESTEY J.: . . . In considering the validity of s. 5(a) it is convenient to deal first with the prohibition of the manufacture and sale of these products.

The prohibition of the manufacture and sale in s. 5(a) directly interferes with the freedom of individuals and corporate bodies to engage in the business of manufacturing or selling the specified food products, including oleomargarine and margarine. As such it is legislation in relation to property and civil rights within the meaning of s. 92(13), with respect to which the Provinces have the exclusive right to legislate, unless the legislation in question may be held to be competent Dominion legislation within the other provisions of the B.N.A. Act.

On behalf of the Dominion it is contended that s. 5(a) is competent Dominion legislation under:

(a) S. 91(2) "The regulation of Trade and Commerce."

(b) S. 91(27) "The Criminal Law . . ."

(c) Peace, Order, and good Government, within the meaning of the opening paragraph of s. 91.

(d) S. 95 ". . . in relation to Agriculture . . ."

This legislation in relation to a specified trade or industry is not competent Dominion legislation within the meaning of s. 91(2) . . .

Moreover, by its express terms this section prohibits rather than regulates the manufacture and sale, and as pointed out by the Privy Council in *Toronto v. Virgo*, [1896] A.C. 88 at p. 93, there is a vast difference between the two in that "a power to regulate and govern seems to imply the continued existence of that which is to be regulated or governed." See also *A.-G. Ont. v. A.-G. Can.*, [1896] A.C. 348 at p. 363. Whether, therefore, the legislation be regarded as part of an enactment to protect and regulate the dairy industry or as merely prohibitory in character, it is in either event not competent Dominion legislation within the meaning of s. 91(2) "The regulation of Trade and Commerce."

It is then contended that as any infraction of the prohibitions under s. 5(a) constitutes an offence for which penalties are provided under s. 10 of the *Dairy Industry Act*, that this is valid criminal legislation within the meaning of s. 91(27). This contention is based upon the oft-quoted statement that the phrase "criminal law" is used in s. 91(27) "in its widest sense"; *A.-G. Ont. v. Hamilton Street R. Co.*, [1903] A.C. 524 and the language of Lord Atkin in *Proprietary Articles Trade Ass'n v. A.-G. Can. (Combines Investigation Act)*, [1931] A.C. 310 at p. 324. . . .

. . . In 1937 Lord Atkin in *A.-G. B.C. v. A.-G. Can. (Reference re S. 498A of the Cr. Code)*, [1937] A.C. 368 at p. 375 referred to his judgment in the *Proprietary Articles* case in these words:

"The basis of that decision is that there is no other criterion of 'wrongness' than the intention of the Legislature in the public interest to prohibit the act or omission made criminal." In both of these cases the legislation was held to be competently enacted under

s. 91(27). While in the latter "intent to do wrong" and that all of the public be immediately affected were negatived as essentials to the constitution of a crime, both cases emphasize that Parliament in enacting criminal law is acting "in the public interest". This last phrase is significant in relation to the limitation suggested in both cases upon the power of the Parliament of Canada, which in the latter is expressed as follows:

"The only limitation on the plenary power of the Dominion to determine what shall or shall not be criminal is the condition that Parliament shall not in the guise of enacting criminal legislation in truth and in substance encroach on any of the classes of subjects enumerated in s. 92. It is no objection that it does in fact affect them. . . ."

These authorities emphasize again that ss. 91 and 92 must be read and construed together, and that it is the substance as distinguished from the form of the legislation that in each case must be considered. The legislation here in question does not disclose that the prohibitions were enacted "in the public interest" in the sense in which that phrase is used in the foregoing authorities. It rather appears that those in s. 5(a) were, as well as many other prohibitions in the *Dairy Industry Act,* enacted for the purpose of protecting and regulating that industry. These prohibitions, as already stated, prevented citizens engaging in the manufacture and sale of these specified food products. As such the legislation is in relation to property and civil rights and therefore within the legislative competence of the Provinces. Legislation so enacted is *ultra vires* the Dominion and it does not become *intra vires* by the inclusion therein of offences and penalties for the purpose of giving coercive and compulsory effect to its provisions. The enactment of such offences and penalties though in form criminal is not in relation to criminal law within the meaning of s. 91(27) and is therefore not competent Dominion legislation under that heading. It was no doubt that the Provinces might have the power to enact compulsory and coercive provisions and thereby give force and effect to legislation enacted in relation to matters assigned to them that s. 92(15) was included in the B.N.A. Act, which enabled the provinces to impose "punishment by fine, penalty, or imprisonment for enforcing any law of the province."

It was submitted that s. 5(a) was competent Dominion legislation under the peace, order and good government clause of s. 91, that while within the provisions of s. 92 the Provinces might prohibit manufacture and sale in a purely local matter "from a provincial point of view," the Dominion possessed in addition thereto a Dominion power to prohibit and thereby deal with such matters as interprovincial trade. This contention appears to be answered by Duff J. (later C.J.) in *The King v. Eastern Terminal Elevator Co.,* [1925] S.C.R. 434 at p. 448, where he stated:

"The other fallacy is . . . that the Dominion has such power because no single province, nor, indeed, all the provinces acting together, could put into effect such a sweeping scheme. The authority arises, it is said, under the residuary clause because of the necessary limits of the provincial authority. This is precisely the view which was advanced in the *Board of Commerce* case, [1922] 1 A.C. 191, and, indeed, is the view which was unsuccessfully put forward in the *Montreal Street R.* case, [1912] A.C. 333, where it was pointed out that in a system involving a division of powers such as that set up by the British North America Act, it may often be that subsidiary legislation by the provinces or by the Dominion is required to give full effect to some beneficial and necessary scheme of legislation not entirely within the powers of either."

Moreover, even if such a power of prohibition did exist, s. 5(a) does not purport to be enacted in relation to interprovincial trade or any aspect in relation to manufacture and sale other than a direct prohibition of the exercise of civil rights within the Provinces.

Neither can this legislation be supported on the basis that it is for the protection of an industry that has attained "such dimensions" or is of such national concern as to give to the Dominion a jurisdiction to validly enact it under the peace, order and good government clause of s. 91 . . .

It would . . . appear that this industry cannot be classified as "unquestionably of Canadian interest and importance" as stated by Lord Watson in the *Liquor License* case, [1896] A.C. 348, nor within the language of Viscount Haldane in the *Board of Commerce* case, [1922] 1 A.C. 191 at p. 197 . . .

Nor does it appear that the language of Viscount Simon in *A.-G. Ont. v. Canada Temperance Federation*, [1946] A.C. 193 at p. 205 in any way alters or affects the jurisdiction of the Parliament of Canada. . .

The importance of the dairy industry in the economy of Canada was not questioned. Nor were the statements to the effect that in the grazing season a surplus of milk is realized that must be disposed of in the manufacture of dairy products, that some Provinces produce a surplus of butter while others must import a portion of their requirements. These, together with those factors of climate that make the conduct of this industry relatively expensive, are of themselves not sufficient in normal conditions to justify the conclusion that the dairy industry has attained "such dimensions" as to give it a Dominion aspect and thereby bring it within the legislative competence of the Parliament of Canada under the peace, order and good government clause of s. 91 as interpreted by the foregoing authorities. If the dairy industry itself has not attained "such dimensions" as to give it a Dominion aspect, s. 5(a) cannot be accepted as competent Dominion legislation in relation thereto.

The Dairy Industry Act, apart from s. 5(a), throughout the hearing of this reference has been accepted as competent Dominion public health legislation under the peace, order and good government clause of s. 91. The products mentioned in s. 5(a), particularly those to which our attention has been directed, being not injurious to health, that section cannot constitute valid public health legislation. It follows that in neither of these aspects can s. 5(a) be accepted as competent Dominion legislation under the opening paragraph of s. 91.

Nor can s. 5(a) be accepted as legislation enacted by the Dominion "in relation to agriculture in all or any of the provinces" within the meaning of s. 95 of the *B.N.A. Act*. As already stated, oleomargarine and margarine are vegetable oil compounds. Legislation with respect to their manufacture and sale is not legislation in relation to agriculture. In *Lower Mainland Dairy Products v. Crystal Dairy Ltd.*, [1933] A.C. 168, the Province of British Columbia enacted legislation under which the sale of milk was regulated. The contention that this was legislation in relation to agriculture was not maintained because it did "not appear in any way to interfere with the agricultural operations of the farmers."

In *The King v. Eastern Terminal Elevator Co., supra*, it was contended that the legislation relative to the sale of grain was legislation in relation to agriculture. Mr. Justice Mignault disposed of this contention: "the subject matter of the Act is not agriculture but a product of agriculture considered as an article of trade."

The prohibition of the importation, manufacture and sale of these manufactured food products might compete with or affect the sale of dairy products, but it does not interfere with the farmers in their agricultural operations within the meaning of s. 95.

The prohibition of importation, unlike that of manufacture and sale, is not in relation to any of the matters assigned exclusively to the Provinces. It is rather a matter of external trade in relation to which the Parliament of Canada possess legislative authority under s. 91(2) "The regulation of Trade and Commerce." . . .

The Parliament of Canada may also enact customs duties under s. 91(3) "The raising of Money by any Mode or System of Taxation." . . .

The attainment of the regulation of trade and commerce by the imposition of customs duties necessarily involves a restriction upon importation which increases as the duty is raised. The difference between the imposition of a duty and complete prohibition is therefore but one of degree rather than principle. The enactment of embargoes and prohibitions, the latter often included in customs legislation, has been a recognized practice in matters of external trade not only in this but in other countries. The Parliament of Canada in legislating under one of the enumerated heads or under the peace, order and good government clause of s. 91 does so as "a fully sovereign state", and upon the basis of the principle underlying the decision of *Croft v. Dunphy*, [1933] A.C. 156, Parliament possesses the power to enact such legislation under s. 91(2).

The considerations that support a prohibition of importation for the regulation and protection of a native industry must often be quite different from those of manufacture and sale, even if both be effected toward the attainment of the same end. Each has a distinct and separate significance, the one affecting external the other domestic trade. In this particular case the vegetable oils which enter into the manufacture of oleomargarine and margarine are largely imported. Moreover, these manufactured products are produced in large quantities in other countries and when the legislation was suspended, as hereinbefore stated, a considerable quantity was imported.

Parliament in 1886 placed the prohibition of importation in the *Customs Act* (1886, c. 37) where it has since remained with some amendments and is now found in s. 214 of the *Customs Tariff Act* (R.S.C. 1927, c. 44, Item 1204 of Sch. C). It was not until 1903 that the prohibition of importation was also included in the *Butter Act* (1903, c. 6). When in the 1914 legislation *supra* the prohibition of margarine was enacted, and though not included in the *Customs Tariff Act*, it was for the attainment of the same end and competent Dominion legislation under s. 91(2). The foregoing indicates that not only has the prohibition of importation a separate and independent significance from that of manufacture and sale, but that to some extent Parliament has so regarded it. It is therefore but reasonable to assume that Parliament would have enacted a prohibition against importation even if it could not have competently included a prohibition against the manufacture and sale of these products. *Reference Re Alberta Bill of Rights*, [1947] A.C. 503. . .

My answer to the question submitted is that s. 5(a) of the *Dairy Industry Act*, R.S.C. 1927 c. 45, is *intra vires* the Parliament of Canada in so far as it prohibits the importation of the products mentioned, but *ultra vires* in so far as it prohibits the manufacture, sale, offering or having in possession for sale the specified products.

[Taschereau and Kellock JJ. also gave reasons which lead them to arrive at the same result as that reached by Rand and Estey JJ. Locke J. gave reasons holding that s. 5(a) was wholly *ultra vires*. On appeal to the Privy Council, *sub nom. Canadian Federation of Agriculture v. A.-G. Que.*, [1951] A.C. 179, [1950] 4 D.L.R. 689, the decision of the majority was affirmed. Lord Morton of Henryton pointed out that it was no longer possible to argue that the purpose of the prohibition was to exclude substances injurious to health; rather the purpose of the challenged legislation was to protect and encourage the dairy industry.

As to the validity of s. 6 of the Dairy Industry Act, referred to by Rinfret C.J.C. *supra*, see *Rex v. Perfection Creameries Ltd.*, [1939] 3 D.L.R. 185, [1939] 2 W.W.R. 139, 47 Man. R. 150.

In *Great West Saddlery Co. v. The King*, [1921] 2 A.C. 91, at p. 118, 58 D.L.R. 1, [1921] 1 W.W.R. 1034, Lord Haldane said the following:

"The only other decision to which their Lordships desire to make reference is that in *Brewers and Maltsters' Association v. A.-G. for Ontario*, [1897] A.C. 231. There the Dominion Legislature had previously and validly regulated the manufacture and wholesale vending of spirituous liquors, and provided for the issue of licences for such manufacture and sale. Ontario had subsequently passed an Act requiring every person so licensed by the Dominion also to obtain a licence for sale from the Province, and to pay a fee for it. It was held in the first place that this was direct taxation for provincial purposes, and therefore within the power of the Province, and secondly that the licence was such as to be authorized among the 'other licences' included in the general words of head 9 of s. 92—'shop, saloon, tavern, auctioneer, and other licences in order to the raising of a revenue for Provincial purposes.' Their Lordships think that what is implied in this decision is that while the Dominion

Legislature had power to place restrictions throughout Canada on the traffic in liquor, the powers conferred by s. 91 did not in any way conflict with the positive powers of taxation and licensing for Provincial objects, expressly and particularly conferred by s. 92. These, in so far as there might have been any interference, had been conferred by the Imperial Parliament on the Provinces by way of exception both from the general power of legislation given to the Dominion by the initial words of s. 91, and from any purely general enumerated head, such as the regulation of trade and commerce."

Can this passage sit with the position taken in the *Margarine* case, *supra?*

"While manufacture is not of itself interstate commerce the shipment of manufactured goods interstate is such commerce and the prohibition of such shipment by Congress is indubitably a regulation of the commerce": *United States v. Darby* (1940), 312 U.S. 100, at p. 113, 61 S. Ct. 451, at p. 457. Is this a proposition which applies in Canada? If so, may the prohibition of shipment be accompanied by regulations that permit such shipment on due compliance?

May it be said, in view of the *Margarine* case, that prohibition of manufacture and, indeed, the regulation of production, is open only to the Province, save in situations which may be brought within the *Russell* case (1882), 7 App. Cas. 829, and that, absent competent federal legislation, it is no answer to such provincial legislation that it will remove goods from interprovincial or foreign trade? Cf. *Mugler v. Kansas* (1887), 123 U.S. 623; *Bayside Fish Flour Co. v. Gentry* (1936), 297 U.S. 422.

Australia had its margarine case in *Grannall v. Marrickville Margarine Proprietary Ltd.* (1955), 93 C.L.R. 55, where an allegation was made that s. 92 of the Constitution was infringed by a State statute prohibiting the manufacture of margarine unless under licence. While it was appreciated that the restriction was in the interests of the dairy industry, the Court found that there was no unconstitutional interference with inter-state trade. The issue here, however, differs from the problem as it arises under the B.N.A. Act.

The Tobacco Restraint Act, R.S.C. 1970, c. T-9 makes it an offence (1) directly or indirectly to sell, give or furnish cigarettes to a person under age 16; (2) for a person under age 16 to smoke in a street or public place or purchase or have tobacco in his possession. Is the Act valid? See *Regina ex rel Barrie v. Stelzer* (1957), 15 D.L.R. (2d) 280, 24 W.W.R. (N.S.) 130, 119 Can. C.C. 305; and cf. *Regina v. Watson* (1890), 17 O.A.R. 221.]

2. Review and Reconsideration

Whether or not one accepts the "collocation" argument in the *Parsons* case or the "provincial autonomy" argument in *Montreal v. Montreal Street Ry., supra,* it is undeniable that they both produced the same inflexibility in measuring the scope of the federal trade and commerce power as was produced by decisions measuring the scope of the federal general power. In both situations, the inflexibility led to extravagance of statement by Lord Haldane in the *Snider* case, and in respect of both there has been a retreat which is still in progress. It will be useful to chart the path of the retreat and to attempt some assessment of its consequences.

The need to reconcile the power to make laws for the peace, order and good government of Canada in relation to the regulation of trade and commerce with the powers reposed in the Provinces cannot be lastingly met by imprisoning either the former or the latter within pre-determined limits which take no account of social and economic change. Lord Porter remarked in *Commonwealth of Australia v. Bank of New South Wales*, [1950] A.C. 235, at p. 310, in reference to an issue of validity raised by competing claims of legislative power that "the problem to be solved will often be not so much legal as political, social or economic, yet it must be solved by a court of law ...". Such an admission, rare in Australian cases in the Privy Council, is even rarer in the Canadian cases, but it is a commonplace of constitutional adjudication in the Supreme Court of United States; and nowhere has it been more emphatically considered than in examination of the scope of Congressional power over interstate commerce: see Murphy J. for the Court in *American Power & Light Co. v. Securities & Exchange Commission* (1946), 329 U.S. 90, at p. 104, 67 S. Ct. 133, at p. 141: "The federal commerce power is as broad as the economic needs of the nation"; *Stern*, The Commerce Clause and the National Economy, (1946) 59 Harv. L. Rev. 645, 883; *Abel*, The Commerce Clause in the Constitutional Convention and in Contemporary Comment, (1941) 25 Minn. L. Rev. 432.

In Australia, the Commonwealth Parliament is empowered by s. 51(i) to make laws, subject to the Constitution, with respect to "trade and commerce with other countries, and among the States". This power is not exclusive of State power, although legislation of the Commonwealth may prevail in case of inconsistency with state legislation; and it has also been held that the Commonwealth power, no less than the State power, is subject to the guarantee in s. 92 that "on the imposition of uniform duties of customs, trade, commerce and intercourse among the States, whether by means of internal carriage or ocean navigation, shall be absolutely free": see *James v. Commonwealth*, [1936] A.C. 578, 55 C.L.R. 1; *Gratwick v. Johnson* (1945), 70 C.L.R. 1; *Hughes & Vale Proprietary Ltd. v. New South Wales (No. 2)* (1955), 93 C.L.R. 127; and see Note, The Commerce Power under the Australian Construction, (1942) 42 Col. L. Rev. 660; *Stone*, A Government of Laws and Yet of Men, being a Survey of Half a Century of the Australian Commerce Power, (1950) 25 N.Y.U.L. Rev. 451. One could not confidently assert, up to the time appeals to the Privy Council were abolished, that federal legislation could embrace regulation of a product as a whole even where the principal market was outside of the province of production; or that federal legislation could embrace regulation of a trade as a whole where it was carried on throughout the country by transactions that ignored provincial boundaries: see *A.-G. B.C. v. A.-G. Can.* (Natural Products Marketing Act case), [1937] A.C. 377, [1937] 1 D.L.R. 691, [1937] 1 W.W.R. 328; *In re Insurance Act of Canada*, [1932] A.C. 41, [1932] 1 D.L.R. 97, [1931] 3 W.W.R. 689. Indeed, at a time when appeals to that body had been already abolished and only pending cases were appealable, the Judicial Committee in the Margarine case (*Canadian Federation of Agriculture v. A.-G. Que.*, [1951] A.C. 179, [1950] 4 D.L.R. 689), reiterated the "autonomy of the provinces" theme as justifying a limitation on the wide scope of the words in s. 91(2).

REFERENCE RE THE FARM PRODUCTS MARKETING ACT, R.S.O. 1950, C. 131, AS AMENDED

In the Supreme Court of Canada. [1957] S.C.R. 198,
7 D.L.R. (2d) 257.

Reference to the Supreme Court of certain questions respecting the validity of certain provisions of and regulations under the Ontario Farm Products Marketing Act. Eight questions were put to the Court. The opinions reproduced here in part concern only the first six questions.

KERWIN C.J.C.—This is a Reference by His Excellency the Governor-General in Council as to the validity of one clause of one section of the *Farm Products Marketing Act,* R.S.O. 1950, c. 131 of the Province of Ontario, of certain Regulations made thereunder, of an Order of the Ontario Hog Producers' Marketing Board, of a proposed amendment to the Act, and of a suggested authorization by the Farm Products Marketing Board if that amendment be held to be *intra vires.* On such a Reference one cannot envisage all possible circumstances which might arise and it must also be taken that it is established that it is not to be presumed that a Provincial Legislature intended to exceed its legislative jurisdiction under the *B.N.A. Act,* although the Court may, on what it considers the proper construction of a given enactment, determine that the Legislature has gone beyond its authority.

Subsequent to the date of the Order of Reference, the Act was amended by c. 20 of the Statutes of 1956, which came into force the day it received Royal Assent, s. 1 of which reads as follows:

"1. *The Farm Products Marketing Act* is amended by adding thereto the following section:

"1a. The purpose and intent of this Act is to provide for the control and regulation in any or all respects of the marketing within the Province of farm products including the prohibition of such marketing in whole or in part."

Without entering into a discussion as to what is a declaratory law, since the term may have different connotations depending upon the matter under review, it is arguable that, for present purposes, this amendment should be read as part of the *Farm Products Marketing Act,* but, in any event, the first question submitted to us directs us to assume that that Act as amended down to the date of the Reference applies only in the case of "intra-provincial transactions". This term means "existing or occurring within a province"; see Shorter Oxford English Dictionary including "intraparochial" as an example under the word "intra". As will appear later, the word "marketing" is defined in the Act, but, in accordance with what has already been stated, I take it as being confined to marketing within the Province.

Question No. 1 is as follows:

"1. Assuming that the said Act applies only in the case of intra-provincial transactions, is clause (*l*) of subsection 1 of section 3 of

The Farm Products Marketing Act, R.S.O. 1950, chapter 131, as amended by Ontario Statutes 1951, chapter 25, 1953, chapter 36, 1954, chapter 29, 1955, chapter 21, *ultra vires* the Ontario Legislature?"

Clause (*l*) of s-s. (1) of s. 3 referred to provides:

"3(1) The Board may,

"(*l*) authorize any marketing agency appointed under a scheme to conduct a pool or pools for the distribution of all moneys received from the sale of the regulated product and requiring any such marketing agency, after deducting all necessary and proper disbursements and expenses, to distribute the proceeds of sale in such manner that each person receives a share of the total proceeds in relation to the amount, variety, size, grade and class of the regulated product delivered by him and to make an initial payment on delivery of the product and subsequent payments until the total net proceeds are distributed."

For a proper understanding of the terms used in this clause and of the provisions of the Act it is necessary to refer to what is proposed by the latter.

The Board is the Farm Products Marketing Board and " 'farm products' includes animals, meats, eggs, poultry, wool, dairy products, grains, seeds, fruit, fruit products, vegetables, vegetable products, maple products, honey, tobacco and such articles of food or drink manufactured or derived in whole or in part from any such product and such other natural products of agriculture as may be designated by the regulations" (s. 1(*b*)). " 'Regulated product' means a farm product in respect of a scheme which is in force" (s. 1(*g*)). Provision is made for the formulation of a scheme for the marketing or regulating of any farm product upon the petition of at least 10% of all producers engaged in the production of the farm product in Ontario, or in that part thereof to which the proposed scheme is to apply. " 'Marketing' means buying, selling and offering for sale and includes advertising, assembling, financing, packing and shipping for sale or storage and transporting in any manner by any person, and 'market' and 'marketed' have corresponding meanings" (s. 1(*e*) as re-enacted by 1955, c. 21, s. 1). The scheme may provide for a "marketing agency" designated by the Board in its regulations. Once the scheme is approved by the Board the latter's Regulations will apply according to the farm products dealt with thereby.

It seems plain that the Province may regulate a transaction of sale and purchase in Ontario between a resident of the Province and one who resides outside its limits; that is, if an individual in Quebec comes to Ontario and there buys a hog, or vegetables, or peaches, the mere fact that he has the intention to take them from Ontario to Quebec does not deprive the Legislature of its powers to regulate the transaction, as is evidenced by such enactments as the *Sale of Goods Act*, R.S.O. 1950, c. 345. That is a matter of the regulation of contracts and not of trade as trade and in that respect the intention of the purchaser is immaterial. However, if the hog be sold to a packing plant or the vegetables or peaches to a cannery, the products of those establishments in the course of trade may be dealt with by the Legislature or by Parliament depending, on the one hand, upon whether all the products are sold or intended for sale within the Province or, on the other, whether some of them are sold or intended for sale beyond provincial limits. It is, I think, impossible to fix any minimum proportion of such last mentioned sales or intended sales as determining the jurisdiction of Parliament. This applies to the sale by the original owner. Once a statute aims at "regulation of trade in matters of interprovincial concern" (*Citizens Ins. Co. v. Parsons* (1881), 7 App. Cas. 96 at p. 113), it is beyond the competence of a Provincial Legislature. The ambit of head 2 of s. 91 of the *B.N.A. Act* —"The Regulation of Trade and Commerce" has been considerably enlarged by decisions of the Judicial Committee and expressions used in some of its earlier judgments must be read in the light of its later pronouncements, as is pointed out by Sir Lyman P. Duff C.J.C. in *Re Alberta Legislation*, [1938] 2 D.L.R. 81 at pp. 96-7, S.C.R. 100 at p. 121 [aff'd [1938] 4 D.L.R. 433, [1939] A.C. 117]. In fact, his judgment in *Reference re Natural Products Marketing Act*, [1936] 3 D.L.R. 622, S.C.R. 398, 66 Can. C.C. 180, which is justly considered as the *locus classicus*, must be read in conjunction with and subject to his remarks in the later case. The concept of trade and commerce, the regulation of which is confided to parliament, is entirely separate and distinct from the regulation of mere sale and purchase agreements. Once an article enters into the flow of interprovincial or external trade, the subject-matter and all its attendant circumstances cease to be a mere matter of local concern. No change has taken place in the theory underlying the construction of the *B.N.A. Act* that what is not within the legislative jurisdiction of Parliament must be within that of the Provincial Legislatures. This, of course, still leaves the question as to how far either may proceed, and, as Lord Atkin pointed out in *A.-G. B.C. v. A.-G. Can.* (*Natural Products Marketing Act* case), [1937] 1 D.L.R. 691 at pp. 694-5, A.C. 377 at p. 389, 67 Can. C.C. 337 at p. 341, neither party may leave its own sphere and encroach upon that of another.

Mr. Robinette suggested that there was an inconsistency between the judgment of Mr. Justice Duff in *Lawson v. Interior Tree Fruit & Vegetable Committee*, [1931] 2 D.L.R. 193, S.C.R. 357, and his judgment in *The King v. Eastern Terminal Elevator Co.*, [1925] 3 D.L.R. 1, S.C.R. 434. However, all that was decided in the latter case was that Parliament had exceeded its jurisdiction while in the former it was held that the British Columbia statute under review was *ultra vires*.

It was contended by Mr. Pepper that the *Combines Investigation Act*, R.S.C. 1952, c. 314, and ss. 411 and 412 of the *Criminal Code*, and the *Agricultural Prices Support Act*, R.S.C. 1952, c. 3, are relevant and prevent the Ontario Legislature from enacting cl. (*l*) of s-s. (1) of s. 3 of the *Farm Products Marketing Act* and therefore the administrative agencies provided for by that Act, from operating. The point is determined against that contention as to the *Combines Investigation Act* by the decision of this Court in *Tolton Mfg. Co. v. Advisory Committee,* [1944] 4 D.L.R. 273, S.C.R. 349, 82 Can. C.C. 129. With respect to that Act and also to the sections of the Criminal Code referred to, it cannot be said that any scheme otherwise within the authority of the Legislature is against the public interest when the Legislature is seized of the power and, indeed, the obligation to take care of that interest in the Province. The *Agricultural Prices Support Act* and in fact all Acts of Canada of a similar nature contain merely provisions for the assistance of agriculture. A final argument was advanced to the effect that the legislation conflicted with s. 25 of the *Live Stock and Live Stock Products Act,* R.S.C. 1952, c. 167, which reads: "25. Notwithstanding anything in this Part, any farmer or drover may sell his own live stock at a stockyard on his own account." This is merely a provision in ease of the other sections of that particular Act.

In view of the wording of Q. 1, I take cl. (*l*) of s-s. (1) of s. 3 of the *Farm Products Marketing Act* as being a successful endeavour on the part of the Ontario Legislature to fulfil its part while still keeping within the ambit of its powers. On the assumption directed to be made and reading the clause so as not to apply to transactions which I have indicated would be of a class beyond the powers of the Legislature, my answer to the first Question is "No".

Question No. 2 asks whether a certain regulation as amended respecting the marketing of hogs is *ultra vires* the Lieutenant-Governor in Council. The Order in Council was made in pursuance of the statute and, as the wording may be construed as contemplating only local trade, the objection, in view of what has already been stated, is without foundation. Nor can I agree (a) that the scheme does not contain substantive terms and therefore is really not a scheme at all; (b) that it is necessary that there should be prior approval by the producers.

I assume that the Regulation of the Farm Products Marketing Board referred to in Q. 3 deals only with the control of the sale of hogs for consumption within the Province, or to packing plants or other processors whose products will be consumed therein. The provision for licensing is not *ultra vires* and a company incorporated by letters patent under the *Companies Act* of Canada [R.S.C. 1952, c. 53], with power to carry on the business of a packing plant throughout the nation, is bound to comply with a general licensing law.

My answer to Q. No. 4 is that the Order of the Ontario Hog Producers' Marketing Board fixing the service charges to be imposed by the marketing agency is not *ultra vires* the Board, as the matter is covered by the decision of the Privy Council in *Shannon v. Lower Mainland Dairy Products Bd.,* [1938] 4 D.L.R. 81, A.C. 708. For the same reason, I think similar answers must be given to Qq. Nos. 5 and 6, the first relating to the marketing of peaches for processing and the latter to the marketing of vegetables for processing. . . .

My answers to the questions are as follows:

Question No. 1:—On the assumption that the Act is restricted to intra-provincial transactions as defined in these reasons, the answer is No.

Question No. 2:—No.

Question No. 3:—Assuming that the Regulation deals only with the control of the sale of hogs for consumption within the Province, or to packing plants or other processors whose products will be consumed therein, the answer is No.

Question No. 4:—No.

Question No. 5:—No.

Question No. 6:—No.

RAND J.: This reference raises questions going to the scope of provincial authority over trade. They arise out of the *Farm Products Marketing Act*, R.S.O. 1950, c. 131, as amended, which deals comprehensively with the matter connoted by its name and out of certain schemes formed under it. Its object is to accord primary producers of farm products the advantages of various degrees of controlled marketing, for which it provides provincial and local machinery.

General jurisdiction over its administration is exercised by the Farm Products Marketing Board; regulation is by way of schemes for marketing of any product; under a scheme, a local board, district committees and county groups are organized; and the marketing may be carried out exclusively by an agency designated by the Board upon the recommendation of the local board.

The questions put, which assume the Act to be limited in application to local trade, call for answers which make it necessary to examine and define the scope of local trade to the extent of the regulation provided. The enquiry must take into account regulatory power over acts and transactions which while objectively appearing to be consummated within the Province may involve or possess an interest of interprovincial or foreign trade, which for convenience I shall refer to as external trade.

The products embraced include "animals, meats, eggs, poultry, wool, dairy products, grains, seeds, fruit, fruit products, vegetable products . . . and such articles of food or drink manufactured or derived in whole or in part from any such product".

"Marketing" means buying, selling, assembling, packing, shipping for sale or storage and transporting in any manner by any person. The Marketing Board may establish negotiating agencies which may adopt or determine by agreement minimum prices and other features of marketing, and prohibit the marketing of any class, variety, grade or size of a product. It may require a licence to be taken out by every person for producing, marketing or processing a product with fees payable at various times and in different amounts. The Board may authorize an agency to control the times and places for marketing, the quantity, grade, class and price of products to be marketed, and to exercise other powers conferred by the statute on the Board.

Although not specifically mentioned in s. 92 of the *B.N.A. Act*. there is admittedly a field of trade within provincial power, and the heads of s. 92 from which it is to be deduced will be considered later. The power is a subtraction from the scope of the language conferring on the Dominion by head 2 of s. 91 exclusive authority to make laws in relation to the Regulation of Trade and Commerce, and was derived under an interpretation of the Act which was found necessary "in order to preserve from serious curtailment, if not from virtual extinction, the degree of autonomy which, as appears from the scheme of the Act as a whole, the Provinces were intended to possess"; *per* Duff J. in *Lawson v. Interior Tree Fruit & Vegetable Committee*. [1931] 2 D.L.R. 193 at p. 200, S.C.R. 357 at p. 366.

In examining the legislation for the purpose mentioned we should bear in mind Lord Atkin's admonition in *A.-G. B.C. v. A.-G. Can.*. [1937] 1 D.L.R. 691 at p. 695, A.C. 377, 67 Can. C.C. 337 at p. 341 that "the legislation will have to be carefully framed, and will not be achieved by either party leaving its own sphere and encroaching upon that of the other".

The définitive statement of the scope of dominion and provincial jurisdiction was made by Duff C.J.C. in *Reference re Natural Products Marketing Act*, [1936] 3 D.L.R. 622 at pp. 633 *et seq.*, S.C.R. 398 at pp. 414 *et seq.*, 66 Can. C.C. 180 at pp. 192 *et seq.* The regulation of particular trades confined to the Province lies exclusively with the Legislature subject, it may be, to Dominion general regulation affecting all trade, and to such incidental intrusion by the Dominion as may be necessary to prevent the defeat of Dominion regulation; interprovincial and foreign trade are correspondingly the exclusive concern of Parliament. That statement is to be read with the judgment of this Court in *The King v. Eastern Terminal Elevator Co.*, [1925] 3 D.L.R. 1, S.C.R. 434, approved by the Judicial Committee in *A.-G. B.C. v. A.-G. Can.*, *supra* at p. 693 D.L.R., p. 387 A.C., p. 339 Can. C.C., to the effect that Dominion regulation cannot embrace local trade merely because in undifferentiated subject-matter the external interest is dominant. But neither the original statement nor its approval furnishes a clear guide to the demarcation of the two classes when we approach as here the origination, the first stages of trade, including certain aspects of manufacture and production.

That demarcation must observe this rule, that if in a trade activity, including manufacture or production, there is involved a matter of extra-provincial interest or concern its regulation thereafter in the aspect of trade is by that fact put beyond provincial power. This is exemplified in *Lawson v. Interior Tree Fruit & Vegetable Committee (supra)* where the Province purported to regulate the time and quantity of shipment, the shippers, the price and the transportation of fruit and vegetables in both unsegregated and segregated local and interprovincial trade movements.

A producer is entitled to dispose of his products beyond the Province without reference to a provincial marketing agency or price, shipping or other trade regulation; and an outside purchaser is entitled with equal freedom to purchase and export. Processing is one of a number of trade services that may be given products in the course of reaching the consumer: milling (as of grain or lumber), sorting, packing, slaughtering, dressing, storing, transporting, etc. The producer or purchaser may desire to process the product either within or beyond the Province and if he engages for that with a local undertaking (using that expression in a non-technical sense), such as a packing plant—and it would apply to any sort of servicing—he takes that service as he finds it but free from such provincial impositions as are strictly trade regulations such as prices or the specification of standards, which could no more be imposed than provincial trade marks. Regulation of that nature could directly nullify external trade vital to the economy of the country. Trade arrangements reaching the dimensions of world agreements are now a commonplace; interprovincial trade, in which the Dominion is a single market, is of similar importance, and equally vital to the economic functioning of the country as a whole. The Dominion power implies responsibility for promoting and maintaining the vigour and growth of trade beyond provincial confines, and the discharge of this duty must remain unembarrassed by local trade impediments. If the processing is restricted to external trade, it becomes an instrumentality of that trade and its control as to prices, movements, standards, etc., by the Dominion follows: *Reference re Validity of Industrial Relations and Disputes Investigation Act,* [1955] 3 D.L.R. 721, S.C.R. 529. The licensing of processing plants by the Province as a trade regulation is thus limited to their operations in local trade. Likewise the licensing of shippers, whether producers or purchasers, and the fixing of the terms and conditions of shipment, including prices, as trade regulation, where the goods are destined beyond the Province; would be beyond provincial power.

Local trade has in some cases been classed as a matter of property and civil rights and related to head 13 of s. 92, and the propriety of that allocation was questioned. The production and exchange of goods as an economic activity does not take place by virtue of positive law or civil right; it is assumed as part of the residual free activity of men upon or around which law is imposed. It has an identity of its own recognized by head 2 of s. 91. I cannot agree that its regulation under that head was intended as a species of matter under head 13 from which by the language of s. 91 it has been withdrawn. It happened that in *Citizens Ins. Co. v. Parsons* (1881), 7 App. Cas. 96, assuming insurance to be a trade, the commodity being dealt in was the making of contracts, and their relation to head 13 seemed obvious. But the true conception of trade (in contradistinction to the static nature of rights, civil or property) is that of a dynamic, the creation and flow of goods from production to consumption or utilization, as an individualized activity.

The conclusive answer to the question is furnished by a consideration of s. 94 which provides for the uniformity in Ontario, New

Brunswick and Nova Scotia of "all or any of the Laws relative to Property and Civil Rights". It is, I think, quite impossible to include within this provision regulation of local trades; that appears to be one feature of the internal economy of each Province in which no such uniformity could ever be expected. What the language is directed to are laws relating to civil status and capacity, contracts, torts and real and personal property in the common law Provinces, jural constructs springing from the same roots, already more or less uniform, and lending themselves to more or less permanence. In some degree uniformity has been achieved by individual provincial action in such legislation, for instance, as that of contributory negligence.

Head 16 contains what may be called the residuary power of the Province: *A.-G. Ont. v. A.-G. Dom.*, [1896] A.C. 348 at p. 365, and it is within that residue that the autonomy of the Province in local matters, so far as it might be affected by trade regulation, is to be preserved. As was recognized in the *Parsons* case *(supra)*, this points up the underlying division of the matters of legislation into those which are primarily of national and those of local import. But this is not intended to derogate from regulation as well as taxation of local trade through licence under head 9 of s. 92, nor from its support under head 13.

It is important to keep in mind, as already observed, that the broad language of head 2 of s. 91 has been curtailed not by any express language of the statute but as a necessary implication of the fundamental division of powers effected by it. The interpretation of this head has undergone a transformation. When it was first considered by this Court in *Severn v. The Queen* (1878), 2 S.C.R. 70 and *City of Fredericton v. The Queen* (1880), 3 S.C.R. 505, the majority views did not envisage the limitation now established; that was introduced by the judgment in the *Parsons* case *(supra)*. The nadir of its scope was reached in what seemed its restriction to a function ancillary to other Dominion powers; but the view has been irretrievably scotched.

The powers of this Court in the exercise of its jurisdiction are no less in scope than those formerly exercised in relation to Canada by the Judicial Committee. From time to time the Committee has modified the language used by it in the attribution of legislation to the various heads of ss. 91 and 92, and in its general interpretative formulations, and that incident of judicial power must, now, in the same manner and with the same authority, wherever deemed necessary, be exercised in revising or restating those formalities that have come down to us. This is a function inseparable from constitutional decision. It involves no departure from the basic principles of jurisdictional distribution; it is rather a refinement of interpretation in application to the particularized and evolving features and aspects of matters which the intensive and extensive expansion of the life of the country inevitably presents.

The reaches of trade may extend to aspects of manufacture. In *A.-G. Ont. v. A.-G. Dom. (supra)* the Judicial Committee dealt with the question whether the Province could prohibit the manufacture within the Province of intoxicating liquor, to which the answer was given that, in the absence of conflicting legislation of Parliament, there would be jurisdiction to that effect if it were shown that the manufacture was carried on under such circumstances and conditions as to make its prohibition a merely local matter in the Province. This involves a limitation of the power of the Province to interdict as a trade matter, the manufacture or production of articles destined for external trade. Admittedly, however, local regulation may affect that trade; wages, workmen's compensation, insurance, taxes and other items that furnish what may be called the local conditions underlying economic activity leading to trade.

The federal character of our Constitution places limits on legislative acts in relation to matters which as an entirety span, so to speak, the boundary between the two jurisdictions. In *The King v. Eastern Terminal Elevator Co. (supra)*, for example, there was a common storage of grain destined both to local and external trade. The situation in *Montreal v. Montreal Street Ry. Co.*, 1 D.L.R. 681, 13 C.R.C. 541, [1912] A.C. 333 was equally striking: there Parliament was held incapable of imposing through rates over a local railway on traffic passing between points on that line and points on a connecting Dominion railway; the only regulation open was declared to be parallel action by Legislature and Parliament, each operating only on its own instrumentality. Although by that means the substantial equivalent of a single administration may be attained, there is a constitutional difference between that co-operating action and action by an overriding jurisdiction.

It follows that trade regulation by a Province or the Dominion, acting alone, related to local or external trade respectively, before the segregation of products or manufactures of each class is reached, is impracticable, with the only effective means open, apart from conditional regulation, being that of co-operative action; this, as in some situations already in effect, may take the form of a single board to administer regulations of both on agreed measures.

On the foregoing interpretation of the scope of provincial regulation of trade, the questions put to us may now be considered.

Three of them go to the validity of two provisions of the Act, s. 3(1) (*l*), authorizing the marketing of a product by means of a pool, and a proposed amendment, para. (*ss*), to s. 7(1) authorizing the purchase of the surplus of a regulated product and its marketing and the use of licence fees to recoup any loss suffered. The remaining five questions go to regulations made in one case by the Lieutenant-Governor in Council, in three cases by the Farm Products Marketing Board, and in one by the Ontario Hog Producers' Marketing Board. [The learned Judge set out s. 3(1) (*l*) of the statute and continued as follows:]

Co-operative disposal may take different forms: it may be that of an exclusive local marketing by an agency, either as owner or agent, by which the products are disposed of and the returns equalized, a form, I should say, within the authority of the Province; or, in the interest of convenience and economy, the producers, as contemplated by the Act here, would make their own sales with all moneys made returnable to the agency, for the recovery of which it may bring suit, and by it equalized and distributed. Since prices can be fixed by the agency, at the point of collecting them the result in both forms becomes the same, and I cannot see any jurisdictional difference between the equalization in the two cases. The exclusion of such an ordinary device of co-operative marketing from provincial power would be a curtailment which I cannot think warranted. As it appears elsewhere in these reasons, indirect taxation is not, under a licensing scheme, a disqualifying factor and in co-operative marketing the essential condition of indirect taxation, the general tendency to pass the tax on to another, is excluded. . . .

On Q. II it is contended that the hog scheme is defective because only a skeleton of machinery is provided, that it does not contain substantive terms without which it is not a scheme at all. What the vote taken under s. 4 [re-enacted 1955, c. 21, s. 3(1)] of the statute is intended to decide is whether or not the product shall be brought under a scheme; and the initial creation of its formal structure appears to be the intendment of the statute. Its approval by the Lieutenant-Governor in Council and the regulations made by the Farm Products Marketing Board furnish its content, similarly envisaged by the statute. The schedule, by its heading, relates the scheme to the Act; and as the language is capable of being confined to local trade it should, in the context, be so construed.

Question III deals with an order of the Farm Products Marketing Board providing by s. 2 that no processor shall commence or continue in the business of processing except under the authority of a licence which the Board may, for any reason deemed by it sufficient, refuse; and by s. 4 prohibiting any person from engaging as a shipper without a licence which a local board may revoke or refuse to renew for failure to observe any order or regulation. This extends to processors or shippers engaged partly or exclusively in external trade. These are trade regulating licences and not for revenue purposes only; and since there is nothing in the regulation to restrict the ordinary meaning of its language, reaching as it does beyond the limits of the statute itself, it is likewise beyond the power of the Farm Products Marketing Board to make.

Section 6 provides for the appointment of a marketing agency through which "all hogs" shall be marketed. This exceeds the authority given the Board. Paragraphs (c) and (d) of s. 8 authorize the imposition of "such service charges as may from time to time be fixed by the local board" and their payment to the local board by the marketing agency. The fees are to be applied to the expenses of administration. This was challenged as involving indirect taxation, a point taken on Qq. IV, V and VI as well and these objections will now be examined together.

Under the hog producers' scheme, the charges are fixed "at the sum of 24 cents per hog and a prorating charge in the sum of 20 cents per producer settlement statement". The scheme for marketing peaches fixes a licence fee at 50 cents for each ton or fraction of a ton of peaches delivered to a processor by a grower; and by the vegetable processing scheme at the rate of 1/2 of 1% of the total sale price due a grower for each ton or fraction of a ton of vegetables delivered to a processor.

On these questions two judgments of the Judicial Committee must be noticed: *Lower Mainland Dairy Products Sales Adjustment Committee v. Crystal Dairy Ltd.*, [1933] 1 D.L.R. 82, A.C. 168 and *Shannon v. Lower Mainland Dairy Products Bd.*, [1938] 4 D.L.R. 81, A.C. 708. In the former the Judicial Committee passed upon legislation of British Columbia purporting to authorize a special exaction from all milk producers in a district proportioned to the quantity of fluid milk sold by them for the purpose of raising a fund to be distributed among the producers whose production was converted into milk products, with a view to equalizing the returns from milk production generally and of bringing about the advantageous distribution of these two classes of commodities. The Committee viewed the issue to be whether the Province, by the means provided, could take money from one group in order to enrich the other and held the impost invalid as indirect taxation. A similar view was taken of the recovery on the same basis of the expenses of the Committee in administering the Act.

The reasons of Lord Thankerton contain no reference to trade regulation: the statute is dealt with as one providing taxation to enable an equalization of price return. The impingement of the tax, related as it was to the volume of products marketed, undoubtedly bore the badge ordinarily held to mark indirect taxation.

In contrast to this was the formation of the issue in *Shannon v. Lower Mainland Dairy Products Bd.*, [1938] 4 D.L.R. 81, A.C. 708. At p. 86 D.L.R., p. 721 A.C., Lord Atkin sums it up: "If regulation of trade within the Province has to be held valid the ordinary method of regulating trade, *i.e.*, by a system of licences, must also be admissible."

There the administering Board was empowered, as here, to control generally the marketing of the regulated product, including the time for marketing, the quantities to be offered by any producer, prohibition of the marketing of any grade, quality or class, the fixing of prices, and marketing through a licensed shipper. Finally there was the authority to collect fees. . . .

The language of Lord Atkin seems to involve the conclusion that fees incidental to provincial regulation of trade by licence are to be considered without reference to the restriction of s. 92(2); and this appears to have been the opinion of Duff J. in *Lawson v. Interior Tree Fruit & Vegetable Committee*, where he says, "and that accordingly imposts which would properly be classed under the general description 'indirect taxation' are not for that reason alone excluded from those which may be exacted under head 9." [[1931] 2 D.L.R. at p. 198].

The power to regulate embraces incidental powers necessary to its effective exercise; and the exaction of fees to meet the expenses of such an administration as that of the schemes, regardless of their incidence, is within that necessity.

The fees in the *Shannon* case were justified on a second ground which supports and supplements the preceding considerations; that they were charges made for services rendered. That is the case here. What the producers received are the benefits of a control that aims at an orderly marketing. The benefit of the organized apparatus is a service rendered by the scheme; and the fees related to either the quantity or the total return are directly proportioned to it.

Mr. Pepper argued that the regulation was in conflict with the provisions of the *Combines Investigation Act* and s. 411 of the *Criminal Code,* but with that I am unable to agree. The provincial statute contemplates coercive regulation in which both private and public interests are taken into account. The provisions of the *Combines Investigation Act* and the *Criminal Code* envisages voluntary combinations or agreements by individuals against the public interest that violate their prohibitions. The public interest in trade regulation is not within the purview of Parliament as an object against which its enactments are directed.

Another conflict was suggested with s. 25 of the *Live Stock and Live Stock Products Act,* R.S.C. 1952, c. 167, which provides: "25. Notwithstanding anything in this part, any farmer or drover may sell his own live stock at a stockyard on his own account." This simply enables a farmer or drover to sell at the stockyard notwithstanding the provisions of that Act; it does not purport to give an absolute right as against other enactments, which if it did it might, as an attempt to control local trade, be so far invalid.

On the assumption that the Act is restricted to intra-provincial transactions as defined in these reasons, I therefore answer the questions put as follows:

Question No.   I: No.
Question No. II: No.
Question No. III: Yes, as indicated.
Question No. IV: No.
Question No.   V: No.
Question No. VI: No.

Locke J.: The order of reference made in this matter by His Excellency the Governor-General in Council, after reciting that questions have arisen respecting the constitutional validity of certain sections of the *Farm Products Marketing Act,* R.S.O. 1950, c. 131, as amended, and the schemes, regulations and orders passed pursuant thereto and that the Government of the Province of Ontario has requested that certain legislation, schemes, regulations and orders be referred to this Court for hearing and consideration, reads:

"AND WHEREAS the Minister of Agriculture for Ontario advises: that under *The Farm Products Marketing Act of Ontario* there are at present in operation 14 marketing schemes covering 21 farm products; that the various schemes are financed by the methods indicated in the questions set out hereunder; that the marketing agency referred to in question number 4 is a co-operative corporation incorporated under Part V of the Corporations Act of Ontario, 1953,

c. 19, and that the by-laws of the marketing agency provide that any surplus of service charges after providing for reserves shall be allocated, credited or paid to those marketing hogs through the agency computed at a rate in relation to the value of the hogs marketed for such person; that in connection with question number 5 one ton peaches makes 144 dozen 20 ounce cans of peaches or 1,728 cans.

"THEREFORE His Excellency the Governor General in Council, under and by virtue of the authority conferred by section 55 of the Supreme Court Act, is pleased to refer and doth hereby refer to the Supreme Court of Canada for hearing and consideration, the following questions:—

"1. Assuming that the said Act applies only in the case of intra-provincial transactions, is clause (*l*) of subsection 1 of section 3 of *The Farm Products Marketing Act,* R.S.O. 1950 chapter 131 as amended by Ontario Statutes 1951, chapter 25, 1953, chapter 36, 1954, chapter 29, 1955, chapter 21 *ultra vires* the Ontario Legislature?

"2. Is Regulation 104 of the Consolidated Regulations of Ontario 1950 as amended by O. Reg. 100/55 and O. Reg. 104/55 respecting the marketing of hogs, *ultra vires* the Lieutenant Governor in Council either in whole or in part and if so in what particular or particulars and to what extent?

"3. Is Ontario Regulation 102/55 respecting the marketing of hogs, *ultra vires* the Farm Products Marketing Board either in whole or in part and if so in what particular or particulars and to what extent?

"4. Is the Order dated the 8th day of June, 1955, made by The Ontario Hog Producers Marketing Board fixing the service charges to be imposed by the marketing agency, *ultra vires* the said Board?

"5. Is regulation 7 of Ontario Reg. 145/54 respecting the marketing of peaches for processing, *ultra vires* the Farm Products Marketing Board?

"6. Is regulation 5 of Ontario Reg. 126/52 respecting the marketing of vegetables for processing, *ultra vires* the Farm Products Marketing Board? . . .

After the Order in Council was made, the Legislature of Ontario by c. 20 of the Statutes of 1956 assented to on March 28, 1956, amended the Act in question by the addition of the following: "1a. The purpose and intent of this Act is to provide for the control and regulation in any or all respects of the marketing within the Province of farm products including the prohibition of such marketing in whole or in part."

The case in this matter contains a copy of an Order in Council made on November 16, 1955, under the provisions of the *Agricultural Products Marketing Act,* R.S.C. 1952, c. 6, whereby certain powers were vested in the Ontario Farm Products Marketing Board, the Ontario Hog Producers' Marketing Board and the Ontario Hog Producers Co-operative, in relation to the marketing of hogs and other products. Since, however, this order is not retrospective in its operation and all of the orders and regulations referred to in Qq. 2 to 6 inclusive were made prior to its date, they can derive no support from it and must depend for their validity entirely upon the provisions of the *Farm Products Marketing Act* as amended.

It should be said at the outset that no useful answer can be made to Qq. 1, 3 and 4 in the absence of some further explanation of what is meant by "intra-provincial transaction" other than that which is to be found in the amendment to the statute made in 1956. This merely says that the purpose and intent of the Act is to provide for the control and regulation of the marketing within the Province of farm products, including the prohibition of such marketing in whole or in part.

"Intra" means within but none of the learned counsel supporting the legislation and the regulations contend that the Legislature is competent to prohibit the marketing of live hogs or other farm products for export. An agreement made in Carleton County between a farmer residing there and a buyer for a packing company operating in Hull, Quebec, is an intra-provincial transaction since it is initiated and completed when the sale is agreed upon and the hog delivered. The farmer is not exporting the hog and it is presumably a matter of indifference to him whether the buyer exports the hog, whether alive or dead, to the Province of Quebec. Yet this transaction would be prohibited if the language of the statute and of the regulation is to be construed literally.

However ineffective the language of the 1956 amendment may be to exclude from the operation of the Act transactions of very great importance and with very wide ramifications which the Province is powerless to regulate (and I think it is quite insufficient), the questions should, in my opinion, be dealt with on the footing that, regardless of the language employed, it was the intention of the Legislature to confine its operation to matters within its own competence. However this procedure may depart from the rules of law applicable to the construction of statutes; this is a reference and, in view of the language of the first question, it is the duty of this Court to endeavour to answer the questions on that basis.

While it is my conclusion that what the *Farm Products Marketing Act* authorizes and what the various boards constituted under its provisions have attempted to do include matters wholly within the jurisdiction of Parliament, all of the necessary powers may be vested in these boards by separate action taken in unison under Dominion and provincial powers and, in answering the questions, I propose to express my opinion as to the respective limits of the jurisdiction of these legislative bodies in matters of this kind, so far as they may be relevant to the matters for consideration.

The main question that has arisen for determination in these matters has been as to the jurisdiction of Parliament under head 2 of s. 91 and that of the Provinces under heads 13 and 16 of s. 92 of the B.N.A. Act. A succession of attempts has been made by various Provincial Legislatures and one by Parliament to regulate and control the sale of natural products and, before attempting to answer the questions, it is of some assistance to consider the principal cases in which the respective powers of the legislative bodies under these heads have been considered. . . .

[The learned Judge dealt at this point with *Lawson v. Interior Tree Fruit & Vegetable Committee,* [1931] S.C.R. 357, [1931] 2 D.L.R. 193; *A.-G. B.C. v. A.-G. Can.,* [1937] A.C. 377, [1937] 1 D.L.R. 691 (The Natural Products Marketing Act Reference); *Shannon v. Lower Mainland Dairy Products Board,* [1938] A.C. 708, [1938] 4 D.L.R. 81, and a number of earlier cases. He then continued as follows:]

The result of the cases in the Judicial Committee appears to me to be most clearly summarized in the judgment of Lord Atkin in *Shannon's case,* [1938] 4 D.L.R. 81 at pp. 84-5, A.C. 708 at p. 719, where it is said: "It is now well settled that the enumeration in s. 91 of 'Regulation of Trade and Commerce' as a class of subject over which the Dominion has exclusive powers does not give the power to regulate for legitimate provincial purposes particular trades or businesses so far as the trade or business is confined to the Province." . . .

Other than in the manner in which this is attempted in the amendment made in 1956 above referred to, the statute does not limit the exercise of the powers which may be vested in the Board under its provisions to natural products marketed for consumption in the Provinces, but includes in its sweeping terms such products which might be sold for export or exported by a producer or one purchasing from him from the Province.

The first question is directed to cl. (*l*) of s-s. (1) of s. 3 of the Act. This authorizes the Board to "authorize any marketing agency appointed under a scheme to conduct a pool or pools for the distribution of all moneys received from the sale of the regulated product and requiring any such marketing agency, after deducting all necessary and proper disbursements and expenses, to distribute the proceeds of sale in such manner that each person receives a share of the total proceeds in relation to the amount, variety, size, grade and class of the regulated product delivered by him and to make an initial payment on delivery of the product and subsequent payments until the total net proceeds are distributed".

Construing the reference to intra-provincial transactions in the question and the words "control and regulation in any or all respects of the marketing within the Province of farm products including the prohibition of such marketing in whole or in part" in the 1956 amendment, as referring to purchases and sales of the controlled product, whether hogs, fruit or vegetables in their natural form, for consumption in the Province, and sales to processors, manufacturers or dealers proposing to sell such products, either in their natural form or after they have been processed by canning, preserving or otherwise treating them, for consumption within the Province, I consider the clause to be within the powers of the Province.

Such transactions are, in my opinion, matters of a merely local or private nature in the Province within head 16 of s. 92, and such regulation is in relation to property and civil rights in the Province within head 13.

The pools authorized by cl. (*l*) appear to be designed to obtain the most favourable prices for the producers as a whole by selling the regulated product through the medium of a marketing agency, a procedure which, it is apparently hoped, will result in better prices being realized for the crop as a whole than would otherwise be possible. I do not consider that the decision of the Judicial Committee in *Lower Mainland Dairy Products v. Crystal Dairy Ltd.,* [1933] 1 D.L.R. 82, A.C. 168, supports a contention that the authority to authorize the proposed pools is beyond provincial powers. In my view, the fact that some of the producers might under such regulations receive less for their product than they would if they were at liberty to sell when the opportunity offers and that others might receive more than they would otherwise receive does not mean that a tax is imposed upon one producer for the benefit of others. The design is apparently to realize what will be over the years better prices for all producers and this, in my opinion, is within the powers given by heads 13 and 16.

In answering this question I exclude sales of produce where the producer himself ships his product to other Provinces or countries for sale by any means of transport, or sells his product to a person who purchases the same for export. To illustrate, I exclude a shipment by a hog producer of his hogs, alive or dead, to the Province of Quebec and transactions between such producer and a buyer for a packing plant carrying on business in Hull who purchases the hog intending to ship it to Hull, either alive or dead, and transactions between a hog producer and a packing plant operating in Ontario purchasing the hog for the purpose of producing pork products from it and exporting them from the Province to the extent that the carcass is so used.

The passage from the judgment in *Lawson's* case which is above quoted makes it clear that to attempt to control the manner in which traders in other Provinces will carry out their transactions within the Provinces, or to prohibit them from purchasing natural products for export, is not a matter of merely provincial concern but also directly and substantially the concern of the other Provinces. I cannot think that from a constitutional standpoint the fact that the buyer for the packing house elects to have the hog killed before it is exported or cut up and, after treatment, exported as hams, bacon or other pork products, can affect the matter. . . .

[The learned Judge then turned to the second and third questions in order and after referring to the regulation mentioned in the third question he continued as follows:]

On the face of it, the regulation assumes to control the marketing of hogs which the producer might wish to export from the Province on his own account, prohibits him, by way of illustration, from selling his hogs to the representative of a packing company in Quebec who proposes to export them from the Province, prohibits the Quebec packing house from buying the hogs from him and packing companies operating in Ontario from purchasing hogs from him for the purpose of manufacturing pork products and exporting them, and from purchasing hogs from any person in Ontario other than the marketing agency and except at prices which may be fixed by the marketing agency and at times determined by them. This, as I have said, is, in my opinion, assuming to regulate trade and commerce in matters which are not merely of concern to the people of Ontario but are directly and substantially the concern of the people of other Provinces and thus beyond the powers which may be vested by the Province in such a board.

To the extent, however, that the regulation assumes to control in this manner hogs sold for consumption within the Province, or to packing plants or other processors purchasing the animals for the manufacture of pork products to be consumed within the Province, the regulation is, in my opinion, *intra vires* as dealing with matters which are merely of a local or private nature in the Province.

The regulation also provides for the licensing of persons shipping or transporting hogs or slaughtering them and, so long as this power is exercised under the licensing power given by head 9 of s. 92 and is not used to prevent those desiring to purchase hogs or pork products for export and thus to regulate inter-provincial trade, I consider it to be within provincial powers. This appears to me to be settled by *Brewers & Maltsters' Ass'n of Ont. v. A.-G. Ont.*, [1897] A.C. 231. It will be noted that the Board, by s. 3 of the regulation, may refuse to grant a licence as a processor "for any reason which the Board may deem sufficient". As every packing company in Ontario must, of necessity, be a processor within the definition contained in the regulation, and since many of the large packing companies are presumably incorporated by letters patent under the Dominion *Companies Act* and have been granted power to carry on their business in all of the Provinces of Canada, the decisions of the Judicial Committee in *John Deere Plow Co. v. Wharton,* 18 D.L.R. 353, [1915] A.C. 330, and in *Gt. West Saddlery Co. v. The King,* 58 D.L.R. 1, [1921] 2 A.C. 91, would in the case of such companies be obstacles in the way of the exercise of such power. The judgments delivered in the Court of Appeal of Saskatchewan in *Re The Grain Marketing Act, 1931* (1931), 25 S.L.R. 273, contain a valuable review of authorities on the question as to the right of the Province to interfere with export by a producer of grain. I refer particularly to the judgments of Turgeon J.A. at p. 282, McKay J.A. at p. 294 and Martin J.A. at p. 309. . . .

[The learned Judge considered the fourth question respecting the validity of service charges imposed for marketing hogs and concluded that "Assuming that the charges are made in respect of hogs sold for consumption in Ontario as mentioned in the answer to Q. 3, in the absence of any evidence to the contrary, it is, in my opinion, to be assumed that these are fair charges for services to be rendered by the marketing agency and the local board. On this footing, I consider the regulation to be a proper exercise of the powers given by heads 13 and 16 of s. 92 and *intra vires* (*Shannon v. Lower Mainland Dairy Products Bd.*, [1938] 4 D.L.R. at p. 87, A.C. at p. 722)." On the fifth question which concerned the validity of certain licence fees payable by growers of peaches for processing and collectible by the processors, he spoke as follows: "The power vested in the Province to legislate in relation to licences in order to the raising of a revenue for provincial, local or municipal purposes under head 9 of s. 92, in my opinion, authorizes this section, even though their imposition in an amount which varies with the quantity sold may tend to increase the sale price. It must, I think, be taken as decided by the judgment of the Judicial Committee in *Shannon's* case that it is not a valid objection to a licence, plus a fee, that it is directed both to the regulation of trade and to the provision of revenue. While the functions of the Marketing Board and the Growers' Committee are not defined in the material, it is proper to assume, in my opinion, that these licence fees are to defray the expenses of these bodies in discharging their duties under the scheme. The fact that the licence fee may be charged in respect of peaches processed for export does not, in my opinion, invalidate the section." For similar reasons he upheld the licence fees referred to in the sixth question. He then continued as follows:]

In my opinion, neither the provisions of the *Combines Investigation Act,* R.S.C. 1952, c. 314 nor of s. 411 of the *Criminal Code* are objections to the schemes in question to the extent that they are within the powers which may be validly granted by the Legislature under the terms of the *B.N.A. Act.* It cannot be said, in my opinion, that within the terms of s. 2(*a*)(vi) of the *Combines Investigation Act* the scheme "is likely to operate to the detriment or against the interests of the public, whether consumers, producers or others". Rather it is a scheme the carrying out of which is deemed to be in the public interest. Furthermore, the offence defined by s. 2 which renders a person subject to the penalties prescribed by s. 32 is a crime against the state. I think that to perform an act which the Legislature is empowered to and has authorized cannot be an offence against the state.

The same reasoning applies, in my opinion, to s. 411 of the *Criminal Code.* I consider that the section has no application to a scheme authorized by a Legislature under its powers conferred by the same statute which, by s. 91, gave to Parliament the power to pass laws in relation to the criminal law. If, indeed, the section could be construed as applying to such an act, I think it would be impossible to say that a scheme deemed by the Legislature to be in the public interest could be held to unduly limit or prevent competition within the meaning of the section.

I have not dealt with the sufficiency of the Hog Producers' Marketing Scheme or any question of severability as it might affect either the statute or the regulations as, in view of the form of the questions, to do so would, in my opinion, serve no useful purpose.

My answers to the various questions are as follows:

Question 1. If the pool for the distribution of moneys received from the sale of the regulated product is limited to such products marketed for use within the province and excludes such products marketed or purchased for export in their natural state or after treatment, clause (*l*) of subs. 1 of s. 3 of the *Farm Products Marketing Act* is not *ultra vires* of the legislature.

Question 2. No.

Question 3.   Yes, except to the extent that the regulation authorizes the control of the marketing of hogs sold for consumption within the province or to packing plants or other processors purchasing the animals for the manufacture of pork products for use within the province. The provision for licensing is *intra vires*, subject to what is said as to the refusal of such a licence.

Question 4. No.

Question 5. No.

Question 6. No. . . .

FAUTEUX J.: . . . Certain general principles, related to the validity of marketing legislation, may expediently be stated before entering into the individual consideration of each of the questions.

The regulation of the marketing of farm products within the Province exclusively is within the legislative competence of the Provincial Legislature and not of Parliament. In *A.-G. B.C. v. A.-G. Can.*, [1937] 1 D.L.R. 691, A.C. 377, 67 Can. C.C. 337, the *Natural Products Marketing Act, 1934,* enacted by Parliament, was held to be *ultra vires* substantially for the reason that it covered transactions completed within the province and having no connection with interprovincial or export trade. Later, in *Shannon v. Lower Mainland Dairy Products Bd.*, [1938] 4 D.L.R. 81, A.C. 708, the *Natural Products Marketing (British Columbia) Act,* 1936, providing for the regulation of marketing within the Province, was held *intra vires.* Such valid regulatory scheme may be carried out and enforced through the means of a licence scheme provided for by a Provincial Legislature for, as stated by Lord Atkin in the *Shannon* case (*supra*) at p. 86 D.L.R., p. 721 A.C.: "If regulation of trade within the Province has to be held valid the ordinary method of regulating trade, *i.e.*, by a system of licences, must also be admissible." Under its licensing power, derived from heads 9, 13 and 16 of s. 92 of the *B.N.A. Act,* a Provincial Legislature may raise money to defray the costs of operation of such valid regulatory scheme. "If licences are granted," says Lord Atkin, immediately following the above quotation from his reasons in the *Shannon* case, "it appears to be no objection that fees should be charged in order either to defray the costs of administering the local regulation or to increase the general funds of the Province, or for both purposes". Again, in the same case, at p. 87 D.L.R., p. 722 A.C., the learned Lord continues: "The impugned provisions can also . . . be supported on the ground accepted by

Martin, C.J.B.C., in his judgment on the reference, *viz.*, that they are fees for services rendered by the Province or by its authorized instrumentalities under the powers given by s. 92(13) and (16). . . . **On these grounds the attack upon the Act based on the powers to exact licence fees must be held to fail"**. Under the authority of the *Shannon* case (*supra*), this Court in *Tolton Mfg. Co. v. Advisory Committee,* [1944] 4 D.L.R. 273, S.C.R. 349, 82 Can. C.C. 129, dealing with a compulsory levy to help to defray the expenses of administering codes of working conditions under the *Industrial Standards Act,* R.S.O. 1937, c. 191, stated at p. 280 D.L.R., p. 359 S.C.R., p. 137 Can. C.C.: "If the assessment be a tax, it is a direct tax, within the meaning of the decisions of the Judicial Committee and of this Court; and, in any event, it may be justified as a fee for services rendered by the Province or by its authorized instrumentalities under the powers given Provincial Legislatures by section 92(13) and 92(16) of the *B.N.A. Act."* Finally, and as such licence fees need not meet the test of direct taxation, the variable character of the amount of the payment is not objectionable. This was affirmed by the Ontario Court of Appeal and the correctness of this affirmation was not questioned by the Privy Council in *Brewers & Maltsters' Ass'n. v. A.-G. Ont.,* [1897] A.C. 231. . . .

[The learned Judge then dealt with certain submissions made in respect of the questions asked and after concluding that the statutory provision involved in the first question was not invalid as authorizing an indirect tax, he turned to the next three questions which concerned a hog marketing scheme. On this matter, he spoke in part as follows:]

The main submission is that the scheme is applicable to the sale of hogs generally, for import and export as well, and as such regulates trade within the meaning of head 2 of s. 91 of the *B.N.A. Act* and therefore is *ultra vires.* In support of this submission, reference was made to sections 1*a* and 1*b* of Sch. 1 reading:

INTERPRETATION

"1*a*. In this scheme

"(*a*) 'hogs' means hogs produced in Ontario except that part thereof comprising the territorial districts and the Provincial County of Haliburton;

"(*b*) 'processing' means the slaughtering of hogs; and

"(*c*) 'producer' means a producer engaged in production of hogs. . . .

APPLICATION OF SCHEME

"1*b*. This scheme applies to hogs marketed either directly or indirectly for processing but does not apply to

"(*a*) hogs sold by a producer

"(i) to a producer or

"(ii) to a consumer, or

"(iii) to a retail butcher, and

"(*b*) hogs resold by a processor who bought the hogs under this scheme."

With respect to importation. It is clear from the above provisions that hogs produced elsewhere than in Ontario are not covered by the scheme. It is equally clear from s. 1*a*(c) read with the provisions of s. 4 of the scheme, which for the whole purpose thereof provides for the grouping of hog producers by districts within the Province, that producers beyond its boundaries are not affected either. In the result, any one in Ontario is free to import therein and one beyond its boundaries to export thereto the regulated product.

With respect to exportation. Were the words "within the Province" expressed or held to be implied after each of the words "marketed" and "processing" appearing in the opening provision of s. 1(*b*), the submission that an Ontario producer is barred from marketing the regulated product elsewhere than in the Province would fail; and in my view it must be so held for the following reasons:

Reference has already been made to the declaratory provision, added to the Act by the Legislature in 1956, and formally stating that: "The purpose and intent of this Act is to provide for the control and regulation in any or all respects of the marketing *within the Province* of farm products including the prohibition of such marketing in whole or in part." This provision imports an all-embracing rule of construction with respect to the Act and also with respect to the legislative provisions authorized to be made thereunder, for expressions used in Orders in Council, Orders, Schemes and Regulations are to be given "the same meaning as those in the Act conferring the power to make them": *Interpretation Act,* R.S.O. 1950, c. 184, s. 6. Thus, the word "marketing" defined in s. 1(*e*) of the Act means "marketing within the Province" and a similar meaning attends the word "marketed" appearing in the opening provisions of s. 1(*b*) of Reg. No. 104. As clearly appears in the latter provisions, the operation, to which the scheme applies, is not that of marketing or that of processing, both *simpliciter*, but that of "marketing for processing", *i.e.,* a form of marketing operation, which cannot here be interpreted as one carried beyond the Province without disregarding the formal statement of the 1956 amendment. The amendment is subsequent to the impugned regulation, but the presumption against construing statutes retrospectively, which was invoked, is inapplicable to an Act which, like the amending Act of 1956, is declaratory in its nature; such Acts, unless providing the contrary, have relation back to the time when the prior Act was passed. *Atty.-Gen. v. Theobald* (1890), 24 Q.B.D. 557; see also Craies on Statute Law, 5th ed., p. 364. The marketing in Ontario of hogs produced in Ontario for processing, *i.e.,* slaughtering, in Ontario, is the sole transaction or particular business controlled and regulated under the scheme.

Other considerations also attend such interpretation. There is a *presumptio juris* as to the existence of the *bona fide* intention of a legislative body to confine itself to its own sphere and a presumption of similar nature that general words in a statute are not intended to extend its operation beyond the territorial authority of the Legislature. These presumptions are not displaced by the language used in the relevant legislative provisions applicable to this scheme when read as a whole. Indeed such provisions consistently imply the intention of the Legislature to restrict the application of the scheme to intra-provincial transactions. . . .

Having reached the view that the transaction covered by the scheme is intra-provincial, I do not find it necessary or expedient to define in general terms what constitutes an intra-provincial transaction. The suggestion that to be intra-provincial a transaction must be completed within the Province, in the sense that the product, object of the transaction, must be ultimately and exclusively consumed or be sold for delivery therein for such consumption, is one, which would, if carried to its logical conclusion, strip from a Province its recognized power to provide for the regulation of marketing within such Province in disregard of the decisions of the Judicial Committee in *A.-G. B.C. v. A.-G. Can.* (*supra*) and in *Shannon v. Lower Mainland Dairy Products Bd.* (*supra*).

That joint action of Parliament and of the Legislature may better solve the difficulties arising in particular cases is well known to those entrusted with the Government of the nation and the Province but provides no answer to the questions here referred for consideration. . . .

It was also argued that these marketing legislative provisions conflict with certain federal laws, namely, (i) the *Combines Investigation Act,* R.S.C. 1952, c. 314 and the provisions of the Criminal Code relating to combines; and (ii) the *Agricultural Prices Support Act,* R.S.C. 1952, c. 3. As to (i): A like submission was unsuccessfully made in *Cherry v. The King ex rel. Wood,* [1938] 1 D.L.R. 156, 69 Can. C.C. 219 and *Tolton Mfg. Co. v. Advisory Committee,* [1944] 4 D.L.R. 273, S.C.R. 349, 82 Can. C.C. 129. The object of Parliament in legislating with respect to private agreements involving monopolies is to protect the public interest in free competition. The adoption by Parliament of an *"Act to Assist and Encourage Co-operative Marketing of Agricultural Products",* R.S.C. 1952, c. 5, does not suggest that marketing schemes devised by Parliament or a Legislature within their respective fields, are *prima facie* to be held to come within the scope of the anti-monopoly legislation. As to (ii): Under the *Agricultural Prices Support Act,* R.S.C. 1952, c. 3, a Board constituted of members appointed by the Governor-General in Council is under certain conditions, given authority to fix the prices at which it may itself, either purchase agricultural products or pay to the producers thereof the difference between such fixed price and the average market price: thus, as the title of the Act suggests, supporting the price of such products. The intent and purpose of both Acts alleged to be in conflict are quite different. Both are intended to assist producers. One however, *i.e.,* the Act here considered, aims at procuring maximum returns by means of orderly marketing, while the other aims at assuring minimum returns, under certain circumstances and conditions. The Ontario Legislature cannot be presumed to have intended its legislation to be operative beyond the limits of its own sphere and contrary to any federal legislation validly adopted.

[The learned Judge then turned to questions 5 and 6 and concluded that the licence fees involved in those questions were valid
service charges. In the result he answered all the six questions in
the negative].

ABBOTT J.:— I have had an opportunity of considering the
exhaustive reasons prepared by my brother Fauteux and I am in
agreement with the views which he has expressed. I desire to add
only a few brief observations.

The *Farm Products Marketing Act,* R.S.O. 1950, c. 131, is in the
usual form of marketing legislation in Canada. With the inclusion
of s. 1(*a*), added in March, 1956, the Act contains in substance, the
same provisions as the *Natural Products Marketing (British Columbia) Act,* R.S.B.C. 1936, c. 165, which was before the Judicial Committee in *Shannon v. Lower Mainland Dairy Products Bd.,* [1938]
4 D.L.R. 81, A.C. 708, and the *Agricultural Products Marketing
(Prince Edward Island) Act,* 1940 (P.E.I.), c. 40, which was before
this Court in *P.E.I. Potato Marketing Bd. v. H. B. Willis Inc.,* [1952]
4 D.L.R. 146, 2 S.C.R. 392.

It might be noted perhaps, that the British Columbia Act covered
"any product of agriculture, of the forest, sea, lake or river" The
Ontario Act is somewhat more limited in its application and relates
only to farm products.

In its essential features, the Ontario Act is, in my opinion, indistinguishable from the British Columbia Act, which was held by the
Judicial Committee in *Shannon's* case to be an Act to regulate particular businesses entirely within the Province and therefore *intra
vires* of the Province. Presumably because of the decision in *Shannon's*
case no question as to the validity of the Prince Edward Island Act
was raised on the Reference to this Court and it was assumed to be
intra vires for the purposes of that Reference. Each marketing
scheme adopted under an Act such as the one under consideration,
and the regulations applicable to such scheme, must, of course, be
looked at, to see whether they come within the authority conferred
by the Act, but as I have stated, I share the view expressed by my
brother Fauteux that the *Farm Products Marketing Act* of Ontario,
including cl. (*l*) of s.-s. (1) of s. 3, is *intra vires* the Ontario Legislature. . . .

It has long been settled that rights, arising out of or in connection with contracts, such as a contract of sale made in a Province
between a producer and a processor, are civil rights within the
meaning of head 13 of s. 92 of the *B.N.A. Act* and as such within
the legislative power of a Province: *Citizens' Ins. Co. v. Parsons,* 7
App. Cas. 96.

In *John Deere Plow Co. v. Wharton,* 18 D.L.R. 353 at p. 358,
[1915] A.C. 330 at p. 339, Viscount Haldane L.C. referring to the
words "civil rights" said: "An abstract logical definition of their
scope is not only, having regard to the context of the 91st and 92nd
sections of the Act, impracticable, but is certain, if attempted, to
cause embarrassment and possible injustice in future cases."

In my opinion it would be equally impracticable and undesirable, to attempt an abstract logical definition of what constitutes inter-provincial or export trade. Each transaction must be looked at, in order to ascertain whether or not, in fact, it involves such trade. It is also dangerous, I think, on a Reference such as this to go beyond the terms of the Reference and to attempt to decide by analogy, questions which are not submitted for the opinion of the Court.

Aside from the attack made on the licence fees imposed under the three schemes, as being indirect taxation, which has been fully dealt with by my brother Fauteux, the principal attack made on the validity of these schemes was that they purport to regulate extra-provincial trade.

It is hard to conceive of any important article of commerce produced in any Province, which would not, to some extent at least, enter into inter-provincial or export trade. Certainly milk, which was the product regulated in *Shannon's* case, in its processed form at any rate, must be exported from British Columbia. Similarly it is common knowledge that potatoes in substantial quantities are shipped out of Prince Edward Island.

The power to regulate the sale within a Province, of specific products, is not, in my opinion, affected by reason of the fact that some, or all, of such products may subsequently, in the same or in an altered form, be exported from that Province, unless it be shown of course, that such regulation is merely a colourable device for assuming control of extra-provincial trade. Similarly, the power to regulate the wages of those engaged in processing such products within a Province, is not affected by the fact that the resulting product may be exported, although it is obvious that the scale of such wages would have a significant effect upon the export price. It is the immediate effect, object or purpose, not possible consequential effects, that are relevant, in determining whether the *Farm Products Marketing Act of Ontario* and the three Schemes adopted under it, which are the subject of the present reference, are laws in relation to a matter falling within provincial legislative competence. As Viscount Simon said in the *Farm Security Act Reference* [*A.-G. Sask. v. A.-G. Can.*], [1949] 2 D.L.R. 145 at p. 149, A.C. 110 at p. 123: "Consequential effects are not the same thing as legislative subject-matter. It is 'the true nature and character of the legislation' —not its ultimate economic results—that matters."

What is regulated under these schemes is not the farm product itself but certain transactions involving that product, and the transaction which is regulated is completed before the product is consumed either in its original or in some processed form. Processing may take many forms and the original product may be changed out of all recognition. The place where the resulting product may be consumed therefore, is not in my opinion conclusive, as a test to determine by what legislative authority a particular transaction involving such farm product, may validly be regulated.

As I have stated, the fact that some, or all, of the resulting product after processing, may subsequently enter into extra-provincial or export trade does not, in my view, alter the fact that the three Schemes submitted in this Reference, regulate particular businesses carried on entirely within provincial legislative jurisdiction, and are therefore *intra vires.*

[The learned Judge then answered all six questions negatively.]

[Taschereau J. concurred with Abbott and Fauteux JJ. The separate opinion of Cartwright J. (who dissented as to the first question on the ground that the legislation imposed indirect taxation, and as to the next three on the ground that no valid scheme was established and who refused to answer the next two questions because of insufficiency of material) is omitted. Nolan J. concurred with Locke J.

Having regard to the *Ontario Farm Products Marketing Act* reference, *supra,* is it open to a Province to set up an exclusive marketing agency for a natural product and to compel all growers to market through that agency? See *Hammerstein v. B.C. Coast Vegetable Marketing Board* (1962), 37 D.L.R. (2d) 153. Would the constitutional position be different if the agency was authorized to set production quotas only, or to do both this and regulate the marketing of the products that resulted from the quotas? *Burns Foods Ltd. v. A.G. Man.*, [1974] 2 W.W.R. 537, 1 N.R. 147, 40 D.L.R. (3d) 731 (Can.) presented the converse situation of things entering a province. It held *ultra vires* as applied to hogs from Saskatchewan regulations under the *Natural Products Marketing Act,* R.S.M. 1970, c. N20 that any hogs prepared for slaughter in Manitoba should have been purchased through the provincial marketing board. The Board equalized prices but set no quotas and did not discriminate between hogs produced in Manitoba or elsewhere.]

MURPHY v. C.P.R. AND A.-G. CAN.

In the Supreme Court of Canada. [1958] S.C.R. 626.

Appeal by plaintiff from (1956), 4 D.L.R. (2d) 443, 19 W.W.R. 57, 672 (Man. C.A.), affirming a judgment of Maybank J., (1955), 1 D.L.R. (2d) 197, 17 W.W.R. 593, dismissing an action challenging the validity of the Canadian Wheat Board Act.

RAND J: This appeal impugns the validity of prohibitory and compulsory features of the *Canadian Wheat Board Act,* R.S.C. 1952, c. 44 as amended. The appellant is a poultry farmer in British Columbia and the president and majority shareholder of a company organized to engage in the business of raising and marketing poultry. Sufficient quantities of feed in wheat, oats and barley to meet the requirements of business of that class are not available from local production and it has become necessary to import from the Prairie Provinces; and it is out of an attempted shipment by the appellant from Manitoba to British Columbia that the dispute arises.

Speaking generally, the scheme of the Act is that primarily all grain entering interprovincial and foreign trade is to be purchased and marketed by the Board, and none purchased directly from the farmers on the Prairies can be shipped to another Province without the production of a licence from the Board. This means that, regardless of the price paid to the producer, for the purpose of private interprovincial movement, the grain is dealt with as if, by the shipper, it had been sold to and thereupon repurchased at the established price from the Board. Sales by the Board for a crop season are pooled and the gross returns less administration expenses equalized among the producers. When the grain is delivered an initial payment is made to the producer with a participation certificate entitling him to share in the ultimate net return. A certificate is likewise given to the individual shipper. In the result the latter is required to pay to the Board the difference between the initial payment and the then selling price. Since the certificate enables him to share in any further return realized, he is treated as a producer selling to the Board and is obliged to share in the administration expenses.

To bring the matter to a test, the appellant in Manitoba bought three sacks of grain, one of wheat, one of oats and one of barley, all grown in that Province, and tendered them to the respondent railway company for carriage to British Columbia. The licence not being forthcoming, the railway declined to accept them and this action was brought. In justification of its refusal, the respondent pleaded the Act and the Regulations made under it and the sufficiency in law of that plea is before us.

The Act consists of six Parts. Part I establishes the Board as a body corporate and an agent of Her Majesty in right of Canada for the object of "marketing" in interprovincial and export trade wheat grown in Canada. Appropriate powers are conferred and the marketing is to be by means of buying from producers, selling and pooling the proceeds.

Part II is a code of provisions dealing with elevators and Dominion railways. By the *Canada Grain Act,* R.S.C. 1952, c. 25 all elevators in the Prairie Provinces are declared to be works for the general benefit of Canada under s. 91(29) of the *B.N.A. Act.* Section 16 of the *Canadian Wheat Board Act* prohibits, except with the permission of the Board, the delivery or acceptance of grain to or by an elevator unless the person delivering (a) is the actual producer of or entitled as a producer to the grain; (b) at the time of delivery produces a permit book under which he is entitled to deliver the grain in the current crop year; and (omitting two requirements not material here) (e) that the quantity delivered does not exceed the quota estimate by the Board for the particular delivery point. Section 17 forbids, without similar permission, the loading of grain into a railway car that is not delivered under a permit book. Even that permission requires the terms of s. 16, unless expressly excepted, to be complied with as in delivery to an elevator. The permit book, by s. 18, authorizes delivery of grain produced on the land of the producer. Various powers in relation to elevators and railways are vested in the Board by s. 20, including the making of Regulations for the delivery to or the receipt of grain into elevators, the delivery out of elevators to railway cars or lake vessels, and the allocation generally of cars on railways to elevators, loading points or persons. By s. 21 the Board is authorized to prescribe terms for delivery and acceptance of grain at elevators or railways by persons other than producers.

Part III deals with voluntary marketing. The Board is bound to buy wheat offered by a producer; a selling pool is provided, and the returns equalized between producers according to the quantity and grade of wheat delivered by them.

The title to Part VI is in these words: "REGULATION OF

INTERPROVINCIAL AND EXPORT TRADE IN WHEAT." By s. 32, except as permitted by Regulation, no person other than the Board may (a) export from or import into Canada wheat or wheat products owned by a person other than the Board; (b) transport or cause to be transported from one Province to another the same commodities so owned; (c) sell or agree to sell those commodities situated in one Province for delivery in another or outside of Canada; and (d) the converse of (c), buy or agree to buy such commodities from one Province for delivery in another or outside of Canada. Section 33 provides for the issue by the Board of licences to ship where that is otherwise forbidden.

In Part V, s. 35 authorizes the Governor in Council by Regulation to extend the application of Parts III or IV or both to oats and barley and thereupon the provisions of those Parts shall be deemed to be re-enacted in Part V including the appropriate expansion of definitions. That was done prior to the tender of the grain for shipment here and the Act was then operative on all three commodities.

In Part VI s. 45 makes the following declaration: "45. For greater certainty, but not so as to restrict the generality of any declaration in the *Canada Grain Act* that any elevator is a work for the general advantage of Canada, it is hereby declared that all flour mills, feed mills, feed warehouses and seed cleaning mills, whether heretofore constructed or hereafter to be constructed, are and each of them is hereby declared to be works or a work for the general advantage of Canada, and, without limiting the generality of the foregoing, each and every mill or warehouse mentioned or described in the Schedule is a work for the general advantage of Canada."

The provisions of the Act embody a policy adopted by Parliament as being in the best interests of the grain producers and the country generally; and the question is whether that administration is within the competence of Parliament to set up, which, in turn, is to be decided on the validity of the substantive enactments of Parts III and IV.

As a preliminary skirmish, it was stressed by Mr. Finkelstein [for the appellant] that the prohibition was equivalent to forbidding a producer in Manitoba from having his own property for his own purposes carried to his home in another Province and this was assumed to be an outrageous thing. That the shipment offered, if carried, would have been an item in interprovincial trade is, I think, beyond question. Whether or not the statute would gather in every conceivable mode of moving goods across a provincial boundary, such as a person transferring his home and belongings from one Province to another, including an ordinary supply of grain for domestic use, or where the farm straddles the borderline of two Provinces, the gathering of crops on one side and storing them in the owner's barns on the other, it is unnecessary to consider. In the situation before us, the intended shipment was to be one of transportation across a provincial line for the purposes and in the course of a business. It makes no difference whether the business is connected or associated with the owner's production of raw material in another Province or with that of strangers; in either case the merchandise and the transportation serve exactly the same purpose, and ownership is irrelevant. The merchandise was to move between interprovincial points in the flow of goods of an economic and business character and that is sufficient.

The main contention was that the legislation and Regulations infringed s. 121 of the Act of 1867 that "all Articles of the Growth, Produce, or Manufacture of any one of the Provinces shall, from and after the union, be admitted free into each of the other Provinces". Assuming this section to be applicable equally to action by Dominion and Province, is the charge exacted as a condition of the shipment an impediment to that free passage for which the section provides? Viewing it in isolation, as a hindrance to interprovincial trade detached from all other aspects, the demand bears the appearance of a violation. Apart from matters of purely local and private concern, this country is one economic unit; in freedom of movement its business interests are in an extra-provincial dimension, and, among other things, are deeply involved in trade and commerce between and beyond Provinces.

But when the exaction is looked at in its true character, as an incident in the administration of a comprehensive extra-provincial marketing scheme, with its necessity of realizing its objective in the returns to producers for all production except for local purposes, interference with the free current of trade across provincial lines disappears. The subjects of trade by their nature embody an accumulation of economic values within legislative jurisdiction, wages, taxes, insurance, licence fees, transportation and others, all going directly or indirectly to make up or bear upon the economic character of those subjects; and the charge here is within that category as one item in a scheme that regulates their distribution.

"Free", in s. 121, means without impediment related to the traversing of a provincial boundary. If, for example, Parliament attempted to equalize the competitive position of a local grower of grain in British Columbia with that of one in Saskatchewan by imposing a charge on the shipment from the latter representing the difference in production costs, its validity would call for critical examination. That result would seem also to follow if Parliament, for the same purpose, purported to fix the price at which grain grown in Saskatchewan could be sold in or for delivery in British Columbia. But burdens for equalizing competition in that manner differ basically from charges for services rendered in an administration of commodity distribution. The latter are items in selling costs and can be challenged only if the scheme itself is challengeable.

Section 121 has been considered in two cases: *Gold Seal Ltd. v. Dom. Express Co. & A.-G. Alta.* (1921), 62 D.L.R. 62, 62 S.C.R. 424 and *Atlantic Smoke Shops Ltd. v. Conlon & A.-G. Can.*, [1943] 4 D.L.R. 81, A.C. 550. In the former a majority of this Court, Duff J., Anglin J. and Mignault J. held that prohibition by Parliament of the importation of intoxicating liquor manufactured in a Province into another where its sale for consumption was illegal did not infringe this section: Duff J. at p. 79 D.L.R., p. 456 S.C.R. said: "The phraseology adopted, when the context is considered in which this section is found, shows, I think, that the real object of the clause is to prohibit the establishment of customs duties affecting inter-provincial trade in the products of any Province of the Union."

A similar view was expressed by Anglin J. at p. 85 D.L.R., p. 466 S.C.R., and by Mignault J. at p. 89 D.L.R., p. 470 S.C.R. who added to customs duties "other charges of a like nature". In *Atlantic Smoke Shops* at p. 92 D.L.R., p. 569 A.C. Viscount Simon L.C. remarked in part on the *Gold Seal* judgment: "The meaning of s. 121 cannot vary according as it is applied to Dominion or to Provincial legislation, and their Lordships agree with the interpretation put upon the section in the *Gold Seal* case."

What was being considered there was a provincial tax to be paid by a person purchasing tobacco at retail for consumption by himself or others. Included in the confirmation was s. 5 which required of residents payment of the tax on tobacco brought in for their personal consumption from other Provinces. Infringement of s. 121 in that case would have been by a tax as distinguished from *Gold Seal,* by prohibition in support of valid provincial law; in neither was it necessary to explore s. 121 beyond those limits.

The case of *James v. Commonwealth of Australia,* [1936] A.C. 578 was strongly urged upon us by Mr. Finkelstein. There the Commonwealth had passed an Act bringing interstate commerce in dried fruits under Regulation. Its effect was to prohibit interstate trade to unlicensed shippers and to restrict it quantitatively when under licence. The latter was the result of a requirement that a determined percentage of the total production by a grower must be exported from Australia or destroyed and that only the balance could be sold either in the grower's own state or in any other state of the Commonwealth. Section 92 of the constitutional *Act,* 63-64 Vict., c. 12, declared: "On the imposition of uniform duties of customs, trade, commerce, and intercourse among the States, whether by means of internal carriage or ocean navigation, shall be absolutely free." The issues were whether the section bound the Commonwealth, and if so, whether the legislation infringed it. The Judicial Committee found the Regulation to be *ultra vires* of the Commonwealth to enact.

Even if the constitutional considerations in that issue were the same as those to be taken into account in this, the difference in character of the restrictions would be a sufficient distinction between them. But those considerations are not the same. . . .

By the Australian Act the Regulation of Trade and Commerce committed by s. 51(i) to the Commonwealth was "subject to this constitution", which drew in s. 92, and was not exclusive; and so far as their legislation did not conflict with that of the Commonwealth, the States could likewise regulate interstate trade.

This diversity in structure and the scope and character of power over interstate trade and commerce, although illuminating in its disclosure of variant constitutional arrangements, suffices to require an independent approach to and appraisal of the question before us. Section 91(2) of the Act of 1867 confides to Parliament, "Notwith-

standing anything in this Act," the exclusive legislative authority
to make laws in relation to "The Regulation of Trade and Commerce".
By what has been considered the necessary corollary of the scheme
of the Act as a whole, apart from general regulations applicable
equally to all trade, and from incidental requirements, this authority
has been curtailed so far but only so far as necessary to avoid the
infringement, if not "the virtual extinction" of provincial jurisdiction
over local and private matters including intra-provincial trade; but
the paramount authority of Parliament is trenched upon expressly
only as it may be affected by s. 121. Pertinent to this is the ruling
in *A.-G. B.C. v. A.-G. Can.*, [1923] 1 D.L.R. 223, 38 Can. C.C. 283,
64 S.C.R. 377 affirmed in [1923] 4 D.L.R. 669, 42 Can. C.C. 398,
[1924] A.C. 222, in which it was held that customs duties imposed
on the import of liquor by British Columbia under s. 91(2) did not
violate s. 125 exempting all property of the Province from taxation.

I take s. 121, apart from customs duties, to be aimed against
trade regulation which is designed to place fetters upon or raise
impediments to or otherwise restrict or limit the free flow of commerce across the Dominion as if provincial boundaries did not exist.
That it does not create a level of trade activity divested of all
regulation I have no doubt; what is preserved is a free flow of trade
regulated in subsidiary features which are or have come to be looked
upon as incidents of trade. What is forbidden is a trade regulation
that in its essence and purpose is related to a provincial boundary.

The scheme of the *Canadian Wheat Board Act* is primarily to
benefit producers of wheat in areas to which that product can now
be said to be indigenous. Its effect is not to reduce the quantity of
either foreign or interprovincial trade; whatever the demands of the
Provinces for these goods, the Board, under its duty to market the
production of the "regulated areas", is bound to supply those requirements. But it is concerned also to spread the furnishing of that supply
equitably among the producers. The individual with grain on hand
may, because of quota be unable to sell at the particular moment
to a buyer in another Province but his neighbour can do so. If the
demands, export and interprovincial, are sufficient, all production
will move into trade; what may be delayed is the particular disposal
by the individual of his excess over the initial quota, not the movement of grain. The Act operates on the individual by keeping him
in effect in a queue but the orderly flow of products proceeds unabated.

Section 121 does not extend to each producer in a Province an
individual right to ship freely regardless of his place in that order.
Its object, as the opening language indicates, is to prohibit restraints
on the movement of products. With no restriction on that movement,
a scheme concerned with internal relations of producers, which, while
benefiting them, maintains a price level burdened with no other
than production and marketing charges, does not clash with the
section. If it were so, what, in these days has become a social and
economic necessity, would be beyond the total legislative power of
the country, creating a constitutional hiatus. As the Provinces are
incompetent to deal with such a matter, the two jurisdictions could

not complement each other by co-operative action: nothing of that nature by a Province directed toward its own inhabitants could impose trade restrictions on their purchases from or sales of goods to other Provinces. It has become a truism that the totality of effective legislative power is conferred by the Act of 1867, subject always to the express or necessarily implied limitations of the Act itself; and I find in s. 121 no obstacle to the operation of the scheme in any of the features challenged.

Objection was taken to s. 33(c) which contemplates a situation where permission is given an individual to export wheat and a charge exacted of such sum as "in the opinion of the Board, represents the pecuniary benefit enuring to the applicant pursuant to the granting of the licence, arising solely by reason of the prohibition of imports or exports of wheat and wheat products without a licence and then existing differences between prices of wheat and wheat products inside and outside of Canada." The subsection, as is seen, is limited to export and is clearly severable; and, being inapplicable to interprovincial trade, its validity is not in question here.

Finally, the contention is made that the purported declarations under the *Canada Grain Act* as well as the *Canadian Wheat Board Act* that all elevators, mills and feed warehouses in the three Prairie Provinces are works for the general advantage of Canada under s. 91(29) of the Act of 1867 are invalid, that declarations under that power must specify the individual work in respect of which considerations for and against have been weighed by Parliament; but we are not called upon to examine this contention. The prohibition of shipment in the case before us is contained in s. 32 of Part IV of the Act and it was in compliance with para. (b) of that section that acceptance of the shipment by the Pacific Railway was refused. The declarations mentioned are pertinent to the application of certain provisions of Part II governing delivery and acceptance of grain at elevators and railways but these are subsidiary to the prohibitions and regulations of carriage under Part IV. It is not suggested that, assuming s. 32 to be valid, the Pacific Railway is not bound by its terms to refuse the shipment as it did, and no elevator is involved. I should add that I am not to be taken as implying that restrictions on local elevators and mills, in relation, among other things, to delivery to carriers of grain for interprovincial transportation could not validly be imposed by Parliament.

I would, therefore, dismiss the appeal with costs.

LOCKE J.: There are, in my opinion, questions as to the power of Parliament to enact certain of the provisions of the *Canadian Wheat Board Act,* one of which is suggested in the judgment of the learned Chief Justice of Manitoba [(1956), 4 D.L.R. (2d) 443, 74 C.R.T.C. 166] which need not be considered in dealing with this appeal except to the limited extent hereinafter referred to. . . .

The appellant is the president and the majority shareholder of a company named Mission Turkey Farms Ltd., incorporated under the laws of British Columbia and which carries on the business of raising turkeys at Mission City and Princeton in that Province. On September 29, 1954 the appellant tendered to the respondent at Winnipeg one sack of wheat, one sack of oats and one of barley, requesting that the grain be conveyed to Princeton and at the time tendered the proper freight charges. It was admitted at the trial that this grain was grown in Manitoba. While the appellant gave evidence, he did not say by whom the grain was owned or how it came into his possession, but it is not suggested that it was grown in Manitoba either by him or by Mission Turkey Farms Ltd. There is no evidence as to the proposed consignee nor any admission as to this. As this does not, in my opinion, affect any issue raised, it may, I think, be assumed that it was proposed to forward the grain to Mission Turkey Farms Ltd.

Other than the allegations as to the tendering of the grain for shipment and the proper freight charges, all of the allegations in the statement of claim were denied in the statement of defence. As to this, the respondent pleaded that it refused to accept the grain for transport and to accept the money tendered as freight since the appellant was prohibited from causing the grain to be so transported and the respondent was prohibited from transporting it by the provisions of the *Canadian Wheat Board Act* and particularly s. 32 and the Regulations made pursuant to that Act.

The constitutional issue was raised by the reply by which it was alleged that the *Canadian Wheat Board Act* was *ultra vires* the Parliament of Canada and that the Regulations referred to were, therefore, invalid. . . .

There are two questions to be determined; the first, as to whether s. 32 of the Act, and the Act as a whole, are in relation to the regulation of trade and commerce: the second, as to whether the regulation infringes the provisions of s. 121 of the *B.N.A. Act*.

The purpose of the *Canadian Wheat Board Act* is made apparent by an examination of its provisions. The Board constituted by the Act is required to buy all wheat, oats and barley produced in the designated area, that area being substantially the three Prairie Provinces. Under Regulations which the Board is empowered to make, deliveries of grain to elevators or to railway cars may be limited and, except with the permission of the Board, no person may deliver grain to an elevator who is not the actual producer of the grain and in possession of a permit book issued by the Board, or load into a railway car any such grain which has not previously been delivered under a permit book and with the Board's permission. The Board is required to undertake the marketing of all the grain delivered either to elevators or railway cars and the producers receive their proportionate share of the moneys realized from the sale of grain of the grade delivered by them less the expenses of the operation of the Board. It is a matter of common knowledge that much the greatest part of the grain delivered to elevators or to railway cars is exported from the Province in which it is grown either to other Provinces of Canada or to foreign countries. Grain consumed upon the farms or retained for use as seed is not, of course, affected by the provisions of the statute.

As the purpose is to pool the amounts realized from the sale of these various kinds of grain in each crop year, it has apparently been considered by Parliament to be essential that complete control of exports should be vested in a body such as the Board. Accordingly, s. 32 which is attacked in the reply to the statement of defence and which appears in Part IV of the Act under the heading "REGU-LATION OF INTERPROVINCIAL AND EXPORT TRADE IN WHEAT" provides that, except as permitted by the Regulations, no person other than the Board shall export from Canada any such grain owned by a person other than the Board or transport or cause to be transported from one Province to another any such products owned by any person other than the Board or sell or agree to sell such grain situated in one Province for delivery in another Province or outside of Canada or buy or agree to buy such grain situated in one Province for delivery in another.

It is further provided by s. 32 that any agreement for the sale of such grain in contravention of any provision of the Act or of any Regulation or order made under its authority shall be void. As part of the plan to vest the desired control in the Wheat Board s. 45 declares that all flour mills, feed mills, feed warehouses and seed cleaning mills theretofore or thereafter constructed are works for the general advantage of Canada and a Schedule to the Act lists a great number of such establishments in the Western Provinces which are affected by the section. By s. 174 of the *Canada Grain Act,* all elevators in Canada are declared to be works for the general advantage of Canada.

Dealing with the first question, it appears to me to be too clear for argument that the *Canadian Wheat Board Act* insofar as its provisions relate to the export of grain from the Province for the purpose of sale is an Act in relation to the regulation of trade and commerce within the meaning of that expression in s. 91. As pointed out by the learned Chief Justice of Manitoba, it has been long since decided that the Provinces cannot regulate or restrict the export of natural products such as grain beyond their borders. . . .

It is contended for the appellant that the power to regulate trade and commerce under head 2 does not enable Parliament to regulate a particular trade, but this is too broad a statement. The result of the cases in the Judicial Committee dealing with this question appear to me to be most clearly summarized in the judgment of Lord Atkin in *Shannon et al. v. Lower Mainland Dairy Products Board,* [1938] 4 D.L.R. 81 at pp. 84-5, A.C. 708, at p. 719, where it was said:—

"It is now well settled that the enumeration in s. 91 of 'The Regulation of Trade and Commerce' as a class or subject over which the Dominion has exclusive legislative powers does not give the power to regulate for legitimate provincial purposes, particular trades or businesses so far as the trade or business is confined to the province."

The *Canadian Wheat Board Act* controls and regulates not one trade or business but several, including the activities of the producer, the railroads, the elevators and flour and feed mills and, except to a very minor extent, it is their activities directed to the export of grain or grain products from the Province, activities which the Province itself is powerless to control.

In the able argument addressed to us by Mr. Finkelstein he has pointed out that, as s. 32 of the Act reads, a producer of grain in Manitoba who is carrying on outside the Province an activity such as that of Mission Turkey Farms Ltd. in British Columbia is prevented from transporting, either by rail or otherwise, his own grain for his own purposes. This appears to be the case as the section declares by para. (*b*) that no other than the Board may transport or cause to be transported from one Province to another Province wheat or wheat products owned by a person other than the Board.

This question, however, is not raised either by the issues defined by the pleadings or by the facts given in the evidence. It is not contended that the appellant produced the grain which he sought to ship by the railway or that the company to whom I have presumed it was consigned was the producer of the grain in Manitoba. It was alleged in the statement of claim but not proven that the appellant was a poultry farmer. All that was proved was that he was the president of a company engaged in that business. The only possible inference to be drawn from the evidence is that the appellant bought the grain from some producer in Manitoba, either on his own behalf or on behalf of the British Columbia company, for the purpose of exporting it from the Province in defiance of the Act and of the Regulations.

If, however, contrary to my view, the question as to the validity of the prohibition of such a movement of a grower's own grain should be considered as having been raised and if it be assumed for the purpose of argument that such prohibition is invalid as being for any reason beyond the powers of Parliament such prohibition would be clearly severable. It would affect only a minute portion of the Western grain crop and it is impossible to sustain an argument that Parliament would not have passed the Act as a whole if it were known that in this respect s. 32 exceeded its powers.

There remains the question as to whether the legislation contravenes the provisions of s. 121 of the *B.N.A. Act*. That section has been construed in the judgments delivered in this Court in *Gold Seal Ltd. v. Dominion Express Co. & A.-G. Alta.* (1921), 62 D.L.R. 62 at p. 79, 62 S.C.R. 424 at p. 456, where Duff J., as he then was, said "that the real object of the clause is to prohibit the establishment of customs duties affecting inter-provincial trade in the products of any Province of the Union" and Anglin J., as he then was agreed (pp. 86-7 D.L.R., p. 466 S.C.R.). This interpretation was accepted by the Judicial Committee in *Atlantic Smoke Shops Ltd. v. Conlon & A.-G. Can.*, [1943] 4 D.L.R. 81 at p. 92, A.C. 550 at p. 569. There is nothing of this nature authorized by the *Canadian Wheat Board Act*.

In my opinion, this appeal fails. . . .

Appeal dismissed.

[Taschereau, Fauteux and Abbott JJ. concurred with Locke J. Cartwright J. concurred in general with Rand and Locke JJ. but added some separate remarks. See *Ballem*, Note, (1956), 34 Can. Bar Rev. 482.

The Manitoba Court of Appeal in *Regina v. Klassen* (1959), 20 D.L.R. (2d) 406, 29 W.W.R. 369, 31 C.R. 275, upheld a conviction for having accepted grain delivery to defendant, a feed mill, without production of the delivery permit book required under the terms of the Canadian Wheat Board Act, R.S.C. 1952, c. 44, now R.S.C. 1970, c. C-12, making such production a condition to a lawful delivery, another section of which declares elevators and feed mills generally to be works for the general advantage of Canada. The feed mill in question, located at an interior point remote from transportation, was not shown to have had any extra-provincial dealings. The court expressly refrained from ruling on the declaratory aspect of the legislation, resting its decision as to the Act's validity on section 91(2). The majority opinion by Tritschler J.A. for himself and Schultz J.A., characterized the provision as to feed mill deliveries as "incidental and ancillary to the achievement of the purpose of the Act, the pith and substance of which is the provision of an export market for surplus grain" and declared it "not relevant . . . that appellant operates his feed mill in a purely legal and provincial manner and it is not engaged in interprovincial or export trading". The Supreme Court refused leave to appeal; see *Laskin*, [1959] 37 Can. Bar Rev. 630. For the decision holding the declaratory feature of the Act *intra vires*, see *Jorgenson v. A.-G. Canada*, [1971] S.C.R. 725, [1971] 3 W.W.R. 149, 3 C.C.C. (2d) 49, 18 D.L.R. (3d) 297, *infra*.

The federal declaratory power under s. 92(10)(c), as applied to a particular feed mill, was held to be sufficient in the context of a statute regulating interprovincial and export trade, *e.g.*, the Canadian Wheat Board Act, to support a requirement that the deliveror of grain to the feed mill produce a permit book in which the delivery must be entered by the feed mill operator, and this notwithstanding that the grain was purchased to prepare it for cattle feed for local consumption: see *The Queen v. Thumlert* (1959), 20 D.L.R. (2d) 335, 28 W.W.R. 481.

The problems of adjustment of local and national interests in trade regulation and marketing are well brought out in numerous decisions in the United States. The absence or presence of Congressional legislation is highly relevant to the constitutionality of state legislation: see *Parker v. Brown* (1943), 317 U.S. 341, 63 S. Ct. 307; *Rice v. Santa Fe Elevator Corp.* (1947), 331 U.S. 218, 67 S. Ct. 1146. Where Congress has spoken clearly, the Supreme Court has upheld its authority over both the interstate and interrelated local market, even though the federal statute extended into production: see *Mulford v. Smith* (1939), 307 U.S. 38, 59 S. Ct. 648; *United States v. Wrightwood Dairy Co.* (1942), 315 U.S. 110, 62 S. Ct. 523; *Wickard v. Filburn* (1942), 317 U.S. 111, 63 S. Ct. 82. The issue of percentages, referred to by Duff J. in the *Eastern Terminal Elevator* case, *supra*, at p. 363, has had an entirely different reception in the United States: see *National Labour Relations Board v. Fainblatt* (1939), 306 U.S. 601; *Santa Cruz Fruit Packing Co. v. National Labour Relations Board* (1938), 303 U.S. 453; and see also *Mabee v. White Plains Publishing Co.* (1946), 327 U.S. 178, 66 S. Ct. 511. For a general review of the issues in this line of cases, see *Southern Pacific Co. v. Arizona* (1945), 325 U.S. 761, 65 S. Ct. 1515.]

CARNATION COMPANY LTD. v. QUEBEC AGRICULTURAL MARKETING BOARD

In the Supreme Court of Canada. [1968] S.C.R. 238, 67 D.L.R. (2d) 1.

The judgment of the Court was delivered by

MARTLAND J.:—This is an appeal from the Court of Queen's Bench for the Province of Quebec (Appeal Side), [[1967] Que. Q.B. 122] which confirmed the judgment given in the Superior Court, upholding the validity of three decisions of the Quebec Agricultural Marketing Board, hereinafter referred to as "the Marketing Board". The question in issue before this Court is as to whether, in making these orders, the Marketing Board had infringed on the exclusive legislative powers of Parliament under s. 91(2) of the *British North America Act* to regulate trade and commerce. Submissions on this issue were made on behalf of the Attorney-General of Canada and the Attorney-General of Alberta, in addition to those presented by the parties to the litigation.

The Marketing Board was created as a corporation by the provisions of the *Quebec Agricultural Marketing Act*, 4-5 Eliz. II, 1955-56 (Que.), c. 37. It was empowered, inter alia, to approve joint marketing plans, and to arbitrate any dispute arising in the course of carrying out a joint marketing plan. The Act provided that ten or more producers of agricultural products in any territory in Quebec could apply to the Marketing Board for approval of a joint plan for the marketing of one or more classes of farm products in such territory, if such plan was supported by a vote of at least 75 per cent in number and value of all producers concerned.

On July 25, 1957, the Marketing Board approved The Quebec Carnation Company Milk Producers' Plan. The administration of the Plan was entrusted to The Quebec Carnation Company Milk Producers' Board. The Plan bound all bona fide milk producers shipping milk and dairy products to any of the plants of the appellant in Quebec. The Producers' Board had power to negotiate with the buyer (the appellant) for the marketing and sale to it of milk and dairy products from the farms of producers bound by the Plan. The Plan provided for a board of arbitration, which might be the Marketing Board, to decide conflicts in the event of a failure to agree with the appellant in the negotiation or execution of a convention.

Agreement was not reached as to the purchase price of milk to be purchased by the appellant from the producers, pursuant to the Plan. The matter was arbitrated by the Marketing Board which, after hearing evidence for both sides, wrote extensive reasons, and determined a price of $3.07 per hundred pounds, on December 18, 1958. Subsequently, on June 11, 1962, after a further arbitration, the Marketing Board decided on a price of $2.78 per hundred pounds.

It is these three orders of the Marketing Board, which approved the Plan, and which determined the price to be paid by the appellant for milk purchased from producers subject to the Plan, which are the subject of the appellant's attack.

The appellant was incorporated under the Canadian *Companies Act*, and has its head office in Toronto. It operates, in Quebec, an evaporated milk plant at Sherbrooke and a receiving station at Waterloo.

During the period concerned, it purchased raw milk from approximately 2,000 farmers, situated mostly in the Eastern Townships. At the Sherbrooke plant it processes raw milk into evaporated milk. The major part of such production is shipped and sold outside Quebec. Milk received at the Waterloo receiving station, during the relevant period, was either sent to the Sherbrooke plant, for processing, or else, skimmed, the butterfat being sold to other manufacturers, and the skim milk being sent to appellant's plant at Alexandria, Ontario, to be processed into skim milk powder.

The appellant, during the relevant period, was the only evaporated milk manufacturer in Quebec, with the exception of the Granby Co-operative, which, as a co-operative, was not subject to the provisions of the *Quebec Agricultural Marketing Act.*

The evidence showed that, since December 18, 1958, the date of the first arbitration award, prices paid by the appellant were about 10 to 25 cents per hundred pounds higher than those paid by other purchasers of raw milk in the same area. . . .

It is clear that [the Act's] provisions relate to the marketing of milk only in the Province of Quebec.

The position taken by the appellant is that the three orders of the Marketing Board are invalid because they enable it to set a price to be paid by the appellant for a product the major portion of which, after processing, will be used by it for export out of Quebec. This, it is contended, constitutes the regulation of trade and commerce within the meaning of s. 91(2) of the *British North America Act*, a field reserved to the Parliament of Canada. . . .

It is now necessary to consider . . . the validity of the three orders which are under attack. . . . The first order, which created The Quebec Carnation Company Milk Producers' Board and empowered it to nego-tiate, on behalf of the milk producers, for the sale of their products to the appellant, is somewhat analogous to the creation of a collective bargaining agency in the field of labour relations. The purpose of the order was to regulate, on behalf of a particular group of Quebec pro-ducers, their trade with the appellant for the sale to it, in Quebec, of their milk. Its object was to improve their bargaining position.

The Producers' Board then undertook, with the appellant, nego-tiations for the sale to it of that milk. The order provided a machinery whereby the price of milk could be determined by arbitration if agree-ment could not be reached. In this respect it differs from most provin-cial legislation governing labour disputes, but there would seem to be no doubt that provincial labour legislation incorporating compulsory arbitration of disputes would be constitutional unless objectionable on some other ground.

The two subsequent orders of the Marketing Board, under attack, contained the decisions which it reached in determining the proper price to be paid to the producers for milk purchased by the appellant.

Are these orders invalid because the milk purchased by the appel-lant was processed by it and, as to a major portion of its product, exported from the province? Because of that fact, do they constitute an attempt to regulate trade in matters of interprovincial concern?

That the price determined by the orders may have a bearing upon the appellant's export trade is unquestionable. It affects the cost of doing business. But so, also, do labour costs affect the cost of doing business of any company which may be engaged in export trade and yet there would seem to be little doubt as to the power of a province to regulate wage rates payable within a province, save as to an undertaking falling within the exceptions listed in s. 92(10) of the *British North America Act*. It is not the possibility that these orders might "affect" the appellant's interprovincial trade which should determine their validity, but, rather, whether they were made "in relation to" the regulation of trade and commerce. This was a test applied, in another connection, by Duff J. (as he then was) in *Gold Seal Limited v. Attorney-General for Alberta* [(1921), 62 S.C.R. 424 at 460, 3 W.W.R. 710, 62 D.L.R. 62].

Thus, as Kerwin C.J. said in the *Ontario Reference* . . . "Once a statute *aims* at 'regulation of trade in matters of inter-provincial concern' it is beyond the competence of a Provincial Legislature."

I am not prepared to agree that, in determining that aim, the fact that these orders may have some impact upon the appellant's interprovincial trade necessarily means that they constitute a regulation of trade and commerce within s. 91(2) and thus renders them invalid. The fact of such impact is a matter which may be relevant in determining their true aim and purpose, but it is not conclusive.

In the *Lawson* case, where the provincial legislation was found to be unconstitutional, the Committee created by the statute was enabled and purported to exercise a large measure of direct and immediate control over the movement of trade in commodities between a province and other provinces. That is not this case.

On the other hand, in the *Shannon* case the regulatory statute was upheld, as it was confined to the regulation of transactions taking place wholly within the province. It was held that s. 91(2) was not applicable to the regulation for legitimate provincial purposes of particular trades or businesses confined to the province.

The view of the four judges in the *Ontario Reference* was that the fact that a transaction took place wholly within a province did not necessarily mean that it was thereby subject solely to provincial control. The regulation of some such transactions relating to products destined for interprovincial trade could constitute a regulation of interprovincial trade and be beyond provincial control.

While I agree with the view of the four judges in the *Ontario Reference* that a trade transaction, completed in a province, is not necessarily, by that fact alone, subject only to provincial control, I also hold the view that the fact that such a transaction incidentally has some effect upon a company engaged in interprovincial trade does not necessarily prevent its being subject to such control.

I agree with the view of Abbott J., in the *Ontario Reference*, that each transaction and each regulation must be examined in relation to its own facts. In the present case, the orders under question were not, in my opinion, directed at the regulation of interprovincial trade. They did not purport directly to control or to restrict such trade. There was no evidence that, in fact, they did control or restrict it. The most that can be said of them is that they had some effect upon the cost of doing business in Quebec of a company engaged in interprovincial trade, and that, by itself, is not sufficient to make them invalid. . . .

Appeal dismissed with costs.

A.-G. FOR MANITOBA v. MANITOBA EGG AND POULTRY ASSOCIATION

In the Supreme Court of Canada. [1971] S.C.R. 689, 19 D.L.R. (3d) 169, [1971] 4 W.W.R. 705.

The Lieutenant Governor in Council for Manitoba referred to the Court of Appeal for hearing and consideration, certain questions as to the legislative competence of the province to authorize a Regulation proposed to be made by the Lieutenant Governor in Council and an Order proposed to be made by the Producer Board to be established by the Regulation. The proposed Regulation and Order would vest in the Producer Board complete control over all eggs whether produced in Manitoba or elsewhere. The opinion of the Court of Appeal for Manitoba was that this was *ultra vires*. The Attorney-General for Manitoba appealed. . . .

MARTLAND J.: . . . The Regulation and the Order, together, constitute what I shall refer to as "the Plan". . . . The Plan . . . contemplates that it shall be applicable to all eggs marketed in Manitoba, whether or not they are produced in that province. While the provincial Legislature could not control, or permit the Producer Board (hereinafter referred to as "the Board") to control the production of eggs in another province, the terms of the Plan are applicable to the produce of another province once it is within Manitoba and available for marketing.

That this is the position is illustrated by the fact that, whereas s. 8(b) of the Regulation authorizes the Board to issue production and marketing quotas to producers, para. (i) of the same section goes on to give a general authority to the Board to establish quotas for production and sale, to prohibit marketing in violation of an established quota and to prohibit the offering for sale of a particular regulated product to ensure the orderly marketing of the regulated product.

Sections 2 and 3 of the Order require a producer to send his whole production to a grading station specified by the Board and to market such production through the Board, acting as his selling agent. Sections 4 and 5 provide that "no person" shall sell or offer for sale any regulated product except through the Board acting as his selling agent and that "no person" shall sell or offer for sale any regulated product not graded, packed and marked in a grading or packing station, the operator of which is under contract with the Board.

These provisions make it clear that the Plan is intended to apply, not only to eggs produced by Manitoba producers, but to any eggs in Manitoba, wherever they may have been produced. This intent is placed beyond doubt by the provisions of ss. 12, 14 and 15 of the Order, which requires the regulated product to be packed in containers provided by the Board, which shall carry an inscription showing the place of origin of the regulated product and indicating whether such place of origin was in Manitoba, in another country, or in another province.

Complete control of the marketing of all eggs in Manitoba is vested in the Board. It is only through the Board, as selling agent, that any eggs may be sold or offered for sale. It has the authority, as already noted, to impose marketing quotas and to prohibit the offering for sale of a particular regulated product to ensure the orderly marketing of the regulated product. No eggs can be sold or offered for sale unless graded, packed and marked by a grading or packing station under contract with the Board. All eggs must be offered for sale to distributors, under contract with the Board, at prices set, from time to time, by the Board.

The Board, to which the Plan proposes to grant these broad powers, is not one which is to be appointed by the Manitoba Government, but is to be elected by the Manitoba producers. Its members must be actively engaged in the production of eggs. The main purposes of the Plan, to be achieved through the Board, is "to obtain for producers the most advantageous marketing conditions for the regulated product".

We have, therefore, a Plan which is intended to govern the sale in Manitoba of all eggs, wherever produced, which is to be operated by and for the benefit of the egg producers of Manitoba, to be carried out by a Board armed with the power to control the sale of eggs in Manitoba, brought in from outside Manitoba, by means of quotas, or even outright prohibition.

The issue which has to be considered in this appeal is as to whether the Plan is *ultra vires* of the Manitoba Legislature because it trespasses upon the exclusive legislative authority of the Parliament of Canada to legislate on the matter of the regulation of trade and commerce conferred by s. 91(2) of *The British North America Act.*

When the Privy Council first addressed itself to the meaning of that provision it was stated that it included "regulation of trade in matters of inter-provincial concern" (*Citizens Insurance Company of Canada v. Parsons* [(1881), 7 App. Cas. 96 at 113]). That proposition has not since been challenged. However, the case went on to hold that the provision did not include the regulation of the contracts of a particular business or trade in a single province.

This limitation on the federal power was reiterated in subsequent decisions of the Privy Council, the effect of which is summarized in *Shannon v. Lower Mainland Dairy Products Board* [[1938] A.C. 708 at 719, 2 W.W.R. 604, 4 D.L.R. 81].... In the judgment of this Court in *Carnation Company Limited v. The Quebec Agricultural Marketing Board* [[1968] S.C.R. 238, 67 D.L.R. (2d) 1] ... our conclusion was that each transaction and regulation had to be examined in relation to its own facts, and that, in determining the validity of the regulatory legislation in issue in that appeal, the issue was not as to whether it might affect the inter-provincial trade of the appellant company, but whether it was made in relation to the regulation of inter-provincial trade and commerce. There was cited the following passage from the reasons of Kerwin C.J. in the *Ontario Reference* (at p. 204):

> Once a statute aims at "regulation of trade in matters of inter-provincial concern" it is beyond the competence of a Provincial Legislature.

It is my opinion that the Plan now in issue not only affects interprovincial trade in eggs, but that it aims at the regulation of such trade. It is an essential part of this scheme, the purpose of which is to obtain for Manitoba producers the most advantageous marketing conditions for eggs, specifically to control and regulate the sale in Manitoba of imported eggs. It is designed to restrict or limit the free flow of trade between provinces as such. Because of that, it constitutes an invasion of the exclusive legislative authority of the Parliament of Canada over the matter of the regulation of trade and commerce.

That being so, I would hold that the Regulation and Order are not ones which are within the legislative competence of the Manitoba Legislature to authorize, and the answer to Question (1) (a) should be: No.

With respect to Question (1) (b), which raises the question of the severability of the Regulation and Order, I agree with the Court of Appeal that they are not severable because those portions which deal with local provincial trade in eggs are inextricably bound up with those which concern inter-provincial trade. My answer to Question (1) (b) would be that the Regulation and the Order are, *in toto,* outside the powers of provincial legislative competence.

The various questions contained in Question (2) are postulated upon the Regulation and the Order, or either of them, being wholly, or in part, within provincial legislative competence. In view of the answers given to Question (1) (a) and (b) these questions are not required to be answered.

In the result, I would dismiss the appeal, and, in answer to the questions referred to the Court of Appeal for Manitoba by the Lieutenant Governor in Council, I would pronounce the opinion:

As to Question 1(a) and (b), that it is beyond the legislative jurisdiction of the Manitoba Legislature to authorize the proposed Regulation and Order in question; and,

As to Question (2), that it does not, by the terms of the Order-in-Council 1083/70 dated November 5, 1970, require an answer. . . .

LASKIN J.—The utility of the Reference as a vehicle for determining whether actual or proposed legislation is competent under the allocations of power made by the *British North America Act* is seriously affected in the present case because there is no factual underpinning for the issues that are raised by the Order of Reference. Marketing data to illuminate those issues might have been set out in the Order itself (as was done, for example, in the *Margarine Reference* [[1949] S.C.R. 1, [1949] 1 D.L.R. 433]), or in an agreed statement of facts, or, indeed, might have been offered to the court to indicate the circumstances which prompted the questions addressed to it.

As it is, I know nothing of the nature of the market for eggs in Manitoba or outside of it, nothing of the production of eggs in that province, nothing of the uses to which the production is put, nothing of the number of producers in Manitoba, nothing of any problems that may have been created in relation to quality, price or otherwise by the entry of out-of-province eggs. I know only, and then in the broad terms set out in the first two recitals in the Order of Reference (and of which matters I could, in any event, have taken judicial notice) that (to quote them) "many Provinces of Canada, including the

Province of Manitoba, have enacted legislation pertaining to the regulation and control of marketing of agricultural products" and "certain of the marketing agencies established under the aforementioned legislation in some of the Provinces assert the right to prohibit, regulate and control the marketing within a Province of agricultural products produced outside that Province".

A knowledge of the market in Manitoba, the extent to which it is supplied by Manitoba producers, and of the competition among them as it reflected in supply, quality and price, would be of assistance in determining the application of the proposed legislative scheme. Thus, if out-of-province eggs were, to put an example, insignificant in the Manitoba market, this would be a factor bearing on a construction of the scheme as operative only in respect of Manitoba producers, retailers and consumers in production, distribution and consumption in Manitoba. Conversely, if such eggs were significant in the Manitoba market, the legislative scheme, not being expressly confined to production, distribution and consumption in Manitoba, could properly be regarded as directed to the out-of-province eggs. In this respect, the issue would be one of its validity or invalidity, and not one of construing it to be applicable only to the distribution and consumption within the province of eggs produced in the province.

The absence of what I regard as relevant data leaves the position as one where, on the face of the legislative scheme and in the light of the arguments thereon addressed to the court, the contemplated regulations and order purport to embrace out-of-province eggs sent or brought into the province. Moreover, the embrace would extend to out-of-province eggs of whatever quantity, and to whatever extent they might engulf the Manitoba retailer and consumer market. On this view of the situation, there is the naked constitutional question to be faced, namely; there being no federal regulatory legislation in force with the same thrust, is the proposed scheme offensive to the legislative power of Parliament in relation to "the regulation of trade and commerce" under s. 91(2) of the *B.N.A. Act*; and, if not or if so, is it, in any event offensive to the prescriptions of s. 121 of that Act?

Previous cases which have been concerned with the validity of provincial regulatory legislation as tested by the scope of s. 91(2) alone (and not also by the concurrent presence of federal regulatory legislation) cannot be dissociated from cases which have been concerned with the validity of federal regulatory legislation and which, accordingly, have dealt affirmatively with the scope of s. 91(2). These two classes are not necessarily opposite sides of the same coin, and hence, the frame of the legislation in each situation has central importance. On the provincial side, a comparison is apt of *Lawson v. Interior Tree Fruit and Vegetable Committee of Direction* [[1931] S.C.R. 357, 2 D.L.R. 193] with *Shannon v. Lower Mainland Dairy Products Board* [[1938] A.C. 708, 2 W.W.R. 604, 4 D.L.R. 81]; and on the federal side, a comparison may be made of *Reference re Natural Products Marketing Act* [[1937] A.C. 377, 1 W.W.R. 328, 67 C.C.C. 337, 1 D.L.R. 691] with *Murphy v. C.P.R.* [[1958] S.C.R. 626, 15 D.L.R. (2d) 145, 77 C.R.T.C. 322].

I adopt the position put by Rand J. in *Reference re Ontario Farm Products Marketing Act* [[1957] S.C.R. 198 at 208-209, 7 D.L.R. (2d) 257], that there is a field of trade within provincial power, such power being a substraction from that comprehended within s. 91(2). The subtraction is, to me, quite rational under the scheme of the *B.N.A. Act*, although stronger terms, referable to a necessary degree of provincial autonomy, have been used in the cases to support it. That there is such subtraction if a provincial regulatory field is to be recognized was obvious to this court in its earliest years. In the very first reported case on the distribution of legislative power, *Severn v. The Queen* [(1878), 2 S.C.R. 70], Strong J., in a dissenting judgment which favoured the validity of the provincial statute that was successfully challenged, pointed out (at p. 104) that, literally, "the regulation of trade and commerce in the Provinces, domestic and internal, as well as foreign and external, [was] by the British North America Act exclusively conferred upon the Parliament of the Dominion". A reduction of this all-embracing authority was effected by this Court in *Citizens Insurance Co. v. Parsons* [(1880), 4 S.C.R. 215], a decision affirmed by the Privy Council [(1881), 7 App. Cas. 96] but with *obiter* remarks that led over the years to almost as much an attenuation of the federal power in relation to s. 91(2) as its literal construction would have led to its aggrandizement. A necessary balance has been coming into view over the past two decades, as is evident from the judgments of this court in *Murphy v. C.P.R.*, already cited (and emphasized by the refusal of leave to appeal in *Regina v. Klassen* [(1959), 20 D.L.R. (2d) 406, 31 C.R. 275, 29 W.W.R. 369; [1959] S.C.R. ix]) and *Carnation Company Ltd. v. Quebec Agricultural Marketing Board* [[1968] S.C.R. 238, 67 D.L.R. (2d) 1].

What this balance points to is a more particular understanding of the meaning of the terms "trade" and "trade and commerce" as they relate respectively to the areas of provincial and federal competence. In *Montreal v. Montreal Street Railway* [[1912] A.C. 333 at 344, 13 C.R.C. 541, 1 D.L.R. 681], the Judicial Committee referred to s. 91(2) as expessing "two of the matters enumerated in s. 91". That provision is perhaps better seen as specifying a single class of subject in words that indicate a stronger source of authority than would be found if "trade" alone was used or "commerce" alone. This view is strengthened by the fact that it is unnecessary here to rely on s. 91(2) for transportation authority (having regard to ss. 92(10) (a) (b), 91(10) and 91(29)), in contradistinction to the judicial history of the commerce power in the United States under clause 3 of Article I of its Constitution and to the evolution of the power of the Commonwealth Parliament under s. 51(i) of the Australian Constitution to make laws with respect to "trade and commerce with other countries and among the States". Etymologically, commerce refers to the buying and selling of goods, and trade has among its meanings (other than commerce) that of mercantile occupation. Although literal application is unthinkable, these meanings do indicate the capacity which inheres in s. 91(2).

Not too often in the history of the interaction of provincial and federal legislation with s. 91(2) have there been attempts to define its terms. An early instance is that by Sedgewick J. in *In re Prohibitory Liquor Laws* [(1895), 24 S.C.R. 170 at 231]. Another instance in which definition or specification was attempted is *In re Canadian Insurance Act, 1910* [(1913), 48 S.C.R. 260, 5 W.W.R. 488, 15 D.L.R. 251], affirmed [[1916] 1 A.C. 588, 26 D.L.R. 288]. The meaning of "trade and commerce" in respect of transactions in goods, as opposed to non-commodity transactions, does not appear to have been elucidated in any reported case, but has been left to inference from the nature of the legislation under review. It has been put beyond doubt that Parliament's power under s. 91(2) is exclusive so far as concerns the prohibition or regulation of exports to and imports from other countries, and that a province may not, as legislator, prohibit or regulate the export of goods therefrom. This last-mentioned proposition, which is exemplified in such decisions as *In re Grain Marketing Act, 1931* [[1931] 2 W.W.R. 146, 25 Sask. L.R. 273], and *Re Sheep and Swine Marketing Scheme* [[1941] 3 D.L.R. 569], does not, however, mean that, in the absence of federal legislation, a province is incompetent to impose any regulation upon transactions in goods produced therein and between persons therein simply because the regulation may have an effect upon ultimate export of the goods from the province, whether in their original or in some processed form.

The stage of dealing at which the regulation is imposed and its purpose, on which economic data would be relevant, are important considerations in assessing provincial competence. This emerges clearly from *Carnation Milk Company Ltd. v. Quebec Agricultural Marketing Board, supra*, where this court rejected a contention that the regulatory scheme, as reflected in three challenged orders, constituted an unlawful invasion of federal power in relation to export. What was there involved was the fixing of prices, by arbitration if agreement could not otherwise be reached, at which milk and dairy products produced in the province were to be sold by provincial producers, contracting under a joint marketing plan, to a distributor and processor in the province. The fact that the processed products were largely distributed and sold outside the province did not react upon the validity of the scheme whose purpose was to improve the bargaining position in the province of provincial producers in their dealings with manufacturers or processors in the province. The regulatory scheme under attack did not involve a marketing control which extended through the various stages of production, distribution and consumption.

What was raised in the *Carnation Milk* case was the meaning, for constitutional purposes, of an intraprovincial transaction where the issue was seen in the context of goods leaving the province. The present Reference raises this question in the context of goods entering the province and their subjection, in consequence, to the same regulatory scheme that operates upon like goods produced in the province. This was a matter which had been considered in the *Shannon* case, *supra*, and in *Home Oil Distributors Ltd. v. Attorney-General of British Columbia* [[1940] S.C.R. 444, [1940] 2 D.L.R. 609], in both of which the impugned schemes were held to be within provincial legislative competence.

There is a passage in the reasons of the judicial Committee in the *Shannon* case which has a bearing on this Reference. Lord Atkin said this (at pp. 718-719 of [1938] A.C.) :

> It is sufficient to say upon the first ground that it is apparent that the legislation in question is confined to regulating transactions that take place wholly within the Province, and are therefore within the sovereign powers granted to the Legislature in that respect by s. 92 of the *British North America Act*. Their Lordships do not accept the view that natural products as defined in the Act are confined to natural products produced in British Columbia. There is no such restriction in the Act, and the limited construction would probably cause difficulty if it were sought at some future time to co-operate with a valid Dominion scheme. But the Act is clearly confined to dealings with such products as are situate within the Province.

The second sentence in this passage must be read in the light of the history of marketing legislation as it evolved in that period. Parliament and provincial legislatures had enacted what they thought was dovetailing legislation only to find that the central piece, the federal enactment, had over-reached in attempting to encompass purely intra-provincial transactions in products grown and marketed in the province, this element of the scheme being founded on the fact that some portion of the product might be exported: see *Attorney-General of British Columbia v. Attorney-General of Canada* [[1937] A.C. 377]. The Privy Council appeared to think in the *Shannon* case that effective co-operation in marketing could better be ensured if the small extra-provincial element was an appendage of provincial legislation. The decision did not foresee the later developments in this area through such legislation as the *Motor Vehicle Transport Act*, 1954 (Can.), c. 59 and the *Agricultural Products Marketing Act*, R.S.C. 1952, c. 6, as amended by 1957 (Can.), c. 15.

In my opinion, the *Shannon* case cannot today have the effect which a literal application of the second sentence of the quoted passage would suggest. Moreover, the fourth and last sentence indicates that the legislation did not purport to apply to out-of-province producers. However, I find this difficult to reconcile with the second sentence unless it be taken that the marketing scheme did not apply to out-of-province products on their mere entry into the province or that any such application was *de minimis* and not an aim of the scheme. If so, the scheme in the *Shannon* case differs from that involved in this Reference.

Home Oil Distributors Ltd. v. Attorney-General of British Columbia [[1940] S.C.R. 444, [1940] 2 D.L.R. 609] concerned not a marketing scheme of the type involved in the *Shannon* case or in the present case, but rather a price fixing scheme, embracing both maximum and minimum prices for coal and petroleum products sold at wholesale or retail in the province or for use in the province. . . .

I cannot see in the *Home Oil* case any parallel with the marketing scheme which the Order of Reference put before the Manitoba Court of Appeal . . .

Neither in the *Shannon* case nor in the *Home Oil* case was there any attempt to examine the various elements or sets of relationships in a marketing or price fixing scheme with a view to elucidating the meaning, for constitutional purposes, of intraprovincial trade and commerce. This exercise fell to this court in the *Ontario Farm Products Marketing Act* Reference, *supra*. What emerges from the various reasons of the members of the court is that (1) individual contracts for the sale and purchase of goods in a province do not engage federal power under s. 91(2) where any applicable provincial legislation relates merely to the terms of the contract; (2) regulation of the marketing, or the processing and marketing, of products in a province for consumption therein is within provincial competence; (3) regulation of the marketing of provincial produce intended for export or sought to be purchased for export is beyond that competence; (4) regulation of production or manufacture must be distinguished from regulation of transactions in the product and it cannot be said that the former is so wholly within provincial regulatory competence as in all cases to cover production or manufacture for export; and (5) even in respect of the latter, it cannot be categorically stated that ultimate extra-provincial destination will foreclose provincial regulation of intermediate steps in the marketing process. The matter was put in the following words by Martland J. speaking for the court in the *Carnation Company* case [[1968] S.C.R. 238 at 253, 67 D.L.R. (2d) 1]:

While I agree with the view of the four judges in the *Ontario Reference* that a trade transaction, completed in a province, is not necessarily, by that fact alone, subject only to provincial control, I also hold the view that the fact that such a transaction incidentally has some effect upon a company engaged in interprovincial trade does not necessarily prevent its being subject to such control.

The *Ontario Farm Products Marketing Act* Reference, although refining the meaning of an intra-provincial transaction, did not expressly address itself to the position of an extraprovincial producer, or a purchaser from him, seeking to bring his production into a province free of a regulatory scheme applicable to local produce. Fauteux J., as he then was, noted in that Reference that the hog marketing scheme which was the subject of the court's concern did not cover hogs produced outside the province nor were producers outside the province affected thereby. "In the result", he said, "any one in Ontario is free to import therein and one beyond its boundaries to export thereto the regulated product" (at p. 254 of [1957] S.C.R.). This is, however, precisely the issue that must be faced in the present Reference.

It must be faced under a scheme which, as set out in the proposed measures attached to the Order of Reference, has the following elements:

(1) A Producer Board is established through which all eggs to be marketed in Manitoba must be sold.
(2) All such eggs must go to grading and packing stations which are to be operated by persons under contract with the Board.

   (3) All such eggs must be graded, packed and marked in the grading and packing stations.

   (4) They are to be packed in containers provided by the Board which are to bear inscriptions of the grade, station number, grading date, place of origin of the eggs and the Board trade mark.

   (5) Only authorized collectors may take delivery of eggs from a producer.

   (6) Production and marketing quotas may be allotted to producers by the Board.

   (7) The Board may establish quotas for production and sale and also fix the time and place of marketing and, equally, may prohibit marketing otherwise or in violation of established quotas or standards.

   (8) The Board may contract with distributors as its intermediaries in sales to retailers.

   (9) Weekly prices for each grade of egg are to be set by the Board and distributors are entitled to buy at those prices.

Although the emphasis is on control of the Manitoba producers and distributors in order (as stated in the proposed measures) "to obtain for producers the most advantageous marketing conditions" and "to avoid overproduction", the scheme brings into its grasp "persons" as well as producers, that is, those outside the province who are either producers or distributors seeking to enter the Manitoba market, or those inside the province who are not themselves producers but who bring in out-of-province eggs for disposition in Manitoba. This view is reinforced by the provision for indicating the origin of eggs, including eggs other than those produced in Manitoba.

There may be a variety of reasons which impel a province to enact regulatory legislation for the marketing of various products. For example, it may wish to secure the health of the inhabitants by establishing quality standards; it may wish to protect consumers against exorbitant prices; it may wish to equalize the bargaining or competitive position of producers or distributors or retailers, or all three classes; it may wish to ensure an adequate supply of certain products. These objects may not all nor always be realizable through legislation which fastens on the regulated product as being within the province. That is no longer, if it ever was, the test of validity. Just as the province may not, as a general rule, prohibit an owner of goods from sending them outside the province, so it may not be able to subject goods to a regulatory scheme upon their entry into the province. This is not to say that goods that have come into a province may not, thereafter, be subject to the same controls in, for example, retail distribution to consumers as apply to similar goods in the province.

Assuming such controls to be open to a province, the scheme before this court is not so limited. It embraces products which are in the current of interprovincial trade and, as noted at the beginning of these reasons, it embraces them in whatever degree they seek to enter the provincial market. It begs the question to say that out-of-province producers who come in voluntarily (certainly they cannot be compelled by Manitoba) must not expect to be treated differently from local producers. I do not reach the question of discriminatory standards applied to out-of-province producers or distributors (that is, the question of a possibly illegal administration of the scheme as bearing on its validity) because I am of opinion that the scheme is on its face an invasion of federal power in relation to s. 91(2).

There are several grounds upon which I base this conclusion. The proposed scheme has as a direct object the regulation of the importation of eggs, and it is not saved by the fact that the local market is under the same regime. Anglin J. said in *Gold Seal Ltd. v. Dominion Express Co.* [(1921), 62 S.C.R. 424 at 465, 3 W.W.R. 710, 62 D.L.R. 62] that "it is common ground that the prohibition of importation is beyond the legislative jurisdiction of the province". Conversely, the general limitation upon provincial authority to exercise of its powers within or in the province precludes it from intercepting either goods moving into the province or goods moving out, subject to possible exceptions, as in the case of danger to life or health. Again, the Manitoba scheme cannot be considered in isolation from similar schemes in other provinces; and to permit each province to seek its own advantage, so to speak, through a figurative sealing of its borders to entry of goods from others would be to deny one of the objects of Confederation, evidenced by the catalogue of federal powers and by s. 121, namely, to form an economic unit of the whole of Canada: see the *Lawson* case [[1931] S.C.R. 357 at 373, 2 D.L.R. 193]. The existence of egg marketing schemes in more than one province, with objectives similar to the proposed Manitoba scheme, makes it clear that interprovincial trade in eggs is being struck at by the provincial barriers to their movement into various provincial markets. If it be thought necessary or desirable to arrest such movement at any provincial border then the aid of the Parliament of Canada must be sought, as was done through Part V of the *Canada Temperance Act*, R.S.C. 1952, c. 30, in respect of provincial regulation of the sale of intoxicating liquor.

I do not find it necessary in this case to invoke s. 121 and hence say nothing about its applicability to the marketing scheme under review.

PIGEON J.—I am in agreement with the reasons and conclusions of my brother Martland subject to the following observations.

In my view, the statement of the Privy Council in *Citizens Insurance Company v. Parsons* [(1881), 7 App. Cas. 96 at 113] must be read in the context of a case in which the actual decision was not as to the extent of federal commerce power but as to the provincial authority over local trade. Furthermore, the statement was immediately followed by this important qualification:

> Their Lordships abstain on the present occasion from any attempt to define the limits of the authority of the dominion parliament in this direction.

Although I fully agree that the Plan in issue is invalid as being aimed at the regulation of interprovincial trade in eggs, I wish to restrict my reason for reaching this conclusion to the following consideration.

An essential part of this scheme designed to obtain for Manitoba egg producers the most advantageous marketing conditions, is not merely to subject eggs brought in from outside the province to the same trade regulations as those produced therein but, in effect, to enable the Manitoba producers through the Board to restrict by means of quotas the local sale of eggs produced elsewhere to whatever extent will best serve their interests, even if this means a complete prohibition of such sale. Thus the Plan is designed to restrict or limit trade between provinces as such.

[Hall J. joined in the opinion of Laskin J.]

CALOIL INC. v. A.-G. CANADA

In the Supreme Court of Canada. [1971] S.C.R. 543, [1971] 4 W.W.R. 37, 20 D.L.R. (3d) 472.

A National Energy Board regulation providing that licences for importation of motor gasoline should be conditioned on the importer's undertaking "not, with the Board's consent, (to) sell or deliver to a third party any 'motor gasoline' except on the condition that it is sold or delivered for consumption east of" the Ontario-Quebec line was declared unconstitutional, *Caloil Inc. v. A.-G. Canada*, [1970] Ex. C.R. 512, 15 D.L.R. (3d) 164. The judgment was not appealed. Instead the regulation was amended to read:

"S. 20(2)   Where the Board is of the opinion that importation of oil that is the subject of an application for a licence to import into Canada will be consistent with the development or utilization of Canadian indigenous oil resources, it may issue a licence to import oil for consumption in the area of Canada specified therein, in such quantities, at such times and at such points of entry into Canada as it may consider appropriate.

"(3)   Any licences issued by the Board pursuant to subsection (2) may be issued under the condition that the oil to be imported will be consumed in the area of Canada specified in the licence."

Based on the amended regulation, the Board refused application to import unless the importer would declare that the oil would be consumed in the areas specified by the Board. A declaratory action was again instituted challenging the regulation's constitutionality. The Exchequer Court sustained the regulation. The company appealed.

PIGEON J.—The appellant did not challenge federal authority over imports as such. The attack was exclusively directed against the regulation of trade in the imported commodity at the level of distribution for consumption. . . . The *Shannon* and *Home Oil* cases both dealt with the validity of provincial regulation of local trades. They hold that provincial authority over transactions taking place wholly within the province is, as a rule, applicable to products imported from another province, as well as to local products. However, it must be borne in mind that the division of constitutional authority under the Canadian Constitution often results in overlapping legislation. . . .

Lord Tomlin's fourth proposition in the *Fish Canneries* case [[1930] A.C. 111 at 118, [1929] 3 W.W.R. 449, [1930] 1 D.L.R. 194] is:

> (4.) There can be a domain in which provincial and Dominion legislation may overlap, in which case neither legislation will be ultra vires if the field is clear, but if the field is not clear and the two legislations meet the Dominion legislation must prevail: . . .

This principle was recently applied by this Court in such cases as *Smith v. The Queen* [[1960] S.C.R. 776, 33 C.R. 318, 128 C.C.C. 145, 25 D.L.R. (2d) 225], *O'Grady v. Sparling* [[1960] S.C.R. 804, 33 C.R. 293, 33 W.W.R. 360, 128 C.C.C. 1, 25 D.L.R. (2d) 145] and *Stephens v. The Queen* [[1960] S.C.R. 823, 33 C.R. 312, 33 W.W.R. 379, 128 C.C.C. 21, 25 D.L.R. (2d) 296]. It is clear, therefore, that the existence and extent of provincial regulatory authority over specific trades within the province is not the sole criterion to be considered in deciding whether a federal regulation affecting such a trade is invalid. On the contrary, it is no objection when the impugned enactment is an integral part of a scheme for the regulation of international or interprovincial trade, a purpose that is clearly outside provincial jurisdiction and within the exclusive federal field of action. The rule must be the same as with respect to criminal law concerning which Duff J. (as he then was) said in *Gold Seal Ltd. v. Attorney General of Alberta* [(1921), 62 S.C.R. 424 at 460, [1921] 3 W.W.R. 710, 62 D.L.R. 62]:

> Most legislation of a repressive character does incidentally or consequentially affect civil rights. But if in its true character it is not legislation "in relation to" the subject matter of "property and civil rights" within the provinces, within the meaning of section 92 of the British North America Act, then that is no objection . . .

In the present case, subs. 2 of s. 20 of the Regulation clearly shows that the policy intended to be implemented by the impugned enactment is a control of the imports of a given commodity to foster the development and utilization of Canadian oil resources. The restriction on the distribution of the imported product to a defined area is intended to reserve the market in other areas for the benefit of products from other provinces of Canada. Therefore, the true character of the enactment appears to be an incident in the administration of an extraprovincial marketing scheme as in *Murphy v. C.P.R.* [[1958] S.C.R. 626, 77 C.R.T.C. 322, 15 D.L.R. (2d) 145. Under the circumstances, the interference with local trade restricted as it is to an imported commodity, is an integral part of the control of imports in the furtherance of an extraprovincial trade policy and cannot be termed "an unwarranted invasion of provincial jurisdiction". . . .

The trial judge did not find it necessary to deal explicitly with the contention that, due to the definition of "import" in para. (*g*) of s.

2 of the Act, s. 20 of the Regulations was not within the scope of s. 85 of the Act. He was clearly right in rejecting it. Nothing shows that the terms and conditions of the licences that may be prescribed by Regulations are to end with the entry of the commodity into Canada and cannot be related to subsequent use. On the contrary, provisions related to the end use of some products have long been a feature of Customs Tariff Acts. . . .

LASKIN J.—I support the dismissal of the appeal, as announced by the Chief Justice at the conclusion of the hearing, and do so on the ground taken by my brother Pigeon that the admitted authority of Parliament to regulate importation of goods from foreign countries was validly exercised in this case in including as part of the regulatory scheme a provision restricting the area of distribution of the goods within Canada by their importer.

[Fauteux C.J. and Abbott, Ritchie, Hall and Spence JJ. joined in the judgment of Pigeon J.; Martland and Judson JJ. concurred with Laskin J.].

3. Business (Non-Commodity) Transactions

It cannot escape notice that just as the liquor cases were the medium through which the federal general power was first examined, so were the insurance cases the medium for initial exposition of the federal trade and commerce power. There is a singular dearth of definition of "trade" or "commerce" in the Privy Council's decisions, perhaps because that tribunal assumed or came to a considered conclusion that the problems in the area lay not so much in the words used to define the power granted but rather in the feasibility of local or national control of economic activities which belonged as much to the Provinces under s. 92(13)(16) of the B.N.A. Act as to the Dominion under s. 91(2). In *In re Sections 4 and 70 of the Canadian Insurance Act, 1910* (1913), 48 S.C.R. 260, at p. 302, 5 W.W.R. 488, at p. 515, Duff J. asserted that s. 91(2) "does not embrace the regulation of occupations as such", and he "[did] not think that the various kinds of businesses which are comprehended under the term 'insurance' . . . can be said to be part of the trade and commerce of the country". Anglin J. was doubtful that the business of insurance could ever be spoken of as a trade, and this doubt was, for him, removed by the association of "trade" with "commerce" in s. 91(2), which made it clear that "trade" did not cover the business of "insurance". No advertence was made or consideration given to insurance as "commerce", not even by the dissenting Judges (Fitzpatrick C.J.C. and Davies J.), both of whom were of opinion that insurance was a "trade". In the *Local Prohibition* case, [1896] A.C. 348, at p. 363, Lord Watson referred to the fact that in the *Parsons* case (1881), 7 App. Cas. 96 insurance was admitted to be a trade. In the *Insurance Reference* case, [1916] 1 A.C. 588, 26 D.L.R. 288, 10 W.W.R. 405, the question whether insurance was a trade for purposes of s. 91(2) was lost in a generalized assertion that federal power was unequal to the regulation by licensing of particular trades carried on in the provinces. The matter has remained in this state, qualified only by recent re-examinations of the trade and commerce power in cases which were concerned with marketing controls.

True, there have been some utterances such as those of Duff C.J.C. in *Reference re Alberta Statutes,* [1938] S.C.R. 100, at p. 121, [1938] 2 D.L.R. 81, at p. 96, which suggest consciousness of the "commerce" side of s. 91(2), but the dominant feature of judicial consideration of s. 91(2) has been preoccupation with the "civil rights" aspects of business regulation, considered as a matter of local provincial concern and as a badge of provincial autonomy. It is worth noting that in the United States where the federal power is expressed in terms of "commerce", it has been held that trade in the sense of transactions between different persons is not a prerequisite to exercise of federal power and that "interstate commerce" embraces such instrumentalities of that commerce as bills of lading: see *United States v. Hill* (1919), 248 U.S. 420, 39 S. Ct. 143; *United States v. Ferger* (1919), 250 U.S. 199, 39 S. Ct. 445. The *Murphy* case, *supra,* at p. 320 raised, on the level of legislative operation, the question whether interprovincial movement of goods by a person for his own use was "trade" (or commerce), a question similar to that in *United States v. Hill,* and the affirmative answer of the Court at least points the way to a more explicit concern with "commerce" under s. 91(2) than has hitherto been the case.

A.-G. ONT. v. RECIPROCAL INSURERS

In the Privy Council. [1924] A.C. 328, [1924] 1 D.L.R. 789, [1924] 2 W.W.R. 397.

Consolidated appeal by special leave from a judgment of the Appellate Division of the Supreme Court of Ontario, 53 O.L.R. 195, upon a reference of certain questions by the Lieutenant-Governor in Council, and upon cases reserved for the opinion of that Court by a police magistrate.

DUFF J.: Availing himself of the provisions of the Provincial statute, c. 85 of R.S. Ont., 1914, the Lieutenant-Governor of Ontario on May 10, 1922, referred to the Appellate Division of the Supreme Court of Ontario three separate questions in the following terms:—

"Question One.—Is it within the legislative competence of the Legislature of the Province of Ontario to regulate or license the making of reciprocal contracts by such legislation as that embodied in the Reciprocal Insurance Act, 1922?

"Question Two.—Would the making or carrying out of reciprocal insurance contracts licensed pursuant to the Reciprocal Insurance Act, 1922, be rendered illegal or otherwise affected by the provisions of ss. 508C and 508D of the Criminal Code as enacted by c. 26 of the Statutes of Canada 7 & 8 Geo. 5, in the absence of a licence from the Minister of Finance issued pursuant to s. 4 of the Insurance Act of Canada 7 & 8 Geo. 5, c. 29?

"Question Three.—Would the answers to questions one or two be affected, and if so how, if one or more of the persons subscribing to such reciprocal insurance contracts is: (A) A British subject not resident in Canada immigrating into Canada? (B) An alien?"

The two Dominion statutes mentioned in the second of these queries were passed on the same day, September 20, 1917 (7 & 8 Geo. 5, c. 29), one entitled the Insurance Act, 1917, and the other (7 & 8 Geo. 5, c. 26), entitled an Act to Amend the Criminal Code respecting insurance. The question whether the first section of the last-mentioned of them, a section professing to bring into force an amendment of the Criminal Code designated as s. 508C, was competently enacted, is the most important question with which their Lordships are concerned on this appeal, and it will be convenient to discuss that question first. It was answered in the affirmative by the Appellate Division.

These two statutes, which are complementary parts of a single legislative plan, are admittedly an attempt to produce by a different legislative procedure the results aimed at by the authors of the Insurance Act of 1910, which in *Attorney-General for Canada v. Attorney-General for Alberta,* [1916] 1 A.C. 588 was pronounced *ultra vires* of the Dominion Parliament.

The Insurance Act of 1917 empowers the Minister of Finance to grant licences to companies, authorizing them to carry on in Canada the business of insurance, except marine insurance, subject to the provisions of the statute and to the terms of the licence. Any company, other than a company already incorporated under the authority of the Dominion Parliament, when licensed under the statute, becomes, and is deemed to be a company incorporated under the laws of Canada. The Minister is also authorized to grant licences to associations of individuals formed upon the plan known as Lloyd's and to associations formed for the purpose of exchanging reciprocal contracts of indemnity upon the plan known as inter-insurance; and in such cases all the provisions and requirements of the statute regulating the business of licensed companies are deemed, so far as applicable, to be terms and conditions of the licence. No provision is made by the statute for licensing individuals or for licensing firms or unincorporated associations other than those falling within the two classes just mentioned.

The enactments of the statute include provisions touching the requirements with which applicants for licences must comply, the terms of licences, the conditions of their cancellation and suspension and a comprehensive system of regulations controlling licensees in relation to the form and terms of contracts of insurance and the business of insurance generally, including (*inter alia*) regulations governing the salaries, allowances and commissions of directors and agents, and the investment of the funds of such companies; to all of which provisions, in so far as applicable, unincorporated associations of the two classes above mentioned, that have received licences, are subject.

In the Insurance Act itself there is no enactment of general application requiring persons carrying on the business of insurance to become licensed under it. Provisions of limited application upon the subject are found in ss. 11 and 12. By s. 11 it is declared to be unlawful for any Dominion company or for any alien, whether a natural person or foreign company, to solicit or accept any risk, to issue or deliver any receipt or policy of insurance, to carry on any business of insurance or to do any of a number of other acts therein enumerated in relation to any such business unless licensed under the Act; and by s. 12 it is declared to be unlawful for any British company or for any British subject not resident in Canada to immigrate into Canada for the purpose of opening or establishing any office or agency for the transaction of any business of or relating to insurance, or doing any of the acts declared to be unlawful by s. 11. Penalties are imposed, for example by ss. 84 and 187, in respect of infringements of the Act.

Broadly speaking, therefore, under the Insurance Act any company, whether British, foreign or Canadian, incorporated for the purpose of carrying on the business of insurance, and any unincorporated association falling within either of the two classes mentioned, may become licensed upon observing the requirements of the Act, and as licensees such company thereupon becomes subject to the provisions of the Act, which, as regards such licensees, receive obligatory force by virtue of the penal clauses already referred to and of the liability of licences to cancellation for non-observance of statutory requirements. But the provisions of the statute contain nothing making it compulsory for any private individual or any unincorporated firm or association to become licensed as a condition of lawfully carrying on or transacting any business of insurance.

It is obvious that, in the absence of some such compulsory enactment, directed against such individuals and unincorporated bodies, the scheme of regulation embodied in the Insurance Act could only be incompletely effectual, and accordingly the authors of the legislation resorted to the expedient of bringing the necessary prohibitions and penalties into force in the form of an amendment to the Criminal Code. That amendment, which is designated as s. 508C of the Criminal Code, is in the following words:

"(1) Everyone shall be guilty of an indictable offence who, within Canada, except on behalf of or as agent for a company thereunto duly licensed by the Minister of Finance or on behalf of or as agent for or as a member of an association of individuals formed upon the plan known as Lloyd's or of an association of persons formed for the purpose of inter-insurance and so licensed, solicits or accepts any insurance risk, or issues or delivers any interim receipt or policy of insurance, or grants in consideration of any premium or payment any annuity on a life or lives, or collects or receives any premium for insurance, or carries on any business of insurance or inspects any risk, or adjusts any loss, or prosecutes or maintains any suit, action or proceeding, or files any claim in insolvency relating to such business or receives directly or indirectly any remuneration for doing any of the aforesaid acts . . .

"Provided that nothing in this section contained shall be deemed to prohibit or affect or to impose any penalty for doing any of the acts in this section described: (A) By or on behalf of a company incorporated under the laws of any Province of Canada for the purpose of carrying on the business of insurance. (B) By or on behalf of any society or association of persons thereunto specially authorized by the Minister of Finance or the Treasury Board. (C) In respect of any policy or risk of life insurance issued or undertaken on or before the thirtieth day of March, one thousand eight hundred and seventy-eight, by or on behalf of any company which has not since the last-mentioned date received a licence from the Minister of Finance. (D) In respect of any policy of life insurance issued by an unlicensed company to a person not resident in Canada at the time of the issue of such policy. (E) In respect of the insurance of property situated in Canada with any British or foreign unlicensed insurance company or underwriters, or with persons who reciprocally insure for protection and not for profit, or the inspection of the property so insured, or the adjustment of any loss incurred in respect thereof if the insurance is effected outside of Canada without any solicitations whatsoever directly or indirectly on the part of the company, underwriters or persons by which or by whom the insurance is made. (F) Solely in respect of marine or inland marine insurance. (G) In respect of any contract entered into or any certificate of membership or policy of insurance issued, before the twentieth day of July, one thousand eight hundred and eighty-five by any assessment life insurance company."

It will be observed that by force of para. (A) of the proviso, Provincial incorporated companies are under no disability. Prohibited acts, though criminal offences when done by an individual on behalf of himself or of an unlicensed unincorporated association or on behalf of an unlicensed company other than a Provincial company, are treated as innocent when done on behalf of a Provincial company, or (in virtue of para. (B)) when done on behalf of a society or association under the special authority of the Minister of Finance or of the Treasury Board. Such acts, by force of para. (F), are likewise innocent when done solely in respect of marine insurance. Subject to these exceptions (the remaining paragraphs of the proviso are of no relevancy) the effect of the enactment, briefly summarized, is that anybody who does, in Canada, any of the acts enumerated, is guilty of an indictable offence unless he is acting on behalf of a company licensed under the Insurance Act or on behalf of or as a member of an association so licensed; and the necessary consequence is that, subject, of course, to the same exceptions, if the enactment be legally operative, contracts of insurance, if lawfully effected, and any business of insurance, if lawfully transacted, are brought, after the passing of the Act, under the dominion of the system of regulations governing licensees under the Insurance Act; and to that extent withdrawn from Provincial control.

In *Attorney-General for Canada v. Attorney-General for Alberta,* it was decided by this Board that it was not competent to the Dominion to regulate generally the business of insurance in such a way as to interfere with the exercise of civil rights in the Provinces.

The provisions relating to licences in the Insurance Act of 1910, which by this judgment was declared to be *ultra vires,* and the regulations governing licences under the Act and applicable to contracts and to the business of insurance, did not, in any respect presently material, substantially differ from those now found in the legislation of 1917; but the provisions of the statute of 1910 derived their coercive force from penalties created by the Insurance Act itself.

The distinction between the legislation of 1910 and that of 1917, upon which the major contention of the Dominion is founded, consists in the fact that s. 508C is enacted in the form of an amendment to the statutory criminal law, and purports only to create offences which are declared to be indictable, and to ordain penalties for such offences. The question now to be decided is whether, in the frame in which this legislation of 1917 is cast, that part of it which is so enacted can receive effect as a lawful exercise of the legislative authority of the Parliament of Canada in relation to the criminal law. It has been formally laid down in judgments of this Board, that in such an inquiry the Courts must ascertain the "true nature and character" of the enactment: *Citizens Insurance Co. v. Parsons* (1881), 7 App. Cas. 96; its "pith and substance": *Union Colliery Co. v. Bryden,* [1899] A.C. 580; and it is the result of this investigation, not the form alone, which the statute may have assumed under the hand of the draughtsman, that will determine within which of the categories of subject matters mentioned in ss. 91 and 92 the legislation falls; and for this purpose the legislation must be "scrutinised in its entirety": *Great West Saddlery Co. v. The King,* [1921] 2 A.C. 91, at p. 117. Of course, where there is an absolute jurisdiction vested in a Legislature, the laws promulgated by it must take effect according to the proper construction of the language in which they are expressed. But where the law-making authority is of a limited or qualified character, obviously it may be necessary to examine with some strictness the substance of the legislation for the purpose of determining what it is that the Legislature is really doing. . . .

A judgment of the Supreme Court of the United States delivered in 1918 in *Hammer v. Dagenhart,* 247 U.S. 251, illustrates the operation of the principle. By the Constitution of the United States the regulation of commerce between the States is committed to Congress, and this authority, it was decided in a series of decisions of the Supreme Court, includes the power to prohibit the transmission, through the channels of inter-State commerce, of any particular class of articles of commerce. The statute of Congress, which the Supreme Court had to consider in the case mentioned, prohibited "the transportation in inter-State commerce" of manufactured goods the product of a factory in which within thirty days prior to their removal therefrom children of certain specified ages had been employed or permitted to work. The authority to enact this statute was rested upon the grounds that the power of Congress in relation to inter-State commerce is an unqualified power, including, as already mentioned, the authority to prohibit the transport of any articles of commerce of any description whatever in inter-State commerce, and that, the legislation impugned, being *ex facie* within the terms of the power, it was not competent to any judicial tribunal to inquire into the purpose or the ultimate or collateral effects, of the enactment. In the course of the judgment delivered by Day J., on behalf of the majority of the Court, holding that the statute could not be supported as legislation regulating inter-State commerce within the true intendment of "the commerce clause," it is said: "A statute must be judged by its natural and reasonable effect. . . . We have neither authority nor disposition to question the motives of Congress in enacting this legislation. The purposes intended must be attained consistently with constitutional limitations and not by an invasion of the powers of the States. This Court has no more important function than that which devolves upon it the obligation to preserve inviolate the constitutional limitations upon the exercise of authority, Federal and State, to the end that each may continue to discharge, harmoniously with the other, the duties entrusted to it by the Constitution. In our view the necessary effect of this act is, by means of a prohibition against the movement in inter-State commerce of ordinary commercial commodities, to regulate the hours of labour of children in factories and mines within the States, a purely State authority. . . . The far-reaching result of upholding the act cannot be more plainly indicated than by pointing out that if Congress can thus regulate matters entrusted to local authority by prohibition of the movement of commodities in inter-State commerce, all freedom of commerce will be at an end, and the power of the States over local matters may be eliminated, and thus our system of Government be practically destroyed."

It is not seriously disputed that the purpose and effect of the amendment in question are to give compulsory force to the regulative measures of the Insurance Act, and their Lordships think it not open to controversy that in purpose and effect s. 508C is a measure regulating the exercise of civil rights. But, on behalf of the Dominion, it is argued that, although such be the true character of the legislation, the jurisdiction of Parliament, in relation to the criminal law, is unlimited, in the sense, that in execution of its powers over that subject matter, the Dominion has authority to declare any act a crime, either in itself or by reference to the manner or the conditions in which the act is done, and consequently that s. 508C, being by its terms limited to the creation of criminal offences, falls within the jurisdiction of the Dominion.

The power which this argument attributes to the Dominion is, of course, a far-reaching one. Indeed, the claim now advanced is nothing less than this, that the Parliament of Canada can assume exclusive control over the exercise of any class of civil rights within the Provinces, in respect of which exclusive jurisdiction is given to the Provinces under s. 92, by the device of declaring those persons to be guilty of a criminal offence who in the exercise of such rights do not observe the conditions imposed by the Dominion. Obviously the principle contended for ascribes to the Dominion the power, in execution of its authority under s. 91, head 27, to promulgate and to enforce regulations controlling such matters as, for example, the solemnization of marriage, the practice of the learned professions and other occupations, municipal institutions, the operation of local works and undertakings, the incorporation of companies with exclusively Provincial objects—and superseding Provincial authority in relation thereto. Indeed, it would be difficult to assign limits to the measure in which, by a procedure strictly analogous to that followed in this instance, the Dominion might dictate the working of Provincial institutions, and circumscribe or supersede the legislative and administrative authority of the Provinces.

Such a procedure cannot, their Lordships think, be justified consistently with the governing principles of the Canadian Constitution, as enunciated and established by the judgments of this Board. [His Lordship proceeded to discuss a number of cases, and then continued as follows:]

. . . In accordance with the principle inherent in these decisions their Lordships think it is no longer open to dispute that the Parliament of Canada cannot, by purporting to create penal sanctions under s. 91, head 27, appropriate to itself exclusively a field of jurisdiction in which, apart from such a procedure, it could exert no legal authority, and that if, when examined as a whole, legislation in form criminal is found, in aspects and for purposes exclusively within the Provincial sphere, to deal with matters committed to the Provinces, it cannot be upheld as valid. . . .

Their Lordships now turn to the examination of the question arising on the first of the interrogatories submitted to the Appellate Division, which concerns the validity of legislation of the character of the Ontario Act (12 & 13 Geo. 5, c. 62) therein mentioned, which by its terms is only to come into force on proclamation to that effect by the Lieutenant-Governor in Council. This Act, as its name imports, is a statute dealing with reciprocal contracts of insurance. The practice of forming groups, for the purpose of exchanging such contracts of insurance, appears to have originated in the United States and to prevail widely there and in Canada. Such groups, described as exchanges in the Act, are usually composed of persons having some common interest, as owners of a particular class of property, for example, or dealers in the same kinds of commodities. The contracts are effected, and the business incidental to them transacted, through the agency of an attorney, who is empowered by each subscriber individually to act for him in making such contracts with other members of the exchange. The exchange, as a whole, undertakes no obligation, the attorney, who receives a commission for his services, in every case acting for the subscriber as an individual, and the obligation of the subscriber being his own individual obligation.

At the date on which the statute of 1922 was assented to, there were, by virtue of the Ontario Insurance Act (R.S. Ont., c. 183), certain prohibitions in force in Ontario which are qualified by that statute. By s. 98 of the Ontario Insurance Act, the transacting or undertaking of insurance (other than guarantee insurance by certain companies), except by a corporation duly registered under s. 66 of that Act, was forbidden, and a penalty was imposed on every person contravening this prohibition. Sections 3 and 4 of the statute of 1922 limit the scope of the prohibition by enacting, first, that it shall be lawful for any person to exchange with other persons, in Ontario or elsewhere, reciprocal contracts of indemnity or inter-insurance, and that no person shall be deemed to be an insurer, within the meaning of the Ontario Insurance Act, by reason of exchanging such contracts with other persons under the provisions of the Act. The making of reciprocal contracts of indemnity or inter-insurance, through an attorney as intermediary, is expressly sanctioned by s. 5. And, by ss. 6 and 7, the Superintendent of Insurance is empowered, upon fulfillment of specified conditions, to grant licences to exchanges, each of which is required to maintain a reserve of specified amount in the hands of its attorney. By s. 14 any one is forbidden to act as an .attorney in the exchange of such contracts, except under the sanction of a licence issued under the Act. And, by s. 15, authority is given for the cancellation or revocation of such licenses, for non-fulfillment of the statutory conditions.

It is alleged upon two grounds, that this statute is illegal. It is said, first, that it is extra-territorial in its operation; and, secondly, that it assumes to deal with subjects not assigned to the Provinces, the subjects of aliens and that of Dominion companies. Their Lordships find nothing in the language of the statute which necessarily gives to its enactments an extra-territorial effect. The enabling provisions of ss. 3 and 4 appear to be designed to exempt the transactions to which they relate from the above-mentioned prohibitions of the Ontario Insurance Act, and the terms of the statute as a whole are, in their Lordships' judgment, capable of receiving a meaning according to which its provisions, whether enabling or prohibitive, apply only to persons and acts within the territorial jurisdiction of the Province. In their opinion it ought to be interpreted in consonance with the presumption which imputes to the Legislature an intention of limiting the direct operation of its enactments to such persons and acts.

As to the second ground of attack, it is only necessary to observe that contracts of insurance form the subject of the statute, a subject peculiarly within the sphere of Provincial control. It is true that its provisions may incidentally affect aliens and Dominion companies who are, or may wish to become, subscribers to an inter-insurance exchange; it is nevertheless not a statute in relation to aliens, as such, or Dominion companies as such. It is unnecessary and undesirable to attempt to say how far, if at all, the Dominion in execution of its powers in relation to the subjects of aliens and Dominion companies may dictate the rules governing contracts of insurance, to which an alien or a Dominion company may be a party. Nothing in s. 91 of the *British North America Act,* in itself, removes either aliens or Dominion companies from the circle of action which the Act has traced out for the Provinces. Provincial statutes of general operation on the subject of civil rights *prima facie* affect them. It may be assumed that legislation touching the rights and disabilities of aliens or Dominion companies might be validly enacted by the Dominion in some respects conflicting with the Ontario statute, and that in such cases the provisions of the Ontario statute, where inconsistent with the Dominion law, would to that extent become legally ineffective; but this, as their Lordships have before observed, is no ground for holding that the Provincial legislation, relating as it does to a subject matter within the authority of the Province, is wholly illegal or inoperative: *McColl v. Canadian Pacific Ry. Co.*, [1923] A.C. 126.

It follows from what has been said that the answer to the first question is in the affirmative, and the answer to the second, in the negative. The provisions of s. 508D have not been specifically referred to, since they do not in their terms purport to prohibit, even upon conditions, the making of the contracts described in the question, and the reference to that section, their Lordships were informed on the argument, was inserted in the question by mistake.

In view of the terms of the third question it is necessary to notice a contention of the respondents that s. 508C can receive a limited effect as applying to aliens within the meaning of s. 1(b) of the Insurance Act, 1917, and to companies and natural persons not aliens immigrating into Canada within the meaning of s. 12, and a parallel contention as to the effect of ss. 11 and 12.

The enactment in question being in substance, notwithstanding its form, an enactment in regulation of contracts of insurance and the business of insurance, subjects not within the legislative sphere of the Dominion, and subject to the proviso which is not here material, being general in its terms, is in their Lordships' opinion invalid in its entirety. Assuming that it would be competent to the Dominion Parliament, under its jurisdiction over the subject of aliens, to pass legislation expressed in similar terms, but limited in its operation to aliens, their Lordships think it too clear for discussion that s. 508C is not an enactment on the subject of aliens (just as the Ontario statute of 1922 is not an enactment on that subject); and that the language of the clause in question cannot be so read as to effect by construction such a limitation of its scope. Such a result could only be accomplished by introducing qualifying phrases, indeed, by rewriting the clause and transforming it into one to which the Legislature has not given its assent.

It follows that the third question must be answered in the negative, but with this qualification, that, in so answering it their Lordships do not express any opinion as to the competence of the Dominion Parliament, by virtue of its authority in relation to aliens and to trade and commerce, to enact ss. 11 and 12, sub-s. 1, of the Insurance Act. This, although referred to on the argument before their Lordships Board, was not fully discussed, and since it is not directly raised by the question submitted, their Lordships, as they then intimated, consider it inadvisable to express any opinion upon it. Their Lordships think it sufficient to recall the observation of Lord Haldane, in delivering the judgment of the Board in *Attorney-General for Canada v. Attorney-General for Alberta*, [1916] 1 A.C. 588, to the effect that legislation, if properly framed, requiring aliens, whether natural persons or foreign companies, to become licensed, as a condition of carrying on the business of insurance in Canada, might be competently enacted by Parliament (an observation which, it may be added, applies also to Dominion companies), and to remark that the second sub-section of s. 12 ascribes an inadmissible meaning to the word "immigrant", which, if governing the interpretation of sub-s. 1, would extend the scope of s. 12 to matters obviously not comprised within the subject of immigration; and that sub-s. 2 is therefore not competently enacted under the authority of the Dominion in relation to that subject. Their Lordships do not think it proper to discuss the limits of that authority, or to intimate any opinion upon the point whether any, or, if any, what effect can be given to the first subsection of s. 12 as an enactment passed in exercise of it.

Appeal allowed.

[*Hammer v. Dagenhart* (1918), 247 U.S. 251, referred to in the *Reciprocal Insurers* case was overruled by *United States v. Darby* (1941), 312 U.S. 100, 61 S. Ct. 451.

In *In re Sections 4 and 70 of the Canadian Insurance Act, 1910* (1913), 48 S.C.R. 260, aff'd *sub nom. A.-G. Can. v. A.-G. Alta.,* [1916] 1 A.C. 588, Duff J. in declaring the Dominion Act *ultra vires* said, *inter alia* (at p. 304): "I do not think that the fact that the business of insurance has grown to great proportions affects the question in the least;" and Anglin J., in reaching the same result, doubted whether insurance was a trade within s. 91(2) but if it was, the *Parsons* case established that "Parliament is not empowered to regulate the conduct of any single trade or business in the provinces or to prescribe the conditions on which it may be carried on." (p. 309). Fitzpatrick C.J. who dissented (as did Davies J.) said, *inter alia* (at p. 264) that "it may be safely stated that the whole report of the *Parsons* case shews that it was assumed by both sides it was within the power of the Parliament of Canada to grant licences." While Davies J. pointed to the fact (at p. 273) that "ever since the year following Confederation, now more than 40 years ago, Parliament has assumed the right so to legislate and the legislation for the past 25 years at least has been substantially in the form the constitutionality of which is now challenged", Duff J. remarked at (p. 305) that "the [Dominion] Act has, until recently at all events, never been enforced except as against Dominion companies and extra-Canadian companies."]

IN RE INSURANCE ACT OF CANADA

In the Privy Council. [1932] A.C. 41, [1932] 1 D.L.R. 97, [1931] 3 W.W.R. 689.

Appeal and cross-appeal from a judgment of the Quebec Court of King's Bench, Appeal Side, 49 Que. K.B. 236, 50 Que. K.B. 176, [1931] 3 D.L.R. 31, on a reference of the following questions:

1. Is a foreign or British insurer who holds a licence under the *Quebec Insurance Act* to carry on business within the Province obliged to observe and subject to ss. 11, 12, 65 and 66 of the Insurance Act of Canada, or are these sections unconstitutional as regards such insurer?

2. Are ss. 16, 20 and 21 of the Special War Revenue Act within the legislative competence of the Parliament of Canada? Would

there be any difference between the case of an insurer who has obtained or is bound to obtain under the Provincial law a licence to carry on business in the Province and any other case?

The answers made by the Court of King's Bench were as follows: To question 1 (by a majority)—in the case of a foreign insurer, "yes" to the first part, "no" to the second part; in the case of a British insurer, "no" to the first part and "yes" to the second part. To question 2 (unanimously)—"yes" to the first part, and "no" to the second part.

In the Privy Council, reference was made to the *Reciprocal Insurers* case, *supra,* and to the fact that following that judgment the Parliament of Canada by an amendment in 1924, repealed s. 12(2) of the Act of 1917. The Act of 1917, as amended, was consolidated in R.S.C. 1927, c. 101 which reproduced the former ss. 11 and 12, and the corresponding penal sections renumbered as 66 and 67; and in the Cr. Code of 1927 the former s. 508C reappeared as s. 507 but with an exception as to reciprocal insurance companies to avoid the direct result of the judgment in the *Reciprocal Insurers* case.

VISCOUNT DUNEDIN: . . . Their Lordships are now in a position to address themselves directly to the first question in this case. It is clear from the quotations from the *Reciprocal Insurers'* case that the question is technically still open, and it is clear from the judgment in the 1916 case that the sections in question can only be justified if to them can be applied what was there said by Lord Haldane in his answer to query 2. Their Lordships will repeat it:—

"To this question their Lordships' reply is that in such a case it would be within the power of the Parliament of Canada, by properly framed legislation, to impose such a restriction. It appears to them that such a power is given by the heads in s. 91, which refer to the regulation of trade and commerce and to aliens." . . .

. . . Their Lordships consider that although the question was studiously kept open in the *Reciprocal Insurers'* case, it was really decided by what was then laid down. The case decided that a colourable use of the Criminal Code could not serve to disguise the real object of the legislation, which was to dominate the exercise of the business of insurance. And in the same way it was decided that to try by a false definition to pray in aid s. 95 of the British North America Act, 1867, which deals with immigration, in order to control the business of insurance, was equally unavailing. What has got to be considered is whether this is in a true sense of the word alien legislation, and that is what Lord Haldane meant by "properly framed legislation". Their Lordships have no doubt that the Dominion Parliament might pass an Act forbidding aliens to enter Canada or forbidding them so to enter to engage in any business without a licence, and further they might furnish rules for their conduct while in Canada, requiring them, *e.g.,* to report at stated intervals. But the sections here are not of that sort, they do not deal with the position of an alien as such; but under the guise of legislation as to aliens they seek to intermeddle with the conduct of insurance business, a business which by the first branch of the 1916 case has been declared to be exclusively subject to Provincial law. Their Lordships have, therefore, no hesitation in declaring that this is not "properly framed" alien legislation.

As regards British subjects, who cannot be styled aliens, once the false definition is gone, the same remark applies as to alien immigrants. This is not a properly framed law as to immigration, but an attempt to saddle British immigrants with a different code as to the conduct of insurance business from the code which has been settled to be the only valid code, i.e., the Provincial Code.

Passing now to the second question, it seems to their Lordships that precisely the same line of reasoning applies. The only section that need be quoted is s. 16, the other sections being only concomitants thereto; that section is as follows:—

"(16). Every person resident in Canada, who insures his property situate in Canada or any property situate in Canada in which he has an insurable interest, other than that of an insurer of such property, against risks other than marine risks; (a) with any British or foreign company or British or foreign underwriter or underwriters, not licensed under the provisions of the Insurance Act, to transact business in Canada; or (b) with any association of persons formed for the purpose of exchanging reciprocal contracts of indemnity upon the plan known as inter-insurance and not licensed under the provisions of the Insurance Act, the chief place of business of which association or of its principal attorney-in-fact is situate outside of Canada; shall on or before the thirty-first day of December in each year pay to the Minister, in addition to any other tax payable under any existing law or statute a tax of five per centum of the total net cost to such person of all such insurance for the preceding calendar year."

Now as to the power of the Dominion Parliament to impose taxation there is no doubt. But if the tax as imposed is linked up with an object which is illegal the tax for that purpose must fall. Section 16 clearly assumes that a Dominion licence to prosecute insurance business is a valid licence all over Canada and carries with it the right to transact insurance business. But it has been already decided that this is not so; that a Dominion licence, so far as authorizing transactions of insurance business in a Province is concerned, is an idle piece of paper conferring no rights which the party transacting in accordance with Provincial legislation has not already got, if he has complied with Provincial requirements. It is really the same old attempt in another way. . . .

Their Lordships will, therefore, humbly advise His Majesty to declare that the proper answers to the questions put are: to the first part of question 1, "No"; and to the second part, "Yes"; to the second question in both branches, "No"—and that the appeal and cross-appeal should be dealt with in accordance with the said declaration.

Judgment varied.

[The second question in *In re Insurance Act of Canada, supra,* was raised again in *Reference re Section 16 of the Special War Revenue Act,*

[1942] S.C.R. 429, [1942] 4 D.L.R. 145, and the same conclusion was reached. The Privy Council refused leave to appeal: [1943] 4 D.L.R. 657. See *Note*, (1942) 20 Can. Bar Rev. 799; *Note*, (1943) 22 Can. Bar Rev. 94.

The relation of the federal taxing power to regulatory power was raised again in *Reference re Employment and Social Insurance Act*, [1936] S.C.R. 427, [1936] 3 D.L.R. 644, aff'd *sub nom. A.-G. Can. v. A.-G. Ont.*, [1937] A.C. 355, [1937] 1 D.L.R. 684, [1937] 1 W.W.R. 312, where a majority of the Supreme Court invalidated a federal unemployment insurance act which provided for compulsory contributions from employers and employees and a contribution from the federal treasury. Duff C.J. and Davies J. dissented in reliance on the then s. 91(1) of the B.N.A. Act ("The public debt and property") and s. 91(3) ("The raising of money by any mode or system of taxation"). The sequal to the case was amendment of the B.N.A. Act by adding "unemployment insurance" to the federal enumerations as s. 91(2A).

In *A.-G. Ont. v. Wentworth Ins. Co.*, [1969] S.C.R. 779, 12 C.B.R. (N.S.) 265, [1969] I.L.R. 1-288, 6 D.L.R. (3d) 545, federal legislation was held to control distribution to creditors on the occasion of an insurance company's insolvency, specially dealt with by the Bankruptcy Act. The Court divided 5-4, the majority rejecting the view that insurance is in effect a provincial "class of subjects" immune from federal regulation.

An interesting comparison with Canada is provided by the constitutional position on insurance regulation in the United States. *Paul v. Virginia* (1868), 75 U.S. 168 was, in effect, the United States *Parsons* case. In *United States v. South-Eastern Underwriters Association* (1944), 322 U.S. 533, 64 S. Ct. 1162, petition for rehearing denied, 323 U.S. 811, a change occurred when the Supreme Court held that inter-state insurance business brought companies engaged therein within the scope of the Sherman Anti-Trust Act, a statute based on the federal interstate commerce power. Shortly thereafter, Congress passed the McCarran Act of 1945 which permitted state regulation and taxation of the insurance business. In *Prudential Insurance Co. v. Benjamin* (1946), 328 U.S. 406, 66 S. Ct. 1142, this cession of Congressional power in favour of state control was regarded as sufficient to entitle a state to impose a tax on foreign companies doing business in the state, although no such tax was imposed on local companies; but see *State Board of Insurance v. Todd Shipyards Corp.* (1962), 370 U.S. 451, 82 S. Ct. 1380 invalidating a state premium tax as a violation of due process where paid out of state on out of state insurance although on property within the state. See *Powell*, Insurance as Commerce in Constitution and Statute, (1944) 57 Harv. L. Rev. 937; *Berke*, Is the Business of Insurance Commerce, (1943) 32 Mich L. Rev. 409; *Note*, Congressional Consent to Discriminatory State Legislation, (1945) 45 Col. L. Rev. 927.]

Note on Securities Regulation

In line with the reasoning in the insurance cases, it has been held that regulation of trading in securities falls within provincial legislative authority and that, moreover, such regulation may operate through a commission empowered to licence brokers and other security dealers and to require full disclosure to the public in the enforcement of honest trading. Federal authority to punish fraudulent dealings in securities under the criminal law power has long been conceded, but not federal authority to regulate security transactions through a licensing or similar control system: see *Smith v. The Queen*, [1960] S.C.R. 776, 25 D.L.R. (2d) 225. Provincial authority is, of course, limited to regulation of business carried on or transactions taking place in the Province, and there is also a special limitation, which can be avoided by drafting (as was indicated in *Lymburn v. Mayland,* [1932] A.C. 318, [1932] 2 D.L.R. 6, [1932] 1 W.W.R. 578), in respect of the issue of securities of a federally incorporated company.

The relevant constitutional issue in this field today is not the scope or limit of provincial power, but the rationale behind a continued preclusion of supervening federal power. Thus, it is of small constitutional consequence that provincial securities legislation may competently encompass promissory notes within its trading provisions when they are used in a defined way in business ventures, (so long as their character and holders' rights under federal legislation are not impaired): see *Duplain v. Cameron,* [1961] S.C.R. 693, 30 D.L.R. (2d) 348, 36 W.W.R. 490. Nor is it surprising that provincial authority should be exercisable against a depository bank by way of a stop order where an investigation into or suspected fraud as to security trading in the Province is involved, even though this goes close to the line where federal power over banks has been exhibited in legislation: see *Gregory & Co. Inc. v. Imperial Bank of Canada and A.-G. Que.,* [1960] Que. S.C. 204. What is ripe for judicial inquiry is whether the ramified national and international character of the securities business deserves constitutional recognition as falling within the trade and commerce power. In *Gregory & Co. Inc. v. Quebec Securities Commission,* [1961] S.C.R. 584, 28 D.L.R. (2d) 721, the question was raised whether provincial competence could reach a securities dealer (having offices in the Province) by an order to cease publication of bulletins which, although produced in the Province, were mailed only to clients outside the Province. The bulletins in fact promoted the sale of shares transferable only in the Province where orders were completed and payment was made. Since all submissions on constitutionality were withdrawn before the Supreme Court the affirmation of the order turned merely on the application of the provincial legislation. However, Cartwright J. stated, speaking for himself alone, that he had difficulty in satisfying himself that the provincial Act, properly construed, authorized the provincial Securities Commission to regulate a business of the sort carried on by the dealer in this case. There is a clear connection here with the question of constitutional power.

Pending any attempt by Parliament to enter this regulatory field, it is reasonable to give the broadest construction to provincial legislation and to apply its policing provisions where acts take place in the Province notwithstanding that they are part of an operation which, overall, is extraprovincial. Thus, in *Regina v. W. McKenzie Securities Ltd.* (1966), 56 D.L.R. (2d) 56, 55 W.W.R. 157, the Manitoba Court of Appeal held that the registration provisions of the Manitoba securities statute validly applied to an Ontario broker-dealer who solicited Manitoba residents by mail and telegraph from Toronto. Hence, that security dealer, having in this way sold shares to a Manitoba resident, could properly be convicted of unlawfully trading in securities, not being registered under the Manitoba legislation.

[For a summary of the constitutional limits of provincial competence in securities regulation, see Report of the Attorney-General's Committee on Securities Legislation in Ontario (1965), Part IX.

It is competent to the Province to provide for administrative investigations into security trading in enforcement of its regulatory legislation; *Re Williams and Williams*, [1961] O.R. 657, 29 D.L.R. (2d) 107; *International Claim Brokers Ltd. v. Kinsey and A.-G. B.C.*, (1966) 57 D.L.R. (2d) 357, 55 W.W.R. 672.

Contrast the situation in the United States as indicated by *Electric Bond & Share Co. v. Securities & Exchange Commission* (1938), 303 U.S. 419, 58 S. Ct. 678; *American Power & Light Co. v. Securities & Exchange Commission* (1946), 329 U.S. 90, 67 S. Ct. 133.

Would it be open to Parliament to invoke its exclusive authority in relation to the "postal service" (s. 91(5) of the B.N.A. Act) and to deny (as Congress has) the use of the mails to security dealers who refuse to register under federal regulatory legislation?

Is there any constitutional objection to provincial legislation excluding use of trading stamps as a merchandising device? Would it make any difference if the exclusion was made a condition of a required retail licence which could be cancelled if the licensee engaged in detrimental practices, e.g. used trading stamps? See *The Queen v. Fleming* (1962), 35 D.L.R. (2d) 483, 38 W.W.R. 513.]

Note on Industrial and Labour Relations

Among the enumerated powers of Parliament are "patents of invention and discovery" and "copyrights" in s. 91(22)(23) of the B.N.A. Act. While "trade-marks" as such are not mentioned and could reasonably be attributed to the federal general power, it has been held that the trade and commerce power could support trade-mark regulation as well as the power of the Dominion to create a national mark (as a form of non-compulsory regulation) and to prescribe the conditions of its use: see *A.-G. Ont. v. A.-G. Can.*, [1937] A.C. 405, [1937] 1 D.L.R. 702, [1937] 1 W.W.R. 333. In dealing in this case with the validity of certain provisions of the Dominion Trade and Industry Commission Act, 1935 (Can.), c. 59 (repealed by 1949 (2nd sess.), c. 31, s. 9) Lord Atkin said, in part:

"There exists in Canada a well established code relating to trade-marks created by Dominion statutes, to be found now in the Trade Marks and Designs Act, R.S.C. 1927, c. 201, amended by S.C. 1928, c. 10. It gives to the proprietor of a registered trade-mark the exclusive right to use the trade-mark to designate articles manufactured or sold by him. It creates, therefore, a form of property in each Province and the rights that flow therefrom. No one has challenged the competence of the Dominion to pass such legislation. If challenged one obvious source of authority would appear to be the class of subjects enumerated in s. 91(2), the Regulation of Trade and Commerce, referred to by the Chief Justice. There could hardly be a more appropriate form of the exercise of this power than the creation and regulation of a uniform law of trade-marks. But if the Dominion has power to create trade-mark rights for individual traders, it is difficult to see why the power should not extend to that which is now a usual feature of national and international commerce—a national mark. It is perfectly true, as is said by the Chief Justice, that the method adopted in s. 18 is to create a civil right of a novel character. Ordinarily, a trade-mark gives rights only when used in connection with goods manufactured or sold by the person who has the right to use the mark. A trade-mark "in gross" would be an anomaly. And it obviously is not contemplated that the Crown should have any proprietary interest in the goods to which the mark vested in the Crown is to be applied. But there seems no reason why the legislative competence of the Dominion Parliament should not extend to the creation of juristic rights in novel fields, if they can be brought fairly within the classes of subjects confided to Parliament by the constitution. The substance of the legislation in question is to define a national mark, to give the exclusive use of it to the Dominion so as to provide a logical basis for a system of statutory licences to producers, manufacturers and merchants. To vest the "exclusive property" in the mark in His Majesty is probably no more than to vest "the use of" the mark in His Majesty. It may afford a useful civil protection for the mark when it is violated in Canada by persons who have not violated the somewhat restricted prohibition of the penal sub-section (which only applies to persons who "apply" the mark to commodities), or violated abroad, where the penal provisions of the law of Canada could not be applied at all. It may be noticed that s. 53 of the Trade Marks and Designs Act, R.S.C. 1927, c. 201, appears to afford protection in Canada to trade-marks owned by foreign associations though held by them "in gross." For the reasons above given the legislation appears to their Lordships to be within the competence of the Dominion Parliament."

(It may be noted that the Supreme Court of Canada to which this case came on a reference, [1936] S.C.R. 379, [1936] 3 D.L.R. 607, held that s. 14 of the Act—providing for approval of agreements for regulating and controlling prices in an industry where there was wasteful or demoralizing competition—was *ultra vires,* and no appeal was taken against this determination.)

Restrictive trade practices, *e.g.,* combinations limiting competition, have been dealt with by the Dominion under its criminal law power: see *P.A.T.A. v. A.-G. Can.,* [1931] A.C. 310, [1931] 2 D.L.R. 1, [1931] 1 W.W.R. 552; *A.-G. B.C. v. A.-G. Can.,* [1937] A.C. 368, [1937] 1 D.L.R. 688, [1937] 1 W.W.R. 317. This is in contrast to the United States where federal anti-trust laws and allied legislation are a projection of the commerce power. In Canada, it has been held permissible to subjoin to combines legislation provisions for initial investigation and report on violation of the prohibitory enactments, with a view to prosecution if thought advisable. Regulation as such has been considered closed to federal legislation, although there would seem to be no reason why such an approach should be incompetent in respect of interprovincial and export trade. So far, however, the Dominion has trod very carefully in dealing (apart from anti-trust measures) with unfair competition, relying mainly on its criminal law power and on its power to enact trade mark legislation: see The Trade Marks Act, R.S.C. 1970, c. T-10, s. 7. *Cf. Good Humor Corp. v. Good Humor Food Products,* [1937] Ex. C.R. 61, [1937] 4 D.L.R. 145.

[The statutory "passing off" action under s. 7(b) of the Trade Marks Act, *supra,* was assumed to have been validly conferred in *Canadian Converters' Co. Ltd. v. Eastport Trading Co. Ltd.* (1968), 70 D.L.R. (2d) 149.]

In the field of employer-employee and labour-management relations, the division of authority between Parliament and provincial
legislatures is based on an initial conclusion that in so far as such
relations have an independent constitutional value they are within
provincial competence; and, secondly, in so far as they are merely a
facet of particular industries or enterprises their regulation is within
the legislative authority of that body which has power to regulate the
particular industry or enterprise: see *Regina v. O.L.R.B., ex parte
Dunn*, [1963] 2 O.R. 302, 39 D.L.R. (2d) 346. Thus, *Minimum Wage
Commission v. Bell Telephone Co. of Canada Ltd.*, [1966] S.C.R. 767,
59 D.L.R. (2d) 145, holds that employer-employee relations in an
enterprise under federal jurisdiction are within Parliament's exclusive competence. While the lower Courts in *Toronto Electric Commissioners v. Snider*, [1925] A.C. 396, [1925] 2 D.L.R. 5, [1925] 1 W.W.R.
785, inclined to the view that an independent constitutional value could
be attributed to measures for settlement of industrial disputes, as
being for the peace, order and good government of Canada, this view
was rejected by the Privy Council. It followed from the Privy Council's
position and from its view of the scope of the trade and commerce
power that Parliament could not enact general regulatory labour relations measures even with respect to industries or enterprises having
interprovincial ramifications. Regulatory control on a federal level
could be exerted only in respect of activities which were within federal
authority by specific enumeration, e.g., interprovincial railways, telegraph and telephone operations and shipping: see *Reference re
Validity of Industrial Relations and Disputes Investigation Act and
Its Applicability to Certain Employees of Eastern Canada Stevedoring
Co.*, [1955] S.C.R. 529, [1955] 3 D.L.R. 721; or those which fell
within the federal general or residuary power, e.g., radio, aerial
navigation and atomic energy (reaching back into uranium production): see *Pronto Uranium Mines Ltd. and Algom Uranium Mines Ltd.
v. Ontario Labour Relations Board*, [1956] O.R. 862, 5 D.L.R. (2d)
341; or those brought within federal authority by a declaration under
s. 92(10)(c) of the B.N.A. Act; or those involved in federal government operations and in federal Crown enterprises: see *Reference re
Legislative Jurisdiction over Hours of Labour*, [1925] S.C.R. 505,
[1925] 3 D.L.R. 1114. Federal regulatory authority in time of war is,
of course, a special case. For some phases of employer-employee
relations the Dominion has resorted to its criminal law power, and
thus was able to make its prohibitions all embracing, as in connection
with picketing (Cr. Code, s. 381) and employment discrimination
because of union activity (Cr. Code, s. 382). See, generally, *Scott,
Federal Jurisdiction over Labour Relations—A New Look* (1960), 6
McGill L.J. 153.

Aside from these areas of federal authority, labour legislation is
a matter for the Provinces which may lawfully enact such legislation
(e.g. collective bargaining enactments or minimum wage statutes or
general factory acts) in relation to industries and enterprises in each
Province, regardless of their economic position vis-à-vis the country

as a whole and regardless of the economic consequences of local regulation. This need not be an ultimate, unchangeable position but the portents of change are not yet clearly visible. The present constitutional position in Canada is in marked contrast to that in the United States: see *N.L.R.B. v. Jones & Laughlin Steel Corp.* (1937), 301 U.S. 1, 57 S. Ct. 615; *West Coast Hotel Co. v. Parrish* (1937), 300 U.S. 379, 57 S. Ct. 578; *United States v. Darby* (1941), 312 U.S. 100, 61 S. Ct. 451. It is in contrast too to the Australian position where, however, the Constitution explicitly empowers the Commonwealth Parliament by s. 51 (xxxv) to make laws with respect to "conciliation and arbitration for the prevention and settlement of industrial disputes extending beyond the limits of any one state"; and see *Wynes*, Legislative, Executive and Judicial Powers in Australia (1956, 2d ed.), pp. 421 ff.

CHAPTER V

PROPERTY AND CIVIL RIGHTS IN THE PROVINCE

1. The Domain of Individual Private Law Relations as a Matter of Legislative Control

Provincial power in relation to "property and civil rights in the Province" may justly be said to have dominated the constitutional thinking of the Privy Council for most of the first half of the twentieth century and, indeed, until the abolition of appeals. A number of questions are suggested by the many cases in which this power has been prominent. Do the Confederation Debates or other historical materials justify the meaning given to the phrase "property and civil rights in the Province"? Is the phrase (often quoted without its concluding words "in the Province") merely a convenient peg upon which to hang a particular view of federalism? Does this view require that s. 92(13) be read not only as conferring power on the Provinces but as excluding power in the Dominion? Is the view of federalism which s. 92(13) seems to express a reflection of the social and economic organization of Canada in the 19th century? Does the interpretation or application of s. 92(13) in the cases represent the actualities in present day Dominion-Provincial governmental relations? How far have the cases which interpreted s. 92(13) ignored the limiting words "in the Province", and are those words of significance in assessing federal power? The judicial opinions on these words as a limitation on provincial legislative power are set out in the cases following this Note.

A historical examination of the phrase "property and civil rights" is to be found in the O'Connor Report, Annex 1, pp. 109 *et seq.* The author amplified his exposition in an article in (1940) 18 Can. Bar Rev. 331. He says, in part (at p. 358) : "The meaning of the expression 'laws in relation to *property* in the province' needs no definition. The meaning of the expression 'laws in relation to *civil* rights in the province' has never been defined. I would not attempt to place any restriction at all upon the authority of a province, acting *bona fide,* to define by statute what shall be civil rights in the province. After all, that is what section 92(13) is for.

"The complaint from the standpoint of the Dominion rests not so much upon erroneous ruling as to what is a *civil right in a province* as upon erroneous ruling as what is a *law in relation* to a civil right, whatever civil right may mean, in a province. No principle of interpretation of the B.N.A. Act has had more consistent lip service than the 'aspect' doctrine, but upon occasions it has been ignored. Let it have its proper effect always and, as was contemplated at confederation, the respective legislative authorities of the Dominion and the provinces will be nurtured and preserved by it. Failure to apply it defeats the intent of the B.N.A. Act. Pursuant to that doctrine if, in pith and substance, a *law in relation to* a matter that comes within section 91 has been enacted it will be, as it ought to be, assigned to section 91. Likewise, if in pith and substance *a law in relation to* a matter that comes within section 92 has been enacted it will be, as it ought to be, assigned to section 92."

According to O'Connor, "civil rights in the province . . . are confined to civil rights as between subject and subject" (18 Can. Bar Rev. at p. 368). There is historical justification for reading s. 92(13) as referring in part to laws governing subjects in their controversies with each other: cf., Property and Civil Rights Act, R.S.O. 1960, c. 310, s. 1; illustrative would be sale of goods legislation or legislation respecting conveyances. For an admirable analysis of this "class of subjects", see generally *Tremblay*, Les Compétences Legislatives au Canada. For the category of individual interests, whether of substance or of personality, see *Stone*, The Province and Function of Law, c. XXI, which may shed clarification in this connection.

Early expressions of opinion by the Supreme Court of Canada on s. 92(13) differ from the pronouncements of the Privy Council; see, for example, *Valin v. Langlois* (1879), 3 S.C.R. 1, per Fournier J. at p. 53; per Henry J. at p. 67 ("The right of the local legislatures to legislate as to civil rights . . . is subordinated to those civil rights not affected by Dominion powers of legislation and to those in the province and not including matters of a general character"); *Fredericton v. The Queen* (1880), 3 S.C.R. 505. The early decisions of the Privy Council on the scope of s. 92(13) differed in degree from those of the Supreme Court of Canada to the extent that they were prepared to sustain provincial legislation in the absence of Dominion legislation but not to use s. 92(13) as a bar to Dominion legislation. This is evident on a comparison of *Citizens Ins. Co. v. Parsons* (1881), 7 App. Cas. 96 and *Russell v. The Queen* (1882), 7 App. Cas. 829. The later decisions of the Privy Council exhibit a difference in kind rather than in degree. Moreover, the Privy Council's views on federalism were rested for purposes of legal justification, on the provincial "property and civil rights" power. This emerges in the cases from the *Local Prohibition* case on, and is made manifest by Lord Haldane's remark during the argument in *John Deere Plow Co. v. Wharton*, [1915] A.C. 330, 18 D.L.R. 353, 7 W.W.R. 706, that "Without expressing a final opinion about it, I should say 'civil rights' was a residuary expression . . ." (quoted in *Lefroy*, Constitutional Law of Canada, p. 246). Yet it should be noted that in his judgment in the *John Deere Plow* case, Lord Haldane expressed the view that s. 92(13) must receive a limited interpretation, a view which may, however, be regarded as related to the scope of s. 92(13) vis-à-vis other classes of subjects in ss. 91 and 92.

Mention may appropriately be made here of s. 94 of the B.N.A. Act which provides as follows: "Notwithstanding anything in this Act the Parliament of Canada may make provision for the uniformity of all or any of the laws relative to property and civil rights in Ontario, Nova Scotia and New Brunswick and of the procedure of all or any of the Courts in those three Provinces, and from and after the passing of any Act in that behalf the power of the Parliament of Canada to make laws in relation to any matter comprised in any such Act shall, notwithstanding anything in this Act, be unrestricted; but any Act of the Parliament of Canada making provision for such uniformity shall not have effect in any Province unless and until it is adopted and enacted as law by the Legislature thereof.

BEDARD v. DAWSON AND A.-G. QUE.

In the Supreme Court of Canada. [1923] S.C.R. 681, [1923] 4 D.L.R. 293, [1923] 3 W.W.R. 412.

Appeal from a judgment of the Quebec Court of King's Bench, Appeal Side, 33 Que. K.B. 246, affirming a judgment of the Superior Court and upholding the validity of a Quebec statute, 10 Geo. V, c. 81.

IDINGTON J.: This action was taken by the respondent Dawson under and by virtue of 10 Geo. V., c. 81 of the Quebec Legislature, entitled "An Act respecting the owners of houses used as disorderly houses," which provides, by sections 2, 3, 4 and 7 as follows:—

2. It shall be illegal for any person who owns or occupies any house or building of any nature whatsoever, to use or to allow any person to use the same as a disorderly house. A certified copy of any judgment convicting any person of an offence under section 228, 228a, 229 or 229a of the Criminal Code shall be *prima facie* proof of such use of the house in respect of which such conviction was had.

3. Any person knowing or having reason to believe that any building or part of a building is being made use of as a disorderly house, may send to the registered owner, or to the lessor, or to the agent of the registered owner, or to the lessee of such building, a notice, accompanied by a certified copy of any conviction as aforesaid, if any there be, by registered mail to the last known address of the said owner, agent or lessee, as the case may be.

4. Ten days after the mailing of such notice, if such building or any part thereof still continues to be used as a disorderly house, any person may apply for and obtain an injunction directed to the owner, lessor, lessee or occupant of such building, or to all such persons, restraining them, their heirs, assigns or successors from using or permitting the use of such building or any other building for the purposes above-mentioned.

7. If the judge finds that the use of such building as a disorderly house continues, he shall by his final judgment, in addition to all other orders he is by law empowered to make, order the closing of the said building against its use for any purpose whatsoever for a period of not more than one year from the date of judgment.

The power of the legislature to so enact having been questioned, by appellant pleading in defence, the Attorney-General for Quebec became an intervenant immediately thereafter. Thereupon the intervenant pleaded, the now appellant answered same, and the intervenant replied.

The case thus constituted was heard by Mr. Justice Maclennan who gave judgment for the respondent and granted the injunction claimed by him as provided in said section 7 of said Act, and for the intervenant with costs maintaining the constitutionality of the Act. . . .

The Court of King's Bench, [on appeal], by a majority, there being a dissenting judge on the question, upheld the constitutionality of the Act and dismissed the appeal as to that issue, with costs to the responding intervenant. . . .

I have long entertained the opinion that the provincial legislatures have such absolute power over property and civil rights, as given them by section 92 of the *B.N.A. Act,* item 13 thereof, that so long as they did not in fact encroach upon the powers assigned by the said Act to the Dominion Parliament it would be almost impossible to question any such exercise of power so given unless by the exercise of the veto power given the Dominion Government. That veto power was originally designed to prevent an improper exercise of legislative power by the provincial legislatures.

I, therefore, do not see that if properly interpreted and construed the said Act now in question herein can be said to be *ultra vires.*

There is, however, one aspect of it which rather disturbs me, and that is this: The Act takes certain sections of the Criminal Code as the basis of its subject-matter and then proceeds to apply convictions thereunder as the basis of its application.

And if, as might well happen, the keeper of the disorderly house so penalized should also be the owner thereof, and this Act applied in such case, it would look very much like adding as a matter of course to the penalties imposed by Parliament for the offence in question, when Parliament alone is endowed with the power and has imposed on it in so doing the sole responsibility of determining what is the proper measure of punishment.

That, however, is not the case presented on the facts in question herein. I point it out as being the possible cause of future embarrassment and would have preferred to see its enactment somewhat differently framed.

As to the argument addressed to us that the local legislatures cannot legislate to prevent crime, I cannot assent thereto for in a very wide sense it is the duty of the legislature to do the ultmost it can within its power to anticipate and remove, so far as practicable, whatever is likely to tend to produce crime; and yet not produce worse forms of it, or tending thereto. . . .

There are many instances of other nuisances which can be better rectified by local legislation within the power of the legislatures over property and civil rights than by designating them crimes and leaving them to be dealt with by Parliament as such. . . .

DUFF J.: The legislation impugned seems to be aimed at suppressing conditions calculated to favour the development of crime rather than at the punishment of crime. This is an aspect of the subject in which the provinces seems to be free to legislate. I think the legislation is not invalid.

ANGLIN J.: . . . I am of the opinion that this statute in no wise impinges on the domain of criminal law but is concerned exclusively with the control and enjoyment of property and the safeguarding of the community from the consequences of an illegal and injurious use being made of it—a pure matter of civil right. In my opinion in enacting the statute now under consideration the legislature exercised the power which it undoubtedly possesses to provide for the suppression of a nuisance and the prevention of its recurrence by civil process. . . .

Appeal dismissed.

[Brodeur and Migneault JJ. also gave reasons upholding the validity of the Act.

In *Rex v. Lamontagne*, [1945] O.R. 606, [1945] 4 D.L.R. 161, a majority of the Ontario Court of Appeal distinguished *Bedard v. Dawson and A.-G. Que., supra*, and held invalid the *Gaming and Betting Act*, 1942 (Ont.), c. 19 in the following circumstances. The Act provided that a Court may on application order the closing for a period up to a year of premises in respect of which there has been, within the previous three months, a conviction under enumerated disorderly house, betting and bookmaking provisions of the Cr. Code. Where a closing order was made and the premises were used in violation of the order, the registered owner and any person found therein at the time (unless such person could prove he was there for a lawful purpose) were to be deemed to have violated the order. A person violating the Act or any order thereunder was guilty of an offence. Certain premises were made the subject of an order closing them for all purposes except use as a private residence or boarding house, and expressly forbidding a violation of the particular Cr. Code provision in respect of use of the premises. While the order was in force one L. was convicted under the Cr. Code of keeping a common bawdy house on the premises. The owner of the premises was also convicted under the Cr. Code of knowingly permitting the premises to be used as a common bawdy house. Thereafter, the owner was charged under the *Gaming and Betting Act* of violating the closing order because of the conviction of L. In affirming the setting aside of a conviction under the Ontario Act the majority held that the statute operated essentially as criminal law in a field already covered by the federal Cr. Code. On the facts, the Act that violated the closing order and exposed the accused to punishment was already an offence under the Cr. Code. McRuer J.A., dissenting, could see no difference in principle between the Ontario statute and the enactment in the *Bedard case*. Do you agree?]

SWITZMAN v. ELBLING AND A.-G. QUE.

In the Supreme Court of Canada. [1957] S.C.R. 285, 7 D.L.R. (2d) 337, 117 Can. C.C. 129.

Appeal from a judgment of the Quebec Court of Queen's Bench (Appeal Side), [1954] Que. Q.B. 421, affirming a judgment of Collins J. and upholding the validity of the Communistic Propaganda Act (Que.).

KERWIN C.J.C.:—I am unable to agree with Mr. Beaulieu's contention that there is in issue the constitutional validity of only part of the statute. The order signed by the Attorney-General of the Province of Quebec, dated January 27, 1949, recites the provisions of both ss. 3 and 12 of that Act and in his intervention the Attorney-General asked the Court to declare the said Act in its entirety constitutional and valid and in full force and effect.

Section 1 provides: "This Act may be cited as *Act Respecting Communistic Propaganda.*"

Sections 3 and 12 read:

"3. It shall be illegal for any person, who possesses or occupies a house within the Province, to use it or allow any person to make use of it to propagate communism or bolshevism by any means whatsoever.

"12. It shall be unlawful to print, to publish in any manner whatsoever or to distribute in the Province any newspaper, periodical, pamphlet, circular, document or writing whatsoever propagating or tending to propagate communism or bolshevism."

Sections 4 to 11 provide that the Attorney-General, upon satisfactory proof that an infringement of s. 3 has been committed, may order the closing of the house; authorize any Peace Officer to execute such order and provide a procedure by which the owner may apply by petition to a Judge of the Superior Court to have the order revised. Section 13 provides for imprisonment of anyone infringing or participating in the infringement of s. 12. In my opinion it is impossible to separate the provisions of ss. 3 and 12.

The validity of the statute was attacked upon a number of grounds, but, in cases where constitutional issues are involved, it is important that nothing be said that is unnecessary. In my view it is sufficient to declare that the Act is legislation in relation to the criminal law over which, by virtue of head 27 of s. 91 of the *B.N.A. Act,* the Parliament of Canada has exclusive legislative authority. The decision of this Court in *Bédard v. Dawson & A.-G. Que.,* [1923] 4 D.L.R. 293, S.C.R. 681, 40 Can. C.C. 404, is clearly distinguishable. As Mr. Justice Barclay points out, the real object of the Act here under consideration is to prevent propagation of Communism within the Province and to punish anyone who does so—with provisions authorizing steps for the closing of premises used for such object. The *Bédard* case was concerned with the control and enjoyment of property. I am unable to agree with the decision of Greenshields C.J. in *Fineberg v. Taub,* [1940] 1 D.L.R. 114, 73 Can. C.C. 37, 77 Que. S.C. 233. It is not necessary to refer to other authorities, because, once the conclusion is reached that the pith and substance of the impugned Act is in relation to criminal law, the conclusion is inevitable that the Act is unconstitutional.

The appeal should be allowed, the judgments below set aside and the action dismissed with costs. . . .

TASCHEREAU J. (dissenting) (approved translation of reasons originally given in French): . . . The appellant admitted having used the building for the propagation of Communistic doctrine, but has specifically pleaded that the law was *ultra vires* of the Legislature of Quebec, as it constitutes an infringement of the legislative power of the federal authority, who alone would be empowered to legislate on the matter. As the constitutionality of the provincial Act was challenged, notice was given to the Attorney-General of the Province of Quebec, pursuant to art. 114 of the *Code of Civil Procedure*, and the latter produced an intervention, in which he supported the total validity of the Act.

Mr. Justice Collins of the Superior Court maintained the action, as well as the intervention of the Attorney-General, cancelled the lease, and consequently upheld the validity of the legislation. This judgment was affirmed by the Court of Queen's Bench, Mr. Justice Barclay dissenting. . . .

The law called *An Act to Protect the Province against Communistic Propaganda* enacts that it is illegal for any person who possesses or occupies a house within the Province, to use it or to allow any person to make use of it to propagate Communism or Bolshevism by any means whatsoever. The law authorizes the Attorney-General, upon satisfactory proof that an infringement has been committed, to order the closing of the house for a period of not more than one year. The recourse conferred by law to the owner of the house, is to make a petition to the Court for a review of the order, by establishing that he was acting in good faith, that he was in ignorance of the house being used in contravention of the Act, or that the house had not been used for illegal purposes.

The appellant contends that this legislation is exclusively within the domain of the criminal law, and that consequently it is without the legislative competency of the provincial authority. I would willingly agree with him, if the Legislature had enacted that Communism was a crime punishable by law, because there would then be clearly an encroachment on the federal domain, which would make the legislation *ultra vires* of the Province. But such is not the case that we have before us. The Legislature did not say that any act constituted a crime, and it did not confer the character of criminalty upon the Communistic doctrine. If the provincial Legislature has no power to create criminal offences, it has the right to legislate to prevent crimes, disorders, as treason, sedition, illegal public meetings, which are crimes under the Criminal Code, and to prevent conditions calculated to favour the development of crime. In order to achieve its aims, I entertain no doubt that it may validly legislate as to the possession and use of property, as this is exclusively within the domain of civil law, and is by virtue of s. 92 of the *B.N.A. Act* (head 13) within the provincial competency.

The case of *Bédard v. Dawson (supra)*, is very similar to the present case. There again, the validity of the provincial law entitled *An Act Respecting the Owners of Houses used as Disorderly Houses*, was challenged. This law enacted that it was illegal for any person who owned or occupied any house or building of any nature whatsoever, to use or to allow any person to use the same as a disorderly house. A certified copy of any judgment convicting any person of an offence under ss. 228, 228a, 229 or 229a, of the old *Criminal Code*, was a *prima facie* proof of such use of the house in respect of which such conviction was had. After notice given to the interested parties, if such building still continued to be used as a disorderly house, an injunction could be obtained directed to the owner or the lessee, restraining them from using or permitting the use of such building for the above purposes. After the expiry of ten days, *the Court could order the closing of the house.*

The Supreme Court of Canada [[1923] 4 D.L.R. 293, S.C.R. 681, 40 Can. C.C. 404], affirming the decision of the Court of King's Bench of the Province of Quebec (*Bédard v. Dawson,* 39 Can. C.C. 175, 33 Que. K.B. 246) held that this law was constitutional, and that although criminal law and rules of procedure were exclusively within the authority of the Federal Parliament, the provincial Legislature had the right to legislate on all civil matters in relation to criminal law and to sanction its enactments with a penalty. . . .

[His Lordship then considered *Lymburn v. Mayland,* [1932] A.C. 318, [1932] 2 D.L.R. 6, [1932] 1 W.W.R. 578, 57 Can. C.C. 311, and *Prov.-Sec. of P.E.I. v. Egan,* [1941] S.C.R. 396, [1941] 3 D.L.R. 305, 76 Can. C.C. 227, and continued as follows:]

I am clearly of opinion that if a Province may validly legislate on all civil matters in relation to criminal law, *that if it may enact laws calculated to suppress conditions favouring the development of crime,* and control properties in order to protect society against any illegal uses that may be made of them, if it has the undeniable right to supervise brokers in their financial transactions in order to protect the public against fraud, if, finally, it has the right to impose civil incapacities as a consequence of a criminal offence, I cannot see why it could not also have the power to enact that all those who extol doctrines, calculated to incite to treason, to the violation of official secrets, to sedition, etc., should be deprived of the enjoyment of the properties from where are spread these theories, the object of which is to undermine and overthrow the established order.

For all these reasons, I am of opinion that this appeal must be dismissed with costs. . . .

RAND J.: By 1937, c. 11, passed by the Legislature of the Province of Quebec entitled *An Act to Protect the Province against Communistic Propaganda* (now R.S.Q. 1941, c. 52) the following provisions are enacted:

"3.   It shall be illegal for any person who possesses or occupies a house within the Province, to use it or allow any person to make use of it to progagate communism or bolshevism by any means whatsoever.

"12.   It shall be unlawful to print, to publish in any manner whatsoever or to distribute in the Province any newspaper, periodical pamphlet, circular, document or writing whatsoever propagating or tending to propagate communism or bolshevism."

The word "house" is defined to extend to any building or other construction whatever. By s. 4 the Attorney-General, "upon satisfactory proof that an infringement of section 3 has been committed, may order the closing of the house against its use for any purpose whatsoever for a period of not more than one year; the closing order shall be registered at the registry office of the registration division wherein is situated such house, upon production of a copy of such order certified by the Attorney-General". When a house is closed, an owner who has not been in possession may apply to the Superior Court to have the order revised upon proving that in good faith he was ignorant of the use being made in contravention of the Act or that the house has not been so used during the 12 months preceding the order. Conversely, after an order has been so modified or terminated, the Attorney-General may, on application to the same Court, obtain a decree reviving it. No remedy by resort to a Court is extended to the person in possession against whom the order has become effective. The Attorney-General may at any time permit re-occupation on any conditions thought proper for the protection of the property and its contents or he may revoke the order.

The action in this appeal was brought by an owner against a tenant to have a lease set aside and for damages on the ground of the use of the leased premises for the illegal purpose so defined and their closure under such an order. As the validity of the Act was challenged by the defence, the Attorney-General intervened and that issue became the substantial question in the proceedings.

In addition to the closure, a large quantity of documentary matter was seized and removed. In the order both ss. 3 and 12 are recited and the concluding paragraph is in these terms: "Je, soussigné, procureur général de la province de Québec, croyablement informé des infractions et violations ci-dessus, vous enjoins de fermer pour toutes fins quelconques, pendant un an à compter de l'exécution de cet ordre, la maison portant le numéro civique 5321 de l'avenue du Parc, dans la cité de Montréal, et de plus, vous êtes par les présentes autorisé, et je vous donne les instructions en conséquence, à saisir et confisquer tout journal, revue, pamphlet, circulaire, document ou écrit quelconque imprimé, publié ou distribué en contravention à la dite loi, en particulier et sans restrictions à saisir et à détruire les exemplaires du journal 'Combat'."

From this it is clear that the order was based upon both sections. . . .

The first ground on which the validity of s. 3 is supported is head 13 of s. 92 of the *B.N.A. Act*, "Property in the Province" and Mr. Beaulieu's contention goes in this manner: by that head the Province is vested with unlimited legislative power over property; it may, for instance, take land without compensation and generally may act as amply as if it were a sovereign state, untrammelled by constitutional limitation. The power being absolute can be used as an instrument or means to effect any purpose or object. Since the objective accomplishment under the statute here is an act on property, its validity is self-evident and the question is concluded.

I am unable to agree that in our federal organization power absolute in such a sense resides in either Legislature. The detailed distribution made by ss. 91 and 92 places limits to direct and immediate purposes of provincial action. Under head 13 the purpose would, in general, be a "property" purpose either primary or subsidiary to another head of the same section. If such a purpose is foreign to powers vested in the Province by the Act, it will invade the field of the Dominion. For example, land could not be declared forfeited or descent destroyed by attainder on conviction of a crime, nor could the convicted person's right of access to provincial Courts be destroyed. These would trench upon both criminal law and citizenship status. The settled principle that calls for a determination of the "real character", the "pith and substance", of what purports to be enacted and whether it is "colourable" or is intended to effect its ostensible object, means that the true nature of the legislative act, its substance in purpose, must lie within s. 92 or some other endowment of provincial power. That a power ostensibly as here under a specific head cannot be exercised as a means directly and immediately to accomplish a purpose not within that endowment is demonstrated by the following decisions of the Judicial Committee: *Union Colliery Co. of B.C. Ltd. v. Bryden,* [1899] A.C. 580, holding that legislative power in relation to employment in a coal mine could not be used as a means of nullifying the civil capacities of citizenship and, specifically, of persons qualifying under head 25 of s. 91, Naturalization and Aliens; *Reference re Validity of Section 5(a) of Dairy Industry Act, Can. Federation of Agriculture v. A.-G. Que.,* [1950] 4 D.L.R. 689, [1951] A.C. 179, holding that the Dominion, under its power in relation to criminal law, could not prohibit the manufacture of margarine for the purpose of benefiting in local trade one class of producer as against another. The heads of ss. 91 and 92 are to be read and interpreted with each other and with the provisions of the statute as a whole; and what is then exhibited is a pattern of limitations, curtailments and modifications of legislative scope within a texture of interwoven and interacting powers.

In support of the legislation on this ground, *Bédard v. Dawson,* [1923] 4 D.L.R. 293, S.C.R. 681, 40 Can. C.C. 404, was relied on. In that case the statute provided that it should be illegal for the owner or occupier of any house or building to use it or allow it to be used as a disorderly house; and procedure was provided by which the Superior Court could, after a conviction under the Criminal Code, grant an injunction against the owner restraining that use of it. If the use continued, the Court could order the building to be closed for a period of not more than one year.

This power is seen to have been based upon a conviction for maintaining a public nuisance. Under the public law of England which underlies that of all the Provinces, such an act was not only a matter for indictment but in a civil aspect the Court could enjoin its continuance. The essence of this aspect is its repugnant or prejudicial effect upon the neighbouring inhabitants and properties.

On that view this Court proceeded in *Bédard.* . . .

That the scene of study, discussion or dissemination of views or opinions on any matter has ever been brought under legal sanction in terms of nuisance is not suggested. For the past century and a half in both the United Kingdom and Canada, there has been a steady removal of restraints on this freedom, stopping only at perimeters where the foundation of the freedom itself is threatened. Apart from sedition, obscene writings and criminal libels, the public law leaves the literary, discursive and polemic use of language, in the broadest sense, free.

The object of the legislation here, as expressed by the title, is admittedly to prevent the propagation of Communism and Bolshevism, but it could just as properly have been the suppression of any other political, economic or social doctrine or theory; and the issue is whether that object is a matter "in relation to which" under s. 92 the Province may exclusively make laws. Two heads of the section are claimed to authorize it: head 13, as a matter of "Civil Rights", and head 16, "Local and Private Matters".

Mr. Tremblay in a lucid argument treated such a limitation of free discussion and the spread of ideas generally as in the same category as the ordinary civil restrictions of libel and slander. These obviously affect the matter and scope of discussion to the extent that it trenches upon the rights of individuals to reputation and standing in the community; and the line at which the restraint is drawn is that at which public concern for the discharge of legal or moral duties and government through rational persuasion, and that for private security, are found to be in rough balance.

But the analogy is not a true one. The ban is directed against the freedom or civil liberty of the actor; no civil right of anyone is affected nor is any civil remedy created. The aim of the statute is, by means of penalties, to prevent what is considered a poisoning of men's minds, to shield the individual from exposure to dangerous ideas, to protect him, in short, from his own thinking propensities. There is nothing of civil rights in this; it is to curtail or proscribe these freedoms which the majority so far consider to be the condition of social cohesion and its ultimate stabilizing force.

It is then said that the ban is a local matter under head 16; that the social situation in Quebec is such that safeguarding its intellectual and spiritual life against subversive doctrines becomes a special need in contrast with that for a general regulation by Parliament. A similar contention was made in the *Reference re Saskatchewan Farm Security Act, 1944, Section 6*, [1947] 3 D.L.R. 689, S.C.R. 394, affirmed in the Judicial Committee [*sub nom. A.-G. Sask. v. A.-G. Can.*], [1949] 2 D.L.R. 145, A.C. 110. What was dealt with there was the matter of interest on mortgages and a great deal of evidence to show the unique vicissitudes of farming in that Province was adduced. But there, as here, it was and is obvious that local conditions of that nature, assuming, for the purpose of the argument only, their existence, cannot extend legislation to matters which lie outside of s. 92.

Indicated by the opening words of the preamble in the Act of 1867, reciting the desire of the four Provinces to be united in a federal union with a Constitution "similar in Principle to that of the

United Kingdom", the political theory which the Act embodies is that of parliamentary Government, with all its social implications, and the provisions of the statute elaborate that principle in the institutional apparatus which they create or contemplate. Whatever the deficiencies in its workings, Canadian Government is in substance the will of the majority expressed directly or indirectly through popular assemblies. This means ultimately government by the free public opinion of an open society, the effectiveness of which, as events have not infrequently demonstrated, is undoubted.

But public opinion, in order to meet such a responsibility, demands the condition of a virtually unobstructed access to and diffusion of ideas. Parliamentary Government postulates a capacity in men, acting freely and under self-restraints, to govern themselves; and that advance is best served in the degree achieved of individual liberation from subjective as well as objective shackles. Under that Government, the freedom of discussion in Canada, as a subject-matter of legislation, has a unity of interest and significance extending equally to every part of the Dominion. With such dimensions it is *ipso facto* excluded from head 16 as a local matter.

This constitutional fact is the political expression of the primary condition of social life, thought and its communication by language. Liberty in this is little less vital to man's mind and spirit than breathing is to his physical existence. As such an inherence in the individual it is embodied in his status of citizenship. Outlawry, for example, divesting civil standing and destroying citizenship, is a matter of Dominion concern. Of the fitness of this order of Government to the Canadian organization, the words of Taschereau J. in *Brassard v. Langevin* (1877), 1 S.C.R. 145 at p. 195 should be recalled: "The object of the electoral law was to promote, by means of the ballot, and with the absence of all undue influence, the free and sincere expression of public opinion in the choice of members of the Parliament of Canada. This law is the just sequence to the excellent institutions which we have borrowed from England, institutions which, as regards civil and religious liberty, leave to Canadians nothing to envy in other countries."

Prohibition of any part of this activity as an evil would be within the scope of criminal law, as ss. 60, 61 and 62 of the *Cr. Code* dealing with sedition exemplify. Bearing in mind that the endowment of parliamentary institutions is one and entire for the Dominion, that Legislatures and Parliament are permanent features of our constitutional structure, and that the body of discussion is indivisible, apart from the incidence of criminal law and civil rights, and incidental effects of legislation in relation to other matters, the degree and nature of its regulation must await future consideration; for the purposes here it is sufficient to say that it is not a matter within the regulation of a Province.

Mr. Scott, in his able examination of the questions raised, challenged also the validity of ss. 4 *et seq.* which vest in the Attorney-General the authority to adjudicate upon the commission of the illegal act under s. 3 and to issue the order of closure; but in view of the conclusion reached on the other grounds, the consideration of this becomes unnecessary.

I would, therefore, allow the appeal, set aside the judgments below, dismiss the action and direct a declaration on the intervention that the statute in its entirety is *ultra vires* of the Province . . .

FAUTEUX J. (translation) : . . . . That the sole legal object of the Act is to prohibit, with penal sanctions, Communistic propaganda, or more precisely to make such propaganda a criminal act, could, I think, not be more manifest.

. . . In this specific instance, the subject-matter of the main provision—prohibition of Communistic propaganda—is certainly one not coming, by itself, within the class of subjects enumerated in s. 92 as being within the competence of the Legislature. Parliament alone, legislating in criminal matters, is competent to enact, define, prohibit and punish these matters of a writing or of a speech that, on account of their nature, injuriously affect the social order or the safety of the state. Such are, for example, defamatory, obscene, blasphemous or seditious libels. In such cases, the rights being encroached upon are not those of an individual entitling him to a monetary compensation. . . .

Two fundamental differences should be pointed out between this Act and the *Act Respecting the Owners of Houses used as Disorderly Houses,* the constitutionality of which was affirmed by this Court in *Bédard v. Dawson (supra)*. In the *Disorderly House Act* [now R.S.Q. 1941, c. 50], there is no provision of the nature of s. 12, as in the statute now under consideration, but merely a provision of the nature of s. 3, *i.e.,* a provision declaring illegal the use of a house as a disorderly one. Moreover, in the *Disorderly House Act,* the Legislature adopted as a definition of the expression "disorderly house", the definition of this expression in the Criminal Code. The existence and the operation of the provincial Act was thus, in its principle and extent, fully subordinated to the existence and operation of the provisions established in the Criminal Code. It was therefore held that the Legislature had not created a crime but had simply provided for civil consequences resulting from the commission of a crime created by competent authority, and suppressed the conditions leading to the commission of that crime. That fundamental feature is obviously missing in the present case; here, the Legislature, not Parliament, created the crime. This aspect of the matter was not present in *Bédard v. Dawson (supra)*; it was present, but was not considered, in *Fineberg v. Taub,* [1940] 1 D.L.R. 114, 73 Can. C.C. 37. For these reasons, neither the decision of this Court in the first case nor the decision of the Superior Court in the second case are authorities supporting the proposition that "Property and Civil Rights in the Province" is the matter in relation to which the law under consideration is enacted . . .

ABBOTT J.: . . . The right of free expression of opinion and of criticism, upon matters of public policy and public administration, and the right to discuss and debate such matters, whether they be social, economic or political, are essential to the working of a parliamentary democracy such as ours. Moreover, it is not necessary to prohibit the discussion of such matters, in order to protect the personal reputation or the private rights of the citizen. That view was clearly expressed by Duff C.J.C. in *Re Alberta Legislation*, [1938] D.L.R. 81 at pp. 107-8, S.C.R. 100 at pp. 132-4 . . .

This right cannot be abrogated by a provincial Legislature, and the power of such Legislature to limit it, is restricted to what may be necessary to protect purely private rights, such as for example provincial laws of defamation. It is obvious that the impugned statute does not fall within that category. It does not, in substance, deal with matters of property and civil rights or with a local or private matter within the Province and in my opinion is clearly *ultra vires*. Although it is not necessary, of course, to determine this question for the purposes of the present appeal, the Canadian Constitution being declared to be similar in principle to that of the United Kingdom, I am also of opinion that as our constitutional Act now stands, Parliament itself could not abrogate this right of discussion and debate. The power of Parliament to limit it is, in my view, restricted to such powers as may be exercisable under its exclusive legislative jurisdiction with respect to criminal law and to make laws for the peace, order and good Government of the nation.

For the reasons which I have given, I would allow the appeal. . . .

Appeal allowed.

[Kellock J. agreed with Rand J. but also delivered a short concurring judgment. Locke J. concurred with Nolan J. who in a concurring judgment concluded that Parliament had exclusive authority to make Communism a crime or to forbid its propagation and hence the provincial statute (which was different from that in *Bédard v. Dawson*) was *ultra vires*. Cartwright J. agreed in a short concurring judgment that the provincial statute invaded the exclusive authority of Parliament in relation to criminal law.]

WALTER v. A.-G. ALTA.

In the Supreme Court of Canada. [1969] S.C.R. 383, 66 W.W.R. 513, 3 D.L.R. (3d) 1. The judgment of the Court was delivered by

MARTLAND J.:—The question in issue in both these appeals is as to the constitutional validity of *The Communal Property Act*, R.S.A. 1955, c. 52, as amended, hereinafter referred to as "the Act". In each of the two actions the real purpose was to obtain a declaration that this statute was ultra vires of the Legislature of the Province of Alberta and they were consolidated for trial.

The facts are not in issue. The appellants, other than the Fletchers, are Hutterians. The Fletchers are owners of land in Alberta which their fellow plaintiffs sought to purchase. The plaintiffs in the other action also sought to purchase Alberta lands. It is conceded that the lands in each case sought to be acquired would be held in common as defined in s. 2(*b*)(i) of the Act and that the operation of the Act prevents the acquisition of the lands. The appellants, other than the Fletchers, in each case formed part of a religious community which based its community life and its holding of property on religious principles.

As of December 31, 1963, Hutterite colonies held approximately 480,000 acres of land in Alberta and over 10,000 acres had been added in 1964. The approximate population of Hutterites in Alberta as of December 31, 1963, was 6,000.

The Act is described as "An Act respecting Lands in the Province Held as Communal Property." "Communal Property" is defined in s. 2 of the Act, which states:

> 2. In this Act,
> (*a*) "colony"
> > (i) means a number of persons who hold land or any interest therein as communal property, whether as owners, lessees or otherwise, and whether in the name of trustees or as a corporation or otherwise,
> > (ii) includes a number of persons who propose to acquire land to be held in such manner, and
> > (iii) includes Hutterites or Hutterian Brethren and Doukhobors;
> (*b*) "communal property" means
> > (i) land held by a colony in such a manner that no member of the colony has any individual or personal ownership or right of ownership in the land, and each member shares in the distribution of profits or benefits according to his needs or in equal measure with his fellow members, and
> > (ii) land held by a member of the colony by personal ownership or right of ownership or under a lease, if the land is used in conjunction with and as part of other land held in the manner described in subclause (i);
> (*c*) "Board" means the Communal Property Control Board established pursuant to this Act.

The general scheme of the Act for controlling the holding of land as communal property is as follows:

Unless otherwise authorized by the Lieutenant Governor in Council in the public interest (s. 5(2)) no colony existing on the 1st day of May, 1947, may increase the holdings of its land beyond its holdings on the 1st day of March, 1944 (s. 4(1)), or, if on that date the holdings were less than 6,400 acres, they may be extended thereto (s. 4(5)). The significance of the dates May 1, 1947, and March 1, 1944, referred to in the statute is as follows: The first Alberta legislation in relation to acquisition of land by Hutterites to come into force was *The Land Sales Prohibition Act*, 1944 (Alta.), c. 15, which came into force on March 1, 1944. In general that statute prohibited the selling of land to and the purchase of land by Hutterites. That Act, as amended, remained the law until it expired on May 1, 1947, and on that date *The Communal Property Act*, 1947 (Alta.), c. 16, came into force. So that between March 1, 1944, and May 1, 1947, no Hutterite could acquire any land in Alberta, but by virtue of the provisions of *The Communal*

Property Act which came into force on the latter date the restrictions on the acquisition of land were lessened somewhat in relation to Hutterites and the new provisions were made applicable to all "colonies", whether Hutterite or otherwise.

The general scheme of the Act goes on to provide as follows:

No "colony" which exists or existed outside the province may acquire land without the consent of the Lieutenant Governor in Council (s. 6).

No land may be acquired for the purpose of establishing a new "colony" without the consent of the Lieutenant Governor in Council (s. 7).

By an amendment to the statute which came into force on May 1, 1951, the Lieutenant Governor in Council was authorized to divide the province into zones and to designate the number of acres a "colony" established after that date may acquire in any zone or class of zones (s. 5(1)). By virtue of an amendment made in 1960, "colonies" established after May 1, 1947, were also limited to the number of acres designated by the Lieutenant Governor for each zone (s. 9).

The Lieutenant Governor in Council is authorized to establish a Communal Property Control Board (s. 3a(1)), which is to hear applications by "colonies" for leave to acquire land. Where the application is for leave to acquire additional lands for a "colony" already holding lands, the Board may grant or refuse the application, subject to an appeal to a judge of a district court by "a person or colony not satisfied with the decision of the Board . .."(s. 13, subss. (1) to (6)).

Where the granting of the application would result in the establishment of a new "colony", the Board is to give public notice of the application, and hold such hearings and make such inquiries as it deems necessary to determine whether the granting of the application would be in the public interest, giving consideration to the location of the lands applied for, the location of existing "colonies", the geographical location of the lands intended for communal use in relation to the lands not so used, and any other factors which the Board may deem relevant.

Following its investigation the Board is to submit a report to the Minister of Municipal Affairs as to its recommendations in the matter. After consideration of the report the Lieutenant Governor in Council may consent or withhold consent as he deems proper in the public interest, irrespective of the Board's recommendation (s. 14).

Dispositions of land to "colonies" which would result in contravention of the provisions of the statute are prohibited (s. 11).

The submission of the appellants is that the Act is legislation in respect of religion and, in consequence, is beyond the legislative powers of a provincial legislature. The respondent contends that the Act is legislation in respect of property in Alberta, controlling the way in which land is to be held, by regulating the acquisition and disposition of land to be acquired by colonies to be held as communal land.

The learned trial judge, Milvain J. (as he then was), held that, in pith and substance, the Act relates to land tenure in the province and is, therefore, intra vires of the Legislature of the Province of Alberta under s. 92(13) of the *British North America Act.*

The judgment was sustained on appeal [(1967), 58 W.W.R. 385, 60 D.L.R. (2d) 253].

In my opinion, the Act was enacted in relation to the ownership of land in Alberta and the Legislature had jurisdiction under s. 92(13) of the *British North America Act,* because it deals with property in the province. The scheme of the legislation indicates that the Legislature considered the use of large areas of land in Alberta for the purposes of communal living was something which, in the public interest, required to be regulated and controlled. The Act restricts, but does not prohibit, the use of land for such purposes.

It would seem to me to be clear that a provincial legislature can enact laws governing the ownership of land within the province and that legislation enacted in relation to that subject must fall within s. 92(13), and must be valid unless it can be said to be in relation to a class of subject specifically enumerated in s. 91 of the *British North America Act* or otherwise within exclusive Federal jurisdiction.

There is no suggestion in the present case that the Act relates to any class of subject specifically enumerated in s. 91.

It was on the basis that the legislation in question in the cases of *Henry Birks & Sons (Montreal) Limited v. The City of Montreal* [[1955] S.C.R. 799, [1955] 5 D.L.R. 321, 113 C.C.C. 135] and *Switzman v. Elbling* [[1957] S.C.R. 285, 117 C.C.C. 129, 7 D.L.R. (2d) 337] related to the subject of criminal law, assigned specifically to the Parliament of Canada by s. 91(27) of the *British North America Act,* that the statutes were held to be ultra vires of the Legislature of the Province of Quebec.

The *Birks* case involved the validity of a statute which empowered municipal councils of cities and towns to pass by-laws to compel the closing of stores on New Year's Day, the festival of Epiphany, Ascension Day, All Saints' Day, Conception Day and Christmas Day. The legislation was supported in argument on the basis that it related to the control of merchandising and the well-being of employees. It was held to be ultra vires of the Legislature of Quebec because it authorized the compulsion of Feast Day observance, and such legislation in England, as in the case of Sunday observance legislation, had been assigned to the domain of criminal law. Legislation in this field was held to relate to the subject of criminal law, assigned specifically to the Parliament of Canada by s. 91(27).

Rand J. went on to add that the legislation was in relation to religion, and beyond provincial competence, and he referred to the *Saumur* case. Kellock and Locke JJ. said that, even if it were not properly "criminal law", it was beyond the competence of the Legislature as being legislation with respect to freedom of religion, a matter dealt with in the statute of the Province of Canada of 1852, 14-15 Vict., c. 175, the relevant portion of which is quoted later in these reasons.

Switzman v. Elbling involved the validity of *The Act Respecting Communistic Propaganda,* R.S.Q. 1941, c. 52, which, inter alia, made it illegal for any person who possessed or occupied a house in the province to use it or to allow any person to make use of it to propagate communism or bolshevism by any means whatsoever. It was attempted to support the legislation on the ground that it dealt with property in the province.

The majority of the Court was of the opinion that the legislation was in respect of criminal law which, under s. 91(27), was within the exclusive competence of the Parliament of Canada.

It was submitted by the appellants that the Act is aimed at preventing the spread of Hutterite colonies in Alberta, that, because the maintenance of such colonies is a cardinal tenet of the Hutterite religion, the Act seeks to deal with religion, and that the subject of religion is within the exclusive jurisdiction of the Parliament of Canada. Their position is stated in the reasons of Johnson J.A., in the Court below, as follows:

> This Act then in its pith and substance is legislation restricting the acquisition by Hutterites of more land in the province.... I find it difficult to say that legislation which is aimed at the restriction of new and existing colonies and the holding of land in common as practised by these colonies when living in such colonies and holding lands in that manner are the principal tenets of Hutterian faith, does not deal with religion.

With respect, I do not share this view . . .

The purpose of the legislation in question here is to control the use of Alberta lands as communal property. While it is apparent that the legislation was prompted by the fact that Hutterites had acquired and were acquiring large areas of land in Alberta, held as communal property, it does not forbid the existence of Hutterite colonies. What it does is to limit the territorial area of communal land to be held by existing colonies and to control the acquisition of land to be acquired by new colonies which would be held as communal property. The Act is not directed at Hutterite religious belief or worship, or at the profession of such belief. It is directed at the practice of holding large areas of Alberta land as communal property, whether such practice stems from religious belief or not. The fact that Hutterites engage in that practice was the circumstance which gave rise to the necessity for the Legislature's dealing generally with the holding of land as communal propery, but that does not mean that legislation controlling the holding of land in that way is not in relation to property in the Province of Alberta.

It is a function of a provincial legislature to enact those laws which govern the holding of land within the boundaries of that province. It determines the manner in which land is held. It regulates the acquisition and disposition of such land, and, if it is considered desirable in the interests of the residents in that province, it controls the extent of the land holdings of a person or group of persons. The fact that a religious group upholds tenets which lead to economic views in relation to land holding does not mean that a provincial legislature, enacting land legislation which may run counter to such views, can be said, in consequence, to be legislating in respect of religion and not in respect to property.

Religion, as the subject-matter of legislation, wherever the jurisdiction may lie, must mean religion in the sense that it is generally understood in Canada. It involves matters of faith and worship, and freedom of religion involves freedom in connection with the profession and dissemination of religious faith and the exercise of religious worship. But it does not mean freedom from compliance with provincial laws relative to the matter of property holding. There has been no suggestion that mortmain legislation by a provincial legislature is incompetent as interfering with freedom of religion . . .

In my opinion, the legislation in question here undoubtedly affects the future expansion and creation of Hutterite colonies in Alberta, but that does not mean it was enacted in relation to the matter of religion. The Act is in relation to the right to acquire land in Alberta, if it is to be used as communal property, and, in consequence, it is within provincial jurisdiction under s. 92(13).

Having reached this conclusion, it is unnecessary for me to express any opinion in respect of the submission of the respondent that legislation in relation to religious freedom falls within the exclusive jurisdiction of provincial legislatures . . .

I would dismiss the appeals with costs. No costs should be paid by or to the intervenant.

Appeals dismissed with costs.

JOHNSON v. A.-G. ALTA.

In the Supreme Court of Canada. [1954] S.C.R. 127, [1954] 2 D.L.R. 625, 108 Can. C.C. 1, 18 C.R. 173.

Appeal from an order of the Alberta Appellate Division, [1953] 1 D.L.R. 284, 7 W.W.R. (N.S.) 193, 105 Can. C.C. 10, 15 C.R. 379, setting aside an order of Egbert J. prohibiting certain proceedings under the *Slot Machine Act (Alta.)*. The appellant had been notified to appear and show cause why certain machines seized by the police should not be confiscated as provided by the Act.

KERWIN J. (dissenting): . . . The *Slot Machine Act* which requires our attention is R.S.A. 1942, c. 333. Section 3 provides: "No slot machine shall be capable of ownership, nor shall the same be the subject of property rights within the Province, and no court of civil jurisdiction shall recognize or give effect to any property rights in any slot machine."

By s. 2(*b*) "Slot machine" means—

"(*i*) any machine which under the provisions of section 986, subsection (4), of *The Criminal Code*, is deemed to be a means or contrivance for playing a game of chance;

"(*ii*) any slot machine and any other machine of a similar nature, the result of one of any number of operations of which is, as regards the operator, a matter of chance and uncertainty, or which as a consequence of any number of successive operations yields different results to the operator, notwithstanding that the result of some one or more or all of such operations shall be known to the operator in advance; and

"(*iii*) any machine or device the result of one of any number of operations of which is, as regards the operator, a matter of chance or uncertainty or which as a consequence of any given number of successive operations yields different results to the operator, notwithstanding that the result of some one or more or all of such operations may be known to the operator in advance."

Section 4 provides in part that upon information on oath by any Peace Officer that there is reasonable ground for believing that any slot machine is kept in any building or premises, it shall be lawful for any Justice of the Peace by warrant under his hand to authorize and empower the Peace Officer to enter and search the building or premises and every part thereof. By s. 5, every Peace Officer executing or assisting in the execution of any such warrant who finds upon the premises mentioned therein any machine or device which he believes to be a slot machine shall forthwith seize and remove it and bring it before a Justice of the Peace; and shall immediately thereafter serve upon the occupant of the premises or the person in whose possession the slot machine was at the time of the seizure a notice requiring the person so served to appear before any Justice and which person shall then be there to show cause why the slot machine so seized should not be confiscated. Section 7 enacts: "At the time and place mentioned in the notice any justice who shall then be there shall hear anything that may be alleged as a cause why the machine should not be confiscated and unless he is by reason of what is so alleged satisfied that the machine is not a slot machine within the meaning of this Act, he shall proceed to make an order declaring the machine to be confiscated to His Majesty to be disposed of as the Attorney-General may direct and shall have power to make such order whether or not the person served with the notice is the owner, bailee or licensee of or otherwise entitled to the possession of the machine."

The necessary steps under ss. 4 and 5 were taken in connection with a number of coin machines or devices but proceedings under s. 7 were prohibited by the order of Egbert J. It is pointed out in the reasons for judgment of W. A. MacDonald J.A., speaking on behalf of the majority of the Appellate Division that, apart from the fact that the machines were placed under seizure, there is no evidence that they are of a type which under valid legislation were liable to confiscation. However, on the argument it was assumed that the machines fall within the definition of "slot machines" in the Act, and on this assumption the first contention was that the subject-matter of the legislation falls under head (27) of s. 91 of the *B.N.A. Act*: "The Criminal Law, except the Constitution of Courts of Criminal Jurisdiction, but including the Procedure in Criminal Matters."

In *Bedard v. Dawson*, [1923] 4 D.L.R. 293, S.C.R. 681, 40 Can. C.C. 404, this Court held that a statute authorizing a Judge to order the closing of a disorderly house was *intra vires* the Quebec Legislature as it dealt with matters of property and civil rights by providing for the suppression of a nuisance and not with criminal law by aiming at the punishment of a crime. . . .

The mere fact that s. 2(*b*)(1) of the *Slot Machine Act* refers to a section of the Criminal Code is not by itself of any importance. . . .

In the present case the Legislature has declared that there is no property in a slot machine. All that the tribunal before which the matter comes has to do is to hear representations that any particular machine is not a slot machine and, unless it is satisfied that such is the case, make an order confiscating it to His Majesty in right of the Province. The legislation impugned is neither criminal law nor incidental thereto. The Legislature was not attempting to create an offence and provide a penalty but was acting within its powers under s. 92 of the *B.N.A. Act,* head (13), "Property and Civil Rights in the Province" and head (16), "Generally all Matters of a merely local or private Nature in the Province". It is not necessary under the Alberta Act that the slot machine be found in a gaming-house. I do not read that Act as aimed at gambling and, therefore, in my opinion it does not cover the same ground as the provisions of the Criminal Code . . .

Counsel referred to several decisions of provincial Courts in which the validity of various provincial *Slot Machine Acts* was in issue. All of these statutes contained sections similar to some of those in the legislation before us but nothing is said about such decisions as in the particular branches of constitutional law with which we are concerned, the line between validity and invalidity is very narrow.

The appeal should be dismissed with costs.

RAND J.:—In this appeal the validity of the *Slot Machine Act,* as amended, of Alberta, is challenged on three grounds: that the true nature of the legislation, directed against a public evil, is criminal law and within the exclusive jurisdiction of Parliament; that the provision for a declaration of confiscation by a Justice of the Peace is in conflict with s. 96 of the *B.N.A. Act,* and as that adjudication is essential to the administration of the Act the whole enactment must fall; and that in any event the field covered by the statute is already occupied by the Criminal Code. In view of the conclusion to which I have come it is unnecessary to deal with more than the last ground.

The definition of "slot machine" in s. 2 of the Act is as follows: [The learned Judge reproduced the provisions already set out in the judgment of Kerwin J., *supra.*]

Section 3 declares that the machines shall not be capable of ownership nor be the subject of property rights within the Province, and that no Court of civil jurisdiction shall recognize or give effect to any rights in them. Sections 4, 5, 6 and 7 provide that, upon information on oath by a Peace Officer that there are reasonable grounds for believing that any slot machine "is kept in any building or premises", a warrant may issue to search and seize and to bring the machine before a Justice of the Peace, and for notice to be served upon the person in possession to show cause why it should not be declared to be confiscated; and unless the Justice is satisfied that the machine is not one within the meaning of the Act, he is to make an order of confiscation to Her Majesty.

In 1938, s. 986(4) of the *Code* was amended [by c. 44, s. 46] to its present form, which, embracing slot machines for any purpose except vending services, declares that "if any house, room or place is found fitted or provided with any such machine there shall be an irrebuttable presumption that such house, room or place is a common gaming house". That presumption arises in any prosecution under s. 229 [re-enacted 1947, c. 55, s. 4] for keeping a disorderly house, which, by s. 226 [re-enacted 1938, c. 44, s. 12], includes a common gaming-house. The prosecution, preceded by an information made under oath, charges the person with being the keeper of a house to which, by the definition in s. 226, persons resort "for the purpose of playing at any game of chance". Once, then, that basis is established and the presence of such a machine is shown, the conviction for keeping a common gaming-house necessarily follows.

We have no facts before us showing the nature of the machines involved in the proceeding taken and we are left, therefore, with the language of the statute and of the Code from which to deduce the limits of inclusion to which the definition can be taken to extend.

It has been decided that slot machines for amusement or entertainment purposes come within the exception to s. 986(4) as vending services: *Laphkas v. The King*, [1942] 2 D.L.R. 47, S.C.R. 84, 77 Can. C.C. 142; they are therefore excluded from subcl. (i) of the definition. In *Regent Vending Machines Ltd. v. Alberta Vending Machines Ltd.*, [1954] S.C.R. 98, [1954] 2 D.L.R. 679, the judgment in which is being delivered with that in this appeal, for the reasons given I was of opinion that the machines in that case which were games or means of entertainment into which skill entered were not within the language of subcl. (ii) or (iii): and the question which is raised at this stage is whether there can be any machine coming within the scope of subcls. (ii) and (iii) to which the provisions of the Code do not extend.

That the object of the statute is to eliminate what is considered to be a local evil is quite apparent—but what evil? I can quite imagine an object of concern to be the waste of time and money, particularly of young persons, in the operation of such machines as were dealt with in the *Regent Vending Machines Ltd.* case, *supra*. Their operation may even be taken to tend to breed a gambling propensity, although that tendency, if it exists at all, must be admitted to be extremely tenuous. But that the legislative purpose is aimed primarily at the evil of gambling is patent from almost the opening words of the statute. There is the incorporation of the instruments falling with s. 986(4) of the *Code* in subcl. (i); subcls. (ii) and (iii) are couched in language which in its technical description of the functional result of the machines is identical with what is contained in that section. The only differences between subcls. (ii) and

(iii) are in the opening words of application in subcl. (ii) "any slot machine and any other machine of a similar nature" against in subcl. (iii) "any machine or device"; in line 5 of subcl. (ii), "any number" against, in lines 4-5 of subcl. (iii), "any given number"; and in line 9 of subcl. (ii) "shall be known" against "may be known" in the second last line of subcl. (iii). If significant differences in the interpretation of the two subclauses exist, they have not been suggested to us. It is therefore, in my opinion, reasonably clear that if the scope of the statute in this respect does go beyond that of s. 986(4), it must be in relation to machines or devices that are of or are used for a gambling nature or purpose.

That being so, what is the scope of the provision of the Code dealing with gaming and gambling instruments? It should be remarked at the outset that, generally, gambling devices are aimed at as the apparatus of gaming-houses. In certain forms they may be found in homes and used if at all in purely private activities beyond the reach of the criminal law. I do not interpret the words of s. 4 of the statute "that any slot machine is *kept* in any building or premises" to extend to an instrument of any kind to be found in a home for family and social entertainment. To be "kept" in the text carries the implication both of keeping in use and for other than purely social purposes. What is intended to be struck at is a public or community evil, not what would involve in its enforcement the invasion of domestic privacy.

In addition to s. 986(4) the provisions of ss. 235 and 641 bear directly on the question. The former makes it an indictable offence to keep in any premises, "any gambling, wagering, or betting machine or device". No definition is given of these machines or devices, and we are left in each case to a determination of fact. Then s. 641 [am. 1947, c. 55, s. 19; 1948, c. 39, s. 17; 1950, c. 11, s. 8] authorizes the seizure within any house, room or place which a Peace Officer believes to be a place kept as a gambling-house, of all instruments of gaming found therein, to be brought before a Justice who, by s-s. (3) is empowered in a proper case to make an order of confiscation. Taken with s. 642 it furnishes the means and the occasion for initiating a prosecution under s. 229.

From this it is seen that the Code has dealt comprehensively with the subject-matter of the provincial statute. An additional process of forfeiture by the Province would both duplicate the sanctions of the Code and introduce an interference with the administration of its provisions. Criminality is primarily personal and sanctions are intended not only to serve as deterrents but to mark a personal delinquency. The enforcement of criminal law is vital to the peace and order of the community. The obvious conflict of administrative action in prosecutions under the Code and proceedings under the statute, considering the more direct and less complicated action of the latter, could lend itself to a virtual nullification of enforcement under the Code and in effect displace the Code so far by the statute. But the criminal law has been enacted to be carried into effect against violations, and any local legislation of a supplementary nature that would tend to weaken or confuse that enforcement would be an interference with the exclusive power of Parliament.

The penalty of the Act, in duplicating forfeiture, is supplementing punishment. That is not legislating either "in relation to" property or to a local object. Every valid enactment made under the authority conferred by means of that phrase is for an object or purpose which is within the power of the enacting jurisdiction, and legislation "in relation to" property is as much subject to that canon as any other head of ss. 91 or 92. Legislation from caprice or perverseness or arbitrary will affecting, say, property, cannot be brought within those words; when of such a nature it passes into another category. That law is reason is in such a sense as applicable to statutes as to the unwritten law. I am unable to agree, therefore, that under its authority to legislate in relation to property the Province can in reality supplement punishment; that it may deal with conditions that conduce to the development of crime where what is proposed is in fact legislation of that character and infringes no legislative field beyond its jurisdiction though undoubted is not in question here.

The result is that since the machines or devices struck at by the statute are the same as those dealt with in similar manner by the Code, it is sufficient to say that the statute is inoperative. . . .

ESTEY J. (dissenting) : . . . Section 3, under which slot machines, as defined, can neither be owned nor be the subject of property rights within the Province, sets forth the basic principle underlying the statute and, as such, is legislation in relation to property and civil rights.

It is, however, the contention of the appellant that when read as a whole the statute makes the possession of these machines and devices an offence and confiscation thereof a penalty; that in reality it is an attempt on the part of the Province to legislate "for the promotion of public order, safety, or morals" and is, therefore legislation in relation to criminal law.

Leaving aside, for the moment, the provisions for seizure and forfeiture, it may be observed that the phrase just quoted appears in the judgment of the Judicial Committee in *Russell v. The Queen* (1882), 7 App. Cas. 829, which, at p. 839, reads: "Laws of this nature designed for the promotion of public order, safety, or morals, and which subject those who contravene them to criminal procedure and punishment, belong to the subject of public wrongs rather than to that of civil rights. They are of a nature which fall within the general authority of Parliament to make laws for the order and good government of Canada, and have direct relation to criminal law."

The submission of the appellant would appear not to give sufficient weight to the words that immediately follow the phrase "public order, safety, or morals," from which it is evident that, in order to give such legislation the quality and character of criminal law, there must be an offence defined and a penalty provided therefor.

Lord Atkin gives expression to the same view when, after stating that the phrase "criminal law" in s. 91(27) of the *B.N.A. Act* is used in its widest sense and is not confined to what was criminal law in 1867, he continues: "The power must extend to legislation to make new crimes. Criminal law connotes only the quality of such acts or omissions as are prohibited under appropriate penal provisions by authority of the State. The criminal quality of an act cannot be discerned by intuition; nor can it be discovered by reference to any standard but one: Is the act prohibited with penal consequences? Morality and criminality are far from co-extensive; nor is the sphere of criminality necessarily part of a more extensive field covered by morality unless the moral code necessarily disapproves all acts prohibited by the State, in which case the argument moves in a circle." *Proprietary Articles Trade Ass'n v. A.-G. Can.*, [1931] 2 D.L.R. 1 at p. 9, A.C. 310 at p. 324, 55 Can. C.C. 241 at pp. 249-50.

The absence of any express provision in the *Slot Machine Act* making possession of these machines or devices an offence and providing a penalty therefor distinguishes it from the legislation of Saskatchewan which expressly included both and as a consequence was declared to be *ultra vires* the Province in *R. v. Karminos*, [1936] 2 D.L.R. 353, 65 Can. C.C. 165. Even in that case Turgeon J.A. would have held the provision, similar to the above-quoted s. 3, competent provincial legislation and severable from that which was criminal in character. In *R. v. Stanley*, [1936] 1 D.L.R. 100, 64 Can. C.C. 385, the Alberta Court of Appeal held that legislation in that Province, prior to that here under consideration, was *intra vires*. It contained a direct prohibition against keeping and operating these machines, but did not provide a penalty therefor. The Appellate Division of the Supreme Court of New Brunswick in *R. v. Lane*, [1937] 1 D.L.R. 212, 67 Can. C.C. 273, 11 M.P.R. 232, held similar slot machine legislation within the legislative competence of the Province.

The appellant cited *Ouimet v. Bazin* (1912), 3 D.L.R. 593, 20 Can. C.C. 458, 46 S.C.R. 502. That case and *A.-G. Ont. v. Hamilton Street Ry.*, 7 Can. C.C. 326, [1903] A.C. 524, upon which it was mainly decided, further emphasize the distinction between legislation in relation to criminal law and the slot machine legislation here in question. In the *Hamilton Street Ry.* case the Privy Council held an Act to prevent the profanation of the Lord's Day legislation in relation to criminal law and, therefore, beyond the competence of the Province to enact. The profanation of the Sabbath was a crime at common law (Encyc. of the Laws of Eng., vol. 13, p. 707) and a statutory offence in Upper Canada prior to Confederation (C.S.U.C. 1859, c. 104). See also *Re Sunday Observance Legislation* (1905), 35 S.C.R. 581. This feature was emphasized by their Lordships of the Privy Council at p. 331 Can. C.C., p. 529 A.C., where it is stated "that an infraction of the Act, which in its original form . . . was in operation at the time of Confederation, is an offence against the criminal law". In the *Ouimet* case the Quebec statute was similar to that in Ontario. It was entitled "An Act Respecting the Observance of Sunday" and it was held to be *ultra vires*.

The slot machine legislation would appear to be more appropriately classified under that type discussed in *Bedard v. Dawson*, [1923] 4 D.L.R. 293, S.C.R. 681, 40 Can. C.C. 404. . . .

[The judgments of Duff and Anglin JJ. in this case] distinguish between legislation which, in effect, prevents the use of property which the legislature has decided is undesirable in the interests of the community from that under which one who commits an offence may be prosecuted and punished therefor.

The Legislature in the *Slot Machine Act,* in effect prevents the use of these machines or devices. That it may prevent the commission of criminal offences may be conceded. That was the precise effect of the legislation in the *Bedard* case. *The Slot Machine Act* goes further and prevents the use of machines and devices which, in the judgment of the Legislature, tend to foster criminal or other tendencies detrimental to the community.

In determining the nature and character of legislation one examines the effect thereof and not its purpose: Viscount Sumner in *A.-G. Man. v. A.-G. Can. (Provincial Sale of Shares Act,)* [1929] 1 D.L.R. 369, A.C. 260. It is here neither the purpose nor the effect of the legislation that offences and penalties are provided with respect to the possession or use of slot machines and devices. The Legislature is not concerned with how and in what manner these machines and devices have been used, but rather that they shall not be used at all within the Province. With that end in view it has defined those it deems undesirable and whether they be slot machines within the language of the *Criminal Code* is not in issue. The only issue under this legislation is whether these machines are within the definition in s. 2. If so, they cannot be owned or made the subject of property rights, but will be confiscated to Her Majesty. The effect of the legislation is to prevent rather than punish. It is, therefore, quite different from that which is classified as criminal law under s. 91(27), or that of creating offences and penalties under s. 92(15). The language used by the Legislature expressly prevents the use of these machines and devices and a construction to that effect should be adopted, rather than one which attributes to the Legislature an effort to indirectly legislate in relation to criminal law. . . .

It is emphasized, in support of the invalidity of the legislation here in question, that the language of the definition in s. 2(b) (ii) and (iii) is almost identical with a portion of s. 986(4) of the *Code*. Before any conclusion should be drawn from this circumstance it should be observed that s. 986(4), as enacted in the Code, is designed to serve two purposes: first, that the automatic or slot machine there defined is "deemed to be a means or contrivance for playing a game of chance" within the meaning of ss. 226 and 229 of the *Code*; second, that any house, room or place fitted or provided with such automatic or slot machines raises an irrebutable presumption that such is a common gaming-house within the meaning of ss. 226 and 229 of the *Code*. The *Slot Machine Act* contains no such provisions. Moreover, s. 986(4) is restricted to automatic or slot machines, while s. 2(*b*) (ii) applies to "any slot machine and any other machine of a similar nature" and subcl. (iii) applies to "any machine or device." This being so, the language of s. 2(*b*) (ii) and (iii) must be construed in its context and in relation to the purposes for which it is there used, rather than the context of s. 986(4).

When regard is had for the true nature and character of this legislation, it is the machine or device, and not the owner or party in possession thereof, against which the legislation is directed. The essential difficulty, therefore, in describing the confiscation here provided for as a penalty is that there is no offence to which it can be attached. "Confiscation" is not a word of art and, while it may be used in association with an offence as constituting part of the penalty, it does not follow that confiscation is always a penalty. In *R. v. Lane*, [1937] 1 D.L.R. at pp. 213-4, 67 Can. C.C. at p. 275, Baxter C.J., after stating that "property can be taken from one person and given to another, or, as by the Act in question, it can be vested in the Crown", goes on to cite *Levin v. Allnutt* (1812), 15 East 267, 104 E.R. 845, and *Re Barnett's Trusts* (1902), 71 L.J. Ch. 408, where the word "confiscation" is used not in the sense of a penalty. The essential feature of the legislation here is that slot machines cannot be owned or subject to property rights and, if the legislation stopped there, the property in these machines would pass, *bona vacantia*, to the Crown. However, the Legislature here provides an opportunity for those who contend that their machines are not within the definition to have that issue judicially determined and, if determined adversely to the party so contending, the Magistrate, under the statute, has no alternative but to direct their confiscation, not as a penalty for an offence, but under the authority of a Province to declare that in respect of property subject to its legislative jurisdiction it may be neither owned nor the subject of property rights and to take possession thereof.

The slot machine legislation, directed as it is to the prevention of the use of these machines and devices within the Province, may be classified under either s. 92(14) or (16). In this connection it is not unimportant to observe that the Province has a right to legislate, as Lord Macnaghten states in *A.-G. Man. v. Man. Licence Holders' Ass'n.*, [1902] A.C. 73 at p. 79, upon "matters which are 'substantially of local or of private interest' in a province—matters which are of a local or private nature 'from a provincial point of view'." At p. 78 Lord Macnaghten states: "In legislating for the suppression of the liquor traffic the object in view is the abatement or prevention of a local evil, rather than the regulation of property and civil rights— though, of course, no such legislation can be carried into effect without interfering more or less with 'property and civil rights in the province'."

In *Lymburn v. Mayland*, [1932] 2 D.L.R. 6, A.C. 318, 57 Can. C.C. 311, it was held that the Alberta *Security Frauds Prevention*

Act (1930, c. 8) was *intra vires*. It was there contended before the
Judicial Committee that "the Act was invalid because under the
colour of dealing with the prevention of fraud in share transactions
it was assuming to legislate as to criminal law". This contention
was not accepted and in the course of their reasons it was stated at
p. 9 D.L.R., p. 324 A.C., p. 314 Can. C.C.: "There is no reason to
doubt that the main object sought to be secured in this part of the
Act is to secure that persons who carry on the business of dealing
in securities shall be honest and of good repute, and in this way
to protect the public from being defrauded."

And at p. 11 D.L.R., p. 326 A.C., p. 316 Can. C.C.: "The provisions of this part of the Act may appear to be far reaching; but
if they fall, as their Lordships conceive them to fall, within the scope
of legislation dealing with property and civil rights the legislature
of the province, sovereign in this respect, has the sole power and
responsibility of determining what degree of protection it will afford
to the public."

These cases are illustrations of the jurisdiction a Province possesses to legislate in respect to morality, order and general welfare,
under the appropriate headings of s. 92, and the imposition of
penalties for infractions thereof, as provided in s. 92(15).

The fact that Parliament has, in legislating in relation to criminal
law, dealt with slot machines does not militate against the jurisdiction
of the Province to prohibit their use. That was expressly decided
in the *Bedard* case. The principle underlying that case would appear
to support the view that in respect to property such as slot machines
a provincial Legislature may, if it deems them undesirable, legislate
to prohibit their use, irrespective of whether Parliament has included
provisions in regard to them in its legislation in relation to criminal
law. A conclusion to the contrary would leave the Province without
legislative capacity to prevent the use of such chattels, however
objectionable or undesirable, in the opinion of the Legislature, they
may be. That the Legislature possesses such a jurisdiction appears
to be established by the authorities mentioned and in my view the
slot machine legislation here in question should be held to be competently enacted.

. . . Under this legislation slot machines can neither be owned by,
nor can individuals obtain a property right or interest therein. As
found they are seized and, upon an order by a Magistrate, confiscated
to the Crown. They come to the Crown, therefore, not because of
property in which there may be diverse claims, but by virtue of these
statutory provisions. . . .

LOCKE J.: . . . In essence, the Act was directed against gambling
and, in my opinion, nothing else, and, in addition to declaring that no
slot machines should be capable of ownership, prohibited any person
from keeping or operating such a machine and permitted its seizure
and confiscation.

. . . The determination of this matter does not, in my opinion, depend alone upon the fact that if the provincial legislation was lawfully

enacted there would be a direct clash with the terms of the Criminal Code: rather is it my opinion that the main reason is that the exclusive jurisdiction to legislate in relation to gaming lies with Parliament under head (27) of s. 91 . . .

I would allow this appeal with costs throughout and declare that the *Slot Machine Act* is *ultra vires* of the Legislature of Alberta.

CARTWRIGHT J.: . . . I am unable to relate the statute in the case at bar to any provincial purpose falling within heads (13) or (16) of s. 92 of the *B.N.A. Act* as the Courts have been able to do in other cases in which the validity of provincial legislation was called in question on the allegation that infringed upon the field of criminal law, as, for example, in the cases of *Provincial Secretary of P.E.I. v. Egan*, [1941] 3 D.L.R. 305, S.C.R. 396, 76 Can. C.C. 227 (the civil regulation of the use of highways), *Bedard v. Dawson*, [1923] 4 D.L.R. 293, S.C.R. 681, 40 Can. C.C. 404 (the suppression of a nuisance and the prevention of its recurrence by civil process) and *Regina v. Wason*, 17 O.R. 58, 17 O.A.R. 221 (the regulation of the dealings of cheese-makers and their patrons). The statute here in question appears to me to be inseverable, to relate only to the prohibition and punishment of keeping contrivances for playing games of chance, that is to criminal law, and to be *ultra vires* of the Legislature *in toto*.

Appeal allowed.

[Taschereau J., dissenting, concurred with Kerwin J. Kellock J. concurred with Cartwright J. In *Deware v. The Queen*, [1954] S.C.R. 182, [1954] 2 D.L.R. 663, in a judgment handed down on the same day as that in the *Johnson* case, the Supreme Court, similarly constituted, split evenly on the validity of the *Slot Machine Act*, R.S.N.B. 1952, c. 212, with Rand J. taking no position on the issue of validity but going off on a question of application of the Act.

Following the *Johnson* case, Alberta enacted a new *Slot Machine Act*, 1954, c. 99, which *inter alia*, defined a slot machine by specification and excluded any machine which under the Cr. Code is deemed to be a means for playing a game of chance. It went on to declare that the maintenance of a slot machine on any premises in the Province is a nuisance. Confiscation was provided for as before, but with jurisdiction in a Supreme Court or District Court Judge. In reliance on the *Johnson* case, the Act was declared *ultra vires* as seeking to suppress gambling not covered by the Cr. Code and thus trespassing on a forbidden field: *Regent Vending Machines Ltd. v. Alberta Vending Machines Ltd. and A.-G. Alta.* (1956), 6 D.L.R. (2d) 144, 19 W.W.R. 509, aff'g [1955] 5 D.L.R. 477, 16 W.W.R. 141.

It is within the power of the Dominion to provide for the forfeiture of vehicles or other things used in the commission of a criminal offence even though the articles are owned by someone other than the convicted person and even though no exculpatory provision is made in respect of the interest of an innocent person: see *Industrial Acceptance Corp. v. The Queen*, [1953] 2 S.C.R. 273, [1953] 4 D.L.R. 369. In *Regina v. McManus ex rel. Globe Mfrers. Agencies Ltd.* (1960), 127 Can. C.C. 220, 32 C.R. 252, 44 M.P.R. 112, it was held to be competent to Parliament to provide for the destruction, on the direction of the Court, of articles seized as evidence of gambling or bookmaking.

Assuming that the Dominion does not provide for the impounding or confiscation of articles used in connection with the commission of (federal) criminal offences, is it open to a Province so to legislate? See *McDonald v. Down*, [1939] 2 D.L.R. 177, 71 Can. C.C. 179, aff'd 75 Can. C.C. 404 (provincial legislation held valid in providing for impounding of automobile in certain circumstances if there has been a conviction under specified provisions of the provincial *Highway Traffic Act* or the federal Cr. Code involving use of the automobile).

A licensing by-law passed in pursuance of provincial legislation provided for the licensing of dance halls on certain conditions, including a stipulation that the licensee must not permit gambling or gaming of any kind on the premises. On appeal by a licensee from his conviction for breach of the by-law in permitting gambling on the licensed premises (although he himself was not present at the time), it was contended that the by-law was *ultra vires*. Do you agree? Would it make any difference if the only sanction for breach of the by-law was revocation of the licence? See *Millar v. The Queen*, [1954] 1 D.L.R. 148, 10 W.W.R. (N.S.) 145, 61 Man. R. 239.

A theatre licensing by-law authorized the cancellation of a licence when an immoral or indecent or profane performance takes place. *Held*, applying the *Johnson* case, the by-law was unconstitutional because it purported to supplement the Cr. Code: *St. Leonard v. Fournier* (1956), 115 Can. C.C. 366, 3 D.L.R. (2d) 315. See also *Hurrell v. Montreal*, [1963] Que. P.R. 89, holding invalid (in view of the obscenity provisions of the Cr. Code) a by-law prohibiting display of pictures of nudes or semi-nudes on news stands without the prior approval of the chief of police.

May a person be convicted of stealing things which by provincial law are declared to be ownerless or incapable of being the objects of property rights? See *Rex v. MacEwen; Rex v. Bell*, [1947] 2 D.L.R. 62, 19 M.P.R. 171.

In *Regina v. Board of Cinema Censors of Quebec, ex parte Montreal Newsdealers Supply Co.* (1967), 69 D.L.R. (2d) 512, a case of first impression, Batshaw J. of the Quebec Superior Court held invalid ss. 4 to 9 of an Act respecting Publications and Public Morals, 1950 (Que.), c. 12 (now R.S.Q. 1964, c. 50) as an invasion of the federal criminal law power being in substance prohibitory legislation dealing with public morals. Under the Act an order of censorship was made, without previous notice, in respect of a certain magazine ("Cavalier") whereby it was declared to be an immoral publication, distributable only on pain of seizure without a warrant, being under the Act hors de commerce and liable to confiscation and destruction upon a certificate of the Board of Censors.

A municipal by-law, authorized by provincial legislation, providing that no person shall create any disturbance in any public place or on any street by screaming, shouting, swearing or singing, or by being drunk or by fighting, was held invalid in view of the provisions of Cr. Code, s. 160, prohibiting the causing of a disturbance in or near a public place by conduct similar to that described in the by-law: *Poole v. Tomlinson* (1957), 118 Can. C.C. 384, 21 W.W.R. 511, 26 C.R. 92. Would the by-law be invalid if there were no Cr. Code, s. 160?

May a Province make it an offence to speculate in the sale of tickets to places of entertainment? See *Regina v. Fink*, [1967] 2 O.R. 132, [1967] 3 C.C.C. 187.

May a provincial legislature make it an offence for a man to register at a hotel with a woman falsely held out to be his wife? Would the validity of the legislation be affected if it provided merely for cancellation of a hotel licence if the proprietor knowingly permitted a man so to register? See *Rex v Hayduk*, [1938] O.R. 653, [1938] 4 D.L.R. 762.

May a provincial legislature provide for committal to jail of a judg-ment debtor if his examination shows that the debt on which the judgment was founded was contracted by false pretences, which is independently punishable under the federal Criminal Code? See *Re Dunn*, [1939] 4 D.L.R. 382, 14 M.P.R. 289.]

SAUMUR v. QUEBEC AND A.-G. QUE.

In the Supreme Court of Canada. [1953] 2 S.C.R. 299,
[1953] 4 D.L.R. 641.

Appeal from a judgment of the Quebec Court of Queen's Bench, Appeal Side, 104 Can. C.C. 106, dismissing an appeal from a judg-ment of the Superior Court holding a certain by-law applicable to Jehovah's Witnesses.

RINFRET C.J.C. (dissenting) (translation of reasons originally given in French):

Stripped of its extravagent build-up and reduced to its true dimensions, this case, in my opinion, is really very simple. It surely does not have the scope and importance that Jehovah's Witnesses have tried to give it through the interpretation of Mr. Laurier Saumur, the appellant, describing himself as a missionary evangelist.

It is a question of the validity of a municipal by-law and there have probably been hundreds and hundreds of cases of this kind since Confederation. If, on the other hand, this type of case has not been very frequently submitted to the Supreme Court of Canada, it is only because of its relative lack of importance and its limited application in each case to the territory of the municipality concerned.

Here is the text of the by-law attacked:

"184(1). It is by the present by-law forbidden to distribute in the streets of the City of Quebec any book, pamphlet, booklet, circu-lar, tract whatever, without having previously obtained for so doing the written permission of the Chief of Police.

"(2) Any one contravening the present by-law shall be liable to a fine, with or without costs, and in default of immediate payment of said fine, with or without costs, as the case may be, to an imprison-ment to be fixed by the Recorder's Court of the City of Quebec, at its discretion, but the said fine shall not exceed one hundred dollars and the imprisonment shall not exceed three months of the calendar. Said imprisonment nevertheless shall cease at any time before the expiration of the term fixed by the said Recorder's Court, upon pay-ment of the said fine or of the said fine and costs, as the case may be, and if said infraction is repeated, said repetition of offence shall constitute day by day, after summons or arrest, a separate offence."

The appellant, pleading his status as subject of Her Majesty the Queen and resident of the City of Quebec, and further alleging that he is a missionary-evangelist and one of Jehovah's Witnesses, declares that he considers it his duty to preach the Bible, either orally or by distributing publications in the form of books, booklets, periodicals, leaflets, etc., from house to house and in the streets.

He claims that By-law 184, reproduced above, in effect renders illegal this distribution of literature without written approval of the Chief of Police of the City of Quebec. He adds that in his capacity as a Canadian citizen he has an absolute right to the expression of his opinions, and that that flows from his right of freedom of speech, freedom of the press and free exercise of his worship of God, as guaranteed by the unwritten British Constitution, by the *B.N.A. Act* generally, and also by the statutes of the Province of Quebec, especially the *Freedom of Worship Act,* R.S.Q. 1941, c. 307.

He alleges that the City of Quebec and the Province of Quebec have no jurisdiction, either in law or constitutionally, to adopt a by-law such as the above, and that the latter is *ultra vires,* unconstitutional, illegal and void. . . .

The respondent, the City of Quebec, has pleaded that By-law 184 was a municipal law lawfully enacted in the exercise of the regulatory powers of the City and according to its incorporating statute; that the law of the Province, by virtue of which the by-law was passed is constitutional. . . .

. . . the by-law in dispute is nothing other than a police regulation; it is based primarily on the fact that the streets should not be used for the purpose of distributing documents. The normal use of the streets is that of circulation on foot or in vehicles (see Dillon on Municipal Corporations, 5th ed., p. 1083; McQuillin on Municipal Corporations, 2nd ed., vol. 3, p. 936 and following; same volume, p. 61, no. 938).

Let us note first of all that the *Charter* of the City of Quebec is anterior to Confederation (29-30 Vict., c. 57). The City is not governed by the *Cities and Towns Act,* R.S.Q. 1941, c. 233, but it is not improper to refer to this law to get a clear idea of the extent of the powers which are bestowed there for the regulation of the streets. . . .:

It is not less clear that in the distribution it makes of legislative powers, the *B.N.A. Act,* by ss. 91 and 92, confers, upon the Legislature in each Province, the exclusive power to make laws relative to the municipal institutions in the Province (s-s. (8)), to property and civil rights in the Province (s-s. (13)), and generally to all matters of a purely local and private nature in the Province (s-s. (16)).

It would be really fantastic to maintain that some of the powers . . . in the *Cities and Towns Act* of the Province of Quebec, could belong to the federal field. I cannot easily picture the Federal Parliament undertaking to adopt laws on any of these matters. (See the judgment of the Privy Council in *Hodge v. The Queen* (1883), 9 App. Cas. 117 at pp. 131, 133-4.)

The difficulty that the appellant is experiencing here results from several reasons:

First: His right to distribute religious pamphlets does not constitute the exercise of worship or religious profession.

Secondly: In any event, the free exercise and enjoyment of religious profession and worship does not, by virtue of s. 2 of R.S.Q. 1941, c. 307, enjoy absolute authorization, but the worship must be exercised "so as the same be not made an excuse for acts of licentiousness, or a justification of practices inconsistent with the peace and safety of the Province."

Thirdly: Freedom of worship is a civil right and consequently falls under s-s. (13) of s. 92 of the *B.N.A. Act*. It is thus provincial domain . . .

Finally, the last point is the question whether freedom of worship is a civil right which is subject to the jurisdiction of the provincial Legislatures. That is what the Provinces of Saskatchewan and Alberta considered when they adopted laws entitled: *An Act to Protect Certain Civil Rights* (1947 (Sask.), c. 35). The object of the law is declared in the preamble as being "to protect Certain Civil Rights" and s. 3 of the law stipulates: "Every person and every class of persons shall enjoy the right to freedom of conscience, opinion and belief, and freedom of religious association, teaching, practice and worship." The Province of Alberta has a similar statute.

On this point it is interesting to refer to the interpretation given by the Privy Council of the expression "civil rights" in the *Quebec Act* of 1774, in the case of *Citizens Ins. Co. of Canada v. Parsons* (1881), 7 App. Cas. 96 at p. 111: "It is to be observed that the same words, 'civil rights,' are employed in the Act of 14 Geo. 3, c. 83, which made provision for the Government of the province of Quebec. Section 8 of that Act enacted that His Majesty's Canadian subjects within the province of Quebec should enjoy their property, usages, and other civil rights, as they had before done, and that in all matters of controversy relative to property and civil rights resort should be had to the laws of Canada, and be determined agreeably to the said laws. In this statute the words 'property' and 'civil rights' are plainly used in their largest sense; and there is no reason for holding that in the statute under discussion they are used in a different and narrower one."

It is sufficient to draw attention to the contradiction of the argument of the attorney for the appellant who on one hand alleges the unconstitutionality of the *Quebec Charter,* while claiming on the other hand that it is in conflict with the *Freedom of Worship Act* of this same Province of Quebec. It is incontestible that the Legislature which has adopted c. 307 had the desired competence to adopt the Charter of the City of Quebec by virtue of which By-law 184 was enacted . . .

KERWIN J.:—In my view the right to practise one's religion is a civil right in the Province under head (13) of s. 92 of the *B.N.A. Act* just as much as the right to strike or lock-out dealt with by the Judicial Committee in *Toronto Elec. Com'rs. v. Snider,* [1925] 2 D.L.R. 5, A.C. 396. . . .

For the same reason I also think that freedom of the press is a civil right in the Province. [The learned judge concluded that, while the by-law was not *ultra vires*, its present application to prevent the appellant's distribution of pamphlets on the highways was not authorized by it and was subject to be enjoined.] . . .

RAND J.:—Strictly speaking, civil rights arise from positive law; but freedom of speech, religion and the inviolabiilty of the person, are original freedoms which are at once the necessary attributes and modes of self-expression of human beings and the primary conditions of their community life within a legal order. It is in the circumscription of these liberties by the creation of civil rights in persons who may be injured by their exercise, and by the sanctions of public law, that the positive law operates. What we realize is the residue inside that periphery. Their significant relation to our law lies in this, that under its principles to which there are only minor exceptions, there is no prior or antecedent restraint placed upon them: the penalties, civil and criminal, attach to results which their exercise may bring about, and apply as consequential incidents. So we have the civil rights against defamation, assault, false imprisonment and the like, and the punishments of the criminal law; but the sanctions of the latter lie within the exclusive jurisdiction of the Dominion. Civil rights of the same nature arise also as protection against infringements of these freedoms.

That legislation "in relation" to religion and its profession is not a local or private matter would seem to me to be self-evident: the dimensions of this interest are nationwide; it is even today embodied in the highest level of the constitutionalism of Great Britain; it appertains to a boundless field of ideas, beliefs and faiths with the deepest roots and loyalties; a religious incident reverberates from one end of this country to the other, and there is nothing to which the "body politic of the Dominion" is more sensitive.

There is, finally, the implication of s. 93 of the *Confederation Act* which deals with education. In this section appear the only references in the statute to religion. Subsection (1) speaks of "Denominational Schools" and preserves their existing rights and privileges. Subsection (2) extends to the separate schools "of the Queen's Protestant and Roman Catholic Subjects" in Quebec the same "Powers, Privileges and Duties" then conferred and imposed upon the separate schools of the "Queen's Roman Catholic Subjects" in Upper Canada. Subsection (3) provides for an appeal to the Governor-General in Council from any act or decision of a provincial authority "affecting any Right or Privilege of the Protestant or Roman Catholic Minority of the Queen's Subjects in relation to Education". Subsection (4) declares that in the event of any failure on the part of the provincial authority to observe or enforce the provincial laws contemplated by the section, Parliament may provide for the execution of the provisions of the section. On the argument advanced, and apart from the question of criminal law, these vital constitutional provisions could be written off by the simple expedient of abolishing, as civil rights and by provincial legislation, the religious freedoms of minorities, and so, in legal contemplation, the minorities themselves. . . .

I would, therefore, allow the appeal. . . .

KELLOCK J.:— . . . The question, . . . which lies at the threshold of the case is as to the true nature and character of the by-law.

Paragraph 1 reads as follows: "It is, by the present by-law, forbidden to distribute in the streets of the City of Quebec, any book, pamphlet, booklet, circular, tract whatever without having previously obtained for so doing the written permission of the Chief of Police."

Paragraph 2 provides a penalty for distribution without licence.

It will be observed that the by-law is perfectly general in its terms and that while it prohibits in the absence of a licence, at the same time it contemplates, fully as much, distribution at the unfettered will of the municipal official to whom is delegated the power to grant or to refuse to grant licences. The by-law affords no guide whatever for the regulation from any standpoint of the prohibition or permission for which it provides.

. . . Assuming, for the purposes of argument, that the by-law here in question might, in actual administration by the official mentioned therein, be administered solely to prevent literature reaching the streets which might cause disturbances or nuisance therein, and that a by-law expressly so limited would be within provincial competence, the present by-law is not so limited in its terms. Its validity is not to be judged from the standpoint of matters to which it might be limited, but upon the completely general terms in which it in fact is couched. . . .

It is undoubted that, under a by-law of the nature of By-law 184, the circulation of such material as the above would be impossible except with permission of the censor. This aspect of religious freedom would thereby be interfered with. The question is, therefore, as to the competency of provincial legislation in this field. In support of the by-law, it is said that this is a subject-matter within the category of "Civil Rights in the Province."

In considering this contention certain historical matters are relevant. Under the *Quebec Act* of 1774, c. 83, provision is made for the government of the Province of Canada, which included, *inter alia*, all of the present Provinces of Ontario and Quebec. By s. 8 it is provided that all His Majesty's Canadian subjects within the Province, with the exception of religious orders and communities, might hold and enjoy "their Property and Possessions, together with all Customs and Usages relative thereto, and all other their *Civil Rights,* in as large, ample and beneficial Manner" as if certain previously made proclamations, etc., had not been made. And it was further provided that in all matters of controversy "relative to *Property and Civil Rights*" resort should be had to the laws of Canada as the rule for decision of the same and that all causes which might thereafter be instituted in any of the Courts of justice should, with respect to "such Property and Rights" be determined agreeably to the said laws and customs of Canada until varied by subsequent enactment.

It is plain from other provisions of the statute that "Property and Civil Rights" do not include the right of exercise and profession of religion, as to which express provision was made elsewhere in the statute.

By s. 5 it is enacted: "That his Majesty's Subjects, professing the Religion of the Church of *Rome* of and in the said Province of *Quebec,* may have, hold, and enjoy, the free Exercise of the Religion of the Church of *Rome,* subject to the King's Supremacy, declared and established by an Act, made in the first Year of the Reign of Queen *Elizabeth* . . . and that the Clergy of the said Church may hold, receive, and enjoy, their accustomed Dues and Rights, with respect to such Persons only as shall profess the said Religion."

Section 6 enacts that: "Provided nevertheless, That it shall be lawful for his Majesty, his Heirs or Successors, to make such Provision out of the rest of the said accustomed Dues and Rights, for the Encouragement of the Protestant Religion, and for the Maintenance and Support of a Protestant Clergy within the said Province, as he or they shall, from Time to Time, think necessary and expedient."

Section 12 provides for the government of the Province by a council, but s. 15 provides that "no Ordinance touching Religion" is to be of any force or effect until the same shall have received the approval of His Majesty. Section 11 confirms English criminal law as the law of the Province.

By s. 17 provision is made for "Courts of Criminal, Civil and Ecclesiastical" jurisdiction.

In 1791 the *Constitutional Act,* c. 31, was passed. This statute provided for the division of the Province into two separate Provinces of Upper and Lower Canada, and for a separate legislative council and assembly for each, with power to make laws for the peace, welfare and good government of each of the Provinces. All laws previously existing were to continue until repealed or varied under the authority of the Act.

Section 42 provided, however, that with respect to any Act or Acts which might be passed by the legislative council or assembly of either of the Provinces varying or repealing the matters covered by ss. 5 and 6 of the Act of 1774 or which "shall in any manner relate to or affect the enjoyment or exercise of any religious form or mode of worship or shall impose or create any penalties, burthens, disabilities, or disqualifications, in respect of the same" or should affect the enjoyment of the dues or rights of any "minister, priest, ecclesiastic, or teacher, according to any religious form or mode of worship, in respect of his said office or function" should, before assent should be given to it, be laid before both Houses of Parliament in Great Britain, and His Majesty was prohibited from assenting to any such Act in case either House within 30 days should present an address to His Majesty to withhold assent therefrom.

In 1792, by 32 Geo. III, c. 1, the Legislature of Upper Canada, after reciting the provision in the Imperial Act of 1774 providing "That in all matters of controversy relative to property and civil rights, resort should be had to the laws of Canada as the rule for the decision of the same", and that that part of the former Province of Quebec then included within Upper Canada having become inhabited principally by persons familiar with the laws of England, this provision was repealed and it was enacted by s. 3 that "from and after the passing of this act, in all matters of controversy relative to *property and civil rights,* resort shall be had to the laws of England, as the rule for the decision of the same." Section 6, however, expressly provided that nothing in the statute should vary or interfere or be construed to vary or interfere with any "of the subsisting provisions respecting *ecclesiastical rights* or dues within this province".

In 1840, by 3-4 Vict., c. 35, the two Provinces were reunited under one legislative council and assembly. Section 42 again provided that whenever any bill should be passed containing any provisions

"which shall in any manner relate to or affect the enjoyment or exercise of any form or mode of religious worship, or shall impose or create any penalties, burdens, disabilities, or disqualifications, in respect of the same,"

every such bill, prior to assent, should be laid before both Houses of Parliament of the United Kingdom, and within 30 days thereof, in case either House of Parliament should address Her Majesty to withhold her assent from any such bill, it should not be lawful for Her Majesty to signify her assent. This section was altered in 1854, by 17-18 Vict., c. 118, s. 6, empowering the Governor to give the Queen's assent.

In the meantime, the Act of 1852, c. 175, was passed by the local Legislature in 1851 and, as required by the statute of 1840, was assented to by Her Majesty at Westminster on May 15, 1852.

It would therefore appear plain from all this legislation that, commencing with the statute of 1774, the phrase "Property and Civil Rights" did not include the right to the exercise and enjoyment of religious profession, that being a matter the subject of special provision in each case, and, by the statute of 1852, made a "fundamental principle" of the *constitution* of the entire country.

It is, of course, well settled that the right to hold any view in matters of religious belief is not a civil right at all except in relation to title to property. [The learned Judge here cited *Forbes v. Eden* (1867), L.R. 1 Sc. & Div. 568.] . . .

The same principle underlies the decision in the *Free Church* case, [1904] A.C. 515; see the judgment of Lord James at p. 655.

This principle was well understood in Canada before 1867. In 1857, by the statute of 20 Vict., c. 43, provision was made for the appointment of Commissioners to reduce into one code "those provisions of the Laws of Lower Canada which relate to *Civil Matters* and are of a general and permanent character". In their second report, dated May 22, 1860, the majority of the Commissioners, in discussing the scope of their terms of reference, refer to a disagreement among the Commissioners on this point.

At p. 149 of vol. I, the majority say:

"On one hand, it is pretended that the laws to be codified are exclusively those upon which the provincial parliament has the right to legislate, and therefore that all those which proceed from or make part of the imperial laws should be omitted. On the other hand it is pretended that the codification required should extend to all classes or categories of laws in force in the province, provided they refer to *civil matters,* from whatever source they come, and that the objection would only be valid in case it should be proposed to repeal or alter these laws, which has never been contemplated; but is without force, for a case like the present, where it is only intended to announce their existence."

The latter view was that of the majority and, while the draft code in its first title is concerned with the enjoyment and loss of "civil rights", it does not deal with the subject-matter of the Act of 1852, although it does deal with the loss of civil rights occasioned by the taking of religious vows upon entry into a religious order. The majority view was adopted by the Legislature in the Code of 1866, the relevant provisions being found in arts. 18, 30 and 34 of the First Title. . . .

In the view of the codifiers, therefore, and in that of the Legislature, freedom of worship and profession was not a "civil right" and certainly not a civil right "within" the Province of Lower Canada.

It has been decided by the Judicial Committee that "Property and Civil Rights" in the Act of 1774, although "used in their largest sense" have exactly the same meaning in the statute of 1867: *Citizens Ins. Co. v. Parsons* (1881), 1 App. Cas. 96 at p. 111, *per* Sir Montague Smith. Section 94 of 1867 authorizes Parliament to make provision for the uniformity of all or any of the laws relative to "Property and Civil Rights" in Ontario, Nova Scotia and New Brunswick with the consent of those Provinces.

As pointed out in the *Parsons* case, at p. 110: "The Province of Quebec is omitted from this section for the obvious reason that the law which governs property and civil rights in Quebec is in the main the French law as it existed at the time of the cession of Canada, and not the English law which prevails in other provinces."

It is equally obvious that so far as the law relating to freedom of worship and profession is concerned, that law was not the French law but rather the statute of 1852, which applied equally to both of the Canadas. . . .

Galipeault J., also, in *Saumur v. Québec* (1948), 26 Can. Bar Rev. at p. 780, in referring to the subject-matter of the very by-law here in question, says (and in my opinion, with respect, perfectly correctly): "And it behooves us to remember that we are here concerned with a matter of public law rather than of 'droit'."

Any contention that the right to the exercise of religion is a mere "civil right" is, therefore, for these reasons quite untenable in my opinion. Even if such a matter could be so regarded, it would not be a civil right "within the Province".

The *B.N.A. Act* itself indicates, in my opinion, that the subject-matter of religious profession is not a matter of provincial legislative jurisdiction within any of the heads of s. 92.

By s. 93 it is enacted that a provincial Legislature may legislate "in relation to" education but subject, *inter alia,* to the provision that:

"(1) Nothing in any law shall prejudicially affect any Right or Privilege with respect to Denominational Schools which any Class of Persons have by Law in the Province at the Union."

The "class" in s-s. (1) must, as stated by the Judicial Committee in *Ottawa Separate School Trustees v. Mackell*, 32 D.L.R. 1 at p. 4, [1917] A.C. 62 at p. 69, be a class determined "according to religious belief". The right or privilege preserved by s-s. (1) to such a class with respect to its denominational schools is such only as existed "by law" at the time of Union. It would in my opinion be absurd to say that a provincial Legislature, while it cannot strike at the right of any such class to impart religious instruction to its adherents, may nevertheless legislate so as to affect or destroy the religious faith of the denomination and thus affect or entirely do away with all necessity for religious instruction in that faith. . . .

ESTEY J.: . . . It will also be observed that in the declaration of this right in the Act of 1851 no penalty is provided for infraction thereof. That would indicate that such was left to the field of criminal law where, in principle, it would seem to belong. The right of the free exercise and enjoyment of religious profession and worship, is a personal, sacred right for which, history records, men have striven and fought. Wherever attained they have resisted restrictions and limitations thereon in every possible manner. In one sense it may be styled a civil right, but it does not follow that it would be included within the phrase "Property and Civil Rights in the Province" within the meaning of s. 92(13) of the *B.N.A. Act*. On the contrary it would rather seem that such a right should be included among those upon which the Parliament of Canada might legislate for the preservation of peace, order and good government.

Moreover, having regard to the nature and character of the right which was, by the *Treaty of Paris,* given "to the inhabitants of the countries ceded" and the legislation of 1851 where it is in the preamble thereto stated "legal equality among all Religious Denominations is an admitted principle of Colonial Legislation" and such "a fundamental principle of our civil polity" that legislative sanction should be given thereto, it would appear that if the draftsmen and those enacting the *B.N.A. Act* intended that legislation in relation to this right should be enacted by the Province and effective in a part, rather than by the Parliament of Canada and, therefore, effective in the country as a whole, that express language to that effect would have been embodied in that enactment, more particularly as by that Act "One Dominion under the Crown . . . with a Constitution similar in Principle to that of the United Kingdom" was created.

Furthermore, if such had not been the intention of those preparing and enacting the *B.N.A. Act* it would seem most unlikely that under s. 93 thereof they would have given, in relation to education, the exclusive legislative authority to the provincial Legislature and then have specifically reserved an appeal "to the Governor General in Council from any Act or Decision of any Provincial Authority affecting any Right or Privilege of the Protestant or Roman Catholic Minority of the Queen's subjects in relation to Education" and given power to the Parliament of Canada to enact legislation, in the absence of appropriate provincial legislation, requisite for the due "Execution of the Provisions" of s. 93 and necessary to give effect to its decision upon any appeal under that section.

It, therefore, appears that legislation in relation to this right comes within the description and classification referred to by Sir Montague E. Smith in *Russell v. The Queen* (1882), 7 App. Cas. 829 at pp. 839-40, where his Lordship, when considering the competence of the Parliament of Canada to enact the *Canada Temperance Act, 1878,* stated: "Law of this nature designed for the promotion of public order, safety, or morals, and which subject those who contravene them to criminal procedure and punishment, belong to the subject of public wrongs rather than to that of civil rights. They are of a nature which fall within the general authority of Parliament to make laws for the order and good government of Canada, and have direct relation to criminal law, which is one of the enumerated classes of subjects assigned exclusively to the Parliament of Canada . . ."

The provision of the enactment of 1851 (assented to in 1852), being legislation under s. 91 of the *B.N.A. Act,* by virtue of s. 129 thereof continued in force after Confederation and thereafter could be repealed, abolished or altered by the Parliament of Canada but not by a provincial Legislature. It has never been repealed or altered by that Parliament and, therefore, remains in force. The enactment, therefore, of s. 2 of c. 307 by the Province of Quebec, being legislation in relation to this right, could not be enacted under either heading (13) (Property and Civil Rights in the Province) or heading (16) (Generally all Matters of a merely local or private Nature in the Province) of s. 92 of the *B.N.A. Act.* . . .

CARTWRIGHT J. (dissenting): . . . In my view, legislation authorizing the City to pass this by-law is *prima facie* in relation to either or both of two subjects within the provincial power which may be conveniently described as (1) the use of highways, and (ii) police regulations and the suppression of conditions likely to cause disorder. I propose to deal with these in the order mentioned.

The judgments of this Court in *O'Brien v. Allen* (1900), 30 S.C.R. 340, and in *Prov. Sec. of P.E.I. v. Egan,* [1941] 3 D.L.R. 305, S.C.R. 396, 76 Can. C.C. 227, established that the use of highways in the Province is a subject-matter within the provincial power. . . .

It appears to me to follow from the judgments in *O'Brien v. Allen, supra,* and *Prov. Sec. of P.E.I. v. Egan, supra,* that the legislative authority to permit, forbid or regulate the use of the highways for purposes other than of passing and repassing belongs to the Province.

Dealing next with the subject of police regulations and the suppression of conditions likely to cause disorder, it appears that this Court has decided that the Province has power to legislate in relation to such matters. [The learned Judge referred here to *Bédard v. Dawson, Reference re Adoption Act,* and *Lymburn v. Mayland*]. . . .

It follows from these authorities that it is within the competence of the Legislature of the Province to prohibit or regulate the distribution, in the streets of the municipalities in the Province, of written matter having a tendency to insult or annoy the recipients thereof with the possible result of giving rise to disorder, and perhaps violence, in the streets.

It is said, however, if I have correctly apprehended the argument for the appellant, that even if the legislation in question appears *prima facie* to fall within the powers of the provincial Legislature under the two heads with which I have dealt above it is in reality an enactment destructive of the freedom of the press and the freedom of religion both of which are submitted to be matters as to which the Province has no power to legislate. In support of such submission counsel referred to a large number of cases decided in the Courts of the United States of America but I am unable to derive any assistance from them as they appear to be founded on provisions in the Constitution limiting the power to make laws in relation to such matters. Under the *B.N.A. Act,* on the other hand, the whole range of legislative power is committed either to Parliament or the provincial Legislatures and competence to deal with any subject-matter must exist in one or other of such bodies. There are thus no rights possessed by the citizens of Canada which cannot be modified by either Parliament or the Legislatures, but it may often be a matter of difficulty to decide which of such bodies has the legislative power in a particular case. . . .

In my view, freedom of the press is not a separate subject-matter committed exclusively to either Parliament or the Legislatures. In some respects, Parliament, and in others, the Legislatures may validly deal with it. In some aspects it falls within the field of criminal law, but in others it has been dealt with by provincial legislation, the validity of which is not open to question, as for example the *Libel and Slander Act,* R.S.O. 1950, c. 204, and the similar Acts in the other Provinces. If the subject-matter of a provincial enactment falls within the class of subjects enumerated in s. 92 of the *B.N.A. Act* such enactment does not, in my opinion, cease to be *intra vires* of the Legislature by reason of the fact that it has the effect of cutting down the freedom of the press. The question of legislative competence is to be determined not by inquiring whether the enactment lays a previous restraint upon publication or attaches consequences after publication has occurred but rather by inquiring whether in substance the subject-matter dealt with falls within the provincial power. I have already indicated my view that the Province has power under the two headings which I have discussed above to authorize the passing of the by-law in question. . . .

It may well be that Parliament alone has power to make laws in relation to the subject of religion as such, that that subject is, in its nature, one which concerns Canada as a whole and so cannot be regarded as of a merely local or private nature in any Province or as a civil right in any Province; but we are not called upon to decide that question in this appeal and I express no opinion upon it. I think it clear that the Provinces, legislating within their allotted sphere, may affect the carrying on of activities connected with the practice of religion. For example, there are many municipal by-laws in force in cities in Ontario, passed pursuant to powers conferred by the provincial Legislature, which provide that no buildings other than private residences shall be erected on certain streets. Such by-laws are, in my opinion, clearly valid although they prevent any religious body from building a church or similar edifice on such streets. Another example of provincial legislation which might be said to interfere directly with the free exercise of religious profession is that under which the by-law considered in *Re Cribbin & Toronto,* 21 O.R. 325, was passed. That was a by-law of the City of Toronto which provided in part: "No person shall on the Sabbath-day, in any public park, square, garden, or place for exhibition in the city of Toronto, publicly preach, lecture, or declaim." The by-law was attacked on the ground, *inter alia,* that it was unconstitutional but it was upheld by Galt C.J. and in my opinion his decision was right. No useful purpose would be served by endeavouring to define the limits of the provincial power to pass legislation affecting the carrying on of activities connected with the practice of religion. The better course is, I think, to deal only with the particular legislation now before us. . . .

To summarize, I am of opinion that it was within the competence of the Legislature to authorize the passing of the by-law in question under its power to legislate in relation to (i) the use of highways, and (ii) police regulations and the suppression of conditions likely to cause disorder; and that such legislation is not rendered invalid because it interferes to the limited extents indicated above with either the freedom of the press or the freedom of religion. It follows that I would dismiss the appeal. . . .

Appeal allowed.

[Locke J. read the by-law as addressed in pith and substance to censorship, hence *ultra vires* under the principles announced by Sir Lyman Duff C.J. in *Re Alberta Legislation,* [1938] S.C.R. 100 at p. 132, 2 D.L.R. 81 at p. 106; affirmed [1939] A.C. 117, [1938] 3 W.W.R. 337, [1938] 4 D.L.R. 433 (*sub nom. A.-G. Alta. v. A.-G. Can.*) Taschereau J., dissenting, concurred with Rinfret C.J.C. and Fauetux J., dissenting, concurred with Cartwright J. The formal judgment of the Court was as follows:

"The appeal is allowed and the judgment of the Court of Queen's Bench (Appeal Side) set aside. It is declared that By-law 184 of the City of Quebec passed on October 27, 1933, does not extend so as to prohibit the appellant as a member of Jehovah's Witnesses from distributing in the streets of Quebec any book, pamphlet, booklet, circular or tract of Jehovah's Witnesses included in the exhibits. The City of Quebec, its officers and agents are restrained from in any way interfering with such actions of the appellant.

The Chief Justice, Taschereau, Cartwright and Fauteux JJ. dissenting would have dismissed the appeal.

Rand, Kellock, Estey and Locke JJ. would have declared the by-law *ultra vires.*

The appellant is entitled to his costs throughout against the City of Quebec, except that nothing is allowed for, or in connection with, his

factum in this Court. No order is made as to costs for or against the intervenant, the Attorney-General of Quebec."
The *Saumur* case is discussed by *Laskin*, Our Civil Liberties—The Role of the Supreme Court, (1955) 41 Queen's Quarterly 455.]

Boyd C. in *Re North Perth, Hessin v. Lloyd* (1891), 21 O.R. 538, at p. 542, after making the obvious statement that "Ontario has no legislative power over the electoral franchise of the Dominion", went on to discuss electoral legislation in general, whether federal or provincial, and assessed it as follows:

> The subjects of this class of legislation are of a political character, dealing with the citizen as related to the Commonwealth (whether province or Dominion), and they are kept distinct in the Federal Constitutional Act from matters of civil rights in the Provinces which regard mainly the *meum* and *tuum* as between citizens. It is in my view rather confusing to speak of the right of voting as comprehended under the 'civil rights' mentioned in sec. 92 sub-s. 13 of the B.N.A. Act. This franchise is not an ordinary civil right; it is historically and truly a statutory privilege of a political nature, being the chief means whereby the people, organized for political purposes, have their share in the functions of government. The question in hand, therefore, falls within the category not of 'civil rights in the Province', but of electoral rights in Canada.

Note on Provincial Regulation of Business

In Canada, as in the United States, there has been judicial acknowledgement that the federal commerce power by its mere existence as such, may preclude provincial or state regulation; but this very acknowledgement makes sense only according to the judicial appreciation of the ambit of the power. While it is difficult to measure the relative generosity or strictness with which the preclusion rule is administered, it is a fair estimate to say that notwithstanding the wider scope given to the commerce power in the United States, its Supreme Court has remained sensitive to local needs both where Congress has not yet legislated and within areas untouched by Congressional legislation: see *Powell*, Vagaries and Varieties in Constitutional Interpretation (1956), chap. V. at pp. 176 ff; see, for example, *Brotherhood of Locomotive Firemen and Enginemen v. Chicago Rock Island & Pacific R. Co.* (1968), 89 S. Ct. 323.

In Canada, the constitutional basis of legislation for local needs, or local market or trade regulation, has been predicated on an *a priori* reduction in the strength of the federal commerce power. In the result, provincial legislation (absent any federal legislation) has been struck down (1) where it avowedly, or as construed, embraced export or import control as a matter of interprovincial or foreign trade movement: see *Lawson v. Interior Tree, Fruit & Vegetable Committee*, [1931] S.C.R. 357, [1931] 2 D.L.R. 193; *Crickard v. A.-G. B.C.* (1958), 14 D.L.R. (2d) 58, 25 W.W.R. 485; and cf. *A.-G. B.C. v. McDonald Murphy Lumber Co.*, [1930] A.C. 357, [1930] 2 D.L.R.

721, [1930] 1 W.W.R. 830; *Rex v. Nat Bell Liquors Ltd.*, [1922] 2
A.C. 128, at p. 136, 65 D.L.R. 1, at p. 6, [1922] 2 W.W.R. 30, at p. 38;
and (2) where the economic facts attending a purported provincial
regulation of marketing or trade revealed that the legislation's only
perceptible effect would be on exports: see *In re Grain Marketing
Act, 1931,* [1931] 2 W.W.R. 146, 25 Sask. L. R. 273; *Re Sheep and
Swine Marketing Scheme.* [1941] 3 D.L.R. 569 (P.E.I. C.A.). While
Severn v. The Queen (1878), 2 S.C.R. 70 went farther in precluding
provincial legislation by reason of the federal commerce power, it
became a discredited authority.

The specifications in s. 92(13) and s. 92(16) have been used, singly
and together, to sustain provincial control of economic activities, but
it has never been made clear when the one may be invoked rather than
the other. As has already been noted, the Privy Council did not conclude until the *Manitoba Licence Holders* case, [1902] A.C. 73, that
provincial liquor licensing legislation was in relation to "matters of a
merely local or private nature in the Province". On the other hand,
marketing regulation, and regulation of trade, and trades in general,
have been ascribed by the Privy Council to power in relation to "property and civil rights in the Province". There are good historical reasons, as well as reasons of context, why regulation of economic activity
by the Provinces should be subsumed under s. 92(16) rather than s.
92(13); and this is the view supported by Rand J. in the *Ontario Farm
Products Marketing Act* reference, [1957] S.C.R. 198, 7 D.L.R. (2d)
257. However, the majority in that case sustained the provincial legislation by reliance on both s. 92(13) and s. 92(16), with advertence by
some to s. 92(9) as well.

2.   Territorial Limitations on Provincial Regulatory Power: The Mean-ing of "In the Province"

The Parliament of Canada was, apparently, precluded from legislating with extra-territorial effect, although this was not explicit in
the *British North America Act* in its case as it was, by and large, in
respect of the provincial legislatures; see *Nadan v. The King,* [1926]
A.C. 482, [1926] 2 D.L.R. 177, [1926] 1 W.W.R. 801, 45 C.C.C. 221.

Section 3 of the *Statute of Westminster,* 1931 (U.K.), Chapter
4 expressly authorized Parliament to legislate with extra-territorial
effect, although it may be doubted in view of *Croft v. Dunphy,* [1933]
A.C. 156, [1933] 1 D.L.R. 225, 59 C.C.C. 141, [1932] 3 W.W.R. 696,
whether this provision was really necessary; see *O'Connell,* The Doctrine of Colonial Extra-territorial Legislative Incompetence, (1959)
75 Law Quarterly Rev. 318; and see *B.C. Electric Railway Company
v. The King,* [1946] A.C. 527, [1946] 4 D.L.R. 81, [1946] 3 W.W.R.
737, 60 C.R.T.C. 105, [1946] C.T.C. 226.

The terms of the *Statute of Westminster,* however, spoke expressly
of "the Parliament of a Dominion", thus leaving unchanged the position of the Canadian provinces as well as of the Australian states. The
beginning words of s. 92, *B.N.A. Act,* reinforced by similar expressions

internally for the listed classes of subjects therein and by like language in other sections, *e.g.* Education, s. 93, Agriculture, s. 95, make it very plain that conduct beyond the borders of a province lies outside of provincial authority to regulate. What official recognition of matters occurring outside shall be extended within the provinces may be another question.

The provincial limitation of taxation to taxation "within the province", s. 92(2), while a branch of the principle against extra-territoriality of provincial authority, has had its own elaborate and particular development, which is discussed *infra*. The cases which follow are illustrative of the operation of the limitation outside the tax sphere.

ROYAL BANK OF CANADA v. THE KING

In the Privy Council. [1913] A.C. 283, 9 D.L.R. 337, 3 W.W.R. 994.

Appeal from a judgment of the Supreme Court of Alberta *en banc*, 1 W.W.R. 1159, affirming a judgment of Stuart J., 1 W.W.R. 1, in favour of respondents.

VISCOUNT HALDANE L.C.: . . . The main controversy is as to the validity of a statute of the Legislature of Alberta passed in 1910 [c. 9], and dealing with the proceeds of sale of certain bonds. These proceeds had been deposited with certain banks, one of them being the appellant bank. The judgment under appeal was given in an action brought by the Government of Alberta against the Royal Bank of Canada, the Alberta and Great Waterways Railway Company, and the Canada West Construction Company, to recover $6,043,083.26, with interest, being the amount of the deposit held by the appellant bank. The Court of first instance and the Court of Appeal of the province have given judgment for the Government.

It is contended by the appellants that the statute in question was not validly enacted. It is said to have been *ultra vires* of the Legislature of the province as attempting to interfere with property and civil rights outside the province, and also as trenching on the field of legislation as to banking, which, by s. 91 of the British North America Act, is reserved to the Parliament of Canada. It is further said that inasmuch as the statute purported to make the deposits part of the general revenue fund of the province, it was inoperative as being an attempt to raise revenue for provincial purposes in a manner not authorized by s. 92 of that Act. In order to determine the points thus raised, it is necessary to examine the transactions to which the legislative action of the Alberta Government was directed.

The appellant railway company was incorporated by an Act of the Legislature of the province, being c. 46 of 1909, for the purpose of constructing and operating a railway to extend from Edmonton in a north-easterly direction, and to be wholly within the province. The capital was to be $7,000,000, and the company was empowered to issue bonds. By another Act of the same session, being c. 16, which received the Royal assent on the same day, February 25, the Government of Alberta was authorized to guarantee the principal and interest of the bonds to be issued by the railway company to the extent of $20,000 a mile up to 350 miles, with a further amount in respect of the cost of terminals. The bonds were to be repayable in fifty years, and were to bear interest at the rate of 5 per cent. By s. 2 it was provided that the bonds so guaranteed were to be secured by mortgage to be made to trustees, which was to cover the railway, its rolling stock and equipment, and its revenues, rights, and powers. By s. 3 the form and terms of the bonds, mortgage, and guarantees were to be approved by the Lieutenant-Governor in Council. By s. 4, when the guarantees were signed on behalf of the Government, the province was to be liable for payment of principal and interest, and no person entitled to the bonds was to be under the necessity of inquiry in respect of compliance with the terms of the Act. By s. 5 all moneys realized by sale, pledge, or otherwise of the bonds were to be paid by the purchaser, subscriber, pledgee, or lender into a bank or banks approved by the Lieutenant-Governor in Council, to the credit of a special account in the name of the Treasurer of the province, or such other credit as the Lieutenant-Governor in Council should direct. The balance at the credit of the special account or accounts was to be credited with interest at such times and at such rate as might be agreed on between the company and the bank holding the same, and such balance was from time to time to be paid out to the company or its nominee, in monthly payments so far as practicable, as the construction of the lines of railway and the terminals was proceeded with to the satisfaction of the Lieutenant-Governor in Council according to specifications to be fixed by contract between the Government and the company and in such sums as an engineer appointed by the Lieutenant-Governor in Council should certify as justified, provided that at the option of the company the moneys so paid into the bank should, instead of being so paid out, be paid to the company on the completion, as certified by the engineer to the satisfaction of the Lieutenant-Governor in Council, of sections and terminals specified. The balance of the proceeds of the bonds which might remain after completion of the railway was to be paid over to the company or its nominee. Sect. 5 concluded with a provision, which appears to have been inaccurately printed, but which their Lordships interpret as bearing the meaning put on it in an Order in Council subsequently made by the Lieutenant-Governor on October 7, 1909, that the balance at the credit of the special account remaining until paid out as above arranged for was to be deemed part of the mortgaged premises under the mortgage, and not public moneys received by the province.

On October 7 two Orders in Council were made by the Lieutenant-Governor. The first of these, after reciting the Incorporating Act and the Guarantee Act above referred to, approved forms of mortgage and a guarantee, authorized the proper officials to execute them, and designated the Standard Trusts Company as the trustee under the mortgage deed. This Order also, pending the preparation of engraved bonds, authorized the guarantee of a single printed bond without coupons for the entire sum to be covered by the bonds, $7,400,000, to be exchanged for the engraved bonds in due course. By the second of these Orders, after reciting that the company had elected to receive the money on completion of sections and of terminals on a progress basis, certain banks, including the appellant bank, were designated as the banks into which the proceeds of the bonds were to be paid in accordance with the Guarantee Act. By an Order made on November 9 the list of banks was varied, but the appellant bank remained included, and the deposit out of the proceeds of the bonds of $6,000,000, being the principal included in the amount sued for, was assigned to it. This Order recited that it was the understanding of the Government that on the proper interpretation of the last-mentioned Act the moneys in question, when paid into the banks, not being public moneys received by the province, could only be withdrawn on the terms stated in the Act. The second Order of October 7 had approved the terms of the preliminary bond in a form which made the principal and interest payable in London at the counting-house of Messrs. Morgan, Grenfell & Co. The terms of the bond provided that it should be secured by a mortgage from the railway company to the Standard Trusts Company and for the guarantee of principal and interest by the province. The bond was to be registered in the books of the company in London, and transfers were to be made in these books.

Shortly after the making of the two Orders in Council of October 7 arrangements were made in London with Messrs. Morgan, Grenfell & Co. for the raising of the money authorized to be borrowed. To enable the transaction to be carried out, the railway company on October 28 entered into a formal contract with the provincial Government for the construction of at least 350 miles of the line. The contract recited the right of the company to issue bonds in proportion to mileage and terminals and the authority of the Government to guarantee principal and interest to the extent of $20,000 a mile and further sums in respect of terminals, and provided, in accordance with the Guarantee Act, that the proceeds arising from the bonds so issued should be paid into the banks approved by the Lieutenant-Governor in Council to the credit of the Treasurer of the province in a special account, and that such proceeds should from time to time by paid out to the railway company on engineers' certificates. The balance of the proceeds after completion of the railway and terminals was to be paid over to the railway company.

By a deed of the same date made between the railway company, the provincial Government, and the Standard Trusts Company, a company incorporated under the law of Manitoba, and having its head office outside the province, the railway company mortgaged its property to the Trusts Company to secure the bonds for the sum of $7,400,000 and interest at 5 per cent., repayable on January 1, 1959, and the Government guaranteed payment of principal and interest. The security expressly included not only the railway and its rolling stock and equipment, but all real and personal property then or thereafter held or acquired for the purpose of the railway. Later on, on November 22, the railway company entered into a contract with the

appellant construction company, which had been incorporated under
Dominion statutes and had its head office outside the province, for
the construction of the railway, and the railway company agreed to
pay to the construction company the net proceeds of the bond issue,
an agreement which was afterwards supplemented by a formal assignment of March 8, 1910.

Under arrangements with Messrs. Morgan, Grenfell & Co., the
preliminary bond for $7,400,000 already referred to was taken up
by them. A letter of October 11, 1909, from the Deputy Provincial
Treasurer of the province to Messrs. J. P. Morgan & Co., of New York,
shews the method adopted by the Government in carrying out the
transaction. The preliminary bond was to be handed to Messrs.
J. P. Morgan & Co. as agents for the Government. That firm was to
transfer to or hold this bond for Messrs. Morgan, Grenfell & Co., the
immediate takers up of the bond issue in London. The purchase-
money was to be deposited to the credit of the Provincial Treasurer in
the Edmonton branches of the designated banks. These arrangements
were carried out in this fashion. As the proceeds of the bond issue
in London came over to New York the money which was to be applied
and secured, in accordance with the statutes, Orders in Council, and
contracts already referred to, was paid in instalments in New York,
the part with which the appellant bank is concerned being received
by its house in New York, and credited to the Provincial Treasurer
to the railway special account. The bank had its head office in
Montreal and was incorporated under Dominion law. The account
at Edmonton in Alberta was opened there in accordance with the
arrangements already referred to. No money in specie was sent to
the branch office which the bank possessed there, but the general
manager in Montreal arranged for the proper credit to the special
account. It is plain that all these transactions were carried out for
the purpose and on the faith of the statutes, Orders in Council,
contracts, and mortgage deed referred to, and were effected for
the purpose of providing for the construction of the railway with the
security and guarantees which had been given. It is not in dispute
that the Government at this period meant the appellants to understand that it would adhere strictly to the terms of its guarantee.

The construction company commenced the works preliminary to
the construction of the line. No part of the sum at the credit of the
special account was paid out for this purpose, but the bank made
advances, and the construction company assigned to the bank as
security its interest in the proceeds of the bond issue.

The second chapter of the history of the events which resulted
in the appeal before their Lordships opened in March, 1910. There
appears to have been public uneasiness about the action of the
Government in entering into the arrangements above described, and
in the event, a Royal Commission of inquiry was appointed. While it
was sitting there was a change of Government. The new Administration introduced and passed two statutes, and on the validity of the
first of these the question to be decided in the appeal turns. This
statute, which became law on December 16, 1910, after setting out in

its preamble that the railway company had made default in payment of interest on the bonds and in the construction of the line, and then ratifying and confirming the guarantee by the province of the bonds, enacted that the whole of the proceeds of sale of the bonds, and all interest thereon, including such part of the proceeds of sale as was then standing in the banks in the name of the Treasurer of the province or otherwise, and comprising, *inter alia*, the $6,000,000 and accrued interest in the appellant bank, should form part of the general revenue fund of the province free from all claim of the railway company or their assigns, and should be paid over to the Treasurer without deduction. It was also provided that notwithstanding the form of the bonds and guarantee the province should as between itself and the railway company be primarily liable on the bonds and should indemnify the company against claims under them. By another statute passed at the same time any person or corporation claiming to have suffered loss or damage in consequence of the passing of the Act just referred to might submit a claim to the Government to be reported on to the Legislature.

On the day of the passing of these Acts a notice was served on behalf of the Treasurer of the province on the appellant bank claiming payment of $6,042,083.26 and interest, and a cheque was presented to and refused by the bank. A claim against the bank as from this date for interest at the rate of 5 per cent. was then made. The action out of which the appeal arises was immediately launched, claiming, on behalf of the Crown and the Provincial Treasurer, the sum above mentioned from the appellant bank, and the railway company and the construction company were subsequently joined as defendants. The main defence pleaded was the invalidity of the first of the two statutes of 1910, and the bank also claimed a lien for advances to the construction company. The case was tried before Stuart J., who held that the proceeds of the bonds were within the province, and that the matter was one of a local nature in the province. He therefore decided that it fell within class 16 of s. 92 of the British North America Act, and not within s. 91 and that accordingly, the statute having been validly passed, there should be judgment for the plaintiffs. The appellants appealed to the Court of Appeal, which unanimously dismissed the appeal. The Chief Justice held that the statute was probably authorized by classes 10 and 16 of s. 92, and certainly by class 13, relating to property and civil rights. He also decided against the appellants on the further points they made that the Act trenched on the subject of banking legislation in s. 91, and that it was invalid as being confiscatory and not an authorized way of raising a provincial revenue. Beck J., Scott J., and Simmons J. decided against the appeal on substantially the same grounds, though the two latter learned judges differed from the rest of the Court on a minor question as to interest.

Their Lordships are not concerned with the merits of the political controversy which gave rise to the statute the validity of which is impeached. What they have to decide is the question whether it was within the power of the Legislature of the province to pass the Act of 1910. They agree with the contention of the respondent that in a case such as this it was in the power of that Legislature subsequently to repeal any Act which it had passed. If this were the only question which arose the appeal could be disposed of without difficulty. But the Act under consideration does more than modify existing legislation. It purports to appropriate to the province the balance standing at the special accounts in the banks, and so to change its position under the scheme to carry out which the bondholders had subscribed their money. Elaborately as the case was argued in the judgments of the learned judges in the Courts below, their Lordships are not satisfied that what appears to them to be the fundamental question at issue has been adequately considered.

It is a well-established principle of the English common law that when money has been received by one person which in justice and equity belongs to another, under circumstances which render the receipt of it a receipt by the defendant to the use of the plaintiff, the latter may recover as for money had and received to his use. The principle extends to cases where the money has been paid for a consideration that has failed. . . .

The present case appears to their Lordships to fall within [this] broad principle . . . The lenders in London remitted their money to New York to be applied in carrying out the particular scheme which was established by the statutes of 1909 and the Orders in Council, and by the contracts and mortgage of that year. The money claimed in the action was paid to the appellant bank as one of those designated to act in carrying out the scheme. The bank received the money at its branch in New York, and its general manager then gave instructions from the head office in Montreal to the manager of one of its local branches, that at Edmonton in the Province of Alberta, for the opening of the credit for the special account. The local manager was told that he was to act on instructions from the head office, which retained control. It appears to their Lordships that the special account was opened solely for the purpose of the scheme, and that when the action of the Government in 1910 altered its conditions, the lenders in London were entitled to claim from the bank at its head office in Montreal the money which they had advanced solely for a purpose which has ceased to exist. Their right was a civil right outside the province, and the Legislature of the province could not legislate validly in derogation of that right. These circumstances distinguish the case from that of *Rex v. Lovitt*, [1912] A.C. 212, where the point decided was in reality quite a different one.

In the opinion of their Lordships the effect of the statute of 1910, if validly enacted, would have been to preclude the bank from fulfilling its legal obligation to return their money to the bondholders, whose right to this return was a civil right which had arisen, and remained enforceable outside the province. The statute was on this ground beyond the powers of the Legislature of Alberta, inasmuch as what was sought to be enacted was neither confined to property and civil rights within the province nor directed solely to matters of merely local or private nature within it.

Other questions have, as already stated, been raised in this appeal as to whether the statute of 1910 infringed the provisions of s. 91 of the British North America Act, by attempting to deal with a question relating to banking, and by trenching on the field already occupied by the Dominion Banking Act. It was also contended that the appropriation of the deposits to the general revenue fund of the province was outside the powers assigned to the provincial Legislature for raising a revenue for provincial purposes. The conclusion already arrived at makes it unnecessary for their Lordships to enter on the consideration of these questions and of other points which were made during the arguments of counsel.

Their Lordships will humbly advise His Majesty that the appeal should be allowed and the action dismissed. The respondents must pay the costs here and in the Courts below.

Appeal allowed.

[For comment on this case, see *Lefroy*, Canada's Federal System, pp. 504 *et seq.* For a purported application of the case, see *Credit Foncier Franco-Canadian v. Ross*, [1937] 3 D.L.R. 365, [1937] 2 W.W.R. 353. *Cf. Workmen's Compensation Board v. C.P.R.*, [1920] A.C. 184, 48 D.L.R. 218, [1919] 3 W.W.R. 167.]

BEAUHARNOIS LIGHT, HEAT & POWER CO. LTD. v. HYDRO-ELECTRIC POWER COMMISSION OF ONTARIO

In the Ontario Court of Appeal. [1937] O.R. 796, [1937] 3 D.L.R. 458.

Appeal by defendants from a judgment of Rose C.J.H.C. in an action to enforce an agreement for the sale of electrical power. The trial judgment was, in part, as follows:

Rose C.J.H.C.: The plaintiff, Beauharnois, Light, Heat and Power Company, hereinafter sometimes referred to as the Beauharnois Company or the company, is a company incorporated by ch. 72 of the Quebec Statutes of 1902, which Act was amended in 1910, 1928, 1930, and 1932. The head office of the company is in Montreal. The plaintiff Beauharnois Power Corporation, Limited, is a company incorporated under the laws of the Dominion of Canada and having its head office in Montreal. The plaintiff Montreal Trust Company is a corporation incorporated under the laws of the Province of Quebec and having its head office at Montreal and branch offices at Toronto and elsewhere; it is the trustee for the holders of bonds issued by the Beauharnois Company and by Beauharnois Power Corporation Limited. The plaintiff Iselin Corporation of Canada is the holder of bonds issued by the Beauharnois Company and also bonds issued by Beauharnois Power Corporation. The defendants are the Attorney-

General of Ontario, the Hydro-Electric Power Commission of Ontario, hereinafter referred to as the Commission, and the Royal Trust Company. The Commission is a corporation organized under the Power Commission Act which is an Act first passed as ch. 15 of the Ontario Statutes of 1906, repealed and with some changes re-enacted as ch. 19 of the Statutes of 1907, and now to be found in ch. 57 of the Revised Statutes of 1927 and some later amendments.

The plaintiffs claim as against all the defendants a declaration of the invalidity of ch. 53 of the Ontario Statutes of 1935 intituled The Power Commission Act, 1935, or of sec. 2(c) whereby a contract or "power agreement", entered into between the Beauharnois Company and the Commission dated November 29, 1929, is "declared to be and always to have been illegal, void and unenforceable as against the Hydro-Electric power Commission of Ontario", and of sec. 3 whereby it is enacted that "No action or other proceedings shall be brought, maintained or proceeded with against the said Commission founded upon any contract by this Act declared to be void and unenforceable, or arising out of the performance or non-performance of any of the terms of the said" contract; and as against the defendant Commission (a) a declaration that the power agreement is valid and binding and still in force, and (b) a declaration that the arbitration provision of the power agreement is binding upon the Commission. As against the Commission, and so far as it is concerned, the Royal Trust Company, the plaintiffs claim a declaration that the Montreal Trust Company, the Royal Trust Company and all holders of bonds issued by the Beauharnois Company or Beauharnois Power Corporation are entitled, notwithstanding the Act of 1935, to exercise the rights and privileges conferred on them by the first and second mortgage trust deeds of the Beauharnois Company and a certain collateral trust deed and supplemental trust deed of the Beauharnois Power Corporation.

The Beauharnois Company claims as against the Commission payment of certain sums which by the terms of the power agreement become due on November 20 and December 20, 1935, and January 20, 1936, respectively, and interest on such sums; or, alternatively, if the Act of 1935 is *intra vires,* (a) a declaration that, notwithstanding the Act, the Commission is liable under the power agreement to the date of the proclamation of the Act, and a reference to take accounts and the payment of the amount found due; and (b) a declaration that the Commission is liable to repay to the Beauharnois Company a sum of $400,000 paid by the Beauharnois Company to the Commission under what the plaintiffs call a "rebate agreement" together with interest. The Beauharnois Power Corporation claims as against the Commission if the Act is *intra vires* a declaration that the Power Corporation is no longer bound by a guarantee which it gave of the obligations of the Beauharnois Company. By consent it was at the trial ordered that the issues raised by the alternative claims just mentioned of the Beauharnois Company against the Commission and the claim just mentioned of the Power Corporation against the Commission should not be tried with the other claims but should stand subject to such directions for trial as might thereafter be made upon application by any of the parties to the action.

The notice required by sec. 32 of The Judicature Act, R.S.O. 1927, ch. 88, when the constitutional validity of an Act of the Legislature is to be brought in question was given to the Attorney-General for Canada, but he did not instruct counsel to appear at the trial. The Attorney-General of Ontario by his statement of defence took the position that he was not properly joined as a defendant, and also that the plaintiffs are prevented by the provisions of sec. 6(4) of The Power Commission Act and by sec. 3 of The Power Commission Act, 1935, from bringing or maintaining this action against the Commission and that none of the relief claimed in the action can be granted in an action to which the Commission is not properly a party; and, without waiving any of his objections that the action is not maintainable against him, he pleaded that the Act of 1935 was *intra vires* the Legislature of Ontario and that, apart from the provisions of that Act, the contract between the Beauharnois Company and the Commission always was illegal, void and unenforceable as declared by the Act. . . .

The power contract is an agreement on the part of the company to keep available for delivery to the Commission and deliver to the Commission when and as required by the Commission specified quantities of horsepower of electrical power and energy, and on the part of the Commission to pay monthly for all power and energy under the agreement at a specified rate. Thirty-five thousand horsepower was to be available and to constitute the "contract demand" from October 1, 1932, and additional amounts were to be available and constitute the contract demand on and from October 1, 1933, October 1, 1934, October 1, 1935, and October 1, 1936. Payment was to be made on the 20th day of each month for the "accrual of the preceding calendar month", and arrears were to bear interest at the rate of 6 per cent. per annum. The quantities that were to be available in 1932, 1933, 1934 and 1935 were made available. Until November, 1935, the Commission paid for the blocks of power made available in October, 1932, October, 1933, and October, 1934; but the statute of 1935 having been passed in April, 1935, the Commission, on September 21, 1935 (although the Act was not brought into force until December 6, 1935), notified the company that payment would not be made for the additional block that was to be ready for delivery on October 1, 1935; and since November 20, 1935, the Commission has not paid for any power. The writ was issued on February 11, 1936, and the statement of claim was delivered on February 28, 1936. At that time there was due, according to the terms of the contract, $573,750 with interest from the days on which the payments respectively became due.

The point of delivery specified in the contract was the boundary between the Provinces of Ontario and Quebec, not farther than five miles from Lake Francis; the company was to instal the suitable and necessary transformers and transmission lines with circuits of all of a number, type and capacity approved by the Commission; all electric power and energy supplied under the agreement was to be measured at the 240,000 volt step-up transformers at the company's station; the power and energy delivered was to be alternating, three-phase, having a controlled average periodicity of 25 cycles per second. In the market for power available to the company in Quebec the power used is 60-cycle power and the company's apparatus installed for the purpose of the contract with the Commission cannot without extensive alteration be made available for delivery of 60-cycle power. . . .

In the preamble to The Power Commission Act, 1935, 25 Geo. V, ch. 53, it is stated that it never was the intention of the Legislature of Ontario that the Commission should have authority to impose financial and other obligations without consent upon the municipal corporations, power users, and taxpayers of the province; and that the Commission, without the consent of the municipalities or the ratepayers, purported to obligate itself to purchase large quantities of power generated without the Province of Ontario, regardless of whether or not the said power was desired or could be used by the municipalities. These statements are not repeated in any statement of defence, and at the trial no evidence in support of them was tendered, counsel for the Attorney-General and the Commission treating the question as to the initial validity of the power contract as a question to be determined, first upon a consideration of the powers which the incorporating Acts professed to confer upon the contracting parties, and, secondly, in case it should be held that the provinces respectively had professed to confer the requisite powers, upon a consideration of the legislative capacity of the provinces to authorize the making of such a contract. . .

At the time of the trial of this action the appeal to the Court of Appeal against the judgment dismissing the similar action brought by Ottawa Valley Power Company and others against the Attorney-General, the Commission, and the trustee for the holders of bonds issued by the Ottawa Valley Company had been argued and was standing for judgment. The judgment has now been pronounced ([1937] O.R. 265 at p. 304), and, to the extent to which a judgment of a Court in Ontario can settle them, it settles many of the questions that were argued in this case.

In the *Ottawa Valley* case the judgment at the trial was based upon the opinion that sec. 6(4) of The Power Commission Act, R.S.O. 1927, ch. 57, was a valid exercise of the provincial legislative power, and that by the judgments in *Beach v. Hydro-Electric Power Commission of Ontario* (1924-5), 56 O.L.R. 35, 57 O.L.R. 603, [1927] S.C.R. 251, the subsection had been given an interpretation which put it out of the power of a Court in Ontario to hold that, rightly interpreted, the subsection does not apply to an action against the Commission founded upon a breach by the Commission itself of a contract entered into by the Commission, but only to an action for something done or omitted by a member (or by members: see The

Interpretation Act, R.S.O. 1927, ch. 1, sec. 28(i)) in the exercise of his (or their) office (or offices). The Court of Appeal (The Chief Justice in Appeal and Riddell J.A., dissenting), has reversed that judgment and has pronounced judgment in favour of the Ottawa Valley Company against the Commission for the amount which, by the terms of the contract sued upon, is payable. The judgment is not a decision that sec. 6(4) of The Power Commission Act is to be given the meaning above suggested; and it is not a decision that sec. 6(4) is for all purposes invalid. But it is a decision that the subsection is not effective to render the obtaining of the consent of the Attorney-General a condition precedent to the institution and prosecution of an action of the kind that was before the Court in the *Ottawa Valley* case; and the present action, being an action of the very same kind, I am bound by the judgment to hold that the want of the consent specified in the subsection is not a bar. Whether the prohibition contained in sec. 3 of The Power Commission Act, 1935, is effective is another question that will be discussed later on.

The Court of Appeal has upheld the initial validity of the contracts that were in question in the *Ottawa Valley* case. Four contracts had been entered into between the Ottawa Valley Company and the Commission. One of them, called the Joint Development Agreement, provided, *inter alia*, that the parties jointly should undertake the development necessary for the utilization of the total power available from and with the use of the waters of the Ottawa River at Chats Falls; that there should be certain works constructed by the parties individually in their respective provinces, and certain joint works; that (with some exceptions) works and rights on the Ontario side of the interprovincial boundary, whether acquired or constructed as a joint expenditure or otherwise, and held or used for and in connection with the joint development should be the separate property of the Commission, and that works and rights on the Quebec side similarly held or used should be the property of the company; and that an executive board of which each party should appoint one-half of the members should approve plans, let contracts, and supervise generally the carrying out of the joint works. Another of the agreements, called the Power Contract, required the company to keep available for the Commission and to deliver to the Commission, when and as required, certain specified quantities of electrical power and energy, the Commission agreeing to pay at specified rates for all power and energy under the contract. The third of the agreements, called the Transformer Agreement, provided for the erection and ownership by the Commission of a transformer station on land owned by the Commission in Ontario and for the payment by the company annually of a certain percentage of the cost of construction and one-half of the costs of maintenance and operation. The fourth of the agreements was called the Operating Contract. By it, the Commission was appointed the company's agent to operate the company's works necessary for the delivery of power to the Commission under the Power Contract.

The claim upon which the Court of Appeal had to pass was the claim of the Ottawa Valley Company against the Commission for the price of power delivered or held in reserve under the Power Contract; but necessarily the Power Contract had to be considered as part of the general agreement for the development and utilization of the water power, which was partly in Ontario and partly in Quebec. It was contended that neither the Commission nor the company, each of them being a provincial corporation, had capacity to enter into the agreements; that the Province of Ontario had not, by The Power Commission Act, professed to endow the Commission with such capacity; that, regard being had to sec. 92(10) (a) of The British North America Act, a province cannot confer power to carry on the operation of transmitting electrical energy across the boundary between two provinces; and that what one province cannot do separately two provinces acting in concert cannot accomplish. But the Court decided that the Power Contract was valid and enforceable; and that decision settles for a trial Judge in Ontario the question as to the initial validity of the contract sued upon in the present case. If it was within the power of the Commission to enter into the Power Contract, tied up as it was with the Joint Development Agreement, by which the Commission bound itself to join in the development and utilization of the water power of an interprovincial river, and with the Operating Contract, by which the Commission bound itself to operate a plant in Quebec, there can be no question of the power of the Commission, by the contract sued upon in this action, to bind itself to pay for power kept available for it and, if demanded, delivered to it by the Beauharnois Company.

The Court of Appeal decided also that it was beyond the power of the Provincial Legislature to pass so much of sec. 2 of the Power Commission Act, 1935, as declares that the "Power Contract" and the "Operating Contract" entered into between the Commission and the Ottawa Valley Company are and always have been illegal, void and unenforceable as against the Commission, the ground of the decision being that the contracts had created rights which were not wholly "in the Province" and which could not be destroyed by the exercise of the power conferred by sec. 92(13) of The British North America Act. If, then, the contract between the Commission and the Beauharnois Company also creates rights which are not wholly in the province, so much of sec. 2 of the Act of 1935 as makes the same declaration concerning that contract must also be held to have been beyond the provincial legislative power.

Now the contract with the Beauharnois Company does not, as did the contract with the Ottawa Valley Company, call for payment to be made in Quebec; it provides for payment by the deposit of money to the credit of the company at such bank or other place in Toronto as may be designated by the company; and the Commission is not by the contract with the Beauharnois Company called upon to construct, or to join in constructing, or to operate works situate in Quebec, as it had to do under the Joint Development Agreement and the Operating Contract made with the Ottawa Valley Company.

There is that much difference between the two cases. But by the contract with Beauharnois Company the Commission acquires many rights in respect of the company's property situate in Quebec. For instance, the company must keep certain specified amounts of power available for delivery to the Commission; the company (clause 1(g)) must instal equipment of a specified capacity and (clause 2(a)) suitable for the delivery of electric energy having a stated "periodicity" and at a stated voltage; the voltage and frequency (clause 2(b)) must, from time to time on the demand of the Commission, be increased or diminished "in order to ensure operation satisfactory to the Commission in parallel with other sources of supply"; and because the high-voltage circuits involved in the agreement are to be physically connected and operated in parallel with those from other power sources, the parties (clause 2(g)) are to co-operate in respect of matters of common interest, including the design of plant and equipment, as will best serve to maintain the system as a whole; access to the company's measuring instruments and transformers shall be free to the Commission at any and all times (clause 4(e)), and the Commission may, after a specified notice, test those instruments and transformers; the company must make certain tests of its meters and adjust any of them that are found to be inaccurate; the Commission (clause 4(g)) may instal duplicate measuring instruments at the company's plant; and representatives of the Commission (clause 6) may from time to time inspect the premises, apparatus, plants, property and records of the company. Thus the Commission took under the contract many rights which were not in the Province of Ontario and which are lost if the contract is made null and void. It is difficult to say whether the words of the Act "as against the Commission" are intended to qualify the words "illegal" and "void", or whether they qualify only the word "unenforceable": that is to say, it seems to be questionable whether the contract is declared to be illegal and void and as against the Commission unenforceable, or whether it is meant that as against the Commission, nothing being said about the company, the contract is illegal, void and unenforceable. It is not clear that one rather than the other of these constructions was adopted by the Court of Appeal, although the judgment of Middleton J.A. seems to indicate that he took the former to be the correct one; but it would be difficult to see how the Commission's rights under the contract could remain unaffected by the termination of the Commission's obligations; and so it seems that, whatever may have been intended, the section, if effective, must operate upon rights which are not in the province. That being so, the decision of the Court of Appeal applies and the section, in so far as it relates to the contract here in question, must be held to be *ultra vires*.

There is a passage in the judgment of Middleton J.A. in the *Ottawa Valley* case which would indicate that the foregoing consideration of the terms of the contract, for the purpose of discovering whether rights over property situate in Quebec are affected by the statute, was unnecessary. Middleton J.A., [1937] O.R. 265, at p. 304, says:

"A contract creates civil rights which, speaking generally, know no territorial limitation. When legislation . . . purports . . . to destroy the contract itself, that legislation does not concern 'Civil Rights in the Province', but is an attempt to destroy civil rights which have no territorial limitation, and, in my view, it is *ultra vires* of the Province."

That statement, however, may be broader than was necessary for the decision of the case in which it was made, and it was not in terms adopted by Masten J.A., or Fisher J.A., and so I have thought it better to deal, not with contracts in general, but with the particular contract here in question and the rights which under it were to be exercised, not in Ontario but in Quebec. The fact that such of those rights as have been mentioned are rights of the Commission rather than of the company, and that the Commission is upholding the validity of the statute, is unimportant; for the question is purely one of legislative power, and legislative power is conferred by The British North America Act, and in no sense by consent. . . .

The Court of Appeal decided that sec. 3 of The Power Commission Act, 1935, 25 Geo. V, ch. 53, was not effective to prevent the prosecution of the Ottawa Valley Company's action, the reason, or one of the reasons, for the decision being, as I understand the judgment, that the Legislature, having no power to destroy the substantive extra-provincial rights arising out of the contracts, was powerless to take away the adjective right of resort to the Courts of Ontario for the enforcement of those substantive rights. That being so, and the rights, or some of the rights, arising out of the contract upon which the present action is founded being civil rights that are not "in the Province", the judgment applies, and it must be held that sec. 3, in so far as it relates to an action founded upon the contract here in question, or arising out of the performance or non-performance of any of the terms of such contract, was beyond the power of the Legislature to enact.

The result then is that the plaintiff, the Beauharnois Light, Heat and Power Company is entitled to judgment against the defendant Commission for the sums which on the day of the issue of the writ were due under the power agreement, with interest upon those sums, at the rate provided by the agreement, from the days on which they respectively became due until judgment. These sums, it was agreed by counsel, are set forth correctly in the statement of claim. . . .

In the judgment at the trial of the *Ottawa Valley* case, as varied by the order of the Court of Appeal, the action against the trustee for bondholders (the Royal Trust Company) is dismissed with costs. The same judgment must be pronounced in this case in respect of the action against the same company as trustee for the holders of bonds issued by Beauharnois Power Corporation, Limited.

The judgment of the Court of Appeal was delivered by

MIDDLETON J.A.: . . . It is not necessary in order to dispose of this appeal that the facts should be elaborated at great length. Plainly, this appeal involves two main questions. First, do the facts in this case differ from those in the *Ottawa Valley* case so as to justify a different conclusion, so that the doctrine of *stare decisis* does not apply? Secondly, does a statute of the Province of Ontario 1937, 1 Geo. VI, ch. 58, which came into force on January 29th, 1937, affect this appeal, having in mind that the action was commenced on the 11th February, 1936, and was tried and disposed of on the 13th January, 1937, before the statute in question came into operation?

Dealing with the first question, a reference to the reasons for judgment will show that the conclusion there arrived at was based upon the opinion that the substantive enactment contained in ch. 53 of the Ontario Statutes of 1935, sec. 2, was *ultra vires* because it assumed to destroy civil rights outside the province, and the Legislature could not, by enactment of adjectival law, preclude the Courts of Ontario from so declaring. Clearly here the legislation affects substantial rights outside the province. The contract was executed in this case within Ontario and the place of payment in the present case is in the City of Toronto, whereas in the *Ottawa Valley* case the contract was executed in the Province of Quebec by some of the parties, and the place of payment named in the contract was the City of Montreal in the Province of Quebec. Neither of these facts affords any ground of distinction. They do not affect the basis of the *Ottawa Valley* decision. In this respect I agree entirely with the learned trial Judge, and in addition I desire to point out that there are rights not enumerated by him, rights which belong to the plaintiff companies, which exist outside of the Province of Ontario. These and the rights conferred upon The Hydro-Electric Commission itself, are a part of that which the Legislature of the Province of Ontario has attempted to destroy. If the decision in the former case is right and is binding upon us, it covers this case entirely.

The second question is as to the effect of the Ontario Statute of 1937, which was in no way dealt with by the former case. The particular Act with which we are mainly concerned is the Ontario Statute, 1937, 1 Geo. VI, ch. 58, which recites that it is expedient that the meaning and effect of subsec. 4 of sec. 6 of The Power Commission Act should be further declared. This Statute enacts, "The meaning and effect of subs. 4 of sec. 6 of *The Power Commission Act* is and always has been that without the consent of the Attorney-General no action of any kind whatsoever shall be brought against The Hydro-Electric Power Commission of Ontario, and that without the consent of the Attorney-General no action of any kind whatsoever shall be brought against any member of The Hydro-Electric Power Commission of Ontario for anything done or omitted by him in the exercise of his office." This Act was assented to on the 29th January, 1937.

The rights of the parties had already passed into judgment, and the legislation has no affect upon this action. It is true the legislation was passed and was in effect when the appeal was heard in this Court, but the duty of an appellate Court is to reconsider the case and to correct any error made, in its opinion, by the trial Judge, and to pronounce the judgment that, in its opinion, the trial Judge ought to have pronounced: see Ontario Judicature Act, R.S.O. 1927, ch. 88, sec. 26.

This principle is recognized in many reported decisions. I refer, for example, to *Eyre v. Wynn-Mackenzie,* [1896] 1 Ch. 135; *Day v. Kelland,* [1900] 2 Ch. 745; *National Trustees Co. v. General Finance Co. of Australasia,* [1905] A.C. 373.

A kindred principle is that laid down by the Supreme Court of the United States in *Fraenkl v. Cerecedo Hermanos* (1910), 216 U.S. Reports, 295. Jurisdiction, it is there said, is determined as of the time of commencing the suit, and legislation subsequently defining the jurisdiction cannot be inquired into for the purpose of determining the propriety of the action at its institution.

The intention of the Legislature is embodied in the formal Act of Parliament and can only be gathered from the words used in that enactment. The Legislature, in matters within its competence, is unquestionably supreme, but it falls to the Courts to determine the meaning of the language used. If the Courts do not determine in accordance with the true intention of the Legislature, the Legislature cannot arrogate to itself the jurisdiction of a further appellate Court and enact that the language used in its earlier enactment means something other than the Court has determined. It can, if it so pleases, use other language expressing its meaning more clearly. It transcends its true function when it undertakes to say that the language used has a different meaning and effect to that given it by the Courts, and that it always has meant something other than the Courts have declared it to mean. Very plainly is this so when, as in this case, the declaratory Act was not passed until after the original Act had been construed, and judgment pronounced.

For these reasons the subsequent legislation has no effect upon this case, and does not enable this Court to say that the trial Judge was not concluded by the earlier decision.

For these reasons the defendants' appeal from the judgment should be dismissed with costs. . . .

Appeal dismissed.

[In determining whether a provincial legislature can interfere with or destroy contract rights, is it material whether any of the contracting parties were or are in the province? Is place of performance relevant? Is provincial power predicated on whether the "proper law" of the contract, in a conflict of laws sense, is the law of the province? Is there a distinction, for constitutional purposes, between destroying the contract "right" and taking away any cause of action in the provincial courts? See Crocket J., dissenting, in *Reference re Debt Adjustment Act (Alta.),* [1942] S.C.R. 31 at p. 49, [1942] 1 D.L.R. 1, at p. 18: "It is not doubted that the right to sue in provincial courts is a civil right in the province, whether the claim sought to be enforced arose in the province or not." To the same effect is *North American Life Ass'ce Co. v. McLean,* [1941] 3 D.L.R. 271, [1941] 1 W.W.R. 430. *Cf. Anspach Co. v. C.N.R.,* [1950] O.R. 317, [1950] 3 D.L.R. 26.

May a provincial legislature enact a statute depriving employees resident in the province, injured in the course of employment outside the province, of any right of action, whether within or without the province, and compelling resort to the provincial workmen's compensation statute? See *Desharnais v.*

C.P.R., [1942] 4 D.L.R. 605, [1942] 3 D.L.R. 594, and *Ching v. C.P.R.*, [1943] S.C.R. 451, [1943] 3 D.L.R. 737

Qualification for benefits under the *Testator's Family Maintenance Act*, R.S.B.C. 1960, c. 378, of persons whose relationship to the decedent rested on relief against defects in solemnization of marriage provided by the *Marriage Act, 1933* (Sask.), c. 59 did not involve giving extraterritorial effect to the provincial legislation; see *Re Howe Louis* (1970), 14 D.L.R. (3d) 49, 75 W.W.R. 1 *(sub nom. Louis v. Louis).*

In *Workmen's Compensation Board v. C.P.R.*, [1920] A.C. 184, 48 D.L.R. 218, [1919] 3 W.W.R. 167, seamen, resident in British Columbia, were drowned when their ship, owned and operated by the C.P.R., sank in the high seas. The right of their dependants to compensation under the provincial *Workmen's Compensation Act, 1916,* (which applied to employers and employed engaged in shipping) was challenged by the C.P.R. on the ground that the Act could not validly apply to accidents outside the Province. The contention was upheld by the British Columbia courts but rejected in the Privy Council where Lord Haldane dealt with it as follows:

"It is said that the purpose is not a provincial one, inasmuch as it is to insure the dependents against accidents to the workmen which may happen, as in the present case, outside the limits of the Province. But in their Lordships' opinion this is not a case in which it is sought to enact any law giving a right to arise from a source outside the Province. The right conferred arises under s. 8, and is the result of a statutory condition of the contract of employment made with a workman resident in the province, for his personal benefit and for that of members of his family dependent on him. Where the services which he is engaged to perform are of such a nature that they have to be rendered both within and without the Province, he is given a right which enures for the benefit of himself and the members of his family dependent on him, not the less that the latter may happen to be non-resident aliens. This right arises, not out of tort, but out of the workman's statutory contract, and their Lordships think that it is a legitimate provincial object to secure that every workman resident within the Province who so contracts should possess it as a benefit conferred on himself as a subject of the Province. When he enters into this contract, it also appears to them to be within the power of the Province to enact that, if the employer does not fully contribute to the accident fund out of which the payment is normally to be made, the employer should make good to that fund the amount required for giving effect to the title to compensation which the workman acquired for himself and his dependants. The scheme of the Act is not one for interfering with rights outside the Province. It is in substance a scheme for securing a civil right within the Province. The case is wholly different from that from Alberta which was before the judicial committee in *Royal Bank of Canada v. The King. . . .*"

An annuity pension contract made in New York State between a resident of Ontario and a New York insurer provided that the validity and effect of the contract would be governed by New York law. Section 134(1) of the Insurance Act, R.S.O. 1950, c. 183 declared that "a contract is deemed to be made in the Province if the place of residence of the insured is stated to be in the Province". The insured named his wife as beneficiary but subsequently submitted another person who was an ordinary beneficiary under Ontario law which required consent of the preferred beneficiary to such a change. *Held,* as a matter of construction, the provisions of the Ontario Act respecting change of beneficiary did not apply to the particular contract and the ordinary beneficiary was entitled to payment thereunder: *Gray v. Kerslake*, [1958]

S.C.R. 3, 11 D.L.R. (2d) 225. Locke J., alone of the members of the Court, took a constitutional ground as follows:

"The situs of the cause of action which would arise on the death of the policyholder or annuitant was clearly in the State of New York. The validity of the finding of the Court of Appeal may perhaps be tested in this manner: Should the respondent bring an action against the Association in the State of New York, where the moneys were payable, would it be an answer to the claim for the Association to say that, in accordance with the terms of the contract, it had paid the moneys to the person entitled under the laws of the State of New York, or could the respondent in such case say that these terms had been changed by an Act of the Legislature of Ontario and that the Association's liability was to be determined under the laws of that Province? It seems to me that to ask the question is to answer it.

"I agree with the contention of the appellant and the Attorney-General that, even if it be assumed that the contract was one of life insurance, s. 134 and s. 132 of *The Insurance Act*, to the extent that it would make s. 134 applicable, do not apply. To hold otherwise would be to say that the Legislature of the Province might affect civil rights the situs of which was outside the Province. . . ."

Section 88 of *The Insurance Act*, R.S.O. 1950, c. 183, provided, *inter alia*, that where the subject-matter of a contract of insurance is an insurable interest of a person resident in Ontario, the contract of insurance if signed, countersigned, issued or delivered in Ontario shall be deemed to evidence a contract made therein and the contract shall be construed according to the law thereof. Is the provision validly applicable to determine by Ontario law the rights of an Ontario insured in respect of a policy of fire insurance on property in Quebec when the policy was issued in Quebec by a Quebec insurer under the Quebec Insurance Act? See *Hubert v. Compagnie Equitable d'Assurance Contre Le Feu* (1958), 12 D.L.R. (2d) 701.]

A.-G. ONT. v. SCOTT

In the Supreme Court of Canada. [1956] S.C.R. 137, 1 D.L.R. (2d) 433, 114 Can. C.C. 224.

Appeal from a judgment of the Ontario Court of Appeal, [1954] O.R. 676, [1954] 4 D.L.R. 546, reversing an order of McRuer C.J.H.C., [1954] O.R. 246, [1954] 2 D.L.R. 465, dismissing an application for prohibition to a magistrate in respect of proceedings under the Reciprocal Enforcement of Maintenance Orders Act, R.S.O. 1950, c. 334. Applicant's wife obtained from a magistrate in London, England, an order for custody of their two children and for payment by applicant of certain sums for maintenance of herself and the children. The orders were declared to be provisional only and to be subject to confirmation by a competent court in Canada. This was in accord with a reciprocal arrangement for enforcement in Ontario, against resident husbands, of provisional maintenance orders for which proceedings had been initiated in a reciprocating jurisdiction by wives resident there. Pursuant to s. 5 of the Act, the Attorney-General received a certified copy of the orders and the depositions of the witnesses and a statement of the grounds on which the orders might have been opposed in England, and he sent the documents to the magistrate's court having jurisdiction in the county where applicant apparently resided, and applicant was there served with a summons to show cause why the orders should not be confirmed. By s. 5(2), "at the hearing it shall be open to the person on whom the summons was served to raise any defence that he might have raised in the original proceedings had he been a party thereto but no other defence . . ." and it also provided that the statement from the English court of the grounds of defence to the order shall be conclusive evidence that those grounds are grounds on which objection might be taken. However, possible objections were not confined to those grounds.

RAND J.: I am unable to appreciate as fatal to this legislation the considerations which have been urged before us. It is said that the matter is one of international comity, that the legislation effects an international treaty, with both of which only Parliament can deal, that it delegates to a foreign Legislature the power to enact provincial law, and that what are involved are civil rights which do not lie within the scope of provincial jurisdiction. Subordinate grounds go to the authority to allocate the issue to an inferior Court or to enable such a Court to deal with a matter involving the currency of a foreign state; that the Magistrate to whom the matter was directed has not been clothed with authority over it; and that in any event there was no jurisdiction over the respondent by reason of non-residence and the absence of any act of wilful neglect in the county in which the proceedings were brought.

Whatever the nature or limits of what is known as "the comity of nations", it ordinarily signifies the respect paid by one state to the laws and to civil rights established by them of another relating to personal or property interests which touch both states.

With this in mind, the principal grounds rest, in my opinion, on a misconception of the true nature of the arrangement. Ontario has territorial jurisdiction over the respondent. His wife, alleging herself to have been deserted and remaining in England, is seeking to compel him to maintain her and their children. The Province, recognizing the practical difficulty of enforcing the rights of a wife so placed, has intimated its willingness to exercise its authority over the husband by compelling him to the performance of a duty which both countries recognize as an incident of the marriage status. In carrying this out, the Province has adopted provisions which the law of England prescribes for the relief of a deserted wife. The effect is to vest in the wife a right to enforce the duty in Ontario in accordance with the provisions adopted.

That the Province can confer such a benefit on a non-resident seems to me to be beyond serious argument. Rights in property and in action in non-residents are created by the law of Ontario in transmissions through death or in the course of business as everyday occurrences. In the former, resort to the foreign law to determine the benefit or the beneficiary is a commonplace. I see no jural distinction between the creation and enforcement of a contract and the recognition and enforcement of a marital duty; the latter in fact arises out of or is attributable to a contract, that of marriage. A civil right within the Province does not require that the Province, in creating it, should have personal jurisdiction over both parties to it; and in its enforcement, the plaintiff by availing herself of the provincial judicature so far submits herself to the authority of the provincial Court; it is the same as if she had come to the Province and enforced a right in the circumstances given her. If these considerations were not recognized, by keeping property in a Province other than that of his own and his creditor's residence, a debtor could effectually put it beyond the reach of the latter: the Province of the *situs* would be powerless, by way of remedial right, to apply it to his debts. Such a restriction upon provincial authority under head (13) of s. 92 would seem to contradict the unquestioned acceptance of the scope of that authority since 1867.

A distinction may properly be made between vesting a right and extinguishing it. The former is, in fact, a declaration that within the jurisdiction making it the attributes of ownership of property or of a claim against a person within the jurisdiction, are available to the non-resident. Generally, the right so declared would be recognized and enforced under the principle of comity by other jurisdictions. But a like declaration purporting to extinguish a right based on jurisdiction over the debtor only could not bind the non-resident creditor—in the case of a Province, even in its own Courts: *Royal Bank of Canada v. The King*, 9 D.L.R. 337, [1913] A.C. 383—outside of that jurisdiction unless otherwise supported by recognized elements furnishing jurisdiction over him or the right. In short, a state, including a Province, does not require jurisdiction over a person to enable it to give him a right *in personam*; but ordinarily, and to be recognized generally, such a jurisdiction is necessary to divest such a right. That is not to say that jurisdiction of this nature is in itself always sufficient to divesting.

That the legislation is within head (16), as a local or private matter, appears to me to be equally clear. No other part of the country nor any other of the several Governments has the slightest interest in such a controversy and it concerns ultimately property, actual or potential, within Ontario in a local sense.

Given, then, a right so created by the law of Ontario, the action taken in England is merely an initiating proceeding looking to effective juridical action in Ontario for the purpose of which it is a means of adducing a foundation in evidence. In the administration of justice the Province is supreme in determining the procedure by which rights and duties shall be enforced and that it can act upon evidence taken abroad either before or after proceedings are begun locally I consider unquestionable. The form which the action in Ontario may take, as here, in the language of the statute, a confirmation of the provisional order, does not touch the substance indicated.

In the converse situation, the initiating step within the Province is simply a local or private matter over which there is plenary jurisdiction, in a setting of cooperative action by two interested states. In that aspect there can be no conflict with Part II of the *Canada Evidence Act,* R.S.C. 1952, c. 307. The latter is a code of provisions of a strictly evidentiary nature concerned with issues raised in existing litigation. The former is more than and different from that: its purpose is to establish the basis for a proceeding elsewhere through the proof of facts within Ontario: an originating proceeding which forms the jurisdictional basis of fact for the supplementary and effective process elsewhere. . . .

Appeal allowed.

[Kerwin C.J.C., Kellock and Cartwright JJ. concurred with Rand J. A separate concurring judgment was delivered by Locke J., and also by Abbott J., with whom Taschereau and Fauteux JJ. concurred. Estey J. did not take part in the judgment. The judgment of Rand J., as edited above, excludes reasons given by him for rejecting arguments based on allegations that the province was party to a treaty, that there was unconstitutional delegation and that the Act violated s. 96 of the B.N.A. Act.

In *McGuire v. McGuire and Desordi,* [1953] O.R. 328, [1953] 2 D.L.R. 394, defendant in a divorce action in Ontario applied for *habeas corpus ad testificandum* to bring her co-defendant, then in prison in a penitentiary in Quebec, to Ontario to give evidence on her behalf. *Held,* the Supreme Court of Ontario had no power, nor could the Ontario legislature give it power over persons outside its territorial jurisdiction, and hence the order for issue of the writ must be set aside.

Has this decision any significance respecting the validity of provincial Rules of Practice and Procedure which provide for issue of a writ of summons or notice thereof outside of the Province? See, for example, Ont. Rule 25.

To what extent, if at all, are constitutional questions involved in the exercise of jurisdiction by the Courts, pursuant to provincial legislation, over persons or property outside the Province? Are English cases on jurisdiction relevant when it is the case that the United Kingdom may legislate extra-territorially but a Province may not? Does it make any difference whether the Court is a superior or inferior Court? See *Regina v. Judges of Vancouver Family Court, ex parte Walker* (1963), 39 D.L.R. (2d) 552, 43 W.W.R. 161; *Elash v. Elash* (1963), 43 D.L.R. (2d) 599, 45 W.W.R. 94. It was said in *Battle Creek Toasted Corn Flake Co. Ltd. v. Kellogg Toasted Corn Flake Co.* (1922), 22 O.W.N. 308 that a Court cannot grant an injunction having extra-territorial operation except where it has jurisdiction over the person of the defendant. Is this a constitutional limitation?

A resident of Ontario failed to answer a Quebec subpoena and a motion was brought in Ontario to commit him for contempt. Is it within Ontario's legislative power so to provide? See *Rideout v. Rideout,* [1956] O.W.N. 644, 4 D.L.R. (2d) 772.

In *Lawson v. Interior Tree, Fruit & Vegetable Committee,* [1931] S.C.R. 357 at p. 361, [1931] 2 D.L.R. 193, at p. 196 Duff J. said: "What, if any, limitations affect the authority of a provincial legislature to determine, for the province, the legal effect within the province of extra-provincial acts, and to prescribe the rules of law which, except in matters governed by s. 91, the provincial courts are to observe in controversies arising in relation to such acts, is a subject of multifarious ramifications, of great importance and, in some respects, not free from difficulty."

A provincial statute prohibits any person not registered thereunder from holding out within the province that he is qualified to practice dentistry either within the province or elsewhere. Are there any objections to its validity? Can it validly apply to non-residents who advertise in the province but do not practise there? See *Cowen v. A.-G. B.C.*, [1941] S.C.R. 321, [1941] 2 D.L.R. 687, aff'g [1941] 1 D.L.R. 565, 55 B.C.R. 506, aff'g [1940] 4 D.L.R. 755, 55 B.C.R. 370.]

CHAPTER VI

TRANSPORT AND COMMUNICATION: WORKS FOR THE GENERAL ADVANTAGE OF CANADA

MONTREAL v. MONTREAL STREET RAILWAY

In the Privy Council. [1912] A.C. 333, 1 D.L.R. 681.

Appeal by special leave from a judgment of the Supreme Court of Canada, 43 S.C.R. 197, setting aside an order of the Board of Railway Commissioners as made without jurisdiction.

LORD ATKINSON: . . . The facts of the case are few and are undisputed. There are in the city of Montreal and the adjacent township two so-called railways. One of these is the Montreal Park and Island Railway, hereafter styled for convenience the Park Railway, and the other the Montreal Street Railway, which is in fact a tramway laid along the streets of that city and its suburbs, and for convenience may be styled the Street Railway. These railways being constructed on the island in the St. Lawrence on which the city of Montreal stands are, of course, situate wholly within the Province of Quebec. They connect physically at several points within and near the limits of the city, and arrangements have been entered into between the companies owning them by which the cars of each railway run over the lines of the other, and passengers are conveyed from points on one system to points on the other over the permanent way of both. It is not disputed that there is conducted over these lines "through traffic" within the meaning of the statute hereinafter referred to.

The Park Railway, though originally constructed and worked under the powers conferred by certain enactments of the provincial Legislature, was, by a statute of the Canadian Parliament (57 & 58 Vict. c. 84), amended by two other similar statutes (59 Vict. c. 28 and 6 Edw. 7, c. 129), declared to be a work for the general advantage of Canada. Railways so declared were in this case called "federal" railways to distinguish them from railways situate wholly within a province, and under the exclusive control of the provincial Legislature styled provincial railways. It is admitted that by this declaration the railway to which it refers was withdrawn from the jurisdiction of the provincial Legislature, that it passed under the exclusive jurisdiction and control of the Parliament of Canada, and, small and provincial though it was, stood to the latter in precisely the same relation, as far as the enactments upon the true construction of which this case turns, as do those great trunk lines, also federal railways, which traverse the Dominion from sea to sea, and where originally constructed and are now worked in exercise of the powers conferred by the statutes of the Parliament of the Dominion of Canada. The Board of Railway Commissioners was created by a Dominion

431

statute (3 Edw. 7, c. 58) entitled "The Railway Act." The Commissioners are officials of the Dominion Government, and in the exercise of their powers are outside the jurisdiction and beyond the control of any provincial Legislature or Government.

A complaint having been made to them that an unjust discrimination had been made by the Park Railway Company in respect of the rates charged and of the service and operation of this railway between the residents of a certain ward in the city of Montreal, named the Mount Royal Ward, and the residents of an outlying township, named the town of Notre Dame de Grace, in both of which localities they have stations, the Order appealed from was made. It purported to have been made under the authority and by virtue of the powers conferred upon the Commissioners by the Railway Act. By it they directed, first, that the Park Railway Company should grant the same "facilities in the way of services and operation including the rates to be charged by it," to the people residing in Mount Royal Ward as it grants to those residing in Notre Dame de Grace, and that it should forthwith enter into the necessary agreements for the purpose of removing the unjust discrimination which they had found in fact to exist; and, secondly, that with respect to "through" traffic over the Street Railway, the Street Railway Company should "enter into any agreement or agreements that may be necessary to enable" the former company to carry out the provisions of this Order.

The Park Railway having by statutory declaration become in the manner mentioned a federal railway, it is admitted that the first portion of this Order dealing with the "unjust discrimination" which it was found to have made was *intra vires*, but the validity of the second part of the Order is challenged, and it has, on behalf of the Street Railway Company, been from the first insisted that the Commissioners had no jurisdiction whatever to make it.

Moreover, it is practically not disputed that the existence in the Commissioners of the jurisdiction challenged depends itself upon the further consideration, namely, whether, having regard to the provisions of the 91st and 92nd sections of the British North America Act, the Parliament of Canada have any jurisdiction, power or authority, express or implied, to enact the 8th section of the before-mentioned Railway Act so far as it affects provincial as distinguished from federal lines. This was in effect the question of law raised by way of appeal from the Order of the Commissioners for the decision of the Supreme Court. It is by the Order of the former body, dated June 8, 1909, framed thus: "Whether upon the true construction of sections 91 and 92 of the British North America Act, and of section 8 of the Railway Act of Canada, the Montreal Street Railway is subject in respect of its through traffic with the Montreal Park and Island Railway Company, to the jurisdiction of the Board of the Railway Commissioners of Canada."

It is to be observed that the question is framed in a general form. The jurisdiction of the Commissioners or of the Dominion Parliament is not made to depend in any way on the character, nature, or volume of the "through" traffic. Nor upon the question whether it is of such a kind as to confer special advantages upon Canada or upon two or more of its provinces. And, indeed, counsel on behalf of the appellants at the hearing before their Lordships boldly contended that once a line of railway, though wholly provincial, i.e., situate wholly within one particular province, and not federal, connects with a federal line, and "through" traffic is conducted over both, the jurisdiction of the Commissioners attaches at least so far as this "through" traffic, whatever its character or amount, is concerned.

The Supreme Court by a majority of its members answered the question so put to them in the negative. The question for the decision of their Lordships is whether their answer is right in point of law.

The 8th section of the Railway Act runs as follows:—

"Every railway, steam, or electric street railway or tramway, the construction or operation of which is authorized by special Act of the Legislature of any province, and which connects with or crosses or may hereafter connect with or cross any railway within the legislative authority of the Parliament of Canada, shall, although not declared by Parliament to be a work for the general advantage of Canada, be subject to the provisions of this Act relating to—

"(a) The connection or crossing of one railway or tramway with or by another, so far as concerns the aforesaid connection or crossing;

"(b) The through traffic upon a railway or tramway and all matters appertaining thereto:

"(c) Criminal matters, including offences and penalties; and

"(d) Navigable waters:

"Provided that, in the case of railways owned by any provincial Government, the provisions of this Act with respect to through traffic shall not apply without the consent of such Government."

It will be observed that if the argument of the appellants be right this section would seem to subject a provincial railway authorized by an Act of the provincial Legislature to all the provisions of this statute of the Canadian Parliament dealing not only with the physical connection or crossing of the two lines and with the through traffic, but also with criminal matters, offences, and penalties, whether connected with the through traffic or not, and further with the relations of the provincial line and its traffic with navigable waters. As to all these matters the jurisdiction and control of the local Legislature is superseded or overborne, comparatively little is left to that authority, and the line itself is placed in this unfortunate position, that its local traffic is put under the jurisdiction and control of the provincial Legislature and the officials of the local Government, and its through traffic, with all these other matters, is subjected to the jurisdiction and control of the Dominion Legislature and the officials of the Dominion Government. A most unworkable and embarrassing arrangement.

Now the effect of sub-s. 10 of s. 92 of the British North America Act, is, their Lordships think, to transfer the excepted works mentioned in sub-heads (a), (b), and (c) of it into s. 91, and thus to place them under the exclusive jurisdiction and control of the Dominion Parliament.

These two sections must then be read and construed as if these transferred subjects were specially enumerated in s. 91, and local railway as distinct from federal railway were specifically enumerated in s. 92.

The matters thus transferred are:

(a)   Lines of steam or other ships, railways, canals, telegraphs, and other works and undertakings, connecting the provinces with any other province or provinces, or extending beyond the limits of the province.

(b)   Lines of steamships between the province and any British or foreign country.

(c)   Works, wholly situate within the province, but declared by the Parliament of Canada to be for the general advantage of Canada or for the advantage of two or more provinces.

These works are physical things, not services. The appropriate number of the group would probably be 29 or 29(a). It has accordingly been strongly urged on behalf of the respondents that if it be desirable in the interest of the Dominion to place the through traffic on a provincial line, such as the Street Railway, under the control of the Railway Commissioners, owing to its nature, character, or amount, the proper course for the Dominion Parliament to take, and the only course it can legitimately take, is by statutory declaration to convert the provincial line into a federal line, thus removing it from the class of subjects placed under the control of the Legislature of the province and placing it amongst the classes of subjects over which it has itself exclusive jurisdiction and control. And further, that there is nothing in the British North America Act to shew that such an invasion of the rights of the provincial Legislature, as is necessarily involved in the establishment of this embarrassing dual control over their own provincial railways, was ever contemplated by the framers of the British North America Act . . .

. . . The Act and Order if justified at all must be justified on the ground that they are necessarily incidental to the exercise by the Dominion Parliament of the powers conferred upon it by the enumerated heads of s. 91. Well, the only one of the heads enumerated in s. 91 dealing expressly or impliedly with railways is that which is interpolated by the transfer into it of subheads (a), (b), and (c) of sub-s. 10 of s. 92. Lines such as the Street Railway are not among these.

In other words, it must be shewn that it is necessarily incidental to the exercise of control over the traffic of a federal railway, in respect of its giving an unjust preference to certain classes of its passengers or otherwise, that it should also have power to exercise control over the "through" traffic of such a purely local thing as a provincial railway properly so called, if only it be connected with a federal railway. The Commissioners have by the 317th section of the Railway Act vast powers over federal railways. They can compel the companies who own such lines to make all the arrangements therein mentioned for receiving and forwarding traffic of all kinds, through or local, and also compel them to conduct their business so as not to give an unjust preference to any person or persons or body or bodies corporate; but it is not to be assumed that the provincial railway companies would in the reasonable conduct of their business refuse to make such agreements with federal railway companies as would enable the latter to discharge the obligations which might be placed upon them under this section, and still less is it to be assumed that the provincial Legislature would fail to exercise their own legislative powers to compel recalcitrant companies over which they had control to enter into such agreements if they refused to do so. As long as it is reasonably probable that the provincial companies will enter into such agreements, or will be coerced to enter into them by the provincial Legislature which controls them, it cannot be held, their Lordships think, that it is necessarily incidental to the exercise by the Dominion Parliament of its control over federal railways that provincial railways should be coerced by its legislation to enter into these agreements in the manner in which it sought to coerce the Street Railway Company in the present case to enter into the agreements specified in the order appealed from. There is not a suggestion in the case that the "through" traffic between this federal and this local line, or between any other federal or local line, had attained such dimensions before the Railway Act was passed as to affect the body politic of the Dominion. If it had been so, the ready way of protecting the body politic was by making such a statutory declaration in any particular case or cases as was made in reference to the Park line. The right contended for in this case is in truth the absolute right of the Dominion Parliament wherever a federal line and a local provincial line connect to establish, irrespective of all consequences, this dual control over the latter line whenever there is through traffic between them, at least of such a kind as would lead to unjust discrimination between any classes of the customers of the former line. In their Lordships' view this right and power is not necessarily incidental to the exercise by the Parliament of Canada of its undoubted jurisdiction and control over federal lines, and is therefore, they think, an unauthorized invasion of the rights of the Legislature of the Province of Quebec.

One of the arguments urged on behalf of the appellants was this: The through traffic must, it is said, be controlled by some legislative body. It cannot be controlled by the provincial Legislature because that Legislature has no jurisdiction over a federal line, therefore it must be controlled by the Legislature of Canada. The answer to that contention is this, that so far as the "through" traffic is carried on over the federal line, it can be controlled by the Parliament of Canada. And that so far as it is carried over a non-federal provincial line it can be controlled by the provincial Legislature, and the two companies who own these lines can thus be respectively compelled by these two Legislatures to enter into such agreement with each other as will secure that this "through" traffic shall be properly conducted; and further that it cannot be assumed that either body will decline to co-operate with the other in a reasonable way to effect an object so much in the interest of both the Dominion and the province as the regulation of "through" traffic.

On the whole, therefore, their Lordships are of opinion that s. 8, sub-s. (b), of the Railway Act is, as regards provincial lines of railway properly so called, *ultra vires* (upon the other sub-sections it is unnecessary to express any opinion).

Appeal dismissed.

LUSCAR COLLIERIES v. McDONALD

In the Privy Council. [1927] A.C. 925, [1927] 3 W.W.R. 454, 33 C.R.C. 399, [1927] 4 D.L.R. 85.

LORD WARRINGTON OF CLYFFE. The appellants, the Luscar Collieries, Ld., are the owners of a short branch line of railway in the Province of Alberta, constructed by them but operated by the Canadian National Railways Company under certain agreements to be mentioned presently. The question in this appeal is whether the appellants' railway is a railway "within the legislative authority of the Parliament of Canada," and therefore a railway to which the Railway Act, 1919, of Canada applies (Railway Act, 1919, s. 5).

The facts giving rise to these questions are as follows:—

In the year 1911 the Grand Trunk Pacific Branch Lines Company, under the authority of an Act of 1909 of the Parliament of Canada, constructed a Coal Branch in the Province from a station on the main line of the Grand Trunk Railway to a point at or near Coalspur. This branch line is now part of the Canadian National Railways.

In the year 1911, by the Act of that year, the Branch Lines Company were authorized by the Parliament of Canada to construct another branch from the branch last mentioned to the Mountain Park Coal Company's collieries.

In the year 1912 the Mountain Park Coal Company, Ld., obtained authority from the Parliament of Alberta to construct, maintain and operate a railway which is either identical with or takes the place of the branch described in the Canadian Act of 1911, and by the same Act of the Parliament of Alberta an agreement set forth in the Schedule to the Act between the Branch Lines Company, the Grand Trunk Company, and the Coal Company was ratified and confirmed, and it was provided that the railway thereby authorized should be operated pursuant to the agreement.

By the said agreement, which is dated January 23, 1912, it was provided in effect that the last mentioned railway should be constructed by and at the expense of the Coal Company, who were to be reimbursed by certain rebates on freight, and that so soon as they had been so reimbursed the Branch Lines Company were to be the absolute owners of the railway. Provision was also made for the operation of the railway by the Grand Trunk Company.

In the year 1921 the appellant company, by an Act of the Parliament of Alberta, were authorized to construct the railway in question to connect with the Mountain Park Company's railway and to enter into an agreement for the operation of the railway by the Canadian National Railways which then comprised both the Branch Lines Company and the Grand Trunk Company, and for the ultimate transfer to or acquisition by the Canadian National Railways of the railway.

By an agreement dated May 10, 1921, made between the Branch Lines Company and the Grand Trunk Company, and the Mountain Park Coal Company, supplemental to the agreement of January 23, 1912, provision was made for the application of the agreement to the railway in question, therein referred to as the Luscar Branch Line, with certain modifications as to the terms of reimbursement, and it was thereby provided that on failure of the coal company to ship over the Luscar Branch Line when constructed the annual quantity of coal therein mentioned, neither the Branch Lines Company nor the Grand Trunk Company should be under any obligation to the coal company to continue the operation of such branch line.

Ultimately, by an agreement dated April 2, 1923, and made between the Mountain Park Company of the first part, the appellant company of the second part, the Branch Lines Company of the third part, and the Grand Trunk Company of the fourth part, the appellant company agreed to submit the Luscar Branch to the operation of the agreements of January 23, 1912, and May 10, 1921, and agreed that the Branch Lines Company and the Grand Trunk Company should have as regards the Luscar Branch all the rights given to them by the Mountain Park Company under the said agreements with regard to the Mountain Park Branch.

Since the construction of the Luscar Branch Line it has been operated under the agreements aforesaid by the Canadian National Railways, and traffic over it can pass without interruption to such parts of the Dominion as are served by the Canadian National Railways.

Under these circumstances the respondent, N. S. McDonald, the owner of a coal lease in the vicinity of the appellants' colliery, made an application to the Board of Railway Commissioners constituted under the Railway Act of 1919, for an order granting him running rights over the Luscar Branch and for an order requiring the Canadian National Railways Company to grant him permission to construct a short track to serve his coal lease.

The appellant company objected to this application on the ground that the Board of Railway Commissioners for Canada had no jurisdiction, asserting that their line was a Provincial railway, to which the Dominion Railway Acts had no application.

The Board of Railway Commissioners overruled the appellants' objection, and on August 14, 1924, made a formal order declaring that in pursuance of the powers conferred by s. 6(c) of the Railway Act, 1919, the Board had power to make the order applied for. In view of the then pending appeal to the Supreme Court of Canada, the Board made no operative order, leaving this to be dealt with after the question of jurisdiction should have been settled.

The Attorney-General of Canada intervened in the appeal to support the jurisdiction of the Board, and by an order dated May 18, 1925, the Supreme Court affirmed the order of the Board and dismissed the appeal.

The appellant company thereupon obtained special leave to appeal to His Majesty in Council. The Attorney-General for Canada and the Attorney-General for Alberta intervened to oppose and support the appeal respectively. The respondent McDonald does not appear.

The material statutory provisions are the following:

By s. 91 of the British North America Act, 1867, it was provided that the exclusive legislative authority of the Parliament of Canada extends to (amongst other subjects thereby enumerated) such classes of subjects as are expressly excepted in the enumeration of the classes of subjects by the Act assigned exclusively to the Legislatures of the Provinces.

Sect. 92, so far as it is material, is as follows: "In each Province the Legislature may exclusively make laws in relation to matters coming within the classes of subjects next hereinafter enumerated, that is to say:— ... 10. Local works and undertakings other than such as are of the following classes: (*a*) Lines of steam or other ships, railways, canals, telegraphs, and other works and undertakings connecting the Province with any other or others of the Provinces or extending beyond the limits of the Province. (*c*) Such works as, although wholly situate within the Province, are before or after their execution declared by the Parliament of Canada to be for the general advantage of Canada or for the advantage of two or more of the Provinces."

The Railway Act, 1919 (Canada), contains the following material provisions:

"Section 2 (4.). 'Company' ... where not otherwise stated or implied means 'railway company' unless immediately preceded by 'any' 'every' or 'all' in which case it means every kind of company which the context will permit of."

"Section 5. This Act shall, subject as herein provided, apply to all ... railways ... within the legislative authority of the Parliament of Canada. ..."

"Section 6. The provisions of this Act shall without limiting the effect of the last preceding section extend and apply to: ... (*c*) Every railway or portion thereof, whether constructed under the authority of the Parliament of Canada or not, now or hereafter owned, controlled, leased or operated by a company wholly or partly within the legislative authority of the Parliament of Canada ... whether such ownership control or ... operation is acquired or exercised by lease agreement or other means whatsoever and whether acquired or exercised under authority of the Parliament of Canada or of the Legislature of any Province or otherwise howsoever; and every railway or portion thereof now or hereafter so owned, controlled, leased or operated shall be deemed and is hereby declared to be a work for the general advantage of Canada."

On this section it is clear that having regard to the definition in s. 2, sub-s. 4, the word "company" means railway company, and does not include a bank or financial company controlling a railway.

The Attorney-General for Canada, in support of the jurisdiction of the Board of Railway Commissioners, relies on two alternative grounds: (1.) That the appellants' railway is, under the circumstances, a railway connecting the Province of Alberta with other Provinces (s. 92, head 10(a)). (2.) That, if this ground fails, then it is a "work" within s. 92, head 10(c), by virtue of s. 6(c), of the Railway Act, 1919, and the declaration therein contained.

Of the judges of the Supreme Court of Canada, three, namely, Anglin, C.J., and Duff and Rinfret, JJ., decided in favour of the jurisdiction on the first ground, but in reference to the second were of opinion that such a general declaration as that contained in s. 6(c) was not a declaration within s. 92, head 10(c), of the British North America Act, 1867; two, namely, Mignault and Newcombe, JJ., accepted the second ground and expressed no option on the first. Idington, J., was for allowing the appeal.

Their Lordships agree with the opinion of Duff, J., that the Mountain Park Railway and the Luscar Branch are, under the circumstances hereinbefore set forth, a part of a continuous system of railways operated together by the Canadian National Railways Company, and connecting the Province of Alberta with other Provinces of the Dominion. It is, in their view, impossible to hold as to any section of that system which does not reach the boundary of a Province that it does not connect that Province with another. If it connects with a line which itself connects with one in another Province, then it would be a link in the chain of connection, and would properly be said to connect the Province in which it is situated with other Provinces.

In the present case, having regard to the way in which the railway is operated, their Lordships are of opinion that it is in fact a railway connecting the Province of Alberta with others of the Provinces, and therefore falls within s. 92, head 10(a), of the Act of 1867. There is a continuous connection by railway between the point of the Luscar Branch farthest from its junction with the Mountain Park Branch and parts of Canada outside the Province of Alberta. If under the agreements hereinbefore mentioned the Canadian National Railways Company should cease to operate the Luscar Branch, the question whether under such altered circumstances the railway ceases to be within s. 92, head 10(a), may have to be determined, but that question does not now arise.

Their Lordships having thus come to a conclusion against the appeal on the first of the two grounds mentioned above, it is unnecessary for them to express any opinion on the second, and in accordance with their usual practice they think it not desirable to do so. But they wish it distinctly to be understood that so far as they are concerned the question as to the validity of s. 6(c) of the Act of 1919 is to be treated as absolutely open.

Counsel for the appellant company raised a question as to the power of the Board of Railway Commissioners to grant the application in the form in which it was framed. This is not a matter going to the jurisdiction of the Board—a Dominion authority as distinct from a Provincial one—and is one which can and ought to be considered by the Board when—its general jurisdiction having been established—it is asked to exercise it in the particular case.

Their Lordships are of opinion that the appeal fails and must be dismissed, but without costs. The respondent McDonald does not appear to ask for costs, and the interveners are not entitled to them. Their Lordships will humbly advise His Majesty accordingly.

[A provincial commuter service to be operated over C.N.R. tracks under an agreement with the C.N.R. is within federal legislative jurisdiction as to tolls and otherwise, regardless of ownership of the rolling stock: *The Queen in right of Ontario v. Board of Transport Commissioners*, [1968] S.C.R. 118, 65 D.L.R. (2d) 425.

Where a company incorporated abroad but licensed to operate street railways in a province also operated under certain agreements with a federal railway company a railway within federal jurisdiction, *held*, in proceedings to subject the local street railway to federal rate jurisdiction, "there is nothing abnormal about its being under provincial jurisdiction in connection with its operation of the one, and under Dominion jurisdiction in connection with its operation of the other". The fact that the local street railway made physical connection with two lines of railway under federal jurisdiction would not bring it also within such jurisdiction when it was not being operated by the federal railways as part of a continuous system but remained under the direction of the foreign company: *B.C. Electric Railway v. C.N.R.*, [1932] S.C.R. 161, [1932] 2 D.L.R. 728.

In *C.P.R. v. Notre Dame de Bonsecours*, [1899] A.C. 367, Lord Watson said (at p. 372) that "The Parliament of Canada has . . . exclusive right to prescribe regulations for the construction, repair and alteration of the railway, and for its management, and to dictate the constitution and powers of the company; but it is, *inter alia*, reserved to the provincial parliament to impose direct taxation upon those portions of it which are within the province in order to the raising of a revenue for provincial purposes. It was obviously in the contemplation of the Act of 1867 that the 'railway legislation' strictly so called applicable to those lines which were placed under its charge should belong to the Dominion Parliament. It therefore appears to their Lordships that any attempt by the Legislature of Quebec to regulate by enactment, whether described as municipal or not, the structure of a ditch forming part of the appellant company's authorized works would be legislation in excess of its powers. If, on the other hand, the enactment had no reference to the structure of the ditch, but provided that, in the event of its becoming choked with silt or rubbish, so as to cause overflow and injury to other property in the parish, it should be thoroughly cleaned out by the appellant company, then the enactment would, in their Lordships' opinion, be a piece of municipal legislation competent to the Legislature of Quebec." See also *G.T.R. v. Therrien* (1900), 30 S.C.R. 485; *A.-G. Alta. v. A.-G. Can.*, [1915] A.C. 363, 22 D.L.R. 501, 7 W.W.R. 634.

Division of tolls for long distance telephone calls, over interconnecting lines of an interprovincial and a provincial telephone call, is not within the jurisdiction of the Canadian Transport Commission to the exclusion of the provincial boards and provincial courts: *Quebec Telephone v. Bell Telephone Co. of Canada*, [1972] S.C.R. 182, 22 D.L.R. (3d) 69.

May provincial legislation impose liability on a Dominion railway for cattle killed or injured on railway tracks by reason of absence of fences? See *Madden v. Nelson and Fort Sheppard Ry.*, [1899] A.C. 626.

"The Dominion Parliament had full power if it thought fit to authorize the use of provincial Crown lands by the company for the purposes of this railway": *A.-G. B.C. v. C.P.R.*, [1906] A.C. 204 at p. 210. May Parliament empower the expropriation of provincial Crown lands for railway purposes?

See *A.-G. Que. v. Nipissing Central Ry.*, [1926] A.C. 715, [1926] 3 D.L.R. 545, [1926] 2 W.W.R. 522.

Where erection of railway works, *e.g.* at level crossings, is ordered under Dominion legislation, is it within federal power to compel municipalities or provincial railways to share the cost of such works? See *C.P.R. v. Toronto Transportation Commission*, [1930] A.C. 686, [1930] 4 D.L.R. 845, [1930] 3 W.W.R. 189; *Toronto Ry. v. Toronto*, [1920] A.C. 426, 51 D.L.R. 55, [1920] 1 W.W.R. 382. See generally *McNairn*, Transportation, Communication and the Constitution, (1969) 47 Can. Bar Rev. 355.]

G.T.R. v. A.-G. CAN.
In the Privy Council. [1907] A.C. 65.

Appeal from a judgment of the Supreme Court of Canada, 36 S.C.R. 136.

LORD DUNEDIN: The question in this appeal is as to the competency of the Dominion Parliament to enact the provisions contained in s. 1 of 4 Edw. 7, c. 31, of the Statutes of Canada. These provisions may be generally described as a prohibition against any "contracting out" on the part of railway companies within the jurisdiction of the Dominion Parliament from the liability to pay damages for personal injury to their servants.

It is not disputed that, in the partition of duties effected by the British North America Act, 1867, between the provincial and the Dominion Legislatures, the making of laws for through railways is entrusted to the Dominion.

The point, therefore, comes to be within a very narrow compass. The respondent maintains, and the Supreme Court has upheld his contention, that this is truly railway legislation. The appellants maintain that, under the guise of railway legislation, it is truly legislation as to civil rights, and, as such, under s. 2, sub.-s. 13, of the British North America Act, appropriate to the province.

The construction of the provisions of the British North America Act has been frequently before their Lordships. It does not seem necessary to recapitulate the decisions. But a comparison of two cases decided in the year 1894—viz., *Attorney-General of Ontario v. Attorney-General of Canada*, [1894] A.C. 189, and *Tennant v. Union Bank of Canada*, [1894] A.C. 31—seems to establish these two propositions: First, that there can be a domain in which provincial and Dominion legislation may overlap, in which case neither legislation will be *ultra vires*, if the field is clear; and, secondly, that if the field is not clear, and in such a domain the two legislations meet, then the Dominion legislation must prevail.

Accordingly, the true question in the present case does not seem to turn upon the question whether this law deals with a civil right— which may be conceded—but whether this law is truly ancillary to railway legislation.

It seems to their Lordships that, inasmuch as these railway corporations are the mere creatures of the Dominion Legislature— which is admitted—it cannot be considered out of the way that the Parliament which calls them into existence should prescribe the terms which were to regulate the relations of the employees to the corporation. It is true that, in so doing, it does touch what may be described as the civil rights of those employees. But this is inevitable, and, indeed, seems much less violent in such a case where the rights, such as they are, are, so to speak, all *intra familiam,* than in the numerous cases which may be figured where the civil rights of outsiders may be affected. As examples may be cited provisions relating to expropriation of land, conditions to be read into contracts of carriage, and alterations upon the common law of carriers.

In the factum of the appellants it is (*inter alia*) set forth that the law in question might "Prove very injurious to the proper maintenance and operation of the railway. It would tend to negligence on the part of employees, and other results of an injurious character to the public service and the safety of the travelling public would necessarily result from such a far-reaching statute."

This argument is really conclusive against the appellants. Of the merits of the policy their Lordships cannot be judges. But if the appellants' factum properly describes its scope, then it is indeed plain that it is properly ancillary to through railway legislation.

Appeal dismissed.

C.P.R. v. A.-G. B.C.

In the Privy Council. [1950] A.C. 122, [1950] 1 D.L.R. 721, [1950] 1 W.W.R. 220.

Appeal by special leave from a judgment of the Supreme Court of Canada, [1948] S.C.R. 373, [1948] 3 D.L.R. 417, affirming a judgment of the British Columbia Court of Appeal, [1947] 1 W.W.R. 927, [1947] 2 D.L.R. 723 holding, on a reference, that the Hours of Work Act, R.S.B.C. 1936, c. 122, as amended, is applicable and binding in respect of employees of a certain hotel owned and operated by the C.P.R.

LORD REID: In 1946 [c. 34] the Legislature of the Province of British Columbia enacted an amendment of the *Hours of Work Act,* R.S.B.C. 1936, c. 122, under which it is provided that the working hours of an employee in any industrial undertaking shall not exceed eight in the day and forty-four in the week. The appellant owns and manages the Empress Hotel in Victoria, B.C. and the definition of industrial undertaking in the *Hours of Work Act* is such as to include a large number of the appellant's employees who work in that hotel. The appellant does not dispute that, in general, regulation of hours of work is a subject exclusively reserved to provincial Legislatures under s. 92 of the *B.N.A. Act;* but it has been contended for the appellant that, for reasons which will appear later, it is not within the power of the provincial Legislature to regulate the hours of work of any of the employees in the Empress Hotel and that the hours of work of these employees must be determined by an agreement between representatives of the appellant's employees and the appellant which is made binding by an Act of the Parliament of Canada (1947 (Can.), c. 28, s. 1). That agreement provides for a

48-hour week. In order to determine this matter an order of reference was made by the Lieutenant-Governor of British Columbia on September 21, 1946, by which the following question was referred to the Court of Appeal for British Columbia for hearing and consideration: "Are the provisions of the 'Hours of Work Act,' being chapter 122 of the 'Revised Statutes of British Columbia, 1936,' and amendments thereto, applicable to and binding upon the Canadian Pacific Railway in respect of its employees employed at the Empress Hotel, and if so to what extent?"

The facts regarding the Empress Hotel are stated in the Order of Reference as follows: "The said Company has further, for the purposes of its lines of railway and steamships and in connection with its said business, built the Empress Hotel at Victoria, which it operates for the comfort and convenience of the travelling public. The hotel is available for the accommodation of all members of the public, as a public hotel. The said hotel caters for public banquets and permits the use of the hotel ballroom for local functions, for reward. The property upon which the said hotel is built is not contiguous to property used by the Company for its line of railway, and is not a terminus for its railway line or steamships. The Company has owned and operated the said hotel for a period of thirty-eight years, and the same provides accommodation for large numbers of travellers and tourists from Canada, the United States of America and elsewhere, having five hundred and seventy-three rooms. The operation of the hotel is a means of increasing passenger and freight traffic upon the Company's lines of railway and steamships. The Company owns and operates other hotels elsewhere in Canada for like purposes. There is a catering department in the hotel wherein the Company employs persons to prepare and serve meals. The Company also employs hotel clerks, bookkeepers and other persons to do clerical work at the hotel." . . .

. . . The determination of this appeal depends on the application to the facts of this case of the provisions of ss. 91 and 92 of the *B.N.A. Act*. The relevant portions of these sections are:

[His Lordship here quoted the opening words of s. 91, clause 29, and the concluding clause thereof, and clauses 10, 13 and 16 of s. 92. He then referred to the four propositions laid down in the *Fish Canneries* case, [1930] A.C. 111, which purported to sum up the inter-relation of ss. 91 and 92 of the B.N.A. Act, and he rejected appellant's argument that its railway system, including its hotels, was a unified system constituting such an extensive and important element in the Canadian economy as to bring it within exclusive federal legislative authority under the opening words of s. 91. He then continued, as follows:]

The second argument submitted for the appellant was on more familiar lines depending on the construction of head (10)(a) of s. 92.

Head (29) of s. 91 brings within the legislative authority of the Parliament of Canada any matter expressly excepted in the enumeration of classes of subjects in s. 92; and, as paras. (a), (b) and (c) of head (10) of s. 92 are exceptions from that head, it follows that if the Empress Hotel can be brought within the scope of any of these paragraphs it must come within the scope of s. 91. If the hotel could be shown to be within the scope of s. 91 that would open the way for an argument that regulation of the hours of work of those who work in it must also be within the scope of that section and therefore a matter within the legislative authority of the Parliament of Canada. Paragraph (b) of head (10) is not relevant in this case but the appellant founded on both paragraphs (a) and (c). The arguments founded on these paragraphs are different and it will be convenient to deal with them separately.

Head (10) (a) begins by specifying four classes "Lines of Steam or other Ships, Railways, Canals, Telegraphs", it then adds another class "and other Works and Undertakings", and then concludes with qualifying words, "connecting the Province with any other or others of the Provinces, or extending beyond the Limits of the Province". Their Lordships have no doubt that these qualifying words apply not only to the words which immediately precede them—"other works and undertakings"—but also to each of the four classes specified at the beginning of the paragraph. A more difficult question is the scope which should be attributed to the words "Lines of" at the beginning of the paragraph: must it be held that the four specified classes are Lines of Steam and other Ships, Lines of Railways, Lines of Canals, and Lines of Telegraphs; or do the words "Lines of" only apply to "Steam and other Ships" so that the other specified classes are not Lines of Railways, etc., but are simply Railways, Canals, and Telegraphs? In their Lordships' judgment the latter construction is correct. The context shows that each of the four specified classes is intended to be a class of "works and undertakings". Head (10) begins by referring to local works and undertakings and the phrase which follows the four specified classes is "other works and undertakings". The latter part of the paragraph makes it clear that the object of the paragraph is to deal with means of inter-provincial communication. Such communication can be provided by organizations or undertakings, but not by inanimate things alone. For this object the phrase "lines of ships" is appropriate: that phrase is commonly used to denote not only the ships concerned but also the organization which makes them regularly available between certain points. But the phrase "lines of railways" would not normally have a similar meaning: it would refer rather to railway tracks and those things which are necessarily incidental to their use and would not be appropriate to denote the undertaking which provides regular travelling facilities. In their Lordships' view the structure of the paragraph does not require that the words "lines of" shall be held to qualify the word "railways"; and to read in those words would tend to defeat the purpose of the paragraph and would introduce a difficult and perhaps unworkable distinction between those parts of a railway undertaking which could properly be denoted by the term "lines of railways" and would therefore be within the legislative authority of the Parliament of Canada, and those parts of the undertaking which could not be so regarded.

The question for decision, therefore, is, in their Lordships' view, whether the Empress Hotel is a part of the appellant's railway works and undertaking connecting the Province of British Columbia with other Provinces or is a separate undertaking. A company may be authorized to carry on and may in fact carry on more than one undertaking. Because a company is a railway company it does not follow that all its works must be railway works or that all its activities must relate to its railway undertaking. By the *Canadian Pacific Railway Act,* 1902 (Can.), c. 52, the appellant was authorized to build and operate hotels (s. 8), to engage in mining and other activities (s. 9), to construct and operate electric generating stations (s. 10) and to exercise the powers of an irrigation company (s. 11). The powers conferred by s. 9 were expressed to be for the purpose of enabling the appellant to utilize its land grant. It was held in *Wilson v. E. & N. R. Co.,* [1922] 1 A.C. 202, that subsidy lands were not held by the company as part of its railway or of its undertaking as a railway company and were not withdrawn from the legislative authority of the provincial Legislature: and it could hardly be suggested that buildings erected on such lands for the purpose of carrying on mining or other activities authorized by s. 9 of the appellant's Act are works coming within the scope of head (10)(a) of s. 92. In the case of other works or other activities it may be difficult to determine whether or not they are part of the company's railway works and undertaking, and the question may depend both on the terms of the section authorizing them and on the facts of the case. Section 8 of the appellant's Act of 1902 is in the following terms: "The Company may, for the purposes of its railway and steamships and in connection with its business, build, purchase, acquire or lease for hotels and restaurants, such buildings as it deems advisable and at such points or places along any of its lines of railway and lines operated by it or at points or places of call of any of its steamships, and may purchase, lease and hold the land necessary for such purposes, and may carry on business in connection therewith for the comfort and convenience of the travelling public, and may lay out and manage parks and pleasure grounds upon the property of the Company and lease the same from or give a lease thereof to any person, or contract with any person for their use, on such terms as the Company deems expedient."

This section limits the places where the appellant may build or operate hotels but it does not limit the classes of hotel business which may be carried on therein. Their Lordships do not read the authority to carry on business "for the comfort and convenience of the travelling public" as requiring the appellant to cater exclusively or specially for those who are travelling on its system. The appellant is free to enter into competition with other hotel-keepers for general hotel business. It appears from the facts stated in the Order of Reference that the appellant has so interpreted its powers and that in the Empress Hotel it does carry on general hotel business. It may be that, if the appellant chose to conduct a hotel solely or even principally for the benefit of travellers on its system, that hotel would be a part of its railway undertaking. Their Lordships do not doubt that the provision of meals and rest for travellers on the appellant's system may be part of its railway undertaking whether that provision is made in trains or at stations, and such provision might be made in a hotel. But the Empress Hotel differs markedly from such a hotel. Indeed there is little if anything in the facts stated to distinguish it from an independently-owned hotel in a similar position. No doubt the fact that there is a large and well-managed hotel at Victoria tends to increase the traffic on the appellant's system: it may be that the appellant's railway business and hotel business help each other, but that does not prevent them from being separate businesses or undertakings.

In dissenting from the judgment of the Court of Appeal in this case, O'Halloran J.A. said [[1947] 2 D.L.R. at pp. 729-30]: "But the undertaking of the C.P.R. is one single undertaking and is not a collection of separate and distinct businesses." His view was that because the hotel provides for the comfort and convenience of travellers it is an integral link in the appellant's transportation system, and that, as the other business done by the hotel cannot be severed from services to the appellant's passengers, the whole must be within the railway undertaking. For the reasons already given their Lordships are unable to agree with this view. In *C.N.R. etc. v. A.-G. Sask.*, [1948] 1 D.L.R. 580, one of the questions decided by the Court of Appeal for Saskatchewan was that the *Hours of Work Act* of that Province did not apply to employees in the appellant's hotels in that Province. MacDonald J.A. in delivering the judgment of the Court adopted the reasoning of O'Halloran J.A. to which reference has already been made and held that the hotels formed an adjunct of the appellant's "works and undertakings". If by that the learned Judge meant that they formed a part of the railway undertaking then their Lordships are unable to reach that conclusion with regard to the Empress Hotel; but, if it was meant that the hotels, though not forming a part of the railway undertaking, were of service to it, then that, in their Lordships' view is not enough to bring them within the scope of the exceptions to head (10) of s. 92.

Their Lordships were referred to a definition of "Pacific Railways" in an Act of the Parliament of Canada (Statutes of Canada 1932-33, c. 33) where the appellant's hotel system was specifically included in that definition. But that Act was passed for a particular purpose and in any event that definition cannot affect the meaning of the word "railways" in the *B.N.A. Act*.

Their Lordships would add that if this hotel, or the appellant's chain of hotels is regarded as separate from its railway undertaking, then those hotels cannot come under the words "other Works and Undertakings connecting the Province with any other or others of the Provinces, or extending beyond the Limits of the Province" because the hotels considered separately from the railway system do not connect one Province with another. Their Lordships therefore hold that the Empress Hotel does not come within the scope of head (10) (a) of s. 92.

The third argument submitted for the appellant sought to bring the Empress Hotel within the scope of head (10) (c) of s. 92. If this argument is to succeed it is necessary to find that the hotel or something which includes the hotel has been declared by the Parliament of Canada to be for the general advantage of Canada or for the advantage of two or more of its Provinces. There is no declaration by the Parliament of Canada which specifically mentions either this hotel or the appellant's hotels generally; but it contended for the appellant that the declaration contained in s. 6(1)(c) of the *Railway Act,* R.S.C. 1927, c. 170, is wide enough to embrace the appellant's hotels including the Empress Hotel. This was not the first declaration by the Parliament of Canada with regard to railways. In an Act of 1883, c. 24 amending the *Consolidated Railway Act,* 1879, it was declared in s. 6 that certain specified lines of railway, including the Canadian Pacific Railway, are works for the general advantage of Canada, and that every branch line or railway then or thereafter connecting with or crossing any of the specified lines of railway is a work for the general advantage of Canada. Declarations in substantially the same terms were contained in the *Railway Act,* R.S.C. 1886, c. 109, s. 121 and the *Railway Act,* 1888 (Can.), c. 29, s. 306. It would be difficult to maintain that these declarations included anything beyond strictly railway works; but that question need not be further considered because in 1919 a wider form of declaration was enacted, and this form of declaration was repeated in 1927 and is still in force. In both the *Railway Act,* 1919, c. 68, and the *Railway Act,* 1927, s. 6(1)(c) is in the following terms:

"6(1) The provisions of this Act shall, without limiting the effect of the last preceding section, extend and apply to

"(c)   every railway or portion thereof, whether constructed under the authority of the Parliament of Canada or not, now or hereafter owned, controlled, leased, or operated by a company wholly or partly within the legislative authority of the Parliament of Canada, or by a company operating a railway wholly or partly within the legislative authority of the Parliament of Canada, whether such ownership, control, or first mentioned operation is acquired or exercised by purchase, lease, agreement or other means whatsoever, and whether acquired or exercised under authority of the Parliament of Canada, or of the legislature of any province, or otherwise howsoever; and every railway or portion thereof, now or hereafter so owned, controlled, leased or operated shall be deemed and is hereby declared to be a work for the general advantage of Canada."

In both the *Railway Act,* 1919 and the *Railway Act,* 1927, s. 2(21) provides that unless the context otherwise requires: " 'Railway' means any railway which the company has authority to construct or operate, and includes all branches, extensions, sidings, stations, depots, wharves, rolling stock, equipment, stores, property real or personal and works connected therewith and also any railway bridge, tunnel or other structure which the company is authorized to construct; and, except where the context is inapplicable, includes street railway and tramway."

It was argued that the Empress Hotel falls within the scope of this definition of railway and therefore within the scope of the declaration in s. 6(1)(c). In their Lordships' judgment that is not so. The fact that it was thought necessary to specify such things as sidings, stations, railway bridges and tunnels as being included in the definition of "railway" indicates that the word "railway" by itself cannot have been intended to have a very wide signification; and in their Lordships' view there is nothing in the definition to indicate that it was intended to include anything which is not a part of or used in connection with the operation of a railway system. The appellant founded on two general phrases which occur in the definition—"property real or personal and works connected therewith" and "other structure which the company is authorized to construct". With regard to the first of these phrases their Lordships are of opinion that the words "connected therewith" qualify the whole phrase and refer back to the preceding words and therefore property which is not connected with the railway system is not included: with regard to the second phrase the context shows that these words were not intended to bring in structures which have no connection with a railway system merely because a railway company was authorized to construct them. The appellant is authorized by the *Canadian Pacific Act,* 1902, to carry on a variety of undertakings including mining, electricity supply and irrigation: it cannot have been intended that structures erected solely for the purposes of these undertakings and having no connection with the railway system should be included within this definition of "railway". Accordingly the Empress Hotel could only come within the scope of the definition if it could be regarded as connected with the appellant's railway system or railway undertaking. Their Lordships have already held that that hotel is not part of the appellant's railway or railway works and undertaking within the meaning of s. 92(10) of the *B.N.A. Act*: for similar reasons they hold that it does not come within the scope of the declaration enacted by the Parliament of Canada in s. 6(1)(c) of the *Railway Act,* 1927. It is therefore unnecessary for their Lordships to consider the argument that this declaration is not a valid declaration. In *Luscar Collieries Ltd. v. McDonald,* [1927] A.C. 925, their Lordships stated that they wished it "distinctly to be understood that so far as they are concerned the question as to the validity of s. 6(c) of the *Railway Act,* 1919, is to be treated as absolutely open". Section 6(1)(c) of the Act of 1927 is in the same terms, and the question of its validity remains absolutely open so far as their Lordships are concerned.

It is also unnecessary for their Lordships to express any opinion on the question whether, if the Empress Hotel could be brought within the scope of either head (10)(a) or head (10)(c) of s. 92 of the *B.N.A. Act,* regulation of the hours of work of persons employed in it would be either within the exclusive legislative authority of the Parliament of Canada or within the domain in which provincial and Dominion legislation may overlap. As their Lordships hold that the general power conferred on the Parliament of Canada by the first part of s. 91 does not apply in this case and that this hotel does not come within the scope of either head (10)(a) or head (10)(c) of s. 92 it follows that regulation of the hours of work of those employed in this hotel is within the exclusive legislative authority of the Legislature of the Province of British Columbia and that the question in the Order of Reference was rightly answered in the affirmative by the Canadian Courts. . . .

Appeal dismissed.

[Are employees of C.N.R. hotels, for labour relations purposes, within the reach of the *Empress Hotel* case, *supra*? See *Re C.N.R. and Can. Brotherhood of Ry. Tpt. and Gen. Wkrs.*, [1973] 2 W.W.R. 700, 35 D.L.R. (3d) 119, aff'd (*sub nom. Lab. Rel. Bd. (Can.) v. C.N.R.*), [1974] 4 W.W.R. 661, 1 N.R. 547, 74 C.L.L.C. 14, 213, 45 D.L.R. (3d) 1 (Can.).

Is provincial legislation respecting rates of pay applicable to an employee of a contractor who takes a contract with a company to design, engineer and manage an interprovincial pipe line? See *Cant v. Canadian Bechtel Ltd.* (1957), 12 D.L.R. (2d) 215. Suppose the pipe line is laid by a contractor in connection with the establishment and servicing of sites for off-shore gas and oil, where the employees work from a barge in erecting a tower and platform at spotted locations in navigable waters which are, however, wholly within a province! Is provincial labour relations legislation applicable to such employees? Would the case for such application be clearer in respect of employees of another contractor who did the actual drilling for oil and gas but had nothing to do with the installations? See *Underwater Gas Developers Ltd. v. Ontario Labour Relations Board*, [1960] O.R. 416, 24 D.L.R. (2d) 673.

It was held in *Bachmeier Diamond & Percussion Drilling Co. Ltd. v. Beaverlodge District of Mine, Mill & Smelter Workers' Local Union 913* (1962), 35 D.L.R. (2d) 241 that merely because a private contractor engages to do work for a federal Crown corporation whose operations are within federal jurisdiction does not *ipso facto* bring that contractor's relations with its employees under federal labour relations legislation, at least in the absence of evidence that such work is integral to the Crown's company's operations. The decision is doubted on the facts rather than on the principle in *Note*, (1963) 41 Can. Bar Rev. 586. Indeed, it appears that subsequently the provincial labour relations board ceded jurisdiction and, in fact, certification proceedings succeeded under the federal statute.]

CAMPBELL-BENNETT LTD. v. COMSTOCK MIDWESTERN LTD. AND TRANS MOUNTAIN PIPE LINE CO.

In the Supreme Court of Canada. [1954] S.C.R. 207, [1954] 3 D.L.R. 481.

Appeal from a judgment of the British Columbia Court of Appeal, [1953] 3 D.L.R. 594, 8 W.W.R. (N.S.) 683, affirming the order of a County Court Judge arising out of negative answers given by him to three questions of law set down for hearing and disposition before trial of an action to enforce a mechanic's lien. The questions were as follows:

(a): Can a lien claimed under the Mechanics' Lien Act, Chap. 205, R.S.B.C. 1948 and amending acts exist or be enforced against the property of the Defendant Trans Mountain Oil Pipe Line Company referred to in the Plaint and Summons in this action under the circumstances therein alleged and having regard to the matters raised by Paragraph 29 of the Dispute Note of the Defendant Trans Mountain Oil Pipe Line Company and Paragraph 27 of the Dispute Note of the Defendant Comstock Midwestern Limited?

(b) If not, can the Plaintiff proceed to obtain Judgment under Section 35 of the Mechanics' Lien Act or otherwise in these proceedings?

(c) : Has this Honourable Court jurisdiction to entertain the matters complained of in this action?

KERWIN J.: . . . There remains for consideration that part of Q. (a) asking whether the lien claimed under the British Columbia *Mechanics' Lien Act* exists, or can be enforced, against the oil pipe-line of Trans Mountain within the County of Yale, having regard to the matters raised by para. 29 of the dispute note of Trans Mountain and para. 27 of the dispute note of Comstock, which paragraphs are in substance the same. It is clear that the work or undertaking of Trans Mountain is a work or undertaking "connecting the Province with any other or others of the Provinces" and therefore within the exclusive authority of Parliament by virtue of s. 91(29), of the *B.N.A. Act*, when read in conjunction with s. 92 10(*a*),—just as much as the work or undertaking of the telephone Company in *Toronto v. Bell Telephone Co.*, [1905] A.C. 52. It is true that this is not a case like *Madden v. Nelson & Fort Sheppard R. Co.*, [1899] A.C. 626, because, there, a provincial enactment specifically imposed a liability upon railway companies declared to be for the general advantage of Canada. Here, the British Columbia *Mechanics' Lien Act* is a law of general application and no work or undertaking under Parliament's jurisdiction is singled out. On the other hand, the present case is distinguishable from *C.P.R. v. Parish of Notre Dame de Bonsecours*, [1899] A.C. 367, "where", according to the *Nelson etc.* case at pp. 628-9, "it was decided that although any direction of the provincial legislature to create new works on the railway and make a new drain and to alter its construction would be beyond the juris-diction of the provincial legislature, the railway company were not exempted from the municipal state of the law as it then existed—that all landowners, including the railway company, should clean out their ditches so as to prevent a nuisance". The result of an order for the sale of that part of Trans Mountain's oil pipe-line in the County of Yale would be to break up and sell the pipe-line piecemeal, and a provincial Legislature may not legally authorize such a result.

We are not called upon to deal with other circumstances that might arise in connection with such a work or undertaking and there-fore nothing is said about them. Confining ourselves to the exact question before us, assistance is obtained in coming to the above conclusion from a consideration of such decisions as *Redfield v. Wickham* (1888), 13 App. Cas. 467; *Central Ont. Ry. v. Trusts & Guar. Co.*, [1905] A.C. 576; *Crawford v. Tilden* (1907), 14 O.L.R. 572; *Johnson & Carey Co. v. C. Nor. R.* (1918), 47 D.L.R. 75, 24 C.R.C. 294, 44 O.L.R. 533.

The *Redfield* case decided that ss. 14 and 15 of the then current *Railway Act of Canada* "do not suggest that according to the policy of Canadian law, a statutory railway undertaking can be disintegrated by piecemeal sales at the instance of judgment creditors or incum-brancers; but they clearly shew that the Dominion Parliament has recognized the rule that a railway or a section of a railway may, as an integer, be taken in execution and sold, like other immeubles, in ordinary course of law" [pp. 476-7]. Provisions analogous to ss. 14 and 15 are found in s. 152 of the present *Railway Act,* R.S.C. 1952, c. 234. These provisions deal with the sale of a railway or any section thereof under the powers contained in a deed or mortgage, and provide for an application by a purchaser to the Minister of Railways and parliamentary sanction for the purchaser to operate the railway. By s. 30 of the *Pipe Lines Act* certain sections of the Railway Act apply to companies authorized by Special Act to construct or operate pipe-lines for the transportation of oil or gas but s. 152 of the *Railway Act* is not one of them.

In the *Central Ont. Ry.* case Lord Davey pointed out at p. 582 that the Courts of Upper Canada had previously decided that the vendee under a sale in pursuance of a bond mortgage could not exercise the franchise by working and operating a railway, and their Lordships saw no reason to doubt the correctness of the law thus laid down. In the case before them, however, their Lordships held that the same result should follow as in *Redfield* because of the provisions of ss. 14, 15 and 16 of the *Railway Act.* The two Ontario cases referred to decide that a lien under the Ontario *Mechanics' and Wage-Earners' Lien Act* could not exist or be enforced against the property of the railway companies there in question.

The absence of any provision such as s. 152 of the present *Railway Act* therefore leaves the matter that it must be taken that the British Columbia *Mechanics' Lien Act* does not even purport to apply to the oil pipe-line of Trans Mountain in the County of Yale. If it does, it is to that extent *ultra vires.* Mr. Campbell agreed that if he failed in his contentions as to Q. (a), it was unnecessary to consider Qq. (b) and (c). . . .

RAND J.:—The respondent, Trans Mountain Oil Pipe Line Company, was incorporated by Dominion statute, 1951, c. 93. It was invested with all the "powers, privileges and immunities conferred by" and, except as to provisions contained in the statute which conflicted with them, was made subject to all the "limitations, liabilities and provisions of any general legislation relating to pipe lines for the transportation of oil" enacted by Parliament. Within that framework, it was empowered to construct or otherwise acquire, operate and maintain interprovincial and international pipe-lines with all their appurtenances and accessories for the transportation of oil.

The *Pipe Lines Act,* R.S.C. 1952, c. 211, enacted originally in 1949, is general legislation regulating oil and gas pipe-lines and is applicable to the company. By its provisions the company may take land or other property necessary for the construction, operation or maintenance of its pipe-lines, may transport oil and may fix tolls therefore. The location of its lines must be approved by the Board of Transport Commissioners and its powers of expropriation are those provided by the *Railway Act.* By s. 38 the Board may declare a company to be a common carrier of oil and all matters relating to traffic, tolls or tariffs become subject to its regulation. Section 10 provides that a company shall not sell or otherwise dispose of any part of its company pipe-line, that is, its line held subject to the authority of Parliament, nor purchase any pipe-line for oil transportation purposes, nor enter into any agreement for amalgamation, nor abandon the operation of a company line, without leave of the Board; and generally the undertaking is placed under the Board's regulatory control.

Is such a company pipe-line so far amenable to provincial law as to subject it to statutory mechanics' liens? The line here extends from a point in Alberta to Burnaby in British Columbia. That it is a work and undertaking within the exclusive jurisdiction of Parliament is now past controversy: *Winner v. S.M.T. (Eastern) Ltd.*, [1951] 4 D.L.R. 529, S.C.R. 887, 68 C.R.T.C. 41, affirmed, with a modification not material to this question, by the Judicial Committee but as yet unreported. The lien claimed is confined to that portion of the line within the County of Yale, British Columbia. What is proposed is that a lien attaches to that portion of the right-of-way on which the work is done, however small it may be, or wherever it may be situated, and that the land may be sold to realize the claim. In other words, an interprovincial or international work of this nature can be disposed of by piecemeal sale to different persons and its undertaking thus effectually dismembered.

In the light of the statutory provisions creating and governing the company and its undertaking, it would seem to be sufficient to state such consequences to answer the proposition. The undertaking is one and entire and only with the approval of the Board can the whole or, I should say, a severable unit, be transferred or the operation abandoned. Apart from any question of Dominion or provincial powers and in the absence of clear statutory authority, there could be no such destruction by means of any mode of execution or its equivalent. From the earliest appearance of such questions it has been pointed out that the creation of a public service corporation commits a public franchise only to those named and that a sale under execution of property to which the franchise is annexed, since it cannot carry with it the franchise, is incompatible with the purposes of the statute and incompetent under the general law. Statutory provisions, such as s. 152 of the *Railway Act*, have modified the application of the rule but the sale contemplated by s. 10 of the *Pipe Lines Act* is a sale by the company, not one arising under the provisions of law and in a proceeding *in invitum*. The general principle was stated by Sir H. M. Cairns L.J. in *Gardner v. London, Chatham & Dover R. Co.* (1867), L.R. 2 Ch. 201 at p. 212: "When Parliament, acting for the public interest, authorizes the construction and maintenance of a railway, both as a highway for the public, and a road on which the company may themselves become carriers of passengers and goods, it confers powers and imposes duties and responsibilities of the largest and most important kind, and it confers and implies them upon the company which Parliament has before it, and upon no other body of persons. These powers must be executed and these duties discharged by the company. They cannot be delegated or transferred."

In the same judgment and speaking of the effect of an authorized mortgage of the "undertaking" he said [p. 217]: "The living and going concern thus created by the Legislature must not, under a contract pledging it as security, be destroyed, broken up, or annihilated. The tolls and sums of money *ejusdem generis*—that is to say, the earnings of the undertaking—must be made available to satisfy the mortgage; but, in my opinion, the mortgagees cannot, under their mortgages, or as mortgagees—by seizing, or calling on this Court to seize, the capital, or the lands, or the proceeds of sales of land, or the stock of the undertaking—either prevent its completion, or reduce it into its original elements when it has been completed."

To the same effect, in the case of execution, are *Peto v. Welland R. Co.* (1862), 9 Gr. 455, and *King v. Alford* (1885), 9 O.R. 643 (an engine house and turn-table of a railway) which followed *Breeze v. Midland R. Co.* (1879), 26 Gr. 225 (a station house).

These considerations, *a fortiori,* become controlling when the question arises as between provincial and Dominion jurisdictions. The mutilation by a Province of a federal undertaking is obviously not to be tolerated in our scheme of federalism, and this from the beginning has been the view taken of provincial legislation of the nature of that before us.

In *Johnson & Carey Co. v. C. Nor. R.,* 47 D.L.R. 75, 24 C.R.C. 294, 44 O.L.R. 533, which followed *Crawford v. Tilden,* 14 O.L.R. 572, as a binding decision, a lien claimed by a subcontractor against a portion of the defendant's railway, under Dominion jurisdiction, was denied. The governing case had gone before both the Divisional Court and the Court of Appeal, and in both the judgment was unanimous. In *Larsen v. Nelson & Fort Sheppard R. Co.* (1895), 4 B.C.R. 151, a similar ruling was made. In *Western Can. Hdwe. Co. v. Farrelly Bros. Ltd.* (1922), 70 D.L.R. 480, 18 A.L.R. 596, the Appellate Division of the Supreme Court of Alberta, speaking through Stuart J.A., found against the application of the *Mechanics' Lien Act* to an irrigation ditch constructed under the authority of Dominion legislation.

In *Bourgoin v. La Compagnie du Chemin de Fer* (1880), 5 App. Cas. 381, the Judicial Committee held that Quebec, even with the consent of the company, could not bring about the dissolution of the undertaking of a railway which had been declared a work for the general advantage of Canada. In *A.-G. Alta. v. A.-G. Can.,* 22 D.L.R. 501, 19 C.R.C. 153, [1915] A.C. 363, Alberta was held incompetent to appropriate in any manner any part of the physical property of a Dominion railway for any purpose even though no interference with the construction or operation of the railway should result. In the case before us we have such a measure by which a physical appropriation is authorized that would completely nullify the object of the legislation of Parliament.

This wide concurrence of opinion, followed in the Courts below, is, if I may say so, the necessary conclusion from the matters that have been accepted as pertinent to the question raised. . . .

Appeal dismissed.

[Fauteux J. concurred with Kerwin J. Kellock, Locke and Cartwright JJ. concurred with Rand J. Estey J. delivered a separate concurring judgment in which he said, *inter alia:*

"Appellant contends that the *Mechanic's Lien Act* became a part of, or was embodied in the contracts made between the parties hereto in a manner that made the position comparable to that under the *Workmen's Compensation Act,* in referring to which the Privy Council stated: "The right conferred arises under s. 8, and is the result of a statutory condition of the contract of employment made with a workman resident in the Province, for his personal benefit and for that of members of his family dependent on him. . . . This right arises, not out of tort, but out of the workman's statutory contract": *Workmen's Compensation Bd. v. C.P.R.,* 48 D.L.R. 218 at pp. 221-2, [1920] A.C. 184.

"It is important to observe an essential difference between the workmen's compensation legislation and that of the mechanics' lien. The former not only creates a contractual term of the contract of employment, but creates a benefit for the employees and their dependants and, in order to provide for that benefit, imposes a tax upon the employers. The *Mechanics' Lien Act* in question is quite different. It merely provides for a lien which the workmen and material men may enforce against the property, but which right ceases to exist unless the lien is registered within the time required by the statute. It is a right created by the statute and, while it arises out of the fact of employment or the furnishing of material, it is not made a provision of the contract of employment or of that under which the material is purchased.

"The appellant submits that the cleaning, grubbing and grading of the construction right-of-way is but incidental to the work and undertaking of Trans Mountain and comparable to the preparation of land for the construction of dwelling-houses, reservoirs and warehouses. The essential difference, however, is that the lien, if effective, here attaches to the pipe-line and its enforcement would, as already stated, substantially destroy the purpose for which the company was incorporated."

In *Re Perini Ltd. v. Can-Met Explorations Ltd. and Guaranty Trust,* [1958] O.W.N. 330, 15 D.L.R. (2d) 375 (appeal quashed for want of jurisdiction, (1959), 17 D.L.R. (2d) 715), it was held that provincial mechanics' lien legislation applied in respect of a uranium mine situate wholly within the Province, although the mine had been declared to be a work for the general advantage of Canada. Is it open to the Dominion to exclude the application of such provincial legislation? *Cf. Loughead v. Shackleton,* [1955] O.W.N. 922, sustaining the validity of s. 208 of the *Canada Shipping Act,* R.S.C. 1952, c. 29 (which provides that wages due or accruing to a seaman are not subject to attachment or arrestment from any court) and declaring that provincial garnishment legislation could not validly apply to seamen employed in Canadian inland waters. This case was followed with hesitation and reluctance in *Re Hamill and C.N.R.* (1960), 27 D.L.R. (2d) 61.

On the other hand, it was held in *Deeks McBride Ltd. v. Vancouver Associated Contractors Ltd.,* [1954] 4 D.L.R. 844, 14 W.W.R. 509, that a province cannot legislate as to federal Crown property any more than it can legislate in respect of federal employees, and hence provincial mechanics' lien legislation is inapplicable to federal Crown land even though the land is registered under the provincial land registry system; see also *Western Canada Hardware Co. Ltd. v. Farrelly Bros. Ltd.,* [1922] 3 W.W.R. 1017, 70 D.L.R. 480; *B.A.C.M. Ltd. v. Parkland Builders Contracting Ltd.* (1971), 18 D.L.R. (3d) 377 (Sask.).

In line with the *Campbell-Bennett* case, *supra,* it was held in *Van Buren Bridge Co. v. Madawaska and A.-G. N.B.* (1958), 15 D.L.R. (2d) 763, 41 M.P.R. 360, that there was no authority in a Province (or in a municipality) to authorize the execution sale of an international bridge; this would mean piecemeal dismemberment.

Is not the result in the *Campbell-Bennett* case, *supra*, now reversed by s. 79 of the National Energy Board Act, R.S.C. 1970, c. N-6 which reads as follows:

"79. It is hereby declared

(a) that nothing in this Act restricts or prohibits any of the following transactions, namely

(i) the sale under execution of any property of a company, or

(ii) the creation of any lien, mortgage, charge or other security on the property of the company or the sale pursuant to an order of a court, of any property of the company to enforce or realize on any such lien, mortgage, charge or other security, and

(b) that a transaction mentioned in para. (a) in respect of any property of the company is subject to the same laws to which it would be subject if the work and undertaking of the company were a local work or undertaking in the Province in which that property is situated."

Absent governing federal legislation, it has been held that general provincial legislation may, in some situations, embrace railways, or other agencies of transportation and communication within federal jurisdiction, in respect of their liabilities and relationships to their employees and others. Thus, it has been the view of the courts that provincial fatal accidents legislation, legislation of a province abolishing the common law fellow servant rule, and even provincial workmen's compensation legislation, may apply to private operators of such transport and communication agencies: see *Can. Southern Ry. v. Jackson* (1890), 17 S.C.R. 316; *Workmen's Compensation Board v. C.P.R.*, [1920] A.C. 184, 48 D.L.R. 218, [1919] 3 W.W.R. 167; *McColl v. C.P.R.*, [1923] A.C. 126, 69 D.L.R. 593, [1922] 3 W.W.R. 859. In *Sincennes-McNaughton Lines Ltd. v. Bruneau*, [1924] S.C.R. 168, [1924] 2 D.L.R. 7 the Supreme Court recognized the paramount authority of Parliament to supersede or oust such provincial legislation in respect of activities subject to federal control under ss. 91(29) and 92(10), but was content there to allow a provincial workmen's compensation statute to apply to a shipping enterprise when there was no competing federal legislation. *Cf. Bonavista Cold Storage Co. Ltd. v. Walters* (1959), 20 D.L.R. (2d) 744.

The central problem here is not the paramountcy of federal legislation, if and when enacted, but the preclusion of provincial legislation by the mere existence of federal power, although unexercised. The problem was clearly noted by the Privy Council in the *Empress Hotel* case, *supra*, at p. 442, but on the facts it was unnecessary to resolve it. It is raised by inquiring whether an interprovincial railway or shipping line or air line must submit to provincial liquor control and licensing legislation where there is no such federal legislation; and by inquiring whether they would have to submit to provincial rate regulation if there were no federal regulation. The answer in this last mentioned situation is quite definitely "no"; in the former, the precedents suggested an affirmative answer. Must a line be drawn between those phases of a s. 91(29) activity which are clearly integral to it and those which are merely peripheral, regardless of the difficulty and artificiality involved? Or is it better to explain the case results by pointing to them as evidence of a working federalism? What assessment then should be made of *Rex v. Pacific Coyle Navigation Co.*, [1949] 3 D.L.R. 157, [1949] 1 W.W.R. 937, holding that a navigation company within federal jurisdiction is not subject to provincial annual holiday legislation in respect to its seamen? (See also *Regina v. Canada Steamship Lines Ltd.*, [1960] O.W.N. 277, holding a municipal smoke by-law inapplicable to a ship in a harbour within federal jurisdiction, and *Regina v. Rice*, [1963] 1 C.C.C. 108, holding that hydroplane racing on a navigable public stream could not be controlled by a municipal anti-noise by-law, although the stream was within the municipal boundaries, because such usage of the waters was within the federal navigation and shipping power.) The result is compatible with a functional view of exclusive federal power and may be contrasted with the startling position taken in *Re Lunenburg Sea Products, Re Zwicker*, [1947] 3 D.L.R. 195, 21 M.P.R. 305, holding federal labour relations legislation inapplicable to the crew of ships although shipping is within federal competence. The *Lunenburg* case must be regarded as of questionable authority, even on its particular facts, in view of the judgment in the *Eastern Canada Stevedoring Co.* reference, [1955] S.C.R. 529, [1955] 3 D.L.R. 721, and also in view of the judgment in the *Empress Hotel* case, *supra*.

Recently, it was held in *Re Etmanski and Taggart Service Ltd.*, [1966] 1 O.R. 473, 54 D.L.R. (2d) 210, that the Ontario Arbitration Act could not be invoked to perfect constitution of an arbitration board under a collective agreement concluded in pursuance of the federal labour relations statute between a trade union and an interprovincial carrier; and this was especially so when the federal enactment itself provided a means of resolving the problem created by a failure of one of the parties to appoint an arbitrator.]

A.-G. CAN. v. C.P.R. AND C.N.R.

In the Supreme Court of Canada. [1958] S.C.R. 285, 12 D.L.R. (2d) 625.

Appeal from a judgment of the Manitoba Court of Appeal, (1956), 2 D.L.R. (2d) 93, 17 W.W.R. 415, on a reference as to the validity of s. 198 of the *Railway Act*, R.S.C. 1952, c. 234. Four questions were referred to the Court, as follows:

"1. Is Section 198 of the *Railway Act ultra vires* of the Parliament of Canada either in whole or in part, and if in part, in what particular or particulars and to what extent?

"2. When title to land without exception of mines and minerals is or was acquired by one of said railway companies without any proceedings being commenced under the compulsory powers given by the *Railway Act* but as a result of agreement made with the owner of such land who also owns or did own the mines and minerals therein and such mines and minerals are or were not excepted or expressly named in the transfer or deed or conveyance of the land, does such railway company own such mines and minerals when that title is or was acquired

"(a) pursuant to said *The Real Property Act*, or

"(b) by deed to which said *The Law of Property Act* applies?

"3. When title to land without exception of mines and minerals is or was acquired by one of said railway companies by purchase after commencement but before completion of proceedings under the compulsory powers given by the *Railway Act* from the owner of such land who also owns or did own the mines and minerals therein and such mines and minerals are or were not excepted or expressly named in the transfer or deed or conveyance of the land, does such railway company own such mines and minerals when that title is or was acquired

"(a) pursuant to said *The Real Property Act,* or

"(b) by deed to which said *The Law of Property Act* applies?

"4.   When title to or ownership of land without exception of mines and minerals is or has been taken by one of said railway companies under the compulsory powers given by the *Railway Act* from the owner of such land who also owns or did own the mines and minerals therein and such mines and minerals are or were not excepted or expressly named in the conveyance of the land, does such railway company own such mines and minerals when that title or ownership is or was acquired

"(a) under said *The Real Property Act,* or

"(b) by virtue of the registration of a vesting order or other authorized evidence of the company acquiring ownership under *The Registry Act, Revised Statutes of Manitoba, 1954,* Chapter 223 or the *Registry Act* for the said Province heretofore from time to time in force within the Province?"

The Manitoba Court of Appeal answered the first question as follows: Section 198(1) and (2) is *ultra vires* except in so far as it prohibits a railway company from expropriating mines and minerals by compulsory proceedings. The Court was also of opinion that s. 198 did not apply to land contracts and transactions by the respondent railway companies because of the terms of their special Acts of incorporation. The Court answered questions 2, 3 and 4 in the affirmative.

RAND J.: The first and the substantial question of law raised by this Reference is whether s. 198 of the *Railway Act,* R.S.C. 1952, c. 234 is in whole or part *ultra vires.* The section is as follows:

"198(1) The Company is not, unless the same have been expressly purchased, entitled to any mines, ores, metals, coal, slate, mineral oils, gas or other minerals in or under any lands purchased by it, or taken by it under any compulsory powers given it by this Act, except only such parts thereof as are necessary to be dug, carried away or used in the construction of the works.

"(2) All such mines and minerals, except as aforesaid, shall be deemed to be excepted from the conveyance of such lands, unless they have been expressly named therein and conveyed thereby."

It appears within a *fasciculus* beginning with s. 192 under the heading "The Taking and Using of Lands". First enacted as s. 132(2) of the *Railway Act* of 1903 [c. 58], which came into force on February 1. 1904, it was continued in c. 37, R.S.C. 1906 as s. 170, in the *Railway Act, 1919* as s. 195 and in c. 170, R.S.C. 1927 as s. 195. The original language has undergone minor changes but in the syntax of the section only. The clause "unless the same have been expressly purchased" was in 1906 transferred from the end of the first sentence (as in s. 132) to its present position, and in the 1952 revision the word "is" was substituted for "shall" in the first line and the word "be" in the second line elided. These changes do not seem to me to be significant and in the interpretation of the present section they may be disregarded.

The section distinguishes between lands "purchased" and lands "taken". In this its text is consistent with the words as used elsewhere in the Act; for example, s. 164(1) (c) clothes the company with power to "purchase, take and hold . . . lands"; s. 202 speaks of land "that may be taken without consent" of the owner; and ss. 207 and 218 exemplify the same distinction. Section 216 expressly contemplates the purchase by agreement of lands which the plan, profile and book of reference deposited in the office of the Registrar of Deeds and other publication give notice will be required for the purpose of the railway and it is only in case of disagreement between the parties that the compulsory proceedings are to be resorted to. The same procedure is envisaged by s. 236; and s. 213 provides for the case of purchase before the plans, etc. are deposited or before the lands required are set out or ascertained.

What s. 198 is designed to do is to prevent the acquisition of minerals unless they are expressly made the subject of agreement with the owner. Among other possible or likely purposes this seems intended to protect the interest of the owner: the minerals are to remain his unless they are made the subject of an express term in the agreement. "Purchase" would include every acquisition of land which the company could, if necessary, take by compulsory measures; that would embrace acquisition following the filing of plans, or under s. 213; but beyond these the form and purpose of acquisition might be of such variety and call for so many assumptions affecting private rights that, for the reasons expressed hereafter, no opinion should be ventured.

Is s. 198, then, so interpreted beyond the authority of Parliament? Reading together the sections dealing with lands, the capacity given to the company to acquire them and the power of expropriating them, it is not seriously arguable—nor was it argued—that prohibition against taking the minerals is *ultra vires:* what it represents is simply the curtailment of an extraordinary power itself created by Parliament which, being its creator, can modify it to whatever extent or in whatever manner may be considered advisable.

But it is contended that in providing in effect, as it is claimed s-s. (2) does, for the interpretation of a provincial instrument of title, Parliament has stepped beyond its legislative boundary. It has, it is said, prescribed the terms of a conveyance which passes property under provincial law and that specifically s-s. (2) conflicts with the statutory law of the Province embodied in the *Real Property Act,* R.S.M. 1954, c. 220 and the *Law of Property Act,* R.S.M. 1954, c. 138.

That Parliament, competent to provide for the acquisition of land for a railway and to limit by conditions the extent of acquisition, cannot also provide the reasonable means for insuring that limitation, would, in the particular circumstances, expose the substantive power to virtual nullification. Powers in relation to matters normally within the provincial field, especially of property and civil rights, are inseparable from a number of the specific heads of s. 91 under which scarcely a step could be taken that did not involve them. In each such case the question is primarily not how far Parliament can trench on s. 92 but rather to what extent are property and civil rights within the scope of the paramount power of Parliament. *Tennant v. Union Bank*, [1894] A.C. 31 in which a provision under the *Bank Act* for taking security for loans made by a bank in disregard of provincial forms of security and registration was upheld is a characteristic example. Here the steps to be taken for expropriation, the payment of money into Court with an authentic copy of the award or the conveyance, or an agreement under s. 213, each of which is declared by s. 236(2) to constitute the title of the company to the lands, are all within the field of railway legislation; and s-s. (2) of s. 198 is simply a means for making effective the condition prescribed.

The law of Parliament declaring such a title is as much a law in force in the Province as an enactment of the Legislature. If the company avails itself of the local law of land titles and presents its conveyance or document of title to the Registrar or other officer, the latter is chargeable with notice of the applicable law including, in the case of a conveyance to a Dominion railway, that provided by s-s. (2). If that instrument does not expressly convey minerals, a certificate of title issuing on it should except them. If this entry were omitted by the registration officer and the minerals subsequently sold by the company to an innocent purchaser, it might be that the original owner would be bound by that error in the certificate; that is a question to be decided when it arises; but so long as the minerals remain in the apparent ownership of the railway company, and assuming that they were not expressly purchased, the certificate remains subject to correction at the instance of the vendor or his transferee: as between these parties the statute is conclusive, subject to any right of reformation of the conveyance which may exist, or in the event of sale, to any trust that may arise.

That the Pacific Company, if the section is valid, is bound by it, is conceded; but the situation of the National Railways is somewhat different. Chapter 13, *Statutes of Canada, 1919* provided for the incorporation of Canadian National Railways Company, and by s. 13 the provisions of the *Expropriation Act* relating to the taking and using of lands were, for the purposes of the company's undertaking, made applicable to the company. The latter was created to embody the ultimate amalgamation of all lines within the National system and the undertaking of the company would therefore depend upon either the absorption by amalgamation of existing lines or the construction by it of new lines. Section 13 in its original form remained in force until 1929 [c. 10] when, in an amendment of s. 17—which it had then become—the words "the taking or using of lands" were omitted. At the same time the company was authorized by s-s. (3) of s. 17 to acquire lands required for any of the companies comprised in the National system, a schedule of which had been annexed to the original enactment. In 1955 [c. 29] the Act was rearranged and modified. By s. 16 all of the provisions of the *Railway Act* were made applicable except certain named sections, including 192 to 195 and 202 to 205, but omitting 198, 199, 200 and 201, all having to do with minerals, and excepting "(b) such other provisions [of the *Railway Act*] as are inconsistent with this Act or with the *Expropriation Act* as made applicable to the National Company by this Act".

Following this, by s. 17 the *Expropriation Act* was made to apply *mutatis mutandis* "subject as follows". What follows are four paragraphs—(a) authorizing the Minister of Transport to sign plans under the *Expropriation Act* and dispensing with the deposit of any description; (b) a declaration that upon the deposit of the plan the title vests in the company for such estate or interest as may be indicated on the plan; and (c) and (d) dealing with compensation.

Prior to 1929 each constituent company of the National system was subject to the *Railway Act* generally. Amalgamations proceeded somewhat slowly commencing with that between the National Company and the Grand Trunk Railway Co. in 1923 and so far ending with that of the National Company, the Canadian Northern Railway Co. and the Grand Trunk Pacific Railway Co. in 1956.

The original s. 13 was before the Judicial Committee in *Boland v. C.N.R.*, [1926] 4 D.L.R. 193 at p. 197, 32 C.R.C. 128 at p. 134, 59 O.L.R. 486 at p. 491, [1927] A.C. 198 at p. 205 of which Viscount Dunedin remarked on its "very involved method of expression", and the distinction was pointed out between the function of the *Expropriation Act* in giving power to take lands and in furnishing machinery for taking them. As s. 17 it was again considered in *Bell Telephone Co. et al. v. C.N.R.*, [1934] 1 D.L.R. 310, 41 C.R.C. 168, [1933] A.C. 563. At p. 322 D.L.R. pp. 181-2 C.R.C., p. 577 A.C. Lord Macmillan, referring to the comment in *Boland*, adds that the amended form "cannot be said to present a more happily inspired example of legislation".

A second proposition advanced by Mr. Guy can be dealt with shortly. Under the charters of many of the constituent companies in the National system power to acquire land for the purposes of the undertaking is conferred. His argument is that by virtue of s. 3 of the *Railway Act* by para. (b) of which it is provided that "where the provisions of this Act and of any Special Act passed by the Parliament of Canada relate to the same subject-matter the provisions of the Special Act shall, in so far as is necessary to give effect to such Special Act, be taken to override the provisions of this Act" the charter power is unaffected by the limitation of s. 198. With this I am unable to agree. The power given under the special Act goes to the capacity generally of the company to acquire and hold land; it does not embrace the taking of land without the owner's consent. Purchases in the course of construction are carried out under a code of sections in the general Act and are within the application of the special Act in no other sense than of capacity. That code contains the element of coercion, in the background of which the purchases are made. To resort to or to take the benefit of the code and that element is action outside of the charter power. The authority under the special Act is admittedly subject to the provisions of the general Act which require plans to be submitted, approved and filed and to those dealing with compensation; but these, on Mr. Guy's contention, would, strictly speaking, seem to "relate to the same subject-matter" and to be restrictions of the charter power. Section 198 does not affect the capacity or the right of the company to acquire minerals, but it does prevent their acquisition directly or indirectly by compulsory action, including purchases that do not carry the express consent of the owner. These provisions, in short, serve to regulate the exercise of the charter capacity as the company moves to construct its railway under the powers, procedures and limitations of the general Act.

The application of ss. 198-201 to the National company is thus seen to involve questions of the time of purchase, of special legislative enactments and of amalgamations of constituent companies, apart from the interpretation of the *National Railways Act* itself. In these circumstances, by answering Qq. 2, 3 and 4 we would be expressing an· opinion that might seriously affect private rights in the absence of those claiming them, a step which would be contrary to the fundamental conception of due process, the application of which to opinions of this nature has long been recognized. . . .

I would, therefore, allow the appeal and answer the questions as follows:

Question No. 1: No;

Question No. 2: Assuming that the question means when title to land on the face of the instrument conveying it is without exception of mines and minerals, and that there was no express agreement to purchase them in the case of the Canadian Pacific Railway Company, subsequent to 1904, and in the case of such constituent companies of the National Railways as were at the time of the acquisition of the land subject to the *Railway Act*, between 1904 and 1919, and as between the railway company and the grantor of lands, the minerals did not pass to the grantee railway; in other cases of the *Canadian National Railways*, for the reasons given I abstain from answering;

Question No. 3: The same answer as to Q. 2;

Question No. 4: The same answer as to Q. 2.

LOCKE J.: . . . No dispute arises as to the power of Parliament to prohibit a railway company of the class mentioned to expropriate mines and minerals, except such as are necessary to be dug, carried away or used in the construction of the work. The exception made in the answer given by the Court of Appeal refers to the prohibition from expropriating mines and minerals as if it were absolute, but this is not entirely accurate. There is, however, no controversy in these proceedings as to this.

The real basis of the attack on the remaining provisions of s. 198 is that as both a transfer of land, the title to which is under the *Real Property Act*, and a deed of Old System lands, to which s. 4 of the *Law of Property Act* applies, convey the entire interest of the transferor or grantor unless a contrary intention is expressed in the instrument, to provide, as does s. 198, that "unless the same have been expressly purchased" and unless they are expressly named in the conveyance, the railway is not entitled to any mines or minerals in or under any land purchased by it is to trespass upon the exclusive provincial power under s. 92 to make laws in relation to property and civil rights in the Province.

In the reasons for judgment delivered by the learned Chief Justice of Manitoba with which the other members of the Court concurred [(1956), 2 D.L.R. (2d) 93, 73 C.R.T.C. 254], after referring to the decisions of the Judicial Committee in *C.P.R. v. Parish of Notre Dame de Bonsecours*, [1899] A.C. 367; *Bank of Toronto v. Lambe*, (1887), 12 App. Cas. 575; *Citizens Ins. Co. v. Parsons* (1881), 7 App. Cas. 96; *John Deere Plow Co. v. Wharton*, 18 D.L.R. 353, [1915] A.C. 330, and *Great West Saddlery Co. v. The King*, 58 D.L.R. 1, [1921] 2 A.C. 91, the following passage appears (pp. 102-3 D.L.R., pp. 264-5 C.R.T.C.):

"These cases hold and make it clear (1) that the land laws of the Province, *i.e.*, the *Real Property Act*, R.S.M. 1954, c. 220, and the *Law of Property Act*, R.S.M. 1954, c. 138, are *intra vires;* (2) that companies incorporated by the Dominion Government are subject to valid provincial laws of general application, such as laws imposing taxes, relating to mortmain, and as to the forms of contracts, so long as such laws do not derogate from the status of such companies and their consequent capacities or as a result of their restriction prevent such companies from exercising powers conferred on them by the Dominion Government."

I am unable, with great respect, to agree with this statement of the law. I think no question arises as to whether the provisions of the *Real Property Act* and the *Law of Property Act* to which reference has been made are within provincial powers. In my opinion, they unquestionably are, but they do not apply to transfers or conveyances of property to railway companies of the classes in question which are referred to in s. 198 since that section came into force. The matter appears to be stated as if to hold that the Dominion legislation is *intra vires*, as I think it is, is to say that the provincial legislation is *ultra vires*. Both are, in my opinion, valid laws in force in Manitoba and have been since they were enacted. . . .

The jurisdiction of Parliament in relation to railways such as the respondent companies is not less extensive than it is in relation to a telephone company such as the Bell Telephone Co. of Canada, with telephone lines connecting various Provinces. The legislation granting powers to that company was considered in *Toronto v. Bell Telephone Co. of Can.*, [1905] A.C. 52. Lord Macnaghten at p. 57, referring to the fact that s. 91 confers on Parliament exclusive legislative authority over all classes of subjects expressly excepted by para. 10*a* of s. 92 such as railways, telegraphs and other works and undertakings connecting the Province with any other or others of the Provinces, said that it would seem to follow that the Bell Telephone Co. acquired from the Legislature of Canada all that was necessary to enable it to carry on its business in every Province of the Dominion and that no Provincial Legislature was or is competent to interfere with its operations as authorized by the Parliament of Canada.

It is said in the passage above quoted from the judgment of the Chief Justice of Manitoba that companies incorporated by the Dominion Government are subject to provincial laws of general application, such as those relating to mortmain. This was decided in the case of trading and certain other companies in *Chaudière Gold Mining Co. v. Desbarats* (1873), L.R. 5 P.C. 277, the company concerned in that matter being a foreign corporation but the statement apparently applying to both foreign and domestic corporations. In the judgment of Viscount Haldane in *Great West Saddlery Co. v. The King*, 58 D.L.R. at pp. 5-6, [1921] 2 A.C. at p. 100, it is said that when a company has been incorporated with powers to trade in any Province it may be subject to provincial laws of general application, such as laws imposing taxes or relating to mortmain.

No one would dispute the fact that the railway companies in question are subject to municipal taxes levied under the powers vested in the Province by head 2 of s. 92 except where such right has been taken away, as in the case of the Canadian Pacific Railway, in respect of part of its operations under the section of the contract between the railway and the Dominion Government, considered by this Court in *C.P.R. v. A.-G. Sask.*, [1951] 1 D.L.R. 721, S.C.R. 190, 67 C.R.T.C. 203 (aff'd [1953] 3 D.L.R. 785, A.C. 594, 70 C.R.T.C. 125]. I think, however, no one would contend that any provincial statute of mortmain would apply to lands purchased or taken by such a railway for the purposes of its undertaking in the Province under the powers conferred by its Act of incorporation or by the *Railway Act*. The reason, of course, is that the legislation authorizing the railway undertaking falling within the exclusive jurisdiction of Parliament, the provincial statute would have no application. . . .

The true view of the matter is, in my opinion, that the sections of the provincial statutes referred to have no application to conveyances made to the railways. If it could be said that the effect of the portion of s. 198 which is attacked is not merely to limit the capacity of the railway company to acquire mines and minerals except in a defined manner, but is rather legislation dealing with the manner in which titles to land may be conveyed to a railway company within Manitoba and the construction to be placed upon conveyances in the statutory form prescribed by the *Real Property Act* or complying with the *Law of Property Act*, the legislation could not, in my opinion, be successfully attacked. . . .

On the argument before us, counsel appearing for the Canadian Pacific R. Co. did not seek to support the finding of the Court of Appeal that s. 198 did not apply to the land contracts and transactions of that company and confined their argument to the issue as to whether the section was *ultra vires*. . . .

[The learned Judge then considered the position of railway companies in the Canadian National System and concluded as follows:]

I would allow the appeal and answer the four questions as follows:

Question 1. No.

Question 2. As to the Canadian Pacific Railway: no. As to the Canadian National Railway Company, as to the properties acquired by the Canadian Northern Railway Company and the two amalgamated companies and the Grand Trunk Pacific Railway Company between February 1, 1904 and June 6, 1919: no.

Question 3. The same answer as to Q. 2.

Question 4. The same answer as to Q. 2. . . .

Appeal allowed.

[Kerwin C.J.C., Taschereau, Kellock, Cartwright and Fauteux JJ. concurred with Rand J. Abbott J. concurred with Locke J. Nolan J. sat at the hearing but died before delivery of judgment. See also *A.-G. Can. v. Toth* (1958), 17 D.L.R. (2d) 273, 27 W.W.R. 230.

TORONTO v. BELL TELEPHONE CO.

In the Privy Council. [1905] A.C. 52.

Appeal from a judgment of the Ontario Court of Appeal, 6 O.L.R. 335, reversing a judgment of Street J., 3 O.L.R. 470, on a special case stated in two actions in which the municipality claimed an injunction against the telephone company.

LORD MACNAGHTEN: . . . The claim was founded upon the contention that the telephone company was not entitled to enter upon the streets and highways of the city and to construct conduits or lay cables thereunder, or to erect poles with wires affixed thereto upon or along such streets or highways without the consent of the corporation.

The company had been incorporated by a Dominion statute of April 29, 1880 (43 Vict. c. 67), for the purpose of carrying on the business of a telephone company. The scope of its business was not confined within the limits of any one province. It was authorized to acquire any lines for the transmission of telephone messages "in Canada or elsewhere," and to construct and maintain its lines along, across, or under any public highways, streets, bridges, watercourses, or other such places, or across or under any navigable waters, "either wholly in Canada or dividing Canada from any other country," subject to certain conditions and restrictions mentioned in the Act which are not material for the present purpose.

The British North America Act, 1867, in the distribution of legislative powers between the Dominion Parliament and provincial legislatures, expressly excepts from the class of "local works and undertakings" assigned to provincial legislatures "lines of steam or other ships, railways, canals, telegraphs, and other works and undertakings connecting the province with any other or others of the provinces or extending beyond the limits of the province": sect. 92, sub-s. 10(a). Section 91 confers on the Parliament of Canada exclusive legislative authority over all classes of subjects so expressly excepted. It can hardly be disputed that a telephone company the objects of which as defined by its Act of incorporation contemplate extension beyond the limits of one province is just as much within the express exception as a telegraph company with like powers of extension. It would seem to follow that the Bell Telephone Company acquired from the Legislature of Canada all that was necessary to enable it to carry on its business in every province of the Dominion, and that no provincial legislature was or is competent to interfere with its operations, as authorized by the Parliament of Canada. It appears, however, that shortly after the incorporation of the company doubts arose as to its right to carry on local business. The question was raised in the province of Quebec, and decided adversely to the company in the case of *Reg. v. Mohr*, 7 Que. L.R. 183. In consequence of this decision, with which their Lordships are unable to agree, the company applied for and obtained from the legislature of Ontario an Act of March 10, 1882 (45 Vict. c. 71, Ontario), authorizing it to exercise within that province the powers which the Dominion Act had purported to confer upon it. This Act, however, according to the construction placed upon it by the corporation (which, for the present purpose, their Lordships assume to be correct), makes the consent of the municipal council a condition precedent to the exercise of the company's powers in cities, towns, and incorporated villages.

The company was proceeding to construct its lines in the city of Toronto without having obtained the consent of the corporation, when the corporation brought the two actions which resulted in the special case the subject of the present appeal. . . .

The view of Street J. apparently was that, inasmuch as the Act of incorporation did not expressly require a connection between the different provinces, the exclusive jurisdiction of the Parliament of Canada over the undertaking did not arise on the passing of the Act, and would not arise unless and until such a connection was actually made. In the meantime, in his opinion, the connection was a mere paper one, and nothing could be done under the Dominion Act without the authority of the legislature of the province. This view, however, did not find favour with any of the learned Judges of Appeal. In the words of Moss C.J.O., "the question of the legislative jurisdiction must be judged of by the terms of the enactment, and not by what may or may not be thereafter done under it. The failure or neglect to put into effect all the powers given by the legislative authority affords no ground for questioning the original jurisdiction." If authority be wanted in support of this proposition, it will be found in the case of *Colonial Building and Investment Association v. Attorney-General of Quebec*, 9 App. Cas. 157, to which the learned Judges of Appeal refer.

Maclennan, J.A. differed from the rest of the Court on one point only. He agreed in thinking that it would not be competent for a provincial legislature of itself to limit or interfere with powers conferred by the Parliament of Canada, but he seems to have thought that the Bell Telephone Company by reason of its application to the Ontario legislature was precluded or estopped from disputing the competency of that legislature, and that the enactment making the consent of the corporation a condition precedent amounted to a legislative bargain between the company and the corporation to the effect that the company would not use the powers conferred upon it by the Dominion Parliament without the consent of the corporation. Their Lordships, however, cannot accept this view. They agree with the Chief Justice in thinking that no trace is to be found of any such bargain, and that nothing has occurred to prevent the company from insisting on the powers which the Dominion Act purports to confer upon it.

Their Lordships, therefore, are of opinion that the appeal must fail.

There are two minor points which ought perhaps to be noticed.

(1) It was argued that the company was formed to carry on, and was carrying on, two separate and distinct business—a local business and a long-distance business. And it was contended that the local business and the undertaking of the company so far as it dealt with local business fell within the jurisdiction of the provincial legislature. But there, again, the facts do not support the contention of the appellants. The undertaking authorized by the Act of 1880 was one single undertaking, though for certain purposes its business may be regarded as falling under different branches or heads. The undertaking of the Bell Telephone Company was no more a collection of separate and distinct businesses than the undertaking of a telegraph company which has a long-distance line combined with local business, or the undertaking of a railway company which may have a large suburban traffic and miles of railway communicating with distant places. The special case contains a description of the company's business which seems to be a complete answer to the ingenious suggestion put forward on behalf of the appellants. . . .

(2) An Act of May 17, 1882 (45 Vict. c. 95), amending the company's Act of incorporation, and passed by the Dominion legislature immediately after the passing of the Ontario Act, was referred to in the course of the argument. This Act seems to have been intended, partly at any rate, to neutralize the effect of the Ontario Act. It declares the Act of incorporation as thereby amended and the works thereunder authorized "to be for the general advantage of Canada." It is not very easy to see what the part of the section declaring the Act of incorporation to be for the general advantage of Canada means. As regards the works therein referred to, if they had been "wholly situate within the province," the effect would have been to give exclusive jurisdiction over them to the Parliament of Canada; but inasmuch as the works and undertaking of the company authorized by the Act of incorporation were not confined within the limits of the province, this part of the declaration seems to be unmeaning. Then the Act of incorporation was amended by the introduction of words giving the engineer or other officer appointed by the municipal council a voice in "the location of the line" as well as in "the opening up of the street." It was contended that this amendment enabled the council to select the course of the line and to determine the streets through which it might be taken. Their Lordships, however, do not think the words introduced by the amendment can have the effect of enabling the council to refuse the company

access to streets through which it may propose to carry its line or lines. They may give the council a voice in determining the position of the poles in streets selected by the company, and possibly in determining whether the line in any particular street is to be carried overhead or underground. . . .

Appeal dismissed.

[See also, to the same effect, *Bell Telephone Co. v. Middlesex County*, [1947] S.C.R. 1, [1947] 1 D.L.R. 248, and *cf. Bell Telephone Co. v. Harwich Township*, [1945] O.R. 852, [1946] 1 D.L.R. 188.

For reasons deducible from *Toronto v. Bell Telephone Co., supra*, and from the *Empress Hotel* case, *supra*, at p. 442 the Bell Telephone Co. is not subject to provincial minimum wage legislation: see *Minimum Wage Commission v. Bell Telephone Co. of Canada Ltd.*, [1966] S.C.R. 767, 59 D.L.R. (2d) 145. On the other hand, a wholly-owned subsidiary engaged in manufacturing certain equipment for which Bell Telephone Co. is the main customer does not become thereby an integral part of Bell's operations so as to escape the application of provincial labour relations legislation in respect of its employees: See *Regina v. Ontario Labour Relations Board, ex parte Dunn*, [1963] 2 O.R. 302, 39 D.L.R. (2d) 346. But *cf. Re Northern Electric Ltd. v. United Steelworkers*, 25 D.L.R. (3d) 368 (Que.).

QUEBEC RAILWAY LIGHT & POWER CO. v. BEAUPORT

In the Supreme Court of Canada. [1945] S.C.R. 16,
[1945] 1 D.L.R. 145.

Two appeals, one from an order of the Board of Transport Commissioners for Canada, 54 C.R.T.C. 120, and the other from a judgment of the Quebec Court of King's Bench, appeal side, [1942] Que. K.B. 110, raising the question whether the matter of the fare or tolls charged by the company in respect of its bus service was within the jurisdiction of the federal Transport Board or within the jurisdiction of the Quebec Public Service Board.

RINFRET C.J.C.: . . . I do not propose to go in detail into the history of the Quebec Railway Light & Power Co., except in so far as it seems to me necessary for the purpose of explaining the grounds upon which I base my conclusions.

The company was originally incorporated by an Act of the legislature of the province of Quebec (Statutes of Quebec, 44-45 Victoria, c. 44) under the name of the Quebec, Montmorency and Charlevoix Railway Company. It was then undoubtedly a local provincial company, operating a railway solely within the province of Quebec.

Later, in 1894, the powers of the company were extended to permit it to operate an electric tramway within the limits of the city of Quebec and this was also done by legislation of the province of Quebec.

But in 1895 the parliament of Canada passed an Act (58-59 Victoria, c. 59) constituting the company a federal corporation and sections (1) and (2) of that Act read as follows:—

(1) The undertaking of the Quebec, Montmorency and Charlevoix Railway Company, a body incorporated as mentioned in the

preamble, and hereinafter called "the Company", is hereby declared to be a work for the general advantage of Canada.

(2) The Company as now organized and constituted under the said Acts of the province of Quebec is hereby declared to be a body politic and corporate within the legislative authority of the Parliament of Canada; and this Act and *The Railway Act* of Canada shall apply to the Company and its undertaking, instead of the said Acts of the province of Quebec and *The Railway Act* of Quebec: Provided that nothing in this section shall affect anything done, any rights or privilege acquired, or any liability incurred under the said Acts of the province of Quebec, prior to the time of the passing of this Act,—to all which rights and privileges the Company shall continue to be subject.

The undertaking of the company was, therefore, "declared to be a work for the general advantage of Canada"; and, furthermore, the company was

declared to be a body politic and corporate within the legislative authority of the Parliament of Canada"; and "this Act (that is to say, the Dominion Act of 1895) and *The Railway Act* of Canada" were declared to apply to the company and its undertaking, instead of the Act of the province of Quebec and *The Railway Act* of Quebec.

The same Act also contained the following section:—

(8) The Company may use and employ for the locomotion and propulsion of its cars, vehicles and rolling stock, where such power is required, electricity in all its forms, steam, and any approved mechanical power or other means, agency or force for such purposes that science or invention may develop—and shall have all rights, powers and privileges necessary and essential to the management, operation and maintenance of its line as an electrical system either in whole or in part; and may acquire, use and develop every kind of electrical force, power and energy required or useful in the working of the undertaking, and apply such agencies and motive power for all its uses and purposes aforesaid.

In 1899 the name of the company was changed to the Quebec Railway Light and Power Company, its present name.

In 1939 the following subsection (2) was added by Parliament to the above section (8) by statute of Canada, 3 Geo. VI, c. 56:—

(2) It is enacted and declared that the Company's now existing powers apart from any limitations with respect to the use of steam, include the power to own, maintain, lease, possess and operate auto busses, trolley busses and all kinds of public or private conveyances whether propelled or moved by oil, vapour or other motor or mechanical power in, over and throughout any of the territory in which it is now authorized to operate, subject to all provincial and municipal enactments, in respect to highways and motor vehicles operated thereon and applicable thereto.

In my mind the legislation already reproduced is all that is necessary to be referred to for the purposes of the decision which we have to render.

As will be noticed, by the amendment of 1939 it was declared that the company's powers "include the power to own, maintain, lease, possess and operate auto busses".

Accordingly, the company applied for an order of the Board of Transport Commissioners approving its tariff of tolls for the carriage of passengers on the motor busses operated by it between the village of Boischatel and the city of Quebec. On the other hand, the town of Beauport petitioned the Quebec Public Service Board for an order prescribing certain improvements in the service of the same auto busses, but mainly with the object of having fixed the rates and tolls on the same line.

The Board of Transport Commissioners dismissed the application of the railway company on the ground that it had no jurisdiction to deal with the company's tariffs of tolls or rates in question here; but on the petition of the town of Beauport to the Quebec Public Service Board, while the President of that Board held that it had jurisdiction to entertain the request of the town, the judgment of the President went before the Court of King's Bench (appeal side) which held that the provincial board had no jurisdiction and that the railway company, in the exercise of its statutory rights, fell under the exclusive jurisdiction of the Board of Transport Commissioners for Canada.

The two decisions being contradictory, the result was that both the town of Beauport appealed to this Court from the judgment of the Court of King's Bench (appeal side) and the Quebec Railway Light and Power Company appealed from the decision of the Board of Transport Commissioners. . . .

It is common ground that the railway company operates its autobus service between Jacques Cartier Square in the city of Quebec and the village of Boischatel, and that it holds a permit from the Public Service Board of the province; but also that, since the legislation of 1895 declaring the undertaking of the company to be a work for the general advantage of Canada, both the steam railway and the tramway system of the Quebec Railway Company are under the legislative jurisdiction of the Dominion. It was so decided in a judgment of this Court in *Quebec Railway, Light & Power Co. v. Montcalm Land Co.*, [1927] S.C.R. 545.

In my opinion the autobus system also comes within the jurisdiction of the Dominion.

In 1895 the Dominion Act (58-59 Victoria, c. 59), declared the "undertaking of the company . . . a work for the general advantage of Canada". Obviously this was done to bring the company under the legislative authority of the Parliament of Canada by force of subsection (10)(c) of section 92 of the *British North America Act*. The effect of such a declaration is to bring the work which is the subject thereof under subsection (29) of section 91 of the Act.

Moreover, the company, by section (2) of the Dominion Act (58-59 Victoria, c. 59) is specifically declared to be "a body politic and corporate within the legislative authority of the Parliament of Canada"; and it is further enacted by the same section that "this

Act and *The Railway Act* of Canada shall apply to the Company and its undertaking, instead of the said Acts of the province of Quebec and *The Railway Act* of Quebec".

It was argued that the declaration that the work was for the general advantage of Canada applied only to the undertaking as it stood in 1895, but, in my view, the declaration extends to the whole of the undertaking of the company, railway, tramway and autobus, for several reasons.

Most of what was said and decided by this Court in the *Montcalm Land* case, [1927] S.C.R. 545, equally applies in the premises. As was said by Mr. Justice Newcombe, at p. 559 of the report of that case:

"One must look to what the respondents' claim involves; it is nothing less than provincial statutory compulsion of a Dominion railway corporation, either to exercise powers which Parliament has not conferred, or, in the exercise of its competent Dominion powers, to submit to provincial review and regulations, followed in either case by a consequence that, for failure to comply with the provincial order, the company may forcibly be deprived of its property, powers, rights and management, and ultimately subjected to an action for its dissolution; and this notwithstanding what is undoubtedly true that neither the constitution and powers of the company nor its authorized undertaking is subject to the legislative authority of the province. It is needless to say that these things cannot be done."

The declaration that the undertaking is for the general advantage of Canada may not be severed; it must be understood to apply to the whole of the undertaking. As was said [by] Mr. Justice Newcombe, it is impossible to admit of a dual control over the essential functions of a federal work.

It may be true that it was only by the Act of 1939 that the power to own, maintain, lease, possess and operate auto busses was for the first time specifically mentioned in the Acts respecting the company, but the Act of 1939 (3 Geo. VI, c. 56) was only declaratory. It must be noted that it is expressed in the following words:

The Company's now existing powers . . . include the power to own, maintain, etc., auto busses.

While it may be said that the word "undertaking" in the Act of 1895 covers all future enterprises of the company and means the railway and works of whatsoever description which the company has authority to construct and to operate (*Railway Act,* section 2-35), it must be noted that the powers of the company, as defined in its original charters, although making no reference to auto busses in particular, are very broad and include the "propulsion of vehicles and rolling stock by any means, agency, or force that science or invention may develop" (section (6) of the statutes of Canada, 58-59 Victoria, c. 59).

It was further argued that a bus line is neither a physical thing nor a work susceptible of being made the subject of a declaration under subsection (10) (c) of section 92 of *The British North America Act;* and that consequently, the declaration that the undertaking of the company was for the general advantage of Canada was ineffective to bring the autobus service under the federal jurisdiction. It was said that a work must have a *locus,* which obviously, it was alleged, the autobus service was utterly incapable of possessing and that, therefore, the declaration contained in the Dominion Act was inappropriate to bring the autobus system under the legislative authority of the Parliament of Canada.

However, I would refer to what was said by Lord Dunedin in *In re Regulation and Control of Radio Communication in Canada,* [1932] A.C. 304, at p. 315:

"Undertaking" is not a physical thing, but is an arrangement under which, of course, physical things are used.

Applying that statement to the situation in the present case, I would be inclined to think that the word "undertaking" as used in the statute comprises the whole of the works of the company, which, upon that interpretation, were all included in the declaration that they were for the general advantage of Canada.

Accordingly, I am of opinion that the auto busses of the company can properly be brought and integrated into the undertaking which was declared to be for the general advantage of Canada. It would appear that it was the intention of Parliament that newly acquired works would fall within the declaration.

Much was made in the argument of the amendment inserted in 1939, whereby the power to operate auto busses was stated to be "subject to all provincial and municipal enactments in respect to highways and motor vehicles operated thereon and applicable thereto."

Undoubtedly it could not be contended that for certain purposes the autobus service is not amenable to the provincial laws, but, in my view, that must mean: provincial laws of general application. (*Lukey v. Ruthenian Farmers' Elevator Co. Ltd.,* [1924] S.C.R. 56; *John Deere Plow Co. Ltd. v. Wharton,* [1915] A.C. 330).

The province has the control of its highways (*Provincial Secretary of Prince Edward Island v. Egan,* [1941] S.C.R. 396). It has to maintain them and to look after the safety and convenience of the public by regulating and controlling the traffic thereon. An instance of the exercise of that control by the province might be the fact that the railway company held a permit from the Quebec Public Service Board; but I do not think that the submission to provincial and municipal enactments can be extended to anything beyond the regulations of the character just mentioned and surely not, in my opinion, to the tariffs of rates and tolls of the company, which are made the subject of special laws and enactments under federal legislation and, in particular, under *The Railway Act* of Canada. Otherwise there would be that dual control, already adverted to and rendering the proper working and operations of the company practically impossible.

Now, *The Railway Act* of Canada deals with tolls and, having regard to all that I have said so far, my conclusions would have been that, in the premises, the Act should apply *mutatis mutandis* to the fixing of rates for the autobus system of the Quebec Railway Light

& Power Co., in respect of which the Board of Transport Commissioners may exercise its jurisdiction.

It is true, nevertheless, that the Dominion *Railway Act* does not specifically refer to the regulation of bus lines and it may be that the specific power to deal with autobus traffic is not given to the Board of Transport Commissioners.

Two of my colleagues who, like me, are of the opinion that there is federal jurisdiction in relation to the autobus tolls have come to the conclusion that the regulation of tolls over services of auto busses is not included in the powers of the Board of Transport Commissioners. In the circumstances, although personally I would be inclined to share the view expressed in his reasons for judgment by the Deputy Chief Commissioner, I will agree with the conclusions of my brothers Kerwin and Rand.

It follows that each appeal should be dismissed with costs, except that there should be no costs to or against either intervenant.

DAVIS J. (dissenting in part): . . . The argument is that the "undertaking" of the company was not validly declared a work for the general advantage of Canada—that the authority of Parliament is by 10(*c*) limited to "Works." A sentence is taken from the judgment of Viscount Dunedin in the *Radio* case, [1932] 2 D.L.R. 81 at p. 86 A.C. 304 at p. 315, 39 C.R.C. 49 at p. 86, as a definition of these words "undertaking" and "works" and applied to the construction of the particular Act of Parliament which is before us. The sentence used by Viscount Dunedin is, " 'Undertaking' is not a physical thing but is an arrangement under which of course physical things are used."

It was argued from that that when the Act of Parliament, 58-59 Vict., c. 59, declared the "undertaking" of the company to be a work for the general advantage of Canada, it did not touch or affect the "works" of the company and, particularly for the argument of these appeals, that the word "undertaking" does not touch or affect the motor busses of the company because they are physical things moving about from place to place. I find it difficult to accept such an interpretation of the particular statute. The effect of the statute would be nugatory on such an interpretation. It seems to me that the word "undertaking" there used involves the totality of the works of the company and that the effect of the statute was that they were declared to be for the general advantage of Canada. Such a declaration was within the competence of the Dominion Parliament when the meaning and scope of the statute is fairly construed. The argument was advanced obviously to put the motor busses of the company beyond Dominion control and place them within provincial control, but I do not think that any such strained construction of the statute as contended for is necessary even to accomplish that end.

Section 2 of the Act of Parliament, 58-59 Vict., c. 59, declares the company "to be a body politic and corporate within the legislative authority of the Parliament of Canada."

In my opinion when Parliament in 1939 amended s. 8 of its original Act of 1895 by adding thereto s-s. (2) above quoted, it extended, or at least expressly defined, the power of the company to own, maintain and operate autobusses in, over and throughout any of the territory in which the company is authorized to operate. But Parliament made a conditional grant of the power—the condition being that the exercise of the power was to be subject to all provincial and municipal enactments in respect of highways and motor vehicles operating thereon and applicable thereto. It might well lead to a state of chaos if a Dominion company had a right to operate motor vehicles on municipal and provincial highways according to its own ideas without reference to the provincial laws, rules and regulations governing the operation of other motor vehicles on the public highways in the Province. For instance, you could not in any practical sense have a Province requiring all motor vehicles to travel on the right-hand side of the road and a Dominion company denying any authority of the Province over it because it was a Dominion company, and asserting the right to run its motor vehicles on the left-hand side of the road. Counsel for the company confronted with such situations, admitted frankly that the company was undoubtedly liable to what he called "all ordinary regulations of general application," respecting motor vehicles on provincial and municipal highways, but contended that that does not include the control or fixing of fares or tolls, because according to his argument you cannot read the word "tolls" into the general words of the subsection to which the power to operate motor busses is made subject. His contention is that the fixing of tolls for the motor busses, because the company itself is a railway company, comes under the Dominion *Railway Act* and the Dominion *Transport Act*, 1938 (Can.), c. 53.

In my opinion the generality of the language of the 1939 amendment imposing a condition on the grant of the power is sufficient to involve the regulation and control by the province of the motor busses on the municipal and provincial highways of the province; and the fixing of fares or tolls, for uniformity or otherwise, by a provincial board comes within the condition of the subsection upon a proper construction thereof.

KERWIN J.: . . . It appears that some time prior to the enactment of the amendment of 1939 the Company had commenced to operate auto busses in the city of Quebec and adjoining territory. The meaning to be ascribed to the word "works" in exception (c) to head 10 of section 92 of *The British North America Act* has been considered in *City of Montreal v. Montreal Street R. Co.*, [1912] A.C. 333, at p. 342; *Wilson v. Esquimalt and Nanaimo Railway Company*, [1922] 1 A.C. 202, at p. 208; *In re Regulation and Control of Radio Communication in Canada*, [1932] A.C. 304, at p. 315. Whatever the precise construction may be, I am satisfied that the busses owned and operated by the Company fall within the meaning of that term so that they would be part of the Company's works as much as the rails and tramcars of the Company's electric tramway system. As to these, it has been decided by this Court in *Quebec Railway, Light and Power Company v. Montcalm Land Company*, [1927] S.C.R. 545, that the Quebec Public Service Commission (now the Public Service Board) had no jurisdiction to order the Company to cause its tramcars to run more frequently. Unless, therefore, the concluding words of the amendment of 1939, "subject to all provincial and municipal enactments in respect to highways and motor vehicles operated thereon and applicable thereto," have the effect of altering the position, the Public Service Board has no jurisdiction to deal with the fares or tolls to be charged by the Company for travel on its auto busses. The words quoted are not, in my opinion, apt to confer such a power. The proviso might apply to such things as the necessity of the busses to carry license plates and of the drivers thereof to obey the provincial or municipal regulations as to traffic, but it does not cover the fixing of fares. It was submitted by the Attorney-General for the Dominion that Parliament would have no power to delegate such authority but, since I deem the proviso inapplicable, it is unnecessary to express any opinion upon the point.

It does not follow that jurisdiction must reside in the Board of Transport Commissioners for Canada. Upon the declaration being made that the works of the Company were for the general advantage of Canada, "the effect of subsection 10 of s. 92 of *The British North America Act* is . . . to transfer the . . . works mentioned . . . into s. 91 and thus to place them under the exclusive jurisdiction and control of the Dominion Parliament. *City of Montreal v. Montreal Street Ry. Co.*, [1912] A.C. 333, at p. 342." It is the "works", however, and not the Company that is thus brought within the jurisdiction of the Dominion. Section 2 of the 1895 Act cannot by itself effect any such result but the "works" being considered as an enumerated head of section 91, Parliament may enact such further legislation as is necessarily incidental to the exercise of its jurisdiction over them, and, in a proper case, it may be necessary to consider how far particular provisions of *The Railway Act* apply to them. Section 323 of that Act was referred to but in my view it has no application. The "tolls" therein mentioned are defined by clause 32 of section 2 but it seems plain that these provisions refer only to tolls for railways as defined in clause 21 of section 2. The word "rolling stock" used in the last mentioned clause, as defined in clause 24, clearly refers only to railways. It is not all charges made, even by a railway company, that fall within the jurisdiction of the Dominion Board. *In re Powers as to Wharfage Charges*, [1931] S.C.R. 431.

HUDSON J. (dissenting): . . . Unlike other legislative powers allocated to the Dominion on the one hand and the provinces on the other, the jurisdiction transferred by declaration under section 92(10)(c) of *The British North America Act* is conferred by an Act of the Parliament of Canada itself and may be repealed, varied, qualified or limited in its application, whenever that Parliament so decides. This is the effect of a decision of the Judicial Committee of the Privy Council in the case of *Hamilton, Grimsby and Beamsville*

Railway Company v. Attorney-General for Ontario, [1916] 2 A.C.
588. There the Hamilton, Grimsby and Beamsville Railway had been
incorporated by an Act of the legislature of Ontario. One of its lines
crossed the railway line of the Grand Trunk Railway Company, a
Dominion railway. By reason of the provision then existing in the
Railway Act, all railways connected with or crossing a Dominion railway were deemed to be works for the general advantage of Canada.
Subsequently, the Dominion *Railway Act* was amended and it was
provided that such provincial railway should be a work for the
general advantage of Canada, in respect only of the connection or
crossing, and certain other matters not here relevant. A provincial
board made an order with respect to sanitary conveniences on the
provincial railway cars. This was contested on the ground that the
railway had become a Dominion railway under the original declaration. However, it was held by the Judicial Committee that this
was not so, that the Act could be repealed, or amended and, as stated
by Lord Buckmaster, "the declaration is a declaration which can be
varied by the same authority as that by which it was made" and
in this instance it was properly varied.

New and subsequently acquired works may fall within such a
declaration but it must appear that Parliament so intended.

In the present case the claim is that a declaration made in 1895
extended to works first authorized by Parliament in 1939.

The operation of autobusses was not necessarily incidental to
the operation of the railway . . .

Neither in the Dominion *Railway Act* nor in any legislation
applicable to this company is there any provision for control of
traffic on the highways in respect of rates or otherwise. It has been
suggested that the regulation of tolls and rates is essentially different
from the control of physical things on the highways. I cannot see
this. The highways are owned by the municipality or the province
and it is the duty of the municipality to maintain them and to
provide for the safety and convenience of the public thereon.

The regulation of rates charged by common carriers using highways is nowadays universally recognized as in the public interest.
The fact that Parliament has not seen fit to make any provision
for such regulation in the present case strongly supports the view
that it was intended that such regulation should be left with the
province, where such regulation was already in force.

My conclusion then is that the declaration of 1895 does not and
never was intended by Parliament to extend to the operation of
autobusses on the highways, either in respect of the regulation of
rates or otherwise.

RAND J.: . . . The autobus services have been integrated with
those of both the railway and the tramway system. The company
has provided for joint carriage by railway and autobus and by tram
and autobus, both within and beyond the city. Questions may,
therefore, arise as to tolls between points on the tramways system
proper, between points on the autobus routes, and between points on

either the railway or the tramway and on the autobus routes, and *vice versa*. Admittedly, all rates confined to the railway and the tramway are within the federal jurisdiction and the application of *The Railway Act* 1919. The question raised is whether the tolls applicable between points on the routes of the autobus services and between those points and points on the tramways are likewise within that exclusive jurisdiction and, if so, whether they come within the scope of that Act.

The works of the company are, in the jurisdictional aspect, to be considered as if they had been specifically set forth in section 91(29) of the B.N.A. Act. Was, then, the legislation of 1939, adding to the powers of the company, within the scope of the legislative field appropriate to the subject-matter of the declaration? I think it was. We cannot deny to such an undertaking modifications in operational means and methods designed more efficiently to carry out its original and essential purposes. The controlling fact is that the identity of the works is preserved: they remain in substance the works of transportation dealt with by the declaration.

Nor do I think there can be attributed to the last clause of that provision an effect which would nullify the operative part of the subsection. What was intended to be and was done was the creation of new powers in the federal works as such, and not merely the addition of a corporate capacity. The contrary view involves the introduction of a dual control over the essential functions of such an undertaking. The concluding language, therefore, must be taken to refer only to provincial regulation arising from ownership and control of highways which might affect features of the autobus operations. It is, at most, a legislative disclaimer of intention to encroach upon an area, in different aspects common to both jurisdictions: but the exclusive field of the Dominion, within which lies the regulation of rates, is unaffected.

The further question arises, however, whether *The Railway Act* 1919 extends to tolls either in respect of the autobus services proper or the joint services of autobus and tramway. By the enactment of 1895, section 2, *The Railway Act* of Canada is to apply to the undertaking of the company, and by section 323 of *The Railway Act* 1919 it is provided:

Nor shall the company charge, levy, or collect any toll or money for any service as a common carrier, except under and in accordance with the provisions of this Act.

Can the regulations of tolls for autobus or joint autobus and tramway services be brought within the language of that legislation?

There can be little question that *The Railway Act* 1919, as its title indicates and as its provisions confirm, is concerned primarily with transportation by railways. Service "as a common carrier," in the absence of a context clearly extending it, means, therefore, as a carrier by railway. All services incidental to that form of transportation are within the clause of section 323 quoted. But autobus services are not incidental to either the railway or the tramway: they are a new form of primary transportation. Now the word "railway" imports locomotion on or over "rails", furnishing a service within fixed and rigid limits: and precise language would be necessary to bring within its scope transportation operations by means of power and vehicles unknown when the legislation was first enacted, with a service of a highly mobile character and involving different considerations of public policy. Closely associated with railway service is carriage by water, but this is the subject of special provisions of the *Railway Act*. That enactment cannot, therefore, be held to embrace the regulation of tolls for autobus transportation, either alone or in conjunction with the tramway.

Then, does the specific application of "The Railway Act of Canada" to the undertaking of the company by the legislation of 1895 add in any way to what otherwise would follow from the declaration? To hold that it does would be to imply a very broad *mutatis mutandis* which is not, in my opinion, warranted. The enactment of 1895 did no more than to apply the Dominion Act to such of the company's activities as were within its ambit.

There is, then, federal jurisdiction in relation to these tolls, but federal legislation is lacking. It is not suggested that there was in force in the province at the time of Confederation any law of carriers adequate or appropriate to fill the hiatus in that legislation. However inconvenient it may appear, therefore, it follows that the regulation of tolls for services in whole or in part by autobus is not within the powers of the Board of Transport; and as *The Provincial Transportation and Communication Board Act* is inapplicable within the exclusive dominion field, these tolls lie outside of any existing statutory control.

The same conclusion follows as to the regulation of the autobus services in the manner proposed.

Appeals dismissed.

[Commenting on the *Beauport* case in *C.N.R. v. A.-G. Sask.*, [1948] 1 D.L.R. 580, [1947] 2 W.W.R. 909, MacDonald J.A. said: "Notwithstanding the lack of legislation by the Dominion on the matter it was held that the Quebec Public Service Board had no jurisdiction to fix tolls."

In *S.M.T. (Eastern) Ltd. v. Ruch*, [1940] 1 D.L.R. 190, 14 M.P.R. 206, Harrison J. of the New Brunswick Supreme Court said that "the regulation of trade and commerce would undoubtedly cover the regulation of means of transportation by which articles of trade or commerce are imported, exported or distributed"; and "an interprovincial freight transportation service by motor vehicle . . . would . . . be excepted from provincial jurisdiction by s. 92(10)(a) as an undertaking connecting the province with others of the provinces".

Is provincial legislative authority over a highway in the province lost if the highway is intended to connect with an international bridge? May the province then expropriate land necessary for the highway? See *Bawtinheimer v. Niagara Falls Bridge Commission and A.-G. Ont.*, [1949] O.R. 788, [1950] 1 D.L.R. 331, aff'd [1950] O.W.N. 507, [1950] 4 D.L.R. 63.]

*Note on the Federal Declaratory Power—Works for the General
Advantage of Canada*

It is an extraordinary power that the Parliament of Canada
possesses under s. 92(10)(c) of the B.N.A. Act to bring within its
legislative jurisdiction "such works as, although wholly situate within
the Province, are before or after their execution declared by the
Parliament of Canada to be for the general advantage of Canada or
for the advantage of two or more of the Provinces": see *Reference re
Waters and Water-Powers,* [1929] S.C.R. 200, [1929] 2 D.L.R. 481.
In remarking on how this authority to clothe itself with jurisdiction
enables Parliament to rearrange the distribution of legislative power,
Duff J. in the *Water-Powers* reference spoke of the decision being
taken by Parliament relative to "the 'work or undertaking' or class
of works or undertakings". Since the term "undertaking" does not
appear in s. 92(10)(c), *quaere* whether this is not just a lapse. In
any event, what is intended by use of the term is not further explained.
The power was included, under different phrasing, but with the
same effect, in the catalogue of federal powers proposed by Sir John
A. Macdonald at the Quebec Conference of 1864 but it was removed in
the course of debate. However, it reappeared in the final Resolutions
adopted by the Conference (see *Pope,* Confederation Documents
(1895), pp. 22-25, 44) and was retained as part of the London (Westminster Palace Hotel) Resolutions, 1866, and ultimately became part
of the B.N.A. Bill. The source of the power is unknown, and what
clues there are to its purpose come down to a concern that "national
works" like the Welland Canal or the St. Lawrence canals should
come under federal control (see Confederation Debates, 1865, at p.
40). It is, however, in its terms, much broader, and unless the courts
assert authority to control federal discretion in invoking s. 92(10)(c),
the only limits on the power depend on what is meant by a "work"
and what is a proper declaration in respect thereof.

There has been a singular reticence in the judicial pronouncements
to explore in any general fashion the scope and meaning of s.
92(10)(c). On a number of things, however, the line of authority is
fairly clear. Parliament may repeal or modify any declaration that
it has made: see *Hamilton Grimsby and Beamsville Ry. Co. v. A.-G.
Ont.,* [1916] 2 A.C. 583, 29 D.L.R. 521. The word "works" in the sub-
paragraph is not in any way limited to the class of works (or limited
in any *ejusdem generis* sense) set out in s. 92(10)(a): see *Rex v. Red
Line Ltd.* (1930), 66 O.L.R. 53, 54 Can. C.C. 271; *The Queen v.
Thumlert* (1959), 20 D.L.R. (2d) 335, 28 W.W.R. 481. A declaration under s. 92(10)(c) must have statutory, enacting force, and
neither a resolution nor a recital nor preamble to a statute will do: see
Montreal v. Montreal Street Railway, [1912] A.C. 333, 1 D.L.R. 681;
St. John & Quebec Ry. Co. v. Jones, 62 S.C.R. 92, 62 D.L.R. 464,
[1921] 3 W.W.R. 327; *Luscar Collieries Ltd. v. McDonald,* [1925]
S.C.R. 460, [1925] 3 D.L.R. 225, aff'd [1927] A.C. 925, [1927] 4
D.L.R. 85, [1927] 3 W.W.R. 454; but cf. *Hewson v. Ontario Power Co.*

(1905), 36 S.C.R. 596. The fact that a certain work or works have been brought by declaration within federal authority does not subject to that authority other works not so declared or other facilities. although belonging to the same enterprise, unless there is some other basis in s. 91 for federal jurisdiction or unless they are an integral part of the work or works brought within federal jurisdiction by declaration: see *Wilson v. Esquimalt & Nanaimo Ry.*, [1922] 1 A.C. 202, 61 D.L.R. 1, [1921] 3 W.W.R. 817. It may be, however, that this last proposition is stated too broadly in view of the judgment in *Quebec Railway Light & Power Co. v. Beauport*, [1945] S.C.R. 16. [1945] 1 D.L.R. 145, which is reproduced above.

A number of more difficult problems remain, and it is desirable to raise them and to consider the possible solutions. The terms of s. 92(10)(c) suggest that Parliament's decision to exercise its declaratory power is not as such reviewable; as Mignault J. put it in *Luscar Collieries Ltd. v. McDonald*, [1925] S.C.R. 460, at p. 480, 484, [1925] 3 D.L.R. 225, at pp. 239, 244, "Parliament is the sole judge of the advisability of making [a] declaration as a matter of policy"; and, again, "the policy or the reason for the declaration is a matter for the consideration of Parliament alone." (See also *The Queen v. Thumlert, supra*.). Yet in the same case Idington J. (at p. 467 S.C.R., p. 229, D.L.R.) stated that it was "quite clear that Parliament was entrusted with the quasi-judicial duty of determining, after hearing all those concerned, whether or not a specific work, either before or after its execution, could properly be declared to be for the general advantage of Canada or of two or more of its Provinces". While, in my submission, the courts have no concern with the occasion or reason for the making of a declaration (subject, perhaps, to an argument of colourability which is suggested as a limitation in *The Queen v. Thumlert, supra*), they undoubtedly have the power to review or define what is a "work".

The suggestion in the *Montreal Street Railway case, supra*, that there must be some "national" dimension before the declaratory power may be exercised cannot be taken seriously. Any local "work" (and, indeed, only a local work: see *Toronto v. Bell Telephone Co.*. [1905] A.C. 52) may be the subject of a declaration. What then is a "work"? Elevators and mills have been so declared without constitutional challenge to the classification. Railways have been similarly brought within federal jurisdiction. In *C.P.R. v. A.-G. B.C.*, [1948] S.C.R. 373, at p. 397, [1948] 3 D.L.R. 417, at p. 430, Rand J. proceeded in that case by "assuming a hotel can be a work", and found that there was no declaration to include it. May land, at least if laid out as a highway or a square, be declared to be a work? It was so indicated by Riddell J.A. in *Rex v. Red Line Ltd.* (1930), 66 O.L.R. 53. 54 Can. C.C. 271, but the proposition remains doubtful. The words "before or after their execution" in s. 92(10)(c) give some clue to what "works" means. Thus, for example, neither a company as such nor its statute of incorporation are "works": see *Toronto v. Bell Telephone Co., supra; Quebec Railway Light & Power Co. v. Beauport*, *supra*. In the *Montreal Street Railway* case, the Privy Council declared that "works are physical things not services", and distinctions have been made in other cases between works and undertakings: see the *Radio* case, [1932] A.C. 304, [1932] 2 D.L.R. 81, [1932] 1 W.W.R. 563, holding that "undertaking" is not a physical thing but is an arrangement under which of course physical things are used; and see also *A.-G. Ont. v. Winner,* [1954] A.C. 541, [1954] 4 D.L.R. 657, 13 W.W.R. (N.S.) 657. It is a fairly easy deduction that "undertakings" as used in s. 92(10) (a) are not within s. 92(10) (c), at least if they are undertakings existing without works: see Rand J. in the *Stevedoring* case, [1955] S.C.R. 529, [1955] 3 D.L.R. 721. What import does this have, especially when Kellock J. in the same case referred to authorities supporting the view that "undertaking" may be used interchangeably with "enterprise" and equated with "organization", while Locke J., also in the *Stevedoring* case spoke (although not directly in a constitutional sense) of "construing the word 'work' as including a commercial enterprise"?

If anything can be gathered from what has been done under s. 92(10) (c), as well as from what has been said about it, the result of a declaration of a "work" to be for the general advantage of Canada must surely be to bring within federal authority not only the physical shell or facility but also the integrated activity carried on therein; in other words, the declaration operates on the work in its functional character: see *The Queen v. Thumlert, supra*. This, of course, raises the question whether a change in function would destroy the effect of the declaration and require the making of a new one to maintain federal jurisdiction. Logically, the answer should be "yes", but there has been little consideration of the problem although it arises peripherally in the *Beauport* case. It must be emphasized that the effect of a declaration is not to nationalize the work; it remains under the same ownership; but if the railway and navigation cases have any relevancy, it would seem to be open to Parliament to expropriate or authorize the expropriation of what it has brought within its jurisdiction. Similarly, it hardly needs saying that Parliament does not have to invoke s. 92(10) (c) in respect of works which are already within its jurisdiction either because of legislative power alone or because they are actually federal public property: see *Rex v. Red Line Ltd., supra*. It may be noted, however, that *Van Buren Bridge Co. v. Madawaska and A.-G. N.B.* (1958), 15 D.L.R. (2d) 763, 41 M.P.R. 360, discloses that Parliament has declared an international bridge to be a work for the general advantage of Canada.

Services as such are clearly outside of the category of "works", yet if function is involved in a declaration there are services connected with the operation of the work. May Parliament then declare a hospital to be a "work"? Or a school, or a university? Or a retail store? In *The Queen v. Thumlert, supra,* the Court refused to deal with this "catch-all" argument. Even if the suggestion be accepted that "works" refers to something of a public or quasi-public character (see speech of Lord Carnarvon in the House of Lords, quoted in the

O'Connor Report, annex 4, at p. 76; Rand J. in the *Stevedoring* case, *supra*) the potential jurisdiction of Parliament is still enormous. In any event, it would seem reasonable to exclude chattels as such from the scope of the term, although they could well be included (as they are in the railway cases) where functionally connected with the operation of a "work".

What form should or must a proper declaration take? There are cases in which the federal declaratory statute has declared "undertakings" to be works (as in the *Beauport* case, *supra*) and others in which "works and undertakings" have been the subject of a declaration: see Atomic Energy Control Act, R.S.C. 1970, c. A-19. Such expressions are technically improper but there is no instance in which a declaration has been invalidated on that ground.

There is a further question involved in s. 92(10)(c), and it is raised by the form of declaration used in s. 6(1)(c) of the Railway Act, R.S.C. 1970, c. R-2, and that in the Canada Grain Act, R.S.C. 1970, c. G-16, s. 174. The question expressly reserved by the Privy Council in *Luscar Collieries v. McDonald, supra*, is as to the effectiveness of a declaration general in terms, and especially when it is expressed to cover works to be constructed as well as existing ones of the class. *Jorgenson v. A.G. Canada*, [1971] S.C.R. 725, [1971] 3 W.W.R. 149, 3 C.C.C. (2d) 49, 18 D.L.R. (3d) 297, has definitely established the validity of such a declaration. In the words of Laskin J., writing for the Court:

> "The substantial point of dispute is ... as to the required specificity of a parliamentary declaration in its bearing (if, indeed, it could embrace them at all) upon elevators not actually in existence at the time the declaration is made. The point arises under the words "before or after their execution", in s. 92(10(c). In my opinion, an individual specification by name or otherwise is not necessary for a valid declaration relating to existing elevators. They may be compendiously brought within federal legislative jurisdiction in respect of their operation by a "class" reference (according to a definition, if that be thought desirable, so long as the Court is satisfied that it refers to "works") which takes in those theretofore constructed. In this aspect of the matter, there is no constitutional infirmity in either s. 174 of the *Canada Grain Act* or in s. 45 of the *Canadian Wheat Board Act*.
>
> Another point lurking in the ... submission was that s. 2(1)(d) pointed only to elevators that were individually covered by a s. 92(10)(c) declaration; and hence, a class declaration, as in the present case, did not bring the elevators in that class within the *Canadian Wheat Board Act*. Support for this point was found in the fact that there were individual listings in the *Canada Grain Act* at the time s. 2(1)(d) was enacted, and this provision was not amended in or after 1950 when the individual listings disappeared. This contention is not convincing. There was a general declaration in the *Canada Grain Act* as well as a listing of specific elevators; and the fact that s. 2(1)(d) speaks in the singular is not a ground for limiting its operation to elevators which have been individually mentioned in a declaration.
>
> A parliamentary declaration operating on works 'after their execution' must identify the works if it is to have any enforceable application.

Since s. 92(10)(c) does not prescribe any special method of identification, there is no reason to select any one method over others as the exclusive yardstick of validity. Hence, provided the declaration refers to a work or works wholly situate within a province, identification as, for example, by location or by description or by both (according to the scope of the declaration), would be open. The question is, simply, this: What existing works wholly situate within the province does the declaration embrace? In a particular case, it may be a proper conclusion on the construction of the declaration, being an Act of Parliament, that a certain work is not within it. Such a conclusion would not mean that the declaration is invalid, even if it proves to be ineffective as to the particular work.

The same approach commends itself to me in respect of works which are made the subject of a declaration "before their execution", that is, before they are completed. The issue of identification *ex post facto* may involve difficulties in precise description that would not arise in respect of executed works, but I do not think that any different principle is involved. The maxim *certum est quod certum reddi potest* has an analogical bearing here. I am satisfied in the present case that s. 2(11) of the *Canada Grain Act* gives sufficient precision to s. 174 of that Act and, through this latter section, to s. 45 of the *Canadian Wheat Board Act* to make them effective vehicles for pre-empting jurisdiction over certain elevators before their execution, but exercisable, of course, only after they have come into existence."

[See, generally, *MacDonald*, Parliamentary Jurisdiction by Declaration, [1934] 1 D.L.R. 1, at pp. 15 ff.; *Lefroy*, Legislative Power in Canada (1897), pp. 604-5 n, referring, *inter alia*, to a resolution of the interprovincial conference of 1887, asking for an amendment to reduce the scope of s. 92(10)(c).

The Act incorporating the Bell Telephone Co., 1880 (Can.), c. 67, was amended by 1882 (Can.), c. 95 to authorize the Company to manufacture telephones and allied apparatus, and by s. 4 it was stated that "the said Act of incorporation as hereby amended and the works thereunder authorized are hereby declared to be for the general advantage of Canada". *Held*, this declaration did not cover telephone apparatus manufacturing operations carried on by another company controlled by Bell: see *Regina v. Ontario Labour Relations Board, ex parte Dunn*, [1963] 2 O.R. 302, 39 D.L.R. (2d) 346. Suppose Bell had itself undertaken the manufacturing but had later sold that part of the business to a wholly-owned subsidiary. Would the declaration still apply?

The fact that an invalid general declaration is made, followed by a specific declaration of particular "works", does not destroy the efficacy of the specific declaration: see *The Queen v. Thumlert, supra.*

Is it open to a provincial legislature to qualify or make defeasible the charter powers or privileges or franchises of a corporation should its "works" be declared by Parliament to be for the general advantage of Canada? See *Lefroy*, Canada's Federal System (1913), p. 370. A provincial legislature cannot, of course, prevent or interfere with the exercise of powers conferred by Parliament in invoking s. 92(10)(c): see *C.N.R. v. Trudeau*, [1962] S.C.R. 398, 32 D.L.R. (2d) 362.

Assuming that Parliament properly declares a certain work to be for the general advantage of Canada, is it then open to Parliament to authorize the owner or operator of such work to expropriate land for the purposes thereof or may Parliament authorize expropriation of the work by the Crown? See *Re Ontario Power Co. of Niagara Falls and Hewson* (1903), 6 O.L.R. 11, aff'd 8 O.L.R. 88, aff'd 36 S.C.R. 596.]

A.-G. ONT. v. WINNER

In the Privy Council. [1954] A.C. 541, [1954] 4 D.L.R. 657,
13 W.W.R. (N.S.) 657.

Appeal and cross-appeal from a judgment of the Supreme Court
of Canada, [1951] S.C.R. 887, [1951] 4 D.L.R. 529, reversing a judgment of the New Brunswick Supreme Court, Appeal Division, [1950]
3 D.L.R. 207, 26 M.P.R. 27, which answered adversely to respondent
certain questions touching his right to operate his bus line in New
Brunswick.

The proceedings arose out of an action by S.M.T. Ltd., a licensee
of the New Brunswick Motor Carrier Board for the operation of buses
between certain points in the Province, for an injunction against
Winner to restrain him from embussing and debussing passengers
within the Province. Winner, who resided in United States, operated a
passenger bus service out of the state of Maine, and he offered service
between Boston and Glace Bay, Nova Scotia, and between intermediate points. The Motor Carrier Board of New Brunswick licensed
his operations over certain highways in the Province from Boston
to Halifax and Glace Bay and return, but he was not to embus or
debus passengers in New Brunswick after a specified date. Winner
continued to embus and debus passengers in New Brunswick, and
indicated that he intended to do so not only in respect of his interprovincial and international operations but also, as incidental thereto,
to pick up passengers in New Brunswick whose destination was also
in the Province.

The Motor Carrier Act, 1937 (N.B.), c. 43, as amended, established a Motor Carrier Board with power to licence the operation
of public motor busses or public motor trucks over specified routes
or between specified points. By s. 11, "except as provided by the
Act, no person . . . shall operate a public motor bus or public motor
truck . . . without holding a licence from the Board authorizing
such operations and then only as specified in such licence and subject
to this Act and the Regulations". It was under this Act that Winner
was given his restricted licence.

The judgment of their Lordships was delivered by

LORD PORTER: . . . The vital question for their Lordships' determination is what restrictions are or can be placed by the Province
of New Brunswick upon inter-state or international undertakings by
reason of the provisions of the *Motor Carrier Act,* and whether the
terms of the licence actually granted to Mr. Winner are authorized
under the Act.

The powers entrusted to the Dominion and Province respectively
are those set out in ss. 91 and 92 of the *B.N.A. Act.* Well known
as those provisions are their Lordships think that the matter is
clarified by setting out the relevant provisions of s. 92, omitting
however s-s. (16) inasmuch as that subsection in the present case
adds nothing to the arguments which depend upon the wording of
s-s. (10).

"92. In each Province the Legislature may exclusively make laws in relation to matters coming within the Classes of Subjects next hereinafter enumerated; that is to say,—

"(10) Local Works and Undertakings other than such as are of the following Classes:

"(a) Lines of Steam or other Ships, Railways, Canals, Telegraphs and other Works and Undertakings connecting the Province with any other or others of the Provinces, or extending beyond the Limits of the Province;

"(b) Lines of Steam Ships between the Province and any British or foreign Country;

"(c) Such Works as, although wholly situate within the Province, are before or after their Execution declared by the Parliament of Canada to be for the general Advantage of Canada or for the Advantage of Two or more of the Provinces.

"(13) Property and Civil Rights in the Province."

It is now authoritatively recognized that the result of these provisions is to leave local works and undertakings within the jurisdiction of the Province but to give to the Dominion the same jurisdiction over the excepted matters specified in cls. (a), (b) and (c) as they would have enjoyed if the exceptions were in terms inserted as one of the classes of subjects assigned to it under s. 91: see *Montreal v. Montreal Street R. Co.*, 1 D.L.R. 681 at pp. 685-6, [1912] A.C. 333 at p. 342, 13 C.R.C. 541 at pp. 550-1.

The Supreme Court of the Province answered all three questions and at the expense of repetition but for the sake of clarity their Lordships again set out the questions inserting the answers given by the Court:

"1. Are the operations or proposed operations of the defendant within the Province of New Brunswick or any part or parts thereof as above set forth, prohibited or in any way affected by the provisions of the *Motor Carrier Act, 1937,* and amendments thereto, or orders made by the said Motor Carrier Board? A.: "Yes, prohibited, until the defendant complies with the provisions of the Act."

"2. Is 13 Geo. VI, Chapter 47 (1949) *intra vires* of the legislature of the Province of New Brunswick?" A.: "Yes, in respect of this defendant." (Richards C.J. and Hughes J. answering simply "Yes.")

"3. Are the proposed operations prohibited or in any way affected by Regulation 13 of the *Motor Vehicle Act,* chap. 20 of the Acts of 1934 and amendments, or under sections 6 or 53 or any other sections of the *Motor Vehicle Act?*" A.: "Yes, until the defendant complies with the provisions of the Act, and the Regulations made thereunder."

From that decision an appeal was taken by Mr. Winner to the Supreme Court of Canada [[1951] 4 D.L.R. 529, S.C.R. 887, 68 C.R.T.C. 41] by leave of the Supreme Court of New Brunswick. Meanwhile the Attorney-General of Canada and of the Provinces of Ontario, Quebec, Nova Scotia, British Columbia, Alberta and Prince Edward Island, together with Canadian National Railway Company, Canadian Pacific Railway Company, Maccam Transport Company and Carwill Transport Limited, intervened.

When the matter came to be considered by the Supreme Court of Canada, that Court pointed out that it was concerned not with a Reference but with an action, that the claim was in its origin made by one motor carrier against another motor carrier asking that he be prohibited by injunction from taking up and setting down passengers in the Province of New Brunswick and that the questions asked involved the consideration of matters outside those involved in the decision of the dispute raised by the pleadings.

The Chief Justice indeed took the view that the only power of the Province was to deal with the appellant under the *Motor Vehicle Act* since (1) by s. 22 the provisions of the *Motor Carrier Act* were to be deemed to be in addition to the provisions of the *Motor Vehicle Act;* (2) the *Motor Vehicle Act* provided for the treatment of non-residents whereas the *Motor Carrier Act* did not; (3) in the case of non-residents therefore the Motor Carrier Board has no authority to give or withhold or limit the terms of a licence; (4) there was no evidence or contention that Mr. Winner had not complied with the provisions of the *Motor Vehicle Act* and (5) there was therefore no ground on which the Court could grant an injunction. The other members of the Court agreed with the Chief Justice that there was no Reference and that the sole question for their determination was whether as between the two parties the one could obtain as against the other an injunction prohibiting him from picking up or setting down passengers within the Province. In their view, however, the provisions of the *Motor Carrier Act* affected the position of a foreigner and the dispute between the parties was as to whether under those provisions or by the terms of their licence the Board had power to prohibit Mr. Winner from embussing or debussing passengers within the Province of New Brunswick. They did not determine that the Board had no power to issue a licence to a non-resident, and accordingly based their decision upon a consideration as to whether the *Motor Carrier Act* or the terms of the licence were authorized by the powers given to a Province under the *B.N.A. Act.*

Their Lordships are not prepared to hold that the Board lack authority to deal with residents in Provinces or countries other than New Brunswick or to decide that the provisions of the *Motor Carrier Act* have no application to the case. Nor indeed was any such contention put before them. They therefore proceeded to discuss the problem whether the *Motor Carrier Act* or the licence is *ultra vires* the jurisdiction of the Province.

It was on this basis that the matter was dealt with by the Supreme Court of Canada and accordingly that Court did not answer the individual questions put to them but summed up their conclusions in the following order:

"And this Court, proceeding to render the judgment which should have been rendered by the said Supreme Court of New Brunswick, Appellate Division, did order and adjudge that the answer to such parts of the questions submitted as it is considered necessary to answer for the disposition of the issues properly in the pleadings is as follows:—

"1. It is not within the legislative powers of the Province of New Brunswick by the statutes or regulations in question, or within the powers of the Motor Carrier Board by the terms of the licence granted by it, to prohibit the appellant by his undertaking from bringing passengers into the Province of New Brunswick from outside said province and permitting them to alight or from carrying passengers from any point in the province to a point outside the limits thereof, or from carrying passengers along the route traversed by its buses from place to place in New Brunswick, to which passenger stop-over privileges have been extended as an incident of the contract of carriage; but except as to passengers to whom stop-over privileges have been extended as aforesaid it is within the legislative powers of the Province of New Brunswick by the Statutes and Regulations in question, and within the powers of the Motor Carrier Board by the terms of the licence granted by it, to prohibit the appellant by his undertaking from carrying passengers from place to place within the said Province incidentally to his other operations."

It will be observed that the order in question adopts a compromise which does not appear to have been contended for by either side, *viz.*, whilst permitting the taking up or setting down of passengers engaged in interprovincial or international journey, it prohibited the carrying of persons between two points where the journey was wholly within the Province.

From that decision there was an appeal by special leave to their Lordships' Board by the Attorney-General of Ontario and others against that part of the judgment which permitted any kind of picking up or setting down within the Province of New Brunswick whether in the course of a journey beginning outside the Province and ending within it or in the course of a journey beginning within it and ending without the Province. There was also a cross-appeal by Mr. Winner and others against the prohibition of purely intra-state traffic, *i.e.*, carriage from one point within the Province to another point also within it.

Before their Lordships when dealing with the matter of the appeal it was urged (1) that Mr. Winner's business did not come within the exception contained in s. 92(10) (*a*), and (2) in any case the Province as owner of or as being in control of its highways had jurisdiction over them not only to license operations upon them but to regulate them in all respects. By virtue, it was said, of the powers of the Province to control provincial highways and traffic, the Motor Carrier Board had power to grant or refuse a licence to Mr. Winner at their discretion. It was acknowledged that it had in fact granted him a licence but asserted that the condition attached to the licence was merely a condition upon which he became entitled to operate upon the highways of the Province, not a regulation of his business or undertaking.

The first proposition involves a close and careful consideration of the terms and effect of s. 92(10) (*a*).

The argument was put in a number of ways. In the first place it was said that works and undertakings must be read conjunctively, that the subsection has no operation unless the undertaking is both a work and an undertaking—the former a physical thing and the latter its use.

There was it was maintained in the present instance no work and the existence of a work was an essential element in order to make the subsection applicable. The necessity for the existence of both elements might, it was said, be illustrated by considering the case of a railway where there was both a track and the carriage of goods and passengers over it, and in construing the words "works and undertakings" regard must be paid to the words associated with them in the subsection.

Their Lordships do not accept the argument that the combination of a work and an undertaking is essential if the subsection is to apply. Perhaps the simplest method of controverting it is to point out that the section begins by giving jurisdiction to the Provinces over local works and undertakings. If then the argument were to prevail, the Province would have no jurisdiction except in a case where the subject-matter was both a work and an undertaking. If it were not both but only one or the other the Province would have no authority to deal with it and at any rate under this section local works which were not also undertakings and local undertakings which were not works would not be subject to the jurisdiction of the Province—a result which so far as their Lordships are aware has never yet been contemplated. Moreover in s-s. (10) (c) the word "works" is found uncombined with the word "undertakings", a circumstance which leads to the inference that the words are to be read disjunctively so that if either works or undertakings connect the Province with others or extend beyond its limits, the Dominion and the Dominion alone is empowered to deal with them.

The case of steamships is an even more potent example of the difficulty of reconciling the suggested construction with the wording of the section. Lines of steamships between the Province and any British or foreign country can carry on their operations without the existence of any works. The only connecting link which they provide is by passing to and fro from the one to the other. Their Lordships must accordingly reject the suggestion that the existence of some material work is of the essence of the exception. As in ships so in buses it is enough that there is a connecting undertaking.

It is true and was contended that it is possible to postulate that s. 92(10) has a limited scope and deals only with matters which are both works and undertakings. Works alone and undertakings alone are in this aspect entrusted to the province under s-s. (13) as being property and civil rights or under s-s. (16) as being matters of a merely local or private nature in the Province. It was argued accordingly that jurisdiction over interconnecting works and undertakings is given to the Dominion under the general words inserted at the beginning and end of s. 91 but not under s. 92(10). In terms however the language of s. 92(10) embraces a wider subject-matter and in their Lordships' view is not confined to so limited a construction. All local works and all local undertakings are included under the phraseology used and it is in their Lordships' opinion immaterial that *ex abundanti cautela* they are again covered by s-s. (13).

If the Province is given authority over both local works and local undertakings it follows that the exceptional works and undertakings in s-s. (10) (*a*) likewise comprise both matters.

Some illumination is, as their Lordships think, given by a consideration of the decision in the *Radio* case (*Re Regulation & Control of Radio Communication*), [1932] 2 D.L.R. 81, A.C. 304, 39 C.R.C. at p. 80, as expressed in the judgment of the Board at pp. 85-6 D.L.R., pp. 84-6 C.R.C., pp. 314-5 A.C. The question in issue was whether the control of radio transmission was in whole or in part within the jurisdiction of the Dominion or of a Province and it was held that the sole authority resided with the Dominion.

Undoubtedly the main contention in that case was that a convention had been entered into between Great Britain, Canada and other Dominions and Colonies on the one part and foreign countries on the other hand and that accordingly under the general powers conferred upon it by s. 91 of the *B.N.A. Act* to make laws for the peace, order and good government of Canada the Parliament of Canada had under the Convention a power similar to that which it would have had under s. 132 if the Convention had been a treaty between the British Empire, as an entitly, and foreign countries.

This aspect of the decision is stressed by their Lordships' Board in the *Labour Convention* case [*Reference re Weekly Rest in Industrial Undertakings Act etc.*], [1937] 1 D.L.R. 673 at pp. 681-2, A.C. 326 at p. 351. But that case was concerned with the effect of s. 132 and except incidentally does not mention s. 92.

The *Radio* case, *supra*, on the other hand expressly applies the provisions of s. 92(10). "Their Lordships" it is said "draw special attention to the provisions of heading (10) of s. 92. Those provisions as has been explained in several judgments of the Board have the effect of reading the excepted matters into the preferential place enjoyed by the enumerated subjects of s. 91". After quoting the words of this subsection, the judgment continues: "Now does broadcasting fall within the excepted matters? Their Lordships are of opinion that it does, falling in (*a*) within both the word 'telegraphs' and the general words 'undertakings connecting the Province with any other or others of the provinces or extending beyond the limits of the Province' ". [p. 85 D.L.R., pp. 94-5 C.R.C.].

Later the judgment proceeds to say " 'undertaking' is not a physical thing but is an arrangement under which of course physical things are used". [p. 86 D.L.R., p. 86 C.R.C.]

In their Lordships' view these expressions are directly applicable to the present case. In the *Radio* case there was no connecting work only a connecting undertaking unless the somewhat fanciful suggestion were to be adopted that the flow of an electric discharge across the frontier of a Province is to be regarded as a physical connection.

It is argued that the Provinces are entrusted with local works and undertakings subject however to the exception that they must be "other than such as are in the following classes", and that on its true construction the section must mean "other than such *local* works and undertakings as are within those exceptions". The submission goes on to maintain that *ex concessis* Mr. Winner's work or undertaking is not local having no anchorage as it were within the Province and for that reason is not within the exception. Their Lordships' Board does not so read the subsection. In their opinion "other than such" merely means such works and such undertakings as are within the categories thereafter set out.

The argument can be tested by considering its effect upon one of the specific subjects mentioned, *e.g.,* railways. A railway is an exception to local works and undertakings because it is included in the words "other than such" etc. But if the appellants' argument is sound the section must mean local works and undertakings other than such local works and undertakings as are in the category of railways: and, as the exception only includes *local* works, it would take local railways out of the jurisdiction of the Province, which it does not, and would not comprehend inter-connecting railways, which have always been held to be included and the inclusion of which is obviously one of the objects of the subsection.

One further point was put forward upon this aspect of the case. It was suggested that, whatever view be taken of the matters which their Lordships have dealt with, yet Mr. Winner's activity never became an undertaking until he received a licence; until then it was but a project; he could not get to work before he had a licence. It is true, the argument went on, that he had obtained a licence but his licence only permitted him to run through New Brunswick without embarking or disembarking passengers. That was his undertaking and so far as New Brunswick was concerned, it could not be enlarged by a claim that it was an interprovincial or international undertaking.

Their Lordships are not prepared to accept the contention that an undertaking has no existence until it is carried into effect or is capable of being lawfully carried out. It may be an undertaking at any rate if the promoter has done everything which was necessary on his part to put it in motion, and has made all the essential arrangements. Indeed the argument that the undertaking did not come into existence until a licence was granted and the transporting actually began is in their Lordships' view inconsistent with the opinion expressed by the Board in *Toronto v. Bell Telephone Co.,* [1905] A.C. 52, . . .

In any case Mr. Winner had obtained a licence and has been exercising a business of transportation under it and has not limited his undertaking to the terms of his licence.

To succeed upon this point the appellants would have to say that this is a local work and undertaking because it makes use of the provincial roads, and that the only existing undertaking is one in which the respondent cannot take up or set down passengers in the Province and that undertaking existed from the initiation of Mr.

Winner's activities and still exists since, whether rightfully or wrong-fully, he has from the start embussed and debussed passengers within the Province. That he does so is stated in the facts and whether the facts and whether the picking up and setting down of passengers is lawful or unlawful is the matter which their Lordships have to determine.

On this part of the case therefore the Board agrees with the majority of the Judges of the Supreme Court; and though it is true that the learned Chief Justice does not find it necessary to consider the point he at least has expressed no opinion against it.

The second contention put forward on behalf of the appellants was that whatever their exact legal position with regard to the roads, they admittedly make, maintain and control them; the roads are local works and undertakings constructed and maintained by the Province; in that capacity it is entitled to regulate their use in any way it pleases and indeed to prohibit their use if it so wishes. The contention is an important one because if it is true, interprovincial undertakings connecting one Province with another are within the jurisdiction of the Dominion, but can be totally sterilized by Acts and Regulations of the Province curtailing or preventing the use of its roads. It was alleged that the roads are property in the Province—as indeed they are—that roads of one Province are divided by an imaginary line from those of another Province or another nation at the point of meeting; there is therefore no connecting work and, their roads being local, the Province has absolute power over their uses, *i.e.,* both the method of use and whether they may or may not be used at all.

Their Lordships are not concerned to dispute either the provincial control of the roads or that it has the right of regulation, but there nevertheless remains the question of the limit of control in any individual instance and the extent of the powers of regulation.

It would not be desirable nor do their Lordships think it would be possible to lay down the precise limits within which the use of provincial highways may be regulated. Such matters as speed, the side of the road upon which to drive, the weight and lights of vehicles are obvious examples but in the present case their Lordships are not faced with considerations of this kind nor are they concerned with the further question which was mooted before them, *viz.,* whether a Province had it in its power to plough up its roads and so make interprovincial connections impossible. So isolationist a policy is indeed unthinkable. The roads exist and in fact form a connection with other Provinces and also, in this case, with another country. Since in their Lordships' opinion Mr. Winner is carrying on an under-taking connecting New Brunswick both with Nova Scotia and the State of Maine there exists an undertaking connecting Province with Province and extending beyond the limits of the Province.

Prima facie at any rate such an undertaking is entrusted to the control of the Dominion and taken out of that of the Province. No doubt if it were not for s. 92(10)(a) of the *B.N.A. Act* the Province, having jurisdiction over local works and undertakings and over property and civil rights within the Province could have prohibited the use of or exercised complete autocratic control over its highways, but the subsection in question withdraws this absolute right where the undertaking is a connecting one. To this limitation some meaning must be given and their Lordships cannot accept the view that the jurisdiction of the Dominion is impaired by the Province's general right of control over its own roads. So to construe this subsection would in their Lordships' opinion destroy the efficacy of the exception.

The limitations of the jurisdiction of Dominion and Province have been many times canvassed and litigated both in the Canadian Courts and in the Privy Council. Undoubtedly the Province has wide powers of regulation. Many instances were adduced in the course of argument and their Lordships may refer to certain of those most relied upon.

In *Colonial Building & Investment Ass'n v. A.-G. Que.* (1883), 9 App. Cas. 157, the provincial mortmain laws were said to be contrary to the jurisdiction given to the Dominion in respect of Dominion companies. The principles relied upon are set out at p. 166 in the following words:—"But the powers found in the Act of Incorporation are not necessarily inconsistent with the provincial law of mortmain, which does not absolutely prohibit corporations from acquiring or holding lands, but only requires, as a condition of their so doing, that they should have the consent of the Crown. If that consent be obtained, a corporation does not infringe the provincial law of mortmain by acquiring and holding lands. What the Act of Incorporation has done is to create a legal and artificial person with capacity to carry on certain kinds of business, which are defined, within a defined area, viz., throughout the Dominion. Among other things, it has given to the association power to deal in land and buildings, but the capacity so given only enables it to acquire and hold land in any province consistently with the laws of that province relating to the acquisition and tenure of land."

Similar propositions were laid down in *Great West Saddlery Co. v. The King*, 58 D.L.R. 1, [1921] 2 A.C. 91, where the gist of the decision may be taken from the [A.C.] headnote where it says: "A Company incorporated by the Dominion under the Companies Act of Canada (R.S.C. 1906, c. 79), with power to trade in any Province may, consistently with ss. 91 and 92 of the *British North America Act*, be subject to Provincial laws of general application, such as laws imposing taxes, or relating to mortmain or requiring licences for certain purposes, or as to the form of contracts."

For the same reasons it was held in *Lymburn v. Mayland*, [1932] 2 D.L.R. 6 at p. 9, A.C. 318 at p. 324, 57 Can. C.C. 311 at pp. 314-5, that a provision prohibiting the selling of the shares of Dominion companies was not *ultra vires* provincial legislation inasmuch as it did not preclude them from selling their shares unless they were registered but merely subjected them to competent provisions applying to all persons trading in securities.

Both the latter cases however are careful to point out that legislation will be invalid if a Dominion company is sterilized in all its functions and activities or its status and essential capacities are impaired in a substantial degree.

What provisions have the effect of sterilizing all the functions and activities of a company or impair its status and capacities in an essential degree will of course depend on the circumstances of each case but in the present instance their Lordships cannot have any doubt but that the Act or the licence or both combined do have such an effect on Mr. Winner's undertaking in its task of connecting New Brunswick with both the United States of America and with the Province of Nova Scotia.

Nor indeed, whatever may be said of the Act, is the licence a provision applying to all persons: It is a particular provision aimed at preventing Mr. Winner from competing with local transport companies in New Brunswick.

But, it is contended, there are two rights—that of the Dominion and that of the Province—one giving power to the one body and the other to the other; and enabling Dominion or Province to pass legislation dealing with its own topic: the Province with its roads and the Dominion with connecting undertakings. So long as the Dominion has not, as it has not, passed legislation dealing with the matter, the powers overlap and the Province is entitled to enact its own provisions which unless and until the Dominion deals with the matter are valid and enforceable. This argument does not appear to have been presented to the Courts in Canada and their Lordships do not agree with it.

The Province has indeed authority over its own roads but that authority is a limited one and does not entitle it to interfere with connecting undertakings. It must be remembered that it is the undertaking not the roads which come within the jurisdiction of the Dominion, but legislation which denies the use of the provincial roads to such an undertaking or sterilizes the undertaking itself is an interference with the prerogative of the Dominion.

Whatever provisions or Regulations a Province may prescribe with regard to its roads it must not prevent or restrict interprovincial traffic. As their Lordships have indicated this does not in any way prevent what is in essence traffic regulation but the provisions contained in local statutes and Regulations must be confined to such matters.

In the present case they are not so confined. They do not contain provisions as to the use of the highways—they are not even general Regulations affecting all users of them. They deal with a particular undertaking in a particular way and prohibit Mr. Winner from using the highways except as a means of passage from another country to another state. It does not indeed follow that a Regulation of universal application is necessarily unobjectionable—each case must depend upon its own facts, but such a Regulation is less likely to offend against the limitation imposed on the jurisdiction of the Province inasmuch as it will deal with all traffic and not with that connecting Province and Province. The question as their Lordships see it, and indeed as it was argued, raises the hackneyed consideration what is the pith and substance of the provision under consideration. Is it in substance traffic regulation or is it an interference with an undertaking connecting Province and Province? Their Lordships cannot doubt but that it was the latter. It obviously sought to limit activities of an undertaking connecting the State of Maine with New Brunswick and New Brunswick with Nova Scotia. It was not mere regulation of road traffic. It is true that the distinction between the jurisdiction of the Dominion and that of a Province may be a fine one as appears from a comparison of two cases both to be found in [1889] A.C., *viz.*: *C.P.R. v. Notre Dame de Bonsecours* at p. 367, and *Madden v. Nelson & Fort Sheppard R. Co.* at p. 626. But except to call attention to the fact that each case must depend on an exact examination of its own facts those decisions are not directly relevant to any point which their Lordships have to decide.

In their Lordships' opinion the action of the Province was an incursion into the field reserved by the *B.N.A. Act* to the Dominion.

In coming to this conclusion their Lordships refrain from deciding whether the Act or the Regulations or both are beyond the powers of the Province. It may be that the Act can be so read as to apply to provincial matters only. If this be so the licence given to Mr. Winner is an unauthorized limitation of his rights because it is for the Dominion alone to exercise either by Act or by Regulation control over connecting undertakings.

On the other hand it may be that the Act itself must be construed as interfering with undertakings connecting Province with Province or with another country.

In either case the Province either through the Act itself or through the licence issued in pursuance of Regulations made under the Act has exceeded its jurisdiction. The licence indeed may be good as a licence but the limitation imposed in it is *ultra vires and of no effect*.

There remains however the further question whether although the licence cannot be limited in the manner imposed by the Board Mr. Winner can nevertheless, as the Supreme Court adjudged be prohibited from taking up and setting down purely provincial passengers, *i.e.,* those whose journey both begins and ends within the Province.

So far as their Lordships are able to judge none of the parties and none of the interveners suggested such a compromise in any of the Courts in Canada.

Their Lordships might however accede to the argument if there were evidence that Mr. Winner was engaged in two enterprises; one within the Province and the other of a connecting nature.

Their Lordships however cannot see any evidence of such a dual enterprise. The same buses carried both types of passenger along the same routes; the journeys may have been different, in that one was partly outside the Province and the other wholly within, but it was the same undertaking which was engaged in both activities.

The Supreme Court however approached the question from a different angle. To them a distinction should be drawn between what was an essential and what was an incidental portion of the enterprise. In their view the portion which could be shed without putting an end to it did not constitute an essential part of the undertaking and therefore could be dealt with by the Province, leaving only the essential part for the Dominion's jurisdiction.

Their Lordships are of opinion that this method of approach results from a misapprehension of the true construction of s. 92(10) (a) of the *B.N.A. Act*. The question is not what portions of the undertaking can be stripped from it without interfering with the activity altogether: it is rather what is the undertaking which is in fact being carried on. Is there one undertaking, and as part of that one undertaking does the respondent carry passengers between two points both within the Province, or are there two?

The view of the Supreme Court is succinctly put by Rand J. when he says: [[1951] 4 D.L.R. at pp. 562-3, S.C.R. at p. 924, 68 C.R.T.C. at pp. 7-8-9]: "Assuming then that the international and inter-provincial components of Winner's service are such an undertaking as head (10) envisages, the question is whether, by his own act, for the purposes of the statute, he can annex to it the local services. Under the theory advanced by Mr. Tennant, given an automobile, an individual can, by piecemeal accumulation, bring within head (10) (a) a day-to-day fluctuating totality of operations of the class of those here in question. The result of being able to do so could undoubtedly introduce a destructive interference with the balanced and co-ordinated administration by the Province of what is primarily a local matter; and the public interest would suffer accordingly. There is no necessary entirety to such an aggregate and I cannot think it a sound con-struction of the section to permit the attraction, by such mode, to Dominion jurisdiction of severable matter that otherwise would belong to the Province."

No doubt the taking up and setting down of passengers journeying wholly within the Province could be severed from the rest of Mr. Winner's undertaking but so to treat the question is not to ask is there an undertaking and does it form a connection with other countries or other Provinces but can you emasculate the actual under-taking and yet leave it the same undertaking or so divide it that part of it can be regarded as interprovincial and the other part as provincial.

The undertaking in question is in fact one and indivisible. It is true that it might have been carried on differently and might have been limited to activities within or without the Province, but it is not, and their Lordships do not agree that the fact that it might be carried on otherwise than it is makes it or any part of it any the less an interconnecting undertaking.

The contention is clearly dealt with by the observations of the Board in the *Bell Telephone* case, [1905] A.C. 52—observations which in their Lordships' opinion have a direct application to the present case and are to be found at p. 59 in the following words: "It was argued that the company was formed to carry on, and was carrying on, two separate and distinct businesses—a local business and a long-distance business. And it was contended that the local business and the undertaking of the company so far as it dealt with local business fell within the jurisdiction of the provincial legislature. But there, again, the facts do not support the contention of the appellants. The undertaking authorized by the Act of 1880 was one single undertaking, though for certain purposes its business may be regarded as falling under different branches or heads. The undertaking of the Bell Telephone Company was no more a collection of separate and distinct businesses than the undertaking of a telegraph company which has a long-distance line combined with local business, or the undertaking of a railway company which may have a large suburban traffic and miles of railway communicating with distant places. The special case contains a description of the company's business which seems to be a complete answer to the ingenious suggestion put forward on behalf of the appellants."

In coming to this conclusion their Lordships must not be supposed to lend any countenance to the suggestion that a carrier who is substantially an integral carrier can put himself outside provincial jurisdiction by starting his activities a few miles over the border. Such a subterfuge would not avail him. The question is whether in truth and in fact there is an internal activity prolonged over the border in order to enable the owner to evade provincial jurisdiction or whether in pith and substance it is interprovincial. Just as the question whether there is an interconnecting undertaking is one depending on all the circumstances of the case so the question whether it is a camouflaged local undertaking masquerading as an interconnecting one must also depend on the facts of each case and on a determination of what is the pith and substance of an Act or Regulation.

Of course, as has so often been pointed out, whether upon the evidence adduced an activity can be adjudged to be local is a matter of law, but once it is decided that it can be local the question whether it is so is one of fact for the relevant tribunal to determine.

In the case under consideration no such question arises. The undertaking is one connecting the Province with another and extending beyond the limits of the Province and therefore comes within the provisions of s. 92(10)(a) and is solely within the jurisdiction of the Dominion.

One note of warning should however be sounded. Their Lordships express no opinion as to whether Mr. Winner could initiate a purely provincial bus service even though it was under the aegis of and managed by his present organization.

No such question however arises or has been raised. As it is their Lordships will humbly advise Her Majesty that the appeal of the Attorneys-General for Ontario, Alberta and Prince Edward Island ought to be dismissed, (2) that the appeal of Israel Winner, Canadian National Railway Company and Canadian Pacific Railway Company ought to be allowed, (3) that the order of the Supreme Court ought to be varied . . .

Appeal dismissed; cross-appeal allowed.

[The jurisdiction declared by the *Winner* case to reside exclusively in Parliament was administratively returned to the Provinces by delegation under the Motor Vehicle Transport Act, 1954 (Can.), c. 59, now R.S.C. 1970, c. M-14. The Act does not, however, permit a province to apply to interprovincial motor carriers the provisions of its legislation with reference to local carriers, giving instead only the licensing (and rate-fixing) functions specified in the Act. *Registrar of Motor Vehicles v. Canadian American Transfer Ltd.*, [1972] S.C.R. 811, 26 D.L.R. (3d) 112. The need for care in drafting the delegating legislation lest an interprovincial carrier find itself obliged to have licences for interprovincial carriage both from the Province of origin and the Province of destination is underscored by *Re Kleysen's Cartage Co. Ltd. and Manitoba Motor Carrier Board* (1965), 48 D.L.R. (2d) 716, 51 W.W.R. 218, rev'g 47 D.L.R. (2d) 244, 49 W.W.R. 577. The Motor Vehicle Transport Act was construed here, on an assessment of its language, in line with the doctrine that a Province cannot prohibit dealing outside the Province; hence a licence for extra-provincial movement of goods was not required from the Province of origin of the movement. But see now The National Transportation Act, R.S.C. 1970, c. N-17, s. 4(e) and Part III, ss. 36-42, under which federal administration is contemplated when Part III is proclaimed.

The *Winner* case only goes as far as to deny provincial power to require an interprovincial bus or trucking line to obtain an operating or business licence; nor may the Province do this indirectly by denying use of provincial (public) highways. However, provincial legislation may (at least in the absence of federal legislation) require drivers employed by the line to obtain a provincial driving permit, may require the vehicles to carry a licence plate, and may similarly impose restrictions directed to proper use of provincial highways, such as those connected with vehicle loads and equipment: see *Regina v. Arrow Transit Lines Ltd.*, [1955] 2 D.L.R. 351, [1954] O.W.N. 538, 109 Can. C.C. 321.

The principle of the *Winner* case was extended by *Re Tank Truck Transport Ltd.*, [1960] O.R. 497, 25 D.L.R. (2d) 161, aff'd without written reasons [1963] 1 O.R. 272, 36 D.L.R. (2d) 636, so as to bring within federal jurisdiction the labour relations of an Ontario company holding extra-provincial and international licences under which, however, only 6 per cent of its activity was extra-provincial, but it was on a regular basis. The company had three terminals in Ontario and one in Quebec, but its payrolls for drivers were made up at two of the Ontario terminals, and employees in the two bargaining units for which union certification was issued under Ontario legislation worked out of two of the Ontario terminals. The extra-provincial and international licences were limited, and the company apparently could not survive save as a local intra-provincial carrier.

Presumably if the company dropped its extra-provincial business, its subjection to the provincial legislation would revive. Does this not suggest that if the union certification under provincial legislation was valid when issued, it should be allowed to remain in force until revoked or displaced by a valid certification under federal legislation? Does the *Bell Telephone Co.* case, *supra*, at p. 464, have any bearing on this matter?

Re Tank Truck Transport Ltd. was followed in *Regina v. Cooksville Magistrates Court, ex parte Liquid Cargo Lines Ltd.*, [1965] 1 O.R. 84, 46 D.L.R. (2d) 700, in respect of an Ontario company which had no extra-provincial terminal and whose extra-provincial business in terms of loads hauled (during a specified 18 month period) was 1.6 per cent of its total business representing 10 per cent of its total mileage. Should the test depend on whether the extra-provincial business, however small, is regular rather than casual? See *Invictus Ltd. v. Manitoba Labour Board* (1967), 62 W.W.R. 150, 65 D.L.R. (2d) 517.

For comparable treatment of the problem of interstate bus operations in the United States, see *Buck v. Kuykendall* (1925), 267 U.S. 307, 45 S. Ct. 324, holding that state licensing not directed to safety or conservation of highways but to a regulation or prohibition of competition is invalid. In *Fry Roofing Co. v. Wood* (1952), 344 U.S. 157, 73 S. Ct. 204, it was held by a bare majority that a non-discretionary permit available on application could be required of interstate carriers before using state highways. See *Kauper*, State Regulation of Interstate Motor Carriers, (1933) 31 Mich. L. Rev. 920.

Does the *Winner* case give any warrant for saying that federal power exists or may be asserted in respect of a provincial highway which connects with a highway of a neighbouring province? Is this a connecting undertaking? See *S.M.T. (Eastern) Ltd. v. Ruch*, [1940] 1 D.L.R. 206, 14 M.P.R. 206. Does it make any difference that the title to the respective highways is in the respective provincial Crowns? Even if there be no interprovincial "undertaking" (in the sense of a business operation), are the two highways not "works" connecting two provinces?

Parliament has dealt with a connecting trans-Canada highway on the basis of grants-in-aid which presuppose federal-provincial agreements and the authority of the provinces over highways within their respective limits: see Trans-Canada Highway Act, R.S.C. 1970, c. T-12.

The National Energy Board Act, R.S.C. 1970, c. N-6 exhibits assertion of undoubted federal control over interprovincial and international pipe lines and international power lines (as well as over the exportation of power or gas and the importation of gas). See, generally, *Ballem*, Constitutional Validity of Provincial Oil and Gas Legislation, (1963) 41 Can. Bar Rev. 199.

Legislative authority in relation to aeronautics has been found in the federal general power, and so too in relation to radio: see Chap. III, *supra*. Television is no less within the federal general power. Is there any area of provincial control in radio and television regulation? Is programme control any different here than it is in respect to motion pictures? In *Re Public Utilities Commission and Victoria Cablevision Ltd.* (1965), 51 D.L.R. (2d) 716, 52 W.W.R. 286, it was held that community antennae television stations, licensed pursuant to the Radio Act, R.S.C. 1952, c. 233, were not subject to provincial legislation requiring compliance with a demand for information under the regulatory power of a provincial public utilities commission. A single integrated undertaking existed in the receiving of programmes by antennae from television stations and relaying them by cable to paying subscribers. Cf. *Note*, State Regulation of Radio and Television, (1959) 73 Harv. L. Rev. 386.

Does federal legislative power embrace independent operators of airport limousine or taxi services or any class of their employees, for example, porters? Would it make a difference if such airport services were controlled by exclusive franchises from the airport authority for access to airport grounds? See *Murray Hill Limousine Services Ltd. v. Batson*, [1965] Que. Q.B. 778; *Re Colonial Coach Lines Ltd. and Ontario Highway Transport Board*, [1967] 2 O.R. 25, 62 D.L.R. (2d) 270, aff'd on other grounds, [1967] 2 O.R. 243, 63 D.L.R. (2d) 198.]

Note on the "Navigation and Shipping" Power and Cognate Matters

Section 91(10) of the B.N.A. Act which gives Parliament exclusive legislative authority in relation to "navigation and shipping" is merely one of a group of federal powers which touch water travel and carriage. The others are in the exceptions in s. 92(10)(a) and (b) ("lines of steam or other ships, railways, canals, telegraphs, and other works and undertakings connecting the province with any other or others of the provinces or extending beyond the limits of the province" and "lines of steam ships between the province and any British or foreign country"), in s. 91(9) ("beacons, buoys, lighthouses. . . ."), and in s. 91(13) ("ferries between a province and any British or foreign country or between two provinces"). The law-making power conferred by these provisions does not transfer any proprietary rights in navigable waters or in ships or in ferries: see *A.-G. Can. v. A.-G. Ont.*, [1898] A.C. 700. However, it has been held that Parliament may give an exclusive right of ferry in accordance with the limits of the power reposed in it under s. 91(13): see *In re International and Interprovincial Ferries* (1905), 36 S.C.R. 206; *Dinner v. Humberstone* (1896), 26 S.C.R. 252. This is in contrast to the denial to the Dominion of any right to give an exclusive right to fish in pursuance of its exclusive power in relation to "seacoast and inland fisheries": see Chapter VII, *infra.* Federal proprietary rights in connection with its navigation and shipping powers depend largely on s. 108 of the B.N.A. Act which transfers to the Dominion the provincial public works and property enumerated in the third schedule to the Act: see Clement, The Canadian Constitution, chapter 29; and see Chapter VII, *infra.*

In *Montreal v. Montreal Harbour Commissioners,* [1926] A.C. 299, [1926] 1 D.L.R. 840, [1926] 1 W.W.R. 398, the Privy Council stated that "there is no doubt that the power to control navigation and shipping conferred on the Dominion by s. 91 is to be widely construed". The association of the terms "navigation" and "shipping" in the one class of subject without limitation posed the question whether local as well as interprovincial or international navigation and shipping fall within exclusive federal authority. The question has been raised, (but not in relation to navigation), whether in view of s. 91(13) and the exceptions in s. 92(10(a) and (b), federal power should not be excluded where local intra-provincial shipping is involved. A majority of the Supreme Court of Canada reached this conclusion in *Reference re Validity of Industrial Relations and Disputes Investigation Act and Its Applicability in respect of Certain Employees of Eastern Canada Stevedoring Co. Ltd.,* [1955] S.C.R. 526, [1955] 3 D.L.R. 721. The Court was concerned with the application of the federal labour relations statute to employees of an independent stevedoring company who, on the accepted facts, were engaged exclusively in the loading and unloading of ships of shipping companies operating between Canadian and foreign ports. The Court held (Rand J. dissenting) that the federal statute applied on the facts not only to the stevedores but also (Locke J. dissenting) to the office staff whose work was connected with the particular stevedoring operations.

In *Agence Maritime Inc. v. Canada Labour Relations Board,* [1969] S.C.R. 851, 12 D.L.R. (3d) 722, the statute was held incapable of applying to labour relations of crews engaged in voyages wholly within the province, such intra-provincial activity being neither "navigation" nor "shipping" within the purview of s. 92(10). Fauteux J., writing for a unanimous Court, said, [translated]

> "In summary and however liberally the power conferred on Parliament by s. 92(10) of the 1867 Act ought to be interpreted, as the Judicial Committee ruled in *City of Montreal v. Montreal Harbour Commissioners*, [*supra*], I am of opinion that in such a case as that which is before us and save as regards the aspect navigation, the dispositions of s. 91(29) and s. 92(10)(a) and (b) considered together have the effect of excluding from the competence of Parliament enterprises of water carriage whose operations are carried out strictly within one province.... Certain exceptions are still evidently to be made for what must be regarded as arising from the aspect navigation. It would clearly not be in order to undertake to define the extent of the field of operation of those exceptions. It is enough to say that they cannot be considered as extending to the case before us."

The cases do not always distinguish and may perhaps not always need to distinguish between the two. Thus the Privy Council held in *Paquet v. Quebec Harbour Pilots Corporation*, [1927] A.C. 1029, 54 D.L.R. 323, that pilot fees earned by pilots whose services were rendered in Quebec Harbour were subject to regulation or control by Parliament as falling within its extensive power in relation to "navigation and shipping". Certain matters can nevertheless be identified as having to do with shipping, for example, ship construction and repair activities: *Ex parte J. B. Porter Co.*, (1968) 68 D.L.R. (2d) 613, and provisions of the *Canada Shipping Act*, R.S.C. 1970, chapter S-9, such as those dealing with the ownership and registry of vessels, cf. *The Queen v. Harper* (1971), 22 D.L.R. (3d) 230, 3 N.B.R. (2d) 655.

The "navigation" power too, is broad. It is a power which enables the Dominion to require its sanction to any works which would interfere with navigability: see *A.-G. Can. v. A.-G. Ont.*, [1898] A.C. 700; *Booth v. Lowery* (1917), 54 S.C.R. 421, 35 D.L.R. 303; and it probably would support the Dominion's right to direct the erection of works or other operations to create as well as to maintain navigability; see *Smith v. Ontario & Minnesota Power Co.* (1918), 44 O.L.R. 43, 45 D.L.R. 266; and cf. *A.-G. Can. v. Brister*, [1943] 3 D.L.R. 50, 17 M.P.R. 93 rev'g [1942] 1 D.L.R. 621. But cf. *Arrow River & Tributaries Slide & Boom Co. Ltd. v. Pigeon Timber Co. Ltd.*, [1932] S.C.R. 495 at p. 502, [1932] 2 D.L.R. 250, at p. 269, per Smith J.: "So far as the rights of the Dominion in connection with navigation are concerned, the provincial jurisdiction to improve the floatability of the non-navigable part of an international stream within the province, except as modified by treaty, does not seem to be different from the jurisdiction to make such improvements in a non-navigable stream wholly within the province." Conversely, provincial legislation is *ultra vires* in so far as it directs or authorizes works which interfere with navigation: *Re Brandon Bridge* (1884), 2 Man. R. 14; *Fleming v. Spracklin* (1921), 50 O.L.R. 289, 64 D.L.R. 382. The Dominion may, of course, expropriate provincial or private property in connection with

the exercise of its "navigation" power, e.g. to permit the erection of
works for navigation purposes: see *Montreal v. Montreal Harbour
Commissioners, supra,* which suggests a requirement of compensation,
at least in the case of provincial Crown lands; and cf. *A.-G. Que. v.
Nipissing Central Ry.,* [1926] A.C. 715, [1926] 3 D.L.R. 545, [1926]
2 W.W.R. 552, and *Reference re Waters and Water-Powers,* [1929]
S.C.R. 200, [1929] 2 D.L.R. 481, which indicate that the position as
to expropriation differs where the Dominion acts under its "railway"
power and where it acts under its "navigation and shipping" power
or its power in relation to Indians and lands reserved for the Indians
(B.N.A. Act, s. 91(24)); see also *Ontario Mining Co. v. Seybold,*
[1903] A. C. 73. Why it should be different is nowhere clearly stated,
although a partial explanation is attempted in the *Water-Powers*
reference. In the *Montreal* case, certain federal legislation appropriating provincial property for harbour works and harbour extension was
held invalid because it did not involve expropriation in relation to
navigation but rather an attempt to enlarge proprietary harbour
rights which under s. 108 of the B.N.A. Act and the third schedule
thereto included only public harbours as they stood at the time of
confederation (at least in relation to the confederating provinces).

Dominion power under s. 91(10) also raises problems in connection
with the so-called public right of navigation. The cases speak of a
public right to navigate high seas and tidal waters; and, in fact, any
waters which are navigable although the bed is owned by some
private person rather than the Crown: see *A.-G. B.C. v. A.-G. Can.,*
[1914] A.C. 153, 15 D.L.R. 308, 5 W.W.R. 878. As to when water is
considered navigable, see *Big Point Club v. Lozon,* [1943] O.R. 491,
[1943] 4 D.L.R. 136. The courts have not found it easy to determine
the basis of this public right in Canada: see *McLaren v. Caldwell*
(1881), 9 App. Cas. 392. Analogies have been drawn to the use of
waters as highways and reliance has been placed on the doctrine of
dedication by user; see *Reference re B.C. Fisheries* (1913), 47 S.C.R.
493, 11 D.L.R. 255, 4 W.W.R. 525, aff'd [1914] A.C. 153, 15 D.L.R.
308, 5 W.W.R. 878; *Maclaren v. A.-G. Que.,* [1914] A.C. 258, 15
D.L.R. 855. There has also been the suggestion that the invitation
to colonists after 1763 to settle in British North America carried an
assurance of the availability of waterways for travel and exploration:
see *Fort George Lumber Co. v. G.T.P. Ry.* (1915), 9 W.W.R. 17,
24 D.L.R. 527. It is not entirely clear whether the federal power
under s. 91(10) enables the Dominion to establish public rights of
navigation over waters where no such rights existed previously.
While this has been acknowledged as against private persons, it has
been denied in relation to waters over provincial Crown lands: see
Fort George Lumber Co. v. G.T.P. Ry., supra. Quaere, whether this
is because the Dominion would be dealing with property rights rather
than exercising regulatory legislative power in respect of existing
public rights! And, if so, would there not be the same objection so
far as private owners are concerned? Where public rights of navigation exist, nothing is clearer than that it is for the Dominion alone
to regulate their exercise, subject, however, to certain qualifications

in the case of waters over provincial Crown lands. The matter is discussed in the case which follows.

[Provincial legislation may competently provide for a system of municipal transportation including a right of ferry, and it is immaterial that the ferry traverses water and touches land owned by the federal Crown (*e.g.* a harbour within the third schedule to the *B.N.A. Act*): see *T.T.C. v. Aqua Taxi Ltd.,* [1957] O.W.N. 65, 6 D.L.R. (2d) 721. The rationale would seem to be (in line with the *Winner* case, *supra*) that a federal waterway is as much a public highway for provincial purposes as a provincial highway is a public facility for the operation of an undertaking within federal competence.

In line with the *Stevedoring* case, *supra,* it was held in *Underwater Gas Developers Ltd. v. Ontario Labour Relations Board,* [1960] O.R. 416, 24 D.L.R. (2d) 673, that employees working from a ship in establishing and servicing off-shore sites for drilling of gas under water (but whose work did not include the actual drilling which was done by another firm using its own employees whom they, however, serviced) were subject, in their relations with their employer, to provincial labour relations legislation. Contrast, *Regina v. Nova Scotia Labour Relations Board, ex parte J. B. Porter Co. Ltd.* (1968), 68 D.L.R. (2d) 613. See also *Swait v. Board of Trustees of Maritime Transportation Unions* (1966), 61 D.L.R. (2d) 317.

In *Rex v. Meikleham* (1905), 11 O.L.R. 366, the Court upheld a conviction against the master of a United States steamer for permitting liquor to be sold thereon in Canadian waters within the limits of Ontario in violation of the provincial liquor licence statute. The ship was, practically speaking, in the harbour, being engaged in running excursions from the harbour a few miles out and back. Suppose the vessel were plying between foreign ports or to a foreign port and back?]

REFERENCE RE WATERS AND WATER-POWERS

In the Supreme Court of Canada. [1929] S.C.R. 200, [1929] 2 D.L.R. 481.

Reference to the Supreme Court of Canada of certain questions touching legislative power and property rights of Dominion and provinces respectively. The questions and the answer thereto given by the Court were as follows:

Question 1(a). Where the bed of a navigable river is vested in the Crown in the right of the province, is the title subordinate to the public right of navigation?

Question 1(b). If not, has the Dominion the legislative power to declare that such title is subordinate to such right?

Answer: The questions as framed postulate the existence of a public right of navigation in the rivers to which they refer, as well as their navigability.

The title to the bed of the river is subject to that public right, except in so far as, at the date of the Union, the Crown possessed by law or has since acquired, under Dominion legislation, a superior right to use or to grant the use of the waters of the river for other purposes, such for example as mining, irrigation or industry.

Question 2. Where the bed of a navigable river is vested in the Crown in the right of the province, has the Dominion power, for navigation purposes, to use or occupy part of such bed or to divert, diminish, or change the flow over such bed (a) without the consent of the province; (b) without compensation?

Question 3. Has the Parliament of Canada the power, by appropriate legislative enactment, to authorize the Dominion Government to expropriate the lands of the Crown in the right of the province for the purposes of navigation with provision or without provision for compensation?

Answer: These questions cannot be answered categorically either in the affirmative or in the negative.

The conditions controlling the exercise of Dominion legislative powers for purposes embraced within the comprehensive phrase, "navigation purposes," depend in part upon the nature of the "purpose," in part upon the nature of the means proposed for accomplishing it, and in part upon the character of the particular power called into play. Reference is respectfully made to the observations in the accompanying reasons, as indicating the governing principles with as much definiteness as is safe or practicable.

Question 4. By section 108 of the *British North America Act, 1867*, and the first item of the Third Schedule thereto, the following public works and property of each province, amongst others, shall be the property of Canada, namely "Canals with lands and waterpower connected therewith."

Has the province any proprietary interest in or beneficial ownership of or legislative control over the water-power which, though connected with the said canals, is created or made available by reason of extensions, enlargements or replacements of said canals made by the Dominion since Confederation and which is not required from time to time for the purposes of navigation?

Question 5. Where the bed of a navigable river is vested in the Crown in the right of the province, has the province any proprietary interest in or beneficial ownership of or legislative control over the water-power created or made available by works for the improvement of navigation constructed thereupon in whole or in part by or under the authority of the Dominion since Confederation which is not required from time to time for the purposes of navigation?

Answer: Whatever subjects are comprehended under the phrase "water-power" in the 1st item of the third schedule, by section 108 passed to the Dominion, there was left to the provinces neither proprietary interest in, nor beneficial ownership of such subjects; and under section 91(1) [now s. 91(1A)] legislative control over them is exclusively committed to the Dominion.

As to water-powers (and these, of course, are not comprised within that item) "created or made available by reason of extensions, enlargements or replacements made by the Dominion since Confederation" or "by works for the improvement of navigation constructed . . . in whole or in part since Confederation," it is impossible to ascertain the respective powers or rights of the Dominion and the provinces in relation thereto, in the absence of a more precise statement as to the character of the works, as to the legislative authority under which the works were executed, and as to the circumstances pertinent to the question whether or not the conditions of such authority were duly observed.

Question 6(a). Has the Dominion exclusive proprietary interest in or beneficial ownership of or legislative control over water-powers created or made available by works authorized by Parliament to be erected in any boundary waters for the purpose of carrying out a treaty between His Majesty and a foreign country providing for the erection of joint works for (1) the improvement of navigation in such waters, or (2) for the development of power, or (3) for both?

The expression "boundary waters" in this question means the waters defined by the preliminary article of the Treaty dated 11th January, 1909, between His Britannic Majesty and the United States of America.

Question 6(b). If the Dominion has not the exclusive proprietary interest in or beneficial ownership of or legislative control over such water-powers, has the province the exclusive proprietary interest in or beneficial ownership of or legislative control over such water-powers?

Answer: The nature and extent of the respective powers, rights and interests of the Dominion and the provinces in, and in respect of such water-powers, would depend upon a variety of facts, including *inter alia*, the terms of the Treaty, and the respective rights of the Dominion and the provinces in, and in relation to, the waters affected. In the absence of information as to such facts, it is impracticable to give an intelligible answer to the questions propounded.

Question 7. Has the Parliament of Canada legislative power to authorize the construction and operation by the Dominion Government of works wholly for powers purposes and the acquisition by purchase or expropriation of the lands and property required for the purposes of such works including lands of the Crown in the right of a province (a) in interprovincial rivers; and (b) in provincial rivers?

"Interprovincial rivers" in this question means rivers flowing along or across the boundaries between provinces.

Answer: As to both "provincial rivers" and "interprovincial rivers," Parliament has jurisdiction in respect of such works, if they fall within the ambit of sec. 92(10a). With reference to the expropriation of provincial Crown lands "for the purposes of such works," the answer to the question would, to some extent, depend upon the particular purpose for which such lands were required. In answering this question, sec. 92(10c) is not taken into account. Reference is respectfully made to what has been said upon that subject in the accompanying reasons.

Question 8. May a province notwithstanding the construction by the Dominion for the purposes of navigation of works in a river the bed of which is within such province, control, regulate and use the waters of such river so long as such control, regulation and use does not interfere with navigation? In the case of a river flowing between two provinces may such provinces jointly control, regulate and use the water in the same manner?

Question 9.   Has a province the right to control or use the waters in provincial rivers and to develop or authorise the development of water-powers within the province provided that in so doing navigation is not prejudiced and that the province complies with Dominion requirements as to navigation?

Answer: These two questions mutually overlap, and it is convenient to deal with them together. If there is no valid conflicting legislation by the Dominion under an overriding power—the power for example bestowed upon the Dominion by sec. 92(10a)—the several provinces have the rights which are the subject of interrogatory number 9.

As to the first branch of the eighth question. The authority of the provinces to "control, regulate and use" such waters, in the circumstances mentioned, is subject to the condition that, in the exercise thereof, the provinces do not interfere in matters the control of which is reserved exclusively for the Dominion, and that all valid enactments of the Dominion, in relation to the navigation works, or in relation to navigable waters, be duly observed.

This condition is not necessarily identical with the condition expressed in the question by the words "so long as such control, regulation and use does not interfere with navigation." The question therefore, in the form in which it is put, cannot be answered in the affirmative; and, as the exercise of legislative jurisdiction, in the comprehensive terms of the question, might encroach upon the exclusive jurisdiction of the Dominion, the proper answer seems to be in the negative.

As to the second branch, considering the variety of meanings which might attach to the phrase "jointly control, regulate and use," no precise or useful answer is possible.

The answers to these questions, conformably to the views adverted to above, also proceed upon the assumption that the questions have no reference to any jurisdiction which might be acquired by the procedure laid down in sec. 92(10c).

Question 10.   (a) If question 4 is answered in the affirmative, what is the nature or extent of such interest or ownership or control?

(b) If question 5 is answered in the affirmative, what is the nature or extent of such interest or ownership or control?

(c) If the answers to both questions 6(a) and 6(b) are in the negative, what are the respective rights and interests of the Dominion and the provinces in relation to such water-powers?

Answer: In view of what has already been stated in response to the 4th, 5th and 6th interrogatories, no answer to this question is called for.

The judgment of the Court in the reference was delivered by Duff J. and a concurring judgment was delivered by Smith J. In his reasons, Duff J. said, *inter alia:* "The 2nd and 3rd questions are broadly expressed. "Navigation purposes" is a sweeping phrase. It has been employed to denote not only regulation and control of ships and shipping, but the control of navigable waters in the interests of shipping, including the improvement of navigability, the execution of works for facilitating navigation, the provision of such aids to navigation as beacons, buoys, and lighthouses; the establishment of harbours and harbour works, such as those considered in the *Montreal Harbour* case, [1926] A.C. 299, which included an embankment and railway on the shore of the harbour, quays, a dry-dock, and a ship-repairing plant. And it was argued on behalf of the Dominion that "navigation and shipping" within the intendment of s. 91(10), would embrace all such matters as those just mentioned, as well as the construction, maintenance and operation of canals and incidental works, and generally all matters relating to transport by water.

It is, at least, doubtful whether the exclusive jurisdiction contemplated by item 10, s. 91, extends to many of the matters, which are above indicated as falling within the scope of the phrase "navigation purposes," when that phrase is given an interpretation so wide as that which counsel for the Dominion ascribe to it. By the 9th head of the same section, exclusive jurisdiction is entrusted to the Dominion in respect of matters falling within the subjects described by the words "beacons, buoys and lighthouses," and, under No. 13 in respect of matters included within the subject "Ferries" between a province and other countries or between two provinces. Exclusive jurisdiction with regard to canals, and to other works of like character, extending beyond the limits of a province, is confined to the Dominion under s. 92(10a); and by sub-heads (a) and (b) of s. 92(10) the subjects of that exclusive jurisdiction comprise all matters falling within the descriptions "Lines of steam or other ships connecting the province with any other or others of the provinces," and "Line of steamships between the province and any British or foreign country." Further, there is much to be said for the view that, subject to the power bestowed upon the Dominion by sub-head (c) of s. 92(10), exclusive authority is committed to the provinces with respect to canals and other similar works (which, according to the contention of the Dominion, would fall within the tenor of the phrase "navigation purposes"), when such works are wholly situated within a province. It is not necessary to decide the point, but it is, at all events, quite open to argument that sub-heads (a) and (b) are intended to define exceptions to the principal clause of head 10, s. 92; and that, consequently, "works and undertakings," under the principal clause, include works and undertakings of the nature of those specified in these sub-heads so long as they are wholly within the boundaries of a province. . . . It is notorious that for many years, probably ever since the formation of the Union, the Dominion Parliament and Government have assumed, and acted on the assumption, that the authority derived from head No. 10 of s. 91 was sufficient to enable Parliament to legislate, in respect of most, if not all, the classes of matters it is now contended fall within the scope of the phrase "navigation purposes"; and in support of that view it may be noticed that the majority of the members of this court took the view in *Booth v. Lowery,* 54 S.C.R. 421, that river improvements, consisting of storage dams and basins, intended to improve the navigability of the river Ottawa and one of its tributaries, were subject to the legislative control of the Dominion under that head. Further, as already observed, the recent pronouncements in the judgments in the Privy Council and this court in the three cases cited above, beginning with the *Montreal Harbour* case, [1926] A.C. 299, give countenance to the view that the Dominion may have an implied authority incidental or ancillary to its exclusive authority under head 10 of s. 91, to legislate in respect of some of the purposes intended to be described as "navigation purposes" in these two questions: although the judgment in the *Montreal Harbour* case seems to say that the exercise of this ancillary or incidental authority is, or may be, conditioned upon the payment of compensation.

The principle of the decision in *Atty.-Gen. for Quebec v. Nipissing Central Ry. Co.,* [1926] A.C. 715, would apply to the authority given by 92(10a) in respect to canals extending beyond a province, which must, for reasons similar to those governing the scope of the authority given by the same sub-head in relation to railways, be held to include the power to determine the route of the canal and make effectual provision for the construction and operation of it on the route determined. Such powers are of the essence of the exclusive authority vested in the Dominion in relation to railways and canals. Obviously, therefore, the 2nd and 3rd questions cannot be answered in the negative. Answers in that sense might convey the impression that the authority of the Dominion, in relation to such a purpose as the construction of a canal, would not in any circumstances involve the power to make use of Provincial Crown property without the consent of the province.

On the other hand, it is impossible to affirm, in respect of every "navigation purpose," within the purport of these questions that the authority in relation thereto, whether derived from s. 92(10) and s. 91(29) or from one of the other heads of s. 91—whether within the exclusive sphere of the Dominion Parliament, or only referable to its incidental or ancillary powers—invests the Dominion with the right to override by its legislation the proprietary rights of the provinces.

There is no general formula for deciding whether or not, in respect of any such given purpose, the nature of the Dominion authority imports the existence of such a right. That can only be determined after an examination of the nature of the purpose, the character of the power involved and the character of the means proposed to be employed in order to effectuate the purpose.

The word "expropriate" in the 3rd question, moreover, would seem to include the act of transferring compulsorily to the Dominion itself, or to the others, the absolute beneficial title of the Crown to lands committed to the control of the provincial legislatures. As already explained, that is an authority which the Dominion did not expressly receive under any of the relevant clauses of s. 91."

[The relation between the public right of navigation and private rights of riparian owners or the extent of the public right of navigation in relation to private property rights in the solum of riparian land is outside the scope of this book. See however, *Rice Lake Fur Co. v. McAllister*, 56 O.L.R. 440, [1925] 2 D.L.R. 506; *Re Snow and Toronto* (1924), 56 O.L.R. 100, [1924] 4 D.L.R. 1023. As to the right of the Court to give relief against interference with the public right of navigation, see *Nicholson v. Moran*, [1949] 4 D.L.R. 571 (right to relief not affected by approval of obstruction under s. 7 of the *Navigable Waters Protection Act*, R.S.C. 1927, c. 140, since this provision is merely permissive).

In the United States, legislative power as to navigation is covered by Congressional power over interstate and foreign commerce: see *Oklahoma v. Atkinson* (1941), 313 U.S. 508, 61 S. Ct. 1050; *U.S. v. Commodore Park Inc.* (1945), 324 U.S. 386, 65 S. Ct. 803.]

Note on Provincial Control over Water and its Uses:
The Limits of the Federal Navigation Power.

Legislative power in respect of water and its uses may be assessed from the standpoint of recognized private and public interests upon which it may intrude; for example, riparian rights of access and use, and public rights of navigation and, to a lesser extent, of fishing. Apart from legislative power arising from federal ownership of land and water lots (including ownership of provincial public works and property that passed under the Third Schedule to the B.N.A. Act), Parliament's regulatory authority rests mainly in the navigation (and shipping) power; it is doubtful whether anything is added by the trade and commerce power. The federal criminal law power is available for prohibitory purposes to safeguard public health (for example, in the field of pollution), and perhaps the agriculture power might be invoked for overriding irrigation control. (It may be noted, however, that there was no mention of the agriculture power in connection with the federal irrigation legislation dealt with in *Western Canada Hardware Co. Ltd. v. Farrelly Bros. Ltd.,* [1922] 3 W.W.R. 1017, 70 D.L.R. 480. This legislation, which had a limited application and was based on power in relation to federal territory and property, was repealed by 1950 (Can.), c. 22, s. 26.) But there has been no indication in the case law that there is any such breadth of federal authority here as exists in the United States where, to quote from *United States v. Appalachian Electric Power Co.* (1940), 311 U.S. 377, at p. 426, 61 S. Ct. 291, at p. 308, "flood protection, watershed development, recovery of the costs of improvements through utilization of power are likewise parts of commerce control", see also *United States v. R. B. Rands* (1967), 389 U.S. 121, 88 S. Ct. 265.

The extensive provincial regulatory authority in respect of water supply and consumption for domestic and industrial uses, in respect of assuring purity against pollution, in respect of development of power projects and in respect of irrigation and reclamation, rests on three heads of legislative power, viz; local works and undertakings under s. 92(10), property and civil rights in the Province under s. 92(13), and matters of a local and private nature in the Province under s. 92(16). In exercising its authority, a Province would be subject to any applicable federal legislation in relation to navigation, but once compliance was made and, depending on its particulars, it would be free to proceed with its own works or schemes. Even in the absence of federal legislation, a Province would have to defer to public rights of navigation which, as such, cannot be impaired save by federal legislation.

The reach of the federal navigation power, supported as it is by s. 91(9) in relation to beacons, buoys, and lighthouses, has not been fully examined in the cases. It is an open question how far the authority in relation to navigation can embrace works or projects which serve navigation purposes and are designed to serve other ends as well. What the question points to is whether federal authority in relation to navigation will support navigation works with which there is an association of power plants, flood control and reclamation. It was said in the United States in *Green Bay & Mississippi Canal Co. v. Patten Paper Co.* (1898), 172 U.S. 58, at p. 80 (in affirming federal jurisdiction over waterpower as a by-product of navigation works) that "in such matters there can be no divided empire". In *Booth v. Lowery* (1917), 54 S.C.R. 421, at p. 424, 35 D.L.R. 303, at p. 305, Fitzpatrick C.J. in a dissenting judgment in a case which did not turn directly on a constitutional issue, said that "whether works for power purposes alone are within the authority of the Dominion Parliament may be doubted", and Duff J., who also dissented, expressed a broader doubt whether works for the improvement of navigation or to facilitate shipping are necessarily within federal jurisdiction for all purposes: see also *Reference re Waters and Water-Powers, supra.*

The suggestion was made by Strong J. in *Queddy River Driving Boom Co. v. Davidson* (1883), 10 S.C.R. 222 that had there been no explicit navigation power in the B.N.A. Act, the trade and commerce power would have filled the gap; and he relied on United States decisions in this connection. Certainly there is no indication that added strength is lent to the one power or the other by the presence of both in the Constitution; the reverse may be true.

Although the *Water-Powers* reference makes it doubtful whether Parliament may expropriate for power development alone, it did intimate that power works extending beyond the limits of a Province or connecting two Provinces may fall within federal jurisdiction under s. 92(10)(a). This proposition was taken up by Lett C.J.S.C. in *British Columbia Power Corporation Ltd. v. A.-G. B.C.* (1963), 44 W.W.R. 65, 47 D.L.R. (2d) 633, in respect of the electrical division of a provincial company's undertaking which had interconnections at the international boundary and cables in United States territorial waters.

Over and above the jurisdiction that may thus reside in Parliament by virtue of s. 92(10)(a), there is the federal declaratory power under s. 92(10)(c) applicable to wholly intraprovincial works, by which jurisdiction may be acquired on a self-serve basis. It would be an important policy decision whether Parliament would invoke this power to enable it to promote a water resources or water power programme which it could not constitutionally carry out under the navigation power alone.

Mention should be made of the constitutional position in respect of interprovincial or international rivers and lakes as such. They are not, in their natural state, works or undertakings so as to come within s. 92(10) (a). So far as navigation thereon is concerned, federal power is incontestible, but the situation is not too clear so far as concerns federal jurisdiction in the case of diversion or construction of works by private persons, as owners or under provincial authority, which affect beneficial uses in a neighbouring province. It is arguable that apart from existing treaties on the matter which by reason of their origin are within federal implementing authority, the issues go beyond s. 92(13) or s. 92(16). But there is no course of decision to support such a view. The central Government may be involved internationally, but this is not presently a basis in itself for domestic legislative jurisdiction. So far as concerns interprovincial relations in respect of waters flowing between two or more Provinces, there is a nice question whether there is any one body of law to which resort can be had to resolve differences between residents of different Provinces or between such Provinces themselves. It is one thing to rest on ordinary tort liability and on the law of the place of trial or place of injury, but a more difficult issue would arise if a Province by statute altered the ordinary riparian law so as to preclude suit. The B.N.A. Act does not contain any provision by which jurisdiction is vested in a Court over litigation between Provinces (as is the case in Australia and in the United States) nor is there provision in the B.N.A. Act (as there is in the United States) for interprovincial compacts. Of course, agreements may be made outside of any constitutional compulsion, and they could be a means of enabling the Courts or a designated Court to fashion applicable law: *Province of Ontario v. Dominion of Canada* (1909), 42 S.C.R. 1, at p. 118.

[The matters discussed above are more fully canvassed in *Laskin,* Jurisdictional Framework for Water Management, in Resources for Tomorrow Conference: Background Papers (1961), Vol. 1, p. 211; and see *LaForest*, Interprovincial Rivers, (1972) 50 Can. Bar Rev. 39.

See the Canada Water Act, R.S.C. 1970, 1st Supp. c. 5.]

CHAPTER VII

PROPRIETARY RIGHTS AND LEGISLATIVE POWER: FISHERIES AND OTHER ILLUSTRATIVE MATTERS.

A.-G. CAN. v. A.-G. ONT. ET AL.

In the Privy Council. [1898] A.C. 700.

Appeal from a judgment of the Supreme Court of Canada, 26 S.C.R. 444, on a reference.

LORD HERSCHELL: The Governor-General of Canada by Order in Council referred to the Supreme Court of Canada for hearing and consideration various questions relating to the property, rights and legislative jurisdiction of the Dominion of Canada and the provinces respectively in relation to rivers, lakes, harbours, fisheries, and other cognate subjects.

The Supreme Court having answered some of the questions submitted adversely to the Dominion and some adversely to the provinces, both parties have appealed. . . .

It is unnecessary to determine to what extent the rivers and lakes of Canada are vested in the Crown, or what public rights exist in respect of them. Whether a lake or river be vested in the Crown as represented by the Dominion or as represented by the province in which it is situate, it is equally Crown property, and the rights of the public in respect of it, except in so far as they may be modified by legislation, are precisely the same. The answer, therefore, to such questions as those adverted to would not assist in determining whether in any particular case the property is vested in the Dominion or in the province. It must also be borne in mind that there is a broad distinction between proprietary rights and legislative jurisdiction. The fact that such jurisdiction in respect of a particular subject-matter is conferred on the Dominion Legislature, for example, affords no evidence that any proprietary rights with respect to it were transferred to the Dominion. There is no presumption that because legislative jurisdiction was vested in the Dominion Parliament proprietary rights were transferred to it. The Dominion of Canada was called into existence by the *British North America Act, 1867*. Whatever proprietary rights were at the time of the passing of that Act possessed by the provinces remained vested in them except such as are by any of its express enactments transferred to the Dominion of Canada.

With these preliminary observations their Lordships proceed to consider the questions submitted to them. The first of these is whether the beds of all lakes, rivers, public harbours, and other waters, or any and which of them situate within the territorial limits of the several provinces, and not granted before confederation, became under the *British North America Act* the property of the Dominion.

510

It is necessary to deal with the several subject-matters referred to separately, though the answer as to each of them depends mainly on the construction of the 3rd schedule of the *British North America Act*. By the 108th section of that Act it is provided that the public works and property of each province enumerated in the schedule shall be the property of Canada. That schedule is headed "Provincial Public Works and Property to be the Property of Canada," and contains an enumeration of various subjects, numbered 1 to 10. The 5th of these is "rivers and lake improvements." The word "rivers" obviously applies to nothing which was not vested in the province. It is contended on behalf of the Dominion that under the words quoted the whole of the rivers so vested were transferred from the province to the Dominion. It is contended, on the other hand, that nothing more was transferred than the improvements of the provincial rivers, that is to say, only public works which had been effected, and not the entire beds of the rivers. If the words used had been "river and lake improvements," or if the word "lake" had been in the plural, "lakes," there could have been no doubt that the improvements only were transferred. Cogent arguments were adduced in support of each of the rival constructions. Upon the whole their Lordships, after careful consideration, have arrived at the conclusion that the Court below was right, and that the improvements only were transferred to the Dominion. There can be no doubt that the subjects comprised in the schedule are for the most part works or constructions which have resulted from the expenditure of public money, though there are exceptions. It is to be observed that rivers and lake improvements are coupled together as one item. If the intention had been to transfer the entire bed of the rivers and only artificial works on lakes, one would not have expected to find them thus coupled together. Lake improvements might in that case more naturally have been found as a separate item or been coupled with canals. Moreover, it is impossible not to be impressed by the inconvenience which would arise if the entire rivers were transferred, and only the improvements of lakes. How would it be possible in that case to define the limits of the Dominion and provincial rights respectively? Rivers flow into and out of lakes; it would often be difficult to determine where the river ended and the lake began. Reasons were adduced why the rivers should have been vested in the Dominion: but every one of these reasons seems equally applicable to lakes. The construction of the words as applicable to the improvements of rivers only is not an impossible one. It does no violence to the language employed. Their Lordships feel justified, therefore, in putting upon the language used the construction which seems to them to be more probably in accordance with the intention of the Legislature.

With regard to public harbours their Lordships entertain no doubt that whatever is properly comprised in this term became vested in the Dominion of Canada. The words of the enactment in the 3rd schedule are precise. It was contended on behalf of the provinces that only those parts of what might ordinarily fall within the term "harbour" on which public works had been executed became vested in the Dominion, and that no part of the bed of the sea did so. Their Lordships are unable to adopt this view. The Supreme Court, in arriving at the same conclusion, founded their opinion on a previous decision in the same Court in the case of *Holman v. Green,* 6 S.C.R. 707, where it was held that the foreshore between high and low water-mark on the margin of the harbour became the property of the Dominion as part of the harbour.

Their Lordships think it extremely inconvenient that a determination should be sought of the abstract question, what falls within the description "public harbour." They must decline to attempt an exhaustive definition of the term applicable to all cases. To do so would, in their judgment, be likely to prove misleading and dangerous. It must depend, to some extent, at all events, upon the circumstances of each particular harbour what forms a part of that harbour. It is only possible to deal with definite issues which have been raised. It appears to have been thought by the Supreme Court in the case of *Holman v. Green* that if more than the public works connected with the harbour passed under that word, and if it included any part of the bed of the sea, it followed that the foreshore between the high and low water-mark, being also Crown property, likewise passed to the Dominion.

Their Lordships are of opinion that it does not follow that, because the foreshore on the margin of a harbour is Crown property, it necessarily forms part of the harbour. It may or may not do so, according to circumstances. If, for example, it had actually been used for harbour purposes, such as anchoring ships or landing goods it would, no doubt, form part of the harbour; but there are other cases in which, in their Lordships' opinion, it would be equally clear that it did not form part of it.

Their Lordships pass now to the question relating to fisheries and fishing rights.

Their Lordships are of opinion that the 91st section of the *British North America Act* did not convey to the Dominion of Canada any proprietary rights in relation to fisheries. Their Lordships have already noticed the distinction which must be borne in mind between rights of property and legislative jurisdiction. It was the latter only which was conferred under the heading, "Sea-Coast and Inland Fisheries" in s. 91. Whatever proprietary rights in relation to fisheries were previously vested in private individuals or in the province respectively remain untouched by that enactment. Whatever grants might previously have been lawfully made by the provinces in virtue of their proprietary rights could lawfully be made after that enactment came into force. At the same time, it must be remembered that the power to legislate in relation to fisheries does necessarily to a certain extent enable the Legislature so empowered to affect proprietary rights. An enactment, for example, prescribing the times of the year during which fishing is to be allowed, or the instruments which may be employed for the purpose (which it was admitted the Dominion Legislature was empowered to pass) might very seriously touch the exercise of proprietary rights, and the extent, character, and scope of such legislation is left entirely to the Dominion Legislature. The suggestion that the power might be abused so as to amount to a practical confiscation of property does not warrant the imposition by the Courts of any limit upon the absolute power of legislation conferred. The supreme legislative power in relation to any subject-matter is always capable of abuse, but it is not to be assumed that it will be improperly used; if it is, the only remedy is an appeal to those by whom the Legislature is elected. If, however, the Legislature purports to confer upon others proprietary rights where it possesses none itself, that in their Lordships' opinion is not an exercise of the legislative jurisdiction conferred by s. 91. If the contrary were held, it would follow that the Dominion might practically transfer to itself property which has, by the *British North America Act,* been left to the provinces and not vested in it.

In addition, however, to the legislative power conferred by the 12th item of s. 91, the 3rd item of that section confers upon the Parliament of Canada the power of raising money by any mode or system of taxation. Their Lordships think it is impossible to exclude as not within this power the provision imposing a tax by way of licence as a condition of the right to fish.

It is true that, by virtue of s. 92, the Provincial Legislature may impose the obligation to obtain a licence in order to raise a revenue for provincial purposes; but this cannot, in their Lordships' opinion, derogate from the taxing power of the Dominion Parliament to which they have already called attention.

Their Lordships are quite sensible of the possible inconveniences, to which attention was called in the course of the arguments, which might arise from the exercise of the right of imposing taxation in respect of the same subject-matter and within the same area by different authorities. They have no doubt, however, that these would be obviated in practice by the good sense of the legislatures concerned.

It follows from what has been said that in so far as s. 4 of the Revised Statutes of Canada, c. 95, empowers the grant of fishery leases conferring an exclusive right to fish in property belonging not to the Dominion, but to the provinces, it was not within the jurisdiction of the Dominion Parliament to pass it. This was the only section of the Act which was impeached in the course of the argument; but the subsidiary provisions, in so far as they are intended to enforce a right which it was not competent for the Dominion to confer, would of course fall with the principal enactment.

Their Lordships think that the Legislature of Ontario had jurisdiction to enact the 47th section of the Revised Statutes of Ontario, c. 24, except in so far as it relates to land in the harbours and canals, if any of the latter be included in the words "other navigable waters of Ontario." The reasons for this opinion have been already stated when dealing with the question in whom the beds of harbours, rivers, and lakes were vested.

The sections of the Ontario Act of 1892, intituled, "An Act for the Protection of the Provincial Fisheries," which are in question, consist almost exclusively of provisions relating to the manner of fishing in provincial waters. Regulations controlling the manner of fishing are undoubtedly within the competence of the Dominion Parliament. The question is whether they can be the subject of provincial legislation also in so far as it is not inconsistent with the Dominion legislation. . . .

. . . Their Lordships feel constrained to hold that the enactment of fishery regulations and restrictions is within the exclusive competence of the Dominion Legislature, and is not within the legislative powers of Provincial Legislatures.

But whilst in their Lordships' opinion all restrictions or limitations by which public rights of fishing are sought to be limited or controlled can be the subject of Dominion legislation only, it does not follow that the legislation of Provincial legislatures is incompetent merely because it may have relation to fisheries. For example, provisions prescribing the mode in which a private fishery is to be conveyed or otherwise disposed of, and the rights of succession in respect of it, would be properly treated as falling under the heading "Property and Civil Rights" within s. 92, and not as in the class "Fisheries" within the meaning of s. 91. So, too, the terms and conditions upon which the fisheries which are the property of the province may be granted, leased, or otherwise disposed of, and the rights which consistently with any general regulations respecting fisheries enacted by the Dominion Parliament may be conferred therein, appear proper subjects for provincial legislation, either under class 5 of s. 92, "The Management and Sale of Public Lands" or under the class "Property and Civil Rights." Such legislation deals directly with property, its disposal, and the rights to be enjoyed in respect of it, and was not in their Lordships' opinion intended to be within the scope of the class "Fisheries" as that word is used in s. 91. . . .

Their Lordships entertain no doubt that the Dominion Parliament had jurisdiction to pass the Act intituled, "An Act respecting certain Works constructed in or over Navigable Waters." It is in their opinion clearly legislation relating to "navigation."

[Further consideration to fishery rights as species of property in their relation to Dominion and provincial legislative power was given by the Privy Council in *A.-G. B.C. v. A.-G. Can.*, [1914] A.C. 153, 15 D.L.R. 308, 5 W.W.R. 878, where certain questions were put as to fishing rights in waters within the railway belt granted by the province to the Dominion. Viscount Haldane said, *inter alia:* "The general principle is that fisheries are in their nature mere profits of the soil over which the water flows, and that the title to a fishery arises from the right to the solum. A fishery may of course be severed from the solum and it then becomes a *profit à prendre in alieno solo* and an incorporeal hereditament. The severance may be effected by grant or by prescription, but it cannot be brought about by custom, for the origin of such a custom would be an unlawful act. But apart from the existence of such severance by grant or prescription the fishing rights go with the property in the solum.

"The authorities treat this broad principle as being of general application. They do not regard it as restricted to inland or non-tidal waters. They recognize it as giving to the owners of lands on the foreshore or within an estuary or elsewhere where the tide flows and reflows a title to fish in the water over such lands, and this is equally the case whether the owner be the Crown or a private individual. But in the case of tidal waters (whether on the foreshore or in estuaries or tidal rivers) the exclusive character of the title is qualified by another and paramount title which is *prima facie* in the public. . . .

". . . The subjects of the Crown are entitled as of right not only to navigate but to fish in the high seas and tidal waters alike. The legal character of this right is not easy to define. It is probably a right enjoyed so far as the high seas are concerned by common practice from time immemorial, and it was probably in very early times extended by the subject without challenge to the foreshore and tidal waters which were continuous with the ocean, if, indeed, it did not in fact first take rise in them. The right into which this practice has crystallized resembles in some respects the right to navigate the seas or the right to use a navigable river as a highway, and its origin is not more obscure than that of these rights of navigation. Finding its subjects exercising this right as from immemorial antiquity the Crown as *parens patriae* no doubt regarded itself bound to protect the subject in exercising it, and the origin and extent of the right as legally cognizable are probably attributable to that protection which gradually came to be recognized as establishing a legal right enforceable in the Courts.

"But to the practice and the right there were and indeed still are limits, or perhaps one should rather say exceptions. . . .

". . . Since the decision of the House of Lords in *Malcolmson v. O'Dea*, 10 H.L.C. 593, it has been unquestioned law that since Magna Charta no new exclusive fishery could be created by Royal grant in tidal waters, and that no public right of fishing in such waters, then existing, can be taken away without competent legislation. This is now part of the law of England, and their Lordships entertain no doubt that it is part of the law of British Columbia.

"Such, therefore, is undoubtedly the general law as to the public right of fishing in tidal waters. But it does not apply universally. To the general principle that the public has a "liberty of fishing in the sea or creeks or arms thereof," Lord Hale [in De Jure Maris] makes the exception, "unless in such places, creeks or navigable rivers where either the King or some particular subject hath gained a propriety exclusive of that common liberty." This passage refers to certain special cases of which instances are to be found in well-known English decisions where separate and exclusive rights of fishing in tidal waters have been recognized as the property of the owner of the soil. In all such cases the proof of the existence and enjoyment of the right has of necessity gone further back than the date of Magna Charta. The origin of these rare exceptions to the public right is lost in the darkness of the past as completely as is the origin of the right itself. But it is not necessary to do more than refer to the point in explanation of the words of Lord Hale, because no such case could exist in any part of British Columbia, inasmuch as no rights there existing could possibly date from before Magna Charta.

"It follows from these considerations that the position of the rights of fishing in the rivers, lakes, and tidal waters (whether in rivers and estuaries or on the foreshore) within the railway belt stand *prima facie* as follows: In the non-tidal waters they belong to the proprietor of the soil, *i.e.*, the Dominion, unless and until they have been granted by it to some individual or corporation. In the tidal waters, whether on the foreshore or in creeks, estuaries, and tidal rivers, the public have the right to fish, and by reason of the provisions of Magna Charta no restriction can be put upon that right of the public by an exercise of the prerogative in the form of a grant or otherwise. It will, of course, be understood that in speaking of this public right of fishing in tidal waters their Lordships do not refer in any way to fishing by kiddles, weirs, or other engines fixed to the soil. Such methods of fishing involve a use of the solum which, according to English law, cannot be vested in the public, but must belong either to the Crown or to some private owner. But we now come to the crux of the present case. The restriction above referred to relates only to Royal grants, and what their Lordships here have to decide is whether the Provincial Legislature has the power to alter these public rights in the same way as a sovereign Legislature, such as that of the United Kingdom, could alter the law in these respects within its territory.

"To answer this question one must examine the limitations to the powers of the Provincial Legislature which are relevant to the question under consideration. They arise partly from the provisions of ss. 91 and 92 of the *British North America Act, 1867*, and partly from the Terms of Union of British Columbia with the Confederation with which we have already dealt. By s. 91 of the *British North America Act, 1867*, the exclusive legislative authority of the Parliament of Canada extends to all matters coming within (amongst other things) "sea coast and inland fisheries." The meaning of this provision was considered by this Board in the case of *Attorney-General for the Dominion v. Attorneys-General for the Provinces*, [1898] A.C. 700, and it was held that it does not confer on the Dominion any rights of property, but that it does confer an exclusive right on the Dominion to make restrictions or limitations by which public rights of fishing are controlled, and on this exclusive right provincial legislation cannot trench. It recognized that the Province retains a right to dispose of any fisheries to the property in which the Province has a legal title, so far as the mode of such disposal is consistent with the Dominion right of regulation, but it held that, even in the case where proprietary rights remain with the Province, the subject-matter may be of such a character that the exclusive power of the Dominion to legislate in regard to fisheries may restrict the free exercise of provincial rights. Accordingly it sustained the right of the Dominion to control the methods and season of fishing and to impose a tax in the nature of licence duty as a condition of the right to fish, even in cases in which the property in the fishery originally was or still is in the Provincial Government.

"The decision in the case just cited does not, in their Lordships' opinion, affect the decision in the present case. Neither in 1867 nor at the date when British Columbia became a member of the Federation was fishing in tidal waters a matter of property. It was a right open equally to all the public and therefore, when by s. 91 sea coast and inland fisheries were placed under the exclusive legislative authority of the Dominion Parliament, there was in the case of the fishing in tidal waters nothing left within the domain of the Provincial Legislature. The right being a public one, all that could be done was to regulate its exercise, and the exclusive power of regulation was placed in the Dominion Parliament. Taking this in connection with the similar provision with regard to "navigation and shipping", their Lordships have no doubt that the object and the effect of these legislative provisions were to place the management and protection of the cognate public rights of navigation and fishing in the sea and tidal waters exclusively in the Dominion Parliament, and to leave to the Province no right of property or control in them. It was most natural that this should be done, seeing that these rights are the rights of the public in general and in no way special to the inhabitants of the Province.

"These considerations enable their Lordships to answer the first question, which reads as follows:

'Is it competent to the Legislature of British Columbia to authorize the Government of the Province to grant by way of lease, licence, or otherwise the exclusive right to fish in any or what part or parts of the waters within the railway belt—(a) as to such waters as are tidal, and (b) as to such waters which, though not tidal, are navigable?'

"The answer to this question must be in the negative. So far as the waters are tidal the right of fishing in them is a public right subject only to regulation by the Dominion Parliament. So far as the waters are not tidal they are matters of private property, and all these proprietary rights passed with the grant of the railway belt, and became thereby vested in the Crown in right of the Dominion. The question whether non-tidal waters are navigable or not has no bearing on the question. The fishing in navigable non-tidal waters is the subject of property, and according to English law must have an owner and cannot be vested in the public generally.

"They now come to the second question, which is: 'Is it competent to the Legislature of British Columbia to authorize the Government of the Province to grant by way of leave, licence, or otherwise the exclusive right, or any right, to fish below low water mark in or in any or what part or parts of the open sea within a marine league of the coast of the Province?'

"Their Lordships have already expressed their opinion that the right of fishing in the sea is a right of the public in general which does not depend on any proprietary title, and that the Dominion has the exclusive right of legislating with regard to it. They do not desire to pass any opinion on the question whether the subjects of the Province might, consistently with s. 91, be taxed in respect of its exercise for the reasons pointed out by Lord Herschell, but no such taxing could enable the Province to confer any exclusive or preferential right of fishing on individuals, or classes of individuals, because such exclusion or preference must import regulation and control of the general right of the public to fish and that is beyond the competence of the Province Legislature.

"In the argument before their Lordships much was said as to an alleged proprietary title in the Province to the shore around its coast within a marine league. The importance of claims based upon such a proprietary title arises from the fact that they would not be affected by the grant of the lands within the railway belt. But their Lordships feel themselves relieved from expressing any opinion on the question whether the Crown has a right of property in the bed of the sea below water mark to what is known as the three-mile limit because they are of opinion that the right of the public to fish in the sea has been well established in English law for many centuries and does not depend on the assertion or maintenance of any title in the Crown to the subjacent land. . . .

"Their Lordships therefore find themselves in agreement with the Supreme Court of Canada in answering the first and second questions in the negative.

"The principles above enunciated suffice to answer the third question, which relates to the right of fishing in arms of the sea and the estuaries of rivers. The right to fish is in their Lordships' opinion a public right of the same character as that enjoyed by the public on the open seas. A right of this kind is not an incident of property, and is not confined to the subjects of the Crown who are under the jurisdiction of the Province. Interference with it, whether in the form of direct regulation, or by the grant of exclusive or partially exclusive rights to individuals or classes of individuals, cannot be within the power of the Province, which is excluded from general legislation with regard to sea coast and inland fisheries."

The application of some of the matters mentioned in the *B.C. Fisheries* case, *supra*, to the province of Quebec was considered in *A.-G. Can. v. A.-G. Que.*, [1921] 1 A.C. 413, 56 D.L.R. 358, where the Privy Council affirmed that the right to fish in tidal waters was a public right subject to exclusive federal control and excluding any licensing power in the province. The following relevant observations were made by Viscount Haldane: "The Dominion Parliament, having exclusive jurisdiction over sea coast and inland fisheries, could regulate the exercise of all fishing rights, private and public alike. As the public right was not proprietary, the Dominion Parliament has in effect exclusive jurisdiction to deal with it. But as to private rights, the provincial Legislature has exclusive jurisdiction so long as these present no other aspects than that of property and civil rights in the Province, or of matter of a local or private nature within it, in the meaning of the words of s. 92.

"The result of this is that a Province cannot grant exclusive rights to fish in waters where the public has the right to fish. Now this right in the public was created by the series of statutes enacted in the old Province of ·Upper and Lower Canada prior to confederation, and as it continued to exist at confederation, only the Dominion could deal with it. As this Board said in the British Columbia case in 1914, the object and effect of the provisions of s. 91 were to place the management and protection of the cognate public rights of navigation and fishing in the seas and tidal waters exclusively in the Dominion Parliament and to leave to the Province no right of property or control in them. These rights, as we observed, are rights of the public in general, and in no way special to the inhabitants of the Province. Even under the guise of their taxing powers the Government of the Province could not confer any exclusive or preferential rights of fishing on individuals or classes of individuals, because such exclusion or preference would import regulation and control of the general right of the public to fish.

"It is true that the public right of fishing in tidal waters does not extend to a right to fix to the solum kiddles, weirs or other engines of the kind. That is because the solum is not vested in the public, but may be so in either the Crown or private owners. It is also true that the power of the Dominion does not extend to enabling it to create what are really proprietary rights where it possesses none itself. But it is obvious that the control of the Dominion must be extensive. It is not practicable to define abstractly its limits in terms going beyond those their Lordships have just employed. The solum and the consequent proprietary title to the fishery may be vested in the Crown in right of the Province or in a private individual, and in so far as this is so it cannot be transferred by regulation. But regulation may proceed very far in limiting the exercise of proprietary rights without ceasing to be regulative."

A.-G. CAN. v. A.-G. B.C.

In the Privy Council. [1930] A.C. 111, [1930] 1 D.L.R. 194, [1929] 3 W.W.R. 449.

Appeal by special leave from a judgment of the Supreme Court of Canada, [1928] S.C.R. 457, [1928] 4 D.L.R. 190, on a reference of certain questions set out below.

LORD TOMLIN: . . . The judgment complained of embodies the conclusions of the Supreme Court upon the questions referred. The questions were as follows:

"(1) Are ss. 7A and 18 of the *Fisheries Act,* 1914, or either of them and in what particular or particulars or to what extent *ultra vires* of the Parliament of Canada?

"(2) If the said provisions of the Fisheries Act, 1914, or either of them be *intra vires* of the Parliament of Canada, has the Minister authority to issue a licence for the operation of a floating cannery constructed on a float or ship, as contradistinguished from a stationary cannery constructed on land, and if so, is he entitled to make the licence subject to any restrictions particularly as to the place of operation of any such cannery in British Columbia?

"(3) Under the provisions of the Special Fishery Regulations for the Province of British Columbia (made by the Governor in Council, under the authority of s. 45 of the *Fisheries Act,* 1914), respecting licences to fish—namely, subs. 3 of s. 14; para. (a) or (b) of subs. 1 of s. 15 or para (a) of subs. 7 of s. 24 of the said Regulations, or under said ss. 7A or 18 of the said Act (if these sections or either of them be *intra vires* of the Parliament of Canada) has: (a) any British subject resident in the Province of British Columbia; or (b) any person so resident who is not a British subject, upon application and tender of the prescribed fee, the right to receive a licence to fish or to operate a fish or salmon cannery in that province, or has the Minister a discretionary authority to grant or refuse such licence to any such person whether a British subject or not?"

The Supreme Court held that the sections mentioned in the first question were *ultra vires* the Parliament of the Dominion, and that in view of this conclusion the second question and so much of the third question as related to the impugned sections required no answer. As to the remainder of the third question a majority of the Court held in effect that under the Regulations there was no discretion in the Minister to grant or refuse a licence to a qualified person. . .

The impugned sections of the Fisheries Act, 1914, are in the following terms:

"7A. No one shall operate a fish cannery for commercial purposes without first obtaining an annual licence therefor from the Minister. Where no other fee is in this Act prescribed for a cannery licence, the annual fee for such licence shall be one dollar (1917, c. 16).

"18. No one shall operate a salmon cannery or salmon curing establishment in British Columbia for commercial purposes except under a licence from the Minister (1-2 Geo. V., c. 9, s. 2).

"(2)—(a) The annual fee for a salmon cannery licence shall be twenty dollars, and in addition, four cents for each case of forty-eight one-pound cans, or the equivalent thereto, of sock-eye salmon, and three cents for each case of forty-eight one-pound cans, or the equivalent thereto, of any other species of salmon, including steel-head (*salmo rivularis*) packed in such cannery during the continuance in force of the licence. The said twenty dollars shall be paid before the licence is issued, and the remainder of the licence fee shall be paid as the Minister may from time to time by regulation prescribe (1924, c. 43, 14-15 Geo. V).

(b) The annual licence fee for a salmon-curing establishment shall be:—

Fifty cents on each ton or fraction thereof of dry-salted salmon put up in the establishment during the season, when the total quantity of dry-salted salmon put up in one season does not exceed ten tons;

Seventy-five cents on each ton or fraction thereof of dry-salted salmon put up in the establishment during the season, when the total quantity of dry-salted salmon put up in one season exceeds ten tons but is not more than twenty tons.

One dollar on each ton or fraction thereof of dry-salted salmon put up in the establishment during the season, when the total quantity of dry-salted salmon put up in one season exceeds twenty tons but is not more than fifty tons.

One dollar and twenty-five cents on each ton or fraction thereof of dry-salted salmon put up in the establishment during the season, when the total quantity of dry-salted salmon put up in one season exceeds fifty tons (12-13 Geo. V, c. 24, s. 1)."

The appellant seeks to support the validity of these sections first upon the ground that their subject-matter is one within the subjects of express enumeration in s. 91, and secondly upon the ground that they consist of provisions necessarily incidental to effective legislation upon an enumerated subject.

The *Fisheries Act,* 1914, is "An Act . . . respecting fisheries and fishing," and contains a body of legislation regulating the fishing industry, and so far as it regulates that industry admittedly within the powers of the Dominion Parliament, inasmuch as sea coast and inland fisheries is one of the subjects enumerated in s. 91.

The appellant contends in the first place that the subject "sea coast and inland fisheries" covers such matters as the regulation of fish cannery or curing establishments, either ashore or afloat, and that the imposition of a licensing system upon such establishments is therefore justified. . . .

. . . The appellant, however, seeks for the word "fisheries" . . . a definition of such amplitude that it will include the operations carried out upon the fish when caught for the purpose of converting them into some form of marketable commodity. He supports his contention by referring to fishery legislation prior to 1867 affecting territories now part of the Dominion, pointing out that in this legislation there are to be found numerous provisions relating to the curing and marketing of fish, and he urges that the *British North America Act,* 1867, must be construed in the light of the earlier legislation, and that the word "fisheries" must be given such a meaning as is wide enough to include at any rate the operations affected by the impugned sections.

Their Lordships are of opinion that the appellant's contention in this respect is not well founded. The fact that in earlier fishery legislation raising no question of legislative competence matters are dealt with not strictly within any ordinary definition of "fishery" affords no ground for putting an unnatural construction upon the words "sea coast and inland fisheries." In their Lordships' judgment, trade processes by which fish when caught are converted into a commodity suitable to be placed upon the market cannot upon any reasonable principle of construction be brought within the scope of the subject expressed by the words "sea coast and inland fisheries." . . .

The second point made by the appellant is that the licensing of fish canning and curing establishments is necessarily incidental to effective legislation under the subject "sea coast and inland fisheries."

It may be, though on this point their Lordships express no opinion, that effective fishery legislation requires that the Minister should have power for the purpose of enforcing regulations against the taking of unfit fish or against the taking of fish out of season, to inspect all fishing canning or fish curing establishments and require them to make appropriate statistical returns. Even if this were so the necessity for applying to such establishments any such licensing system as is embodied in the sections in question does not follow. It is not obvious that any licensing system is necessarily incidental to effective fishery legislation, and no material has been placed before the Supreme Court or their Lordships' Board establishing the necessary connection between the two subject-matters. In their Lordships' view, therefore, the appellant's second contention is not well founded.

The impugned sections confer powers upon the Minister in relation to matters which in their Lordships' judgment *prima facie* fall under the subject "property and civil rights in the province", included in s. 92 of the British North America Act, 1867. As already indicated, these matters are not in their Lordships' opinion covered directly or indirectly by any of the subjects enumerated in s. 91. It is not suggested that they are of national importance and have attained such dimensions as to affect the body politic of the Dominion.

In their Lordships' judgment, therefore, the impugned sections deal with matters not within the legislative competence of the Parliament of the Dominion and cannot be supported.

Having regard to the view which their Lordships take of the first question, the second question requires no answer.

It remains to deal with the third question.

So far as this question deals with the sections which are the subject of the first question it now requires no answer. That part of it, however, which deals with certain provisions of the Special Fishery Regulations for the Province of British Columbia must be considered. The validity of these provisions is not attacked; their construction only is in question. . . .

The regulations in question affect both public and private rights of fishing. There is no express provision for withholding a licence where a qualified applicant submits a proper application and pays the small prescribed fee, and in their Lordships' judgment there is nothing in the language of the regulations giving rise to a necessary implication that the Minister has a discretion to grant or withhold the licence. Their Lordships agree with the answer which the majority of the Supreme Court gave to the third question.

Appeal dismissed.

[For application of the distinction between exclusive Dominion regulatory authority as to the time or mode or manner of fishing and provincial proprietary rights, see *Rex v. Wagner*, [1932] 2 W.W.R. 162, [1932] 3 D.L.R. 679 (provincial statute making it an offence to have in possession fish caught during closed season declared *ultra vires*) and *Rex v. Tomasson*, [1932] 2 W.W.R. 176, [1932] 3 D.L.R. 693 (similar Dominion statute sustained); see also *Regina v. Wold* (1956), 19 W.W.R. 75, 24 C.R. 332.

What conditions may a province, as owner of the solum, attach to a licence granting a right to fish? Under s. 92(5) of the *B.N.A. Act* provincial legislative power covers the management of public lands belonging to the province. May it not then restrict the use thereof to certain seasons or to certain modes of user? Cf. *Brooks-Bidlake and Whittall Ltd. v. A.-G. B.C.*, [1923] A.C. 450, [1923] 2 D.L.R. 189, [1923] 1 W.W.R. 1150.

Does it follow from the *Fish Canneries* case, *supra*, and, indeed, from the other cases on fisheries, that it would be incompetent to Parliament to expropriate or authorize the expropriation of fishing areas or to grant franchises in such number as it may determine? (Of course, no problem of federal-provincial power would arise in respect of fishing on the high seas outside of provincial territorial waters: see *Gavin v. The Queen* (1956), 3 D.L.R. (2d) 457, 115 Can. C.C. 315.) If Parliament may grant railway, radio and television franchises and authorize expropriation of land in those respects, why not in relation to seacoast and inland fisheries? Surely the reference to the exclusive right of fishing, as a profit à prendre, and as within provincial competence, is significant only in the absence of federal legislation. If Parliament may take the fee simple in land, or authorize its taking, why is there any difficulty about overriding such a lesser interest as a profit when acting within exclusive legislative authority? Or, is the "fishery" power different in quality from the other enumerated powers? In *The Queen v. Robertson* (1882), 6 S.C.R. 52, at p. 120, Ritchie C.J. observed that "legislation in regard to 'inland and sea fisheries' contemplated by the British North America Act was not in reference to 'property and civil rights' —that is to say not as to the ownership of the beds of the rivers, or of the fisheries, or the rights of individuals therein, but to subjects affecting the fisheries generally, tending to their regulation, protection and preservation, matters of a national and general concern and important to the public, such as forbidding fish to be taken at improper seasons in an improper manner, or with destructive instruments, laws with reference to the improvement and increase of the fisheries; in other words, all such general laws as enure as well to the benefit of the owners of the fisheries as to the public at large, who are interested in the fisheries as a source of national or provincial wealth; in other words, laws in relation to the fisheries, such as those which the local legislatures were, previously to and at the time of confederation, in the habit of enacting for their regulation, preservation and protection, with which the property in the fish or the right to take the fish out of the water to be appropriated to the party so taking the fish has nothing whatever to do, the property in the fishing, or the right to take the fish, being as much the property of the province or the individual, as the dry land or the land covered with water. I cannot discover the slightest trace of an intention on the part of the Imperial Parliament to convey to the Dominion Government any property in the beds of streams or in the fisheries incident to the owner-ship thereof, whether belonging at the date of confederation either to the provinces or individuals, or to confer on the Dominion Parliament the right to appropriate or dispose of them, and receive therefor large rentals which most unequivocally proceed from property, or from the incidents of property in or to which the Dominion has no shadow of claim . . .".]

Note on Legislative Power in relation to "Indians and Lands Reserved for the Indians"

Parliament's exclusive power under s. 91(24) of the *B.N.A. Act* to legislate in relation to "Indians" as well as in relation to "Lands reserved for the Indians" has, of course, historical roots, and in its specification that Indians as a class should be under federal protection it may be compared with exclusive federal power in relation to "aliens" under s. 91(25). Historical evidence has been relied on to determine who is properly classified as an Indian; and the Supreme Court has decreed that the Eskimo inhabitants of Quebec are included in the aboriginal groups covered by s. 91(24): see *Re Eskimos*, [1939] S.C.R. 104, [1939] 2 D.L.R. 417. There is no doubt but that Parliament alone has authority to regulate the lives and affairs of Indians on a reservation and, indeed, to control the administration of a reservation; provincial laws are inapplicable on a reservation (save as they may be referentially introduced through federal legislation): see *Rex v. Jim* (1915), 26 B.C.R. 106, 26 Can. C.C. 236; *Rex v. Rodgers*, [1923] 3 D.L.R. 414, [1923] 2 W.W.R. 353; *Warman v. Francis* (1958), 20 D.L.R. (2d) 627, 43 M.P.R. 197; *cf. The Indian Act*, R.S.C. 1970, c. I-6. Federal power extends to the subjecting of Indians to federal regulatory legislation even though it be in derogation of "treaty" rights previously or subsequently accorded to the Indians; and the question in such cases is not so much constitutional as one of construction of the federal legislation: see *Sikyea v. The Queen*, [1964] S.C.R. 642, [1965] 2 Can. C.C. 129, 50 D.L.R. (2d) 80. The doubt expressed in *Regina v. George*, [1964] 1 O.R. 24, 41 D.L.R. (2d) 31, aff'd [1964] 2 O.R. 429, 45 D.L.R. (2d) 709, whether there is legislative power at all to take away Indian treaty rights granted before Confederation stands rejected by the Supreme Court's affirmation of federal power in this connection in reversing the judgments below: see *Regina v. George*, [1966] 3 Can. C.C. 137, 47 C.R. 382, 55 D.L.R. (2d) 386.

Parliament cannot compulsorily create or expropriate for reservations. Its legislative power in relation to such lands depends on their establishment otherwise, e.g. by federal-provincial agreement or under pre-confederation or post-confederation "treaty"; and what the Indians have in such lands is a usufructuary interest with the ultimate title (if the land is in a Province) resting in the Crown in right of the Province: see *Ontario Mining Co. v. Seybold*, [1903] A.C. 73. While Parliament may provide for the surrender of reserved Indian lands (see *Logan v. Styres*, [1959] O.W.N. 361, 20 D.L.R. (2d) 416), the surrender if effected is to the Province in which the lands are situate: see *St. Catherines Milling & Lumber Co. v. The Queen* (1889), 14 App. Cas. 46; *A.-G. Can. v. A.-G. Ont.*, [1897] A.C. 199. Provincial taxation of a non-Indian occupier of reservation land was sustained in *Sammartino v. A.-G. B.C.*, 22 D.L.R. (3d) 194, [1972] 1 W.W.R. 24, as being neither a regulation of Indian lands nor taxation of federal property forbidden by *B.N.A. Act*, s. 125.

The more difficult problem in this area is the extent to which Indians off their reservations are subject to provincial legislation and the extent to which Parliament may free them from subjection to such legislation. In terms of aspect, it may be found, as was the case in *Rex v. Commanda,* [1939] O.W.N. 466, [1939] 3 D.L.R. 635, that competent provincial legislation for the protection of game and fish on provincial lands applied to Indians in respect of surrendered Indian lands which passed to the province after Confederation. (It was also held in that case that the privilege to hunt and fish reserved by the treaty of surrender in 1850 did not fall within s. 109 of the *B.N.A. Act,* and that even if it did, it was subject to competent provincial legislation for the protection of game and fish). Compare *R. v. Cardinal,* 22 D.L.R. (3d) 716, 5 C.C.C. (2d) 193, 17 C.R.N.S. 110, [1972] 1 W.W.R. 536 (*sub nom. A.-G. Alta. v. Cardinal*). Would it however, be open to a province to deny certain working opportunities to Indians, as was attempted in respect of "aliens" in *Union Colliery Co. v. Bryden,* [1899] A.C. 580, which held the provincial legislation to be *ultra vires?* Such indications as the few cases on the subject afford suggest that in the absence of federal legislation to the contrary, Indians off the reservation are subject to general provincial property and regulatory legislation: see *Sanderson v. Heap* (1909), 11 W.L.R. 238, 19 Man. R. 122; *Rex v. Hill* (1907), 15 O.L.R. 406. While judgments may hence go against them or convictions be registered under valid provincial legislation, the Indian as a person is not subject to attachment nor may he be taken under provincial process: see *Re Caledonia Milling Co. v. Johns* (1918), 42 O.L.R. 338; *Ex parte Tenasse,* [1931] 1 D.L.R. 806, 2 M.P.R. 253; *Re Kane,* [1940] 1 D.L.R. 390. Federal legislation, as in the Indian Act, may, of course, remove this immunity or may visit other disabilities which would be controlling: cf: *Regina v. Little Bear* (1958), 122 Can. C.C. 173, 26 W.W.R. 335; *Geoffries v. Williams* (1958), 16 D.L.R. (2d) 157, 26 W.W.R. 323.

Does *R. v. Drybones,* [1970] S.C.R. 282, 3 C.C.C. 555, 10 C.R.N.S. 334, 71 W.W.R. 161, 9 D.L.R. (3d) 473, setting aside, as repugnant to the prohibition in the *Canadian Bill of Rights* of "discrimination by reason of race", a conviction under the *Indian Act,* R.S.C. 1952, c. 149, s. 94 for conduct which would not have been punishable for a non-Indian, effectively erase the first branch of s. 91(24) from the *British North America Act?* If classification of Indians as a separate category for legislative treatment is impermissible, can any statute be drawn that has a matter falling within the class of subjects "Indians"?

These questions were explored in *A.G. Can. v. Lavelle; Isaac v. Bedard* (1973), 23 C.R.N.S. 197, 11 R.F.L. 333, 38 D.L.R. (3d) 481 (Can.), though because of the diverse opinions and of the fact that it like the *Drybones* case primarily involved questions of application of the Canadian Bill of Rights, as to which see *infra,* p.   , the answers are still somewhat unclear.

[See *Lysyk,* The Unique Constitutional Position of the Canadian Indian, (1967) 45 Can. Bar Rev. 513.]

Note on Property Provisions of the B.N.A. Act

Part VIII of the B.N.A. Act, ss. 102 to 117 and s. 126, provided for the apportionment between Dominion and provinces of the property and revenues, assets and liabilities, of the confederating provinces. S. 117 has been regarded as the key to the property clauses since it provides that "the several provinces shall retain all their respective public property not otherwise disposed of in this Act, subject to the right of Canada to assume any lands or public property required for fortifications or for the defence of the country." (*Quaere* whether this *proviso* adds anything to federal legislative power in relation to "militia, military and naval service, and defence" under s. 91(7)! It has, however, been held to be an executive and not a legislative power: see *A.-G. Que. v. Nipissing Central Ry.*, [1926] A.C. 715, [1926] 3 D.L.R. 545, [1926] 2 W.W.R. 552.) This residuary provision is emphasized by s. 109 under which "all lands, mines, minerals and royalties belonging to the several provinces. . . at the union. . . . shall belong to the several provinces of Ontario, Quebec, Nova Scotia and New Brunswick in which the same are situate or arise, subject to any trusts existing in respect thereof, and to any interest other than that of the province in the same." On British Columbia's entry as a province, it transferred to the Dominion a large area in connection with the construction of the C.P.R. (the Railway Belt), but otherwise it was in the same position as the original confederating provinces. However, s. 109 had no application to any but the original confederating provinces. The three western provinces which were carved out of the territories acquired by the Dominion from the Hudson's Bay Company had no rights over Crown land within their boundaries until 1930 when by virtue of agreements in 1929 and 1930 with the Dominion and of an amendment to the *B.N.A. Act* their "natural resources" were returned to them; at the same time the Dominion re-transferred to British Columbia, its remaining interest in the "Railway Belt": see B.N.A. Act, 1930 (Imp.), c. 26 and schedules thereto; *In re Transfer of Natural Resources to Saskatchewan*, [1932] A.C. 28, [1931] 4 D.L.R. 712, [1931] 3 W.W.R. 488; *Spooner Oils Ltd. v. Turner Valley Gas Conservation Board*, [1933] S.C.R. 629, [1933] 4 D.L.R. 545. Prince Edward Island had granted away almost all of its Crown land before being admitted as a province and some concessions by way of increased subsidy and otherwise were made to it on this account. See *Clement,* The Canadian Constitution, chap. 29, for a discussion of the "property" position of the provinces and Dominion. The terms of union with Newfoundland conformed generally to the property provisions of the B.N.A. Act, 1867: see 1949 (Imp.), c. 22 and schedule, especially ss. 31, 33, 35 and 37 of the terms of union set out in the schedule.

Disputes about the respective property interests of Dominion and provinces provided a good deal of the constitutional business of the courts in the first three or four decades after Confederation. It is sufficient here to advert to a few special points; for a general discussion see *Clement, op. cit., supra. Mercer v. A.-G. Ont.* (1883), 8 App. Cas. 767 established the right of the provinces rather than of the Dominion to take land by escheat, a right deemed to be covered by "royalties" in s. 109. (In the western provinces, escheat to the Crown meant, until 1930, escheat to the Crown in right of the Dominion.

It was, however, held to be competent to a western province to alter its laws respecting devolution although this would affect escheat in favour of the Dominion: see *A.-G. Can. v. Stone and A.-G. Sask.*, [1924] S.C.R. 682, [1925] 1 D.L.R. 60). So, too, the province took personalty as *bona vacantia:* see *A.-G. Alta. v. A.-G. Can.*, [1928] A.C. 475, [1918] 3 D.L.R. 849, [1928] 3 W.W.R. 97; *Rex v. A.-G. B.C.*, [1924] A.C. 213, [1923] 4 D.L.R. 690, [1923] 3 W.W.R. 1252. In other cases (some of which are set out in this and in the preceding chapter), the Privy Council drew the lines between legislative power and proprietary right, making it clear that it was the Crown (Province) rather than the Crown (Dominion) in which, except as provided expressly in the B.N.A. Act, public property vested and that federal legislative power did not *per se* give the Crown (Dominion) any proprietary rights in connection with the classes of subjects listed in s. 91, save as the Dominion might have acquired such rights otherwise.

Public or Crown property which at Confederation was transferred to the Dominion is that referred to in s. 108 of the B.N.A. Act providing that "the public works and property of each province enumerated in the third schedule to this Act, shall be the property of Canada."

Some of the items in this schedule are considered in a number of the cases set out in this and in the preceding chapter. See also *A.-G. Can. v. Western Higbie and Albion Investments Ltd. and A.-G. B.C.*, [1945] S.C.R. 385, [1945] 3 D.L.R. 1 ("public harbours"); *A.-G. Can. v. Ritchie Contracting & Supply Co.*, [1919] A.C. 990, 48 D.L.R. 147, [1919] 3 W.W.R. 347 ("public harbours"); *The King v. A.-G. Ont. and Forrest*, [1934] S.C.R. 133, [1934] 1 D.L.R. 657 ("public harbours"); *La Forest*, The Meaning of "Public Harbours" in the Third Schedule to the British North America Act, (1963) 41 Can. Bar Rev. 519; *A.-G. B.C. v. A.-G. Can.*, [1906] A.C. 552 (military establishments).

Under s. 91(1A) (formerly s. 91(1)) of the B.N.A. Act, Parliament has legislative power in relation to "the public debt and property". This does not, of course, have any reference to the public debt or property of the provinces. They are entitled under s. 92(5) to manage their own (Crown) lands; and whether it be under s. 92(13) or s. 92(16) or perhaps under s. 92(3), the provinces are equally empowered to deal with and dispose of other assets belonging to them, assets to which provincial title is confirmed by ss. 109 and 126 of the *B.N.A. Act.* The power given by s. 91(1A) enables Parliament to condition any dispositions of its property, e.g. by way of exempting it, at least when still in the hands of the Dominion or subject to a Dominion claim, from provincial laws which might otherwise be applicable, e.g. registry and execution laws: see *The King v. Powers*, [1923] Ex. C.R. 121; *Re McManus*, [1939] 4 D.L.R. 759; *Re Young*, [1955] 5 D.L.R. 225. Indeed, as Duff C.J.C. said in a dissenting judgment in *Reference re Employment and Social Insurance Act*, [1936] S.C.R. 427, at p. 444, [1963] 3 D.L.R. 644, at p. 658 (a case in which federal

unemployment insurance legislation was held invalid by the Supreme
Court majority as well as by the Privy Council: see [1937] A.C. 355,
[1937] 1 D.L.R. 684, [1937] 1 W.W.R. 312) "no province possesses any
authority to legislate in relation to the application of . . . a [Dom-
inion public] fund". Moreover, federal authority respecting property
of any kind acquired by the Crown in right of Canada has been the
basis of a widely-used technique of non-compulsory regulation through
federal grants-in-aid, given upon compliance with conditions prescribed by Parliament.

Federal legislative power in relation to the Dominion's own debt
and property is but part of the picture of immunity of such debt and
property from provincial legislation: see *Persons v. The Queen* [1966]
Ex. C.R. 538, at p. 545. It follows from the principle of the *Liquidators*
case, [1892] A.C. 437 that the distribution of authority between
central and provincial legislatures and governments was a distribution
which covered executive as well as legislative power, and this necessarily left the Crown in right of the Province as much in enjoyment
of prerogatives *qua* provincial interests as was the Crown in right
of Canada entitled to assert prerogatives in federal interests. Of
course, these prerogatives were subject to control by competent legislation, and it seems clear that here (by virtue both of federal exclusive
authority and of the principle of paramountcy) the federal Crown
cannot be deprived of its prerogatives by provincial legislation and, *à
fortiori*, provincial legislation cannot competently deal with or subject
federal public property to provincial regulation: see *Gauthier v. The
King* (1918), 56 S.C.R. 176, 40 D.L.R. 355; *Deeks McBride Ltd. v.
Vancouver Associated Contractors Ltd.*, [1954] 4 D.L.R. 844, 14
W.W.R. 509; *Re Director of Soldier Settlement* (1960), 25 D.L.R. (2d)
463, 31 W.W.R. 647; *B.A.C.M. Ltd. v. Parkland Builders Contracting
Ltd.* (1971), 18 D.L.R. (3d) 377.

On the federal Crown prerogative side of the problem under
discussion, there is one Privy Council judgment which, however
explained or rationalized as to result, appears to be wrong in principle,
unless a distinction be drawn between Crown prerogatives and Crown
property with a consequential holding that the federal Crown may
only assert its prerogatives, e.g. priority as a creditor, in conformity
with provincial legislation validly governing a situation in which the
prerogative claim is asserted. There is no strong indication that
such distinction is recognized, although there are cases holding that
the federal Crown in choosing to resort to provincial legislation must
take that legislation with its burdens as well as its advantages: see
Reid v. Canadian Farm Loan Board, [1937] 4 D.L.R. 248, 45 Man. R.
357, [1937] 3 W.W.R. 1; and see *Gordon,* How Far Privative or
Restrictive Enactment Binds the Crown, (1940) 18 Can. Bar Rev.
751. It is doubtful, however, whether provincial legislation can validly
have the effect of destroying or denying a federal crown prerogative
which exists apart therefrom.

The questionable Privy Council judgment is in *Exchange Bank of
Canada v. The Queen* (1886), 11 App. Cas. 157, where there were

claims by both the federal and provincial (Quebec) Crowns as well as by other unsecured creditors against a bank which was in liquidation. The two Crowns did not oppose each other but were in fact jointly represented by counsel in claiming priority against other creditors. In denying the priority as being subject to overriding Quebec legislation, Lord Hobhouse stated that "their Lordships think it clear not only that the Crown is bound by the [Quebec] Codes but that the subject of priorities is exhaustively dealt with by them, so that the Crown can claim no priority except what is allowed by them". No distinction was made in the position of the Crown in right of Canada and in right of Quebec. The case may be explicable on the ground that the Crown was treated as "one and indivisible" (a not very satisfactory explanation), but in the *Liquidators* case Lord Watson referred to the *Exchange Bank* case as one where the Judicial Committee "negatived the preference claimed by the Dominion Government upon the ground that by the law of the province of Quebec the prerogative was limited to the case of the common debtor being an officer liable to account to the Crown for public moneys collected or held by him". If this is intended to suggest that provincial law may control federal Crown prerogatives, it is contrary to other authority as well as to constitutional principle. It was held in *Emerson v. Simpson* (1962), 32 D.L.R. (2d) 603, 38 W.W.R. 466, that the prerogative of the federal Crown could not be defeated by provincial legislation and that the filing of a writ of extent against the debtor's land under the legislation did not amount to abandonment of the prerogative; to the same effect is *The Queen v. Hamilton* (1962), 37 D.L.R. (2d) 545, 39 W.W.R. 545. But see *Re Mendelsohn* (1960), 25 D.L.R. (2d) 778, rev'g by consent of counsel for the Dominion (1959), 22 D.L.R. (2d) 748. This result was questioned in *Stroud v. Imperial Oil Ltd.* (1961), 28 D.L.R. (2d) 366, 35 W.W.R. 4. A position contrary to *Re Mendelsohn* was taken in a similar fact situation in *Re Sternschein* (1965), 50 D.L.R. (2d) 762.

In re *Silver Bros. Ltd.*, [1932] A.C. 514, [1932] 2 D.L.R. 673, [1932] 1 W.W.R. 764, holds that in the absence of federal legislation expressly giving the federal Crown a priority over the Crown in right of a Province in a matter which is within federal authority, e.g., upon a bankruptcy, the prerogative of the provincial Crown may be asserted *pari passu* with the federal Crown; and see also *Re Walter's Trucking Service Ltd., The Queen v. A.-G. Can.* (1965), 50 D.L.R. (2d) 711, 51 W.W.R. 407. This is because of the principle that the Crown is not bound unless expressly or necessarily included in the applicable legislation. What the *Silver Bros.* case does is to give this principle a constitutional significance by requiring specific inclusion of the provincial Crown in restricting federal legislation. Thus, there is no doubt of the legislative power of Parliament, when acting under s. 91, to determine the order in which priorities may be claimed and to give the federal Crown a preference against the Crown in right of a Province: see *A.-G. B.C. v. A.-G. Can.* (1922), 21 Ex. C.R. 281, 63 D.L.R. 82, aff'd 64 S.C.R. 377, [1923] 1 W.W.R. 241, [1923] 1 D.L.R. 223, aff'd [1924] A.C. 222, [1923] 4 D.L.R. 669, [1923] 3

W.W.R. 1249; *Industrial Development Bank v. Valley Dairy Ltd. and MacDonald*, [1953] O.R. 70, [1952] 1 D.L.R. 788. The converse situation does not hold true, although one might urge that it is not logical to deny to a provincial legislature power to bind the federal Crown in matters within provincial legislative authority. Cf. *Uther v. Federal Commissioner of Taxation* (1947), 74 C.L.R. 508; *Commonwealth of Australia v. Cigamatic Pty. Ltd.* (1962), 108 C.L.R. 372; and see *Sawer*, State Statutes and the Commonwealth (1961), 1 Univ. of Tas. L. Rev. 580. The effective answer is that nothing in the provincial catalogue of powers justifies any claim to bind the Crown in right of Canada, even where no federal Crown property is involved but only prerogative claims; see *Gauthier v. The King, supra;* and *cf. The King v. Murphy*, [1948] S.C.R. 357, [1948] 3 D.L.R. 1. The *Exchange Bank* case cannot sensibly be explained on the basis of continuing pre-Confederation legislation which was operative thereafter by virtue of s. 129 of the *B.N.A. Act*. The federal Crown was newly created by the *B.N.A. Act* and could not be said to be caught by pre-Confederation legislation; see *Re D. Moore Co. Ltd.*, 61 O.L.R. 434, [1928] 1 D.L.R. 383; *Toronto and Toronto Electric Com'rs. v. Wade*, [1931] O.R. 470, [1931] 4 D.L.R. 928, aff'd [1932] O.R. 500, [1932] 3 D.L.R. 509; *Holmstead v. Minister of Customs and Excise*, [1927] Ex. C.R. 68. Any reference to the Crown in provincial legislation (*e.g. Trustee Act*, R.S.O. 1970, c. 70, s. 50) can be no more than a reference to the provincial Crown: see *Gauthier v. The King supra;* but see *Re Mendelsohn, supra;* cf. *Bowers v. Hollinger*, [1946] O.R. 526, at p. 536, [1946] 4 D.L.R. 186, at p. 196; *The King v. Star Kosher Sausage Mfg. Co.*, [1940] 4 D.L.R. 365, [1940] 3 W.W.R. 127, 48 Man. R. 147; *The King ex rel. A.-G. Can. v. Sanford*, [1939] 1 D.L.R. 374, 13 M.P.R. 469.

Federal legislative authority in relation to federal public property clearly operates defensively to preclude provincial legislation against such property: see *Spooner Oils Ltd. v. Turner Valley Gas Conservation Board*, [1933] S.C.R. 629, [1933] 4 D.L.R. 545; *Burrard Power Co. v. The King*, [1911] A.C. 87; *cf. Regina v. Hughes* (1958), 122 Can. C.C. 198 (provincial highway traffic legislation applicable in national park because of referential federal legislation). Provincial legislation could not restrict the rights of lessees or licensees of federal Crown lands any more than it could do so if the federal Crown was itself in occupation: see *Spooner Oils Ltd.* case, *supra*. It was held in *Re Armstrong and Van Der Weyden*, a 1956 case reported in [1965] 1 O.R. 68, 46 D.L.R. (2d) 629, no written reasons being given, that Parliament could validly provide in s. 5(3) of the *Veterans' Land Act*, R.S.C. 1952, c. 280 that grants of land by the Director under the Act (being land of or acquired by the federal Crown) constitute new titles with the same effect as if they were grants of previously ungranted Crown lands. It is an adaptation of the foregoing principle to hold that a contractor engaged by the federal Crown (or an agency thereof) to build on federal Crown land in a municipality is not obliged to obtain a municipal building permit: see *Ottawa v. Shore & Horowitz Construction Co. Ltd.*, [1960] O.W.N.

137, 22 D.L.R. (2d) 247. To what extent however, may Parliament legislate in respect of its property, however acquired, to confer or create rights which might operate affirmatively against existing provincial legislation? In principle, there would seem to be no bar to such federal legislation, accepting that it has acquired full title or seeks to deal only with such interest as it has. Section 5(2) of the *Veterans' Land Act,* R.S.C. 1952, c. 280 raises the problem envisaged here by providing that "all conveyances from the Director constitute new titles to the land conveyed and have the same and as full effect as grants from the Crown of previously ungranted Crown lands". *Quaere,* whether Parliament can thus give a better title than it has! Cf. *Re Harpell,* [1968] 2 O.R. 600, 70 D.L.R. (2d) 165.

[There is no unconstitutional interference with federal property rights where a privately-owned boat house, standing on federal Crown land and permitted by the lessee of the federal Crown to be placed there, is subject to removal as a nuisance under a properly authorized municipal by-law: *Re Wheatley, Re Kodak and Marsh* (1958), 24 W.W.R. 323 (B.C.).

Similarly, a municipality may properly require a retail vendor's licence from a person who sells to the public although he is on federal (National Harbours Board) property when there is no preclusion either in federal legislation or in regulations thereunder: *Regina v. Karchaba* (1965), 52 D.L.R. (2d) 438, 51 W.W.R. 314; accord, *Re Mowat & Lorne Murphy Foods Ltd.,* [1972] 1 O.R. 559, 23 D.L.R. (3d) 543.

In *Lab. Rel. Bd. (Can.) v. C.N.R.,* [1974] 4 W.W.R. 661, 1 N.R. 547, 74 C.L.L.C. 14, 213, 45 D.L.R. (3d) 1 (Can.), construction of the relevant federal legislation left undecided constitutional issues relating to provincial legislation authority over property situated in a national park which was held under lease and operated by a federally owned Crown corporation.

Until recently, there had been no authoritative determination of the limits of territorial jurisdiction or ownership in a Province, vis-a-vis the Dominion, over or in lands lying under adjacent (territorial) waters. Apart from international law questions touching proprietary rights in the maritime belt, the proprietary interests as between Canada and any Province would depend not only on boundary considerations but on the constitutional distribution of legislative power and property rights, already considered herein. There was a discussion of this matter in the context of a municipal assessment appeal respecting submarine workings of coal companies within the three-mile limit from the Nova Scotia coast: see *Re Dominion Coal Co. Ltd. and County of Cape Breton* (1963), 40 D.L.R. (2d) 593, 48 M.P.R. 174. For a comment on this case, see *LaForest,* in (1964), 2 Can. Year Book of Int. Law 233. Since then the Supreme Court of Canada has decided in *Reference re Offshore Mineral Rights of British Columbia,* [1967] S.C.R. 792, 65 D.L.R. (2d) 353, that as between Canada and British Columbia, it is the former that has ownership of the bed of the territorial sea adjacent to British Columbia and the right to explore and exploit the minerals and other natural resources thereof, as well as having legislative jurisdiction in relation thereto; and moreover the same result must be recognized in respect of the continental shelf beyond the area of the territorial sea. See *Head,* The Canadian Offshore Minerals Reference: The Application of International Law to a Federal Constitution (1968), 18 U. of T.L.J. 131.

For a consideration of these problems in the United States, see *United States v. California* (1947), 332 U.S. 19, 67 S. Ct. 1658; *United States v. Louisiana* (1960), 363 U.S. 1, 121, 80 S. Ct. 961, 1026.]

CROWTHER v. A.-G. CAN.

In (1959) 17 D.L.R. (2d) 437, 42 M.P.R. 296 (N.S.).

Appeal from a judgment of Ilsley C.J., 15 D.L.R. (2d) 204, upholding a claim of the Crown (Dominion) to priority of payment.

DOULL J.: This is an appeal from a decision of the Chief Justice who decided that the Crown in the right of Dominion of Canada had a claim in priority to other claimants upon a sum of $5,000 paid into Court by the defendant Canadian Mercantile Insurance Company under the following circumstances.

Following a collision between motor vehicles, the plaintiff recovered judgment against Nathaniel Martin Patterson for damages incurred in the collision, amounting to $9,100 and costs which were taxed at $403.15.

The Attorney-General of Canada also obtained a judgment against Nathaniel Martin Patterson for loss of services of one Joseph Content, a member of the armed forces of Canada who was injured in the same collision, for $10,954.57.

On April 16, 1958, the plaintiff issued a writ in the present action claiming: "as a judgment creditor under Section 26(1) of the Automobile Insurance Act, being Chapter 18, R.S.N.S. 1954, against the defendant as insurer to have the money payable under an owner's policy issued by the defendant to Nathaniel Patterson applied in or towards satisfaction of plaintiff's judgment and of a judgment of the Attorney-General of Canada." The Attorney-General of Canada notified the defendant's solicitor that he claimed for the Crown priority in the application of the fund.

The defendant thereupon applied for and obtained an order directing it to pay the amount of its insurance policy into Court and that further action against it be stayed and that the issue between the claimants be disposed of in a summary manner. This order was dated May 23, 1958, and the money was paid into Court on the same date. . . .

Section 26(1) of the *Automobile Insurance Act*, R.S.N.S. 1954, c. 18, is as follows:

> "Any person having a claim against an insured, for which indemnity is provided by a motor vehicle liability policy, shall, notwithstanding that such a person is not a party to the contract, be entitled, upon recovering a judgment therefor against the insured, to have the insurance money payable under the policy applied in or towards satisfaction of his judgment and of any other judgments or claims against the insured covered by the indemnity and may, on behalf of himself and all persons having such judgments or claims, maintain an action against the insurer to have the insurance money so applied." Before the enactment of this section there was no way in which a party who sustained injury by an owner of an automobile could recover directly from the owner's insurer. . . .

The fact is that the plaintiff brought an action under that section. The Act gives the plaintiff the right "to have the insurance money payable under the policy applied in or towards satisfaction of his judgment and of any other judgments or claims against the insured covered by the indemnity and may on behalf of himself and all persons having such judgments or claims, maintain an action against the insurer to have the insurance money so applied": *Northern Ass'ce Co. v. Brown*, 3 D.L.R. (2d) 705 at pp. 706-7, [1956] S.C.R. 658 at pp. 660-1, I.L.R. 1064.

The question is whether the money so recovered for the benefit of all judgment creditors is to be divided *pro rata* as would be the case if the creditors were of the same degree, or is it to be paid to the Crown in priority, leaving in this case nothing for the plaintiff who brought the action and sued for the benefit of himself and others.

It is argued that the claim of the Crown in this case is only by virtue of the Nova Scotia statute and that the Crown suing under that statute must take its place as one of the "others" on behalf of whom the plaintiff has brought his action.

In other words the Crown must take the burden of the statute with the benefit.

For this proposition, the appellant cites the case of *Food Controller et al. v. Cork*, [1923] A.C. 647. This is a decision of the House of Lords. It was a case of the winding-up of a company and was decided by a consideration of sections of the *Companies Act* (Eng.) and applicable sections of the *Bankruptcy Act*, which gave certain priorities and were held to have the effect of destroying any other priority than such as the statute provided.

There are, however, pronouncements that the Crown has no right to priority when the so-called Crown debt arises out of some commercial project in which the Crown has engaged. This was a case of the purchase and sale of frozen rabbits and the Crown through its agent acted in the same way as an ordinary trader. . . .

I find myself unable to hold, however, that the Crown in the present case is a person engaged in a commercial undertaking. The services which the Crown lost and of which the loss was sued for, were lost to the Armed Forces of the Crown, a vital part of the Government. . . .

I think all creditors who come in take such priority as the law gives them. If the Crown in the right of this Province were claiming a priority, it might be a question whether or not it could succeed in such a claim; there are no clear words that change the rule that the Crown comes first. But if there is any such implication from some of the phrases, it can not be effectual against the Crown's priority in the right of the Dominion: *Gauthier v. The King* (1918), 40 D.L.R. 353, 56 S.C.R. 176; *Re Dominion Income Tax, The King v. Lithwick & Cole, Assignee of Defendant's Insolvent Estate* (1921), 57 D.L.R. 1, 20 Ex. C.R. 293.

I can see no reason to hold that because the Crown has laid claim in Provincial Courts and that the money has been paid because of Provincial legislation that it follows that the Crown has abandoned its priority. . . .

MacDONALD J.: . . . The sole issue is: (1) whether the sum of $5,000 paid into Court by the insurer should be paid out *pro rata* to the two judgment creditors—as the plaintiff claims; or (2) whether it should be paid out in its entirety to the Attorney-General by virtue of the prerogative of the Crown Dominion—as the Attorney-General claims, and as the learned Chief Justice has ordered.

It may be of use to note that prior to the institution of the present action the Attorney-General had demanded payment of the whole sum from the insurer. He took no proceedings in furtherance of this demand until having been brought into these proceedings at the instance of the plaintiff and on the trial of the issue in question he contended that the whole sum was payable to the Crown Dominion as a matter of prerogative right. I agree that there has been no abandonment or waiver of whatever prerogative right the Crown may have. (*N.S.W. Taxation Com'rs. v. Palmer* [1907] A.C. at p. 185; *The Queen v. Bank of Nova Scotia* (1885), 11 S.C.R. 1).

In view of s. 13 of the *Interpretation Act*, R.S.N.S. 1954, c. 136 and the entire absence of any reference to the Crown in s. 26 of the *Insurance Act*, it is clear that the latter provision cannot operate to bind the Crown Dominion or to curtail any of its prerogative rights.

There is, of course, difficulty in applying those parts of the common law which create or recognize prerogative powers, rights, privileges or immunities to new situations created by new types of statutory enactment. Hence I think it is desirable to point out that the prerogative claimed by the Crown Dominion is that described in the Attorney-General's factum herein as "the prerogative which provides that, whenever the right of the Crown and the right of the subject with respect to the payment of debts or claims of equal degree come into competition, the right of the Crown prevails . . . to the exclusion or postponement of other claimants of equal degree." This is well established and has been held to apply to the Crown in the right of Canada or of a Province where not excluded by competent legislation. . . .

Put in the usual form as the right of the Crown as creditor to priority over other creditors, difficulty is encountered at once in this case; for, as contended by the plaintiff, neither the Crown nor the plaintiff can be regarded as creditors of the insurer—or the latter as their debtor—in the normal sense. By virtue of the statute, each has a new but qualified right (as judgment creditor of an insured person) to maintain an action against the insurer to have the insurance money payable under the policy applied in or towards satisfaction of his judgment and of any other judgments against the insured. (It is only by such a "class action" that the insurance money can be reached (*Knudsen v. Gore District Mutual Fire Ins. Co.*, [1958] I.L.R. 1431). Perhaps a permissible analysis is that the insurer is a *trustee* of the insurance fund for the benefit of proper claimants under the statute.

These difficulties largely disappear if regard is had to the fact that the prerogative to priority of payment of debts is but an instance of a wider prerogative right.

This appears clearly by reference to the oft cited judgment of Macdonald C.B. in *R. v. Wells,* 16 East 278 at p. 282: (1) "This appears to me to go a great way to shew what prerogatives of the Crown it was to which the statute (33 Henry 8) applies: that it was to the prerogative of having first execution . . . and not to any prerogative which goes to determine the preference between two executions, one of the Crown and the other of the subject subsisting at the same time. (2) This latter prerogative will be found to depend upon another principle, perfectly distinct from this, and far more general; determining a preference in favour of the Crown in all cases, and touching all rights of what kind soever, where the Crown's and the subject's right concur, and so come into competition. (3) I take it to be an incontrovertible rule of law, that where the King's and the subject's title concur, the King's shall be preferred." (Numerals inserted by me.)

In *N.S.W. Taxation Com'rs. v. Palmer, supra,* the Privy Council (*per* Lord Macnaghten) in upholding the prerogative right of the Crown to priority of payment as against other creditors in bankruptcy, referred (p. 182) to the rule of law in passage 3 as "one of universal application". Later (p. 185) he said: "The prerogative, the benefit of which the Crown is now claiming [*i.e., priority of payments between creditors*], depends, as explained by Macdonald C.B. in *The King v. Wells,* upon a principle 'perfectly distinct . . . and far more general'," and quoted the remainder of passage (2) *supra.*

Accordingly it may be taken that the prerogative right of priority of payment is but an illustration of a larger principle that wherever a right of the Crown and that of a subject come into competition, the former is preferred (see 7 Hals., 3rd ed., para. 701, pp. 326-7; Broom's Legal Maxims, 9th ed., p. 48; Bell's Crown Proceedings, p. 42).

There is another instance of this generic rule, namely, where the right of the Crown and a subject under proceedings by way of distress or execution come into competition.

In *Atty.-Gen. v. Leonard,* 38 Ch. D. 622, a distress levied by the Crown came into competition with one previously levied by a subject but the latter of which had not been executed by sale. The Crown sought an injunction to prevent such a sale. Chitty J. dealt with the case solely in terms of the prerogative. He quoted extensively from the judgment of Macdonald C.B. in *R. v. Wells, supra.* He concluded that the rule that where two executions (the King's and that of a subject) subsist at the same time, the former is preferred, is but an illustration of the general nature of the Crown's prerogative "that where the King's and the subject's title concur, the King's shall be preferred". He held that proceeding by way of extent or the Statute of 33 Hen. 8, c. 39 "has nothing to do with the Crown's title under an execution or under a distress coming in competition with the title of the subject under an execution or a distress. Directly those two titles concur, then the Crown's priority of title attaches, and the . . . Crown's priority is not displaced until . . . the property in goods is changed". [p. 626] This was followed in *Re Corley* (1889),

23 L.R. Ir. 249. Robertson on Civil Proceedings, 1908, sums up these cases at p. 163: "The prerogative right of the Crown to priority is not limited to proceedings by writ of extent, but equally attaches to proceedings by distress or to the recovery of the amount found due to the Crown on a *scire facias* on a bond . . . These principles must be read into the decisions which follow."

The nature of the right given to a third party under s. 26 of the *Automobile Insurance Act* is not too clear. The Supreme Court of Canada has held that the action contemplated is not an action on the policy of insurance but is one arising on the statute and is therefore not caught by a statutory condition prescribing, a one-year limitation period "against an insurer under a contract" (*Northern Ass'c. Co. v. Brown*, 3 D.L.R. (2d) 705, [1956] S.C.R. 658, I.L.R. 1064). In that case after an analysis of s. 214 of the Ontario *Insurance Act* (identical with s. 26 quoted above) Rand J. said (pp. 707-8 D.L.R., p. 661 S.C.R.): "The statute not only gives a right to sue but it creates its substantive basis, a right against the contractual liability as *an asset available, in effect, for execution purposes*. . . . The right given is a charge upon the insurance money. But the statutory provisions contemplate insurance with a limit of liability. . . . The total claims in one accident . . . may easily exceed the total amount of the insurance or the limits furnished . . . and this fact excludes, except conceivably where there is only one claimant, an ordinary money judgment."

Here I think the Crown and the plaintiff may be regarded as competing judgment creditors of a common debtor (Patterson) and the fund of $5,000 as constituting assets of that debtor segregated from his other assets and designated by law as the assets to satisfy the claims to indemnity.

The effect of a class action by a judgment creditor is to make the insurance money available for the satisfaction, or *pro tanto* satisfaction, of all persons having judgments or claims against the statutory fund as a species of execution.

With the bringing of this action both the plaintiff and the Crown became possessed of a statutory right to share in this fund. The title of each is concurrent with that of the other. It is a clear case of subsisting and competing claims by the Crown and a subject.

In this situation I think the Crown is entitled to assert its prerogative right (1) as a creditor to priority of payment as against other creditors on the principles first mentioned; or (2) as founding a preferential claim as against other execution creditors on the larger principle enunciated in the third passage quoted from *R. v. Wells*, *supra*, and the special application of it to competing executions made in *Atty.-Gen. v. Leonard, supra*. . . .

Appeal dismissed.

[Currie and Patterson JJ. concurred with Doull J. Parker J. concurred with MacDonald J. See also *Gandy & Allison Ltd. v. Erectors & Constructors Ltd.* (1963), 43 D.L.R. (2d) 461. Crown priority was denied in *The Queen v.*

Workmen's Compensation Board (1962), 36 D.L.R. (2d) 166 because the claim arose out of an ordinary business transaction.]

Note on the Federal Government in Business: The Federal Expropriation Power

The federal "property" power enables the Government of Canada to go into business free of provincial regulatory legislation but, without any power to compel dealing or to exclude competitors, unless it is engaged in an activity falling otherwise with s. 91. Thus, it is open to the Canadian government to sell insurance, which it in fact does under its offer of annuities as a facet of the operations of the Department of Labour: see *Government Annuities Act*, R.S.C. 1970, c. G-6; cf. also *Crop Insurance Act*, R.S.C. 1970, c. C-36. Similarly, the Government of Canada is engaged through the Canadian Wheat Board in the purchase and sale of wheat: see *Canadian Wheat Board Act*, R.S.C. 1970, c. C-12.

The validity of the Government Annuities Act was sustained in *Porter v. The Queen*, [1965] 1 Ex. C.R. 200 in a judgment which struggled to distinguish it from the type of legislation governing the annuities trade or the insurance business, so often held to be within exclusive provincial competence as such. The judgment rightly posed the problem (and rightly said it was one of difficulty and importance on which there was no previous authority) "whether Parliament can authorize the federal executive to carry on such a business, or conversely, whether a provincial legislature can authorize the provincial executive to carry on a business that is subject to regulation exclusively by Parliament". It was enough for the case at hand to support the federal legislation as authorizing the Crown in right of Canada or the federal Government to enter into contracts with volunteering persons; and surely this is the basis for any federal government venture into activities which from a regulatory standpoint are ordinarily within provincial competence.

It is engaged also in the production and sale of synthetic rubber and allied products through a Crown corporation, Polymer Corporation Ltd., referred to as a "proprietary corporation" for purposes of Part VIII of the *Financial Administration Act*, R.S.C. 1970, c. F-10, a statute which lists, and regulates the operations of, the various federal Crown corporations. Indeed, there is no obstacle (premising proper acquisition of authority as an integral parliamentary question) to the government acquiring property of any kind by voluntary purchase or to its entry into business. Where the property or business operations are in the hands of the Crown proper or of a Crown agency (as contrasted with an independent government-sponsored corporation) there is a resulting tax immunity under s. 125 of the *B.N.A. Act* as well as under accepted constitutional principles implicit in the Act. For a discussion of this matter and a list of the business operations of the federal government under enumerated authorizing legislation, see *Hodgetts*, The Public Corporation in Canada, at pp. 201 ff; *Friedmann and Garner*, Government Enterprise (1970); *Ashley and Smalls*, Canadian Crown Corporations (1965). In the United States there have been similar adventures of the federal government in business in pursuance of the federal property power there: see U.S. Constitution, art. 4, s. 3; *Ashwander v. Tennessee Valley Authority* (1936), 297 U.S. 288, 56 S. Ct. 466; *Note*, Power of the Federal Government to Compete with Private Enterprise, (1935) 83 U. of Pa. L. Rev. 662; *Lilienthal and Marquis*, The Conduct of Business Enterprises by the Federal Government, (1941) 54 Harv. L. Rev. 545. The position in Australia is not as clear, and there is doubt as to how far the Commonwealth may support the carrying on of business activity under its limited property power: see *Commonwealth v. Australian Shipping Board* (1926), 39 C.L.R. 1; *A.-G. Victoria v. Commonwealth* (1935), 52 C.L.R. 533; and see *Wynes*, Legislative, Executive and Judicial Powers in Australia (1956 2nd ed.), pp. 162, 264-5.

Although there is a case to be made for the proposition that when the Dominion acts as a private citizen, *e.g.* engages in business, it may be required to act according to applicable provincial legislation (subject, of course, to any express constitutional immunity), common law principles respecting Crown immunity from legislation have been raised to constitutional stature in the Canadian federal scheme to deny provincial legislative authority to bind the federal Crown: see *Gauthier v. The King* (1918), 56 S.C.R. 176, 40 D.L.R. 353, and material at p. 527, *supra*. Moreover, in respect of certain kinds of businesses at least, the federal Crown is disposing of Crown property, and this is clearly caught by s. 91(1A) of the *B.N.A. Act*. It follows, hence, that the fact that a federal Crown business operation is carried on in the teeth of a provincial regulatory system or in derogation of a provincial franchise scheme would not affect its validity. Different questions arise, however, where the federal Crown purports compulsorily to acquire a business or property rather than to obtain it by ordinary purchase in the market. What, in other words, is the nature and scope of the federal expropriation power? There is no explicit reference to any power of "eminent domain" in the *B.N.A. Act* (other than the special defence provision in s. 117) as there is in the Constitution of the United States which in the Fifth Amendment forbids the taking of private property for public use without just compensation (and in the Fourteenth Amendment forbids any State to deprive any person of property without due process of law). As Duff J. pointed out in *Reference re Waters and Water-Powers*, [1929] S.C.R. 200, [1929] 2 D.L.R. 481, in speaking of alleged federal power to take compulsorily lands committed to the control of the provincial legislatures, "that is an authority which the Dominion did not expressly receive under any of the relevant clauses of s. 91".

Provincial power to take land in the province (other than federal Crown land) is clear under s. 92(13) of the *B.N.A. Act*, and whether or not compensation is made is a matter of policy rather than constitutional obligation: see *Florence Mining Co. Ltd. v. Cobalt Lake*

Mining Co. Ltd. (1908), 18 O.L.R. 275 (aff'd on appeal, and aff'd further (1910), 43 O.L.R. 474 (P.C.)), where Riddell J. said in reference to a provincial legislature: "The prohibition 'Thou shalt not steal' has no legal force upon the sovereign body. And there would be no necessity for compensation to be given". There is equally, no doubt, of the power of Parliament to expropriate in connection with objects or activities which fall within s. 91: see *Reference re Waters and Water-Powers, supra;* and see p. 499, *supra.* Moreover, it seems probable that Parliament may assert a power of expropriation consequent upon a declaration of a work to be for the general advantage of Canada under s. 92(10)(c): see *Re Ontario Power Co. of Niagara Falls and Hewson* (1903), 6 O.L.R. 11, aff'd 8 O.L.R. 88, aff'd 36 S.C.R. 596. The difficult question is whether federal power of compulsory taking extends beyond these limits and embraces what in the United States would be any "public use", a term whose content is, in any ultimate sense, subject to judicial review but in respect of which the courts are disposed to defer to the legislative judgment: see *United States ex rel. Tennessee Valley Authority v. Welch* (1946), 327 U.S. 546, 66 S. Ct. 715; *Note,* (1946), 20 So. Calif. L. Rev. 99. It should be noted that in Australia the Commonwealth Parliament has an express power of expropriation under s. 51(xxxi) of the Constitution but it is limited to acquisition "on just terms . . . for any purpose in respect of which the Parliament has power to make laws": see *Wynes,* Legislative, Executive and Judicial Powers in Australia (1956 2nd ed.), pp. 461 ff. While the Parliament of Canada, unlike the Congress of the United States and the Commonwealth Parliament, is not a body with enumerated powers only, it may be doubted that it has a power of expropriation beyond purposes otherwise falling within its legislative authority.

In *Shepherd v. Regina,* [1964] Ex. C.R. 274, Dumoulin J. rejected an attack on the validity of the federal Expropriation Act relative to the registration of a servitude on land adjoining an airport so as to prohibit the erection thereon of buildings above a certain height, and asserted that "the fundamental answer is that a Government shorn of such a power would lack one of the essential attributes of sovereignty, one pertaining to the peace, order and generally speaking, to the good government of the country (cf. B.N.A. Act, 1867, s. 91) and to its defence". Although the language is general, there is the fact that the case involved resort to expropriation in relation to a matter clearly within federal competence.

The Expropriation Act, R.S.C. 1970, c. E-19 is geared in its substance and machinery to the taking land for "public works" which is defined in s. 2 to mean and include "the dams, hydraulic works, hydraulic privileges, harbours, wharfs, piers, docks and works for improving the navigation of any water, the lighthouses and beacons, the slides, dams, piers, booms and other works for facilitating the transmission of timber, the roads and bridges, the public buildings, the telegraph lines, Government railways, canals, locks, dry-docks, fortifications and other works of defence and all other property, that now belong to Canada, and also the works and properties acquired, constructed, extended, enlarged, repaired or improved at the expense of Canada, or for the acquisition, construction, repairing, extending, enlarging or improving of which any public moneys are voted and appropriated by Parliament, and every work required for any such purpose, but not any work for which the money is appropriated as a subsidy only". The Act embraces the taking of provincial Crown land, as is made clear by s. 15. In so far as this Act authorizes expropriation in connection with the federal navigation power no doubt exists of its validity. This is equally true of expropriation in relation to defence. The statute, however, goes further and appends a power of expropriation as auxiliary to any federal public property or property on which federal money is expended. Justification for this may conceivably be found in s. 91(1A) of the *B.N.A. Act.* If so, this means that the Dominion, on acquiring property by voluntary purchase may subsequently extend it by compulsory acquisition. This is not a very tenable proposition.

What, however, is to be said of the federal power of expropriation conferred by s. 13 of the *National Capital Act,* R.S.C. 1970, c. N-3, which empowers the National Capital Commission (established under the Act) to take (with government approval) land compulsorily for the development of the "National Capital Region" (an area defined in the Act)? If it is necessary to find explicit authority in the *B.N.A. Act* for such expropriation it can only be found (having regard to the provisions of s. 16 of the *B.N.A. Act* which establishes Ottawa as the Canadian capital) in federal power to legislate for the peace, order and good government of Canada. See generally, *Lajoie,* Expropriation et Federalisme au Canada (1972).

[In *The King v. O'Halloran,* [1934] Ex. C.R. 67, where land was taken for penitentiary purposes (which fall within s. 91(28)) a bare suggestion that the *Expropriation Act* is *ultra vires* was rejected, and the Court declared (at p. 84) that "the true construction of [s. 2(g)] is . . . that 'public work' includes undertakings, public buildings or properties which the Government of Canada is authorized to construct, acquire, extend or maintain for any authorized public purpose". Assuming the Court is right as a matter of statutory construction, is it right from the standpoint of constitutional power?

In *The King v. Toronto,* [1946] Ex. C.R. 424, the Court concluded that land held by the federal Crown under a lease could be expropriated under power conferred by the *Expropriation Act.* Is this a tenable constitutional conclusion irrespective of the use made of the land by the Crown or the purpose to which it was devoted? In the particular case the land had on it a post office building owned by the federal Crown.

May Parliament validly prescribe the legal effect of provisions of a contract to which the federal Crown is a party? Must the contract be with respect to a matter within federal legislative competence? See *Dimensional Investments Ltd. v. The Queen,* [1966] Ex. C.R. 761.]

CHAPTER VIII

INCORPORATION AND REGULATION OF COMPANIES

1. The "Dominion" Company in the Provinces

GREAT WEST SADDLERY CO. v. THE KING

In the Privy Council. [1921] 2 A.C. 91, 58 D.L.R. 1,
[1921] 1 W.W.R. 1034.

Consolidated appeals by special leave from two judgments of the Supreme Court of Canada, 59 S.C.R. 19 and 35, and a judgment of the Ontario Appellate Division, 41 O.L.R. 475, on the validity of Saskatchewan, Manitoba and Ontario legislation in so far as it purported to apply to Dominion companies.

VISCOUNT HALDANE: In this case their Lordships are called on to interpret and apply the implications of a judgment, delivered by the Judicial Committee on November 2, 1914, in *John Deere Plow Co. v. Wharton,* [1915] A.C. 330. It was there laid down that the *British North America Act of 1867* had so enabled the Parliament of the Dominion to prescribe the extent of the powers of companies incorporated under Dominion law with objects which extended to the Dominion generally, that the status and powers so far as there in question of one of the three appellant companies could not as matter of principle be validly interfered with by the Provincial Legislature of British Columbia. It was held that laws which had been passed by the Legislature of that Province, and which sought to compel a Dominion company to obtain a certain kind of Provincial licence or to be registered in the way brought before the Judicial Committee, as a condition of exercising its powers in the Province or of suing in the Courts, were *ultra vires.* The reason given was that their Lordships interpreted what had been done by the Province in that case as interfering in a manner not consistent with the principles laid down with the status and corporate capacity of a company with Dominion objects to which the Parliament of Canada had given powers to carry on its business in every part of the Dominion.

In the consolidated appeals now before their Lordships analogous questions are raised by legislation in varying forms enacted in three other Provinces, Saskatchewan, Manitoba, and Ontario.

Since the decision in 1914 the Province of Saskatchewan has passed an Act, in 1915, which supersedes its earlier Companies Acts, and apparently seeks to avoid the features in these which might conflict with the decision of this Committee in *John Deere Plow Co. v. Wharton* as to the British Columbia legislation. The question raised as regards Manitoba arises out of older legislation of 1913 (subsequently amended and re-enacted in 1916), and as regards Ontario under an older Ontario Companies Act and the Extra-Provincial Corporations Act of 1914. No question is raised from

British Columbia, or from any Provinces other than Saskatchewan, Manitoba and Ontario, on this occasion.

The proceedings out of which the present appeals arise concern several Dominion companies, and are, as to Saskatchewan, two cases before a magistrate for infraction of the provisions of the Provincial Companies Act, and an action by a shareholder in one of the Dominion companies concerned, to restrain it from attempting to carry on its business without complying with the requirements of the Companies Act of the Province. The main issue in all these proceedings is substantially the same. In Manitoba an analogous question was raised in a shareholders' action, and also in an action by the Attorney-General of the Province. The main issue in Ontario was similar to that in Saskatchewan, but there was also raised a question as to whether a Dominion company could hold land in the Province without being authorized to do so by its Government, in accordance with Ontario statute law. In the proceedings referred to judgments were delivered in the Courts of first instance and by the appellate Courts in Saskatchewan and Manitoba and by the Courts of first instance and the appellate Court in Ontario. In the cases in the two former Provinces there was an appeal to the Supreme Court of Canada, but in the Ontario litigation the appeal has been brought directly to the King in Council from the judgment of the appellate Court of the Province. On August 18, 1919, special leave to appeal to the Privy Council was granted, and it was ordered that the appeals, six in number, from judgments which had been adverse to the Dominion companies concerned, should be consolidated and heard together. The Attorneys-General for Canada and for the Provinces have intervened throughout.

It will be convenient, having regard to the course taken in the argument, to consider in the first place the appeal from the Court of Appeal in Ontario.

In order to ascertain the real points now in controversy, it is important to refer in some detail to what was actually decided in 1914 in *John Deere Plow Co. v. Wharton*. The British Columbia Companies Act had provided that, in the case of an incorporated company which was not one incorporated under the laws of the Province, and was called in the Act an extra-provincial company, certain conditions must be complied with. If such a company had gain for its object it must be licensed or registered under the law of the Province, and no agent was to carry on its business until this had been done. If this condition were complied with, such an extra-provincial company might sue in the Courts of the Province and hold land there. Such a company might also, if it were only duly incorporated under the laws of, among other authorities, the Dominion, and if authorized by its charter to carry out purposes to which the legislative authority of the Province extended, obtain from the Registrar, under the general Companies Act of the Province, a licence to carry on business within the Province on complying with the provisions of the Act and paying a proper licence fee. It was then to have the same powers and privileges in the Province as though incorporated under the Provincial Act. If such a company carried on business without a licence it was made liable to penalties, and its agents were similarly made liable. So long as unlicensed, the company could not sue in the Courts of the Province in respect of contracts in connection with its business made within the Province. The Registrar might refuse a licence where the name of the company was identical with or resembled that by which a company, society or firm in existence was carrying on business or had been incorporated, licensed or registered, or where the Registrar was of opinion that the name was calculated to deceive, or disapproved of it for any other reason.

Their Lordships pointed out that, under the Dominion Companies Act, which they held to have been validly passed, the charter of the John Deere Plow Company incorporated it with the powers to which the legislative authority of the Parliament of Canada extended. The Dominion Interpretation Act provided that the meaning of such an incorporation included this, that the corporate body created should have power to sue, to contract in its corporate name, and to acquire and hold personal property for its purposes. There was in the Dominion Companies Act a provision that such a company should not be incorporated with a name likely to be confounded with the name of any other known company, incorporated or unincorporated, and it gave the Secretary of State the discretion in this connection. On incorporation the company was to be vested with all the powers, privileges, and immunities, requisite or incidental to the carrying on of its undertaking. It was to have an office in the city or town in which its chief place of business in Canada was situated, which should be its legal domicile in Canada, and could establish other offices and agencies elsewhere. No person acting as its agent was to be subjected, if acting within his authority, to individual penalty.

Their Lordships made reference to the circumstance that the concluding words of s. 91 of the British North America Act, "Any matter coming within any of the classes of subjects enumerated in this section shall not be deemed to come within the class of matters of a local or private nature comprised in the enumeration of the classes of subjects by this Act assigned exclusively to the Legislatures of the Provinces," render it necessary to do more than ascertain whether the subject-matter in question apparently falls within any of the heads of s. 92; for if it also falls within any of the enumerated heads of s. 91, then it cannot be treated as covered by any of those in s. 92. As is now well settled the words quoted apply, not only to the merely local or private matters in the Province referred to in head 16 of s. 92, but to the whole of the sixteen heads in that section: *A.-G. for Ontario v. A.-G. for Canada,* [1896] A.C. 348. The effect, as was pointed out in the decision just cited, is to effect a derogation from what might otherwise have been literally the authority of the Provincial Legislatures, to the extent of enabling the Parliament of Canada to deal with matters local and private where, though only where, such legislation is necessarily incidental to the exercise of the enumerated powers conferred on it by s. 91.

If therefore in legislating for the incorporation of companies under Dominion law and in validly endowing them with powers, the Dominion Parliament has by necessary implication given these companies a status which enables them to exercise these powers in the Provinces, they cannot be interfered with by any Provincial law in such a fashion as to derogate from their status and their consequent capacities, or, as the result of this restriction, to prevent them from exercising the powers conferred on them by Dominion law. Their Lordships, however, observed that when a company has been incorporated by the Dominion Government with powers to trade in any Province it may not the less, consistently with the general scheme, be subject to Provincial laws of general application, such as laws imposing taxes, or relating to mortmain, or even requiring licences for certain purposes, or as to the forms of contracts; but they were careful not to say that the sanctions by which such Provincial laws might be enforced could validly be so directed by the Provincial Legislatures as indirectly to sterilize or even to effect, if the local laws were not obeyed, the destruction of the capacities and powers which the Dominion had validly conferred. To have said so would have been to misread that scheme of the *British North America Act,* which is one that establishes interlacing and in-dependent legislative authorities. Within the spheres allotted to them by the Act the Dominion and the Provinces are rendered on general principle co-ordinate Governments. As a consequence, where one has legislative power the other has not, speaking broadly, the capacity to pass laws which will interfere with its exercise. What cannot be done directly cannot be done indirectly. This is a principle which has to be kept closely in view in testing the validity of the Provincial legislation under consideration as affecting Dominion companies. . . .

The general Companies Act of Ontario was passed before the decision of the *John Deere Plow* case, and has no special bearing on the question in this appeal. The important statute is the *Extra-Provincial Corporations Act,* which was also passed before that decision. The purpose of the latter statute is to provide that certain classes of extra-Provincial corporations (which mean corporations created otherwise than by or under the authority of an Act of the Ontario Legislature), including those created under any Act of the Dominion and authorized to carry on business in Ontario, must take out a licence (s. 4) under the Ontario statute. On complying with its provisions a corporation coming within these classes is entitled to receive a licence (s. 5) to carry on its business and exercise its powers within Ontario. In the absence of such a licence it is forbidden to do so (s. 7), and its agents are subjected to a like prohibition. A penalty of $20 a day is imposed for any contravention of this provision. An extra-Provincial corporation coming within the classes referred to may apply to the Lieutenant-Governor in Council for a licence to carry on its business and exercise its powers in Ontario, and no limitations or conditions are to be included in any such licence which would interfere with the rights of such a corpora-

tion—for example, a Dominion company—to carry on in Ontario all
such part of its powers as by its Act or charter of incorporation it
may be authorized to carry on and exercise there (s. 9, sub-ss. 1 and
2). A corporation receiving a licence may, subject to the limitations
and conditions of the licence, and the provisions of its own constitution, hold and dispose of real estate in Ontario, just as an Ontario
company might (s. 12). A corporation receiving a licence may be
called on to make returns comprising such information as is required
from an Ontario company (s. 14). The Lieutenant-Governor in
Council may make regulations for, among other things, the appointment and continuance by the extra-Provincial company of a representative in Ontario on whom service of process and notices may
be made (s. 10, sub-s. 1(b)). If such a company, having received a
licence, makes default in complying with the limitations and conditions of the licence or of the provision as to returns, or the regulations
respecting the appointment of a representative, its licence may be
revoked (s. 15). If such a corporation carries on in Ontario without
a licence any part of its business, it is to incur a penalty of $50 a day,
and is rendered incapable of suing in the Ontario Courts in respect
of any contract made in whole or in part within Ontario in relation
to business for which it ought to have been licensed (s. 16). The
Lieutenant-Governor in Council may prescribe fees on the transmission of the statement or return required under s. 14. Such fees are
to vary with the capital stock of the company (s. 20).

It is obvious that the Act thus summarised assumes that the
Legislature of the Province can impose on a Dominion company
conditions which, if not complied with, will restrict the exercise of
its powers within the Province. These conditions do not appear to
their Lordships to be merely a means for the attainment of some
exclusively Provincial object, such as direct taxation for Provincial
purposes. They apparently assume a general right to limit the
exercise of the powers of extra-Provincial companies if they seek
to exercise these powers within Ontario. A question of principle is
thus raised broadly. . . .

Their Lordships turn next to the case which has been brought
forward as regards the legislation on the subject in Manitoba. In
the Courts of that Province analogous questions were raised in a
shareholder's action. The Attorney-General of the Province intervened in the course of the subsequent appeal.

In Manitoba there was passed in 1913 a general *Companies Act,*
of which Part IV deals with extra-Provincial companies and includes
Dominion corporations. Under s. 108 every such corporation
is required to take out a licence under this part of the Act, and
by s. 109 (*inter alia*) such a corporation, on complying with the
provisions of that part and with the regulations made under the Act,
is entitled to receive a licence to carry on its business and exercise
its powers in Manitoba. By s. 111 (*inter alia*) such a corporation
may apply to the Lieutenant-Governor in Council "for a licence to
carry on its business or part thereof, and exercise its powers or
part thereof, in Manitoba, and upon the granting of such licence

such corporation may thereafter, while such licence is in force, carry on in Manitoba the whole or such parts of its business and exercise in Manitoba the whole or such parts of its powers as may be embraced in the licence; subject, however, to the provisions of this part and to such limitations and conditions as may be specified in the licence." On such an application the corporation is to file certain evidence and a power of attorney to someone in the Province appointing him to accept service. This is not to apply if the head office is within the Province (s. 114, sub-s. 3). By s. 118 no such corporation is to carry on within Manitoba any of its business, and no agent is to act for it, until a licence has been granted to it, and then only so long as this is in force. Sect. 120 requires annual returns of information to be made. By s. 121 the Lieutenant-Governor in Council may suspend or revoke the licence for default in observing the provisions of the Act. Sect. 122 provides, as in the case of the Ontario statute, for penalties for the carrying on of business in the absence of the licence, and incapacitates the corporation from suing without it in the Courts of the Province. Sect. 126 enables the Lieutenant-Governor to fix the fees to be paid. These are for the exchequer of the Province, and are to vary in part according to the nature and importance of the business to be carried on in the Province, and in part according to the amount of the entire capital stock of the corporation. In addition to these provisions, s. 112 enables a duly licensed corporation to hold real estate in the Province, but limited, in its licence, by s. 113 to such annual value as may have been deemed proper, as fully as if it had been a Manitoba company under the general Act. There is no Mortmain Act in the Province, but the registration of titles to land requires a licence and the registration of title to real estate in the case of extra-Provincial companies.

Thus there does not appear to be anything in the form or substance of the *Manitoba Act* which differentiates it materially from the corresponding Ontario Act. . . .

The four *Saskatchewan Companies Acts,* now operative, differ from those of Ontario and Manitoba in the circumstance that they were passed in 1915, 1916 and 1917, after the decision in *John Deere Plow Co. v. Wharton* by this Committee. It is the first of these four Acts that alone is important for the purposes of the present question. This is a general Companies Act, the provisions in which have nothing unusual in them, but which extends to (*inter alia*) Dominion companies having gain for their object, and carrying on business in the Province. The effect of s. 23 is that a Dominion company of this nature must be registered under the Act, and that if it does not register, the Dominion company and its representatives are liable to penalties for carrying on business in the Province. The effect of s. 24 is that registration cannot be refused to a Dominion company. By s. 25 the company may, on complying with the provisions of the Act, receive an annual licence, for which it is to pay fees to the Government of the Province, and may then carry on its business, subject to the provisions of the instrument creating it, as if it had been incorporated under the Act; but a company carrying on business without a licence is liable to penalties. By s. 27 the Lieutenant-Governor in Council may prescribe such regulations as he may deem expedient for the registration of all companies, and for fixing the fees payable. By s. 29 if the registrar thinks that a company registered has ceased to carry on business he may, after finding on inquiry that this is so, strike the company off the register, whereupon it is dissolved; but by an amending Act passed since the commencement of these proceedings the provision as to dissolution is to take effect only as to Saskatchewan companies. By s. 30 if the prescribed fee is not paid the company may be struck off the register.

Proceedings were taken in Saskatchewan before a Justice of the Peace against a Dominion company for not being licensed or registered, and an action was brought by a shareholder, as in the cases of the other Provinces already referred to. The substantial question was again the validity of the Provincial statute. . . .

. . . . Can the relevant provisions of all or any of the three sets of Provincial statutes be justified as directed exclusively to the attainment of an object of legislation assigned by s. 92 to the Legislatures, such as is the collection of direct taxes for Provincial purposes; or do these provisions interfere with such powers as are conferred on a Dominion company by the Parliament of Canada to carry on its business anywhere in the Dominion, and so affect its status? The question is one primarily of the interpretation of the *British North America Act* and in the second place of the meaning of the principle already laid down by this Committee in the *John Deere Plow* case. The constitution of Canada is so framed by the *British North America Act* that the difficulty was almost certain to arise. For the power of a Province to legislate for the incorporation of companies is limited to companies with Provincial objects, and there is no express power conferred to incorporate companies with powers to carry on business throughout the Dominion and in every Province. But such a power is covered by the general enabling words of s. 91, which, because of the gap, confer it exclusively on the Dominion. It must now be taken as established that s. 91 enables the Parliament of Canada to incorporate companies with such status and powers as to restrict the Provinces from interfering with the general right of such companies to carry on their business where they choose, and that the effect of the concluding words of s. 91 is to make the exercise of this capacity of the Dominion Parliament prevail in case of conflict over the exercise by the Provincial legislatures of their capacities under the enumerated heads of s. 92. It is clear that the mere power of direct taxation is saved to the Province, for that power is specifically given and is to be taken, so far as necessary, on a proper construction to be an exception from the general language of s. 91, as was explained by Sir Montague Smith in delivering the judgment of the Judicial Committee in *Citizens Insurance Co. v. Parsons,* 7 App. Cas. 96. Nevertheless, the methods by which the direct taxation is to be enforced may be restricted to the bringing of an action, with the usual consequences, which was all that was decided to be legal in *Bank of Toronto v. Lambe,* 12 **App. Cas.** 575. It does not follow that because the Government of the Province can tax it can put an end to the existence or even the powers of the company it taxes for non-compliance with the demands of the tax-gatherer. Their Lordships find themselves unable to agree with an observation made by Meredith C.J. towards the conclusion of his judgment [in 41 O.L.R. 475]. "It is," he says, "I think to be regretted that at the outset it was not determined that the authority of the Parliament of Canada to incorporate companies was limited to creating them and endowing them with capacity to exercise such powers as it might be deemed proper that they should possess, but leaving to each Province the power of determining how far, if at all, those powers should be exercised within its limits." Such a construction would have left an hiatus in the *British North America Act,* for there would have been in the Act so read no power to create a company with effective powers directed to other than merely Provincial objects. It was decided as long ago as 1883, in *Colonial Building Investment Association v. A.-G. for Quebec,* 9 App. Cas. 157, that there was no such hiatus. Nor does it appear, if reference may be made as matter of historical curiosity to the resolutions on which the British North America Act was founded, and which were passed at Quebec on October 10, 1864, for the guidance of the Imperial Parliament in enacting the Constitution of 1867, that these resolutions gave countenance to the idea that a different construction on the point in question was desired. The learned Chief Justice refers to them without quoting their language. But, in connection with the topic in controversy, all that was desired by the words of these resolutions to be assigned to the Provincial Legislatures was "the incorporation of Private or Local Companies, except such as relate to matters assigned to the General Parliament.". . . .

The principle of interpretation to be followed in applying the test laid down in the *John Deere Plow Co.* case, that Provincial legislation cannot validly destroy the status and powers conferred on a Dominion company by Act of the Parliament of Canada, does not appear to be obscure when read in this light. Turning to its application, the first thing to be observed is the nature of the question to be answered. Their Lordships will dispose in the first place of a subsidiary matter, which is whether a Dominion company can be precluded from acquiring and holding land in a province by a Provincial law of the nature of a general Mortmain Act. It is clear, both on principle and from previous decisions, that it is within the competence of a Provincial Legislature to enact such legislation, and the question is therefore answered in the affirmative. If there be a provision to this effect, occuring even in a statute which in other respects is *ultra vires,* and that provision be severable, it is valid. In the Ontario case there is therefore no doubt that the broad result of the contention of the Province under this head is well founded; for there the Legislature has passed a Mortmain Act of General application, and in regard to this Act a Dominion company is in no better position than any other corporation which desires to hold land.

In Manitoba there is no general Mortmain Act, but s. 112 of the *Manitoba Companies Act* enables a corporation receiving a licence under Part IV of the Act, relating to extra-Provincial companies, to acquire and hold land as freely as could any company under Part I of the Act. Even if the provision as to the licensing of extra-Provincial companies is held to be *ultra vires*, so as to prevent such a provision from being operative, as being inseverable, it is plain that the substance of a provision which is of the character of a mortmain law is within the power of the Province.

In Saskatchewan there is no general Mortmain Act, but the *Companies Act* of 1915, by s. 19, enables a company incorporated under the law of the Province to hold land. By s. 25 a company not so incorporated (and this includes a Dominion company) may, if it has been licensed, carry on its business as if it had been incorporated under the law of the Province. This enables it to hold land unless the provisions as to the grant to it of a licence are inoperative. Their Lordships do not think that s. 29 of the Companies Act of Canada, which purports to enable a Dominion company to acquire and hold real estate requisite for the carrying on of its undertaking, can prevail against any severable provision by a Provincial Legislature restricting the power of corporations generally to acquire or hold real estate in the Province.

Their Lordships now pass to the question of a more general order, which is the main one in these appeals. Had the Provinces of Ontario, Manitoba and Saskatchewan power to impose on Dominion companies the obligation to obtain a licence from the Provincial Government as a condition of the exercise in those Provinces res-pectively of the powers conferred on them by the Dominion?

If the condition of taking out a licence had been introduced, not so as to affect the status of the Dominion company, but simply for the purpose of obtaining payment of a direct tax for Provincial purposes, or of securing the observance of some restriction as to contracts to be observed by the public generally in the Province, or of causing the doing, by that public generally, of some act of a purely local character only under licence, their Lordships would, for reasons already given, have been prepared to regard the condition as one which it was within the power of the Province to impose. Even then it would have been requisite to see, as was pointed out by Lord Herschell, in delivering the judgment of the Judicial Committee in the *Brewers and Maltsters* case, that the Provincial Legislature was not, under the guise of imposing such direct taxation in the form of which he was speaking as being within their power, really doing something else, such as imposing indirect taxation. As to any inquiry in the future whether this or anything analogous has been in substance attempted, their Lordships hold themselves unfettered. If, for example, such a question were to arise hereafter, involving consideration of whether the real effect of the licence required by a Provincial law has been to abrogate capacity which it was within the power of the Parliament of Canada to bestow, or whether for a breach of conditions a Provincial Legislature could impose, not an ordinary penalty but one extending to the destruction of the status of the company and its capacity in the Province, nothing that has been here said is intended to prejudice the decision of such a question, should it occur. It is sufficient to observe once more that in such matters what cannot be done directly can no more be effected by indirect methods.

What remains is to apply the principle of the decision in the *John Deere Plow* case as so interpreted to the actual Provincial legislation challenged.

As to Ontario, the statute impugned is the Extra-Provincial Corporations Act in its application to Dominion companies. Their Lordships have come to the conclusion that the real effect of this Act, as expressed or implied by its provisions, is to preclude companies of this character from exercising the powers of carrying on business in Ontario, to the same extent as in other parts of Canada, unless they comply with a condition sought to be imposed, that of obtaining a licence to do so from the Government of the Province. By s. 7 such companies are expressly prohibited from doing so, and the provision in s. 9, sub-s. 2, that no limitations or conditions are to be included in such a licence as would limit a Dominion company, for example, from carrying on in the Province all such parts of its business, or from exercising there all such parts of its powers, as its Act or charter of incorporation authorizes, does not in their Lordships' opinion sufficiently mend matters. For the assertion remains of the right to impose the obtaining of a licence as a condition of doing anything at all in the Province. By s. 11 the grant of the licence is made dependent on compliance with such regulations as may happen to have been made by the Lieutenant-Governor in Council under ss. 2 and 10 of the Act. By s. 16, and also under s. 7 itself an extra-Provincial corporation required to take out a licence is to be fined for not doing so, and, under s. 16, is to be incapable of suing in the Courts of the Province. Their Lordships are of opinion that these provisions cannot be regarded as confined only to such limited purposes as would be legitimate, and that they are therefore *ultra vires*.

Taking next the *Companies Act of Manitoba*, Part IV of this Act deals with extra-Provincial corporations, including Dominion companies. The effect of the scheme of this part does not appear to their Lordships to differ in any feature that is material from that of the Ontario Act. *Inter alia*, a Dominion company must take out a licence, which it is entitled to receive if it complies with the provisions of the Act and with regulations to be made by the Lieutenant-Governor in Council. There may, under s. 111, be limitations and conditions specified in the licence, and if the company makes default in complying with these or certain other provisions, the licence may be revoked under s. 121. Unless the company obtains a licence it cannot, nor can any of its agents carry on business in Manitoba. Penalties are imposed for carrying on business without a licence, and so long as unlicensed the company cannot invoke the jurisdiction of the Courts of the Province. It does not alter the scope of these provisions that by s. 126 fees are payable for the licence, to be applied to the benefit of the revenue of the Province.

Their Lordships are unable to take the view that these sections regarded together are directed solely to the purposes specified in s. 92. They interpret them, like those of the Ontario statute, as designed to subject generally to conditions the activity within the Province of companies incorporated under the Act of the Parliament of Canada. The restrictions in this statute as to the holding of land cannot be severed from the general provisions as to licensing so as to make those restrictions enforceable as being in the nature of Mortmain legislation.

The statute remaining to be considered is that passed by the Legislature of Saskatchewan in 1915, a general Companies Act which, however, contains provisions applicable to Dominion companies. By s. 23, if such companies carry on business in Saskatchewan, they must be registered under this Act, and if they carry on business without registering, the companies, and also the agents acting for them, are made liable on summary conviction to penalties. By s. 24 such companies are entitled to be registered on complying with the provisions of the Act and on paying the prescribed fees. There are also payable annual fees. By s. 25 such companies may upon certain conditions receive a licence to carry on business in Saskatchewan, and if they carry on business without a licence are guilty of an offence and liable to penalties. By s. 29, where the Registrar satisfies himself in the prescribed manner that a company registered under the Act has ceased to carry on business, he may strike the company off the register, and it is then to be dissolved. By s. 30, if the registration fees prescribed by the regulations made by the Lieutenant-Governor in Council be not paid, the Registrar is to strike the company off the register.

Here again their Lordships think that the Provincial Legislature has failed to confine its legislation to the objects prescribed in s. 92, and has trenched on what is exclusively given by the *British North America Act* to the Parliament of Canada. If the Act had merely required a Dominion company, within a reasonable time after commencing to carry on business in Saskatchewan, to register its name and other particulars in the Provincial register and to pay fees not exceeding those payable by Provincial companies, and had imposed upon it a daily penalty for not complying with this obligation, it could (their Lordships think) be supported as legitimate machinery for obtaining information and levying a tax. But the effect of imposing upon such a company a penalty for carrying on business while unregistered is to make it impossible for the company to enter into or to enforce its ordinary business engagements and contracts until registration is effected, and so to destroy for the time being the status and powers conferred upon it by the Dominion. Further, if it is the intention and effect of the Act that a Dominion company when registered in the Province shall be subject (by virtue of the definition section or otherwise) to the general provisions of the *Saskatchewan Companies Act* or shall become liable to dissolution under s. 29, the Act would be open to question on that ground; but it is right to say that such a construction was disclaimed by counsel for the Attorney-General of Saskatchewan and (as regards the liability to dissolution) has been excluded by an amending Act passed while these proceedings were pending. Sect. 25 of the *Saskatchewan Act*, which requires a Dominion company to obtain a licence, stands on the same footing as the enactments in Ontario and Manitoba which have been held void as *ultra vires*; and in this case also the restrictions on the holding of land are not severable from the licensing provisions and are invalid on that ground.

The result is that their Lordships take the view which commended itself to a minority of the judges in the Courts below, and find themselves unable to agree on the main question argued, either with the preponderating opinion expressed in the Supreme Court of Canada on the Saskatchewan and Manitoba legislation, or with that of the majority of the Appellate Division in Ontario on the validity of the statute of that Province, but that on the subsidiary question as to the Mortmain Act of Ontario they agree with the Ontario Courts.

Appeals allowed.

[The cases on legislative authority in relation to companies are discussed in *Wegenast*, Canadian Companies, chap. 3. For a general survey, see *Ziegel*, Constitutional Aspects of Canadian Companies, chap. 5 of *Ziegel* (ed.), Studies in Canadian Company Law (1968).

A foreign incorporated company does not enjoy the same constitutional protection against certain kinds of provincial legislation as does a federally incorporated company: see *Van Buren Bridge Co. v. Madawaska and A.-G. N.B.* (1958), 15 D.L.R. (2d) 763, 41 M.P.R. 360.

Is provincial mortmain legislation applicable to a Dominion company incorporated for the purpose only of dealing in and holding land? See *Citizens Insurance Co. v. Parsons* (1881), 7 App. Cas. 96. Must a bank have a provincial licence in mortmain?

Mortmain legislation should be examined to determine whether a company's title or power to convey a good title is affected by failure to take out a licence in mortmain. See *Joslin*, Mortmain Legislation in Canada and the United States, (1951) 29 Can. Bar Rev. 621; *Re Garner and Gavan*, [1952] O.R. 385, [1952] 2 D.L.R. 804. Cf. Mortmain and Charitable Uses Act, R.S.O. 1970, c. 280, and Escheats Act, R.S.O. 1970, c. 149.

Assuming the immunity of "Dominion" companies from provincial general licensing legislation, it does not cover particular licences required for engaging in a controlled activity in the Province. Thus, a federally incorporated company authorized to engage in or practise engineering could not by reason only of such incorporation claim to take engineering work without complying with provincial licensing legislation; and this would be equally true as to other controlled professions or activities, even if there were a licensing requirement for any type of business: see *Motor Car Supply Co. v. A. G. Alta.*, [1939] 3 D.L.R. 660, [1939] 3 W.W.R. 65. If this is so, does it mean that a province may competently exclude a corporation, whether federally incorporated or not, from engaging in particular kinds of business for which a licence is required? See *Giffels & Vallet of Canada Ltd. v. The King*, [1952] 2 D.L.R. 720, [1952] O.W.N. 196, aff'g [1952] 1 D.L.R. 620.

In *Public Accountants Council for Ontario v. Premier Trust Co.*, [1964] 1 O.R. 386, 42 D.L.R. (2d) 411, the question arose whether a federally incorpor-

ated trust company empowered by its charter to execute the offices of accountant and auditor in connection with its primary business of trustee and
fiduciary, was caught by the *Public Accountancy Act*, R.S.O. 1960, c. 317 which
forbade a corporation to practice public accountancy. Schatz J. said that "the
restriction upon the defendant operating as a public accountant does not
'impair the status and essential capacities of the company in a substantial
degree' and that the defendant is not sterilized in all its functions and activities", because the business of acting as public accountant was not contemplated as a basic or substantial part of the company's activities. Hence the
Act was properly applicable. Would it matter if public accountancy was the
main or only authorized activity of the federal company?

If a licence for a particular business or activity is available to corporations in general, is there a constitutional right in a federally incorporated
company to obtain a licence when the power to issue it is discretionary?

Accepting that a Dominion company no less than a foreign company
operating in a Province is subject to provincial taxing legislation, is there
any tenable constitutional objection in either case against discriminatory
taxation? See *Van Buren Bridge Co. v. Madawaska and A.-G. N.B., supra;
Charlottetown v. Foundation Maritime Ltd.*, [1932] 1 D.L.R. 453, 3 M.P.R. 196,
aff'd [1932] S.C.R. 589, [1932] 3 D.L.R. 353. Does it make any difference if
the Dominion company is an ordinary trading company or is a bank? See
A.-G. Alta. v. A.-G. Can., [1939] A.C. 117, [1938] 4 D.L.R. 433, [1938] 3
W.W.R. 337.

Flowing from the foregoing is the question whether there is any limitation on the objects or powers with which a company may be incorporated
by the Dominion. Presumably, it could not incorporate a municipality within
a Province, but are there any other limitations on its power to incorporate?
It is the Provinces that are limited in their powers of incorporation under
s. 92(11) of the B.N.A. Act. Is it not open then to the Parliament of Canada
to authorize the incorporation of a college or a university? See *The Frontier
College Act*, 1922 (Can.), c. 77, which empowers the incorporated college to
grant degrees in arts. But cf. *In re the Brothers of the Christian Schools in
Canada* (1876), Cout. S.C. 1.

How far if at all may the Dominion in incorporating a company regulate
its domestic administration? May it circumscribe the kind or range of investments? Or the liability of the company or its directors to creditors? See
Reference re Section 110 of the Dominion Companies Act, [1934] S.C.R. 653,
[1934] 4 D.L.R. 6; and cf. *Letain v. Conwest Exploration Co.* (1960), 23 D.L.R.
(2d) 444, 31 W.W.R. 638.

May the Dominion in its company legislation validly restrict the transfer
of shares by or to certain persons or companies or generally? May it compel
minority shareholders to sell if a prescribed majority approves of a proposed
sale of the company's shares or any class thereof? See *Rathie v. Montreal
Trust Co.*, [1952] 3 D.L.R. 61, 5 W.W.R. (N.S.) 675, aff'd [1952] 4 D.L.R. 448,
6 W.W.R. (N.S.) 652, rev'd on other grounds [1953] 2 S.C.R. 204, [1953]
4 D.L.R. 289; *Esso Standard (Inter-America) Inc. v. J. W. Enterprises Inc. and
Morrisroe*, [1963] S.C.R. 144, 37 D.L.R. (2d) 598.

The fact that a federally incorporated company confines its activities to
one province does not affect the validity of its constitution: see *Colonial
Building & Investment Assoc. v. A.-G. Que.* (1883), 9 App. Cas. 157. Is there
any constitutional objection then to a federal incorporation which limits
territorially the operations of the company?

In a number of cases it has been held that a provincial Attorney-General
may (apart from any authority in federal legislation) take proceedings by
way of *scire facias* to revoke the charter of a federally incorporated company:
see *Guimond v. National Real Estate & Investment Co.* (1915), 16 Que. P.R.

328. Some reliance has been placed for this result on s. 130 of the *B.N.A. Act,* but it is difficult to see how this helps in the case of a post-confederation federally incorporated company: see *Loranger v. Montreal Telegraph Co.* (1882), 5 L.N. 429. If provincial legislation is incompetent to destroy the status and capacity of a Dominion company, what justification is there for permitting this through exercise of a provincial executive or prerogative authority? The issue was convassed in *People's Holding Co. v. A.-G. Que.,* [1931] S.C.R. 452, [1931] 4 D.L.R. 317 and the right of the provincial Attorney-General to seek forfeiture of the charter of a federally incorporated company was upheld, subject to any contrary federal legislation. However, the Supreme Court refrained from passing on the question whether the courts could order the dissolution or winding-up of a Dominion company at the instance of the provincial Attorney-General. The fact that the Dominion company has been a constant violator of provincial law is surely no basis for supporting the result reached by the Supreme Court. In view of recent decisions precluding dismemberment of interprovincial (federal) undertakings through resort to provincial legislation, how can the *People's Holding Co.* case stand as an untarnished authority?

Section 80 of the *Canada Corporations Act,* R.S.C. 1970, c. C-32 imposes liability (in stated circumstances and subject to possibility of exculpation) upon directors of a federally incorporated company to make compensation to any person who subscribes for securities of the company and who suffers loss or damage by reason of any untrue statement in a prospectus. Does this provision (which is clearly valid) affect, in relation to Dominion companies the validity of s. 142 of the *Securities Act,* R.S.O. 1970, c. 426, which similarly (subject to exculpation) makes directors liable to pay compensation for loss or damage resulting from a material false statement in a prospectus? Is the principle established by *Smith v. The Queen,* [1960] S.C.R. 776, 25 D.L.R. (2d) 225, in reference to criminal liability for furnishing false information in a prospectus, applicable here?]

LYMBURN v. MAYLAND

In the Privy Council. [1932] A.C. 318, [1932] 2 D.L.R. 6,
[1932] 1 W.W.R. 578.

Appeal from a judgment of the Alberta Appellate Division, [1931] 2 D.L.R. 698, [1931] 1 W.W.R. 735, 25 Alta. L.R. 310, holding, *inter alia,* that s. 9 of the Security Frauds Prevention Act (Alta.), c. 8, could not apply to a Dominion company.

LORD ATKIN: This is an appeal from the Supreme Court of Alberta in proceedings taken by the plaintiffs to challenge powers sought to be exercised by the Attorney-General of Alberta under the provisions of the Security Frauds Prevention Act, 1930 (Alberta), Statutes of Alberta, 20 Geo. V, c. 8. Under the terms of s. 9 of that Act the Attorney-General or any delegate appointed by him has power to examine any person or company at any time in order to ascertain whether any fraudulent act as defined by the statute or any offence against the Act or the regulations has been, is being, or is about to be, committed. The Attorney-General, Mr. Lymburn, had appointed the defendant, Mr. Frawley, to hold the examination in question, and Mr. Frawley had summoned the plaintiff, Mr. Mayland, to attend him for examination on an inquiry amongst other things into items appearing in the balance sheet of the other plaintiff, Mercury Oils, Ltd., as at December 31, 1930. Mr. Frawley also give notice that he intended to inquire into a transaction between Solloway Mills & Co., Ld., and the plaintiff Mayland respecting the exchange of certain shares and the assumption by Mayland of an underwriting agreement entered into between Solloway Mills & Co., Ld., and Mill City Petroleums Ld. All the companies mentioned are incorporated under the provisions of the *Dominion Companies Act....*

[It was alleged before the Board that] the whole Act was invalid so far as it related to Dominion companies, because it destroyed their status by making it impossible for them to issue their share capital. In this respect it was said the case was covered by the decision of this Board in *Attorney-General for Manitoba v. Attorney-General for Canada,* [1929] A.C. 260. It was further contended that apart altogether from Dominion companies the Act was invalid because under the colour of dealing with the prevention of fraud in share transactions it was assuming to legislate as to criminal law, a class of subject reserved to the Dominion. Apart from invalidity, it was further said that if the terms of the Act were examined the three Dominion companies in question, as well as the plaintiff Mayland, did not carry on any business as brokers in shares; and it was only to transactions by brokers that the provisions of s. 9 applied. Their Lordships cannot accept any of these contentions.

When the framework of the Act is examined it will be found that after an elaborate definition clause it is divided into five parts. The material definitions are those of broker, which includes every person, other than a "salesman" as defined, who is engaged in the business of "trading" in securities, and "trading" includes the solicitation or obtaining a subscription to any security. "Salesman" includes every person employed by a company to trade in securities. Part I is entitled "Registration of brokers and salesmen," and provides in substance that no person may trade in securities unless he is registered as a broker or salesman. The prohibition is confined to "persons" which by the definition clause does not include corporations. A corporation may however be registered, in which event its officials do not need separate registration. Registration is made subject to the approval of the Attorney-General, who may direct that registration be refused for any reason which he may deem sufficient. Registered persons must enter into a personal bond, and may be required to enter into a surety bond each in the sum of $500, conditioned for payment if the registered person, amongst other events, is (in the former bond) "charged with," (in the latter bond) "convicted of," a criminal offence, or found to have committed an offence against the Act or the regulations made thereunder. It was contended on behalf of the Attorney-General for the Dominion that to impose a condition making the bond fall due upon conviction for a criminal offence was to encroach upon the sole right of the Dominion to legislate in respect of the criminal law. It indirectly imposed an additional punishment for a criminal offence. Their Lordships do not consider this objection well founded. If the legislation be otherwise *intra vires,* the imposition of such an ordinary condition in a bond taken to secure good conduct does not appear to invade in any degree the field of criminal law.

There is no reason to doubt that the main object sought to be secured in this part of the Act is to secure that persons who carry on the business of dealing in securities shall be honest and of good repute, and in this way to protect the public from being defrauded. Incidentally the net has been drawn so wide as to cover the issue of shares by a public company, with the result that a company cannot issue its shares to the public unless for that purpose it employs a registered broker or salesman, or unless the company itself is registered. It is said that these provisions so far as they affect Dominion companies are *ultra vires* according to the principles adopted by this Board in *John Deere Plow Co. v. Wharton; Great West Saddlery Co. v. The King; and Attorney-General for Manitoba v. Attorney-General for Canada.* In those cases there was a general prohibition to companies either to trade at all or to issue their capital unless the company was registered. The legislation was held *ultra vires* because the legislative powers of the Province are restricted so that "the status and powers of the Dominion company as such cannot be destroyed" (*John Deere Plow Co.* case) and legislation will be invalid if a Dominion company is "sterilized in all its functions and activities" or "its status and essential capacities are impaired in a substantial degree" (*Great West Saddlery Co.* case). It appears to their Lordships impossible to bring this legislation within such a principle. A Dominion company constituted with powers to carry on a particular business is subject to the competent legislation of the Province as to that business and may find its special activities completely paralysed, as by legislation against drink traffic or by the laws as to holding land. If it is formed to trade in securities there appears no reason why it should not be subject to the competent laws of the Province as to the business of all persons who trade in securities. As to the issue of capital there is no complete prohibition, as in the Manitoba case in 1929; and no reason to suppose that any honest company would have any difficulty in finding registered persons in the Province through whom it could lawfully issue its capital. There is no material upon which their Lordships could find that the functions and activities of a company were sterilized or its status and essential capacities impaired in a substantial degree.

Their Lordships have discussed this part of the Act because the attack of the respondents was mainly directed to it, partly because it was said that the pith and substance of the Act was contained in it and that by sterilizing Dominion companies it was inseverably invalid; and partly because it was said that, even if severable so far as registration of Dominion companies was concerned, inasmuch as inquiry could be made under Part II, as to an offence against the Act, an inquiry under Part II might be directed to an alleged offence invalidly created, and therefore the inquiry provisions of Part II themselves were invalid. This brings their Lordships to the consideration of Part II, and it will be found that once the main attack on registration has failed there is little to be said against this part of the Act.

Sect. 9, under which the examination in dispute in these proceedings was ordered, empowers the Attorney-General or any delegate appointed by him to examine any person or company in order to ascertain whether any fraudulent act or any offence against the Act or regulations has been, is being, or is about to be, committed. The definition of "fraudulent act" appears to be very wide, in some cases having no relation to securities or dealing in securities; and it is possible that if the question becomes relevant a limited construction would be put upon the very general terms used. But this has no bearing upon the question of validity. The examination is not confined to questions of registration, nor are the persons or companies to be examined limited to persons or companies who themselves trade in securities. It seems obvious that the object of the section would be defeated unless the powers of examination extended to persons who might have relevant knowledge, including companies and the officials of companies whose securities might be or be about to be the subject of dealings with the public. The provisions of this part of the Act may appear to be far-reaching; but if they fall, as their Lordships conceive them to fall, within the scope of legislation dealing with property and civil rights the legislature of the Province, sovereign in this respect, has the sole power and responsibility of determining what degree of protection it will afford to the public. There appears to be no reason for excluding Dominion companies from the inquiries of the Attorney-General under this section; and no inconsistency between this legislation and the powers of inquiry under the Dominion Companies Act made on application of members of a company and for a limited purpose—namely, the investigation of the affairs of the company. Their Lordships are unable to agree with the view which was adopted by the Appellate Division that in respect of the subject-matter under discussion the legislature of the Province has only a limited right to require information.

Part III of the Act provides for the appointment of auditors to audit the accounts of brokers and to advise the executive committees of stock exchanges in the Province. Their appears to be no ground for disputing the validity of these provisions.

Part IV by s. 14 contains a provision making it an offence for a broker in certain transactions for customers to place beyond his control securities he may be carrying for customers, and ss. 15 and 16 provide for the necessary records of such transactions. The penal provisions of s. 14 have been subsequently incorporated into the Criminal Code of the Dominion by 20 & 21 Geo. V, c. 11 (Canada), s. 5, which now presumably occupies the field so far as the criminal law is concerned. The substantive provisions of the section avoiding the impugned transaction at the option of the customer and the provisions of the other sections of this part cannot be attacked. Part V has general provisions which need not be noticed except as to the argument of the respondents founded on the words of s. 20, which provide (*inter alia*) that any person who does any fraudulent act not punishable under the provisions of the Criminal Code of Canada shall be liable to fine and imprisonment. It is said that this encroaches on the exclusive legislative power of the Dominion as to criminal law. Having regard to the wide definition of "fraudulent act" above referred to, it may well be that this argument is well founded. But so far as the section is invalid it appears to be clearly severable. In any case it appears to their Lordships, after reviewing the whole Act, that there is no ground for holding that the Act is a colourable attempt to encroach upon the exclusive legislative power of the Dominion as to criminal law. They have already given their reasons for holding that the Act cannot be considered invalid as destroying the status of Dominion companies. The provisions therefore of Part II of the Act appear to be competent Provincial enactments dealing with property and civil rights and have to be obeyed by persons subject to them.

In the result the order of the Appellate Division should be set aside. . . .

Appeal allowed.

[In *A.-G. Man. v. A.-G. Can.*, [1929] A.C. 260, [1929] 1 D.L.R. 368, [1929] 1 W.W.R. 136, where provincial legislation was held *ultra vires* in so far as it prohibited a Dominion company from selling its shares without obtaining a licence, Lord Sumner said, *inter alia*: "The capacity of a Dominion company to obtain capital by the subscription or so-called sale, of its shares, is essential in a sense in which holding particular kinds of property in a province or selling particular commodities, subject to provincial conditions or regulations, is not. Neither is the legislation which is in question saved by the fact that all kinds of companies are aimed at and that there is no special discrimination against Dominion companies. The matter depends upon the effect of the legislation and upon its purpose." See also *Lukey v. Ruthenian Farmers' Elevator Co. Ltd.*, [1924] S.C.R. 56, [1924] 1 D.L.R. 706, [1924] 1 W.W.R. 577. On the applicability of provincial legislation to Dominion companies, see *Rex v. Arcadia Coal Co. Ltd.*, [1932] 2 D.L.R. 475, [1932] 1 W.W.R. 771; *Re Chromex Nickel Mines Ltd.*, 16 D.L.R. (3d) 273, [1971] 1 W.W.R. 163 (*sub nom. Re Hretchka and Chromex Invts. Ltd.*; appeal quashed (1971), 19 D.L.R. (3d) 1 (*sub nom. Hretchka v. A.-G. B.C.*).

Despite the holding in *Lymburn v. Mayland, supra,* would it be open to the Dominion to enact federal securities legislation applicable at least to the marketing of the shares and bonds of federally incorporated companies?

May a province condition the right of a Dominion lending company to enforce its claims in the provincial courts by requiring the prior consent of (a) an administrative board; or (b) the Lieutenant-Governor in Council; or (c) a Judge? See *Reference re Debt Adjustment Act, 1937 (Alta.)*, [1942] S.C.R. 31, [1942] 1 D.L.R. 1, aff'd on other grounds, [1943] A.C. 356, [1943] 2 D.L.R. 1, [1943] 1 W.W.R. 378.

Do any of the principles respecting subjection of federally incorporated companies to provincial legislation apply to federal Crown corporations? May a province at least compel such a corporation to make statistical returns?]

LA COMPAGNIE HYDRAULIQUE DE ST. FRANCOIS v. CONTINENTAL HEAT AND LIGHT CO.

In the Privy Council. [1909] A.C. 194.

Appeal from a judgment of the Quebec Court of King's Bench, Appeal Side, 16 Que. K.B. 406, affirming a judgment of the Superior Court dismissing appellants' action for an injunction.

SIR ARTHUR WILSON: A statute, 60 & 61 Vict. c. 72, of the Parliament of Canada incorporated the respondent company and enacted that (s. 7) it might manufacture, supply, sell, and dispose of gas and electricity, with other powers.

Subsequent provincial statutes of Quebec incorporated the appellant company and granted it the exclusive privilege of producing and selling electricity within a radius of thirty miles from the village of Disraeli, in the province of Quebec.

The statute further enacted that "No company shall exercise any privileges, franchises, or rights of a like nature to those conferred upon the St. Francis Water Power Company by the Act 2 Edward VII, chapter 76, in the territory designated in the said Act without first obtaining the consent of the said St. Francis Water Power Company, and that of the companies mentioned in the following clause."

The respondents took steps to act under their charter by establishing works within thirty miles from Disraeli. The appellants applied for an injunction to restrain them from so doing. The Courts in Canada refused the injunction, and against that refusal the present appeal has been brought.

The contention on behalf of the appellant company was that the only effect of the Canadian Act was to authorize the respondent company to carry out the contemplated operations in the sense that its doing so would not be *ultra vires* of the company, but that the legality of the company's action in any province must be dependent on the law of that province.

This contention seems to their Lordships to be in conflict with several decisions of this Board. Those decisions have established that where, as here, a given field of legislation is within the competence both of the Parliament of Canada and of the provincial Legislature, and both have legislated, the enactment of the Dominion Parliament must prevail over that of the province if the two are in conflict, as they clearly are in the present case.

Appeal dismissed.

The brief Privy Council opinion, reproduced here in full, fails to set out the facts. They are reported in the Quebec judgment. It shows that several provincial companies, named in the Act, were privileged to engage in the activity from which it sought to exclude the Dominion company, also that the Dominion charter antedated the Provincial. The latter was in the form of a special Act and so, on general principles for construing statutes, inoperative to prejudice existing rights under elder legislation.

If the province establishes a government monopoly of a certain business and the Dominion incorporates a company empowered to carry on such a business, what is the constitutional basis for prohibiting the Dominion company from operating in the province? Take, for example, the retail sale of liquor or electric power. May the province constitutionally withdraw from competition all businesses not falling within s. 91? May a province discriminate against a Dominion company by franchise legislation? Suppose the discrimination is in the administration of the legislation?

The position of the province as owner of property (*e.g.* timber, minerals) may be different from its position when exercising legislative authority: see *Brooks-Bidlake and Whittall Ltd. v. A.-G. B.C.*, [1923] A.C. 450, [1923] 2 D.L.R. 189, [1923] 1 W.W.R. 1150.

The limitations on provincial power to interfere with the operations of Dominion companies apply to pre-confederation companies which were given a corporate existence throughout the former province of Canada: *Dobie v. Temporalities Board* (1881), 7 App. Cas. 136. Only the Dominion can deal with the constitution of such companies. Can the province add to the powers of such companies where there is no inconsistency with their "federal" charter? See *Sun Life Assurance Co. v. Sisters Adorers of the Precious Blood*, [1942] O.R. 708, [1943] 1 D.L.R. 596.]

Note on the Favoured Position of the Dominion Company Under the B.C. Power Case

The unusually lengthy judgment of the late Chief Justice Lett of the British Columbia Supreme Court in *British Columbia Power Corp. Ltd. v. A.-G. B.C.* (1963), 44 W.W.R. 65, 47 D.L.R. (2d) 633 makes the federally incorporated company a pampered darling of Canadian constitutional law; it is accorded an advantage not enjoyed by a human. The settlement of the hard-fought dispute in the matter avoided an appeal, and the trial judgment stands as a monument to detailed diligence perhaps unsurpassed in Canadian constitutional litigation. It also amounts to a considerable extension of the line of cases which had theretofore defined the scope of the undoubted federal power to incorporate companies. Stripped of a number of entangling elements which were relevant to a total assessment of the constitutional issues raised in the case, the decision stands for this proposition: a federally-incorporated company which exercises its powers by limiting itself to ownership of all the common shares of a provincially-incorporated company engaged in public utility operations in electricity, gas and transportation, and which has no other business but the management of its wholly-owned subsidiary, may not constitutionally be divested of ownership of the common shares of the provincial company by the Legislature of the province of incorporation. Although the adequacy of the compensation may be said to have been an element in the decision, it was not the determinant in a conclusion that is difficult to reconcile with a long line of decision on the federal incorporation power. The conclusion was arrived at by a considerable sentence parsing by Lett C.J.S.C. of earlier judgments, and by analogical application of abstract propositions.

From the *Parsons* case on, a distinction has been drawn between the federal power to incorporate a company and federal power to regulate its activities; the one did not necessarily carry the other, unless, as in the case of banking, interprovincial railways and aviation (to take a few examples), the activity was otherwise within federal regulatory competence. The evolution of doctrine in respect of the federal company cases from *John Deere Plow v. Wharton* through to the *Great West Saddlery* case and down to *Lymburn v. Mayland* showed a recognition that federal companies *qua corporate* entities were entitled to become established as such, and without limitation or discrimination against them in achieving corporate life through the raising of capital by the issue of shares and debentures. But they had no constitutional guarantee of being entitled to carry on any particular business within provincial regulatory power in the teeth of provincial requirements. If such businesses were open to private entry or competition, the federal company could ask no more than to be treated in the same way as a provincial company or private individual. If the business was one in which a limited number of franchises for it were available, the federal company had no preferential claim to a grant. Moreover, if the business was one which was withdrawn from competition and was a government or public monopoly, federal incorporation would be of no avail to shatter the provincial policy.

Some of the language of some of the cases no doubt went beyond these propositions; an example is found in the judgment of Duff C.J.C. in *Reference re Alberta Debt Adjustment Act,* [1942] S.C.R. 31, [1942] 1 D.L.R. 1. On the other hand, standards formulated to help assess the validity of provincial legislation in relation to Dominion companies have been erected into rigid canons and given a different context than that in which they originated. This is true of the phrase "laws of general application" as pointing to subjection of Dominion companies to regulatory legislation equally applicable to other persons or corporations in the regulated field. It could not rationally be applied to preclude a Province from expropriating shares of a company which it incorporated merely because such shares constituted the only assets of a federal company. To say, as did the Judge in the *B.C. Power* case, that the expropriating provincial legislation was not a law of general application but was in truth selective legislation directed against a Dominion company, was simply to play a game of numbers without regard to the pervasiveness of the provincial company's business and the provincial government's policy in relation thereto. The object of the expropriation of the shares was to gain operating control for the government of a power business in furtherance of a policy to make the generation and distribution of power a government enterprise. This was an object within provincial competence over and above competence to deal with the shares of a creature of the Province.

Ownership of the shares of a provincial company and regulation of the business or activities of the company are different things. If it be the case that a provincial company engages in business which as such is within federal jurisdiction, federal regulatory power is not excluded by reason of compulsory change of ownership of the shares; not even if they became vested in the Crown in right of the Province. The fact that the business was managed by a federal company by reason of its ownership of the provincial company's shares has in truth very little to do with the issue of provincial competence to take the shares. It would be no different if the federal company was concerned only in the management of land which it owned in a Province and asserted a right of immunity from that Province's expropriation legislation. The tenability of the assertion would depend not on the fact of federal company ownership but on whether the land was connected with, if it was not an integral part of, a business or undertaking which as such was within federal competence. If, as has been held, a federal company dealing only in land is subject to provincial mortmain legislation, it would be equally subject to provincial expropriation legislation. And why would a federal company dealing in shares of provincial companies or in the shares of only one provincial company be in any different position?

It is difficult to conceive how ownership of all the shares of a provincial company as a federal company's choice of business can go to the matter of its incorporation. The argument of "impairment of the status and capacities of a federal company in a substantial degree" cannot go beyond protection of the federal company's right to become launched as a corporation by raising capital. Does a federal company by limiting itself to one line of business within provincial competence obtain a constitutional right to be left alone in its ownership, thus enjoying an advantage not open to a natural person?

[The case is fully discussed by *Yule*, Constitutional Aspects of the B.C. Power Expropriation Case, (1964) 22 Univ. of Tor. Fac. of Law Rev. 5; and cf. *Strayer*, Constitutional Aspects of Nationalization of Industry (1964), 7 Can. Bar Jo. 226; *Lederman*, Legislative Power to Create Corporate Bodies and Public Monopolies in Canada, in *Lang* (ed), Contemporary Problems of Public Law in Canada (1968), p. 108.

Quaere, as to the correctness of *Regina v. New Westminster, ex parte Canadian Wirevision Ltd.* (1965), 55 D.L.R. (2d) 613, 54 W.W.R. 238, holding that a federally-incorporated company was subject to a general municipal by-law requiring trades licences to be obtained, where the company's business was cable television, a matter within exclusive federal competence! Does the application of the licensing by-law depend on the authority given to the company in its federal incorporation or on the reach of provincial (or municipal) legislation to businesses within exclusive federal regulatory power?]

2. The "Provincial" Company Outside its Home Province

BONANZA CREEK GOLD MINING CO. LTD. v. THE KING

In the Privy Council. [1916] 1 A.C. 566, 26 D.L.R. 273, 10 W.W.R. 391.

Appeal by special leave from a judgment of the Supreme Court of Canada, 50 S.C.R. 534, 21 D.L.R. 123, 31 W.L.R. 43, affirming the judgment of the Exchequer Court, 6 W.W.R. 1056, dismissing a petition of right for damages for breach by the Crown (Dominion) of the terms of mining leases held by appellants, an Ontario company.

VISCOUNT HALDANE: This is an appeal from a judgment of the Supreme Court of Canada in a petition of right which gave rise to questions of constitutional importance as to the position of joint stock companies, incorporated within the provinces, but seeking to carry on their business beyond the provincial boundaries.

The appellants were incorporated in Ontario by letters patent dated December 23, 1904, and issued under the authority of the *Ontario Companies Act,* and by virtue of any other authority or power then existing, in the name of the Sovereign and under the Great Seal of the province, by its Lieutenant-Governor. The letters patent recite that this Act authorizes the Lieutenant-Governor in Council by letters patent under the Great Seal to create and constitute bodies corporate and politic for any of the purposes or objects to which the legislative authority of the province extends. They go on to incorporate the company to carry on the business of mining and exploration in all their branches, and to acquire real and personal property, including mining claims, with incidental powers. There are no words which limit the area of operation or prohibit the company from carrying out its objects beyond the provincial boundaries.

In the years 1899 and 1900 the Crown, through the Minister of the Interior of the Dominion, had granted to predecessors in title of the appellants leases of certain tracts of land, in what is now the Yukon district, for the purpose of hydraulic mining. Two of these leases contained exclusions of so much of the tracts as had been taken up and entered for placer mining claims. In the year 1900 the Crown entered into agreements with these predecessors in title to the effect that, if any of the placer mining claims within the tracts should be forfeited or surrendered, the Crown would include them in the tracts by supplementary leases. The original leases having subsequently been assigned to the appellants, and certain of the placer mining claims having reverted, the Crown purported in 1907 to demise to the appellants these claims, and to agree to demise to them such other of the claims as might thereafter revert for the same terms of years as those for which the original leases were granted.

In 1906 the Minister of the Interior of the Dominion had purported to issue to the appellants a free miner's certificate. This certificate was issued in conformity with certain regulations under an Order in Council made under the provisions of the Dominion Lands Act, which gives the right to a free miners' certificate to persons of over eighteen and to joint stock companies, the latter being defined to include any company incorporated "for mining purposes under a Canadian charter or licensed by the Government of Canada."

When the Yukon district was, by the statute passed by the Dominion Parliament in 1899, made a separate territory, power to make ordinances was conferred on the Commissioner of the territory. Under this power the Foreign Companies Ordinance was passed, under which any company, incorporated otherwise than by or under the authority of an ordinance of the territory or an Act of the Parliament of Canada, was required to obtain a licence under the ordinance to carry on its business in the Yukon territory. Such a licence when issued was made sufficient evidence in the Courts of the territory of the due licensing of the company. In September, 1905, the appellants obtained such a licence.

In 1908 the appellants presented a petition of right in the Exchequer Court of Canada, alleging that, in breach of the agreement entered into by the Crown, placer mining claims which had reverted to the Crown and should have been leased to the appellants had been wrongly withheld from the appellants, and that by reason of this and other breaches of the agreement the appellants had suffered heavy damage, for which they as suppliants prayed compensation. The respondent delivered an answer to the petition of right, the first two paragraphs of such answer being as follows: "1. The respondent denies that the suppliant has now or ever had the power, either under letters patent, licence, free miner's certificate, or otherwise, to carry on the business of mining in the district of the Yukon, or to acquire any mines, mining claims, or mining locations therein, or any estate or interest by way of lease or otherwise in any such mines, mining claims, or locations. 2. Should a free miner's certificate have been issued to the suppliant, the respondent claims that the same is and always has been invalid and of no force or effect, that there was no power to issue a free miner's certificate to the suppliant, a company incorporated under provincial letters patent, and that there was no power vested in the suppliant to accept such a certificate."

[His Lordship then discussed the views of the Courts below and concluded that the question raised by the second paragraph, *supra,* should be answered in favour of appellants because "if they possessed legal capacity to receive such a Dominion certificate, [they] had it validly bestowed on them and that, if so, they subsequently obtained a good title to the mining locations and also to the Yukon licence to carry on business which was granted to them."]

Their Lordships accordingly turn to the larger question raised by the first of the two paragraphs, a question which is of far-reaching importance. It is whether a company incorporated by provincial letters patent, issued in conformity with legislation under s. 92 of the *British North America Act,* can have capacity to acquire and exercise powers and rights outside the territorial boundaries of the province. In the absence of such capacity the certificates, licences, and leases already referred to were wholly inoperative, for if the company had no legal existence or capacity for purposes outside the boundaries of the province conferred on it by the Government of Ontario, by whose grant exclusively it came into being, it is not apparent how any other Government could bestow on it rights and powers which enlarged that existence and capacity. The answer to this question must depend on the construction to be placed on s. 92 of the *British North America Act* and on the *Ontario Companies Act.*

Section 92 confers exclusive power upon the provincial Legislature to make laws in relation to the incorporation of companies with provincial objects. The interpretation of this provision which has been adopted by the majority of the judges in the Supreme Court is that the introduction of the words "with provincial objects" imposes a territorial limit on legislation conferring the power of incorporation so completely that by or under provincial legislation no company can be incorporated with an existence in law that extends beyond the boundaries of the province. Neither directly by the language of a special Act, nor indirectly by bestowal through executive power, do they think that capacity can be given to operate outside the province, or to accept from an outside authority the power of so operating. For the company, it is said, is a pure creature of statute, existing only for objects prescribed by the Legislature within the area of its authority, and is therefore restricted, so far as legal capacity is concerned, on the principle laid down in *Ashbury Railway Carriage and Iron Co. v. Riche,* L.R. 7 H.L. 653.

Their Lordships, however, take the view that this principle amounts to no more than that the words employed to which a corporation owes its legal existence must have their natural meaning, whatever that may be. The words of the *British Companies Act* were constructed as importing that a company incorporated by the statutory memorandum of association which the Act prescribes could have no legal existence beyond such as was required for the particular objects of incorporation to which that memorandum limited it. A similar rule has been laid down as regards companies created by special Act. The doctrine means simply that it is wrong, in answering the question what powers the corporation possesses when incorporated exclusively by statute, to start by assuming that the Legislature meant to create a company with a capacity resembling that of a natural person, such as a corporation created by charter would have at common law, and then to ask whether there are words in the statute which take away the incidents of such a corporation. This was held by the House of Lords to be the error to which Blackburn, J., and the judges who agreed with him had fallen when they decided in *Riche v. Ashbury Railway Carriage and Iron Co.,* L.R. 9 Ex. 224, in the Court below that the analogy of the status and powers of a corporation created by charter, as expounded in the *Sutton's Hospital Case,* (1663) 10 Rep. 1a. should in the first instance be looked to. For to look to that analogy is to assume that the Legislature has had a common law corporation in view, whereas the wording may not warrant the inference that it has done more than concern itself with its own creature. Such a creature, where its entire existence is derived from the statute, will have the incidents which the common law would attach if, but only if, the statute has by its language gone on to attach them. In the absence of such language they are excluded, and if the corporation attempts to act as though they were not, it is doing what is *ultra vires* and so prohibited as lying outside its existence in contemplation of law. The question is simply one of interpretation of the words used. For the statute may be so framed that executive power to incorporate by charter, independently of the statute itself, which some authority, such as a Lieutenant-Governor, possessed before it came into operation, has been left intact. Or the statute may be in such a form that a new power to incorporate by charter has been created, directed to be exercised with a view to the attainment of, for example, merely territorial objects, but not directed in terms which confine the legal personality which the charter creates to existence for the purpose of these objects, and within territorial, limits. The language may be such as to show an intention to confer on the corporation the general capacity which the common law ordinarily attaches to corporations created by charter. In such a case a construction like that adopted by Blackburn, J., will be the true one.

Applying the principle so understood to the interpretation of s. 92 and of the *Ontario Companies Act* passed by virtue of it, the conclusion which results is different from that reached by the Court below. For the words of s. 92 are, in their Lordships' opinion, wide enough to enable the Legislature of the province to keep the power alive, if there existed in the Executive at the time of confederation a power to incorporate companies with provincial objects, but with an ambit of vitality wider than that of the geographical limits of the province. Such provincial objects would be of course the only objects in respect of which the province could confer actual rights. Rights outside the province would have to be derived from authorities outside the province. It is therefore important to ascertain what were the powers in this regard of a Lieutenant-Governor before the *British North America Act* passed, and in the second place what the *Ontario Companies Act* has really done.

The Act which was passed by the Imperial Parliament in 1840, 3 & 4 Vict. c. 35, in consequence of the report on the state of affairs in Canada made by Lord Durham, united the Provinces of Upper and Lower Canada under a Governor-General, who had power to appoint deputies to whom he could delegate his authority. This Act established a single Legislature for the new United Province of Canada, and shortly after it had passed responsible government was there set up. In 1867 the *British North America Act* modified the Constitution so established. . . . It is to be observed that the *British North America Act* has made a distribution between the Dominion and the provinces which extends not only to legislative but to executive authority. The executive government and authority over Canada are primarily vested in the Sovereign. But the statute proceeds to enact, by s. 12, that all powers, authorities, and functions which by any Imperial statute or by any statute of the provinces of Upper Canada, Lower Canada, Canada, Nova Scotia, or New Brunswick are at the Union vested in or exercisable by the respective Governors or Lieutenant-Governors of these provinces shall, "as far as the same continue in existence and capable of being exercised after the Union in relation to the government of Canada," be vested in and exercisable by the Governor-General. Section 65, on the other hand, provides that all such powers, authorities, and functions shall, "as far as the same are capable of being exercised after the Union in relation to the government of Ontario and Quebec respectively, be vested in and exercisable by the Lieutenant-Governors of Ontario and Quebec respectively." By s. 64 the constitution of the executive authority in Nova Scotia and New Brunswick was to continue as it existed at the Union until altered under the authority of the Act.

The effect of these sections of the *British North America Act* is that, subject to certain express provisions in that Act and to the supreme authority of the Sovereign, who delegates to the Governor-General and through his instrumentality to the Lieutenant-Governors the exercise of the prerogative on terms defined in their commissions, the distribution under the new grant of executive authority in substance follows the distribution under the new grant of legislative powers: In relation, for example, to the incorporation of companies in Ontario with provincial objects the powers of incorporation which the Governor-General or Lieutenant-Governor possessed before the Union must be taken to have passed to the Lieutenant-Governor of Ontario so far as concerns companies with this class of objects. Under both s. 12 and s. 65 the continuance of the powers thus delegated is made by the implication to depend on the appropriate Legislature not interfering.

There can be no doubt that prior to 1867 the Governor-General was for many purposes entrusted with the exercise of the prerogative power of the Sovereign to incorporate companies throughout Canada, and such prerogative power to that extent became after confederation, and so far as provincial objects required its exercise, vested in the Lieutenant-Governors, to whom provincial Great Seals were assigned as evidences of their authority. Whatever obscurity may at one time have prevailed as to the position of a Lieutenant-Governor appointed on behalf of the Crown by the Governor-General has been dispelled by the decision of this Board in *Liquidators of the Maritime Bank of Canada v. Receiver-General of New Brunswick,* [1892] A.C. 437. It was there laid down that "the act of the Governor-General and his Council in making the appointment is, within the meaning of the statute, the act of the Crown; and a Lieutenant-Governor, when appointed, is as much the representative of Her Majesty for all purposes of provincial government as the Governor-General himself is for all purposes of Dominion government." . . .

Their Lordships have now to consider the question whether legislation before or after confederation has been of such a character that any power of incorporation by charter from the Crown which formerly existed has been abrogated or interfered with to such an extent that companies so created no longer possess that capacity which the charter would otherwise have attached to them.

Prior to confederation the granting of letters patent under the Great Seal of the province of Canada for the incorporation of companies for manufacturing, mining, and certain other purposes was sanctioned and regulated by the Canadian statute of 1864, 27 & 28 Vict. c. 23 (Province of Canada). This statute authorized the Governor in Council to grant a charter of incorporation to persons who should petition for incorporation for the purposes of the enumerated kinds of business. Applicants for such a charter were to give notice in the *Canadian Gazette* of, among other things, the object or purpose for which incorporation was sought. By s. 4 every company so incorporated under that Great Seal for any of the purposes mentioned in this Act was to be a body corporate capable of exercising all the functions of an incorporated company as if incorporated by a special Act of Parliament. Their Lordships construe this provision as an enabling one, and not as intended to restrict the existence of the company to what can be found in the words of the Act as distinguished from the letters patent granted in accordance with its provisions. It appears to them that the doctrine of *Ashbury Railway Carriage and Iron Co. v. Riche,* L.R. 7 H.L. 653, does not apply where, as here, the company purports to derive its existence from the act of the Sovereign and not merely from the words of the regulating statute. No doubt the grant of a charter could not have been validly made in contravention of the provisions of the Act. But, if validly granted, it appears to their Lordships that the charter conferred on the company a status resembling that of a corporation at common law, subject to the restrictions which are imposed on its proceedings. There is nothing in the language used which, for instance, would preclude such a company from having an office or branch in England or elsewhere outside Canada.

The *Dominion Companies Act* (c. 79 of the Revised Statutes of 1906), is, so far as Part I is concerned, framed on the same principle, although the machinery set up is somewhat different. Part II stands on another footing. This part deals only with companies directly incorporated by special Act of Parliament of Canada, and to these it is obvious that other considerations may apply. But the companies to which Part I applies are, like those under the old statute, to be incorporated by letters patent, the only material difference being that the Act enables these to be granted by the Secretary of State under his own seal of office. When granted by s. 5 they constitute the shareholders a body corporate and politic for any of the purposes and objects, with certain exceptions, to which the legislative authority of the Parliament of Canada extends. The Sovereign, through the medium of the Governor-General, in this way delegates the power of incorporation, subject to restrictions on its exercise, to the Secretary of State, and it is by the exercise of the executive power of the Sovereign that the company is brought into existence.

The *Ontario Companies Act,* which governs the present case, is c. 191 of the Revised Statutes of the province, 1897. The principle is similar, save that the letters patent are to be granted directly by the Lieutenant-Governor of the province under the Great Seal of Ontario. Excepting in this respect, the provisions of s. 9, which corresponds to s. 5 of the Dominion Act, are substantially the same as those of the latter section so that, subject to the express restrictions in the statute, it is by the grant under the Great Seal and not by the words of the statute, which merely restrict the cases in which such a grant can be made, that the vitality of the corporation is to be measured. It will be observed that s. 107 enables an extra-provincial company desiring to carry on business within the province of Ontario to do so if authorized by licence from the Lieutenant-Governor, a provision which bears out the view indicated.

It was obviously beyond the powers of the Ontario Legislature to repeal the provisions of the Act of 1864, excepting in so far as the *British North America Act* enabled it to do this in matters relating to the province. If the Legislature of Ontario had not interfered the general character of an Ontario company constituted by grant would remain similar to that of a Canadian company before confederation.

The whole matter may be put thus: The limitations of the legislative powers of a province expressed in s. 92, and in particular the limitation of the power of legislation to such as relates to the incorporation of companies with provincial objects, confine the character of the actual powers and rights which the provincial Government can bestow, either by legislation or through the Executive, to powers and rights exercisable within the province. But actual powers and rights are one thing and capacity to accept extra-provincial powers and rights is quite another. In the case of a company created by charter the doctrine of *ultra vires* has no real application in the absence of statutory restrictions added to what is written in the charter. Such a company has the capacity of a natural person to acquire powers and rights. If by the terms of the charter it is prohibited from doing so, a violation of this prohibition is an act not beyond its capacity, and is therefore not *ultra vires,* although such a violation may well give ground for proceedings by way of *scire facias* for the forfeiture of the charter. In the case of a company the legal existence of which is wholly derived from the words of a statute, the company does not possess the general capacity of a natural person and the doctrine of *ultra vires* applies. Where, under legislation resembling that of the *British Companies Act* by a province of Canada in the exercise of powers which s. 92 confers, a provincial company has been incorporated by means of a memor-andum of association analogous to that prescribed by the *British Companies Act,* the principle laid down by the House of Lords in *Ashbury Railway Carriage and Iron Co. v. Riche,* of course, applies. The capacity of such a company may be limited to capacity within the province, either because the memorandum of association has not allowed the company to exist for the purpose of carrying on any business outside the provincial boundaries, or because the statute under which incorporation took place did not authorize, and there-fore excluded, incorporation for such a purpose. Assuming, however, that provincial legislation has purported to authorize a memoran-dum of association permitting operations outside the province if power for the purpose is obtained *ab extra,* and that such a memo-randum has been registered, the only question is whether the legis-lation was competent to the province under s. 92. If the words of this section are to receive the interpretation placed on them by the majority in the Supreme Court the question will be answered in the negative. But their Lordships are of opinion that this interpre-tation was too narrow. The words "legislation in relation to the incorporation of companies with provincial objects" do not preclude the province from keeping alive the power of the Executive to incor-porate by charter in a fashion which confers a general capacity analogous to that of a natural person. Nor do they appear to preclude the province from legislating so as to create, by or by virtue of statute, a corporation with this general capacity. What the words really do is to preclude the grant to such a corporation, whether by legislation or by executive act according with the distribution of legislative authority, of powers and rights in respect of objects out-side the province, while leaving untouched the ability of the corpora-tion, if otherwise adequately called into existence, to accept such powers and rights if granted *ab extra.* It is, in their **Lordships'** opinion, in this narrower sense alone that the restriction to provincial objects is to be interpreted. It follows, as the Ontario Legislature has not thought to restrict the exercise by the Lieutenant-Governor of the prerogative power to incorporate by letters patent with the result of conferring a capacity analogous to that of a natural person, that the appellant company could accept powers and rights conferred on it by outside authorities.

The conclusions at which their Lordships have thus arrived are sufficient to enable them to dispose of this appeal; for, according to these conclusions, the appellant company has a status which enabled it to accept from the Dominion authorities the right of free mining, and to hold the leases in question and take the benefit of the agreements relating to the locations in the Yukon district, as well as of the licence from the Yukon authorities. . . .

Appeal allowed.

[It may be noted that in the concluding part of his judgment, not reproduced here, Viscount Haldane considered the question whether the Governor-General or Lieutenant-Governors were in the position of viceroys rather than mere representatives of His Majesty. He concluded that this was not so. Is the conclusion valid today in respect of the Governor-General? See *Kennedy*, Office of Governor-General of Canada, (1953), 31 Can. Bar Rev. 994.

While there is an obvious territorial limitation on provincial incorporating power, is the province also limited (as to objects or activities with which it can endow its creatures) by the scheme of distribution of legislative power in ss. 91 and 92 of the B.N.A. Act? Cf. *Cudney*, Incorporation of Companies, (1948) 26 Can. Bar Rev. 1182. In *In re International and Interprovincial Ferries* (1905), 36 S.C.R. 206, Taschereau J. said (at p. 209): "No provincial legislature could incorporate a company to run a ferry between . . . two provinces and no provincial government could itself be granted by its legislature the power to run an exclusive ferry between . . . two provinces".

In any case, a charter mentioning only provincial objects is not impaired by failure expressly to exclude operations falling within federal competence, which operations, it is contemplated, will be involved in the company's acting under its charter; see *Kootenay & Elk Ry. Co. v. C.P.R.*, 28 D.L.R. (3d) 385.

Accepting the view of the *Bonanza Creek* case as to the capacity of a letters patent company to engage in activities outside of the province of incorporation, is it open to the incorporating province to legislate so as to control any such extra-provincial activities (apart, that is, from any limitations in the letters patent)? For example is it open to Ontario to enforce its securities legislation against an Ontario company operating in the North West Territories?

Was it really necessary in the *Bonanza Creek* case to make a constitutional distinction between companies incorporated by letters patent and so-called statutory or memorandum of association companies, so far as concerns capacity to accept powers which a foreign jurisdiction wishes to confer? Why should there be any difference when the exercise of powers in a foreign jurisdiction depends on the laws thereof? Issues may arise, as between an incorporating jurisdiction and a foreign jurisdiction relative to the status of a company, its continuing existence and operation, but these are matters which are independent of any question of capacity arising from the form of incorporation: see *National Trust Co. v. Ebro Irrigation & Power Co. Ltd.*, [1954] O.R. 463, [1954] 3 D.L.R. 326.

Under the *Bonanza Creek* case, and under other cases it is clear that "capacity" may be conferred on a statutory company to accept powers *ab extra* without any violation of the constitutional limits of s. 92(11), and moreover this "capacity" may be conferred by implication as well as expressly: *see Honsberger v. Weyburn Townsite Co.,* [1919] 3 W.W.R. 783, 59 S.C.R. 281, 50 D.L.R. 147. Must the powers so conferred be limited to those set out in the incorporating instrument? See *C.P.R. v. Ottawa Fire Ins. Co.,* (1907), 39 S.C.R. 405; *In re Incorporation of Companies in Canada* (1913), 48 S.C.R. 331, 15 D.L.R. 332, 5 W.W.R. 299, varied [1916] 1 A.C. 598, 26 D.L.R. 293, 10 W.W.R. 410.

Following the judgment in *Bonanza Creek,* the Ontario Legislature enacted by 1916, c. 35, s. 6 what is now s. 304 of the *Corporations Act,* R.S.O. 1970, c. 89 which states: "A corporation unless otherwise expressly provided in the Act or instrument creating it, has and shall be deemed to have had from its creation the capacity of a natural person and may exercise its powers beyond the boundaries of Ontario to the extent to which the laws in force where the powers are sought to be exercised permit, and may accept extra-provincial powers and rights". In *Walton v. Bank of Nova Scotia,* [1964] 1 O.R. 673, 43 D.L.R. (2d) 611, aff'd on other grounds, [1965] S.C.R. 681, 52 D.L.R. (2d) 506, Schroeder J.A. commented on the *Bonanza Creek* case as follows: "Whether the correct deduction from the opinion of Viscount Haldane is that a provincial company being a common law company, could carry on any business that a natural person could, or that the judgment must be read as deciding no more than that a provincial company could carry on business and had the capacity to carry on business outside of the incorporating jurisdiction and that anything beyond this concept is pure dictum is of very little importance for immediately following the decision of the Privy Council there were enactments in nearly all the Provinces which settled the point". After referring to the 1916 legislation above mentioned, he continued: "In *Edwards v. Blackmore* (1918), 42 O.L.R. 105, 42 D.L.R. 280, it was held that by virtue of the provisions of that section a company thus incorporated was endowed with all the capacity which a corporation created by charter had at common law—that is, almost unlimited capacity to contract; the statements in the letters patent defining the objects of incorporation did not take away that capacity; and even express restrictions in the charter did not take it away, but should be treated as a declaration of the Crown's pleasure in reference to the purposes beyond which the capacity of the corporation was not to be exercised, a breach whereof gave the Crown a right to annul the charter. That judgment has been followed consistently in Ontario ever since. . . . In my opinion, the word 'expressly' is used in s. 287 in this sense—meaning that a provision of the Act or instrument creating the corporation does not have the effect sought to be attributed to it unless it is stated in express and positive terms, directly, and not merely by implication from the language used."

Does the right of a company incorporated in one province or jurisdiction to sue in another depend on whether it is a letters patent company where there is no prohibitory legislation of the forum? See *Aetna Factors Corp. Ltd. v. Breau* (1958), 15 D.L.R. (2d) 326, 41 M.P.R. 288; *Aetna Factors Corp. Ltd. v. Hachey* (1957), 8 D.L.R. (2d) 105.

In *Hague v. Cancer Relief and Research Institute,* [1939] 4 D.L.R. 191, [1939] 3 W.W.R. 1, 47 Man. R. 325, Dysart J. declared, *intra alia,* that "there can be no corporation . . . unless and until there is first a group or series of natural persons to compose or constitute the corporation, because although later corporations may be formed of existing corporations, these component corporations in the first instance must consist exclusively of natural persons".

Hence, where a corporation was created by provincial statute without named corporators and without members, and a separate board of trustees was established to manage the affairs of the corporation, Dysart J. held that the corporation "was nothing". Is this a limitation on constitutional power under s. 92(11), and if so what is its basis? And if it is such a limitation, does it or could it equally apply to the federal power of incorporation?

A common law municipal corporation is also unaffected by the doctrine of *ultra vires*: see *A.-G. N.B. v. St. John*, [1948] 3 D.L.R. 693, 22 M.P.R. 389. To what extent, having regard to s. 92(8) of the B.N.A. Act, may a municipal corporation exercise powers conferred by federal legislation? Must it obtain "capacity" from the province? See *G.T.R. v. Toronto* (1900), 32 O.R. 120.]

Note on Foreign Companies in Canada

In so far as any foreign company purports to engage in activities falling within federal or provincial authority it would be subject to regulation by Dominion or Province as the case may be. Is there any federal authority over foreign companies which are in a business that falls within provincial authority? It has already been pointed out that a foreign company does not enjoy protection against provincial legislation (within the *Great West Saddlery* doctrine) that is accorded to federally incorporated companies. In *A.-G. Can. v. A.-G. Alta.*, [1916] 1 A.C. 588, 26 D.L.R. 288, 10 W.W.R. 405 in answer to the question whether the Dominion has power to require a foreign company to take out a licence as a condition of doing business, even if the company wishes to confine its business to a single province, Viscount Haldane said that "in such a case it would be within the power of the Parliament of Canada, by properly framed legislation, to impose such restriction. It appears . . . that such a power is given by the heads in s. 91 which refer to the regulation of trade and commerce and to aliens." This observation was referred to by the Privy Council in *A.-G. Ont. v. Reciprocal Insurers*, [1924] A.C. [1924] 1 D.L.R. 789, [1924] 2 W.W.R. 397. It was qualified, however, in *In re Insurance Act of Canada*, [1932] A.C. 41, [1932] 1 D.L.R. 97, [1931] 3 W.W.R. 689, where the Privy Council said that the Dominion cannot under the guise of legislation in relation to aliens inter-meddle with the conduct of a business which is exclusively subject to provincial laws, e.g., insurance. Is the Dominion then limited to conditioning merely the entry of foreign companies into Canada without attempting to licence them to carry on a "provincial" business? May it require guarantees of solvency? May it control their range of investments?

Note on Inter-Jurisdictional Reincorporation and Amalgamation

A provincial Legislature may competently provide for the amalgamation of corporations originally created under its laws, and Parliament may similarly provide for amalgamation of Dominion companies. This proposition must, however, be qualified to exclude provincial power in this connection to destroy or limit extra-provincial rights of creditors, and also to exclude federal power in this connection to interfere with rights of creditors save where this may be done when the businesses or undertakings are as such within federal legislative jurisdiction.

Inter-jurisdictional reincorporation and amalgamation raises different and more difficult problems, both where the corporations of two different Provinces are involved and where a provincial and a federal corporation are involved. Company legislation in some of the Provinces, e.g. Manitoba and Ontario, provides for the reincorporation in the Province of extra-provincial corporations if authorized by the laws of the incorporating jurisdiction; and, conversely, permits the reincorporation (or continuing incorporation) of a creature of the Province under the laws of another jurisdiction whereupon it ceases to be a creature of the Province of original incorporation or ceases to be subject to its companies legislation: see *Companies Act*, R.S.M. 1970, c. C-160, ss. 129 and 130; *Corporations Act*, R.S.O. 1970, c. 89, s. 343. The theory appears to be that reincorporation of an extra-provincial corporation will domesticate it, and amalgamation with a local corporation can then follow without liability to constitutional pitfalls.

The pitfall at the level of reincorporation and amalgamation as between corporations of different Provinces is the prohibition against extra-territorial exercise of legislative power. It is arguable that this prohibition, which affects all provincial legislative power, is not dissolved merely because of permissive legislation of the Province whose creature is to be reincorporated in another Province. No direct comfort can be derived from *A.-G. Ont. v. Scott, supra*, at p. 426 on this question; but the point can be made, independently of that case, that if a provincial corporation may properly exercise powers in and under the laws of another Province, it may be stamped with corporate identity under such laws. The matter is not, however, free from doubt.

Extraterritoriality is not a factor in federal legislative power but there is a problem in the fact that provincial powers of incorporation are limited to the incorporation of companies with provincial objects. Inter-jurisdictional reincorporation and amalgamation of a provincial and a federal company could not, in any event, involve on the part of a Province reincorporation of a federal company whose business or undertaking is within exclusive federal legislative power. Where the federal company carries on a business which is subject to provincial regulatory authority, and provincial reincorporation is permitted under federal legislation, the situation should be as constitutionally manageable as it would be between two corporations of different Provinces. Federal reincorporation of a provincial company, where permitted by provincial legislation, should give rise to even less doubt of its constitutional propriety.

The two-step procedure of, first, reincorporation and then amalgamation (if desired) at least blunts an attack that would be harder to meet if there was an attempt at direct amalgamation between two companies incorporated by different Provinces or between a federal and a provincial company; and there is an additional counter to any argument of invalidity in the permission of the jurisdiction of original incorporation so to deal with its creature. However, the legislation on the matter still remains to be tested in judicial decision.

[Federal company legislation provides for the amalgamation of federal companies: see the *Canada Corporations Act*, R.S.C. 1970, c. C-32, s. 137(1). A proposal to provide for inter-jurisdictional amalgamation was dropped.]

CHAPTER IX

PROBLEMS RELATING TO THE CREDIT SYSTEM AND CREDIT TRANSACTIONS

1. Banking and Credit

The *B.N.A. Act* contains overwhelming internal evidence of the conviction that money, banking and credit (in its public aspect) should be exclusively of federal concern. Among the enumerated classes of subjects in s. 91 are (1) currency and coinage (head 14); (2) banking, incorporation of banks and issue of paper money (head 15); (3) savings banks (head 16); (4) bills of exchange and promissory notes (head 18); (5) interest (head 19); and (6) legal tender (head 20); these are in addition to federal power in relation to bankruptcy and insolvency (head 21). From the outset, the courts took a broad view of the federal banking power. In *Tennant v. Union Bank of Canada*, [1894] A.C. 31, 5 Cart. B.N.A. 244, the Privy Council declared that "banking" was "wide enough to embrace every transaction coming within the legitimate business of a banker"; and see also *Merchants Bank v. Smith* (1884), 8 S.C.R. 512. Its opinion did not vary over the years as is indicated in *Reference re Alberta Bill of Rights Act, A.-G. Alta. v. A.-G. Can.*, [1947] A.C. 503, [1947] 4 D.L.R. 1, [1947] 2 W.W.R. 401, where it reaffirmed a consistent course of decision that what is fairly included within the conception of 'banking' is a matter reserved exclusively for Parliament, and this without any limitation to the extent and kind of business that was carried on by banks in Canada in 1867.

REFERENCE RE ALBERTA STATUTES

In the Supreme Court of Canada. [1938] S.C.R. 100, [1938] 2 D.L.R. 81.

Reference to the Supreme Court of Canada to determine the validity of three bills passed by the legislative assembly of Alberta in 1937 but reserved by the Lieutenant-Governor for the signification of the Governor-General's pleasure. The three bills were: Bill No. 1, "An Act respecting the Taxation of Banks"; Bill No. 8, "An Act to Amend and Consolidate the Credit of Alberta Regulation Act"; and Bill No. 9, "An Act to ensure the Publication of Accurate News and Information." The judgment as reproduced below refers only to the first two bills.

DUFF C.J. (for himself and for Davis J.) : The three Bills referred to us are part of a general scheme of legislation and in order to ascertain the object and effect of them it is proper to look at the history of the legislation passed in furtherance of the general design.

It is no part of our duty (it is, perhaps, needless to say) to consider the wisdom of these measures. We have only to ascertain whether or not they come within the ambit of the authority entrusted by the constitutional statutes (the *British North America Act* and the *Alberta Act* to the legislature of Alberta and our responsibility is rigorously confined to the determination of that issue. As judges, we do not and cannot intimate any opinion upon the merits of the legislative proposals embodied in them, as to their practicability or in any other respect.

It will be necessary, first of all, to examine with some care the central measure which is *The Alberta Social Credit Act*, and to arrive at a proper conception of its character from the constitutional point of view.

Various declarations throughout the enacting provisions of this statute, as well as in the preamble, leave no room for doubt as to its objects. We cite *verbatim* some of these declarations because we think it is important to have before us the language selected by the Legislature itself to describe the purpose of the legislation and the general nature and functions of the machinery which is to be put into operation.

To appreciate the significance of these declarations, however, it is necessary to advert to the constitution and nature of the three bodies set up by the statute for the administration of the Acts as well as to the statutory definition of "Alberta Credit."

There is, first, a Board which is designated simply as "The Board"; the first members of which are named by the statute, their successors being appointed by the Legislature. Then there is the Provincial Credit Commission which is to be appointed by the Board; and here it is convenient to mention the duties of the Commission in determining the value of "Alberta Credit." "Alberta Credit" is defined by section 2(a) as,

> the unused capacity of the industries and people of the province of Alberta to produce wanted goods and services.

By section 5(1) there is to be an account in the treasury of the province known as the Provincial Credit Account. The Commission is to determine, in the manner prescribed by the Act, the value for each year of the

> unused capacity of the industries and people of the province of Alberta to produce wanted goods and services;

in other words, the value in money (section 2(k)) of "Alberta Credit." This amount is to be credited to the Provincial Credit Account and "at the end of each year the amount" in this account "which shall not have been drawn upon in that year shall be written off." The decisions of the Board and of the Commission in the determination of the annual money value of this "unused capacity" are to be final and are to govern the Provincial Treasurer in the establishment and maintenance of the "Provincial Credit Account." It is this "Alberta Credit" annually determined and credited to the Provincial Credit Account which constitutes, according to the plan of the statute, a fund of credit that is to be employed and put into circulation through the machinery set up by the Act in order to facilitate the exchange of goods and services and generally to effectuate the purposes of the Act.

Then, there is the Alberta Credit House which is a department of the provincial administration, constituted by the Commission and a body corporate; and which is to maintain branches throughout the province.

A reference is also necessary to Treasury Credit Certificates. These are issued by the Provincial Treasurer against the Provincial Credit Account from time to time through the Credit House system. [The Chief Justice then referred to certain declarations in the preamble and other parts of the statute expounding its purpose, and continued:] These declarations enable us to affirm with certainty (1) that the evil as the Legislature conceives it with which the statute is intended to grapple is the inability of the people of Alberta to attain to a proper standard of living by reason of the inadequate supply or the unfair distribution of purchasing power; and (2) that, broadly speaking, the enactments in the statute are designed, to employ the phraseology of the authors of the legislation, to equate purchasing power or effective demand with productive capacity; and, moreover, it is easily susceptible of demonstration by reference to the provisions of this statute in detail and to those of the cognate legislation that these measures proceed upon this fundamental postulate, viz., that the economic ills which they aim at curing arise primarily from financial causes and, particularly, from the circumstance that bank credit, which constitutes in the main, in point of volume, the circulating medium of payment and exchange in this country, is issued through private initiative for private profit. And, speaking in general terms, the statute sets up the machinery of a financial system which is to be administered by statutory authority and the predominant function of which is to provide a form of credit designated as "Alberta Credit" which is to be made accessible to consumers and others through the channels created by the Act, and which is to circulate as a medium of exchange and payment.

Alberta credit (the nature of which is described as explained above) is distributed by the Provincial Treasurer by means of Treasury Credit Certificates; and it is his duty to issue through the Credit House system Treasury Credit Certificates in such amounts and at such times as may be required for the purposes of the statute. In particular, it is his duty to issue such certificates to the branches or other agencies for the purpose of providing the credits established pursuant to the requirements of section 13 for, that is to say,

    (a) a discount on prices to consumers at retail;
    (b) government services;
    (c) interest free loans;
    (d) debt payments;
    (e) export subsidies;
    (f) provincial consumers' dividends;
    (g) such other purposes as the Lieutenant-Governor in Council at the request of the Board may by order so declare.

As to the purposes mentioned in section 13(g), it should be noticed that, by section 36(a), in addition to the other powers conferred by the Act, the Commission is empowered to transfer Treasury Credit Certificates in any manner consistent with the purpose of this Act.

The Commission is, moreover, specifically authorized by section 5(3) to advance Alberta credit to persons engaged in

agriculture or manufacturing or industry . . . and . . . to defray the costs of the building of a home or for establishing or maintaining any business, vocation, calling or for public service.

It is also authorized to negotiate any transfer to Alberta credit with any person, firm or corporate body "entitled to Alberta credit."

Then the Lieutenant-Governor in Council is authorized (section 10),

on the advice of the Board . . . (to) declare that all claims against the province for the payment of any money out of any appropriation of public money made by the Legislative Assembly . . . shall be satisfied by the transfer to such person of an amount of Alberta credit

equivalent to the amount of such claim, with a proviso that, in the case of contractual obligations, all parties must agree.

Municipal corporations (by s. 12) are authorized to accept transfers of Alberta credit in satisfaction of any claim and to transfer such Alberta credit to persons who are willing to accept the same in satisfaction or partial satisfaction of their claims for the carrying out of any public work.

Two principle methods are provided for securing access to Alberta Credit by the population generally as individuals. One of the means adopted for this purpose is designated the "Consumers' Dividend,"— a monthly grant of Alberta credit to everybody falling within the designation of "persons entitled to Alberta credit," which includes virtually everybody who is twenty-one years of age, a British subject, resident and domiciled in Alberta, the amount of which is determined by the Commission. The payment of these dividends is provided by Treasury Certificates issued to each branch for the amount that branch has to disburse and the branch issues credit vouchers to the recipients of the dividend in payment thereof.

The second method is by use of the retail discount rate, which constitutes, perhaps, the cardinal feature of the statutory plan. This is a rebate by which purchasers of goods and services are subsidized through a reduction of price compensated by a corresponding credit to the retailer. It is applicable to sales of goods and services to ultimate consumers by persons qualified to "dispense" the discount. In order to qualify for this purpose, a retailer must enter into an agreement with the Commission, one term of which, if the Commission so requires, is that he will deal only with wholesalers and primary producers who have entered into agreements with the Commission pursuant to the provisions of the statute. The discount rate is fixed by the Commission and is determined by the ratio of the money value of the "unused productive capacity" of Alberta to the value of the total capacity.

For augmenting purchasing power, the principal agency appears to be this retail discount rate. A subsidy in this form, by way of reduction of price, it is, perhaps, assumed, will not be attended with the same risk of consequential inflation as a direct subsidy to consumers; especially as the rate, being fixed by reference to the ratio between the value of unused capacity for production and the value of total capacity may be supposed to diminish with augmentation of production. A condition of the operation of this device is, of course, the provision of some means for compensating the seller for the reduction in price and, since the province of Alberta has no legislative control over the creation of currency or legal tender or bank credits, compensation in any of these forms would ordinarily be supplied by means of taxation, or in other words, ultimately from the pockets of people living in Alberta or owning property there. Such difficulties the statutory plan proposes to avoid by the establishment of Alberta credit as a fund of credit for employment, as we have seen, as a means of exchange and payment.

The statute recognizes that extra-provincial debts will in most cases have to be paid in currency and declares that they shall be so paid when desired by the "other party"; and certain enactments of the statute appear to be intended to make provisions for this. It is recognized, in other words, that it would not be practicable for Alberta to establish a system under which legal tender is wholly dispensed with.

As regards intra-provincial transactions, authority is given to everybody to receive Alberta credit in payment of goods and services, but here again the Legislature has obviously recognized its lack of authority to make such acceptance compulsory by direct legislative enactment. Nevertheless, it is clear from the declarations above quoted, as well as from the statute as a whole that the substitution generally in internal commerce of Alberta credit for bank credit and legal tender as the circulating medium is of the very essence of the plan.

The object being to provide increased purchasing power, it is, as explained, of the essence of the scheme that this shall be brought about, not by subsidizing consumers directly, but, mainly by a rebate in prices through the application of the retail discount rate. As that necessarily involves the provision of some means for compensating the seller, and since the compensation provided is compensation out of Alberta credit, it is clear enough that this device could only be made practicable in connection with transactions where the price is paid in Alberta credit, and the discount rate will itself, of course, be paid in the same way.

The practicability of the scheme, the feasibility of it as a means of accomplishing the declared purpose of the legislation, postulates, therefore, a willingness on the part of sellers of goods and services, in Alberta transactions, to accept Alberta credit in payment; in other words, acceptance generally in Alberta of Alberta credit as the circulating medium.

The Credit House is, as already observed, the agent of the Provincial Treasurer through which Alberta credit circulates. The Credit House is to accept deposits of currency and securities, to transfer credit, to receive deposits of credit vouchers and of transfers of Alberta credit. It can convert currency and negotiable instruments on demand into Alberta credit. It is to issue credit vouchers in payment of the consumers' dividend. It is probably intended to issue discount vouchers. Alberta credit on deposit with a branch may be drawn against by a customer by means of an instrument in the form prescribed by the Commission. The forms of credit vouchers and discount vouchers and of transfers are to be settled by regulation by the Commission.

It is expressly provided that a transfer of credit becomes effective on delivery; that is to say, on presentation to a branch of the Credit House. In other words, it is equivalent to an order which is to be honoured on demand. Bankers' credit may be described as the "right to draw cheques on a bank"; and the practical exercise of this right involves either the transfer of credit to another on the books of the same bank, or on the books of another bank, or payment to the payee in legal tender at his discretion. A customer of the Credit House has no right to require payment of legal tender at his discretion, unless his deposit is a currency deposit, and cannot transfer such a right to another, but, save in that respect, he is and must necessarily be, if the system is really to be operative, in relation to his account in the Credit House, in the same position as the customer of a bank.

The question arises: Is legislation of this type competent to a province. . . .?

. . . The general character of the classes of subjects enumerated in section 91, especially . . . Trade and Commerce, Currency and Coinage, Banks and Banking, Legal Tender, is important. A comparison of the nature of these subjects with the subjects included in section 92 seems to suggest that credit (including credit in this novel form) as a medium for effecting the exchange of goods and services, and the machinery for issuing and circulating it, are among the matters assigned to the Dominion under section 91 and not among those intended to be assigned to the provinces under any of the categories of section 92.

The categories (of s. 91) mentioned having been committed for legislative action to Parliament, which represents the people of Canada as a whole, we find it difficult to suppose that it could have been intended, under the general headings Property and Civil Rights, Matters merely local or private, that a single province might direct its powers of legislation under section 92 to the introduction, maintenance and regulation of this novel apparatus for all commercial, industrial and trading operations.

For our present purpose, we are, once again, not in the least concerned with any question of the practicability of the scheme;

which will necessarily depend, as we have seen, upon the general acceptance, by the people of Alberta, of Alberta credit as a medium of payment in intra-provincial transactions. In order to test the validity of the legislation we must, we think, envisage the plan in practice as the statute contemplates it.

Our conclusion is that it is not within the power of the province to establish statutory machinery with the functions for which this machinery is designed and to regulate the operation of it. Weighty reasons could be urged for the conclusion that, as subject-matter of legislation, in part at least, it comes within the field designated by "Currency" (no. 14 of section 91). We think the machinery in its essential components and features comes under head no. 15, Banks and Banking; and if the legislation is not strictly within the ambit of no. 14 or no. 15, or partly in one and partly in the other, then we are satisfied that its subject-matter is embraced within category no. 2, Trade and Commerce, and that it does not come within section 92.

First, as to banking. A banker has been defined as "a dealer in credit." True, in ordinary speech, bank credit implies a credit which is convertible into money. But money as commonly understood is not necessarily legal tender. Any medium which by practice fulfils the function of money and which everybody will accept in payment of a debt is money in the ordinary sense of the word even although it may not be legal tender; and this statute envisages a form of credit which will ultimately, in Alberta, acquire such a degree of confidence as to be generally acceptable, in the sense that bank credit is now acceptable; and will serve as a substitute therefore . . . .

In substance, we repeat, this system of administration, management and circulation of credit (if, and in so far as it does not fall under the denomination "Currency") constitutes in our view a system of "banking" within the intendment of section 91; and the statute in our opinion is concerned with "banking" in that sense.

There is, if the subject-matter of the statute is not strictly "currency" or "banking," or both, an alternative view of the character of it. Employing the words in their ordinary sense and detached from their context in the *British North America Act,* nobody would hesitate to say that *The Alberta Social Credit Act* is concerned with "trade and commerce." It provides the machinery for a novel system of credit and contemplates the separation of intra-provincial industry, commerce and trade from the existing system of finance (in which bank credit and legal tender constitute the media of payment); and the conduct of industrial, commercial and trading activities by the instrumentality of this new system of credit through this statutory machinery; and this would appear to involve profound and far-reaching changes in the operations of commerce and trade. In this connection the comprehensive terms of section 36(b) should be recalled. Any proposal reported to the Board by the Commission pursuant to that section can, under the powers of section 42, be given the force of statute by the Lieutenant-Governor in Council, even though that should involve an amendment of the Act. These two sections afford striking evidence of the penetrating and far-reaching character of the activities of the Board and the Commission in relation to commerce, industry and trade which the authors of the legislation had in view.

Such legislation, if not legislation in respect of banking or currency, would appear to be concerned with the regulation of trade and commerce, rather than with property and civil rights or matters merely local or private in the province. . . .

We come now to the bills submitted. The first to be considered is Bill no. 8, *"The Credit of Alberta Regulation Act, 1937."*

In view of what has already been said, this statute is *ultra vires* on a narrow ground. It is a licensing statute, not in the sense that it imposes taxation by way of licence, but in the sense that the licensing authority is used for the purpose of regulating the institutions to which the statute relates; that is the pith of it, and the licensing authorities are the Provincial Credit Commission and the Social Credit Board, the commission and the board constituted under *The Alberta Social Credit Act;* and the narrow point is this: In the view already expressed, *The Alberta Social Credit Act* is *ultra vires.* The machinery it professes to constitute cannot, therefore, come into operation. Consequently, *The Credit of Alberta Regulation Act* which can only take effect through that machinery must necessarily be inoperative. Furthermore, it is quite plain, not only from the preamble of *The Credit of Alberta Regulation Act,* but also from its enacting provisions, that it is a part of the general scheme of legislation of which *The Alberta Social Credit Act* is really the basis; and that statute being *ultra vires,* ancillary and dependent legislation falls with it.

The broader ground upon which we think this legislation is *ultra vires* is this: First, it is legislation in relation to the regulation of trade and commerce within the meaning of section 91(2) of *The British North America Act.*

The statute contains no express definition of "credit." Nevertheless, the language itself in which the enactments of the statute are expressed appears to afford indicia from which it is not difficult to ascertain the kind of credit the statute contemplates. First, we have the declaration that a "credit institution" is a person or corporation whose business or any part of whose business is the business of dealing in credit. The credit we are concerned with, therefore, is something which is dealt with as part of a business.

Then, by clause (b), a business of this kind consists in transactions whereby such "credit is created, issued, lent . . . provided . . . by means of bookkeeping entries" or "dealt in" by such means. Further, the credit is of such a character that these transactions occur in relation to it: "the payment of cheques (which have been) made, drawn or paid in by customers," the payment of other negotiable instruments which have been similarly dealt with by customers and "the making of advances and the granting of overdrafts."

We are concerned, for the present, with ascertaining the effect of clause (a) and of clause (b) minus the last member.

Perhaps it is convenient at the outset to refer to the recital which is in these words:

Whereas the extent to which property and civil rights in the province may be enjoyed depends upon the principles governing the monetization of credit and the means whereby such credit is made available to the province and to the People collectively and individually of the province.

"Monetization of credit" does not seem to be a very precise expression, but it does point to the conclusion that the credit with which the statute is concerned is credit in a form in which it can be employed for the purposes of money.

Now, the language of clause (b), excluding, of course, the last member, is perfectly sensible as applied to bank credit. . . .

. . . Speaking generally, bank credit transferable on demand and so available for commercial purposes is evidenced by bookkeeping entries, and it is upon the evidence and authority of such entries that the banker and his employees daily and hourly act in the business of the bank. Such entries are for practical purposes the record as well as the evidence of the creation of bank credit and it is by means of them that such credit as a medium of payment and exchange is transferred, disbursed and dealt in.

Then, the transactions enumerated in the second member of the clause are all defined as transactions relating to "credit created, issued, lent, provided or dealt in by means of bookkeeping entries" in course of the business of dealing in credit. In this country, the functions of temporary lending and the provisions of transferable credits as a means of payment are performed together as a matter of course.

But it is important to emphasize that, while the payment of customers' cheques and other negotiable instruments and the making of advances and the granting of overdrafts are enumerated in the second member of the clause, they are all transactions having relation to some "credit created . . . or dealt in by means of bookkeeping entries."

The essential feature of the business of dealing in credit, therefore, is, by this definition, the creation of credits and the dealing in credits by means of bookkeeping entries and these related transactions. It should be noted also that, from the persons carrying on the business of dealing in credits so defined is excepted the Bank of Canada; and clause (b), with the last member left out of consideration, has unquestionably the effect of designating transactions which are the transactions of somebody who is carrying on business in banking. We are unable to read this language as extending to transactions which are not of that character. It was suggested that the trans-actions of a bill broker or a person engaged in discounting bills or making advances on the credit of bills or promissory notes would fall within it, but this leaves entirely out of account the all important limitation that the business of dealing in credit, by definition, is the business of somebody who is engaged in transactions of the kind specified but with the qualification that such transactions are effectuated by means of "bookkeeping entries." Such language, properly understood, finds, as we have seen, a reasonable application in designating the transactions of a banker but, so far as we are aware, it has no application to the business of a bill broker or to that of a money lender who is not a banker.

It should be observed that the statute applies only to credit institutions which are carrying on business when the Act comes into force, that is, when assented to.

We come now to the final member expressed in these words: "but does not include transactions which are banking within the meaning of the word 'banking' as used in subhead 15 of section 91 of *The British North America Act, 1867.*"

We repeat, clause (b) consists of a single sentence containing what professes to be a definition of "business of dealing in credit" as employed in the statute. The words just quoted are part of that definition. If effect is given to them, they completely destroy everything which precedes them in that definition. They reduce the definition to the single proposition that the "business of dealing in credit" in the Act "does not include transactions which are banking within the meaning of the word 'banking' as used in subhead 15 of section 91 of *The British North America Act, 1867.*"

We have come to the conclusion that we have here one of those cases in which there is a repugnancy of such a character that the last words, if any effect is to be given them, really empty the clause of all meaning as a definition and the statute of its intended effect and must be disregarded. (*The Case of Alton Woods* (1600), 1 Co. Rep. 40b, at 47b; *Clelland v. Ker* (1843), 6 Ir. Eq. 35).

If we should be wrong in this view of the construction of section 2(b), in other words, if, giving full effect to the last sentence, there is still some content left in the phrase "business of dealing in credit" then the subject-matter of the statute would appear to be within the category Regulation of Trade and Commerce within the meaning of section 91(2). We think it plain that "credit" (if not strictly confined to bank credit) here means credit which is dealt in as bank credit is dealt in, not such a credit, for example, as is created by a purchase of goods on credit in the ordinary course of business, but credit which is created, issued and so forth for the purpose of being dealt with as such.

In our opinion, legislation regulating credit from the aspect and with the purpose disclosed by the provisions of the statute as a whole, read in light of the preamble and of the cognate statutes and bills (if it is not banking legislation) is legislation respecting matters which fall strictly within Trade and Commerce and not within any of the matters contemplated as subjects of provincial legislation within the meaning of section 92. . . .

The answer, therefore, to the question concerning this Bill is that it is *ultra vires.*

The next Bill to be considered is that respecting the Taxation of Banks: The question to be determined in relation to this Bill is this:

Is it an enactment in exercise of the provincial power to raise a revenue for provincial purposes by direct taxation, or is it legislation which, in its true character, relates to Incorporation of Banks and Banking. . . .

The rate of taxation is an annual rate of one-half of one per cent of the paid-up capital and one per cent upon the amount of the reserves as well as upon the amount of the undivided profits. It is proper, we think, to test the effect of the legislation by considering the case of a bank—the Bank of Montreal, for example—which carries on business in every province of Canada as well as in many other places in North America and elsewhere.

The population of Alberta, in round numbers, is 800,000 and that of the Dominion, in round numbers, 10,000,000. The ratio of the first figure to the second is expressed by the fraction two twenty-fifths. It is not, we think, for our present purposes an inaccurate assumption that the volume of business carried on by such a bank in Alberta would bear a ratio to the total business of the bank in Canada not materially greater than the ratio of the Alberta population to the population of the Dominion. The annual tax, therefore, in the case of such a bank of one-half of one per cent upon the paid-up capital may be regarded as a charge upon two twenty-fifths of its total business; and, in respect of its reserves and undivided profits, one per cent, borne by the same part of its business. Indeed, it is pretty obvious that the fraction two twenty-fifths expresses a considerably higher ratio than a figure strictly in accord with the facts. This would appear to give a fair and reasonable point of view for obtaining a just idea of the practical effect of such taxation.

It is plain, of course, that if such a bank were subjected to such a levy in each of the provinces but on a scale varying with the business done in the province, or the population of the province, the total levy charged upon its business throughout the Dominion would amount to an annual impost of six and one-quarter per cent upon its paid-up capital and twelve and one-half per cent upon each of the other funds—the reserves and the undivided profits.

In our opinion, it requires no demonstration to show that such a rate of taxation must be prohibitive in fact and must be known to the Alberta legislature to be prohibitive. It is our duty, as judges, to take judicial notice of facts which are known to intelligent persons generally; and any suggestion that the profits of banking as carried on in Canada could be such as to enable banks to pay taxes to the provinces of such magnitude, having regard to the other burdens, such as municipal rates, which are levied upon them in Canada, as well as the taxes paid in foreign countries, would be incontinently rejected by anybody possessing the most rudimentary acquaintance with affairs.

Now this tax upon banks is of proportions which have no parallel in the Alberta system of taxation. In the same year there was no substantial increase in the taxes levied upon corporations generally, including banks. This levy now in question which was imposed later is directed exclusively against banks.

Such legislation, in effect prohibitive, although in form relating to taxation is, in truth, legislation "directed to," to quote the phrase of Lord Haldane in *Wharton's* case, [1915] A.C. 343, controlling the banks in the conduct of their business, by forcing upon them a discontinuance of business, or otherwise. Such legislation, notwithstanding its form, is not within the powers of the provinces under section 92 because its subject-matter in truth is the Incorporation of Banks and Banking, one of the enumerated heads of section 91 (No. 15). . . .

The chartered banks in Alberta exercise their powers under the authority of a Dominion statute, the *Bank Act*. By that statute, a system of banking is set up by the Parliament of Canada and provision is made for the incorporation of individual banks which, on compliance with the statutory conditions, are entitled to carry on business subject to the provisions of the statute. This system of banking has been created by the Parliament of Canada in exercise of its plenary and exclusive authority in relation to that subject, and any legislation by a province which, to quote . . . the phrase of Lord Haldane, is "so directed by the provincial legislatures" as either directly or indirectly to frustrate the intention of the Bank Act by preventing banks carrying on their business or controlling them in the exercise of their powers must be invalid (*G. W. Saddlery v. The King,* [1921] 2 A.C. 91, at p. 100).

This view of the effect of the legislation is greatly strengthened by the obvious relation of the Bill to the scheme of legislation to which the other Bills already discussed belong. This relation between the Bill in question and the Social Credit legislation as a whole enables us in some degree to understand a measure which would otherwise be simply incomprehensible.

There are two other points to which we think it advisable to refer briefly. As regards the excessive magnitude of the tax, the question may be asked: Where are you to draw the line? The answer to that is, any attempt to draw an abstract line is difficult and, in dealing with questions of the kind before us, it is inadvisable to attempt it unless it be absolutely necessary. This case presents no such necessity. It is plain on the face of the Bill that the purpose of it is not to raise a revenue for provincial purposes, and equally plain that taxation of this character throughout Canada, if operative, would completely frustrate the purposes of the *Bank Act*.

[His Lordship then proceeded to distinguish *Bank of Toronto v. Lambe* (1887), 12 App. Cas. 575, and he concluded as follows:] The specific ground on which, in our opinion, this legislation is invalid is: It is not competent to the provinces of Canada, by the exercise of their powers of taxation, to force banks which are carrying on business under the authority of the *Bank Act* to discontinue business; and taxation by one province on a scale which, in a practical business sense, is manifestly prohibitive is not a valid exercise of provincial legislative authority under section 92. Such legislation, though in the form of a taxing statute, is "directed to" the frustration of the system of banking established by the *Bank Act,* and to the controlling of banks in the conduct of their business.

The answer, therefore, to the question concerning this Bill is that it is *ultra vires. . . .*

[Cannon J., Kerwin J. (Crocket J. concurring) and Hudson J. gave separate reasons for reaching the same conclusions as Duff C.J. On appeal to the Privy Council on Bill No. 1 alone, the judgment of the Supreme Court was affirmed: [1939] A.C. 117, [1938] 4 D.L.R. 433, 3 W.W.R. 337.

Federal legislative power in relation to banks empowers Parliament to regulate registration and transfer of bank shares, although their *situs* for succession duty purposes is thereby affected: *Smith v. Provincial Treasurer of N.S.* (1918), 58 S.C.R. 570, 47 D.L.R. 108.

Under the *Bank Act,* R.S.C. 1970, c. B-1, s. 157 it is an offence to use the word "bank" to describe a business unless under the authority of Parliament.

How far does federal power in relation to the credit system enable Parliament to regulate credit buying? Clearly, Parliament may control credit through regulating the supply of money and restrictions on the powers and activities of banks. May it do so by direct interference in the relations of retailer and consumer? See the *Consumer Credit (Temporary Provisions) Act,* 1950-51 *(Can.),* c. 3, am. 1951 (1st sess.), c. 14, providing for the restriction of consumer credit under regulations made by the government. The Act had an expiry date of July 31, 1952, with provision for continuation which was not acted upon. It was enacted as a companion measure to the *Essential Materials (Defence) Act,* 1950-51 *(Can.),* c. 6 which was repealed by s. 40 of the milder *Defence Production Act,* 1951 (Can. 1st sess.), c. 4, which replaced it. *Quaere,* whether the constitutional basis of the statute was defence or the power to control the credit system or both!]

RE BERGETHALER WAISENAMT

In the Manitoba Court of Appeal. [1949] 1 D.L.R. 769, [1949] 1 W.W.R. 323, 57 Man. R. 66.

Appeal from a judgment of Dysart J., [1948] 1 D.L.R. 761, [1948] 1 W.W.R. 305, reversing an order of the Master and directing that certain depositor creditors of a bankrupt company were not entitled to rank *pari passu* with other creditors.

RICHARDS J.A.: The Bergethaler Waisenamt was incorporated by a special Act of the Legislature, 1907 (Man.), c. 50. The English translation of the name is "Bureau for Orphans of Bergethaler Community".

The powers given to the corporation were to act as administrator or executor, guardian of any minor, or committee for any lunatic or person of unsound mind, and to hold real and personal property upon trust. The special Act provided further that the *Manitoba Trustee Act* [R.S.M. 1902, c. 170] should apply to the corporation and that the corporation should have the power to invest such moneys as may come into its hands upon such securities as are authorized by the said Act.

The Act further provided that the corporation should not be entitled to do business until authorized by an Order in Council. The Order in Council was not passed until October 1919. But in the meantime the corporation engaged in business and acted as executor, administrator and trustee, as well as borrowing or receiving moneys on deposit and lending money. There was no express authority to receive money on deposit or to borrow money.

In the year 1920 by c. 160 and again in 1922 by c. 72, the Manitoba Legislature passed special Acts validating all acts of the corporation purporting to be done in pursuance of the powers given it,. and in particular the receipt of money on deposit and the lending of money on securities. In 1922, the corporation was authorized to receive money on deposit, to lend money on real and personal securities and to borrow money on its own assets.

In February 1930, the corporation required ready money and borrowed $42,000 from the Monarch Life Ass'ce Co. on the security of the best mortgages, lands and agreements of sale which it owned or controlled. Shortly afterwards the corporation, being unable to meet its current liabilities, made an assignment in bankruptcy and was ordered to be wound up. . . .

[The learned Judge referred here to certain steps in the winding-up proceedings and to claims of certain creditors to rank ahead of depositor creditors because the claims of the latter arose out of banking business which the company could not lawfully be authorized to conduct. He then continued as follows:]

Evidence was taken as to the business carried on by the corporation and the learned Judge found that it had carried on a banking business for about 23 years, from the time of its incorporation until the assignment in bankruptcy, and held that the claims of the deposit creditors were based upon banking transactions which the corporation had no right to engage in because they were not authorized by the Parliament of Canada which had the exclusive legislative authority over "Banking" and "Incorporation of Banks", and were invalid as against those whose claims arose from the legitimate estate business of the corporation; and that the deposit creditors were entitled to be paid only after the estate claimants had been paid in full.

The learned Judge relied on the well-known case of *Sinclair v. Brougham*, [1914] A.C. 398. In that case it was established beyond question that the Birkbeck Permanent Benefit Bldg. Soc. carried on for many years a very extensive banking business contrary to the provisions of the *Building Societies Act, 1836*, under which it was formed. The society was popularly known as the Birkbeck Bank and used that title in connection with its banking business.

The learned trial Judge referred to the amendments to the Bergethaler Waisenamt Charter made by the Manitoba Legislature in 1920 and 1922, as purporting to ratify and confirm previous banking transactions, and to authorize the continuance of them and other such transactions into the future, and he said that such ratification was wholly ineffectual to legalize the corporation's banking business. I think the amending validating Acts do not bear any such meaning.

In any event the Legislature had the right, I think, without doubt, under its authority over property and civil rights, to enact legislation affecting the respective interests of persons and parties in Manitoba as between themselves, regardless of how such interests came into being or whether they were valid or invalid because of acts of the corporation which might or might not have been *ultra vires*. Such legislation does not mean or purport to mean the validation of banking business.

The right of a provincial Legislature to incorporate a loan, trust or financial corporation without authority to do a banking business is not questioned. That is all the Legislature purported to do here. The conduct of a banking business was not contemplated.

In *Reference re Alberta Bill of Rights Act, A.-G. Alta. v. A.-G. Can.,* [1947] A.C. 503, Viscount Simon, in discussing operations which fall within the connotation of "Banking" as that word is used in s. 91 of the *B.N.A. Act,* made a statement which is very pertinent to any consideration of what is banking business. He is reported, at p. 516 A.C. as saying: "The question is not what was the extent and kind of business actually carried on by banks in Canada in 1867, but what is the meaning of the term itself in the Act." He pointed out, too, that actually the business of banking has developed since Confederation.

Expert opinion was not given in evidence in this case as to what is banking business, but it is common knowledge that during the period of the corporation's operations banking did include the following: (1) Receiving money on deposit from its customers. (2) Paying a customer's cheques or drafts on it to the amount on deposit by such customers, and holding Dominion Government and Bank notes and coin for such purpose. (3) Paying interest by agreement on deposits. (4) Discounting commercial paper for its customers. (5) Dealing in exchange and in gold and silver coin and bullion. (6) Collecting notes and drafts deposited. (7) Arranging credits for itself with banks in other towns, cities and countries. (8) Selling its drafts or cheques on other banks and banking correspondents. (9) Issuing letters of credit. (10) Lending moneys to its customers: (a) on the customers' notes; (b) by way of overdraft; (c) on bonds, shares and other securities.

The business of a Canadian chartered bank is wider still because of the statutory rights and powers given to a bank under the provisions of the *Bank Act.*

The evidence of A. D. Friesen, joint manager of Bergethaler Waisenamt from 1915 until it went into bankruptcy, shows that the corporation did not carry on any of the above-listed functions except to borrow money on deposit and to pay interest thereon, and in turn to lend money to others who, as a rule, were not its deposit customers. In particular it did not pay customers in cash across its counter. The customers called in person and, on their oral requests, were given the cheques of the corporation on the Canadian Bank of Commerce which did all the banking business effected. It did not discount or lend on commercial paper but only on direct indebtedness. It collected as executor or administrator a few notes for estates but, otherwise, did not make a practice of making collections for customers. It did not deal in exchange or in gold or silver bullion. It had no Canadian or foreign banking correspondents. Any remittances to other countries or cities were sent, without charge, as secretary or agent for the remitter of the money and any banking business in connection therewith was done by the Canadian Bank of Commerce which sold and made charges for the drafts. The total amount remitted in this manner for the year 1927 was only $1,467.30. The evidence does not show what, if any, was remitted in other years. It did not issue letters of credit. It did not make a practice of lending by way of overdraft.

The learned Judge quoted a number of authorities defining or referring to the meaning of the business of banking. None, however, gave a complete list of the usual functions of a bank. Many of them do, however, state that the bank is bound to honour any cheques or orders for the payment of money which the customer may send to it to the extent of the sum deposited. In other words, as stated in the Oxford Dictionary, the bank's "essential duty is the payment of the orders given on it by its customers". . . .

In *A.-G. Can. v. A.-G. Que., Bk. of Montreal v. A.-G. Que.,* [1947] A.C. 33 at p. 44, Lord Porter, who delivered the judgment of the Judicial Committee of the Privy Council, is reported as saying: "The relation between banker and customer who pays money into the bank is stated in words which have ever since been accepted in *Foley v. Hill* (1848), 2 H.L.C. 28, 9 E.R. 1002, as 'the ordinary relation of debtor and creditor, with a superadded obligation arising out of the custom of bankers to honour the customer's drafts'."

In 1 Hals., 2nd., s. 1299, p. 793, after stating that Acts of 1844 and 1857 restricted banking associations to not more than six persons and then to not more than ten, in note (f) it is said: "It is not clear whether the restriction applies only to combinations formed for the exclusive purpose of banking, or whether it would include combinations carrying on banking business *as part* of their undertaking, *or what precisely constitutes banking business.* See *Re District Savings Bank, Ltd., Ex parte Coe* (1861), 3 DeG. F. & J. 335: 3 Digest 134, 97, where a society formed to receive deposits and conduct emigration operations was held not a banking company within the *Joint Stock Companies Act* and 21 & 22 Vict. c. 91 (1858). . . . Probably the real test is the receiving money *to be withdrawn by cheque."*

The business carried on by most banks includes the totality of the functions I have enumerated, but, of course, a banking business can be carried on without performing all of them and most corporations and individuals engaged in a financial business of any kind are required to carry on or perform some of them, and it does not follow from the fact that banks perform them that every exercise of one or more of the functions is a form of banking.

The common business and callings of life, the ordinary trades and pursuits which are innocent of themselves and have been followed for a long time, are free to all, subject to any restrictions or prohibitions of law.

Here many important functions, including the important or essential duty or obligation to pay the customers' orders, were lacking.

The acts of the corporation were, in my opinion, no more than those of a loan or trust company, or a combined loan and trust company and did not amount to carrying on a banking business.

The answer to the question whether the corporation was engaged in "banking" decides this case I think. The learned Judge based his decision on that point alone and it does not appear to be necesary to consider or discuss further, in the event of the Court holding the corporation was engaged in banking, whether the acts of the corporation were *ultra vires* or whether *Sinclair v. Brougham*, [1914] A.C. 398, as interpreted by the Court of Appeal in *Re Diplock*, [1948] 1 Ch. 465 [aff'd *sub nom. Ministry of Health v. Simpson*, [1950] 2 All E.R. 1137], applies.

Appeal allowed.

[McPherson C.J.M. and Williams C.J.K.B. *(ad hoc)* concurred. Coyne J.A. and Adamson J.A. delivered separate concurring judgments.

In the light of this judgment, see The Treasury Branches Act, R.S.A. 1970, c. 370 (first enacted in 1938). In *Breckenridge Speedway Ltd. v. The Queen in right of Alberta*, [1970] S.C.R. 174, 70 W.W.R. 481, 9 D.L.R. (3d) 142, where its validity was challenged, the Court found itself able to dispose of the case without passing on that issue.

Under s. 92(3) of the *B.N.A. Act*, a provincial legislature may pass laws in relation to "the borrowing of money on the sole credit of the province." To what extent, if at all, does this enable a province to establish a banking system? See *In re Dominion Trust Co.*, [1918] 3 W.W.R. 1023 (B.C.); *Winnipeg Trustee v. Kenny*, [1924] 1 D.L.R. 952 (Man.). Cf. *Agricultural Development Finance Act*, R.S.O. 1970, c. 11.

Is "gold clause" legislation competent to a Province in so far as it provides for discharge in legal tender of any obligation which gives the obligee a right to require payment in gold or in a particular kind of currency? See *The Gold Clauses Act*, R.S.O. 1970, c. 193. Is it competent to Parliament to legislate to this effect? See *Gold Clauses Act*, R.S.C. 1970, c. G-4. See also *Norman v. B. & O. Ry.* (1935), 294 U.S. 240, 55 S. Ct. 407; *Perry v. U.S.* (1935), 294 U.S. 330, 55 S. Ct. 432.

Does the federal banking power preclude provincial legislation in respect of money lending? Cf. *The Credit Unions Act*, R.S.O. 1970, c. 96, as amended, authorizing the incorporation of credit unions for the purpose of receiving money on deposit from members and the making of loans to members with or without security; and see, as to validity, *La Caisse Populaire Notre Dame Ltée v. Moyen* (1967), 61 D.L.R. (2d) 118, 59 W.W.R. 129.

For a non-constitutional discussion of what is "banking", see *United Dominion Trust Ltd. v. Kirkwood*, [1966] 1 All E.R. 968.

In *A.G. Can. v. A.-G. Que.*, [1947] A.C. 33, [1947] 1 D.L.R. 81, [1946] 3 W.W.R. 659, rev'g [1943] Que. K.B. 543, it was held that provincial legislation appropriating unclaimed bank deposits (being merely debts of the bank) was invalid, whether the Province purports to hold such choses in action for the owners or not. Should there be any difference in result if the Crown in right of a Province claims such choses as *bona vacantia?* May the Province define what constitutes *bona vacantia* in such a way as to cover unclaimed bank deposits? *Cf. Treasurer of Manitoba v. Minister of Finance; A.-G. Man. v. Minister of Finance*, [1943] S.C.R. 370, [1943] 3 D.L.R. 673. For the position on these problems in the United States where there is no exclusive federal banking power, see *Anderson National Bank v. Luckett* (1944), 321 U.S. 233, 64 S. Ct. 599 and *Roth v. Delano* (1949), 338 U.S. 226, 70 S. Ct. 22, upholding state authority in respect of unclaimed bank deposits so long as there is no interference with the federal banking system.

A provincial legislature has no authority to require a bank to have a provincial licence as a condition of doing business. Nor may it seek to regulate or require that deposits be backed by a specified amount or percentage of reserves: see *A.-G. Alta. v. A.-G. Can.* (Reference re Alberta Bill of Rights Act), [1947] A.C. 503, [1947] 4 D.L.R. 1, [1947] 2 W.W.R. 401; *La Brie*, Note, (1947) 25 Can. Bar Rev. 888.

To what extent, absent federal legislation, are banks subject to provincial legislation of general application, *e.g.*, provincial registry laws respecting land, conditional sale and chattel mortgage legislation, and garnishment legislation? See *Re Victor Varnish Co.* (1908), 16 O.L.R. 338; *Brantford v. Imperial Bank of Canada*, 65 O.L.R. 625, [1930] 4 D.L.R. 658.

Section 3 of the *Mechanics' Lien Act*, R.S.O. 1970, c. 267 establishes a statutory trust of money received on account of the contract price by a builder, contractor or subcontractor and forbids its conversion by them save to the extent to which workmen, suppliers and subcontractors have been paid. How does this provision affect a bank, in which a contractor has a current account to which he has deposited money received on the contract price, where the bank applies the money to an overdraft? Does the statutory trust operate against the bank in view of s. 96(1) of the *Bank Act*, R.S.C. 1970, c. B-1 which provides that "the bank is not bound to see to the execution of any trust, whether express, implied or constructive, to which any deposit made under the authority of this Act is subject"? See *Fonthill Lumber Ltd. v. Bank of Montreal*, [1959] O.R. 451, 19 D.L.R. (2d) 618. Does it, or should it make any difference whether the contract money is actually deposited with the bank or is claimed by the bank under, say, a general assignment of book debts given to the bank by a contractor debtor? See *Canadian Bank of Commerce v. T. McAvity & Sons Ltd.*, [1959] S.C.R. 478, 17 D.L.R. (2d) 529.

Is it competent for a Province to empower a landlord to distrain on goods of a tenant which are covered by an assignment to a bank by way of security? No doubt Parliament could protect the bank's security by affirmative legislation but in the absence thereof should provincial legislation apply where it operates to deny the effect of security taken before distress is levied? See *Re Newmarket Lumber Co. Ltd., International Wood Products Ltd. v. Royal Bank of Canada*, [1951] O.R. 642, [1951] 4 D.L.R. 720.]

2. Bankruptcy, Insolvency and Debt Adjustment

A.-G. B.C. v. A.-G. CAN.

In the Privy Council. [1937] A.C. 391, [1937] 1 D.L.R. 695, [1937] 1 W.W.R. 320.

Appeal by special leave from a judgment of the Supreme Court of Canada, [1936] S.C.R. 384, [1936] 3 D.L.R. 610, on a reference to determine the validity of the *Farmers' Creditors Arrangement*

Act, 1934 (Can.), c. 53, amended 1935, c. 20. The Supreme Court, Cannon J. dissenting, held that the Act was valid. Counsel for appellants argued in part as follows: The effect of the Act has been upheld as bankruptcy legislation coming under head 21 of s. 91 of the *British North America Act, 1867*—"Bankruptcy and Insolvency." The submission of all the Provinces is the same, namely, that the Act is not in its pith and substance bankruptcy, but is colourable legislation. If it is bankruptcy legislation, then it involves the right to interfere incidentally with property and civil rights in the Province. If, on the other hand, it is not bankruptcy legislation as such, but is only colourable, then the matter undoubtedly comes within property and civil rights in the Province. The fundamental characteristic of bankruptcy and insolvency legislation is that it is designed in the interests of creditors as a class. It is to provide for the rateable distribution of the assets of the debtor among his creditors whether or not the debtor is willing. The present Act, on the contrary, has none of the characteristics of bankruptcy and insolvency legislation for the following reasons: (a) It is designed for the purpose of keeping the farmer on his farm, and not to distribute his assets. (b) It is not bankruptcy but the prevention of bankruptcy. (c) The proceedings of the Act are not in course of bankruptcy proceedings, but before such proceedings. (d) An act of bankruptcy is not the basis of the proceedings but follows only thereafter in case of a failure to carry out a compromise under the Act. (e) The proposal of "compromise" so-called is not an ancillary of bankruptcy proceedings, but antecedent to and independent thereof. (f) The essential proposal for a compromise is in its features not a voluntary arrangement but a compulsory arrangement imposed by a Board on the creditors. (g) Such a scheme is made with a view not of the creditors' welfare as a class, or to distribution among them. It is made to defeat distribution. It may be without regard to their interests and solely in the interests of the debtor and with a view to protecting the value of the farm. (h) The scheme is not for the protection of the creditors, but at their expense. (i) It deals not with the assets of the debtor for the benefit of the creditors, but with the assets of the creditors for the benefit of the debtor. (j) The references in the Act to the *Dominion Bankruptcy Act* are colourable and establish no substantial connection between the two enactments. (k) The scheme treats a subject-matter which in part in some aspects may be ancillary to bankruptcy and insolvency legislation as itself the principal or primary subject-matter of legislation. (l) It has no general relation to bankruptcy and insolvency but is special legislation relative to farmers, and is or may be restricted to certain Provinces. . . . The Act sets up a new scheme which in its purpose is not to administer the farmer's property as the assets of his creditors, but to administer it in defiance of that.

[Citation of authorities.] If those authorities, which show that in all schemes of bankruptcy the basis of the scheme is the distribution of the assets of the debtor among the creditors, are sound, the present Act came in as an independent Act with its own recital for the purpose not to distribute the assets among creditors, but to prevent that in order to promote production in Canada by moneys taken from the secured creditors and given for the benefit of the farmer. . . . The Dominion of Canada does not acquire jurisdiction in regard to property and civil rights of the farmers merely because they are unable to pay their obligations as they arise: the Dominion can only deal with the farmer in that connection in the limited field of bankruptcy. It is not claimed that legislation must conform to what was bankruptcy at federation: it is not contended that matters not strictly bankruptcy legislation may not be included as ancillary or necessarily incidental. Legislation which is the antithesis of bankruptcy, however, such as the present, cannot be ancillary, and still remains within the field of the Province. There is no severable clause in the Act and the legislation is bad *in toto*.

Counsel for the Dominion were not called upon.

LORD THANKERTON: . . . The appellant raises no question as to s. 17 of the Act, which relates to interest, and falls under head 19 of s. 91 of the *British North America Act of 1867*, but he maintains that the rest of the Act does not truly form legislation relating to "bankruptcy and insolvency," but is an invasion of the sphere of the Provincial Legislatures in relation to "property and civil rights in the Province" or "matters of a merely local or private nature in the Province," which is secured to them by heads 13 and 16 of s. 92 of the *British North America Act*.

The appellant submitted that the fundamental characteristic of legislation in relation to bankruptcy and insolvency is that it is conceived in the interests of the creditors as a class, and provides for distribution of the debtor's assets among them, and he maintained that the Act here in question is not only lacking in such a characteristic, but is inconsistent therewith, and he gave twelve reasons which may be compendiously stated as follows: The Act is mainly designed to keep the debtor farmer on the land at the expense of his creditors; it deals with a stage prior to bankruptcy and insolvency, and is designed to prevent bankruptcy by means of a composition which is compulsory on creditors and defeats their interests; it deals with assets belonging to creditors for the benefit of the debtor; the references to bankruptcy are merely ancillary to the main design; and the Act has no general relation to bankruptcy and insolvency, as it refers to farmers only, and may refer to certain Provinces only.

The long title of the Act of 1934 is "An Act to facilitate compromises and arrangements between farmers and their creditors." The relevant sections of the Act of 1934, as amended by the Act of 1935, may now be referred to. [His Lordship then set out various provisions of the Act governing compositions and continued:]

In a general sense, insolvency means inability to meet one's debts or obligations; in a technical sense, it means the condition or standard of inability to meet debts or obligations, upon the occurrence of which the statutory law enables a creditor to intervene, with the assistance of a Court, to stop individual action by creditors and to secure administration of the debtor's assets in the general interest of creditors; the law also generally allows the debtor to apply for the same administration. The justification for such proceeding by a creditor generally consists in an act of bankruptcy by the debtor, the conditions of which are defined and prescribed by the statute law. In a normal community it is certain that these conditions will require reconsideration from time to time. Their Lordships are unable to hold that the statutory conditions of insolvency which enabled a creditor or the debtor to invoke the aid of the bankruptcy laws, or the classes to which these laws applied, were intended to be stereotyped under head 21 of s. 91 of the *British North America Act* so as to confine the jurisdiction of the Parliament of Canada to the legislative provisions then existing as regards these matters.

Further, it cannot be maintained that legislative provision as to compositions, by which bankruptcy is avoided, but which assumes insolvency, is not properly within the sphere of bankruptcy legislation. (*In re Companies' Creditors Arrangement Act,* [1934] S.C.R. 659.)

It will be seen from the sections above quoted that the Āct here in question relates only to a farmer who is unable to meet his liabilities as they become due, and enables him to make a proposal for a composition, extension of time or scheme of arrangement either before or after an assignment has been made, for which a precedent existed in the *Canadian Bankruptcy Act of 1919.* As defined in s. 2, an assignment means an assignment made under the *Bankruptcy Act* by a farmer. If the creditors fail to approve of the farmer's proposal, the Board of Review, on written request of a creditor or the debtor, is to endeavour to formulate "an acceptable proposal" for submission to the creditors and the debtor; if the creditors or the debtor decline to approve the Board's proposal, the Board may nevertheless confirm their proposal, and it is to bind the creditors and the debtor.

Subject to the contention by the appellants, now to be dealt with, their Lordships are of opinion that these provisions fall within head 21 of s. 91 of the *British North America Act.*

The appellant maintains that the real object of these provisions is to keep the farmers on the land for the benefit of agricultural production, and that this object is to be attained by the operations of the Board of Review, who have power to sacrifice the interests of the creditors for the benefit of the debtor farmer; he further maintains that under s. 7 the secured creditor may be deprived of that which is his property. To deal first with the last contention, their Lordships are clearly of opinion that s. 7 does not enable any creditor to be deprived of his security, but does enable the proposal for composition to provide for the reduction of the debt itself, or the extension of time for its payment, which is a familiar feature of compositions.

The appellant laid stress on the provisions of sub-s. 8 of s. 12, but that does not appear to their Lordships to be an illegitimate or unusual element to be taken into account in the consideration of composition schemes, and, indeed, the retention of the business under the management of the debtor may well be a consideration in the interests of the creditors as well as of the debtor. Its fair application appears to be well secured by the provisions of sub-ss. 3, 4 and 9. A judicial Chief Commissioner is provided for under sub-s. 3; under sub-s. 4 the Board's proposal is to be designed as an acceptable one to both parties, and this element is emphasized by sub-s. 9. Their Lordships are unable to accept the contention that the Act is not genuine legislation relating to bankruptcy and insolvency. . . .

Appeal dismissed.

[In *In re Companies' Creditors Arrangement Act*, [1934] S.C.R. 659, [1934] 4 D.L.R. 25, Duff C.J., in upholding the validity of the federal statute, declared that "legislation in respect of compositions and arrangements is a natural and ordinary component of a system of bankruptcy and insolvency law"; and further: "Matters normally constituting part of a bankruptcy scheme but not in their essence matters of bankruptcy and insolvency may, of course, from another point of view and in another aspect be dealt with by a provincial legislature; but when treated as matters pertaining to bankruptcy and insolvency, they clearly fall within the legislative authority of the Dominion."

Provincial legislative power in relation to voluntary assignments was recognized in *A.-G. Ont. v. A.-G. Can.*, [1894] A.C. 189. Dominion legislation would, of course, prevail in case of conflict. See also *L'Union St. Jacques de Montréal v. Belisle* (1874), L.R. 6 P.C. 31; *Cushing v. Dupuy* (1880), 5 App. Cas. 409.

"The exclusive authority . . . given to the Dominion Parliament to deal with all matters arising within the domain of bankruptcy and insolvency enables that Parliament to determine by legislation the relative priorities of creditors under a bankruptcy or an authorized assignment": *A.-G. Que. and Royal Bank v. Larue and A.-G. Can.*, [1928] A.C. 187, [1928] 1 D.L.R. 945, [1928] 1 W.W.R. 534. The Dominion may, hence, by its legislation limit or take away the priority or immunity of the Crown in right of a province (see, for example, *Re Clemenshaw* (1962), 33 D.L.R. (2d) 524, 38 W.W.R. 426), but unless it does so expressly the Crown in right of a province may assert its common law priority or immunity: *In re Silver Bros. Ltd., A.-G. Que. v. A.-G. Can.*, [1932] A.C. 514, [1932] 2 D.L.R. 673, [1932] 1 W.W.R. 764; *Re Navilla Ice Cream Co.*, [1934] O.R. 772, [1934] 4 D.L.R. 741. Federal power embraces not only the order of priorities on a bankruptcy but also the extent: see *Re Gingras Automobile Ltée*, [1962] S.C.R. 676, 34 D.L.R. (2d) 751.

Where a provincially-incorporated insurance company has become insolvent and a winding-up order has been made against it under the federal Winding-up Act, may provincial legislation be applied to the distribution of the proceeds of convertible securities deposited by it as a condition of provincial licensing? If the federal Winding-up Act prescribes a different order of distribution will it prevail? See *Re Wentworth Insurance Co.*, [1968] 2 O.R. 416, 69 D.L.R. (2d) 448, affirmed (*sub nom. A.-G. Ont. v. Wentworth Insurance Co.*) [1969] S.C.R. 779, 6 D.L.R. (3d) 545, 12 C.B.R. (N.S.) 265, [1969] I.L.R. 1-288.

LADORE v. BENNETT

In the Privy Council. [1939] A.C. 468, [1939] 3 D.L.R. 1, [1939] 3 All E.R. 98.

Appeal from a judgment of the Ontario Court of Appeal, [1938] O.R. 324, [1938] 3 D.L.R. 212, affirming a judgment of Hogg J. in an action involving the validity of an Ontario statute providing for the amalgamation of four municipalities and for a refunding of their debts through the retirement of existing debentures by the issue of new debentures of the new municipality of the same nominal amount but at a reduced rate of interest.

LORD ATKIN: . . . The questions raised in the case arise out of the affairs of four adjoining municipalities, the city of Windsor, the city of East Windsor, the town of Sandwich and the town of Walkerville. Before the year 1935 they were each an independent municipality exercising local government over their inhabitants. They had each of them raised loans for local purposes, amounting in the aggregate to many millions of dollars, which were represented by debentures. These debentures were simple acknowledgements of debt and gave no charge upon municipal property. In the case of East Windsor some of them were made payable outside the Province of Ontario, that is to say, in Montreal, in the Province of Quebec, and in New York. Large amounts were held by holders resident outside the Province. Closely associated with the affairs of the municipalities were various public utility corporations, the Walkerville-East Windsor Water Commission, the Walkerville Hydro-Electric Commission, and the Essex Borders Utilities Commission, whose functions need not be particularly described. They had each issued debentures which, in the case of the Essex Borders Utilities Commission and of the Walkerville-East Windsor Water Commission, for instance, purported to create a charge upon properties named therein. These debentures were in many cases held by persons resident outside the Province. These commissions had all been incorporated pursuant to statutes of the Ontario Legislature. By 1935 financial difficulties of these municipalities and their commissions had become acute. In October, 1931, East Windsor defaulted in payment of debenture interest and maturing principal. In March and December, 1932, they were followed by Sandwich and the city of Windsor, and in December, 1934, by Walkerville. Meanwhile, in 1933, the Essex Borders Commission had defaulted, while in June, 1936, the Walkerville-East Windsor Water Commission stopped payment of interest. In December, 1934, by Order in Council, a Royal Commission was appointed to inquire into the municipal and other local affairs of the four municipalities in question, particularly with regard to acts to be done and steps to be taken in connection with their amalgamation. The Commission reported in April, 1935. In the Courts of Canada the report, when tendered in evidence by the plaintiffs, was objected to by the defendants, and the objection was upheld. Before the Board the objection was withdrawn, and by consent of both parties the report was placed before their Lordships. The report disclosed a serious financial position. Commercial conditions had so changed in recent years that, in 1934, 29 per cent. of the total population was, on a daily average, in receipt of relief. Assessments had fallen in value by 38 per cent. of the peak value in 1930; taxation was at breaking point, and something like total default was threatened. The provision for maintenance in every department was entirely inadequate, while, if adequate maintenance was received in existing conditions, the credit of the area, both public and private, would be destroyed. Neither public money for improvements nor mortgage money for private building would be obtainable, nor would present mortgages be renewable, unless under some form of Government compulsion.

Their Lordships do not cite this report as evidence of the facts there found, but as indicating the materials which the Government of the Province had before them before promoting in the Legislature the statute now impugned, c. 74 of 1935, "an Act to amalgamate The City of East Windsor, The Town of Walkerville, The City of Windsor and the Town of Sandwich." The Act amalgamated the four municipalities into one municipality which was incorporated under the name of "The Corporation of The City of Windsor." As from a named date the existing municipal corporations were dissolved. A special body entitled the Windsor Finance Commission was constituted with interim powers of administering the affairs of the new city. By s. 6, sub-s. 1, it was to "have and exercise the same rights, authorities, powers and duties as by the provisions of Part III of the Department of Municipal Affairs Act, 1935, are conferred upon the said department," and the provisions of Part III were to apply to the new city. The Finance Commission, by s. 7(c), were to "undertake the preparation and submission of a plan for funding and refunding the debts of the amalgamated municipalities, upon the general basis that the debt of each of the amalgamated municipalities shall be discharged by the imposition of rates upon the rateable property in that area of the new city which formerly comprised such municipality." As far as the public utility commissions were concerned, a new commission was constituted by s. 12, sub-s. 1, entitled "The Windsor Utilities Commission." Certain powers were confided to it by s. 12, sub-s. 1, and s. 16. The Essex Borders Utilities Commission, the Waterworks Commission and Hydro-Electric Commission of the amalgamated municipalities, including the Walkerville-East Windsor Water Commission, were dissolved and ceased to exist. In pursuance of the Act the Finance Commission prepared a plan for submission to the Ontario Municipal Board. In 1936, however, an amending Act [The City of Windsor (Amalgamation) Amendment Act, c. 66 of 1936] was passed which did away with the Windsor Finance Commission and transferred its duties to the Department of Municipal Affairs for Ontario. Sects. 5, 6, 7 and 9 of the principal Act were repealed. The plan prepared by the Finance Commission for funding and refunding the debt was taken under consideration by the Municipal Board. After formulating what appears to have been an interim decision in December, 1936, the Board heard objections from creditors and others, and eventually, on June 15, 1937, made an order, which had received the consent of the new city and the majority of creditors, approving the final scheme. It is unnecessary to state the details of the scheme: generally it may be said that the former creditors receive debentures of the new city of equal nominal amount to those formerly held, but the interest is scaled down in various classes of debentures. Arrears of interest were dealt with by paying a composition in cash. It is not quite clear whether the scheme derives its statutory power from the provisions of the Amalgamation Acts of 1935 and 1936 or from the provisions of Part III of the Department of Municipal Affairs Act, 1935, or from both sources. It was prepared under s. 7 of the Amalgamation Act of 1935, but that section was repealed by the Act of 1936. It becomes necessary, in any case, to discuss the provisions of Part III of the Department of Municipal Affairs Act, 1935, for that Part is attacked by the plaintiffs as invalid, and it is expressly applied by the Amalgamation Acts to the new city and its affairs.

The Department of Municipal Affairs Act, 1935, is a general Act setting up a Department of Municipal Affairs whose duty it was to administer all acts in respect of municipal institutions and affairs. By an Act of the same date, an Act to amend the Ontario Municipal Board Act, 1932, 1935, c. 51, Part VI of the Ontario Municipal Board Act, 1932, the heading of which is "Special Jurisdiction over Defaulting Municipalities" was repealed, and the Department of Municipal Affairs Act of 1935 contained in Part III corresponding provisions under the same heading. In substance, the provisions are that if the Ontario Municipal Board is satisfied after request and upon inquiry that a municipality has failed to meet its debentures or interest when due, or failed to meet any of its other debts or liabilities, when due, owing to financial difficulties affecting the municipality, or has, or may, become financially involved or embarrassed so that default or unusual difficulty in meeting debts or obligations may ensue (as amended by the Department of Municipal Affairs Amendment Act, 1936, c. 15, c. 5), the Board may exercise the special jurisdiction and powers conferred by the Act. The powers extend to control over all the affairs of the corporation (s. 27, sub-s. 2) and include, in s. 33, powers in respect to the debenture debt and debentures of the municipality, and interest thereon, and also other indebtedness. These powers include power to order (a) the consolidation of the whole or any portion; (b) issue of debentures in payment and satisfaction of the whole or any portion of such other indebtedness, and compulsory acceptance of such debentures in payment and satisfaction thereof; (f) terms, conditions, places and times for exchange of new debentures for outstanding debentures; (g) postponement of or variation in the terms, times and places for payment of the whole or any portion of the debenture debt and outstanding debentures and other indebtedness and interest thereon and variation in the rates of such interest. It should be noticed that by s. 2(f) of the Act, "municipality" includes any local board thereof; and by s. 2(b) of the Ontario Municipal Board Act, 1932, "Local Board" includes any public utility commission. Counsel for the plaintiffs attacked the whole of the proceedings in connection with these municipalities on three grounds. He said that the relevant statutes and the authorities which they purported to give were *ultra vires* the Legislature of Ontario because they invaded the field of the Dominion as to: (1) Bankruptcy and Insolvency (s. 91

(21) of the *British North America Act,* 1867), (2) Interest (s. 91(19)); and were not within the exclusive powers of the Province because (3) they affected private rights outside the Province . . .

It appears to their Lordships that the Provincial legislation cannot be attacked on the ground that it encroaches on the exclusive legislative power of the Dominion in relation to [bankruptcy and insolvency]. Their Lordships cannot agree with the opinion of Henderson J.A. that there is no evidence that these municipalities are insolvent. Insolvency is the inability to pay debts in the ordinary course as they become due; and there appears to be no doubt that this was the condition of these corporations. But it does not follow that because a municipality is insolvent the Provincial Legislature may not legislate to provide remedies for that condition of affairs. The Province has exclusive legislative power in relation to municipal institutions in the Province: s. 92(8) of the *British North America Act,* 1867. Sovereign within its constitutional powers, the Province is charged with the local government of its inhabitants by means of municipal institutions. If local government in any particular area becomes ineffective or non-existent because of the financial difficulties of one or more municipal institutions, or for any other reason, it is not only the right, but it would appear to be the duty, of the Provincial Legislature to provide the necessary remedy, so that the health of the inhabitants and the necessities of organized life in communities should be preserved. If corporation A or B or C is unable to function satisfactorily it would appear to be elementary that the Legislature must have power to provide that the functions of one or all should be transferred to some other body or corporation. For this purpose, as the corporation could be created by the Province, so it could be dissolved, and a new corporation created as a municipal institution to perform the duties performed by the old. The result of dissolution is that the debts of the dissolved corporation disappear. Amalgamation of municipalities for the purpose of more effective administration, whether for financial or other reasons, is a common incident of local government. It is necessarily accompanied by an adjustment of financial relations. Where the former bodies are dissolved it is inevitable that the old debts disappear, to be replaced by new obligations of the new body. And in creating the new corporation with the powers of assuming new obligations it is implicit in the powers of the Legislature (sovereign in this respect) that it should place restrictions and qualifications on the obligations to be assumed. Efficient local government could not be provided in similar circumstances unless the Province were armed with these very powers, and if for strictly Provincial purposes debts may be destroyed and new debts created, it is inevitable that debtors [creditors?] should be affected whether the original creditors reside within or without the Province. They took for their debtor a corporation which at the will of the Province could lawfully be dissolved, and of its destruction they took the risk. That for the purpose of keeping control over municipal institutions the Legislature provided that a department of the Provincial government should have the means of ascertaining whether a particular municipal body was solvent or insolvent does not make its legislative provision in that regard an encroachment on the general powers of the Dominion over bankruptcy and insolvency. It is of the essence of its control over local government administered by municipalities that it should have these powers of inquiry and decision. In other words, the pith and substance of both the *Amalgamation Acts* and the *Municipal Board Act, 1932*, and the *Department of Municipal Affairs Act, 1935*, are that the Acts are passed in relation to municipal institutions in the Province. They would also, so far as the public utility commissions are concerned, be justified as having been passed in relation to local works and undertakings under s. 92(10) of the *British North America Act*.

It was suggested in argument that the impugned provisions should be declared invalid because they sought to do indirectly what could not be done directly—namely, to facilitate repudiation by Provincial municipalities of obligations incurred outside the Province. . . . But in the present case nothing has emerged even to suggest that the Legislature of Ontario at the respective dates had any purpose in view other than to legislate in times of difficulty in relation to the class of subject which was its special care—namely, municipal institutions. For the reasons given the attack upon the Acts and scheme on the ground either that they infringe the Dominion's exclusive power relating to bankruptcy and insolvency, or that they deal with civil rights outside the Province, breaks down. The statutes are not directed to insolvency legislation; they pick out insolvency as one reason for dealing in a particular way with unsuccessful institutions; and though they affect rights outside the Province they only so affect them collaterally, as a necessary incident to their lawful powers of good government within the Province.

The question of interest does not present difficulties. The above reasoning sufficiently disposes of the objection. If the Provincial Legislature can dissolve a municipal corporation and create a new one to take its place, it can invest the new corporation with such powers of incurring obligations as it pleases, and incidentally may define the amount of interest which such obligations may bear. Such legislation, if directed *bona fide* to the effective creation and control of municipal institutions, is in no way an encroachment upon the general exclusive power of the Dominion Legislature over interest.

Appeal dismissed.

[See also *Quebec Municipal Commission v. Aylmer,* [1933] 2 D.L.R. 638 (Que.); *Day v. Victoria,* [1938] 4 D.L.R. 345, [1938] 3 W.W.R. 161, 53 B.C.R. 140.]

A.-G. SASK. v. A.-G. CAN.

In the Privy Council. [1949] A.C. 110, [1949] 2 D.L.R. 145,
[1949] 1 W.W.R. 742.

Appeal by special leave from a judgment of the Supreme Court of Canada, [1947] S.C.R. 394 [1947] 3 D.L.R. 689 (Taschereau J. dissenting), invalidating on a reference s. 6 of the *Farm Security Act, 1944* (Sask. 2nd sess.), c. 30, as amended.

The *Farm Security Act,* 1944, of Saskatchewan was entitled "An Act for the protection of certain mortgagors, purchasers and lessees of farm land," and the main object of the Act was to lighten the contractual obligations of a mortgagor or purchaser of farm land in the event of the yield of grain grown on the land falling below a prescribed minimum. The earlier sections of the Act provided for relief of that nature being granted also to lessees, who rented such land on the terms that the lessor was to receive a share of the crop, but s. 6 was concerned only with the modification of the contractual rights of mortgagees or vendors of farm land in respect of the contractual payments due to them in the event of a "crop failure".

Sub-section 1 of s. 6 defined "crop failure" as meaning a "failure of grain crops grown in any year on mortgaged land or on land sold under agreement of sale, due to causes beyond the control of the mortgagor or purchaser, to the extent that the sum realized from the said crops is less than a sum equal to six dollars per acre sown to grain in such year on such land." The sub-section also contained a definition commencing on the first day of August in the year in which the crop failure occurs and ending on the thirty-first day of July in the next succeeding year." Sub-section 2 of s. 6 ran as follows:

"(2) Notwithstanding anything to the contrary, every mortgage and every agreement of sale shall be deemed to contain a condition that, in case of crop failure in any year and by reason only of such crop failure:

1. the mortgagor or purchaser shall not be required to make any payment of principal to the mortgagee or vendor during the period of suspension.

2. payment of any principal which falls due during the period of suspension and of any principal which thereafter falls due under the mortgage or agreement of sale shall become automatically postponed for one year;

3. the principal outstanding on the fifteenth day of September in the period of suspension shall on that date become automatically reduced by four per cent. thereof or by the same percentage thereof as that at which interest will accrue immediately after the said date on the principal then outstanding, whichever percentage is the greater; provided that, notwithstanding such reduction, interest shall continue to be chargeable, payable and recoverable as if the principal had not been so reduced."

VISCOUNT SIMON: In the view which their Lordships take on the constitutional validity of sub-s. 2, and on its relation to the rest of s. 6, it is not necessary to set out the remaining sub-ss. of s. 6, though they have been carefully examined to see if they throw further light on sub-s. 2. The contention of the respondents is that para. 3 of sub-s. 2 is *ultra vires* of the provincial legislature of Saskatchewan because it is an encroachment in relation to "interest"—a matter which, by s. 91, head 19, of the *British North America Act* is within the exclusive legislative power of the Dominion Parliament. It is further contended by the respondents that the impeached provision conflicts with provisions of the *Interest Act* of Canada. Reliance was also placed on head 21 of s. 91, which confers on the Dominion Parliament the exclusive power to legislate in relation to "Bankruptcy or Insolvency." On this last point their Lordships would be disposed to agree with Taschereau J. (who alone deals with it) that the respondents' contention is unsound, but the real difficulty in the appellant's way lies elsewhere.

The appellant argues that the "pith and substance" of para. 3 is "property and civil rights," a matter in relation to which the provincial legislature has an exclusive legislative power, and that in so far as para. 3 affects "interest" it does so only incidentally. In support of this view the Attorney-General for Saskatchewan relies on *Ladore v. Bennett,* [1939] A.C. 468, and especially on the concluding passage of Lord Atkin's judgment. A further ground on which the appellant contends that the impeached paragraph is *intra vires* of the Province is that its "pith and substance" is "agriculture in the Province" within the meaning of s. 95 of the *British North America Act,* and that it is not repugnant to any Act of the Parliament of Canada such as is referred to in that section.

It is convenient to deal first with this last contention, which provided a chief ground on which the dissenting judgment of Taschereau J. was based. There was abundant evidence that agriculture is the main industry of Saskatchewan and that it is the principal source of revenue of its inhabitants. It is moreover clear that the result of the impeached legislation, if it is validly enacted, would be to relieve in some degree a certain class of farmers from financial difficulties due to the uncertainties of their farming operations. But, as Rand J. points out, there is a distinction between legislation "in relation to" agriculture and legislation which may produce a favourable effect on the strength and stability of that industry. Consequential effects are not the same thing as legislative subject-matter. It is "the true nature and character of the legislation"—not its ultimate economic results—that matters (*Russell v. The Queen,* 7 App. Cas. 829, at p. 840). Here what is sought to be statutorily modified is a contract between two parties one of which is an agriculturist but the other of which is a lender of money. However broadly the phrase "agriculture in the Province" may be construed, and whatever advantages to farmers the re-shaping of their mortgages or agreements for sale might confer, their Lordships are unable to take the view that this legislation can be regarded as valid on the ground that it is enacted in relation to agriculture.

A more difficult question is raised by the alternative contention that the legislation is in relation to civil rights in the Province. Contractual rights are, generally speaking, one kind of civil rights and, were it not that the Dominion has an exclusive power to legislate in relation to "interest," the argument that the provincial legislature has the power, and the exclusive power, to vary provisions for the payment of interest contained in contracts in the province could not be overthrown. But proper allowance must be made for the allocation of the subject-matter of "interest" to the Dominion legislature under head 19 of s. 91 of the *British North America Act.* There is another qualification to the otherwise unrestricted power of the provincial legislature to deal with civil rights in head 18 "Bills of Exchange and Promissory Notes." The Dominion power to legislate in relation to interest cannot be understood to be limited to a power to pass statutes dealing with usury such as were repealed in the United Kingdom in 1854 (17 & 18 Vict., c. 90). So restricted a construction was rejected by the Judicial Committee in *Board of Trustees of Lethbridge Irrigation District v. Independent Order of Foresters and Attorney-General for Canada,* [1940] A.C. 513, at pp. 530-1, for reasons stated by Viscount Caldecote. The validity of the *Interest Act* of the Parliament of Canada (R.S.C. 1927, c. 102) has not been challenged in any particular. Section 2 of this statute provides: "Except as otherwise provided by this or by any other Act of the Parliament of Canada, any person may stipulate for, allow and exact, on any contract or agreement whatsoever, any rate of interest or discount which is agreed upon." It is therefore clear that a provincial statute which varies the stipulation in a contract as to the rate of interest to be exacted would not be consonant with the existence and exercise of the exclusive Dominion power to legislate in respect of interest. The Dominion power would likewise be invaded if the provincial enactment was directed to postponing the contractual date for the payment of interest without altering the rate, for this would equally be legislating in respect of interest.

There thus remain two questions to be considered: first, does the provincial statute now under consideration operate to the above effect? And secondly, even if it does, can the consequent invalidity be avoided because this result should be regarded as merely incidental to the achievement of the real and valid statutory purpose, so that, although the topic of interest is trenched upon, the subject of interest is not the pith and substance of the Act? The first of these questions must be answered in the light of an established rule of construction in such cases, namely, that regard must be had to the substance and not to the mere form of the enactment, so that "you cannot do that indirectly which you are prohibited from doing directly" (per Lord Halsbury in *Madden v. Nelson and Fort Sheppard Ry. Co.,* [1899] A.C. 626, at p. 627). If, under colour of an arrangement which purports to deal only with the principal of a debt, it is really the contractual obligation to pay interest on the principal which is modified, the enactment should be regarded as dealing with interest. With this rule in mind, their Lordships have examined the language and effect of s. 6 of the *Farm Security Act* with much care, and they have been greatly assisted in this task by the arguments of counsel on either side. Sub-section 2 of s. 6 provides in effect that, in the event of crop failure, (a) the mortgagor or purchaser shall not be required to make any payment of principal during the period of suspension, (b) the payment of any principal which is contractually due during that period and any principal which thereafter falls due shall be postponed for one year, (c) the principal outstanding on September 15 in the period of suspension shall on that date become automatically reduced by 4 per cent. thereof "or by the same percentage thereof as that at which interest will accrue immediately after the said date on the principal then outstanding, whichever percentage is the greater," but (d) notwithstanding such reduction, interest shall continue to be chargeable, payable and recoverable as if the principal had not been so reduced.

It is not in dispute that mortgages or agreements to defer payment of purchase money of land in Saskatchewan, practically without exception, provide for interest on outstanding principal at a rate greater than 4 per cent. per annum. The effect, therefore, is to reduce the outstanding principal, in the event of crop failure, by an amount equal to the amount of interest called for under the contract, but to require this same amount of interest to continue to be paid as though the outstanding principal had not been reduced. If the sub-section had said in plain terms that for the period of suspension there should be no interest charged and that the payment of outstanding principal should be postponed, the result (at any rate in the first year of suspension) to the mortgagee or vendor would be the same. Moreover, such agreements normally stipulate for a "rate" of interest on outstanding principal, and a "rate" is the ratio which the sum payable as interest bears to the amount of such outstanding principal. To provide that principal is to be reduced by statute but that the amount to be paid as interest is to remain unaltered is necessarily to increase the rate on the principal outstanding. But provincial legislation which alters a stipulated rate of interest would conflict with s. 2 of the *Interest Act*. These considerations lead their Lordships to confirm the conclusion at which the majority of the Supreme Court has arrived, that para. 3 of sub-s. 2 of s. 6 trenches upon the Dominion field. It is obvious that the language used has been ingeniously chosen in an endeavour to avoid a conflict with Dominion powers and legislation, but in the view of their Lordships the endeavour is not successful. This view of the matter renders it unnecessary to determine what would be the correct application of the words used in the difficult situation of successive years of suspension analysed in the judgment of Kellock J.

Secondly, can the remaining argument be upheld that this interference with the topic of interest none the less remains valid because it is merely incidental to the exercise of a valid power to legislate for a modification of principal debts? On this, it is to be observed that there is not only an exclusive power to legislate in relation to interest vested in the Dominion Parliament, but that such legislation has been enacted in the *Interest Act*. . . . Apart, however, from the obstacle created by the existence of the *Dominion Interest Act*, their Lordships are unable to take the view that the dealing with interest is only incidental, for it lies at the heart of the matter. Their Lordships are not called on to discuss, and do not pronounce on, a case where a provincial enactment renders null and void the whole contract to repay money with interest. Here the contracts survive, and once the conclusion is reached that, as Kerwin J. said, "the legislation here in question is definitely in relation to interest," reliance on such a decision as *Ladore v. Bennett* is misplaced. The provincial legislation there considered was legislation in relation to "municipal institutions in the Province," and, as Viscount Caldecote pointed out in the *Lethbridge* case: "having come to the conclusion that the pith and substance of the legislation in question related to one or more of the classes of subjects under s. 92, the Board had no difficulty in holding that the regulation of the interest payable on the debentures of the new City was not an invasion of Dominion powers under head 19 of s. 91."

Lastly, does the invalidity of para. 3 involve the consequence that s. 6 is *ultra vires* as a whole? Their Lordships agree with the Supreme Court that it does. . . .

Appeal dismissed.

[Having regard to this decision, is there any substance at all in the concurrent "agriculture" power? And is not the conclusion that the legislation is in relation to "interest" a negation of a basic assumption of the legislation that the farmer must look to his crop yield to pay off the debt on his farm?

Section 38 of the *Judicature Act, R.S.O. 1970,* c. 228 provides that "interest is payable in all cases in which it is now payable by law or in which it has been usual for a jury to allow it". For an application of this provision without any reference to its constitutionality, see *Toronto Ry. Co. v. Toronto,* [1906] A.C. 117.

Is provincial legislation providing for interest on unpaid taxes *intra vires?* See *The Queen v. Harper* (1971), 22 D.L.R. (3d) 230, 3 N.B.R. (2d) 655.]

A.-G. ONT. v. BARFRIED ENTERPRISES LTD.

In the Supreme Court of Canada. [1963] S.C.R. 570, 42 D.L.R. (2d) 137.

Appeal from a judgment of the Ontario Court of Appeal, [1962] O.R. 1103, 35 D.L.R. (2d) 449, reversing an order of Clark Co. Ct. J. and declaring The Ontario *Unconscionable Transactions Relief Act* to be invalid.

JUDSON J. (for Taschereau C.J.C., Fauteux and Hall JJ. as well as for himself):

The Attorney-General for Ontario appeals from a judgment of the Ontario Court of Appeal which declared The *Unconscionable Transactions Relief Act,* R.S.O. 1960, c. 410, to be unconstitutional. The Attorney-General for Quebec has intervened and supports the appeal. No other province is represented. The appeal is opposed by Barfried Enterprises Ltd., the lender under the impugned transaction, and by the Attorney-General of Canada.

One Ralph Douglas Sampson, the borrower, applied in the County Court of the County of Wellington, to have revised a certain mortgage transaction with the respondent Barfried. The mortgage is dated September 3, 1959, and was for a face amount of $2,250 with interest at 7 per cent. per annum. The sum actually advanced was $1,500 less a commission of $67.50. The difference between the $1,500 and the face amount of $2,250 was made up of a bonus and other charges. The County Judge set aside the mortgage in part and revised it to provide for payment of a principal sum of $1,500 with interest at 11 per cent. per annum. No constitutional issue was raised before him.

Barfried raised this issue for the first time in the Court of Appeal. Briefly, The *Unconscionable Transactions Relief Act* empowers the Court to grant specified relief in respect of money lent where it finds that the 'cost of the loan' is excessive and the transaction harsh and unconscionable. 'Cost of the loan' is defined in the Act to mean, among other things, 'the whole cost to the debtor of money lent and includes interest, discount, subscription, premium, dues, bonus, commission, brokerage fees and charges.' This was held by the Court of Appeal to be legislation in relation to interest, its essential purpose being to afford a remedy to a borrower to have the contract of loan modified, by having interest, 'in the broad sense of the term as compensation for the loan', reduced. The Court also held that the Act was in direct conflict with s. 2 of the *Interest Act*, R.S.C. 1952, c. 156.

The essence of the judgment appealed from is contained in the following passage from the reasons for judgment of the Court of Appeal:

"The statute is applicable to only one kind of contract—a money-lending contract. Its essential purpose and object is to provide a remedy to a borrower to enable him to have the terms of such a contract modified. The end result of an application to the Court in accordance with its provisions, if the borrower is entitled to succeed, must be that the interest in the broad sense of that term, payable as compensation for the loan will be reduced. It matters not, in my opinion, whether this result is achieved through the intervention of a provision in the Act itself fixing a stated rate or scale of interest. In either case it is unquestionably legislation in relation to interest under the pith and substance rule, and, in my opinion, clearly invalid as an infringement of the exclusive legislative power committed to Parliament. Moreover it is in direct conflict with the provisions of s. 2 of the *Interest Act*, R.S.C. 1952, c. 156. Accordingly, it is beyond the province's legislative competence to enact."

Both provinces submit common grounds of error:

(a) That the Act is legislation in relation to a matter coming within s. 92(13) of the *British North America Act*, Property and Civil Rights in the Province, the subject-matter being rescission and reformation of a contract of loan under the conditions defined by the Act;

(b) That in so far as the Act affects any matter coming within the Classes of Subjects assigned by the *British North America Act* to the exclusive legislative authority of the Parliament of Canada, it does so only incidentally;

(c) That there is no conflict or repugnancy between the provisions of the Act and any validly enacted federal legislation.

The powers of the Court are stated in s. 2 of the Act, which reads:

'2. Where in respect of money lent, the court finds that, having regard to the risk and to all the circumstances, the cost of the loan is excessive and that the transaction is harsh and unconscionable, the court may,

(a) re-open the transaction and take an account between the creditor and the debtor;

(b) notwithstanding any statement or settlement of account or any agreement purporting to close previous dealings and create a new obligation, re-open any account already taken and relieve the debtor from payment of any sum in excess of the sum adjudged by the Court to be fairly due in respect of the principal and the cost of the loan;

(c) order the creditor to repay any such excess if the same has been paid or allowed on account by the debtor;

(d) set aside either wholly or in part or revise or alter any security given or agreement made in respect of the money lent, and, if the creditor has parted with the security, order him to indemnify the debtor.'

The terms 'money lent' and 'cost of the loan' are defined as follows:

'"Money lent" includes money advanced on account of any person in any transaction that, whatever its form may be, is substantially one of money-lending or securing the repayment of money so advanced and includes and has always included a mortgage within the meaning of *The Mortgages Act*, R.S.O. 1950, c. 402, s. 1; 1960 c. 127, s. 1.

'"Cost of the loan" means the whole cost to the debtor of money lent and includes interest, discount, subscription, premium, dues, bonus, commission, brokerage fees and charges, but not actual lawful and necessary disbursements made to a registrar of deeds, a master or local master of titles, a clerk of a county or district court, a sheriff or a treasurer of a municipality.'

In my opinion all these submissions are well founded and the Act is within the power of the provincial Legislature. The foundation for the judgment under appeal is to be found in the adoption of a wide definition of the subject-matter of interest used in the *Saskatchewan Farm Security Act* reference, [1947] S.C.R. 394 at 411, [1947] 3 D.L.R. 689. The judgment of this Court in that case was affirmed in the Privy Council, [1949] A.C. 110, [1949] 1 W.W.R. 742, [1949] 2 D.L.R. 145. Interest was defined:

'In general terms, the return or consideration or compensation for the use or retention by one person of a sum of money, belonging to, in a colloquial sense, or owed to, another.'

This is substantially the definition running through the three editions of Halsbury. However, in the third edition (27 Hals. 3rd. ed., p. 7) the text continues:

'Interest accrues *de die in diem* even if payable only at intervals, and is, therefore, apportionable in point of time between persons entitled in succession to the principal.'

The day-to-day accrual of interest seems to me to be an essential characteristic. All the other items mentioned in *The Unconscionable Transactions Relief Act* except discount lack this characteristic. They are not interest. In most of these unconscionable schemes of lending the vice is in the bonus.

In the cases decided in this Court under s. 6 of the *Interest Act,* it is settled that a bonus is not interest for the purpose of determining whether there has been compliance with the Act. Section 6 reads:

'. . . whenever any principal money or interest secured by mortgage of real estate is, by the same, made payable on the sinking fund plan, or on any plan under which the payments of principal money and interest are blended . . . no interest whatever shall be . . . recoverable . . . unless the mortgage contains a statement showing the amount of such principal money and the rate of interest chargeable thereon, calculated yearly or half-yearly, not in advance.'

Schroeder J.A. cited *Singer v. Goldhar* (1924), 55 O.L.R. 267, [1924] 2 D.L.R. 141, as defining interest in wide terms. In *Singer v. Goldhar* there was no provision for interest in the mortgage but there was a very big bonus. The Court of Appeal held that this infringed s. 6 of the *Interest Act,* the bonus being the same thing as interest. But in *Asconi Building Corporation v. Vocisano,* [1947] S.C.R. 358 at 365, Kerwin J. pointed out that *London Loan and Savings Co. of Canada v. Meagher,* [1930] S.C.R. 378, 2 D.L.R. 849, had overruled *Singer v. Goldhar.* It is now established that in considering s. 6 of the *Interest Act,* a bonus is not interest and the fact that interest may be payable on a total sum which includes a bonus does not involve an infringement of s. 6 of the Act. This was recognized in all the reasons delivered in the *Asconi* case. It was in this context that the wide definition of interest above referred to was used in the *Saskatchewan Reference* case. The Court held that the subject-matter of the legislation was interest and that to call it a reduction of principal did not change its character.

There is, therefore, error in the judgment of Schroeder J.A. in following *Singer v. Goldhar* in holding that interest in the wide sense includes bonus instead of following the subsequent cases which over-rule it.

The *Lethbridge Northern Irrigation* case, [1940] A.C. 513, 1 W.W.R. 502, 2 D.L.R. 273, and the *Saskatchewan Farm Security* case, [1947] S.C.R. 394, 3 D.L.R. 689, do not govern the present case. In the first of these cases, provincial legislation reduced the rate of interest on provincial debentures or provincially-guaranteed debentures. This legislation was concerned with interest in its simplest sense and nothing more and was held to be *ultra vires.*

The *Saskatchewan Farm Security* case was treated as being on the same subject or matter. Legislation which provided that in case of crop failure as defined by the Act, the principal obligation of the mortgagor or purchaser of a farm should be reduced by 4 per cent. in that year but that interest should continue to be payable as if the principal had not been reduced, was held to be legislation in relation to interest.

Day v. Victoria, [1938] 3 W.W.R. 161, 53 B.C.R. 140, [1938] 4 D.L.R. 345, and *Ladore v. Bennett,* [1939] A.C. 468, [1939] 2 W.W.R. 566, [1939] 3 D.L.R. 1, come much clcser to the present problem. In *Day v. Victoria,* legislation altering the rate of interest of municipal debentures was held to be incidental to a recasting of the city debt structure and was within the competence of the province under s. 92(8) 'Municipal Institutions in the Province', and s. 92(13) 'Property and Civil Rights in the Province.' In *Ladore v. Bennett* a reduction in the rate of interest on municipal debentures was incidental to an amalgamation of four municipalities and a consolidation of their separate indebtedness and the issue by the new municipality of its own debentures in place of the old but at a reduced rate of interest.

The issue in this appeal is to determine the true nature and character of the Act in question and, in particular, of s. 2 above quoted. The Act deals with rights arising from contract and is *prima facie* legislation in relation to civil rights and, as such, within the exclusive jurisdiction of the province under s. 92(13). Is it removed from the exclusive provincial legislative jurisdiction by s. 91(19) of the Act, which assigns jurisdiction over interest to the federal authority? In my opinion, it is not legislation in relation to interest but legislation relating to annulment or reformation of contract on the grounds set out in the Act, namely, (a) that the cost of the loan is excessive, and (b) that the transaction is harsh and unconscionable. The wording of the statute indicates that it is not the rate or amount of interest which is the concern of the legislation but whether the transaction as a whole is one which it would be proper to maintain as having been freely consented to by the debtor. If one looks at it from the point of view of English law it might be classified as an extension of the doctrine of undue influence. As pointed out by the Attorney-General for Quebec, if one looks at it from the point of view of the civil law, it can be classified as an extension of the doctrine of lesion dealt with in articles 1001 to 1012 of the *Civil Code*. The theory of the legislation is that the Court is enabled to relieve a debtor, at least in part, of the obligations of a contract to which in all the circumstances of the case he cannot be said to have given a free and valid consent. The fact that interference with such a contract may involve interference with interest as one of the constituent elements of the contract is incidental. The legislature considered this type of contract as one calling for its interference because of the vulnerability of the contract as having been imposed on one party by extreme economic necessity. The Court in a proper case is enabled to set aside the contract, rewrite it and impose the new terms.

This legislation raises the very case which the Privy Council refrained from deciding in the *Saskatchewan Farm Security* case when it said, at p. 126 A.C.:

> 'Their Lordships are not called on to discuss, and do not pronounce on, a case where a provincial enactment renders null and void the whole contract to repay money with interest. Here the contracts survive, and once the conclusion is reached that, as Kerwin J. said, 'the legislation here in question is definitely in relation to interest,' reliance on such a decision as *Ladore v. Bennett* is misplaced.'

Under the Ontario statute an exercise of judicial power necessarily involves the nullity or setting aside of the contract and the substitution of a new contractual obligation based upon what the Court deems it reasonable to write within the statutory limitations. Legislation such as this should not be characterized as legislation in relation to interest. I would hold that it was validly enacted, that no question of conflict arises.

I would therefore reverse the order of the Court of Appeal for Ontario and hold that the *Unconscionable Transactions Relief Act* is within the powers of the Legislature of the Province of Ontario. . . ."

CARTWRIGHT J.: . . . The *Unconscionable Transactions Relief Act* appears to me to be legislation in relation to Property and Civil Rights in the Province and the Administration of Justice in the Province, rather than legislation in relation to Interest. Its primary purpose and effect are to enlarge the equitable jurisdiction to give relief against harsh and unconscionable bargains which the Courts have long exercised; it affects, but only incidentally, the subject-matter of Interest specified in head 19 of s. 91 of the *British North America Act*. For this reason and for the reasons given by my brother Judson I agree with his conclusion that The *Unconscionable Transactions Relief Act* is not *ultra vires* of the Legislature of Ontario.

Particular cases may arise in which the provisions of the Provincial Act will come into conflict with those of the Dominion Act. In such cases the Dominion Act will of course prevail. The case at bar does not appear to me to be such a case. It has not been suggested that the applicant could have obtained any relief from a bargain to pay interest at 7 per cent. on the amount actually advanced to him. It is of the items other than interest making up the 'cost of the loan' that complaint is made. . . ."

MARTLAND J. (for himself and Ritchie J.), (dissenting): . . . It is the contention of the appellant, the Attorney-General for Ontario, supported by the intervenant, the Attorney-General of Quebec, that this legislation is within the jurisdiction of the Province to enact, under subss. 13 and 16 of s. 92 of the *British North America Act,* as relating to Property and Civil Rights in the Province and to Matters of a merely local or private Nature in the Province.

Whether or not this contention could be maintained successfully, in the absence of legislation by the Parliament of Canada in the same field, it is unnecessary for me to consider, since I have reached the conclusion that the provisions of the Act under consideration come into conflict directly with the provisions of s. 2 of the *Interest Act,* R.S.C. 1952, c. 156, which provides as follows:

'2. Except as otherwise provided by this or by any other Act of the Parliament of Canada, any person may stipulate for, allow and exact, on any contract or agreement whatsoever, any rate of interest or discount that is agreed upon.'

That the validity of the provisions of the *Interest Act,* under s. 91(19) of the *British North America Act,* is unquestionable was stated by Viscount Caldecote, L.C. in *Board of Trustees of the Lethbridge Northern Irrigation District v. Independent Order of Forresters,*

[1940] A.C. 513 at 531. Section 2 of that Act, above quoted, provides that, except as provided by that Act or any other Act of the Parliament of Canada, a person may not only stipulate for any rate of interest or discount that is agreed upon, but may exact the same. Parliament has, therefore, given to a creditor, who has agreed with his debtor upon a rate of interest or discount, the legal right to demand and to enforce payment of the same. . . .

The power of the Court to act under [the Ontario] Act arises only if it has found that the cost of the loan is excessive. It is true that it must also find the transaction to be harsh and unconscionable, but it may happen, as it did in the present case, that the judge who hears the case decides that the transaction is harsh and unconscionable because of the excessive cost of the loan. The result is that the very Court to which a creditor must resort in order to enforce payment of the interest or discount which the Interest Act says he may exact is, by the Provincial legislation, empowered to decide whether that interest or discount is, in all the circumstances, excessive. Furthermore, if that Court decides that it is excessive and that the transaction is harsh and unconscionable, it may relieve the debtor of the obligation of paying that portion of his obligation which it considers to be excessive, and thus is in a position to relieve him from the payment of an obligation which the Parliament of Canada has stated the creditor is entitled to exact from him.

In these circumstances there is a direct conflict between the two statutes, and, that being so, the legislation of the Canadian Parliament, validly enacted, must prevail. . . .

In my opinion, therefore, the legislation in question is *ultra vires* of the Ontario Legislature. . .''

Appeal allowed.

[The *Saskatchewan Farm Security Act* case and the *Barfried* case represent the dilemmas for provincial legislatures arising from the federal interest power. Can the two cases stand together? The problem raised by these cases was adumbrated in the early decision of *Lynch v. Canada North-West Land Co.* (1891), 19 S.C.R. 204, where the Supreme Court sustained a provincial statute providing, *inter alia*, that if municipal taxes were paid after a stipulated date, 10 per cent of the amount of the tax was to be paid in addition. After stating that the federal power in relation to interest encompassed contractual interest, Ritchie C.J. said, with reference to the 10 per cent penalty provision, that "had it been specifically named as interest I am of opinion that it was an incident to the right of taxation vested in the municipal authority, and though more than the rate allowed by the Dominion statute in matters of contract, in no way in conflict with the authority secured to the Dominion Parliament over interest by the British North America Act, but must be read consistently with that as within the power given to the local legislature under its power to deal with municipal institutions. . . ."

A different kind of case is *Lethbridge Northern Irrigation District Trustees v. I.O.F. and A.-G. Can.; The King v. I.O.F. and A.-G. Can.,* [1940] A.C. 513, [1940] 2 D.L.R. 273, [1940] 1 W.W.R. 502, where provincial legislation which simply halved the interest payable on provincial debentures and provincially guaranteed debentures was held *ultra vires*. The Court rejected an argument that the legislation respecting the provincial debentures was supportable under s. 92(3) of the B.N.A. Act respecting "the borrowing of money on the sole credit of the Province". Would it have made any difference in this case if the legislation had provided for compulsory refunding and a lower rate of interest as part of the refinancing programme?

The *Lethbridge* case reasserted that federal competence in relation to interest covered contractual interest and, rejecting an argument that it was limited to usurious interest, the Court stated that the Dominion "might very well include in an Act dealing generally with the subject of interest provisions to prevent harsh transactions". *Quaere,* in view of the *Barfried* case, *supra,* is there room for the concurrent operation of the *Small Loans Act,* R.S.C. 1970, c. S-11, s. 2 (raising the limit of its application to $1,500) which defines "cost of a loan" in terms similar to those in the Ontario *Unconscionable Transactions Relief Act,* and stipulates the maximum that may be charged by a money-lender on pain of a summary conviction penalty? In *Regina v. Exchange Realty Co. Ltd.* (1963), 42 D.L.R. (2d) 682, 45 W.W.R. 346, the Act was held to be valid federal legislation in relation to interest and to have paramount effect when it was challenged by an unlicensed money-lender who refused to permit inspection of his books under s. 9 which provides for such inspection for assurance of compliance with the Act.]

REFERENCE RE ALBERTA DEBT ADJUSTMENT ACT

In the Supreme Court of Canada. [1942] S.C.R. 31,
[1942] 1 D.L.R. 1.

Reference to the Supreme Court of Canada to determine the validity of the *Debt Adjustment Act,* 1937 (Alta.), c. 9, as amended. The Act was in four parts, but Part II had been replaced. There was a preliminary part containing definitions, including one stating that a " 'resident debtor' means a person who is a debtor and who is an actual resident of and personally living in the province, and includes the personal representative or representatives, son, daughter, widow or widower, of a deceased resident debtor, and includes a family corporation which is a debtor" as therein mentioned. There was also a definition of "resident farmer." In s. 3 there was provision for the constitution of a Debt Adjustment Board, to consist of one, two or three members appointed by the Lieutenant-Governor in Council. The powers of the board could be exercised by any single member or by any person designated by the board with the approval of the Lieutenant-Governor. Under s. 6 the board had power to make "inquiries . . . with regard to the property of any resident debtor or resident farmer," and might examine the debtor or any other persons under oath and had the same power as a commissioner under *"The Public Inquiries Act."*

Part I of the Act began with s. 8 which in its first subsection enacted as follows:

"8. (1) Unless the board or any person designated by the board under the provisions of this Act, issues a permit in writing giving consent thereto:—(a) no action or suit for the recovery of any money which is recoverable as a liquidated demand or debt in respect of any claim enforceable by virtue of any rule of law or equity or by virtue of any statute, except money payable in respect of rates and taxes payable pursuant to any statute, and debts owing to a hospital for hospital service; and (b) no proceedings by way of execution, attachment or garnishment; and (c) no action or proceeding for the sale under or foreclosure of a mortgage on land, or for cancellation, rescission or specific performance of an agreement for sale of land or for recovery of possession of land, whether in court or otherwise; and (d) no action or proceeding to sell land under or in satisfaction of any judgment or mechanic's lien; and (e) no seizure or distress under an execution or under any lease or any tenancy howsoever created, lien, chattel mortgage, conditional sale agreement, crop payment agreement or an attornment as tenant under any agreement for sale or mortgage, and no sale or other proceedings thereunder either by virtue of rights of property at common law or under a statute passed prior to this Act; (f) no proceedings by a lessor, mortgagee, vendor, or other person claiming possession of a share of crop in any case where the provisions of *The Crop Payments Act* apply; and (g) no action respecting such other class of legal or other proceedings as may be brought within the provisions of this section by order of the Lieutenant-Governor in Council,—shall be taken, made or continued by any person whomever against a resident debtor in any case." Sub-sec. 3 provided that the section should not apply to any contract made or entered into by a debtor where the whole of the original consideration for the contract arose on or after July 1, 1936, but should apply to (among other things) any judgment obtained before July 1, 1936. By sub-s. 5: "the board may at any time in its discretion cancel or suspend any permit which has been previously issued under the section by the board." Under s. 9 no permit was to be granted in respect of any proceedings on a mortgage of farm lands or an agreement for sale thereof, if those proceedings led to foreclosure by reason only of the temporary impossibility owing to abnormal depreciation in values of realizing the probable normal value of the security. Under s. 10 a creditor might apply for a permit to commence or continue any action against a resident debtor, and the board in that case must make its proper inquiries, and thereupon might issue a permit, or refuse, or adjourn the application for such period as it thought fit. By s. 11 it was provided that the time during which proceedings were prohibited by the board did not run against the creditor under the *Limitation of Actions Act, 1935*.

Part III of the Act related to negotiations for agreements for the adjustment of debts of resident debtors. Section 21 provided that any resident debtor, or the creditor of any resident debtor, could by written application call on the board to investigate the resident debtor's financial position, and to endeavour to negotiate an agreement for the settlement of the debtor's debts, either in full or by a composition. The board was to have all the extensive powers of inquiry conferred by the Act. Any agreement between a resident debtor and a creditor made through the agency of the board, however informal, was to be binding (s. 22) and the board (s. 23) was to endeavour to bring about an agreement between the resident debtor and his creditors whereby the secured and unsecured debts of the debtor were reduced to an amount which, in the opinion of the board, was in accordance with the ability of the debtor to pay, either presently or in the future, having regard to the productive capacity of the farm and its equipment and the average net prices of agricultural produce between the date of the debt being incurred and the date of adjustment (see ss. 22 and 23).

Part IV contained provisions specially applicable to resident farmers. Section 26 provided that a resident farmer who was in default on a proposal formulated and confirmed under the *Farmers' Creditors Arrangement Act, 1934* (a Federal Act: 1934, S.C. 24-25, Geo. 5, c. 53) could not be proceeded against by his creditor by any of the proceedings set out in s. 8 of the *Debt Adjustment Act, 1937,* unless the board issued a written consent under that section. Section 27 provided that a chattel mortgage given by a resident farmer after May 1, 1934, to secure a past debt should be invalid unless approved by the board within sixty days. By s. 28 a resident farmer could be authorized by the board, in order to supply his own necessities or fodder or seed grain, to sell free of encumbrance any goods or chattels subject to a chattel mortgage given by him. By s. 29 a resident farmer who was a lessee of land under a crop share lease might be authorized by the board to retain for his own use crop deliverable to the lessor.

Part V contained miscellaneous provisions, of which, s. 36 was the most noticeable. It provided for an appeal by any person who deemed himself aggrieved by the action of the board in granting or refusing a permit or its other orders "to a judge of the Supreme Court sitting with a jury of six persons." Sub-section 8 provided that the question as to the action of the board in withholding or granting a permit, or in giving any direction under the Act was to "be a question of fact for the determination of the jury under proper instructions from the judge and there shall be no appeal from such determination or from any judgment or order made thereon." The question of fact was nowhere defined. Section 32 provided for the imposition of a penalty, namely, a fine not exceeding two hundred and fifty dollars and, in default of payment, a term of imprisonment with hard labour not exceeding three months, or both, on any person who "wilfully takes or continues any action or proceeding or makes or continues any seizure or sells or disposes of a chattel in violation of the provisions of this Act or the regulations."

DUFF C.J. (for himself, Rinfret, Davis, Kerwin, Hudson and Taschereau JJ.): By section 8, sub-section 1(a), of the *Debt Adjustment Act*, a legal right which the owner of it is entitled to enforce is converted into a conditional right, enforceable only by grace of a permit from the Board granting to the owner of it a dispensation from the incidence of the general rule.

The authority of the Board may be considered with reference to debts arising by virtue of statutes, or legal rules, that the legislature is powerless to repeal or vary, as well as with reference to creditors whose powers and status it is incompetent to impair, or whose undertakings, or business, the legislature is incompetent to regulate.

It is most important, I think, not to lose sight of the arbitrary nature of the Board's authority. The powers of the Board, it will be noticed, may be exercised by any single member of the Board, or by any person designated by the Board, with the approval of the Lieutenant-Governor in Council. *Ex hypothesi* the debt or liquidated demand, which the Board has to consider on any application for a permit, may be one which, but for the statute, would admittedly be enforceable by law; and in discussing the operation of the enactment I shall assume that we are dealing with a debt, or demand, admittedly so enforceable.

The statute prescribes no rule, or principle, by which the Board, or its designated agent, is to be guided in granting, or refusing, a permit; nor does it give any clue to the considerations upon which the Board is to act. I do not think that any Court can, with any confidence, form a judgment as to the reasons by which the Board will be guided, except that the Board may be assumed to act in accordance with its own conception of its duty in each particular case. It is the duty of the Board, under section 10 of the Act, to make such enquiries as it may deem proper into the circumstances, but that section makes it clear, I think, that it is for the Board exclusively to decide what are the considerations by which it ought to be influenced in granting, or refusing, an application for a permit, or adjourning the application for such period as it "may deem advisable under the circumstances." In effect the Board is empowered to exercise in each particular case an arbitrary determination. The appeal to a jury, given by the amending statute, on which it is to decide as a question of fact whether the determination of the Board is to stand, or is to be changed, merely gives an appeal from the arbitrary determination of one authority to the arbitrary determination of another. The consequence of all this is that all creditors who are the owners of debts, or liquidated demands, that apart from the statute, would be presently enforceable by law, have their rights in respect of their enforceability by action, or suit, taken away, and for them they have substituted the possibility of obtaining from this authority permission to enforce them.

The distinction between right and remedy is often a useful distinction, but an enactment which takes away the remedy by action, which the law otherwise would give to the creditor in respect of his debt, and substitutes therefor the chance of obtaining, by the arbitrary act of a public authority, permission to enforce a remedy is, I think, something more than an enactment relating to procedure. It strikes, I think, at the substance of the creditor's rights. The enactment is repugnant to the provisions of Dominion statutes relating to matters within the exclusive jurisdiction of the Dominion Parliament, provisions creating or directly giving rise to, or recognizing, obligations in the nature of debts and liquidated demands: for example, certain provisions of the *Bills of Exchange Act*, section 125 of the *Bank Act*, and provisions in respect of calls made by a Dominion company upon the holders of unpaid shares (see section 44, *Companies Act*.) Such instances could be multiplied.

There is another class of cases that I have just alluded to, the consideration of which leaves it, I think, very clear that in attempting to establish an authority of this character a provincial legislature is exceeding its authority. Section 91 of the *British North America Act* gives to the Parliament of Canada exclusive control over certain types of businesses and undertakings. I particularly refer to two classes of business only. The first of these, that of banks, perhaps illustrates the point most strikingly. The lending of money is a principal part of the business of any bank. A debt arising from a loan by a bank to a customer will, speaking generally, fall within section 8(1)(a), and the bank's right to enforce repayment is by the enactment conditioned upon the existence of a permit. It is in the power of the Board to refuse a permit in all such cases, or in the case of any particular debt. This power of selection seems to involve a considerable power of regulation of the business of the banks. It is, I think, incompetent to the legislature to establish any such authority. I think the case of banking is, perhaps, from this point of view, the most striking case, although the application of the authority of the Board to companies engaged in operating Dominion undertakings, such as Dominion railway companies and companies engaged in operating lines of ocean shipping, might well exceed the ambit of provincial authority.

What I have said is sufficient, in my opinion, to show that subsection (1)(a) of section 8 is *ultra vires*. I assume that debts and liquidated demands falling entirely (that is to say, exclusively) under the regulative authority of the province, as being "civil rights within the province," could be dealt with by a province by an enactment having the characteristics of section 8(1)(a), but limited to such debts and demands. It is not necessary to decide it, but I assume that to be so. I do not think that section 8(1)(a) can properly be construed as limited in its application to such debts and demands and is, therefore, I think, entirely destitute of effect.

Subsection 1(b) of section 8 presents a different question, but it is, in my opinion, *ultra vires* by reason of considerations of much the same character. It is no answer to say that the authority extends to all judgments; because the Board can arbitrarily refuse to grant a permit in any particular case. The Board is authorized to refuse a permit for a writ of execution where the debt sued upon is one which it has no power to regulate and to do so for any reason which to it may appear sufficient; and, of course, to discriminate in this respect between debts which it has power to regulate and debts in respect of which it has no such power.

We are not required to consider the authority of a provincial legislature to restrict the jurisdiction of the provincial Courts to giving declaratory judgments and to deprive them of the power to grant any consequential relief. This legislation affects the jurisdiction of the provincial Courts, but the pith and substance of it is to establish a provincial authority which is empowered to exercise the discriminatory control just mentioned. While in form this is legislation in relation to remedy and procedure, in substance this provision which attempts to regulate the remedial incidents of the right in this manner must, when it is read in light of the context in which it stands in this section 8(1), be regarded as a step in a design to regulate the right itself.

There is a class of creditors occupying a special position which must be considered. I refer to companies incorporated by the Dominion. It is settled that in the case of companies with objects other than provincial objects, the exclusive power to legislate in relation to incorporation is vested in Parliament, and that by the joint operation of the residuary power under section 91 of the *Confederation Act* and the powers conferred upon Parliament in relation to the enumerated subject, the regulation of trade and commerce, this power extends to the status and powers of the company. True, where the business of the company is subject to provincial legislative regulation, the provincial legislature may legislate in such a manner as to affect the business of the company by laws of general application in relation to the kind of business in which the company engages in the province; but the provisions of this statute giving to the Board the authority to interfere with the affairs of creditors in the manner set forth in section 8 would not appear to be a general law in this sense.

A company, for example, incorporated by the Dominion with authority to carry on the business of lending money upon various kinds of security in the province, may find itself in a position, under the operation of subsections 1(a) and (b) of section 8, in which it and other Dominion companies are precluded from enforcing their securities in the usual way. In my view, such legislation is not competent and, accordingly, paragraphs (c), (d), (e) and (f) would appear to be incompetent, as well as paragraphs (a) and (b).

As regards interest, subsection (1) of section 8 is plainly repugnant to section 2 of the *Interest Act*. In truth, the scope of subsection (1) of section 8 is indicated by paragraph (g) thereof and by section 41 which withdraws from the operation of the Act debts owing to The Canadian Farm Loan Board or to The Soldiers' Settlement Board and proceedings for enforcing the payment of any such debts. I think we must conclude that subsection (1) must be treated as a whole, that is to say, that it is valid or invalid as a whole, and for the reasons I have given it is, I think, invalid. The provisions of subsection (3) limiting the application of section 8 in the manner there mentioned do not, it appears to me, affect the force of what has been said. The whole of section 8 is *ultra vires*.

As to section 26, the matters dealt with by this enactment, in my opinion, are so related to the subject-matter of *The Farmers' Creditors Arrangement Act* as to be withdrawn from provincial jurisdiction by force of the last paragraph of section 91.

There remains the contention of the Attorney-General of Canada that the statute as a whole constitutes an attempt to legislate in relation to bankruptcy and insolvency. I have very carefully considered this contention and the first thing that strikes one is that the effect of section 8(1) is, as regards debts where the creditor and debtor reside in the province and the contract has been made in the province and the debt is payable in the province, that the creditor is deprived of his right to present a bankruptcy petition. As appears from what has already been said, section 8(1) does not merely suspend the remedy—it takes away the remedy given by law and substitutes therefore a remedy dependent upon the arbitrary consent of the Board, or the arbitrary determination of a jury. As I have already said, this, in my opinion, strikes at the debt itself and I do not think that in any Court governed by this legislation it could be successfully contended that in respect of an obligation to which the statute applies there is a "debt owing" to the creditor, within the meaning of section 4 of the *Bankruptcy Act*. Moreover, I find it impossible to escape the conclusion that Part III contemplates the use of the Board's powers under section 8(1) to enable it to secure compulsorily the consent of the parties to arrangements proposed by it for composition and settlement. Bankruptcy is not mentioned, but normally the powers and duties of the Board under Part III will come into operation when a state of insolvency exists. It is not too much to say that it is for the purpose of dealing with the affairs of debtors who are pressed and unable to pay their debts as they fall due that these powers and duties are created. Indeed the whole statute is conceived as a means of protecting embarrassed debtors who are residents of Alberta. Most people would agree that in this point of view the motives prompting the legislation may be laudable ones. But the legislature, in seeking to attain its object, seems to have entered upon a field not open to it. The statute, if valid, enables the Board (invested with exclusive possession of the key to the Courts) to employ its position and powers coercively in compelling the creditors of an insolvent debtor and the debtor himself to consent to a disposition of the resources of the debtor prescribed by the Board. In this way the statute seeks to empower the Board to impose upon the insolvent debtor and his creditors a settlement of his affairs, which the creditors must accept in satisfaction of their claims. I cannot escape the conclusion that the statute contemplates the use of the powers of the Board in this way. I think this is an attempt to invade the field reserved to the Dominion under Bankruptcy and Insolvency.

It may be that by apt legislation strictly limited to enactments relating exclusively to matters within the legislative jurisdiction of a province, a Board might lawfully be constituted having some of the powers which the Debt Adjustment Board receives under this legislation. As already intimated, it is unnecessary to express any opinion upon that. In view of that question, it is impossible in this legislation to disentangle what a provincial legislature might competently enact from the principal enactments of the statute constituting this Board with authority to exercise powers that the legislature is incompetent to confer upon it; and indeed, if this were possible and the *Debt Adjustment Act* could be re-written excluding what is *ultra vires* from what I assume might be *intra vires*, there can be no probability that the legislature would have enacted the statute in this truncated form. The competent elements of the legislation, if such there be, not being severable from the incompetent enactments constituting the Board with the powers conferred upon it, the statute is, as a whole, *ultra vires*.

CROCKET J. (dissenting): The whole purpose of the statute, as it plainly appears to me from an examination of all its provisions, is to regulate and control the enforcement of contractual obligations for the payment of money so as to safeguard during a period of financial stress the interests of unfortunate resident debtors, who, through no fault of their own, but entirely owing to the general depreciation of values brought about by abnormal economic conditions, find themselves in such a position that the stringent enforcement of their creditors' claims might entail irreparable loss upon them. Its provisions are predominantly directed to procedure in civil matters in provincial courts, in relation to the constitution and organization of which courts the provinces, within the limits already indicated, unquestionably possess sovereign legislative powers, as each province does, in relation to property and civil rights within its territorial jurisdiction. It is not doubted that the right to sue in provincial courts is a civil right in the province, whether the claim sought to be enforced arose in the province or not. None of the provisions of the provincial statute are directed to insolvency legislation or to banks or banking legislation, nor to the contracts of Dominion companies carrying on business either within or without the province, though they may affect these subjects and these rights collaterally as a necessary incident to the attainment of the obvious object of the statute, *viz.*, the granting of relief to hard pressed resident debtors. How, then, can it be said that the impugned statute is entirely beyond the constitutional competency of the province because it provides that no action for the recovery of money in respect of a liquidated demand or debt shall be commenced or continued, and no proceedings by way of execution, attachment, etc., taken, and no warrant of distress, chattel mortgage, conditional sale agreement or power of sale contained in a mortgage on land enforced against a resident debtor unless the Debt Adjustment Board issues a permit giving consent thereto? . . .

It is contended, however, that the impugned statute, by authorizing the Debt Adjustment Board to grant or refuse permits, gives it the unreasonable and arbitrary power to deny a creditor all access to the established Courts of the Province. Whether the Board is given power arbitrarily and without investigation of the conditions and circumstances in any particular case or not does not in my opinion affect the constitutionality of the enactment. That has been laid down in so many cases as to admit of no doubt. It is emphasized particularly by Lord Herschell in his judgment in the 1898 case at p. 713, and is strikingly illustrated by . . . *Ladore v. Bennett*. That consideration may possibly bear on the question as to whether the provincial enactment is a mere colourable device or mere pretence, by which the Legislature has sought to do indirectly what it could not do directly. Many attacks have been made against Dominion as well as provincial legislation on this ground, and some of them have succeeded. Once, however, it becomes clear from an examination of the provisions of an enactment that it is within the constitutional competency of the enacting Legislature, the Courts have no concern as to the reasonableness or injustice of those provisions. . . . I may add that a study of the whole Act has convinced me that it was not the intention of the Legislature that the Debt Adjustment Board should exercise the powers committed to it without any investigation or consideration of the facts and circumstances in any case coming before it, and that I cannot agree with the suggestion that the appeal for which the Act provides was intended to be an appeal merely to a jury of laymen. The appeal is in point of fact to a Judge of the Supreme Court sitting with a jury, which can only determine the issue under proper instructions from the Judge. See s. 3(d) and ss. 6, 9, 10, 21, 23, 33 and 36(1), (3), (4), (5), (7), (8) and (10).

As to the suggestion that the Act was a colourable device to reach out at something which was beyond the competence of the Legislature I need only refer, I think, to s. 39, which distinctly provides that the Act "shall not be so construed as to authorize the doing of any act or thing which is not within the legislative competence of the Legislative Assembly".

I differ also from my brethren in their conclusion that the *Debt Adjustment Act* is not an Act of general application in the Province of Alberta within the meaning of the authorities. . . .

[The Act is valid] except in so far as its provisions may conflict with any existing Dominion legislation strictly relating to any of the classes of subjects specially enumerated in s. 91 of the *B.N.A. Act* or as being necessarily incidental to the particular subject-matter, upon which the Parliament of Canada has undertaken to legislate as falling within one or other of the said enumerated heads. . . .

Act declared invalid.

[The judgment was affirmed by the Privy Council, *sub nom. A.-G. Alta. v. A.-G. Can.,* [1943] A.C. 356, [1943] 2 D.L.R. 1, [1943] 1 W.W.R. 378 on the two grounds that "the Act as a whole constitutes a serious and substantial invasion of the exclusive legislative powers of the Parliament of Canada in relation to bankruptcy and insolvency, and, on the other hand, that it obstructs and interferes with the actual legislation of that Parliament on those matters". The Privy Council refused to say anything on the matters discussed and decided by the Supreme Court. See *Note,* (1942) 20 Can. Bar Rev. 343; *Note,* (1943), 21 Can. Bar Rev. 310. See also, *Bastedo,* Constitutional Limitations of Provincial Debt Adjustment Legislation, (1941), 6 Sask. Bar Rev. 1.

In *Reference re Legal Proceedings Suspension Act,* [1942] 3 D.L.R. 318, [1942] 2 W.W.R. 536, the Alberta Appellate Division, by a majority, held *ultra vires* a temporary enactment of the legislature which would have had the effect of keeping alive the then recently invalidated *Debt Adjustment Act, 1937,* pending a final decision on its validity by the Privy Council. In *Roy and A.-G. Alta. v. Plourde,* [1943] S.C.R. 262, [1943] 3 D.L.R. 81, where Alberta legislation extended the period of redemption in pending and prospective mortgage foreclosure and specific performance actions but excepted from the statute actions in which a permit was not required under the *Debt Adjustment Act* or in which a permit was obtained, the Supreme Court upheld the legislation by severing the excepting clause as having no effect by reason of the invalidity of the *Debt Adjustment Act.*

In the earlier case, *A.-G. Alta and Winstanley v. Atlas Lumber Co.,* [1941] S.C.R. 87, [1941] 1 D.L.R. 625 the Supreme Court held that s. 8(1)(a) of the Act could not validly apply to actions on bills of exchange and promissory notes, particularly because it was repugnant to s. 74 of the *Bills of Exchange Act.* R.S.C. 1927, c. 16, in requiring a permit as a condition of suit. See *Note,* (1940) 18 Can. Bar Rev. 725.

If provincial legislation requiring a permit to sue on a bill of exchange or promissory note is invalid, may a province validly enact a statute of limitations applicable to bills and notes? In any event, on what ground does general provincial limitations legislation apply to actions on bills and notes (as is the assumption: see, for example, *Weingarden v. Moss,* [1955] 4 D.L.R. 63, 15 W.W.R. 481, 63 Man. R. 243) when there is no referential federal enactment making such provincial legislation applicable? See *Dorfer v. Winchell,* [1941] 2 D.L.R. 772, [1941] 1 W.W.R. 541 and *Costley v. Allen,* [1941] 4 D.L.R. 754, [1941] 3 W.W.R. 742, rev'd on other grounds [1942] 3 D.L.R. 76, [1942] 2 W.W.R. 239; *Note,* (1942) 20 Can. Bar Rev. 60. Cf. *Note,* (1945) 58 Harv. L. Rev. 738.

Provincial conditional sales legislation limits a conditional seller to his "lien" upon the chattel and to repossession and sale upon the buyer's default. It this legislation effective against an assignee of the conditional seller so as to preclude such assignee from recovering for any deficiency where he is holder in due course of a promissory note given to the conditional seller? See *Traders Finance Corp. Ltd. v. Casselman,* [1960] S.C.R. 242, 22 D.L.R. (2d) 177, aff'g 16 D.L.R. (2d) 183, 25 W.W.R. 289, which rev'd 11 D.L.R. (2d) 622, 22 W.W.R. 625.

Provincial legislation, *e.g., The Gaming Act,* R.S.O. 1970, c. 187 declares that a bill or note given in connection with gaming is deemed to be given for an illegal consideration and that where any person who makes or draws or gives such a bill or note pays to any holder, endorsee or assignee money secured thereby the money is deemed to be paid on account of the person to whom the bill or note was originally given and to be a debt owing to the person who paid it and shall be recoverable by action. Is this legislation competent to a province? See *McGillis v. Sullivan,* [1947] O.R. 650, [1947] 4 D.L.R. 113, aff'd [1949] S.C.R. 201, [1949] 2 D.L.R. 305.]

Note on the Federal Insolvency Power and Provincial Moratorium Legislation

The decision in the *Alberta Debt Adjustment Act* case had significance for Manitoba and Saskatchewan as well as for Alberta because all three provinces had similar legislation. One immediate result was the promulgation by the federal government of Order-in-Council P.C. 3243 of April 20, 1943, applicable to the three Provinces and empowering the Courts, where mortgage actions and actions by vendors of land were brought against farmers, to order a stay, postpone payments and prescribe terms which would; during the war period, retain on the land efficient and industrious farmers of good faith; and the Courts were also charged, so far as possible and consistent with this purpose, to protect the interests of other persons in the land: see *Note,* (1943) 21 Can. Bar Rev. 416. While the Order-in-Council was a war measure (and easily supportable on that ground) it raised the question, which recent cases have brought into sharper focus, whether a Province is precluded (in view of exclusive federal power in relation to insolvency as well as bankruptcy) from enacting not only compulsory debt adjustment legislation but general moratorium legislation.

Apart from the debt adjustment legislation invalidated by the Courts, other Provinces, *e.g.* Ontario and British Columbia, had enacted moratorium legislation in the early 1930's, applicable to mortgages and sales of land: see *Mortgagors' and Purchasers' Relief Act,* 1932 (Ont.), c. 49; *Mortgagors' and Purchasers' Relief Act,* 1934 (B.C.), c. 49. These statutes were envisaged as temporary and were re-enacted over successive periods until becoming spent in 1946 and 1949 respectively. Administration was confided to the Courts whose leave was required to enforce mortgages and sales of land where there was default of principal or interest (in British Columbia) or of principal only in (Ontario). In British Columbia provision was made for preliminary inquiry and report by the Court registrar in connection with an application for leave, and in Ontario a debtor was entitled to apply for relief by way of postponement of payments of interest, rent or taxes (apart from the protection afforded him where interest was paid up but principal only was in default).

The distinction between such legislation and the invalidated debt adjustment legislation lay in the administrative machinery in the latter for effecting a composition of debts through withholding a permit to sue. That the effect of Court control in the former type of legislation might be to persuade the parties to a voluntary composition was not, apparently, enough to taint it constitutionally, especially when regard was had to its restricted and temporary nature. Indeed, to borrow a phrase from the Privy Council's earliest decision on the federal bankruptcy and insolvency power, the British Columbia and Ontario relief legislation could be sustained because it did not provide for the administration of the estates of persons who were bankrupt or insolvent: see *L'Union St. Jacques v. Belisle* (1874), L.R. 6 C.P. 31. Although the *Voluntary Assignments* case, [1894] A.C. 189, which sustained provincial legislation respecting administration of estates under a voluntary assignment for benefit of creditors, may be regarded as of doubtful authority to-day, moratorium legislation which involves postponement only, without accompanying provisions for enforcing a composition, is supportable on a provincial level; and additional support may be found in the analogy of a stay of proceedings under the rules of procedure of provincial courts.

Admittedly, the line is thin between effective provincial moratorium legislation (which would generally be operable where a condition of insolvency exists) and an invasion of the federal bankruptcy and insolvency power; and, no doubt, Parliament could competently enter the field. As Rand J. pointed out in *Canadian Bankers Association v. A.-G. Sask.,* [1956] S.C.R. 31, [1955] 5 D.L.R. 736, a Province cannot justify legislation in relation to bankruptcy or insolvency on the ground that the conditions aimed at by the legislation are of a local or private nature. Two other statements in his judgment bare the nature of the issue presented by provincial legislative concern for hard-pressed debtors: (1) "If the Province steps in and actively assumes the general protection of [an insolvent] debtor, by whatever means, it is acting in relation to insolvency, and assuming the function of Parliament; it is so far administering, coercively as to creditors, the affairs of insolvent debtors. In this it is frustrating the laws of the Dominion in relation to the same subject". (2) "That the Province may in certain circumstances and in proper aspects, enact moratorium legislation . . . may be accepted; its validity will depend upon the facts, circumstances and means adopted, determining its true character". In the same case Locke J. rationalized provincial debt legislation against federal power by declaring that "power to declare a moratorium for the relief of residents of a Province generally in some great emergency, such as existed in 1914 and in the days of the lengthy depression in the thirties is one thing, but power to intervene between insolvent debtors and their creditors irrespective of the reasons which have rendered the debtor unable to meet his liabilities, is something entirely different". The recession from earlier case law conceding some scope for provincial administration of estates of self-declared insolvent persons is shown also by *A.-G. Alta. v. Nash* (1964), 50 W.W.R. 155, aff'g 48 W.W.R. 420, holding invalid the Alberta Fraudulent Preferences Act, R.S.A. 1955, c. 120. (But see *Allison & Burnham Concrete Ltd v. Mountain View Construction Ltd.* (1965), 53 W.W.R. 274, 54 D.L.R. (2d) 67.)

The *Canadian Bankers Association* case may usefully be contrasted for the problem at hand with the earlier case of *Abitibi Power & Paper Co. Ltd. v. Montreal Trust Co.*, [1943] A.C. 536, [1943] 4 D.L.R. 1, [1943] 3 W.W.R. 33. In the *Abitibi* case, an action was begun in Ontario to enforce a bond mortgage on which there had been default by the company. Shortly afterwards the company was declared insolvent at the instance of a creditor and a winding-up order was made. Under s. 21 of the *Winding-up Act*, R.S.C. 1927, c. 213, no action could be commenced or continued after the making of a winding-up order except by leave of the proper provincial Court. Leave to continue with the action on the bond mortgage was obtained, but during the course of the action a provincial commission of inquiry into the affairs of the company was appointed, and in consequence of its report a special moratorium Act was passed staying proceedings for a fixed period to enable consideration to be given to a proposed plan for rehabilitating the company. The Act was renewed after one year's force by another temporary Act expiring in the succeeding calendar year. The validity of these temporary moratorium statutes was successfully attacked in the provincial Courts as an invasion of the federal bankruptcy and insolvency power and as an interference with federal winding-up legislation. The Privy Council reversed and sustained the provincial enactments, holding that the action against the company had begun and continued (once leave had been given) as a provincial action and could be subjected to provincial control. The core of the matter is found in the following passage of the judgment: "It was pressed on their Lordships that the real substance of the legislation was an attempt to coerce the bondholders into accepting a plan of reconstruction, and that arrangements such as were contemplated by the report of the Royal Commission were within the exclusive field of the Dominion. So they are, but this Board must have cogent grounds before it arising from the nature of the impugned legislation before it can impute to a provincial legislature some object other than what is to be seen on the face of the enactment itself. In the present case their Lordships see no reason to reject the statement of the Ontario legislature, contained in the preamble to the Act, that the power to stay the action is given so that an opportunity may be given to all the parties concerned to consider the plan submitted in the report of the Royal Commission".

The *Canadian Bankers Association* case was markedly different from the *Abitibi* case and, in substance, the Province of Saskatchewan sought to achieve through two statutes what had been struck down when combined in the *Alberta Debt Adjustment Act*. Under the *Moratorium Act,* R.S.S. 1953, c. 98, enacted in 1943, the Lieutenant-Governor in Council was empowered to make general or particular orders postponing payment of debts or suspending process for a period not exceeding two years. Coupled with this Act was the *Provincial Mediation Board Act,* R.S.S. 1953, c. 40, also enacted in 1943, under which, on a debtor's application, the Board was authorized to try to effect a compromise with his creditors. Force could be lent to the Board's efforts by a government order under the moratorium statute. In invalidating this Saskatchewan scheme, the Supreme Court reinforced the *Alberta Debt Adjustment Act* decision. It refused to find any constitutional distinction in the fact that while a permit to sue was necessary under the legislation in the *Alberta* case no such requirement was included in the Saskatchewan legislation. The reason for this refusal was that the possibility of a suspension order hung over a creditor; and he would thus be "coerced" for two years to arrive at some compromise under the aegis of the Mediation Board just as in the Alberta case the Debt Adjustment Board could bring similar pressure by denying a permit to sue; and nothing of substance turned on the fact that in the Alberta case the permit to sue could be denied without limit of time.

[Is there any constitutional objection to provincial legislation which requires a secured creditor to submit to supervision of the realization of his security, where such legislation is applicable whether the debtor be insolvent or not? See *Montreal Trust Co. v. Abitibi Power & Paper Co.,* [1938] O.R. 81, [1938] 1 D.L.R. 548, aff'd on other grounds [1938] O.R. 589, [1938] 4 D.L.R. 529; *Canada Trust Co. v. Hanson,* [1950] 1 D.L.R. 375, [1949] O.W.N. 803, aff'd [1951] S.C.R. 366, [1951] 1 D.L.R. 402.

Is it open to a Province to create a statutory trust in favour of certain creditors, as has been done by s. 2 of the *Mechanics' Lien Act,* R.S.O. 1970, c. 267, and thus colour the term "trust" as used in s. 47(a) of the *Bankruptcy Act,* R.S.C. 1970, c. B-3; so as to remove certain assets of a person who subsequently becomes bankrupt from the claims of creditors generally? See *John M. M. Troup Ltd. v. Royal Bank of Canada,* [1962] S.C.R. 487, 34 D.L.R. (2d) 556.]

REFERENCE RE VALIDITY OF THE ORDERLY PAYMENT OF
DEBTS ACT, 1959 (ALTA.), C. 61.
In the Supreme Court of Canada. [1960] S.C.R. 571,
23 D.L.R. (2d) 449.

Appeal from a judgment of the Alberta Appellate Division, 20
D.L.R. (2d) 503, 29 W.W.R. 435, holding, on a reference, that the
Alberta Orderly Payment of Debts Act is invalid. It was urged
before the Supreme Court that the Act was competent to the Province
under s. 92(13), (14) and (16). The argument against the validity
of the Act was founded on s. 91(21), and on s. 91(15), (18) and (19),
and it was additionally contended that the Act gave to the clerk of
a District Court the powers of a s. 96 Judge.

KERWIN C.J.C.: . . . I agree with the Appellate Division that
the Act is *ultra vires* on the ground that in pith and substance it is
bankruptcy and insolvency legislation and that it is therefore unnecessary to consider the other grounds of attack.

Section 3 of the Orderly Payment of Debts Act provides:—

3. (1) This Act applies only

(a) to a judgment for the payment of money where the amount
of the judgment does not exceed one thousand dollars,

(b) to a judgment for the payment of money in excess of one
thousand dollars if the creditor consents to come under this
Act, and

(c) to a claim for money, demand for debt, account, covenant or
otherwise, not in excess of one thousand dollars.

(2) This Act does not apply to a debt due, owing or payable to
the Crown or a municipality or relating to the public revenue or one
that may be levied and collected in the form of taxes or, unless the
creditor consents to come under this Act,

(a) to a claim for wages that may be heard before, or a judgment
therefor by, a magistrate under *The Masters and Servants Act,*

(b) to a claim for a lien or a judgment thereon under *The
Mechanics' Lien Act,* or

(c) to a claim for a lien under *The Garagemen's Lien Act.*

(3) This Act does not apply to debts incurred by a trader or
merchant in the usual course of his business.

Provision is then made whereby a debtor may apply to the Clerk
of the District Court of the judicial district in which he resides for a
consolidation order, showing by affidavit all his creditors together
with the amount he owes to each one, his income from all sources
and, if he is married, the amount of the income of his wife, the
number of persons dependent upon him, the amount payable for
board or lodging or rent or as payment on home property and whether
any of his creditors' claims are secured, and if so, the nature and
particulars of the security held by each. The Clerk is to settle an
amount proposed to be paid by the debtor into court periodically

or otherwise on account of the claims of his creditors and provide for hearing objections by the latter. After such a hearing, if necessary, a consolidation order is to be made, which order is a judgment of the Court in favour of each creditor, and provision is made for a review by the Court of any such order.

Sections 12, 13 and 14 are important and read as follows:—

12. The Court may, in deciding any matter brought before it, impose such terms on a debtor with respect to the custody of his property or any disposition thereof or of the proceeds thereof as it deems proper to protect the registered creditors and may give such directions for the purpose as the circumstances require.

13. Upon the making of a consolidation order no process shall be issued in any Court against the debtor at the instance of a registered creditor or a creditor to whom this Act applies
(a)   except as permitted by this Act or the regulations, or
(b)   except by leave of the Court.

14. (1) The clerk may at any time require of, and take from the debtor an assignment to himself as clerk of the Court of any moneys due, owing or payable or to become due, owing or payable to the debtor or earned or to be earned by the debtor.

(2) Unless otherwise agreed upon the clerk shall forthwith notify the person owing or about to owe the moneys of the assignment and all moneys collected thereon shall be applied to the credit of the claims against the debtor under the consolidation order.

(3) The clerk may issue a writ of execution in respect of a consolidation order and cause it to be filed with the sheriff of a judicial district and at any land titles office.

While the Act applies only to claims or judgments which do not exceed one thousand dollars, unless in the case of a judgment for the payment of money in excess of one thousand dollars the creditor consents to come under the Act, I can read these provisions in no other way than showing that they refer to a debtor who is unable to pay his debts as they mature. Why else is authority given the Court to impose terms with respect to the custody of his property or any disposition thereof or of the proceeds thereof as it deems proper to protect the registered creditors (s. 12)? And why else may no process be issued in any court against the debtor at the instance of a registered creditor or a creditor to whom the Act applies, except as stated (s. 13)? Section 14 authorizing the Clerk to require an assignment to him by the debtor of any monies due, owing or payable or to become due, owing or payable to the debtor, or earned or to be earned by the debtor is surely consonant only with the position of an involvent debtor. In fact a debtor under the Act is ceasing to meet his liabilities generally as they become due and therefore falls within s. 20(1) (j) of *The Bankruptcy Act,* R.S.C. 1952, c. 14.

In *Attorney-General for British Columbia v. Attorney-General for Canada et al.,* [1937] A.C. 391, Lord Thankerton speaking for the Judicial Committee states at p. 402:—

> In a general sense, insolvency means inability to meet one's debts or obligations; in a technical sense, it means the condition or standard of inability to meet debts or obligations, upon the occurrence of which the statutory law enables a creditor to intervene, with the assistance of a Court, to stop individual action by creditors and to secure administration of the debtor's assets in the general interest of creditors; the law also generally allows the debtor to apply for the same administration. The justification for such proceeding by a creditor generally consists in an act of bankruptcy by the debtor, the conditions of which are defined and prescribed by the statute law.

This was said in an appeal affirming the decision of the majority of this Court in the *Reference as to the Validity of The Farmers' Creditors Arrangement Act of the Dominion,* as amended, [1936] S.C.R. 384.

In *Canadian Bankers' Association v. Attorney-General of Saskatchewan,* [1956] S.C.R. 31 this Court held that *The Moratorium Act* of Saskatchewan was *ultra vires* as being in relation to insolvency. There the decision of the Judicial Committee in *Abitibi Power and Paper Company v. The Montreal Trust Company,* [1943] A.C. 536 was relied upon, but, for the reasons given by Mr. Justice Locke, it was held that it had no application. As was pointed out, the Judicial Committee in the 1943 case held that the purpose of the impugned legislation was to stay proceedings in the action brought under the mortgage granted by the Abitibi Company until the interested parties should have an opportunity of considering such plan for the reorganization of the company as might be submitted by a Royal Commission appointed for that purpose. For the same reason that decision is inapplicable here. The older decision of the Privy Council in *Attorney-General for Ontario v. The Attorney-General of Canada,* [1894] A.C. 189, dealing with *The Ontario Assignments and Preferences Act,* is quite distinguishable, although in my view it is doubtful whether in view of later pronouncements of the Judicial Committee it would at this date be decided in the same sense, even in the absence of Dominion legislation upon the subject of bankruptcy and insolvency.

The Act in question is not legislation for the recovery of debts. It has no analogy to provincial bulk sales legislation because there the object is to make sure that when a person sells his stock of goods, wares, merchandise and chattels, ordinarily the subject of trade and commerce, the creditors will not be placed in any difficulty because of the disappearance of the proceeds of the sale. It is unnecessary to express any opinion as to the validity of s. 156 of *The Division Courts Act of Ontario,* R.S.O. 1950, c. 106, apparently introduced for the first time in 1950 by c. 16 of the statutes of that year, which provides for a consolidation order.

The debtor under *The Orderly Payment of Debts Act* is not in the same position as the appellant in *L'Union St. Jacques de Montréal v. Bélisle* (1874), L.R. 6 P.C. 31, and the appellant can gain no comfort from *Ladore v. Bennett*, [1939] A.C. 468. . . . The legislation in question in each of these cases was quite different from the effort by Alberta in *Board of Trustees of the Lethbridge Northern Irrigation District v. I.O.F.*, [1940] A.C. 513.

The appeal should be dismissed.

LOCKE J.:—The *Orderly Payment of Debts Act* was passed by the Legislature of Alberta and appears as c. 61 of the Statutes of 1959. By s. 22 it is declared that the Act is to come into force on a date to be fixed by proclamation. We are informed that, pending the determination of the reference, it has not been proclaimed.

In my opinion, of the various grounds upon which it is contended that the Act is *ultra vires* the legislature it is necessary to consider only that as to whether it infringes upon the exclusive jurisdiction of Parliament to make laws in relation to bankruptcy and insolvency under head 21 of s. 91.

While "bankruptcy" and "insolvent person" are defined in s. 2 of the *Bankruptcy Act* (c. 14, R.S.C. 1952) it is rather the meaning that these words commonly bear that is to be given to them in construing the words in s. 91. In *Parker v. Gossage* (1835), 5 L.J. Ex. 4, Parke B. said that an insolvent in the ordinary acceptation of the word is a person who cannot pay his debts. In *Reg. v. Saddlers Company* (1863), 10 H.L.C. at p. 425, Willes J. adopted what had been said by Baron Parke as to the meaning assigned to the term "insolvent" and said that the words "in insolvent circumstances" had always been held to mean not merely being behind the world, if an account were taken, but insolvency to the extent of being unable to pay just debts in the ordinary course of trade and business.

In *Attorney-General of British Columbia v. Attorney-General of Canada*, [1937] A.C. 391, at 402, referring to the words in head 21, Lord Thankerton said that, in a general sense, insolvency means inability to meet one's debts or obligations.

When the *Bankruptcy Act* was first enacted in 1919 (c. 36) "insolvent person" and "insolvent" were declared to include a person who is for any reason unable to meet his obligations as they respectively become due, or who has ceased paying his current obligations in the ordinary course of business, thus substantially adopting what had been said by Parke B. and Willes J. The meaning commonly borne by the terms employed in head 21 of s. 91 did not differ in 1867 from their present day meaning.

The statute to be considered does not refer in terms either to bankruptcy or insolvency and this, while not decisive, is a matter to be considered in determining the question as to what is its true nature.

The Act is declared by s. 3 to apply to a judgment not in excess of one thousand dollars, to a judgment in excess of that amount if the creditor consents to come under the Act and to a claim for money, demand for debt, account, covenant or otherwise, not in excess of one thousand dollars. Debts due to the Crown or to a municipality or relating to the public revenue, claims for wages that might be heard before a magistrate under the *Masters and Servants Act,* claims for a lien or a judgment thereon under the *Mechanics Lien Act,* claims for a lien under the *Garagemen's Lien Act* and debts incurred by a trader or merchant in the usual course of business are exempted from the operation of the Act.

As in the case of a proposal made by a debtor under the provisions of s. 27 of the *Bankruptcy Act* or s. 7 of the *Farmers' Creditors Arrangement Act* (c. 111 R.S.C. 1952), proceedings under this statute are initiated by the debtor who may apply to the clerk of the district court of the judicial district in which he resides for what is called a consolidation order. With the application the debtor is required to file an affidavit in the prescribed form setting forth, *inter alia,* particulars of the debts owing by him, of the nature and extent of his property, the amount of the income of himself and his wife and the number of persons dependent upon him.

Section 5 requires the clerk to file the affidavit and the particulars in a register and:

> upon reading the affidavit and hearing the debtor settle an amount proposed to be paid by the debtor into court, periodically or otherwise, on account of the claims of his creditors and enter particulars thereof in the register or, if so proposed, enter in the register a statement that the present circumstances of the debtor do not warrant the fixing of any amount.

The clerk is then required to give notice of the application to each of the creditors and fix a date on which he will hear objections. If no objections are received within twenty days after the notices are mailed, the clerk is required to note the fact in the register and issue a consolidation order.

By s. 7 it is provided that any creditor may within the time limited file an objection with the clerk either to the amount entered in the register as the amount owing to him or to any other creditor or to the amount "fixed to be paid into court by the debtor or the times of payment thereof or to the statement fixing no amount." Upon such objection being filed the clerk is required to notify the debtor and any other creditor whose claim is objected to.

By s. 8 the clerk is empowered to bring in and add to the register the name of any creditor of the debtor of whom he has notice and who is not disclosed in the affidavit of the debtor.

Section 9 reads:—

(1) At the time appointed for the hearing the clerk shall consider all objections filed with him in accordance with this Act and

> (a) if an objection is to the claim of a creditor and the parties are brought to agreement or if the creditor's claim is a judgment of a court and the only objection is to the amount paid thereon, he may dispose of the objection in a summary manner and determine the amount owing to the creditor.

(b) if an objection is to the proposed terms or method of payment of the claims by the debtor or that terms of payment are not but should be fixed, he may dispose of the objection summarily and determine as the circumstances require the terms and method of payment of the claims, or that no terms be presently fixed, or

(c) in any case he may on notice of motion refer any objection to be disposed of by the court or as the court otherwise directs.

(2) The clerk shall enter in the register his decision or the decision of the court, as the case may be, and shall issue a consolidation order.

Section 10 provides that the consolidation order shall state the amount owing to each creditor, the amount to be paid into court by the debtor and the times of payment, and declares that a consolidation order is a judgment of the court in favour of each creditor for the amount stated and is an order of the court for the payment by the debtor of the amounts specified.

Section 11 provides that on notice of motion a judge of the district court may review a consolidation order made by the clerk and vary it or set it aside. Under the provisions of s. 12 the judge may impose such terms on a debtor with respect to the custody of his property or any disposition thereof as he deems proper to protect the registered creditors and give such directions for that porpose as the circumstances require.

Section 13 declares that upon the making of a consolidation order no process shall be issued in any court against the debtor at the instance of a registered creditor or a creditor to whom the Act applies, except as permitted by the Act or the regulations, or by leave of the court.

Section 14 enables the clerk at any time to require the debtor to assign to him any moneys owing to or to become owing or to be earned by the debtor and authorizes him to issue a writ of execution "in respect of a consolidation order" and to file it with the sheriff or at any land titles office.

Section 15 permits an application to be made by a creditor whose claim is not entered in the consolidation order to have it entered in the register and provides the manner of settlement of any dispute as to its amount.

Section 16 declares that a registered creditor holding security for his claim may, at any time, elect to rely upon his security and if the security is realized any excess above the amount of the creditor's claim is to be paid to the clerk and applied in payment of other judgments against the debtor.

By s. 17 provision is made, *inter alia,* for an application by any registered creditor where a debtor defaults in complying with an order for payment or any other order or direction of the court, or where any other proceeding for the recovery of money has been brought against the debtor, or where a judgment is recovered against him for an amount in excess of one thousand dollars and the judgment creditor refuses to permit his name to be added to the register for leave to take proceedings on behalf of all of the registered creditors to enforce the consolidation order. The section further provides for an *ex parte* application to the court where a debtor is about to abscond or has absconded or, with intent to defraud his creditors, is about to remove his property from Alberta.

Section 18 provides that the debtor or any registered creditor may at any time apply *ex parte* to the clerk for a further examination of the debtor as to his financial circumstances and, after notice has been given to all parties to the consolidation order, vary the order as to the time, amount and method of payment.

Section 19 requires the clerk to distribute the moneys paid into court on account of the debts of a debtor at least once every three months *pro rata* among the registered creditors.

While, according to s. 3, the Act applies only to judgments or claims which do not exceed one thousand dollars, the total of such claims is not mentioned so that the Act can be applied irrespective of the aggregate amount of the debts. While the debtor may be required by the clerk under the provisions of s. 14 to assign any moneys due, owing, payable, or to become due or earned by the debtor, there is no express provision for the conveyance of the debtor's other assets to the clerk, though the powers of the district court judge under s. 12 would permit such an order to be made.

Persons engaged in farming in Alberta, as that expression is defined in the *Farmers' Creditors Arrangement Act,* who are entitled to make a proposal to their creditors under the terms of s. 7 of that Act are among those to whom the *Orderly Payment of Debts Act* will be applicable.

The language of s. 5 is that the clerk, upon an application being filed, after reading the affidavit required by s. 4 and hearing the debtor (apparently *ex parte*) shall "settle an amount proposed to be paid by the debtor into court periodically or otherwise on account of the claims of his creditors" or, "if so proposed" (presumably by the debtor) enter in the register a statement that the present circumstances of the debtor do not warrant the fixing of any amount. This language, while lacking in clarity, appears to indicate that, at least in the first instance, the clerk is to accept the debtor's estimate as to what, if anything, he can pay to his creditors and record this in the court records. Providing no objections are received within twenty days, this estimate appears to be conclusive by virtue of s. 6 and a consolidation order will issue.

Where objections are filed, they are to be dealt with under s. 9 which gives to the clerk power to settle the amount payable under any judgment if the amount is in dispute and, where the proposed scheme of payment is objected to, he may dispose of the objection summarily and decide upon the terms of the consolidation order.

This procedure may be compared with that provided for dealing with proposals which may be made to a trustee in bankruptcy by an insolvent person under the provisions of Part III of the *Bankruptcy Act* where the proposal is submitted to a meeting of the creditors and, if accepted by them and approved by the court having jurisdiction in bankruptcy under the terms of s. 34, becomes binding upon the parties concerned. Under the Act in question, where the proposal is objected to by a creditor whose claim does not exceed one thousand dollars, the wishes of the creditors may be disregarded by the clerk. The provisions of s. 13 which prohibit the taking of any proceedings by a registered creditor or a creditor to whom the Act applies are after a consolidation order has been made as to these creditors, similar in their effect to the provisions of s. 40 of the *Bankruptcy Act* and s. 11 of the *Farmers' Creditors Arrangement Act* relating to bankruptcy and to proposals. While s. 4 details certain information that is to be contained in the debtor's affidavit, the form of the affidavit which may be prescribed by the Lieutenant-Governor in Council by regulation is not before us. Whether that affidavit is to contain a statement that the debtor is unable to meet his debts as they become due, or whether the clerk who is required to act by s. 5 is to do so upon the unsworn statement of the debtor that he is in insolvent circumstances, does not appear.

While the Act does not require that the debtor who applies must be insolvent in the sense that he is unable to pay his debts as they become due, it must, in my opinion, be so construed since it is quite impossible to believe that it was intended that the provisions of the Act might be resorted to by persons who were able to pay their way but do not feel inclined to do so. In my opinion, this is a clear invasion of the legislative field of insolvency and is, accordingly, beyond the powers of the legislature.

There have been bankruptcy laws in England since 1542 dealing with the estates of insolvent persons, and the terms of statutes in force in England prior to 1867 may be looked at as an aid in deciding what subject-matters were generally regarded as included in these terms.

The *Bankruptcy Consolidation Act* of 1849 (c. 106, 12-13 Vict.), which consolidated the law relating to bankrupts, contained in ss. 201 to 223 provisions by which a trader unable to meet his engagements with his creditors might petition the court to approve a composition or scheme of arrangement for the payment of his debts and declared the manner in which such a proposal might be submitted to the creditors and, if approved, to the court for its approval.

The manner in which disputes between the official assignee and the creditors as to the carrying out of a deed of composition or arrangement were to be settled was further dealt with in 1861 in s. 136 of an *Act to amend the law relating to bankruptcy and insolvency in England* (c. 134, 24-25 Vict.).

Compositions and schemes of arrangement have thus for more than 100 years past been treated as subject-matters falling within the scope of the statutes relating to bankruptcy and insolvency. The provisions dealing with this subject at the present day in England are to be found in the *Bankruptcy Act of 1914* as amended (see *Williams on Bankruptcy*, 17th ed. p. 92). When the *Bankruptcy Act* was enacted in Canada in 1919 it contained in s. 13 provisions whereby an insolvent debtor who wished to make a proposal to his creditors for a composition in satisfaction of his debts or an extension of time for payment thereof or a scheme of arrangement of his affairs might, either before or after the making of a receiving order against him or the making of an authorized assignment by him, require in writing an authorized trustee to convene a meeting of his creditors for the consideration of such proposal and provisions whereby the scheme, if approved, might become binding upon the parties concerned. Similar provisions for dealing with such a proposal, a term which is defined to include a proposal for a composition, an extension of time, or for a scheme of arrangement, are contained in the *Bankruptcy Act* as it is today.

These provisions are made applicable to proposals by farmers in Alberta, Manitoba and Saskatchewan by the *Farmers' Creditors Arrangement Act* above mentioned. The Act under consideration appears to be an attempt to substitute for the provisions of the *Bankruptcy Act* and the *Farmers' Creditors Arrangement Act* relating to proposals for an extension of time or a scheme of arrangement which are submitted to the interested creditors for their approval and, if approved, thereafter to the judge in bankruptcy, a scheme whereby the propriety of accepting such a proposal is to be determined by the clerk of the district court and with regard, apparently, only to the claims of those creditors the debts owing to whom are less than one thousand dollars in amount and those to whom greater amounts are owing who consent to come under the Act, leaving other creditors whose claims are greater to resort to such remedies as they may be advised to take for the enforcement of their claims. The provisions of the Provincial Act thus conflict with those in the legislation passed by Parliament dealing with the same matters.

In *Attorney-General of British Columbia v. Attorney-General of Canada*, [1937] A.C. 391, where the *Farmers' Creditors Arrangement Act*, 1934 of the Parliament of Canada, as amended by the *Farmers' Creditors Arrangement Act Amendment Act*, 1935 was considered, Lord Thankerton said in part (p. 403) :—

> it cannot be maintained that legislative provision as to compositions, by which bankruptcy is avoided, but which assumes insolvency, is not properly within the sphere of bankruptcy legislation.

and referred to the judgment of this Court in the matter of the *Companies' Creditors Arrangement Act*, [1934] S.C.R. 660, where Sir Lyman Duff, delivering the judgment of the majority, said that the history of the law seems to show clearly that legislation in respect of compositions and arrangements is a natural and ordinary component of a system of bankruptcy and insolvency law.

Some support for the validity of this legislation is sought in the judgment of the Judicial Committee in *Attorney General of Ontario v. Attorney-General of Canada*, [1894] A.C. 189. The question in that appeal was as to whether s. 9 of c. 124, R.S.O. 1887, was within the powers of the legislature. The Act was entitled *"An Act respecting assignments and preferences by insolvent persons."* A majority of the members of the Court of Appeal who considered the question had found the section to be *ultra vires*. In an earlier case, *Clarkson v. Ontario Bank* (1890), 15 A.R. 166, Haggarty C.J.O. and Osler J.A. had held the Act as a whole to be *ultra vires* as legislation relating to bankruptcy and insolvency, while Burton and Patterson JJ.A. considered it to be *intra vires* as being in relation to property and civil rights in the province.

Prior to the passing of that statute the *Insolvency Act of 1875* (c. 16) had been repealed by Parliament by c. 1 of the Statutes of 1880 and there was no Bankruptcy or Insolvency Act of the Dominion.

The judgment allowing the appeal was delivered by Herschell L.C. The Act, the first two sections of which dealt with fraudulent preferences by insolvents or those knowing themselves to be on the eve of insolvency, permitted a debtor—solvent or otherwise—to make an assignment of his exigible assets to a sheriff for the purpose of realization and distribution *pro rata* among his creditors. Section 9 provided that such an assignment should take precedence of all judgments and all executions not completely executed by payment. There were no provisions permitting proposals for a composition or extensions of time for payment of debts. It was said that the effect to be given to judgments and executions and the manner and the extent to which they might be enforced was *prima facie* within the legislative powers of the legislature and that the validity of the assignment and the application of s. 9 did not depend on whether the assignor was or was not insolvent. Such an assignment, their Lordships said, did not infringe on the exclusive legislative power of Parliament under head 21. The concluding portion of the judgment reads (pp. 200-201):—

> Their Lordships do not doubt that it would be open to the Dominion Parliament to deal with such matters as part of a bankruptcy law, and the provincial legislature would doubtless be then precluded from interfering with this legislation inasmuch as such interference would affect the bankruptcy law of the Dominion Parliament. But it does not follow that such subjects, as might properly be treated as ancillary to such a law and therefore within the powers of the Dominion Parliament, are excluded from the legislative authority of the provincial legislature when there is no bankruptcy or insolvency legislation of the Dominion Parliament in existence.

As Parliament has dealt with the matter, the concluding portion of this judgment would be fatal to the appellant's contention, even if the subject of bankruptcy and insolvency were one in relation to which the province might legislate in the absence of legislation by the Dominion. But the language of s. 91 is that the exclusive legislative power of the Parliament of Canada extends to all matters in relation to, *intra alia,* bankruptcy and insolvency, and the provinces are excluded from that field. . . .

CARTWRIGHT J.: . . . I think I am right in saying that in every decision of the Judicial Committee or of this Court in which provincial legislation, impugned on the ground that it affected the rights and obligations of an insolvent entity and its creditors and thereby trenched on the subject matter comprised in head 21 of s. 91, has been upheld it appears that in the view of the court two conditions were found to exist; (i) that the impugned legislation was not in truth and substance primarily in relation to Bankruptcy and Insolvency but rather in relation to one or more of the matters enumerated in s. 92; and (ii) that in so far as it affected the rights and obligations of an insolvent and its creditors it did not conflict with existing valid legislation of Parliament enacted in exercise of the power contained in head 21 of s. 91.

In the case at bar, as is shown in the reasons of my brother Locke, neither of these conditions exists. . . .

Appeal dismissed.

[Taschereau, Fauteux, Abbott, Judson and Ritchie JJ. concurred with Kerwin C.J.C. and Martland J. concurred with Locke and Cartwright JJ.].

CHAPTER X

TAXING POWERS

1. The Scope of Dominion and Provincial Taxing Powers: Taxing and Regulation: Spending

It will be convenient to list at the outset those provisions of the *B.N.A. Act* which confer upon the Dominion and the Provinces authority to raise money and which, conversely, limit that authority. The Dominion's powers are in s. 91(3) ("the raising of money by any mode or system of taxation") and s. 122 ("the customs and excise laws of each province shall subject to the provisions of this Act continue in force until altered by the Parliament of Canada"). It is a tenable conclusion that s. 122 is now spent and that customs and excise laws are, independently of s. 122, competent to the Dominion under s. 91(2) and s. 91(3). *Cf. MacDonald*, Taxation Powers in Canada, (1941) 19 Can. Bar Rev. 75, at p. 95; *A.-G. B.C. v. Kingcome Navigation Co. Ltd.*, [1934] A.C. 45, [1934] 1 D.L.R. 31, [1933] 3 W.W.R. 353; and *cf. Rex v. Shearwater Co.*, [1934] S.C.R. 197, [1934] 3 D.L.R. 544. In any event, s. 122 may be regarded as confirmatory of some of the things covered by s. 91(3): see *P.A.T.A. v. A.-G. Can.*, [1931] A.C. 310, [1931] 2 D.L.R. 1, [1931] 1 W.W.R. 552. The provincial powers are in s. 92(2) ("direct taxation within the province in order to the raising of a revenue for provincial purposes") and s. 92(9) ("shop, saloon, tavern, auctioneer and other licences in order to the raising of a revenue for provincial, local or municipal purposes"). Two limiting provisions may be noted: s. 121 ("all articles of the growth, produce or manufacture of any one of the provinces shall from and after the Union be admitted free into each of the other provinces") and s. 125 ("no lands or property belonging to Canada or any province shall be liable to taxation"). The effect of these sections has been partly treated in Chap. IV, *supra*.

While the primary concern here is to consider the legal aspects of federal and provincial revenue powers, the issues raised by the scope of the respective powers, considered in conjunction with the various subsidy arrangements, first under s. 118 (repealed by 1950 (U.K.), c. 6) and later under the B.N.A. Act, 1907 (U.K.), c. 11 and also under federal legislation, transcend legalism and go to the heart of a working federalism. *Cf. Maxwell*, A Flexible Portion of the *B.N.A. Act*, (1933) 11 Can. Bar Rev. 149, on the changes in the provision for federal subsidies to the provinces; see also the *Provincial Subsidies Act*, R.S.C. 1970, c. P-26; the *Maritime Provinces Additional Subsidies Act*, 1942 (Can.), c. 14; B.N.A. Act, 1949, No. 1, 1949 (U.K.), c. 22, Terms of Union with Newfoundland, and 1949 (Can.), c. 1. It has become a truism of Canadian constitutional law that judicial interpretation of the *B.N.A. Act* has given the provinces substantive legislative authority (especially in respect of social services) that far exceeds their financial resources and their money-raising power, while it has left the Dominion with financial resources through an ample taxing power overshadowing its regulatory authority. Having regard to this result of the legal division of powers, and to the disparate economic strength of the various provinces *inter se,* it is understandable why the financial relations of Dominion and provinces have become a central issue in Canadian federalism—an issue in which the strict legal position is of secondary importance: see Report of Royal Commission on Dominion-Provincial Relations, 1940, Book I, Chaps. 8 and 9; Book II, chap. 1; Proceedings of Constitutional Conference of Federal and Provincial Governments, 1950; Proceedings of Constitutional Conference of Federal and Provincial Governments (Second Session), 1950; Report of the Dominion-Provincial Conference on Fiscal Relations, 1957; Federal-Provincial Relations, 1958 (A Symposium), (1958) 1 Can. Pub. Adm., No. 3, pp. 1-25. The amendments to the *B.N.A. Act* respecting unemployment insurance and old age pensions and supplementary benefits are indicative of piecemeal solutions on a political level which, no doubt, may be extended into other areas where social pressure for governmental action becomes insistent. But these special and particular amendments have left the general legal framework of financial and taxing powers otherwise unimpaired. Within this framework, Dominion and provinces have had to meet and satisfy the claims and demands for various forms of public assistance. Hence, the development of grants in aid by Dominion to provinces, and the growth of what may be called a federal "spending" power involving disbursement of money on stipulated conditions but without any right of compulsory direction or regulation of the beneficiaries: see *Gouin and Claxton,* Legislative Expedients and Devices Adopted by the Dominion and the Provinces (Royal Commission Study, Appendix 8), chap. III; *Gettys,* Administration of Canadian Conditional Grants; *Smiley,* Conditional Grants and Canadian Federalism (1963); *Cheffins,* The Constitutional Process in Canada, pp. 143-146 (1969); and *cf. The Family Allowances Act,* R.S.C. 1970, c. F-1.

The Dominion's right to spend money which it has raised through a proper exercise of its taxing power is confirmed, if confirmation be necessary, by s. 91(1A) of the *B.N.A. Act* ("the public debt and property"). "We are satisfied", said Duff C.J. in his dissenting judgment in *Reference re Employment and Social Insurance Act,* [1936] S.C.R. 427, at p. 432, [1936] 3 D.L.R. 644, at p. 647, "that if Parliament out of public monies exclusively were to constitute a fund for the relief of unemployment and to give to unemployed persons a right to claim unemployment benefits, to be paid out of that fund upon such conditions as Parliament might see fit to prescribe, no plausible argument could be urged against the validity of such legislation". An issue of validity does arise, however, where the legislation is not a mere spending enactment (*e.g. The Family Allowances Act*) but purports to be an exercise of the taxing power or combines taxation (*i.e.* compulsory exactions) with a scheme of disbursement (*e.g. The Employment and Social Insurance Act of 1935*). In *In re*

Insurance Act of Canada, [1932] A.C. 41, at p. 52, [1932] 1 D.L.R. 97, at p. 106, [1931] 3 W.W.R. 689, at p. 697, reproduced, *supra*, at p. 356, the Privy Council stated the problem as follows: "Now as to the power of the Dominion Parliament to impose taxation there is no doubt. But if the tax as imposed is linked up with an object which is illegal, the tax for that purpose must fall". This principle is, of course, as applicable to provincial taxing measures as it is to federal enactments: see *A.-G. Alta. v. A.-G. Can.,* [1939] A.C. 117, [1938] 4 D.L.R. 433, [1938] 3 W.W.R. 337. As to Dominion statutes, the problem has been whether the Dominion may exercise its plenary taxing power towards achievement of a regulatory purpose which it cannot realize through direct regulation, either by licensing or otherwise. Thus, in the *Employment and Social Insurance Act* case, Rinfret J. took the position ([1936] S.C.R. 427, at p. 453, [1936] 3 D.L.R. 644, at p. 666) that "the contributions (or the taxes if we are to call them so) are mere incidents of the regulation" of employment service and unemployment insurance, forbidden (at that time) to the Dominion. When the case came before the Privy Council ([1937] A.C. 355, [1937] 1 D.L.R. 684, [1937] 1 W.W.R. 312), that body went a little farther—too far, perhaps—in warning against an overreaching of the federal taxing power. Said Lord Atkin: "But assuming that the Dominion has collected by means of taxation a fund, it by no means follows that any legislation which disposes of it is necessarily within Dominion competence. It may still be legislation affecting [sic] the classes of subjects enumerated in s. 92 and, if so, would be *ultra vires*". This statement has not had any noticeable effect upon Dominion spending. Indeed, the rejection of an attack on the constitutionality of the *Family Allowances Act* lends emphasis to the view that the Courts have no concern with the disbursement of public funds which have been validly raised: see *Angers v. Minister of National Revenue,* [1957] Ex. C.R. 83. It ought to be said that in contrasting taxation and regulation, the courts have not been influenced so much by a belief in "pure taxation" (*i.e.* taxation which produces revenue but has no economic effects—an imaginary situation in the modern world) as by a legal view of the distribution of legislative power and of the "pith and substance" doctrine.

Whether legislation imposes a tax is a question which is as important for the provinces as it is for the Dominion. Its relevance for the provinces is in respect of their limitation to direct taxation under s. 92(2). For example, are employer contributions to a provincial workmen's compensation fund taxes which must meet the test of "direct taxation"? Or, are they in the nature of premiums statutorily exacted to insure employees against employment hazards, and hence a matter of the exercise of provincial regulatory authority under s. 92(13)? The Privy Council indicated in *Workmen's Compensation Board v. C.P.R.,* [1920] A.C. 184, 48 D.L.R. 218, [1919] 3 W.W.R. 167, that such contributions were taxes. In the course of his judgment for the Board, Lord Haldane remarked: "Nor can it be successfully contended that the Province had not a general power to impose direct taxation in this form on the respondents if for provincial purposes"; see also *Workmen's Compensation Board v. Bathurst Co.*, [1923] 4 D.L.R. 84, 50 N.B.R. 246; *Royal Bank of Canada v. Workmen's Compensation Board of N.S.*, [1936] S.C.R. 560, [1936] 4 D.L.R. 9 (assessments on employers held to be direct taxation). This view, and its consequence, should be compared with the attitude of the Privy Council in the *Employment and Social Insurance Act* case, *supra*, and the consequence for the Dominion of the view that the contributions there were not taxes. Having regard to the limitations on federal regulatory power, reliance on the plenary taxing power was necessary. This proved adequate in *Reader's Digest Assoc. (Canada) Ltd. v. A.-G. Can.* (1962), 37 D.L.R. (2d) 239, aff'd. (1965), 59 D.L.R. (2d) 54 to sustain a federal excise tax on the value of advertising material in so-called special editions (as defined) of non-Canadian periodicals published in Canada, although it was clear that the tax was designed to aid or had the effect of aiding Canadian periodicals. The matter has come up in several other cases with respect to provincial legislation. In *Ontario Boys Wear Ltd. v. Advisory Committee and A.-G. Ont.*, [1944] S.C.R. 349, [1944] 4 D.L.R. 273 an issue arose whether the compulsory levy to help defray the expenses of administering codes of working conditions under the *Ontario Industrial Standards Act* was a tax, and, if so, whether it was direct. Kerwin J., speaking for the Court stated that "if the assessment be a tax, it is a direct tax . . .; and, in any event, it may be justified as a fee for services rendered by the Province or by its authorized instrumentalities under the powers given provincial legislatures by sections 92(13) and 92(16) of the *B.N.A. Act*". See, to the same effect, *Shannon v. Lower Mainland Dairy Products Board*, [1938] A.C. 708, [1938] 4 D.L.R. 81, [1938] 2 W.W.R. 604. In *A.-G. B.C. v. E. & N. Ry.*, [1950] A.C. 87, [1950] 1 D.L.R. 305, [1949] 2 W.W.R. 1233, the Privy Council had to consider, *inter alia*, whether s. 124 of the *Forest Act*, R.S.B.C. 1948, c. 128, providing for the creation of a forest protection fund through an annual levy on owners of timber lands and through annual provincial grants, imposed a tax or merely a service charge for fire protection services. Although imposed on a defined and limited class of persons, and applicable to a special purpose without ever falling into the general mass of proceeds of taxation, the levy was held to be a tax. The decision on tax or service charge had to be made in this case to determine whether the railway company was exempt from the levy because of a statutory exemption from "taxation". In two other cases the courts held that certain equalization levies designed to effectuate provincial schemes of price fixing as an aid to orderly marketing were really taxes which were unconstitutional because indirect: see *Lower Mainland Dairy Products Sales Adjustment Committee v. Crystal Dairy Ltd.*, [1933] A.C. 168, [1933] 1 D.L.R. 82, [1932] 3 W.W.R. 639; *Lower Mainland Dairy Products Board v. Turner's Dairy Ltd.*, [1941] S.C.R. 573, [1941] 4 D.L.R. 209. The problem raised by these cases is considered below, but it may be said here that their authority was somewhat attenuated by the Supreme Court's judgment in *Reference re The Farm Products Marketing Act, R.S.O. 1950, c. 131, as Amended*, [1957] S.C.R. 198,

7 D.L.R. (2d) 257, and was effectively undermined by the Supreme Court's more recent judgment in *Crawford and Hillside Farm Dairy Ltd. v. A.-G. B.C.*, [1960] S.C.R. 346, 22 D.L.R. (2d) 321; see *R. v. Ont. Milk Marketing Board; ex p. Channel Islands Breeds Milk Producers Association*, [1969] 1 O.R. 309, 4 D.L.R. (3d) 490; aff'd [1969] 2 O.R. 121, 4 D.L.R. (2d) 490. In *Children's Aid Society v. Salmon Arm*, [1941] 1 D.L.R. 532, [1941] 1 W.W.R. 68, 55 B.C.R. 495, it was held that a provincial enactment authorizing the making of an order fixing a municipality with responsibility for maintaining a neglected child, did not impose a tax; hence there was no question of "direct" or "indirect" to be determined.

While it would seem to be a necessary consequency of these cases that there is a legally definable thing called a "tax", it is difficult to square the results of the cases with the indicia of taxation which they lay down. Perhaps the pioneer effort at definition was that made by Duff J., as he then was, in *Lawson v. Interior Tree, Fruit & Vegetable Committee*, [1931] S.C.R. 357, [1931] 2 D.L.R. 193, which involved the validity of provincial marketing legislation authorizing an administrative agency to impose levies on any products marketed to defray expenses of operation. According to Duff J., the levies were taxes because they were (1) enforceable by law; (2) imposed under the authority of the legislature; (3) imposed by a public body; and (4) made for a public purpose. It followed in this case that they were invalid because indirect in violation of s. 92(2). It is a fair question whether they would not today be considered valid under s. 92(9) if enacted under a licensing system established by provincial marketing legislation: see *Shannon v. Lower Mainland Dairy Products Board, supra*. In *A.-G. B.C. v. E. & N. Ry., supra*, it appeared to be enough to mark the forest protection fund levy as a tax that (to use the words of the Privy Council) "it [was] imposed compulsorily by the State and [was] recoverable at the suit of the Crown" ([1950] A.C. 87, at p. 121); the special features of the levy, already noted, did not matter. This much is clear; a tax under the *B.N.A. Act* is not confined to an exaction for the support of the government.

The tests of a tax, indicated in the *Lawson* case and in the *E. & N. Ry.* case were applied by Egbert J. in *Re Unearned Increment Tax Act*, [1953] 1 D.L.R. 657, 6 W.W.R. (N.S.) 657. There a statute imposed a tax of ten per cent (payable on the registration under the *Alberta Land Titles Act* of any transfer of land) on the increase in value of the land at the time of such registration over and above the last preceding value, excluding cost of improvements or of development work. Despite the language of the statute which spoke of a "tax" the learned Judge held that the exaction was not a tax because not imposed directly upon anyone, not made compulsory, nor was it enforceable by law when the only penalty for non-payment was refusal to register a transfer; indeed, a purchaser could escape the consequence of non-payment by registering a caveat. Egbert J. held that exaction was a confiscation or capture of a capital gain, but he went on to hold that if he should be wrong in this and the levy was a tax, it was direct. The Alberta Appellate Division affirmed in a few words, holding the exaction to be a tax and to be direct.

[Are water rates taxes in respect of federal Crown property? See *A.-G. Can. v. Toronto* (1893), 23 S.C.R. 514.]

A few other features of federal and provincial taxing powers may be noted here. The Dominion under s. 91(3) may impose a licence tax in connection with matters falling within its regulatory authority, *e.g.* "seacoast and inland fisheries": *A.-G. Can. v. A.-G. Ont.*, [1898] A.C. 700. Since the *Statute of Westminster*, 1931 (Imp.), c. 4, s. 3, the Dominion may give its tax legislation an extraterritorial operation: see *B.C. Electric Ry. Co. v. The King*, [1946] A.C. 527, [1946] 4 D.L.R. 81, [1946] 3 W.W.R. 737. While provincial taxing power under s. 92(2) is limited both in kind and in area, neither of these limitations affects the plenary authority of the Dominion under s. 91(3). The necessary reconciliation of these two grants of power (adverted to in *Citizens Insurance Co. v. Parsons* (1881), 7 App. Cas. 96, at p. 108 and in *Bank of Toronto v. Lambe* (1887), 12 App. Cas. 575 at p. 585) has, however, withdrawn from Dominion authority any power of direct taxation within a province to raise revenue for provincial purposes—a limitation on Dominion power which is quite inconsequential. Whether the Dominion can impose indirect taxation within a province to raise revenue for provincial purposes was considered to be an improbable event in *Caron v. The King*, [1924] A.C. 999, [1924] 4 D.L.R. 1005, [1924] 3 W.W.R. 417. It has been suggested that in principle this should fall to the provinces under s. 92(16): see *Kennedy and Wells,* Law of the Taxing Power in Canada (1931), p. 152. This would, no doubt, be a welcome proposition to the provinces but the courts have not hitherto accorded to the provinces any revenue raising authority save as given by s. 92(2) and s. 92(9). In the case of the latter, it appears to be the law that licence fees need not conform to the test of direct taxation: see *Shannon v. Lower Mainland Dairy Products Board, supra.* The problem raised by *Caron v. The King* as to federal authority to impose indirect taxation for provincial purposes is considered below in a Note on "The End of the Crystal Dairy Doctrine: A Superfluous Federal Legislative Cure".

Because the taxing powers of Dominion and Provinces are independent of each other, there is no constitutional objection to double taxation: see *Forbes v. A.-G. Man.*, [1937] A.C. 260, [1937] 1 D.L.R. 289, [1937] 1 W.W.R. 167, where Lord Macmillan said: "Both [*i.e.* Dominion and provincial] income taxes may co-exist and be enforced without clashing. The Dominion reaps part of the field of the Manitoba citizen's income. The Province reaps another part of it." What the constitutional position would be if Dominion and provincial income taxation aggregated over 100 per cent. has not yet been decided, but the situation would invite the application of the "paramountcy" doctrine to tax collection: *cf. In re Silver Bros., A.-G. Que. v. A.-G.*

Can., [1932] A.C. 514, [1932] 2 D.L.R. 673, [1932] 1 W.W.R. 764.
Despite the absence of constitutional difficulty, the existence of
common tax fields (as in the case of income tax) has induced
Dominion-provincial co-operation in income taxation, both in the
interests of economy of administration and of relieving the taxpayer
from making multiple returns. Thus, by tax agreements with the
Dominion the provinces have undertaken, in return for payments to be
made to them by the Dominion, to refrain from levying specified taxes.
No delegation of power is involved because the Dominion is clearly entitled in any event to levy such taxes. And it is to be doubted that the
Dominion-Provincial tax arrangements can be attacked as involving
direct taxation by the Dominion within a Province to raise revenue for
provincial purposes. The law on the matter is, however, enmeshed in
economic and political considerations which go to the very heart of
Canadian federalism: see *Scott,* the Constitutional Background of
Taxation Agreements, (1955) 2 McGill L.J. 1. Indeed, the taxation
agreements are not legally enforceable against the Dominion except
as they may involve legislative acceptance of jurisdiction for their
implementation: see *In re Taxation Agreement between Saskatchewan and Canada,* [1946] 1 W.W.R. 257. (*Quaere,* however, whether
it is not open to the Crown in one aspect to sue the Crown in another
on a contract between them!) Moreover, it is open to a Province to
pass valid legislation in derogation of the agreements: see *Van Buren
Bridge Co. v. Madawaska and A.-G. N.B.* (1958), 15 D.L.R. (2d) 763,
41 M.P.R. 360; *Re Lofstrom & Murphy* (1971), 22 D.L.R. (3d)
120 (Sask.). The contrary intimation in *Alworth Jr. v. A.-G. B.C.*
(1959), 20 D.L.R. (2d) 544 (B.C.) (affirmed on appeal with express
exclusion of any determination on this point (1960), 24 D.L.R. (2d)
71) is incompatible with well-understood constitutional principle. No
so-called contract between Dominion and Province can operate as a
constitutional limitation on provincial taxing power to the advantage
of a person caught by a provincial statute which violates the contract.

[In *Caron v. The King,* [1924] A.C. 999, at p. 1004, [1924] 4 D.L.R. 105,
at p. 108, [1924] 3 W.W.R. 417, at p. 420, Lord Phillimore said: "Upon any
view there is nothing in section 92 to take away the power to impose any
taxation for Dominion purposes which is *prima facie* given by head 3 of
section 91. It is not therefore *ultra vires* on the part of the Parliament of
Canada to impose a Dominion income tax for Dominion purposes"; see too
Duff C.J. (dissenting) in *Reference re Employment and Social Insurance Act,*
[1936] S.C.R. 427, at p. 433, [1936] 3 D.L.R. 644, at p. 648: "The authority,
it will be noticed, is an authority to legislate in relation to the raising of
money. There is no limitation in those words as respect the purpose or
purposes to which the money is to be applied." Note the use of the federal
"spending" power in connection with the marketing of wheat by the offer
of a fixed price to farmers which they are not, however, legally obliged to
accept; and see Chap. IV, *supra.* It is similarly open to the Dominion to
spend money on education or on any other objects, either by conditional or
unconditional grants.]

2. Direct Taxation Within the Province

BANK OF TORONTO v. LAMBE

In the Privy Council. (1887), 12 App. Cas. 575.

Appeal from a judgment of the Quebec Court of Queen's Bench upholding the validity of certain Quebec taxing legislation referred to below.

LORD HOBHOUSE: In the year 1882 the Quebec legislature passed a statute entitled "An Act to impose certain direct taxes on certain commercial corporations." It is thereby enacted that every bank carrying on the business of banking in this province; every insurance company accepting risks and transacting the business of insurance in this province; every incorporated company carrying on any labour, trade, or business in this province; and a number of other specified companies, shall annually pay the several taxes thereby imposed upon them. In the case of banks the tax imposed is a sum varying with the paid-up capital, and an additional sum for each office or place of business.

The appellant bank was incorporated in the year 1855 by an Act of the then parliament of Canada. Its principal place of business is at Toronto, but it has an agency at Montreal. Its capital is said to be kept at Toronto, from whence are transmitted the funds necessary to carry on the business at Montreal. The amount of its capital at present belonging to persons resident in the province of Quebec, and the amount disposable for the Montreal agency, are respectively much less than the amount belonging to other persons and the amount disposable elsewhere.

The bank resists payment of the tax in question on the ground that the Quebec legislature had no power to pass the statute which imposes it. Mr. Justice Rainville sitting in the Superior Court took that view, and dismissed an action brought by the government officer, who is the respondent. The Court of Queen's Bench, by a majority of three judges to two, took the contrary view, and gave the plaintiff a decree. The case comes here on appeal from that decree of the Court of Queen's Bench.

The principal grounds on which the Superior Court rested its judgment were as follows: That the tax is an indirect one; that it is not imposed within the limits of the province; that the parliament has exclusive power to regulate banks; that the provincial legislature can tax only that which exists by their authority or is introduced by their permission; and that if the power to tax such banks as this exists, they may be crushed out by it, and so the power of the parliament to create them may be nullified. The grounds stated in the decree of the Queen's Bench are two, viz., that the tax is a direct tax, and that it is also a matter of a merely local or private nature in the province, and so falls within class 16 of the matters of provincial legislation. It has not been contended at the bar that the provincial legislature can tax only that which exists on their authority or permission. And when the appellant's counsel were proceeding to argue that the tax did not fall within class 16, their Lordships intimated that they would prefer to hear first what could be said in favour of the opposite view. All the other grounds have been argued very fully, and their Lordships must add very ably, at the bar.

To ascertain whether or not the tax is lawfully imposed, it will be best to follow the method of inquiry adopted in other cases. First, does it fall within the description of taxation allowed by class 2 of sect. 92 of the Federation Act, *viz.*, "Direct taxation within the province in order to the raising of a revenue for Provincial purposes"? Secondly, if it does, are we compelled by anything in sec. 91 or in the other parts of the Act so to cut down the full meaning of the words of sect. 92 that they shall not cover this tax?

First, is the tax a direct tax? For the argument of this question the opinions of a great many writers on political economy have been cited, and it is quite proper, or rather necessary, to have careful regard to such opinions, as has been said in previous cases before this Board. But it must not be forgotten that the question is a legal one, *viz.*, what the words mean, as used in this statute; whereas the economists are always seeking to trace the effect of taxation throughout the community, and are apt to use the words "direct", and "indirect", according as they find that the burden of a tax abides more or less with the person who first pays it. This distinction is illustrated very clearly by the quotations from a very able and clear thinker, the late Mr. Fawcett, who, after giving his tests of direct and indirect taxation, makes remarks to the effect that a tax may be made direct or indirect by the position of the taxpayers or by private bargains about its payment. Doubtless, such remarks have their value in an economical discussion. Probably it is true of every indirect tax that some persons are both the first and the final payers of it; and of every direct tax that it affects persons other than the first payers; and the excellence of an economist's definition will be measured by the accuracy with which it contemplates and embraces every incident of the thing defined. But that very excellence impairs its value for the purposes of the lawyer. The legislature cannot possibly have meant to give a power of taxation valid or invalid according to its actual results in particular cases. It must have contemplated some tangible dividing line referable to and ascertainable by the general tendencies of the tax and the common understanding of men as to those tendencies.

After some consideration Mr. Kerr [counsel for appellant] chose the definition of John Stuart Mill as the one he would prefer to abide by. That definition is as follows:

"Taxes are either direct or indirect. A direct tax is one which is demanded from the very persons who it is intended or desired should pay it. Indirect taxes are those which are demanded from one person in the expectation and intention that he shall indemnify himself at the expense of another; such are the excise or customs.

"The producer or importer of a commodity is called upon to pay a tax on it, not with the intention to levy a peculiar contribution upon him, but to tax through him the consumers of the commodity, from whom it is supposed that he will recover the amount by means of an advance in price."

It is said that Mill adds a term—that to be strictly direct a tax must be general; and this condition was much pressed at the bar. Their Lordships have not thought it necessary to examine Mill's works for the purpose of ascertaining precisely what he does say on this point; nor would they presume to say whether for economical purposes such a condition is sound or unsound; but they have no hesitation in rejecting it for legal purposes. It would deny the character of a direct tax to the income tax of this country, which is always spoken of as such, and is generally looked upon as a direct tax of the most obvious kind; and it would run counter to the common understanding of men on this subject, which is one main clue to the meaning of the legislature.

Their Lordships then take Mill's definition above quoted as a fair basis for testing the character of the tax in question, not only because it is chosen by the appellant's counsel, nor only because it is that of an eminent writer, nor with the intention that it should be considered a binding legal definition, but because it seems to them to embody with sufficient accuracy for this purpose an understanding of the most obvious indicia of direct and indirect taxation, which is a common understanding, and is likely to have been present to the minds of those who passed the Federation Act.

Now whether the probabilities of the case or the frame of the Quebec Act are considered, it appears to their Lordships that the Quebec legislature must have intended and desired that the very corporations from whom the tax is demanded should pay and finally bear it. It is carefully designed for that purpose. It is not like a customs' duty which enters at once into the price of the taxed commodity. There the tax is demanded of the importer, while nobody expects or intends that he shall finally bear it. All scientific economists teach that it is paid, and scientific financiers intend that it shall be paid, by the consumer; and even those who do not accept the conclusions of the economists maintain that it is paid, and intend it to be paid, by the foreign producer. Nobody thinks that it is, or intends that it shall be, paid by the importer from whom it is demanded. But the tax now in question is demanded directly of the bank apparently for the reasonable purpose of getting contributions for provincial purposes from those who are making profits by provincial business. It is not a tax on any commodity which the bank deals in and can sell at an enhanced price to its customers. It is not a tax on its profits, nor on its several transactions. It is a direct lump sum, to be assessed by simple reference to its paid-up capital and its places of business. It may possibly happen that in the intricacies of mercantile dealings the bank may find a way to recoup itself out of the pockets of its Quebec customers. But the way must be an obscure and circuitous one, the amount of recoupment cannot bear any direct relation to the amount of tax paid, and if the bank does manage it, the result will not improbably disappoint the intention and desire of the Quebec Government. For these reasons their Lordships hold the tax to be direct taxation within class 2 of sect. 92 of the *Federation Act.*

There is nothing in the previous decisions on the question of direct taxation which is adverse to this view. In the case of *Queen Insurance Co.,* 3 App. Cas. 1090, the disputed tax was imposed under cover of a license to be taken out by insurers. But nothing was to be paid directly on the license, nor was any penalty imposed upon failure to take one. The price of the license was to be a percentage on the premiums received for insurances, each of which was to be stamped accordingly. Such a tax would fall within any definition of indirect taxation, and the form given to it was apparently with the view of bringing it under class 9 of sect. 92, which relates to licenses. In *Reed's* case, 10 App. Cas. 141, the tax was a stamp duty on exhibits produced in courts of law, which in a great many, perhaps most, instances would certainly not be paid by the person first chargeable with it. In *Severn's* case, 2 S.C.R. 70, the tax in question was one for licences which by a law of the legislature of Ontario were required to be taken for dealing in liquors. The Supreme Court held the law to be *ultra vires,* mainly on the grounds that such licences did not fall within class 9 of sect. 92, and that they were in conflict with the powers of parliament under class 2 of sect. 91. It is true that all the judges expressed opinions that the tax, being a licence duty, was not a direct tax. Their reasons do not clearly appear, but, as the tax now in question is not either in substance or in form a licence duty, further examination of that point is unnecessary.

The next question is whether the tax is taxation within the province. It is urged that the bank is a Toronto corporation, having its domicile there, and having its capital placed there; that the tax is on the capital of the bank; that it must therefore fall on a person or persons, or on property, not within Quebec. The answer to this argument is that class 2 of sect. 92 does not require that the persons to be taxed by Quebec are to be domiciled or even resident in Quebec. Any person found within the province may legally be taxed there if taxed directly. This bank is found to be carrying on business there, and on that ground alone it is taxed. There is no attempt to tax the capital of the bank, any more than its profits. The bank itself is directly ordered to pay a sum of money; but the legislature has not chosen to tax every bank, small or large, alike, nor to leave the amount of tax to be ascertained by variable accounts or any uncertain standard. It has adopted its own measure, either of that which it is just the banks should pay, or of that which they have means to pay, and these things it ascertains by reference to facts which can be verified without doubt or delay. The banks are to pay so much, not according to their capital, but according to their paid-up capital, and so much on their places of business. Whether this method of assessing a tax is sound or unsound, wise or unwise, is a point on which their Lordships have no opinion, and are not called on to form one, for as it does not carry the taxation out of the province it is for the Legislature and not for Courts of Law to judge of its expediency.

Then is there anything in sect. 91 which operates to restrict the meaning above ascribed to sect. 92? . . . Their Lordships adhere to [the] view, and hold that, as regards direct taxation within the province to raise revenue for provincial purposes, that subject falls wholly within the jurisdiction of the provincial legislatures.

It has been earnestly contended that the taxation of banks would unduly cut down the powers of the parliament in relation to matters falling within class 2, *viz.* the regulation of trade and commerce; and within class 15, *viz.*, banking, and the incorporation of banks. Their Lordships think that this contention gives far too wide an extent to the classes in question. They cannot see how the power of making banks contribute to the public objects of the provinces where they carry on business can interfere at all with the power of making laws on the subject of banking, or with the power of incorporating banks. . . .

Then it is suggested that the legislature may lay on taxes so heavy as to crush a bank out of existence, and so nullify the power of parliament to erect banks. But their Lordships cannot conceive that when the Imperial Parliament conferred wide powers of local self-government on great countries such as Quebec, it intended to limit them on the speculation that they would be used in an injurious manner. People who are trusted with the great power of making laws for property and civil rights may well be trusted to levy taxes. There are obvious reasons for confining their power to direct taxes and licences, because the power of indirect taxation would be felt all over the Dominion. But whatever power falls within the legitimate meaning of classes 2 and 9, is, in their Lordships' judgment, what the Imperial Parliament intended to give; and to place a limit on it because the power may be used unwisely, as all powers may, would be an error, and would lead to insuperable difficulties, in the construction of the Federation Act. . . .

Appeal dismissed.

[See also *A.-G. Que. v. Imperial Oil Ltd.*, [1945] C. Tax C. 233.

In *A.-G. Que. v. Reed* (1884), 10 App. Cas. 141, referred to in the *Lambe* case, the Privy Council asserted that "the question whether it is a direct or an indirect tax cannot depend upon those special events which may vary in particular cases; but the best general rule is to look to the time of payment; and if at the time the ultimate incidence is uncertain then, as it appears to their Lordships, it cannot in this view, be called direct taxation . . ." (at p. 144). In *A.-G. B.C. v. Kingcome Navigation Co. Ltd.*, [1934] A.C. 45, at p. 52, [1934], 1 D.L.R. 31, at p. 35, [1933] 3 W.W.R. 353, at p. 356, the Privy Council, referring to the foregoing passage in the *Reed* case said: "It is clear that 'ultimate incidence' is not there used in the sense of the political economists, but refers to the ultimate incidence among the parties to the transaction in respect of which the tax is imposed". Mill's definition of direct and indirect taxation as applied in the *Lambe* case was approved in *Brewers and Maltsters' Association of Ontario v. A.-G. Ont.*, [1897] A.C. 231 where legislation imposing a flat licence fee of $100 on brewers and distillers engaged in wholesale selling was upheld under s. 92(2) and s. 92(9) of the *B.N.A. Act.* Since the fee had no relation to the quantity of goods sold and in the ordinary course there was no intention or expectation of recoupment from customers, it satisfied the accepted test of direct taxation. In *Cotton v. The King,* [1914] A.C. 176, 15 D.L.R. 283, 5 W.W.R. 662, "direct taxation" as used in s. 92(2) was held to be settled in meaning by Mill's definition.

Although the *Reed* case was the first in which Mill's definition was mentioned, there was an earlier reference in *A.-G. Que. v. Queen Ins. Co.* (1878), 3 App. Cas. 1090 to the fact that at least two encyclopedias had been produced in support of the conclusion that both the popular and technical use of the term "direct tax" excluded a stamp tax.

In *A.-G. Man. v. A.-G. Can.,* [1925] A.C. 561, [1925] 2 D.L.R. 691, [1925] 2 W.W.R. 60, the Privy Council invalidated the *Manitoba Grain Futures Taxation Act,* 1923, which (although exempting sales where the seller is the grower or either party to the contract is owner or tenant of the land on which the grain is to be grown) imposed a tax on the seller or his broker or agent in respect of every contract of sale of grain for future delivery. Lord Haldane said that "it is impossible to doubt that the tax was imposed .in a form which contemplated that some one else than the person on whom it was imposed should pay it. The amount will, in the end, become a charge against the amount of the price which is to come to the seller in the world market, and be paid by some one else than the persons primarily taxed. The class of those taxed obviously includes an indefinite number who would naturally indemnify themselves out of the property of the owners for whom they were acting".]

FORTIER v. LAMBE

In the Supreme Court of Canada. (1895), 25 S.C.R. 422.

Appeal from a judgment of the Quebec Superior Court sitting in review, 5 Que. S.C. 355, affirming a judgment of the Superior Court, 5 Que. S.C. 47, directing defendant to pay the licence fee imposed by provincial legislation on manufacturers and traders. In this case the tax demanded was the double licence fee arising under provisions which required every trader doing business in Montreal by wholesale, or by wholesale and retail, to take out an annual licence at a cost of $100 if his stock in trade exceeds $500; and in certain situations, of which the present case was one, double licence fees were payable.

SIR HENRY STRONG C.J.: This judgment is in my opinion free from error. If I was at liberty to do so, I might hold according to the opinion I expressed in *Severn v. The Queen,* that a licence of this kind came within the words "other licences" in subsect. 9, sec. 92 *British North America Act,* but I am precluded from doing this by the judgment of this court in that case.

I am, however, of opinion that this is the case of a direct tax and is governed by the decision of the Privy Council in the *Bank of Toronto v. Lambe,* 12 App. Cas. 576, and that it is not an indirect tax within *Attorney-General v. Queen Insurance Co.,* 3 App. Cas. 1090. I quite agree with the courts below in the definition which they give of a direct tax. In order that a tax may be indirect it must appear clearly that it was one not to be ultimately borne by the person by whom it is to be paid in the first instance. I cannot say that a tax upon a man's business is one which must necessarily be borne by the persons who make purchases from him.

This distinction between a direct and an indirect tax depending on the incidence of the tax is well pointed out by Professor Sidgwick in his work on Political Economy, 2d ed. p. 57, where he says:

> We have now to note a new element of imperfection and uncertainty in the equalization of taxation due to the fact that we can only partially succeed in making the burden of either direct or indirect taxes fall where we desire; the burden is liable to be transferred to other persons when it is intended to remain where it is first imposed, and on the other hand when it is intended to be transferred the process of transference is liable to be tardy and incomplete. Indeed this process is often so complicated and obscure that it is a problem of considerable intricacy and difficulty to ascertain where the burden of a tax actually rests; and it is not even a simple matter to state accurately the general principle for determining the incidence of a tax supposing all the facts to be known.

And in a note he adds:

> The common classification of taxes as direct and indirect appears to me liable to mislead the student by ignoring the complexity and difficulty of the problem of determining the incidence of taxation.

If the tax was imposed without the device of a licence it would be precisely identical with that in question in *Bank of Toronto v. Lambe,* and I cannot see that the circumstance that the persons affected by the tax are, for convenience of the government in collecting it, required to take out a licence can make any difference. It is a direct tax to all intents and purposes, and within the powers expressly conferred upon the legislature.

The objection of want of uniformity which was so strongly pressed is no legal objection. Granting that the legislatures have the power of imposing such taxes it is for them to say how it is to be distributed.

We have not in the *British North America Act* any such provision as that contained in the constitution of the United States, which requires that all taxes, excises and imposts shall be uniform throughout the United States.

The cases cited in support of this contention were principally American authorities which had reference to this express constitutional provision requiring uniformity. . . .

TASCHEREAU J.: The contention of the appellant based on the ground that this tax has not been legally apportioned, and is null for want of uniformity and equality, is, in my opinion, untenable. Whenever political economists and other writers may say on this subject I know of no law in the Dominion that in any way puts any restriction, limitation or regulation of that kind on the powers of the federal or provincial authorities in relation to taxation within their respective spheres.

In the United States a provision on the subject is to be found in the federal constitution, but there is no similar enactment in the *British North America Act.*

The appellant's other contention, that this tax involves a regulation of trade and commerce, and is therefore *ultra vires,* is also untenable. A similar point was urged in *Citizens Ins. Co. v. Parsons,* 7 App. Cas. 96, and in *Bank of Toronto v. Lambe,* and declared unfounded. The reasoning of their Lordships of the Privy Council upon that point in those cases applies here. In fact, if this is a direct tax, *cadit questio,* this statute is *intra vires;* the fact that it might involve in a certain degree a regulation of trade and commerce cannot deprive the provincial legislature of the right to raise a revenue by means of direct taxation, or impair such right in any way. . . .

The cases of *Reg. v. Taylor,* 36 U.C.Q.B. 183; *Severn v. The Queen; Attorney-General v. The Queen Ins. Co.; Attorney-General v. Reed; Bank of Toronto v. Lambe,* though not directly in point, contain all that can be said, and almost all the authorities and writers that can be cited, on this question. It would be, however, useless for me, in the view I take of the present case, and fettered by authority as I deem myself to be, to enter into a renewed consideration of the different aspects of the question in relation to the *British North America Act.* I mean, of course, as a question of law, not as one of statesmanship or political economy. Assuming that licences, generally speaking, constitute indirect taxation, a proposition that in law I would now very much doubt as applicable to the *British North America Act,* I hold that though the Quebec legislature has resorted to a system of licenses as a means to raise the tax in question yet this statute is not to be taken as a license Act.

It is evident, by its terms, that it contains no prohibition whatever as to manufacture or trade. Therefore no license, no permit (*lices licere*) is necessary in the province as a condition precedent to legally manufacture or legally trade, and all contracts entered into by the manufacturer or trader in the course of his business are perfectly lawful and enforceable at law. The *Liquor License Acts,* on the contrary, as did also the Act under consideration in *Severn v. The Queen,* absolutely prohibit the selling of any liquor without having first obtained a license to do so. Under that class of statutes, every time a sale without license is made the penalty is incurred; each sale is a distinct offence, and is altogether unlawful. Under the statute now under consideration the double license fee is exigible only once a year, and the sale or manufacture without a license is not unlawful in the sense that a sale of liquor without a license is under a prohibitory law. This is, it seems to me, as direct a tax as the tax under consideration in the *Bank of Toronto* case, which by the Privy Council has been declared to constitute direct taxation. In fact it is nothing else but an extension to private individuals of that statute which applied only to corporations. Now, if this tax was a direct one when imposed upon commercial corporations, is it the less direct when imposed upon private individuals? And can the form of collecting the tax alter its nature? We have the high authority of the Privy Council in *Attorney-General v. The Queen Insurance Co.* for the proposition that it does not. And in the same sense Mr. Justice Clifford, delivering the judgment of the United States Supreme Court in *Scholey v. Rew,* 23 Wall. 331, in answering negatively the argument that the tax in question in that case was a tax on land because the act creating it made it a lien on the land, said: "Nor is the tax in question affected in the least by the fact that the tax or duty is made a lien upon the land, as the lien is merely an appropriate regulation to secure the collection of the exaction."

In my opinion the license in question here is likewise merely an appropriate regulation to secure the collection of a direct tax.

I would dismiss the appeal. If the question was *res integra* I would be inclined to think that the words "direct taxation" in subsec. 2 of sec. 92 of the *British North America Act* were not intended to give to the provinces the very large powers of taxation that are claimed by the respondent here, and which the judgments of the courts below concede them, either directly or inferentially. However, in view of the decision of the Privy Council, I have to refrain from giving my own opinion on the question submitted.

GWYNNE J. (after holding that the case was governed by *Bank of Toronto v. Lambe*): . . . As to the contention of the appellant on the one side that the Act was *ultra vires* of any jurisdiction conferred by item 9 of sec. 92, and that of the respondent on the other hand that the Act was *intra vires* of that item, and that the authority of *Severn v. The Queen,* was so shaken by the judgment of this court in *Molson v. Lambe* 15 S.C.R. 253, that it should no longer be followed, I decline to express any opinion, for the reason already given, as to whether this case is or is not governed by *Severn v. The Queen,* or whether that case was well or ill decided. It certainly has not been judicially overruled, and until it shall be it is, I presume, binding upon this court, and it is not necessary for the decision of the present case to bring it within *Severn v. The Queen,* and as to its being shaken by *Molson v. Lambe,* a perusal of the report of that case will show that the only question raised and submitted to the court in that case was as to the right of a party to proceedings in an inferior jurisdiction, by the law of the province of Quebec. to prohibit the judge of the inferior jurisdiction from proceeding to judgment upon issues joined in the matter before him; and the judgment of the court was that as the matter in which the issues were joined was within the jurisdiction of the Superior Court proceedings in prohibition could not be instituted according to the law of the province of Quebec to prevent the judge proceeding to judgment in the case, and that if he should render an erroneous judgment in the matter it could be reviewed upon a *certiorari.*

Appeal dismissed.

[Sedgewick and King JJ. concurred.

The principal case was followed in *Colpitts Ranches v. A.-G. Alta.*, [1954] 3 D.L.R. 121, 11 W.W.R. (N.S.) 301, sustaining the validity of a municipal business tax on fox farming, as authorized by provincial legislation, where the tax was payable whether or not the fox was pelted or sold or kept for breeding or for show purposes. The authorizing legislation provided for the passing of by-laws for assessing the business of fur farming on the basis of the number and kind of fur bearing animals kept for the purpose of the business at any amount per animal, not exceeding that fixed by the Lieutenant-Governor in Council. The municipality in this case exacted the limit of the permitted amount. Cairns J. held that this was clearly a tax on a business, a tax on plaintiff's personal property imposed with the intention that he should bear it even if in the course of business he might pass it on; consequently it was a direct tax.]

THE KING v. CALEDONIAN COLLIERIES LTD.

In the Privy Council. [1928] A.C. 358, [1928] 3 D.L.R. 657.
[1928] 2 W.W.R. 417.

Appeal by special leave from a judgment of the Supreme Court of Canada, [1927] S.C.R. 257, [1927] 2 D.L.R. 70, reversing a judgment of the Alberta Appellate Division, [1926] 2 W.W.R. 280, [1926] 2 D.L.R. 1070, and holding that the *Alberta Mine Owners Tax Act*, 1923, was *ultra vires*.

LORD WARRINGTON OF CLYFFE: The question raised by this appeal is whether the *Mine Owners Tax Act*, 1923, of the Province of Alberta, which imposes upon mine owners as therein defined a percentage tax upon the gross revenues of their coal mines is *ultra vires* the Province as an attempt to impose indirect taxation . . .

The Act in question was passed by the Legislature of Alberta on April 21, 1923. It contained the following material provisions: "Section 3. Every mine owner shall from the last day of May, 1918, be subject to a tax upon the gross revenue received by him from his mine. Section 4. The said tax shall not be more than 2 per cent. of the said revenue and as determined by the Lieut.-Governor in Council under the provisions of this Act. Section 6. On or before the last day of each month each mine owner shall forward to the Minister a sum of money equal to 2 per cent. of the gross revenue received by him from his mine during the next preceding month."

The Act repealed a previous Act of the Province—the *Mine Owners Tax Act*, 1918—which also imposed a tax upon gross revenue, taking the form in that Act of 5 c. per ton of the coal removed from the mine premises. The validity of this tax had been disputed by the mine owners who had in many cases refused to pay it.

On August 14, 1925, the Lieutenant-Governor by and with the advice of the Executive Council ordered that the tax in question should be 2 per cent. of the gross revenue received by the mine owner from his mine.

The respondent company is a mine owner within the definition of that term contained in the Act in question. They began business in

November, 1923. They refused to pay the tax, and on August 21, 1925, the action, in which the order under appeal was made, was commenced for the purpose of recovering the amount of the tax alleged to be due from them. . . .

The question whether a tax is direct or indirect has on many occasions been the subject of decision by this Board, but it is unnecessary to refer to any of these decisions except that of *Bank of Toronto v. Lambe,* in which Lord Hobhouse, in delivering the judgment of the Board, made some useful observations as to the mode in which the question should be approached. . . .

What then is the general tendency of the tax now in question?

First it is necessary to ascertain the real nature of the tax. It is not disputed that, though the tax is called a tax on "gross revenue", such gross revenue is in reality the aggregate of sums received from sales of coal, and is indistinguishable from a tax upon every sum received from the sale of coal.

The respondents are producers of coal, a commodity the subject of commercial transactions. Their Lordships can have no doubt that the general tendency of a tax upon the sums received from the sale of the commodity which they produce and in which they deal is that they would seek to recover it in the price charged to a purchaser. Under particular circumstances the recovery of the tax may, it is true, be economically undesirable or practically impossible, but the general tendency of the tax remains.

It is said on behalf of the appellant that at the time a sale is made the tax has not become payable, and therefore cannot be passed on. Their Lordships cannot accept this contention; the tax will have to be paid, and there would be no more difficulty in adding to the selling price the amount of the tax in anticipation than there would be if it had been actually paid.

Appeal dismissed.

[In *Charlottetown v. Foundation Maritime Ltd.,* [1932] S.C.R. 589, [1932] 3 D.L.R. 353, a by-law under authorizing legislation was held invalid as imposing an indirect tax where it required all non-resident contractors to pay a graduated tax by way of a percentage of the contract price on every contract for work within the municipality. See also *Reference Re Agricultural Land Relief Act (Alta.),* [1938] 4 D.L.R. 28, [1938] 3 W.W.R. 186.

A tax on net profits is, of course, distinguishable from a tax on gross revenue, and it was held in *Nickel Rim Mines Ltd. v. A.-G. Ont.,* [1966] 1 O.R. 345, 53 D.L.R. (2d) 290, aff'd [1967] S.C.R. 270, 60 D.L.R. (2d) 576 that s. 3 of the *Mining Tax Act,* R.S.O. 1960, c. 242, imposed valid direct taxation not only in respect of annual profits received from output sold during the year but also in respect of profits, pre-estimated according to a statutory formula, on unsold ore severed from the mine and treated at the mine or elsewhere.

Where a Province has validly imposed a land tax, it is equally valid to make the tax a special or first lien on the crops grown on the assessed land, although there may be a question of priority if there is competing valid federal legislation: See *Reference re Section 31 of the Municipal District Act Amendment Act,* 1941 (Alta.), [1943] S.C.R. 295, [1943] 3 D.L.R. 145.]

A.-G. B.C. v. McDONALD MURPHY LUMBER CO.

In the Privy Council. [1930] A.C. 357, [1930] 2 D.L.R. 721,
[1930] 1 W.W.R. 830.

Appeal by special leave from a judgment of Morrison C. J. of the
Supreme Court of British Columbia, [1929] 2 W.W.R. 529, declaring
invalid certain provincial taxing legislation set out below.

LORD MACMILLAN: The controversy in this appeal relates to the
validity of an enactment of the legislature of the Province of British
Columbia imposing a tax on timber cut within the Province.

The tax was originally imposed in 1903 in substantially its present
form by a Provincial statute of that year, and was subsequently
re-enacted with unimportant alterations until in s. 58 of the Forest
Act, being s. 93 of the revised statutes of British Columbia, 1924, it
assumed the form in which its legality is now for the first time
challenged.

The section reads as follows: "58. There shall be due and payable
to His Majesty a tax upon all timber cut within the Province, save
and except that upon which a royalty is reserved by this Act or the
'Timber Royalty Act', or that upon which any royalty or tax is
payable to the Government of the Dominion, which tax shall be in
accordance with the following Schedules:" The first schedule deals
with "timber suitable for the manufacture of lumber and shingles",
which it classifies into three grades, to be taxed respectively at $2,
$1.50 and $1 per 1,000 feet, board measure, "provided that a rebate
of all the tax over one cent per thousand feet board measure, shall
be allowed when the timber upon which it is due or payable is manufactured or used in the Province." Schedule No. 2 deals with piles,
poles and crib timber, schedule No. 3 with railway-ties, mining props
and lagging, pulp-wood and cordwood, and schedule No. 4 with shingle
or other bolts of cedar, fir or spruce, taxes of varying amount being
assigned to the different categories. To each of these other schedules, as to the first, is appended a *proviso* remitting, by way of rebate,
all the tax over one cent when the timber is used in the Province.

Sect. 62 of the statute prohibits, under a penalty, the export or
removal from the Province of any timber in respect of which any tax
is payable to His Majesty in right of the Province unless a permit is
obtained from an officer of the Forest Board certifying that all taxes
so payable in respect thereof have been paid and confers on the
Minister of Lands drastic powers for the enforcement of the Act.

Sect. 127 requires every owner of granted lands and every holder
of a timber lease or licence on lands whereon any timber is cut in
respect of which any tax is payable, and every person dealing in any
timber cut from any such lands and every person operating a mill or
other industry which cuts or uses timber upon which any tax is
payable, to keep correct books of account of all timber cut for or
received by him and to render monthly statements to the district
forester, "and the owner, lessee or licensee or person dealing in the
timber or operating the mill or other industry as aforesaid shall pay

monthly all such sums of money as are shown to be due, to the Minister."

The respondent company are engaged in the business of logging, and sell both locally and for export timber which they cut upon lands granted to them or their predecessors. Having entered into a contract to sell a consignment of their logs to a purchaser in the State of Washington, U.S.A., they applied to the customs officials of the Dominion government for clearance which was refused on the ground that they did not hold an export permit from the Provincial government. The officers of the forest branch of the Provincial government declined to grant an export permit except on payment of the tax now in question. Thereupon the respondent company instituted the present proceedings against the Attorney-General for British Columbia claiming a declaration that they were under no obligation to pay the tax demanded, and that the relative provisions of the statute were *ultra vires* of the Provincial legislature.

The case was heard in the Supreme Court of British Columbia by Morrison C.J. sitting alone, who, after hearing evidence, gave judgment declaring s. 58 of the Forest Act and ss. 62 and 127 "in so far as they purport to implement any tax levied by the said s. 58", to be *ultra vires* of the Provincial legislature. From that judgment the present appeal is taken.

The validity of the tax was maintained by the appellant on the ground that it was competently imposed by the Provincial legislature as being "direct taxation within the Province in order to the raising of a revenue for Provincial purposes", which is the second class of subjects upon which Provincial legislatures have by s. 92 of the British North America Act, 1867, exclusive power to make laws.

The respondent company, on the other hand, impugned the tax mainly on two grounds—namely: (1.) that it was an indirect tax, and, therefore, not within the competence of the Provincial legislature; and (2.) that it violated ss. 121, 122, 123 and 124 of the Act of 1867. Sect. 121 provides for the free admission into each of the other Provinces of all articles of the growth, produce or manufacture of any one of the Provinces. Sect. 122 enacts that "the customs and excise laws of each Province shall, subject to the provisions of this Act, continue in force until altered by the Parliament of Canada." Sec. 123 deals with customs duties in relation to exportation and importation as between two Provinces. Sect. 124 saves the right of New Brunswick to levy but not to increase certain lumber dues in operation at the Union, "but the lumber of any of the Provinces other than New Brunswick shall not be subjected to such dues."

Their Lordships have on many occasions been called upon to determine questions relating to the constitutional validity of fiscal legislation under the British North America Act and have laid down the principle that in every case the first requisite is "to ascertain the real nature of the tax": *Rex v. Caledonian Collieries*, [1928] A.C. 358, 362. Now, in the present case, the real nature of the tax in question is transparently obvious. While the statute sets out to impose a tax on all timber cut within the Province it proceeds in the relative schedules to reduce the tax by rebate to an illusory amount in the case of timber used in the Province, leaving it to operate to its full effect only on timber exported. The best evidence that the tax was intended to be to all intents and purposes an export tax is afforded by the fact that since 1914 the minute rebated tax on timber used within the Province has not been collected. Indeed, the tax has come to be known as "the timber tax on export", and is so described in the final report of the Royal Commission of Inquiry on Timber and Forestry, 1909-10, extracts from which are among the exhibits in the case. The economic effect and, presumably, the object of the tax is to encourage the utilization within the Province of its home-grown timber and to discourage its exportation. The success of the tax, if this be its object, will thus be measured inversely by the revenue which it yields, which is not the normal characteristic of a tax imposed "in order to the raising of a revenue for Provincial purposes."

Once it is ascertained that the tax is in its real nature an export tax, as their Lordships are satisfied that it is, the task of justifying its imposition by the Provincial legislature becomes one of great difficulty. The appellant admitted that the imposition of customs and excise duties is a matter within the exclusive competence of the Dominion parliament, as, indeed, plainly appears from s. 122 of the *British North America Act*. The reason for this is, no doubt, that the effect of such duties is not confined to the place where, and the persons upon whom, they are levied, which is perhaps just another way of saying that they are indirect taxes. If then an export tax falls within the category of duties of customs and excise there is an end of the question. Their Lordships are of opinion that according to the accepted terminology and practice of fiscal legislation and adminis-tration export duties are ordinarily classed as duties of customs and excise. In Wharton's Law Lexicon "Customs" are defined as "duties charged upon commodities on their importation into or exportation out of a country", and a similar definition is given in Murray's New English Dictionary. An early example of this usage is to be found in Comyn's Digest, 5th ed., 1822, p. 468, where, under the heading of "Customs of tonnage and poundage", there is mentioned poundage "on all goods carried out of the King's dominions", with a citation of 12 Car. 2, c. 4, while a modern instance is provided by the Finance Act, 1901, in which s. 3, imposing an export duty on coal, is included in Part I of the Act, headed "Customs and Excise."

Mr. Lawrence, however, contended that although the tax might accurately be described as an export duty, this did not necessarily negative its being a direct tax within the meaning of the Act. Without reviewing afresh the niceties of discrimination between direct and indirect taxation it is enough to point out that an export tax is normally collected on merchantable goods in course of transit in pursuance of commercial transactions. Whether the tax is ultimately borne by the exporting seller at home or by the importing buyer abroad depends on the terms of the contract between them. It may be borne by the one or by the other. It was said in the present case that the conditions of the competitive market in the United States compelled the exporter of timber from British Columbia to that country to bear the whole burden of the tax himself. That, however, is a matter of exigencies of a particular market, and is really irrelevant in determining the inherent character of the tax. While it is no doubt true that a tax levied on personal property, no less than a tax levied on real property, may be a direct tax where the taxpayer's personal property is selected as the criterion of his ability to pay, a tax which, like the tax here in question, is levied on a commercial commodity on the occasion of its exportation in pursuance of trading transactions, cannot be described as a tax whose incidence is, by its nature, such that normally it is finally borne by the first payer, and is not susceptible of being passed on. On the contrary, the existence of an export tax is invariably an element in the fixing of prices, and the question whether it is to be borne by seller or purchaser in whole or in part is determined by the bargain made. The present tax thus exhibits the leading characteristic of an indirect tax as defined by authoritative decisions.

Their Lordships are accordingly of opinion, without entering upon other topics which were discussed at the hearing, that the timber tax in question is an export tax falling within the category of duties of customs and excise, and as such, as well as by reason of its inherent nature as an indirect tax, could not competently be imposed by the Provincial legislature.

Appeal dismissed.

[See also *Security Export Co. v. Hetherington,* [1923] S.C.R. 539, [1923] 3 D.L.R. 519, rev'd on other grounds, [1924] A.C. 988, [1924] 3 D.L.R. 779; *Texada Mines Ltd. v. A.-G. B.C.,* [1960] S.C.R. 713, 24 D.L.R. 2d 81, 32 W.W.R. 37. In *Lawson v. Interior Tree Fruit and Vegetable Committee,* [1931] S.C.R. 357, [1931] 2 D.L.R. 193, where the Supreme Court of Canada invalidated the British Columbia Produce Marketing Act, 1927, on the principal ground that it invaded federal legislative power in relation to trade and commerce, Cannon J. in a concurring judgment (to the principal one delivered by Duff J.) said, *inter alia,* (at p. 373): "By the Produce Marketing Act of 1927, the province of British Columbia imposed levies on the fruits or vegetables grown or produced in a large area, including appellant's farm, and obliged all shippers to secure a licence to market and sell products of the province anywhere within the Dominion under a penalty for each contravention. Even leaving aside the licence, and considering only the levy, I believe, as pointed out by my brother Duff, that such imposts on commodities, on trade in commodities, have always been regarded as indirect taxes for a public purpose and come under the head of "taxation"—which is dealt with in Part VIII of the British North America Act, where is found article 121. It may be considered as an excise tax which necessarily has a tendency to affect, and affects, the price of the product to the customer in another province. To use the words of Lord MacMillan, in *Attorney-General for British Columbia v. McDonald Murphy Lumber Company,* [1930] A.C. 357, at 363, the levy in question 'is an export tax falling within the category of duties of customs and excise, and as such, as well as by reason of its inherent nature as an indirect tax, could not competently be imposed by the provincial legislature.' I therefore, reach the conclusion that this legislation is an attempt to impose by indirect taxation and regulations an obstacle to one of the main purposes of Confederation, which was, ultimately, to form an economic unit of all the provinces in British

North America with absolute freedom of trade between its constituent parts."
Cf., on the question when goods become "exports", the *Ontario Farm Products
Marketing Act Reference, supra*, at p. 296; and see *Richfield Oil Corp. v. State
Board of Equalization* (1946), 329 U.S. 69, 67 St. Ct. 156; Note, (1946) 59 Harv.
Law Rev. 627.]

A.-G. B.C. v. KINGCOME NAVIGATION CO. LTD.

In the Privy Council. [1934] A.C. 45, [1934] 1 D.L.R. 31, [1933] 3 W.W.R. 353.

Appeal from a judgment of the British Columbia Court of Appeal,
[1933] 3 D.L.R. 364, 47 B.C.R. 114, affirming a judgment of Morrison
C.J., [1933] 1 D.L.R. 688, and holding the British Columbia Fuel-oil
Tax Act, 1930, as amended, *ultra vires*.

LORD THANKERTON: The material provisions of the Act of 1930,
as amended by the Act of 1932, are as follows:

2. For the raising of a revenue for Provincial purposes every
person who consumes any fuel-oil in the Province shall pay to the
Minister of Finance a tax in respect of that fuel-oil at the rate of
one-half cent a gallon.

3. The tax imposed by this Act shall be paid and collected at
such times and in such manner as the regulations may prescribe.

4. The amount of any tax imposed by this Act may be recovered
by action in any Court as for a debt due to the Crown in right of the
Province, and the Court may make an order as to the costs of the
action in favour of or against the Crown. (2) In every action for the
recovery of any tax imposed by this Act, the burden of proving the
quantity of fuel-oil consumed by the defendant, and of proving that
the tax has been paid in respect of the fuel-oil in question, shall be
upon the defendant. (1932, c. 51, s. 2.)

5. (1) Upon the expiration of thirty days after the commencement of this Act no person shall keep for sale or sell fuel-oil in the
Province unless he is the holder of a licence issued pursuant to this
section in respect of each place of business at which fuel-oil is so kept
for sale or sold by him. (2) The manner of application and the forms
of application and of the licence shall be as prescribed in the regulations. A licence fee of one dollar shall be payable in respect of each
licence. (3) The Minister of Finance may, without holding any
formal or other hearing, cancel any licence issued pursuant to this
section if the licensee is convicted of any offence against this Act,
and may during the period of twelve months next succeeding the
cancellation of that licence refuse to issue any new licence to the
person so convicted.

6. (1) Every collector, constable, and every person authorized
in writing by the Minister of Finance to exercise the powers of
inspection under this section may without warrant enter upon any
premises on which he has cause to believe that any fuel-oil is kept
or had in possession, and may inspect the premises and all fuel-oil
found thereon, and may interrogate any person who is found on the
premises or who owns, occupies or has charge of the premises. (2)

Every person interrogated under this section who refuses or fails to answer any question put to him respecting the fuel-oil kept or had on the premises, or who refuses or fails to produce for inspection or to permit inspection of any book, record or document, or any barrel, tank, or receptacle in his possession or under his control which he is required to produce for inspection or of which he is required to permit inspection, shall be guilty of an offence against this Act.

7. (1) Every person who consumes any fuel-oil in the Province and every person who keeps for sale or sells fuel-oil in the Province shall keep such books and records and shall make and furnish such returns as are prescribed in the regulations. (2) Every person who refuses or fails to keep any book or record or to make and furnish any return prescribed by the regulations or who withholds any entry or information required by the regulations to be made or entered in any book, record, or return, or who makes any false or deceptive entry or statement in any such book, record, or return, shall be guilty of an offence against this Act.

The respondent challenges the validity of the tax on three grounds —namely: (a) that in its nature it is either an import duty or a duty of excise, and therefore falls into the category of indirect taxes; (b) that it is not direct taxation in respect that the burden may be passed on; and (c) that it invades the legislative sphere of the Dominion parliament in regard to regulation of trade and commerce.

The respondent's first contention is that the tax in question is a customs or excise duty, according to the general understanding current in 1867, and that all customs and excise duties are outside the competence of a Provincial legislature, apart from any question whether the tax is "demanded from the very persons who it is intended or desired should pay it." For this construction he prays in aid s. 122 of the Act of 1867, and, in order to establish that the present tax was in the nature of a customs or excise duty, he relied on the definitions of political economists and the course of custom and excise legislation in this country up to 1867. In their Lordships' opinion this contention is inconsistent with the decisions of this Board, which go back to the year 1878, and have settled that the test to be applied in determining what is "direct taxation" within the meaning of s. 92, head 2, of the Act of 1867 is to be found in Mill's definition of direct and indirect taxes.

[His Lordship here discussed *A.-G. Que. v. Queen Insurance Co.* (1878), 3 App. Cas. 1090; *A.-G. Que. v. Reed* (1884), 10 App. Cas. 141; *Bank of Toronto v. Lambe* (1887), 12 App. Cas. 575; *Brewers and Maltsters' Association of Ontario v. A.-G. Ont.*, [1897] A.C. 231, and *Cotton v. The King*, [1941] A.C. 176. He quoted from Lord Moulton's judgment in the *Cotton* case the statement that decided cases have established that "the meaning to be attributed to the phrase 'direct taxation' in s. 92 . . . is substantially the definition quoted . . . from the treatise of John Stuart Mill, and that this question is no longer open to discussion." He then continued as follows:]

These decisions, in their Lordships' opinion, make clear that if the tax is demanded from the very person who it is intended or desired should pay it, the taxation is direct, and that it is none the less direct even if it might be described as an excise tax, for instance, or is collected as an excise tax. Among the numerous subsequent decisions of the Board, the respondent was only able to refer to two, as containing any suggestion to the contrary—namely, *City of Halifax v. Fairbanks' Estate,* [1928] A.C. 117 and *Attorney-General for British Columbia v. McDonald Murphy Lumber Co.*

In *Fairbanks'* case a city charter, enacted by the Provincial legislature, imposed a "business tax" to be paid by every occupier of real property for the purposes of any trade, profession or other calling carried on for the purposes of gain. Where the property was let to the Crown or to any person exempt from taxation, the owner was to be deemed to be the occupier, and was to be assessed for business tax according to the purposes for which it was occupied. The property in question was let to the Crown, and the respondent estate, as owner, had been assessed to the tax. It was held that the tax was direct taxation even though the owner probably would seek to pass it on to the tenant. Lord Cave, who delivered the judgment of the Board, stated in regard to the Act of 1867: "The framers of that Act evidently regarded taxes as divisible into two separate and distinct categories—namely, those that are direct and those which cannot be so described, and it is to taxation of the former character only that the powers of a Provincial government are made to extend. From this it is to be inferred that the distinction between direct and indirect taxes was well known before the passing of the Act; and it is undoubtedly the fact that before that date the classification was familiar to statesmen as well as to economists, and that certain taxes were then universally recognized as falling within one or the other category. Thus, taxes on property or income were everywhere treated as direct taxes. . . . On the other hand, duties of customs and excise were regarded by every one as typical instances of indirect taxation. When therefore the Act of Union allocated the power of direct taxation for Provincial purposes to the Province, it must surely have intended that the taxation, for those purposes, of property and income should belong exclusively to the Provincial legislatures, and that without regard to any theory as to the ultimate incidence of such taxation. To hold otherwise would be to suppose that the framers of the Act intended to impose on a Provincial legislature the task of speculating as to the probable ultimate incidence of each particular tax which it might desire to impose, at the risk of having such tax held invalid if the conclusion reached should afterwards be held to be wrong.

"What then is the effect to be given to Mill's formula above quoted? No doubt it is valuable as providing a logical basis for the distinction already established between direct and indirect taxes, and perhaps also as a guide for determining as to any new or unfamiliar tax which may be imposed in which of the two categories it is to be placed; but it cannot have the effect of disturbing the established classification of the old and well-known species of taxation, and making it necessary to apply a new test to every particular member of those species. The imposition of taxes on property and

income, of death duties and of municipal and local rates is, according
to the common understanding of the terms, direct taxation, just as
the exaction of a customs or excise duty or commodities or of a
percentage duty on services would ordinarily be regarded as indirect
taxation; and although new forms of taxation may from time to time
be added to one category or the other in accordance with Mill's
formula, it would be wrong to use that formula as a ground for
transferring a tax universally recognized as belonging to one class to
a different class of taxation". . . .

As has already been pointed out the ultimate incidence of the tax,
in the sense of the political economist, is to be disregarded, but where
the tax is imposed in respect of a transaction, the taxing authority is
indifferent as to which of the parties to the transaction ultimately
bears the burden, and, as Mill expresses it, it is not intended as a
peculiar contribution upon the particular party selected to pay the
tax. Similarly, where the tax is imposed in respect of some dealing
with commodities, such as their import or sale, or production for sale,
the tax is not a peculiar contribution upon the one of the parties
to the trading in the particular commodity who is selected as the
taxpayer. This is brought out in the second paragraph of Mill's
definition, and is true of the typical customs and excise duties referred
to by Lord Cave [in *Fairbanks'* case]. Again, taxes on property and
income are imposed in respect of the particular taxpayer's interest in
property or the taxpayer's own income, and they are a peculiar contribution upon him, and it is intended and desired that he shall pay it,
although it is possible for him, by making his own arrangements to
that end, to pass the burden on in the sense of the political economists.
The decision in *Fairbanks'* case is in accordance with the principles
already stated by their Lordships as those to be derived from the
earlier decisions of the Board.

In the *McDonald Murphy Lumber Co.'s* case a Provincial tax
upon all timber cut in the Province, with a rebate of nearly the whole
tax in the case of timber used or manufactured in the Province
was held to be in its nature an export tax "levied on a commercial
commodity on the occasion of its exportation in pursuance of trading
transactions." The tax was held to be *ultra vires* . . .

It is clear that this decision applied Mill's definition, as adopted by
the previous decisions of the Board, as the test, and that the result
was in accordance with those decisions. The present respondent
relied on the reference to s. 122 of the Act of 1867 as being of assistance to his argument. In their Lordships' opinion the customs or
excise duties on commodities ordinarily regarded as indirect taxation,
referred to in the judgment in *Fairbank's* case and the *McDonald
Murphy Lumber Co.'s* case, are duties which are imposed in respect
of commercial dealings in commodities, and they would necessarily
fall within Mill's definition of indirect taxes. They do not extend, for
instance, to a dog tax, which is clearly direct taxation, though the
machinery of the excise law might be applied to its collection, or to a
licence duty, such as was considered in *Lambe's* case. Customs and
excise duties are, in their essence, trading taxes, and may be said to be
more concerned with the commodity in respect of which the taxation

is imposed than with the particular person from whom the tax is exacted. Sect. 122 of the Act merely provided for the temporary continuation of the then existing legislation as regards customs and excise, and the respondent was unable to point to anything in that legislation which would fall outside the above definition of customs and excise duties. It follows that the tax here in question must be tested by Mill's definition, as adopted by the decisions of the Board.

Turning then to the provisions of the *Fuel-Oil Act* here in question, it is clear that the Act purports to exact the tax from a person who has consumed fuel-oil, the amount of the tax being computed broadly according to the amount consumed. The Act does not relate to any commercial transaction in the commodity between the taxpayer and someone else. Their Lordships are unable to find, on examination of the Act, any justification for the suggestion that the tax is truly imposed in respect of the transaction by which the taxpayer acquires the property in the fuel-oil nor in respect of any contract or arrangement under which the oil is consumed, though it is, of course, possible that individual taxpayers may recoup themselves by such a contract or arrangement; but this cannot affect the nature of the tax. Accordingly their Lordships are of opinion that the tax is direct taxation within the meaning of s. 92, head 2, of the *British North America Act.* [His Lordship concluded by rejecting the argument that the Act invaded the federal "trade and commerce" power.]

Appeal allowed.

[The *Gasoline Tax Act*, R.S.O. 1970, c. 190, as amended, imposes a tax on the "purchaser" not the "consumer". Does this affect its validity? *Cf. A.-G. B.C. v. C.P.R.*, [1927] A.C. 934, [1927] 4 D.L.R. 113, [1927] 3 W.W.R. 460, where the Privy Council held invalid a previous British Columbia fuel-oil taxing statute, the *Fuel-oil Tax Act,* R.S.B.C. 1924, c. 251. The *C.P.R.* case is not referred to in the Privy Council's *Kingcome* judgment.]

ATLANTIC SMOKE SHOPS LTD. v. CONLON AND A.-G. CAN.

In the Privy Council. [1943] A.C. 550, [1943] 4 D.L.R. 81, [1943] 3 W.W.R. 113.

Appeal by special leave from a judgment of the Supreme Court of Canada, [1941] S.C.R. 670, [1941] 4 D.L.R. 129, varying a judgment of the New Brunswick Supreme Court, Appeal Division, [1941] 1 D.L.R. 416, 15 M.P.R. 278, and upholding the validity of the *New Brunswick Tobacco Tax Act,* 1940, save as to certain provisions making an agent of a consumer liable for the tax. The relevant sections of the Act read as follows:

"2. In this Act, unless the context otherwise requires, (a) 'consumer' or 'consumer of tobacco' means any person who, within the province, purchases from a vendor tobacco at a retail sale in the province for his own consumption or for the consumption of other persons at his expense or who, within the province, purchases from a vendor tobacco at a retail sale in the province on behalf of or as agent for a principal who desires to require such tobacco for consumption by such principal or other persons at the expense of such principal. (d) 'Purchaser' means any person who, within the province, purchases from a retail vendor tobacco at a retail sale in the province. (e) 'Retail sale' means a sale to a consumer for purposes of consumption and not for resale. (f) 'Retail vendor' means any person who, within the province, sells tobacco to a consumer. (g) 'Tobacco' means tobacco in any form in which tobacco is consumed and includes snuff. (h) 'Vendor' includes both wholesale vendor and retail vendor. (i) 'Wholesale vendor' means any person who, within the province, sells tobacco for the purpose of resale.

3. (2) No person shall sell any tobacco in the province at a retail sale unless he holds a retail vendor's licence issued to him under authority of this Act and such licence is in force at the time of sale.

4. Every consumer of tobacco purchased at a retail sale in the province shall pay to His Majesty the King in right of the province for the raising of a revenue, at the time of making his purchase, a tax in respect of the consumption of such tobacco, and such tax shall be computed at the rate of ten per centum of the retail price of the tobacco purchased.

5. Every person residing or ordinarily resident or carrying on business in New Brunswick, who brings into the province or who receives delivery in the province of tobacco for his own consumption or for the consumption of other persons at his expense or on behalf of or as agent for a principal who desires to acquire such tobacco for consumption by such principal or other persons at his expense shall immediately report the matter to the minister and forward or produce to him the invoice, if any, in respect of such tobacco and any other information required by the minister with respect to the tobacco and shall pay the same tax in respect of the consumption of such tobacco as would have been payable if the tobacco had been purchased at a retail sale in the province at the same price.

10. A consumer shall be and remain liable for the tax imposed by this Act until the same has been collected."

VISCOUNT SIMON L.C.: This appeal from a judgment of the Supreme Court of Canada raises the important and difficult question whether the *Tobacco Tax Act* of New Brunswick, 1940, (4 Geo. 6, c. 44), and the regulations made thereunder are within the powers of the provincial legislature as constituting "direct taxation within the province", or whether on the contrary, all or any part of these provisions must be held to be *ultra vires* having regard to the distribution of legislative powers effected by the *British North America Act, 1867,* and to the bearing of ss. 121 and 122 of the Act on provincial taxing powers.

The New Brunswick *Tobacco Tax Act* is entitled "An Act to provide for imposing a tax on the consumption of tobacco". . . . There are . . . four applications of the tax provided for by ss. 4 and 5: (a) In its main and simplest form the tax is to be paid by anyone who purchases tobacco, as defined, for his own consumption (or for the consumption of other persons at his expense) from a retail vendor in the province. The tax amounts to ten per cent. on the retail price charged on the sale. By regulations made under s. 20 of the Act it is to be collected by the retail vendor, who is constituted an agent of the minister for the collection of the tax, and has to give a receipt for the tax to the customer and account to the Tobacco Tax Commissioner for the tax thus collected, subject to the allowance of three per cent. as remuneration. (b) If the purchase from the retail vendor is made by an agent acting for a principal, who desires to acquire such tobacco for his own consumption (or for the consumption of other persons at his expense), the tax is payable by the agent. It is, however, clear that if the agent has not already been put in funds by his principal, he will be entitled to be indemnified by his principal for the tax, no less than for the purchase price. In both cases ((a) and (b)) the tax is payable at the time of making the purchase. (c) If a person residing or ordinarily resident or carrying on business in New Brunswick brings into the province such tobacco or receives delivery of it in the province, for his own consumption (or for the consumption of other persons at his expense), he is to report the matter to the minister, with any invoice and other information required, and he becomes liable to pay the same tax as would have been payable if the tobacco had been purchased at a retail sale in the province. (d) Lastly, if such a person as is last described brings the tobacco into the province, or receives delivery there, as agent for a principal who desires to acquire it for his own consumption (or for the consumption of other persons at his expense), the agent is put under a similar obligation to report and to pay an equivalent tax. It may be noted that in this last case the principal is not in express terms limited to a principal within the province. This is perhaps implied, but, in any event, the instance of an agent within the province acting for a principal outside can seldom occur.

A striking difference of opinion has disclosed itself in the Canadian courts as to the validity of this taxing legislation. In the Supreme Court of New Brunswick, Baxter C.J. and his two colleagues, Grimmer and Richards JJ., held that the tax was valid. . . . On appeal to the Supreme Court of Canada, conflicting views were expressed, and these need to be carefully analysed. On the first and main form of the tax Duff C.J. and Davis J. held that the tax was not direct. The Chief Justice considered that the tax was a tax on tobacco in respect of the commercial dealing between the retail vendor and the purchaser. He says that "the payment of the tax is not only a condition of legal purchase; it is an integral element in the transaction of sale and purchase passing from the purchaser to the vendor as part of the price to the purchaser." ([1941] S.C.R. 670, at p. 679). In effect, the argument is that this is a sales tax and that, being a sales tax, it is necessarily indirect. Rinfret J. and Crocket J. maintained the opposite view, and agreed with the judgment of the Supreme Court of New Brunswick that the tax in all its forms was *intra vires*. Kerwin J. took up an intermediate position. He considered that the tax in the form (a) was valid, but that the attempt to impose the tax on an agent failed as being indirect taxation. He further held that the tax in the forms (c) and (d) was also invalid as being an infringement of s. 121 of the *British North America Act*. Hudson J. held that the tax was valid, save so far as it imposed a liability on an agent, *i.e.,* that (a) and (c) were valid, but that (b) and (d) were not, and Taschereau J. took the same view. In the result, therefore, the majority of the Supreme Court of Canada decided that the tax in the forms (a) and (c) was valid, but that it was invalid in the forms (b) and (d), since these latter forms involved taxation of an agent, whereas the burden of the taxation would fall on his principal. The arguments addressed to the Board, which included arguments on behalf of the Attorney-General for Canada, supporting the appellants, and of other interveners representing Quebec and five other provinces supporting the respondents, ranged over all aspects of the tax, and their Lordships are requested to reach a conclusion as to the validity or nonvalidity of the tax in all its forms.

Their Lordships must first consider whether the tax in the form (a) is a valid exercise of provincial legislative powers. It has been long and firmly established that, in interpreting the phrase "direct taxation" in head 2 of s. 92 of the Act of 1867, the guide to be followed is that provided by the distinction between direct and indirect taxes which is to be found in the treatise of John Stuart Mill. The question of course, as Lord Herschell said in *Brewers and Maltsters' Association of Ontario v. Attorney-General for Ontario,* is not what is the distinction drawn by writers on political economy, but in what sense the words were employed in the *British North America Act.*' Mill's Political Economy was first published in 1848, and appeared in a popular edition in 1865. Its author became a member of parliament in this latter year and commanded much attention in the British House of Commons. Having regard to his eminence as a political economist in the epoch which the Quebec Resolutions were being discussed and the Act of 1867 was being framed, the use of Mill's analysis and classification of taxes for the purpose of construing the expression now under review is fully justified. In addition to the definition from Mill's Political Economy already quoted, citation may be made of two other passages as follows: "Direct taxes are either on income or on expenditure. Most taxes on expenditure are indirect, but some are direct, being imposed not on the producer or seller of an article, but immediately on the consumer" (bk. V. ch. 3). And again, in ch. 6, in discussing the comparative merits of the two types of tax, he takes as the essential feature of direct taxation that "under it everyone knows how much he really pays." Their Lordships, therefore, consider that this tobacco tax in the form they have called (a) would fall within the conception of a "direct" tax, and ought so to be treated in applying the *British North America Act.* It is a tax which is to be paid by the last purchaser of the article, and, since there is no question of further re-sale, the tax cannot be passed on to any other person by subsequent dealing. The money for the tax is found by the individual who finally bears the burden of it. It is unnecessary to consider the refinement which might arise if the taxpayer who has purchased the tobacco for his own consumption subsequently changes his mind and in fact resells it. If so, he would, for one thing, require a retail vendor's licence. But the instance is exceptional and far-fetched, while for the purpose of classifying the tax, it is the general tendency of the impost which has to be considered. So regarded, it completely satisfies Mill's test for direct taxation. Indeed, the present instance is a clearer case of direct taxation than the tax on the consumer of fuel-oil in *Attorney-General for British Columbia v. Kingcome Navigation Co.*, [1934] A.C. 45, for fuel-oil may be consumed for the purpose of manufacture and transport, and the tax on the consumption of fuel-oil might, as one would suppose, be sometimes passed on in the price of the article manufactured or transported. Yet the Privy Council held that the tax was direct. In the case of tobacco, on the other hand, the consumer produces nothing but smoke. Mr. Pritt urged that the tax is a sales tax, and that a sales tax is indirect because it can be passed on. The ordinary forms of sales tax are, undoubtedly of this character, but it would be more accurate to say that a sales tax is indirect when in the normal course it can be passed on. If a tax is so devised that (as Mill expresses it) the taxing authority is not indifferent as to which of the parties to the transaction ultimately bears the burden, but intends it as a "peculiar contribution" on the particular party selected to pay the tax, such tax is not proved to be indirect by calling it a sales tax. Previous observations by this Board as to the general character of sales taxes, or of taxes on commercial dealings, ought not to be understood as denying the possibility of this exception.

There remains, on this first head, the question whether, notwithstanding that the tax in the form (a) is "direct" within Mill's test, it is none the less beyond the powers of the province to impose as being in the nature of "excise" in the sense that the attempted imposition would be an alteration of the "excise laws" of New Brunswick which the provincial legislature is debarred from affecting under s. 122 of the *British North America Act*. "Excise" is a word of vague and somewhat ambiguous meaning. Dr. Johnson's famous definition in his dictionary is distinguished by acerbity rather than precision. The word is usually (though by no means always) employed to indicate a duty imposed on home-manufactured articles in the course of manufacture before they reach the consumer. So regarded, an excise duty is plainly indirect. A further difficulty in the way of the precise application of the word is that many miscellaneous taxes, at any rate in this country, are classed as "excise" merely because they are for convenience collected through the machinery of the Board of Excise—the tax on owning a dog, for example. Their Lordships do not find it necessary in the present case to determine whether this tobacco tax in the form (a) is for any purpose analogous to an excise duty, for it is enough to accept and apply the proposition laid down on behalf of this Board by Lord Thankerton in the *Kingcome* case, namely, "that if the tax is demanded from the very persons who it is intended or desired should pay it, the taxation is direct, and that it is none the less direct, even if it might be described as an excise tax". In the course of reaching this conclusion, Lord Thankerton carefully examined the only two cases which might be thought to contain any suggestion to the contrary effect, namely, *City of Halifax v. Fairbanks' Estate* and *Attorney-General for British Columbia v. McDonald Murphy Lumber Co.*, and pointed out that the customs or excise duties on commodities ordinarily regarded as indirect taxation referred to in the judgments in these two cases are duties which are imposed in respect of commercial dealings in commodities in such a form that they would necessarily fall within Mill's definition of indirect taxes. Their Lordships are of opinion that Lord Cave's reference in his judgment in the *Fairbanks'* case to "two separate and distinct categories" of taxes, "namely, those that are direct and those which cannot be so described" ([1928] A.C. at p. 124), should not be understood as relieving the courts from the obligation of examining the real nature and effect of the particular tax in the present instance, or as justifying the classification of the tax as indirect merely because it is in some sense associated with the purchase of an article. With the greatest respect to the view of the Chief Justice of Canada, their Lordships are unable to take the view that a valid distinction is to be found between the directness of the tax in the *Kingcome* case and the quality of the tax in the present instance on the ground that in the former case the tax was on every person who had consumed fuel-oil whereas the tax in the present case is on every person who buys tobacco in order to consume it. In both instances the circumstance which makes the tax direct is the same, namely, that the person who pays the tax is the person who actually bears it, and this arises necessarily from the circumstance that purchase for re-sale is not taxed. Their Lordships, therefore, conclude that the tax in form (a) is valid.

Next comes the question whether the tax, though "direct" when the principal deals personally with the retail vendor across the counter, ceases to be "direct" if the purchase is made by an agent acting for his principal. Their Lordships have already pointed out that in this case also the person who bears the tax is really the principal, either because he has already given his agent the money to pay it or because he is bound forthwith to repay his agent for the expense incurred with his authority and on his behalf. This indemnification does not follow because there is any fresh transaction analogous to re-sale after the purchase by the agent has been made. It is part and parcel of a single transaction. The agent pays the tax for and on behalf of his principal. If, indeed, the agent gave the name of his principal to the vendor the contract of sale would be with the principal. If there was anything to complain of in the quality of the article it would be the principal, whether named or not, who might have a remedy against the vendor. It is said that the tax in this second form is not direct because the agent, who is personally liable for the tax and has to pay it when receiving the tobacco, is distinct from the principal who bears the burden of the duty, but, in their Lordships' opinion, this circumstance does not, according to the distinction laid down by Mill, prevent the tax from being a direct tax. There is an obvious distinction between an indirect tax, like an ordinary customs or excise duty, which enters into the cost of an article at each stage of its subsequent handling or manufacture, and an impost laid on the final consumer, as "the particular party selected to pay the tax", who produces the money which his agent pays over. This is mere machinery, and resembles the requirements in British income tax that in certain cases A is assessed for tax which B really bears— a circumstance which does not make income tax "indirect". The test for indirect taxation which Mill prescribed is the passing on of the burden of a duty by the person who first pays it through subsequent transactions to future recipients in the process of dealing with the commodity, or, at any rate, the tendency so to pass on the burden. Here the position is quite different. It is really the principal who in this case also both pays the tax and bears it. Their Lordships find it impossible to suppose that, in applying the economic distinction which is at the bottom of Mill's contrast, it would be correct to call this tax "direct" if a man bought a packet of cigarettes over the counter by putting his hand in his pocket and paying price and tax himself to the vendor, but "indirect" if he stood outside the shop and gave his wife the necessary amount to get the cigarettes and pay the tax for him. It is argued that the decision of this Board in the *Grain Futures* case, *Attorney-General for Manitoba v. Attorney-General for Canada,* goes to show that a tax imposed on agents dealing in a commercial article for their principals must be indirect. Their Lordships are of opinion that the actual decision does not justify so wide and general a deduction. The tax in the *Grain Futures* case, as Lord Haldane pointed out, became a charge against the amount of the price which was to come to the seller in the world market, and was thus indirect. Similar considerations governed the view taken by this Board in *Lower Mainland Dairy Products Sales Adjustment Committee v. Crystal Dairy Ltd.,* [1933] A.C. 168; *Attorney-General for British Columbia v. Canadian Pacific Ry. Co.,* [1927] A.C. 934; and *Rex x. Caledonian Collieries,* [1928] A.C. 358. In all these instances the tax was indirect because of its tendency to affect the price paid by persons other than the taxpayer for the commodity as an article of trade. Nothing of the sort happens here. The production of the money to pay the tax by the agent is a mere piece of machinery unconnected with any subsequent commercial dealing with the tobacco. Notwithstanding that an agent is employed, it is the principal who really finds the money for the tax and he throughout bears the burden of it. *Qui facit per alium facit per se.* Their Lordships, therefore, take the view that the tax imposed by s. 4 of the Act is valid both in the form (a) and in the form (b).

For the same reasons, and apart from other considerations which apply only to s. 5, their Lordships are of opinion that the tax is valid in the forms (c) and (d), but the tax imposed by s. 5 raises difficulties of a different order. It is manifest that s. 5 is enacted merely as a supplementary provision, to guard against the methods of avoidance of s. 4 which might otherwise remain available. At the same time, the validity of s. 5 must be judged according to its terms, and, if its enactment by the provincial legislature be beyond the powers of that legislature, it cannot be justified on the ground that it is needed to make the whole scheme watertight. Objection is taken to the validity of s. 5 on the alleged ground that it offends against ss. 121 and 122 of the *British North America Act*. When the scheme of Canadian federation is considered as a whole, the purpose and effect of these two sections seem plain enough. Previous to the date of federation, each province was a separate unit raising part of its revenue by customs duties on certain commodities imported from outside—it might even be from another province. One essential purpose of federating such units is that they should cease to maintain customs barriers against the produce of one another, and hence s. 121, supplemented by s. 123, established internal free trade from July 1, 1867, which was the date proclaimed for the Union. It was not, however, practicable to abolish provincial customs entirely on that date. Ordinary customs and excise are, as Mill's treatise shows, the classical examples of indirect taxation, and thus fell thenceforward within the exclusive legislative competence of the Dominion Parliament. But until the Dominion had imposed and collected sufficient taxes on its own account, it was desirable to continue to gather in the revenue arising from the customs and excise laws of the provinces (with the exception of the inter-provincial import duties), though it would appear from s. 102 of the *British North America Act* that after federation the proceeds passed into the consolidated revenue fund of the Dominion. A dominion tariff has long since been enacted and the customs and excise laws of the different provinces have been brought to an end by dominion legislation. The question, therefore, on this part of the case, which has to be determined is whether s. 5 of the New Brunswick Act is invalid as amounting to an attempt by the province to tax in disregard of the restrictions contained in ss. 121 and 122 of the constitution. If s. 5 purports to impose a duty of customs, it is wholly invalid, and, if it denies free admission of tobacco into New Brunswick, it is invalid so far as this refers to tobacco manufactured in another province of Canada. Their Lordships have reached the conclusion that s. 5 does not impose a customs duty, and they adopt the reasoning on this point of Rinfret J. and Crocket J. The argument to the contrary is the argument that failed in the *Kingcome* case. Lord Thankerton pointed out the distinction in his judgment in that case when he said: "Customs and excise duties are, in their essence, trading taxes, and may be said to be more concerned with the commodity in respect of which the taxation is imposed than with the particular person from whom the tax is exacted", [1934] A.C. 45, at p. 59. Here the tax is not imposed on the commodity as such at all, and is not imposed on anyone as a condition of its lawful receipt. The "particular person" from whom the tax is exacted is the recipient in the province only if he is the prospective smoker, and, as Lord Hobhouse said in *Bank of Toronto v. Lambe,* "any person found within the province may legally be taxed there if taxed directly." Their Lordships agree with the majority of the Supreme Court that this is not a duty of customs.

Similar considerations dispose of the contention that, as applied to the recipient of tobacco manufactured in another province, the tax offends s. 121. Here again, it is important to remember the special feature of the tax that it is imposed as a direct tax on the consumer. Section 121 was the subject of full and careful exposition by the Supreme Court of Canada in *Gold Seal, Ltd. v. Attorney-General for Alberta* (1921), 62 S.C.R. 424, where the question arose whether the parliament of Canada could validly prohibit the importation of intoxicating liquor into those provinces where its sale for beverage purposes was forbidden by provincial law. The meaning of s. 121 cannot vary according as it is applied to dominion or to provincial legislation, and their Lordships agree with the interpretation put on the section in the *Gold Seal* case. . . .

That the tax is taxation within the province is, their Lordships think, clear for the reasons given by Taschereau J.

Their Lordships will humbly advise His Majesty that the appeal fails and that the *Tobacco Tax Act, 1940*, is in all respects a valid exercise of the powers of the legislature of the province of New Brunswick.

Judgment varied

[See *Note*, (1942) 20 Can. Bar Rev. 157; *Note*, Enforcing State Consumption Taxes on Out of State Purchases, (1951) 65 Harv. L. Rev. 301. Has "direct" taxation become merely a matter of proper drafting used as a method of tax collection? See *A.-G. B.C. v. E. & N. Ry.*, [1950] A.C. 87, [1950] 1 D.L.R. 305, [1949] 2 W.W.R. 1233, rev'g in part [1948] S.C.R. 403, [1949] 3 D.L.R. 343; and see *Note*, (1950) 28 Can. Bar Rev. 577.

In *Re Rush and Tompkins Construction Ltd.* (1961), 28 D.L.R. (2d) 441, 35 W.W.R. 264, a provincial consumption or use tax on persons residing or ordinarily resident or carrying on business in the Province who bring in tangible personalty, acquired for value, for consumption or use therein (and being the same tax that would be payable if the property was purchased at a retail sale in the Province), was held properly exacted from a non-resident contractor who entered the Province to carry out a construction contract with the federal Crown in a national park in the Province vested in the federal Crown. The tax liability was held to be a personal one arising when the property was brought into the Province, and hence it was immaterial that under the contract the property vested in the Crown when brought to the site.

Although a Province may, both constitutionally and practically, be able to enforce a consumer sales tax by licensing retailers who carry on business in the Province and oblige them to collect the tax, what is its constitutional and practical position with respect to extra-provincial retailers who solicit in the Province by catalogue or mail or by a representative therein? A consumer in the Province who brings taxable goods in from outside may validly be embraced by tax, as determined in the *Conlon* case, but collection depends on the reporting of the purchase or other means of ascertaining that it was made. If the goods purchased from an outside vendor are shipped or delivered to the provincial purchaser-consumer rather than brought in by him, is there a constitutional means by which the Province may enforce payment of the tax by such consumer through the imposition of duties or requirements on the outside retailer? May such retailer be prohibited by the Province from shipping goods into the Province or from delivering them therein, unless he registers with the Province? Would this not be regulating inter-provincial trade or, at least, imposing an import control? Is it open to the Province to constitute such outside retailer an agent of the Province for collection of the tax, or to prohibit suit for recovery of the price of goods sold to a provincial consumer unless the retailer complies with prescribed requirements, or to require security from him? Would s. 121 of the B.N.A. Act be violated in any of the foregoing circumstances? See the excellent note by *Beck,* Sales Tax on Interprovincial Transactions—Collection from Non-Resident Retailers —Reciprocal Enforcement of Tax Claims, (1964) 42 Can. Bar Rev. 490, commenting on the Quebec Retail Sales Tax Act, now R.S.Q. 1964, c. 71, and especially ss. 2(13), 3, 4, 5, 8, 11 and 12.]

Note

The taxing technique used in the *Kingcome* and *Conlon* cases in respect of consumables like gasoline and tobacco was tested in the Supreme Court of Canada in its application to non-consumables (or durable goods) in *Cairns Construction Ltd. v. Government of Saskatchewan,* [1960] S.C.R. 619, 24 D.L.R. (2d) 1, aff'g 16 D.L.R. (2d) 465, 27 W.W.R. 297, rev'g 9 D.L.R. (2d) 721, 22 W.W.R. 193. The *Cairns* case involved the validity of a provincial statute imposing a tax on consumers and users of tangible personalty purchased at retail in the Province from a licensed vendor who was required to collect the tax at the time of the retail sale. The "agency" transaction covered by the legislation in the *Conlon* case was similarly embraced by the legislation in the *Cairns* case, as was the case of the provincial resident bringing into the Province or receiving therein tangible personalty for his own consumption or use. The thin line in the "direct taxation" cases between the validity of the statute (construed in terms of its general tendency) and its application to a particular person was forcibly demonstrated in the *Cairns* case where the tax was demanded of a building contractor who purchased tangible personalty (being pre-fabricated building materials) for incorporation into houses built on the contractor's land for general sale or built on lands of others under a fixed contract price or on a cost-plus basis. The statute pinpointed the elusive division between constitutionality and particular application by its definition of "retail sale" as "a sale to a consumer or user for purposes of consumption or use and not for resale as tangible personal property". The building contractor purchased the materials for resale, but not for resale as personalty; and, considered in terms of general tendency there was no more reason to hold the tax indirect in this case than it would be to hold a gasoline tax to be indirect in respect of a trucking company for which the tax was part of its general overhead. However, accepting the constitutional validity of the tax even as applied to the building contractor, it might still be arguable that as a matter of statutory construction the contractor was outside the enactment because he was buying for resale, even though he was at the same time a consumer or user of the building materials. This was not something that could be said in respect of consumables like tobacco and gasoline, so far as concerned a consumer or user of such products. It was this dilemma that was sought to be cured by defining "retail sale" in the terms above set out, terms which permit tax exoneration of a particular purchaser only where the resale of the personalty is in its form as such. Clearly, the legislature was entitled to limit tax exemption in this way as a mere matter of statutory coverage; and any constructional evasion of the limitation would be really a return to a constitutional argument. The Court was hence quite justified (on the given basis of the *Kingcome* and *Conlon* cases) in upholding both the validity of the provincial statute and its particular application to the building contractor.

[See also *A.-G. Nfld. v. Avalon Telephone Co. Ltd.* (1962), 33 D.L.R. (2d) 402, 47 M.P.R. 165. It is clear from the case law that a tax is no less indirect where it is passed back than where it is passed on: see *A.-G. Man. v. A.-G. Can.*, [1925] A.C. 561, [1925] 2 D.L.R. 691, [1925] 2 W.W.R. 60; *A.-G. B.C. v. E. & N. Ry.* [1950] A.C. 87, [1950] 1 D.L.R. 305, [1949] 2 W.W.R. 1233; *Prov. Treas. of Alta. v. Kerr*, [1933] A.C. 710, [1933] 4 D.L.R. 81, [1933] 3 W.W.R. 38.]

C.P.R. v. A.-G. SASK.

In the Supreme Court of Canada. [1952] 2 S.C.R. 231, [1952] 4 D.L.R. 11.

Appeal and cross-appeal from a judgment of the Saskatchewan Court of Appeal, [1951] 4 D.L.R. 21, 2 W.W.R. (N.S.) 424, reversing in part a judgment of Thomson J., [1951] 3 D.L.R. 362, 1 W.W.R. (N.S.) 193, upholding the validity of the *Mineral Taxation Act* (Sask.).

RINFRET C.J.C. (dissenting): The appellants sought to have the *Mineral Taxation Act* and amendments of the Province of Saskatchewan declared *ultra vires*. There were other conclusions in their statement of claim and some of them were passed upon by the Court of Appeal of the Province of Saskatchewan, but before this Court the only point discussed was whether the tax imposed ought to be classed as an indirect tax and, therefore, outside the powers of the Legislature of the Province of Saskatchewan.

The task of deciding the point, to my mind, is not an easy one. In *Halifax v. Fairbanks*, [1927] 4 D.L.R. 945, [1928] A.C. 117, Viscount Cave L.C., delivering the judgment of their Lordships of the Privy Council, insisted upon the fact that in considering the question raised it was important to bear in mind that the problem to be solved was one of law and that the framers of the *B.N.A. Act* evidently regarded taxes as divisible into two separate and distinct categories—namely, those that are direct and those which cannot be so described. From this he inferred that the distinction between direct and indirect taxation was well known before the passing of the *B.N.A. Act* and, he says, it is undoubtedly the fact that before that date the classification was familiar to statesmen as well as to economists, and that certain taxes were then universally recognized as falling within one or the other category. Viscount Cave stated that the well known formula of John Stuart Mill no doubt was valuable as providing a logical basis for the distinction already established between direct and indirect taxes, and perhaps also as a guide for determining as to any new or unfamiliar tax which may be imposed in which of the two categories it is to be placed.

That judgment was handed down in 1928, but the Judicial Committee in *A.-G. B.C. v. Esquimalt & Nanaimo R. Co.*, [1950] 1 D.L.R.

305 at p. 324, A.C. 87 at p. 119, 64 C.R.T.C. 165 at p. 186, said this about Viscount Cave's judgment in the *Fairbanks* case: "Viscount Cave L.C. in delivering the judgment of the Board used expressions which if not correctly understood might appear to lay down too rigid a test for the classification of taxes; but as is pointed out by Viscount Simon L.C. in the judgment of the Board in the later case of *Atlantic Smoke Shops Ltd. v. Conlon,* [1943] 4 D.L.R. 81 at pp. 88-9, A.C. 550, those expressions 'should not be understood as relieving the Courts from the obligation of examining the real nature and effect of the particular tax in the present instance, or as justifying the classification of the tax as indirect merely because it is in some sense associated with the purchase of an article'."

In *Bank of Toronto v. Lambe* (1887), 12 App. Cas. 575 Lord Hobhouse, delivering the judgment of the Board, made some useful observations as to the mode in which the question should be approached, and stated that the drafters of the *B.N.A. Act* "must have contemplated some tangible dividing line referrable to and ascertainable by the general tendencies of the tax and the common understanding of men as to those tendencies". [p. 582]

This language was approved by the Board in *The King v. Caledonian Collieries Ltd.,* [1928] 3 D.L.R. 657, A.C. 358.

In view of these pronouncements of the Judicial Committee, I feel that Lord Cave's suggested classifications should not be strictly adhered to. . . .

In the present case there are really only two sections of the *Mineral Taxation Act* (1948 (Sask.), c. 24, as amended by 1949 (Sask.), c. 23, and 1950 (Sask.), c. 22) which have to be considered. These are s. 3 imposing a tax at the rate of three cents for every acre on "every owner of minerals . . . not situated within a producing area", and s. 22 imposing a tax at the rate of fifty cents for every acre of land on the "owner of minerals . . . within, upon or under any land situated within a producing area".

By force of s. 5 of the Act "producing areas" are those which are so declared by order of the Lieutenant-Governor in Council, and the latter may designate the mineral or minerals in respect of which the portion of the Province therein described is constituted a "producing area". For those areas so designated assessors are provided to assess "at their fair value minerals within, upon or under any parcel of land" so constituted. They prepare an assessment roll in which shall be set out as accurately as may be a brief description of each such parcel of land, a brief description of the minerals assessed, the names and addresses of the owners of the minerals and the assessed value thereof.

Section 7 deals with the method of assessment and s. 6, dealing with the imposition of the tax, states: "Every owner whose name appears on the assessment roll mentioned in section 7 shall be liable for and shall on or before the thirty-first day of December in each year pay to the minister a tax at such rate as the Lieutenant-Governor in Council may from time to time prescribe not exceeding ten mills on the dollar of the assessed value of his minerals as shown on the assessment roll subject to any changes made on appeal."

We were told that so far no assessment has been made under these sections and we need not trouble ourselves with the question as to how the assessors are to arrive at the "fair value" of minerals which are within, upon or under the land and, indeed, which may not exist at all, for, it should be mentioned, that apparently the Act is to apply whether there are or are not minerals within, upon or under the land.

What we have to consider for the purpose of this appeal is, therefore: What is the true nature of the tax imposed under s. 3 or under s. 22 of the Act, the first applying to every owner at the rate of three cents for every acre, and the second to the owners of minerals, within a producing area at the rate of fifty cents for every acre of land in respect of which they are such owners? Of course, we are not concerned about the question of how the Act may be made to work, or even whether it is workable at all. The only point is whether it is *ultra vires* of the Legislature of Saskatchewan. The answer to be given is not helped by the definition of the word "mineral" in the Act. Subsection (4) of s. 2 is as follows: " 'Mineral' means the right existing in any person by virtue of a certificate of title to work, win and carry away any mineral or minerals within, upon or under the area described in the certificate of title, and also any mineral or minerals within, upon or under any land."

Then there are certain exceptions with which we need not concern ourselves for the purpose of the present decision.

The peculiarity of that definition is:

(1) It comprises an incorporeal right and a corporeal thing, to wit, the right to work, win and carry away minerals and also the mineral itself.

(2) It proceeds to define "mineral" by the same word.

We are told that "mineral" is a "mineral" and while one might say that such a definition is clearly insufficient, it might also be pointed out that defining a word by the same word is hardly a way of indicating the meaning of the word.

On the other hand, the word "land" is not defined in the Act and I fail to see how, for the purpose of knowing what the Legislature has in mind, we may go to some other statute where that word may be defined. In the latter case the definition is evidently that given as usual for the purpose of that particular Act and it may not be imported into the *Mineral Taxation Act* of 1948. It does not matter that the "certificate of title" as set out in s-s. (2) of s. 2 is stated to mean "a certificate of title granted pursuant to the provision of *The Land Titles Act*". We are asked to say that the tax provided for by the legislation which is the subject of the appeal is a tax on land, and when "land" is not defined in the statute under consideration it seems to me to be contrary to the usual canons of construction to look for the meaning of the word "land" in a different statute.

Here we are dealing with the *Mineral Taxation Act*, 1948, and, therefore, with taxation on minerals. The least that we can say is that the attempt to tax a right existing in any person by virtue of a certificate of title to work, win and carry away any mineral or minerals within, upon or under the area described in the certificate of title, is certainly a tax which, at the time of Confederation, could not find its place in the two categories of taxation spoken of in the *Fairbanks* case; and from all points of view it should be considered as a new species of taxation, sufficient to satisfy Viscount Cave in the *Fairbanks* case and obliging the Court to apply the Mill's formula "as a guide for determining as to any new or unfamiliar tax which may be imposed in which of the two categories it is to be placed": *Halifax v. Fairbanks,* [1927] 4 D.L.R. at p. 949, [1928] A.C. at p. 125. It is clearly a tax which does not belong to the "established classification of the old and well known species of taxation" and which "makes it necessary to apply a new test to every particular member of those species".

We are not called upon here to transfer a tax universally recognized as belonging to one class to a different class of taxation in accordance with the Mill's formula. It is undoubtedly a new form of taxation, the nature of which must be ascertained in order to decide whether it is direct or indirect.

As I said before, the obvious intention of the Act is to tax minerals. Not only must we gather this from the title of the Act itself, but from its whole purport. Of course, the owner of the minerals is taxed and that is in accordance with the observations of Lord Thankerton in *Provincial Treasurer of Alta. v. Kerr,* [1933] 4 D.L.R. 81 at pp. 83-4, A.C. 710 at p. 718, where he says: "Generally speaking, taxation is imposed on persons, the nature and amount of the liability being determined either by individual units, as in the case of a poll tax, or in respect of the taxpayers' interests in property or in respect of transactions or actings of the taxpayer. It is at least unusual to find a tax imposed on property and not on persons."

But it is clear from the Act that the subject-matter of the tax is not the person of the owner, but the minerals and, in the circumstances, I find some difficulty in assimilating the tax with which we are concerned to a tax on land. With respect, I repeat that we cannot, for that purpose, look for the definition of the word "land" in some other statute. The *Mineral Taxation Act* does describe the words "parcel of land", but the definition there given applies to a different subject.

If it is correct to look at the tax as a tax on minerals and not as a tax on land, then it cannot be taken as belonging to the obvious category of direct taxation; and the nature of the tax is rather to be assimilated to what was under consideration in the *Caledonian Collieries* case, [1928] 3 D.L.R. 657, A.C. 358. Indeed, as it happened in that case, coal was the subject-matter of the tax, and both in this Court and in the Judicial Committee the tax was considered to apply to a commodity and to the sale of that commodity. . . .

Much reliance was placed by the respondents on the decision of the Privy Council in *A.-G. B.C. v. E. & N.R. Co.,* [1950] 1 D.L.R. 305, A.C. 87, 64 C.R.T.C. 165. I may say that I am not at all embarrassed by the decision of the Judicial Committee in that appeal. First, it must be remembered that that judgment was given on a Reference and it has been invariably stated that judgments on References are not necessarily binding, because in a concrete case the circumstances might alter the general application of the principle laid down in such judgments; and, secondly, in the *Nanaimo* case the Reference was not made on existing legislation, but the question was only whether the proposed legislation might be adopted by the Legislature of British Columbia along the lines of the report of Chief Justice Sloan. As to that Lord Greene had this to say at p. 319 D.L.R., p. 181 C.R.T.C., p. 114 A.C.: "In construing questions of this nature which do not purport to give more than an outline of the proposed legislation the method applicable in construing a statute must not, in their Lordships' opinion, be too rigidly applied. In the completed legislation many sections of an explanatory or machinery nature would be included. Ambiguities would be cleared up, gaps would be filled and it may often be necessary in construing what is no more than a 'projet de loi' to assume a reasonable intention in that regard on the part of the legislature."

And at p. 318 D.L.R., pp. 179-80 C.R.T.C., p. 113 A.C. Lord Greene repeated: "The answer to the question whether the tax is or is not a direct tax is to be found in their opinion primarily by an examination of the nature and effect of the tax as collected from the language describing it."

Moreover, the *Nanaimo* judgment insists upon the fact that the Judicial Committee is there dealing with what was undoubtedly a tax on land. . . .

It will be seen, therefore, that the foundation of the judgment in the *Nanaimo* case was that their Lordships came to the conclusion that it was the land which was to be assessed and that the tax was imposed on the land; and they quoted from the judgment of O'Halloran J.A., who dissented in the Court of Appeal for British Columbia, as follows [p. 320 D.L.R., p. 182 C.R.T.C., p. 115 A.C.]: " 'Because land bears a tax which is measured by the reflected value of its products is no reason to say that the tax on the land is a colourable tax on its products, and that such a tax is not in truth a tax on the land itself.' "

All that was said because the contention on behalf of the respondent, the Esquimalt & Nanaimo R. Co.—a contention which found favour in this Court—was that it was in reality a tax on timber and not a tax on land. On the contrary, in the present case there is no question of taxing the land. The acreage tax under s. 3 is upon the owner of minerals and not upon the owner of land, and so it is under s. 5 and still more so under ss. 6 and 7, because what the assessor is to ascertain is the "fair value of all minerals within, upon or under any parcel of land situated within a producing area". The assessor is to give a "brief description of the minerals assessed"; and the tax prescribed by s. 6, if the occasion should occur, is to be at a certain rate "not exceeding ten mills on the dollar of the assessed value of his minerals as shown on the assessment roll". Then, if we turn to s. 22, we find that "every owner of minerals . . . shall be liable for and shall, on or before the thirty-first day of December in each year in which such minerals have not been assessed under the provisions of this Act, pay to the minister a tax at the rate of fifty cents for every acre and every fraction of an acre of such land in respect of which he is such owner". This remark is strengthened by the very definite definition of the word "mineral" in s-s. (4) of s. 2, where it is stated to mean "the right existing in any person by virtue of a certificate of title to work, win and carry away any mineral or minerals within, upon or under the area described in the certificate of title, and also any mineral or minerals within, upon or under any land".

I would think that it is significant that the Act itself does not give any definition of the word "land". It is to the "minerals" and not to the "land" that the Act is directed. I am of the opinion, therefore, that the present case is distinguishable from the *Nanaimo* judgment and, on the contrary, falls within the *Caledonian Collieries* judgment. If that be so, as I think it is, I would agree with Gordon J.A., in the Court of Appeal for Saskatchewan, and declare the Act *in toto ultra vires* of the Legislature of the Province of Saskatchewan. Of course, incidentally I also agree with that part of the judgment of Martin C.J.S., concurred in by Proctor J.A., insofar as they declare *ultra vires* that part of the Act which relates to the "producing area".

In view of my conclusion it becomes unnecessary to pass upon the question of severability.

I would, therefore, allow the appeal with costs throughout and dismiss the cross-appeal with costs against the respondent.

KERWIN J.: The appellants are the Canadian Pacific Railway Company and certain other companies who brought an action against the respondents, the Attorney-General for the Province of Saskatchewan and the Minister of Natural Resources and Industrial Development of the Province of Saskatchewan, in the King's Bench in Saskatchewan [[1951] 3 D.L.R. 362], for a declaration that the *Mineral Taxation Act, 1944* (Sask. 2nd Sess.), c. 27, and amendments were *ultra vires* the Legislature of the Province, and for certain other relief. At the date of the trial this Act and the amendments thereto had been repealed and replaced by the *Mineral Taxation Act, 1948* (Sask.), c. 24, and the appellants were permitted to amend their statement of claim so that the important question raised was whether the last mentioned Act (as amended in 1949, after the commencement of the action but before the trial) was *ultra vires*. In 1950, after the conclusion of the trial and before judgment, other amendments were enacted but it is not contended that the latter are not relevant since, by express provision, they were made retroactive. What we are called upon to decide, therefore, is whether the 1948 Act as thus amended in 1949 and 1950 is *ultra vires*. . . .

The 1948 *Mineral Taxation Act* and the amendments thereto of 1949 and 1950 (hereafter referred to compendiously as the Act) provide for the imposition of taxes. Under the general scheme of the Act all the land in the Province of Saskatchewan may be divided into two categories, one of which, for convenience, may be termed the non-producing area, and the other of which will mean producing areas or a producing area. In the non-producing area a tax is imposed by s. 3 on the owner of minerals within, upon, or under any land, at the rate of three cents per acre or fraction thereof.

A producing area is established by a declaration of the Lieutenant-Governor in Council under the authority of s-s. (1) of s. 5, which also delegates to that body the power to increase, decrease or abolish any producing area. In any such declaration, the Lieutenant-Governor in Council may, by virtue of s-s. (2) of s. 5, designate the mineral or minerals in respect of which the designated area is being, or was, constituted a producing area. Provision is made for the appointment of an assessor who, by s. 7, is to assess at their fair value all minerals upon or under any parcel of land situated within a producing area and within the boundaries of which land minerals are then being produced or to the knowledge of the assessor have at any time been produced. By s. 6, everyone whose name appears on the assessment roll, prepared by the assessor, shall be liable for and shall on or before December 31st in each year pay to the Minister a tax at such rate as the Lieutenant-Governor in Council may from time to time prescribe, not exceeding ten mills on the dollar of the assessed value of his minerals. By s. 22, every owner of minerals within, upon or under any land situated within a producing area shall be liable for and shall, on or before December 31st, in each year *in which such minerals have not been assessed,* pay to the Minister a tax at the rate of fifty cents per acre or fraction thereof. What happened was that by successive orders of the Minister of Natural Resources and Industrial Development upon whom the powers were conferred by the 1944 Act (and also the 1948 Act before amendment), a certain area was declared a producing area; that area was increased; coal was designated as the only mineral; and, finally, the producing area was decreased. No assessment was ever made in the producing area. In the result, therefore, under s. 22 a tax was imposed of fifty cents per acre on every "owner" of the "mineral" coal in the producing area, while in the non-producing area, in which is included all other owners, a tax of three cents per acre became payable under. s. 3. However, the terms of the Act providing for a tax at an annual rate on the dollar must be considered together with the other relevant provisions.

The trial Judge, Thomson J. [[1951] 3 D.L.R. 362], declared that all classes of taxation were valid and in the Court of Appeal [[1951] 4 D.L.R. 21, 68 C.R.T.C. 232] Culliton J.A. (with whom McNiven J.A. agreed) came to the same conclusion. The Chief Justice (with whom Procter J.A. agreed) considered that only the taxation in the non-producing area was valid while Gordon J.A. considered the Act *ultra vires in toto.*

The main contention is that the Act does not impose direct taxation within the Province under s. 92(2) of the *B.N.A. Act* but in my view that argument is not sound. Dealing first with a non-producing area, s. 3 imposes the three cents per acre tax upon "every owner of minerals, whether of all kinds or only one or more kinds, within, upon or under any land". By para. 6 of s-s. (1) of s. 2, " 'owner' means a person who is registered in a land titles office as the owner of any mineral or minerals whether or not the title thereto is severed from the title to the surface". By para. 4 of s-s. (1) of s. 2: " 'Mineral' means the right existing in any person by virtue of a certificate of title to work, win and carry away any mineral or minerals within, upon or under the area described in the certificate of title, and also any mineral or minerals within, upon or under any land."

By para. 2 of s-s. (1) of s. 2: " 'Certificate of title' means a certificate of title granted pursuant to . . . *The Land Titles Act*". The *Land Titles Act* is presently R.S.S. 1940, c. 98, and under s. 2(1) thereof " 'certificate of title' means the certificate (form A) granted by the registrar and entered and kept in the register". By s. 2(10) of the *Land Titles Act*: " 'Land' or 'lands' means lands, messuages, tenements and hereditaments, corporeal and incorporeal, of every nature and description, and every estate or interest therein, whether such estate or interest is legal or equitable, together with paths, passages, ways, watercourses, liberties, privileges and easements appertaining thereto, and trees and timber thereon, and mines, minerals and quarries thereon or thereunder lying or being, unless any such are specially excepted."

These provisions make it plain that the tax in the non-producing area is imposed upon the owner of any mineral or minerals within, upon or under any land, or the owner of the right to work, win and carry away such minerals. Where a person appears from a certificate of title under the *Land Titles Act* as the owner of the mines or minerals or has the right to work, win and carry them away, he is liable to the tax of three cents per acre whether there be minerals in the land or not. This is a land tax and is clearly direct taxation: *Halifax v. Fairbanks*, [1927] 4 D.L.R. 945, [1928] A.C. 117; *A.-G. B.C. v. E. & N. R. Co.*, [1950] 1 D.L.R. 305, A.C. 87, 64 C.R.T.C. 165. In substance this is the view of all, save one, of the members of the Courts below who have considered the matter.

If, in the Act, no provisions had been made in producing areas for an assessment roll and the imposition of a tax at an annual rate on the dollar, and s. 22 had merely provided that every owner of minerals within a producing area should pay a tax at the rate of fifty cents per acre, the same result would follow. The mere fact that provision is made for an assessment roll, etc., does not in my opinion change the character of the tax. Section 7 provides that the assessor is to assess at their fair value all minerals within, upon or under any parcel of land situated within a producing area and within the boundaries of which land minerals are then being produced, or to the knowledge of the assessor have at any time been produced. In such assessment roll there is to be set out, among other things, a brief description of each such parcel of land and of the minerals assessed. "Parcel of land" is defined by para. 7 of s-s. (1) of s. 2

as meaning: " 'Parcel of land' means all the separately described areas, within the boundaries of a section according to the system of surveys under *The Land Surveys Act* or within the boundaries of a river lot, which are contiguous and in respect of which the same person is the owner of the minerals. For the purpose of this paragraph, separately described areas which have at least part of their boundaries in common or which are separated only by a highway, road or railway right of way shall be deemed to be contiguous, and separately described areas adjoining at only one point shall be deemed to be not contiguous."

This is not a tax on production. In the *E. & N.R. Co.* case, Lord Greene, speaking for the Judicial Committee, adopted, at p. 320, D.L.R., p. 182 C.R.T.C., p. 115 A.C., as correct what had been said by O'Halloran J.A. in that case: " 'Because land bears a tax which is measured by the reflected value of its products is no reason to say that the tax on the land is a colourable tax on its products, and that such a tax is not in truth a tax on the land itself.' "

These remarks apply with equal force to the problem now under consideration and it was for these reasons that the trial Judge and McNiven and Culliton JJ.A. came to the same conclusion.

Finally, there is nothing to indicate that the Legislature was not in truth doing what it purported to do, that is, impose a direct tax for the raising of a revenue for provincial purposes. On this point I am content to adopt the reasoning of those members of the Courts below who so held.

The appeal of the plaintiffs should be dismissed with costs and the cross-appeal of the defendants should be allowed with costs. The judgment at the trial should be restored.

RAND J.: This is an appeal arising out of the *Mineral Taxation Act*, 1948, of Saskatchewan. The Province has purported to tax all minerals within its boundaries except those within, upon or under railway lands, the land within any city, town or village, or within any registered subdivision of lots for residential or business purposes or for a cemetery.

"Mineral" is defined by s. 2(4) as meaning "the right existing in any person by virtue of a certificate of title to work, win and carry away any mineral or minerals within, upon or under the area described in the certificate of title, and also any mineral or minerals within, upon or under any land."

The tax scheme imposes, first, a general annual levy of three cents on every taxable acre or fractional part of an acre not within what may be declared to be a "producing area". The language of s. 3, providing this initial tax, is "Every owner of minerals, whether of all kinds or only one or more kinds, within, upon or under any land not situated within a producing area, shall be liable for and shall on or before the thirty-first day of December in each year pay to the Minister a tax at the rate of three cents for every acre and every fraction of an acre of such land in respect of which he is such owner".

Then, by s. 5, the Lieutenant-Governor in Council is authorized from time to time to declare any portion of the Province to constitute a "producing area", and, in any manner to modify or abolish such an area.

Section 7 directs an assessment each year "at their fair value" of all minerals "within, upon or under any parcel of land situated within a producing area and within the boundaries of which land minerals are then being produced or to the knowledge of the assessor have at any time been produced, and shall prepare an assessment roll in which shall be set out as accurately as may be a brief description of each such parcel of land, a brief description of the minerals assessed, the names and addresses of the owners of the minerals and the assessed value thereof". Subsection (2) authorizes him to resort to all available information pertinent to that value. Section 2(7) defines "parcel of land" to mean: "all the separately described areas, within the boundaries of a section according to the system of surveys under *The Land Surveys Act* or within the boundaries of a river lot, which are contiguous and in respect of which the same person is the owner of the minerals. For the purpose of this paragraph, separately described areas which have at least part of their boundaries in common or which are separated only by a highway, road or railway right of way shall be deemed to be contiguous, and separately described areas adjoining at only one point shall be deemed to be not contiguous".

Finally, by s. 22, it is provided that: "Subject to subsection (2) of section 5, every owner of minerals, whether of all kinds or only one or more kinds, within, upon or under any land situated within a producing area shall be liable for and shall, on or before the thirty-first day of December in each year in which such minerals have not been assessed under the provisions of this Act, pay to the minister a tax at the rate of fifty cents for every acre and every fraction of an acre of such land in respect of which he is such owner."

The appellants are the owners of minerals, both severed and unsevered in title from the fee simple, and have brought this action for a declaration that the statute is *ultra vires;* and the narrow question presented is whether the annual tax of mineral *in situ,* as a component of the soil, having a special discrete value to be realized upon some manner of removal from the soil, is direct taxation within the meaning of these words as used in head (2) of s. 92 of the *B.N.A. Act*.

The argument assumed that there is mineral of some nature and quantity in all lands, and the tax has, therefore, in fact in all cases a real subject-matter. The contention of the appellants is, moreover, that the three categories of tax must stand or fall together. Mr. Leslie, in his able and frank argument, urged that, although for the purposes of taxing land as such, the value of all its component parts, ascertained by some means or other, may be reflected, yet when a mineral component is segregated as a subject-matter of tax, that becomes equivalent to the taxation of an article in commerce, an article, in effect, on its way to market, in which the tax is gathered up as part of the charges intended and expected to be recouped in the price.

That, for the purposes of a land tax, the assessed value of land can reflect the value of its products, such as timber, even though the timber represents substantially the entire value, was laid down by the Judicial Committee in the case of *A.-G. B.C. v. E. & N.R. Co.,* [1950] 1 D.L.R. 305, A.C. 87, 64 C.R.T.C. 165. This Court had held the proposed imposts to be a tax in substance on the timber as and when severed, but that view was rejected. I can see no difference, for this purpose, between the reflected value of a "growing" product and one, such as mineral, of a somewhat disparate character and of a limited quantity or existence: they are all, in contemplation of law, part of the soil.

The reflected value of a severable portion of land can only be determined, in a practical sense, by estimating its worth *in situ* in relation to its market worth as a commodity, after making allowance for all costs and risks: to which, for the total tax on the land, would be added the residual value of the soil, that is, of such part as was not involved in realizing the value of the severable portion: at least, counsel could suggest no other means or method by which, as in the *Nanaimo* case, the land tax could be computed, and none has occurred to me; and the market price of the land as an entirety would be based on the same factors. If, then, these can be so combined and treated as a single tax on the land, what is there in the nature of taxation or the subject-matter of taxation to prevent the two components from having their individual value ascertainments carried right into the same or different assessments so long as the tax is against each only as it is *in situ?* Since a mineral occupies space, its taxation includes the space it fills, and in every sense is directed against the land.

In the *E. & N.R. Co.* case, Lord Greene takes as a significant consideration the fact that the tax was charged upon the land only and did not attach to the severed timber. That is the effect of s. 23a [enacted 1950 (Sask.), c. 22, s. 3(1)] here: the tax is in respect of materials *in situ,* and only against them as they form part of the land does the charge apply.

Lord Greene in the same case speaks of the "fundamental difference" between the "economic tendency" of an owner to try to shift the incidence of a tax and the "passing on" of the tax regarded as the hall mark of an indirect tax. In relation to commodities in commerce, I take this to lie in the agreed conceptions of economists of charges which fall into the category of accumulating items; and the question is, what taxes, through intention and expectation, are to be included in those items? If the tax is related or relatable, directly or indirectly, to a unit of the commodity or its price, imposed when the commodity is in course of being manufactured or marketed, then the tax tends to cling as a burden to the unit or the transaction presented to the market. However much, in any case, these may be actually "intended" or "expected" to be passed on, it is now settled that they are to be so treated: *A.-G. B.C. v. C.P.R.,* [1927] 4 D.L.R.

113, A.C. 934; *The King v. Caledonian Collieries Ltd.,* [1928] 3 D.L.R. 657, A.C. 358.

In the case, on the other hand, of any large public undertaking, the taxes on its fixed assets might wipe out any operating profit and its revenues have to be increased to avoid such a result; but that, obviously, would not convert them into indirect taxes.

Here we have an intermediate case: a capital asset which, in the course of its business exploitation, becomes used up. The tax is not in any way related to the course of that exploitation. It is an annual levy on the total quantity then existing; and that capital tax could not, in the sense of a general tendency, be taken to be intended and expected to be passed on to the consumer as an element of the price; it might be paid for years before a ton of mineral was removed. There might be the "economic tendency" to transfer some of it to price, but that is as irrelevant here as in *E. & N.R. Co.*

The tax, at the moment of imposition, is in fact against land; it is an annual impost; the charge securing it is limited to land; and it is not an item related to or recognized as reflected in the cluster of charges intended and expected to be recouped in the price of the marketed commodity. It is of the nature of a fixed asset tax rather than a transaction tax; and it is therefore direct. That being so in the case of the tax based on an annual assessment of value, it is much more clearly so in the cases of the flat acreage rates.

I would therefore dismiss the appeal, allow the cross-appeal and restore the judgment at trial. . . .

LOCKE J.: . . . The right of the owner of minerals found on or under the surface of land, whether held in conjunction with the ownership of the surface rights or separately from such rights, is an interest or estate in land. It is in respect of the ownership of such interest that this taxation is imposed. A tax so imposed is not to be distinguished, in my opinion, from a tax upon the interest of the owner of the surface of the land in the sense of being direct unless, under the guise of taxing the interest, the Legislature is really attempting to impose a tax upon the minerals as commodities after they have been mined. The question is not, in my opinion, concluded by the language of the taxing section and the fact that the tax is imposed in respect of an interest in land, since, as was said by Viscount Haldane in *A.-G. Man. v. A.-G. Can.,* [1925] 2 D.L.R. 691 at p. 694, A.C. 561 at p. 566, the question of the nature of a tax is one of substance and does not turn only upon the language used by the local Legislature which imposes it, but on the provisions of the Imperial Statute of 1867.

This is on the face of it a tax upon land and thus a tax of a kind which was at the time of the passing of the *B.N.A. Act* everywhere treated as a direct tax. The tax is imposed annually and whether or not such minerals as exist may ever be mined or removed. In like manner the taxes imposed by municipalities upon owners of surface rights are payable, whether or not the land be put to any use. While it may well be true that as and when the minerals or the right to mine them are sold by the present owners, the tendency will be to endeavour to obtain recoupment of the amounts paid as mineral tax to the Province by increasing the price demanded, this fact does not itself establish that the legislation contemplated that the tax be thus borne in whole or in part by others or be in any sense imposed upon the minerals or commodities as and when they were removed.

Taxes of a like nature have been imposed by several of the Provinces of Canada and in one for a long period of years. By the *Placer Mining Act,* R.S.B.C. 1897, c. 136, s. 152, there was imposed upon the owner of every mineral or placer claim of which a Crown grant had been issued an annual tax of twenty-five cents on every acre and fractional part of an acre conveyed by the grant. Taxation of this nature has been continuously imposed in that Province since that time and is now imposed upon every owner of a mineral claim, with certain defined exceptions by the *Taxation Act,* R.S.B.C. 1948, c. 332, ss. 55-6. An acreage tax was imposed upon the owner of all mining rights in Ontario by the *Mining Tax Act,* R.S.O. 1914, c. 26, s. 15. In Manitoba, by the *Mining Tax Act,* the owner, holder, lessee or occupier of every mineral claim is liable to an annual tax of $5, R.S.M. 1940, c. 207, s. 3. In Alberta, by the *Mineral Taxation Act,* 1947, c. 10, taxation of a similar nature to that imposed by the Saskatchewan statute here in question is imposed. The fact that the legislation in British Columbia, Ontario and Manitoba has not, so far as I am aware, been attacked on the ground that it is *ultra vires* as being indirect taxation, does not, of course, establish its validity. It is not without significance, however, that a tax of this nature is apparently regarded by those engaged in the mining industry as a proper exercise of provincial powers to tax land and interests in lands and as a direct tax.

I think the decision of the Judicial Committee in *A.-G. B.C. v. E. & N.R. Co.,* [1950] 1 D.L.R. 305, A.C. 87, 64 C.R.T.C. 165, does not assist in determining the present matter. The proposed taxes referred to in Qq. 5 and 6 which are mentioned at pp. 316-7 D.L.R., pp. 178-9 C.R.T.C. were to be imposed upon the land but in the case of Q. 5 to be payable only as and when the merchantable timber was cut and severed from the land, and in the case of Q. 6 at the election of the taxpayer only as the timber was cut. The time at which these taxes were to become payable and the fact that if the timber was not cut they would never become payable lent support to the view that, while expressed as a land tax the real intention was to impose taxation upon the commodity after it had been severed from the land. Had it been proposed that the taxes be levied annually and upon the owner in respect of its ownership of the timber and the right to cut and remove it as an incidence of that ownership and thus a tax upon an interest in land (*Glenwood Lbr. Co. v. Phillips,* [1904] A.C. 405 at p. 408), the decision in the matter would have directly touched the question with which we are concerned. . . .

Appeal dismissed; cross-appeal allowed.

[Taschereau, Cartwright and Fauteux JJ. concurred with Kerwin J. Separate concurring judgments were delivered by Kellock and Estey JJ.

The principal case was followed in *Utah Co. of the Americas and Texada Mines Ltd. v. A.-G. B.C.* (1959), 19 D.L.R. (2d) 705, 29 W.W.R. 529, rev'g 17 D.L.R. (2d) 16, 26 W.W.R. 481. The British Columbia Court of Appeal rejected the holding at trial that the challenged statute, the *Mineral Property Taxation Act*, was bound up with the *Iron Bounty Act*, and was *ultra vires* as imposing an export tax. The Supreme Court of Canada reversed, and restored the trial judgment: see *Texada Mines Ltd. v. A.-G. B.C.*, [1960] S.C.R. 713, 24 D.L.R. (2d) 81, 32 W.W.R. 37.

In *Re Unearned Increment Tax Act*, [1953] 1 D.L.R. 657, 6 W.W.R. (N.S.) 657, Alberta legislation provided, *inter alia*, that "there shall be payable upon the registration under the *Land Titles Act* of any transfer of land a tax of ten per cent. on the increase in value at the time of registration of the said land over and above the value thereof according to the last preceding value for the purposes of this Act, excluding in all cases the cost of improvements or of development work actually made or done upon or in connection with the land". It also forbade the registration of any transfer until the tax was paid. While the tax was not expressly imposed on any particular person, the statute contemplated that it would be borne by the transferor who had the benefit of the increment. The trial Judge held that the Act did not impose a tax at all but was rather a confiscation of a portion of a capital asset. However, if the exaction be regarded as a tax, it was a direct tax; not a tax on land, but a tax on capital profits and a direct tax on the same principle as an income tax is regarded as a direct tax. On appeal, in a two line judgment, it was held that the statute validly imposed a direct tax on the increase in value of the land since the last valuation. It may be noted that the Act was later repealed: see *Perry*, The Alberta Unearned Increment Tax, (1947) 12 Univ. of Tor. L.J. 94.

In *The Mobile Homes Park Fee Act*, 1971 (B.C.), c. 35, a fee calculated according to the number of mobile homes located in a park and charged against the owner, was assimilated to a tax on land and so sustained as direct, even if both novel and shiftable; see *R. v. Churchill*, [1972] 6 W.W.R. 107, 29 D.L.R. (3d) 368.]

3. Indirect Taxation or Regulation and Price Fixing

LOWER MAINLAND DAIRY PRODUCTS SALES ADJUSTMENT COMMITTEE v. CRYSTAL DAIRY LTD.

In the Privy Council. [1933] A.C. 168, [1933] 1 D.L.R. 82, [1932] 3 W.W.R. 639.

Appeal from a judgment of the British Columbia Court of Appeal, [1932] 2 D.L.R. 277, affirming a judgment of Murphy J. dismissing an action against respondent dairy in which the validity of the *Dairy Products Sales Adjustment Act*, 1929 (B.C.), c. 20, as amended, was brought in question.

LORD THANKERTON: This appeal arises out of an action by the appellants for a *mandamus* commanding the respondents, as a "distributor" as defined by s. 2 of the *Dairy Products Sales Adjustment Act*, being c. 20 of the Statutes of British Columbia, 1929, as amended by the Statutes, 1930, c. 13, and 1931, c. 14 (hereinafter called "the Act of 1929"), to make forthwith to the appellants, an incorporated

Committee appointed under the Act of 1929, returns of all milk or manufactured products purchased or received by the respondents from dairy farmers as defined by the Act and for damages. . . .

Section 3 of the Act of 1929 authorizes the Lieutenant-Governor in Council upon a petition supported by 66 per cent. of the dairy farmers present at a meeting held in terms of s. 4, to appoint an Adjustment Committee, in such portion of the Province as may be set forth in the order, to ascertain and apportion between the dairy farmers the returns received from the sale of milk on the fluid market and the sale of manufactured products, which are defined as any product manufactured wholly from, or derived by any form of treatment from milk.

The appellant Committee were so appointed in 1929 for the Lower Mainland District of the Province. The chief market for disposal of fluid milk in that district is in the cities of Vancouver and New Westminster.

It is common ground that disposal of milk in its fluid form affords a better return to the dairy farmer than its disposal in manufactured form, and, as the Act makes clear, the purpose of the legislature was to relieve congestion in the fluid milk market, caused by a shortage of demand. Broadly stated, this object is attained by the Committee fixing monthly the standard prices for fluid milk and manufactured products respectively and the weight and quantity of each sold or disposed of by all the farmers in the district, based on returns compulsorily obtained from them, and thereafter apportioning the difference between the total value of sales of each, calculated at the respective standard prices, over the whole body of farmers, in proportion to the weight of fluid milk sold or disposed of by each farmer. Each farmer is then bound to contribute his share of the apportionment to the Committee, who apportion and pay the total amount so received to the farmers who have sold or disposed of the manufactured products. This contribution by the farmers is hereinafter called the "adjustment levy".

The expenses of the Committee are met by a compulsory levy collected from the farmers, hereinafter called the "expenses levy".

The adjustment levy and the expenses levy are both recoverable by the Committee as a debt (s. 11), and the Committee may also require from the farmer an order for their amount on the purchaser of the farmer's milk or manufactured products (s. 9(g)).

The main question at issue between the parties is whether the imposition of these levies, or either of them, involves taxation within the meaning of ss. 91 and 92 of the *British North America Act, 1867,* and, if so, whether they constitute direct taxation within the meaning of s. 92, head 2, of the Act. Both the Courts below have held that both these levies are taxes and do not constitute direct taxation, and that the legislation is *ultra vires* of the Province. . . .

In the first place, it is clear, in the opinion of their Lordships, that the substantive provision of the Act of 1929 is to transfer compulsorily a portion of the returns obtained by the traders in the fluid milk market to the traders in the manufactured products market;

the other statutory provisions afford the machinery by which this is enabled to be done. The decision of this appeal turns mainly, if not entirely, on whether such a compulsory transfer is within the legislative competence of the Province.

The appellants based their contention that the Act was *intra vires* of the Province (a) on head 13 of s. 92 of the Act of 1867—"property and civil rights in the Province"; (b) on head 16—"Generally all matters of a merely local or private nature in the Province", and (c) on s. 95 of the Act of 1867, which empowers the legislature in each Province to make laws in relation to agriculture in the Province, so long as they are not repugnant to any existing law of the Dominion Parliament.

The respondents founded (a) on head 3 of s. 91 of the Act of 1867, claiming that the Act of 1929 operated as taxation, and was not direct taxation, which is lawful to the Province under head 2 of s. 92 of the Act of 1867; (b) that the Act of 1929 was an attempt to regulate trade in infringement of the reservation of trade and commerce to the Dominion under head 2 of s. 91 of the Act of 1867; and (c) that it dealt with the merchanting of commodities and was not local in its operation, and was repugnant to existing legislation as to trade combines.

In the first place, the contention of the appellants that the Act of 1929 is a law relating to agriculture under s. 95 of the Act of 1867 may be disposed of as untenable, for the Act of 1929 does not appear in any way to interfere with the agricultural operations of the farmers, and s. 21 of the Act expressly prohibits the Committee from fixing prices at which milk or manufactured products may be sold, and from directing in what quantity, to whom or when milk or manufactured products may be sold or disposed of by a dairy farmer.

The main issue of this appeal is whether the adjustment levies are taxes, and, if so, whether they are direct taxes. . . .

In the opinion of their Lordships, the adjustment levies are taxes. They are compulsorily imposed by a statutory Committee consisting of three members, one of whom is appointed by the Lieutenant-Governor in Council, the other two being appointed by the dairy farmers within the district under s. 6 of the Act. They are enforceable by law, and a certificate in writing under the hand of the chairman of the Committee is to be *prima facie* evidence in all courts that such amount is due by the dairy farmer (s. 11). A dairy farmer who fails to comply with every determination, order or regulation made by a Committee under the Act is to be guilty of an offence against the Act (s. 13), and to be liable to a fine under s. 19. Compulsion is an essential feature of taxation: *City of Halifax v. Nova Scotia Car Works Ltd.*, [1914] A.C. 992. Their Lordships are of opinion that the Committee is a public authority, and that the imposition of these levies is for public purposes. Under s. 22 the Lieutenant-Governor in Council has power to suspend the functions of a Committee, if its operations are adversely affecting the interest of consumers of milk or manufactured products, and the Committee is to report annually to the Minister and to send him every three months the auditor's report on their accounts (s. 12, sub-s. 2, and

s. 8a). The fact that the moneys so recovered are distributed as a bonus among the traders in the manufactured products market does not, in their Lordships' opinion, affect the taxation character of the levies made. The district here affected is a considerable part of the whole Province, but the Act might have still wider application within the Province. While not saying that these elements are exhaustive of the elements which might be found in other cases to point to the same conclusion, their Lordships are of opinion that they are sufficient to characterize the adjustment levies in the present case as taxes. . . .

It seems to follow that the expenses levies in the present case, which are ancillary to the adjustment levies, must also be characterized as taxes.

The principles on which taxes are to be classified as direct or indirect are now well established by decisions of this Board, which it is quite unnecessary to recapitulate. They are summarized in *Attorney-General for British Columbia v. Canadian Pacific Ry. Co.* The adjustment levies are imposed on traders in the fluid milk market in proportion to the weight sold or disposed of by each of them calculated at the standard price; the expenses levies are imposed "on milk and (or) manufactured products sold or disposed of." In effect, both levies are imposed on the sale of commodities by the persons taxed, and, in their Lordships' opinion there can be little doubt that such taxes have a tendency to enter into and affect the price which the taxpayer will seek to obtain for his commodities, as is the case with excise and customs. That tendency is likely to be enhanced in the present case by the limitation of competition among the dealers in the fluid milk market, which seems to follow from the compensating bonus given to those who deal in the less remunerative market for manufactured products.

The distinction between the present class of tax and that class of direct tax of which the assessments for the workmen's compensation fund were an example (*Workmen's Compensation Board v. Canadian Pacific Ry. Co.*, [1920] A.C. 184), is pointed out in the judgment of the Board in that case. . . .

The tax in that case was assessed according to the amount of the employers' pay-rolls. The tax here is imposed on the proceeds of particular transactions. Their Lordships are of opinion that both the levies here are indirect taxes. It is therefore unnecessary to consider the remaining contentions of the respondents.

Appeal dismissed.

[British Columbia sought to avoid the tax pitfall of the *Crystal Dairy* case through a new scheme of milk marketing involving the establishment of a central agency with exclusive power to buy from producers and sell to dairies. A cardinal feature of the scheme was price-fixing authority which was exercised to fix the price payable to producers for fluid milk and the price payable by dairies. The scheme was held to be invalid as falling within the *Crystal Dairy* doctrine; it was a "colourable" attempt to use provincial marketing and price-fixing authority to carry out an equalization policy which amounted to indirect taxation: *Lower Mainland Dairy Products Board v. Turner's Dairy Ltd.*, [1941] S.C.R. 573, [1941] 4 D.L.R. 209, aff'g [1941] 2 D.L.R. 279, [1941] 3 W.W.R. 342.

In *Prince George Gas Co. Ltd. and Prince George v. Inland Natural Gas Co. Ltd. (No. 2)* (1958), 25 W.W.R. 337, 14 D.L.R. (2d) 247, Davey J.A. refused to apply the Crystal Dairy doctrine "to a process of rate fixing in the quite different field of public utility regulation, a process which in this respect contains no element of taxation."]

CRAWFORD AND HILLSIDE FARM DAIRY LTD., ET AL. v. A.-G. B.C. ET AL.

In the Supreme Court of Canada. [1960] S.C.R. 346, 22 D.L.R. (2d) 321.

Appeal from a judgment of the British Columbia Court of Appeal, 17 D.L.R. (2d) 637, on a reference as to the validity of the *British Columbia Milk Industry Act*, 1956, and of an Order of the Milk Board thereunder.

The judgment of the full Court was delivered by

LOCKE J.:—Under the provisions of the *Constitutional Questions Determination Act* (c. 66, R.S.B.C. 1948) His Honour the Lieutenant-Governor in Council of British Columbia referred to the Court of Appeal, for hearing and consideration, the following questions:—

1. Is the *Milk Industry Act*, c. 28 of the Statutes of British Columbia 1956, in its pith and substance a statute to regulate the production, distribution and marketing of milk and manufactured products within British Columbia and within the competence of the Legislative Assembly of British Columbia to enact or is it in its pith and substance a taxing statute to impose indirect taxation and *ultra vires* of the said Legislative Assembly and if it is *ultra vires* in what particular or particulars and to what extent?
2. Is Order No. 5 of the Milk Board under the said Act, dated the 18th day of January, 1957, *intra vires* of the said Milk Board and if not in what particular or particulars and to what extent?

The opinion of the Court as certified to the Lieutenant-Governor in Council, reads:—

1. That the *Milk Industry Act*, being Chapter 28 of the Statutes of British Columbia, 1956, is in its pith and substance a statute to regulate the production, distribution and marketing of milk and manufactured milk products within British Columbia and is within the competence of the Legislative Assembly of British Columbia to enact.
2. That, subject to the question of whether it infringes upon the legislative jurisdiction of the Parliament of Canada in relation to trade and commerce, Order No. 5 of the Milk Board under the said Act, dated the 18th day of January, 1957, is *intra vires* of the said Milk Board.

Davey J.A. dissented as to Question 2, certifying his opinion as being that the said order is completely beyond the powers of the

Milk Board because it is based upon indirect taxes to be collected from vendors in the form of adjustment levies.

The *Milk Industry Act* repealed, *inter alia,* the *Milk Act* (c. 208, R.S.B.C. 1948) and the *Creameries and Dairies Regulation Act* (c. 80, R.S.B.C. 1948). The statute contains 72 sections, almost all of which are designed to ensure that milk offered for sale in the Province shall be produced under sanitary conditions from cattle free from disease and that it be sold in the condition and in the manner best calculated to protect the public health. No one contends that these provisions are beyond the powers of the Province. The attack upon the statute is directed against part of one section alone, *i.e.* s-ss. (h) to (q) inclusive of s. 41, and the order made by the Milk Board purporting to act under the authority vested in it by these sub-sections.

By a commission issued under the provisions of the *Public Inquiries Act* (c. 162, R.S.B.C. 1948) the Honourable Mr. Justice Clyne was directed to inquire, *inter alia,* into any matters relating to the production, marketing and distribution of milk in the Province which, in his opinion, ought to be investigated in the public interest, and to make such recommendations as he might think proper. After a lengthy inquiry the Commissioner made an exhaustive report in which the difficulties of the producers of milk in the lower mainland of British Columbia were reviewed and recommendations for legislation were made.

The preamble to the *Milk Industry Act,* which is to be deemed as part of the Act intended to assist in explaining its purport and object (the *Interpretation Act,* c. 1, R.S.B.C. 1948, s. 23(5)) reads in part:—

> WHEREAS it has been made to appear to the Government of British Columbia that, as a result of instability in the production and marketing of milk in British Columbia and particularly on the Lower Mainland of the Province and on Vancouver Island, there has been uncertainty that producers of milk would receive a reasonable return therefor, and there have been lacking the incentives necessary to ensure to consumers continuity of supply of safe, clean milk in fluid form:

> And whereas it has appeared that, due to the lack of proper and adequate pricing and an unjust and discriminatory marketing system, unwarranted surpluses have been encouraged and improper trade practices have existed which threatened the whole price structure and endangered the continuity of a supply to consumers of safe, clean fluid milk as aforesaid.

After referring to the inquiry conducted by Clyne J. and the fact that by his report certain findings and recommendations had been made to His Honour the Lieutenant-Governor in Council, the preamble continues:—

> And whereas the Legislative Assembly of British Columbia has considered the contents of the said report and is of the opinion:—

(a) That it is necessary to consolidate the present legislation dealing with milk and to enact further measures in relation thereto to safeguard the public health:

(b) That all milk for human consumption in fluid form must, in respect of qualities of safety and cleanliness, meet a common standard:

(c) That at the present time the total volume of such milk available for the fluid market greatly exceeds the demand therefor, but that in the foreseeable future, owing to increases in population and the limited area in which milk can be produced, the demand for such fluid milk may exceed the possible supply thereof:

(d) That the price of milk of such standard for consumption on the fluid market in British Columbia is affected only by local supply and demand, whereas the price for milk for manufacturing purposes is fixed by world market conditions in respect of the manufactured product:

(e) That, in order to ensure to the consuming public of British Columbia a continuity of supply of safe and clean fresh fluid milk meeting such standard, it is necessary that a premium be offered to producers thereof, but because of market conditions aforesaid the price which all producers shall receive for the total volume of such milk must be conditioned by the price paid for the surplus supply which is sold at the world market price, resulting in a return to the producers of a blended price for all milk produced by them.

(f) That in this Province the history of production and distribution of milk for consumption in fluid form shows an inequality in bargaining strength as to price between producers and distributors, and that the fixing of prices to be paid to producers for such milk is therefore necessary:

(g) That, for the foregoing reasons and for other reasons referred to in the report, it is essential that prices which the producer shall receive for all milk which he has produced under conditions qualifying it for the fluid market be fixed at a level which will ensure an adequate but not an excessive supply of milk qualified for the fluid market.

By s. 2 "qualifying milk" is defined to mean milk which is produced on an approved fluid-milk dairy-farm or an approved raw-milk dairy-farm, certified as such, which meets such standards for such milk as may be prescribed by regulation made under the statute.

Part III of the Act constitutes the Milk Board which is declared to be a body corporate and defines its functions.

Section 41, so far as it need be considered, reads:—

For the purpose of controlling and regulating under this Act the marketing of milk produced in British Columbia, the Board shall, so far as the legislative authority of the Province extends, have power to make orders in relation to the said marketing, and, without limiting the generality of the foregoing, shall have power to make orders:—

(a) Providing for the classifying of any or all persons engaged in the production, supplying, processing, distribution, or sale of milk within the Province, and providing for the licensing of persons in any or all of such classes and for the qualifications for such licences, and defining standards and grades in relation to the quality of any such milk:

.   .   .   .   .

(c) Prescribing the form of licences and the term of such licences, and the terms and conditions upon which the same shall be issued, renewed, suspended, or revoked:

(d) Prohibiting any person from engaging in the production, supplying, processing, distribution, or sale of milk, or of any class or classes, grade or grades thereof, within the Province unless he is the holder of a current licence from the Board which has not been suspended or revoked:

(e) Providing for classes of milk according to acceptability for utilization in each of such classes:

(f) Prescribing the terms and times of payment for milk supplied to vendors by producers thereof:

.   .   .   .   .

(h) Fixing the minimum value at which vendors shall account to producers for milk which is sold on the fluid market, which value shall be set by formula as hereinafter provided:

(i) Determining the minimum value at which vendors shall account to producers for milk used in manufactured milk products, which value shall be determined on the basis of current market yields:

(j) Fixing the price which shall be paid to all producers for all milk marketed by them and qualifying for the fluid market, which price shall be a blended price, taking into account the quantity of milk which has been sold on the fluid milk market and the quantity of such milk surplus to fluid-milk requirements and which must be sold on the market for manufactured milk products and the values applicable to the said quantities respectively in accordance with clauses (h) and (i) hereof:

(k) Apportioning the quantity of milk which has been sold as fluid milk among all producers qualifying for the fluid market and fixing the price for milk qualifying for the fluid market so that each producer of such qualifying milk receives:—

(i) The fluid-milk value as determined in clause (h) for the proportion of all milk qualifying for the fluid market marketed by him which is equal to the proportion that total fluid milk sales is of the total quantity of milk which qualifies for the fluid market received by licensed vendors in each area of production; and

(ii) The value as determined in clause (i) for the remainder of the milk marketed by him which qualifies for the fluid market;

and providing for the distribution of the total proceeds of milk which qualifies for the fluid market accordingly:

(l) Ordering that the proceeds of the total quantity of milk qualifying for the fluid market and produced by all producers in each area of production and sold on both the said markets shall be pro-rated among all such producers so that each producer shall receive his proportionate share of the total proceeds in accordance with the quantity of milk qualifying for the fluid market supplied by him:

(m) Establishing and adopting a formula for the purpose of the fixing of values hereunder in each area of production or for the Province as a whole, which formula shall take into account relevant economic factors, including changes in the general price level, changes in the price of any or all factors of production, and the quantity of milk which is sold on the fluid market in relation to the total quantity of milk which qualifies for the fluid market. The said formula shall be such as to provide a reasonable premium for the production of milk for the fluid market to ensure an adequate but not an excessive supply of milk which qualifies for such market:

.   .   .   .   .

(o) Directing that accounts be given by vendors to producers of the milk received by such vendors from such producers, which accounts shall contain particulars of the quantity of milk received, the total value thereof, and the amount due to each such producer at the values and prices from time to time fixed and determined by the Board, and the basis (as to butter-fat content or on other basis) on which such values and prices have been fixed and determined:

(p) Directing the payment of the amounts due by vendors to producers in accordance with the said accounts:

(q) From time to time designating the vendor to whom or through whom a producer shall market his milk, and requiring every such vendor to accept milk from such producers as the Board may determine:

.   .   .   .   .

(t) Establishing or designating an agency to or through which all fluid milk shall or may be delivered or sold:

It was under the powers assumed to have been vested in the Milk Board that Order No. 5, the validity of which is questioned, was made.

The term "producer" is defined in s. 2 of the Act as meaning any dairy farmer who produces milk for human consumption and the term "vendor" as meaning, *inter alia,* any person dealing in milk, whether by purchase or sale or on the basis of delivery on consignment for sale, but not a producer as such. Section 3 of Order 5 provides for the issue of licences to vendors and producers, and by s. 4 no person shall act in either capacity unless he is in possession of a current licence. The fee for such licence is $1.00.

Section 15 requires that qualifying milk shall be classified at the premises of the vendor where it is received from the producer on the basis of utilization as follows:—

(a) Class I Milk shall be all qualifying milk to be utilized by a vendor for sale in fresh fluid form to:—

(i) Wholesale or retail customers in any part of the Province:
(ii) Other vendors in any part of the Province:

(b) Class II milk shall be all qualifying milk sold in the Province to a vendor and surplus to his fluid requirements and utilized in the Province for the manufacture of canned evaporated milk or for the manufacture of concentrated fresh fluid milk:

(c) Class III milk shall be all qualifying milk sold in the Province to a vendor and surplus to his fluid requirements and utilized in the Province for any purpose other than those set forth in subsections (a) and (b) of this section.

Section 16 declares the manner in which the minimum value of the various classes of milk, as defined in the order, is to be determined. To the figures which result there may be additions or subtractions, dependent on the butter fat content as provided by s. 17. It is the resulting figures which are used for the purpose of the computations directed in the two succeeding sections of the Order.

Section 18 provides the manner in which the total value of qualifying milk received during any month at each plant by each vendor shall be computed, and s. 19 the manner in which the "producer price" per hundred weight for qualifying milk shall be determined. It is unnecessary for the purpose of this opinion to state in more exact detail the manner in which this value is determined.

Section 24, which contains the provision for what is referred to by the appellants as a levy or tax, reads as follows:—

For the purposes of milk regulation contemplated by the Act:—

(a) Each producer shall market his qualifying milk in each class in the same proportion that the total sales by all vendors of qualifying milk in each class bears to the total volume of qualifying milk received by them from all producers in each area of production. For the purpose of avoiding the unnecessary cost to vendors, producers, or consumers resulting from the movement of qualifying milk pursuant to the foregoing provisions of this section, and in lieu of requiring vendors to transfer to other vendors such quantity of qualifying milk in any class received by them from their producers as will ensure that each vendor shall market the same proportion of the volume of each class of qualifying milk, the producer price resulting from the computations mentioned in sections 19, 20, 22, 23 and 25 hereof is fixed as one price for qualifying milk so that each vendor will pay to each producer the same price for qualifying milk:

(b) As in complying with the order for payment of the said price some vendors may be required to pay to producers more and other vendors may be required to pay to producers less than the total value of the volume of qualifying milk received by them as computed in section 18 hereof:—

(i) On or before the fifteenth day after the end of the month during which the milk was received, every vendor shall pay to the Board the amount by which the value of milk received by him as calculated under section 18 hereof is greater than the amount which he must pay to producers in complying with sections 19, 20, 22, 23 and 25 hereof:

(ii) On or before the seventeenth day after the end of the month during which the milk was received, the Board shall pay to every vendor the amount by which the value of milk received by him as calculated under section 18 hereof is less than the amount which he must pay to producers in complying with sections 19, 20, 22, 23 and 25 hereof.

Section 25(a), so far as it need be considered, reads:—

On or before the nineteenth day after the end of each month each vendor shall make payment to each producer for qualifying milk received at the plant of such vendor from such producer during the previous month:—

(i) Where the provisions of section 22 have not become applicable, at not less than the price for all qualifying milk adjusted for butter-fat differential as provided in section 20 hereof:

Section 22 relates to the payment where quotas have been established and we were informed that none such have been established by the Board.

Section 29 provides that the Board shall announce monthly the minimum accounting value determined for each month for each of the three classes of milk delivered by producers during the preceding month.

It will be seen from the foregoing that, so far as the producers (other than producer-vendors) are concerned, the milk is sold to the vendors at a price to be determined in the following month. The vendors are required to report monthly to the Milk Board showing the amount of qualifying milk purchased during the month and the extent to which it has been sold as Class I, Class II, or Class III milk, as defined by s. 15.

With this information from all of the vendors, including presumably producer-vendors, the Board, in accordance with the formula stated in the Order, determines the value of the milk sold in each of the three classes. The value of the milk sold in the fluid market is placed at a higher figure than that sold for manufacturing purposes which is said to provide the incentive for continued production of qualifying milk. The vendor realizes his profits in handling such milk from the amount added by him to the amount for which he is liable to the Board. While the value placed upon milk sold for consumption in fluid form is an arbitrary figure when computed in accordance with the formula, the value of Class II and Class III milk can be more closely determined from the prices ruling in the manufacturing market during the month in question.

Having arrived at the total of the values of all qualifying milk in the manner directed by s. 18 of Order No. 5, the producer price is determined in the manner prescribed by s. 19. It is upon the footing that the respective rights and obligations of the parties are to be those defined in the Order that the parties contract. As between the producer and the vendor, the obligation of the latter is twofold; he must account for the full determined value of all the milk he has received and he must pay to the producer the blended producer price. In order that this may be done in the case of all the producers, the vendor is obligated to pay to the Board any amount by which the value of the milk purchased by him, determined in the prescribed manner, exceeds the amount to be paid for it at the blended price, computed as aforesaid, on the assumption that all vendors discharge this obligation. The amount paid to the Board in these circumstances is in satisfaction of a contractual obligation. It is in no sense a levy.

Some illustrations of the manner in which these adjustments as between the Board and the vendors are made are to be found in the reasons for judgment of Davey J.A. As between the Board and the vendors the payments are made to and by the Board which accounts to the producers on behalf of what is in essence a pool operated on behalf of all the producers in the production area who have been supplied qualifying milk during the period.

The attack upon s. 41 and Order 5 is based upon the judgment of the Judicial Committee in *Lower Mainland Dairy Products v. Crystal Dairy Ltd.*, [1933] A.C. 168. Due to the fact that the production of milk in what is now defined by s. 40 of the Act as the Vancouver area of production has been for a very long time in excess of the demand for fluid milk, various attempts have been made by legislation to provide a means whereby the benefit of the available high price on the fluid market should be shared by all of the producers. In the *Crystal Dairy* case, the legislature had passed the *Dairy Products Sales Adjustment Act 1929,* which authorized the appointment of a committee which would be empowered to require the producers to make returns to it of the milk sold by them, and those selling fluid milk were required to pay a levy assessed according to the quantity sold. The total of these levies was to be apportioned by the committee among the farmers who had sold milk to be used for manufacturing purposes at lower prices. The committee was further authorized to make a levy upon the producers to pay its expenses. It was held that both levies were taxes and it was held that, as they would tend to affect the price of commodities, they were indirect taxes and the Act was *ultra vires* the Province.

In a later case decided in this Court, *Lower Mainland Dairy Products Board v. Turner's Dairy Ltd.,* [1941] S.C.R. 573, orders made by a marketing board established under the *Natural Products Marketing (B.C.) Act,* c. 165, R.S.B.C. 1936, which required the producers in the area to sell their milk to a company incorporated at the instance of the Board at prices fixed by it and directed that the proceeds of the resale of the milk should be divided *pro rata* among all of the producers, were held to be invalid as being merely a colourable attempt to impose indirect taxes upon those producers whose milk might otherwise be disposed of as fluid milk at prices in excess of what they would receive under the orders of the Board. It had been held at the trial that the real purpose of the impugned orders was to take from the producer supplying the fluid market a portion of his real returns and to contribute the same to other producers and that the sale and resales directed by the order were mere shams, and these findings were upheld in this Court.

In my view, neither of these cases affect the issue to be decided in the present matter. Apart from any objection that might be made to the legislation and the Order on the ground that, to the extent that they may trespass upon the powers of Parliament in relation to the regulation of trade and commerce under Head 2 of s. 91 of the *British North America Act,* they are *ultra vires* (and we are asked not to deal with this point), the parts of s. 41 which are questioned and the Order both deal, in my opinion, with matters of a merely local or private nature in the province within Head 16 of s. 92 and with property and civil rights in the province within Head 13.

In my opinion, in dealing with the sale of milk for consumption within the Province, the Legislature might provide for the operation of a pool by a designated body to which all milk produced should be delivered and by which it would be sold and the net proceeds, after deduction of the operating expenses, divided among the producers of milk of equal quality in the proportion that the quantities delivered by each bears to the total quantity sold. I consider that s. 41 of the Act authorizes, and Order No. 5 provides, the machinery for the carrying out of what is in essence such a pool but operated in a manner which effects, for the benefit of the producers and consumers, a large saving of expense by avoiding to a large extent the cost which would be incurred in delivering milk from the eastern and southern portion of the production area to the large market for fluid milk in the cities of Vancouver and New Westminster. The practical effect of the legislation is that each producer receives his proportionate share of the higher value of milk on the fluid market, which is paid to him in the blended price that he receives from the vendor. It is true that he does not receive the full amount realized on the fluid milk market, as he would if the milk was sold on behalf of the pool to which he delivers his milk, since by the method followed the price paid by the vendors must, of necessity, enable them to sell milk on the fluid market at a profit. The fact that the Legislature considers that this method is preferable in the interests of the milk industry as a whole cannot have any bearing upon the validity of the legislation.

I agree with the argument advanced by counsel for the Attorney-General of British Columbia that the legislation and the Order do not authorize or impose any levy or tax. In so far as the producer is concerned, the legislation authorizes the Board to fix the price which the vendor is to pay to him from month to month, this being the blended price referred to in the preamble, and the accounting value mentioned in the Order which is the value mentioned in paragraphs (h) (i) and (j) of s. 41.

In so far as the vendors are concerned, the contention that the amounts they may be required to pay to the Milk Board under the provisions of paragraph (b) of s. 24 of Order No. 5 is a levy or tax appears to me to be based upon a misapprehension of the real nature of the transaction between the producers and the vendors.

As appears from the reasons for judgment of the Chief Justice and of Sidney Smith and Coady JJ.A., it was contended in the Court of Appeal that s-ss. (h) to (q), inclusive, of s. 41, and Order No. 5, as they apply to producer-vendors, are *ultra vires*.

A producer-vendor is defined in s. 2 of the Act as being any person who distributes milk produced only by his own cattle.

Section 44, so far as it need be considered, reads:—

In the application of the provisions of this Act, a producer-vendor shall be entitled to all the rights and privileges and be subject to all the duties and obligations given to and imposed on a producer and on a vendor.

Order No. 5, s. 3, provides for the licensing of vendors and of producers, but not of producer-vendors as such. They are not mentioned elsewhere in the Order and, if there is some other order of the Milk Board regulating the manner in which such dealers shall operate, it is not before us.

As producers they are required by s. 24(a) of Order No. 5 to market their qualifying milk in each of the three classes defined by s. 15 in the proportions stated. In the factum filed on behalf of the appellant Hay Bros Farms Ltd. in this Court, it is stated that the whole of the production of a producer-vendor is sold in the fluid market. As to do this would, upon the material before us, render the dealer liable to the heavy penalties prescribed by s. 63 of the Act and to a suspension of his licence under s. 13 of Order No. 5, it is apparent that in some manner such dealers are relieved of the obligation of complying with s. 24(a). We are not informed as to how this has been done.

The language of s. 44 of the Act must be construed as imposing upon a producer-vendor such of the obligations of a vendor as are by their nature applicable. The relation between a producer and a vendor, such as above referred to, is that of vendor and purchaser and the obligation imposed by s. 24 rests upon a vendor *qua* purchaser. Since one cannot contract with oneself, this portion of the Order cannot refer to a producer-vendor.

Whether there is anything done by the Board in its dealings with producer-vendors which may be objectionable as beyond its powers cannot be determined upon the material before us.

A further contention made on behalf of the appellants is that Order No. 5 goes beyond the powers vested in the Milk Board by s. 41. In my opinion, ample powers are given to the Board by the subsections of s. 41 which are above quoted to make the said order.

While the form in which Question 1 is stated asks the opinion of the Court as to the constitutional validity of the *Milk Industry Act* as a whole, the answer made should be restricted, in my opinion, to that portion of the Act which it is contended is *ultra vires* and as to which we have heard argument. Whether or not any of the other 71 sections of the Act deal with matters beyond the powers of the Province is a matter which I consider, should not be determined without argument.

I would, accordingly, substitute for the answer made by the Court of Appeal to the first question the following:—

> Subject to the question of whether they infringe upon the legislative jurisdiction of the Parliament of Canada in relation to trade and commerce, subsections (a), (d), (e), (f), (h), (i), (j), (k), (l), (m), (o), (p), (q) and (t) of s. 41 of the *Milk Industry Act* are *intra vires* the Legislature of British Columbia.

I agree with the answer made by the majority of the Court of Appeal to the second question.

Subject to the qualification to the answer to Question 1 as above mentioned, I would dismiss this appeal.

Appeal dismissed, with a variation.

[For subsequent proceedings in this matter, see *Milk Board v. Hillside Dairy Ltd.* (1963), 40 D.L.R. (2d) 731, 43 W.W.R. 131.]

Note, The End of the Crystal Dairy Doctrine: A Superfluous Federal Legislative Cure

The *Crawford and Hillside Farm Dairy Ltd.* case may properly be regarded as writing "finis" to the *Crystal Dairy* doctrine. A few years after the *Crystal Dairy* case was decided its principle was somewhat attenuated where a licensing scheme was used as a means of conjoint regulation and revenue-raising: see *Shannon v. Lower Mainland Dairy Products Board*, [1938] A.C. 708, [1938] 4 D.L.R. 81, [1938] 2 W.W.R. 604. The marketing scheme in the *Shannon* case did not have to meet the test of direct taxation because the legislation did not involve the type of adjustment levy found in the *Crystal Dairy* case; and the Court was able to sustain the scheme without reference to s. 92(2). But it did involve licence fees bound up with marketing administration, and thus reflected on the alternative majority position taken by the Supreme Court in respect of the expenses levy associated with the marketing scheme in *Lawson v. Interior Tree Fruit and Vegetable Committee of Direction*, [1931] S.C.R. 357, [1931] 2 D.L.R. 193. The holding of Duff J. for the majority that the expenses levy was taxation (and invalid because indirect) was taken up in the *Crystal Dairy* case which, however, involved an adjustment levy as well as an expenses levy. Certainly, so far as an expenses or administration levy is concerned, case law since the *Shannon* case has followed that case rather than the *Lawson* case: see *Ontario Boys' Wear Ltd. v. Advisory Committee*, [1944] S.C.R. 349, [1944] 4 D.L.R. 273; *P.E.I. Potato Marketing Board v. H. B. Willis Inc.*, [1952] 2 S.C.R. 392, [1952] 4 D.L.R. 146; *Reference re the Ontario Farm Products Marketing Act*, [1957] S.C.R. 198, 7 D.L.R. (2d) 257.

What then of the presence of an adjustment or apportionment levy in a scheme of marketing regulation? On what basis may it be said that it is segregable as a taxing measure which in provincial legislation must meet the test of a direct tax? An examination of the *Crystal Dairy* case shows that the Privy Council devoted more attention to the question whether the marketing levies were direct or indirect taxes than to the question whether they were taxes at all. Rand J. noted this in his judgment in the *Ontario Farm Products Marketing Act* reference when he remarked that "the reasons of Lord Thankerton contain no reference to trade regulation; the statute is dealt with as one providing taxation to enable an equalization of price return". Moreover, the *Crystal Dairy* decision showed a complete indifference of the Privy Council to the language of the provincial taxing power on which it relied. Section 92(2) stipulates that it is direct taxation within the province *"in order to the raising of a revenue for provincial purposes"*. An equalization scheme or one for adjustment of returns as between classes or groups of producers subjected to marketing regulation is a far cry from any association with the raising of revenue for provincial purposes.

It is a striking comment on *stare decisis*—there is no other rational explanation—that not only in the *Turner's Dairy Ltd.* case, [1941] S.C.R. 573, [1941] 4 D.L.R. 209, but also in *P.E.I. Potato Marketing Board v. H. B. Willis Inc.*, [1952] 2 S.C.R. 392, [1952] 4 D.L.R. 146 (see the judgments of Rand J. and of Estey J.), the Supreme Court was content with an uncritical acceptance of the *Crystal Dairy* doctrine. With appeals to the Privy Council gone, the Court took a closer look at the doctrine in the *Ontario Farm Products Marketing Act* reference, *supra*, but even there the Court at once distinguished it and applied it. It found that the doctrine did not apply to a marketing scheme involving merely the pooling of products and returns by producers engaged in a statutorily-directed scheme of co-operative disposal of their products. In this respect the scheme did not contemplate (to use the language of Fauteux J.) that one producer or one class of producers should contribute part of his or its returns to another producer or class. This was not taxation; and indeed, the Supreme Court re-emphasized the fact that a mere pooling scheme is not taxation when it reviewed the pooling arrangements in the federal *Canadian Wheat Board Act* in *Murphy v. C.P.R.,* [1958] S.C.R. 626, 15 D.L.R. (2d) 145. To have characterized the pooling arrangement as a taxing device might have involved a collision with s. 121 of the *B.N.A. Act,* although, apart from this risk of invalidity, the Dominion might have as safely argued taxation as regulation of interprovincial and export trade. The importance of the *Murphy* case lies precisely in the fact that the Court regarded the federal enactment constitutionally as what it was in fact, *i.e.* a marketing measure.

The application and acceptance of the *Crystal Dairy* doctrine in the *Ontario Farm Products Marketing Act* reference came in answer to a question whether it would be permissible for the Province to authorize a marketing board to use licence fees to equalize or adjust returns to producers. In the *Crystal Dairy* sense, this was not merely a question of pooling products and returns but of compulsory transfer of returns from one producer to another. Even so, as Rand J. pointed out, cooperative disposal may take different forms, one of which may be exclusive marketing by an agency by which the products are disposed of and the returns equalized. Even if confiscation is involved as regards some producers for the benefit of others, this affords no ground for characterizing the programme as one of taxation rather than marketing or price-fixing. It is worth noting that Locke J., who spoke for the Court in the *Crawford and Hillside Farm Dairy Ltd.* case prefaced his acceptance of the *Crystal Dairy doctrine* in the *Ontario Farm Products Marketing Act* reference "on the assumption that the producer sells his own product on the market". In such case (he continued) "a licence designed to raise moneys not merely for the expenses of the Board but to cover losses incurred by it in its market operations or to equalize or adjust returns received by all the producers would . . . be *ultra vires*". The assumption suggests a distinction between a scheme of self-marketing and one of centralized marketing through or by direction of a marketing agency. A tenuous case could be made that exaction of licence fees by a public board from profit-making producers for remittance to loss-incurring producers involves taxation which, if so, would be clearly indirect. The public purse is not, of course, enriched nor is the scheme of adjustment directed to such an end; the matter is still connected with a conception of orderly marketing. But, be that as it may, the assumption made by Locke J. finds no factual support in the scheme which was before him in the *Crawford and Hillside Farm Dairy Ltd.* case. Moreover, it is difficult to see why the interposition or not of an exclusive marketing agency should make a difference as to whether an equalization aspect of a total regulatory scheme may properly be separated and evaluated in taxation terms.

There is, of course, no explicit language in the *Crawford and Hillside Farm Dairy Ltd.* case which depreciates the *Crystal Dairy* doctrine. But it is a fair conclusion that the Supreme Court has

broken loose from the tax assumption of the *Crystal Dairy* doctrine
and that it recognizes implicitly that whether a compulsory marketing scheme provides for a simple pooling of products and returns in
proportion to products pooled, or goes further and embraces a
formula for adjustment of returns as between classes of regulated
products, the gist of the matter is trade regulation. If there is any
vice in such provincial regulation it can only be in an overreaching
of the legislation to encompass interprovincial or export trade. See *R.
v. Ont. Milk Marketing Board; ex p. Channel Islands Breeds Milk Producers Association*, [1969] 1 O.R. 309, 4 D.L.R. (3d) 490; aff'd [1969]
2 O.R. 121, 4 D.L.R. (2d) 490; cf. *Brant Dairy Co. v. Ontario Milk
Commission*, (1972) 30 D.L.R. (3d) 559.

If the foregoing estimate of the by-passing of the *Crystal Dairy*
doctrine is valid, then the federal assistance lent to the Province to
escape its consequences is no longer necessary. After the decision in
the *Ontario Farm Products Marketing Act* reference, the Parliament
of Canada amended its *Agricultural Products Marketing Act*, R.S.C.
1952, c. 6, so that s. 2 of R.S.C. 1970, c. A-7 reads as follows:

2.   (1) The Governor in Council may by order grant authority to any
board or agency authorized under the law of any province to exercise powers
of regulation in relation to the marketing of any agricultural product locally
within the province, to regulate the marketing of such agricultural product
in inter-provincial and export trade and for such purposes to exercise all
or any powers like the powers exercisable by such board or agency in
relation to the marketing of such agricultural product locally within the
province.

(2) The Governor in Council may by order grant to any board or agency
mentioned in subsection (1) authority,

(a) in relation to the powers granted to such board or agency under the
laws of any province with respect to the marketing of any agricultural product locally within the province, and

(b) in relation to the powers that may be granted to such board or
agency under this Act with respect to the marketing of any agricultural product in inter-provincial and export trade,

to fix, impose and collect levies or charges from persons engaged in the
production or marketing of the whole or any part of any agricultural
product and for such purpose to classify such persons into groups and fix
the levies or charges payable by the members of the different groups in
different amounts, to use such levies or charges for the purposes of such
board or agency, including the creation of reserves, and the payment of
expenses and losses resulting from the sale or disposal of any such agricultural product, and the equalization or adjustment among producers of any
agricultural product of moneys realized from the sale thereof during such
period or periods of time as the board or agency may determine.

(3) The Governor in Council may by order revoke any authority granted
under this section.

There is, of course, no constitutional impropriety in delegation of
executive or administrative authority. However, what Parliament
did was to authorize the imposition of the specified levies by a
provincial marketing board not only in relation to interprovincial

or export trade (matters clearly within Parliament's authority) but in relation to purely intraprovincial trade which as such is beyond regulation by Parliament. The justification, of course, is in the limitation on provincial taxing power which, as expressed in the *Crystal Dairy* case, extends to intraprovincial marketing; and it rests too on the proposition that the B.N.A. Act exhausts the range of legislative power. In *Caron v. The King*, [1924] A.C. 999, at p. 1004, [1924] 4 D.L.R. 105, at p. 108, [1924] 3 W.W.R. 417, at p. 420 the Privy Council referred to "the not very probable event of the Parliament of Canada desiring to raise money for provincial purposes by indirect taxation". Parliament did the improbable by its 1957 enactment, purporting to fill the gap left by the limited terms in which provincial taxing power is expressed in s. 92(2).

On the submissions already made in this Note, it is clear that the amendment to the federal Agricultural Products Marketing Act is superfluous. But there is, in any event, a deeper reproach to this federal solution to the judicial frustration of provincial marketing policy. Having regard to developed constitutional principles in respect of revenue or taxing measures, (principles emphasized by ss. 54 and 90 of the *B.N.A. Act*), it is odd indeed that governmental initiative (if not responsibility) for the raising of revenue for provincial purposes should be exercised by the federal ministry.

[For a more extended discussion of the matters considered in the foregoing Note, see *Laskin*, Provincial Marketing Levies: Indirect Taxation and Federal Power, (1959) 13 Univ. of Tor. L.J. 1.

Whatever its operation as to equalization levies, the federal delegation to provincial marketing boards does not authorize a province to impose an export levy on the commodities covered, *P.E.I. Potato Marketing Board v. Sunny Isles Farms* (1969), 7 D.L.R. (3d) 263.

In *United States v. Butler* (1935), 297 U.S. 1, where the federal Agricultural Adjustment Act was struck down as relating to agricultural production which was beyond Congressional power, the Court rejected an argument founded on the federal taxing power, saying in part (at p. 61): "A tax, in the general understanding of the term, and as used in the Constitution, is an exaction for the support of the Government. The word has never been thought to connote the expropriation of money from one group for the benefit of another. We may concede that the latter sort of imposition is constitutional when imposed to effectuate regulation of a matter in which both groups are interested and in respect of which there is a power of legislative regulation. But manifestly no justification for it can be found unless as an integral part of such regulation. The exaction cannot be wrested out of its setting, denominated an excise for raising revenue and legalized by ignoring its purpose as a mere instrumentality for bringing about a desired end. To do this would be to shut our eyes to what all others than we can see and understand." What was unconstitutional regulation in the *Butler* case was unconstitutional taxation in the *Crystal Dairy* case. The two cases represent an interesting problem in comparative federalism.]

4. Taxation Within the Province

The territorial limitation of provincial taxing power under s. 92(2) invites examination of the charging sections of provincial taxing statutes to determine who or what is being taxed. This question assumes added importance when regard is had to the settled proposition, easier to state than it is at times to apply, that the constitutionality of a tax imposed within the province (and being, of course, a direct tax) is not affected if extra-provincial attributes are used to measure its amount: see *Bank of Toronto v. Lambe* (1887), 12 App. Cas. 575; *Minister of Finance (B.C.) v. Royal Trust Co.*, 61 S.C.R. 127, 56 D.L.R. 226, [1920] 3 W.W.R. 600, rev'd on other grounds [1922] 1 A.C. 87, 61 D.L.R. 194, [1921] 3 W.W.R. 749; *Gunn,* Provincial Taxation of Paid-up Capital of Foreign Corporations, (1941) 19 Can. Bar Rev. 31; and see also *A.-G. B.C. v. E. & N. Ry.,* [1950] A.C. 87, at p. 115, [1950] 1 D.L.R. 305, at p. 320, [1949] 2 W.W.R. 1233, at p. 1249, where Lord Greene said: "It simply is not the case that a tax on land is the same thing as a tax on timber, however minute or even non-existent may be the difference in value of the land and of the timber. . . . Their Lordships are in agreement with what was said by O'Halloran J.A. on this topic in the following passage: 'Because land bears a tax which is measured by the reflected value of its products is no reason to say that the tax on the land is a colourable tax on its products, and that such a tax is not in truth a tax on the land itself.' " The constitutional problem thus often dissolves into a matter of statutory construction: Is the tax on a person or on a thing or on some transaction or benefit within the province? *Kerr v. Superintendent of Income Tax,* [1942] S.C.R. 435, [1942] 4 D.L.R. 289, is illustrative, for there an Alberta resident was taxed under Alberta legislation in respect of income deposited to her credit outside of Alberta. The central issue, decided adversely to the taxpayer, was whether the taxing statute charged persons in Alberta or income in Alberta. See, to the same effect, *C.P.R. v. Prov. Treas. of Man.,* [1953] 4 D.L.R. 233, 10 W.W.R. (N.S.) 1, 61 Man. R. 283. In *International Harvester Co. v. Provincial Tax Commission,* [1949] A.C. 36, [1949] 1 D.L.R. 1, [1948] 2 W.W.R. 1037, rev'g [1941] S.C.R. 325, [1941] 3 D.L.R. 65, the Saskatchewan taxing statute in question charged the income of non-residents carrying on business in the province, and defined it as "the net profit or gain arising from the business . . . in Saskatchewan." The Privy Council noted the distinction between taxing profits *received* in a province and profits *arising* from the business therein; and it agreed with the argument, accepted by Duff C.J. in his dissenting judgment below, that the assessed company could properly exclude a "manufacturing" profit on sales in Saskatchewan attributable to its factory operations in another province. See also *Prov. Treas. of Man. v. Wm. Wrigley Jr. Co.,* [1950] A.C. 1, [1950] 1 D.L.R. 1, [1949] 2 W.W.R. 1089. Similarly, a question of construction, both of a statute and of a contract, faced the courts which dealt with *Firestone Tire & Rubber Co. of Canada Ltd. v. Com'r of Income Tax,* [1942] S.C.R. 476, [1942] 4 D.L.R. 433, where a British Columbia statute taxed "income earned within the province" by non-residents. An Ontario manufacturing company had entered into a "distributor's warehouse" contract in Ontario with a distributor in British Columbia to whom it granted the exclusive right to handle its products in that province. The Supreme Court of Canada decided that the contract was one of sale rather than of agency, with the result that the company did not earn any profits in British

Columbia. While the Court proceeded on the view that the alternatives were to find a sale to the distributor in Ontario or a sale by the company to purchasers in British Columbia through the distributor, the terms of the contract would support the argument that the distributor remained a bailee until he effected a sale in British Columbia, a transaction which would involve both a purchase by him from the company and a resale by him: see *Note,* (1943) 21 Can. Bar Rev. 61.

The phrase "within the province" in s. 92(2) presents no particular difficulty of application to persons or firms or corporations or tangible things. The difficult problems in this connection have arisen in determining the situs of intangibles and in defining the conditions in which a province may levy succession duties or gift taxes in respect of estates of deceased persons, especially where the assets are intangibles. The cases which follow illustrate these problems.

THE KING v. NATIONAL TRUST CO.

In the Supreme Court of Canada. [1933] S.C.R. 670,
[1933] 4 D.L.R. 465.

Appeal from a judgment of the Quebec Court of King's Bench, Appeal Side, 54 Que. K.B. 351, [1933] 2 D.L.R. 474, affirming a judgment of the Superior Court which dismissed appellant's action.

The judgment of the Court was delivered by

DUFF C.J.: The statutory enactments under consideration are sections 3 and 5 of the Quebec Succession Duties Act. So far as pertinent, the provisions of these sections are as follows:

"3. All property, moveable or immoveable, the ownership, usufruct, or enjoyment whereof is transmitted owing to death, shall be liable to the following taxes calculated upon the value of the property transmitted, after deducting debts and charges existing at the time of death. . . .

5. The word 'property' within the meaning of this division includes all property, moveable or immoveable, actually situate within the province, and all debts which were owing to the deceased at the time of his death, or are payable by reason of his death, and which are either payable in the province, or are due by a debtor domiciled therein; the whole whether the deceased at the time of his death had his domicile within or without the province, or whether the transmission takes place within or without the province."

The property in respect of which the dispute arises consists of certain bonds or debentures of the Grand Trunk Pacific Railway Company and the Canadian National Railway Company respectively, guaranteed by the Government of the Dominion of Canada. These bonds were the property of Sir Clifford Sifton who, at the time of his death on the 17th of April, 1929, was domiciled in the province of Ontario where the bonds were in his possession.

The enactments of the statute purport to impose a tax upon property transmitted owing to death; and, therefore, they only affect subjects having a situs within the province (*Woodruff v. Attorney-General for Ontario*, [1908] A.C. 508; *Rex v. Lovitt*, [1912] A.C. 212; *Toronto General Trusts Corporation v. The King*, [1919] A.C. 679; *Brassard v. Smith*, [1925] A.C. 371; *Provincial Treasurer of Alberta v. Kerr*, [1933] A.C. 710).

The question we have to consider is whether or not these bonds have, in the relevant sense, a local situation within that province.

Some propositions pertinent to that issue may, we think, be collected from the judgments of the Judicial Committee of the Privy Council, if not laid down explicitly, at least, as implicit in them. First, property, whether moveable or immoveable, can, for the purposes of determining situs as among the different provinces of Canada in relation to the incidence of a tax imposed by a provincial law upon property transmitted owing to death, have only one local situation. In applying this proposition, of course, it is necessary to distinguish between a tax upon property and a tax upon persons domiciled or resident in the province. (*Toronto General Trusts Corp. v. The King; Brassard v. Smith; Provincial Treasurer of Alberta v. Kerr*).

Then, it seems to be a corollary of this proposition that situs, in respect of intangible property (which has no physical existence) must be determined by reference to some principle or coherent system of principles; and again, the courts appear to have acted upon the assumption that the British Legislature, in defining, in part, at all events, by reference to the local situation of such property, the authority of the province in relation to taxation, must be supposed to have had in view the principles of, or deducible from, those of the common law. (*The King v. Lovitt; Toronto General Trusts Corp. v. The King; Brassard v. Smith; Royal Trust Co. v. Attorney-General for Alberta*, [1930] A.C. 144.)

We think it follows that a provincial legislature is not competent to prescribe the conditions fixing the situs of intangible property for the purpose of defining the subjects in respect of which its powers of taxation under s. 92(2) may be put into effect.

On this appeal we are concerned with debts, or obligations to pay money. As is well known, rules for the determination of such situs for various purposes have been drawn from those which defined the jurisdiction of the ecclesiastical tribunals respecting probate. (*Royal Trust Co. v. Attorney-General for Alberta; English, etc., Bank v. The Commissioners of Inland Revenue*, [1932] A.C. 238 at p. 242.) In those rules, a broad distinction was observed between specialties and simple contract debts. The latter were *bona notabilia* in the jurisdiction in which the debtor had his personal residence; the former, where the instrument constituting the specialty was found at the death of the testator. The case of judgment debts which were deemed to be situated where the judgment was recorded, may be regarded as a special one.

Situs has been ascribed in conformity with these rules to such property, when regarded as items in a succession, "for the purposes of representation and collection", for the purpose of giving effect to testamentary dispositions, of ascertaining the incidence of stamp duties and of determining the incidence of death duties. (*English, etc. Bank v. The Commissioner of Inland Revenue.*)

In the *Royal Trust Co. v. Atty.-Gen. for Alberta* the rule in relation to specialties was held to govern, for the now relevant purpose, the local situation of "statutory obligations of the Dominion of Canada evidenced by bonds" which were "authenticated in the manner prescribed by the Legislature"; and which were by statute (*The Consolidated Revenue Act,* s. 7) charged upon the Consolidated Revenue Fund; and it was there decided that the locality of such statutory obligations, evidenced by particular bonds, was at the place where the bonds were found at the death of the testator.

In the evolution of the legal principles derived from the rules governing the earlier practice and their application to new states of fact, novel questions will naturally arise. A corporation debtor may have more than one residence, and, consequently, it may be necessary to determine which of these is the residence of the corporation for the purpose of the inquiry. The reason given by Lord Field in *Commissioner of Stamps v. Hope* for assigning the locality of the debt to the place of the personal residence of the debtor is that there the assets for paying the debt may be presumed to be. Another reason has been given, *viz.,* that there, in the ordinary course, payment of the debt may be enforced, or that there the debt is "properly recoverable. (*N.Y. Life Ins. Co. v. Public Trustee,* per Atkin L.J.; Westlake 7th ed. 209; Dicey, p. 342).

The circumstances of a particular case may be such that, to them, none of the rules as formulated and applied in decided cases or books of authority is strictly appropriate; and then one must have recourse to analogy, and to the principles underlying the decisions or the rules as formulated or deducible therefrom. (*N.Y. Life Ins. Co. v. Public Trustee,* [1924] 2 Ch. 101.)

Applying the rules and principles so ascertained, is it established that these bonds are locally situated in the province of Quebec?

The Crown puts its case on two grounds: First, it is said that the domicile in each case, of the primary debtor, is in Quebec and that the locality of the obligation is, therefore, there. The contention of the respondent, that the situs of the obligation is determined in each case by the fact that it is a specialty, is met by the argument that the obligation receives its character from the law of Quebec, and the institution of the common law, known as specialty, is not recognized by the law of that province. Secondly, it is argued that the bonds, in both cases, being registered in Quebec, and being, as the Crown contends, transferable only on the company's register in that province, the situs of the obligation is, by virtue of that circumstance, in that province, even assuming that the rule as to specialties would otherwise be applicable, and that the facts do not bring the case within the rule under which residence is the criterion.

It is convenient to examine first the last mentioned contention.

The Crown argues that, as the bonds were transferable only on the company's register in the province of Quebec, the situs is fixed in that province by force of the rule laid down in the judgment of the Judicial Committee in *Brassard v. Smith*. The subjects of taxation in respect of which the controversy in that case arose were shares in the capital stock of the Royal Bank of Canada. It was held that, since, by the provisions of the Bank Act, the place of registration of the shares was in Nova Scotia, and there, and only there, except in circumstances having no relevancy, the shares could be validly transferred, they had locality in that province, and not in Quebec. The test applied is stated in the judgment of Lord Dunedin at p. 376 as, "the circumstance that the subjects in question could be effectively dealt with within the jurisdiction" (that is to say, in Nova Scotia.)

It is an important rule that the scope of a decision should not, speaking generally, be determined by reference to expressions in the judgment, and without regard to the subject-matter upon which the court is pronouncing. Judgments must be read, as the phrase is, *secundum subjectam materiem*. The Lordships in *Brassard v. Smith* were not dealing with debts. They were dealing with shares in the capital stock of a corporation, a different kind of property, and the judgment of the Judicial Committee in the *Royal Trust Co. v. Attorney-General for Alberta* requires us, we think, to hold that the decision of the matter now in debate is not ruled by the observation just quoted from the judgment of their Lordships in *Brassard v. Smith*.

"It was sought to liken (says Lord Merrivale in the course of the judgment in the *Royal Trust Co.'s* case) the bonds to the shares of a joint stock company so as to apply the principal affirmed in *Brassard v. Smith,* that in the case of such shares the test of local situation is supplied by the question, "Where could the shares be effectively dealt with?" But these securities were statutory bonds and not shares. The conditions of the bonds as to registration are in no way analogous to the provisions in articles of association for the incorporation of shareholders in a joint stock company by the entry of their names on the register of shareholders at its authorized place of being."

It may not be out of place to observe that the phrase cited by Lord Dunedin from the judgment in this court in *Smith v. Levesque,* [1923] S.C.R. 578 is, in the latter judgment, shewn to be a quotation from Mr. Dicey's book at p. 342, and that in the passage in that book where the phrase quoted occurs, the situs as determined by the test expressed in that phrase, when applied to debts, is "the country where" the debt is "properly recoverable or can be enforced"; which, it may be added, is the test given in the judgment of Atkin L.J. in *New York Life Ins. Co. v. Public Trustee.*

The judgment in *Attorney-General v. Bouwens* (1838), 4 M. & W. 171 . . . distinguishes simple contract debts from debts by specialty, as well as from debts embodied in negotiable instruments, that is to say, instruments the delivery of which effects a transfer of the debt. Negotiable instruments are treated as instruments "of a chattel nature capable of being transferred by acts done here, and sold for money here" as "in fact a simple chattel"; therefore, it is said, "such an instrument follows the nature of other chattels as to the jurisdiction to grant probate." The criterion expressed in Mr. Dicey's words may fairly be said to be that approved in the judgment in *Attorney-General v. Bouwens* as respects negotiable instruments and other kinds of intangible property which are "dealt with" ordinarily and naturally by transferring them. But, we do not doubt (independently of the binding force of the judgment in the *Royal Trust Co. v. Attorney-General for Alberta*) that there is nothing in the judgment in *Brassard v. Smith*, or in the judgment in *Attorney-General v. Bouwens*, the principle of which that judgment adopts, to justify the conclusion that a specialty debt, non-negotiable, has (either necessarily, or *prima facie*) its situs at a place where some formality has to be observed in order effectually to transfer it.

On the contrary, the rules by which the courts have uniformly governed themselves in ascertaining the locality of specialties or simple contract debts (except in the case of negotiable instruments) have been those already stated, unless the circumstances have been such (as, for instance, in *Toronto General Trusts Corporation v. The King*) as to make them inapplicable. If the criterion adopted in *Brassard v. Smith* were to be considered appropriate to debts (other than specialties and negotiable instruments) then the words "the place where it can be effectively dealt with" must be understood, as Mr. Dicey uses them, in relation to such debts, as denoting "the place where it is properly recoverable or can be enforced." (See *Attorney-General v. Glendinning* (1905), 92 L.T. 87, per Phillimore J.) .

The bonds now under consideration were, in neither case, negotiable (transferable by delivery) at the date of the testator's death. As regards the bonds of the Grand Trunk Pacific Railway Company, we shall presently give our reasons for the conclusion that they are specialties. As regards the bonds of the Canadian National Railway, somewhat different considerations come into play. We are not satisfied that the obligation of the company itself, under these bonds is a specialty debt; but the argument of the Crown, immediately under discussion, as respects these bonds, fails, nevertheless, on the facts. The clause dealing with the subject of registration is in the following terms:

"Unless registered this bond shall pass by delivery. This bond may be registered as to the principal sum in the name of the holder on the books of the company at the head office of the corporate trustee in the borough of Manhattan city and state of New York, or at the office of the company in the city of Montreal, Dominion of Canada, such registration being noted thereon. After such registration no transfer shall be valid unless made at one of said offices by the registered holder in person or by his attorney duly authorized, and similarly noted hereon, but this bond may be discharged from registration by being in like manner transferred to bearer, and thereupon transferability by delivery shall be restored; and this bond may again from time to time be registered or transferred to bearer as before."

We have quoted the pertinent provision in its entirety. It is quite plain that a bond registered in Montreal may be transferred in New York, and a bond registered in New York transferred in Montreal. Duplicate registers are obviously contemplated. Registration at either place is registration in both. The language of the bond is explicit and cannot properly be read as requiring transfer at the place of registration.

It is worth while, perhaps, to compare the language of this bond with the language of the Grand Trunk Pacific Railway Company's bond, in which it is unequivocally stated that, after registration of the bond, transfer can be effectuated only "on the company's books at the office where such registration was made."

Coming then to the contentions (a) that the rule as to specialties is irrelevant, and (b) that the locality of the obligation is determined, in each case, by the residence of the corporation.

We shall first consider whether the bonds are, in the present connection, to be treated as specialties.

The view to which we have already referred, *viz.*, that the rules for determining situs, in applying the enactment of s. 92(2) of the *B.N.A. Act,* must rest upon the principles of the common law in England, does not, by any logical necessity, involve the consequence that an obligation in its scope and nature governed by the rules of the law of Quebec is, for this purpose, a specialty, merely because such obligation created in like circumstances in one of the other provinces of the Dominion and having *inter partes* the like scope and effect, would, by the rules of the common law, fall within the category of specialty. It is unnecessary now to discuss or consider any such question.

The bonds with which we are concerned are the guaranteed bonds of Dominion railway companies. There can, we think, be no controversy as to the power of the Parliament of Canada to authorize a Dominion railway company to execute specialties. Normally, the undertaking of such a company is a work extending through two or more provinces of Canada; and such companies must, frequently, in the ordinary course, become concerned in transactions in provinces other than Quebec, which involve the execution of deeds of conveyance and deeds of covenant. The authority of the Dominion must necessarily extend to empowering such companies to execute instruments having the effect of a common law specialty, and the exercise of this power cannot be affected by the circumstance that the head office of the company is fixed by statute in Quebec.

It is unnecessary to consider what restrictions may affect the exercise of the power as respects transactions which, apart from Dominion legislation, would, ordinarily, under the accepted principles of private international law, be governed by the civil law of Quebec. There can be no doubt that, as regards bonds charged by trust deed or otherwise upon the company's undertakings as a whole, Parliament is competent to empower the company to execute transfers by deed having the effect of a deed at common law, to execute covenants having the force of, and being, specialties, at common law, and to give the same effect to the bonds and debentures to which securities attach; as well as to bonds and debentures not so secured, issued in the exercise of the borrowing powers of the Company. Nor have we any doubt that such is the effect of the statutes and Orders in Council by which the bonds now in question were authorized.

First of the Grand Trunk Pacific Railway Company. That company's bonds were guaranteed by the Government of Canada pursuant to the provisions of a statute known as the *Grand Trunk Pacific Guarantee Act, 1914* (c. 34 of the statutes of that year)....

The bonds are under the seal of the company. A seal is not necessary for compliance with the forms and conditions prescribed by the *Railway Act* (s. 132(2), c. 170, R.S.C. 1927). It cannot be presumed that the execution of the bonds under seal, as prescribed by the Governor in Council, was an idle ceremony merely. The bonds must, we think, as respects the obligation of the company, be considered specialties.

As to the guarantee of the Government of Canada, the Parliament of Canada has exclusive jurisdiction by force of the enactments of s. 91(1) to make laws in relation to the subject of the "Public Debt." We see no reason to think that the subject defined in these words does not include the form and effect of the instruments authorized by Parliament to evidence the public obligations; and the case already cited (*Royal Trust Co. v. Attorney-General for Alberta*) is conclusive authority for the proposition that debentures authorized by Parliament and charged by statute upon the Consolidated Revenue Fund have the character of specialties.

[His Lordship here referred to s. 6 of the *Guarantee Act*, to the form of the guarantee certificate and to certain stipulations in the bonds and in the mortgage securing them.]

From all this it is quite clear that . . . His Majesty is liable "as guarantor for the payment of principal and interest" of each of the bonds "according to the tenor thereof"; and that "the said payment", that is to say, "the payment of principal and interest" of the bonds, forms "a charge upon the Consolidated Revenue Fund."

The debt under the guarantee is, therefore, not only the debt of His Majesty, it is a debt by statute and as such is charged upon the Consolidated Revenue Fund. As regards the guarantee, these circumstances bring the obligation plainly within the principle of the *Royal Trust Co. v. Attorney-General for Alberta*.

As to the situs of the specialty—the bond was in the possession of the testator in the province of Ontario. The copy of the guarantee endorsed upon the bond in compliance with the terms of the approval of the Governor in Council, acting under statutory authority, together with the certificate of the trustee in the form approved by the Governor in Council acting under the same authority, constituted, and were intended to constitute, a representation to persons dealing in the bonds that the conditions of the statutory guarantee had been complied with, and that the charge, conditionally created by the statute, was operative. (*Ex parte Asiatic Banking Corp.*, L.R. 2 Ch. App. 391; *Bhugwandass v. Netherlands etc. Insce. Co.*, 14 App. Cas.

83.) The bond, in the hands of the holder, in itself, constitutes the evidence, and it alone constitutes the evidence, of the holder's individual right to demand payment in execution of the guarantee. Again, on the principle of the *Royal Trust Co. v. Attorney-General for Alberta,* the proper conclusion seems to be that the specialty had its situs in Ontario. . . .

The Grand Trunk Pacific Railway Company's bonds are, therefore (as respects both the obligation of the company and the guarantee of the Government) specialties which had their situs in Ontario at the critical date.

Secondly, of the Canadian National Railway Company's bonds. These bonds were executed by the Canadian National Railway Company, under the authority conferred by s. 26 of c. 13 of the Dominion statutes of 1919; and, pursuant to an Order in Council of the 13th of September, 1924, a guarantee was signed by the acting Minister of Finance on behalf of His Majesty. This Order in Council, and the guarantee given pursuant to it, were authorized by the *Appropriation Act* (No. 3) of 1924, being c. 75 of the statutes of that year and schedule "A" thereto. . . .

The form of the bonds, and of the trust deed referred to in it, were duly approved by the Order in Council mentioned. By the trust deed, an original counterpart of the guarantee is to be deposited with the corporate trustee, and a copy of it to be endorsed upon all the bonds with the same effect as if the original guarantee were endorsed thereon; the guarantee, when deposited with the corporate trustee, is to be absolute and unconditional; it is unnecessary for the trustees or for any holders of the bonds to take any steps or proceedings for enforcing their rights against the company in order to preserve or enforce their rights against the Government.

The bond itself declares the "payment of the principal and interest of the bonds of this issue as and when the same become respectively due and payable is unconditionally guaranteed by His Majesty the King acting in right of the Dominion of Canada, by guaranty, a copy of such guarantee being hereon endorsed with the same effect as if the original guarantee were hereon endorsed."

It is also stipulated that the bonds shall not be obligatory for any purpose until authenticated by the certificate of the corporate trustee under the trust agreement endorsed thereon.

The nature of the guarantee clearly appears to be that of an unconditional obligation resting upon His Majesty to pay the principal and interest of the bonds according to their tenor. The approval of the form of the bond and of the trust agreement by the Governor in Council, acting as the delegate of the legislature, and its direction to the Minister of Finance to execute the guarantee have the same effect as if such approval and direction formed part of an Act of Parliament. The debt incurred is a debt created by statute. And, once again, the individual right of the holder is evidenced by the bond, and by the bond alone, that is to say, by the instrument as a whole, the promise of the company, the declarations contained in the bond and the copy of the guarantee attached to, and the certificate of the trustee endorsed upon it. The instrument, in so far as it embodies an obligation of His Majesty unconditionally to pay principal and interest when due according to the terms of the bond, seems clearly, on the principle to which effect was given in the *Royal Trust Co. v. Attorney-General for Alberta,* to be a specialty and to have had its situs, where it was at the testator's death, in his possession in the province of Ontario.

It is necessary, however, to consider the nature of the obligation of the company, which is not under the company's seal.

First, we think the obligation of the company itself is not a specialty debt. It is not a specialty in form; and the obligation is clearly not a debt by statute within the meaning of the rule applied in the *Royal Trust Co.'s* case.

Then, treating the company's obligation as a simple contract debt. The company has its head office in Montreal. The company has, therefore, a residence there. The bonds as we have seen were registered there. On both grounds, as we have already noticed, it is argued that the situs of this obligation was in Quebec.

The effect of registration in Montreal has been discussed.

What weight is to be attached to the fact that the head office of the company is in Quebec?

The evidence afforded by the public statutes and the evidence in the appeal book touching the amalgamation of the Canadian National Railway Company with the Grand Trunk Pacific Railway Company require us to take notice of the fact that the Canadian National Railway Company carries on business in other provinces, including Ontario, as well as in Quebec. The debt of the company is primarily payable in New York. But the company is bound to provide for payment of the bonds at Toronto and at Ottawa as well as in New York and Montreal. Payment is not, moreover, contemplated at the head office of the company, or indeed at any office of the company. In each of the places mentioned the bonds are payable at the principal office of the Bank of Montreal.

Either of the reasons, above mentioned, for the rule fixing the situs of simple contract debts by reference to the residence of the debtor, would justify the assignment of locality to the bonds in Toronto or Ottawa as well as in Montreal. New York is, as mentioned, the primary place of payment, and, again, there is sufficient evidence in the public statutes that the Canadian National Railway Company carried on business in the state of New York at the pertinent date, to require us to take judicial notice of that fact; although we cannot judicially know, however notorious it may be, that the Canadian National Railway Company at that date carried on business in New York City.

In the light of these facts, the residence of the debtor, in the circumstances stated, does not seem to afford, in itself, a criterion for the selection of any one among these jurisdictions as the situs of the bonds.

On the other hand, there are other considerations derived from the circumstances that are not without considerable weight.

The guaranteed bond is the sole evidence of the holder's individual right as against the company as well as against the Crown. Since the instrument embodies a specialty debt, that of the Crown, and since, being in Ontario, it was an asset there; and it could not justifiably be dealt with there, possession of it, for the purpose of transferring it, could not lawfully be assumed there, except by sanction of an Ontario probate, or an Ontario grant of administration (*Attorney-General v. N. Y. Breweries,* [1899] A.C. 62.) Moreover, as an asset having its situs in Ontario, it could not justifiably be reduced into possession in Ontario, for presentation on behalf of the estate of Sir Clifford Sifton for payment in New York or Montreal, except under such sanction.

Probate or administration in Ontario would not, of course, alone entitle the executors to receive payment elsewhere than in Ontario. But the point I am now emphasizing is that, if the bond became due on the date named in it, or by the happening of any of the events having that effect under the trust deed, payment would, in the ordinary course, be provided for in Ontario, where Sir Clifford Sifton resided in his lifetime, and where on his death his legal personal representative in Ontario would be entitled to receive payment; and, in the last mentioned event, nobody would be entitled to take possession of it in Ontario for the purpose of presenting it for payment but such legal personal representative. Moreover, on fulfilment of the conditions entitling the holder of the bond to enforce payment directly against the company, the debt would be "properly recoverable", in every sense, in Ontario.

Furthermore, the primary right of the holder of the bond, on default, is not to enforce the obligation directly against the company; it is to call upon the trustees to proceed on behalf of the holders of all the outstanding bonds. That right would appear to be a right primarily exercisable and situate in New York where the trustees are.

Again, in the event of default continuing for sixty days, the trustees are entitled to require payment to themselves in New York. The rights of the trustees could be asserted in Ontario or in New York as well as in Quebec.

It is unnecessary, therefore, for the purpose either of transfer or of collection, to resort to the province of Quebec, while for the purpose of asserting the holder's primary rights in case of default, resort to the trustees in New York is necessary, and, for the purpose of getting possession of the bond, probate or administration in Ontario in the event of death, is necessary.

The question before us is a question as to the locality of certain assets of the estate of the testator. These assets are guaranteed bonds. In assessing the assets to succession duty no attempt has been made, and probably such an attempt would be merely idle, to segregate the value of the obligation of the company from the value of the obligation of the Government, as an asset. In point of fact, the company was empowered only to issue a guaranteed bond, the payment of which was charged upon the Consolidated Revenue Fund. In view of the considerations just mentioned, it seems to be difficult to assign one situs to the bond as guarantee and another to the simple contract obligation of the company. There is a sense in which it may be said that the obligation of the company, if that obligation had a separate situs in Quebec, would receive its value from the fact that it is guaranteed by a statutory charge and that the situs of this charge is *non ad rem*; but the value derived from the statutory charge is nevertheless a value primarily attaching to something in Ontario; and, at the date of the event which happened, the event on which succession duties became payable, *viz.*, the death of Sir Clifford Sifton, this thing was part of the *bona notabilia* of his estate in Ontario, and could not rightfully be taken possession of or realized except by an executor or administrator acting under the sanction of Ontario law.

For these reasons it seems to be more conformable to the rules determining the situs of *bona notabilia* from which the principles by which we are governed are derived, to hold that this asset had not a situs in Quebec.

The appeal should be dismissed with costs.

Appeal dismissed.

THE KING v. WILLIAMS

In the Privy Council. [1942] A.C. 541, [1942] 3 D.L.R. 1, [1942] 2 W.W.R. 321.

Appeal from a judgment of the Ontario Court of Appeal, [1940] O.R. 403, [1941] 1 D.L.R. 22, affirming a judgment of McTague J.A., [1940] O.R. 320, [1940] 3 D.L.R. 73, holding that certain fully paid shares in Lake Shore Mines Ltd., an Ontario letters patent company, which were owned by one Williams, an American citizen who died in Buffalo, State of New York, where he was domiciled, having there the share certificates endorsed in blank, were not property situate in Ontario within s. 6(1) of the *Ontario Succession Duty Act, 1934.* The company whose head office was in Ontario had, by resolutions, established two offices, one in Toronto and one in Buffalo, where transfers of its shares could be made on books of the company. Other relevant facts are stated in the judgment reproduced below.

VISCOUNT MAUGHAM: In this case there is no question of a transmission within Ontario, and it is admitted that the deceased was domiciled in the State of New York. The question, then, is the simple one: Were the shares in question properly situated in Ontario? If they were, the appellant is entitled to the duty in right of the province. If they were not, the sum paid ($65,336) for duty in respect of the shares with interest was rightly ordered to be repaid to the respondents by the judgment under appeal and the judgment should be affirmed. It was contended on behalf of the appellant that the company had no power to provide that its shares could effectively be transferred in the city of Buffalo. If this contention is well founded the appeal should succeed. If it fails other questions will arise for decision.

Shares in a company are "things in action" which have in a sense no real situs, but it is now settled law that for the purposes of taxation under such a statute as the *Succession Duty Act* they must be treated as having a situs which may be merely of a fictional nature. The decision of this Board in *Brassard v. Smith,* [1925] A.C. 371 has been treated as laying down a correct test for ascertaining for fiscal purposes the situs of such shares. That was a claim by the collector of succession duty in the Province of Quebec in respect of certain bank shares, and it may be noted that the Treasurer for the Province of Nova Scotia had already recovered judgment for succession duty in respect of the same shares. In effect, therefore, it was a contest between the authorities of the two provinces, each of which could only levy "direct taxation within the province in order to the raising of a revenue for provincial purposes": *British North America Act, 1867,* s. 92, sub-s. 2. The shares were those of the Royal Bank of Canada, whose head office was at Montreal. The deceased died resident and domiciled in Nova Scotia, and intestate. The bank, however, had power by a Dominion statute to maintain in any province a registry office at which alone shares held by residents of that province could be registered and validly transferred. The Judicial Committee held that the ownership of the shares could only be effectively dealt with in Nova Scotia, and, therefore, were not property in Quebec for succession duty purposes, although the head office of the bank was at Montreal. . . .

Some five years later *Erie Beach Co. v. Attorney-General for Ontario,* [1930] A.C. 161, came before the Board. At first sight it strongly resembled the present case, for it related to shares in a company incorporated under the *Ontario Companies Act,* having its head office in that province. The deceased was one F. V. E. Bardol, and he was domiciled in the State of New York. He was the person chiefly concerned in the undertaking which was carried on at Fort Erie on the Canadian side. All the meetings of the company were held at Buffalo; its business was conducted from its office there; and all its books and records, including its records of share transfers, were kept there, regardless, apparently, of Canadian law. It is a fair inference that Mr. Bardol kept the certificates for the shares issued to him in Buffalo, but nothing is said in the report as to this. The claim on behalf of the Attorney-General of Ontario was for succession duty under s. 7 of the Act. The company had no legal transfer office in the State of New York. It had in fact passed a by-law, No. 22, in these terms: "Shares of stock in the company shall not be transferable without the consent and approval of a quorum of the Board of Directors. The shares of the company shall only be transferable by the recording on the stock book of the company at the head office of the company, or at the office of the company's transfer agents, if any, by the shareholder or his or her attorney, of the transfer thereof and the surrender of the certificate of such share, if any certificate shall have been issued in respect thereof, and upon the making of such transfer in the books of the said company the transferee shall be entitled to all the privileges and subject to all the liabilities of the original shareholder, provided that the directors, in case any certificate of share shall have been lost, may in their discretion accept and cause to be recorded the said transfer without the production of the original certificate." But no transfer agents in Buffalo were ever appointed, and Lord Merrivale, in delivering the judgment of the Board, after referring to certain sections of the *Ontario Companies Act,* had no difficulty in deciding that the shares in question, following the decision in *Brassard v. Smith*, could only be effectively dealt with in Ontario, and were, therefore, property situate there for the purposes of the *Ontario Succession Duty Act.* The maxim *mobilia sequuntur personam* was held to have no application in such case. . . . Their Lordships . . . agree with the learned [trial] judge that the *Erie Beach* case is not an authority for holding that the provisions of the *Ontario Companies Act* altogether preclude a company subject to its provisions from legally establishing a transfer office in some place outside the province or inside it at some place other than at the head office.

This is a question their Lordships have now to consider. They observe at this point that the two decisions of the Board, which have repeatedly been followed in Canada, relate to cases where there was a single province in which alone shares could be effectively dealt with, though, of course, the principle may have a limited operation in certain other cases. The legal position of the company as regards transfer offices and the registration of share transfers must depend mainly on the *Ontario Companies Act* and the by-laws of the company, for it is not suggested that there is anything in the letters patent incorporating the company which limits its common law powers in those respects. It should, however, be mentioned that the letters patent provide (*inter alia*) that the head office of the company is to be situate at the town of Haileybury in the Province of Ontario. In fact, the head office for some time past has been at Kirkland Lake. The letters patent also authorized the holding of meetings outside of the Province of Ontario. . . .

On December 21, 1916, the directors of the company passed a resolution appointing The Trusts and Guarantee Company, Ltd., transfer agent and registrar of the capital stock of the company in the City of Toronto. On May 21, 1925, the directors of the company passed a resolution appointing the Royal Trust Company registrar of its stock in the City of Toronto. On May 18, 1927, the directors of Lake Shore Mines, Ltd., passed the following resolution: "That the company hereby designate and appoint Manufacturers & Traders Trust Company of Buffalo, New York, as an additional registrar and transfer agent at which office shareholders may have their stock registered and transferred within the United States of America." Their Lordships agree with all the judges in Canada that this resolution was within the powers of the directors, if the company had such a power. In 1914 the company had passed a by-law, No. 2, para. 17 of which related to transfers of stock. It was in the following terms: "17. A stock transfer book shall be provided in such form as the board of directors may approve of and all transfers of stock in the capital of the company shall be made in such book and shall be signed by the transferor or by his attorney duly appointed in writing. Stock certificates shall be in such form as the Board may approve of and shall be under the seal of the company and shall be signed by the president or vice-president and the secretary or such other officer in place of the secretary as the board may by resolution authorize." It is not in dispute that since the directors' resolution of May 18, 1927, American shareholders of the company have completed transfers of their shares through the Buffalo agency on books belonging to the company, and have had new certificates issued to and registered in the names of purchasers. Shares are transferable in either Buffalo or Toronto irrespective of where the certificates were issued. Careful steps are taken to prevent an over-issue of shares by daily reports being made by the officials of the company in Toronto and Buffalo as to the various transfers which are being effected day by day in the two cities respectively, and as to the issue of new certificates to new members.

It is contended by the appellant that, in the circumstances stated and in view of the *Ontario Companies Act* provisions, the company could not establish an agency office in the State of New York where transfers of its shares might be made in its books pursuant to ss. 56 and 60 of the Act, R.S.O. 1937, c. 251. The point is not free from difficulty, and it has been elaborately argued. The contention on behalf of the appellant is mainly based on the view that the transfer books of the company, on which according to s. 56, sub-s. 1, the shares are transferable, must be included in the books mentioned in s. 101, in one of which books "must be recorded" the date and other particulars of all transfers of shares in their order, for all such books must (under s. 102) be kept at the head office of the company within Ontario. The Lieutenant-Governor in Council might have relieved the company from that provision if he thought fit under s. 102, sub-s. 3, but he has not done so. There are some sections in the Act which at first sight seem to assist the appellant's contention, but, on the whole, their Lordships are satisfied that it cannot prevail. It is important to observe that the company could set up a transfer office out of Ontario unless there is in the *Companies Act* under which it was created an express declaration to the contrary: s. 217 of the Act. Is there such a declaration? It is reasonably plain that the purpose of s. 101 is widely different from that of ss. 56 and 60. The first, like s. 107, is aimed at providing information to shareholders and creditors who are given a right of inspection under s. 105 "at the head office or chief place of carrying on its undertaking." The objects of ss. 56 and 60 are mainly devoted to the rights of shareholders, and relate in particular to the regulations as to transfers of shares. Provided books are kept complying in all respects with s. 101 it is difficult to see why other books should not be kept elsewhere, outside of Ontario if so desired, in which shares shall be transferable as provided in s. 56. There is, at any rate, no express provision to the contrary, and it is significant in this connection that s. 102 is in terms confined to books mentioned in ss. 101 and 107, and does not include those mentioned in s. 56 or s. 60.

The conclusion on this point must, therefore, be in agreement with all the judges in Canada who have dealt with the matter, namely, that the company had legally established a transfer agency in Buffalo and that the shares in question at and before the death of the testator were transferable both in Ontario and in Buffalo. The answer, then, to the question where the shares could be effectively dealt with, must be either in Ontario or in the State of New York, and further reasons must be found to justify a preference being given to one or the other. . . .

[His Lordship then considered and rejected the argument that the share certificates were specialties because they were under the seal of the company.]

Their Lordships are concerned here merely with the question whether the certificates being under seal can be treated as establishing that the shares of the testator must be regarded as situate where the certificates were found at the death of the testator. They plainly are not specialty debts. They do not contain any express obligation or promise. As Lord Cairns observed in *Shropshire Union Railways & Canal Co. v. The Queen,* L.R. 7 H.L. 496, at p. 509, the certificate was not the title, but evidence of the title, to the shares: see also *Attorney-General v. Higgins* per Martin B., 2 H. & N. 339. Being little more than pieces of paper evidencing the right to shares in the company it is impossible to regard them as taking the modern place of "notable goods". The ancient rules as to situs of specialty debts have no real application in such a case. It should be added that the view that ordinary certificates for shares are not specialty debts has been assumed to be correct in a number of decided cases both in Canada and in England and in a much greater number of cases where there has been no litigation. The rule laid down in *Brassard v. Smith* would in practice be useless if the place where the certificates for shares were found at the time of the death should be taken to be necessarily the situs of the shares. Their Lordships have no hesitation in holding that the situs of the certificates is not, taken alone, sufficient to afford a solution to the present problem.

Before going further it is necessary to call attention to a circumstance which seems not to have been previously mentioned. Their Lordships noted that the only stock certificates proved in evidence of which complete copies were produced were two in number (exhibits 10 and 14), the first relating to 1,000 shares in the name of A. D. Williams, and the second to 100 shares in his name. Each bears the usual endorsement on the back of forms of transfer of the shares and the appointment of an attorney for the purpose. The endorsements are signed, one of them "Alexander Duncan Williams", and the other "A. D. Williams". The names of the transferees and of the attorneys are left in blank. . . . Counsel for the appellant before their Lordships admitted that it must be taken in the circumstances that the testator had signed the endorsements on all the certificates in his name leaving the names of the transferees and of the attorneys in blank in the way usual both in the Dominion and in the United States. This had the admitted result of making a delivery of the certificates with the endorsements signed in blank a good assignment of the shares, since it passed a title to the assignees both legal and equitable, with a right as against the company to obtain registration and to obtain new certificates: *Colonial Bank v. Cady and Williams*, 15 App. Cas. 267. It must be accepted, therefore, as a fact, that the certificates were currently marketable in the State of New York as securities for the shares, and that they were documents necessary for vouching the title of the testator to the shares. . . .

There remains the question whether, accepting the view, first, that there were two places in which the shares could properly be registered (of which one was outside Ontario) and, secondly, that the certificates are not of the nature of specialties, the shares must be regarded as "property situate in Ontario" at the date of the death. It may be useful here to make some general remarks on the meaning and effect of the principle laid down in *Brassard v. Smith* and in the *Erie Beach* case. The first observation is that the phrase used in laying down the principle clearly means "where the shares can be effectively dealt with as between the shareholder and the company, so that the transferee will become legally entitled to all the rights of a member", *e.g.*, the right of attending meetings and voting and of receiving dividends. If the phrase only meant "effectively dealt with as between transferor and transferee of shares", the test would obviously be almost completely useless, since the rights of a share- holder as between himself and a transferee can, speaking generally, effectively be transferred in any part of the world. The second observation is that the test, where applicable, is concerned merely with the place where the shares are to be taken to be situate. The late owner in the normal case was absolutely entitled to the shares as the registered owner of them in the books of the company, and, if resident in a country or province different from that in which the shares can be effectively dealt with, could nevertheless have sold the shares and completed the transaction by an attorney or otherwise. That, however, does not touch the question of situs. Moreover, in relation to succession duties imposed by the provinces of Canada, some other propositions are well-founded . . . [In *The King v. National Trust Co.*, [1933] S.C.R. 670] in what their Lordships take leave to describe as a very luminous judgment of the Supreme Court, Chief Justice Duff formulated as the result of the authorities certain propositions pertinent to the question of situs of property with which their Lordships agree. First, property, whether movable or im- movable, can, for the purpose of determining situs as among the different provinces of Canada in relation to the incidence of a tax imposed by a provincial law upon property transmitted owing to death, have only one local situation. Secondly, situs in respect of intangible property must be determined by reference to some principle or coherent system of principles, and the courts appear to have acted on the assumption that the legislature in defining in part at all events by reference to the local situation of such property the authority of the province in relation to taxation, must be supposed to have had in view the principles deducible from the common law. Thirdly, a provincial legislature is not competent to prescribe the conditions fixing the situs of intangible property for the purpose of defining the subjects in respect of which its powers of taxation under s. 92, sub-s. 2, of the *British North America Act* may be put into effect.

Their Lordships are now in a position to deal with the problem arising from the existence of two valid registries, one in Ontario and one in Buffalo. They observe that the solution must be the same in this case as it would have been if the testator had been domiciled in another province of Canada, say in Quebec, instead of in New York, and if all the other facts had been as they were in fact, including the existence of a separate registry in Quebec. It has been argued that in a case where shares can be effectively dealt with in registries existing in different fiscal areas, a possible view is that the case of *Brassard v. Smith* and following decisions, above referred to, have no application, and that a completely different test or tests of situs should be applied, *e.g.,* that of head office or principal place of business, or domicile, leaving out of account the principle laid down in *Brassard v. Smith*. Their Lordships do not accept this view. The principle seems to them not to have lost all weight even if in certain cases a choice has to be made as between more than one place where the shares can effectively be transferred. Moreover, to search through all the surrounding circumstances for a completely new ground for attributing a situs to the shares would certainly not be keeping within the "coherent system of principles" by which the courts ought to be guided in such a case. One or other of the two possible places where the shares can be effectively transferred must therefore be selected on a rational ground.

Their Lordships have come to the conclusion that the existence in Buffalo at the date of the death of certificates in the name of the testator endorsed by him in blank must be decisive in the present case. They must reject the notion that the domicile of the deceased has anything to do with the situs of the property, or that the maxim *"mobilia sequuntur personam"* has any relevance. . . . The certificates endorsed and signed as they were cannot be regarded as mere evidence of title. They were valuable documents situate in Buffalo marketable there, and a transferee was capable of being registered as holder there without leaving the State of New York or performing any act in Ontario. On the testator's death his legal personal representatives in the State of New York became the lawful holders of the certificates, entitled to deal with them there. Any sale by them would be "in order" and the purchaser could obtain registration in the Buffalo registry. If we contrast the position in Ontario the difference is obvious. Nothing effective could lawfully be done there without producing the certificates, and the legal personal representatives in Buffalo could not be compelled to part with them to enable the transfers to be effected in Ontario rather than at Buffalo. In a

business sense the shares at the date of the death could effectively
be dealt with in Buffalo and not in Ontario.

Their Lordships do not think it would be right for them to express
any opinion as to the conclusion which they would have come to if the
certificates had not been endorsed and signed in blank by the testator,
for that point does not arise for decision, and there are some obvious
distinctions arising in cases where the endorsement on certificates
has not been signed by the registered holder.

Appeal dismissed.

[See *Laskin*; Taxation and Situs: Company Shares, (1941) 19 Can. Bar
Rev. 617; *Note*, (1942) 20 Can. Bar Rev. 471; *Note*, (1942) 20 Can. Bar
Rev. 640. Does the *Williams* case deny power to a province to include share
certificates within a definition of property subject to taxation if found within
the province? *Cf. Stern v. The Queen*, [1896] 1 Q.B. 211. In *In re Brookfield
Estate, Royal Trust Co. v. The King*, [1949] S.C.R. 329, [1949] 2 D.L.R. 153,
[1949] C.T.C. 59, rev'g [1948] 4 D.L.R. 210, 22 M.P.R. 140, [1949] C.T.C. 50, the
deceased, domiciled in Nova Scotia, had registered certain shares in United
States companies, which had no share transfer registries in Nova Scotia, in
the names of Nova Scotia nominees. The certificates, endorsed in blank, with
attached declarations of trust by the registered owners, were held by a Nova
Scotia trust company subject to the deceased's instructions. The Supreme
Court of Canada held that the deceased's beneficial interest in the shares was
not property situate in Nova Scotia within ss. 3(1) and 8(a) of the *Succession
Duty Act*, 1945 (N.S.), c. 7. Rand J. said, *inter alia*: "Under a law-making
sovereignty the subject-matter of taxation may in fact be anything on which
power can be exerted or in respect of which the payment of money can be
made the condition of the doing of an act or exercising a right within its
territorial boundaries. In the *Stern* case there were street certificates within
England which were essential to an entry of transfer on the register outside
of England; and the legislative authority of England extended in effect to
restrain the use of these certificates until, or to charge other property
admittedly in England with, the payment of certain monies related to them.
Whether these monies are taken to be probate or estate duties or legacy
or succession duties does not, for purposes of jurisdiction in taxes, appear
to be material.

"But a province of the Dominion is not apparently in that degree of
sovereignty. The power of 'direct taxation within the province', interpreted
as it has been by the authorities cited, is to be exercised on the footing
that there is only one *situs* for every class of property and that that *situs*
must be within the province. And for shares, there can be no such division
of interest or powers in or annexed to them as would in the result attribute
to them a *situs* in two or more places.

"It is not suggested that the law of New York has embodied the visible
and exclusive evidence of these rights in one tangible and moveable symbol
to be looked upon and dealt with as a chattel as in *Attorney-General v.
Bouwens* (1838), 4 M. & W. 171, and that being so, we are remitted to the
considerations by which the shares are localized in the place where they may
be effectually dealt with. But it is conceded that an entry of the purchaser's
name on the registry of the shares in New York would be essential to
admitting him to membership in the company and the case comes then
directly within the principles laid down."

Would it be competent to a Province, which permits companies incorporated therein to establish share transfer registries outside, to declare that

shares of a deceased shareholder are transferable only on the registry in the Province? See *Re Wolfenden*, [1971] 5 W.W.R. 168, 21 D.L.R. (3d) 118; affirmed (*sub nom. First Nat. Bank of Nevada v. Minister of Finance*) [1972] 5 W.W.R. 443, 28 D.L.R. (3d) 756 (B.C.); *Note*, (1944) 22 Can. Bar Rev. 838; *Note* (Correspondence), (1945) 23 Can. Bar Rev. 77; *Note*, (1945) 23 Can. Bar Rev. 167.]

TREASURER OF ONTARIO v. BLONDE; TREASURER OF ONTARIO v. ABERDEIN

In the Privy Council. [1947] A.C. 24, [1946] 4 D.L.R. 785, [1946] 3 W.W.R. 683.

Appeals from two judgments of the Ontario Court of Appeal, [1941] O.R. 227, [1941] 3 D.L.R. 225, and [1945] O.R. 206, at p. 213, [1945] 2 D.L.R. 37, holding that certain shares of deceased owners were not situated in Ontario. In the *Blonde* case, the deceased who died domiciled and resident in Ontario, owned shares in Michigan companies having their head office in Detroit and share transfer agencies in Michigan and New York but none in Ontario. At his death the share certificates were in his possession unendorsed. In the *Aberdein* case, the deceased who died domiciled and resident in Massachusetts owned shares in a Dominion company and was also joint owner with his wife of shares in an Ontario company. The head office of each company was in Ontario and each had share transfer registries in Toronto and New York. At his death the share certificates were in Massachusetts unendorsed.

LORD UTHWATT: These appeals from the Court of Appeal for Ontario relate to the question of the situs to be attributed to registered shares in companies for the purposes of the Succession Duty Acts of Ontario. They may be conveniently dealt with together. . . . The authorities which bear on the situs of registered shares were recently reviewed by their Lordships in *Rex v. Williams*, and it is unnecessary again to review them. It is now settled beyond dispute that for the purpose of death duties a local situation is to be attributed to shares in a company and that (leaving aside the case of "street certificates") the first matter to be ascertained in an inquiry as to the situs of registered shares is the place in which the shares can be effectively dealt with as between the shareholders and the company so that the transferee will become legally entitled to all the rights of a member. The authorities before *Rex v. Williams* establish that, if such a place be found within a particular jurisdiction, the shares are situate within that jurisdiction, but in none of those cases was there present the feature that there were two places where the shares could effectively be dealt with, one within and the other outside the jurisdiction. That situation arose in *Rex v. Williams*, where shares could be transferred indifferently in Toronto, Ontario and in Buffalo, New York. The principle laid down and applied in that case was if it were possible on rational grounds to prefer one of the alternative places to the other as the place of transfer for the shares in question, the selection should be made accordingly.

A just estimation is, in their Lordships' opinion, first to be made of all matters which relate to the transfer of the shares under consideration. If sufficient reason for a choice of one place then appears, the problem is solved. It is only where a solution on these lines is not possible that the need for resort to some other principle for determining situs arises.

The adoption of place of transfer as the leading consideration in determining locality involves, in their Lordships' view, the corollary that, if there be, outside the jurisdiction in which it is suggested the shares are situate, several places where transfers can be effectively carried through in the ordinary course of business, and there is no place within the jurisdiction where a transfer can be carried through, the shares cannot be situate within the jurisdiction. The inquiry at the outset is "Are the shares situate in the jurisdiction or not?" The inability of the jurisdiction to satisfy the test removes it from the arena. The circumstance that alternative places of transfer exist in what happen to be two different states outside the jurisdiction is for the purpose in hand no more relevant than the circumstance that two places of transfer exist in one state outside the jurisdiction.

These considerations are sufficient to dispose of *Blonde's* case. It is clear that the shares could be transferred outside Ontario in the ordinary course of business and could not be transferred within Ontario at all. The shares were therefore not situate in Ontario. The domicile of the testator, grant of probate in Ontario and the presence in Ontario of the share certificates, are irrelevant.

Aberdein's case cannot be disposed of so summarily. Effective transfers were possible both in Ontario and outside Ontario. The other matters bearing on transfer must therefore be considered. In argument two matters were referred to as helping the view that the shares were situate in Ontario. First, it was said that under the law of New York, the shares were not situate in New York. The field was therefore left open for Ontario, and the absence of a competitor, if not conclusive in favour of Ontario as the situs of the shares, at least tipped the scale in its favour. In their Lordships' opinion the view taken by the law of New York as to the situs of the shares is irrelevant. The question at issue is what is the situs according to the law of Ontario, and on that topic the law of New York has no bearing. A situs in New York according to the law of Ontario is consistent with the absence of that situs according to the law of New York. It may be added that it was not suggested that the lack, according to the law of New York, of situs in New York in any way impeded operations on the register of transfers maintained in New York. Secondly, it was suggested, in the case of the shares in the [Ontario] Company, that as the Ontario Companies Act required a register of members to be kept in Ontario and the maintenance of a register of members and a transfer office in New York was facultative, primacy should be accorded to the Ontario office. In their Lordships' opinion there is no substance in this point. The New York transfer office was no fleeting phantom and, as regards its functions, it stood in all respects on a parity with the Ontario transfer office.

The other features that bear on transfer are that the shares were freely marketable both in New York and in Ontario; that the registered owners were domiciled and resident in Massachusetts; that the share certificates were in Massachusetts; that probate in Ontario was not necessary in order to enable Aberdein's executors to be registered on the New York register, and that there were clear advantages to executors in choosing New York rather than Ontario as the place of transfer (see *Rex v. Globe Indemnity Company of Canada Ltd.*, [1945] O.R. 190.) The common feature of these matters is that none of them points to Ontario, and all point to New York, as the place at which in the ordinary course of affairs the shares would be dealt with by the registered owner. That owner, domiciled and living in Massachusetts and with alternative markets open to him, would be little likely when desiring to deal with his shares to choose a market and place of transfer which subjected him to the necessity of transferring the share certificates to a place outside the U.S.A. and of receiving Canadian dollars on a sale. On transmission on death both as regards shares held jointly as well as the shares held by Aberdein solely, New York and not Ontario would in the ordinary course be selected as the place for completing the formalities incident to the new ownership. In substance for transfer purposes New York occupied the field so far as these shares were concerned. Without leaving the region of transfer there is, in their Lordships' view, sufficient ground here (though there is not present, as in *Rex v. Williams,* any blank endorsement of the certificate) to enable a selection to be made between New York and Ontario. In their Lordships' view the shares were not, according to the law of Ontario, situate in Ontario.

Appeals dismissed.

[On the question of the situs of "street" certificates, which Lord Uthwatt seemed to treat as open, see Rand J. in *In re Brookfield Estate, Royal Trust Co. v. The King,* [1949] S.C.R. 329, at p. 339, [1949] 2 D.L.R. 153, at p. 161, [1949] C.T.C. 59, at p. 67, where after referring to *Brassard v. Smith* and the *Williams* case, he said: "These pronouncements, re-affirmed in *Treasurer of Ontario v. Blonde,* treat mere transferability or merchantability of the right to become a shareholder, in the initial stages of the inquiry, as having little if any relevance to situs, but they recognize as matters of a determinative nature what the law creating the shares has provided to evidence their characteristics as property. Registration in a book and representation by a certificate are tangible badges which set conditions to complete transferability of the shares as well as facilitate dealings with them. If, as in the case of bearer shares, in analogy to bearer bonds, the issuing jurisdiction has in effect embodied in a certain instrument the exclusive symbol of the total rights created, then, certainly, as a rule, the situs is taken to be the locality in which the instrument may at any time be".]

The rules governing the situs of various kinds of intangibles are discussed by *Falconbridge,* Essays on the Conflict of Laws (1954 2d ed.), chap. 20. The following illustrative cases may be noted:

1. Simple contract debts: *Rex v. Lovitt,* [1912] A.C. 212; *In re Muir Estate, Standard Trust Co. v. Treas. of Man.* (1915), 51

S.C.R. 428, 23 D.L.R. 811, 9 W.W.R. 1226; *Bitter v. Secretary of State for Canada,* [1944] Ex. C.R. 61, [1944] 3 D.L.R. 482 (corporation debtor with several residences).

2. Specialty debts: *Royal Trust Co. v. A.-G. Alta.,* [1930] A.C. 144, [1930] 1 D.L.R. 868, [1929] 3 W.W.R. 633; *Toronto General Trusts Corp. v. The King,* [1919] A.C. 679, 46 D.L.R. 318, [1919] 2 W.W.R. 354.

3. Judgment debts: *A.-G. v. Bouwens* (1838), 4 M. & W. 171, 150 E.R. 1390.

4. Negotiable instruments: *Crosby v. Prescott,* [1923] S.C.R. 446, [1923] 2 D.L.R. 937, [1923] 2 W.W.R. 569.

5. Bank deposit receipts: *Prov. Treas. of Man. v. Bennett,* [1937] S.C.R. 138, [1937] 2 D.L.R. 1.

6. Bonds: *Re Moore,* [1937] 2 D.L.R. 746 (Ont.); *Re Mathews,* [1938] 2 D.L.R. 763 (Ont.); *The King v. Sanner and Bank of Montreal* (1936), 74 Que. S.C. 42.

7. Debts due from the Crown and statutory government obligations: *The King v. National Trust Co.,* [1933] S.C.R. 670, [1933] 4 D.L.R. 465.

8. Mortgages: *Toronto General Trusts Corp. v. The King, supra; Royal Trust Co. v. Prov. Sec.-Treas. of N.B.,* [1925] S.C.R. 94, [1925] 2 D.L.R. 49; *Treas. of Ont. v. Pattin* (1910), 22 O.L.R. 184.

9. Agreements for sale of land: *In re Muir Estate, Standard Trust Co. v. Prov. Treas. of Man., supra; Vaughn v. A.-G. Alta.,* [1924] 3 D.L.R. 467, [1924] 2 W.W.R. 821; *Schmidt v. Prov. Treas. of Alta.,* [1935] 4 D.L.R. 752, [1935] 3 W.W.R. 498.

10. Trusts: *A.-G. N.S. v. Davis,* [1937] 3 D.L.R. 673. Cf. *A.-G. Ont. v. Fasken,* [1935] O.R. 288, [1935] 3 D.L.R. 100; *In re Brookfield Estate, Royal Trust Co. v. The King,* [1949] S.C.R. 329, [1949] 2 D.L.R. 153, [1949] C.T.C. 59.

11. Life insurance policies: *In re Corlet Estate* [1939] 4 D.L.R. 111, [1939] 2 W.W.R. 478 (Alta.); *Re Lawton,* [1944] 3 D.L.R. 51, [1944] 2 W.W.R. 265, aff'd [1945] 4 D.L.R. 8, [1945] 2 W.W.R. 529 (Man.).

12. Interests in estates: *In re Steed and Raeburn Estates, Minister of National Revenue v. Fitzgerald,* [1949] S.C.R. 453, [1949] 3 D.L.R. 497, [1949] C.T.C. 101; *In re Lunn Estate,* [1925] 2 W.W.R. 608, 35 B.C.R. 411.

Some of the foregoing cases are discussed in *Farwell,* Law of Succession Duties in Ontario (1942), pp. 67-79; *Quigg,* Succession Duties in Canada (2d ed. 1937), chap. IX; *Jameson,* Ontario Succession Duties (1959), chap. 4; and see also *Perry,* Taxation in Canada (1951), chap. 8. It may be noted that the *Estate Tax Act,* R.S.C. 1970, c. E-9, s. 42, fixes the situs of various kinds of property in places differing from those fixed by the common law rules. The Dominion is not, of course, affected by the constitutional and territorial limitations governing the provinces, and certainly not in respect of federally incorporated companies (see *Hunt v. The Queen*, [1968] S.C.R. 323, 67 D.L.R. (2d) 373), but the federal rules take on importance for the provinces in the light of Dominion-Provincial tax agreements.

[Where provincial legislation prohibits the transfer of shares into the name of the beneficiary without a succession duty clearance is the legislation valid with respect to the transfer of shares in a Dominion company where Dominion legislation declares that the right of the shareholder to transfer his shares shall not be restricted? See *Christie v. British American Oil Co. Ltd.*, [1947] O.R. 842, [1947] 4 D.L.R. 672.]

PROV. TREAS. OF ALTA. v. KERR

In the Privy Council. [1933] A.C. 710, [1933] 4 D.L.R. 81, [1933] 3 W.W.R. 38.

Appeal and cross-appeal from a judgment of the Alberta Appellate Division, [1933] 1 D.L.R. 88, [1932] 2 W.W.R. 705, relating to the validity of Alberta succession duty legislation in its application to personal property of an Alberta domiciliary.

LORD THANKERTON: The late Isaac Kendall Kerr died on December 3, 1929, domiciled and resident in the Province of Alberta. He left a large estate, and the respondents in the original appeal, both of whom are resident in the city of Calgary, obtained letters probate as executrix and executor of his will. Thereafter duties amounting to $54,754.21 were assessed under the Alberta Succession Duties Act by the Provincial Treasurer in respect of the property of the deceased, and the respondents, along with a surety, entered into the bond afterwards referred to in order to secure payment of these duties.

The respondents challenged the validity of the imposition of these duties by the Province and a special case was agreed to by the parties, which was referred, pursuant to the Alberta Rules of Court, to the Appellate Division of the Supreme Court of Alberta. In this case two questions were referred for determination, and the decision of the Appellate Division, given July 22, 1932, has led to the original appeal by the Provincial Treasurer and the Attorney-General for Alberta (hereinafter called "the Province"), and a cross appeal by the executrix and executor (hereinafter called "the executors").

The property in respect of which the duties were imposed is described in the special case as follows:

"(2.) The property owned by the said Isaac Kendall Kerr at the time of his death consisted of—(a) certain personal property of the aggregate value of $265,703.58 composed of shares and other securities of various companies which had no head office in the Province of Alberta, and none of which had any registration or transfer office within the said Province, together with other personal property locally situate outside of the said Province. The share certificates and other documents evidencing such shares and other securities were found in the City of Calgary, in the Province of Alberta. (b) Certain real property and personal property having an aggregate value of $274,697.03. The real property is situate within the Province of Alberta and the personal property consists of shares and other securities in companies with head office and transfer office situate within the Province of Alberta, and other personal property locally situate within the said Province. (3.) Within the two years prior to his death the said Isaac Kendall Kerr transferred to Clara E. Kerr, one of the plaintiffs, certain real estate situate within the Province of Alberta, together with certain personal estate."

No question is raised as to the duties in respect of the property in para. 3, and the following questions were submitted for the opinion of the Court: "(1.) Whether or not the succession duties levied in respect of the property mentioned in sub-s. (a) in para. 2 of the special case are valid and payable to the defendants or either of them. (2.) Whether or not the succession duties levied in respect of the property mentioned in sub-s. (b) in para. 2 of the special case are valid and payable to the defendants or either of them."

The determination of the validity of the imposition of the duties depends on the application of the limits placed upon the taxing powers of a Province by s. 92 of the *British North America Act, 1867*—namely, "Direct taxation within the Province in order to the raising of a revenue for Provincial purposes" to the provisions of the Alberta Succession Duties Act. As regards the first question, which relates to personal property locally situate outside the Province, the issue is twofold—namely, whether the taxation is direct and whether it is within the Province. On the second question, which covers real and personal property situate within the Province, the issue is whether the taxation is direct.

Dealing first with the question of taxation "within the Province", the general law as to the power of taxation of a sovereign state has been thus stated; *Blackwood v. The Queen:* (8 App. Cas. 82, at p. 96) "There is nothing in the law of nations which prevents a Government from taxing its own subjects on the basis of their foreign possessions. It may be inconvenient to do so. The reasons against doing so may apply more strongly to real than to personal estate. But the question is one of discretion, and is to be answered by the statutes under which each state levies its taxes, and not by mere reference to the laws which regulate successions to real and personal property."

There can be no doubt that the Alberta Succession Duties Act purports to impose taxation on the basis (*inter alia*) of personal property situate outside the Province, and therefore, if it possessed unlimited sovereign power, it would be entitled to impose such taxation on its subjects. Accordingly, the present question only arises because of the limitations placed on the legislative powers of the Province by s. 92 of the *British North America Act,* 1867, and, for this reason, the cases on legacy and succession duties in England are of little assistance for the present purpose. Generally speaking, taxation is imposed on persons, the nature and amount of the liability being determined either by individual units, as in the case of a poll tax, or in respect of the taxpayers' interest in property or in respect of transactions or actings of the taxpayers. It is at least unusual to find a tax imposed on property and not on persons—in any event, the duties here in question are not of that nature. In considering the limits placed on Provincial taxation, the Courts have invariably had regard to the basis or subject-matter in respect of which the taxation is imposed, and their Lordships agree with the statement of Anglin J. in *Rex v. Cotton,* 45 S.C.R. 469, at p. 536, where he said: "in order that a Provincial tax should be valid under the British North America Act, in my opinion the subject of taxation must be within the province."

The Province maintained in the first place, that under the Alberta Succession Duties Act the subject-matter of taxation was the transmission of the property and not the property itself, and fell within the principle of the decision of this Board in *Alleyn v. Barthe.*

In their Lordships' opinion, the principle to be derived from the decisions of this Board is that the Province, on the death of a person domiciled within the Province, is not entitled to impose taxation in respect of personal property locally situate outside the Province, but that it is entitled to impose taxation on persons domiciled or resident within the Province in respect of the transmission to them under the Provincial law of personal property locally situate outside the Province.

In *Lambe v. Manuel,* [1903] A.C. 68, a claim was made by the Province of Quebec for succession duties on movable property locally situate in that Province, which formed part of the succession of a testator domiciled in Ontario. The claim was rejected on the view that, on its true construction, the Quebec Succession Duty Act only applied, in the case of movables, to transmissions of property resulting from the devolution of a succession in the Province of Quebec. Sect. 1191B of the Quebec Act of 1892, on which the issue turned, provided as follows: "All transmissions, owing to death, of the property in, usufruct, or enjoyment of, moveable and immoveable property in the province shall be liable to the following taxes . . ." Thus the taxes were held to be imposed in respect of transmissions.

The Quebec Act of 1892 and the later Act of 1906, which reenacted the words above quoted with alterations immaterial to this point, were considered in the case of *Cotton v. Rex,* and were construed as imposing the duties in respect of the transmission of the property. It was held, on construction, that neither of these Acts imposed any duty upon the transmission of moveable property outside the Province, and also that the taxation was not direct, in respect that it was imposed on "someone who was not intended himself to bear the burden but to be recouped by someone else."

In *Woodruff v. Att.-Gen. for Ontario,* [1908] A.C. 508, the deceased having died domiciled in the Province of Ontario, that Province claimed succession duty in respect of movable property locally situate in the United States. It was held to be an attempt to levy

a tax on property locally situate outside the Province, which was
beyond their competence. The Ontario Act of 1897, s. 4, sub-s. 1,
provided "the following property shall be subject to a succession
duty", which clearly was not a tax in respect of the transmission
of a succession.

The case of *Rex v. Lovitt,* [1912] A.C. 212 provides an interesting contrast to *Lambe's* case, [1903] A.C. 68. The testator, who
died domiciled in Nova Scotia, was possessed of certain personal
property locally situate in the Province of New Brunswick, in respect
of which the latter Province claimed succession duty. It was held
that, although called a succession duty, the tax in question was laid
on the corpus of the property, and its payment was made a term of
the grant of ancillary probate, and the claim to duty was upheld.
The *New Brunswick Succession Duty Act, 1896,* s. 5, sub-s. 1, enacted:
"All property, whether situate in this province or elsewhere, . . .
passing either by will or intestacy . . . shall be subject to a succession
duty."

In *Alleyn v. Barthe,* [1922] 1 A.C. 215, 62 D.L.R. 515, [1922]
1 W.W.R. 100, though an argument to the contrary was submitted,
the judgment clearly proceeds on the footing that the taxation was
imposed in respect of the transmission, and it may be noted that
by the *Quebec Succession Duty Act, 1909,* as revised in 1914, s. 1387B,
"All transmissions within the Province, owing to the death of a
person domiciled therein, of movable property locally situate outside
the Province at the time of such death", were made liable to the
duties; this provision is substantially the same as that under construction in *Lambe's* case. The main question in *Alleyn's* case was
whether the taxation was direct, but, in delivering the judgment of
this Board, Lord Phillimore, after referring to the statutory provisions, states: "The conditions therein stated upon which taxation
attaches to property outside the Province are two: (1) that the
transmission must be within the Province; and (2) that it must be
due to the death of a person domiciled within the Province. The
first of these conditions can, in their Lordships' opinion, only be
satisfied if the person to whom the property is transmitted is, as
the universal legatee in this case was, either domiciled or ordinarily
resident within the Province; for, in the connection in which the
words are found no other meaning can be attached to the words
'within the Province' which modify and limit the word 'transmission.'
So regarded, the taxation is clearly within the powers of the
Province."

The identification of the subject-matter of the tax is naturally
to be found in the charging section of the statute, and it will only
be in the case of some ambiguity in the terms of the charging section
that recourse to other sections is proper or necessary. In the present
case, s. 7, sub-s. 1, is the charging provision, and as amended provided
as follows:

"7.—(1) Save as otherwise provided, all property of the owner
thereof situate within the Province, and in the case of an owner
domiciled in the Province, all the personal property of the owner

situate outside the Province, and passing on his death, shall be subject to succession duties at the rate or rates set forth in the following table, the percentage payable on the share of any beneficiary being fixed by the following, or by some one or more of the following considerations, as the case may be:

(a) the net value of the property of the deceased;

(b) the place of residence of beneficiary;

(c) the degree of kinship or absence of kinship of the beneficiary to the deceased."

In their Lordships' opinion, the terms of this section, which is very similar to that considered in *Lovitt's* case, clearly show that the subject matter of the taxation is the property and not the transmission of property; it is in marked contrast to the terms of the Quebec section considered in the cases of *Lambe* and *Alleyn*. It may be added that s. 9 of the Alberta Act, on which the Province sought to rely, does not modify this view, but merely provides a particular liability for payment of the tax.

The Province next contended that, although locally situate outside the Province, the personal property of a person, who dies domiciled within the Province, is to be treated as "within the Province" for the purposes of s. 92 of the *British North America Act,* by reason of the application of the rule embodied in the maxim *"mobilia sequuntur personam."* This argument appears to proceed on a misunderstanding of the meaning and effect of that rule. If A dies domiciled in the United States of America, leaving movable property locally situate in England, the latter country has complete jurisdiction over the property, but the law of England, in order to decide on whom the property devolves on the death of A, will not apply English law of succession, but will ascertain and apply the American law. In other words, it is the law of England—not the law of America—that applies the principle of *mobilia sequuntur personam* in exercising its jurisdiction over the movable property in England, the locus of the latter remaining unchanged; in no sense could the property be described as "within America".

The Province further maintained that, as the bond given by the executors limited their liability to the duties in respect of property "coming into their hands", and the property here in question had admittedly come into their hands, the taxation was in respect of property within the Province; but, in their Lordships' opinion, the bond merely defines the extent of the security taken from the executors, and its terms cannot affect the validity or invalidity of the duties imposed under s. 7 of the Act. While that is sufficient to dispose of the contention, it may well be doubted whether "coming into their hands" means anything more than that the executors have completed their title to the property in question, the local situation of the property remaining unchanged.

Accordingly, their Lordships are of opinion that the duties under s. 7, so far as imposed on personal property locally situate outside the

Province, did not come within the limits placed on Provincial taxation by s. 92 of the *British North America Act*.

There remains the question of "direct taxation". The principle to be applied in such cases is now well settled. Is the duty imposed on the very person whom the legislature intended or desired should pay it, without any expectation or intention that he should indemnify himself at the expense of some other person? Under the *Alberta Succession Duties Act* the duties in question were imposed on the executors on their application for probate, and letters probate could not be issued without the consent of the Provincial Treasurer, whose duty was to secure payment of the duties or obtain security therefor by a statutory bond before giving such consent. There can be no doubt that normally the application for probate will be by executors, and the issue is whether the legislature intended or desired that an executor should pay the duties without any expectation that such executor should indemnify himself at the expense of some other person. In their Lordships' opinion the determination of this issue depends on the answer to a simple test, which was applied in the cases of *Cotton* and *Alleyn*, already referred to—namely, whether the executor is personally liable for the duties. If the executor is so liable, then the tax is imposed on the executor, with the obvious intention that he should indemnify himself out of the beneficiaries' estate, and the taxation is indirect. If the executor is not personally liable for the duties, then the tax is truly imposed on the beneficiaries and the taxation is direct.

In *Cotton's* case, the provisions of the *Quebec Succession Act, 1906,* were construed by this Board as entitling the collector of inland revenue to collect the whole of the duties on the estate from the person making the declaration and as providing, in the ordinary case, for payment of the duties by some one who was not intended himself to bear the burden but to be recouped by some one else, and the taxation was held to be indirect. . . .

In principle also the local situation of the property comprised in the estate of the deceased appears to be irrelevant to the issue whether the executor is personally liable for payment of the duties, in the absence of any distinction in this respect drawn by the Act itself as regards duties in respect of different classes of property. In the Quebec Act, which was a tax on transmission, no such distinction was drawn, nor is any such distinction to be found in the present case.

In *Burland v. The King,* [1922] 1 A.C. 215, 62 D.L.R. 515, [1922] 1 W.W.R. 100, the testator had died in 1907, and the Quebec Act was again in question. It was held that certain amendments to the Act which had followed immediately after the decision in *Cotton's* case, were insufficient to avoid the applicability of that decision, and the taxation was held to be indirect. But in *Alleyn's* case, which was decided at the same time as *Burland's* case, the testator died in 1913, by which time further important amendments had been enacted, which led to a contrary conclusion. In their Lordships' opinion, it is clear that the reason for this conclusion was the new provision in art. 1387g of the Quebec Act, which was in the following terms: "No notary, executor, trustee or administrator shall be personally liable for the duties imposed by this section. Nevertheless the executor, the trustee or the administrator may be required to pay such duties out of the property or money in his possession belonging or owing to the beneficiaries, and if he fails to do so may be sued for the amount thereof, but only in his representative capacity, and any judgment rendered against him in such capacity shall be executed against such property or money only."

The *Alberta Succession Duties Act* contains no similar clause excluding personal liability of an executor, etc., and, in their Lordships' opinion, it is clear, under ss. 11 and 12 of the Act, that an executor who applies for probate becomes personally liable for the amount of the duties determined by the Provincial Treasurer, and must either pay them or give security for their payment by a bond in the statutory form, and, further, that under the terms of the bond the executor is personally liable for payment of the duties in respect of any of the property coming into his hands. It follows that the taxation is indirect and beyond the competency of the Province.

Reliance was placed in the Court below on the case *In re Cust*, 8 Alb. L.R. 308, but it will be clear from the views their Lordships have expressed as to the principle laid down by the cases of *Cotton* and *Alleyn*, that the decision of the Court which decided *Cust's* case on appeal was erroneous, and must be taken as overruled. *Rex v. Lovitt*, referred to in that decision, was the case of a local probate duty charged by the Province, where the property was locally situate, for the collection or local administration of the particular property, and was not a case of pure taxation, as in *Cotton's* case and the present one. The question of direct or indirect taxation is not referred to in the judgment, and the only reference to it in the argument was in a contention that the tax was imposed on a transmission in another Province and was therefore not direct; but it was held that the tax was not on transmission but on the corpus of the property.

Their Lordships are therefore of opinion that the succession duties levied in respect of the property mentioned in both sub-ss. (a) and (b) in para. 2 of the special case are not valid. In the case of sub-s. (a) the taxation is neither direct nor within the Province, and in the case of sub-s. (b) the taxation is not direct.

Appeal dismissed; cross-appeal allowed.

[See also *A.-G. Ont. v. Baby*, [1927] 1 D.L.R. 1105, 60 O.L.R. 1, aff'g. [1926] 3 D.L.R. 928, 59 O.L.R. 181; *In re Dalrymple Estate, Hogg v. Provincial Tax Commission*, [1941] 2 W.W.R. 253, aff'd [1941] 3 W.W.R. 605 (Sask.); and see *Note*, (1941) 19 Can. Bar Rev. 746; *Col v. A.-G. B.C.*; *In re Promis and Frank Estates*, [1934] 3 D.L.R. 488, [1934] 2 W.W.R. 481 (B.C.). *Cf. Quigg*, Constitutionality of Succession Duties, (1938) 16 Can. Bar Rev. 344; *Anderson*, Succession Duties—Double Taxation, (1937) 15 Can. Bar Rev. 620.

Is there not an internal inconsistency in the *Kerr* case as to the subject matter of the tax?

Having regard to the *Kerr* case, is it competent to a province in its succession duty legislation to tax a beneficiary in the province in respect of benefits received, regardless of deceased's domicile and of the situs of his estate? Would this not be valid as a tax on a person in the province as indicated in *Bank of Toronto v. Lambe* (1887), 12 App. Cas 575? What reasons are there to doubt provincial competence to use domicile as a basis of death duty legislation? See *Laskin*, Ontario Succession Duties: Constitutional Implications (Canadian Tax Foundation Paper, 1960).]

RE FLAVELLE ESTATE

In the Supreme Court of Ontario. [1943] O.R. 167,
[1943] 1 D.L.R. 756.

A motion by the executors and trustees of the estate of Sir Joseph Flavelle for the advice and direction of the Court. The deceased died domiciled and resident in Ontario, having during his lifetime made many gifts (or "dispositions") in respect of which a question arose as to succession duty liability under the *Succession Duty Act,* 1934 (Ont.), c. 55 as amended by 1937 (Ont.), c. 3 and 1937 (Ont. 2nd sess.), c. 1.

ROSE C.J.H.C. . . . The charging section of the Ontario Act as amended reads as follows:

"9.   At the date of the death of any person—

(a)   all property situate in Ontario passing on the death of such person, whether such person was at the time of his death domiciled in Ontario or elsewhere;

(b)   every transmission within Ontario owing to the death of any person domiciled therein of personal property locally situate outside Ontario;

(c)   every disposition of any property (other than realty situate outside Ontario) made within Ontario by any such person during his lifetime, on or after the 1st day of July, 1892;

(d)   every person to whom a disposition of any personal property (other than the property mentioned in clause *g* of section 10) was made after the date of the coming into force of this Act by the deceased in his lifetime outside Ontario, in respect of such personal property, when such deceased person was domiciled within Ontario at the time of such disposition and at the time of his death, and when the person to whom such disposition was made was resident or domiciled within Ontario at the time of such disposition and at the time of the death of the deceased person;

shall be subject to duty."

By s. 10(*g*) the property passing on the death of the deceased (and by s. 9(*a*) declared to be subject to duty) is declared to include for all purposes of the Act:

"(g)   any property in respect of which a disposition was made by the deceased person outside Ontario during his lifetime, where such deceased person was domiciled in Ontario at the time of the disposition and at the date of his death and which property was situate within Ontario and owned by the person to whom such dispotion was made at the date of the death of such deceased person, or any other property into which such property has become directly converted, or which, exclusive of income, has been derived therefrom, when such other property was situate within Ontario and owned by the person to whom such disposition was made, at the date of the death of the deceased person;" ...

We are not concerned in this case with any property disposed of outside Ontario or with transmissions within Ontario of personal property locally situate outside Ontario, or with persons to whom dispositions were made by the testator during his lifetime outside Ontario, because the papers produced do not indicate that the testator in his lifetime disposed outside Ontario of any property or that there was on his death any transmission in Ontario of personal property locally situate outside Ontario. The inquiry, then, so far as s. 9 is concerned, has to do only with dispositions made within Ontario on or after July 1, 1892 (s. 9(c)).

Section 9(c) is attacked on several grounds. The first of these to be considered is the ground that the subject-matter of the tax is dispositions made before the death of the testator and at a time when there was no law making them subject to duty; that such dispositions (whatever may be the fact as to the property disposed of) have no existence either in Ontario or elsewhere at the time of the death; and therefore that the enactment that they shall be subject to duty at the date of the death of the testator cannot be justified as taxation within the province. ...

The change from s. 6 of the statute of 1934—which ... declared that all property situate in Ontario passing on the death. of any person should be subject to duty, and that property passing on the death of the deceased should be deemed to include any property taken under a disposition made since July 1, 1892—to the statute of 1937—which professed to make subject to duty every disposition of any property (other than realty situate outside Ontario) made within Ontario by any "such" person—was, as the whole of the Act of 1937 shows, made deliberately. It was made not very long after the Judicial Committee of the Privy Council in *Provincial Treasurer of Alberta et al. v. Kerr et al.*, [1933] A.C. 710, had clarified the distinction to be drawn, in the consideration of provincial succession duty Acts, between transmissions and the property transmitted. Apparently it was made in the endeavour to take advantage of a similar distinction between the disposition and the property disposed of; but whatever the motive for the change may have been, the distinction between the disposition and the property disposed of as the subject-matter of taxation is made very clear; property, transmissions, dispositions and persons, are severally declared to be subject to duty; by s. 12(c) the provisions of s. 9 are to apply notwithstanding that the property in respect of which there is a disposition may not be in existence at the date of the death or owned at that date by the person to whom the disposition was made; and in s. 19(1) the disponee is declared to be liable for the duty if any in respect of the disposition. My opinion upon the reading of all of these sections is that the subject-matter of the taxation imposed by the charging s. 9(c) is the disposition and not the property or the disponee, and that, as in *Provincial Treasurer of Alberta v. Kerr,* the sections which profess to provide a particular liability for payment of the tax do not affect the question as to the validity of the tax. . . .

If a transmission within the Province may be (as, undoubtedly, upon the authorities, it can be) the subject-matter of provincial taxation, there seems to be no reason for saying that a disposition made within the Province cannot be such a subject-matter. Indeed, it was not contended that it would be beyond the power of the Legislature to make a disposition bear a tax at the time at which it was made; what was attacked was the validity of the attempt to make it the subject-matter of taxation at the death of the disponer. The idea of the continued existence of the disposition is not easy to grasp, but it seems to have been the idea of the draughtsman of s. 9(c) of the Act of 1937. Thus in s. 19 he declares to be liable for the duty a person in whose favour a disposition *is* made, and I do not think that by the use of the present tense he intends to make liable only a person in whose favour a disposition is made after the effective date of the Act of 1937. He appears to treat a disposition, whenever made after 1892 by a person who dies after the effective date of the Act of 1937, as something that can be spoken of in the present tense. The idea is a new one, and the declaration that a notional thing like a disposition shall be subject to duty may lead to practical difficulties, or may, in many instances, be ineffective as a revenue-producing measure; for instance, a disposition cannot be seized or sold for non-payment of the duty to which it is declared to be subject, and at the death of the disponer the disponee may be no longer living, or if living, may not be domiciled or even resident in the taxing Province. Nevertheless it seems to be difficult to say that because the disposition had its effect once and for all at the time at which it was made, and because in that sense it has no longer any situs within the Province, there can be applied in respect of it such a statement as was made by Anglin J. (as he then was) in *The King v. Cotton et al.* (1912), 45 S.C.R. 469 at 536, and approved by Lord Thankerton in *Provincial Treasurer of Alberta et al. v. Kerr et al.,* [1933] A.C. 710 at 718. When Anglin J. said that in order that a provincial tax should be valid under the *British North America Act* the subject of the taxation must be within the Province, he was speaking of physical property and its situs; he was not thinking of or discussing any question as to whether a transaction that had taken place within the province could, at a later time, be made subject to duty in the Province, and his statement, as I understand it, can have no bearing upon the point now under consideration. Theoretically, if the notional thing, the disposition, is in the Province originally, and therefore is a permissible subject-matter of provincial taxation, the Province does not go beyond its borders in making it the subject-matter of taxation on the death of the disponer; and so I think that whatever may be said as to other grounds of attack upon the validity of s. 9(c) of the Ontario Act, it cannot be said that it is invalid just because the thing which it declares to be subject to duty is not in the Province. . . .

Another reason advanced for saying that s. 9(c) was beyond the provincial power was that the imposition of the duties was not taxation in the sense in which the word is used in s. 92(2) of the *British North America Act*. It was said that real taxation involves a proportional levy, proportional, for instance, to the benefit that the person taxed has received (as in local improvement taxes) or to ability to pay; that there must be certainty; that there must be generality of application, and not, as in this case, an imposition of liability upon those disponees who happen to outlive the disponer, while those who died in his lifetime, or their estates, go scot-free; and in connection with the suggestion that this tax is not proportionate to the benefit received by the disponee, attention was directed to s. 12 which makes the value of the disposition depend (subject to certain provisoes) upon the market value, at the date of the death of the disponer, of the property in respect of which the disposition was made. It was pointed out that property, for instance, shares of stock which had little value at the time of the disposition, may, through the disponee's skilful management become very valuable by the time of the death of the disponer, and that the disponee, if he is made to pay the duty, will, in comparison with a disponee whose property has not increased in value, be treated quite unfairly. It was said that succession duty properly so-called is good taxation because it is upon a succession which takes place under the protection of the law, the class taxed being composed of those who succeed; but that when you come to disponees you have no class at all of persons who have something in common; that to enact that every disponer shall pay a tax, no matter how computed, is one thing, but that to say that some disponees shall pay a tax, making disponees from one disponer, or disponees who outlive the disponer, liable, but leaving disponees from another disponer, or (the estates of) disponees who predecease their disponer, free, is not taxation but arbitrary confiscation. . . .

It may be that some of the inequalities and hardships that may follow upon the application of the Ontario statute are inseparable from any statute which has for one of its objects the frustration of any attempt of the owners of property to free their families of the obligation to pay succession duties, or death taxes, or whatever they may be called, by disposing of the property *inter vivos,* and especially may this be so in the case of a statute which, to use the words used by Lord Hanworth M.R. in *Attorney-General for Ontario v. National Trust Company, Limited,* [1931] A.C. 818, "looks back over a span of more than a full generation of years"; and in my opinion there is no warrant in any of the decided cases for saying that because of the existence of the inequalities, uncertainties, and hardships to which attention has been directed, the statute as amended in 1937 is beyond the legislative power of the Province. Indeed, I think it can be said that the general trend of the authorities is to ignore the economists' discussion of the question as to what a tax ought to be, and to treat as valid taxation, within the meaning of s. 92(2) of the *British North America Act,* measures adopted by the Province, even if, because of the method of computation of the amounts payable or for the other reasons, they are of unequal or even unfair application, provided, of course, that they stand the tests of directness and do not transgress the territorial limitation.

Another attack upon the constitutional validity of the Act calls attention to the sweeping nature of the charging section and the sections which provide for the collection of the duty to which, *inter alia,* the dispositions made within Ontario are declared to be subject. In part s. 9(c) is somewhat difficult to construe: it is hard to say who is meant by the expression "any such person." Section 9 begins, "At the date of the death of any person,—"; then in clause (a) it mentions property passing on the death of "such" person, whether such person was at the time of his death domiciled in Ontario or elsewhere; in (b) it mentions every transmission within Ontario owing to the death "of any person domiciled therein" of personal property locally situate outside Ontario; in (c) every disposition of any property (other than realty situate outside Ontario) made within Ontario by any "such" person; and in (d) every person to whom a disposition of personal property (other than the property deemed to pass on the death) was made outside Ontario when the deceased person was domiciled and the disponee was resident or domiciled within Ontario at the relevant times; and then it closes with the words "shall be subject to duty". The words "any such person" in clause (c) may refer back to the words "any person domiciled" within Ontario in clause (b) or they may relate back to the opening words of the section, "At the date of the death of any person". To construe them as relating to the person domiciled in Ontario, who is the person immediately before mentioned, would be natural but for the fact of the use of the similar expression in (a) where obviously, and as, indeed, is stated expressly, they mean any person wherever domiciled. But it is not clear to me that very much depends on ascertaining which of the readings is correct; for even if (c) professes to make subject to duty a disposition made within Ontario by a person not therein domiciled, I think that, for the reasons already given in connection with the discussion of the question whether a past disposition is something that can be made subject to duty, the clause is not, for that reason alone, to be held to be invalid. In the course of the argument it was suggested that even if s. 9(c) professes to touch dispositions made within Ontario by persons not domiciled therein, it ought to be read as applying only to dispositions made by persons so domiciled to others also so domiciled or ordinarily resident. This suggestion was based in part upon what Lord Phillimore said in *Burland et al. v. The King; Alleyn et al. v. Barthe,* [1922] 1 A.C. 215 at 228. But what Lord Phillimore was there discussing was the Quebec statute, 4 Geo. V, c. 10 (art. 1387b) by which it was enacted that "All transmissions within the Province, owing to the death of a person domiciled therein, of moveable property locally situate outside the Province at the time of such death, shall be liable to the following taxes . . .", and (art. 1387(g)) that "Every person to whom as heir, universal legatee, legatee by general or particular title, or donee under a gift in contemplation of death, moveable property outside the

Province is transmitted, is personally liable for the duties in respect of such property." He said that the conditions stated in the statute upon which taxation attaches to property outside the Province are two: (1) that the transmission must be within the Province, and (2) that it must be due to the death of a person domiciled within the Province, and he went on to say that the first of these conditions could only be satisfied if the person to whom the property was transmitted was either domiciled or ordinarily resident within the Province; "for in the connection in which the words are found no other meaning can be attached to the words 'within the Province' which modify and limit the word 'transmission'." But a transmission takes place by reason of the relevant law, whereas a disposition is the act of the parties, and my opinion is that what Lord Phillimore said about transmissions is not applicable to dispositions. In my opinion a disposition is within the Province if, at the time at which it is made, the disponer and the disponee, wherever domiciled or ordinarily resident, are there present; and that is my reason for thinking that even if s. 9(c) professes to make subject to duty a disposition made within Ontario by a person not therein domiciled, it is not, for that reason alone, to be held to be beyond the provincial legislative power.

The making of a notional thing like a disposition subject to duty does not advance the Province very far in the effort to collect revenue: the real effectiveness of the attempt must depend upon the part of the enactment which renders some one liable for the payment of the duty to which the disposition is made subject. Therefore, in the present case (assuming the correctness of my holding that s. 9(c) is valid) the important sections appear to be ss. 16 and 19.

[His Lordship here discussed s. 16 which levied duty at particular rates and s. 19 which declared the liability of the disponee in respect of dutiable dispositions.] . . .

Section 19 is not, in words, restricted to professing to impose liability upon heirs, legatees, persons to whom property passes, or persons in whose favour a disposition is made who are, at the time of the death of the deceased person, domiciled or resident in Ontario. Of course it must be ineffective as regards such of those persons as are not subject to the legislative jurisdiction of the Legislature of Ontario, and it was suggested that because it was not, in words, made applicable only to persons who are so subject, it was invalid *in toto*. This suggestion is, in my opinion, completely met by the decision in *Macleod v. Attorney-General for New South Wales,* [1891] A.C. 455. . . .

[The constitutional problems besetting provincial succession duty legislation do not, of course, affect federal legislation of that kind: see *Estate Tax Act,* R.S.C. 1970, c. E-9 as amended. The Dominion is free to define succession or transmission or disposition, as the case may be, without being limited by their meanings under provincial law. But see *Mignault,* The Dominion Succession Duty Act—Its Effect on the Succession Law of Quebec, (1941) 19 Can. Bar Rev. 719; and see reply by C. F. Elliott, (1942) 20 Can. Bar Rev. 141.]

Note on "for provincial purposes" in Section 92(2)

In *Reference re Employment and Social Insurance Act,* [1936] S.C.R. 427, at p. 434, [1936] 3 D.L.R. 644, at p. 649, Duff C.J.C. put the matter as follows: "If you read head No. 2 of s. 92 with s. 126, and by the light of the observations of Lord Watson in *St. Catherine's Milling & Lumber Co. v. The Queen* (1888), 14 App. Cas. 46 there is . . . solid ground for the conclusion that the words 'for provincial purposes' mean neither more nor less than this: the taxing power of the legislature is given to them for raising money for the exclusive disposition of the legislature". The Courts have scotched any notion that the taxing authority in s. 92(2) extended only to the raising of money for *general* provincial purposes, *i.e.* by province-wide taxation for the general purposes of the whole province. In *Dow v. Black* (1875), L.R. 6 P.C. 272 the Privy Council stated (at p. 282) that s. 92(2) "must be taken to enable the provincial legislature . . . to impose direct taxation for a local purpose upon a particular locality within the province".

5. The Provincial Licensing Power

Under s. 92(9) of the *B.N.A. Act* the provinces may legislate in relation to "shop, saloon, tavern, auctioneer and other licences in order to the raising of a revenue for provincial, local or municipal purposes." The main problems which this head of power raises are these: (1) Is the phrase "other licences" to be read *ejusdem generis* with the preceding enumeration? (2) Must the revenue-raising provisions of licensing legislation conform to the standards of direct taxation? (3) May the province license for regulatory rather than, or for regulatory as well as, for revenue purposes?

It is well established that the *ejusdem generis* rule does not apply to "other licences": *Brewers and Maltsters Assoc. of Ont. v. A.-G. Ont.,* [1897] A.C. 231; *Shannon v. Lower Mainland Dairy Products Board,* [1938] A.C. 708, [1938] 4 D.L.R. 81, [1938] 2 W.W.R. 604. Moreover, the provinces enjoy an omnibus licensing power within the limits of s. 92. This power, in its regulatory character, can be supported under s. 92(13) and s. 92(16). In so far as a licensing system established for regulatory purposes also exhibits a revenue purpose by reason of the exaction of licence fees, it now appears that resort may be had to s. 92(9); and in this connection, it is unnecessary to meet the requirements of direct taxation. In *Lawson v. Interior Tree Fruit and Vegetable Committee,* [1931] S.C.R. 357, [1931] 2 D.L.R. 193, involving, *inter alia,* the validity under provincial legislation of marketing licences and fees authorized in connection therewith and also of certain levies authorized to defray the expenses of operating the marketing scheme, Duff J. spoke for the majority of the Court as follows: "This brings us to the question whether the levies complained of are levies which can be brought under head No. 9 of s. 92 . . . The question has never yet been decided whether or not the revenue contemplated by this head can in any circumstances be raised by a fee which operates in such a manner as to take it out of the scope of 'direct taxation'. *Prima facie,* it would appear, from inspection of the language of the two several heads, that the taxes contemplated by No. 9 are not confined to taxes of the same character as those authorized by No. 2, and that accordingly imposts which would properly be classed under the general description 'indirect taxation' are not for that reason alone excluded from those which may be exacted under head 9. On the other hand, the last mentioned head authorizes licences for the purpose of raising a revenue, and does not, I think contemplate licences which, in their primary function, are instrumentalities for the control of trade—even local or provincial trade. Here, such is the primary purpose of the legislation. The imposition of these levies is merely ancillary, having for its object the creation of a fund to defray the expenses of working the machinery of the substantive scheme for the regulation of trade. Even the licence fee is discretionary with the Committee. This part of the statute would appear to be *ultra vires.* The levy authorized is not within s. 92(2), and the licence is not within s. 92(9)." *Cf. Russell v. The Queen* (1882), 7 App. Cas. 829, where the Privy Council indicated that s. 92(9) could not be invoked for regulation. That part only of Duff J.'s statement which viewed the licensing power as essentially a revenue raising power was rejected by the Privy Council in *Shannon v. Lower Mainland Dairy Products Board, supra;* and Lord Atkin said *inter alia:* "If regulation of trade within the Province has to be held valid, the ordinary method of regulating trade, *i.e.,* by a system of licences, must also be admissible. A licence itself merely involves a permission to trade subject to compliance with specified conditions. A licence fee, though usual, does not appear to be essential. But, if licences are granted, it appears to be no objection that fees should be charged in order either to defray the costs of administering the local regulation or to increase the general funds of the Province, or for both purposes. The object would appear to be in such a case to raise a revenue for either local or Provincial purposes. On this part of the case their Lordships, with great respect, think that the present Chief Justice, then Duff J., took a somewhat narrow view of the Provincial powers under s. 92(9) in *Lawson v. Interior Tree Fruit and Vegetable Committee of Direction.* . . . It cannot, as their Lordships think, be an objection to a licence plus a fee that it is directed both to the regulation of trade and to the provision of revenue. It would be difficult in the case of saloon and tavern licences to say that the regulation of the trade was not at least as important as the provision of revenue. And, if licences for the specified trades are valid, their Lordships see no reason why the words 'other licences' in s. 92(9) should not be sufficient to support the enactment in question." See also *Motor Car Supply Co. v. A.-G. Alta.,* [1939] 3 W.W.R. 65. In *Nelson v. City of Dartmouth* (1964), 45 D.L.R. (2d) 183, the principle thus expounded was applied to sustain a licence tax on owners of mobile home parks, regardless of the fact that it was

indirect in its incidence. It would appear that the Privy Council in the
Shannon case intended, by its criticism, to do no more than give a
basis of support to licence taxes where the purpose was as much
regulatory as fiscal. It was certainly unnecessary, even if the explicit
terms thereof be overlooked, to extend s. 92(9) to cover purely regulatory licences because power to this end exists in other heads of s.
92; *cf. Cherry v. The King*, [1938] 1 D.L.R. 156, [1938] 1 W.W.R. 12.
For a general discussion, see *MacDonald*, The Licensing Power of the
Provinces, (1939) 17 Can. Bar Rev. 240.

6.   Express Limitations on the Taxing Powers

The meaning of s. 121 of the *B.N.A. Act* was considered in *Gold
Seal Ltd. v. Dominion Express Co. and A.-G. Alta.*, 62 S.C.R. 424,
62 D.L.R. 62, [1921] 3 W.W.R. 710, reproduced, *supra*, at p. 245,
and in *Atlantic Smoke Shops Ltd. v. Conlon, et al.*, [1941] S.C.R.
670, [1941] 4 D.L.R. 129, varied [1943] A.C. 550, [1943] 4 D.L.R.
81, [1943] 3 W.W.R. 1131, reproduced, *supra*, at p. 662. Additional
consideration was given to s. 121 in the *Murphy* case reproduced
supra, at p. 320, and Rand J. there suggested a wider view of the
provision.

The tax immunity given by s. 125 to "lands or property belonging
to Canada or any province" is an immunity in favour of lands or
property vested in the Crown in right of the Dominion or of a province: see *St. Catherine's Milling & Lumber Co. v. The Queen* (1888),
14 App. Cas. 46. Section 125 does not operate to confer any immunity
on private persons who have some interest in Crown land or other
property; nor does it operate to give them any immunity where the
Crown acquires some interest in land or other property belonging
to such persons. Section 125 in terms deals only with taxes charged
on lands or property and not with "personal" taxes. But, it probably
also covers taxation on the Crown in right of the Dominion or of a
province in respect of lands or property in which the Crown has an
interest. In other words, it ought reasonably to be construed as
giving immunity from a tax charged on Crown property or on the
Crown itself in respect of its interest in such property. In *Halifax
v. Halifax Harbour Commrs.*, [1935] S.C.R. 215, [1935] 1 D.L.R.
657, a case involving municipal assessment of a federal Crown
agency in respect of its occupation of Crown property, Duff C.J. said
that any attempt to tax the Dominion Government or the property
of the Dominion Government must fail as *ultra vires* a provincial
legislature. The converse should be equally true. However, the constitutional protection of s. 125 does not extend to shield a provincial
Crown from other types of federal taxation, such as customs duties
connected with the regulation of trade and commerce. The statement
by *Clement*, The Canadian Constitution (3rd ed.), p. 643, that s. 125
"would operate no doubt to exempt from customs duties goods purchased abroad by a provincial government" was later proved wrong
by the Privy Council in *A.-G. B.C. v. A.-G. Can.*, [1924] A.C. 222,

[1923] 4 D.L.R. 669, [1923] 3 W.W.R. 1249, reproduced, *supra*, at p. 251.

Most of the cases in which arguments were raised based on s. 125 really turned on the construction of the taxing statute in order to ascertain whether the interest of the Crown was being taxed or the interest of a private person, or whether the tax was on the Crown or on a private person in respect of a property interest. It has been held that a tax may be validly levied on an owner of land leased to the Crown (*Halifax v. Fairbanks Estate*, [1928] A.C. 117, [1927] 4 D.L.R. 945, [1927] 3 W.W.R. 493; *Vancouver v. A.-G. Can.*, [1944] S.C.R. 23, [1944] 1 D.L.R. 497); or on a tenant or occupant of Crown land (*Smith v. Vermillion Hills*, [1916] 2 A.C. 569, 30 D.L.R. 83, [1917] 1 W.W.R. 108; *Montreal v. A.-G. Can.*, [1923] A.C. 136, 70 D.L.R. 248; or on an occupant of Crown land residing thereon in virtue of his employment by the federal Crown (*Phillips and Taylor v. Sault Ste. Marie*, [1954] S.C.R. 404, [1954] 3 D.L.R. 81); or on a purchaser under an agreement of sale with the Crown (*Southern Alberta Land Co. v. McLean* (1916), 53 S.C.R. 151, 29 D.L.R. 403, 10 W.W.R. 879. Attempts to realize such taxes must, of course, stop short of interfering with the Crown's rights in the property affected: see *Calgary & Edmonton Land Co. v. A.-G. Alta.* (1911), 45 S.C.R. 170. In *Spooner Oils Ltd. and Spooner v. Turner Valley Gas Conservation Board and A.-G. Alta.*, [1933] S.C.R. 629, at p. 645, [1933] 4 D.L.R. 545, at p. 559, Duff C.J. referred to these matters as follows: "The occupant of Dominion lands under a legal right may be taxed [by a province] in respect of his occupancy. But it is necessary to be cautious in inferring from this that such taxation can in every case be enforced by remedies involving the sale or appropriation of the occupant's right, without regard to the nature of that right. Where the right is equivalent to an equitable title in fee simple, probably no difficulty would arise . . . , but if the enforcement of a tax imposed by provincial legislation, would involve a nullification in whole or in part of competent Dominion legislation under which the right is constituted, then it is, to say the least, doubtful, whether such provisions could take effect".

In some cases, the question has arisen whether a corporate body or agency claiming tax immunity when occupying Crown land, is the Crown or a servant or agent of the Crown; and here, too, questions of construction may arise in assessing the character of the corporation or agency to determine whether it is a servant or agent of the Crown: see *Halifax v. Halifax Harbour Commrs.*, [1935] S.C.R. 215, [1935] 1 D.L.R. 657; *Re Toronto and C.B.C.*, [1938] O.W.N. 507; *Recorder's Court v. C.B.C.*, [1941] 2 D.L.R. 551, 70 Que. K.B. 65; *Northern Saskatchewan Flying Training School v. Buckland*, [1944] 1 D.L.R. 825, [1943] 3 W.W.R. 609 (Sask.); *Montreal v. Montreal Locomotive Works*, [1947] 1 D.L.R. 161, [1946] 3 W.W.R. 748 (P.C.); *Regina Industries Ltd. v. Regina*, [1947] S.C.R. 345, [1947] 3 D.L.R. 81. Similarly, it may be necessary to determine whether occupation of private land is an occupation of or for the Crown or in the private interest of the occupant: see *Stinson v.*

Middleton Tp.; Wright v. Middleton Tp., [1949] O.R. 237, [1949] 2 D.L.R. 328. In *Bennett & White (Calgary) Ltd. v. Sugar City,* [1951] A.C. 786, [1951] 4 D.L.R. 129, 3 W.W.R. (N.S.) 111, it was held as a matter of interpretation that under a construction contract between appellant and the Crown, certain property was owned by the Crown and, further, that although appellant was in possession for the purposes of the contract, nevertheless only an owner or an owner in possession was taxed, and hence appellant was not subject to tax measured by the value of the Crown property.

It has been held that s. 125 only prohibits Dominion taxation of provincial property and provincial taxation of Dominion property. It does not prohibit them from taxing their own property; for example, a province may competently authorize municipal taxation of property vested in a corporate servant of the Crown in right of that province: see *Re Taxation of University of Manitoba Lands,* [1940] 1 D.L.R. 579, [1940] 1 W.W.R. 145, 240; *B.C. Power Commission v. Victoria,* [1951] 2 D.L.R. 480, 1 W.W.R. (N.S.) 700. Moreover, the unqualified terms of s. 125 indicate that the tax immunity extends to property of any province (*i.e.* vested in the Crown in right thereof) as against taxation by another province. While neither the Dominion nor any province can legally destroy the immunity conferred by s. 125 (short of an amendment to that effect), either can "waive" it and submit to taxation through a voluntary payment of money in the exercise of a spending power: see *The Municipal Grants Act,* R.S.C. 1970, c. M-15; and *cf. Ottawa Public School Board v. Ottawa,* [1953] O.R. 122, [1953] 1 D.L.R. 692.

[A municipality's cost of repairing a sidewalk on failure of the fronting owner to repair, when recoverable as a tax, is within the immunity of section 125: see *The Queen v. Breton,* [1967] S.C.R. 503, 65 D.L.R. 2d 76.]

There is no express constitutional immunity from taxation of the property of a foreign state; the question would appear to turn on the application of recognized principles of international law in the construction of the taxing statute: see *Reference re Powers to Levy Rates on Foreign Legations and High Commissioners' Residences,* [1943] S.C.R. 208, [1943] 2 D.L.R. 481; *Yin-Tso Hsiung v. Toronto,* [1950] O.R. 463, [1950] 4 D.L.R. 209; and see *Note,* (1943) 21 Can. Bar Rev. 560. The Crown in right of Great Britain should stand in no different position; see *Jennings v. Whitby Tp.,* [1943] O.W.N. 170.]

Note on Taxation of Dominion or Provincial "Instrumentalities"

In *Caron v. The King,* [1924] A.C. 999, at p. 1006, [1924] 4 D.L.R. 105, at p. 110, [1924] 3 W.W.R. 417, at p. 422, Lord Phillimore, adverted to a proposition laid down in *Great West Saddlery Co. v. The King,* [1921] 2 A.C. 91, 58 D.L.R. 1, [1921] 1 W.W.R. 1034, that "no provincial legislature could use its special powers as an indirect means of destroying powers given by the Parliament of Canada"; and, he added, "by parity of reason the Parliament of Canada could not exercise its powers of taxation so as to destroy the capacity of officials lawfully appointed by the province". Subject to these principles, Canadian constitutional law does not recognize any immunity of federal or provincial functionaries from valid taxation imposed by province or Dominion, as the case may be. The *B.N.A. Act* gives power to the Dominion under s. 91(8) in relation to "the fixing of and providing for the salaries and allowances of civil and other officers of the government of Canada"; and by s. 92(4) gives power to the provinces in relation to "the establishment and tenure of provincial offices and the appointment and payment of provincial officers". These provisions do not carry the implication that the respective salaries may not be diminished by valid taxation. Thus, in the *Caron* case, in upholding the power of the Dominion to exact income taxes from the Quebec Minister of Agriculture in respect of his salary as minister and his sessional indemnity as a member of the provincial legislative assembly, Lord Phillimore asserted that "their Lordships can see no reason in principle why any of the sources of income of a taxable citizen should be removed from the power of taxation given to the Parliament of Canada". Similarly, an officer of the armed forces and a Dominion civil servant are liable to pay provincial income tax: *Worthington v. A.-G. Man.*; *Forbes v. A.-G. Man.*, [1936] S.C.R. 40, [1936] 1 D.L.R. 465. While two Judges of the Supreme Court dissented on the ground that the provincial tax was imposed on funds in the hands of the Dominion—a view which the majority rejected—and that, admittedly, the province cannot tax Dominion funds, this position raises a drafting problem rather than a constitutional issue. However, one of the dissenting Judges, Cannon J., took a specific constitutional ground in elaborating the proposition that a provincial legislature cannot interfere with the salary fixed by the Dominion for an officer of the permanent forces and a full-time civil servant; moreover, the provincial taxing legislation would interfere with the relationship which under law exists between the Government and its servants by compelling a portion of their services to be given gratuitously with a consequent adverse effect on the efficiency of the federal civil service. The difficulty in the way of this proposition was not only the *Caron* case but also an earlier judgment of the Supreme Court of Canada in *Abbott v. City of St. John* (1908), 40 S.C.R. 597, which affirmed the liability of a Dominion employee to pay municipal taxes levied under provincial legislation. In the *Abbott* case the Supreme Court abruptly halted the development of a principle of immunity which had been earlier asserted in *Leprohon v. City of Ottawa* (1878), 2 O.A.R. 522. The general position may now be considered as settled, in the terms of the *Abbott* case, by the Privy Council's judgment on an appeal by Forbes from the Supreme Court's decision: see *Forbes v. A.-G. Man.*, [1937] A.C. 260, [1937] 1 D.L.R. 289, [1937] 1 W.W.R. 167; and see also *Reference re Alberta Statutes*, [1938] S.C.R. 100, per Duff C.J. at pp. 130-1, and per Cannon J., at pp. 138-141; *Paquin v. Warden King Ltd. and A.-G. Que.* (1941), 71 Que. K.B. 425 (execution against federal civil servant). There remains, however, the qualification stated at the beginning of this Note—and noticed also in the *Abbott* case and in the *Forbes* case—that the respective taxing powers of Dominion and provinces may not be used by either of them to sterilize powers conferred by the other upon its functionaries or substantially to impair their status. A particular application of this principle has already been illustrated in connection with taxation of banks: see *A.-G. Alta. v. A.-G. Can.,* [1939] A.C. 117, [1938] 4 D.L.R. 433, [1938] 3 W.W.R. 337. The principle has also had a wide application in the "company" cases: see Chap. VIII, *supra;* and *cf. Reference re Debt Adjustment Act,* [1942] S.C.R. 31, [1942] 1 D.L.R. 1, reproduced *supra,* at p. 612.

Judges, too, are subject to taxation imposed by Dominion or province. It matters not whether they are County or District Court Judges: see *City of Toronto v. Morson* (1917), 40 O.L.R. 227, 38 D.L.R. 224; or Supreme Court Judges: see *The Judges v. A.-G. Sask.* (1937), 53 T.L.R. 464. Nor is it material that they are members of provincial or Dominion courts. Although Judges of the provincial superior courts have, by s. 99 of the *B.N.A. Act,* a constitutionally protected tenure (subject now to compulsory retirement at age 75), the Privy Council in *The Judges v. A.-G. Sask., supra,* did not think that their independence would be affected by requiring them to pay taxes in respect of their salaries which are for the Dominion to fix and provide under s. 100 of the *B.N.A. Act.* The judgment of the Privy Council proceeded, in part, as follows: "An argument had apparently been addressed to the Court [below, the Saskatchewan Court of Appeal, [1936] 2 W.W.R. 443] based on the word "fixed" in section 100. The same word is used in section 91(8) of the *British North America Act* in defining the powers of the Parliament of Canada with respect to the salaries of civil servants, and the Court had before it two decisions of the Supreme Court of Canada— namely, *Abbott v. City of St. John,* 40 S.C.R. 597, and *Forbes v. A.-G. Man.,* [1936] S.C.R. 40, in which a provincial income-tax on such salaries was upheld. The latter of these two cases was appealed to His Majesty in Council: [1937] A.C. 260. The decision of the Supreme Court was affirmed, and the argument under discussion is therefore not now open. This, in effect, disposes of the present case also, unless judicial emoluments are in a class apart, protected by some paramount principle making inapplicable to that form of income a tax imposed by a statute in terms wide enough to include it. There is no foundation in the realities of the situation for any such conception. Neither the independence nor any other attribute of the judiciary can be affected by a general income-tax which charges their official incomes on the same footings as incomes of other citizens. The Court below, agreeing with, though not bound by, two decisions in other Dominions —namely, *Cooper v. Com'r of Income Tax for Queensland* (1907), 4 C.L.R. 1, 304, before the High Court of Australia, and *Krause v. Com'r for Inland Revenue,* [1929] S.A.R. (A.D.) 286, in the Supreme Court of South Africa—found no reason for exempting judicial emoluments from income-tax. Their Lordships are of the same opinion."

One question remains. Would it be competent to the Dominion to legislate expressly against any diminution by provincial taxation of the salaries of Judges or of Dominion functionaries? Would this not be valid legislation under ss. 91(8) and 100 which would prevail against any provincial taxing measure?

[*Cf. Lederman*, The Independence of the Judiciary, (1956) 34 Can. Bar Rev. 1139, at p. 1165: "The words 'fixed and provided' are specially entrenched in the constitutional sense as part of section 100 of the *B.N.A. Act* and hence confer a guarantee of salary to superior court judges that cannot be impaired by an ordinary federal statute". The reference is to impairment apart from general income tax legislation applicable to all recipients of income. See *Holdsworth*, The Constitutional Position of Judges, (1932) 48 Law Q. Rev. 25; *Wade*, His Majesty's Judges, (1932) 173 L. T. 246, 267; *Holdsworth*, Reply, 173 L.T. 336; and see (1933) 176 L.T. 103.]

CHAPTER XI

ADMINISTRATION OF JUSTICE

1. Constitution and Jurisdiction of Provincial Courts: Appointment of Judges

REFERENCE RE AUTHORITY TO PERFORM FUNCTIONS VESTED BY THE ADOPTION ACT, THE CHILDREN'S PROTECTION ACT, THE CHILDREN OF UNMARRIED PARENTS ACT, THE DESERTED WIVES' AND CHILDREN'S MAINTENANCE ACT OF ONTARIO

In the Supreme Court of Canada. [1938] S.C.R. 398, [1938] 3 D.L.R. 497.

Reference to determine whether County or District Court Judges, Juvenile Court Judges, police magistrates and justices of the peace have authority to perform the functions vested in them by the four provincial statutes above-mentioned. The circumstances leading to the reference are set out in the order of reference as follows:

In several of the provinces of Canada in the case of certain social legislation, the legislatures have purported to confer extensive judicial powers upon officials appointed by the Lieutenant-Governor in Council to be members of tribunals constituted under the said legislation.

Questions have been raised whether these judicial powers are such as were theretofore exercised only by the Superior and District and County Courts of the provinces, in which event doubt arises as to whether the said judicial powers have been validly conferred. It has been held by the Courts of Appeal of Alberta and Ontario in two recently decided cases that only persons appointed by the Governor General were capable of exercising the powers so conferred [*Kazakewich v. Kazakewich*, [1937] 1 D.L.R. 548, [1936] 3 W.W.R. 699; *Clubine v. Clubine*, [1937] O.R. 636, [1937] 3 D.L.R. 754.] In one of these cases, the Honourable the Chief Justice of Ontario described the question of jurisdiction as being of great public interest and importance and stated that it was desirable that it should be settled by the Court of final resort.

The Attorney-General of Ontario has represented to the Minister of Justice that there are four Ontario Statutes of widespread application in relation to which this question arises, namely—the *Adoption Act*; the *Children's Protection Act*; the *Children of Unmarried Parents Act*; and the *Deserted Wives' and Children's Maintenance Act*, and that judicial powers under these Acts are exercisable by Justices of the Peace, Magistrates and Juvenile Court Judges, and in some cases, concurrently with these officials, County or District Court Judges.

The Attorney-General of Ontario further represents that the effective administration of the aforesaid statutes has been greatly impeded by the doubt that has been raised as to the validity of their provisions relating to the exercise of judicial powers and has requested that the same be referred to the Supreme Court of Canada in order that the doubt may be set at rest.

The judgment of the Court was delivered by

DUFF C.J.: The starting point for the consideration of the statutes referred to us is this: In point of substantive law it is not disputed that the matters which are the subjects of this legislation are entirely within the control of the legislatures of the provinces. We are not concerned with any ancillary jurisdiction in respect of children which the Dominion may possess in virtue of the assignment to the Dominion Parliament by section 91 of the subject Marriage and Divorce. Whatever may be the extent of that jurisdiction, we are not concerned with it here and I mention it only to put it aside . . .

The responsibility of the state for the care of people in distress (including neglected children and deserted wives) and for the proper education and training of youth, rests upon the province; in all the provinces the annual public expenditure for education and the care of indigent people is of great magnitude, a magnitude which attests in a conclusive manner the deep, active, vigilant concern of the people of this country in these matters. Moreover, while, as subject-matter of legislation, the criminal law is entrusted to the Dominion Parliament, responsibility for the administration of justice and, broadly speaking, for the policing of the country, the execution of the criminal law, the suppression of crime and disorder, has from the beginning of Confederation been recognized as the responsibility of the provinces and has been discharged at great cost to the people; so also, the provinces, sometimes acting directly, sometimes through the municipalities, have assumed responsibility for controlling social conditions having a tendency to encourage vice and crime.

The statutes before us constitute a part of the legislative measures in Ontario directed to these various ends. It would be competent to the Province of Ontario to put in effect a Poor Law system modelled upon that which prevails in England today. The province has not seen fit to do that but in some important respects the statutes that we have to consider embody features of the Poor Law System . . .

Now, it seems to be indisputable that sections 96 and 97 of the *British North America Act* contemplate the existence of provincial courts and judges other than those within the ambit of section 96. Indeed, it would be a non-natural reading of those sections to construe them as applying to such courts of summary jurisdiction as magistrates and justices of the peace. Besides, such a construction, having regard to the circumstances, even if the language in its ordinary sense extended to such judicial officers, would seem to be excluded by the fact that all judges appointed by the Governor General are to be selected from the bars of the respective provinces. That the statesmen responsible for Confederation could in fact have contemplated such a restriction upon the appointment of magistrates and justices of the peace would be a supposition that nobody having any knowledge of the circumstances of the country could countenance.

Nor so far as I know, has it been contended since 1892 that magistrates and justices of the peace and courts presided over by them at the time of Confederation fell within the intendment of section 96. Nevertheless, the argument before us in support of the attack on the constitutionality of the legislation based upon some dicta and decisions of the last few years appears logically to involve the conclusion that magistrates and justices of the peace exercising civil jurisdiction are within the purview of sections 96 and 97 and it is necessary to examine the validity of this position.

In the early years of Confederation, the view was advanced and found vigorous support for nearly a quarter of a century that, since the appointment of all judges, including technically magistrates and justices of the peace, was matter of prerogative (and since, as was contended, every prerogative has been vested exclusively in the Governor General as the sole representative of the Sovereign in the Dominion), the Lieutenant-Governors possessed strictly in point of law no authority to appoint such functionaries and the legislatures none to legislate with regard to such appointments.

Shortly after the *B.N.A. Act* came into force, the view was put forward by the Department of Justice in reporting on provincial legislation that no prerogative rights of property and no prerogative power passed to the provinces and that the provinces had no legislative jurisdiction in respect of such rights or powers. Notwithstanding the convincing argument set forth in a memorable state paper by Mr. Mowat, in which he expounded the views of the government of Ontario touching the relation of the provincial executive to the Crown; notwithstanding the decision in *Regina v. Coote* (1873), L.R. 4 P.C. 599, affirming the unanimous judgment of the Court of Queen's Bench for Quebec; notwithstanding the decisions of the Ontario judges supporting the doctrine advocated by Mr. Mowat on which the Ontario legislation was based (*Regina v. Wason*, 17 O.A.R. 221; *A.-G. for Canada v. A.-G. for Ontario*, 20 O.R. 222; 19 O.A.R. 31), the Department of Justice did not yield the ground it had taken up in this controversy until the decision of the Privy Council in the *Maritime Bank's* case, [1892] A.C. 437. That decision gave final judicial sanction to the views of Ontario as expounded by Mr. Mowat nearly twenty years before. In the meantime, the authority of the provinces in respect of the appointment of justices of the peace and other judicial officers of summary jurisdiction had come before the courts. In 1877, the Supreme Court of New Brunswick (in *Ganong v. Bayley*, 2 Cart. 509) had to consider the validity of provincial legislation constituting a small debts court with limited jurisdiction in contract and in tort presided over by judicial officers designated as commissioners. The legislation was sustained by the majority of the court; but the minority, the Chief Justice and Duff J., held it unconstitutional upon the ground that it dealt with matter of prerogative over which the province had no jurisdiction, and declared at the same time that another statute of that province, passed in 1873, dealing with the appointment of justices of the peace, was *ultra vires* because that matter, the appointment of justices of the peace, being likewise matter of prerogative, was also beyond the powers of provincial legislatures under the subject, the administration of justice and constitution of courts.

This view expressed by the minority of the Supreme Court of New Brunswick met with no concurrence in the Canadian courts until, in the year 1890, Drake J., of the Supreme Court of British Columbia, pronounced a decision in *Burk v. Tunstall*, 2 B.C.R. 12, based in part at least upon the same grounds, a decision which has assumed a great importance in the discussion of these matters and to which particular reference will be made later.

In the meantime, in Ontario, judicial authority and opinion had pronounced themselves finally against this view of the minority of the New Brunswick court. The subject of the authority of the provinces in relation to the appointment of justices of the peace came before a Divisional Court in Ontario in 1888 (Armour C.J., Street J. and Falconbridge J.) in *Regina v. Bush,* 15 O.R. 398. Street J., a judge of exceptional experience in such matters, reviewed the subject in an admirable judgment in the course of which he said that, subject to sections 96, 100 and 101, the words of paragraph 14 of section 92

> confer upon the Provincial Legislatures the right to regulate and provide for the whole machinery connected with the administration of justice in the Provinces, including the appointment of all the judges and officers requisite for the proper administration of justice in the widest sense, reserving only the procedure in criminal matters. . . .
>
> It is clearly the intention of the Act that the Provincial Legislatures shall be responsible for the administration of justice within their respective provinces, excepting in so far as the duty was cast upon the Dominion Parliament. The only duty cast upon the Dominion Parliament in the matter is contained in the clauses to which I have referred, by which the appointment of the judges of certain courts is reserved to it. The administration of justice could not be carried on in the Provinces effectually without the appointment of justices of the peace and police magistrates, and the conclusion seems to me to be irresistible that it was intended that the appointment of these and other officers, whose duty it should be to aid in the administration of justice, should be left in the hands of the Provincial Legislatures. (pp. 403-405)

In 1896, in *In re Small Debts Act,* 5 B.C.R. 246, the full court of the Supreme Court of British Columbia had to pass upon a controversy touching the validity of a statute investing justices of the peace with small debts jurisdiction up to $100. The argument based upon the absence of authority in the provinces to legislate touching the prerogative was rejected on the authority of the *Maritime Bank's* case, which had, in the meantime, been decided. I do not dwell upon the able judgments delivered by McCreight and Walkem JJ. but it is necessary to take note of that of Drake J., in view of the importance that has been attached to some language of his in the earlier judgment, already mentioned, delivered some six years before in 1890 and before the decision in the *Maritime Bank's* case. In his judgment in 1896, Mr. Justice Drake makes it plain that in his view sections 96 and 97 of the *British North America Act* recognize provincial courts and judges other than those enumerated in section 96; and at the conclusion of his judgment he uses these words:

> In holding this particular Act *intra vires*, I do not intend to lay down any strict line of demarcation between the courts over which the Dominion Government have the power of appointing and paying the judges, and those other smaller and inferior courts which the Provincial Legislatures may establish. No line can be drawn; every case must depend on the particular circumstances, and will be dealt with when the necessity to do so arises.

I consider it important to call attention to these words because a construction has been put upon a passage which has been cited and relied upon in his earlier judgment in *Burk v. Tunstall* which would give to section 96 a wider scope and make it applicable to all provincial courts. The discrepancy is easily understood when the judgment in *Burk v. Tunstall* is read as a whole. In that case, which was an application for a writ of prohibition, nobody appeared in opposition to the application and there was no argument in support of the validity of the impugned legislation. The controversy concerned the Mining Court of British Columbia, a court established prior to Confederation. After Confederation the jurisdiction of this Court has been increased by successive increments until the jurisdiction exercised by the Mining Court was vastly more important than that exercised by any County Court in Canada. In British Columbia from the beginning there were officials styled Gold Commissioners who within their respective districts were charged with very important administrative functions under the *Mineral Act,* under other statutes and in still other respects. By the Act constituting the Mining Court, the Gold Commissioner of the District was made the judge of that Court. Mr. Justice Drake undoubtedly held the view that the Mining Court as constituted in 1890, was a court within the contemplation of s. 96; but it is right to point out that there is no sort of resemblance between the jurisdiction and powers of the Mining Court of British Columbia at that date and the jurisdiction of the tribunals we have now to consider. The Mining Court was a court of record and was in explicit words invested with the authority of a court of law and equity to deal with all manner of disputes concerning mining lands, mining property, mining rights, and in respect of claims for supplies against free miners (who would virtually constitute every corporation and individual of the population of a mining district) without restriction as to amount or value, with authority to issue writs of *ca. sa., ne exeat* and so on. I do not doubt that the actual decision of Mr. Justice Drake in that case was right.

A passage from his judgment expressing certain views as to the construction of section 96 is quoted with approval in the judgment of the Judicial Committee of the Privy Council in *Martineau v. Montreal City,* [1932] A.C. 113, at 121. Their Lordships' observations are in these words:

But by s. 92, head 13, of the Act, as is well remembered, there is conferred upon the Provincial legislature the exclusive right of making laws in relation to property and civil rights in the Province and (by head 14) in relation to the administration of justice in the Province, including the constitution, maintenance and organization of Provincial Courts, both of civil and criminal jurisdiction, and including procedure in civil matters in these Courts. These exclusive Provincial powers have made it extremely difficult in many cases to draw the line between legislation which is within the competence of the Province under s. 92 of the Act, and legislation which is beyond its competence by reason of s. 96. This observation may be illustrated by two instances, neither of them remote from the present case, the first on the one side of the line and the second on the other. In *Regina v. Coote*, L.R. 4 P.C. 599, it was held by this Board, in an appeal upon which, it must be noticed, the respondent was not represented, that certain statutes of Quebec appointing officers named "fire marshals," with power to examine witnesses under oath and to inquire into the cause and origin of fires and to arrest and commit for trial in the same manner as a justice of the peace, were within the competence of the Provincial legislature. On the other hand, in a British Columbia case in 1890—*Burk v. Tunstall*, (1890) 2 B.C.R. 12,—it was held by Drake J. that while it was within the competence of the Province to create mining courts and to fix their jurisdiction, it was not within its competence to appoint any officer thereof with other than ministerial powers. The learned judge, in the course of his judgment, referring to s. 96 of the Act, observes, as their Lordships think with reason:

> "It is true that the language used in that section is limited to the judges of the superior, district and county Courts in each Province, and it might be contended that these Courts having been expressly named, all other Courts were excluded. If this were so the Provincial legislature would only have to constitute a Court by a special name to enable them to avoid this clause. But in the section itself, after the special Courts thus named, the Courts of probate in Nova Scotia and New Brunswick are excepted from the operation of the clause, thus showing that s. 96 was intended to be general in its operation."

This passage in their Lordships' judgment is the basis on which the argument directed against the jurisdiction of courts of summary jurisdiction in this and in other cases of recent years, has mainly rested. It has, I venture to think, been misunderstood but it has been cited again and again as authority for the proposition that it is incompetent to the provincial legislatures to legislate for the appointment of any officer of any provincial court exercising other than ministerial functions, and for the proposition that s. 96 is general in its character in the sense that all provincial courts come within its scope, including courts of summary jurisdiction such as justices of the peace, and that, as regards all such courts exercising, at all events, civil jurisdiction, the appointment of judges and officers presiding over them is vested exclusively in the Dominion.

It is quite clear, I think, that this is a wholly unwarranted view of *Martineau's* case and I shall revert to the judgment of their Lordships a little later. It is necessary, I think, before doing so, to consider a little further the judgment of Mr. Justice Drake in *Burk v. Tunstall*.

That judgment is based on two grounds. One ground is that the appointment of all judges, without distinction, being matter of prerogative right, is, conformably to the view of the minority of the judges of the Supreme Court of New Brunswick in *Ganong v. Bayley* (which in 1890 was still the view of the Department of Justice), entirely outside the ambit of provincial jurisdiction in relation to the administration of justice and the constitution of courts. The judgment is also put on the ground indicated in the passage quoted above from the Judicial Committtee in *Martineau's* case that the Mining Court was a court within the purview of section 96. Mr. Justice Drake did, I am convinced, intend to say that, under its powers in relation to the administration of justice and of constitution of courts of the province, a province has no power to appoint any officer of any such court other than officers charged with strictly ministerial functions. The view he then held touching the pre-'rogative necessarily excluded from the authority of the provinces power to appoint judges of provincial courts, including judicial officers such as magistrates and justices of the peace, which he considered was vested exclusively in the Governor General; and he intended to say that this exclusive authority was in no way restricted by section 96. He would not have taken this view had his attention been called to *Regina v. Coote;* but, as mentioned above, he had not the benefit of any argument in support of the legislation.

As I have already observed, his views had changed in 1896 and his judgment of that year gives the simple explanation, *viz.*, that he loyally accepted, as, of course, it was his duty to do, the judgment of the Judicial Committee in the *Maritime Bank's* case as negativing the views he had formerly held with regard to the prerogative. He points out in the later judgment that the views of the Chief Justice and of Duff J., in the New Brunswick case (*Ganong v. Bayley*), touching the prerogative had necessarily been displaced by the *Maritime Bank's* case. Therefore, he definitely recognized, as appears from the passage I have quoted, the authority of the Province to constitute courts to which section 96 has no application and to appoint the judges or judicial officers to preside over them.

After the decision in the *Maritime Bank's* case down to the judgment of the Judicial Committee in *Martineau's* case in 1932, the view, to which effect was given in *Regina v. Bush* in 1888, and in the British Columbia case, *In re Small Debts Act,* in 1896, was generally accepted in Canada; the view, that is to say, that it is competent to the provinces to legislate for the appointment of justices of the peace and invest them as well as other courts of summary jurisdiction with civil and criminal jurisdiction. Even the Department of Justice accepted this view, as appears from the report of Mr. Fitzpatrick, as Minister of Justice, of December 31st, 1901, where, in referring to the district courts of the Province of New Brunswick invested with a jurisdiction to deal with claims in contract up to $80 and in tort up to $40, he says:

These courts appear, however, to be intended to take the place of the parish courts and magistrates' courts, having limited civil jurisdiction, heretofore established, and they are not courts in the opinion of the undersigned having the dignity of the district courts intended by the *British North America Act*.

In 1917 there was a reference by the Lieutenant-Governor in Council of Alberta touching the validity of the *Small Debts Recovery Act* of that province, [1917] 3 W.W.R. 698. The question was fully discussed in the judgments of Harvey C.J. and Beck J. and determined in the sense of the British Columbia decision of 1896.

The attack on the validity of such provincial legislation based upon the argument drawn from the Justice Department's theory as to prerogative powers having received its quietus from the decision in the *Maritime Bank's* case, justices of the peace of almost every province of Canada, along with other courts of summary jurisdiction, exercised without question civil jurisdiction in the character of small debts courts and otherwise until the judgment of the Privy Council in *Martineau's* case which seemed to start a fresh series of attacks upon the provincial jurisdiction in relation to the administration of justice.

Now, I think the observations of the Judicial Committee in *Martineau's* case were not directed to magistrates' courts and courts of justices of the peace or, indeed, to courts of summary jurisdiction of any kind; and, when the whole of the passage in Lord Blanesburgh's judgment on pages 121 and 122 is read, this seems to be clear. It is quite true it is observed that the respondent was not represented in *Regina v. Coote*, but it must be noticed that in that case the Court of Queen's Bench in Quebec had unanimously held the legislation in question there, which provided for the appointment of fire marshals, with the powers of justices of the peace, and with authority to investigate and report on the origin of fires and to commit persons for trial if the facts should warrant that course, to be within the competence of the provincial legislature and this their Lordships appear to have considered, as did the Court of Queen's Bench, a question upon which it was necessary to pass; and they did so by expressly approving the decision of the Court of Queen's Bench.

But their Lordships' judgment in *Martineau's* case does not profess to overrule the previous decision in *Regina v. Coote* which, it may be observed, was decided by a board that included Sir Montague Smith.

I have already said that, in my view, Drake J. in the earlier case did mean to say that section 96 applies to all provincial courts of every description because his view as touching the prerogative necessarily excluded the authority of the province; but it is equally clear to me that their Lordships in the Privy Council, had not their attention called to this aspect of the subject and are not giving their sanction to the words of Drake J. in the extended sense in which I think he intended to employ them. Indeed, it is quite plain that they could not do so consistently with the previous decision in *Regina v. Coote* which explicitly recognized the authority of the provinces to legislate for the appointment of judicial officers with the powers of justices of the peace; and, as I humbly think, it cannot be supposed that their Lordships could have given their adherence to a pronouncement at variance with all Canadian decisions and all Canadian practice since 1892 without some reference to such decisions and practice.

It cannot, therefore, be seriously disputed that, on enactment of the *British North America Act,* and on the subsequent extension of the Act to the provinces of British Columbia and Prince Edward Island, magistrates and justices of the peace remained outside the scope of section 96. Some more or less obvious consequences follow from that.

At the date of the Union, in Upper Canada, justices of the peace exercised jurisdiction in civil matters; in respect notably of claims for wages and of orders for the protection of the earnings of married women. In Nova Scotia they possessed a small debts jurisdiction up to $80 in contract and to a lower limit in tort. In British Columbia, they possessed jurisdiction in respect of protection orders, in respect of claims for ferry tolls, in respect of line fences; and in disputes respecting the ownership of stolen cattle. At least in the Maritime provinces, in Quebec and British Columbia there was, under the *Seamen's Acts* and under the *Merchants Shipping Act,* jurisdiction to entertain claims for seamen's wages. . . .

. . . The *B.N.A. Act,* . . . by its express terms [s. 129] provided for the continuance of courts possessing civil jurisdiction which were not within the scope of section 96 and concerning the powers of which the provinces had exclusive authority in virtue of section 92(14).

The provinces acquired plenary authority, not only to diminish the jurisdiction of such courts, but also to increase it, subject only to any qualification arising in virtue of s. 96.

My view of the effect of s. 96 as regards such courts existing at the date of Confederation (that is to say, outside the scope of that section) is this: the provinces became endowed with plenary authority under s. 92(14), but, a province is not empowered to usurp the authority vested exclusively in the Dominion in respect of the appointment of judges who, by the true intendment of the section, fall within the ambit of s. 96, or to enact legislation repugnant to that section; and it is too plain for discussion that a province is not competent to do that indirectly by altering the character of existing courts outside that section in such a manner as to bring them within the intendment of it while retaining control of the appointment of the judges presiding over such courts. That, in effect, would not be distinguishable from constituting a new court, as, for example, a Superior Court, within the scope of section 96 and assuming power to appoint the judge of it. In principle, I do not think it is possible to support any stricter limitation upon the authority of the provinces, and I do not think what I am saying is in substance inconsistent with what was laid down by Lord Atkin speaking on behalf of the Judicial Committee in *Toronto v. York,* [1938] A.C. 415.

One of the contentions of the appellants in that case was that the Ontario Municipal Board was invalidly constituted as being a Superior Court constituted in violation of sections 96, 99 and 100 of the *British North America Act.* The conclusion of their Lordships in the Privy Council on this contention was that the Municipal Board is primarily in "pith and substance," an administrative body. As to Part III of the Act (22 Geo. V, 1932, chap. 27), especially sections 41-46, 54 and 59, . . . their Lordships said it was difficult to avoid the conclusion that the sections in question purport to clothe the Board with the functions of a Court, and to vest in it judicial powers, and held that

> so far, therefore, as the Act purports to constitute the Board a Court of Justice, analogous to a Superior, District, or County Court it is *pro tanto* invalid.

But it is obvious that their Lordships were not considering, because there was no occasion to do so, the distinction between the courts that come within the intendment of section 96 of the *British North America Act* and other courts or tribunals.

In effect, it was argued before us that provincial legislation is repugnant to section 96 if in any particular the jurisdiction of one of these courts of summary jurisdiction existing at the date of Confederation is increased. That, in my view, is quite inadmissible in principle as it is incompatible with practice and authority since Confederation with the exception of one or two decisions in very recent years which are put upon the authority of *Martineau's* case.

Before proceeding further, it will be convenient to advert to some general considerations. In the argument addressed to us there is an underlying assumption that the interest of the people of this country in the independent and impartial administration of justice has its main security in sections 96, 97 and 99. Now, there were weighty reasons, no doubt, for those sections, and a strict observance of them as regards the judges of courts within their purview is essential to the due administration of justice. But throughout the whole of this country magistrates daily exercise, especially in the towns and cities, judicial powers of the highest importance in relation more particularly to the criminal law, but in relation also to a vast body of law which is contained in provincial statutes and municipal by-laws. The jurisdiction exercised by these functionaries, speaking generally, touches the great mass of the people more intimately and more extensively than do the judgments of the Superior Courts; and it would be an extraordinary supposition that a great community like the province of Ontario is wanting, either in the will or in the capacity, to protect itself against misconduct by these officers whom it appoints for these duties; and any such suggestion would be baseless in fact and altogether fallacious as the foundation of a theory controlling the construction of the *B.N.A. Act.*

Moreover, except in the case of the Superior Court judges of the province, who, by force of section 99, hold office during good conduct and are removable only by the Governor General on address by the Senate and the House of Commons, the *British North America Act* provides no security of tenure for judges coming within s. 96.

It is very clear to me, therefore, that, if you were justified in holding that by force of s. 96 the provinces have been disabled since Confederation from adding to the jurisdiction of judges not within that section, there would be equally good ground for holding that by force of s. 99 the provinces are disabled from extending the jurisdiction of the County Courts and the District Courts in such a way as to embrace matters which were then exclusively within the jurisdiction of Superior Courts.

Now, the pecuniary limit of claims cognizable by County Court judges has been frequently enlarged since Confederation and nobody has ever suggested so far as I know that the result has been to transform the County Court into a Superior Court and to bring the County Court judges within s. 99. . . .

If the provinces have no authority to increase the jurisdiction of the County Courts without depriving them of their character as such, then no such jurisdiction exists anywhere. As Mr. Justice Strong, speaking for this Court, said in *Re County Courts of British Columbia,* 21 S.C.R. 446 at p. 453:

> . . . The jurisdiction of parliament to legislate as regards the jurisdiction of provincial courts is, I consider, excluded by subsection 14 of s. 92, before referred to, inasmuch as the constitution, maintenance and organization of provincial courts plainly includes the power to define the jurisdiction of such courts territorially as well as in other respects. This seems to me too plain to require demonstration.

In answer to the suggestion that a territorial increase of jurisdiction ought to be followed by a fresh commission to the judge of the County Court, he observed that the suggestion was a "preposterous" one.

There is a strong current of authority against the proposition I am discussing. Small debts courts presided over by judges appointed by the provinces were established in New Brunswick in 1877, in British Columbia in 1895, in Alberta in 1917, and, no doubt, elsewhere, and the validity of this legislation has been uniformly sustained. The jurisdiction of the Nova Scotia magistrates in such matters (vested in them before Confederation) is still exercised without challenge.

In *French v. McKendrick,* 66 O.L.R. 306, the Court of Appeal in Ontario unanimously held the Division Courts, courts established before Confederation, exercising jurisdiction in contract and in tort within defined limits as to amount and value, presided over, by the statute constituting them, by a County Court judge or by a member of the bar named as deputy by one of the judges, not to be courts within the scope of s. 96. The Court of Appeal unanimously took the view that the enactment authorizing the appointment of a deputy judge from the bar by a County Judge was competent and also that legislation enlarging the pecuniary limits of jurisdiction was competent.

I agree with the view expressed by Mr. Justice Drake, in his judgment in *Re Small Debts Act,* that it is inadvisable to attempt to draw an abstract line for the purpose of classifying courts as falling within section 96 or otherwise. I think, with respect, that this is not in the least inconsistent with Lord Atkin's observations in *Toronto v. York,* [1938] A.C. 415.

Then, it should be observed that, if you have a provincial court outside the scope of s. 96 and the province enlarges its jurisdiction or its powers, but not in such a manner as to constitute a court of a class within the intendment of s. 96, I, as a judge, charged solely with the application of the law, have no further concern with what the legislature has done. It is no part of my function as a judge to consider whether, if the province should go on enlarging the jurisdiction and powers of the court, it might arrive at a point when the tribunal would cease to be one outside the ambit of s. 96. I have nothing to do with that. It may be a very excellent ground for disallowance of the legislation by the Governor General. Even if I am satisfied that there is something in the nature of an abuse of power, that in itself is no concern of mine. If, in its true character the legislation is legislation concerning the administration of justice and the constitution of provincial courts and is not repugnant to the *B.N.A. Act* as a whole, that is the end of the matter. . . .

I am unable to accept the view that the jurisdiction of inferior courts, whether within or without the ambit of s. 96, was by the *B.N.A. Act* fixed forever as it stood at the date of Confederation.

Coming now to the legislation before us. I do not intend to examine it in detail. Let me first observe that the jurisdiction of the Legislature to pass the *Adoption Act* appears to me too clear for discussion and I add nothing to that.

The remaining three statutes fall into two classes. As regards the *Children of Unmarried Parents Act* and the *Deserted Wives' and Children's Maintenance Act,* these statutes, broadly speaking, aim at declaring and enforcing the obligations of husbands and parents to maintain their wives and children and these, self-evidently, are peculiarly matters for provincial authority. As regards the maintenance of illegitimate children and deserted wives and children, the public responsibility, as already mentioned, rests exclusively with the provinces and it is for the provincial legislatures, and for them alone, to say how the incidence of that responsibility shall be borne. The enactments are closely analogous to certain of the enactments forming part of the Poor Law system as it has developed in England since the time of Elizabeth; and the jurisdiction vested by these statutes in magistrates and judges of the Juvenile Court is not in substance dissimilar to the jurisdiction of magistrates under that system. I agree with the Supreme Court of British Columbia in *Dixon v. Dixon,* 46 B.C.R. 375, that there is no little analogy between the pre-Confederation legislation in British Columbia and in Ontario by which the earnings of the wife, which are the property of the husband, can be taken from the husband by a protection order and placed under the control of the wife. I agree with that, on the assumption upon which the argument against this legislation proceeded, that a maintenance order against a delinquent husband at the instance of a deserted wife is to be treated as on the some footing as alimony.

I think, with great respect, however, that the matter is of little importance. The subject is envisaged by these statutes from a different point of view. It is dealt with from the point of view of the obligation of the community and of the husband to the community. That is to say, it recognizes, first, the obligation of the community to protect women and children afflicted by misfortune through the default of their natural protector in the discharge of his natural obligations and, as one means of securing that end, it imposes upon the defaulting father and husband the legal duty enforceable by summary proceedings to support his children and his wife. The statute places the obligation to care for the deserted wife and children on the shoulders of that member of the community whose duty it is to the community as well as to his family to bear the burden. . . .

One further point made against this feature of the statute is that there is no pecuniary limit. This again I regard as of small importance. The jurisdiction is not without limit; it is necessarily limited by the purpose for which the order is made. . . .

. . . With the greatest possible respect, I am unable to concur in the decisions in *Clubine v. Clubine* and *Kazakewich v. Kazakewich*.

In *Rex v. Vesey*, 12 M.P.R. 307, the Supreme Court of New Brunswick pronounced a decision based upon the view that such legislation was not beyond the competence of a provincial legislature.

Looking at the question in controversy from the point of view most favourable to the attack, the question one must ask oneself is this: does the jurisdiction conferred upon magistrates under these statutes broadly conform to a type of jurisdiction generally exercisable by courts of summary jurisdiction rather than the jurisdiction exercised by courts within the purview of s. 96? There can be only one answer to that question. . . .

Coming to the *Children's Protection Act*. Having regard to the purpose of the Act and its machinery, it appears to me to be precisely the kind of legislation which might be described as the modern counterpart of the Poor Law legislation in those features of it which are concerned with the care of neglected children. With great respect, I am unable to perceive any ground upon which it can be validly affirmed that magistrates exercising jurisdiction under this statute are entering upon a sphere which, having regard to legal history, belongs to the Superior Courts rather than to courts of summary jurisdiction; or that in exercising the functions attributed to them by this legislation they come within any fair intendment of section 96. . . .

Having given my reasons for thinking that these statutes are validly enacted in respect of the jurisdiction vested in the magistrates and justices of the peace as such, I come now to the Juvenile Court.

There is one general observation which must first be made. If you have a jurisdiction which can be exercised by a tribunal not within section 96, that is to say, by a tribunal presided over by a judge or officer appointed by the province, it is entirely for the province to say how the tribunal shall be constituted and by what name judicial officers presiding over it shall be called. *Regina v. Coote* is, on this point, conclusive.

Now, the Juvenile Court is recognized and, to my mind, properly beyond all doubt recognized as a properly constituted court for the purpose of dealing with offences under the Dominion *Juvenile Delinquents Act, 1929* (19-20 Geo. V, ch. 46) and the amendments of 1935 and 1936 (25-26 Geo. V, ch. 41, and 1 Edw. VIII, ch. 40).

Jurisdiction under the old law of the Province of Canada in respect of offences by juvenile delinquents was exercisable by two justices of the peace, by a recorder, or by a stipendiary magistrate. A Juvenile Court constituted for exercising this jurisdiction in respect of juvenile offenders is plainly to my mind a court not within s. 96 and it does not become so by virtue of the fact that the officers presiding over it are invested with further jurisdiction of the same character as is validly given to magistrates and justices of the peace. . . .

Questions answered in affirmative.

[In line with the *Adoption Act reference, supra,* it was held in *A.-G. Ont. v. Scott,* [1956] S.C.R. 137, 1 D.L.R. (2d) 433, that a provincially-appointed family court Judge could constitutionally be authorized to make "provisional" maintenance orders in favour of a resident wife and children against a non-resident husband (such orders being enforceable in a reciprocating state), and also to enforce in the Province against resident husbands "provisional" maintenance orders made in reciprocating states.

The problems raised by s. 96 of the *B.N.A. Act* and the case law thereon are discussed and reviewed by *Willis,* Section 96 of the *British North America Act,* (1940) 18 Can. Bar Rev. 517, and by *Laskin,* Municipal Tax Assessment and Section 96 of the *British North America Act: The Olympia Bowling Alleys* case, (1955) 33 Can. Bar Rev. 993.]

Note

The relation of s. 96 (in terms an appointing power respecting certain classes of provincial courts) to s. 92(4) of the *B.N.A. Act* ("The establishment and tenure of provincial offices and the appointment and payment of provincial officers") and to s. 92(14) ("The administration of justice in the province, including the constitution, maintenance and organization of provincial courts both of civil and criminal jurisdiction, and including procedure in civil matters in those courts") has a relevance both for provincial "court" and "administrative board" organization and functioning. For a comprehensive review and thoughtful analysis of the authorities on this and related issues, see *Pepin,* Les Tribunaux Administratifs et la Constition (1969).

It has been suggested by *Lederman*, The Independence of the Judiciary, (1965) 34 Can. Bar Rev. 1139, at pp. 1175 ff. that the limitations of ss. 96 to 100 of the *B.N.A. Act* may properly be imported into s. 101 so as to restrict federal courts in the same way; but there is no tenable ground of history or text or context to support the suggestion. Indeed, it was rejected in *Regina v. Canadian Labour Relations Board, ex parte Federal Electric Corp.* (1964), 44 D.L.R. (2d) 440, 47 W.W.R. 391.

The clash of provincial legislation respecting organization and jurisdiction of inferior courts with s. 96 is exhibited in the following illustrative cases:

1.   Establishment of provincial court and appointment of presiding officer vested with authority formerly exercised by a "section 96" court: *Seminary of Chicoutimi v. A.G. Quebec*, (1973) 27 D.L.R. (3d) 356 (provincial court not validly empowered to quash municipal by-laws); *Burk v. Tunstall* (1890), 2 B.C.R. 12 and *Re McLean Gold Mines Ltd. and A.-G. Ont.*, 54 O.L.R. 573, [1924] 1 D.L.R. 10 (provincial mining commissioner incompetent to exercise conferred jurisdiction); *Rimmer v. Hannon*, [1923] 3 W.W.R. 1, 60 D.L.R. 637, 14 Sask. L.R. 387 (provincially appointed surrogate court Judge competent to exercise surrogate jurisdiction); *Re Ritchie and Ritchie* (1968), 3 D.L.R. (3d) 676 (B.C.) (enforcement by provincial Judge of alimony orders of superior court); and *Armich v. Armich*, [1971] 1 W.W.R. 207, 3 R.F.L. 207, 16 D.L.R. (3d) 326 (B.C.) (revision of alimony orders not incident to divorce).

2.   Authorizing provincial court officer to do the work of a "section 96" court: *A.-G. Ont. and Display Service Co. Ltd. v. Victoria Medical Bldg. Ltd.*, [1960] S.C.R. 32, 21 D.L.R. (2d) 97 (Master incompetent to try (where not by way of a reference) mechanics' lien actions); see also *C. Huebert Ltd. v. Sharman*, [1950] 2 D.L.R. 344, [1950] 1 W.W.R. 682, 58 Man. R. 1; and *cf. Maitre v. Chisvin and Chisvin* (1958), 15 D.L.R. (2d) 120, 25 W.W.R. 664, dealing with curing legislation consequent upon the *Sharman* case; *Polson Iron Works v. Munns* (1915), 24 D.L.R. 18, 9 W.W.R. 231 (Master may competently be empowered to strike out defence and give leave to sign summary judgment); *Colonial Investment and Loan Co. v. Grady* (1915), 24 D.L.R. 176, 8 W.W.R. 995, 8 Alta. L.R. 496 (Master incompetent to receive authority to try mortgage actions or actions on agreements for sale of land); *Schrier v. Bernstein and Latour Terrace Ltd.* (1962), 33 D.L.R. (2d) 305, 47 M.P.R. 401 (invalidity of Rules of Court authorizing Judge to appoint Master to try a cause). See *Lefroy*, Annotation, (1915) 24 D.L.R. 22.

3.   Assigning and altering jurisdiction and functions of and among "section 96" courts: *In re County Courts of B.C.* (1892), 21 S.C.R. 446 and *Rex v. Brown* (1907), 41 N.S.R. 293, 13 Can. C.C. 133 (provincial legislation may validly extend the territorial jurisdiction of county court Judges); *A.-G. Ont. v. A.-G. Can.*, [1925] A.C. 750, [1925] 2 D.L.R. 753, [1925] 1 W.W.R. 1131 (provincial legislation

invalid in purporting to authorize designation of Judges as Chief Justices or assignment of Judges to established divisions of provincial Supreme Court); and *cf. Scott v. A.-G. Can.*, [1923] 4 D.L.R. 647, [1923] 3 W.W.R. 929, 40 T.L.R. 6; *Regina v. Carker* (1965), 52 D.L.R. (2d) 763, 53 W.W.R. 559 (provincial legislation valid in designating County Court as a Court of General Sessions of the Peace).

4. Establishment of provincial inferior courts of a kind known in 1867 and appointing incumbents: *Ganong v. Bailey* (1877), 17 N.B.R. 324 (provincial legislation establishing small claims courts presided over by provincial appointees held valid); *The King v. Sweeney* (1912), 1 D.L.R. 476, 45 N.S.R. 494 (provincial legislation competent to authorize appointment of stipendiary magistrates); *French v. McKendrick*, [1931] 1 D.L.R. 696, 66 O.L.R. 306 (provincial *Division Courts Act* validly authorizing Judge to appoint barrister as deputy to try cases); and see also *In re Queen's Counsel* (1896), 23 O.A.R. 792, aff'd *sub nom. A.-G. Can. v. A.-G. Ont.*, [1898] A.C. 247.

See, generally, the *Adoption Act* case, *supra,* for a review of the history and case-law.

5. Increasing jurisdiction of provincial inferior courts; *Regina v. Coote* (1873), L.R. 4 P.C. 599 (criminal jurisdiction of justices of the peace validly conferred on fire marshals in respect to fires); *Re Small Debts Recovery Act*, [1917] 3 W.W.R. 698, 37 D.L.R. 170, 12 Alta. L.R. 32 (small debt jurisdiction validly conferred on justices of the peace); *French v. McKendrick, supra* (extension of jurisdiction of Division Court upheld); *Reference re the Magistrate's Court of Quebec, A.-G. Que. v. Bar of the Province of Quebec and A.-G. Can.*, [1965] S.C.R. 772, 55 D.L.R. (2d) 701 (pecuniary limit of jurisdiction of magistrate's court validly raised from $200 to $500); and see also *Adoption Act* case, *supra.*

6. Reposing confiscatory authority in provincial inferior courts: *Re Johnson*, [1953] 1 D.L.R. 284, 7 W.W.R. (N.S.) 193, 105 Can. C.C. 10, rev'd on other grounds [1954] S.C.R. 127, [1954] 2 D.L.R. 625, 108 Can. C.C. 1 (jurisdiction to order confiscation of slot machines competently conferred on justices of the peace); and *cf. Rex v. Nat Bell Liquors Ltd.*, [1922] 2 A.C. 128, 65 D.L.R. 1, [1922] 2 W.W.R. 30.

Since s. 96 reposes only an executive appointing power in the Governor-General and gives no legislative power to Parliament (see *Re Judges Act*, [1923] 2 D.L.R. 604, 52 O.L.R. 105), is it open to Parliament to limit the range or kind of duties exercisable by section 96 Judges or to deny them powers conferred by provincial legislation? See *Re Winnipeg and Cross*, [1927] 3 D.L.R. 1072, [1927] 2 W.W.R. 644, 37 Man. R. 40.

Does the fact that an appointment under s. 96 carries with it certain conceptions of function operate to preclude a province from reposing "non-judicial" duties in a section 96 Judge? Put another way, is some variant of a separation of powers doctrine applicable to section 96 Judges? *Cf. A.-G. Australia v. The Queen and The*

Boilermakers' Society of Australia, [1957] A.C. 288, [1957] 2 All E.R. 45.

Note on Legislative Power to Curtail Jurisdiction of Provincial Superior Courts: Denial of Judicial Review of Administrative Adjudications

"There is no constitutional rule against taking away the jurisdiction of the higher courts . . .": see *Willis* in (1940) Can. Bar Rev. 517, at p. 523. This proposition is surely not open to challenge in relation to substantive original and appellate jurisdiction where curtailment is by the competent legislature. It does not controvert the common law rule that a superior court is (apart from appeal) not accountable to any other judicial tribunal, and hence may properly determine its own jurisdiction: see *Holdsworth,* Immunity for Judicial Acts, (1924), 1 Jo. S.P.T.L. 17. This determination, if done as an exercise in fashioning common law, is subject to legislative control; and the competent legislature may confer or curtail, may shape or condition jurisdiction of a court.

There is nothing in the *British North America Act* which expressly protects the courts in any claim to particular jurisdiction against both Parliament and provincial Legislatures. Implicit in the Act is, of course, a guaranteed jurisdiction to rule on the validity of legislation. Although general rules of procedure may operate to prescribe the conditions and time limits for bringing challenging actions, it has been held that an inferior tribunal cannot validly preclude a superior Court from entertaining constitutional objections to its proceedings by promulgating rules that limit the time within which such objections can be made: see *Regina v. Ontario Labour Relations Board, ex parte Dunn,* [1963] 2 O.R. 301, 39 D.L.R. (2d) 346. The *British North America Act,* moreover, assumes but without explicitly so declaring, that provincial superior Courts have a constitutional existence. Since their existence is expressive of function, there has been from time to time reference in the case law to inherent jurisdiction. This has become particularly significant with respect to superior court supervisory jurisdiction over adjudications of inferior courts and, especially, of administrative agencies.

There have been a series of holdings that deny to a legislature in Canada power to preclude curial review of administrative board action or decision alleged to be taken or given without or in excess of statutory jurisdiction: see Rinfret C.J.C. in *L'Alliance des Professeurs Catholiques de Montreal v. Labour Relations Board of Quebec,* [1953] 2 S.C.R. 140, at p. 155, [1953] 4 D.L.R. 161, at p. 175; *Dauphin v. Director of Public Welfare* (1956), 5 D.L.R. (2d) 274, 19 W.W.R. 97. The matter was put boldly by Roach J.A. in *Bradley v. Canadian General Electric Co. Ltd.,* [1957] O.R. 316, 8 D.L.R. (2d) 65, as follows:

". . . though Parliament or the Legislature may by adequate legislation take that remedy (*certiorari*) away for every other purpose, it cannot take it away as a remedy where the inferior tribunal has acted without or in excess of its jurisdiction . . . because in such a case the inferior tribunal has not brought itself within the terms of the statute taking it away."

This position of the Courts, which is more than a constructional conclusion, is supported by *Lederman, op. cit.* 34 Can. Bar Rev. at p. 1174, who blends it with his thesis that there is a guaranteed core of jurisdiction that must be reposed in superior courts as against administrative tribunals.

It can hardly be reconciled, however, with *Woodward v. Minister of Finance*, [1972] C.T.C. 385, [1972] 5 W.W.R. 581, 27 D.L.R. (3d) 608, (Can.) where a statutory formula enacted by the British Columbia legislature was held to make the Minister's determination immune to challenge even for want of jurisdiction over objections that it was *ultra vires* under sections 96-100 of the British North America Act.

Although this asserted constitutional guarantee of a reviewing power on questions of jurisdiction has not been as positively asserted in relation to preclusive legislation respecting decisions of inferior courts (see, for example, *Re Ambeau* (1964), 46 D.L.R. (2d) 517, where a statute denying *certiorari* was applied literally with respect to an order of a Family Court Judge), there was an attempt to extend it even further in respect of administrative boards by invoking s. 96 of the *British North America Act* to deny finality to the determination of questions of law by such boards. In *Regina v. Ontario Labour Relations Board, ex parte Ontario Food Terminal Board*, [1963] 2 O.R. 91, 38 D.L.R. (2d) 530 it was, moreover, said that:

"When the question of jurisdiction or any other question of pure law is raised in a proceeding before a tribunal . . . constituted (under provincial legislation), the proceeding should be stayed until such question has been finally determined by a Court of competent jurisdiction."

Not only has this latter position been rejected in other cases (see *Regina v. Ontario Labour Relations Board, ex parte Taylor*, [1964] 1 O.R. 173, 41 D.L.R. (2d) 456, aff'd [1964] 1 O.R. 207, 42 D.L.R. (2d) 320; *Re Armstrong Transport and Ontario Labour Relations Board*, [1964] 1 O.R. 358, 42 D.L.R. (2d) 217), but the supposed limitation of s. 96 of the *British North America Act* has been rejected by the Supreme Court of Canada. In *Farrell v. Workmen's Compensation Board and A.-G. B.C.*, [1962] S.C.R. 48, 31 D.L.R. (2d) 177, 37 W.W.R. 39 the Supreme Court was concerned, *inter alia,* with an attack on the validity of s. 76(1) of the *Workmen's Compensation Act*, R.S.B.C. 1948, c. 370 (a privative enactment covering questions of fact and law); the attack was two pronged: (1) that the Legislature had no power to deny access to the Courts by prohibiting review of questions of law; and (2) that such prohibitory legislation in favour of decisions of an administrative board contravened s. 96 of the *British North America Act*. Judson J., for a unanimous Court, adverted to the fact that the objection based on s. 96 was abandoned and he commented that in view of the cases "it is very questionable whether there could be any profitable argument on this point", and he concluded as follows:

"If an argument based upon s. 96 of the *B.N.A. Act* is untenable, the other argument based upon right of access to the courts falls with it. Its rejection as far as this Board is concerned is implicit in the judgments in the *Dominion Canners* case ([1923] S.C.R. 46, [1923] 1 D.L.R. 551) and in the *Alcyon* case ([1961] S.C.R. 299, 27 D.L.R. (2d) 775). The restrictions on the legislative power of the Province to confer jurisdiction on Boards must be derived by implication from the provisions of s. 96 of the *B.N.A.* Act. Short of an infringement of this section, if the legislation is otherwise within the provincial power, there is no constitutional rule against the enactment of s. 76(1)."

Having regard to the *Farrell* case, there is no constitutional prohibition against vesting provincial administrative boards with final authority to determine questions of law involved in the exercise of jurisdiction committed to them. *Quaere,* whether it is equally open to a provincial legislature to deny curial power to examine administrative board decisions on so-called collateral matters whose determination is a precondition of their otherwise admitted jurisdiction! See *Re Kinnaird v. Workmen's Compensation Board* (1962), 34 D.L.R. (2d) 110, 39 W.W.R. 177. See, generally, *Laskin, Note,* Provincial Administrative Tribunals and Judicial Power—The Exaggeration of Section 96 of the *British North America Act,* (1963) 41 Can. Bar Rev. 446.

May then a provincial legislature properly withdraw jurisdiction from a "superior" court and vest it in a county court? Would that involve a violation of s. 99 of the *B.N.A. Act* which gives only superior Court Judges tenure during good behaviour? Or, would there be an appointment within s. 96? See the *Adoption Act* case, *supra.* There are many illustrations of provincial legislation conferring on county courts concurrent jurisdiction with superior courts: see, for example, *Conveyancing and Law of Property Act,* R.S.O. 1970, c. 85, s. 38; *Vendors and Purchasers Act,* R.S.O. 1970, c. 478, s. 3.

Is the Dominion under any enforceable duty to appoint Judges to Courts established by a Province? Or, is it under any enforceable duty to provide their salaries as is prescribed by s. 100 of the *B.N.A. Act?* Is it competent for Parliament to reduce the salaries of existing Judges of provincial superior courts? See *Valin v. Langlois* (1879), 3 S.C.R. 1, at p. 81; and see *Lederman, op. cit.* 34 Can. Bar Rev. at pp. 1160-1166. Is it competent for a Province to prescribe an oath of office to be taken by a federally-appointed Judge? See *Re Law Society of Upper Canada and Robinette,* [1954] O.R. 349, [1954] 2 D.L.R. 692.

Are ss. 96-100 of the *B.N.A. Act* protected against amendment by the Parliament of Canada acting under s. 91(1) of the *B.N.A. Act?* Was it obligatory to go to the British Parliament to amend the original s. 99 to provide for compulsory retirement of provincial superior court Judges at age 75?

LABOUR RELATIONS BOARD OF SASKATCHEWAN v. JOHN EAST IRON WORKS LTD.

In the Privy Council. [1949] A.C. 134, [1948] 4 D.L.R. 673, [1948] 2 W.W.R. 1055.

Appeal from a judgment of the Saskatchewan Court of Appeal, [1948] 1 D.L.R. 652, [1948] 1 W.W.R. 81, quashing certain orders of the Saskatchewan Labour Relations Board on the ground that

s. 5(e) of the *Trade Union Act, 1944* (Sask. 2nd sess.), c. 69 was *ultra vires*.

LORD SIMONDS: . . . The facts of the case upon which the question arises are not in dispute and can be shortly stated.

On May 15, 1947, the respondent, John East Iron Works Ltd., which carries on business in Saskatchewan, dismissed from its employment six of its employees. Thereupon the United Steel Workers of America, a trade union, complaining that the respondent in dismissing these employees had been guilty of an unfair labour practice within the meaning of s. 8(1) (e) of the Act applied to the appellant, the Labour Relations Board of Saskatchewan, for orders requiring the respondent to reinstate them and to pay them the monetary loss suffered by them by reason of their dismissal. On the 10th, 11th and 12th June, 1947, the union's applications were heard by the appellant Board and in the course of the hearing the application in respect of one of the six employees was withdrawn. Both the union and the respondent appeared by counsel before the appellant Board and called evidence. The appellant Board, having heard evidence and argument, found that the respondent had discriminated "against each of the five employees in regard to tenure of employment with a view to discouraging membership in or activity in or for a labour organization (the applicant trade union)" and had discharged them contrary to the provisions of the Act.

On July 8, 1947, the appellant Board issued orders requiring the respondent to reinstate each of the five employees and to pay each of them the sum of $200.80, being the sum which each of them would have received for his services if he had remained in the employment of the respondent continuously from May 23, 1947 (up to which date he had been paid) until the date of that decision.

On November 6, 1947, the respondent filed a notice of motion in the Court of Appeal for Saskatchewan giving notice of intention to move the Court for an order quashing the orders of the appellant Board. The notice stated six grounds of application of which only one has been considered by the Court of Appeal and by their Lordships. That ground is that the Act in so far as it purports (a) to make the orders of the appellant Board enforceable as orders of the Court of King's Bench, and (b) to give to the appellant Board the power to make any order under s. 5(e) of the Act is *"ultra vires* of the Legislature of Saskatchewan as being legislation setting up a Superior, District or County Court or tribunal analogous thereto, the Judges or members of which are not appointed by the Governor-General of Canada in Council and as purporting to confer judicial power upon a body not so appointed."

On December 15, 1947, the Court of Appeal . . . upholding this appeal, gave judgment quashing the orders of the appellant Board. Hence this appeal to His Majesty in Council.

It is now necessary to recur to the terms of the Act the validity of which is impeached, but before doing so it is proper to recall the salient provisions of the *B.N.A. Act.* Under that Act, while by s. 92

there was exclusively reserved to the provincial Legislatures *legislative* power in respect of "(14) The Administration of Justice in the Province, including the Constitution, Maintenance, and Organization of Provincial Courts, both of Civil and of Criminal Jurisdiction, and including Procedure in Civil matters in those Courts", yet by Part VII, entitled "Judicature", the following provisions are made, which must be stated in full:

"S. 96. The Governor General shall appoint the Judges of the Superior, District, and County Courts in each Province, except those of the Courts of Probate in Nova Scotia and New Brunswick.

"S. 97. Until the Laws relative to Property and Civil Rights in Ontario, Nova Scotia, and New Brunswick, and the Procedure of the Courts in those Provinces, are made uniform, the Judges of the Courts of those Provinces appointed by the Governor General shall be selected from the respective Bars of those Provinces.

"S. 98. The Judges of the Courts of Quebec shall be selected from the Bar of that Province.

"S. 99. The Judges of the Superior Courts shall hold Office during good Behaviour, but shall be removable by the Governor General on Address of the Senate and House of Commons.

"S. 100. The Salaries, Allowances, and Pensions of the Judges of the Superior, District, and County Courts (except the Courts of Probate in Nova Scotia and New Brunswick), and of the Admiralty Courts in Cases where the Judges thereof are for the Time being paid by Salary, shall be fixed and provided by the Parliament of Canada."

It is in the application of these sections to the constitution and functions of the appellant Board that the problem lies which their Lordships have to determine and they would at the outset emphasize that its solution is not to be found by answering the question whether in certain of its functions the appellant Board exercises judicial power. It may do so and yet have constitutional validity. For, whatever doubts may at one time have been entertained, two propositions cannot now be challenged (1) that it is not only Courts which are designated "Superior" or "District" or "County" Courts that are within the ambit of the sections that have been cited, (2) that not all tribunals which exercise judicial power are within their ambit. It is this consideration that led the respondent in challenging the orders made by the appellant Board to use the expression "a tribunal analogous t' ereto", thus echoing the language used by Lord Atkin in deliveri g the opinion of their Lordships in *Toronto v. York*. [1938] A.C. 415. The question for determination is therefore a double one (a) whether the appellant Board exercises judicial power and (b), if so, whether in that exercise it is a tribunal analogous to a Superior, District or County Court.

The Act, as amended by c. 108 of the Statutes of 1945, c. 98 of the Statutes of 1946 and c. 102 of the Statutes of 1947, had as its original title "An act respecting Trade Unions and the Right of Employees to organize in Trade Unions of their own choosing for the Purpose of Bargaining Collectively with their Employers". Herein its purpose is apparent, a purpose, it may be observed, that would have sounded strange to the ears of the Legislature of 1867.

Section 2 contains certain definitions of which the following may be noted: [The Board here quoted the definitions of "bargaining collectively"; "board"; "collective bargaining agreement"; and "employee".] . . .

Section 3 gives employees the right to organize in trade unions and to bargain collectively through representatives of their own choosing and provides that the representatives selected for the purpose of bargaining collectively by the majority of employees in a unit appropriate for such purpose shall be the exclusive representatives of all employees in such unit for the purpose of bargaining collectively.

Section 4 (which is all important for the purpose of this appeal) prescribes that there shall be a Board to be known as the Labour Relations Board composed of seven members appointed by the Lieutenant-Governor in Council at such salaries or remuneration as he deems fit, that the Lieutenant-Governor in Council shall name a Chairman and Vice-Chairman of the Board, and that the members of the Board shall be equally representative of organized employees and employers, and, if the Lieutenant-Governor in Council deems it desirable, of the general public. The same section lays down rules of procedure for the Board.

Section 5 defines the power of the Board. It has power to make orders

"(a) determining whether the appropriate unit of employees for the purpose of bargaining collectively shall be an employer unit, craft unit, plant unit or a subdivision thereof or some other unit;

"(b) determining what trade union, if any, represents a majority of employees in an appropriate unit of employees;

"(c) requiring an employer to bargain collectively;

"(d) requiring any person to refrain from violations of this Act or from engaging in any unfair labour practice;

"(e) requiring an employer to reinstate any employee discharged contrary to the provisions of this Act and to pay such employee the monetary loss suffered by reason of such discharge;

"(f) requiring an employer to disestablish a company dominated organization;

"(g) rescinding or amending any order or decision of the board."

Sections 6 and 7 give directions as to the mode of ascertaining what trade union represents a majority of employees in an appropriate unit.

Section 8 defines in great detail what is an unfair labour practice for (1) an employer or his agent and (2) an employee or any person acting on behalf of a labour organization respectively. It is necessary for the present purpose to refer only to s-s. (1)(e) [am. 1947, c. 102, s. 4(1)] by which it is made an unfair labour practice for an employer or his agent: "To discriminate in regard to hiring or tenure of employment or any term or condition of employment or to use coercion or intimidation of any kind with a view to encouraging or discouraging membership in or activity in or for a labour organization or participation of any kind in a proceeding under this Act; and if an employer or employer's agent discharges an employee from his employment and it is alleged by a trade union that such employer or employer's agent has thereby committed an unfair labour practice within the meaning of this clause, it shall be presumed, unless the contrary is proved, that such employer or employer's agent has discriminated against such employee" in manner aforesaid.

Section 9 provides that a certified copy of any order or decision of the Board shall within one week be filed in the office of the Registrar of the Court of King's Bench and shall thereupon be enforceable as a judgment or order of the Court, but the Board may nevertheless rescind or vary any such order.

Section 10 [am. 1947, c. 102, s. 5(1), (3)] provides (1) that in any application to the Court arising out of the failure of any person to comply with the terms of any order filed in pursuance of s. 9, the Court may refer to the Board any question as to the compliance or non-compliance of such person or persons with the order of the Board and (2) that the application to enforce any order of the Board may be made to the Court by and in the name of the Board, any trade union affected or any interested person, and upon such application being heard the Court shall be bound absolutely by the findings of the Board and shall make such order or orders as may be necessary to cause every party with respect to whom the application is made to comply with the order of the Board and (3) that the Board may in its own name appeal from any judgment, decision or order of any Court affecting any of its orders or decisions.

Section 11 provides for the imposition of penalties on any person who takes part in, aids, abets, counsels or procures any unfair labour practice, s. 12 for the appointment by the Lieutenant-Governor in Council in certain events of the controller of a business, and s. 13 for the making of rules and regulations.

Section 14 gives to the Board and the members thereof the power of a Commissioner under the *Public Inquiries Act* with liberty to receive and accept such evidence and information on oath, affidavit or otherwise as in its discretion it may deem fit and proper whether admissible as evidence in a Court of law or not.

Finally, s. 15 enacts that there shall be no appeal from an order or decision of the Board under the Act and that the Board shall have full power to determine any question of fact necessary to its jurisdiction and that its proceedings, orders and decisions shall not be reviewable by any Court of law or by any certiorari, mandamus, prohibition, injunction or other proceeding whatsoever.

Their Lordships have thought it proper to set out in some detail the relevant provisions of the impugned Act inasmuch as upon the question that they must determine it is inevitable that fine distinctions should be drawn. The borderland in which judicial and administrative functions overlap is a wide one and the boundary is the more difficult to define in the case of a body such as the appellant Board, the greater part of whose functions are beyond doubt in the administrative sphere. Nor can a more difficult question be posed (but their Lordships can find no easier test) than to ask whether one Court is "analogous" to another.

The question for determination has been stated as a double one. And so logically it is. For it should first be asked whether the appellant Board when it makes an order under s. 5(e) of the Act is exercising judicial power. If it is not, then it is not a Court at all and cannot be a "Superior, District or County Court," or a Court analogous thereto.

Their Lordships, however, think it unnecessary finally to answer this question. Without attempting to give a comprehensive definition of judicial power, they accept the view that its broad features are accurately stated in that part of the judgment of Griffith C.J. in *Huddart, Parker & Co. Proprietary Ltd. v. Moorehead* (1908), 8 C.L.R. 330 at p. 357, which was approved by this Board in *Shell Co. of Australia Ltd. v. Federal Com'r of Taxation*, [1931] A.C. 275. Nor do they doubt, as was pointed out in the latter case, that there are many positive features which are essential to the existence of judicial power, yet by themselves are not conclusive of it, or that any combination of such features will fail to establish judicial power if, as is a common characteristic of so-called administrative tribunals, the ultimate decision may be determined not merely by the application of legal principles to ascertained facts but by considerations of policy also.

Whether in the present case the power exercised by the appellant Board under s. 5(e) of the Act is a judicial power, their Lordships do not decide. For the elements in its constitution and functions which at least make it doubtful whether it is in the strict sense a Court exercising judicial power at all appear to lead conclusively to the opinion that it is not a Superior, District or County Court or a Court analogous thereto.

It is a truism that the conception of the judicial function is inseparably bound up with the idea of a suit between parties, whether between Crown and subject or between subject and subject, and that it is the duty of the Court to decide the issue between those parties, with whom alone it rests to initiate or defend or compromise the proceedings. Here at once a striking departure from the traditional conception of a Court may be seen in the functions of the appellant Board. For, as the Act contemplates and the Rules made under it prescribe, any trade union, any employer, any employers' association or any other person directly concerned may apply to the Board for an order to be made (a) requiring any person to refrain from a violation of the Act or from engaging in an unfair labour practice, (b) requiring an employer to reinstate an employee discharged contrary to the provisions of the Act and to pay such employee the monetary loss suffered by reason of such discharge, (c) requiring an employer to disestablish a company-dominated organization or (d) requiring two or more of the said things to be done. Other Rules provide for the discharge by the Board of other functions. It is sufficient to refer only to (b) *supra*, which clearly illustrates that, while the order relates solely to the relief to be given to an individual, yet the controversy may be raised by others without his assent, and, it may be, against his will, for the solution of some far-reaching industrial conflict. It may be possible to describe an issue thus raised as a *lis* and to regard its determination as the exercise of judicial power. But it appears to their Lordships that such an issue is indeed remote from those which at the time of Confederation occupied the Superior or District or County Courts of Upper Canada.

In the Court of Appeal for Saskatchewan the learned Chief Justice (in whose opinion the other Judges concurred) accepted the view that the Board exercised a judicial power analogous to that of the Courts named on the ground that such Courts always had jurisdiction in connection with the enforcement of contracts of hiring and awarding damages for the breaches thereof. But, as their Lordships think, this view ignores the wider aspects of the matter. The jurisdiction of the Board under s. 5(e) is not invoked by the employee for the enforcement of his contractual rights: those, whatever they may be, he can assert elsewhere. But his reinstatement, which the terms of his contract of employment might not by themselves justify, is the means by which labour practices regarded as unfair are frustrated and the policy of collective bargaining as a road to industrial peace is secured. It is in the light of this new conception of industrial relations that the question to be determined by the Board must be viewed, and, even if the issue so raised can be regarded as a justiciable one, it finds no analogy in those issues which were familiar to the Courts in 1867.

This matter may be tested in another way. If the appellant Board is a Court analogous to the Superior and other Courts mentioned in s. 96 of the *B.N.A. Act*, its members must not only be appointed by the Governor-General but must be chosen from the Bar of Saskatchewan. It is legitimate therefore to ask whether, if trade unions had in 1867 been recognized by the law, if collective bargaining had then been the accepted postulate of industrial peace, if, in a word, the economic and social outlook had been the same in 1867 as it became in 1944, it would not have been expedient to establish just such a specialized tribunal as is provided by s. 4 of the Act. It is as good a test as another of "analogy" to ask whether the subject-matter of the assumed justiciable issue makes it desirable that the Judges should have the same qualifications as those which distinguish the Judges of Superior or other Courts. And it appears to their Lordships that to this question only one answer can be given. For wide experience has shown that, though an independent President of the tribunal may in certain cases be advisable, it is essential that its other members should bring an experience and knowledge acquired extra-judicially to the solution of their problems. The members of the Board are to be equally representative of organized employees and employers and in a certain event of the general public. That does not mean that bias or interest will lead them to act otherwise than judicially, so far as that word connotes a standard of conduct, but it assuredly means that the subject-matter is such as profoundly to distinguish such a tribunal from the Courts mentioned in s. 96.

It is relevant too to consider the alleged judicial function of the Board under s. 5(e) of the Act in relation to its other duties. It is not impossible, as the case of *Toronto v. York*, [1938] A.C. 415, illustrates, for a body to be validly established for administrative purposes and yet to be unconstitutionally clothed with a judicial power. It is not therefore conclusive of the constitutionality of the Board that in the main it is an administrative instrument and that its judicial function is designed to implement administrative policy. But, once more seeking an analogy with the Courts mentioned in s. 96, their Lordships must observe that the feature of the Board's constitution, which is conspicuously shown in the power vested in it by s. 10(3) of the Act to appeal in its own name from any judgment of any Court affecting any of its orders or decisions, emphasises the dissimilarity from those Courts.

On behalf of the respondent stress was laid upon the provisions of s. 15 of the Act. It was urged that a tribunal, whose decisions were not subject to appeal and whose proceedings were not reviewable by any Court of law or by any *certiorari* or other proceedings whatsoever, must be regarded as a "Superior" Court or a Court analogous thereto. But the same considerations which make it expedient to set up a specialized tribunal may make it inexpedient that that tribunal's decisions should be reviewed by an ordinary Court. It does not for that reason become itself a "Superior" Court. Nor must its immunity from *certiorari* or other proceedings be pressed too far. It does not fall to their Lordships upon the present appeal to determine the scope of that provision but it seems clear that it would not avail the tribunal if it purported to exercise a jurisdiction wider than that specifically entrusted to it by the Act.

At this stage their Lordships reach the conclusion that the jurisdiction exercisable by the Board is not such as to constitute it a Court within s. 96 of the *B.N.A. Act*. They do not think it necessary to consider whether it is a jurisdiction more nearly analogous to that exercised at the time of Confederation by Justices of the Peace—a matter to which much argument was directed—nor would they pursue the comparison with the jurisdiction of the Workmen's Compensation Board, which was also pressed upon them by counsel. It is sufficient to say that it is not in their opinion analogous to that of a Superior, District or County Court.

But before parting with the case their Lordships think it proper to observe upon two cases which have recently come before them, *O. Martineau & Sons Ltd. v. Montreal*, [1932] A.C. 113, and *Toronto v. York*, *supra*, of which passing mention has already been made, and more particularly also upon *Reference Re Adoption Act, etc.* [1938] S.C.R. 398, in which will be found a judgment of Sir Lyman P. Duff, lately Chief Justice of Canada, so exhaustive and penetrating both in historical retrospect and in analysis of this topic, that their Lordships would respectfully adopt it as their own, so far as it is relevant to the present appeal.

In *Martineau's* case, where the question was as to the constitutionality of the Quebec Public Service Commission in that its members exercised certain judicial functions but were not appointed by the Governor-General, it would appear that the decision of this Board in favour of the validity of the awards made by the Commission was largely determined by the fact that this Commission was itself the successor of a body which was in existence at the date of Confederation and then exercised a similar jurisdiction. Apart therefore from any other consideration its constitutionality appeared to be preserved by s. 129 of the *B.N.A. Act*. But in the course of delivering the judgment of the Board Lord Blanesburgh, referring to a decision of Drake J. in a British Columbia case, *Burk v. Tunstall* (1890), 2 B.C.R. 12, approved the following words used by that learned Judge: "But in the section itself, after the special Courts thus named, the Courts of Probate in Nova Scotia and New Brunswick are excepted from the operation of the clause, thus showing that section 96 was intended to be general in its operation."

It appears from cases cited upon the present appeal and from the judgment of Duff C.J.C. in *Re Adoption Act* that this passage has been made the basis for the proposition that it is incompetent for provincial Legislatures to legislate for the appointment of any officer of any provincial Court exercising other than ministerial functions. Their Lordships agree with the learned Chief Justice in thinking that this is a wholly unwarranted view of *Martineau's* case, which was directed neither to Courts of summary jurisdiction of any kind nor to tribunals established for the exercise of jurisdiction of a kind unknown in 1867.

In *Toronto v. York* it was decided that the Ontario Municipal Board was primarily an administrative body but that certain sections of the Act by which it was established purported to clothe it with the functions of a Court and to vest in it judicial powers and that *pro tanto,* since its members were not appointed by the Governor-General, the Act was invalid. But it is clear that in that case the question did not arise for argument, as it arises in the case under appeal, whether, upon the assumption that judicial power was vested in the Board, the Board was thereby brought within the ambit of s. 96. It is true that at an early stage in the judgment delivered by Lord Atkin the question was asked "Is, then, the Municipal Board of Ontario a Superior Court, or a tribunal analogous thereto?" But it seems to have been assumed by their Lordships that if the power vested in it was judicial, it was such a tribunal, for (as Duff C.J.C. pointed out in the case cited) it is obvious that their Lordships did not consider, because presumably there was no occasion to do so, the distinction between the Courts that come within the intendment of s. 96 of the *B.N.A. Act* and other Courts and tribunals.

Finally, in *Re Adoption Act* it fell to the Supreme Court of Canada to determine the constitutionality of a number of Acts which beyond question purported to vest judicial power in various judicial officers to be designated by the Lieutenant-Governor in Council. In point of substantive law the subject-matter of these Acts lay within the legislative power of the Provinces just as does the subject-matter of the present appeal. The question then was, whether the judicial bodies thus established were Courts within the intendment of s. 96, and the answer was in the negative. It was sufficient for the purpose of that case for the learned Chief Justice to pose this question: "Does the jurisdiction conferred upon magistrates under these statutes broadly conform to a type of jurisdiction generally exercisable by Courts of summary jurisdiction rather than the jurisdiction exercised by Courts within the purview of s. 96?" and, answering that question in the affirmative, to pronounce for the validity of the statutes. And, if in this case the same alternative was presented to their Lordships, they might well answer it in the same way, for at least from the earliest times the administrative and judicial duties of Justices of the Peace have been curiously blended: that feature a Court of summary jurisdiction has in common with the appellant Board. But they would prefer to put the question in another way, which may be more helpful in the decisions of similar issues, *viz.*: "Does the jurisdiction conferred by the Act upon the appellant Board broadly conform to the type of jurisdiction exercised by the Superior, District or County Courts?" In their view, for the reasons already stated, it does not do so. They do not think it necessary to say whether it conforms more nearly to any other jurisdiction existing in 1867.

Their Lordships conclude that the judgment of the Court of Appeal for Saskatchewan cannot be maintained. But that does not end the matter. For apart from the plea of unconstitutionality of the Act the respondent claimed to have the orders of the appellant Board quashed on two other grounds (a) that in their assessment of the monetary loss suffered by the discharged employees the Board proceeded upon an error in law so fundamental as to deprive the Board of jurisdiction, and (b) that the conduct of the Chairman of the Board disqualified him by bias or the reasonable apprehension of bias from taking part in the enquiry and the Board as constituted at the hearing was thereby also disqualified. The Court of Appeal, being in favour of the respondent on the constitutional plea, did not think it necessary to consider these grounds and their Lordships are not prepared to do so until at least the Court of Appeal has pronounced upon them. Therefore, while the present appeal must be allowed, the case must be remitted to the Court of Appeal for rehearing upon the footing that the Act is not *ultra vires* and that the Board and its members are constitutionally established. Their Lordships will humbly advise His Majesty accordingly.

Appeal allowed.

[On the re-hearing by the Saskatchewan Court of Appeal, the impugned orders of the Board were again quashed on the ground, *inter alia,* that the Board had failed to take into consideration the principle of mitigation: see [1949] 3 D.L.R. 51, [1949] 1 W.W.R. 842. That Court refused leave to appeal to the Supreme Court of Canada: [1949] 3 D.L.R. 488, [1949] 2 W.W.R. 39. The Supreme Court itself also refused leave, but for want of jurisdiction:

[1949] S.C.R. 677, [1949] 3 D.L.R. 851. The issues in the *John East* case and its relevance for s. 96 are discussed by *Shumiatcher,* Section 96 of the *B.N.A. Act* Re-examined, (1949) 27 Can. Bar Rev. 131.]

A. E. DUPONT v. INGLIS

In the Supreme Court of Canada. [1958] S.C.R. 535, 14 D.L.R. (2d) 417.

Appeal from a judgment of the Ontario Court of Appeal, [1957] O.R. 377, 8 D.L.R. (2d) 193, reversing a judgment of Ferguson J., [1957] O.R. 193, 8 D.L.R. (2d) 26, and directing prohibition to the Ontario Mining Commissioner in respect of the hearing of an appeal from an order of the Mining Recorder.

The judgment of the Court was delivered by

RAND J.: The issue here goes to the constitutional validity of a tribunal established under the *Mining Act,* R.S.O. 1950, c. 236, as amended by 1956, c. 47, s. 7. The attack is made on the ground that the tribunal is or, in the proceedings out of which this appeal arises, was attempting to exercise the jurisdiction of a Court within the meaning of s. 96 of the *B.N.A. Act.*

The *Mining Act* is primarily legislation providing for the administration of mining resources owned by the Province in the way of promoting their development and exploitation in private ownership, according to provisions, Rules and Regulations contained in the Act or made by the Lieutenant-Governor in Council. The administration is under the general direction of the Minister of Mines, with a deputy, a departmental organization and a number of statutory officers.

The Act specifies in detail the acts to be performed by licensees as conditions of rights reaching ultimately to a patent in fee simple or a renewable lease of either land including minerals or the latter alone. Licences are obtainable by any person over 18 years of age on payment of a fee. The initial step is the staking of a claim by means of posts set down in a prescribed manner on which certain information is inscribed. By s. 57: "Substantial compliance as nearly as circumstances will reasonably permit with the requirements of this Act as to the staking out of mining claims shall be sufficient." Within a fixed time the staking is to be recorded at the office of the Recorder for the district within which the claim lies. A sketch or plan of the claim showing the posts and distances is forwarded with the application together with other information sufficient to enable the Recorder to indicate the location of the claim on the office map, and to record the day and hour when staked, the date of application and the inscriptions or markings made. Required also is a certificate, verified by affidvait, that there was nothing on the lands to indicate that they were not open for staking, such as buildings, clearings or improvements. Particulars of every application which the Recorder "deems to be in accordance with this Act" are entered unless a prior application is already recorded and subsisting for the lands or "any substantial portion" of them. The application, with its accompanying documents, is filed with the office records; and the recording is to be deemed to be made as of the moment when the application is received in the office. Within six months, the licensee is required to affix to each of the corner posts of the claim metal tags, supplied by the Recorder, impressed with the numbers and letters of the claim. On a written report by an inspector that the tags have not been so attached, the Recorder is to cancel the claim, and to notify the licensee accordingly.

In case of rejection, if the licensee desires it, the Recorder, under s. 61(2), shall "file" the application pending adjudication of its sufficiency. For that purpose, the licensee must, within 60 days, bring the matter before the Recorder or the Commissioner, but this step is not deemed a "dispute" of a recorded claim, to which particular reference appears later.

Up to this point the functions of the Recorder are ministerial and administrative, that is, possessing some measure of discretion. But in the competition of licensees, challenges to alleged stakings and other required acts are inevitable which must be settled without delay, more or less informally, in some proximity to the situs of the claims, and by persons made familiar by experience with the substance of those practical details. They are what the history and the exigencies of prospecting and mineral discovery have shown to be best suited to the orderly and efficient utilization of the resources, and in large measure are embodied in the statute. At the same time that experience has furnished a similar acquaintance with the practices, attitudes and tendencies of those who push discovery into these remote and difficult regions.

Provision is therefore made for filing with the Recorder a "dispute" alleging the invalidity of a recorded claim; if the disputant claims to be entitled to be recorded in whole or part, a note of the filing is entered on the record of the claim. Unless it is otherwise ordered by the Commissioner or a transfer is made to the Commissioner by the Recorder, the controversy is, in the first instance, decided by the Recorder whose decision, unless an appeal is taken to the Commissioner, is, by s. 123(5) [re-enacted 1956, c. 47, s. 7] "final and binding". By s. 124 [re-enacted 1956, c. 47, s. 7] the Recorder "may give directions for the . . . carrying on of proceedings before him, and in so doing he shall adopt the cheapest and simplest methods of determining the questions raised before him".

Section 63 [re-enacted by 1954, c. 53, s. 3] provides for a "certificate of record". This certificate is issued after a claim has been recorded for 60 days or more and the Recorder, among other things, "is satisfied that the requirements of the Act have been met". In the absence of mistake or fraud, it is conclusive evidence that, except for work to be done on the claim, those requirements have been met, but it may be set aside by the Commissioner on the grounds mentioned. When a certificate of work has been granted the conditions of a right to obtain a title have been met. In cases of forfeiture, the Commissioner may give relief on such terms as he considers just.

The Commissioner is appointed by the Lieutenant-Governor in Council and his authority touches the entire administration. He may decide any claim, question, dispute or other matter and so far supersede the Recorder. On appeal from the latter, the Commissioner is to make "such order in the premises as he deems just": s. 127 [re-enacted 1956, c. 47, s. 7]. He may require or admit new evidence, or may retry the matter; he is to decide questions "without unnecessary formality", select the place deemed most convenient for the parties, and his decisions on subsidiary issues are final and not appealable. He may obtain the assistance of "engineers, surveyors or other scientific persons" to examine the property and make such use of their opinions or reports as he thinks proper: s. 131 [re-enacted 1956, c. 47, s. 7]. He may view the property and make use of any special skill or knowledge he possesses, in which case he is to make a statement of the fact sufficiently full to enable a judgment to be made of the weight to be given it. When the parties consent in writing, he may proceed wholly on a view and his decision so based is, again, final. The order made by him, with the evidence, exhibits, statements, reports and reasons, is filed in the department or the office of the Recorder as he directs. Subject to the provisions for finality, by s. 144 [re-enacted 1956, c. 47, s. 7] an appeal from a decision by him lies to the Court of Appeal.

In the issue before us, some months after the recording of an alleged staking by the respondents, an application to record for the same area was made by the appellants; but in view of the prior entry the application was "filed". Following an inspector's adverse report on the respondents' claims, an enquiry was held by the Recorder, who found that the staking had not been made as alleged and expunged the record of it; at the same time he recorded the application of the appellants. On appeal to the "Judge", as under the existing legislation the appeal functionary was called, the dispute was aired *de novo;* but before decision, the statute was amended and a Commissioner was substituted for the Judge without affecting the appeal jurisdiction. Steps were then taken to reinstate the appeal before the Commissioner, upon which the respondents applied for a writ of prohibition. For the purposes of the issue of fact raised, Ferguson J. [8 D.L.R. (2d) 26, [1957] O.R. 193] held the appointment of the Commissioner to have been within the legislative authority of the Province and refused the writ. The Court of Appeal, speaking through Schroeder J.A. [8 D.L.R. (2d) 193, [1957] O.R. 377], took the view that the adjudication by the Commissioner infringed s. 96 of the *B.N.A. Act,* a view based largely, if not exclusively, on the fact of the provision for appeal from the Recorder to the Commissioner, and directed the writ to issue.

I think it desirable to enquire first into the real character and content of the rights which the statute creates and the means it furnishes to give them recognition. The statute is dealing primarily with Crown lands; it would, in my opinion, be within Provincial power to dispose of that land, over which legislative jurisdiction is exclusive, on any terms or conditions to be determined by, or in the absolute judgment or discretion of, any functionary whatever; the award or adjudication, in that case, would itself be a constituent element in the rights created. Does the Act here evidence such an intendment? Its language creates rights but *sub modo*; consistently with equality of treatment, tribunals have been set up with officers, *ex officio* Justices of the Peace, to make determinations while the land still remains within the title of the Crown. The Recorder is an officer of the Department; the Commissioner, although not declared a department officer is a statutory officer. His decisions on disputes are only part of a general supervising function. This comprehensive administration taken with the provisions expressly excluding resort to the ordinary Courts, except by appeal under s. 144, indicates that the determinations by the statutory officers are integrated in the rights provided; that, including those given by the Court of Appeal, they inhere in the rights as conditions of their creation: *Florence Mining Co. v. Cobalt Lake Mining Co.* (1910), 54 O.L.R. 474 at p. 475 where Lord Collings uses this language: "They [the plaintiffs] have completely failed to establish their claim to have made a discovery within the provisions of the *Mines Act* to the satisfaction of the officer charged with the duty of seeing that the regulations are duly observed."

The first Provincial mining statute was the *Gold Mining Act*, 1864 (Can.), c. 9. The machinery set up, though not so elaborate, was, for such an issue as that here, in substance what is now provided. By s. 3 the officers, likewise Justices of the Peace, had power to "settle summarily all disputes as to extent or boundary of claims, use of water, access thereto, damage by licensees to others, forfeitures of licenses, and generally to settle all difficulties, matters or questions which may arise under this Act" and no case was to be removed into any Court by *certiorari*. The Superior Courts, those mentioned in s. 96 of the *B.N.A. Act* were excluded from any feature of that administration. The determinations of fact, so far as they might be taken as possessing a judicial quality, were made by Justices of the Peace, inferior tribunals. The practical competence called for and, by experience, acquired is of the character implied by Lord Simonds in *Labour Relations Board of Sask. v. John East Iron Works Ltd.*, [1948] 4 D.L.R. 673 at p. 682, [1949] A.C. 134 at p. 151 where he says: "It is as good a test as another of 'analogy' to ask whether the subject-matter of the assumed justiciable issue makes it desirable that the Judges should have the same qualifications as those which distinguish the Judges of Superior or other Courts."

The adjudications by the Recorder and the Commissioner are not to be treated in isolation; the special elements of experienced judgment and discretion are so bound up with those of any judicial and ministerial character that they make up an inseverable entirety of administration in the execution of the statute. To introduce into the regular Courts with their more deliberate and formal procedures what has become summary routine in disputes of such detail would create not only an anomalous feature of their jurisdiction but one of inconvenience both to their normal proceedings and to the expeditious accomplishment of the statute's purpose.

By s. 129 of the Confederation Act, all laws, Courts and all "legal Commissions, Powers, and Authorities, and all Officers, Judicial, Administrative, and Ministerial" existing in Ontario at the Union were continued subject to be repealed, abolished or altered by Parliament or Legislature according to the authority of each. Within this continuity was the *Gold Mining Act*; and the function of deciding the sufficiency of compliance with the statutory requirements, as, for example, of staking, by the officer, was either an integral part of the rights arising, or, if of a judicial character, of a type not then exercised by the Superior Courts.

If judicial power was conferred and it is to be held to be of the type exercised by Superior Courts, then either the officers under the Act, for all purposes of this administrative statute, would be required to be appointed by the Dominion, or the adjudicatory function notionally segregated and held to be beyond exercise by a Provincial appointee. That question would arise on the death or cesser of tenure of the functionary so continued in office. In the latter alternative those sections of the statute providing for the determination of disputes would at that moment automatically cease to have force, and resort, if any were open, would be to the Superior Courts: it would be a constitutional absurdity that the Dominion should appoint, in accordance with ss. 96, 99 and 100, the officer of such a tribunal for his role as adjudicator of incidental disputes and the Province appoint the same person for all other purposes. I cannot accept a view that produces such a result as the effect of s. 129.

The interpretation of s. 96 has been authoritatively given by this Court in *Reference re Adoption Act, etc.,* [1938] 3 D.L.R. 497, S.C.R. 398, 71 Can. C.C. 110 and by the Judicial Committee in *Martineau & Sons Ltd. v. Montreal,* [1932] 1 D.L.R. 353, A.C. 113, 52 Que. K.B. 542, and in *Labour Relations Bd. of Sask. v. John East Iron Works Ltd., supra.* The Province, under its authority over the administration of justice, including the establishment of Courts, may and is in duty bound to maintain judicial tribunals and define their jurisdiction. The restriction of s. 96, with ss. 99 and 100, provisions vital to the judicature of Canada, is confined to Courts endowed with jurisdiction conforming broadly to the type of that exercised in 1867 by the Courts mentioned in the section or tribunals analogous to them. A distinction is here necessary between the character of a tribunal and the type of judicial power, if any, exercised by it. If in essence an administrative organ is created as in *Toronto v. York Tp.,* [1938] 1 D.L.R. 593, A.C. 415, 1 All E.R. 601, 47 C.R.C. 361, there may be a question whether Provincial legislation has purported to confer upon it judicial power belonging exclusively to Courts within s. 96. Judicial power not of that type, such as that exercised by inferior Courts, can be conferred on a Provincial tribunal whatever its primary character; and where the administrative is intermixed with *ultra vires* judicial power, the further question arises of severability between what is valid and what invalid.

With the greatest respect to the Court of Appeal, I cannot take the fact of a right of appeal to have any significant bearing on the issue. The Commissioner, by the terms of the statute, is not strictly an appeal Court; his function in appeal is essentially the same as that of the Recorder, but on a review level; and its purpose is obviously to furnish the confirmation of a superior and here a possibly more independent functionary. That confirmation lies behind the appeal to the Court of Appeal, the precise nature or scope of which may call for some consideration. Since the Province can create and appoint Justices of inferior Courts, there is no reason in the nature of things why it cannot establish an inferior Court of review or appeal; it is the subject-matter rather than the apparatus for adjudication that is determinative. Appeals in criminal matters from Justices of the Peace to quarter sessions were established procedure prior to Confederation in Ontario, in which, also, an appeal was long provided to the Division Court, the Judge of which was appointed by the Province. In *Shell Co. of Australia Ltd. v. Federal Com'r of Taxation*, [1931] A.C. 275 at p. 295, Lord Sankey L.C. quotes with approval the reasons of Starke J. in the High Court (1926), 38 C.L.R. 153, from the judgment of which the appeal was taken: " 'A right of appeal in itself does not establish the vesting of judicial power either in the Commissioner or in a Board of Review'." And equally it does not of itself show judicial power of a Superior Court character within the meaning of s. 96. On the same page the Lord Chancellor quotes the definition of "judicial power" given by Griffith C.J. in *Huddart, Parker & Co. v. Moorehead* (1909), 8 C.L.R. 330 at p. 357 in which it is said: " 'The exercise of the power does not begin until some tribunal which has the power to give a binding and authoritative decision (whether subject to appeal or not) is called upon to take action.' "

It was contended that several provisions of the Act purported to confer jurisdiction over matters affecting private rights beyond the administration of Crown lands, and ss. 115 and 119 [re-enacted 1956, c. 47, s. 7] were cited. In the former no action is to be taken in any Court on any "matter or thing concerning any right, privilege or interest conferred by or under the authority of this Act". Section 118 [re-enacted 1956, c. 47, s. 7] expressly removes from the jurisdiction of the Commissioner any "power or authority to declare forfeited and void or to cancel or annul any Crown patent issued for lands, mining lands, mining claims or mining rights". This limits the scope of s. 115 to rights, privileges or interests arising up to the issue of patent. Confirmatory of that is the declaration by s. 66(1) of the interest of a licensee prior to the issue of a certificate of record as that only of a "licensee of the Crown" in the ordinary sense of the word "licensee", and after the issue and until patent, "a tenant at will of the Crown". These are preceded by the declaration that: "The staking out or the filing of an application for, or the recording of a mining claim, or all or any of such acts, shall not confer upon a licensee any right, title, interest or claim in or to the mining claim, *other than the right to proceed,* as in this Act provided to obtain a certificate of record and a patent from the Crown." (The italics are mine.)

In *Clarkson & Forgie v. Wishart & Myers*, [1913] A.C. 828, the "right to proceed" was held to be within the *Execution Act* and that a purchaser was entitled to be substituted as owner of that right; but as between the licensee and the Crown there is only the licence or tenancy.

Section 119 contemplates proceedings which involve private civil and property rights and provides that a party may apply for an order transferring the proceedings to the Supreme Court. I should say that once that situation appears an order should go unless the party applying is willing to accept the Commissioner as an arbitrator. By reason of its terms s. 119 is clearly a severable provision and would be so apart from the provision for transfer.

Other sections, by general suggestion, were said to be similarly tainted, but nothing was specifically pointed out which if encroaching on the judicial power of Superior Courts, was so bound up with valid jurisdiction as to drag the latter down with it. The precise issue raised in this proceeding, which alone is in question, is clearly within Provincial power and, contained in an administration statute with the scope of valid action clearly ascertainable, the separation of other encroachments, if any, would present no difficulty.

It was urged that the issue was in reality between the respondents and the individual appellants, but that confuses the matter. The question is the validity of the alleged first staking, and that is a matter between the licensee and the Crown. Its adjudication may affect a subsequent staking by another licensee; but there is no *vinculum juris* and no *lis* between the two licensees, and the disputant is before the tribunal only as he is permitted by the statute to have the claim of another put in question before the Recorder. In the enquiry the subsequent staking is irrelevant, and the decision should be the same as if no such action had taken place.

Under the statute immediately before the amendments in 1956, R.S.O. 1950, c. 236, the Judge, before whom the appeal here was brought, had been appointed by the Lieutenant-Governor in Council of Ontario. This was confirmed by a commission issued under an order of the Governor-General in Council. The purpose of the latter was to provide against the contingency that the appointment by the Province should be held to be *ultra vires*. The order of confirmation recites that in the view of His Excellency's Government the responsibility for the appointment did not rest with that Government and that the commission was to be for the purpose of confirming the appointment only so far as it was competent to His Excellency to do so. In my opinion the appointment by the Lieutenant-Governor was valid and the confirmatory action by the Governor-General in Council of no effect. . .

Appeal allowed.

[In *Re McLean Gold Mines Ltd. and A.-G. Ont.*, 54 O.L.R. 573, [1924] 1 D.L.R. 10, a case not mentioned by Rand J., the Ontario Appellate Division held that a provincially-appointed mining commissioner could not constitutionally be empowered to deal with disputes respecting mining claims, arising *before or after patent* between contesting claimants or between the Crown and a claimant. *Quaere,* whether the authority of this case is shaken by *Dupont v. Inglis?*

Work certificates issued in respect of certain mining leases were cancelled by the Minister of Mines under s. 271 of the *Placer-Mining Act,* R.S.B.C. 1948, c. 214, on being satisfied after investigation and report that they had been obtained in violation of the Act. *Held,* the Minister was discharging an administrative function with the management of lands and was not exercising a power which would be incompetent to him under s. 96 of the *B.N.A. Act.* The fact that he was authorized to cancel or make such orders as he deemed just, subject in either case to appeal to the Courts, did not alter the nature of his action: *Grevas v. The Queen* (1957), 10 D.L.R. (2d) 500, 23 W.W.R. 577.

In line with the attitude reflected in *Dupont v. Inglis,* is the judgment of the Supreme Court in *Brooks v. Pavlick,* [1964] S.C.R. 108, 42 D.L.R. (2d) 572, which applied the test of the *John East* case (*i.e.,* whether the jurisdiction in question was exercised by superior courts at 1867), and concluded that it was competent to a Province to invest the Master of Titles with jurisdiction to determine the validity of an objection to the boundary line on an application for the first registration of a title under the *Land Titles Act,* now R.S.O. 1960, c. 204, and consequently to decide whether a fee simple title should be registered for the land in question. Although the Master of Titles was obliged to act judicially in determining what documents should be registered on the title, and who should be protected in a guaranteed title, and who had the right to claim against the assurance fund created by the Act, he was not thereby discharging a function caught by s. 96 of the *B.N.A. Act.*

In *Rossignol and Rossignol v. Hart,* [1956] S.C.R. 314, 1 D.L.R. (2d) 705, a workman's claim for compensation for injury allegedly suffered in the course of employment was rejected by the Workmen's Compensation Board which held that no injury was in fact suffered. In a negligence action by the workman against a fellow employee, who had allegedly caused the injury complained of, a question was raised as to the binding effect of the Board's finding. On the assumption that the workmen's compensation statute made the finding conclusive (although in fact the Court held that it did not) the Supreme Court (per Rand J.) declared: "It would . . . in any case be a novel procedure that a claimant or a third party, employee or employer, must submit to the adjudication of such an administrative body on an essential element of his common law right or liability. It would in ordinary cases be *ultra vires* of the Province to confer that power on a provincial tribunal. Even assuming that the issue of negligence could ever be committed to an inferior Court, beyond petty jurisdiction, the Judges, for such purpose, must, by the Confederation Act, be of Dominion appointment".

In *Calgary & Edmonton Corp. Ltd. v. British American Oil Co.* (1963), 40 D.L.R. (2d) 964, 41 W.W.R. 413, aff'd 40 D.L.R. (2d) at p. 972, 44 W.W.R. 416, Milvain J. in the Court of first instance (the point not being taken on appeal) said: "I have doubt of the gravest character as to whether the Province can set up a tribunal with power to interpret contracts and so settle a dispute between the contracting parties as to the proper construction to be placed upon the agreements which bind them". Does the context in which such power is given make any difference?

Apart from any question involving s. 96 of the *B.N.A. Act,* there is no constitutional impropriety in a Dominion-Provincial Agreement, given legislative effect, by which the appointments to an administrative tribunal are made partly by the one government and partly by the other; *cf. Lake of the Woods Control Board Act,* 1921 (Can.), c. 10.

In an action against a municipality to restrain the pollution of a stream on plaintiff's land by defendant's sewage disposal plant, objection to the Court's jurisdiction was taken under s. 106(16) of the *Public Health Act,* R.S.O. 1950, c. 306 reading as follows: "The jurisdiction of the Ontario Municipal Board under this section [dealing with sewerage projects] shall be conclusive and all claims for injury or damages or any other matter arising under . . . this section relating to the construction by an urban municipality of a sewerage project in a township municipality shall be heard and determined by the Board". Is the objection tenable? See *Stephens v. Richmond Hill,* [1955] O.R. 806, [1955] 4 D.L.R. 572, aff'd on other grounds, [1956] O.R. 88, 1 D.L.R. (2d) 569.

A provincial statute authorized the passing of by-laws, with the approval of the Ontario Municipal Board, for the assumption by a metropolitan municipality of any land or building that it might require for police purposes and which was vested in any area or constituent municipality and at least 40 per cent. of which was used on a specified date for police force purposes in such area or constituent municipality. Any dispute or doubt as to whether any land or building was used at least 40 per cent. for police force purposes was to be determined, with final effect, by the Ontario Municipal Board. *Held,* while it was competent to require Board approval of a by-law, it was beyond provincial power to commit to the Board the determination of a question on which the jurisdiction to pass a by-law depended. It involved construction of a statute on which the legal right to retention of property depended: see *Forest Hill v. Metropolitan Toronto,* [1958] O.R. 254, 14 D.L.R. (2d) 136. *Quaere,* whether this is not merely committing to the Board determination of a "jurisdictional fact" which, at least in the first instance, may be vested in an administrative agency, although its determination may be reviewable!

The Ontario Municipal Board was a competent body to determine the award of compensation for loss of a utility franchise occasioned by municipal annexation; the adjustment of financial arrangements on account of amalgamation in 1867 was dealt with by arbitrators and not by courts. *Re Local Lines (Sudbury) Ltd. and Sudbury,* [1969] 2 O.R. 740, 6 D.L.R. (3d) 644.]

Note on Municipal Tax Assessment and Section 96—A Case Study

The illumination provided by the *Adoption Act* case and by the *John East* case has been but faintly admitted to the determination of a series of municipal assessment cases originating in Ontario. What is wanting in this area of decision is an explicit renunciation of *Toronto v. York,* [1938] A.C. 415, [1938] 1 D.L.R. 593, [1938] 1 W.W.R. 452, a case which, arguably, has been effectively undermined by the *John East* case. Because, however, *Toronto v. York* deals with the Ontario Municipal Board, a key agency in the administration of Ontario municipal assessment, it has remained to plague the numerous assessment cases which have been raised under s. 96.

The use of s. 96 as a stultification of effective provincial administration of municipal tax assessment is based on concepts which have been rejected for other purposes, a fact made clear by the *John East* case. Long before *Toronto v. York,* there had been lower court utterances that saw in s. 96 a limitation on exercise of "judicial power" by provincial administrative agencies, but this was coupled with a reluctance to interfere with the operation of those agencies; see for example, *Sandwich East v. Union Natural Gas Co.*, [1925] 2 D.L.R. 707, 56 O.L.R. 399, aff'd [1925] 4 D.L.R. 795, 57 O.L.R. 656. When *Toronto v. York* was before the Ontario Court of Appeal, [1937] O.R. 177, [1937] 1 D.L.R. 175, Rowell C.J.O. reviewed the existing authorities and lent emphasis to the view that a provincial tribunal may not be empowered "to determine purely judicial questions such as are normally determined by Courts of Justice" and that it was *ultra vires* the provincial legislature to confer on such a board "judicial functions". The Privy Council gave its imprimatur to this view, although a decade later in the *John East* case it was made clear that *Toronto v. York* had proceeded on a consideration of only the first of the two relevant questions under s. 96 and had, indeed, assumed that the exercise of a "judicial power" was sufficient to raise the ban of s. 96.

The shape of things to come emerged in the judgment of Roach J.A. in *Re Imperial Leaf Tobacco Co. of Canada and Mersea Township*, [1949] O.R. 665, [1949] 4 D.L.R. 65, a case which involved the proper statutory tax classification of the company. It was conceded that the company was assessable for business tax; otherwise, said Roach J.A., there would arise "a pure question of law, the determination of which would require the exercise of judicial power". However, since the company was assessable, "the problem of classifying it within the Act is a matter of administration [involving] a conclusion of fact", although admittedly this conclusion was itself dependent on questions of law, *viz.*, the construction of the statute and whether there was evidence upon which the business could be classified as it was. In *Quance v. Ivey & Sons Ltd.*, [1950] O.R. 397, [1950] 3 D.L.R. 656, it was held that a provincial board could not constitutionally determine a person's liability to assessment and, indeed, neither could the Court of Appeal sitting as a designated tribunal of appeal under the assessment statute. This was a question which at Confederation had been subject to superior Court adjudication. *Quance. v. Ivey & Sons Ltd.* indicated that it must remain irrevocably with s. 96 Courts, a conclusion at variance with the *Adoption Act* case and dependent on the same sort of half answer to the problem of s. 96 that characterized *Toronto v. York*.

Quance v. Ivey & Sons Ltd. was not appealed and it fixed the pattern of subsequent decisions in Ontario on the question of initial assessability: see *Re Tp. of Cornwall Assessments*, [1955] 1 D.L.R. 547, [1954] O.W.N. 920. Ten years earlier a similar issue of assessability by a provincial tribunal was raised in Nova Scotia and there determined in favour of the tribunal's competence: see *Dartmouth v. R.C. Episcopal Corp. of Halifax*, [1950] 2 D.L.R. 309, 15 M.P.R. 47. If effect were given to the argument of s. 96, said the Court in the *Dartmouth* case, "it would frustrate the whole system of assessment". The shaky basis of *Quance v. Ivey & Sons Ltd.* is evident, apart from more germane considerations, in the mere fact that if at Confederation some province had experience with determination of assessability by a provincial functionary or board, that would have resolved the matter in favour of a continuation of that authority despite s. 96. The "mystique" of the state of the statute book as of 1867 is disclosed by the Ontario Court of Appeal's decision in *Hamilton v. Firestone Tire and Rubber Co.*, [1954] O.R. 493, [1954] 3 D.L.R. 685, holding that it was competent to the Province to invest courts of revision and the Ontario Municipal Board with power to order a refund of taxes already paid, this being something never done by s. 96 Courts and being also a valid extension of a pre-confederation power of courts of revision to remit or reduce taxes that were due although not yet paid. In a companion case, *London Railway Commission v. Port Stanley*, [1954] O.R. 486, [1954] 3 D.L.R. 475, the same Court sustained the statutory power of the above-mentioned tribunals to direct a refund of taxes already paid where the claim for refund was grounded on the fact that the property had become exempt. "Tweedledum" in *Quance v. Ivey & Sons Ltd.* was "tweedledee" in the two last-mentioned cases.

In 1955, the Supreme Court of Canada faced for the first time the *Quance v. Ivey & Sons Ltd.* problem, and its judgment in *Toronto v. Olympia Edward Recreation Club Ltd.*, [1955] S.C.R. 454, [1955] 3 D.L.R. 641 was (despite the five to four division of the Court) a clear affirmation of that decision. Regrettably, it appears that the constitutional issue of the relation of s. 96 to provincial assessment administration was intertwined with constructional matters, such as whether the assessment statute made resort to its machinery exclusive and precluded resort to a superior court for relief by way of declaration or *certiorari* on the legal question of assessability. Two earlier cases, one in the Privy Council and one in the Supreme Court (but neither turning on any constitutional principle), influenced the result reached both by the majority and the minority in the *Olympia* case.

The Privy Council judgment was *Toronto Ry. Co. v. Toronto*, [1904] A.C. 809 where a taxpayer who had exhausted the scheme of assessment review (including resort to the Court of Appeal) but without success, brought a declaratory action to establish exemption from taxation. Although the assessment statute empowered the court of revision to try all complaints in regard to persons wrongly placed on or omitted from the assessment roll or assessed at too high or too low a sum, the Privy Council held that the statute did not (on its proper construction) cover questions of liability to assessment. A few years later the Ontario legislature amended the statute to declare that the assessment tribunals (the court of revision, the County Judge, the Ontario Municipal Board, as it now is, and the Court of Appeal) "have and always have had . . . jurisdiction to determine . . . all questions as to whether any persons or things are or were assessable or are or were legally assessed or exempted from assessment": 1910 (Ont.), c. 88, s. 19. It follows from the *Olympia* case that it is incompetent for a provincial legislature to confer such jurisdiction on the designated agencies and Courts. The Supreme Court in the *Olympia* case had to consider, however, its earlier judgment in *Bennett & White (Calgary) Ltd. v. Sugar City*, [1950] S.C.R. 450, [1950] 3 D.L.R. 81, rev'd [1951] A.C. 786, [1951] 4 D.L.R. 129, 3 W.W.R. (N.S.) 111. There the Alberta statute, while not providing for assessment review by the Courts, gave express authority to provincial tribunals to determine assessability. Rand J. held (speaking for the majority, and he was sustained in this view by the Privy Council) that the Alberta enactment could and should be construed as permitting determination of assessability in relation only to the administrative function of assessment and not as vesting judicial authority to determine questions of jurisdiction arising out of provisions declaring exemptions; otherwise, he said, a serious question of *ultra vires* would arise. In other words, the supervening jurisdiction of the ordinary Courts to determine liability to assessment was not excluded by the Alberta statute.

This view was raised to constitutional significance in the *Olympia* case. The majority held that assessability could not be finally determined by a non-section 96 Court (nor apparently even by a section 96 Court acting under statutory provisions for appeal from the provincial assessor or other assessment tribunal). The minority took the position expounded in the *Sugar City* case; it was open to a Province to permit its tribunals to determine assessability in the administration of their task of assessment but not to determine it in any conclusive sense so as to foreclose any claim of exemption by a taxpayer who may have exhausted the statutory review procedure. The majority took a cleaner line, rejecting the duality of the minority's position, and holding unconstitutional the statutory conferment of jurisdiction on provincially-appointed tribunals to determine assessability.

The significance of this result for assessment administration was obvious; and the legislature, moving to fill the void created by the majority's decision, adopted the procedure implicit in the minority's position. It limited the court of revision, the County Judge and the Ontario Municipal Board to review of the assessment with a further appeal to the Court of Appeal which then became seized of the matter as a Court of original jurisdiction to determine assessability: see 1956 (Ont.), c. 3, ss. 12, 13, 14. Under this scheme, the Ontario Municipal Board must decline jurisdiction on any question of assessability: see *Assessment Commissioner for Metropolitan Toronto v. Eglinton Bowling Co.*, [1957] O.R. 621, 11 D.L.R. (2d) 195. Section 96 is being used here to place assessment matters on a particular jurisdictional plane associated with determination of questions of law: see *Ontario Motor League v. Toronto*, [1960] O.R. 38, 20 D.L.R. 2d 216. Surely this is inconsistent with the *John East* case and unnecessarily raises constitutional principle in a situation which could be handled more simply by admitting review by appeal (where given) or by certiorari or even declaratory action, unless expressly and effectively excluded. (After all, there is no constitutional principle which forbids curtailment of superior court jurisdiction).

In *Topping v. L. J. McGuinness & Co. Ltd.*, [1960] O.W.N. 208, 23 D.L.R. 2d 86, it was held to be constitutionally proper to allow the court of revision (and the County Judge and Ontario Municipal Board on appeal) to determine whether a person is wrongly placed on the assessment roll in respect of school support. The conclusion was based on the fact that such jurisdiction was a matter of pre-Confederation record. Surely this points to the emptiness of the result reached in *Quance v. Ivey & Sons Ltd.* and in the *Olympia* case. As was said elsewhere (see Municipal Tax Assessment and Section 96 of the *British North America Act*: The *Olympia Bowling Alleys* case, (1955) 33 Can. Bar Rev. 993, at p. 1017):

"Assessment must be considered in all its ramifications in determining whether it should be administered by section 96 courts or by provincial administrative tribunals. If the duties connected with assessment be taken as a whole, there could be no justification for suggesting that they are properly 'section 96' duties rather than duties open for assignment to a provincially appointed tribunal. In the making up of an assessment roll, determination of assessability of a person or of exemption of some piece of property is part and parcel of the routine of the task, and of no greater significance than questions of valuation or of classification. To put labels of 'judicial power' or 'question of law' on assessability or exemption, and labels of 'administrative power' or 'question of fact' on valuation or classification may well serve the necessities of a limited statutory right of appeal or of permissible resort to prerogative writs. But to move from this to a constitutional prohibition is a needless artificiality. In my view, the form of administration, whether by section 96 court or by board, is simply a policy question for the provincial legislature. Nothing in section 96 compels any other conclusion or dictates any such constitutional division of function as is indicated in the majority and minority opinions in the *Olympia* case. Assessment is so intimately connected with municipal government that, even apart from the authorities, one finds it difficult to associate exclusive superior court jurisdiction with any phase of the matter, be it assessability or exemption therefrom. That the association should be given a constitutional protection is stranger still, especially when it means that original consideration must come from a section 96 court as opposed to simply an opportunity for review by appeal (or by prerogative writ), which is open on the legislation as it stands. Beyond this, the *John East* case supports the view that the totality of the assessment function should be measured against the compulsion of section 96, and not a mere fragment."

[That the *Olympia Bowling Alleys* case rests heavily on the Supreme Court on the issue of assessability is evident from *Copper Cliff v. Department of Municipal Affairs of Ontario*, [1961] S.C.R. 324, 27 D.L.R. (2d) 756.]

Note

The provincial "board" cases arising under s. 96 of the *B.N.A. Act* involve the following representative administrative agencies:

1. Workmen's compensation boards: *Tremblay v. Kowhanko,* [1920] 1 W.W.R. 787, 51 D.L.R. 174, 30 Man. R. 198 (Manitoba statute validly providing for appointment and exercise of powers by Board); *A.-G. Que. v. Slanec and Grimstead,* [1933] 2 D.L.R. 289, 54 Que. K.B. 230 (Quebec statute with similar effect upheld).

2. Expropriation tribunals: *O. Martineau & Sons Ltd. v. Montreal,* [1932] A.C. 113, [1932] 1 D.L.R. 353, [1932] 1 W.W.R. 302 (assessment of compensation payable on expropriation by municipality validly reposed in provincial appointee as continuation of pre-confederation procedure).

3. Public utility and other regulatory boards: *Winnipeg Electric Ry. v. Winnipeg,* [1917] 1 W.W.R. 9, 30 D.L.R. 159, 26 Man. R. 584; *Winnipeg v. Winnipeg Electric Ry.,* [1920] 3 W.W.R. 246, 54 D.L.R. 445 (public utilities commission validly appointed in respect of powers conferred); *Toronto Ry. v. Toronto,* [1920] A.C. 446, 51 D.L.R. 69, [1920] 1 W.W.R. 755, rev'g 44 O.L.R. 381, 46 D.L.R. 547 (valid imposition by railway board of authorized penalty for railway's failure to comply with order); *Sandwich East v. Union Natural Gas Co.,* [1925] 2 D.L.R. 707, 56 O.L.R. 399, aff'd [1925] 4 D.L.R. 795, 57 O.L.R. 656 (appointment and powers of board authorized to fix rates for supply of natural gas upheld); *The King ex rel. Stamford v. McKeown,* [1935] O.R. 109, [1935] 2 D.L.R. 157 (general attack on constitution and appointment of Ontario Municipal Board rejected although some powers conferred on it might properly belong to s. 96 Court); *Spooner Oils Ltd. v. Turner Valley Gas Conservation Board,* [1932] 4 D.L.R. 750, [1932] 3 W.W.R. 477, rev'd on other grounds, [1933] S.C.R. 629, [1933] 4 D.L.R. 545 (natural gas conservation board competently appointed and authorized); *Board of Public Utility Commrs. v. Model Dairies,* [1937] 1 D.L.R. 95, [1936] 3 W.W.R. 601 (public utility board validity constituted); *Toronto v. York,* [1938] A.C. 415, [1938] 1 D.L.R. 593, [1938] 1 W.W.R. 452 (Ontario Municipal Board validly established as administrative board but improperly authorized to construe and vary water agreement between municipalities).

4. Assessment boards: *Dartmouth v. R.C. Episcopal Corp. of Halifax,* [1940] 2 D.L.R. 309, 15 M.P.R. 47 (assessment officer and assessment board competent to determine liability to municipal assessment); *Quance v. Ivey & Sons Ltd.,* [1950] O.R. 397, [1950] 3 D.L.R. 656 (questions of disputed liability to assessment, as opposed to questions of quantum, properly determinable by s. 96 Courts and not by provincially appointed officers); *Re Minister of Municipal Affairs v. L'Evêque d'Edmundston,* 4 N.B.R. (2d) 567, 24 D.L.R. (3d) 534 (applying Olympia Edward doctrine); and

see Note on Municipal Tax Assessment and Section 96—A Case Study, *supra*.

5. Local government boards: *Toronto v. York, supra* (Ontario Municipal Board competently established to discharge enumerated local government functions); *Re Gordon and De Laval Co.,* [1938] O.R. 462, [1908] 3 D.L.R. 263 (power of a provincial functionary to determine validity of a municipal by-law questioned).

6. Land registry agencies: *Re Marcella Smith,* [1925] 2 D.L.R. 556, 19 Sask. L.R. 577 (issue of certificate of title by registrar not a s. 96 function); *Re Winter,* [1962] O.R. 402, 32 D.L.R. (2d) 429 (Master of Titles not empowered to determine question of law by striking out, as being void, a condition subsequent attached to a reserved right of way, and thus purporting to exercise a s. 96 function); *Heller v. Registrar, Vancouver Land Registration District,* [1963] S.C.R. 229, 38 D.L.R. (2d) 1, 41 W.W.R. 641 (*semble,* Land Titles Registrar cannot adjudicate on contested rights where he must consider and weigh evidence, this being a s. 96 function; but may be empowered to correct, at his discretion, errors in register on the material in his own records); but see *Brooks v. Pavlick,* [1964] S.C.R. 108, 42 D.L.R. (2d) 572, referred to *supra,* at p. 783.

7. Domestic tribunals of professional associations: *Re Ashby,* [1934] O.R. 421, [1934] 3 D.L.R. 565 (province competent to establish tribunal to govern and discipline members of a profession).

8. Labour relations boards: *Tremblay v. Quebec Labour Relations Board,* [1967] S.C.R. 697, 64 D.L.R. (2d) 484 (s. 96 not violated by reposing power in provincial labour relations board to order dissolution of employer dominated employees' association).

If, by provincial legislation, orders of a board, on being filed, are enforceable as orders of a superior court, does the board become in that respect a s. 96 Court? Cf. *Bruton v. Regina City Policemen's Assoc.,* [1945] 3 D.L.R. 437, [1945] 2 W.W.R. 273; and cf. *John East* case, *supra*.

2. Establishment of Dominion Courts: Dominion Legislation Affecting Jurisdiction of Provincial Courts

CONSOLIDATED DISTILLERIES LTD. ET AL v. THE KING

In the Privy Council. [1933] A.C. 508, [1933] 3 D.L.R. 1, [1933] 2 W.W.R. 430.

Consolidated appeals by special leave from three judgments of the Supreme Court of Canada, [1932] S.C.R. 419, [1932] 2 D.L.R. 631, affirming judgments of the Exchequer Court, [1932] Ex. C.R. 85, [1931] 2 D.L.R. 879, in favour of the Crown (Dominion) on bonds given to the Crown pursuant to the *Inland Revenue Act,* R.S.C. 1906, c. 51 and regulations thereunder. Two questions fell to be determined: (1) whether the Exchequer Court had jurisdiction; (2) whether appellants' liability on the bonds had been discharged. The Privy Council agreed with the Supreme Court that there was jurisdiction but reversed the Court's judgment on the second question. The opinion of the Privy Council is noted on the question of jurisdiction only.

LORD RUSSELL OF KILLOWEN: . . . The question of jurisdiction depends upon a consideration of the *British North America Act, 1867,* and the *Exchequer Court Act* (R.S., Can., 1927, c. 34). The matters in regard to which the Provincial legislatures have exclusive power to make laws include, under the *British North America Act,* s. 92, head 13—"Property and civil rights in the province" and s. 92, head 14—"The administration of justice in the province including the constitution, maintenance and organization of provincial courts, both of civil and of criminal jurisdiction, and including procedure in civil matters in those courts." Section 101, however, provides that: "The Parliament of Canada may notwithstanding anything in this Act, from time to time provide for the . . . establishment of any additional courts for the better administration of the laws of Canada."

The Exchequer Court of Canada was constituted in the year 1875 in exercise of this power. It was conceded by the appellants (and rightly, as their Lordships think) in the argument before the Board, that the Parliament of Canada could, in exercising the power conferred by s. 101, properly confer upon the Exchequer Court jurisdiction to hear and determine actions to enforce the liability on bonds executed in favour of the Crown in pursuance of a revenue law enacted by the Parliament of Canada. The point as to jurisdiction accordingly resolves itself into the question whether the language of the *Exchequer Court Act* upon its true interpretation purports to confer the necessary jurisdiction. The relevant section is s. 30, which is in the following terms:

"30. The Exchequer Court shall have and possess concurrent original jurisdiction in Canada (a) in all cases relating to the revenue in which it is sought to enforce any law of Canada, including actions, suits and proceedings by way of information to enforce penalties and proceedings by way of information in *rem,* and as well in *qui tam* suits for penalties or forfeiture as where the suit is on behalf of the Crown alone; (b) in all cases in which it is sought at the instance of the Attorney-General of Canada to impeach or annul any patent of invention, or any patent, lease or other instrument respecting lands; (c) in all cases in which demand is made or relief sought against any officer of the Crown for anything done or omitted to be done in the performance of his duty as such officer; and (d) in all other actions and suits of a civil nature at common law or equity in which the Crown is plaintiff or petitioner. R.S., c. 140, s. 31."

By virtue of s. 2(a) the Crown means the Crown in right or interest of the Dominion of Canada.

The learned President held that the Exchequer Court had jurisdiction, inasmuch as the bonds were required to be given by a law enacted by the Parliament of Canada in respect of a matter in which it had undoubted jurisdiction. The subject matter of the actions directly arose from legislation of Parliament in respect of excise.

The Chief Justice thought that the cases fell clearly within s. 30(d), and probably also within s. 30(a). Duff J., while suggesting a possible doubt as to the application of sub-s. (a) held that the cases were plainly within sub-s. (d).

Their Lordships are anxious to avoid expressing any general views upon the extent of the jurisdiction conferred by s. 30, beyond what is necessary for the decision of this particular case. Each case as it arises must be determined in relation to its own facts and circumstances. In regard to the present case their Lordships appreciate that a difficulty may exist in regard to sub-s. (a). While these actions are no doubt "cases relating to the revenue," it might perhaps be said that no law of Canada is sought to be enforced in them. Their Lordships, however, have come to the conclusion that these actions do fall within sub-s. (d). It was suggested that if read literally, and without any limitation, that sub-section would entitle the Crown to sue in the Exchequer Court and subject defendants to the jurisdiction of that Court in respect of any cause of action whatever, and that such a provision would be *ultra vires* the Parliament of Canada as one not covered by the power conferred by s. 101 of the *British North America Act*. Their Lordships, however, do not think that sub-s. (d) in the context in which it is found, can properly be read as free from all limitations. They think that in view of the provisions of the three preceding sub-sections the actions and suits in sub-s. (d) must be confined to the actions and suits in relation to some subject-matter, legislation in regard to which is within the legislative competence of the Dominion. So read, the sub-section could not be said to be *ultra vires*, and the present actions appear to their Lordships to fall within its scope. The Exchequer Court accordingly has jurisdiction in the matter of these actions. . . .

Appeal allowed on other grounds.

["Laws of Canada" in s. 101 of the *B.N.A. Act* refers to legislation enacted by, and within the legislative competence of, the Dominion: see *In re Board of Commerce Act, etc.*, [1922] 1 A.C. 191, at p. 199, 60 D.L.R. 513, at p. 518, [1922] 1 W.W.R. 20, at pp. 25-26; *Rex v. Hume*; *Consolidated Distilleries Ltd. v. Consolidated Exporters Corp. Ltd.*, [1930] S.C.R. 531, [1930] 3 D.L.R. 704 (claim by defendant against a third party for indemnity in an action in the Exchequer Court brought by the Crown on certain bonds held to be outside the competence of the Exchequer Court); *Kellogg Co. v. Kellogg*, [1941] 1 D.L.R. 766, rev'd [1941] S.C.R. 242, [1941] 2 D.L.R. 545 (jurisdiction of Exchequer Court to determine right to invention as between inventor and employer doubted in Court below, although arising in patent proceedings, but broader view taken by Supreme Court without definitive decision on the point).

"Laws of Canada" must also include common law which relates to the matters falling within classes of subjects assigned to the Parliament of

Canada. This proposition is elaborated in the following note; and see the exposition of a related theme by *Dixon,* The Common Law as an Ultimate Constitutional Foundation, (1957) 31 Aust. L.J. 240.]

Note on Federal Jurisdiction and Federal Common or Decisional Law

The common law in the various provinces and the civil law in Quebec are both subject to ultimate exercise of legislative authority according to the distribution of legislative power ordained by the *B.N.A. Act.* It is a pertinent, even if trite, observation that the unifying role of the Supreme Court of Canada (differing in this respect from the role of the Supreme Court of the United States) makes possible an overall uniformity in the common law in the various Provinces (excluding Quebec), save, of course, in respect of those exceptional cases where the common law on a particular point has been received in one Province but not in another. In this context it is a correct observation that there is no such thing as federal as contrasted with provincial common law: see, generally, *Willis,* Securing the Uniformity of Law in a Federal System—Canada, (1944) 5 Univ. of Tor. L.J. 352. But because the common law is potentially subject to overriding legislative power, there is federal common or decisional law and provincial common or decisional law according to the matters respectively distributed to each legislature by the *B.N.A. Act.*

This is not, however, the central theme of this Note. Rather is it concerned with the possible jurisdiction that may be reposed in federal courts of first instance and with the law (whether common law or civil law or statute law) which may be administered in such Courts. There is no doubt of the power of Parliament to establish federal Courts to administer matters falling within exclusive federal competence: see *Valin v. Langlois* (1879), 3 S.C.R. 1, per Taschereau J., at pp. 74-5; leave to appeal refused (1879), 5 App. Cas. 115. This power extends to the constitution of courts of original criminal jurisdiction, notwithstanding that s. 92(14) authorizes provincial courts of criminal jurisdiction, while s. 91(27) expressly excludes criminal courts from federal competence. The paramount force of s. 101 compels this conclusion: see *A.-G. Ont. v. A.-G. Can.,* [1947] A.C. 127, [1947] 1 D.L.R. 801, [1947] 1 W.W.R. 305.

The *Exchequer Court Act* vesting only a limited and specialized jurisdiction in the Court which it established left room for many questions as to the capacity of courts established by the provinces under section 92(14) to entertain claims grounded on federal law or as to which the Dominion was an interested party, whether they did so independently of or pursuant to explicit provincial legislation. *The Federal Court Act,* R.S.C. 1970, c. 10 (2nd Supp.) has conferred a comprehensive jurisdiction over such matters in the Federal Court, including by section 26(1) all matters within the jurisdiction of the Exchequer Court, but extending well beyond that. Besides the provisions as to review of federal administrative action, discussed *infra,* there are others having to do with many specific and a number of general classes of suits. The Act should be consulted for the comprehensive list but a few sections are here set out to illustrate the breadth of the grant.

17.(1) The Trial Division has original jurisdiction in all cases where relief is claimed against the Crown and, except where otherwise provided, the Trial Division has exclusive original jurisdiction in all such cases.

17.(4) The Trial Division has concurrent original jurisdiction
(a) in proceedings of a civil nature in which the Crown or the Attorney General of Canada claims relief; and
(b) in proceedings in which relief is sought against any person for anything done or omitted to be done in the performance of his duties as an officer or servant of the Crown.

23. The Trial Division has concurrent original jurisdiction as well between subject and subject as otherwise, in all cases in which a claim for relief is made or a remedy is sought under an Act of the Parliament of Canada or otherwise in relation to any matter coming within the class of subject of bills of exchange and promissory notes . . . aeronautics, and works and undertakings connecting a province with any other province or extending beyond the limits of a province, except to the extent that jurisdiction has been otherwise specially assigned.

The provision of section 19, vesting jurisdiction "where the legislature of a province has passed an Act agreeing that the Court . . . has jurisdiction in cases of controversies . . . (b) between such province and in other province or provinces that have passed a like Act", successor to a like provision in the *Exchequer Court Act*, R.S.C. 1970 c. E-11, s. 30(1), raises the questions, How can the provinces bestow such consent to jurisdiction, *i.e.* how is administration of justice "in the Province" involved? And how can Parliament accept and implement it, *i.e.*, what are the "laws of Canada" to be applied?

Grants of "jurisdiction" on "concurrent jurisdiction" rather than "exclusive jurisdiction would seem at a minimum to maintain the status of provincial courts respecting the proceedings they deal with as it was before the *Federal Court Act*. Are they to be read as going further? In recognizing concurrent provincial court jurisdiction do they affirmatively direct that it be taken? One matter that has certainly been clarified by the *Federal Court Act* is that there is no longer any gap to be supplied by implication as to the existence of a forum for hearing claims with a federal element.

There would seem to be no reason in principle why a Province could not, in the absence of federal legislation specifying the proper forum, make its Courts available to handle by original suit causes arising out of federal legislation in the same way as they now handle common law actions involving matters that fall within exclusive federal power. (*Quaere*, whether this would extend to fixing, in the absence of federal legislation, rules of jurisdiction involving matters of status, as, for example in relation to marriage and divorce; or, are such rules bound up with the substantive law in these matters which only Parliament may enact?)

The foregoing proposition is implicit if not explicit in *A.-G. B.C. v. McKenzie,* [1965] S.C.R. 490, 51 D.L.R. (2d) 623, 51 W.W.R. 528 where provincial legislation conferring jurisdiction on County Court Judges as Local Judges of the provincial Supreme Court to try actions for divorce and other matrimonial causes was held valid in the absence of federal legislation on the matter. The issue of s. 96 of the *B.N.A. Act* was, of course, covered because County Court Judges are federal appointees. At first blush this view might appear to be inconsistent with *In re Storgoff,* [1945] S.C.R. 526, [1945] 3 D.L.R. 673 where the Supreme Court held that a provincial enactment could not validly confer jurisdiction on a provincial appellate court to hear an appeal in respect of *habeas corpus* arising out of a detention under a federal criminal conviction. However, the *Storgoff* case fell within exclusive federal authority under s. 91(27) in relation to "procedure in criminal matters", and this covered appeals, whether in the provincial court system or in the federal court system: see also *In re Nagy,* [1926] 3 W.W.R. 759, 21 Sask. L.R. 292, 46 Can. C.C. 333; *Northwest Mortgage Co. v. Com'r of Excise,* [1945] 1 D.L.R. 561, [1945] 1 W.W.R. 182. In the result, the power of provincial legislatures to endow provincial Courts with jurisdiction to administer federal law is subject not only to the paramount authority of Parliament but is limited by the exclusion of authority to deal with procedure in criminal matters. It was held recently that the pre-Confederation authority of the Quebec Superior Court to entertain prohibition in a criminal matter had been implicitly ousted by the Criminal Code: see *Minister of National Revenue v. Lafleur,* [1964] S.C.R. 412, 46 D.L.R. (2d) 439. It is, hence, immaterial whether the phrase in s. 92(14) "procedure in civil matters" is read as embracing only such civil matters as fall within provincial competence substantively. While this is not a necessary construction, it may be regarded as subordinate to a more encompassing authority in the opening words "administration of justice in the Province".

It follows from the terms of the *B.N.A. Act* that such a principle as is represented for the United States in *Erie Railroad Co. v. Tompkins* (1938), 304 U.S. 64, has no place in Canadian constitutional law. While a dual system of Courts is possible in Canada, the duality does not embrace application of local and federal law in the federal courts, as is the case in the federal court system of the United States. *Cf. Mitchell Wendell,* Relations Between Federal and State Courts (1949); and for the position in Australia, see *Cowen,* Federal Jurisdiction in Australia (1960), especially chapter V. Federal Courts of first instance or of intermediate appeal in Canada may administer only federal law. Nor does the duality affect the final authority of the Supreme Court of Canada (if an appeal lies) to resolve contested issues of provincial law as well as federal law. That Court is in no way limited to constitutional questions and to questions arising under exercise of federal powers. It is not bound by the views of the highest provincial court as to the provincial law.

It has been suggested, particularly because of the exposed position of the Quebec civil law and also because of the variations in the common law systems in the other Provinces, that the Supreme Court of Canada should as a matter of policy accept the views of the final provincial Court as to what is the law on matters falling within provincial legislative jurisdiction; the Supreme Court, it is argued, should concentrate on questions of federal law and constitutional law: see *Abel*, The Role of the Supreme Court in Private Law Cases, (1965) 4 Alta. L. Rev. 39. This is not put forward as a constitutional imperative—indeed, it could not be under present circumstances— but as a prudent bow to the differing needs and sentiments of the Provinces. At bottom, this is an appeal to curtail the appellate juris- diction of the Supreme Court. (For a contrary view, see *Gibson*, Federalizing the Judiciary, (1966) 44 Can. Bar Rev. 674.). Since there is no such thing in Canada as federal court jurisdiction based on diversity of citizenship as there is in the United States, compulsory acceptance of provincial court determination of the law can only be realized at the Supreme Court level, and then only by refusal of leave to appeal where such leave is necessary, or by elimination of appeals as of right, a matter for Parliament alone.

There is, of course, the possibility of adoption by the Dominion of provincial law for federal purposes, an adoption exemplified in the Crown Liability Act, R.S.C. 1970, c. C-38; and see *Schwella v. The Queen*, [1957] Ex. C.R. 226, 9 D.L.R. (2d) 137. That, however, is a different thing from the intimation, and, indeed, assertion in some cases originating in the Exchequer Court that provincial statute law is properly applicable even though not referentially adopted. Thus, in *LeVae and Ilott and Crooks v. S.S. Giovanni Amendola*, [1956] Ex. C.R. 55, 1 D.L.R. (2d) 117, Sidney Smith D.J.A. said in an undocu- mented statement, which was *obiter*, that "I see no reason why recog- nition should not be given in the Exchequer Court to provincial legislation defining substantive law." (The dictum had reference to a situation where federal legislation was wanting on the matter in question in the Exchequer Court. The same Judge recognized in a later case the governing effect of federal legislation: see *New England Fish Co. of Oregon and Woods v. Britamerican Ltd.*, [1959] Ex. C.R. 327, 20 D.L.R. (2d) 29.)

With respect, such recognition depends not on the *ipse dixit* of an Exchequer Court Judge nor even on the statutory jurisdiction of the Court, but on the substantive law declared by Parliament under s. 101 of the *B.N.A. Act* to be applicable therein or, failing such statutory declaration, on the common law (or admiralty law as well) applicable to the assigned jurisdiction. Provincial statute law cannot apply unless there is some federal statutory basis for finding that it was incorporated into federal law for federal purposes. There is, on this view, some difficulty in appreciating the judgments of the Supreme Court of Canada in *T.T.C. v. The King*, [1949] S.C.R. 510, [1949] 3 D.L.R. 161 and *Gartland Steamship Co. and La Blanc v. The Queen* (1960), 22 D.L.R. (2d) 385. While the result therein would have been understandable if the actions were brought in provincial Courts, a different situation prevails in a federal Court.

Both cases involved claims by the federal Crown brought in the Exchequer Court to recover for damage to its property resulting from negligence. In each case there was contributory negligence, and under the applicable common law the Crown would have failed for failure to show that defendants' negligence alone caused the damage. But the Crown was held entitled to recover by invoking the apportionment provisions of provincial contributory negligence legislation. "The choice", said the Court in the *Gartland* case, "is between no recovery at all and a recovery under the *Ontario Negligence Act*. This is a common law action for damages under s. 29(d) of the *Exchequer Court Act* and . . . the Crown as plaintiff is entitled to the advantage of the Ontario Act." But how can this be so in a Court which, by s. 101 of the *B.N.A. Act*, may administer only federal law?

The most comprehensive treatment of the matter so far found in the cases is that of Jackett P. in *The Queen v. Murray*, [1965] 2 Ex. C.R. 663, aff'd [1967] S.C.R. 262, 60 D.L.R. (2d) 647, reproduced in part below.

It differs from the cases above-mentioned in that the federal Crown's claim was cut down by subjecting it to provincial negligence legislation rather than being allowed in full under the common law position. The judgment fails to make clear whether the provincial law had referentially or otherwise become federal law applicable as such in a suit in the Exchequer Court or whether s. 101 of the *B.N.A. Act* is to be read in a different way where a claim by the federal Crown (as opposed to a claim against the federal Crown) is made in that Court. There is the intimation that because the suit arose out of an injury to a member of the armed forces the legislative power of Parliament was engaged, but how far this goes was not made explicit.

There is no tenable ground for giving the federal Crown a preferred constitutional position in a suit in a federal Court unless we hold that it is not bound by s. 101. The principle that the Crown may take advantage of legislation was developed outside of any limitations of federalism. No doubt, the question of liability of the federal Crown is a matter for Parliament, and it may condition or limit that liability as it chooses. Thus, it may decree that the Crown may be sued only in a particular Court or only in a specified class of cases. The situation is different, however, where the Crown is plaintiff. True, it is permissible to apply, even for *B.N.A. Act* purposes, the doctrine that the federal Crown may sue in any Court having jurisdiction in the particular matter. But does it follow that Parliament may compel any subject to submit to the jurisdiction of a particular Court, *e.g.* the Federal Court, merely because the federal Crown is suing and regardless of what the cause of action may be? Where the matter on which the federal Crown founds its actions is within federal legislative power then, clearly, jurisdiction may be reposed in a federal court. Where, however, the matter so in issue is within provincial competence (and there is no question of imposing liability on the federal Crown), how can jurisdiction to try the matter be reposed in a federal Court? Cf. *C.N.R. v. North-West Telephone Co.*, [1961] S.C.R. 178, 26 D.L.R. (2d) 628.

The answer given in *Farwell v. The Queen* (1894), 22 S.C.R. 553 is far from satisfying. There the federal Crown filed an information in the Exchequer Court respecting land in the British Columbia railway belt of which the title had been vested in the Dominion. While there would be a tenable ground of jurisdiction in respect of federal public property (and this was mentioned by the Court), the Supreme Court dealt with a challenge to jurisdiction on another ground. Referring to a provision in the *Exchequer Court Act* giving the Court original jurisdiction "in all actions and suits of a civil nature at common law or equity in which the Crown is plaintiff or petitioner", King J. for the majority (Taschereau J. being doubtful on the question of jurisdiction) adverted to the Crown's privilege of suing in any Court it pleases. Proceeding from this, he said:

> It follows, in my mind, that the Crown by and with the advice and consent of the Houses of Parliament, must have the right (a right which it would need clear words to take away) to enact that all actions and suits of a civil nature at common law or equity, in which the Crown in right of the Dominion is plaintiff or petitioner, may be brought in the Exchequer Court—the right to establish which with its other branches of jurisdiction is undisputed and indisputable.

This, with respect, is a non-sequitur under a federal scheme such as that embodied in the *B.N.A. Act*. Indeed, in the *Consolidated Distilleries* case, reproduced *supra*, at p. 790, the Privy Council treated the head of Exchequer Court jurisdiction relied on in *Farwell v. The Queen* as referable to matters falling within federal legislative power. The conclusion is warranted that the Dominion cannot require a private person to submit to the jurisdiction of the Exchequer Court merely because the federal Crown is plaintiff; there must be a basis of jurisdiction in the matter in issue. It is otherwise, of course, where the federal Crown's liability is in issue; that, in itself, is a federal matter for the purpose of entitling the Dominion to designate the forum as well as to determine how far to relax the Crown's immunity from liability.

[The Crown (Dominion) may be sued in a provincial Court only if federal legislation permits. Cf. *Grant v. St. Lawrence Seaway Authority*, [1960] O.W.N. 249, 23 D.L.R. (2d) 252. May the Crown in right of a Province be sued in a federal Court? See the *Dominion Courts Act*, R.S.O. 1970, s. 134 s. 1(*a*), giving jurisdiction to the Supreme Court of Canada and to the Exchequer Court, according to the federal *Supreme Court Act* and the *Exchequer Court Act*, "in controversies between the Dominion of Canada and Ontario". This legislation complements s. 19(*a*) of the *Federal Court Act*, R.S.C. 1970, c. 10 (2d Supp.). See *Mundell*, Legal Nature of Federal and Provincial Executive Governments, (1960) 2 Osgoode Hall L.J. 56, at pp. 70 ff.

If the federal Crown sues in a provincial Court, as it properly may, to what extent is it bound by provincial legislation? See, *Note on Property Provisions of the B.N.A. Act, supra*, at p. 524 referring to *Gauthier v. The King* (1918), 56 S.C.R. 176, 40 D.L.R. 353; and see also *Bowers v.*

Hollinger & Co. Ltd., [1949] O.R. 526, [1946] 4 D.L.R. 186; *A.-G. Can. v. Tombs*, [1946] 4 D.L.R. 516; *The King v. Murphy*, [1948] S.C.R. 537, [1948] 3 D.L.R. 1.]

THE QUEEN v. MURRAY

In the Supreme Court of Canada. [1967] S.C.R. 262, 60 D.L.R. (2d) 647.

Appeal from a judgment of Jackett P., [1965] 2 Ex. C.R. 663 in an action by the federal Crown, tried upon an agreed statement of facts, to recover for loss of services of a member of the armed forces injured by the combined negligence of the driver of a car in which he was a gratuitous passenger and the driver of another car. The latter only was sued along with the owner because legislation in Manitoba where the accident occurred denies liability to a gratuitous passenger unless there has been gross negligence or wilful or wanton misconduct of the driver contributing to the injury or loss (s. 99(1) of the *Highway Traffic Act*), and denies recovery of damages from any person for the portion of the loss caused by such driver when there is no cause of action against him (s. 5 of the *Tortfeasors and Contributory Negligence Act* which by s. 9(2) declares that it "applies to actions by and against the Crown and Her Majesty is bound thereby and has the benefit thereof"). The proportions of fault assigned to the two negligent drivers here were 75 per cent. and 25 per cent. respectively. The defendants contended, accordingly, that they were liable for only 25 per cent. of the Crown's loss but the Crown claimed full recovery. Jackett P. upheld the defendant's contention.

The judgment of the Court was delivered by

MARTLAND J.:—The appellant instituted proceedings in the Exchequer Court against the respondents claiming damages to the full amount of the loss sustained by Her Majesty as a result of being deprived of the services of one Robert James Briggs, a member of the Canadian armed forces. He sustained personal injuries in a highway traffic accident in the Province of Manitoba, while being transported, as a guest without payment, in a motor vehicle owned by one Reykdal. That vehicle was in collision with another motor vehicle owned by the respondent company and operated by its servant, the respondent Murray. It is agreed that the collision resulted from the negligence of both Reykdal and Murray, and that the former was responsible for it to the extent of 75%.

Section 99(1) of the *Highway Traffic Act*, R.S.M. 1954, c. 112 [since rep. & sub. 1966, c. 29, s. 145(1)], provides that:

99(1) No person transported by the owner or operator of a motor vehicle as his guest without payment for transportation shall have a cause of action for damages against the owner or operator for injury, death, or loss, in case of accident, unless the accident was caused by the gross negligence or wilful and wanton misconduct of the owner or operator of the motor vehicle and unless the gross negligence or wilful and wanton misconduct contributed to the injury, death, or loss for which the action is brought.

Sections 5 and 9(2) of the *Tortfeasors and Contributory Negligence Act,* R.S.M. 1954, c. 266, provide:

5. Where no cause of action exists against the owner or operator of a motor vehicle by reason of section 99 of The Highway Traffic Act no damages or contribution or indemnity shall be recoverable from any person for the portion of the loss or damage caused by the negligence of such owner or operator and the portion of the loss or damage so caused by the negligence of such owner or operator shall be determined although such owner or operator is not a party to the action.

9(2) This Act applies to actions by and against the Crown, and Her Majesty is bound thereby and has the benefit thereof.

There is no suggestion of gross negligence or of wilful or wanton misconduct on the part of Reykdal.

The question in issue is as to whether s. 5 of the latter Act is effective so as to limit the appellant's claim to 25% of the damages sustained by Her Majesty because of the loss of Briggs' services, or whether, notwithstanding that provision, there can be recovery of the total loss.

The position taken by the appellant is that the Crown in the right of Canada cannot be bound by this provincial legislation because it was never intended to be made applicable to the appellant, and that, if it had been so intended, it would have been *ultra vires* of the Legislature of Manitoba.

The learned President decided the issue in favour of the respondents and from that decision the present appeal is brought. His position is stated in his reasons for judgment as follows [[1965] 2 Ex. C.R. 663 at p. 671]:

It follows that, as long as the Sovereign relies upon Her common law status as a person to take advantage of a cause of action available to persons generally in the province, and not upon some special right conferred on Her by Parliament, She must take the cause of action as She finds it when Her claim arises and, if the legislature of the province has changed the general rules applicable as between common subjects, the Sovereign must accept the cause of action as so changed whether the change favours Her claim or is adverse to it.

To put the matter in other terms, I have reached the conclusion that this case should be decided against the view put forward by the Attorney General, and in favour of that put forward by the defendant, because I am of opinion that, under our constitution, when the Sovereign in right of Canada relies upon a right in tort against a common person, She must, in the absence of some special prerogative or statutory right to the contrary, base Herself upon the general law in the province where the claim arises governing similar rights between common persons.

In *The King v. Richardson and Adams,* [1948] 2 D.L.R. 305, [1948] S.C.R. 57, this Court decided that the relationship of master and servant between the Crown and a member of the armed forces was settled by the provision which is now s. 50 of the *Exchequer Court Act, R.S.C.* 1952, c. 98, which provides that:

50. For the purpose of determining liability in any action or other proceeding by or against Her Majesty, a person who was at any time since the 24th day of June, 1938, a member of the naval, army or air forces of Her Majesty in right of Canada shall be deemed to have been at such time a servant of the Crown.

The constitutional validity of this section was challenged in *A.-G. Can. v. Nykorak*, 33 D.L.R. (2d) 373, [1962] S.C.R. 331, 37 W.W.R. 660, and the provision was declared by this Court to be valid.

These cases do not go further than to hold that Parliament has properly declared the existence of a certain legal relationship between the Crown and members of the armed forces for the purpose of determining liability in an action by or against Her Majesty. Section 50 does not purport to establish what shall be the consequences of the relationship in any such action.

In *A.-G. Can. v. Jackson*, [1946] 2 D.L.R. 481, 59 C.R.T.C. 273, [1946] S.C.R. 489, it was held, in a case where a member of the armed services had been injured while travelling as a guest passenger in a motor vehicle, that the Crown could not recover damages from the driver of that vehicle because a provision of the *Motor Vehicles Act* of New Brunswick declared that the owner or driver of a motor vehicle not operated in the business of carrying passengers for hire or gain should not be liable for loss or damage sustained by a person being carried in such vehicle. This Court held that the Crown, as master, could not claim damages for injury to the servant where the latter had no right of action himself. The servant had no cause of action because of the effect of the provincial statute.

It was decided, in *The Queen v. Sylvain,* 52 D.L.R. (2d) 607, [1965] S.C.R. 164, that, the common law action *per quod servitium amisit* not existing in the civil law, the Crown could not succeed in a claim under art. 1053 of the *Civil Code* for injuries sustained by members of the armed forces in a collision, in the Province of Quebec, between a military vehicle and that of the respondent, driven by his son.

In each of these cases the liability of a defendant to the Crown, in its capacity of master, was determined on the basis of the law of the Province in which the injuries were sustained.

The applicability of provincial legislation to the federal Crown in a damage claim based upon negligence was also considered by this Court in *Toronto Transportation Com'n v. The King*, [1949] 3 D.L.R. 161, 63 C.R.T.C. 289, [1949] S.C.R. 510. As a result of a collision between a street car and a Royal Air Force truck, an aircraft, loaded on the truck, was damaged. The trial Judge [[1947] 1 D.L.R. 657, 62 C.R.T.C. 252, [1946] Ex. C.R. 604] found both drivers to be negligent and apportioned the responsibility equally between them. It was held by this Court that while, if the common law alone were applicable, the Crown's claim would fail, because it failed to prove that the negligence of the street car driver alone caused the damage, the Crown could take advantage of the Ontario *Negligence Act,* R.S.O. 1937, c. 115, and could, pursuant to that statute, recover one-half of its damages.

Kerwin, J. (as he then was), delivering the judgment of the majority of the Court, said, at pp. 165-6:

> The Crown coming into Court could claim only on the basis of the law applicable as between subject and subject unless something different in the general law relating to the matter is made applicable to the Crown. . . . Here, if the common law alone were applicable, the Crown would have no claim by reason of the fact that it failed to prove that the negligence of the Commission's servants caused the damage. . . .
>
> The Crown is able to take advantage of the Ontario *Negligence Act* and is therefore entitled to one-half of the damages.

This was, of course, a case in which the Crown took advantage of a statutory provision which was in its favour. The right of a defendant, in an action by the Crown, to take advantage of a statute limiting the extent of liability was, however, considered by this Court in *Gartland Steamship Co. and LaBlanc v. The Queen,* 22 D.L.R. (2d) 385, 80 C.R.T.C. 254, [1960] S.C.R. 315, in which the Crown claimed in respect of damage caused to its bridge by negligence in the operation of the appellant's vessel. One of the issues involved was as to whether the appellant could limit its liability to pay damages in accordance with ss. 649 and 651 of the *Canada Shipping Act,* 1934 (Can.), 44. The respondent contended that these sections could not be relied upon as against Her Majesty because the statute did not specifically apply to the Crown.

Locke, J., who, while he dissented on the apportionment of responsibility, delivered the unanimous opinion of the Court on this issue, said, at p. 400:

> The effect of the sections of the *Canada Shipping Act,* however, are to declare and limit the extent of the liability of ship owners in accidents occurring without their own fault and privity. It cannot be said, in my opinion, that the Royal prerogative ever extended to imposing liability upon a subject to a greater extent than that declared by law by legislation lawfully enacted. The fact that liability may not be imposed upon the Crown, except by legislation in which the Sovereign is named, or that any of the other prerogative rights are not to be taken as extinguished unless the intention to do so is made manifest by naming the Crown, does not mean that the extent of the liability of a subject may be extended in a case of a claim by the Crown beyond the limit of the liability effectively declared by law.

In my opinion this proposition of law is applicable to the circumstances of the present case, and the fact that, in the *Gartland* case, the statute in question was a federal enactment, while in the present case it is provincial, does not affect the position. The words "limit of the liability effectively declared by law" at the end of the statement must mean, in a federal state, effectively declared by that legislative body which has jurisdiction to declare such limit.

The Manitoba Legislature has created, in favour of the owner and the driver of a motor vehicle in that Province, the right, in the event that injury is caused by that motor vehicle to a gratuitous passenger in another vehicle, the driver of which is not legally responsible to such passenger because of s. 99(1) of the *Highway Traffic Act,* to have their legal responsibility to pay damages limited to that portion of the loss or damage caused by the negligence of the driver of that motor vehicle. That right is a civil right created by statute enacted by the legislative body which had the necessary jurisdiction. This legislation did not affect any previously existing right of the Crown in the right of Canada created by competent federal legislation. Nor did it affect any prerogative right of the Crown. The appellant would have had no right of recovery at all had it not been for s. 50 of the *Exchequer Court Act.* But, as has already been noted, that section did not create a right of recovery. It merely established a relationship from which certain results might flow.

To put the matter in another way, this is not a case in which a provincial Legislature has sought to "bind" the federal Crown, in the sense of imposing a liability upon it or of derogating from existing Crown prerogatives, privileges or rights. The situation is that as a result of s. 50 of the *Exchequer Court Act*, Parliament enabled the Crown, in the event of an injury to a member of the armed services, to enforce such rights as would be available to a master seeking compensation for loss of the services of his injured servant. What those rights may be can only be determined by the law in force at the time and the place when and where the injury to the servant occurred.

The appellant placed reliance upon the decision of this Court in *Gauthier v. The King* (1918), 40 D.L.R. 353, 56 S.C.R. 176, which was given careful consideration by the learned President. In that case, the Federal Government agreed to purchase from the appellant certain fishing rights, the price to be settled by arbitration. Each party selected an arbitrator and those two chose a third, but, before proceedings were taken, the Government revoked the submission and declared its intention to abandon the purchase. Section 5 of the Ontario *Arbitration Act*, R.S.O. 1914, c. 65, made a submission to arbitration irrevocable except by leave of the Court. Section 3 provided that the Act should apply to an arbitration to which His Majesty was a party. The question in issue was as to whether the Government could revoke the submission and pay damages for breach of the government to arbitrate or whether the Crown was bound by the arbitration award, which had been made, after the withdrawal of the Government ap-

pointed arbitrator, by other arbitrators. It was held in this Court that
s. 5 did not apply to a submission by the Crown in the right of Canada.

In my opinion that case is not analogous to the present one. The
Gauthier case was one in which it was sought to impose a contractual
liability upon the federal Crown by virtue of a provincial statute which
had changed the common law with respect to the revocation of a
submission to arbitration. Anglin, J., who delivered the reasons
accepted by the majority of the Court, drew a distinction between
cases falling within s. 19 (now s. 17) of the *Exchequer Court Act* and
those falling within s. 20 (now s. 18) of that Act. Section 19 gave
to the Exchequer Court jurisdiction to deal with liabilities (*in posse*)
of the Crown already existing. With regard to those, he said, there
was no ground for holding that the Crown had renounced prerogative
privileges theretofore enjoyed and submitted its rights to be disposed
of according to the law in like cases applicable as between subject and
subject.

The claim in issue, being one of contract, was within s. 19, and the
law to be applied, the cause of action having arisen in Ontario, was
the common law, except as modified by a statute binding upon the
federal Crown. He regarded the common law right to revoke the
authority of an arbitrator as being a privilege of the Crown, which
could not be taken away or abridged by provincial legislation.

On the other hand, he recognized that s. 20 of the Act had created
and imposed new liabilities on the Crown, and that the authorities had
decided that in cases falling within that section the Crown's liability
would be determined according to the existing general law applicable
as between subject and subject. The reason for this was that "No other
law than that applicable between subject and subject was indicated in
the Exchequer Court as that by which these newly created liabilities
should be determined". (See p. 363).

It may be noted that it was s. 20 which imposed a liability upon
the Crown in respect of injury caused by the negligence of a servant
of the Crown.

The present case deals with a claim in negligence by the Crown
against a subject. It could arise only because of the master and
servant relationship deemed to exist between the Crown and members
of the armed services by virtue of s. 50 of the *Exchequer Court Act*.
In my view that section likewise did not indicate that the legal consequences ensuing from that legislation would be determined by any
law other than the provincial law applicable between subject and
subject.

For that reason, even if the decision reached on the facts of the
Gauthier case be accepted (as to which, as the learned President
points out, some question is raised by the later decision of the Privy
Council in *Dominion Building Corp. Ltd. v. The King*, [1933] 3 D.L.R.
577 at pp. 589-91, 41 C.R.C. 117, [1933] A.C. 533, [1933] 2 W.W.R.

417, respecting the application of a provincial statute to a contract made by the federal Crown), it does not assist the appellant in this case.

In my opinion the appeal should be dismissed with costs.

Appeal dismissed.

[Jackett P. in the above case expressly refused to follow *A.-G. Can. v. Patterson and Content* (1958), 13 D.L.R. (2d) 90, which decided that the federal Crown was not bound by Nova Scotia legislation similar to that of Manitoba considered in the *Murray* case. Where "The Crown" simpliciter is mentioned in a federal statute does it necessarily mean only the federal Crown? Does the notion of the indivisibility of the Crown apply in Canada's federal system so that "The Crown" (unless particularized) covers the federal and provincial, which then represents "two statutory purses"? See *Nickel Rim Mines Ltd. v. A.-G. Ont.*, [1967] S.C.R. 672, 63 D.L.R. (2d) 688.

Do the provisions of the *Crown Liability Act*, R.S.C. 1970, c. C-38, equating the liability of the federal Crown to that of private persons, subject it to provincial requirements as to the time for and manner of suing municipalities? See *The Queen v. Montreal* (1972), 27 D.L.R. (3d) 349 (Fed. Ct.).]

IN RE VANCINI

In the Supreme Court of Canada. (1904), 34 S.C.R. 621.

Appeal from a decision of Killam J. in Chambers refusing a writ of *habeas corpus*. Appellant was charged with theft before a police magistrate, consented to be tried summarily by him, and, on a plea of guilty, was sentenced to imprisonment. He sought *habeas corpus*, contending, *inter alia*, that the Dominion cannot give jurisdiction to a provincial court to try criminal offences unless the provincial court has been so empowered by provincial legislation.

The judgment of the Court was delivered by

SEDGEWICK J.: . . . As to the second point in our view "the Dominion Parliament can, in matters within its sphere, impose duties upon any subjects of the Dominion, whether they be officials of provincial courts, other officials or private citizens; and there is nothing in the *British North America Act* to raise a doubt about the power of the Dominion Parliament to impose new duties upon the existing provincial courts, or to give them new powers, as to matters which do not come within the subjects assigned exclusively to the legislatures of the provinces, or to deprive them of jurisdiction over such matters. (Lefroy on Legislative Power in Canada, page 510.)" This statement of the law is mainly founded upon the celebrated decision of this court in *Valin v. Langlois*, 3 S.C.R. 1, where it was held that the *Dominion Controverted Elections Act (1874)* was not *ultra vires* of the Dominion Parliament, and whether or not the Act established a Dominion court, the Dominion Parliament had a perfect right to give to the courts of the respective provinces and the judges thereof the power thereby created, and did not, in utilizing judicial officers and establishing [established?] courts to discharge the duties assigned to them by that Act, in any particular invade the rights of the local legislatures; and the majority of the court, Ritchie C.J. and Taschereau and Gwynne JJ., held that the Act established a Dominion court as authorized by section 101 of the *British America Act*.

The question is most fully treated by Mr. Justice Taschereau, now Chief Justice of this court, and it is unnecessary now to do more than refer to that opinion. The judgment of this court, in that case, was affirmed by the Judicial Committee of the Privy Council upon the grounds stated, 5 App. Cas. 115.

This court again affirmed the same principle in *Attorney-General v. Flint,* 16 S.C.R. 707, which, however, related to a jurisdiction imposed by the Parliament of Canada upon the imperially created Court of Vice-Admiralty, in Nova Scotia.

Where once the Parliament of Canada has given jurisdiction to a provincial court whether superior or inferior, or to a judicial officer, to perform judicial functions in the adjudicating of matters over which the Parliament of Canada has exclusive jurisdiction, no provincial legislation, in our opinion, is necessary in order to enable effect to be given to such parliamentary enactments.

Appeal dismissed.

[See also, *Regina v. Stewart, ex parte Shatford,* [1965] 1 Can. C.C. 9, 44 C.R. 10.

The doctrine of the *Vancini* case embraces federal power to give a right of appeal to a provincial Court in respect of matters arising under federal legislation, and where this is done provincial appeal procedures would, although otherwise competent, be by-passed: see *Re International Petroleum Co. Ltd.,* [1962] O.R. 705, 33 D.L.R. (2d) 658, aff'd on other grounds, [1963] S.C.R. 144, 37 D.L.R. (2d) 598. If federal legislation is silent but does not preclude an appeal, would not provincial legislation apply (subject to the principle of *In re Storgoff*) if broad enough in terms to give jurisdiction to the provincial appellate Court? See *Deputy A.-G. Can. v. Brown,* [1964] C.T.C. 483, where the question was raised but not decided.

The Dominion may vest power in a magistrate to admit a person to bail after his committal for trial. Authority for this resides in s. 91(27) of the *B.N.A. Act:* see *Regina v. McDonald,* [1958] O.R. 373, 120 Can. C.C. 198,

The same basis supported the Criminal Code authorization for court appointment of counsel for an indigent defendant, R.S.O. 1970, c. C-34, s. 612, see *Regina v. Happeney,* 2 N.B.R. (2d) 699, 12 C.R.N.S. 116, 2 D.L.R. (3d) 538, [1970] 5 C.C.C. 353.

May a provincial legislature give jurisdiction to Dominion Courts or impose duties on Dominion officers? *Clement,* The Canadian Constitution states (at p. 435): "But the principle of the cases cited above is equally applicable to uphold such provincial legislation in relation to subjects within its competence". This view, it is submitted, is erroneous: see *Union Colliery Co. of B.C. v. A.-G. B.C.* (1897), 27 S.C.R. 637: cf. *Irwin v. A.G. Ont.,* [1932] O.R. 490, [1932] 3 D.L.R. 668.

The *Dominion Courts Act,* R.S.O. 1970, c. 134 provides by s. 1(c) that "the Supreme Court of Canada . . . according to the *Supreme Court Act (Canada)* . . .has jurisdiction in actions or proceedings in which the parties thereto by their pleadings have raised the question of the validity of an Act of the Parliament of Canada or of an Act of the Legislature of Ontario, when in the opinion of a judge of the court in which the same are pending the question is material, and in such case the judge shall, at the request of the parties, and may without such request, if he thinks fit, order the case to be removed to the Supreme Court of Canada, in order that the question may be decided." See *P.E.I. Potato Marketing Board v. H. B. Willis and A.-G. Can.*, [1952] 1 D.L.R. 321 (Can.). Would it be competent to a Province to confer jurisdiction on the Supreme Court without enabling federal legislation? Would it be competent to Parliament to provide for removal of causes from provincial Courts to the Supreme Court without enabling provincial legislation?

There is no doubt about the power of the Dominion to curtail or withdraw jurisdiction of provincial Courts in respect of matters within federal competence: *Valin v. Langlois* (1879), 3 S.C.R. 1, at p. 74; *Nanaimo Community Hotel v. Board of Refrerees*, [1945] 3 D.L.R. 225, [1945] 2 W.W.R. 145.

For comparison, see *Note*, Utilization of State Courts to Enforce Federal Penal and Criminal Statutes, (1947) 60 Harv. L. Rev. 966; *Note*, State Enforcement of Federally Created Rights, (1960) 73 Harv. L. Rev. 1551.]

CROWN GRAIN CO. v. DAY

In the Privy Council. [1908] A.C. 504.

Appeal by special leave from an order of the Supreme Court of Canada, 39 S.C.R. 258, dismissing a motion to quash an appeal from the Manitoba Court of King's Bench *en banc*.

LORD ROBERTSON: By the 101st section of the British North America Act, 1867, the Parliament of Canada was authorized to provide for "the constitution, maintenance, and organization of a general Court of Appeal for Canada"; and by Act of the Dominion Parliament the Supreme Court of Canada was accordingly established, the existing statute being Rev. Stat. Canada, 1906, c. 139. It is inconceivable that a Court of Appeal could be established without its jurisdiction being at the same time defined; and this statute contains these provisions:—

"The Supreme Court shall have, hold, and exercise an appellate civil and criminal jurisdiction within and throughout Canada" (s. 35).

"Except as hereinafter otherwise provided an appeal shall lie to the Supreme Court from any final judgment of the highest Court of final resort now or hereafter established in any province of Canada" (s. 36).

If this Dominion statute be the governing enactment in *hac re,* it unquestionably allows the appeal to the Supreme Court of Canada, the competency of which was challenged in this case.

The question now in dispute is whether that enactment has been affected, and so far defeated, by an Act of the Legislature of Manitoba which admittedly purports to apply to the suit in which the appeal was brought, and which makes the judgment of the provincial Court final and conclusive. The Manitoba statute relates to liens; and it is in regard to suits about liens that appeal is excluded.

Liens are admittedly in the region of legislation appropriated to provincial Legislatures by the *British North America Act*. It is incidentally to the subject of liens that the Manitoban legislation provides that the judgment of the Court of King's Bench on suits relating to liens shall be final and binding, and that no appeal shall lie therefrom. This enactment is in direct conflict with the general provisions of appeal in the Dominion Act; and the question is, which enactment prevails?

The appellants maintain that the implied condition of the power of the Dominion Parliament to set up a Court of Appeal was that the Court so set up should be liable to have its jurisdiction circumscribed by provincial legislation dealing with those subject-matters of litigation which, like that of contracts, are committed to the provincial Legislatures. The argument necessarily goes so far as to justify the wholesale exclusion of appeals in suits relating to matters within the region of provincial legislation. As this region covers the larger part of the common subjects of litigation, the result would be the virtual defeat of the main purposes of the Court of Appeal.

It is to be observed that the subject in conflict belongs primarily to the subject-matter committed to the Dominion Parliament, namely, the establishment of the Court of Appeal for Canada. But, further, let it be assumed that the subject-matter is open to both legislative bodies; if the powers thus overlap, the enactment of the Dominion Parliament must prevail. This has already been laid down in *Dobie v. Temporalities Board*, 7 App. Cas. 136, and *Grand Trunk Ry. Co. of Canada v. Attorney-General of Canada*, [1907] A.C. 65.

For these reasons their Lordships on July 9 last agreed humbly to advise His Majesty that the appeal ought to be dismissed. . . .

Appeal dismissed.

[The Supreme Court of Canada has long held that a provincial legislature cannot confer or limit or abrogate a right of appeal to that Court: see *Clarkson v. Ryan* (1890), 17 S.C.R. 251; *Union Colliery Co. of B.C. v. A.-G. B.C.* (1897), 27 S.C.R. 637. It is immaterial that the matter in issue is within provincial legislative competence. The *Crown Grain Co.* case settled any doubts that there might be on the question. See, however, O'Halloran J.A. in *Gill v. Ferrari*, [1951] 1 D.L.R. 647, 1 W.W.R. (N.S.) 94 where he sought to revive the issue.

Where the Supreme Court has been vested with appellate jurisdiction Parliament may properly provide for certifying its judgment to the proper officer of the Court of original jurisdiction, albeit a provincial Court, and for the taking in that Court of all subsequent proceedings on the judgment: see *Bowes v. Bamford* (1957). 9 D.L.R. (2d) 83.

Does the term "general court of appeal for Canada" in s. 101 contemplate that the Dominion may provide for appeals to the Supreme Court only from "section 96 courts" or tribunals analogous thereto? May the Dominion properly give an appeal from or provide for review of a decision of a provincial administrative agency? See *Théberge Ltée v. Syndicat National des Employes de l'Aluminum d'Arvida Inc.*, [1966] S.C.R. 378, 58 D.L.R. (2d) 764.

May a provincial appellate court, in the exercise of an inherent jurisdiction or under provincial legislation or rules of court, stay execution on a judgment pending an appeal to the Supreme Court of Canada despite federal statutory provision on the matter or, at least, where the stay would not be inconsistent with the federal statute? See *Buxton v. Carriss* (1958), **13** D.L.R. (2d) 671, 25 W.W.R. 225. If Parliament has spoken on the question of a stay of execution pending an appeal to the Supreme Court, does not its legislation govern? See *Downsview Meadows Ltd. v. Wright-Winston Ltd.*, [1965] 2 O.R. 566, 51 D.L.R. (2d) 396.]

Note on Jurisdiction to Review Decisions of Federal Agencies or Officers

The *Federal Court Act*, R.S.C. 1970, c. 10 (2nd Supp.) effectively vests review of federal administrative officials exclusively in the Federal Court. The principal provision is section 18:

> The Trial Division has exclusive original jurisdiction (*a*) to issue an injunction, writ of *certiorari*, writ of prohibition, writ of *mandamus* or writ of *quo warranto*, or grant declaratory relief, against any federal board, commission or other tribunal; and (*b*) to hear and determine any application or other proceeding for relief in the nature of relief contemplated by paragraph (*a*), including any proceeding brought against the Attorney General of Canada, to obtain relief against a federal board, commission or other tribunal.

Under the Act, section 2, " 'federal board, commission or other tribunal' means any body or any person or persons having, exercising or purporting to exercise jurisdiction or powers conferred by or under an Act of the Parliament of Canada, other than any such body constituted or established by or under a law of a province or any such person or persons appointed under or in accordance with a law of the province or under section 96 of the *British North America Act, 1867*".

There are in addition in relation to particular categories of federal competence—members of the Canadian Forces acting abroad (sec. 17(5)), patents (section 20), appeals under the *Canadian Citizenship Act* (section 21)—specific grants of exclusive jurisdiction.

With the enactment of this legislation, there remains little occasion to consider the questions which attracted a good deal of judicial attention earlier as to the powers and duties of provinces in connection with such review. Those questions would seem, however, to have been in large part resolved by the judgment in *Three Rivers Boatman Ltd. v. Canada Labour Relations Board*, [1969] S.C.R. 607, 12 D.L.R. (3d) 710, holding the Board subject to supervisory review by the Quebec Superior Court notwithstanding the definition of that Court's jurisdiction by the Code of Civil Procedure as extending to review of tribunals under the jurisdiction of the Quebec Legislature. The Superior Court, speaking through Fauteux J. said:

"At the moment of its creation in 1849, the Superior Court received fully the civil jurisdiction of first instance and in particular the supervisory jurisdiction theretofore exercised by the Court of King's Bench, cf. 12 Vic. c. 38, s. VII. At the same time, it was provided that the prerogative writs involved in the exercise of that supervisory jurisdiction should issue thenceforth from the Superior Court, cf. 12 Vic. c. 41, s. 16. The Superior Court thus became vested with the supervisory power based on the common law which the Court of King's Bench in England exercised, on which our Court of King's Bench was modelled. The law of the judicial control of tribunals, political bodies or corporations exercising judicial or quasi judicial powers, comes to us from English public law introduced into Quebec at the time of and consequent on the cession . . .

"It was in 1957 by the Act of 5-6 Eliz. II, c. 16, s. 1, that the Quebec Legislature amended section 50, Code of Civil Procedure— section 33 of the present Code—to provide expressly that the Superior Court's right of supervision or revision of lower tribunals should be limited to tribunals *falling under the jurisdiction of the Quebec Legislature.* A legislature is presumed to legislate within the limits of its competence. The Legislature of Quebec has no authority to modify and nothing indicates that it intended to modify by the 1957 amendment the power of supervision and control that the Superior Court has possessed since before Confederation, as well by virtue of its governing statute as of the powers inherent to its functions, over the agencies which fall now under the jurisdiction of Parliament and which act judicially or quasi-judicially on provincially situated activities and render decisions which are there carried into the effect. Alone authorized to do so, since 1867, cf. s. 129 of the British North America Act, Parliament has not, generally at least, assigned to any other court this right of control and supervision. It follows that the Superior Court still possesses that authority which it inherited, by statute, from the Court of King's Bench of 1849, so that anyone who claims that his rights have been infringed through a federal agency's exceeding its jurisdiction can, in order to establish them and insure that they will be respected, have recourse to it.

"In fact as the draftsmen of the new Code have noted, section 846 combines the provisions of sections 1003 and 1292 of the previous Code, concerning prohibition and *certiorari* respectively. . . . So notwithstanding its twofold function, the remedy spoken of in section 846 is not new. Different in form but not in essence, the remedy is not substantially different from those used only then to protect in a summary and effective way against excesses of jurisdiction by administrative tribunals.

"I should say then, following Dorion C.J., that the Superior Court has jurisdiction to control the execution of a quasi-judicial decision by the Canadian Board, when this decision would affect the rights of parties in the province of Quebec and to be put into effect there. In the absence of a specification of appeal procedures to the Superior Court, the parties can, in conformity with the provisions of section 20, Code of Civil Procedure, use the procedure applicable as to administrative tribunals coming under the jurisdiction of the Quebec Legislature".

[Editor's translation]

3. Procedure in Provincial and Dominion Courts

Note on Constitutional Aspects of Procedure in Courts

By express provision of the *B.N.A. Act,* procedure in civil matters in provincial courts is within the exclusive legislative authority of the provinces (s. 92(14)), and procedure in criminal matters is within exclusive federal competence (s. 91(27)). No constitutional question arises in respect of the power of the Dominion to control and dictate the procedure in federal courts; and where a provincial court is seized of a "federal" cause of action the Dominion may, if it chooses, prescribe the procedure through which it is to be enforced therein. As Rinfret J. said in *A.-G. Alta. and Winstanley v. Atlas Lumber Co.,* [1941] S.C.R. 87, [1941] 1 D.L.R. 625, "it has long been decided that with respect to matters coming within the enumerated heads of s. 91, the Parliament of Canada may give jurisdiction to provincial Courts and regulate proceedings in such Courts to the fullest extent". If federal legislation is silent, the question then arises whether and to what extent provincial procedure in provincial courts is applicable.

The ordinary rule is that, where no other procedure is prescribed, a litigant suing on a federal matter in a provincial court takes the procedure of that court as he finds it: see *Alexander v. Vancouver Harbour Commrs.,* [1922] 1 W.W.R. 1254, 65 D.L.R. 355, 31 B.C.R. 11; *Morris v. Morris,* [1950] O.R. 697, [1951] 1 D.L.R. 38. Indeed, there is no reason to doubt provincial competence to alter existing procedure as it applies to federal causes of action, at least when no pre-confederation or federal post-confederation procedure associated with such causes of action is in force in the province: see *Davidson v. Davidson,* [1953] 1 D.L.R. 297, 7 W.W.R. (N.S.) 272; *Adler v. Adler,* [1966] 1 O.R. 732, 55 D.L.R. (2d) 113.

This being so, a central question arises as to what is meant by "procedure" in this connection. It is undoubted that a province is incompetent to legislate in relation to the substance (or substantive law) of a matter within the federal catalogue of powers: *cf. Reference re Debt Adjustment Act,* [1942] S.C.R. 31, [1942] 1 D.L.R. 1, aff'd [1943] A.C. 356, [1943] 1 W.W.R. 378; see *Notes,* (1945) 23 Can. Bar Rev. 159, 265. It was held in *Re Etmanski and Taggart Service Ltd.,* [1966] 1 O.R. 473 that a substantive rather than a procedural matter was involved in the constitution of an arbitration board pursuant to a collective agreement stemming from federal labour relations legislation; hence, the provincial *Arbitration Act* could not be invoked to permit a Judge to appoint an arbitrator thereunder for one of the parties to the collective agreement upon its failure to make an appointment. In any event, the federal Act itself provided a remedy for this problem and provincial legislation was precluded, whether or not a matter of procedure or substance was involved. But where "procedure" is concerned, there are lower Court decisions holding, or at least suggesting, that provincial enactments apply in provincial courts to federal causes of action even though there is federal legislation on the particular procedural issue: see *Stafford v. Stafford and Cope,* [1945] O.W.N. 52, [1945] 1 D.L.R. 263; *Davison v. Davison,* [1954] 1 D.L.R. 567, 10 W.W.R. (N.S.) 423. This appears to be an overreaching: *cf. Regina v. Fox* (1889), 18 P.R. 343; and also *Klein v. Bell,* reproduced *infra.*

Several illustrative problems may be put. In a divorce action, may a Province prescribe what shall be sufficient proof of a matrimonial offence defined by federal legislation? See *Andrews v. Andrews and Roberts,* [1945] 1 D.L.R. 595, [1945] 1 W.W.R. 113; *Chambers v. Chambers,* [1947] O.W.N. 927. Is this a question of procedure or of substantive divorce law, and, even if the former, what if federal legislation prescribes a lower standard of proof? Is a question of non-access as it arises in a divorce action a matter of evidence (as being part of the procedure in the action) or a matter of substantive divorce law? See *Schiedl v. Schiedl and Upton,* [1949] 4 D.L.R. 630, [1949] 2 W.W.R. 403, rev'd [1950] 1 D.L.R. 656, [1950] 1 W.W.R. 168.

Are provincial statutes of limitation applicable to federal causes of action in the provincial courts, and, if so, on what principle? See *Burton v. Burton,* [1946] 1 D.L.R. 315, [1945] 3 W.W.R. 765; *Weingarden v. Moss,* [1955] 1 D.L.R. 747, 13 W.W.R. (N.S.) 161, aff'd [1955] 4 D.L.R. 63, 15 W.W.R. 481. In an action on a bill of exchange or promissory note, may a Province impose conditions on the right to sue beyond any that are included in federal legislation governing such instruments? See *Atlas Lumber Co. v. A.-G. Alta. and Winstanley,* [1940] 3 D.L.R. 648, [1940] 2 W.W.R. 437, aff'd [1941] S.C.R. 87, [1941] 1 D.L.R. 625.

Since "procedure in criminal matters" is exclusively for Parliament, the problem here as related to provincial courts is to determine what are matters of criminal procedure as distinguished from matters connected with the constitution and organization of provincial courts. Thus, it has been determined that *habeas corpus,* considered in popular terms to be a bulwark of "civil liberty", falls to be regulated by the Dominion in respect of any right of appeal in provincial courts where the resort to the writ arises out of a conviction under federal criminal legislation. The Province cannot provide for an appeal even if Parliament has remained silent: *In re Storgoff,* [1945] S.C.R. 526, [1945] 3 D.L.R. 673; *Gordon,* Note, (1945) 23 Can. Bar Rev. 595; see also *Re Wattebled,* [1953] Que. Q.B. 108, 106 Can. C.C. 200, 16 C.R. 301 (*habeas corpus* in extradition proceedings). The same holds true with respect to any power to award costs in *habeas corpus* proceedings arising out of detention under the federal criminal law: see *Re Christianson,* [1951] 4 D.L.R. 462, 3 W.W.R. (N.S.) 133. (Some of the discussion in the *Storgoff* case would warrant the conclusion that it goes beyond a determination of what is "procedure in criminal matters", and indeed would exclude provincial competence in respect of *habeas corpus* (although there be no federal legislation) if the matter out of which the writ arises is itself within federal competence. This is, it is submitted, too broad a proposition as applied to non-criminal matters). The *Storgoff* doctrine as limited to "procedure in criminal matters" applies to the other prerogative writs: see, as to prohibition, *Re Rex v. Thompson*, [1946] O.R. 560, [1946] 4 D.L.R. 591; and as to *mandamus, Marathon Paper Mills of Canada Ltd. v. The King*, [1947] O.R. 532, 89 Can. C.C. 59, 4 C.R. 16; and as to *certiorari, Burrows v. Gilding*, [1954] 3 D.L.R. 357, 11 W.W.R. (N.S.) 89. Of course, where the offence arises under competent provincial legislation, it is for the Province to provide for the procedure (including rights of appeal) in the provincial courts: see *Rex v. McIlree*, [1950] 1 W.W.R. 894, 97 Can. C.C. 89, 9 C.R. 447.

The *Storgoff* rule must be considered applicable to *habeas corpus* in respect of preventive justice, *i.e.* binding over to keep the peace under Cr. Code, s. 745, although no nominate offence has been committed. The abolition of common law offences by s. 8 of the Cr. Code must be taken to have excluded any common law of preventive justice which had theretofore been in force in any Province (see *MacKenzie v. Martin*, [1952] O.R. 849, [1953] 1 D.L.R. 161, aff'd [1954] S.C.R. 361, [1954] 3 D.L.R. 417), and although the opinion had been expressed that there is a provincial area of preventive justice, with consequential authority in the province to prescribe procedure, e.g., in respect of *habeas corpus* and appeals therefrom (see *Rex v. MacKenzie*, [1945] O.R. 787, [1946] 1 D.L.R. 584; and cf. O'Halloran J.A. *in Frey v. Fedoruk*, [1949] 2 W.W.R. 604, 95 Can. C.C. 206, 8 C.R. 373, rev'd on other grounds, [1950] S.C.R. 517, [1950] 3 D.L.R. 513), this is not a tenable proposition. The substantive field is surely a matter falling within the criminal law power, and any procedure or appeal in respect thereof is within exclusive federal authority under s. 91(27): cf. *Regina v. Wright*, [1953] 4 D.L.R. 193, 9 W.W.R. (N.S.) 214 (Province incompetent to abridge time prescribed by Cr. Code for launching an appeal; provincial appeal rules inapplicable). There is a preventive side to the federal criminal law power (see *Goodyear Tire & Rubber Co. of Canada Ltd. v. The Queen*, [1956] S.C.R. 303, 2 D.L.R. (2d) 11) no less than there is to other heads of federal legislative authority (see *A.-G. Ont. v. Canada Temperance Federation*, [1946] A.C. 193, [1946] 2 D.L.R. 1, [1946] 2 W.W.R. 1, where the Privy Council said: "To legislate for prevention appears to be on the same basis as legislation for cure.")

The Supreme Court of Canada has applied the *Storgoff* rule to contempt proceedings by holding in *Poje v. A.-G. B.C.*, [1953] 1 S.C.R. 516, [1953] 2 D.L.R. 785, that where contempt is properly characterized as criminal contempt (rather than civil) provincial rules of Court and provincial provisions for appeal are inapplicable, and this notwithstanding that the contempt arises out of matters or proceedings which are within provincial legislative authority. Under the Criminal Code, s. 9 a right of appeal in respect of summary contempt convictions is as follows: (1) Where there is a conviction for contempt of court committed in the face of the court, an appeal lies against the punishment imposed; and (2) where there is a conviction for contempt of court not committed in the face of the court an appeal lies from conviction or against the punishment imposed. The conclusion follows that the provision presupposes, in accordance with the *Poje* case, a constitutional significance in the distinction between criminal and civil contempt of court, and applies only to the former.

The mode of trial, whether jury or non-jury, involves constitutional questions where federal matters are triable in provincial courts. While in the absence of specific federal legislation, provincial modes of trial will apply to federal civil causes of action or proceedings, the express reservation to the Dominion of procedure in criminal matters has resulted in a number of problems respecting the use of grand and petit juries in criminal proceedings. It is clear that it is for Parliament alone to determine whether jury trial should be available in criminal prosecutions and, if so, the number to constitute the jury and the number by whom a verdict shall be given: see *Rex v. Preusantanz,* [1936] 2 D.L.R. 421, [1936] 1 W.W.R. 520, 44 Man. R. 33; *Rex v. McGavin Bakeries Ltd.,* [1951] 4 D.L.R. 806, 2 W.W.R. (N.S.) 1. Equally is it for Parliament to determine whether a special jury shall be available in a criminal trial: see *Rex v. McPherson,* [1952] O.R. 273, [1952] 4 D.L.R. 512. The situation should be no different in respect of the use of a grand jury, but it has been held that while the selection or qualification and summoning of grand jurors, and the number by whom a bill may be found is a matter for Parliament alone (see *Regina v. O'Rourke* (1882), 32 U.C.C.P. 388, 1 O.R. 464; *Sproule v. The Queen* (1886), 1 B.C.R. (Pt. 2) 219; *Regina v. Plante* (1891), 7 Man. R. 537), the number of jurors returned to serve on a grand jury is a matter for the Province as pertaining to the constitution of the provincial court (see *Regina v. Cox* (1898), 31 N.S.R. 311, 2 Can. C.C. 207; *Rex v. Walton* (1906), 12 O.L.R. 1, 11 Can. C.C. 204). The *Cox* and *Walton* cases express the law on the subject in the absence of federal legislation and a like principle applies as to coroners' juries, see *Re Wilson; Whitelaw v. McDonald,* 66 W.W.R. 522, 2 D.L.R. (3d) 298, [1969] 3 C.C.C. 4 (B.C. C.A.). It is certainly open to Parliament to determine the number of grand jurors no less than the number of petit jurors. Similarly, it is for Parliament to say, if it will, whether there is a right to inspect the jury panel in criminal causes (see *In re Chantler* (1905), 9 O.L.R. 529, 9 Can. C.C. 465). The fact that Parliament has, in respect of jury matters, legislated by reference to or adoption of provincial legislation (see Cr. Code, s. 534) does not militate against its independent competence.

[In a criminal appeal in a provincial court, one of the five appellate Judges died after the hearing and the others delivered judgment as permitted by provincial legislation. It was alleged that this legislation was *ultra vires* because in allowing the majority to act, it precluded the possibility of a further appeal, as given by federal legislation, where there was a dissent. Do you agree? See *Re Rex v. Imperial Tobacco Co.,* [1942] 2 D.L.R. 167, [1942] 1 W.W.R. 625.]

KLEIN v. BELL

In the Supreme Court of Canada. [1955] S.C.R. 309, [1955]
2 D.L.R. 513.

Appeal by special leave from a judgment of the British Columbia
Court of Appeal, [1954] 4 D.L.R. 273, 12 W.W.R. (N.S.) 272,
reversing an order of Clyne J., [1954] 1 D.L.R. 225, 10 W.W.R. (N.S.)
324 and ordering answers to certain questions on discovery, notwithstanding that such answers might tend to criminate.

KERWIN C.J.C.: . . . The appellants argued that examinations
for discovery are not included in or covered by s. 5 of the *Evidence
Act,* R.S.B.C. 1948, c. 113, which is in these terms: "No witness
shall be excused from answering any question upon the ground that
the answer to the question may tend to criminate him, or may tend
to establish his liability to a civil proceeding at the instance of the
Crown or of any person, and if but for this section the witness would
therefore have been excused from answering the question, then,
although the witness shall be compelled to answer, yet the answer
so given shall not be used or receivable in evidence against him in
any criminal trial or other criminal proceeding against him thereafter
taking place other than a prosecution for perjury in giving such
evidence."

Order 31a, M.R. 370c of the British Columbia Supreme Court
Rules provides: "A party to an action or issue, whether plaintiff or
defendant, may, without order, be orally examined before the trial
touching the matters in question by any party adverse in interest,
and may be compelled to attend and testify in the same manner,
upon the same terms, and subject to the same rules of examination
of a witness except as hereinafter provided.

"(1)   In the case of a corporation, any officer or servant of such
corporation may, without any special order, and any one who has
been one of the officers of such corporation may, by order of a Court
or a Judge, be orally examined before the trial touching the matters
in question by any party adverse in interest to the corporation, and
may be compelled to attend and testify in the same manner and upon
the same terms and subject to the same rules of examination as a
witness, save as hereinafter provided. Such examination or any
part thereof may be used as evidence at the trial if the trial Judge
so orders."

We were not referred to any exception "hereinafter provided"
and, in view of the express terms that a party, officer or servant may
be compelled to attend and testify "in the same manner, upon the
same terms, and subject to the same rules of examination of [or as]
a witness", the person being examined is subject to the direction
contained in s. 5 of the Act and, of course, is entitled to the privilege.
Order 31a is modelled from the Ontario Rules, 1897 and amendments,
and in *Chambers v. Jaffray* (1906), 12 O.L.R. 377, it was so held,
although in the Divisional Court the majority apparently did so

because they considered themselves bound by *R. v. Fox* (1899), 18 P.R. (Ont.) 343. Without expressing any opinion as to the latter, the result arrived at in the *Chambers* case is, in my view, the correct one. . . .

It is now necessary to deal with the point taken by the appellants for the first time in this Court that s. 5 of the *Evidence Act,* R.S.B.C. 1948, c. 113, is *ultra vires* the provincial Legislature. It should be noted that the earliest Evidence Acts of the Canadian Parliament had no provision such as is found in s. 5 of the *Canada Evidence Act.* R.S.C. 1952, c. 307. The forerunner of that section first appeared in c. 31 of the Statutes of 1893 and read as follows:

"5. No person shall be excused from answering any question upon the ground that the answer to such question may tend to criminate him, or may tend to establish his liability to a civil proceeding at the instance of the Crown or of any other person: Provided, however, that no evidence so given shall be used or receivable in evidence against such person in any criminal proceeding thereafter instituted against him other than a prosecution for perjury in giving such evidence."

This Act was amended by c. 36 of the Statutes of 1901 by adding thereto the following as s-s. (2) of s. 5:

"5(2) The proviso to subsection 1 of this section shall in like manner apply to the answer of a witness to any question in which pursuant to an enactment of the legislature of a province such witness is compelled to answer after having objected so to do upon any ground mentioned in the said subsection, and which, but for that enactment, he would upon such ground have been excused from answering."

In the Revised Statutes of Canada 1906, c. 145, s. 5 of the *Canada Evidence Act* appeared as follows:

"5(1) No witness shall be excused from answering any question upon the ground that the answer to such question may tend to criminate him, or may tend to establish his liability to a civil proceeding at the instance of the Crown or of any person.

"(2) If with respect to any question a witness objects to answer upon the ground that his answer may tend to criminate him, or may tend to establish his liability to a civil proceeding at the instance of the Crown or of any person, and if but for this Act, or the act of any provincial legislature, the witness would therefore have been excused from answering such question, then although the witness is by reason of this Act, or by reason of such provincial act, compelled to answer, the answer so given shall not be used or receivable in evidence against him in any criminal trial, or other criminal proceeding against him thereafter taking place, other than a prosecution for perjury in the giving of such evidence."

In 1894 the British Columbia Legislature revised its *Evidence Act* [c. 13] and therein enacted verbatim s. 5 of the federal Act of 1893 set out above. The provincial statutes were again revised in 1897, when s. 6 of the *Evidence Act,* c. 71, appeared in the same form as s. 5 of the Act of 1894. They were consolidated in 1911 when, for the first time, s. 5 of the *Evidence Act,* c. 78, appeared in practically the same form as the section now before us, R.S.B.C. 1948, c. 113.

It has been pointed out that in 1894 the British Columbia Legislature enacted the same provision as Parliament had passed in 1893. The enactment in 1911 in British Columbia was an endeavour to carry out the idea underlying s. 5 of c. 145 of R.S.C. 1906. I have no doubt that this was done with the object of taking care of cases where the proper objection to testify was taken in proceedings over which the Legislature had jurisdiction and then providing that such evidence might not be used later either in civil cases or a criminal trial. Looking at s. 5 as it appeared in the 1894 provincial enactment and considering its history since then, I am driven to the conclusion that "criminal proceeding" is not confined to what are known as provincial crimes, particularly when that part of the statute is followed by the words "other than a prosecution for perjury". The decision of the British Columbia Court of Appeal on this point in *Staples v. Isaacs,* [1940] 3 D.L.R. 473, 74 Can. C.C. 204, 55 B.C.R. 189 (which, in fact, was overruled by the Court of Appeal in the present case) cannot be supported. Canada, of course, could only provide with reference to all proceedings over which it had legislative authority and the provincial Legislature with reference to proceedings over which it had such authority. I am unable to agree with the contention on behalf of the respondent and the Attorney-General of British Columbia that the proviso in the provincial enactment may be disregarded, because I am unable to hold that even if the constitutional point had been brought to the attention of the Legislature it would have enacted the section without some proviso and it is impossible to say what that proviso would have contained. Reliance was placed by the respondents and the Attorney-General of British Columbia upon s. 36 of the *Canada Evidence Act,* which is in these terms:

"36. In all proceedings over which the Parliament of Canada has legislative authority, the laws of evidence in force in the province in which such proceedings are taken, including the laws of proof of service of any warrant, summons, subpoena or other document subject to this and other Acts of the Parliament of Canada, apply to such proceedings."

This, however, cannot assist, because, if s. 5 of the British Columbia Act is of no effect, it is not part of the provincial law of evidence. Section 5 must, therefore, be declared *ultra vires.* This conclusion is to be regretted, but the situation is not beyond remedy by the Legislature.

In the absence of any such remedial legislation the common law applies as well to an officer taking the objection on behalf of his company as to an individual litigant. In both cases, however, the objection must be made on the oath of the person under examination that, to the best of his belief his answer would tend to criminate him, or the company, as the case may be. Such person is not entitled to object to answer ordinary questions about his residence, place of business, etc., nor is he entitled to rest on a statement that on the advice of his solicitor, or the solicitor for the company, he refuses to answer any questions on the ground that the answers might tend to criminate him, or it. He must pledge his oath in his belief that his answers to particular questions *seriatim* would so tend: *Power v. Ellis* (1881), 6 S.C.R. 1. What occurred on the examinations for discovery in this case is not sufficient. . . .

RAND J.: . . . This [s. 5 of the provincial Act], originally passed in 1894, was given its present form in 1897. In 1893 what is now s. 5 of the *Canada Evidence Act,* in enacting that, in criminal and other proceedings respecting which Parliament has jurisdiction, no person should be excused from answering any question on the ground of crimination, provided that no evidence so given should "be used or receivable in evidence against such person in any criminal proceeding thereafter instituted against him other than a prosecution for perjury in giving such evidence". This was the law of Parliament at the time of the enactment of s. 5 of the provincial Act, and it will be observed that its immunity does not reach one who has been compelled to answer by provincial law. It was not until 1901 that the protection of the Dominion Act was extended to evidence so adduced; and the critical question is, what was the law regarding compulsion to answer, say, in 1898? This depends upon the interpretation of s. 5 of the provincial Act and whether or not the proviso can be severed from the main clause.

The language employed does not vary materially from that of s. 5 of the Dominion Act of 1893. The provincial Act came before the Court of Appeal in the case of *Staples v. Isaacs,* [1940] 3 D.L.R. 473, 74 Can. C.C. 204, 55 B.C.R. 189. The effect of the judgment was that, in both its compulsory and protective features, the section was limited to matters that relate to what are called "provincial crimes", for example, breaches of municipal by-laws or violations of the provincial Government *Liquor Control Act.* This is made clear in the reasons of Sloan J.A. (now C.J.B.C.). The view expressed was that as the party examined could be afforded no safeguard by the provincial Act in a prosecution under the Criminal Code, the Legislature could not be taken to have abrogated the privilege generally. At the same time it was held that the word "witness" in s. 5 of the Dominion Act did not extend to a person being examined on discovery.

To attribute such a limited scope to s. 5 of the provincial Act would, of course, dispose of this appeal without more; the matters of incrimination here have nothing to do with provincial offences. But the Court of Appeal has declined to follow *Staples v. Isaacs, supra,* and it becomes necessary to examine the statutory language more closely. The proviso declares that the answer "shall not be used or receivable in evidence against him in any criminal trial or other criminal proceeding against him thereafter taking place other than a prosecution for perjury in giving such evidence". I think it would be distorting the natural meaning of these words to say that they are restricted to provincial crimes. The opening clause of the section is equally broad: the witness is not to be excused from answering any question upon the ground of crimination.

I entertain no doubt that a Province cannot exclude from testimony in a criminal prosecution admissions made in the course of discovery or of trial in a civil proceeding; to do so would be to legislate in relation to procedure in criminal matters which is within the exclusive jurisdiction of Parliament. Can the proviso be taken in the sense that the compulsory feature is to be effective where and when under any law the answer is not available for use in criminal proceedings against the person making it? The amendment made in 1901 would in that case feed the proviso and bring into operation the compulsory clause. But the language excludes such a construction. The purpose and intention were to create by force of what was looked upon as effective legislation a protection complementary to the broadest compulsion.

Is the proviso, then, severable? Can it be taken not as a condition bound up with the preceding clause, but as an independent and consequential declaration which may be struck out without affecting it? The Act, as declared in s. 3, undoubtedly includes proceedings over which the Legislature has jurisdiction, and a residue can be found in the proviso for purely provincial matters which would leave the general compulsion intact. But if the question had arisen in 1895, can any one doubt what the answer would have been? Considering the obvious purpose of the legislation, in a radical departure from the ancient rule, such an interpretation would be repugnant to the vital considerations the Legislature had in mind. The entire section consequently was inoperative *ab initio*.

That being so in 1894, it could not be revived by the amendment of 1901; nor could the general revisions of the Act made since that time furnish any efficacy to the section. It seems quite evident that the significance of the amendment in relation to the provincial Act was not appreciated. The result is unfortunate, but I see no way of escaping it. . . .

Appeal allowed.

[Taschereau, Estey and Fauteux JJ. concurred with Kerwin C.J.C. See also *Regina v. Hambleton,* [1955] 5 D.L.R. 773, 17 W.W.R. 153, holding that a British Columbia statute compelling criminating answers in an administrative inquiry, subject only to such privilege as was given by the provincial *Evidence Act* and by the *Canada Evidence Act,* was not *ultra vires* under *Klein v. Bell.* The statute had been enacted after the *Canada Evidence Act* provided protection against subsequent use in criminal proceedings of answers compelled in civil (provincial) proceedings. Thus, the reference therein to the provincial Evidence Act could be regarded as mere surplusage and there was no reason to hold that an invasion of the criminal law power was involved in the provincial statute.

Statements, compelled by provincial legislation, but declared thereby not to be admissible "in any trial" (although serving administrative purposes), are not by that reason alone inadmissible in criminal proceedings; the question of admissibility depends on federal law: see *Marshall v. The Queen,* [1961]

S.C.R. 123, 26 D.L.R. (2d) 459; *Regina v. Eftoda*, [1963] 2 C.C.C. 75, 41 W.W.R. 245, 39 C.R. 324.

Do you agree with the intimation of Kerwin C.J.C., in *Klein v. Bell*, *supra*, that the Parliament of Canada, in compelling criminating answers, could not give protection or immunity against their use in any subsequent proceedings which were within provincial competence? Is there a difference, constitutionally, between federal legislation precluding use of certain evidence in a provincial civil proceeding and precluding a cause of action? See *Note*, (1941) 19 Can. Bar Rev. 379.]

Note on Self-Crimination and Compellable Testimony: *Federal Legislative Power*

Just as it is not open to a Province to exclude from subsequent criminal proceedings evidence given in civil or other proceedings that are within provincial legislative jurisdiction, so is it not open to a Province to abrogate the common law rule against self-crimination so far as it relates to offences within federal jurisdiction. Hence, a witness in a civil case may properly refuse to answer criminating questions referable to federal offences unless the protection of the common law rule is removed by federal legislation: see *Sweezey v. Crystal Chemicals Ltd. and Clark* (1963), 38 D.L.R. (2d) 505.

Equally, of course, it is not open to a provincial Legislature to make an accused or, indeed, any person a compellable witness, whether for the Crown or defence, in a criminal proceeding that is within federal legislative power. This proposition was involved in *Batary v. A.-G. Sask.*, [1965] S.C.R. 465, 52 D.L.R. (2d) 125, 51 W.W.R. 449, where certain provisions of a provincial Coroners Act were held to be unconstitutional in providing that a person accused of a crime referable to another's death is a compellable witness for the Crown at an inquest into such death. As Cartwright J., speaking for the Court (save for Fauteux J. who dissented on non-constitutional grounds) said in the *Batary* case, "any legislation purporting to make [a person charged with murder compellable to give evidence at an inquest on the body of the victim] or to abrogate or alter the existing rules which protect a person charged with a crime from being compelled to testify against himself, is legislation in relation to the criminal law including the procedure in criminal matters and so within the exclusive legislative authority of the Parliament of Canada. . . ."

The difference between Cartwright J. and Fauteux J. turned on whether, under the applicable federal law, a person charged with an offence should be considered as an accused even for purposes of an inquest (and hence to be not a compellable witness thereat) or whether he should be considered to be simply a witness for inquest purposes (and hence compellable as such under s. 5 of the Canada Evidence Act, subject to being protected thereunder in the use of his answers in any subsequent criminal proceedings). On the view of Cartwright J., s. 5 of the Canada Evidence Act applies only to a person who becomes a witness and in itself does not compel testimony; and there is no federal enactment which obliges an accused person to give testimony at an inquest or, indeed, in any criminal proceedings.

[For different views as to compellability at an inquest of a person not yet charged, see *Re Wyshynski*, [1966] 2 C.C.C. 199, 53 W.W.R. 422 and *Regina v. McDonald, ex parte Whitelaw* (1968), 2 D.L.R. (3rd) 298, 66 W.W.R. 522 (sub nom. *Re Wilson*).

In view of the *Batary* case, is it open to Parliament to supersede provincial legislation respecting coroners and inquests by them and to establish federal coroners' "courts," and appoint the coroners as well as prescribe the procedure to be followed at an inquest?]

CHAPTER XII

CRIMINAL LAW

In *A.-G. Ont. v. Hamilton Street Ry.*, [1903] A.C. 524, 7 Can. C.C. 326, the Privy Council stated that "it is . . . the criminal law in its widest sense that is reserved" for the exclusive authority of the Dominion under s. 91(27) of the *B.N.A. Act.* Earlier, in the *Russell* case, 7 App. Cas. 829, the Judicial Committee had pointed out that provincial authority in relation to property and civil rights in no way prevented the Dominion from enacting that certain uses of property and certain acts in relation to property were criminal. Illustrations were given of laws making it a criminal offence for a man wilfully to set fire to his own house, or to overwork his horse; or laws restricting the sale or exposure of cattle having a contagious disease. "Laws of this nature," said the Privy Council, "designed for the promotion of public order, safety or morals, and which subject those who contravene them to criminal procedure and punishment, belong to the subject of public wrongs rather than to that of civil rights." In the *Board of Commerce* case, [1922] 1 A.C. 191, 60 D.L.R. 513, [1922] 1 W.W.R. 20, Lord Haldane introduced a limited view of federal power under s. 91(27) by referring to it "as enabling the Dominion Parliament to exercise exclusive legislative power where the subject matter is one which by its very nature belongs to the domain of criminal jurisprudence." In the context in which he spoke it would have been enough to say (as the Privy Council later said in the *Reciprocal Insurers* case, [1924] A.C. 328, [1924] 1 D.L.R. 789, [1924] 2 W.W.R. 397) that merely to attach penal sanctions to designated activity does not necessarily foreclose judicial inquiry into whether the legislation is in pith and substance in relation to the criminal law. In *P.A.T.A. v. A.-G. Can.*, [1931] A.C. 310, [1931] 2 D.L.R. 1, [1931] 1 W.W.R. 552, the Privy Council found it necessary expressly to dissociate itself from Lord Haldane's view of the criminal law power. In that case, the Privy Council upheld federal legislation making it an offence to combine in restraint of trade, and Lord Atkin speaking for the Judicial Committee restated a broad view of the criminal law power as follows:

"In their Lordships' opinion s. 498 of the *Criminal Code* and the greater part of the provisions of the *Combines Investigation Act* fall within the power of the Dominion Parliament to legislate as to matters falling within the class of subjects, 'the criminal law including the procedure in criminal matters' (s. 91, head 27). The substance of the Act is by s. 2 to define, and by s. 32 to make criminal, combines which the legislature in the public interest intends to prohibit. The definition is wide, and may cover activities which have not hitherto been considered to be criminal. But only those combines are affected 'which have operated or are likely to operate to the detriment or against the interest of the public, whether consumers, producers or others'; and if Parliament genuinely determines that commercial activities which can be so described are to be suppressed in the public interest, their Lordships see no reason why Parliament should not make them crimes. 'Criminal law' means 'the criminal law in its widest sense': *Attorney-General for Ontario v. Hamilton Street Ry. Co.* It certainly is not confined to what was criminal by the law of England or of any Province in 1867. The power may extend to legislation to make new crimes. Criminal law connotes only the quality of such acts or omissions as are prohibited under appropriate penal provisions by authority of the State. The criminal quality of an act cannot be discerned by intuition; nor can it be discovered by reference to any standard but one: Is the act prohibited with penal consequences? Morality and criminality are far from co-extensive; nor is the sphere of criminality necessarily part of a more extensive field covered by morality—unless the moral code necessarily disapproves all acts prohibited by the State, in which case the argument moves in a circle. It appears to their Lordships to be of little value to seek to confine crimes to a category of acts which by their very nature belong to the domain of 'criminal jurisprudence'; for the domain of criminal jurisprudence can only be ascertained by examining what acts at any particular period are declared by the State to be crimes, and the only common nature they will be found to possess is that they are prohibited by the State and that those who commit them are punished."

A few years later the Privy Council returned to the exposition of the criminal law power with a qualification of the loose formula of the *P.A.T.A.* case. *A.-G. B.C. v. A.-G. Can.,* [1937] A.C. 368, [1937] 1 D.L.R. 688, [1937] 1 W.W.R. 317, sustained the validity of s. 498A of the *Dominion Criminal Code,* penalizing stipulated acts of unfair competition (*e.g.* discriminatory discounts or rebates; unreasonably low selling prices to destroy competition), and Lord Atkin stated that "the basis of [the P.A.T.A.] decision is that there is no other criterion of 'wrongness' than the intention of the Legislature in the public interest to prohibit the act or omission made criminal." Moreover the public interest may be sufficiently served in this connection although the prohibition has in view only the protection of individual competitors of a vendor of goods. However, Lord Atkin added: "The only limitation on the plenary power of the Dominion to determine what shall or shall not be criminal is the condition that Parliament shall not in the guise of enacting criminal legislation in truth and in substance encroach on any of the classes of subjects enumerated in s. 92. It is no objection that it does in fact affect them. If a genuine attempt to amend the criminal law, it may obviously affect previously existing civil rights. The object of an amendment of the criminal law as a rule is to deprive the citizen of the right to do that which, apart from the amendment, he could lawfully do. No doubt the plenary power given by s. 91(27) does not deprive the Provinces of their right under s. 92(15) of affixing penal sanctions to their own competent legislation. On the other hand, there seems to be nothing to prevent the Dominion, if it thinks fit in the public interest, from applying the criminal law generally to acts and omissions which so far are only covered by provincial enactments. In the present case there seems to be no reason for supposing that the Dominion are using the criminal law as a pretence or pretext, or that the legislature is in pith and substance only interfering with civil rights in the Province."

This Privy Council conception of the criminal law power has been carried into later judgments of the Supreme Court of Canada. In a recent pronouncement on the subject the Supreme Court independently scotched the Haldane notion that there is a "domain of criminal law": see *Lord's Day Alliance v. A.-G. B.C.*, [1959] S.C.R. 497, 19 D.L.R. (2d) 97. In an earlier case, *Prov. Sec. of P.E.I. v. Egan*, [1941] S.C.R. 396, [1941] 3 D.L.R. 305, Duff C.J.C. referred to the subject of criminal law as being "necessarily an expanding field," and in the *Margarine* case, [1949] S.C.R. 1, [1949] 1 D.L.R. 433, Rand J. put the following test and gave the following answer on the scope of the criminal law power: "Is the prohibition . . . enacted with a view to a public purpose which can support it as being in relation to criminal law? Public peace, order, security, health, morality: these are the ordinary though not exclusive ends served by that law. . . ." The contrast was with an economic object, such as the giving of trade protection in the production and distribution of articles of trade. The criminal law may, of course, serve an economic interest. To quote Rand J. again: "A crime is an act which the law, with appropriate penal sanctions, forbids; but as prohibitions are not enacted in a vacuum, we can properly look for some evil or injurious or undesirable effect upon the public against which the law is directed. That effect may be in relation to social, economic or political interests; and the legislature has had in mind to suppress the evil or to safeguard the interest threatened." The other side of the coin is represented by Judson J.'s statement in *O'Grady v. Sparling*, [1960] S.C.R. 804, 25 D.L.R. (2d) 145, 33 W.W.R. 360 that "a provincial enactment does not become a matter of criminal law merely because it consists of a prohibition and makes it an offence for failure to observe the prohibition."

Resort to the criminal law power to proscribe undesirable commercial practices is to-day as characteristic of its exercise as has been resort thereto to curb violence or immoral conduct. It is not a necessary condition of such use of the criminal law power that the offences be defined in terms of conspiracy. Thus, for example, resale price maintenance as such may properly be the subject of a criminal prohibition by Parliament, even without a requirement of proof of harm to the public, when viewed from the standpoint of the public interest in preserving free and equal competition. In *Regina v. Campbell*, [1964] 2 O.R. 487, 46 D.L.R. (2d) 83, a majority of the Ontario Court of Appeal deferred to Parliament's opinion that resale price maintenance should be suppressed in the public interest, but the dissenters felt that the mere imposition of a sanction against a commercial practice did not amount to a valid exercise of the criminal law power when there was nothing to indicate that harm to the public was an element of the offence.

Whatever be the proper standards for attributing federal legislation to an exercise of the criminal law power, or, correlatively, denying validity to provincial legislation as an invasion of that power, certain propositions in this area are well established. Federal authority in relation to criminal law encompasses not only the creation of new crimes but the legalization of conduct or activity which was criminal at Confederation or which was subsequently proscribed as criminal: see *Toronto Ry. v. The King,* [1917] A.C. 630, at p. 639, 38 D.L.R. 537, at p. 541; *A.B.C. v. Herman,* 65 O.L.R. 296, [1930] 2 D.L.R. 513. Thus, the Dominion has made it an offence to publish, distribute, sell or have in possession a "crime comic" (*Cr. Code,* s. 159(1)(*b*), (7)): see *Regina v. Superior Publishers Ltd. and Zimmermann,* [1954] O.R. 981, 110 Can. C.C. 115, 20 C.R. 51. It is an offence to sell or give cigarettes or tobacco to a person under age 16 (*Tobacco Restraints Act,* R.S.C. 1970, c. T-9): see *Regina ex rel. Barrie v. Stelzer* (1957), 15 D.L.R. (2d) 280, 24 W.W.R. 130, 119 Can. C.C. 305. The Dominion may validly provide for indeterminate preventive detention of habitual criminals (as defined by federal legislation); see *Brusch v. The Queen,* [1953] 1 S.C.R. 373, [1953] 2 D.L.R. 707; and it may equally provide for indeterminate preventive detention of criminal sexual psychopaths: see *Regina v. Neil,* [1957] S.C.R. 685, 119 Can. C.C. 1. While generally prohibiting the keeping of a gaming house and book-making, the Dominion may exempt (*i.e.* permit) pari-mutuel betting at race courses: see *Cr. Code,* s. 188 which exhibits regulatory aspects to what is formally merely an exemption from a criminal prohibition: and *cf. Re Race-Tracks and Betting* (1921), 49 O.L.R. 339, 61 D.L.R. 504. In other words, federal criminal legislation may be absolute or conditional in operation, may be punitive after the event and also preventive. Where the Dominion has enacted prohibitions, whether absolute or qualified, it is incompetent, of course, for a Province to relax them: see *Re Morrison and Kingston,* [1938] O.R. 21, [1937] 4 D.L.R. 740; *Regina v. Stanley* (1952), 104 Can. C.C. 31; *A.-G. Can. v. Prince Albert,* [1952] 1 D.L.R. 195, 3 W.W.R. (N.S.) 646, 13 C.R. 303. It is equally incompetent for a Province to supplement the punishment prescribed by the Dominion, at least where the Province is acting only to strengthen enforcement of the federal prohibition: see *Prov. Sec. of P.E.I. v. Egan,* [1941] S.C.R. 396, [1941] 3 D.L.R. 305; *cf. Boyce v. The Queen* (1959), 22 D.L.R. (2d) 555, 125 Can. C.C. 305. There are a number of border-line situations which arise in this connection.

Notice was taken in the preceding chapter (see p. 813) of the authority of Parliament to legislate in relation to preventive criminal law; as, for example, by binding over a person to keep the peace. Parliament's power extends more obviously to the detention of an accused who has been acquitted on the ground of insanity at the time the offence charged was committed: see *Rex v. Trapnell* (1910), 22 O.L.R.

219. Equally, it encompasses authority to order and supervise detention of an accused who is unfit, by reason of mental incompetency, to
stand trial for a federal offence. In *Green v. Livermore,* [1940] O.R.
381, [1940] 4 D.L.R. 678 it was held that the Province could validly
provide for the committal to a mental institution of a person charged
with an "offence" (which was the term then used in the Ontario
legislation and is the term still used). In rejecting the argument that
this was an invasion of the criminal law power, the Court declared
that "the action of the magistrate in sending the plaintiff to the
hospital does not arise from any crime. . . . It is a step in the control
of persons who have always been dealt with by the Province in legislation of the nature of the Mental Hospitals Act." In fact, the person
so committed had been charged with a provincial offence and the case
left open the question how far, if at all, the provincial enactment could
be validly used in respect of a person charged under the federal
criminal law.

This question was partly answered by the judgment in *Fawcett v.
A.-G. Can.,* [1964] S.C.R. 625, 45 D.L.R. (2d) 579. The *Fawcett* case
allowed a complementary resort to the provincial legislation where the
original remand to a mental institution of a person accused of a federal
offence was made under the *Cr. Code.* Criticism of this reliance on
provincial legislation in the *Fawcett* case can, to some extent at least,
be supported by the earlier judgment of the Supreme Court of Canada
in *Re Trenholm,* [1940] S.C.R. 301, [1940] 1 D.L.R. 497. Although *Re
Trenholm* is distinguishable because there was an attempt there to
detain an accused after his remand on a federal criminal charge had
expired, and because the reliance for his continued detention before
expiry of the remand was on a clause of the provincial statute limited
to imprisonment for a provincial offence, nonetheless the case indicates
a concern not to mix up the provincial and federal powers of detention.

Be that as it may, the Ontario Court of Appeal in *Kennedy v.
Tomlinson* (1959), 20 D.L.R. (2d) 273, at p. 305 felt it necessary to distinguish *Re Trenholm* (and it is doubtful that this was done on a
tenable ground) after properly noticing that the legislation considered
in *Green v. Livermore* "is not by its terms limited to offences against
provincial enactments." In effect, it was held in *Kennedy v. Tomlinson*
that an original committal under the provincial Mental Hospitals Act
could be made of a person charged under the federal *Cr. Code.* This
decision, if correct, fills the gap left by *Green v. Livermore;* and,
indeed, provides a more direct route to committal of a person charged
with a federal criminal offence than that taken in the *Fawcett* case.
In the face of the provisions of the *Cr. Code* for original committal to
a mental institution of a person charged with a federal offence,
Kennedy v. Tomlinson is more open to criticism than is the *Fawcett*
case.

Having regard to its exclusive authority in relation to criminal
procedure as well as substantive criminal law, it is for Parliament
alone to legislate in respect of the disposition of fines imposed for
violations of federal criminal law: *Toronto v. The King,* [1932] A.C.
98, [1932] 1 D.L.R. 161, [1931] 3 W.W.R. 698; it is for Parliament

alone to provide for payment of fees to witnesses and functionaries in connection with criminal proceedings: *A.-G. Que. v. A.-G. Can.,* [1945] S.C.R. 600, [1945] 4 D.L.R. 305; it is for Parliament alone to deal with costs in criminal proceedings, whether in respect of prosecutions under the federal criminal law or in respect of resort to prerogative writs directed to enforcement of that law: *Re Bence,* [1954] 4 D.L.R. 460, 108 Can. C.C. 373. See, on the claim of a defendant to a trial in the French language, *Re Poulin,* 64 W.W.R. 705, 69 D.L.R. (2d) 526 (*sub nom. R. v. Watts; Ex p. Poulin*),[1968] 4 C.C.C. 221 (B.C.) (claim grounded on British North America Act, s. 133, rejected as to prosecution before magistrate); and *R. v. Lajoie,* [1971] 1 W.W.R. 157, 13 C.R.N.S. 92, 2 C.C.C. (2d) 89, 15 D.L.R. (3d) 365 (B.C.) (claim grounded on the *Official Languages Act,* R.S.C. 1970, c. O-2, s. 11, rejected on basis of referential exemption, recognizing provincial procedure.

Federal criminal law power does not extend to the mere attaching of penalties to offences defined by valid provincial legislation. There is a category of so-called "provincial crimes" (see *Rex v. Nat Bell Liquors Ltd.,* [1922] 2 A.C. 128, 65 D.L.R. 1, [1922] 2 W.W.R. 30), and by s. 92(15) of the *B.N.A. Act* exclusive authority is vested in the Provincial legislatures to enforce those offences by appropriate sanction.

While it is clearly settled that the imposition of a penalty does not *ipso facto* validate federal legislation, there has been no settled course of decision on the question whether the character of a penalty may result in invalidation of an otherwise valid provincial enactment. For example, would it be open to a Province to prescribe life imprisonment or whipping or, as an ultimate, hanging, for violation of a provincial enactment? Putting the matter another way, what are the limitations if any, that reside in the words "imposition of punishment by fine, penalty or imprisonment" in s. 92(15)?

In *Regina v. Wason* (1890), 17 O.A.R. 221 it was stated by members of the Court that provincial enforcement power extended to penalty without limit in amount and to imprisonment without limit in duration; or, as Osler J.A. put it (at p. 240) "the competency of the [provincial] enactment cannot be tested by the severity of the sanction so long as the latter is limited to fine, penalty or imprisonment"; see also *Regina v. Chief* (1963), 42 D.L.R. (2d) 712, 46 W.W.R. 57, aff'd. 44 D.L.R. (2d) 108, [1964] 3 Can. C.C. 347. "Penalty" would presumably include forfeiture of property (see the *Nat Bell* case, *supra*) and hard labour as an adjunct of imprisonment (see *Hodge v. The Queen* (1883), 9 App. Cases 117), but would not include capital punishment.

[Cr. Code, s. 116 makes it an offence to disobey, without lawful excuse, a lawful order of a court of justice or of any person or body authorized by any Act to make or give the order (other than an order for payment of money), unless some penalty or punishment or other mode of proceeding is expressly provided by law. Is this provision validly applicable to an order made by a provincial magistrate or administrative board acting under provincial legislation? See *Rex v. Clement,* (1947), 90 Can. C.C. 284.

May a Province validly provide for compulsory sterilization of persons who are convicted of certain offences?

On the scope of s. 91(27) see *Symposium*, The Criminal Law Power in Canada, (1957) 15 Univ. of Tor. Faculty of Law Rev. 1 ff.]

GOODYEAR TIRE & RUBBER CO. OF CANADA LTD.
v. THE QUEEN

In the Supreme Court of Canada. [1956] S.C.R. 303, 2 D.L.R. (2d) 11.

Appeal from a judgment of the Ontario Court of Appeal, [1954] O.R. 377, [1954] 4 D.L.R. 61, affirming with variations an order of prohibition by Treleaven J., [1953] O.R. 856, under s. 31(1) of the *Combines Investigation Act* (Can.).

LOCKE J.: . . . The appellants were indicted together on the charge that they "during the period from 1936 to the 31st day of October 1952, both inclusive, within the jurisdiction of this Honourable Court, did unlawfully conspire, combine, agree or arrange together and within one another and with BARRINGHAM RUBBER & PLASTICS LIMITED; G. L. GRIFFITH & SONS, LTD.; VICEROY MANUFACTURING COMPANY LIMITED; FIRESTONE TIRE & RUBBER COMPANY OF CANADA, LIMITED and CANALCO LIMITED, to unduly prevent or lessen competition in the production, manufacture, purchase, barter, sale, transportation or supply in the City of Toronto, in the County of York, and other places throughout the Province of Ontario, and in the City of Montreal, in the Province of Quebec, and other places throughout the Province of Quebec and elsewhere in Canada where the articles or commodities hereinafter mentioned are offered for sale, of articles or commodities which may be the subject of trade or commerce, to wit (then followed a description of the commodities), contrary to the provisions of the Criminal Code, Section 498, subsection 1(d)."

Section 31 of the *Combines Investigation Act* reads:

"31(1) Where a person has been convicted of an offence under section thirty-two or thirty-four of this Act or under section four hundred and ninety-eight or four hundred and ninety-eight A of the *Criminal Code*

"(*a*) the court may, at the time of such conviction, on the application of the Attorney-General of Canada or the attorney-general of the province, or

"(*b*) a superior court of criminal jurisdiction in the province may at any time within three years thereafter, upon proceedings commenced by information of the Attorney-General of Canada or the attorney-general of the province for the purposes of this section,

and in addition to any other penalty imposed on the person convicted, prohibit the continuation or repetition of the offence or the doing of any act or thing by the person convicted or any other person directed towards the continuation or repetition of the offence and where the conviction is with respect to the formation or operation of a merger, trust or monopoly, direct the person convicted or any other person to do such acts or things as may be necessary to dissolve the merger, trust or monopoly in such manner as the court directs.

"(2) Where it appears to a superior court of criminal jurisdiction in proceedings commenced by information of the Attorney-General of Canada or the attorney-general of the province for the purposes of this section that a person is about to do or is likely to do any act or thing constituting or directed towards the commission of an offence under section thirty-two or thirty-four of this Act or section four hundred and ninety-eight or four hundred and ninety-eight A of the *Criminal Code,* the court may prohibit the commission of the offence or the doing of any act or thing by that person or any other person constituting or directed towards the commission of such an offence.

"(3) A court may punish any person who contravenes or fails to comply with a prohibition or direction made or given by it under this section by a fine in the discretion of the court, or by imprisonment for a term not exceeding two years.

"(4) Any proceedings pursuant to an information of the Attorney-General of Canada or the attorney-general of a province under this section shall be tried by the court without a jury, and the procedure applicable in injunction proceedings in the superior courts of the province shall, in so far as possible, apply.

"(5) This section applies in respect of all prosecutions under this Act or under section four hundred and ninety-eight or four hundred and ninety-eight A of the *Criminal Code* whether commenced before or after the coming into force of this section and in respect of all acts or things, whether committed or done before or after the coming into force of this section.

"(6) In this section 'superior court of criminal jurisdiction' means a superior court of criminal jurisdiction as defined in the *Criminal Code."* [re-enacted 1952, c. 39, s. 3]

All of the appellants pleaded guilty to the charge and Crown counsel, representing the Attorney-General of Canada and the Attorney-General of Ontario, then applied for an order under the provisions of s. 31 and on September 24, 1953, the learned trial Judge imposed a fine of $10,000 upon each of the accused and directed that an order of prohibition issue, as permitted by the section.

On September 25, 1953, an order issued out of the Supreme Court of Ontario which, after reciting the conviction, read:

"1. This Court doth prohibit the continuation or repetition of the said offence by the persons convicted.

"2. This Court doth further prohibit the doing of any act or thing by the persons convicted or by any other person directed towards the continuation or repetition of the said offence."

The appellants obtained leave to appeal to the Court of Appeal and contended before that Court that s. 31 was *ultra vires* of Parliament. That appeal was dismissed, the Court, however, directing that para. (2) of the order be altered so that it reads:

"This Court doth further prohibit the doing of any act or thing by the persons convicted, and/or their directors, officers, servants and agents, directed towards the continuation or repetition of the said offence."

While, pursuant to the direction of this Court, all of the provincial Attorneys-General were notified of the questions to be raised on the appeal, none were represented before us, the argument in support of the validity of the legislation being made on behalf of the Attorney-General of Canada.

Stated shortly, the contention of the appellants is that s. 31 is either wholly or partially *ultra vires* of Parliament, being a colourable attempt, under the guise of enacting legislation in relation to criminal law, to trench upon the field of property and civil rights in the Province assigned exclusively to the Legislature by head (13) of s. 92 of the *B.N.A. Act*. A subsidiary point is that the Court of Appeal erred in interpreting the reference in s.-ss. (1) and (2) of s. 31 to "any other person" as meaning only those who stood in such a relation to the accused that a prohibitory order against them would affect the accused and be a penalty on the accused.

Counsel for the Attorney-General supports the legislation as a valid exercise of the powers of Parliament under head (27) of s. 91 as criminal law, and under head (2) as the regulation of trade and commerce.

Since 1888 there has been legislation in Canada prohibiting the offences referred to in s. 498 of the *Code*. In substantially the same form, that section appeared as s. 520 when the *Code* was first enacted in 1892 (c. 29).

Following the decision of the Judicial Committee finding the *Board of Commerce Act* and the *Combines and Fair Prices Act*, enacted in 1919, to be *ultra vires* (54 D.L.R. 354, 60 S.C.R. 456, [1922] 1 A.C. 191), the *Combines Investigation Act*, 1923 (Can.), c. 9, which repealed the said statutes, was enacted.

In 1929 the Governor-General in Council referred to this Court the question as to whether that Act, either in whole or in part, and s. 498 of the *Cr. Code* were *ultra vires*. Both the statute and the section were held to be within the power of Parliament, [1929] 2 D.L.R. 802, S.C.R. 409, 52 Can. C.C. 223, and that decision was upheld by the Judicial Committee in *Proprietary Articles Trades Ass'n v. A.-G. Can.,* [1931] 2 D.L.R. 1, A.C. 310, 55 Can. C.C. 241. . .

Section 31 was not part of the Act in 1929, having been first enacted by c. 39 of the Statutes of 1952. It is not a valid objection, in my opinion, to that portion of the section which has been invoked in the present matter, that, since the offence is prohibited by s. 498 of the *Code* and penalties are provided both by the *Code* and by the *Combines Investigation Act*, the power to deal with the matter under head (27) is exhausted. It is to be noted that the making of a prohibitory order is authorized "in addition to any other penalty", being thus treated as a penalty. The power to legislate in relation to criminal law is not restricted, in my opinion, to defining offences and providing penalties for their commission. The power of Parliament extends to legislation designed for the prevention of crime as well as to punishing crime. It was, apparently, considered that to prohibit the continuation or repetition of the offence by order, a breach being punishable under s-s. (3) of s. 31, would tend to restrain its repetition. As to the language "or the doing of any act or thing by the person convicted . . . directed toward the continuation or repetition of the offence", this appears to me to be properly construed as forbidding the taking of any step by the person to whom the order is directed, looking to the continuation of the offence dealt with by the conviction or its repetition by forming another combine, and I do not think it is intended to deal only with attempts to commit the offence. The language appears to me to permit the prohibition of any act such as a preliminary proposal to others regarding the formation of a combine which, in itself, might not fall within the definition of an attempt under s. 72. As Parliament apparently considered that such an order might be of use in preventing the formation of such combines, I think the matter to be wholly within its powers.

This view is supported, in my opinion, by a passage from the judgment of Sir Lyman P. Duff C.J.C. in *Provincial Secretary of P.E.I. v. Egan,* [1941] 3 D.L.R. 305, S.C.R. 396, 76 Can. C.C. 227. Section 285(7)(a) of the *Code* provides that, where a person is convicted of an offence defined by s-ss. (1), (2), (4) or (6) of that section, the Court may "in addition to any other punishment provided for such offence, make an order prohibiting such person from driving a motor vehicle or automobile anywhere in Canada during any period not exceeding three years".

Dealing with the argument that the making of such a prohibitory order did not fall under head (27), the Chief Justice said (p. 308 D.L.R., p. 230 Can. C.C.): "I may say at once I cannot agree with this view. . . . It appears to me to be quite clear that such pro-hibitions may be imposed as punishment in exercise of the authority vested in the Dominion to legislate in relation to criminal law and procedure."

In *A.-G. Ont. v. Can. Temperance Federation,* [1946] 2 D.L.R. 1, A.C. 193, 85 Can. C.C. 225, Viscount Simon L.C. referring to and rejecting an argument that Parliament was without power to re-enact provisions with the object of preventing a recurrence of a state of affairs which had been deemed to necessitate the passage of an earlier statute, said that to legislate for prevention appears to be on the same base as legislation for cure.

Whether or not it can properly be said that the language referred to was intended to define a new offence, or whether it should be construed as merely providing the means of preventing the com-mission of the offence, it is, in my opinion, equally within the power of Parliament under head (27) of s. 91.

It is further contended that the power to make a prohibitory order directed to the person convicted "or any other person" is not legis-lation authorized by head (27). While, literally construed and divorced from the context, these words would permit the making of an order against persons quite unconnected with those against whom a conviction has been made, it is impossible that this was the intention of Parliament and I agree with the learned Judges of the

Court of Appeal that it should properly be construed as meaning, in cases such as this where the accused are corporations, the directors, officers, servants and agents of the various companies.

The appellants further submitted that that part of s-s. (1) which reads "and where the conviction is with respect to the formation or operation of a merger, trust or monopoly, direct the person convicted or any other person to do such acts or things as may be necessary to dissolve the merger, trust or monopoly in such manner as the court directs", is *ultra vires*.

This power was not exercised by the Court in the present case and as, in my opinion, this portion of the subsection is clearly severable from that portion which has been invoked, the point as to whether this is within the powers of Parliament should not, in my opinion, be determined. This is not a Reference to the Court in which we are asked to determine the validity of s. 31 as a whole, but rather that portion of it purporting to give to the Court the powers which have been exercised in making the order complained of.

In view of my conclusion that the impugned legislation is *intra vires* of Parliament under head (27), it is unnecessary to consider the question as to whether it might not also fall within head (2). . .

Appeal dismissed.

[Kerwin C.J.C., Taschereau, Kellock and Fauteux JJ. concurred with Locke J. A separate concurring judgment was delivered by Rand J. who said, *inter alia*, that "it is accepted that head (27) of s. 91 . . . is to be interpreted in its widest sense, but that breadth of scope contemplates neither a static catalogue of offences nor order of sanctions". Estey J. took no part in the judgment.

For an exposition of the range of s. 31(1) of the *Combines Investigation Act*, see *Regina v. Howard Smith Paper Mills Ltd.*, [1954] O.R. 633, [1954] 4 D.L.R. 517. See, generally, *Blair*, Combines, Control or Competition, (1953) 31 Can. Bar Rev. 1083, at pp. 1091 ff.

May the Dominion confer upon an informer the right to recover by civil action penalties imposed for breach of the criminal law? See *Doyle v. Ball* (1884), 11 O.A.R. 326; and see Cr. Code, s. 652.]

TRANSPORT OIL CO. LTD. v. IMPERIAL OIL CO. LTD.

In the Ontario Court of Appeal. [1935] O.R. 215, [1935] 2 D.L.R. 500.

Appeal from a judgment of Hope J., [1935] O.R. 111, determining adversely to plaintiff a point of law raised by the pleadings.

The judgment of the Court was delivered by

MIDDLETON J.A.: . . . Paragraph 9 of the statement of claim reads as follows:

"The defendants unlawfully operated a combine contrary to the provisions of The Combines Investigation Act, Revised Statutes of Canada 1927, Chapter 26, by entering into an arrangement detrimental to the interest of the public and particularly the plaintiff and having or designing to have the effect of:

(a) Limiting the facilities for supplying motor gasoline; and/or

(b) fixing a common price for motor gasoline; and/or

(c) enhancing the price thereof; and/or

(d) lessening competition therein; and/or

(e) otherwise restraining trade therein;

by reason of which the plaintiff has suffered great loss and damage in addition to the damage sustained by it as a member of the public."

The paragraphs of the respective statements of defence are as follows:

"7. Further as to said paragraph 9 of the said statement of claim, this defendant submits that the allegations raised in the said paragraph, even if proved, do not give the plaintiff any right of action against this defendant by reason thereof."

"10. In further reply to said paragraph nine of the said statement of claim this defendant says that the same discloses no reasonable cause of action against this defendant."

Mr. Justice Hope in a careful judgment is of the opinion that *The Combines Investigation Act* does not in any way contemplate, nor was it the intention of Parliament to confer, any private right of action.

With this conclusion we agree. . . .

The Combines Investigation Act, R.S.C. 1927, ch. 26, sec. 32, provides that everyone is guilty of an indictable offence and liable to a penalty not exceeding $10,000.00, or to two years' imprisonment, or, if a corporation, to a penalty not exceeding $25,000.00, who is a party or privy to or knowingly assists in the formation or operation of a combine within the meaning of the statute, and that no prosecution for any offence under this section shall be commenced, otherwise than at the instance of the Solicitor-General of Canada, or of the Attorney-General of a Province.

A combine is by the interpretation section of the Statute (sec. 2(1)) a combine likely to operate to the detriment or against the interest of the public, whether consumers, producers or others. The whole scope and trend of the Act indicate that the legislative intention was to create a criminal offence punishable as indicated by the section itself by a limited penalty and a limited term of imprisonment, and a further safeguard requires all prosecutions under the Act to be initiated by the Solicitor-General or the Attorney-General of a Province. There is nothing from which any intention to give a private right of action could possibly be inferred.

When it is remembered that we have a dual legislative system, the Parliament of Canada possessing exclusive jurisdiction over criminal law and the Provincial Legislature exercising sole jurisdiction over property and civil rights, I think it is plain that the Parliament of Canada in passing this Act intended it to be an exercise by it of the power to legislate with respect to crime and criminal law, and that it did not intend to interfere with the Provincial jurisdiction over property and civil rights. The Act was attacked as being beyond the competence of the Dominion Parliament, but its validity was upheld as an exercise of the right to deal with crime. See *Proprietary*

Articles Trade Association v. Attorney-General for Canada, [1931] A.C. 310.

The appeal fails and should be dismissed with costs.

Appeal dismissed.

[In *Gordon v. Imperial Tobacco Sales Co.,* [1939] O.R. 122, [1939] 2 D.L.R. 27, McFarland J., relying in a similar situation on the *Transport Oil* case, stated that "the principle is quite clearly established that Dominion legislation cannot trespass upon or create any civil right in a province". *Quaere* whether any constitutional principle is raised where the Dominion criminal legislation is silent on whether a civil action arises upon a breach of the criminal enactment! See *Finkleman,* Note, (1935) 13 Can. Bar Rev. 517, at p. 521: "The right of action for injury caused by a conspiracy, arises not by virtue of any federal legislation but by operation of the common law doctrine which gives a right of action to anyone injured by a criminal conspiracy, in this case a conspiracy to violate a Dominion statute". In *Floyd v. Edmonton City Dairy Ltd.,* [1935] 1 D.L.R. 754, [1934] 3 W.W.R. 326 (Alta.), Ford J. stated (at p. 756) that "a proven violation of s. 498 of the Criminal Code, if it results in damage, is actionable at the suit of the individual damnified"; and see *Wasney v. Jurazsky,* [1933] 1 D.L.R. 616 (Man.). Cf. Duff C.J. in *Philco Products Ltd. v. Thermionics Ltd.,* [1940] S.C.R. 501, at p. 504, [1940] 4 D.L.R. 1, at p. 3: "If B commits an indictable offence and the direct consequence of that indictable offence is that A suffers some special harm different from that of the rest of His Majesty's subjects, then, speaking generally, A has a right of action against B. As at present advised, I think it is not obvious that this well settled doctrine does not apply to indictable offences under section 498 of the Criminal Code." See, too, *Note,* (1941) 19 Can. Bar Rev. 51; *Placatka v. Thompson,* [1941] 1 W.W.R. 528 (Alta.); *Pullan v. McLellan,* [1946] 2 D.L.R. 606 (B.C.).

In *Direct Lumber Co. Ltd. v. Western Plywood Co. Ltd.,* [1962] S.C.R. 646, 35 D.L.R. (2d) 1, 29 W.W.R. 43, which affirmed dismissal of an action for damages based on alleged discriminatory treatment in violation of pro-hibitions of the federal criminal law respecting monopolies and illegal trade practices, Judson J. for the Supreme Court commented as follows: "I recognize that there may be a difference between a common law action for damages based on conspiracy and one based on price discrimination. The common law itself imposes liability for harm caused by combinations to injure by unlawful means but the common law never gave any cause of action for price dis-crimination unaccompanied by conspiracy. To this extent some of the *dicta* in the *Transport Oil* case, which was a conspiracy case, may be open to question, and it may well be doubted whether any constitutional principle is raised when Dominion criminal legislation is silent upon the question whether a civil action arises upon breach of its terms. This doubt has been expressed by *Wright* in Cases on the law of Torts, 2nd Ed., p. 279; *Laskin,* Canadian Constitutional Law, 2nd Ed., p. 863; and *Finkelman,* (1935) 13 Can. Bar Rev. 517, and it is probably the basis for the statement of Duff C.J.C. in *Philco Products Ltd. v. Thermionics Ltd. . . ."* Whether federal criminal legislation could give or support a civil action (apart from one based on conspiracy) did not have to be decided in this case.

In *St. Catharines General Hospital v. Sviergula,* [1961] O.R. 164, 26 D.L.R. (2d) 455 it was held that Cr. Code, s. 186 which imposed a legal duty to provide necessaries of life to, *inter alia,* a child under age 16, did not create any civil liability; and the Court added, "if it did so it might well be challenged as unconstitutional because property and civil rights are involved."

See also *Note,* Implying Civil Remedies from Federal Regulatory Statutes, (1963) 77 Harv. L. Rev. 285, alluding to one of the theories underlying liability imposed by the cases as being that "a new cause of action implied from a federal statute creates a federal right." Would this be applicable under Canadian federal regulatory statutes as opposed to criminal enactments?]

Note on Criminal Proceedings and Civil Actions

The *Transport Oil* case, *supra,* and the comment thereon in the *Direct Lumber Co.,* case touch but one of a number of problems with constitutional implications where, whether by common law or by legislation, civil actions are permitted or restricted in reference to acts or conduct which is criminal. Parliament provided by what was formerly Cr. Code s. 734 that a person acquitted on a charge of common assault or who, if convicted, has paid or suffered the penalty awarded against him, shall be released from all further civil or criminal proceedings for the same cause. The enactment, which has disappeared from the present Cr. Code, understandably gave rise to a division of opinion as to its validity in so far as it purported to release a person from civil liability for conduct which, as a tort matter, was subject to provincial legislative authority: see *Rice v. Messenger,* [1929] 2 D.L.R. 669, 60 N.S.R. 399 and *Dawson v. Muttart,* [1941] 2 D.L.R. 341, 15 M.P.R. 451, holding s. 734 to be invalid; and see, holding s. 734 to be *intra vires, Wilson v. Codyre* (1886), 26 N.B.R. 516; *Flick v. Brisbin* (1895), 26 O.R. 423; *Trinea v. Duleba,* [1924] 3 D.L.R. 636, [1924] 2 W.W.R. 1177, 20 Alta. L.R. 493; *Dowsett v. Edwards,* [1926] 3 D.L.R. 367, [1926] 3 W.W.R. 447, 22 Alta. L.R. 292; *Nykiforuk v. Kohut,* [1949] 3 D.L.R. 399, [1949] 1 W.W.R. 708 (Sask.). What was s. 734 was taken from English legislation where it had no constitutional implications: see *Note,* (1948) 26 Can. Bar Rev. 1001. The better reasoning would be against the validity of such a provision as the former s. 734: see *Note,* (1941) 19 Can. Bar Rev. 379. Mere initial resort to the criminal law cannot alone be a basis for federal control or denial of civil rights of action otherwise open to an injured person under provincial common or statute law. Certainly, it could not be argued that a Province could control criminal proceedings by making initial resort to a civil action a bar to criminal prosecution.

There is, however, a case to be made for the validity of federal legislation in limiting or even excluding the civil liability of police officers or others for acts done in the enforcement of the federal criminal law. Parliament has, indeed, acted in this area. Cr. Code, s. 717 goes far in providing for an order of protection from civil liability where there has been an excess of jurisdiction; such an order may be made without the proof of good faith which is a requirement of the justification conferred by the general terms of s. 25(2) where there has been a defect of jurisdiction in the execution of process. In *Re Royal Canadian Legion (Branch 177)* (1964), 48 D.L.R. (2d) 164, 48 W.W.R. 481, the Court assumed their validity in giving an order of protection to a justice of the peace who wrongly issued a search warrant, and in refusing such an order in favour of policemen who executed it in indiscriminate fashion. Certainly there is no doubt as to federal authority to give them immunity from criminal liability, and it is also a proper conclusion that no civil liability can arise from the exercise of powers, *e.g.*, of arrest and search, expressly conferred by federal legislation in connection with enforcement of the criminal law; see for example, *Woodward v. Begbie*, [1962] O.R. 60, 31 D.L.R. (2d) 22, which accepted this conclusion where the conduct of the police fell within the protective terms of Cr. Code, s. 25(4); see also *Fletcher v. Collins*, [1968] 2 O.R. 618. It follows, of course, that an expansion of their powers would enlarge the area of civil immunity of police and others, even if no express federal legislation were enacted on the question of immunity from civil suit: see Cr. Code, ss. 25-31; and cf. *Frey v. Fedoruk*, [1949] 2 W.W.R. 604, 96 Can. C.C. 206, 8 C.R. 373, rev'd. on other grounds [1950] S.C.R. 517, [1950] 3 D.L.R. 513; *Priestman v. Colangelo and Smythson*, [1959] S.C.R. 615, 19 D.L.R. (2d) 1; *Kennedy v. Tomlinson* (1959), 20 D.L.R. (2d) 272 (Ont. C.A.).

Similarly, there is a tenable argument for the validity, as an exercise of the criminal law power, of legislation providing for the return of stolen goods to their owner or for restitution of property or money realized therefrom by a thief: see Cr. Code, ss. 654, 655; and see *Benesiewicz v. Dionne*, [1946] 1 D.L.R. 426, [1945] 3 W.W.R. 297.

But even without legislation the Courts could be expected to assert jurisdiction to order return of money or other property to their owners or to persons from whom it was taken, even if such persons be accused who were acquitted, or are convicted persons from whom property was taken which had no connection with their crime: see *Regina v. Hargreaves* (1959), 124 Can. C.C. 167, 31 C.R. 182; *Regina v. Doig*, [1963] S.C.R. 3, [1963] 1 Can. C.C. 292, 38 C.R. 373. It is more doubtful, however, whether Parliament may empower the convicting criminal court (as it purports to do in Cr. Code, s. 653) to order the accused "to pay . . . an amount by way of satisfaction or compensation for loss of or damage to property suffered . . . as a result of the commission of the offence. . . ." The validity of this provision was assumed in *Regina v. Scherstabitoff*, [1963] 2 Can. C.C. 208, 39 C.R. 233, where on an appeal against an order to pay compensation to the victim of an offence the Court, in affirming the order, said shortly that once the order is made "it then becomes an enforcement on the civil side."

In *Hurley v. Foreman* (1962), 35 D.L.R. (2d) 596, where an order to pay the medical expenses of an aggrieved person was made as a condition of a recognizance under Cr. Code, s. 638, on suspension of a sentence for assault, it was held that the order did not preclude a civil action for the same assault since it did not amount to a judgment enforceable by plaintiff against defendant; failure to obey the order would merely expose defendant to liability to sentence for the offence of which he was convicted. Even if it is not a judgment, would it not be open to the aggrieved person to sue on the order, as indicated in the *Scherstabitoff* case? The compensation provisions of the Cr. Code whose validity is assumed in the cases are illustrations of the Code giving rise directly to civil liabilities enforceable by action.

[Cr. Code, s. 10 provides that "no civil remedy for an act or omission is suspended or affected by reason that the act or omission is a criminal offence". This provision does away with the rule of public policy by which a civil action based on facts also constituting a crime was suspended until the plaintiff had prosecuted the defendant. The validity of the section was questioned by Duff J. in *MacKenzie v. Palmer* (1921), 62 S.C.R. 517, at p. 520, 63 D.L.R. 362, [1922] 1 W.W.R. 880, at p. 882. See also *Kozlowski v. Workers' Benevolent Society*, [1934] 1 D.L.R. 237, at p. 241, [1933] 3 W.W.R. 566, at p. 571.

In *Lamb v. Benoit*, [1959] S.C.R. 321, 17 D.L.R. (2d) 369, Cartwright J. raised, and left unanswered, the question whether the law governing an action for malicious prosecution was part of the criminal law defining the privilege or condition of immunity of a person who sets the criminal proceedings in motion or whether it was simply part of the law of torts and hence definable under provincial law. What is the answer? Is the situation any different from that which would arise if a Province purported to deny or confer a civil cause of action consequent upon a criminal conviction or acquittal?

In *Priestman v. Colangelo and Smythson*, [1959] S.C.R. 615, 19 D.L.R. (2d) 1, Cartwright J. raised the question, initially one of construction, whether the justification accorded to a police officer under Cr. Code, s. 25(4) (in respect of the use of force where a person whom the officer is proceeding lawfully to arrest takes flight) operates only as between the officer and the alleged offender or also extends to injuries suffered by innocent bystanders by reason of the force that is used. He answered it as follows:

"The words of the subsection appear to me to be susceptible of either interpretation and that being so I think we ought to ascribe to them the more restricted meaning. In my opinion, if Parliament intended to enact that grievous bodily harm or death might be inflicted upon an entirely innocent person and that such person or his dependants should be deprived of all civil remedies to which they would otherwise have been entitled in circumstances such as are present in this case, it would have used words declaring such intention without any possible ambiguity."

Where a question arises in civil proceedings whether a party thereto has committed a crime, is there any constitutional reason to doubt the power of the provincial court to make an affirmative determination? In *Re Nordstrom, Nordstrom v. Bauman*, [1962] S.C.R. 147, 31 D.L.R. (2d) 255, 37 W.W.R. 16, where the question was whether a wife who had set fire to premises in which her husband died could claim an intestate share in his estate, and this depended on whether she was insane at the time, a majority of the British Columbia Court of Appeal when the case was before it (27 D.L.R. (2d) 634, 34 W.W.R. 556) held that a finding of crime could not properly be made on an originating summons concerning insanity or criminality. O'Halloran J.A. said that "in view of the divisional heads in ss. 91 and 92 of the B.N.A. Act . . . a provincially constituted court is without jurisdiction to determine in civil proceedings whether or not a person has committed a crime." The Supreme Court of Canada reversed; and Locke J., addressing himself to the constitutional point, remarked that "if it were not permissible in civil actions to make findings of fact which if proven in criminal proceedings would be held criminal, the due administration of justice would be gravely impeded."

Section 23 of the Evidence Act, R.S.O. 1970, c. 151, provides that "a witness may be asked whether he has been convicted of any crime . . ." *Held,* on an issue to determine whether a witness in a civil action may be questioned as to a provincial offence, "crime" in s. 23 means an offence under the federal criminal law: *Street v. Guelph,* [1964] 2 O.R. 421, 45 D.L.R. (2d) 652.]

Adulteration Legislation

REX v. PERFECTION CREAMERIES LTD.

In the Manitoba Court of Appeal. [1939] 3 D.L.R. 185, [1939] 2 W.W.R. 139, 47 Man. R. 150.

Appeal by way of stated case from dismissal of a charge of unlawfully manufacturing butter in violation of s. 6(2) of the *Dairy Industry Act,* R.S.C. 1927, c. 45. The charge was dismissed on the ground that s. 6(2) was unconstitutional. The impugned provision reads as follows:

"No person shall manufacture any butter containing over sixteen per centum of water, or less than eighty per centum of milk fat."

TRUEMAN J.A.: . . . The learned Magistrate considered that s. 6(2) deals solely with "Property and Civil Rights", a subject exclusively within the jurisdiction of the Provinces. My reading of the section and the accompanying provisions leads me to a different opinion. I find therein a clear indication of the public evil aimed at. It is that butter can be affected in its weight and quality by the methods therein stated, and that the purpose of the section is to protect the public from dishonesty or fraud in weight and quality of butter so brought about. The legislation is thus in pith and substance "criminal law" within s. 91(27) of the *B.N.A. Act.* The Act, 1889, c. 43 of the Parliament of Canada . . . provided, *inter alia,* that "No person shall sell, supply or send to any cheese or butter or condensed milk manufactory, or to the owner or manager thereof or to any maker of butter, cheese or condensed milk, to be manufactured, milk diluted with water, or in any way adulterated, or milk from which any cream has been taken, or milk commonly known as skimmed milk." No difficulty was experienced by the Court in *Regina v. Stone* (1892), 23 O.R. 46, in pronouncing the Act to be *intra vires.* Similar legislation, with a sufficient distinction, enacted by the Legislature of Ontario, was upheld in *Regina v. Wason* (1890), 17 O.A.R. 221, as a law in relation to "Property and Civil Rights in the Province." . . .

See . . . *Re Combines Investigation Act and S. 498 of the Cr. Code,* [1929] S.C.R. 409, aff'd [1931] A.C. 310, where Duff J., as he then was, said (at p. 413 S.C.R.): "Fraud, for example, may be of such a character as to constitute an actionable wrong or a criminal offence. The law in relation to civil rights, while necessarily concerned with defining the elements of the wrong entailing the civil responsibility of the wrong-doer, is primarily concerned with the victim's right of reparation, while the criminal law deals with the fraud as such, as something deserving of punishment at the hands of the State."

Pertinent to the case at bar are *R. v. Lee* (1911), 23 O.L.R. 490, and particularly, *Standard Sausage Co. v. Lee, Proctor v. Standard Sausage Co.,* [1933] 4 D.L.R. 501, [1934] 1 D.L.R. 706, 47 B.C.R. 411, where the constitutionality of the *Food and Drugs Act,* R.S.C. 1927, c. 76, was affirmed by the Court of Appeal.

Having the opinion that the provisions in question are strictly criminal law, there being no evidence or material before the Court to show that this not their true nature, I am unable to deal with Mr. Williams' submission that percentage of water or butter fat relates solely to grade, quality or standard of butter, and thus that the legislation is a colourable invasion of the provincial field. . . .

ROBSON J.A.: I adhere to the opinion I expressed in *R. v. Brodsky,* [1936] 1 D.L.R. 578, 65 Can. C.C. 4, 43 Man. R. 522. I think s-s. (2) of s. 6 of the *Dairy Industry Act,* R.S.C. 1927, c. 45, is within the powers of the Dominion. I would therefore set aside the order of dismissal and remit the case to the Magistrate for continuance of the trial.

Appeal allowed.

[Prendergast C.J.M., Dennistoun and Richards JJ.A. agreed. In *Standard Sausage Co. v. Lee,* referred to in the *Perfection Creameries* case, Macdonald J.A. of the British Columbia Court of Appeal, dealt with the facts and issues as follows: "In this appeal the right of the Dominion Parliament to enact the *Food and Drugs Act,* R.S.C. 1927, c. 76, and specifically ss. 3, 4 and 23 thereof and regulations thereunder is questioned. Appellant used an adulterant in the manufacture of sausages, *viz.,* sulphur dioxide to the extent of 0.46 parts to every 2,000 parts of meat product. This quantity is not injurious to health. It is submitted that he was unlawfully enjoined from using this drug as a preservative on the ground that the sections of the Act referred to and regulations passed thereunder are *ultra vires* of the Federal Parliament.

"The sample sausage, submitted for analysis, found to contain the adulterant, was sold as "fresh sausage". By spreading sulphur dioxide over it, or mixing it with the sausage, it stops fermentation and makes it fit for consumption and therefore saleable for from 12 to 18 hours longer than would otherwise be the case. [His Lordship here quoted the pertinent statutory provisions, and then continued as follows.]

"It will be observed that it is an offence to use an adulterant even although it may not be injurious to health. The penalty however is greater if it is injurious in that respect. This raises the question in issue—is it within the power of the Dominion Parliament to declare that a harmless act is criminal?

"By ss. 3 and 4 adulteration (the alleged criminal offence) is defined by regulations passed pursuant thereto. By Order in Council it is provided (IX(2)) that, 'Preservatives other than those mentioned in class 1 section XII, or colouring matter, shall not be used in or upon meat or meat products.

"By referring to Class 1 of s. 12 of the regulations it will be found that sulphur dioxide is not included in the list of permissible preservatives. It follows therefore that unless the sections referred to and regulations are *ultra vires* of the Federal Parliament the appeal must be dismissed.

"These sections (and regulations) are valid, if at all, under s. 91(27) of the *British North America Act* giving exclusive authority to the National Government to legislate in respect of 'The Criminal Law . . . including the Procedure in Criminal Matters.'

"Acts of a similar nature respecting food adulteration appear in the Dominion statutes, practically since Confederation, standing often side by side with somewhat similar legislation, of a more restricted character, enacted by the Provinces. In *Reg. v. Wason* (1890), 17 O.A.R. 221, a provincial Act to provide against frauds in supplying milk to cheese or butter manufactories (held *intra vires*) was considered in its relation to the Dominion *Adulteration Act* of that day and as Rose J. stated in *Reg. v. Stone* (1893), 23 O.R. 46, at p. 49, where the Dominion *Adulteration Act* was held to be *intra vires* of the Dominion Parliament, the reported argument of Mr. Edward Blake, in the *Wason* case correctly outlined the law where the jurisdictions of the provincial and Dominion Legislatures appear to overlap.

"The cases have been so often reviewed that extended references should not be necessary. The Dominion Parliament cannot acquire jurisdiction by attaching penalties to the commission of acts otherwise within the exclusive legislative control of the provinces subject to this—that it is not precluded from creating offences merely because the subject-matter, in another aspect, may fall under one of the sub-heads of s. 92. The limitation is that the Dominion Parliament cannot under the guise of criminal law legislate for the purpose of assuming, or with the object of securing, control over activities properly local and provincial in character. This however is not the avenue of approach in considering the case at bar. We start with the fact that the selling of food, not only unfit for human consumption but *dangerous* was a criminal offence at common law. If death followed, the vendor, if he knew it was unfit or 'dangerous', might be indicted for manslaughter.

"Section 224 of the Code makes it a criminal offence to knowingly sell food unfit for consumption. Food may be rendered unfit or potentially dangerous by adulteration. This case arises only because the mixing of sulphur dioxide with meat to the extent disclosed in evidence is not injurious to health. But the subject of legislation is adulteration of food (properly classified as a crime) and what constitutes adulteration must, at least within reasonable limits, be left to the judgment of Parliament in the light of the best knowledge available at the time. The subject of food purity, free from adulteration by the admixture of baser ingredients, is so important and the need to preserve its purity so great to prevent widespread calamity that precautions of the most detailed character must be taken to ensure it. These restrictions may be unnecessarily wide and open to criticism but that does not affect the principle. By the regulations Parliament entrusted to the Governor in Council the power and duty to make regulations prescribing what preservatives might or might not be used in or upon meat or meat products. Eight are permitted, *viz.*, common salt, sugar, saltpetre, wood smoke, vinegar, spices, alcohol and refined sodium nitrate. Greater scientific knowledge may induce Parliament or the Governor in Council to add sulphur dioxide to the list. In that event it would doubtless be necessary to prescribe the quantities that could safely be used. This might involve the danger that careless manufacturers would use too much or too little and for aught we know excessive quantities might be injurious to health.

"In the meantime, it is reasonable to provide in dealing with a product in which it is essential to maintain purity, that with other preservatives available, sulphur dioxide may not be used at all. We may assume that the framers of the regulations were aware of the facts disclosed in evidence, *viz.*, that this preservative is used, at least in part, to enable the dealer to offer the product for sale from 12 to 18 hours later than he otherw se could if no preservatives, permissible preservatives, were used. What happens if the dealer should be careless and sell after 20 hours elapse: or if a larger quantity should be used than 0.46 to 2,000 parts? The meat inspector stated that this quantity 'so far as a poison is concerned' would be inert but he does not state possible results if by mistake or design a larger proportion should be used.

"These considerations point to the conclusion that, granted the general subject of the adulteration of food may be the subject of legislation by the Dominion Parliament under the heading 'criminal law', it must follow, reasonably and necessarily, that it may define precisely the ingredients that may or may not be used. Nor is it any less a crime because it may be shown scientifically that some of the ingredients prescribed may not, if used in proper quantities, be deleterious at all. It is not a *sine qua non*, as many provisions of the Criminal Code show, that injury to property or to the person must necessarily follow the commission of the unlawful act. This contingency is recognized inasmuch as the penalty is less severe if injurious results do not follow. . . .

"The primary object of this legislation is the public safety—protecting it from threatened injury. If that is its main purpose—and not a mere pretence for the invasion of civil rights—it is none the less valid because it may be open to a criticism, from which few acts are free, that its purpose would be served equally well by accepting the opinion of others, *viz.*, that sulphur dioxide might with safety be added to the list of usable preservatives. Tampering with food by the introduction of foreign matter, however good the intentions, should properly be regarded as a public evil and it may properly be regarded as highly dangerous to lower the bars, or to remove restrictions which, rightly or wrongly, Parliament in its wisdom thought fit to prescribe.

"I think, too, if further support is required, the Act may be upheld because its purpose is not only to protect the consumer, but also to suppress fraud, in its criminal aspect, in the distribution of food products. The product was 'sold as fresh sausage'. It is in fact the substitution of an article treated with a preservative for one free from extraneous matter. If a dealer sold sausages as 'fresh' and then treated them in this way he would obtain money by fraud and false pretences and the customer would not be appeased by the assurance of the meat inspector that this 'keep 'em' process, as the butchers call it, is wholly effective. However it is not necessary to rely on this view. The drug in limited quantities may be safe; it is necessary to convince Parliament on that point."

Contrast the *Margarine* case, [1949] S.C.R. 1, [1949] 1 D.L.R. 433 aff'd. [1951] A.C. 179, [1950] 4 D.L.R. 689, reproduced at p. 269, *supra*.

The validity of federal adulteration legislation was recognized by the Privy Council in its unreported judgment in the *McCarthy Act* case, 1885, where in invalidating the Dominion *Liquor License Act*, 1883, it stated that the provisions of this Act as to adulteration, if separated, would be *intra vires*. For a recent illustration of adulteration legislation, see *Maple Products Industry Act*, R.S.C. 1970, c. M-2. The authority of the provinces in the matter recognized in *Regina v. Wason* (1890), 17 O.A.R. 221, illustrates the aspect doctrine; Dominion legislation would govern where it "occupied the field".

If it is open to the Dominion to establish or prescribe standards of purity or wholesomeness above scientifically tested safety levels (as *Standard Sausage Co. v. Lee* indicates), would it be within its power to require the fluoridation of water?]

Note on the Criminal Law Power and the Juvenile Offender

A series of cases, one of which reached the Supreme Court of Canada, has taken the position that the Parliament of Canada may competently exercise its criminal law power against juveniles by asserting a paramount authority over their conduct, whether it be violative of federal criminal law or provincial penal law, and thus exclude a Province's enforcement of its own penal legislation where the offender is a juvenile as defined by federal law. The cases are recent, beginning with *Re Dunne,* [1962] O.R. 595, 33 D.L.R. (2d) 190, which sustained the validity of s. 20(2) of the *Juvenile Delinquents Act,* R.S.C. 1960, c. 160 under which the designated Court could make an order against the parents of an adjudged juvenile delinquent or against his or her municipality (with a right in the latter to recover from the parents) to contribute to the child's support. This imposition of a "civil" obligation to support a "criminal" adjudication is not in itself very heretical if the criminal law power be conceived as broad enough to embrace social responsibility for rehabilitation of juvenile offenders.

There is no doubt as to the power of the Province to impose obligations on parents and municipality for the care of neglected or deprived children, to provide for their proper custody in institutions or elsewhere if parents neglect or abuse them, and to prescribe education and training for them. This is clearly so in the absence of federal legislation; and the question to be answered is whether Parliament may pre-empt part or all of this field of jurisdiction. Certainly, it may exercise control over juveniles through custody and required training as by-products of their violation of federal criminal law. What arises from *Re Dunne* and other cases discussed below is the question whether federal authority extends to the supervision of juveniles on the broader basis of violation of provincial or even of municipal legislation, or of immoral conduct which may not itself be against the law. The *Juvenile Delinquents Act* asserts federal jurisdiction on this broader basis by creating an offence of "delinquency" which covers violations of federal, provincial or municipal law and covers also "sexual immorality or any similar form of vice" and the commission of any other act rendering a juvenile liable to be committed to any reformative institution or refuge for children or juvenile reformatory under any federal or provincial statute.

In *Regina v. Kelleher,* [1964] 3 C.C.C. 299, 43 C.R. 257, this assertion of federal jurisdiction was upheld by the quashing of a magistrate's conviction of a juvenile for a provincial motor vehicle offence; this was held to be a delinquency over which the jurisdiction of the Juvenile Court was exclusive. Although this ruling, as a matter of construction, was not new, it was supported by an obiter approval of *Re Dunne* and the conclusion that the *Juvenile Delinquents Act* was within the federal criminal law power. The constitutional point came squarely before the British Columbia Court of Appeal in *A.-G. B.C. v. Smith* (1965), 53 D.L.R. (2d) 713, 53 W.W.R. 129, and by a bare majority the validity of the Act was sustained in relation to a fact situation similar to that present in the *Kelleher* case. On a further appeal to the Supreme Court of Canada, this majority view was affirmed: see [1967] S.C.R. 702, 65 D.L.R. (2d) 82.

Under present constitutional doctrine there can be no basis other than the federal criminal law power for support of the *Juvenile Delinquents Act*, R.S.C. 1970, c, J-3. It is somewhat incongruous, therefore, to find the Act expressing its key philosophy in s. 3(2) in these terms: "Where a child is adjudged to have committed a delinquency he shall be dealt with, not as an offender, but as one in a condition of delinquency and therefore requiring help and guidance and proper supervision." This expression is fortified by s. 38 which enjoins liberal construction of the Act "to the end that its purpose may be carried out, namely, that the care and custody and discipline of a juvenile delinquent shall approximate as nearly as may be that which should be given by its parents, and that as far as practicable every juvenile delinquent shall be treated, not as a criminal, but as a misdirected and misguided child, and one needing aid, encouragement, help and assistance." If these provisions were related to general child welfare legislation detached from delinquency as such, there would be little doubt of invalidity of the legislation as a federal measure. Is then the constitutional position advanced by tying it to a definition of delinquency which embraces violation of provincial and municipal law and, indeed, extends to conduct which is not elsewhere defined as an offence?

What is involved is the assumption of authority over the conduct of persons on the basis of age; persons are caught by the *Juvenile Delinquents Act* if they are apparently or actually under age 16 or, where so proclaimed (as in British Columbia), apparently or actually under age 18. The question is not whether the conduct as such is within the criminal law power, but whether it comes within it by reason of the age of the offender. It may not be germane to ask whether Parliament might, for the purposes of the criminal law, claim jurisdiction over the conduct of persons according to sex or occupation, as it has purported to do on the basis of age; criminal law systems have not been so based. But neither can it be controlling for constitutional law purposes that criminologists and sociologists support the theory of the *Juvenile Delinquents Act;* other means than an illegal exercise of legislative power would have to be found to realize it, such as complementary federal and provincial action based on respect for constitutional limitations.

Age presently plays a role in the federal criminal law by reason of the immunity given by s. 12 of the *Cr. Code* to persons under age 7, and of the qualified immunity given to persons under age 14 by s. 13. But these are immunities from criminal liability properly imposed for conduct which, as such, falls within the criminal law power. So far as such prohibited conduct is concerned, it would be clearly open to Parliament to prescribe a special or particular procedure for the trial and punishment or treatment of juvenile offenders. The *Juvenile Delinquents Act* cannot, however, be supported on this ground. Having regard to its terms, such a basis of constitutional justification would beg the very question of the validity of the substantive prohibitions to which the procedure of the Act is addressed; and, moreover, of their validity relative to juvenile offenders. The reasons of the Supreme Court in the *Smith* case amount to an assertion that the preventive side of the federal criminal law power enables Parliament to enact a comprehensive criminal code for children, covering all breaches of statute or by-law and immoral behaviour by them, and to supersede provincial legislation at the level of law enforcement. Fauteux J. for the Court said:

"Briefly and in scope the Act deals with juvenile delinquency in its relation to crime and crime prevention, a human, social and living problem of public interest, in the constituent elements, alleviation and solution of which jurisdictional distinctions of constitutional order are obviously and genuinely deemed by Parliament to be of no moment."

There are two supporting considerations for the *Juvenile Delinquents Act* that are suggested by its terms. First, the Act could be viewed as an exercise of federal power to legislate for prevention of crime, a power which Parliament enjoys along with that of legislating for cure. Second, the definition of "delinquency" might be considered as the creation of federal offences, in part by incorporation by reference. Both considerations are adverted to in the dissenting judgments of Davey and Norris JJ.A. in the *Smith* case in the British Columbia Court of Appeal. Although there is cogency in the argument of prevention, it is in truth a subordinate factor to the issue of scope of the Act as reflected in the conception of delinquency. Incorporation by reference has significance only as it is appendant to a base of jurisdiction otherwise open to Parliament; it cannot by itself be a justification for incorporating provincial and municipal enactments into federal criminal law. The same reasoning applies to delegation; and there is the additional practical consideration that the variation in substantive liability that results from making provincial and local legislation the touchstone, shows that Parliament is not advancing any policy of its own in relation to the prohibited conduct save that based of an offender's age. See (1968) 46 Can. Bar Rev. 473.

The argument for validity on that basis is not advanced by s. 39 of the Act which provides, *inter alia*, that nothing therein shall be construed to effect the repeal of or override any provincial enactment intended for the protection or benefit of children; and which provides also that a juvenile delinquent may be dealt with under the *Juvenile Delinquents Act* or under a provincial Act, as may be in his best interests, where his conduct does not involve an indictable offence under the Cr. Code but comes within the provincial Act. This is conditional legislation which amounts to an assertion of federal power. As a matter of construction, it was held in *Regina v. Kelleher, supra,* in line with earlier authority, that a provincial *Summary Convictions Act* could not be said to be legislation for the protection or benefit of children so as to be applicable in the circumstances of that case by the self-denial of the federal enactment.

The *Juvenile Delinquents Act* has been in force in substantially its present form since 1908, and it may be surprising that there had been no constitutional attack upon it for over half a century. An article on it by *W. L. Scott* in (1908) 28 Can. Law Times 892 when it was first enacted said nothing about its validity. There was a preamble to the original Act reading as follows: "Whereas it is inexpedient that youthful offenders should be classed or dealt with as ordinary criminals, the welfare of the community demanding that they should, on the contrary, be guarded against association with crime and criminals and should be subjected to such wise care, treatment and control as will tend to check their evil tendencies and to strengthen their better instincts." This truly emphasizes the preventive side of the criminal law power but it does not clearly answer the embrace by the Act of provincial and municipal penal legislation, save on the principle of a general sweep.

[Some background to the *Juvenile Delinquents Act* is provided by *Laycock*, Juvenile Courts in Canada, (1943) 21 Can. Bar Rev. 1, who states, inter alia, that in order to bring the Act within federal competence delinquency had to be dealt with as an act, and not as a state, and made an offence. *Sed quaere!*]

Note on Sunday and Other Religious Observance Legislation

A particular illustration of the federal criminal law power as encompassing, *inter alia,* control of human conduct or behaviour under penal sanction is afforded by so-called Lord's Day legislation. In *A.-G. Ont. v. Hamilton Street Ry.*, [1903] A.C. 524, 7 Can. C.C. 326, the Privy Council in a brief judgment invalidated a provincial Sunday observance statute as being legislation in relation to criminal law. The matter was raised again on a reference to the Supreme Court of Canada, *In re Jurisdiction of a Province to Legislate Respecting Abstention from Labour on Sunday* (1905), 35 S.C.R. 581, where the Court amplified the *Hamilton Street Ry.* decision as follows (at p. 592): ". . . . it appears to us that the day commonly called Sunday . . . is recognized in all Christian countries as an existing institution, and that legislation having for its object the compulsory observance of such day or the fixing of rules of conduct (with the usual sanctions) to be followed on that day is legislation properly falling within the views expressed by the Judicial Committee in the *Hamilton Street Ry.* reference and is within the jurisdiction of the Dominion Parliament." Following these two cases, the federal Lord's Day Act was enacted in 1906 as a prohibitory measure. A history of the statute is given by *Waterman,* The Lord's Day Act in a Secular Society, (1965), 11 Can. Jo. Theol. 108. The jurisdiction, in respect of such prohibitory legislation is, of course, exclusive. *Cf. St. Prosper v. Rodrigue* (1917), 56 S.C.R. 157. It is often difficult, however, to determine whether provincial regulatory legislation (or municipal by-laws under provincial authorization) dealing, for example, with closing hours of public places and covering Sunday closing, is not invalid as being criminal law, *i.e.,* as being directed to Sunday observance by people of the community rather than to the "secular" object of regulating the conduct of certain businesses; see *Rex v.*

Epstein, [1931] O.R. 726; *Rex v. Bachynski*, [1938] 2 D.L.R. 691, 46 Man. R. 1; *Re Gregory and Hamilton*, [1942] 4 D.L.R. 735; *Rex v. Paling*, [1946] 3 D.L.R. 54 (provincial prohibition of hunting on Sunday upheld as game protection measure). The difficulty is one, however, which is largely curable by proper drafting in the case of municipal by-laws; and in the case of a comprehensive provincial regulatory statute, such as a liquor control statute or a wage and hour statute, the nature of the legislation is itself a sufficient answer to any contention that compulsory Sunday or other religious observance is involved in what is truly a secular scheme: see *Lieberman v. The Queen*, [1963] S.C.R. 643, 41 D.L.R. (2d) 125; *Regina v. Court of Sessions of the Peace, ex parte Pilon*, [1964] Que. Q.B. 919, 45 D.L.R. (2d) 59; *Regina v. Court of Sessions of the Peace, ex parte Richstone Bakeries Inc.*, (1963), 40 D.L.R. (2d) 246.

The Dominion *Lord's Day Act*, now R.S.C. 1970, c. L-13 raises some problems relative to its general prohibition of Sunday work (with the usual exceptions in cases of necessity), which is followed by an exculpatory clause reading, "except as provided in any provincial Act or law now or hereafter in force." It hardly needs stating that this excepting clause is not a delegation of power for that would be unconstitutional: see *A.-G. N.S. v. A.-G. Can.*, [1951] S.C.R. 31, [1950] 4 D.L.R. 369. Rather, it operates by way of conditional legislation, and provincial enactments contemplated by that clause must be directed to some object or purpose competent to the province. Hence, prohibitory legislation respecting Sunday observance would be invalid: see *Ouimet v. Bazin* (1912), 46 S.C.R. 502. On the other hand, provincial regulatory legislation which, standing alone, would be valid (although subject, of course, to be overridden or forestalled by Dominion legislation "occupying the field"—as for example, unconditional Sunday observance legislation), may properly operate under the excepting clause of the Dominion *Lord's Day Act:* see *Lord's Day Alliance v. A.-G. Man.*, [1925] A.C. 384, [1925] 1 D.L.R. 561, [1925] 1 W.W.R. 296; *Lord's Day Alliance v. A.-G. B.C.*, [1959] S.C.R. 497, 19 D.L.R. (2d) 97; *Lord's Day (Ontario) Act*, R.S.O. 1970, c. 259.

The Sunday observance cases have been held applicable to preclude as well any provincial prohibitory legislation requiring compulsory observance of other religious (or feast) days: see *Henry Birks & Sons (Montreal) Ltd. v. Montreal and A.-G. Que.*, [1955] S.C.R. 799, [1955] 5 D.L.R. 321. Compulsory recognition of religious values, at least through observance legislation, falls within exclusive federal competence—certainly as within the criminal law power and also, in the view of some members of the Supreme Court, as being in relation to religion, considered as a separate constitutional value which is beyond provincial legislative power: see the opinions of Rand J. and of Kellock J. (Locke J. concurring) in the *Birks* case, *supra*. These opinions give a direct "civil liberties" basis to questions of religious observance; and if the power to legislate in relation to religion is federal (as it must be if the theory of exhaustiveness of the range of legislative power is accepted) then the traditional liberties are matters within the federal general power: see *Note*, (1956) 34 Can. Bar Rev. 81. For a comparative reference, see *Note*, State Sunday Laws and the Religious Guarantees of the Federal Constitution, (1960) 73 Harv. L. Rev. 729.

The matter has arisen in the context of the *Canadian Bill of Rights* which supports its hortatory affirmation of certain freedoms, including freedom of religion, by stipulating that every federal enactment, whether enacted before or after the *Canadian Bill of Rights*, shall be "construed and applied" so as not to abridge any of the declared freedoms unless it be expressly stated by Parliament that the enactment shall operate notwithstanding the *Canadian Bill of Rights*. The *Lord's Day Act* was alleged in this setting to be inoperative but the contention was rejected in *Robertson and Rosetanni v. The Queen*, [1963] S.C.R. 651, 41 D.L.R. (2d) 485, where the majority of the Court found it possible to reconcile the Act with the *Canadian Bill of Rights*. It did this (over the dissent of Cartwright J.) by holding in effect that freedom of religion was not abridged by state support of particular religious tenets (Christian in this case) so long as there was no compelled observance thereof by others; and the fact that these others were obliged to close their businesses on Sunday was a secular consequence. Of course, the *Lord's Day Act* could not be supported as valid federal legislation if it had a secular purpose; and in this respect the recent line of decisions in the United States, of which *McGowan v. Maryland* (1961), 366 U.S. 420, 81 S. Ct. 1101 is illustrative, provided no analogy in holding that Sunday legislation had become secular in object so as not to offend the religious guarantees of the first amendment of the Constitution of the United States.

The result of the *Robertson and Rosetanni* case was not only to curtail the efficacy of the *Canadian Bill of Rights* but also to suggest a limitation on the constitutional authority of Parliament in relation to freedom of religion; unless, of course, it be the case that Parliament's exclusive authority is larger in the constitutional sense than the scope of freedom of religion in the *Canadian Bill of Rights*. See, generally, *Barron*, Sunday in North America, (1965) 79 Harv. L. Rev. 42; *Laskin*, Note, Freedom of Religion and the Lord's Day Act— The Canadian Bill of Rights and The Sunday Bowling Case, (1964) 42 Can. Bar Rev. 147.

While it may be said with confidence that a Province is without authority to compel religious observance, it is still an unsettled question whether a Province may constitutionally interfere with exercise of religion: see *Saumur v. Quebec and A.-G. Que.*, [1953] 2 S.C.R. 299, [1953] 4 D.L.R. 641. The better opinion is that a Province has no such power, at least where the challenged legislation is characterized as being in relation to religious exercise or profession. In *Chaput v. Romain*, [1955] S.C.R. 834, 1 D.L.R. (2d) 241, an action for damages arising out of the dispersal by the police of a religious gathering of Jehovah's Witnesses on private premises, Taschereau J. (who spoke also for Kerwin C.J.C. and Estey J.) gave voice to an utterance which, while capable of having constitutional import, was not squarely addressed to such an end; he said:

In our country, there is no state religion. All religions are on an
equal footing, and Catholics as well as Protestants, Jews and
other adherents to various religious denominations enjoy the most
complete liberty of thought. The conscience of each is a personal
matter and the concern of nobody else. It would be distressing to
think that a majority might impose its religious views upon a
minority, and it would also be a shocking error to believe that one
serves his country or his religion by denying in one Province,
to a minority, the same rights which one rightly claims for oneself in another Province.

[*The Holidays Act*, R.S.C. 1970, c. H-7 provides that July 1 in every year
(or July 2 if July 1 is a Sunday) shall be a legal holiday throughout Canada
and be kept and observed as such. What is the constitutional basis for the
enactment? See *Re Canadian Westinghouse Co. Ltd. and United Electrical,
Radio & Machine Workers*, [1962] O.R. 20, at p. 24, 30 D.L.R. (2d) 676, at
p. 680].

CHAPTER XIII

CULTURAL GUARANTEES

ROMAN CATHOLIC SEPARATE SCHOOL TRUSTEES FOR TINY
v. THE KING

In the Privy Council. [1928] A.C. 363, [1928] 3 D.L.R. 753,
[1928] 2 W.W.R. 641.

Appeal by special leave from a judgment of the Supreme Court
of Canada, [1927] S.C.R. 637, [1927] 4 D.L.R. 857, affirming on
equal division a judgment of the Ontario Appellate Division, 60 O.L.R.
15, [1927] 1 D.L.R. 913, which affirmed a judgment of Rose J., 59
O.L.R. 96, dismissing a petition of right by appellants.

VISCOUNT HALDANE: Their Lordships are fully aware that this
appeal is among the most important that have come before them
from Canada in recent years. It relates to the interpretation of the
Constitution of Canada in regard to the separate schools of a large
part of her Roman Catholic population, and to the character of the
rights conferred on them by the legislative settlement made at the
time of Confederation under the *British North America Act.* So far
as concerns the question brought before the Judicial Committee of
the Privy Council, it will be found to be a question of pure law, turning on the interpretation and application of words in that Act. . . .

These proceedings took the form of a petition of right presented
by the appellants to the Supreme Court of Ontario. The petition
claimed that certain Acts of the legislature of that Province, and
certain regulations purporting to have been passed under these Acts,
prejudicially affected the rights conferred by the *British North
America Act* on the appellants and were *ultra vires.* The appellants
asked for a declaration that the Acts of the legislature, which had
sought to alter the basis of distribution of legislative grants which
existed at the date of Confederation, were *ultra vires* so far as concerned separate schools, and for judgment for a sum equal to the
difference between the amount paid to the trustees of the Roman
Catholic School for school section No. 2 in the Township of Tiny, out
of the legislative grant of the Province for 1922, and the amount that
would have come to it if effect had been given to the *Separate School
Act,* 1863, which was in force at Confederation, and created (it is
claimed) a right which the legislature of the Province had no power
after Confederation to affect prejudicially. The appellants also
claimed that they had the right to establish and conduct in their
own schools courses of study and grades of education such as were
being conducted in continuation schools, collegiate institutes and
high schools, and that all regulations purporting to affect that right
were invalid. They asked for a further declaration that the supporters of Roman Catholic separate schools were exempt from the
rates imposed for the support of the former kind of schools, unless
established or conducted by boards of trustees of Roman Catholic
separate schools.

All of these claims were traversed by the Attorney-General of Ontario on behalf of the Government of Ontario.

The question which has to be decided is one of far-reaching magnitude. To understand its scope it is necessary to have in mind the history of education in Canada, including that of s. 93 of the *British North America Act,* 1867. That section embodies a compromise. The language proposed by the conferences of delegates from the various parts of Canada, which passed resolutions at Quebec on October 10, 1864, was not adopted, so far as the final arrangement was concerned, in the form in which the resolutions were passed: see Cartwright's Cases on the B.N.A. Act, vol. ii, Quebec resolution No. 43. Resolution 43 proposed to give power to the local legislatures to make laws as to education, saving the rights and privileges which the Protestant and Catholic minority in both Canadas might possess as to their denominational schools at the time when the Union came into operation. In the *British North America Act,* as passed by the Imperial Parliament, the substance of this resolution is not included in s. 92, but is embodied in a separate section, 93. The separate section enacts that in and for each Province the legislature may exclusively make laws in relation to education, subject and according to certain provisions. These provisions were: (sub-s. 1) that nothing in such law should prejudicially affect any right or privilege with respect to denominational schools which any class of person had by law in the Province at the Union; (sub-s. 2) all the powers, privileges and duties at the Union, conferred and imposed in Upper Canada on the separate schools and school trustees of the Queen's Roman Catholic subjects are extended to the dissentient schools of the Queen's Protestant and Roman Catholic subjects in Quebec (on this sub-section no question arises in the present appeal); and by sub-s. 3, as follows: "Where in any Province a system of separate or dissentient schools exists by law at the Union or is thereafter established by the legislature of the Province, an appeal shall lie to the Governor-General in Council from any Act or decision of any Provincial authority affecting any right or privilege of the Protestant or Roman Catholic minority of the Queen's subjects in relation to education." The fourth sub-section enacts that if a Provincial law which seems to the Governor-General in Council requisite to give effect to his decision is not made or the decision is not executed, then the Parliament of Canada may make the necessary remedial law.

It will be observed that sub-s. 3 goes further than sub-s. 1 in material respects. In the first place, it applies not merely to what exists at the time of Confederation, but also to separate or dissentient schools established afterwards by Provincial legislatures. In the second place, the word "prejudicially", in sub-s. 1, is dropped out from before the expression "affecting", in subs-3. In the third place, the right or privilege is not confined to one in respect of denominational schools, but is given in respect of education. Their Lordships think that these changes in language are significant. They show that the protection given by sub-s. 1 was deemed, if taken by itself, to be insufficient. It was not considered to be enough protection for the denominational schools to apply to them a restriction which only rendered *ultra vires* of the Provinces a law which took away what was an existing legal right or privilege at the time of Confederation in respect of denominational schools. Sub-s. 3 contemplates that within the powers of the Provincial legislature Acts might be passed which did affect rights and privileges of religious minorities in relation to education, and gives a different kind of remedy, which appears, as has already been pointed out, to have been devised subsequently to the Quebec resolutions of 1864, and before the bill of 1867 was agreed on. Whenever an Act or decision of a Provincial authority affecting any right or privilege of the minority, Protestant or Roman Catholic, in relation to education is challenged, an appeal is to lie to the Governor-General in Council, as distinguished from the Courts of law. No doubt if what is challenged is challenged on the ground of its being *ultra vires*, the right of appeal to a Court of law remains for both parties unimpaired. But there is a further right not based on the principle of *ultra vires*. That this is so is shown by the extension of the power to challenge to any system of separate or dissentient schools established by law after Confederation and which accordingly could not be confined to rights or privileges at the time of Confederation. The omission of the word "prejudicially" in sub-s. 3 tends to bear out the view that something wider than a mere question of legality was intended, and the language of sub-s. 4 enabling the Dominion Parliament to legislate remedially for giving effect, "so far only as the circumstances of each case require", to the decision of the Governor-General in Council, points to a similar interpretation. What is to be dealt with is a right or privilege in relation to education.

Their Lordships are of opinion that where the head of the executive in council in Canada is satisfied that injustice has been done by taking away a right or privilege which is other than a legal one from the Protestant or Roman Catholic minority in relation to education, he may interfere. The step is one from mere legality to administrative propriety, a totally different matter. But it may be that those who had to find a new constitution for Canada when the *British North America Act* was passed in 1867, came to the conclusion that a very difficult situation could be met in no other way than by transferring the question from the region of legality to that of administrative fairness.

There is no question before their Lordships in this case concerning any appeal to the Governor-General in Council, and they abstain from saying anything as to the principles on which, if invoked, he may think fit to proceed. But the view that the rights of the appellants are not necessarily confined to rights under sub-s. 1 has an important bearing on the construction of that sub-section, inasmuch as it no longer takes away all remedy in cases to which the principle of *ultra vires* does not apply. It may even be that the power conferred on the Governor-General in Council enables him to take into account the considerations arising out of what had been done in the course of *de facto* administration, which James L.J. excluded in delivering the judgment of the Judicial Committee in 1874, in *Maher v. Town of*

Portland, reported in Wheeler's Confederation Law of Canada, and quoted by the late Lord Chancellor in delivering his recent judgment of the Committee in *Hirsch v. Protestant School Commissioners of Montreal,* [1928] A.C. 200 on February 2 last. The question is one of administrative policy, and it is not before their Lordships. They desire, however, to observe that the view now expressed as to the relations of sub-ss. 1 and 3 of s. 93 is substantially the same as that taken in *Brophy v. Attorney-General of Manitoba,* [1895] A.C. 221. In that case the question arose under the *Constitution Act of Manitoba,* 1870, a Dominion Act under which, as subsequently confirmed by Imperial statute, Manitoba became one of the Provinces of the Dominion of Canada. The Act contains in s. 22 provisions which for present purposes are identical with those of sub-ss. 1, 3 and 4 of s. 93 of the *British North America Act.* It is true that in the second and corresponding sub-section of the *Manitoba Act* the appeal is expressly stated to lie against any Act or decision of the legislature of the Province as well as of any Provincial authority, thus in words saying more than in sub-s. 3 of s. 93 of the Act of 1867. But Lord Herschell in *Brophy's* case expressed his dissent from the argument that the insertion of the additional words in the Manitoba Act showed that in the Act of 1867 it could not have been intended to comprehend the legislatures under the words "any Provincial authority". Their Lordships agree with his view, and they are of opinion that the legislatures are so comprehended. The point may prove to be one of great importance if there is hereafter an appeal to the Governor-General in Council. In *Brophy's* case the Roman Catholic minority in Manitoba appealed to the Governor-General in Council under sub-s. 2 of s. 22 of their Constitutional Act on the ground that rights and privileges of theirs in relation to education had been affected by two statutes of the legislature of Manitoba passed in 1890, which set up a general system of non-sectarian education. The schools of the Roman Catholic minority were deprived of their previously existing proportionate share of the money contributed for school purposes out of the taxes, while for the new non-sectarian schools they were both taxed and assessed for rates. It had been held, in *City of Winnipeg v. Barrett,* [1892] A.C. 445, that the statutes of 1890 did not affect any right or privilege with respect to their schools which the Roman Catholics of Manitoba had by law or practice in their Province at the Union in 1870. The only right or privilege which they then possessed was to establish and maintain for the use of members of their own Church such schools, at their own expense, as they pleased. In *Barrett's* case this was the only question before the Judicial Committee, and it was held that the Acts of 1890 were not *ultra vires.*

But in *Brophy's* case the question was the wholly different one, whether the rights and privileges of Roman Catholics in relation to education had not been so affected by the Acts of 1890 as to enable an appeal to the Governor-General in Council in a quasi administrative capacity. It was held that there was such affection, in fact although not in law, inasmuch as Roman Catholics were to be taxed and rated for the upkeep of schools which were obnoxious to their religious opinion in regard to education. It was no point of illegality. What was decided was that the Governor-General in Council had power to entertain such an appeal under sub-s. 2 of s. 22 of the Constitutional Act, corresponding, as their Lordships have already stated, to sub-s. 3 of s. 93 of the *British North America Act,* 1867.

Their Lordships have dwelt on what was decided in *Brophy's* case in reference to the scope of the appeal against the affection of rights or privileges within the meaning of sub-s. 3 of s. 93 of the *British North America Act,* with a view to bringing out the limitation which has to be placed on the expressions used in sub-s. 1. The rights and privileges there referred to must be such as are given by law, and the redress which may be given in respect of prejudice to them, caused by laws made by the Provincial legislatures which, in other respects, have the exclusive power of legislation in relation to education, is a redress based on the principles of *ultra vires.* Such redress can therefore, for the reasons given in *Brophy's* case, be sought from the Courts of law alone. The other remedy which sub-ss. 3 and 4 afford not only supplements the former but affords cogent reasons why sub-s. 1 should be construed as being confined strictly to questions of *ultra vires.* Were the Acts and regulations complained of in the petition of right assailable under this principle? In order to answer this question it is necessary to understand clearly what was their nature, and to understand this it is essential to see what has been the development of the system of education in Upper Canada.

Before 1867 there were in Canada schools of three principal classes—common schools, grammar schools and separate schools. Since Confederation there have come into existence continuation schools, collegiate institutes and high schools, which have developed out of the three kinds of school last mentioned. The claim of the appellants is that, in 1867, Roman Catholics in Upper Canada enjoyed by law the right to establish denominational schools, to be conducted by boards of trustees chosen by themselves; that, as regards selection of text-books and courses of study, the control of these belonged to the boards of trustees who could sanction in their schools courses of study co-extensive in scope with those, since Confederation, pursued in high schools, collegiate institutes and continuation schools. The case made was that the trustees could do this in the separate schools, inasmuch as these, although common schools, were not under the old order of things, restricted in their scope as regards education of pupils up to twenty-one years of age. It is argued for the appellants that under s. 93, sub-s. 1, the Roman Catholics of Ontario continued to enjoy these autonomous rights, coupled with a consequential right of exemption from taxation for the purposes of the high schools, collegiate institutes and continuation schools, which, it is said, are mere forms of what fall within the scope of existing separate schools, and are, therefore, of a kind for which the Roman Catholics were exempt from taxation.

Their Lordships may say at once that if such a right was really conferred on the boards of separate schools, the right and the title to grants dependent on it were not interrupted by the Act of 1867. . . .

Section 93 was, . . . obviously meant to apply to the future as well as to the past, and to the new Province of Ontario.

This consideration leads up to the crucial point in this appeal. Did the trustees of the separate Roman Catholic schools secure at Confederation a right to maintain, free from control or regulation by the legislature of Ontario, as respects the scope of instruction, denominational schools which could embrace the subjects formerly taught in the separate schools on their higher sides, and afterwards taught in the undenominational high schools, collegiate institutes and continuation schools, as developed after Confederation, or analogous subjects taught in the Roman Catholic separate schools before Confederation, and to exemption from taxation for the support of such undenominational educative organizations? And did the trustees secure a title to receive a share of every grant by the legislature for common school purposes, construed as extending to the maintenance of education of the type given in post-Confederation secondary schools, as well as in those that were merely elementary, based on the number of pupils attending the separate schools, and independant of the subjects taught, or the text-books used, every separate school being entitled to its share, calculated according to a statutory rate, however advanced, however rudimentary, the education and books might be? If these questions are answered in the affirmative then it was *ultra vires* of Ontario to take away the right either to regulate the schools in a manner inconsistent with this freedom, or to diminish the grants or to tax for the support of the undenominational schools, by legislation, or administratively, so far as control was concerned, by State regulation.

The question is a very serious one. Before Confederation the common schools and with them the separate schools were left free, by statute (see *Upper Canada Common Schools Act, 1859, s. 16*), to educate pupils up to the age of twenty-one, and some of them were in the habit of giving to the older pupils advanced teaching such as would fit them to enter the University. But Roman Catholics find a great difficulty in sending their sons and daughters to the higher schools which have now been established for the purposes of this advanced teaching. As the Chief Justice of Canada has said, undenominational education is based on the idea that the separation of secular from religious education may be advantageous. But Roman Catholics, at least, hold that religious instruction and influence should always accompany secular training.

What, then, were the rights of the supporters of the separate schools at the time of Confederation? To answer this, and the question of *ultra vires* which arises out of it, it is necessary to look at the history of the development of education in Canada. [His Lordship here reviewed certain statutes dealing with education in Upper Canada and, after 1840, in the province of Canada.] . . .

In 1859 a Consolidating Act was passed by what had become the Legislative Council and Assembly for the now United Province of Canada. This Act related to common schools. It did not make any important changes in the law, but aimed, for most part, at bringing together the existing statutory provisions relating to common schools. Many of the provisions of this Act were embodied by reference in the Act respecting separate schools passed in the same years as stated below. The office of Chief Superintendent of Education was reconstituted. He was to be under the direction of the Governor. The duty of the Chief Superintendent under the *General Consolidating Act* now cited was among other things, under s. 106, to apportion in each year "all monies granted or provided by the legislature for the support of common schools in Upper Canada, and not otherwise appropriated by law, to the several counties, townships, cities, &c.," according to ratio of population.

There was also to be a Council of Public Instruction of nine persons, appointed by the Governor. Among other things it was to make regulations for the organization, government and discipline of common schools, for the classification of schools and teachers, and for school libraries, and to examine, and at its discretion to recommend or disapprove of text-books for the use of schools or school libraries. By s. 120 the Governor could authorize the expenditure, in Upper Canada, out of the share of the legislative school grant and the additional moneys granted in aid of common and grammar schools "and not otherwise expressly appropriated by law" of certain sums for purposes which were not connected with the separate schools. By s. 121, the whole of the remainder of the grants mentioned in s. 120 and not exclusively appropriated in its sub-sections, were to be expended in aid of the common schools according to the provisions of the Act. There was a conscience section (129) in the Act.

In the same year (1859) the *Separate Schools Act*, already referred to, was passed. The main provisions of the *Common Schools Act* of 1859 were thereby made applicable to the separate schools, but the new Act was designed in ss. 18 to 36 to make clear what was the position in particular of Roman Catholic separate schools. The existing provisions for these were repeated with variations, and it was enacted that the trustees of each separate school should perform the same duties and be subject to the same penalties as trustees of common schools. By s. 33 every separate school was again to be entitled to a proportionate share in the annual grant for common schools. The trustees were to report the names and attendance of the children attending these schools to the Chief Superintendent, who was thereupon to determine what they were entitled to receive out of the legislative grant.

It is now necessary to refer to the final *Separate Schools Act*, passed in 1863, which substituted a new set of provisions in the Act of 1859, in place of ss. 18 to 36, which were by this Act repealed. Amongst those new provisions was s. 20, a re-enactment with additions of the old s. 33 of the Act of 1859; and a section which their Lordships set out later in their judgment.

The appellants contend that the words in s. 106 of the *Common Schools Act* of 1859 "not otherwise appropriated by law" includes the share of the apportioned fund to which they are entitled under

s. 20 of the Act of 1863, and shows that they are not excluded from
sharing in all the moneys appropriated outside those "granted or
provided by the legislature for the support of common schools." But
their Lordships think that this is erroneous and that the learned
judges were right who thought that the separate schools are only
entitled to share in the moneys "granted by the legislature for the
support of common schools not otherwise appropriated by law", and
also by the Act of 1863 in all other public grants made for common
school purposes. The appropriations form in short a first debit item
against the money grant. After that, after the appropriations have
been made and the debit item satisfied, comes the second stage—
namely, that of apportionment; and it is in this apportionment that
the separate schools have their share. The apportionment mentioned
in s. 106, sub-s. 2, is not that of the total fund, but only of that fund
after the trustees of the separate schools had received their share.
This their Lordships regard as the true meaning of the Act.

This statute of 1863 is an important one. Its declared purpose was
to restore to Roman Catholics in Upper Canada certain rights in
respect of separate schools, and to bring the law respecting separate
schools more into harmony with the law respecting common schools.
It was in force at Confederation, and it has been spoken of as the
charter of the denominational schools. The chief points in it were
that separate school sections, whether in the same or in adjoining
municipalities (not only, as in the earlier Act, the schools in one
ward of a city or town), might be joined in a separate school union
section. The teachers of separate schools were to be subject to the
same examinations, and to receive certificates of qualification in the
same way as common school teachers generally. Supporters of
separate schools were to be exempt from payment of municipal rates
for common schools and libraries, while they continued to be supporters of separate schools, and not merely for the current year, as
under the old legislation. The Roman Catholic separate schools were
to be subject to such inspection as might be directed by the Chief
Superintendent of Education, and were to be subject also to such
regulations as might be imposed from time to time by the Council
of Public Instruction for Upper Canada. All judges, members of the
legislature, heads of local municipal bodies, the Chief Superintendent
and the local superintendent of common schools, and clergymen of
the Roman Church, were to be visitors of these separate schools.

Section 20 is a section to which much of the argument at their
Lordships' bar was directed. It is in these terms: "Every separate
school shall be entitled to a share in the fund annually granted by
the legislature of this Province for the support of common schools,
and shall be entitled also to a share in all other public grants, investments and allotments for common school purposes now made or
hereafter to be made by the Province or the municipal authorities,
according to the average number of pupils attending such school
during the twelve next preceding months, or during the number of
months which may elapse from the establishment of a new separate
school, as compared with the whole average number of pupils attending school in the same city, town, village or township."

By s. 21, local assessments for common school purposes were excluded from the money to which the separate schools were to be entitled. By s. 26 the Roman Catholic separate schools were to be subject to such inspection as might be directed from time to time by the Chief Superintendent and were to be "subject also to such regulations as might be imposed from time to time by the Council of Public Institution for Upper Canada."

The questions which arise on this Act are, first of all, whether, having regard to the provisions quoted, laws have been enacted by the Province which prejudicially affect any legal right or privilege with respect to denominational schools which the Roman Catholic community (a class of persons) had obtained under these statutes at the Union. The second question is whether under these statutes the Roman Catholic schools had become entitled at the Union to grants which were fixed and could not be taken away or interfered with by the authorities of the Province. It has been to render the nature of these questions clear that their Lordships have considered it necessary to examine at some length the history and character of the legislation before Confederation.

The petition of right claims that the suppliants have a legal title to establish and conduct courses of study, with grades of education, such as are now conducted in what are designated as continuation schools, collegiate institutes, and high schools, and that any statutes and regulations purporting to limit or prejudicially affect this title are *ultra vires*. The petition further claims that the class of persons represented by the petitioners are exempt from payment of rates imposed for the support of these organizations when not established by trustees of Roman Catholic separate schools. Consequently on their claim the petitioners ask that the trustees of the Roman Catholic separate schools for section 2, Township of Tiny, may have paid to them certain moneys to which it is said that they would have been entitled on the footing that the general claim as to validity is properly established.

The appellants say that the old common schools were allowed to give such education as was found suitable to pupils up to twenty-one, who were thereby prepared for the University, and that the separate schools enjoyed the right thus permitted, and possessed it at Confederation. For this purpose the classes in the schools were in point of fact "graded". The Courts of Ontario have held in the present case that while this grading was *de facto* permitted it was always subject to the regulations by which the State authorities might from time to time alter and define the work in the common (including the separate) schools. Subject to this supervision, "grading" might take place either in the classes of a single school, or by distributing the teaching where there was a group of schools, as in urban municipalities. It is said for the appellants that the only rival of the common and separate schools as they were up to and after Confederation, was the grammar school, which was not under the common school Acts, but was always organized under separate statutes. The appellants further argued that an Act passed after Confederation in

Ontario in 1871 for the improvement of the common and grammar schools really transformed both the common and grammar schools. They were re-arranged in two divisions, in one of which free education was to be given up to the age of twelve, such division to be called a "public school". The other division was to be a "high school", and to give higher instruction with the aid of the old grammar school grant, and of contributions from local revenues by the municipal authorities. The Boards of Grammar school trustees were to take over these high schools, and to administer them under regulation.

The appellants contend that the common school was at the Union entitled to provide for the public, other than separate school supporters, education of every kind which in the judgment of its trustees it was desirable to give and that some of the urban common schools were then known as high schools, in which the teaching extended as far as that in the grammar schools, and was substantially that prescribed for the new high schools after the Act of 1871. The new public and high schools were, it is argued, just divisions of pre-Confederation common schools, with compulsory taxation for the new high schools. From such taxation, it is said, the Roman Catholic separate school supporters must be exempt, and they cannot be affected by the combination brought about by the Act of 1871.

Of the post-Confederation continuation schools, which were established by statutes of 1896 and 1908, it is said that these began by being only continuation classes in public schools in municipalities in which no high school had been established, but were by the Act of 1908 made into continuation schools supported by grants and rates. In any view, as they cannot be given the form of separate schools, Roman Catholics should be free from taxation for them. Of collegiate institutes, it is said that they are only certain high schools to which a special name has been given.

The petition also claims that certain sections in various statutes which infringe the principles thus contended for are *ultra vires*.

The Provincial Legislature is supreme in matters of education, excepting so far as s. 93 of the *British North America Act* restricts its authority. Sub-s. 1 preserves as they stood any rights and the privileges given in relation to denominational schools by law in 1867. The question, therefore, is whether the Province could then as the law stood so control the courses of study and the general range and quality of the text-books used, as to enable the educational authorities of the Province to prescribe the graduation of the separate school and the stages in which instruction should be given in it. Examination of the statutes and of the history of the subject have satisfied their Lordships that, while a settlement was come to in 1863 with both Roman Catholics and Protestants, a settlement which in so far as it remained unaltered at Confederation, must be strictly maintained, the Province showed in the wording of the successive earlier statutes the intention to preserve for the rest the power to mould the 'educational system in the interests of the public at large, as distinguished from any section of it, however important. . . .

The examination of the series of statutes relating to education from 1807 onwards has led their Lordships to the view that the Province did provide for the regulation, in the full sense, of its common or public schools. . . .

It is this principle and purpose which appear to their Lordships to be dominant through the statutes, and the language used . . . has brought this Committee to the conclusion that the power of regulation must be interpreted in a wider sense than that given to it in the judgment of the Chief Justice of Canada. They are not at one with him in thinking that separate school trustees could give secondary education in their schools otherwise than by the permission, express or implied, of the Council of Public Instruction. The separate school was only a special form of common school, and the Council could in the case of each determine the courses to be pursued and the extent of the education to be imparted. A full power of regulation, such as the purpose of the statutes quoted renders appropriate, is what suggests itself, and this is the natural outcome of a scheme which never appears to have really varied. Such expressions as "organization", "government", "discipline" and "classifiication", do, in their Lordships' interpretation of them, imply a real control of the separate schools. The duty of the Judicial Committee is simply to interpret the words used. It may be that even if the contention of the appellants as to the scope of sub-s. 1 is shut out, there will remain to them a remedy of a wholly different kind in the shape of an appeal under sub-s. 3 to the Governor-General in Council in an administrative capacity. That question does not arise in this appeal and is in no way prejudiced by the conclusion to which their Lordships have come.

What has been said on the subject of *ultra vires* in regard to regulation also applies to the title to fixed grants. The appellants rely on s. 20 of the *Separate Schools Act* of 1863. . . . It declares every separate school to be entitled to a share in the fund annually granted by the legislature for the support of common schools, and also to a share in all other public grants, investments and allotments for common school purposes, according to a defined proportion. It is argued that their share of these grants is being withheld from the appellants and from the Roman Catholic separate schools generally. But the question really turns on whether the authorities of the Province had power to make apportionments and payments out of the funds granted before the balance was arrived at which should be available for common school purposes. In their Lordships' opinion it is clear that there was such power. Section 106 of the *Common Schools-Act* of 1859 defined as the duty of the Chief Superintendent to apportion the moneys granted or provided by the legislature "and not otherwise appropriated by law" in a manner analogous to that subseouently provided by s. 20 of the Act of 1863. Section 120 of the 1859 Act enabled the Governor to make a number of appropriations out of the sums granted, and s. 121 provides that the whole of the remainder of the grants mentioned and not exclusively appropriated in the earlier sub-sections are to be expended in aid of the common schools according to the provisions of the Act.

In their Lordships' view, in the face of the provisions referred to, it is impossible to contend successfully that it was *ultra vires* after Confederation to make new appropriations out of the grants which would diminish what would otherwise have come to the appellants. Whether the case is looked at from the point of view of regulation, or whether it is regarded from that of discretion in power of appropriation, the result is the same. It is indeed true that power to regulate merely does not imply a power to abolish. But the controversy with which this Board has to deal on the present occasion is a long way from abolition. It may be that the new laws will hamper the freedom of the Roman Catholics in their denominational schools. They may conceivably be or have been subjected to injustice of a kind that they can submit to the Governor-General in Council, and through him to the Parliament of Canada. But they are still left with separate schools, which are none the less actual because the liberty of giving secondary and higher education in them may be abridged by regulation. Such an abridgement may be in the usual course when a national system of education has attained a certain stage in its development, and it would be difficult to forego this power if the grading which may be essential is also to be possible. Their Lordships do not think grading is in itself inconsistent with such rights to separation of schools as was reserved at Confederation. . . .

Appeal dismissed.

[See also *Ottawa Separate School Trustees v. Mackell*, [1917] A.C. 62, 32 D.L.R. 1. As to the position of Protestant separate schools in Quebec and the extent to which Quebec legislation could give Jews status in the Protestant school system, see *Hirsch v. Protestant School Com'rs of Montreal*, [1928] A.C. 200, [1928] 1 D.L.R. 1041. As to the compellability of German Lutherans in Alberta to send their children to public schools, see *Rex v. Ulmer*, [1923] 1 D.L.R. 304 (Alta.). As to the application of s. 93 of the *B.N.A. Act* in Saskatchewan, see *McCarthy v. Regina and Regina Public School Trustees*, [1917] 1 W.W.R. 1105, 32 D.L.R. 741, aff'd [1918] A.C. 911, 43 D.L.R. 112.

In *Reference re Adoption Act, etc.*, [1938] S.C.R. 398, at p. 402, [1938] 3 D.L.R. 497, at p. 498, Duff C.J. speaking for the Court said: "It is well not to forget . . . that by section 93 (subject to provisions having for their purpose the protection of religious minorities) education is committed exclusively to the responsibility of the [provincial] legislatures; and that, as regards that subject, the powers of the legislatures are not affected by the clause at the end of section 91. We should perhaps also recall that section 93 (as is well known) embodies one of the cardinal terms of the Confederation arrangement. Education, I may add, is, as I conceive it, employed in this section in its most comprehensive sense." See, in support, Quebec Resolution 43(6).

Note that by the terms of union with Newfoundland a different provision is substituted for s. 93 and declared to be applicable in its stead: see s. 17 of the Terms of Union, appended as a schedule to 1949 (Can. 1st sess.), c. 1 and the *British North America Act* (No. 1) 1949 (Imp.), c. 22.

The "education" power is discussed in detail in *Lefroy*, Canada's Federal System, chap. 26 and *Clement, The Canadian Constitution* (3rd ed.), chap. 38.

In speaking of the application of s. 93 of the *B.N.A. Act* to British Columbia, New Brunswick, Nova Scotia and Prince Edward Island, *Clement* says (at p. 782): "Only in the event of the future establishment of a system of separate or dissentient schools by any of these provinces can their full autonomy in relation to educational matters be interfered with by the parliament of Canada. In none of these provinces could the claim to a 'right or privilege' [with respect to denominational schools which any class of persons have by law in the province at the union—s. 93(1)] existing at the time of the Union be more strongly supported than in New Brunswick; and, as to that province, it has been held by the Privy Council [in *Maher v. Town of Portland* (1874), 2 Cart. 486n, approving *Ex parte Renaud* (1873), 14 N.B.R. 273; more fully reported in Wheeler's Confederation Law of Canada, p. 362] that no such right or privilege existed there." See also *Lefroy*, Annotation, 24 D.L.R. 490; *Scott*, The Privy Council and Minority Rights, (1930) 37 Queen's Quarterly 668. For a historical study of separate schools in the various provinces see *Sissons*, Church and State in Canadian Education (1959).

Provincial legislative authority in relation to education is not incompatible with federal activity in the field by way of grants in aid or institutional contributions. *Cf.* Report of the Royal Commission on National Development in the Arts, Letters and Sciences, 1951, pp. 7-8; "There is no general prohibition in Canadian law against any group, governmental or voluntary, contributing to the education of the individual in its broadest sense. Thus, the activities of the Federal Government and of other bodies in broadcasting, films, museums, libraries, research institutions and similar fields are not in conflict with any existing law. . . . If the Federal Government is to renounce its right to associate itself with other social groups, public and private, in the general education of Canadian citizens, it denies its intellectual and moral purposes, the complete conception of the common good is lost and Canada, as such, becomes a materialistic society. . . . We are convinced that our activities have in no way invaded the rights of the provinces but may rather have been helpful in suggesting means of co-operation." For a wider view of federal power in relation to higher education, see *Corry* Higher Education in Dominion-Provincial Relations, (1966) 8 University Affairs. No. 2, at p. 3.

Is religious conviction a tenable ground for refusal to obey provincial compulsory school attendance legislation in the absence of any exemption given on that ground by the legislation? See *Perepolkin v. Superintendent of Child Welfare* (1958), 11 D.L.R. (2d) 417, 23 W.W.R. 592; *cf. Donald v. Hamilton Board of Education*, [1945] O.R. 518, [1945] 3 D.L.R. 424.

Is it open to parents to send their children to a public school and yet claim exemption on religious grounds from certain religious instruction and acts of devotion prescribed as part of the curriculum of the school? See *Chabot v. School Commissioners of Lamorandiere*, [1957] Que. Q.B. 707, 12 D.L.R. (2d) 796; and see *Scott*, *Note*, (1958) 36 Can. Bar Rev. 248; *Note*, (1958) 4 McGill L.J. 268.

JONES v. A.-G. CAN.

In the Supreme Court of Canada. (1974), 7 N.B.R. 2nd 526, 1 N.R. 582 (*sub nom.*) *Reference Re Official Languages Act*, 16 C.C.C. (2d) 297, 45 D.L.R. (3d) 583.

The judgment of the Court was delivered by

LASKIN C.J.C.: This appeal and cross-appeal arise out of a Reference by the Lieutenant-Governor in Council of New Brunswick of five questions to the New Brunswick Supreme Court, Appeal Division, pursuant to O.C. 72-536, dated July 19, 1972, made under s. 24A of the *Judicature Act*, R.S.N.B. 1952, c. 120 as amended. . . .

The questions that were referred for answer were as follows:

1. Are subsections (1), (3) and (4) of section 11 of the Official Languages Act, R.S.C. 1970, c. O-2, within the legislative competence of the Parliament of Canada, in so far as they purport to be applicable to proceedings in criminal matters in courts of criminal jurisdiction in the Province of New Brunswick?

2. Is section 23C of the Evidence Act, R.S.N.B. 1952, c. 74, within the legislative competence of the Legislature of New Brunswick?

3. Is section 14 of the Official Languages of New Brunswick Act, S.N.B. 1969, c. 14, within the legislative competence of the Legislature of New Brunswick?

4. If subsections (3) and (4) of section 11 of the Official Languages Act and section 23C of the Evidence Act are intra vires the Parliament of Canada and the Legislature of New Brunswick, respectively, does section 23C of the Evidence Act have the effect of making subsections (1) and (3) of section 11 of the Official Languages Act operative in New Brunswick?

5. If question 4 is answered in the negative and section 14 of the Official Languages of New Brunswick Act is intra vires the Legislature of New Brunswick, will section 14 of the said Act, when proclaimed, have the effect of making subsections (1) and (3) of section 11 of the Official Languages Act operative in New Brunswick?

It will be convenient to set out at this point the legislative provisions which were the subject of the questions referred for determination. Section 11(1), (3) and (4) of the *Official Languages Act*, R.S.C. 1970, c. O-2, reads as follows:

11(1) Every judicial or quasi-judicial body established by or pursuant to an Act of the Parliament of Canada has, in any proceedings brought or taken before it, and every court in Canada has, in exercising in any proceedings in a criminal matter any criminal jurisdiction conferred upon it by or pursuant to an Act of the Parliament of Canada, the duty to ensure that any person giving evidence before it may be heard in the official language of his choice, and that in being so heard he will not be placed at a disadvantage by not being or being unable to be heard in the other official language.

(3) In exercising in any proceedings in a criminal matter any criminal jurisdiction conferred upon it by or pursuant to an Act of the Parliament of Canada, any court in Canada may in its discretion, at the request of the accused or any of them if there is more than one accused, and if it appears to the court that the proceedings can effectively be conducted and the evidence can effectively be conducted and the evidence can effectively be given and taken wholly or mainly in one of the official languages as specified in the request, order that, subject to subsection (1), the

proceedings be conducted and the evidence be given and taken in that language.

(4) Subsections (1) and (3) do not apply to any court in which, under and by virtue of section 133 of *The British North America Act, 1867,* either of the official languages may be used by any person, and subsection (3) does not apply to the courts of any province until such time as a discretion in those courts or in the judges thereof is provided for by law as to the language in which, for general purposes in that province, proceedings may be conducted in civil causes or matters.

Section 23C of the *Evidence Act,* R.S.N.B. 1952, c. 74, as enacted by 1967, c. 37, s. 1, is in these terms:

23C. In any proceeding in any court in the Province, at the request of any party, and if all the parties to the action or proceedings and their counsel have sufficient knowledge of any language, the Judge may order that the proceedings be conducted and the evidence given and taken in that language.

And s. 14 of the *Official Languages of New Brunswick Act,* 1969 (N.B.), c. 14, is as follows:

14(1) Subject to section 16, in any proceeding before a court, any person appearing or giving evidence may be heard in the official language of his choice and such choice is not to place that person at any disadvantage.

(2) Subject to subsection (1), where
(a) requested by any party, and
(b) the court agrees that the proceedings can effectively be thus conducted;

the court may order that the proceedings be conducted totally or partially in one of the official languages.

Although only part of one section of the *Official Languages Act* was made the subject of the Reference, it is an integral part of that Act in advancing its over-all purpose as stated in s. 2. This section reads:

2. The English and French languages are the official languages of Canada for all purposes of the Parliament and Government of Canada, and possess and enjoy equality of status and equal rights and privileges as to their use in all the institutions of the Parliament and Government of Canada.

This deliberate limitation of the official character of English and French to their use in the institutions of the Parliament and Government of Canada is relevant to any issue of the concurrent authority of the provincial Legislatures in relation to the use of English and French in provincial governmental agencies or, indeed, in respect of activities that fall within exclusive provincial competence. In short, no question arises as to the power of the Parliament of Canada to give official status and equality to English and French throughout Canada and in respect of any operations or activities which are otherwise within exclusive provincial competence; Parliament has not attempted to go that far. Of course, the limitation expressed in s. 2 aforesaid does not relieve this Court from the duty of examining particular provisions of the *Official Languages Act* which are challenged as unconstitutional, either because they do not conform to the limitation generally expressed in s. 2 or because they are in any event beyond federal legislative power.

The appellant has mounted a challenge in this last-mentioned aspect on two main grounds. It was contended by his counsel that s. 133 of the *British North America Act, 1867* foreclosed the Parliament of Canada from enacting not only s. 11(1), (3) and (4) of the *Official Languages Act* but also the Act as a whole. The second main contention was that s. 91(1) of the *British North America Act, 1867,* enacted by 1949 (U.K.), c. 81, not only preserved the foreclosing effect of s. 133 but, independently, precluded Parliament from enacting the *Official Languages Act. . . .*

Apart from the effect of s. 133 and s. 91(1), to be considered later in these reasons, I am in no doubt that it was open to the Parliament of Canada to enact the *Official Languages Act* (limited as it is to the purposes of the Parliament and Government of Canada and to the institutions of that Parliament and Government) as being a law "for the peace, order and good Government of Canada in relation to [a matter] not coming within the Classes of Subjects . . . assigned exclusively to the Legislatures of the Provinces". The quoted words are in the opening paragraph of s. 91 of the *British North America Act, 1867;* and, in relying on them as constitutional support for the *Official Languages Act,* I do so on the basis of the purely residuary character of the legislative power thereby conferred. No authority need be cited for the exclusive power of the Parliament of Canada to legislate in relation to the operation and administration of the institutions and agencies of the Parliament and Government of Canada. Those institutions and agencies are clearly beyond provincial reach.

In so far as s. 11(1), (3) and (4) of the *Official Languages Act* concerns the use of English and French as official languages in proceedings before judicial or quasi-judicial bodies competently established under federal authority, and in criminal proceedings before any Court in Canada whose exercise of criminal jurisdiction is competently authorized by the Parliament of Canada (these bodies and Courts not being dependent institutions or agencies of Parliament or the Government of Canada), it is similarly necessary to determine whether the language provisions so made invade provincial jurisdiction. As to that, I am likewise in no doubt that it was within Parliament's authority under the opening words of s. 91, already quoted, under s. 101 of the *British North America Act, 1867,* and particularly under s. 91(27) so far as s. 11(3) of the *Official Languages Act* is concerned, to enact the challenged s. 11(1), (3) and (4). . . .

One matter that was canvassed before the New Brunswick Supreme Court, Appeal Division, but not before this Court was the allegation of unconstitutional delegation, said to reside in s. 11(4) of the *Official Languages Act.* I need say no more than was said on this point by Chief Justice Hughes who invoked the principle expressed in *Lord's Day Alliance of Canada v. A.-G. B.C.* (1959), 123 C.C.C. 81, 19 D.L.R.

(2d) 97, [1959] S.C.R. 497, and on this basis rightly rejected the allegation.

In making a specific attack upon the validity of s. 11(3) of the *Official Languages Act,* counsel for the appellant submitted that it was colourable legislation whose purpose was to evade the constitutional limitation upon language legislation said by him to reside in s. 133 of the *British North America Act, 1867.* This is part of the over-arching contention urged by the appellant against the *Official Languages Act* as a whole, but subject to the merit of that contention which I shall examine later in these reasons, I am of the opinion that the respondent and the intervenors were correct in supporting the conclusion of the New Brunswick Supreme Court, Appeal Division, that s. 91(27) of the *British North America Act, 1867* provided adequate support for the enactment of s. 11(3). I point out, in addition, that it is within federal legislative competence to impose duties upon provincially-appointed judicial officers in respect of matters falling within federal legislative authority, as for example, the criminal law and its administration: see *Re Vancini* (1904), 34 S.C.R. 621. A *fortiori,* it is within federal competence to repose a discretion in such officers in relation to the administration of the federal criminal law, albeit in Courts established under provincial legislation.

It was the submission of counsel for the Attorney-General of Canada, which I accept, that the language in which criminal proceedings are conducted, whether documents are involved or oral conduct only or both, may be brought within the legislative authority conferred by s. 91(27) of the *British North America Act, 1867*; and so far as s. 91(27) is alone the source of authority for the specification of language in which the criminal law is to be written or in which criminal proceedings thereunder are to be conducted, Parliament's authority is paramount.

I come now to the submissions on ss. 133 and 91(1) of the *British North America Act, 1867.* The submission as to s. 133 by counsel for the appellant is that that provision is exhaustive of constitutional authority in relation to the use of English and French, and that a constitutional amendment is necessary to support any legislation which, like the *Official Languages Act*, would be beyond it. I do not accept that submission which, in my opinion, is unsupportable under the language of s. 133, unsupportable as a matter of such history thereof as is available, and unsupportable under the scheme of distribution of legislative power as established by the *British North America Act, 1867* and as construed by the Courts over a long period of time.

I do not think that any assistance on the scope or effect of s. 133 can be obtained from such governmental documents as "A Canadian Charter of Human Rights" published in 1968, or "Federalism for the Future", also published in 1968, or the Final Report of the Royal Commission on Bilingualism and Biculturalism, vol. 1, "The Official Languages", published in 1967. What those documents recommend, in relation to what I may term linguistic rights and going beyond the specifications of s. 133, is constitutional entrenchment, but that is hardly a support for the contention that there can be no advance upon s. 133 without constitutional amendment. Certainly, what s. 133 itself gives may not be diminished by the Parliament of Canada, but if its provisions are respected there is nothing in it or in any other parts of the *British North America Act, 1867* (reserving for later consideration s. 91(1) that precludes the conferring of additional rights or privileges or the imposing of additional obligations respecting the use of English and French, if done in relation to matters within the competence of the enacting Legislature.

The words of s. 133 themselves point to its limited concern with language rights; and it is, in my view, correctly described as giving a constitutionally based right to any person to use English or French in legislative debates in the federal and Quebec Houses and in any pleading or process in or issuing from any federally established Court or any Court of Quebec, and as imposing an obligation of the use of English and French in the records and journals of the federal and Quebec legislative Houses and in the printing and publication of federal and Quebec legislation. There is no warrant for reading this provision, so limited to the federal and Quebec legislative chambers and their legislation, and to federal and Quebec Courts, as being in effect a final and legislatively unalterable determination for Canada, for Quebec and for all other Provinces, of the limits of the privileged or obligatory use of English and French in public proceedings, in public institutions and in public communications. On its face, s. 133 provides special protection in the use of English and French; there is no other provision of the *British North America Act, 1867* referable to the Parliament of Canada (apart from s. 91(1)) which deals with language as a legislative matter or otherwise. I am unable to appreciate the submission that to extend by legislation the privileged or required public use of English and French would be violative of s. 133 when there has been no interference with the special protection which it prescribes. I refer in this respect particularly to s. 11(4) of the *Official Languages Act,* already quoted.

History does not support the appellant's contention. I need go back no farther than s. 41 of the Act of Union 1840 (U.K.), c. 35, which reads as follows:

It is Enacted,

41. That from and after the said re-union of the said two provinces, all writs, proclamations, instruments for summoning and calling together the Legislative Council and Legislative Assembly of the province of Canada, and for proroguing and dissolving the same, and all writs of summons and election, and all writs and public instruments whatsoever relating to the said Legislative Council and Assembly, or either of them, and all returns to such writs and instruments, and all journals, entries, and written or printed proceedings, of what nature soever, of the said Legislative Council and Legislative Assembly, and of each of them respectively, and all written or printed proceedings and reports of committees of the said Legislative Council and Legislative Assembly respectively, shall be in the English language only: Provided always, that

this enactment shall not be construed to prevent translated copies of any such documents being made, but no such copy shall be kept among the records of the Legislative Council or Legislative Assembly, or be deemed in any case to have the force of an original record.

This provision for the use of English only was repealed by 1848 (U.K.), c. 56, s. 1, and judicial notice may be taken of the fact that following that repeal statutes of the Province of Canada were enacted in both English and French.

Among the Quebec Resolutions that were approved at the Conference in 1864, which was a prelude to Confederation in 1867, was Resolution 46, which became Resolution 45 at the London (Westminster Palace Hotel) Conference in 1866. It was as follows:

Both the English and French languages may be employed in the general Parliament and in its proceedings and in the local Legislature of Lower Canada, and also in the Federal courts and in the courts of Lower Canada.

As it emerged in s. 133, this Resolution had an obligatory aspect added to its provision for the use of English or French. In establishing equality of use of the two languages, s. 133 did so in relation to certain proceedings of a public character in specified legislative operations and in specified Courts, but it went no farther.

I am unable to agree that an implicit constitutional limitation must be read into the *British North America Act, 1867* as a deduction from the enactment of s. 133. This is the burden of the appellant's submission and, in my opinion, it runs counter to the principles of exhaustiveness which the Courts have ascribed to the distribution of legislative power under the *British North America Act, 1867*.

That principle was stated by the late Mr. Justice Rand in *Murphy v. C.P.R.* (1958), 15 D.L.R. (2d) 145 at p. 153, [1958] S.C.R. 626, 77 C.R.T.C. 322, as follows: "It has become a truism that the totality of effective legislative power is conferred by the Act of 1867, subject always to the express or necessarily implied limitations of the Act itself." Section 91(1) aside, there are no express limitations on federal legislative authority to add to the range of privileged or obligatory use of English and French in institutions or activities that are subject to federal legislative control. Necessary implication of a limitation is likewise absent because there would be nothing inconsistent or incompatible with s. 133, as it relates to the Parliament of Canada and to federal Courts, if the position of the two languages was enhanced beyond their privileged and obligatory use under s. 133. It is one thing for Parliament to lessen the protection given by s. 133; that would require a constitutional amendment. It is a different thing to extend that protection beyond its present limits.

Heavy reliance was placed by the appellant upon the canon of interpretation expressed in the maxim *expressio unius est exclusio alterius*. This maxim provides at the most merely a guide to interpretation; it does not pre-ordain conclusions. I find it inapt as a measure of what s. 133 embraces; indeed, it serves no purpose to that end. There is no attempt in the present case to bring something within s. 133 which is not expressly there; there is no attempt here to add to the constitutional reach of s. 133. It stands unimpeached, and it is rather outside of it, and under the grants of legislative power which leave it untouched, that Parliament has acted. Lord Dunedin's statement in *Whiteman v. Sadler*, [1910] A.C. 514 at p. 527 (which the appellant invoked) that "It seems to me that express enactment shuts the door to further implication. 'Expressio unius est exclusio alterius' " is a conclusion upon his construction of a particular section of a statute. It does not assist in the present case.

It remains to consider the effect of s. 91(1) of the *British North America Act, 1867* which confers legislative power upon Parliament in relation to the "amendment from time to time of the Constitution of Canada" except, *inter alia*, "as regards the use of the English or French language". The contention of the appellant is that this exception was designed not only to maintain the integrity of s. 133 but went beyond it to enlarge the limitations thereof by embracing any use of the English or French language beyond what s. 133 itself prescribed. This contention would turn the exception from a grant of a new power under s. 91(1) into a general substantive limitation unrelated to that power, and it is untenable. I am not called upon here to state exhaustively what is comprehended within the phrase in s. 91(1) "the Constitution of Canada". It certainly includes the *British North America Act, 1867* and its amendments, and hence includes s. 133. What is excepted from Parliament's amending power under s. 91(1) includes an exception as regards the use of the English or French language. Parliament is forbidden to amend the Constitution of Canada as regards the use of either of the languages, and s. 91(1) therefore points to the provisions of the Constitution dealing therewith, and thus to s. 133: see Scott, "The British North America (No. 2) Act, 1949" (1950), 8 Univ. of Tor. L.J. 201 at p. 205.

I turn finally to the answers that I would give to the questions referred to the New Brunswick Supreme Court, Appeal Division. For the reasons I have already given, I would answer Question 1 in the affirmative. Question 2, respecting the validity of s. 23C of the provincial *Evidence Act* should also be answered in the affirmative. In my view, in the absence of federal legislation competently dealing with the language of proceedings or matters before provincial Courts which fall within exclusive federal legislative authority, it was open to the Legislature of New Brunswick to legislate respecting the languages in which proceedings in Courts established by that Legislature might be conducted. This includes the languages in which evidence in those Courts may be given. Section 92(14) of the British North America Act, 1867 is ample authority for such legislation. For the same reason I would answer Question 3, respecting the validity of s. 14 of the *Official Languages of New Brunswick Act,* in the affirmative.

In *R. v. Murphy, Ex. p. Belisle and Moreau,* [1968] 4 C.C.C. 229, 69 D.L.R. (2d) 530, 5 C.R.N.S. 68, the New Brunswick Supreme Court, Appeal Division, held that s. 23C could not have any application to criminal proceedings in a provincial Court, in the absence of federal legislation making it applicable. The holding was that it would not apply of its own force despite its general wording ("In any proceeding in any Court in the Province"), and was not made applicable by s. 36 of the *Canada Evidence Act*, R.S.C. 1952, c. 307, because it was not a law of evidence within that provision. What the New Brunswick Supreme Court, Appeal, Division, did in effect was to limit the scope of s. 23C to civil and penal matters within provincial legislative jurisdiction, in accordance with the principle expressed by this Court in *McKay v. The Queen* (1965), 53 D.L.R. (2d) 532, [1965] S.C.R. 798. I do not think that there is the same antinomy in the present case as existed in the *McKay* case; rather, the situation here is one for the application of a doctrine of concurrency of legislative authority subject to the paramountcy of federal legislation.

In summary, the answers I would give to the questions which were the subject of the reference by the Lieutenant-Governor in Council of New Brunswick are as follows:

> Question 1: Yes.
> Question 2: Yes.
> Question 3: Yes.
> Question 4: Yes.
> Question 5: No answer required.

It follows from my answers that I would dismiss the appeal and allow the cross-appeal. This is not a case for any order as to costs.

Appeal dismissed; cross-appeal allowed.

[See *Honsberger*, Bi-Lingualism in Canadian Statutes (1965), 43 Can. Bar Rev. 315. In *Regina v. Watts ex parte Poulin* (1968), 69 D.L.R. (2d) 526, 64 W.W.R. 705 aff'd (1968), 1 D.L.R. (3d) 239, it was held that an accused on trial before a provincially appointed magistrate in British Columbia on a criminal charge has no right to require that the proceedings be conducted in French, the only language of the accused. The applicable law of British Columbia provided for English only.]

CHAPTER XIV

NATURALIZATION AND ALIENS: IMMIGRATION, EXCLUSION, AND DEPORTATION.

Introductory Note

Although by s. 91(25) of the *B.N.A. Act* the Dominion has exclusive legislative authority in relation to "naturalization and aliens" and by s. 95 it has concurrent but overriding authority in relation to immigration, there is no specific reference in the Act to citizenship or nationality. The reason is, of course, obvious. However, the right of the Dominion, under its general power to define the national status of persons in Canada, to regulate admission into and exclusion and deportation from Canada is undeniable. *Cf.* Rand J. in *Winner v. S.M.T. (Eastern) Ltd. and A.-G. Can.*, [1951] S.C.R. 887, at p. 919, [1951] 4 D.L.R. 529, at p. 558. Prior to the *Statute of Westminster*, 1931 (Imp.), s. 4, Dominion authority in relation to nationality was limited by Imperial legislation applicable to Canada; for example, see the *Naturalization Act*, 1847 (Imp.), c. 83; *Naturalization Act*, 1870 (Imp.), c. 14; *British Nationality and Status of Aliens Act*, 1914 (Imp.), c. 17; and see the discussion in *Clement*, The Canadian Constitution, chaps. 9 and 31. Since the *Statute of Westminster* it has become possible (in view of the power given to the Dominion to repeal British legislation applicable to Canada) to deal with and give full meaning to Canadian citizenship as opposed to British nationality; see the *Canadian Citizenship Act*, first enacted in 1946, and now R.S.C. 1970, c. C-19; and see *Tamaki*, The Canadian Citizenship Act, 1946, (1947) 7 Univ. of Tor. L.J. 68.

Federal power in relation to national status, and to aliens and immigration, clearly enables the Dominion to make freedom of movement throughout Canada an attribute not only of citizenship but of lawful presence in Canada: see *Note*, (1941) 19 Can. Bar Rev. 750, discussing the United States case of *Edwards v. People of State of California* (1941), 314 U.S. 160. Nor is there any doubt about federal power to exclude or deport either aliens or naturalized persons (usually upon revocation of their naturalization under stipulated circumstances), or even natural-born persons, although this raises questions of international law relative to the reception of such persons abroad: see *A.-G. Can. v. Cain; A.-G. Can. v. Gilhula*, [1906] A.C. 542; *Co-operative Committee on Japanese Canadians v. A.-G. Can.*, [1947] A.C. 87, [1947] 1 D.L.R. 577. Any doubt about extra-territorial power has, of course, been removed by s. 3 of the Statute of Westminster; see also *Croft v. Dunphy*, [1933] A.C. 156, [1933] 1 D.L.R. 225, [1932] 3 W.W.R. 696. Whatever the scope of provincial power to condition entry into a province under s. 95 of the *B.N.A. Act*, it is still subordinate to federal power conferred by the same section. The question may be asked, however, whether conditions of entry related not to immigration as such but to some regulatory policy otherwise competent to a province are not similarly subject to overriding Dominion legislation. For a particular illustration of provincial legislation of this character (now repealed) aimed at national and international trade unionism; see *Forsey*, The Prince Edward Island Trade Union Act, 1948, (1948) 26 Can. Bar Rev. 1159; and *cf. Mercier*, Immigration and Provincial Rights, (1944) 22 Can. Bar Rev. 856.

Difficult questions remain which admit of no categorical answer. Is any special significance to be attached to the fact that Dominion power under s. 91(25) is in relation to "naturalization", not naturalized persons; and "aliens", not alienage? Or should the courts read the terms as if they were "naturalization and naturalized persons and aliens and alienage"? What is the extent of Dominion power to legislate as to the consequences of citizenship or nationality or alienage, in the light of provincial legislative authority, especially in relation to property and civil rights in the province? How far can a provincial legislature regulate or limit the activities of or deny privileges to naturalized persons or aliens? Does the *B.N.A. Act* protect such classes of persons from discriminatory treatment only? Or, are they protected against provincial legislation even where a natural-born person would not be protected?

[See, *Head*, The Stranger in Our Midst: A Sketch of the Legal Status of the Alien in Canada, in 2 Canadian Yearbook of International Law (1964), p. 107.]

UNION COLLIERY CO. OF BRITISH COLUMBIA LTD. v. BRYDEN

In the Privy Council. [1899] A.C. 580.

Appeal from a judgment of the British Columbia Supreme Court *en banc*, affirming a judgment of Drake J. upholding the validity of s. 4 of the *Coal Mines Regulation Act*, 1890, now s. 4 of R.S.B.C. 1897, c. 138.

LORD WATSON: The appellant company carries on the business of mining coal by means of underground mines, in lands belonging to the company, situated near to the town of Union in British Columbia. The company have hitherto employed, and still continue to employ, Chinamen in the working of these underground mines.

By s. 4 of the *Coal Mines Regulation Act*, 1890, it is expressly enacted that, "no boy under the age of twelve years, and no woman or girl of any age, *and no Chinaman*, shall be employed in or allowed to be for the purpose of employment in any mine to which the Act applies, below ground."

By the Act of 1890, the words "and no Chinaman" were added to the 4th section of the then existing *Coal Mines Regulation Act*, which was chapter 84 of the Consolidated Statutes of 1888, and now, as amended, is chapter 138 of the Revised Statutes of British Columbia, 1897. It is sufficiently plain, and it is not matter of dispute, that the provisions of the Act of 1890 were made to apply, and so far as competently enacted do apply, to the underground workings carried on by the appellant company.

The present action was instituted, in the Supreme Court of British Columbia, by the respondent, John Bryden, against the appellant company of which he is a shareholder. It concludes (1) for a declaration that the company had and has no right to employ Chinamen in certain positions of trust and responsibility, or as labourers in their mines below ground, and that such employment was and is unlawful, and (2) for an injunction restraining the company from employing Chinamen in any such position of trust and responsibility, or as labourers below ground, and from using the funds of the company in paying the wages of the said Chinamen. The respondent averred in his statement of claim that the employment of Chinamen in positions of trust and responsibility, and as labourers underground, was a source of danger and injury to other persons working in the mines, which involved the liability of the company for damages, and was also injurious and destructive to the mines. He also pleaded that the employment of Chinamen in these capacities was contrary to the statute law of the province.

The appellant company, by their statement of defence, denied that there was any risk of injury arising either to other workmen in their mines, or the mines, from the employment of Chinamen as underground miners. They pleaded that, in so far as they related to adult Chinamen, the enactments of s. 4 of the *Coal Mines Regulation Act* were void as being *ultra vires* of the legislature of the Province of British Columbia. . . .

. . . It appeared from the evidence that the appellant company, in working some of their underground seams of coal, employed no workmen except Chinamen who were of full age, and that, in those parts of their workings where miners other than Chinamen were employed, no Chinamen occupied a position of trust or responsibility, such as were alleged in the statement of claim. The consequence was that, in the subsequent conduct of the litigation, the Courts below, and their Lordships in this appeal, have only been invited to consider the conclusions of the action in so far as these bear upon the legality of employing Chinese labour in violation of the express enactments of s. 4 of the Revised Statute No. 138 of 1897. In other words, the controversy has been limited to the single question—whether the enactments of s. 4, in regard to which the appellant company has stated the plea of *ultra vires*, were within the competency of the British Columbian Legislature. . . .

There can be no doubt that, if s. 92 of the Act of 1867 had stood alone and had not been qualified by the provisions of the clause which precedes it, the provincial legislature of British Columbia would have had ample jurisdiction to enact s. 4 of the Coal Mines Regulation Act. The subject-matter of that enactment would clearly have been included in s. 92, sub-s. 10, which extends to provincial undertakings such as the coal mines of the appellant company. It would also have been included in s. 92, sub-s. 13, which embraces "Property and Civil Rights in the Province."

But s. 91, sub-s. 25, extends the exclusive legislative authority of the Parliament of Canada to "naturalization and aliens." Sect. 91 concludes with a proviso to the effect that "any matter coming within any of the classes of subjects enumerated in this section shall not be deemed to come within the class of matters of a local or private nature comprised in the enumeration of the classes of subjects by this Act assigned exclusively to the legislatures of the provinces."

Sect. 4 of the Provincial Act prohibits Chinamen who are of full age from employment in underground coal workings. Every alien when naturalized in Canada becomes, *ipso facto,* a Canadian subject of the Queen; and his children are not aliens, requiring to be naturalized, but are natural-born Canadians. It can hardly have been intended to give the Dominion Parliament the exclusive right to legislate for the latter class of persons resident in Canada; but s. 91, sub-s. 25, might possibly be construed as conferring that power in the case of naturalized aliens after naturalization. The subject of "naturalization" seems *prima facie* to include the power of enacting what shall be the consequences of naturalization, or, in other words, what shall be the rights and privileges pertaining to residents in Canada after they have been naturalized. It does not appear to their Lordships to be necessary, in the present case, to consider the precise meaning which the term "naturalization" was intended to bear, as it occurs in s. 91, sub-s. 25. But it seems clear that the expression "aliens" occurring in that clause refers to, and at least includes, all aliens who have not yet been naturalized; and the words "no Chinaman," as they are used in s. 4 of the Provincial Act, were probably meant to denote, and they certainly include, every adult Chinaman who has not been naturalized. . . .

The provisions of which the validity has been thus affirmed by the Courts below are capable of being viewed in two different aspects, according to one of which they appear to fall within the subjects assigned to the provincial parliament by s. 92 of the British North America Act, 1867, whilst, according to the other, they clearly belong to the class of subjects exclusively assigned to the legislature of the Dominion by s. 91, sub-s. 25. They may be regarded as merely establishing a regulation applicable to the working of underground coal mines; and, if that were an exhaustive description of the substance of the enactments, it would be difficult to dispute that they were within the competency of the provincial legislature, by virtue either of s. 92, sub-s. 10, or s. 92, sub-s. 13. But the leading feature of the enactments consists in this—that they have, and can have, no application except to Chinamen who are aliens or naturalized subjects, and that they establish no rule or regulation except that these aliens or naturalized subjects shall not work, or be allowed to work, in underground coal mines within the Province of British Columbia.

Their Lordships see no reason to doubt that, by virtue of s. 91, sub-s. 25, the legislature of the Dominion is invested with exclusive authority in all matters which directly concern the rights, privileges, and disabilities of the class of Chinamen who are resident in the provinces of Canada. They are also of opinion that the whole pith and substance of the enactments of s. 4 of the Coal Mines Regulation Act, in so far as objected to by the appellant company, consists in establishing a statutory prohibition which affects aliens or naturalized subjects, and therefore trench upon the exclusive authority of the Parliament of Canada. The learned judges who delivered opinions in the Full Court noticed the fact that the Dominion legislature had passed a "Naturalization Act, No. 113 of the Revised Statutes of Canada, 1886," by which a partial control was exercised over the rights of aliens. Walkem J. appears to regard that fact as favourable to the right of the provincial parliament to legislate for the exclusion of aliens being Chinamen from underground coal mines. The abstinence of the Dominion Parliament from legislating to the full limit of its powers, could not have the effect of transferring to any provincial legislature the legislative power which had been assigned to the Dominion by s. 91 of the Act of 1867.

Their Lordships will therefore humbly advise Her Majesty to reverse the judgment appealed from; to find and declare that the provisions of s. 4 of the British Columbia *Coal Mines Regulation Act,* 1890, which are now embodied in chapter 138 of the Revised Statutes of British Columbia, 1897, were, in so far as they relate to Chinamen, *ultra vires* of the provincial legislature, and therefore illegal. . . .

Appeal allowed.

CUNNINGHAM AND A.-G. B.C. v. TOMEY HOMMA AND A.-G. CAN.

In the Privy Council. [1903] A.C. 151.

Appeal from a judgment of the British Columbia Supreme Court *en banc,* affirming a judgment of the County Court which reversed a decision of a collector of votes and ordered that the name of Tomey Homma be placed on the register of voters for the Vancouver electoral district to enable him to vote in a provincial election. Tomey Homma was a native of the Japanese empire not born of British parents but a naturalized British subject. Sect. 8 of the *Provincial Elections Act,* R.S.B.C. 1897, c. 67 provided that "no Chinaman, Japanese, or Indian shall have his name placed on the register of voters for any electoral district, or be entitled to vote at any election." By s. 3 the term "Japanese" was defined to include "any native of the Japanese empire or its dependencies not born of British parents, and shall include any person of the Japanese race naturalized or not."

EARL OF HALSBURY L.C.: In this case a naturalized Japanese claims to be placed upon the register of voters for the electoral district of Vancouver City, and the objection which is made to his claim is that by the electoral law of the province it is enacted that no Japanese, whether naturalized or not, shall have his name placed on the register of voters or shall be entitled to vote. Application was made to the proper officer to enter the applicant's name on the register, but he refused to do so upon the ground that the enactment in question prohibited its being done. This refusal was overruled by the Chief Justice sitting in the county court, and the appeal from his decision to the Supreme Court of British Columbia was disallowed. The present appeal is from the decision of the Supreme Court.

There is no doubt that, if it is within the capacity of the province to enact the electoral law, the claimant is [dis]qualified by the express language of the statute; but it is contended that the 91st and 92nd sections of the British North America Act have deprived the province of the power of making any such provision as to disqualify a naturalized Japanese from electoral privileges. It is maintained that s. 91, sub-s. 25, enacts that the whole subject of naturalization is reserved to the exclusive jurisdiction of the Dominion, while the Naturalization Act of Canada enacts that a naturalized alien shall within Canada be entitled to all political and other rights, powers, and privileges to which a natural-born British subject is entitled in Canada. To this it is replied that, by s. 92, sub-s. 1, the constitution of the province and any amendment of it are placed under the exclusive control of the provincial legislature. The question which their Lordships have to determine is which of these two views is the right one, and, in determining that question, the policy or impolicy of such an enactment as that which excludes a particular race from the franchise is not a topic which their Lordships are entitled to consider.

The first observation which arises is that the enactment, supposed to be *ultra vires* and to be impeached upon the ground of its dealing with alienage and naturalization, has not necessarily anything to do with either. A child of Japanese parentage born in Vancouver City is a natural-born subject of the King, and would be equally excluded from the possession of the franchise. The extent to which naturalization will confer privileges has varied both in this country and elsewhere. From the time of William III down to Queen Victoria no naturalization was permitted which did not exclude the alien naturalized from sitting in Parliament or in the Privy Council.

In Lawrence's Wheaton, p. 903 (2nd annotated ed. 1863), it is said that "though (in the United States) the power of naturalization be nominally exclusive in the Federal Government, its operation in the most important particulars, especially as to the right of suffrage, is made to depend on the local constitution and laws." The term "political rights" used in the Canadian Naturalization Act is, as Walkem J. very justly says, a very wide phrase, and their Lordships concur in his observation that, whatever it means, it cannot be held to give necessarily a right to the suffrage in all or any of the provinces. In the history of this country the right to the franchise has been granted and withheld on a great number of grounds, conspicuously upon grounds of religious faith, yet no one has ever suggested that a person excluded from the franchise was not under allegiance to the Sovereign.

Could it be suggested that the province of British Columbia could not exclude an alien from the franchise in that province? Yet, if the mere mention of alienage in the enactment could make the law *ultra vires,* such a construction of s. 91, sub-s. 25, would involve that absurdity. The truth is that the language of that section does not purport to deal with the consequences of either alienage or naturalization. It undoubtedly reserves these subjects for the exclusive jurisdiction of the Dominion—that is to say, it is for the Dominion to determine what shall constitute either the one or the other, but the question as to what consequences shall follow from either is not touched. The right of protection and the obligations of allegiance are necessarily involved in the nationality conferred by naturalization; but the privileges attached to it, where these depend upon residence, are quite independent of nationality.

This, indeed, seems to have been the opinion of the learned judges below; but they were under the impression that they were precluded from acting on their own judgment by the decision of this Board in the case of *Union Colliery Co. v. Bryden,* [1899] A.C. 580. That case depended upon totally different grounds. This Board, dealing with the particular facts of that case, came to the conclusion that the regulations there impeached were not really aimed at the regulation of coal mines at all, but were in truth devised to deprive the Chinese, naturalized or not, of the ordinary rights of the inhabitants of British Columbia, and, in effect, to prohibit their continued residence in that province, since it prohibited their earning their living in that province. It is obvious that such a decision can have no relation to the question whether any naturalized person has an inherent right to the suffrage within the province in which he resides.

For these reasons their Lordships will humbly advise His Majesty that the order of the Chief Justice in the county court and the order of the Supreme Court ought to be reversed. . . .

Appeal allowed.

[Are *Union Colliery Co. v. Bryden* and *Cunningham v. Tomey Homma* reconcilable? See *Lefroy,* Canada's Federal System, p. 308. Cf. *In re the Coal Mines Regulation Act* (1904), 10 B.C.R. 408, following the *Bryden* case and distinguishing the *Tomey Homma* case. Is there a tenable distinction between provincial legislation which confers a privilege, e.g. the right to vote, and provincial legislation which denies to persons advantages which are ordinarily available, e.g. work in coal mines? Is it open to a province to make distinctions or discriminate on account of race or ethnic origin and thus circumvent any limitation arising from s. 91(25)?

May a provincial legislature exclude aliens, who are otherwise qualified, from practising a profession in the province simply because of alienage? It is clearly open to a provincial legislature to provide for self-regulation of a profession, but may the regulatory body, when granted a general authority, exclude persons because they are, for example, communists? See *Martin v. Law Society of British Columbia,* [1950] 3 D.L.R. 173, aff'g [1949] 1 D.L.R. 105. May it similarly exclude aliens? Would it make any difference if the Dominion purported to give aliens equal rights and privileges with all natural-born or naturalized persons? Could the Dominion validly so legislate to supersede or foreclose provincial legislation?

May a province validly enact that no one may change his name save under a prescribed procedure and then exclude aliens from any right to resort to that procedure? See *Change of Name Act,* R.S.O. 1970, c. 60; *Note,* (1940) 18 Can. Bar Rev. 69.

How far, if at all, may a province deny to aliens access to provincial courts? Cf. Harrison J. in *S.M.T. (Eastern) Ltd. v. Winner*, [1950] 3 D.L.R. 207, 26 M.P.R. 27 (N.B.) (foreign national has no status to attack constitutionality of provincial legislation), rev'd [1951] S.C.R. 887, [1951] 4 D.L.R. 529, which was varied (on other grounds), [1954] A.C. 541, [1954] 4 D.L.R. 657, 13 W.W.R. (N.S.) 657.

The relation of this problem to Dominion and foreign companies is discussed in chapter VIII, *supra.*]

QUONG-WING v. THE KING

In the Supreme Court of Canada. (1914), 49 S.C.R. 440,
18 D.L.R. 121, 6 W.W.R. 270.

Appeal from a judgment of the Saskatchewan Supreme Court 12 D.L.R. 656, 4 W.W.R. 1135, affirming on appeal by way of stated case, a conviction of appellant on a charge of employing white females in violation of 1912 (Sask.), c. 17.

FITZPATRICK C.J.: The appellant, a Chinaman and a naturalized Canadian citizen, was convicted of employing white female servants contrary to the provisions of chapter 17 of the statutes of Saskatchewan, 1912, and, for his defence, he contends that the Act in question is *ultra vires* of the provincial legislature.

It is urged that the aim of the Act is to deprive the defendant and the Chinese generally, whether naturalized or not, of the rights ordinarily enjoyed by the other inhabitants of the Province of Saskatchewan and that the subject-matter of the Act is within the exclusive legislative authority of the Parliament of Canada.

The Act in question reads as follows:—

1. No person shall employ in any capacity any white woman or girl or permit any white woman or girl to reside or lodge in or to work in or, save as a *bona fide* customer in a public apartment thereof only, to frequent any restaurant, laundry or other place of business or amusement owned, kept or managed by any Chinaman.

2. Any employer guilty of any contravention or violation of this Act, shall, upon summary conviction be liable to a penalty not exceeding $100 and, in default of payment, to imprisonment for a term not exceeding two months.

In terms the section purports merely to regulate places of business and resorts owned and managed by Chinese, independent of nationality, in the interest of the morals of women and girls in Saskatchewan. There are many factory Acts passed by provincial legislatures to fix the age of employment and to provide for proper accommodation for workmen and the convenience of the sexes which are intended not only to safeguard the bodily health, but also the morals of Canadian workers, and I fail to understand the difference in principle between that legislation and this.

It is also undoubted that the legislatures authorize the making by municipalities of disciplinary and police regulations to prevent disorders on Sundays and at night, and in that connection to compel tavern and saloon keepers to close their drinking places at certain hours. Why should those legislatures not have powers to enact that women and girls should not be employed in certain industries or in certain places or by a certain class of people? This legislation may affect the civil rights of Chinamen, but it is primarily directed to the protection of children and girls.

The Chinaman is not deprived of the right to employ others, but the classes from which he may select his employees are limited. In certain factories women or children under a certain age are not permitted to work at all, and, in others, they may not be employed except subject to certain restrictions in the interest of the employee's bodily and moral welfare. The difference between the restrictions imposed on all Canadians by such legislation and those resulting from the Act in question is one of degree, not of kind.

I would dismiss the appeal with costs.

DAVIES J.: The question on this appeal is not one as to the policy or justice of the Act in question, but solely as to the power of the provincial legislature to pass it. There is no doubt that, as enacted, it seriously affects the civil rights of the Chinamen in Saskatchewan, whether they are aliens or naturalized British subjects. If the language of Lord Watson, in delivering the judgment of the Judicial Committee of the Privy Council in *Union Colliery Company of British Columbia v. Bryden,* [1899] A.C. 580, was to be accepted as the correct interpretation of the law defining the powers of the Dominion Parliament to legislate on the subject-matter of "naturalization and aliens" assigned to it by item 25 of section 91 of the "British North America Act, 1867," I would feel some difficulty in upholding the legislation now under review. . . .

But in the later case of *Cunningham v. Tomey Homma,* [1903] A.C. 151, the Judicial Committee modified the views of the construction of sub-section 25 of section 91 stated in the *Union Colliery* decision. . . .

Reading the *Union Colliery* case, therefore, as explained in this later case, and accepting their Lordships' interpretation of sub-section 25 of section 91, that "its language does not purport to deal with the consequences of either alienage or naturalization", and that, while it exclusively reserves these subjects to the jurisdiction of the Dominion in so far as to determine what shall constitute either alienage or naturalization, it does not touch the question of what consequences shall follow from either, I am relieved from the difficulty I would otherwise feel.

The legislation under review does not, in this view, trespass upon the exclusive power of the Dominion legislature. It does deal with the subject-matter of "property and civil rights" within the province, exclusively assigned to the provincial legislatures, and so dealing cannot be held *ultra vires,* however harshly it may bear upon Chinamen, *naturalized or not,* residing in the province. There is no inherent right in any class of the community to employ women and children which the legislature may not modify or take away altogether. There is nothing in the "British North America Act" which says that such legislation may not be class legislation. Once it is decided that the subject-matter of the employment of white women is within the exclusive powers of the provincial legislature and does not infringe upon any of the enumerated subject-matters assigned to the Dominion, then such provincial powers are plenary. . . .

I think the pith and substance of the legislation now before us is entirely different [from that in the *Bryden* case]. Its object and purpose is the protection of white women and girls; and the prohibition of their employment or residence, or lodging, or working, etc., in any place of business or amusement owned, kept or managed by any Chinaman is for the purpose of ensuring that protection. Such legislation does not, in my judgment, come within the class of legislation or regulation which the Judicial Committee held *ultra vires* of the provincial legislatures in the case of *The Union Collieries v. Bryden*.

The right to employ white women in any capacity or in any class of business is a civil right, and legislation upon that subject is clearly within the power of the provincial legislatures. The right to guarantee and ensure their protection from a moral standpoint is, in my opinion, within such provincial powers and, if the legislation is *bona fide* for that purpose, it will be upheld even though it may operate prejudicially to one class or race of people.

There is no doubt in my mind that the prohibition is a racial one and that it does not cease to operate because a Chinaman becomes naturalized. It extends and was intended to extend to all Chinamen as such, naturalized or aliens. Questions which might arise in cases of mixed blood do not arise here. . . .

The prohibition against the employment of white women was not aimed at alien Chinamen simply or at Chinamen having any political affiliations. It was against "any Chinaman" whether owing allegiance to the rulers of the Chinese Empire, or the United States Republic, or the British Crown. In other words, it was not aimed at any class of Chinaman, or at the political status of Chinamen, but at Chinamen as men of a particular race or blood, and whether aliens or naturalized.

For these reasons I would dismiss the appeal with costs.

IDINGTON J. (dissenting): . . . The Act, by its title, refers to female labour and then proceeds to deal with only the case of white women.

In truth, its evident purpose is to curtail or restrict the rights of Chinamen.

In view of the provisions of the "Naturalization Act," under and pursuant to which the appellant, presumably, has become a naturalized British subject, one must have the gravest doubt if it ever was intended to apply such legislation to one so naturalized.

The "Naturalization Act," in force long before and at the time of the creation of the Province of Saskatchewan, and ever since, provided by section 4 for aliens acquiring and holding real and personal property, and by section 24, as follows:—

24. An alien to whom a certificate of naturalization is granted shall, within Canada, be entitled to all political and other rights, powers and privileges, and be subject to all obligations to which a natural-born British subject is entitled or subject within Canada, with this qualification, that he shall not, when within the limits of the foreign state of which he was a subject previously to obtaining his certificate of naturalization, be deemed to be a British subject unless he has ceased to be a subject of that state in pursuance of the laws thereof, or in pursuance of a treaty or convention to that effect.

These enactments rest upon the class No. 25 of the classification of subjects assigned, by section 91 of the "British North America Act, 1867," to the exclusive jurisdiction of the Dominion Parliament, and which reads as follows: "Naturalization and Aliens." The political rights given any one, whether naturalized or natural-born British subjects, may in many respects be limited and varied by the legislation of a province, even if discriminating in favour of one section or class as against another. Some political rights or limitations thereof may be obviously beyond the power of such legislature. But the "other rights, powers and privileges" (if meaning anything) of natural-born British subjects to be shared by naturalized British subjects, do not so clearly fall within the powers of the legislatures to discriminate with regard to as between classes or sections of the community. . . .

Again, it may also be well argued that, within the exclusive powers given to the Dominion Parliament over the subject of naturalization and aliens, there is implied the power to guarantee to all naturalized subjects that equality of freedom and opportunity to which I have adverted. And I ask, has it not done so by the foregoing provision of the "Naturalization Act"? . . .

The appellant having, under the "Naturalization Act" (as I think fair to infer) become a British subject, he has presumably been certified to as a man of good character and enjoying the assurance, conveyed in the section thereof which I have quoted, of equal treatment with other British subjects, I shall not willingly impute an intention to the legislature to violate that assurance by this legislation specially aimed at his fellow-countrymen in origin. Indeed, in a piece of legislation alleged to have been promoted in the interests of morality, it would seem a strange thing to find it founded upon a breach of good faith which lies at the root of nearly all morality worth bothering one's head about. . . .

Looked at from this point of view I am constrained to think that this Act must be construed as applicable only to those Chinamen who have not become naturalized British subjects, and is not applicable to the appellant who has become such.

Whether it is *ultra vires* or *intra vires* the alien Chinamen is a question with which, in this view, I have nothing to do.

DUFF J.: . . . There can be no doubt that, *prima facie*, legislation prohibiting the employment of specified classes of persons in particular occupations on grounds which touch the public health, the public morality or the public order from the "local and provincial point of view" may fall within the domain of the authority conferred upon the provinces by section 92(16). Such legislation stands upon precisely the same footing in relation to the respective powers of the provinces and of the Dominion as the legislation providing for the local prohibition of the sale of liquor, the validity of which legislation has been sustained by several well-known decisions of the Judicial Committee. . . .

I think that, on the proper construction of this Act (and this appears to me to be the decisive point), it applies to persons of the races mentioned without regard to nationality. According to the common understanding of the words "Japanese, Chinaman or other Oriental person," they would embrace persons otherwise answering the description who, as being born in British territory (Singapore, Hong Kong, Victoria or Vancouver, for instance), are natural-born subjects of His Majesty equally with persons of other nationalities. The terms Chinamen and Chinese, as generally used in Canadian legislation, point to a classification based upon origin, upon racial or personal characteristics and habits, rather than upon nationality or allegiance. The "Chinese Immigration Act," for example, R.S.C. 1906, ch. 95 (sec. 2(d) and sec. 7) particularly illustrates this; and the judgment of Mr. Justice Martin, *In re "The Coal Mines Regulation Act"*, 10 B.C.R. 408, at pages 421 and 428, gives other illustrations. Indeed, the presence of the phrase "other Oriental persons" seems to make it clear, even if there could otherwise have been any doubt upon the point, that the legislature is not dealing with these classes of persons according to nationality, but as persons of a certain origin or persons having certain common characteristics and habits sufficiently indicated by the language used. *Prima facie,* therefore, the Act is not an Act dealing with aliens or with naturalized subjects as such. It seems also impossible to say that the Act is, in its practical operation, limited to aliens and naturalized subjects. . . .

Orientals are not prohibited in terms from carrying on any establishment of the kind mentioned. Nor is there any ground for supposing that the effect of the prohibition created by the statute will be to prevent such persons carrying on any such business. It would require some evidence of it to convince me that the right and opportunity to employ white women is, in any business sense a necessary condition for the effective carrying on by Orientals of restaurants and laundries and like establishments in the Western provinces of Canada. Neither is there any ground for supposing that this legislation is designed to deprive Orientals of the opportunity of gaining a livelihood.

There is nothing in the Act itself to indicate that the legislature is doing anything more than attempting to deal according to its lights (as it is its duty to do) with a strictly local situation. In the sparsely inhabited Western provinces of this country the presence of Orientals in comparatively considerable numbers not infrequently raises questions for public discussion and treatment, and, sometimes in an acute degree, which in more thickly populated countries would excite little or no general interest. One can without difficulty figure to one's self the considerations which may have influenced the Saskatchewan Legislature in dealing with the practice of white girls taking employment in such circumstances as are within the contemplation of this Act; considerations, for example, touching the interests of immigrant European women, and considerations touching the effect of such a practice upon the local relations between Europeans and Orientals; to say nothing of considerations affecting the administration of the law. And, in view of all this, I think, with great respect, it is quite impossible to apply with justice to this enactment the observation of Lord Watson in the *Bryden* case, that "the whole pith and substance of it is that it establishes a prohibition affecting" Orientals. For these reasons, I think, apart altogether from the decision in *Cunningham v. Tomey Homma,* to which I am about to refer, that the question of the legality of this statute is not ruled by the decision in *Bryden's Case.*

I think, however, that in applying *Bryden's* case we are not entitled to pass over the authoritative interpretation of that decision which was pronounced some years later by the Judicial Committee itself in *Cunningham v. Tomey Homma,* [1903] A.C. 151. The legislation their Lordships had to examine in the last mentioned case, it is true, related to a different subject-matter. Their Lordships, however, put their decision upon grounds that appear to be strictly appropriate to the question raised on this appeal. Starting from the point that the enactment then in controversy was *prima facie* within the scope of the powers conferred by section 92(1), they proceeded to examine the question whether, according to the true construction of section 91(25), the subject-matter of it really fell within the subject of "aliens and naturalization"; and, in order to pass upon that point, their Lordships considered and expounded the meaning of that article. . . .

It should not be forgotten that the very eminent judges (Lord Halsbury, Lord Macnaghten, Lord Davey, Lord Robertson and Lord Lindley), constituting the Board which heard the appeal in *Cunningham's* case, had that case before them for something like six months after it had been very fully argued by Mr. Blake against the provincial view; and, in delivering the considered judgment of the Board, Lord Halsbury, as we have seen, examines and sums up the effect of the decision in *Bryden's* case, which the courts in British Columbia had believed themselves to be following in passing upon *Cunningham's* case. In these circumstances, whatever might otherwise have been one's view of their Lordships' judgment in *Bryden's* case, we should not be entitled to adopt and act upon a view as to the construction of item 25 of section 91 ("B.N.A. Act"), which was distinctly and categorically rejected in the later judgment.

There is one more point to be noted. Section 24 of the "Naturalization Act," ch. 77, of the Revised Statutes of Canada, 1906, provides as follows: [The section is set out in the judgment of Idington J., *supra.*]

It is unnecessary to consider whether or not this section goes beyond the powers of the Dominion in respect of the subject of naturalization, or whether "the rights, powers and privileges" referred to therein ought to be construed as meaning those only which are implied by the "protection" that is referred to as the correlative of allegiance in the . . . judgment of the Judicial Committee in *Cunningham's* case. This much seems clear: The section cannot fairly be construed as conferring upon persons naturalized under the provisions of the "Naturalization Act," a status in which they are exempt from the operation of laws passed by a provincial legislature in relation to the subjects of section 92 of the "British North America Act, 1867," and applying to native-born subjects of His Majesty in like manner as to naturalized subjects and aliens. If the enactment in question had been confined to Orientals who are native-born British subjects it would have been impossible to argue that there was any sort of invasion of the Dominion jurisdiction under section 91(25); and it seems equally impossible to say that this legislation deprives any Oriental, who is a naturalized subject, of any of "the rights, powers and privileges" which an Oriental, who is a native-born British subject, is allowed to exercise or retain.

Appeal dismissed.

[Anglin J. agreed with Davies J. *The Canadian Citizenship Act*, R.S.C. 1970, c. C-19, s. 22 provides as follows: "A Canadian citizen other than a natural-born Canadian citizen is, subject to the provisions of this Act, entitled to all the rights, powers and privileges and is subject to all obligations, duties and liabilities to which a natural-born Canadian citizen is entitled or subject and, on and after becoming a Canadian citizen, subject to the provisions of this Act, has a like status to that of a natural-born Canadian citizen." Consider the affirmative effect, if any, of this provision: see also s. 24 which removes the property disabilities of aliens; and *cf. Re Kvasnak*, [1951] 3 D.L.R. 412; *Re Lukac, Hayzel v. Public Trustee* (1963), 40 D.L.R. (2d) 120, 44 W.W.R. 582.

The limitations on provincial legislative power arising from s. 91(25) do not obtain where the provincial legislature acts in a proprietary capacity, e.g., in relation to Crown lands. However, the position may be affected by overriding competent Dominion legislation; see *Brooks-Bidlake and Whittall Ltd. v. A.-G. B.C.*, [1923] A.C. 450, [1923] 2 D.L.R. 189, [1923] 1 W.W.R. 1150, and *A.-G. B.C. v. A.-G. Can.*, [1924] A.C. 203, [1923] 4 D.L.R. 698, [1923] 3 W.W.R. 945. In the former case, Lord Cave said, *inter alia*, that "sect. 91(25) reserves to the Dominion Parliament the general right to legislate as to the rights and disabilities of aliens and naturalized persons; but the Dominion is not empowered by that section to regulate the management of the public property of the province, or to determine whether a grantee or licensee of that property shall or shall not be permitted to employ persons of a particular race. These functions are assigned by s. 92, head 5, and s. 109 of the [B.N.A.] Act to the Legislature of the Province; and there is nothing in s. 91 which conflicts with that view." The latter case is set out *infra*.]

A.-G. B.C. v. A.-G. CAN.

In the Privy Council. [1924] A.C. 203, [1923] 4 D.L.R. 698, [1923] 3 W.W.R. 945.

Appeal from a judgment of the Supreme Court of Canada, 63 S.C.R. 293, 65 D.L.R. 577, [1922] 2 W.W.R. 429, on a reference to determine the validity of 1921 (B.C.), c. 49, being "An Act to validate and confirm Orders in Council and provisions relating to the employment of persons on Crown property." The majority of the Supreme Court held that the statute was *ultra vires*.

VISCOUNT HALDANE: . . . The relevant facts are briefly these: In 1902 two minutes passed in the Executive Council of the Province and were approved by the Lieutenant-Governor. The Executive Council set out in these minutes resolutions passed by the Legislative Assembly, and recommended, in accordance with these resolutions, that all tunnel and drain licences issued under s. 58 of the *Minerals Act* and s. 48 of the *Placer Mining Act,* and all leases granted under Part VII of the latter Act, should contain provisos that they were granted on the express condition that no Chinese or Japanese should be employed in or about the tunnels, drains or premises to which the licences or leases related, and that a similar provision should also be inserted in all instruments relating to a number of enumerated leases and licences which should be issued by the officers of the Provincial Government.

In 1913 a treaty was made between His Majesty the King and the Emperor of Japan by which it was, among other things, agreed that the subjects of each of the High Contracting Parties should have full liberty to enter, travel and reside in the territories of the other, and in all that relates to the pursuit of their industries, callings, professions and educational studies, should be placed in all respects on the same footing as the subjects or citizens of the most favoured nation.

Section 132 of the *British North America Act* provides that the Parliament and Government of Canada shall have all powers necessary or proper for performing the obligations of Canada or any Province thereof, as part of the British Empire, towards foreign countries. On April 10, 1913, the Parliament of the Dominion passed the *Japanese Treaty Act* of that year. The Act provided that the Treaty just referred to should be thereby sanctioned and declared to have the force of law in Canada.

On April 2, 1921, the Legislature of British Columbia proceeded to pass the *Oriental Orders in Council Validation Act*. This statute purported to validate and confirm the two Orders in Council of the Province already referred to, and passed in the form of recommendations of the Provincial Executive Council approved by the Lieutenant-Governor in May, 1902. The statute further provided that the Orders should be deemed to have been valid and effectual according to their tenor as from the dates of the approval, and that where in any instrument referred to in the said Orders in Council, or in any instrument of a similar nature to any of those so referred to, issued by any minister or officer of any department of the Government of the Province, any provision had heretofore been inserted or was thereafter inserted relating to or restricting the employment of Chinese or Japanese, that provision should be deemed to have been and to be valid, and always to have had the force of law according to its tenor. It was further enacted that every violation of or failure to observe any such provision on the part of any licensee, or other person in whose favour the instrument operated, should be sufficient ground for the cancellation of the instrument by the Lieutenant-Governor.

This is the statute the validity of which has been the subject of decision by the Supreme Court of Canada. Before, however, proceeding to the questions there discussed reference must be made to certain recent proceedings which resulted in an appeal to the Sovereign in Council and a decision which restricts the questions that are still open.

In 1912 licences had been granted by the Minister of Lands of British Columbia to certain persons, enabling them to cut and carry away timber on lands belonging to the Province. Each of these licences was granted for a year only, but under a provision in the *Crown Lands Act* the licences were renewable from year to year if [their] terms and conditions had been complied with. Among these was the stipulation, inserted in accordance with the Orders in Council of 1902, that no Chinese or Japanese were to be employed in connection with the licence. The stipulation had been violated by the grantees, but notwithstanding this the licences had been renewed down to 1920.

In that year the Lieutenant-Governor of the Province referred to the Court of Appeal for British Columbia the question whether the stipulation was valid, having regard to head 25 of s. 91 of the *British North America Act,* which reserves for the Dominion Parliament the exclusive power to legislate with reference to "naturalization and aliens," and also to possible repugnancy to the Dominion Japanese Treaty Act of 1913. The Court of Appeal of British Columbia held the stipulation to be invalid on both grounds. However, the licences were in fact renewed for another year, and meantime the *Oriental Orders in Council Validation Act* was passed in April, 1921. Apparently relying on the new statute the Minister of Lands called the attention of the grantees to their breach of the stipulation, and threatened to cancel the licences.

The grantees or the persons who had succeeded them in title then commenced an action in the Supreme Court of British Columbia claiming a declaration that, notwithstanding the stipulation, they were entitled to employ Chinese and Japanese on the timber lands, and an injunction against interference with their employment under the licences. On an interlocutory motion, the judge of first instance, holding himself bound by the opinion previously given by the Court of Appeal, granted an injunction. The Provincial Government, by arrangement, appealed directly to the Supreme Court of Canada. While this appeal was pending the Governor-General referred to the Supreme Court the questions in the appeal now before their Lordships, as to the validity of the Provincial statute. The Supreme Court heard the two matters before it together, and gave successive judgments in them. As already stated, the majority held the Provincial statute to be invalid. But on the appeal in the action (63

S.C.R. 466) they allowed the appeal and dismissed the action itself, mainly on the ground that, even though the stipulation as to not employing Oriental labour were void, it not the less formed one of the conditions of the licences, and could not be treated as struck out of them, with the result that the only right to renewal was one which, being founded on a condition which was its foundation notwithstanding any illegality, must fail.

This last question was brought on appeal to the Privy Council. Their Lordships considered both of the points made. They held, first, that the stipulation was not void as violating s. 91 of the *British North America Act*. For it related only to the way in which the Province claimed to be free to manage its own property as distinguished from a claim to regulate the general status of aliens. Whatever might be said about the stipulation as affecting this in the case of Japanese labour, there was nothing in the *Treaty Act* which affected the status of Chinese labour, and it was therefore only under s. 91 that the stipulation as to Chinese labour, which was severable, could be struck at. As their Lordships were of opinion that this particular stipulation was not inconsistent with s. 91, the appellants had no right to renewal. The point as to the *Treaty Act* thus became immaterial, and their Lordships did not deal with it, but dismissed the appeal on the ground just stated.

That decision (*Brooks-Bidlake and Whittall v. Attorney-General for British Columbia*, [1923] A.C. 450) thus leaves the question now before their Lordships for decision untouched. The views taken of it by the learned judges in the Supreme Court of Canada were divergent. Davies, C.J., thought that the Provincial Act of 1921 was *ultra vires* (1) as infringing the provisions of s. 91 of the *British North America Act,* and (2) as conflicting with the provisions of the *Treaty Act,* 1913, by prohibiting the employment of Japanese subjects. Idington, J., (who dissented from the conclusion of the majority) was of opinion that the powers of the Provincial Government over the lands of the Province were as extensive as those of private owners, and that a private owner could have determined not to have Japanese subjects on his property, and could have stipulated to that effect. He thought that, this being so, the terms of the Treaty must be construed as leaving intact the right of the Province to exercise that liberty of a private owner, which he held the Treaty not to touch. Duff, J., devoted the first part of an exhaustive judgment to the question whether the Provincial statute of 1921 was *ultra vires* as being an attempt at legislation in regard to aliens, the capacity for which was conferred exclusively on the Dominion Parliament by s. 91. He came to the conclusion that the statute was not such an attempt, but was so far a legally valid exercise by the Provincial Legislature of a power confided to it of making provision for settlement on Provincial property of a suitable population. He pointed out that the two Orders in Council and the condition which they imposed related only to specific and limited kinds of such property. What was excluded was not the employment of subjects of foreign Powers, in particular, but that of Chinese and Japanese, whether aliens, naturalized subjects or native-born subjects, under particular circumstances. But when the learned judge passed to s. 132 he came to the conclusion that the *Treaty Act* was the exercise of an authority to the Dominion to deal with subjects of imperial and national concern as distinguished from matters of strictly Dominion concern only. He thought the scope of the section broad enough to support the *Treaty Act,* and to put Japanese subjects in the same position before the law as the subjects of the most favoured nation. The statute of 1921 he held to contravene the right so given to Japanese subjects, by excluding them from employment in certain definite cases. And this was not the less so in that the Province in so doing was administering its own corporate and economic affairs. The new Provincial law was repugnant to the Treaty and could not stand. Since the statute of 1921 treats Chinese and Japanese as constituting a single group, the learned judge thought that it was inoperative, not merely as regards Japanese subjects, but *in toto.* Anglin, J., based his opinion entirely on s. 91, which he held the statute of 1921 to contravene. It was in substance a statute passed to deprive Chinese and Japanese of general capacity. He expressed no opinion about the effect of the *Treaty Act.* Mignault J., delivered judgment to the same effect as Anglin, J. Brodeur J., thought the Provincial statute *ultra vires* so far as Japanese subjects were concerned, as conflicting with the provisions of the Treaty Act. He considered it, however, to be *intra vires* as regards the Chinese.

As the result of the opinion delivered in the Supreme Court of Canada, the Governor-General in Council on March 31, 1922, being within the year from the passing of the statute of 1921, during which his power of disallowance remained operative, disallowed it.

Leave to appeal to the Sovereign in Council against the judgment of the Supreme Court was subsequently given. On the decision in the present appeal depends, therefore, the ascertainment of the limits within which the Legislature of the Province can attempt further legislation on the subject. What their Lordships have to consider is whether the statute of 1921 is invalid on any of the grounds alleged. The main reasons submitted in favour of its invalidity are, first that s. 91, head 25, of the *British North America Act* has debarred the Provincial Legislature from enacting what was really in its pith and substance legislation dealing with the rights of aliens. It is said that although the statute contains provisions regulating the mode of dealing with its own property by the Province, it not the less is a statute which affects radically the status of classes of aliens. Whether it relates to Chinese or Japanese it thus equally trenches to an extent which cannot be exhaustively defined on the subject-matter assigned to the Dominion by s. 91, head 25. The principle which applies is alleged to be that laid down in *Union Colliery Co. v. Bryden,* and not that applied in *Cunningham v. Tomey Homma.*

In the appeal in the *Brooks-Bidlake* case what their Lordships decided was that the stipulation in the licences against the employment of Chinese was a severable stipulation which had been broken, with the result that the licensees could not claim a renewal. Such a stipulation was held to be in itself consistent with s. 91, head 25, and so far as Chinese labour was concerned no question could arise under the Japanese Treaty.

On the present occasion a wholly different question presents itself. The statute of 1921 not only confirms the stipulations provided for in the Orders in Council of 1902, but it enacts that where in any instrument of a similar nature to any of those referred to in these Orders a provision is inserted relating to or restricting the employment of Chinese or Japanese, the provision is to be valid and to have the force of law, and failure to observe it is to be ground for cancellation by the Provincial Government of the licence or other instrument. Their Lordships observe that this provision may not altogether unreasonably be looked on as containing an approach to the laying down of something more than a mere condition for the renewal of the right to use Provincial property. Still, the question is far from free from difficulty, for the reasons assigned by Duff, J., in his judgment in the Supreme Court.

In the view, however, which their Lordships take of the bearing of the *Treaty Act* on the statute it becomes unnecessary for them to express any opinion about it, and they refrain from doing so in accordance with the practice which they have repeatedly laid down for their own guidance of deciding no more than is necessary in appeals relative to the interpretation of the *British North America Act*.

As regards the question arising as to the application of the Treaty Act itself, they entertain no doubt that the Provincial statute violated the principle laid down in the Dominion Act of 1913. This conclusion does not in any way affect what they decided on the previous appeal as to the title to a renewal of the special licences relative to particular properties. It is concerned with the principle of the statute of 1921, and not with that of merely individual instances in which particular kinds of property are being administered.

The statute has been disallowed, and if re-enacted in any form will have, in their Lordships' opinion, to be re-enacted in terms which do not strike at the principle in the Treaty that the subjects of the Emperor of Japan are to be in all that relates to their industries and callings in all respects on the same footings as the subjects or citizens of the most favoured nation. They are unable to accept the view that as the terms of the statute stand they do not infringe this principle so far as concerns subjects of the Emperor. That others who are not such subjects happen to be included can make no difference to this conclusion. . . .

Appeal dismissed.

CHAPTER XV

LEGISLATIVE POWER IN RELATION TO MATRIMONIAL MATTERS

IN RE MARRIAGE LEGISLATION IN CANADA

In the Privy Council. [1912] A.C. 880, 7 D.L.R. 629.

Appeal by special leave from a judgment of the Supreme Court of Canada, 46 S.C.R. 132, 6 D.L.R. 588, on a reference of three questions set out below.

VISCOUNT HALDANE L.C.: The questions to be decided arise on an appeal, for which special leave was given, from the answers returned by the Supreme Court of Canada to certain questions submitted by the Government of Canada pursuant to s. 60 of the Supreme Court Act.

The questions so submitted were the following:

1. (a) Has the Parliament of Canada authority to enact, in whole or in part, Bill No. 3 of the First Session of the Twelfth Parliament of Canada, intituled "An Act to amend the Marriage Act"?

The Bill provides as follows:

"(1.) The Marriage Act, Chapter 105 of the Revised Statutes, 1906, is amended by adding thereto the following section:

"3. Every ceremony or form of marriage heretofore or hereafter performed by any person authorized to perform any ceremony of marriage by the laws of the place where it is performed, and duly performed according to such laws, shall everywhere within Canada be deemed to be a valid marriage, notwithstanding any differences in the religious faith of the persons so married and without regard to the religion of the person performing the ceremony."

"(2.) The rights and duties, as married people of the respective persons married as aforesaid, and of the children of such marriage, shall be absolute and complete, and no law or canonical decree or custom of or in any Province of Canada shall have any force or effect to invalidate or qualify any such marriage or any of the rights of the said persons or their children in any manner whatsoever."

(b) If the provisions of the said Bill are not all within the authority of the Parliament of Canada to enact, which, if any, of the provisions are within such authority?

2. Does the law of the Province of Quebec render null and void, unless contracted before a Roman Catholic priest, a marriage that would otherwise be legally binding, which takes place in such Province,

(a) between persons who are both Roman Catholics, or

(b) between persons one of whom, only, is a Roman Catholic?

3. If either (a) or (b) of the last preceding question is answered in the affirmative, or if both of them are answered in the affirmative, has the Parliament of Canada authority to enact that all such marriages, whether

(a) heretofore solemnized, or

(b) hereafter to be solemnized,
shall be legal and binding?

The answers of the learned judges of the Supreme Court were in substance to the following effect:

1. As to the first question the Chief Justice, Davies J., Duff J., and Anglin J. were of opinion that the proposed legislation was *ultra vires* of the Parliament of Canada. Idington J. differed.

2. As to the second question all the learned judges concurred in holding that the law of Quebec does not render null and void unless contracted before a Roman Catholic priest a marriage which takes place in that province between persons one of whom only is a Roman Catholic. As to the validity of such marriages between persons who are both Roman Catholics the Chief Justice asked permission to decline to answer. Sir Louis Davies, Idington, and Duff JJ. were of opinion that they were valid, and Anglin J. held that they were null and void.

3. As to the third question, all the judges except Idington J. were of opinion that the Parliament has no power to enact such remedial legislation.

The decision of these questions turns on the construction to be placed on ss. 91 and 92 of the *British North America Act,* 1867. Section 91 enacts that the Parliament of the Dominion may make laws for the peace, order, and good government of Canada in relation to all matters not coming within the classes of subjects by the Act assigned exclusively to the Legislatures of the provinces, and, for greater certainty, but not so as to restrict the generality of the foregoing terms of the section, declares that, notwithstanding anything in the Act, the exclusive legislative authority of the Parliament of the Dominion extends to all matters coming within the classes of subjects enumerated. One of these is marriage and divorce. The section concludes with a declaration that any matter coming within any of the enumerated classes shall not be deemed to come within the class of matters of a local or private nature comprised in the enumeration of the classes of subjects by the Act assigned exclusively to the Legislatures of the provinces.

Section 92 enacts that in each province the Legislature may exclusively make laws in relation to matters coming within the classes of subjects enumerated in this section. Among these is the solemnization of marriage in the province. The enumeration also includes, *inter alia,* property and civil rights, and generally matters of a merely local or private nature in the province.

In the course of the argument it became apparent that the real controversy between the parties was as to whether all questions relating to the validity of the contract of marriage, including the conditions of that validity, were within the exclusive jurisdiction conferred on the Dominion Parliament by s. 91. If this is so, then the provincial power extends only to the directory regulation of the formalities by which the contract is to be authenticated, and does not extend to any question of validity. This was the view contended for by one set of the learned counsel who argued the case at their

Lordships' Bar. The other learned counsel contended that the power conferred by s. 92 to deal with the solemnization of marriage effected a distribution of powers under which the Legislature of the province had the exclusive capacity to determine by whom the marriage ceremony might be performed, and to make the officiation of the proper person a condition of the validity of the marriage.

If the latter view is taken, it is clear how the question must be answered. For it was agreed between counsel that the Bill referred to in the first question was intended to enable a person with any authority to perform the ceremony to perform it validly whatever the religious faith of those married by him. On the footing indicated the Bill would therefore be *ultra vires* of the Dominion Parliament. The third question would also be disposed of, for the Parliament of Canada would, in the events indicated in the question, have no authority. The second question consequently becomes not only unimportant, but superfluous.

Notwithstanding the able argument addressed to them, their Lordships have arrived at the conclusion that the jurisdiction of the Dominion Parliament does not, on the true construction of ss. 91 and 92, cover the whole field of validity. They consider that the provision in s. 92 conferring on the provincial Legislature the exclusive power to make laws relating to the solemnization of marriage in the province operates by way of exception to the powers conferred as regards marriage by s. 91, and enables the provincial Legislature to enact conditions as to solemnization which may affect the validity of the contract. There have doubtless been periods, as there have been and are countries, where the validity of the marriage depends on the bare contract of the parties without reference to any solemnity. But there are at least as many instances where the contrary doctrine has prevailed. The common law of England and the law of Quebec before Confederation are conspicuous examples, which would naturally have been in the minds of those who inserted the words about solemnization into the statute. *Prima facie* these words appear to their Lordships to import that the whole of what solemnization ordinarily meant in the systems of law of the provinces of Canada at the time of Confederation is intended to come within them, including conditions which affect validity. There is no greater difficulty in putting on the language of the statute this construction than there is in putting on it the alternative construction contended for. Both readings of the provision in s. 92 are in the nature of limitations of the effect of the words in s. 91, and there is, in their Lordships' opinion, no reason why what they consider to be the natural construction of the words "solemnization of marriage", having regard to the law existing in Canada when the *British North America Act* was passed, should not prevail.

Appeal dismissed.

[The second question in the above case which was left unanswered was necessarily considered in *Despatie v. Tremblay,* [1921] 1 A.C. 702, 58 D.L.R. 29, rev'g 43 Que. S.C. 59, which involved the validity of a marriage of two Roman Catholics celebrated in Quebec before a Roman Catholic priest. The parties were unaware at the time that they were cousins in the fourth degree and the dispensation required by ecclesiastical law was not obtained. Subsequently, the husband obtained an ecclesiastical decree that the marriage was invalid because of an ecclesiastical impediment. The Quebec courts, on an application for a like declaration, held that the Quebec Civil Code adopted ecclesiastical impediments as part of the civil law. The Privy Council came to a different conclusion on its construction of Quebec marriage law, holding that ecclesiastical impediments were not imported into the civil law, and hence the marriage was valid. See also *Howard v. Bergeron and Kriklow*, [1941] 4 D.L.R. 360. *In re Marriage Legislation in Canada* was followed in *Gilham (falsely called Steele) v. Steele*, [1953] 2 D.L.R. 89, 8 W.W.R. (N.S.) 62, in upholding the validity of provincial legislation that a marriage solemnized by an unregistered minister is a nullity.

In *Re Howe Louis* (1970), 14 D.L.R. (3d) 49, 75 W.W.R. 1 (*sub nom. Louis v. Louis*), the British Columbia Court of Appeal held that one who had contracted an informal marriage *à la mode de Chine* in Saskatchewan was entitled to benefits under the British Columbia testator's family dependent legislation, by virtue of a Saskatchewan statute which validated prior informal marriages as far as they were within provincial jurisdiction; the statute being read as dealing in pith and substance with the solemnization of marriage, although incidentally affecting the marriage status.]

KERR v. KERR AND A.-G. ONT.

In the Supreme Court of Canada. [1934] S.C.R. 72, [1934] 2 D.L.R. 369.

Appeal by plaintiff from a judgment of the Ontario Court of Appeal, [1932] O.R. 601, [1932] D.L.R. 288, reversing a judgment of Logie J., [1932] O.R. 289, [1932] 2 D.L.R. 349, and dismissing his action for a decree of nullity.

DUFF C.J.: I concur with the view of the Appellate Division that s. 17(1) of the *Marriage Act* is *intra vires* of the Provincial Legislature. I have no doubt that, in exercise of its jurisdiction in relation to the subject reserved to the provinces by s. 92(12), "Solemnization of Marriage", the legislature of a province may lawfully prescribe the consent of the parents or guardian to the marriage of a minor as an essential element in the ceremony of marriage itself. Nor have I any doubt that by s. 17(1) the consents required are prescribed as elements in the ceremony. These requirements apply to all marriages celebrated in Ontario, and to no marriages but those celebrated in Ontario, whether the parties to the marriage be domiciled in Ontario or elsewhere. The legislature is, I think, dealing with the solemnities of marriage and not with the capacity of the parties.

It is not suggested that, according to the practice prevailing in the different provinces of Canada at the time of Confederation, the giving of such consents pursuant to the requirements of the law, would not properly have been regarded as belonging to such solemnities. The province, therefore, has power to require such consents as a condition of the validity of the solemnization of marriages within the province. But, it should be observed that the jurisdiction of the province is not limited to that. The authority with regard to the subject "Solemnization of Marriage" is plenary. Lord Watson, in

Liquidators of the Maritime Bank of Canada v. Receiver-General of New Brunswick, [1892] A.C. 437 at p. 442, said:

"In so far as regards those matters which, by s. 92, are specially reserved for provincial legislation, the legislation of each province continues to be free from the control of the Dominion, and as supreme as it was before the passing of the Act."

The authority of the provinces, therefore, extends not only to prescribing such formalities as properly fall within the matters designated by "Solemnization of Marriage"; they have the power to enforce the rules laid down by penalty, by attaching the consequence of invalidity and by attaching such consequences absolutely or conditionally. It is within the power of a province to say that a given requirement shall be absolute in marriages of one class of people, while it may be dispensed with in other marriages. This, of course, is always subject to the observation that a province cannot, under the form of dealing with the "solemnization of marriage", enact legislation which, in substance, relates to some part of the subject of "marriage" which is not reserved to the provinces as a subject of legislative jurisdiction.

I must not be understood as expressing the view that it would not be competent to the Dominion, in exercise of its authority in relation to the subject of "marriage", in matters which do not fall within the subject of "solemnization of marriage", to deprive minors domiciled in Canada of the capacity to marry without the consent of their parents. No such question arises here, and it is quite unnecessary to pass an opinion upon it. The authority of the Dominion to impose upon intending spouses an incapacity which is made conditional on the absence of certain nominated consents is not in question. . . .

Nor is it necessary to consider whether or not the requirements of s. 34, which, admittedly, control the courts of Ontario in exercising the jurisdiction thereby conferred, have the effect of qualifying any rule of substantive law in respect of the invalidity of marriages which may be established by s. 17(1) and s. 34. The point might be of considerable practical importance, but it does not arise on this appeal. The province unquestionably has authority (whether in relation to the Administration of Justice (s. 92(14)), or in relation to Solemnization of Marriage (s. 92(12)), it is needless to determine) to prescribe rules governing the courts of the province in exercising the jurisdiction conferred upon these courts by s. 34. That power is vested in the province, first, because *prima facie* it affects matters falling within the subject "Solemnization of Marriage", or the subject "Administration of Justice"; and second, because the authority to prescribe rules governing the courts of Ontario, in exercising the jurisdiction conferred upon them by the legislature of Ontario, for giving effect by remedial process to rules of substantive law relating to "Solemnization of Marriage", a subject within the exclusive jurisdiction of the legislature, could not be brought under any jurisdiction appertaining to the Dominion Parliament under any of the enumerated heads of s. 91. For our present purpose, we may assume that some jurisdiction is vested in the Dominion in respect of remedial process touching matters within "Marriage", and not within either "Divorce" or "Solemnization of Marriage". But, as regards process designed to give effect to substantive rules of law competently enacted by a province, in execution of the exclusive authority belonging to it in virtue of s. 92(12), the Dominion would be powerless to intervene in any way with a view to sanctioning or controlling any jurisdiction or procedure established for that purpose by a province. If there is no such authority vested in the Dominion, it follows that it must be vested in the province. . . . This alone is fatal to the appeal.

Nor do I think the Dominion statute of 1930 [The *Divorce Act (Ontario)*, 1930] (20 & 21 Geo. V., c. 14) affects any matter in controversy. Minors above the ages of consent (14 in males, and 12 in females) were undoubtedly capable of contracting marriages under the law of England as it existed on the 15th of July, 1870. As I have already pointed out, the provisions of the legislation before us do not affect this matter of capacity—a matter which is not touched by them. They deal exclusively with matters which are properly treated as comprised within the solemnities of marriage. If the effect of the Dominion Act is to make available the procedure of the probate and divorce court in England for the purpose of obtaining a declaration of invalidity on the ground that, under the provisions of s. 17(1) and s. 34, a marriage is void for want of observing the formalities therein prescribed (formalities comprised within the subject "Solemnization of Marriage") then, as already indicated, to that extent, the Dominion statute is *ultra vires*. The Dominion, to repeat, has no power to prescribe such a procedure for such a purpose, either explicitly or referentially.

But I am by no means satisfied that such is the effect of the Act of 1930. The phrase "annulment of marriage" may not unreasonably be read as restricted to proceedings impeaching a marriage on grounds other than some defect in "solemnization" within the meaning of s. 92 which would vitiate *ab initio* the ceremony itself by force of the law of the province alone. In view of the then existing state of Ontario law, the qualification "in so far as it can be made to apply in the province of Ontario", may, perhaps, be paraphrased "in so far as it can properly be made to apply to that province by the Dominion legislation" and this consideration may afford, as Riddell J.A. thinks, a good ground for so construing the words "annulment of marriage".

The appeal must be dismissed with costs.

SMITH J.: (for himself, Rinfret and Cannon JJ.) The facts and secs. 17 and 34 of the Ontario *Marriage Act,* R.S.O. 1927, ch. 181, are set out in the reasons of my brother Lamont.

The appellant, in his statement of claim, pleads the provisions of *The Divorce Act (Ontario),* 1930, being Statutes of Canada, 20-21 Geo. V., ch. 14, and amendments thereto, and the provisions of the Ontario *Marriage Act*; and claims, by virtue of these Acts, a decree declaring the ceremony of marriage celebrated between the parties null and void.

The *Divorce Act* referred to does not deal in any way with the solemnization of marriage, which is a matter entirely within provincial jurisdiction. It is applicable to divorce and to the annulment of marriages where there has been valid solemnization. A marriage validly solemnized may, under the English law, be void or voidable on grounds other than those giving a right to divorce. The facts established in this case would not, under the English law, constitute a ground for annulment of a validly solemnized marriage, for the reasons stated by the learned Chief Justice of Ontario.

The question of whether or not there was a validly solemnized marriage in this case depends entirely upon the provisions of the Ontario *Marriage Act*. If, under the terms of that Act, there was a valid solemnization of marriage, the appellant's action necessarily fails. That question turns upon the construction to be given to the provisions of sec. 17 when read in conjunction with subsec. 2 of sec. 34, which reads as follows:

(2) The Court shall not declare a marriage void where carnal intercourse has taken place between the parties before the ceremony.

If this subsection is to be construed as dealing with jurisdiction without any other signification, and sec. 17 is to be regarded as alone dealing with the question of validity and as making the marriage void under the circumstances of this case, then we have the peculiar situation of an enactment making a marriage void and at the same time forbidding the court so to declare in an action between the parties. It is difficult to understand what object would be served by such prohibition.

On the other hand, if sec. 17 and this subsec. 2 are to be read together, it may be that the proper construction is that subsec. 2 makes an exception to the provision of sec. 17 requiring consent and making consent a condition, in which event the marriage would be valid, notwithstanding the provisions of sec. 17. If such is the proper construction, there can be no doubt that such a provision is *intra vires* because the legislature clearly has jurisdiction to provide that the stipulated consent must be had under certain circumstances but shall not be necessary under certain other circumstances.

It is pointed out, however, that it is not necessary in this particular action to pass upon the question of the validity of the marriage, because the appellant cannot succeed unless the marriage was void, and the court, by the statute, is expressly prohibited, in this kind of an action, from making any such declaration.

There seems to be no doubt that the court has no inherent jurisdiction to entertain an action of this kind between the parties to the marriage ceremony, and that the jurisdiction rests entirely upon the provisions of the statute. That being so, subsec. 2 excludes jurisdiction under the circumstances of this case.

I am therefore refraining from expressing an opinion as to the proper construction to be placed upon the provisions of sec. 17 and subsec. 2 of sec. 34. I concur in the view that in any event the court had no jurisdiction to declare the marriage void, as prayed in the statement of claim, and that the appeal should be dismissed. There will be no order as to costs.

LAMONT J.: . . . The facts of the case are not in dispute. The parties first met in April, 1930, and sexual intercourse took place between them on some four occasions. In September, 1930, Frances Margaret Smith found herself to be pregnant and she and some of her friends urged the appellant to marry her. He objected, claiming that he was not the cause of her condition. Yielding, however, to their importunities, the appellant, on December 2nd, 1930, went through a form of marriage with her at Hamilton, Ontario, where they both resided. To obtain the marriage licence Frances Margaret Smith made an affidavit that she was eighteen years of age, although she was then only seventeen. When the affidavit was made both the appellant and Miss Smith knew that the statement therein contained as to her age was false, and knew also that it was made for the purpose of procuring the marriage licence. The ceremony was performed without the knowledge of the parents or family of either of the parties. No consent to the marriage was obtained from the mother of Frances Margaret Smith as required by section 17 of the *Marriage Act* (R.S.O. 1927, ch. 181). The marriage was never consummated and the parties, since the ceremony, have not cohabited or lived together as man and wife. . . .

The appeal turns upon the construction to be placed upon sections 17 and 34 of the *Marriage Act*. The relevant parts of these sections are:

17. (1) Save in cases provided by subsections 3 and 4 of this section and by section 18, where either of the parties to an intended marriage, not a widower or a widow, is under the age of eighteen years, the consent in writing of the father if living, or, if he is dead, or living apart from the mother and child, and is not maintaining or contributing to the support of such child, the consent in writing of the mother if living, or of a guardian if any has been duly appointed, shall be obtained from the father, mother or guardian before the licence is issued . . . and such consent shall be deemed to be a condition precedent to a valid marriage, unless the marriage has been consummated or the parties have after the ceremony cohabited and lived together as man and wife.

34. (1) Where a form of marriage is gone through between persons either of whom is under the age of eighteen years without the consent of the father, mother or guardian of such person, when such consent is required by the provisions of this Act, . . . such form of marriage shall be void and the Supreme Court shall have jurisdiction and power to entertain an action by the person who was at the time of the ceremony under the age of eighteen years, to declare and adjudge that a valid marriage was not effected or entered into, and shall so declare and adjudge if it is made to appear that the marriage has not been consummated and that such persons have not, after the ceremony, cohabited and lived together as man and wife, and that the action is brought before the person bringing it has attained the age of nineteen years.

(2) The Court shall not declare a marriage void where carnal intercourse has taken place between the parties before the ceremony.

The contention of the appellant is:

1.   That section 17(1) is competent provincial legislation in so far as it requires the consent of the parents or guardians of a contracting party—not a widower or a widow—to an intended marriage before the issue of the licence if the party is under the age of eighteen years, and also in so far as it enacts that such consent shall be a condition precedent to a valid marriage.

2.   That section 34 is *ultra vires* of the provincial legislature, as it is legislation on the subject of marriage and divorce which, by section 91(26) of the *British North America Act,* 1867, is exclusively assigned to the Dominion Parliament.

3.   That, as the consent required by section 17(1) was not obtained, and as section 34 is *ultra vires,* the marriage should be held null and void by virtue of *The Divorce Act (Ontario),* 1930, enacted by the Dominion Parliament. . . .

Solemnization of marriage within the meaning of section 92 includes not only the essential ceremony by which the marriage is effected, but also parental consent where such consent is required by law. In *Sottomayor v. DeBarros,* 3 P.D. 1, at p. 7, Cotton, L.J., says:

"It only remains to consider the case of *Simonin v. Mallac* (1860), 2 Sw. & Tr. 67. The objection to the validity of the marriage in that case, which was solemnized in England, was the want of consent of parents required by the law of France, but not under the circumstances by that of this country. In our opinion, this consent must be considered a part of the ceremony of marriage, and not a matter affecting the personal capacity of the parties to contract marriage."

The provincial legislature is, therefore, competent by apt legislation to make the preliminaries, leading up to the marriage ceremony, conditions precedent to the solemnization of the marriage. From this it follows, in my opinion, that the legislature is also competent to declare that in the event of these conditions precedent not being complied with no valid marriage has taken place.

Section 17, however, does not make consent a condition precedent to a valid marriage in every case where a contracting party is under the age of eighteen years. The legislation does not apply to cases coming within subsections 3 and 4 of this section, nor where the contracting party is a widow or widower, nor does it apply where the marriage has been consummated, or the parties have, after the ceremony, cohabited and lived together as man and wife.

Then are subsections 1 and 2 of section 34 competent provincial legislation?

It will be observed that subsection 1 deals, not with marriage, but with a "form of marriage", which indeed is all that the performing of the ceremony can be where no valid marriage takes place.

Section 34(1) declares that if the consent, required by section 17, has not been obtained "such form of marriage shall be void."

The object of these two sections is, I think, clear. By them the legislature was endeavouring:

1.   To provide that a failure to furnish the consent to an intended marriage, required by section 17 in case of a contracting party thereto

under the age of eighteen years who has gone through a form of marriage, would in certain cases have the effect of preventing a valid marriage from taking place, and

2. To bestow on the Supreme Court of Ontario jurisdiction to entertain an action and to declare and adjudge that the going through of such a form of marriage, under the circumstances, would not constitute a valid marriage.

This jurisdiction was bestowed on the court only in those cases in which the conditions prescribed by the statute had been complied with. That is to say where:

1. The action is brought by a contracting party who at the time of the ceremony was under the age of eighteen years, and who brought the action before he or she reached the age of nineteen years.

2. It is made to appear that the marriage had not been consummated and that such persons have not, after the ceremony, cohabited and lived together as man and wife.

The onus of establishing each of these requisites is on the person bringing the action and if the onus is not discharged the court has no jurisdiction to declare that a valid marriage has not taken place.

Apart, therefore, from enacting that the furnishing of the consent should be a condition precedent to a valid marriage and that when a form of marriage had been gone through without such consent being obtained such form should be null and void—which it is not disputed is within the competence of the legislature—the whole enactment in these two sections concerns the bestowal of jurisdiction on the Supreme Court of Ontario to try an action and make a declaration that there has been no valid marriage in certain cases and under certain conditions, and the withholding of such jurisdiction in others, particularly subsection 2 where the Act expressly states that the court should not declare a marriage void where carnal intercourse has taken place between the parties before the ceremony. Is it within the competence of the legislature to give jurisdiction to the court in some cases and withhold or deny it in others?

In the case of a marriage void by the law of the place where it was celebrated, on account of lack of essential formalities, a declaration that it is invalid has been described as "merely a judicial ascertainment of facts." It ascertains but does not change the status of the parties. If that is so, and I think it is, it is difficult to see why the Legislature should not be competent to invest the courts with jurisdiction to ascertain a fact. The jurisdiction of the Supreme Court of Ontario is statutory. Without this enactment the court would have no jurisdiction to declare null and void the going through of a form of marriage.

In my opinion the bestowing upon the court jurisdiction to entertain an action to make a finding of fact thereon and to make a declaration in accordance with that fact, is clearly within the competence of the legislature under section 92(14) which, subject to section 101 of the Act, assigns to the legislature the exclusive power to make laws respecting the "Administration of Justice in the Province, including the Constitution, Maintenance and Organization of Provincial Courts, both of Civil and of Criminal jurisdiction, and including Procedure in Civil Matters in those Courts." This includes the power to define the jurisdiction of the courts as well as the jurisdiction of the judges who constitute the same. (*In re County Courts of British Columbia,* 21 S.C.R. 446). It also includes the power to enlarge, alter or diminish such jurisdiction. (*Regina v. Levinger,* 22 O.R. 690.)

If we examine sections 91 and 92 it will be seen, speaking generally, that the power to legislate in respect of practice and procedure (adjective law) has been exclusively assigned to the provincial legislatures except so far as relates to divorce and criminal law, subject of course, to s. 101 of the Act; that in matters relating to the subjects over which exclusive legislative jurisdiction has been, by section 91, assigned to the Dominion Parliament, whenever it was intended that Parliament should also legislate as to the practice and procedure to be adopted, an express statement to that effect is found in section 91. In this case I have no doubt that the provincial legislature had full power, under section 92(14), to enact the impeached legislation.

It was also contended that the marriage should be annulled on the ground that the marriage licence was obtained by the false affidavit of the respondent, Frances Margaret Kerr, as to her age. A similar contention was made in *Plummer v. Plummer,* [1917] P. 163. In that action, although the notice of declaration required by the Acts contained statements false to the knowledge of both parties, it was held that a marriage by licence was not to be invalidated by reason of a false statement in the notice. The same principle, in my opinion. applies here.

The appeal should therefore be dismissed.

CROCKET J. (dissenting in part): I regret that I cannot agree with my brethren upon the question of the constitutionality of the provisoes of sec. 34 of the Ontario *Marriage Act* as it stood in that statute at the time of the commencement and trial of this action.

The impugned section deals with two distinct subjects. The first part concerns the requirement of the consent of a parent or guardian to the marriage of a person under the age of 18 years and unqualifiedly enacts that a form of marriage gone through by such a person without such consent shall be void. The remainder of that section deals entirely with the jurisdiction of the Supreme Court to pronounce a decree of annulment in the case of such a marriage. It purports to empower the court to entertain an action for annulment only by the person who was at the time of the marriage ceremony under the age of 18 years, and then to adjudge that a valid marriage was not effected or entered into only "if it is made to appear that the marriage has not been consummated and that such persons have not, after the ceremony, cohabited and lived together as man and wife, and that action is brought before the person bringing it has attained the age of nineteen years." It then, by subsec. 2, expressly prohibits the court from declaring a marriage void where carnal intercourse has taken place between the parties before the ceremony.

The consent of a parent or guardian of the person under the age of 18 years, concerning, as it intrinsically does, the subject-matter of the solemnization of marriage (see *Sottomayor v. De Barros*), unmistakably falls under sec. 92(12) of the *British North America Act*, and is a subject respecting which the legislature by that section is given exclusive capacity to legislate, by way of exception to the exclusive legislative authority which sec. 91(26) vests in the Parliament of Canada in relation to all other matters pertaining to the larger subject of Marriage and Divorce.

The report of the Judicial Committee of the Privy Council in the Canadian *Marriage Reference* of 1912 distinctly laid down the principle that sec. 92(12) enables the provincial legislature "to enact conditions as to solemnization which may affect the validity of the contract" of marriage. I have no doubt that in accordance with the principle of this decision, this exclusive legislative authority in the provincial legislature comprises not only the power to declare void a marriage for want of the required consent of a parent or guardian in the case of a marriage solemnized between persons, one of whom is under the age of 18 years, but the power to confer upon the Supreme Court jurisdiction to pronounce a decree of nullity for want of such consent in such case, or for any other reason which in reality pertains to the subject-matter of the solemnization of marriage.

I find it impossible, however, to assent to the view that the conditions prescribed by the provisoes in sec. 34 as conditions, not as to the validity or invalidity of the marriage ceremony, but as conditions to the right of the court to pronounce a decree of nullity in the case of such a marriage, are conditions which do pertain in any way to the subject-matter of the solemnization of marriage. The manifest intent, and the real pith and substance of these provisoes, is to prevent the Supreme Court from declaring void any marriage ceremony for want of the required consent of a parent or guardian of a person under the age of 18 years, except at the instance of the party to the marriage ceremony who was under the prescribed age at the time of the performance of that ceremony; and, even where an action for annulment is brought by such party, to prohibit the court from granting such a decree if, after the ceremony, there has been consummation and cohabitation as husband and wife between the parties; or if the plaintiff has failed to bring his or her action for such annulment before attaining the age of 19 years; or, further, if the parties to the marriage have had carnal intercourse before the performance of the ceremony. The provisoes prescribe conditions which, whether they do or do not themselves strictly affect the validity of the marriage contract, make a judicial declaration or judgment of annulment impossible in such a case. They are an absolute bar to such a decree, and in reality dispense with the requirement of a parent's or guardian's consent to the solemnization of the marriage ceremony, which the statute has previously enacted as a condition of validity, making, as they do, the neglect or laches of the party under age to bring his or her action for annulment before attaining the age of 19 years, or carnal intercourse between the parties, either before or after the marriage ceremony, conclusive, so far as the court is concerned, of a valid marriage relationship quite irrespective of the required consent of parent or guardian or of the solemnization of the marriage ceremony at all. None of these conditions pertain to any of the requisite preliminaries or formalities of the marriage ceremony. They treat of matters which are wholly extraneous thereto, *i.e.*, the conduct of the parties before and after the ceremony. Consummation and cohabitation as husband and wife are, no doubt, the natural consequences of a marriage ceremony, but obviously, whether consummation or subsequent cohabitation take place or not, could not conceivably affect the right of any person, possessing the requisite governmental authority for the purpose, to solemnize or perform the ceremony, or even the right or capacity of the parties themselves to have it solemnized; neither could the neglect or laches of either party to bring an action for annulment before attaining the age of 19 years. In my opinion, they go entirely beyond the subject-matter of the solemnization of marriage and consequently invade the exclusive legislative authority of the Dominion Parliament in relation to all other matters pertaining to the larger subject of Marriage and Divorce. . . .

It seems to me that if it is now to be held that the provincial legislatures can validly impose any such restrictions as are here in question upon the right of the Supreme or any other provincial court to grant decrees of annulment for want of the requisite consent of a parent or guardian to the solemnization of a marriage ceremony, they may quite as logically impose any other imaginable restrictions, not only as conditions to the granting of such decrees, but as conditions to the validity of a marriage, and thus exhaust and effectively control the whole field of validity. If they can prescribe the fact of no previous carnal intercourse having taken place between the parties to the solemnization of a marriage ceremony, either as a condition of the validity of the marriage or as a condition of the power of the court to grant a decree of annulment, why may they not likewise, for instance, prescribe the condition that the parties be not related by consanguinity or that there is no impotence upon the part of either as further conditions of validity or of the jurisdiction of the court to pronounce a decree of annulment in such a case?

In the Province of New Brunswick, the legislature, long before Confederation, constituted a Court of Divorce and Matrimonial Causes which, by virtue of sec. 129 of the *British North America Act*, still exists, for the determination of all matters and questions touching and concerning marriage and contracts of marriage, and divorce, as well from the bond of matrimony as divorce and separation from bed and board, and alimony. The statute establishing this court prescribes as the only causes for divorce from the bond of matrimony and of dissolving and annulling marriage frigidity or impotence, adultery and consanguinity within the prohibited degrees. Whether consanguinity and impotence are regarded as grounds of divorce from the bond of matrimony or as grounds of annulment, I venture to think that neither is a matter which concerns Solemnization of Marriage within the contemplation of sec. 92(12) of the *British North America*

Act, and that, since that Act came into operation, only the Parliament of Canada could validly legislate with respect to them, either as grounds of divorce or as grounds of annulment. The provincial legislatures may enact conditions as to solemnization which may affect validity, but such conditions must not go beyond those matters which in reality pertain either to the act or ceremony of solemnization itself or to the preliminary steps leading thereto. They cannot, by annexing to a condition which does thus concern the solemnization of marriage, such as the consent of a parent or guardian of one under age, further conditions, which do not themselves pertain to solemnization, but have to do with the capacity of the parties and their conduct as well after as before the performance of the marriage ceremony, as conditions either of validity of the ceremony or of the rights of the parties to obtain judicial declarations of annulment, trench upon that field which the *British North America Act* has exclusively reserved for the Parliament of Canada, *viz.:* Marriage and Divorce, except the Solemnization of Marriage. Such further conditions, as I have indicated, either concern or they do not concern the subject-matter of the solemnization of marriage. If they are to be regarded as concerning that subject-matter, the words "marriage and" in enumeration 26 of the classes of subjects with respect to which sec. 91 of the *British North America Act* provides that the Parliament of Canada may exclusively make laws, would, in my opinion, be rendered meaningless and of no effect, and the provincial legislatures enabled to occupy the entire field of validity of marriage, for, as I have already endeavoured to point out, there would be no condition which they could not enact as a prerequisite of the valid solemnization of a marriage, whether such condition concerned the capacity of the parties or not. "Solemnization of marriage in the province", as enumerated in sec. 92(12), would not operate "by way of exception" to the powers conferred on the Parliament of Canada by sec. 91(26) to make laws in relation to "marriage and divorce", as held by the Judicial Committee on the Reference of 1912, but by way of a complete abrogation of those powers, in so far as "marriage" is concerned.

For these reasons I think the enactment that a marriage ceremony solemnized between persons, one of whom is under the age of 18 years, without the consent of a parent or guardian of such person, shall be void, is valid as touching a matter which directly pertains to the solemnization of the marriage ceremony, and that it is severable from the rest of the section, which deals with another distinct subject, *viz.:* the conditions upon which the Supreme Court may exercise its jurisdiction to pronounce decrees of annulment; and that the rest of that section is *ultra vires* of the provincial legislature. . . .

If I am right in the view that the unqualified nullification enactment for want of the consent of a parent or guardian of the party to the marriage who was under the age of 18 years is valid and severable from the rest of the section, and the rest of the section *ultra vires,* it follows that it is or was at the time of the commencement and trial of the action enacted as substantive law in the Province of Ontario that the solemnization of such a marriage ceremony without the required consent was absolutely void. But where, apart from the enactments of sec. 34, does the Supreme Court of Ontario derive its authority to pronounce a decree of annulment?

It is argued that *The Divorce Act (Ontario)*, enacted by the Dominion Parliament in 1930, conferred the necessary jurisdiction. This Act reads as follows:

1.   The law of England as to the dissolution of marriage and as to the annulment of marriage, as that law existed on the fifteenth day of July, 1870, in so far as it can be made to apply in the province of Ontario, and in so far as it has not been repealed, as to the province, by any Act of the Parliament of the United Kingdom or by any Act of the Parliament of Canada or by this Act, and as altered, varied, modified or affected, as to the province, by any such Act, shall be in force in the province of Ontario.

2.   The Supreme Court of Ontario shall have jurisdiction for all purposes of this Act.

By the law of England a marriage was not on the date mentioned void for want of consent of a parent or guardian of a person under the age of .18 years nor has it since been so enacted. In any event the law of Ontario, in so far as it was validly enacted in relation to the solemnization of marriage, would not be affected thereby. In relation to any conditions affecting the validity of marriage or the annulment of marriage other than conditions as to solemnization the law of England, in my opinion, would apply by virtue of the Dominion Act. The conferring of jurisdiction upon the Supreme Court of Ontario by sec. 2 of the Dominion Act "for all purposes of this Act" does not therefore, I think, cover any jurisdiction to grant a decree of annulment for any cause which the provincial legislature has validly declared as a cause of annulment in exercise of its exclusive legislative authority upon the subject-matter of the solemnization of marriage.

It is contended also that the Supreme Court, apart from the provisions of sec. 34 of the provincial *Marriage Act*, possessed inherent jurisdiction as His Majesty's Supreme Court of Judicature for the Province, without any express authorization, to apply and give judicial effect to any substantive law competently enacted by the provincial legislature, such as the enactment now in question, unqualifiedly declaring void any marriage ceremony gone through by a person under the age of 18 years without the consent of a parent or guardian of such person. I confess that I have felt considerable doubt upon this question in view of the judgment of the Judicial Committee of the Privy Council in *Board v. Board*, [1919] A.C. 956, an Alberta case involving the jurisdiction of the Supreme Court of that Province, in which the substantive law enacted by the *English Matrimonial Causes Act*, 1857, had been introduced, to give effect to that law in the absence of any specific statutory authority to try matrimonial causes. After anxious consideration of the reasons for that decision, as stated by Viscount Haldane, and of the reasons for judgment of the Court of Appeal of Ontario in *Vamvakidis v. Kirkoff*, 64 O.L.R. 585, in which the history of the several courts, established in Upper Canada and in the Province of Ontario, which were finally "consolidated" as the Supreme Court of Ontario in 1881, and their jurisdiction, were exhaustively considered in the light of the reasons for the decision in *Board v. Board*, [1919] A.C. 956, I have reached the conclusion, though not without some difficulty, that it cannot be presumed in the case of the Supreme Court of Ontario, that it possessed inherent authority to entertain a suit for the declaration of nullity of marriage, and that no statutory authority existed whereby the learned trial judge could validly adjudge, as he did, that a valid marriage was not effected between the parties in this case.

Appeal dismissed.

[The *Kerr* case was followed in *A.-G. Alta. and Neilson v. Underwood*, [1934] S.C.R. 635, [1934] 4 D.L.R. 167, where Rinfret J., speaking for the Court, said *inter alia*: "The whole question depends upon the distinction to be made between the formalities of the ceremony of marriage and the status or capacity required to contract marriage. Solemnization of marriage is not confined to the ceremony itself. It legitimately includes the various steps or preliminaries leading to it. The statute of Alberta, in its essence, deals with those steps or preliminaries in that province. It is only territorial. It applies only to marriages solemnized in Alberta and it prescribes the formalities by which the ceremony shall be celebrated in that province (*Brook v. Brook*, 9 H.L.C. 193). It does not pretend to deprive minors domiciled in Alberta of the capacity to marry outside the province without the consent of their parents. Moreover, it requires that consent only under certain conditions and it is not directed to the question of personal status.

"Under the provisions of that statute, no clergyman shall solemnize marriage, unless the parties to the intended marriage produce to him the marriage licence prescribed for by the Act, or a certificate of the due publication of banns (sec. 4). The manner in which banns of marriage shall be published and the conditions under which marriage licences are to be issued are dealt with in separate sections of the Act. And among the preliminaries required before the publication of the banns, or before the issue of the licence, or at all events before any marriage is contracted or solemnized, it is enacted by sec. 20 that if either of the parties to the intended marriage is under the age of twenty-one years, a certain consent in a certain prescribed form shall be deposited with the issuer of the marriage licence, or with the clergyman who is to solemnize the marriage. That consent is required according to circumstances, from the father and mother, or from one of them, or from a lawfully appointed guardian, or from the acknowledged guardian. And it is expressly enacted that the consent so required 'shall be deemed to be a condition precedent to a valid marriage', except in certain events not material in the premises. Under the circumstances, the parental consent is a requirement similar in quality to the other requirements concerning the banns or the marriage licences. It is one of the forms to be complied with for the marriage ceremony, and it does not relate to capacity.

"It is a requirement which a provincial legislature may competently prescribe in the exercise of its jurisdiction in relation to the solemnization of marriage in the province and to which it may 'attach the consequence of invalidity absolutely or conditionally' (*Kerr v. Kerr*; *Marriage Reference*).

"In this case, parental consent was required 'as a condition of the validity of the solemnization of the marriage within the province.' Such enactment being legislation within the province's authority and the required consent not having been obtained, it follows that the ceremony itself was void *ab initio* and that no valid marriage has taken place. The appellant was therefore entitled to the declaration prayed for and her action ought to have been maintained.

"Unlike the case of *Kerr v. Kerr*, the jurisdiction of the Alberta courts to grant a declaration of nullity is not questioned. It is common ground that the jurisdictional limitations of the courts of Ontario, discussed in the *Kerr* case, present no problem in this appeal.

"It must further be understood that our judgment does not express any view as to the competency of the Dominion, in the exercise of its proper authority, to legislate in relation to the capacity to marry of persons domiciled in Canada. In the absence of legislation by the Dominion, that question does not arise here and is fully reserved. All that we decide in regard to it is that the Dominion legislation, as it stands, does not affect the present case." See also *Graham v. Graham*, [1938] 1 D.L.R. 778, [1938] 1 W.W.R. 155 (Sask.); *Ross v. MacQueen*, [1948] 2 D.L.R. 536, [1948] 1 W.W.R. 258 (Alta.); *Clause v. Clause*, [1956] O.W.N. 449, 4 D.L.R. (2d) 286.

The self-asserted jurisdictional limitation of the Ontario courts to make a declaration of nullity (see *Vamvakidis v. Kirkoff*, 64 O.L.R. 585, [1930] 2 D.L.R. 877) was removed, so far as it was within Dominion power so to do, by the *Divorce Act (Ontario)*, 1930 (Can.), c. 14, now *Annulment of Marriage Act (Ontario)*, R.S.C. 1970, c. A-14. As to their power to make a declaration of nullity based on a ground of invalidity under competent provincial legislation, see the *Matrimonial Causes Act*, R.S.O. 1970, c. 265, s. 11.]

Unlike the English law of nullity, the English law of divorce was never part of the law of Ontario because there was no such law in England until 1857. It has been held that the Dominion Act of 1930 did not introduce into Ontario the English procedure in divorce causes but only the substantive law (apart from conferring jurisdiction on the Ontario Supreme Court): see *Morris v. Morris*, [1950] O.R. 697, [1951] 1 D.L.R. 38; *Davies v. Davies*, [1940] O.R. 267, [1940] 3 D.L.R. 334; *Adler v. Adler*, [1966] 1 O.R. 732.

To what extent does provincial legislative power in relation to solemnization of marriage enable a Province to add to or remove existing grounds of annulment? Cf. *Alspector v. Alspector* [1957] O.R. 454, 9 D.L.R. (2d) 679, where Roach J.A. for the Ontario Court of Appeal said, *inter alia*: "The issuance of a licence or special permit and the publication of banns as pre-ceremonial requirements are formalities within the matters designated by 'solemnization of marriage'". It follows that a Province may make invalidity of the marriage a consequence of non-observance of its valid requirements. Similarly, a provincial legislature may validly condition the issue of a licence and the celebrating of a marriage on the attainment by the parties of a specified age: see *Ross v. MacQueen*, [1948] 2 D.L.R. 536, [1948] 1 W.W.R. 258 (Alta.).

May a provincial legislature repose in a provincial officer, empowered to issue or authorize issue of a marriage licence, authority to determine whether a foreign divorce obtained by an applicant for a licence was effective to dissolve his or her previous marriage? See *Regina v. Provincial Secretary, ex parte Walden*, [1960] O.R. 165,

23 D.L.R. (2d) 159. May the legislature authorize such officer to refuse a licence to persons who are within prohibited degrees of affinity as determined by the officer? See *Re Schepull and Bekeschus and The Provincial Secretary*, [1954] O.R. 67, [1954] 2 D.L.R. 43, recognizing that legislative power in respect of prohibited degrees of affinity is within exclusive federal competence. This does not mean, however, that a Province may not condition grants of a licence on compliance with prohibited degrees as federally prescribed.

For over a century after Confederation, Parliament refrained from enacting general legislation bearing on the subject of divorce. With the adoption of the *Divorce Act* in 1968, now R.S.C. 1970, c. D-8, a comprehensive measure was adopted, with the effect of relegating to history much of the intervening case law. This had been extensive and complicated, turning on variations amongst the provinces dependent upon what the state of the law, whether special to the province or under English law as received in the particular province was at the time of the province's entry into Canada, see *McKee,* Annotation, Law of Divorce in Canada (1922), 62 D.L.R. 1. In the face of Parliamentary inaction and hence of divorce proceedings being dealt with on whatever basis was legally relevant by courts whose constitution and procedure was prescribed by the provinces under section 92(14) of the British North America Act, the cases were often at the interface of substance and procedure. The *Divorce Act's* specification of rules governing both has obviated consideration of many of the issues formerly of concern but a few of the decisions established principles of continuing vitality. Thus *Hellens v. Densmore*, [1957] S.C.R. 768, 10 D.L.R. (2d) 561, involving the bringing into operation of a disqualification to marry until after expiration of the statutory time for appeal from a divorce decree, as a preliminary issue, represented an acceptance by a court unanimous on this point, although divided on other issues, that that was a matter within Parliament's competence as going to substance and as having to do with the capacity to marry. Being such, a province could not validate the marriage of a divorced person that took place within the prohibited period, which in fact expired without an appeal against the divorce having been taken: see *Forsythe v. Forsythe* (1965), 51 W.W.R. 257, 51 D.L.R. (2d) 262; aff'd on this point but rev'd on other grounds, (1965) 54 W.W.R. 577, 56 D.L.R. (2d) 322 (B.C.).

Legislative power to deal with the substantive law of alimony has been held to belong to the Provinces: see *Rousseau v. Rousseau*, [1920] 3 W.W.R. 384 (B.C.); *Holmes v. Holmes*, [1923] 1 D.L.R. 294, [1923] 1 W.W.R. 86, 16 Sask. L.R. 390. So too, legislative power in relation to maintenance: see *Langford v. Langford*, [1936] 1 W.W.R. 174, 50 B.C.R. 303. Equally, it is within provincial legislative power to deal with the protection of children and with their custody and support, or the support of spouses *inter se*: see *Reference re Adoption Act*, [1938] S.C.R. 398, [1938] 3 D.L.R. 497. But this has been in the absence of federal legislation on those matters which can be considered as involved in federal power in relation to marriage and divorce. See *Lee v. Lee*, [1920] 3 W.W.R. 530, 54 D.L.R. 608

(Alta.); and note the suggestion in the *Adoption Act* reference, [1938] S.C.R. 398, at p. 402, [1938] 3 D.L.R. 497, at p. 498, as to the "ancillary" jurisdiction of Parliament in respect of children arising under its "marriage and divorce" power. The new Divorce Act provides for interim orders for alimony or an alimentary pension for maintenance and for maintenance and custody of children, and also provides for maintenance and custody orders after decree nisi.

Are judicial separation and decrees for the restitution of conjugal rights within exclusive provincial authority or within exclusive federal authority, or are they susceptible of treatment either by Province or Dominion, subject to the principle of federal paramountcy? See Power on Divorce (2nd ed. 1964), pp. 1-6.

May the Province or the Dominion confer or control rights of action for damages against an adulterer, or against a co-respondent in a divorce action? See *Mitchell v. Mitchell,* [1936] 2 D.L.R. 374, [1936] 1 W.W.R. 553, 44 Man. R. 23; *Mowder v. Roy,* [1946] O.R. 154, at p. 157, [1946] 2 D.L.R. 427, at p. 432.

CHAPTER XVI

CIVIL LIBERTIES, CONSTITUTIONAL GUARANTEES,
AND THE CANADIAN BILL OF RIGHTS

REFERENCE RE ALBERTA STATUTES

In the Supreme Court of Canada. [1938] S.C.R. 100,
[1938] 2 D.L.R. 81.

Reference to the Supreme Court of Canada to determine the
validity of three bills passed by the legislative assembly of Alberta
in 1937 but reserved by the Lieutenant-Governor for the signification
of the Governor-General's pleasure. The three bills were: Bill No. 1,
"An Act respecting Taxation of Banks"; Bill No. 8, "An Act to
Amend and Consolidate the Credit of Alberta Regulation Act"; and
Bill No. 9, "An Act to ensure the Publication of Accurate News and
Information". The judgments as reproduced below refer only to the
last mentioned bill. Portions of the judgment dealing with the first
two bills are reproduced, *supra*, at p. 574.

DUFF C.J. (for himself and Davis J.): . . . We now turn to Bill
No. 9.

This Bill contains two substantive provisions. Both of them
impose duties upon newspapers published in Alberta which they are
required to perform on the demand of "the Chairman", who is, by
the interpretation clause the Chairman of "the Board constituted by
section 3 of *The Alberta Social Credit Act.*"

The Board upon the acts of whose Chairman the operation of
this statute depends, is, in point of law, a non-existent body (there
is, in a word, no "board" in existence "constituted by section 3 of
The Alberta Social Credit Act") and both of the substantive
sections, sections 3 and 4, are, therefore, inoperative. The same
indeed, may be said of sections 6 and 7 which are the enactments
creating sanctions. It appears to us, furthermore, that this Bill is
a part of the general scheme of Social Credit legislation, the basis
of which is *The Alberta Social Credit Act;* the Bill presupposes, as
a condition of its operation, that *The Alberta Social Credit Act* is
validly enacted; and, since that Act is *ultra vires,* the ancillary and
dependent legislation must fall with it.

This is sufficient for disposing of the question referred to us but,
we think, there are some further observations upon the Bill which
may properly be made.

Under the constitution established by *The British North America
Act,* legislative power for Canada is vested in one Parliament consisting of the Sovereign, an upper house styled the Senate, and the
House of Commons. Without entering in detail upon an examination
of the enactments of the Act relating to the House of Commons, it
can be said that these provisions manifestly contemplate a House of
Commons which is to be, as the name itself implies, a representative
body; constituted, that is to say, by members elected by such of the

900.1

population of the united provinces as may be qualified to vote. The preamble of the statute, moreover, shows plainly enough that the constitution of the Dominion is to be similar in principle to that of the United Kingdom. The statute contemplates a parliament working under the influence of public opinion and public discussion. There can be no controversy that such institutions derive their efficacy from the free public discussion of affairs, from criticism and answer and counter-criticism, from attack upon policy and administration and defence and counter-attack; from the freest and fullest analysis and examination from every point of view of political proposals. This is signally true in respect of the discharge by Ministers of the Crown of their responsibilities to Parliament, by members of Parliament of their duty to the electors, and by the electors themselves of their responsibilities in the election of their representatives.

The right of public discussion is, of course, subject to legal restrictions; those based upon considerations of decency and public order, and others conceived for the protection of various private and public interests with which, for example, the laws of defamation and sedition are concerned. In a word, freedom of discussion means, to quote the words of Lord Wright in *James v. Commonwealth,* [1936] A.C. 578 at p. 627, "freedom governed by law."

Even within its legal limits, it is liable to abuse and grave abuse, and such abuse is constantly exemplified before our eyes; but it is axiomatic that the practice of this right of free public discussion of public affairs, notwithstanding its incidental mischiefs, is the breath of life for parliamentary institutions.

We do not doubt that (in addition to the power of disallowance vested in the Governor-General) the Parliament of Canada possesses authority to legislate for the protection of this right. That authority rests upon the principle that the powers requisite for the protection of the constitution itself arise by necessary implication from *The British North America Act* as a whole (*Fort Frances Pulp & Power Co. Ltd. v. Manitoba Free Press Co. Ltd.,* [1923] A.C. 695); and since the subject-matter in relation to which the power is exercised is not exclusively a provincial matter, it is necessarily vested in Parliament.

But this by no means exhausts the matter. Any attempt to abrogate this right of public debate or to suppress the traditional forms of the exercise of the right (in public meeting and through the press) would, in our opinion, be incompetent to the legislatures of the provinces, or to the legislature of any one of the provinces, as repugnant to the provisions of the *British North America Act,* by which the Parliament of Canada is established as the legislative organ of the people of Canada under the Crown, and Dominion legislation enacted pursuant to the legislative authority given by those provisions. The subject-matter of such legislation could not be described as a provincial matter purely; as in substance exclusively a matter of property and civil rights within the province, or a matter private or local within the province. It would not be, to quote the words of the judgment of the Judicial Committee in *Great West*

Saddlery Co. v. The King, [1921] 2 A.C. 91, at p. 122, "legislation directed solely to the purposes specified in section 92"; and it would be invalid on the principles enunciated in that judgment and adopted in *Caron v. The King,* [1924] A.C. 999 at p. 1005.

The question, discussed in argument, of the validity of the legislation before us, considered as a wholly independent enactment having no relation to the *Alberta Social Credit Act,* presents no little difficulty. Some degree of regulation of newspapers everybody would concede to the provinces. Indeed, there is a very wide field in which the provinces undoubtedly are invested with legislative authority over newspapers; but the limit, in our opinion, is reached when the legislation effects such a curtailment of the exercise of the right of public discussion as substantially to interfere with the working of the parliamentary institutions of Canada as contemplated by the provisions of *The British North America Act* and the statutes of the Dominion of Canada. Such a limitation is necessary, in our opinion, "in order" to adapt . . . words . . . from the judgment in *Bank of Toronto v. Lambe,* 12 App. Cas. 575, "to afford scope" for the working of such parliamentary institutions. In this region of constitutional practice, it is not permitted to a provincial legislature to do indirectly what cannot be done directly (*Great West Saddlery Co. v. The King*).

Section 129 of *The British North America Act* is in these words:

"129. Except as otherwise provided by this Act, all Laws in force in Canada, Nova Scotia or New Brunswick, at the Union, and all Courts of Civil and Criminal Jurisdiction, and all legal Commissions, Powers, and Authorities, and all Officers, Judicial, Administrative, and Ministerial, existing therein at the Union, shall continue in Ontario, Quebec, Nova Scotia, and New Brunswick respectively, as if the Union had not been made; subject nevertheless (except with respect to such as are enacted by or exist under Acts of the Parliament of Great Britain or of the Parliament of the United Kingdom of Great Britain and Ireland), to be repealed, abolished, or altered by the Parliament of Canada, or by the Legislature of the respective Provinces, according to the Authority of the Parliament or of that Legislature under this Act."

The law by which the right of public discussion is protected existed at the time of the enactment of *The British North America Act* and, as far as Alberta is concerned, at the date on which the Alberta Act came into force, the 1st of September, 1905. In our opinion (on the broad principle of the cases mentioned which has been recognized as limiting the scope of general words defining the legislative authority of the Dominion) the Legislature of Alberta has not the capacity under section 129 to alter that law by legislation obnoxious to the principle stated.

The legislation now under consideration manifestly places in the hands of the Chairman of the Social Credit Commission autocratic powers which, it may well be thought, could, if arbitrarily wielded, be employed to frustrate in Alberta these rights of the Crown and the people of Canada as a whole. We do not, however, find it necessary to express an opinion upon the concrete question whether or not this particular measure is invalid as exceeding the limits indicated above.

The answer to the question concerning this Bill is that it is *ultra vires*.

CANNON J.: . . . The third question put to us is the following:

Is Bill No. 9, entitled *An Act to ensure the Publication of Accurate News and Information,* or any of the provisions thereof and in what particular or particulars or to what extent *intra vires* of the legislature of the province of Alberta? . . .

The preamble of the bill, which I will hereafter call the "Press Bill" recites that it is "expedient and in the public interest that the newspapers published in the Province should furnish to the people of the Province statements made by the authority of the Government of the Province as to the true and exact objects of the policy of the Government and as to the hindrances to or difficulties in achieving such objects to the end that the people may be informed with respect thereto."

Section 3 provides that any proprietor, editor, publisher or manager of any newspaper published in the province shall, when required to do so by the Chairman of the Board constituted by section 3 of the *Alberta Social Credit Act,* publish in that newspaper any statement furnished by the Chairman which has for its object the correction or amplification of any statement relating to any policy or activity of the government of the province published by that newspaper within the next preceding thirty-one days.

And section 4 provides that the proprietor, etc., of any newspaper upon being required by the Chairman in writing shall within twenty-four hours after the delivery of the requirement "make a return in writing setting out every source from which any information emanated, as to any statement contained in any issue of the newspaper published within sixty days of the making of the requirement and the names, addresses and occupations of all persons by whom such information was furnished to the newspaper and the name and address of the writer of any editorial, article or news item contained in any such issue of the newspaper."

Section 5 denies any action for libel on account of the publication of any statement pursuant to the Act.

Section 6 enacts that in the event of a proprietor, etc., of any newspaper being guilty of any contravention of any of the provisions of the Act, the Lieutenant-Governor-in-Council, upon a recommendation of the Chairman, may by order prohibit,

(a) the publication of such newspaper either for a definite time or until further order;

(b) the publication in any newspaper of anything written by any person specified in the order;

(c) the publication of any information emanating from any person or source specified in the order.

Section 7 provides for penalties for contraventions or defaults in complying with any requirement of the Act.

The policy referred to in the preamble of the Press bill regarding which the people of the province are to be informed from the government standpoint, is undoubtedly the Social Credit policy of the government. The administration of the bill is in the hands of the Chairman of the Social Credit Board who is given complete and discretionary power by the bill. "Social Credit," according to sec. 2(b) of ch. 3, 1937, second session, of the *Alberta Social Credit Amendment Act* is "the power resulting from the belief inherent within society that its individual members in association can gain the objectives they desire;" and the objectives in which the people of Alberta must have a firm and unshaken belief are the monetization of credit and the creation of a provincial medium of exchange instead of money to be used for the purposes of distributing to Albertans loans without interest, per capita dividends and discount rates to purchase goods from retailers. This free distribution would be based on the unused capacity of the industries and people of the province of Alberta to produce goods and services, which capacity remains unused on account of the lack or absence of purchasing power in the consumers in the province. The purchasing power would equal or absorb this hitherto unused capacity to produce goods and services by the issue of Treasury Credit certificates against a Credit Fund or Provincial credit account established by the Commission each year representing the monetary value of this "unused capacity"—which is also called "Alberta credit."

It seems obvious that this kind of credit cannot succeed unless every one should be induced to believe in it and help it along. The word "credit" comes from the latin: *credere,* to believe. It is, therefore, essential to control the sources of information of the people of Alberta, in order to keep them immune from any vacillation in their absolute faith in the plan of the government. The Social Credit doctrine must become, for the people of Alberta, a sort of religious dogma of which a free and uncontrolled discussion is not permissible. The bill aims to control any statement relating to any policy or activity of the government of the province and declares this object to be a matter of public interest. The bill does not regulate the relations of the newspapers' owners with private individual members of the public, but deals exclusively with expression of opinion by the newspapers concerning government policies and activities. The pith and substance of the bill is to regulate the press of Alberta from the viewpoint of public policy by preventing the public from being misled or deceived as to any policy or activity of the Social Credit Government and by reducing any opposition to silence or bring upon it ridicule and public contempt.

I agree with the submission of the Attorney-General for Canada that this bill deals with the regulation of the press of Alberta, not from the viewpoint of private wrongs or civil injuries resulting from any alleged infringement or privation of civil rights which belong to individuals, considered as individuals, but from the viewpoint of public wrongs or crimes, *i.e.*, involving a violation of the public rights and duties to the whole community, considered as a community, in its social aggregate capacity.

Do the provisions of this bill, as alleged by the Attorney-General for Canada, invade the domain of criminal law and trench upon the exclusive legislative jurisdiction of the Dominion in this regard?

The object of an amendment of the criminal law, as a rule, is to deprive the citizen of the right to do that [which], apart from the amendment, he could lawfully do. Sections 120 to 136 of the Criminal Code deal with seditious words and seditious publications; and sect. 133(a) reads as follows:

No one shall be deemed to have a seditious intention only because he intends in good faith,—

(a) to show that His Majesty has been misled or mistaken in his measures; or

(b) to point out errors or defects in the *government* or constitution of the United Kingdom, or of any part of it, or of Canada or *any province thereof*, or in either House of Parliament of the United Kingdom or of Canada, or *in any legislature*, or in the administration of justice; or to excite His Majesty's subjects to attempt to procure, by lawful means, the alteration of any matter of state; or

(c) to point out, in order to their removal, matters which are producing or have a tendency to produce feelings of hatred and ill-will between different classes of His Majesty's subjects.

It appears that in England, at first, criticism of any government policy was regarded as a crime involving severe penalties and punishable as such; but since the passing of *Fox's Libel Act* in 1792, the considerations now found in the above article of our Criminal Code that it is not criminal to point out errors in the Government of the country and to urge their removal by lawful means have been admitted as a valid defence in a trial for libel.

Now, it seems to me that the Alberta legislature by this retrograde Bill is attempting to revive the old theory of the crime of seditious libel by enacting penalties, confiscation of space in newspapers and prohibitions for actions which, after due consideration by the Dominion Parliament, have been declared innocuous and which, therefore, every citizen of Canada can do lawfully and without hindrance or fear of punishment. It is an attempt by the legislature to amend the Criminal Code in this respect and to deny the advantage of sect. 133(a) to the Alberta newspaper publishers.

Under the British system, which is ours, no political party can erect a prohibitory barrier to prevent the electors from getting information concerning the policy of the government. Freedom of discussion is essential to enlighten public opinion in a democratic State; it cannot be curtailed without affecting the right of the people to be informed through sources independent of the government concerning matters of public interest. There must be an untrammelled publication of the news and political opinions of the political parties contending for ascendancy. As stated in the preamble of the *British North America Act*, our constitution is and will remain, unless radically changed, "similar in principle to that of the United Kingdom." At the time of Confederation, the United Kingdom was a democracy. Democracy cannot be maintained without its foundation: free public opinion and free discussion throughout the nation of all matters affecting the State within the limits set by the Criminal Code and the common law. Every inhabitant in Alberta is also a citizen of the Dominion. The province may deal with his property and civil rights of a local and private nature within the province; but the province cannot interfere with his status as a Canadian citizen and his fundamental right to express freely his untrammelled opinion about government policies and discuss matters of public concern. The mandatory and prohibitory provisions of the Press Bill are, in my opinion, *ultra vires* of the provincial legislature. They interfere with the free working of the political organization of the Dominion. They have a tendency to nullify the political rights of the inhabitants of Alberta as citizens of Canada, and cannot be considered as dealing with matters purely private and local in that province. The federal Parliament is the sole authority to curtail, if deemed expedient and in the public interest, the freedom of the press in discussing public affairs and the equal rights in that respect of all citizens throughout the Dominion. These subjects were matters of criminal law before Confederation, have been recognized by Parliament as criminal matters and have been expressly dealt with by the Criminal Code. No province has the power to reduce in that province the political rights of its citizens as compared with those enjoyed by the citizens of other provinces of Canada. Moreover, citizens outside the province of Alberta have a vital interest in having full information and comment, favourable and unfavourable, regarding the policy of the Alberta government and concerning events in that province which would, in the ordinary course, be the subject of Alberta newspapers' news items and articles.

I would, therefore, answer the question as to Bill No. 9 in the negative.

KERWIN J. (for himself and Crocket J.): . . . the Press Bill is part of the same legislative plan that, in my opinion, is outside the powers conferred upon the provinces, and . . . the part must suffer the fate of the whole.

Other objections against the validity of the Press Bill were urged but I refrain from expressing any opinion upon them. They raise important constitutional questions, the consideration of which I prefer to postpone until the need to do so arises.

HUDSON J.: . . . I concur in the views of the other members of the Court that the bill entitled "An Act to ensure the publication of accurate news and information" is *ultra vires,* because it is ancillary to and dependent upon the *Alberta Social Credit Act,* but refrain from expressing any views as to the boundaries of legislative authority as between the provinces and the Dominion in relation to the press. It is a problem with many facets with which I hesitate to deal until presented to us in a more concrete form.

[An appeal to the Privy Council proceeded on Bill No. 1 alone: [1939] A.C. 117, [1938] 4 D.L.R. 433, [1938] 3 W.W.R. 337.

See the criticism by *Tollefson,* Freedom of the Press, in *Lang* (ed.), Contemporary Problems of Public Law in Canada (1968), p. 49.]

WINNER v. S.M.T. (EASTERN) LTD. AND A.-G. CAN.

In the Supreme Court of Canada. [1951] S.C.R. 887,
[1951] 4 D.L.R. 529.

RAND J.: This appeal raises the question of the extent and nature of the provincial jurisdiction over highways of New Brunswick. As now constituted, the action is brought by S.M.T. (Eastern) Ltd. as relator on behalf of the Attorney-General. That company is a carrier of passengers by bus under a licence to operate on named highways which include one running from St. Stephen near the international boundary bordering the State of Maine, through the cities of Saint John and Moncton and on to the boundary with Nova Scotia. The appellant, Winner, is an American citizen of Maine, who conducts a bus line which for some time prior to 1949 had been operating between Boston and Halifax over the highway mentioned. In June, 1949, he was granted a licence under the *Motor Carrier Act* for the operation of his buses, subject to the restriction that no passengers could be set off or taken on in the Province. The result was that only an operation across the Province was authorized. In disregard of that limitation, he is taking up and setting down passengers without reference to originating point or destination. . . . .

The claim made for provincial control is, in my opinion, excessive. The first and fundamental accomplishment of the constitutional Act was the creation of a single political organization of subjects of His Majesty within the geographical area of the Dominion, the basic postulate of which was the institution of a Canadian citizenship. Citizenship is membership in a state; and in the citizen inhere those rights and duties, the correlatives of allegiance and protection, which are basic to that status.

The [B.N.A.] *Act* makes no express allocation of citizenship as the subject-matter of legislation to either the Dominion or the Provinces; but as it lies at the foundation of the political organization, as its character is national, and by the implication of head (25), s. 91, "Naturalization and Aliens", it is to be found within the residual powers of the Dominion: *Canada Temperance* case [*A.-G. Ont. v. Can. Temperance Federation*], [1946] 2 D.L.R. 1 at p. 5, A.C. 193 at p. 205, 85 Can. C.C. 225 at p. 230. Whatever else might have been said prior to 1931, the *Statute of Westminster,* coupled with the declarations of constitutional relations of 1926, out of which it issued, creating, in substance, a sovereignty, concludes the question.

But incidents of status must be distinguished from elements or attributes necessarily involved in status itself. British subjects have never enjoyed an equality in all civil or political privileges or immunities as is illustrated in *Cunningham v. Tomey Homma,* [1903] A.C. 151, in which the Judicial Committee maintained the right of British Columbia to exclude a naturalized person from the electoral franchise. On the other hand in *Bryden's* case [*Union Colliery Co.*

of B.C. v. Bryden], [1899] A.C. 580, a statute of the same Province that forbade the employment of Chinamen, aliens or naturalized, in underground mining operations, was found to be incompetent. As explained in *Homma's* case [p. 157], that decision is to be taken as determining "that the regulations there impeached were not really aimed at the regulation of coal mines at all, but were in truth devised to deprive the Chinese, naturalized or not, of the ordinary rights of the inhabitants of British Columbia and, in effect, to prohibit their continued residence in that province, since it prohibited their earning their living in that province".

What this implies is that a Province cannot, by depriving a Canadian of the means of working, force him to leave it: it cannot divest him of his right or capacity to remain and to engage in work there: that capacity inhering as a constituent element of his citizenship status is beyond nullification by provincial action. The contrary view would involve the anomaly that although British Columbia could not by mere prohibition deprive a naturalized foreigner of his means of livelihood, it could do so to a native-born Canadian. He may, of course, disable himself from exercising his capacity or he may be regulated in it by valid provincial law in other respects. But that attribute of citizenship lies outside of those civil rights committed to the Province, and is analogous to the capacity of a Dominion corporation which the Province cannot sterilize.

It follows, *a fortiori*, that a Province cannot prevent a Canadian from entering it except, conceivably, in temporary circumstances, for some local reason as, for example, health. With such a prohibitory power, the country could be converted into a number of enclaves and the "union" which the original Provinces sought and obtained disrupted. In a like position is a subject of a friendly foreign country; for practical purposes he enjoys all the rights of the citizen.

Such, then, is the national status embodying certain inherent or constitutive characteristics, of members of the Canadian public, and it can be modified, defeated or destroyed, as for instance by outlawry, only in Parliament.

Highways are a condition of the existence of an organized state: without them its life could not be carried on. To deny their use is to destroy the fundamental liberty of action of the individual, to proscribe his participation in that life: under such a ban, the exercise of citizenship would be at an end. A narrower constitutional consideration arises. Civil life in this country consists of inextricably intermingled activities and relations within the legislative jurisdiction of both Parliament and Legislature; and deprivation of the use of highways would confound matters appertaining to both. To prevent a person from engaging in business as a post office or a customs house or a bank by forbidding him the use of highways is, so far, to frustrate a privilege imbedded in Dominion law. These considerations are, I think, sufficient to demonstrate that the privilege of using highways is likewise an essential attribute of Canadian citizenship status.

The Province is thus seen to be the *quasi*-trustee of its highways to enable the life of the country as a whole to be carried on; they are furnished for the Canadian public and not only or primarily that of New Brunswick. Upon the Province is cast the duty of providing and administering them, for which ample powers are granted; and the privilege of user can be curtailed directly by the Province only within the legislative and administrative field of highways as such or in relation to other subject-matter within its exclusive field. The privilege of operating on the highway **now** enjoyed by Winner so far constitutes therefore the equivalent of a right-of-way. . . .

[See also the judgment of Estey J., who said, in part:

"While it was contended by certain of the Attorneys-General that the Province possesses the power to prohibit an international and interprovincial bus to pass and repass upon its highways, no authority was cited to that effect. The Dominion of Canada was created by the *B.N.A. Act* as "one Dominion under the Name of Canada" (s. 3); and there shall be "one Parliament for Canada" (s. 17). Moreover, there is but one Canadian citizenship and, throughout, the *B.N.A. Act* contemplates that citizens, and all others who may be for the time being in Canada, shall enjoy freedom of passage throughout the Dominion, subject to compliance with competent provincial legislation."

The judgment of the Privy Council in this case, reversing in part the judgment of the Supreme Court is reproduced at p. 509. It makes no reference to the issues raised by Rand and Estey JJ. in the portions of their judgments quoted above.

Is it competent to a Province to licence associations, *e.g.*, trade unions, and to exclude from the Province or to deny existence to any that are affiliated with groups elsewhere or which admit non-residents to membership? Would it make any difference if the licence or exclusion were referable only to privileges conferred by provincial legislation? See *Forsey*, The Prince Edward Island Trade Union Act, 1948, (1948) 26 Can. Bar Rev. 1159.

In view of explicit provision in s. 95 of the *B.N.A. Act* for concurrent power in the Provinces and the Dominion (but subject to federal paramountcy) to legislate in relation to immigration, is it arguable that a Province may exclude persons holding certain opinions from entering the Province, at least where there is no superseding affirmative federal legislation? Is there a "right" of interprovincial movement of people no less than of goods which is beyond provincial restriction? *Cf. Edwards v. California* (1941), 314 U.S. 160, 62 S. Ct. 164; *Note* (1942) 55 Harv. L. Rev. 873; and see *Note* (1941) 19 Can. Bar Rev. 750.]

DISTRICT OF KENT v. STORGOFF et al. and A.-G. B.C.

In the Supreme Court of British Columbia. (1962), 38 D.L.R. (2d) 362, 41 W.W.R. 301, 40 C.R. 16.

Motion by the provincial Attorney-General to dissolve an interlocutory injunction restraining violation of a by-law (see 40 W.W.R. 278), and, by consent, treated as trial of the action.

WHITTAKER J.: This action is brought by the Corporation of the District of Kent (hereinafter referred to as "Kent") against Florence

Storgoff and Marie Shlakoff and the class that they represent being the Sons of Freedom Sect of the Doukhobors. The Attorney-General of British Columbia is also named as a defendant.

The plaintiff's claim is for an injunction restraining the defendants (other than the Attorney-General) from violating the terms and provisions of plaintiff's By-law No. 399 passed on September 18, 1962. My brother Munroe, on October 9, 1962, granted an injunction until trial. In his reasons for judgment Munroe J., was careful to express no opinion as to the validity of the by-law. . . .

At the outset of the present hearing, Mr. Wilson, counsel for Kent, admitted that certain portions of the by-law were bad for uncertainty. Counsel for the Attorney-General conceded that those portions could properly be severed. The preamble and operative sections of the by-law, with the offending portions deleted, read:

> WHEREAS the Council of the District of Kent is reliably informed that an organized group of several hundred members of the Doukhobor sect known as Sons of Freedom is rapidly approaching the District of Kent with the intention of remaining in that District for an indefinite period.
>
> AND WHEREAS many children of school age are within the approaching group.
>
> AND WHEREAS the group has neither the financial resources necessary to enable the members to acquire dwelling houses nor the intention of acquiring or maintaining dwelling houses within the district.
>
> AND WHEREAS members of the sect are addicted to nudism, arson and the illegal use of dynamite and explosive devices.
>
> AND WHEREAS the District of Kent lacks school accommodation to take care of the children of school age within the group.
>
> AND WHEREAS the District of Kent lacks facilities for the accommodation of a group of this magnitude under healthful and sanitary conditions.
>
> AND WHEREAS the arrival of a group of this kind in the District of Kent will disorganize the educational system of the School District, will be a menace to health and is likely to lead to breaches of the peace and the possible break-down of law and order in the District.
>
> AND WHEREAS the powers and authorities vested in or conferred upon the Council are inadequate to deal with the emergency created by these conditions.
>
> NOW THEREFORE the Council of the District of Kent in open meeting duly assembled enacts as follows:
>
> 1. The council of the District of Kent declares that by reason of the matters set forth in the preamble hereto an emergency exists.

2. No person . . . being a part of the group of Doukhobors presently moving from the Kootenay area or the Grand Forks area to Agassiz or the District of Kent with the intention of remaining close to the Mountain Prison for Doukhobors and no person who is . . . a member of . . . the Doukhobor sect known as Sons of Freedom shall enter the District of Kent during the continuance of this emergency.

3. Any person who contravenes any provision of the By-law shall be liable to arrest without warrant and on summary conviction to a fine of up to $500.00 or to imprisonment for up to six months or both together with costs.

This by-law was passed by Kent in purported exercise of the powers conferred upon municipal bodies by s. 218(2) of the Municipal Act, R.S.B.C. 1960, c. 255. The subsection is as follows:

(2) Notwithstanding any other provision of this Act, when the powers and authorities vested in or conferred upon the Council of a municipality are inadequate to deal with an emergency, the Council may, by by-law adopted by an affirmative vote of at least two-thirds of all the members thereof, declare that an emergency exists and exercise such powers as are necessary to deal effectively with the emergency.

It is not for me to say whether such an emergency existed as would justify the exercise by Kent of the rather wide powers conferred by s. 218(2). The council evidently felt that the authorities vested in them were inadequate to meet the situation and declared that an emergency existed. That would appear to conclude the question as to whether or not an emergency did in fact exist. If, however, that were a question for me to decide, I would have no hesitation in saying that Kent was, and still is, confronted with an emergency of alarming proportions. In what is known as the Mountain Prison in Kent Municipality some sixty-eight Freedomites are serving sentences for such offences as arson, bombing and possession of explosives. In August or early September of this year there was a mass migration of Freedomites, men, women and children from their homes in the Kootenays approximately 400 miles distant from Kent, with the expressed intention of "going where our destiny lies, with our fathers, husbands, brothers and sons at Buchenwald". Before leaving on this trek many burned their own homes. Eventually the trekkers arrived at Hope, only a few miles from Kent, where they are now camped. There are approximately 1,000 persons in this group, including about 160 children.

On September 10, 1962, representatives of the Freedomite marchers read the following document at a meeting of the Kent municipal council:

To Give the General Public A Clear Understanding of Our Present Mission, We Would Like to Publish Our Side of the Present Situation. We Take Full Responsibility for the Following Statement.

First—Our Destination

We are going where our destiny lies, with our fathers, husbands, brothers and sons at Buchenwald.

Second—Why We Are Going

John L. Lebedoff, who has the protection of the R.C.M.P., has been threatening our people with loss of life if we did not comply with his wishes, which are: *the burning of homes voluntarily.* If this was not carried out, he stated that the homes would be levelled to the ground with bulldozers supplied by the R.C.M.P. He further stated that Krestova would be razed to the ground; the old would be destroyed, the new would be created.

This shows us how Lebedoff and the Government of British Columbia have been working hand-in-hand to create the present situation. While the Government were building the fireproof and indestructible Buchenwald of Mountain Prison at Agassiz, Lebedoff was instigating the terrorism for the complete destruction of Krestova and the other districts of Sons of Freedom.

This accomplishes the plans of Lebedoff and the Government by fulfilling the purpose of Buchenwald, which is the transplanting of the Sons of Freedom from their homes to a concentration camp.

This terrorism and the consequent use of the Mountain Prison has left us destitute and homeless.

Now, we, the mothers, wives, children, the aged are going there to complete the transplanting. Why we the children follow in line with our fathers and mothers? Because we fear we will be taken again from our parents and will undergo again the same experience, cold hunger and separation as we have went through in the New Denver Dormetory.

Have you built this Buchenwald for us or for yourselves? If for us, then let us go there to join our brethren. If you find that the Mountain Prison will not be satisfactory for all of us, will not accommodate all of us, then build us a duplicate at Krestova. You make claims that the Mountain Prison is only for terrorists and wrongdoers. We ask all of you who the wrongdoers in Germany were—the Fascists and Hitlerites, those who built Buchenwald and allowed it to be built, or those who were imprisoned in it? If you judge that those who built and allowed it to be built, are the guilty party, then by comparison you likewise are the wrongdoers. By remaining silent, you share the guilt.

You consider us third-class citizens, not worthy of having homes or land, or having a family and our own way of lives, of having children and bringing them up satisfactorily according to our religious convictions. You wish to solve our problems with the complete liquidation of our group. If that is your true desire, Good! Do with us as you wish. Do with our bodies as you think necessary—soap, fertilizer, handbags, lampshades and bind your books with our hides.

The population of Kent is about 2,200. The prospect facing this small municipality was its invasion by 1,000 people belonging to a sect with a history of violence and the expressed present intention of joining those members of the sect then inmates in the Mountain Prison. These people were without housing and had no financial resources. Problems of housing and sanitation would inevitably arise. Schools would have to be provided for the children. The residents of Kent might well fear a break-down of law and order following the frustration of the Freedomites' expressed purpose of joining their imprisoned brethren. These are the urgent problems which the residents of Kent have sought to forestall by the passage of the by-law in question.

Said s. 218(2) is, in my opinion, wide enough to confer upon a municipal council the power, in an emergency, to adopt such measures as could be exercised by the Provincial Government. It cannot, however, authorize the enactment of legislation in a field assigned exclusively to the Parliament of Canada. . . .

. . . it seems clear that Kent has, by ss. 2 and 3 of the by-law, made, or attempted to make it a crime for any Freedomite to enter the municipality. This is an invasion of the exclusive legislative authority of the Parliament of Canada, unless it can be said that the imposition of punishment was for the purpose of enforcing a law coming within any of the classes of subjects enumerated in . . . s. 92.

It is true that in the preamble the by-law refers to anticipated problems of housing, education and health. Those are local problems, but the penalties imposed are not for the breach of any law relating to those subjects. The by-law is designed to prevent conditions arising which may lead to their breach. This is a laudable object, if it could be achieved by the exercise of powers within the jurisdiction of the municipality or the Province, but Kent has sought to meet the situation by the creation of a new crime. This is clearly beyond its powers.

The by-law is also designed to prevent conditions arising which may lead to a breach of the peace or unlawful assembly. These are matters relating to the criminal law and as such are within the exclusive legislative jurisdiction of the Parliament of Canada. Both are covered by the *Criminal Code,* 1953-54 (Can.), c. 51; breach of the peace by ss. 30 and 31, and unlawful assembly by s. 64. . . .

I am of the opinion that for the reasons mentioned the by-law must be declared invalid and the interim injunction dissolved. There were a number of other points of attack on the by-law which I need not consider. I may say that I have been greatly assisted by the able arguments of counsel on both sides.

If I am right in the decision I have given it would appear that Kent, acting alone, is helpless in the face of the emergency with which it is threatened. One does not like to think that the law is so inadequate that higher authority also finds itself powerless to come to Kent's assistance. [The learned Judge then referred to *Criminal Code,* ss. 64, 27 and 435 respecting unlawful assembly, preventive use of force, and power to arrest without warrant. He concluded as follows:]

These preventive measures could be taken as soon as the Freedomites show signs of leaving their present camping grounds for their march on Kent.

Anything I have said which is unnecessary for my decision on the validity of the by-law is said solely for consideration by the proper authorities, and is not intended as a judicial pronouncement. It is not for me to say what Government policy should be. Nevertheless, every citizen must be concerned, as I have been while writing these reasons, because of the problems facing the people of Kent if the Freedomites are permitted to enter their municipality.

Action dismissed.

Note on Federal Political Rights and Provincial Legislative Power

Long before the *Alberta Press Bill* reference, Boyd C. in *Re North Perth, Hessin v. Lloyd* (1891), 21 O.R. 538, at p. 542, anticipated some of the issues that were canvassed in it. After making the obvious statement that "Ontario has no legislative power over the electoral franchise of the Dominion", he went on to discuss electoral legislation in general, whether federal or provincial, and assessed it as follows:

> The subjects of this class of legislation are of a political character, dealing with the citizen as related to the Commonwealth (whether province or Dominion), and they are kept distinct in the Federal Constitutional Act from matters of civil rights in the Provinces which regard mainly the *meum* and *tuum* as between citizens. It is in my view rather confusing to speak of the right of voting as comprehended under the 'civil rights' mentioned in sec. 92 sub-s. 13 of the B.N.A. Act. This franchise is not an ordinary civil right; it is historically and truly a statutory privilege of a political nature, being the chief means whereby the people, organized for political purposes, have their share in the functions of government. The question in hand, therefore, falls within the category not of 'civil rights in the Province', but of electoral rights in Canada.

It would be taking the case too far to see in this quotation any recognition of federal power over provincial electoral matters; but, as in the case of the *Alberta Press Bill* reference in the judgments of Duff C.J.C. (Davis J. concurring) and of Cannon J., there is the intimation that public debate on political matters, whether federal or provincial, cannot be trammelled by provincial legislation. Moreover, the contrast drawn in *Re North Perth* between political and civil rights for *B.N.A. Act* purposes is relevant to a consideration of the divided judgments of the Supreme Court of Canada in *Oil, Chemical & Atomic Workers International Union, Local 16-601 v. Imperial Oil Ltd.,* [1963] S.C.R. 584, 41 D.L.R. (2d) 1, 45 W.W.R. 1, and *McKay v. The Queen,* [1965] S.C.R. 798, 53 D.L.R. (2d) 532. A bare majority of a seven-Judge Court in the first of these two cases upheld provincial legislation on principles which were denied by a bare majority of the full nine-Judge Court in the second in giving a limited construction to a municipal zoning by-law.

Although this may be stating the opposing results too broadly and without the caution that is always demanded in assessing constitutional decisions based on different pieces of legislation, it does reflect the different approaches of Cartwright J. (and Judson J.) who dissented in the *Imperial Oil Ltd.* case in which Martland J. (and Ritchie J.) carried the majority, and of the latter, who dissented in the *McKay* case in which Cartwright J. carried the majority.

The *Imperial Oil Ltd.* case involved the validity and, alternatively, the reach of an amendment to the British Columbia Labour Relations Act which prohibited a trade-union, as the beneficiary of a revocable check-off of union dues under the Act or under a collective agreement, or of dues paid as a condition of membership in the trade union, from distributing or expending any of such money to or on behalf of any political party or candidate for political office. Ancillary provisions to fortify the prohibition were included in the amendment, but it is unnecessary to detail them; and it is a sufficiently accurate characterization of the amendment for the purposes of this Note to say that it left a trade union free to make voluntary collections only for political purposes when made outside of the machinery of the Act and outside of the framework of a collective agreement.

In sustaining this legislation in its application both to federal and provincial political activity and elections, the majority saw it as a protection of the civil (industrial and political?) rights of individual employees which it was open to the Province to give in the particular context. The Province had undoubted power to regulate labour relations in enterprises within provincial jurisdiction and could fix the conditions upon which the certification and compulsory collective bargaining advantages of the Labour Relations Act would be accorded. Indeed, the assumption of the majority was that because the machinery of the Act was geared to certification so that trade unions seeking its advantages could be put on terms, it was open to the Province to embrace voluntary collective bargaining within the political ban, and, equally, to extend it to trade unions soliciting membership outside of contemporaneous resort to the advantages of the Act. In effect, trade unions operating in the Province in respect of enterprises within provincial legislative jurisdiction were held properly subject to provincial legislative control in the use of dues paid by members, a control extending to prohibition of support for federal political activity.

In thus interfering in the relations of trade unions and employers, and of trade unions and members, without conditioning the interference on the conferment of privileges that go with certification, or without limiting the political ban to check-off money received in virtue of some statutory compulsion visited upon employers or upon employees or both, the Province, in the view of the dissenting Judges, shed any nexus with labour relations. Moreover, it had legislated in general terms that were broad enough to encompass federal political activity. On this view, the challenged amendment was in relation to political activity, and invalid at least in its purported application to federal politics. This was so whether the purpose was to protect the political freedom of choice of individual employees or to limit trade union participation in federal politics through the use of union funds.

The case raised the same type of dilemma that confronted the Supreme Court in *Saumur* which had come to an inconclusive result on the constitutional issue. With the *Switzman* case (and the earlier *Birks* case), it was arguable that the Supreme Court had shown its preference for protecting the traditional political freedoms against general restrictive provincial legislation, in line with the Rand, Kellock, Estey and Locke JJ. approach in *Saumur*. Only Taschereau, Cartwright and Fauteux JJ. of the *Saumur* Court were still on the bench when the *Imperial Oil Ltd.* and *McKay* cases were decided. Taschereau J. (later C.J.C.) alone dissented in the *Switzman* case, whereas he had the companionship of dissent by Cartwright and Fauteux JJ. in the *Saumur* case. Both he and Fauteux J. remained faithful to their *Saumur* philosophy in the *Imperial Oil Ltd.* case; Cartwright J. obviously did not feel that that philosophy had any application. In the *McKay* case, Taschereau C.J.C. by joining in Cartwright J.'s judgment for the majority, enabled the Court (with the two newest Judges, Spence and Hall JJ. dividing for the Cartwright J. and Martland J. views respectively) to return to the *Saumur* approach of Rand J. and Company.

This approach was a two-fold one; first, to view the impugned provincial legislation in terms of the reach of its language; and, second, to recognize in the political freedoms an independent constitutional value which could not be submerged in general provincial legislation merely because there was a constitutional peg on which the legislation could hang. Of the by-law in the *McKay* case it could be said, as Kellock J. said of the by-law in the *Saumur* case, that "its validity is not to be judged from the standpoint of matters to which it might be limited but upon the completely general terms in which it in fact is couched". The zoning by-law in the *McKay* case forbade the display on certain residential property of all signs except those expressly permitted. Election signs were not within the permitted class, and the simple question was whether the by-law should be construed to embrace in its prohibition signs concerned with promoting candidates for election to the federal House of Commons.

The majority saw the case as involving the well known situation where general provincial or provincially authorized enactments must be limited in their reach to objects to which provincial competence extends. The Province had no authority to regulate federal election campaigning, and hence the zoning by-law could properly be construed as not extending thereto. To sweep federal election activity into the ban of the by-law merely because of the generality of its language was to denigrate the federal constitutional value involved. A Province clearly cannot extend its legislation to federal Crown property, either in general or in specific terms; nor can it do so in respect of federal Crown enterprises; and it may even be doubted whether general provincial or provincially-authorized zoning legislation could restrict the use of land for purposes (e.g. airports) within exclusive federal competence; certainly not, in the face of affirmative federal legislation.

These considerations have a bearing on the question which the dissenting Judges saw as the pivotal one. Speaking through Martland J. they considered that the effect of the zoning by-law on federal electioneering was only incidental. It is unnecessary to dwell on the thesis of the *Alberta Bank Taxation* case that the particular zoning restriction in the *McKay* case should be writ large in order to assess its constitutionality, and envisaged therefore as applicable throughout all the Provinces. It is enough to view it in the context of federal candidacy in a single constituency in which the restriction applied. The values involved in the opposing judgments emerge no less clearly on such an appraisal.

[The *Liquor Control Act*, R.S.O. 1960, c. 217, provides in s. 93(3) that "no person unless authorized by the Board, shall exhibit, publish or display any . . . advertisement or any other announcement, publication or price list of or concerning liquor or where or from whom the liquor may be had, obtained or purchased." It was argued in *Regina v. Toronto Magistrates, ex parte Telegram Publishing Co.*, [1960] O.R. 518, 25 D.L.R. (2d) 471, that this prohibition went beyond the regulatory objects of the statute, that it would, for example, prevent publications by temperance organizations, and that it was consequently invalid as an interference with freedom of speech and freedom of the press. *Held*, the prohibition should be construed as relating to advertising of the sale of liquor, and it was consequently valid.]

SAUMUR v. QUEBEC AND A.-G. QUE.

In the Supreme Court of Canada. [1953] 2 S.C.R. 299, [1953] 4 D.L.R. 641.

Appeal from a judgment of the Quebec Court of Queen's Bench, Appeal Side, 104 Can. C.C. 106, dismissing an appeal from a judgment of the Superior Court holding a certain by-law applicable to Jehovah's Witnesses. Extracts from this judgment are reproduced at pp. 395 *et seq.*, supra.

[Following the *Saumur* decision, the *Quebec Freedom of Worship Act*, R.S.Q. 1941, c. 307 was amended by 1953-54, c. 15 to provide in effect that it is not freedom of religious profession and worship to distribute the kind of pamphlets that Jehovah's Witnesses were passing out, *i.e.* pamphlets attacking the religious beliefs of others, or to make speeches involving such attacks. The amendment creates a summary conviction offence in these respects and also provides for injunction proceedings. Does the amendment effectively cure in favour of the Province the situation produced by the view of Kerwin J. that the by-law in the *Saumur* case must give way before the *Freedom of Worship Act?* An attempt to obtain a ruling on the validity of the amended statute was rejected in *Saumur v. A.-G. Que.*, [1964] S.C.R. 252, 45 D.L.R. (2d) 627 on the ground that the plaintiff had no status to sue for a declaratory judgment.

The *Saumur* case, and especially the judgment of Kellock J., was relied on in *Regina v. Beattie*, [1967] 2 O.R. 488, 64 D.L.R. (2d) 207 to invalidate a municipal by-law which purported to regulate the use of parks and pro-hibited the use of language likely to stir up hatred against any member of the public distinguished by colour, race, religion, ethnic or national origin. Is this decision consistent with *Re Cribbin and Toronto,* referred to on p. 406?

In *R. v. Harrold,* [1971] 3 W.W.R. 365, 3 C.C.C. (2d) 387, 19 D.L.R. (3d) 471 (B.C. C.A.) the accused, a member of a religious group which would gather in the city streets and chant sounds to the accompaniment of a small drum and a few cymbals, was convicted of violating a City of Vancouver anti-noise by-law. The British Columbia Court of Appeal in upholding the conviction applied the dictum of Cartwright J. in *Saumur,* (see pp. 404 *et seq., supra*) and held:

> the right to freedom of religion does not permit anyone, acting under the umbrella of his religious teachings and practices, to violate the law of the land, whether that law be Federal, Provincial or Municipal.

Leave to appeal to the Supreme Court of Canada was refused.]

SWITZMAN v. ELBLING AND A.-G. QUE.

In the Supreme Court of Canada. [1957] S.C.R. 285, 7 D.L.R. (2d) 337, 117 Can. C.C. 129.

Appeal from a judgment of the Quebec Court of Queen's Bench (Appeal Side) [1954] Que. Q.B. 421, affirming a judgment of Collins J. and upholding the validity of the Communistic Propaganda Act (Que.). Extracts from this judgment are reproduced at pp. 369 *et seq., supra.*

[In *Oil, Chemical & Atomic Workers International Union Local 16-601 v. Imperial Oil Ltd.,* [1963] S.C.R. 584, 41 D.L.R. (2d) 1, 45 W.W.R. 1, Abbott J., dissenting, cautiously reaffirmed his views in the *Switzman* case, *supra.*

The Labour Relations Act, R.S.Q. 1941, c. 162A, s. 6, am. 1953 (2nd sess.), c. 10, s. 1 provided that an association which tolerated a communist among its organizers or officers should be denied recognition. Is this provision (now repealed; the Labour Relations Act has been replaced by the Labour Code, R.S.Q. 1964, c. 141, as amended) valid in the face of the *Switzman* case?

The *Labour Relations Act,* R.S. Nfld. 1952, c. 258, am. 1960, c. 58, s. 5 provided by s. 6A that where on an application by the Attorney-General, the Supreme Court is satisfied that a substantial number of the superior officers, agents or representatives of a trade union or any body, group or organization of trade unions outside the province has been convicted of any crime such as trafficking in narcotics, manslaughter, extortion, embezzlement or perjury and any or all of them remain as officers, agents or representatives, the Court shall order that on the expiration of three months from the order any trade union in the province which is a branch, local or affiliate of that trade union or body, group or organization of trade unions shall be dissolved unless within that time it ceases to be such a branch, local or affiliate. Does this provision (which was repealed by 1963, c. 82, s. 2) offend the principles expressed by Rand J. in the *Winner* case, *supra,* or the ratio of the *Switzman* case? *Cf. McWhinney,* Mr. Justice Rand's "rights of the Canadian citizen"—The "Pad-lock" case, (1958) 4 Wayne L. Rev. 115.

A municipal charter authorized suspension of a business licence for gross misconduct on an inspector's opinion. May this power be validly invoked to suspend the licence for publication of a newspaper at a certain address because of disapproval of its contents? See *Hlookoff v. Vancouver* (1968), 67 D.L.R. (2d) 119, 63 W.W.R. 129.

In the fall of 1970 the Lieutenant Governor of British Columbia approved an Order in Council which declared as public policy that no teachers in an educational institution receiving government support

> shall continue in the employment of the educational institution if they advocate the policies of Le Front de Liberation du Quebec, or the overthrow of democratically elected governments by violent means.

Is the Order in Council *ultra vires*? In *Jamieson v. A.G. B.C.*, [1971] 5 W.W.R. 600, 21 D.L.R. (3d) 313 (B.C.) an attempt to obtain such a declaration failed because it was held the plaintiffs had no status to sue.

The Communal Property Act, R.S.A. 1955, c. 52; am. 1960, c. 16; 1962, c. 8 (since repealed by 1972 (Alta.), c. 103), limited to its holding at a specified date the amount of land that might be held by a "colony" (defined to mean a number of persons who hold land as communal property and as including Hutterites and Doukhobors), prohibited the acquisition of land by a colony without the consent of the Lieutenant-Governor in Council who might by regulation designate the number of acres that a colony established after certain dates might hold in any zone determined thereby, and created the Communal Property Control Board to which a colony might apply for leave to acquire land. The Act extended its prohibitions to prospective sellers of land to a colony; and, in addition to invalidating contracts or sales in violation of the Act, it created a summary conviction offence for contravention of any of its terms. It was held in *Walter v. A.-G. Alta.* (1966), 60 D.L.R. (2d) 253, 58 W.W.R. 385, aff'd by the Supreme Court of Canada, 3 D.L.R. (3d) 1, 66 W.W.R. 513, that the Act was valid as being in relation to land tenure in the Province, notwithstanding that it involved interference with communal living as a tenet of persons of certain religious faiths.

Compare the approach of the United States Supreme Court in *Wisconsin v. Yoder*, 406 U.S. 205. For a fuller discussion of the Hutterite way of life see *Hofer v. Hofer*, [1970] S.C.R. 958, 73 W.W.R. 644, 13 D.L.R. (3d) 1, where the majority of the Supreme Court of Canada (Pigeon J. dissenting) held that a member of the Hutterite colony expelled for changing his views to those of a faith incompatible with Hutterite tenets could not move to dissolve the Colony and distribute its assets rateably among the contributing members.

See, generally, *Sanders*, The Hutterites: A Case Study in Minority Rights, (1964) 42 Can. Bar Rev. 225.]

Note on Civil Liberties and Legislative Power

Apart from the dictum by Abbott J. in the *Switzman* case, *supra*, there is no high authority which places civil liberties beyond the legislative reach of both Parliament and the provincial Legislatures. There are no explicit guarantees of civil liberties in the B.N.A. Act— nothing comparable to the Bill of Rights (the first ten amendments) in the Constitution of the United States, which, within the limits and on conditions prescribed by the Supreme Court as ultimate expounder of the meaning and range of the Constitution, prohibits both federal and state action infringing, *inter alia*, freedom of religion, of speech, of the press and of assembly: see *Greenawalt*, Legal Aspects of Civil Liberties in the United States and Recent Developments, (1959) 2 Jo. of Int. Comm. of Jurists 81; *Covington*, The Dynamic American Bill of Rights, (1948) 26 Can. Bar Rev. 638. There is a vast literature on constitutional guarantees in the United States, and a discernible growing relevance of such matters for Canada warrants a few references: see *Chafee,* Free Speech in the United States (1948); *Abel,* The Bill of Rights in the United States: What Has It Accomplished? (1959) 37 Can. Bar Rev. 147; *Freund,* The Supreme Court and Civil Liberties, (1951) 4 Vand. L. Rev. 533; *Cushman,* Clear and Present Danger in the Free Speech Cases (1948); *Meiklejohn,* Free Speech and its Relation to Self-Government (1948); *Donnelly,* Government and Freedom of the Press, (1950) 45 Ill. L. Rev. 31; *Pear,* The United States Supreme Court and Religious Freedom, (1948) 12 Mod. L. Rev. 167; *MacKinnon,* Freedom? Or Toleration: The Problem of Church and State in the United States [1959] Public Law 374; *Allen,* The Wolf Case: Search and Seizure, Federalism and Civil Liberties, (1950) 45 Ill. L. Rev. 271; *Frank and Munro,* Original Understanding of "Equal Protection of the Laws", (1950) 50 Col. L. Rev. 131; *Note,* The Federal Bill of Rights and The Fourteenth Amendment, (1938) 26 Geo. L.J. 439; *Pound,* The Development of Constitutional Guarantees of Liberty (1957).

In Canada, as the generality of judicial doctrine indicates, the constitutional issue in "civil liberties" legislation is simply whether the particular suppression or enlargement is competent to the Dominion or to the Province, as the case may be. Certainly, since the *Statute of Westminster* there are no constitutional limitations in the field arising under any external considerations (*e.g.* British legislation) which prohibit both federal and provincial action. Legislative supremacy, diluted though it is in Canada by the distribution of law-making power, is nonetheless occasionally resisted by the Courts beyond mere resort to constructional expedients for evading distasteful enactments. Thus, in *Rex v. Hess (No. 2),* [1949] 4 D.L.R. 199, [1949] 1 W.W.R. 586, O'Halloran J.A. denied to Parliament power to authorize the detention of a person, acquitted on an appeal, pending the determination of a further appeal by the Crown to the Supreme Court of Canada. His principal concern was with the power of the Courts, a matter underlined in more recent cases by dicta denying legislative power to oust judicial review of administrative action: see Chap. XIII, *supra.* But O'Halloran J.A. went farther, as brief reference to his language shows. He said, in part:

> "It is part of the common law of England that Parliament shall respect the decisions of the Courts. If Parliament may assume the power to set aside a decision of the Court or interfere with the enforcement of its judgments because it does not like a decision or a judgment then there is really no use for Courts at all in our constitutional sense, for then the people would be saddled with a judiciary whose first law would be to decide a case in accordance with the wishes of the dominant party then in control of the machinery of the State. It would break down the independence of the judiciary and destroy the judicial system Canada and its common law provinces have inherited".

From this conception the learned Judge proceeded to the view that the preamble to the *B.N.A. Act,* expressing the desire for federal union "with a Constitution similar in principle to that of the United Kingdom", had incorporated the written constitution of the United

Kingdom, as reflected in Magna Carta, the Petition of Right, the Bill of Rights and the Act of Settlement; hence the impugned federal legislation. *Cr. Code,* s. 1025A, "is contrary to the Canadian Constitution and beyond the competence of Parliament or any provincial Legislature to enact so long as our Constitution remains in its present form of a constitutional democracy".

It is a measure of the political character of constitutional law, even under Canadian federalism, that both O'Halloran J.A., *supra,* and Abbott J. in the *Switzman* case should find inspiration for their innovations in constitutional limitations in the preamble to the *B.N.A. Act*—a statement which not only lacks enacting force but in substance refers to the political traditions of a unitary state possessing in law an omnipotent legislature. The "freedoms" in Great Britain (and in this Canada has followed the same course) are protected in the main by common law rules providing redress in civil actions against illegal governmental action, and procedural safeguards in criminal prosecutions: see *Dicey,* Law of The Constitution (10th ed. 1959), Introduction, s. 3; chaps. 4-7; appendix, sec. 2; *Jennings,* The Law and The Constitution (5th ed. 1959), chap. 8; *Wade and Phillips,* Constitutional Law (7th ed. 1965), Part II, chaps. 35-40. The private litigation aspect of civil liberties in Canada is exemplified in such judgments of the Supreme Court of Canada as *Chaput v. Romain,* [1955] S.C.R. 834, 1 D.L.R. (2d) 241: *Lamb v. Benoit,* [1959] S.C.R. 321, 17 D.L.R. (2d) 369; and *Roncarelli v. Duplessis,* [1959] S.C.R. 121, 16 D.L.R. (2d) 689. The relation of these common law rules to superseding legislation has, at least until recent constitutional litigation, raised political rather than legal issues, save in so far as there might be a question whether the overriding legislation was competent to the Dominion or to a Province. This is apart, of course, from rules of construction applied by the Courts to minimize the impact of the statute on the traditional common law. In this latter respect, the problem is one for the draftsman to consider in seeking to implement in words the policy which is being legislated.

Some of the common law protection of the "freedoms" has passed into statute law, and in Canada this is especially so in the field of criminal law and procedure. Again, the only legal issue which usually arises is that of the construction and scope of the statute. *Cf. Rex v. Mazerall,* [1946] O.R. 511, [1946] 4 D.L.R. 336, aff'd [1946] O.R. 762, [1946] 4 D.L.R. 791; *Rex v. Tass,* [1946] 3 D.L.R. 804, [1946] 2 W.W.R. 97. In Saskatchewan, a provincial *Bill of Rights Act,* R.S.S. 1953, c. 345 was successfully invoked to qualify a municipal by-law in so far as it purported to prohibit distribution of religious handbills: see *Rex ex rel. Mackie v. Naish,* [1950] 1 W.W.R. 987, 97 Can. C.C. 19, 10 C.R. 65; and see *Note,* (1941) 19 Can. Bar Rev. 49; Note, (1949) 27 Can. Bar Rev. 1248. This is a parallel situation to the decision in the later *Saumur* case, *supra,* and to the recent judgment of the Supreme Court in *McKay v. The Queen,* [1965] S.C.R. 798, 53 D.L.R. (2d) 532. A particular example is afforded by *Donald v. Hamilton Board of Education,* [1945] O.R. 518, [1945] 3 D.L.R. 424, raising the question (which was decided favourably to the parents and pupils concerned) whether a statutory guarantee of freedom of religion in school legislation was being abridged by a disciplinary requirement of singing the "national anthem" and saluting the flag. The case may usefully be compared with the "flag salute" decisions in the United States where constitutional guarantees were invoked: see *Minersville School District v. Gobitis* (1940), 310 U.S. 586; *West Virginia State Board of Education v. Barnette* (1943), 319 U.S. 624; and see *Note*, (1944) 22 Can. Bar Rev. 840. Another comparison is provided by the respective approaches of the Courts in Canada and United States to racial restrictive covenants. While in the United States reliance could be placed on a constitutional prohibition against judicial enforcement of such covenants—this being state action prohibited under the equal protection terms of the 14th amendment to the Constitution—in Canada the argument against enforcement of such covenants turned on conceptions of public policy and on rules of property law: see *Shelley v. Kramer; McGhee v. Sipes* (1948), 334 U.S. 1, 68 S. Ct. 836; *Barrows v. Jackson* (1953), 346 U.S. 249, 73 S. Ct. 1031; *Re Drummond Wren*, [1945] O.R. 778, [1945] 4 D.L.R. 674; *Noble and Wolf v. Alley*, [1951] S.C.R. 64, [1951] 1 D.L.R. 321; and See *Note*, Equal Protection and the Racial Restrictive Covenant (1955) 30 Ind. L.J. 366. Provincial legislatures have recently intervened affirmatively in this field: see *Conveyancing and Law of Property Act*, R.S.O. 1960, c. 66, s. 22; *Law of Property Act*, R.S.M. 1954, c. 138, s. 7; *Bill of Rights Act*, R.S.S. 1953, c. 345, am. 1956, c. 67, ss. 10 and 16.

A less fragile support for a constitutional limitation than the preamble to the *B.N.A. Act*—at least in respect of freedom of speech and of public debate and discussion—is suggested by Professor Scott in appealing to ss. 11, 20 and 50 of the *B.N.A. Act,* with special reliance on s. 20 requiring an annual session of Parliament: see *Scott,* Civil Liberties and Canadian Federalism (1959), at p. 21. This, however, does not go to the heart of the question of civil liberties in their constitutional significance, as Professor Scott himself recognizes: *op. cit., supra,* pp. 28ff.

There are at least three questions which must be faced. One is indicated by the judgment of Cartwright J. in the *Saumur* case, asserting that freedom of speech and freedom of religion are not separate constitutional values in relation to the distribution of power under the *B.N.A. Act.* This is surely an inadmissible proposition unless the learned Justice means only that the freedoms in question are not a class of subject. (This may easily be conceded without conceding that they are not also "matters" coming within a class of subject.) The second question is whether civil liberties are within exclusive federal or exclusive provincial competence or within the competence of both or neither. The cases have not yet given a definitive answer to this question, because, as is evident from the *Imperial Oil Ltd.* case and the *McKay* case, discussed *supra,* in a Note, at p. 917, it is still fighting ground whether civil liberties issues are segregable from otherwise valid provincial legislation in which they are involved. The third question, which in a sense should precede the other two, is one of determining what is meant by or should be comprehended within the term "civil liberties" or any analogous term. An answer to this question is a necessary basis for evaluating issues of legislative power addressed to freedoms of one sort or another.

There is nothing in the Privy Council decisions on the Canadian Constitution that gives an answer to any of the three questions that have been put. Strangely enough, the Privy Council was never required to face squarely any issue of legislative power in respect of the traditional political freedoms. If the theory of exhaustiveness of legislative power under the *B.N.A. Act* has any validity, then civil liberties, however classified, must be within the keeping of either Dominion or the Provinces as to all or some of them respectively, and this, whether or not they are independently "matters" coming within the specified heads of power. Classification is important in this context so as to permit an attribution of responsibility to a particular source, *i.e.* Parliament or a Provincial Legislature or, conceivably, both in some respects. Because, apart from the phrase "civil rights in the Province" in s. 92(13), there is no language in ss. 91 and 92 which even remotely expresses civil liberty values, the problem of classification for legislative power purposes involves as well an assessment of the relative scope of the heads of power. It may be too simple a solution to say that because civil liberties are not mentioned expressly either in ss. 91 or 92 they fall necessarily within the federal general power. "Civil liberties" is not a term of art in law, and certainly not in Canadian constitutional law which has had only recent concern with the problems posed by that concept.

A convenient classification of civil liberties, based on political and social experience, is to recognize four different meanings in the term. There are, first, the traditional political liberties, *i.e.* freedom of association, of assembly, of utterance, of communication and of conscience and religion. Second, there is legal liberty, such as freedom from arbitrary arrest, or arbitrary search and seizure; protection from self-crimination and protection of fair and impartial adjudication. Third, there is economic civil liberty, involving a transfer to the economic sphere of the notion of individual rights developed in the political sphere. Fourth, there is civil liberty in the egalitarian or human rights sense, involving not state abstention but affirmative intervention to secure such things as equality of employment opportunity or of access to services or amenities without discrimination on account of religion or colour or origin. For an elaboration of these classifications, referable to legislative power in Canada, see *Laskin, An Inquiry into the Diefenbaker Bill of Rights*, (1959) 37 Can. Bar Rev. 77. They do not all stand on the same footing so far as legislative power is concerned. Despite the *Saumur* case, it may be asserted that the traditional political liberties are within the legislative power of Parliament alone, at least so far as their protection is concerned if not also so far as their restriction is concerned. As has been admirably and exhaustively demonstrated by Rand, Kellock and Estey JJ. in the *Saumur* case, there is no tenable basis on which it may be said that the term "civil rights in the Province" in s.

92(13) comprehends the traditional political liberties: see also *Laskin, op. cit., supra,* at pp. 113 ff.

In terms of legislative power, the political liberties represent independent constitutional values which are exclusively in federal keeping. The same cannot be said of economic liberty or liberty in the egalitarian sense or even legal liberty. Whatever their content, they are respectively subject to either federal or provincial legislation, on to both concurrently, according to whether the activities or proceedings with which these classes of liberties are connected are themselves within the power of the Dominion or of a Province, or according to the aspect from which they are treated. Thus, it is competent to a Province to enact non-discriminatory fair employment practices legislation relative to industries or establishments within provincial legislative control: see *Regina ex rel. Nutland v. McKay* (1956), 5 D.L.R. (2d) 403, 115 Can. C.C. 104. But it is equally competent to Parliament to deal with discrimination, *e.g.* on the ground of colour or origin, from the standpoint of criminal law: see, for example, *Cr. Code,* s. 367 forbidding discrimination in employment because of union activity.

Note on the Development of the Canadian Bill of Rights

Over the years there has been discussion in Canada and sporadic pressure for the inclusion of a "Bill of Rights" in the *B.N.A. Act:* see W. *Glen How,* The Case for a Canadian Bill of Rights, (1948) 26 Can. Bar Rev. 759. The matter was examined in part by a Joint Parliamentary Committee on Human Rights and Fundamental Freedoms, established in 1947, in relation to Canada's obligations under the United Nations Universal Declaration of Human Rights: see (1948) 26 Can. Bar Rev. 706. A more extensive examination was made by a Senate Committee on Human Rights and Fundamental Freedoms which reported in 1950, after taking considerable evidence, on the desirability at least of the enactment by the federal Parliament of a Declaration of Human Rights covering matters within federal legislative authority. The Committee added that were it not for constitutional difficulties which presently prevent it, the most desirable step would be to write basic rights into the constitution "so that they may be administered in our Courts and so that they may become binding and obligatory alike upon individuals and upon government." For similar conclusions, see *Scott,* Dominion Jurisdiction over Human Rights and Fundamental Freedoms, (1949), 27 Can. Bar Rev. 497. If constitutional limitations in the United States sense are envisaged, there is no overriding need to appraise classes of civil liberties in the present context of legislative power. The slate could be considered relatively clean from the standpoint (even making allowance for Abbott J.'s dictum in the *Switzman* case), and the problem would be more the political one of determining what to enshrine in the fundamental instrument. Existing limits of legislative power are however, important if some statutory declaration or protection of "basic freedoms" is contemplated. They are important not only to inform the enacting legislature of what it may not do, but also to inform it of what it may do. In this setting, the question of the form of the enactment, its machinery of enforcement, if any, has merely a constructional significance for the Courts, and leaves the citizen or resident to whatever range of protection is provided by either the affirmative benefits given or the self-limitations accepted by the enacting legislature, which may be temporary only in either case.

The government of Canada chose in 1958 to move Parliament to enact an essentially declaratory Canadian Bill of Rights, operative on a federal level and without effect on provincial legislatures despite the fact that in respect of some of the matters covered by the Bill there is good ground to contend that Parliament could bind the Provinces. The Bill enacted in 1960 after intermediate study, is set out in Appendix II to this book. It is addressed to Parliament itself and to the Courts, admonishing the former not to enact, and the latter not to construe, federal legislation in derogation of the declared rights. As first presented in 1958 (and it was little changed) it was the subject of an extensive symposium examination in (1959) 37 Can. Bar Rev. 1-236; 247-262, including some comparative evaluations, especially on the position in the United States.

Section 1 of the Bill is declaratory of certain fundamental freedoms which are said to have existed and are to continue to exist without discrimination by reason of race, national origin, colour, religion or sex. Section 1 is then given operative force by its referential incorporation into s. 2 which in turn commands the courts to construe and apply federal legislation so as not to abridge the declared freedoms; and s. 2 itself contains a whole set of additional guarantees. These are essentially a statement of procedural safeguards mainly, but not completely, related to the criminal trial process.

It is now beyond dispute, particularly in light of s. 5(2), that the Canadian Bill of Rights did not freeze the federal statute book as of the date of its enactment. Nor is it open to question that federal legislation enacted after the date of the Bill as well as pre-existing law may run afoul of its prescriptions.

What have emerged as central issues in the development of the Canadian Bill of Rights are the following:

i. The role of the Canadian Bill of Rights when measured against federal legislation and the overriding issue of the relationship between the Canadian Bill of Rights and the British North America Act.

ii. The situations in which the Bill of Rights will have operative force and the related question of the effect of an infringement of one or more of its guarantees.

iii. The relationship between the prohibited kinds of discrimination in s. 1 and the enumerated freedoms in s. 1(a)-(f).

iv. The elaboration of the content of the specific guarantees and freedoms and in particular the due process clause in s. 1(a) and the guarantee of equality before the law in s. 1(b).

Robertson and Rosetanni v. The Queen, [1963] S.C.R. 651, 41 D.L.R. (2d) 485 (discussed at p. 847, *supra*), was the first decision on the Canadian Bill of Rights to reach the Supreme Court of Canada. In that case the Court took the narrow position that "construed and applied" in s. 2 meant only that existing federal legislation was to be interpreted in a way compatible with the Bill of Rights, but if it could not be so interpreted then s. 2 was spent and the prior federal legislation prevailed. On this basis the Canadian Bill of Rights could at best be an interpretation statute providing rules of construction of federal statutes, but with little, if any, substantive effect. The turning point came in *R. v. Drybones*, [1970] S.C.R. 282, 10 C.R.N.S. 334, 71 W.W.R. 161, 9 D.L.R. (3d) 473, [1970] 3 C.C.C. 355, rejecting an earlier decision of the British Columbia Court of Appeal in *R. v. Gonzales* (1962), 37 C.R. 56, 37 W.W.R. 257, 132 C.C.C. 237, 32 D.L.R. (2d) 290 (B.C. C.A.).

At issue in *Drybones* was a clash between the provisions of s. 94 of the Indian Act, R.S.C. 1952, c. 149, and s. 19 of the North-West Territories Liquor Ordinance, R.O.N.W.T. 1956, c. 60 (a law of Canada), the aggregate effect of which was that in the North-West Territories it was not an offence for anyone except an Indian to be intoxicated elsewhere than in a public place. Two important propositions resulted from the decision. First, in the language of Ritchie J., delivering the majority opinion in [1970] S.C.R. 282 at 294: "It seems to me that a more realistic meaning must be given to the words in question and they afford, in my view, the clearest indication that s. 2 is intended to mean and does mean that if a law of Canada cannot be 'sensibly construed and applied' so that it does not abrogate, abridge or infringe one of the rights and freedoms recognized and declared by the Bill, then, such law is inoperative 'unless it is expressly declared by an Act of the Parliament of Canada that it shall operate notwithstanding the *Canadian Bill of Rights*'."

While the court did not depart explicitly from its holding in *Robertson and Rosetanni*, it had nonetheless elevated the Canadian Bill of Rights beyond a mere interpretation statute whose terms would yield to a contrary intention; the Bill now had paramount force when a federal enactment conflicted with its terms and it was the incompatible federal enactment which had to give way. It is perhaps worth noting that Cartwright C.J.C., who had been unable to agree with the majority on this issue in *Robertson and Rosetanni*, now decided his earlier decision had been wrong and thereby found himself dissenting in *Drybones* as well.

The second point decided in *Drybones* (and it flowed from the first) was that the accused Indian in being convicted and punished under s. 94 of the Indian Act was denied equality before the law contrary to s. 1(*b*) of the Bill of Rights because in the words of Ritchie J., in [1970] S.C.R. 282 at 297: "I think that s. 1(*b*) means at least that no individual or group of individuals is to be treated more harshly than another under that law, and I am therefore of opinion that an individual is denied equality before the law if it is made an offence punishable at law, on account of his race, for him to do something which his fellow Canadians are free to do without having committed any offence or having been made subject to any penalty."

While not in any way retreating in principle from the pre-eminent role which it gave to the Bill of Rights in *Drybones*, nonetheless the Supreme Court of Canada has curtailed its actual impact in subsequent cases. Of these the most significant have been *A.G. Can. v. Lavell; Isaac v. Bedard* (1973), 11 R.F.L. 333, 23 C.R.N.S. 197, 38 D.L.R. (3d) 481 (Can.). These cases involve conflicting provisions of the Indian Act alone — under s. 12(1)(b) of that Act an Indian woman who marries a non-Indian loses her Indian status (and all the incidental rights which that status confers) whereas no such disability is visited on an Indian man registered under s. 11(1)(b) who then marries a non-Indian. In a 5-4 decision the Court held that the impugned provision did not offend the guarantee of equality before the law. It is not easy to distill the ratio of *Lavell*; nor is it easy to see any such difference in principle between *Lavell* and *Drybones* as would yield opposite results. It would seem however that the case at least stands for these propositions:

(1) equality before the law means only equality in the administration or application of the law before the ordinary courts of the land — it is not in any way concerned with the internal regulation of the status of Indians on the reserve. This is a narrow treatment indeed, one which was specifically rejected by the minority and one which holds little prospect for a fertile application of s. 1(b) of the Bill of Rights in the future. Indeed in *R. v. Burnshine*, [1974] 4 W.W.R. 49, 2 N.R. 53, 25 C.R.N.S. 270, 15 C.C.C. (2d) 505, 44 D.L.R. (3d) 584 (Can.) the Court narrowed the guarantee even further by holding that the right to equality before the law in s. 1 (b) of the Bill did not mean that all federal statutes must apply equally to all individuals in all parts of Canada. Federal legislation which applied to a particular group of class of people (here young offenders who were differently dealt with in Ontario and British Columbia than in any of the other provinces) did not offend s. 1(b) if it was enacted to achieve a valid federal objective.

(2) The Canadian Bill of Rights must be subject to and cannot detract from the effective exercise by Parliament of its exclusive authority to legislate in relation to Indians under s. 91(24) of the B.N.A. Act. Applying this principle to *Lavell* and *Drybones* the enactment of laws establishing qualifications for Indian status is indispensable to the exercise of legislative power under s. 91(24), whereas the enactment of laws pertaining to liquor offences is not. In a wider perspective there is reflected here the concern that were *Lavell* decided differently it is but a short step to the conclusion that the Bill of Rights would render the whole Indian Act inoperative, thereby virtually suppressing federal legislation over Indians. The answer to that contention may simply be, as Laskin J. stated in the minority opinion in *Lavell* (1973), 23 C.R.N.S. 197 at 228: "discriminatory treatment on the basis of race or colour or sex does not inhere in that grant of legislative power" and one cannot resort to the British North America Act to escape the force

of the Bill of Rights when the latter statute makes no differentiation among the various heads of legislative power under the former.

The majority of the court however, reaffirmed its position in *Lavell* in *A.G. Can. v. Canard*, [1975] 3 W.W.R. 1, holding 5-2 that ss. 42 to 44 of the Indian Act, which vest the administration of estates of deceased Indians in the responsible Minister, do not infringe the Bill of Rights. Thus to this date *Drybones* stands alone as the only case in which the Supreme Court of Canada has rendered federal legislation inoperative.

It is worthwhile to note that the Bill of Rights does not only apply to situations where the provisions of two federal statutes are in conflict (e.g. *Drybones*) or to situations where various provisions of one statute may clash (e.g. *Lavell*) so as to raise an issue of incompatibility with the Bill. It may also apply in a case where a statute or provision thereof alone must be measured against the standards of the Bill of Rights and must conform to its guarantees. This is effectively what the court was doing in *Lowry v. The Queen*, [1974] S.C.R. 195, 19 C.R.N.S. 315, [1972] 5 W.W.R. 229, 6 C.C.C. (2d) 531, 26 D.L.R. (3d) 224 as well as in *Curr v. The Queen*, [1972] S.C.R. 889, 18 C.R.N.S. 281, 7 C.C.C. (2d) 181, 26 D.L.R. (3d) 603, and *Brownridge v. The Queen*, [1972] S.C.R. 926, 18 C.R.N.S. 308, 7 C.C.C. (2d) 417, 28 D.L.R. (3d) 1, and less obviously what it was also called upon to do in *Canard*.

One situation where the Bill of Rights does not, of course, apply is in resolving a direct conflict between the provisions of a federal statute on the one hand and a provincial statute on the other (see *e.g. Re Birth Registration No. 67-09-022272*, [1974] 3 W.W.R. 363, 14 R.F.L. 396, 44 D.L.R. (3d) 718 (sub. nom. *Re Adoption Act* (B.C. C.A.)). The interesting issue which arose in *Canard* was whether the Bill of Rights can govern where the subject matter of the impugned federal legislation (administration of estates) was generally the subject of provincial legislation, but where the latter was not directly in issue. In principle there seems no reason why it cannot where the federal legislation operates prohibitively against a specified class and the court is simply called upon to assess whether that legislation in view of its purpose denies the affected class the protection of the Bill of Rights. More precisely it involves no more than measuring the federal legislation in its own terms against the standards of the Bill of Rights. This conclusion is implicit even in the reasons of Beetz J. for the majority, and explicit in the dissenting judgment of Laskin C.J.C.

There is not in the Canadian Bill of Rights itself any sanction for an infringement of its provisions, either in terms of the effect on the impugned federal legislation or on the individual who has successfully invoked one of its guarantees. Accordingly it has been left to the courts to provide the sanction. It is perhaps too obvious to state that the Canadian Bill of Rights in no sense repeals a piece of federal legislation under attack—that is a matter for Parliament. It either renders the legislation inoperative as in *Drybones*, or, as in *Brownridge v. The Queen, supra*, federal legislation may become inapplicable in a particular fact situation while otherwise remaining operative. For an individual the relevant question, at least in the field of criminal law, is whether an infringement of the Canadian Bill of Rights automatically vitiate a conviction. The answer in Canada as opposed to the United States has generally been no. There can be no real quarrel with that result where there is admissible evidence, apart from the evidence obtained through a violation of the Bill, to sustain a conviction. Conversely, in a case such as *Brownridge*, where the accused was denied the right to retain and instruct counsel contrary to s. 2(c)(ii) of the Bill and thereupon refused to take a breathalyzer test, it was only logical that his conviction under s. 235(2) of the Criminal Code for refusing to take the test be set side because in the words of Laskin J., [1972] S.C.R. 926 at 955, "the violation in this case was the very basis upon which the accused was charged." A middle ground is represented by *Hogan v. The Queen* (1974), 26 C.R.N.S. 207, 2 N.R. 343, 9 N.S.R. (2d) 145, 18 C.C.C. (2d) 65, 48 D.L.R. (3d) 427 (Can.), where the accused was also denied his right to speak to his counsel before taking a breathalyzer test. However, upon being told he would be charged with failing to take the test, and lacking the fortitude of Mr. Brownridge, he submitted, whereupon he was charged with and convicted of driving with a blood alcohol level greater than .08, contrary to s. 236 of the Criminal Code. The majority of the Supreme Court of Canada sustained the conviction essentially on the basis of the Anglo-Canadian common law position relating to the admissibility of illegally obtained evidence. The minority position reflects the importance of the Canadian Bill of Rights as a quasi-constitutional document, and indeed one wonders what primacy the Bill can really have in safeguarding the rights of the individual unless the sanction for an invasion of one of its guarantees is the exclusion of the evidence thereby obtained.

Most of the unresolved issues concerning the guarantees themselves are found in s. 1 of the Bill. In *Curr v. The Queen*, [1972] S.C.R. 889, 18 C.R.N.S. 281, 7 C.C.C. (2d) 181, 26 D.L.R. (3d) 603, Laskin J., in delivering the majority opinion of the Supreme Court of Canada in [1972] S.C.R. 889 at 896, considered the reach of that section: "the prohibited discrimination is an additional lever to which federal legislation must respond. Putting the matter another way, federal legislation which does not offend s. 1 in respect of any of the prohibited kinds of discrimination may nonetheless be offensive to s. 1 if it is violative of what is specified in any of the clauses (a) to (f) of s. 1. It is, *a fortiori*, offensive if there is discrimination by reason of race so as to deny equality before the law. That is what this Court decided in *R. v. Drybones* and I need say no more on this point."

However, in *A.G. Can. v. Lavell, supra*, at p. 900.28, Ritchie J. (writing the majority judgment) explained the above passage as follows in (1973), 23 C.R.N.S. 197 at 209: "it follows, in my view, that those sections cannot be invoked unless one of the enumerated rights and freedoms has been denied to an individual Canadian or group of Canadians. . . . There is no language anywhere in the Bill of Rights stipulating that the laws of Canada are to be construed without discrimination unless that discrimination involves the denial of one of the guaranteed rights and freedoms."

It therefore now appears that a prohibited discrimination alone which does not result in a denial of equality before the law (as that phrase was defined in *Drybones* and narrowed by the majority in *Lavell*) cannot amount to an infringement of the Bill of Rights. In fact such a finding was essential to the majority result in *Lavell*. It is no doubt also true that the extent to which federal legislation can discriminate on grounds not enumerated in s. 1, for example age or literacy, will depend solely on whether such discrimination amounts to a denial of s. 1(*b*).

While there has been fairly extensive invocation of the Bill since its enactment, not unnaturally the increase in Bill of Rights cases since the decision in *Drybones* has been considerable. (For example, between *Robertson and Rosetanni* and *Drybones*, i.e. between 1963 and 1970, the Supreme Court of Canada dealt with only six other cases involving a Bill of Rights issue. Since *Drybones* that figure has doubled.) Much of the jurisprudence has been given to developing the content and meaning of the specific guarantees and freedoms. A detailed discussion of that subject is beyond the scope of this book. Suffice it to say that s. 1(*a*) and (*b*) has raised the most difficult questions of interpretation and has warranted the most detailed examination. (S. 1(*c*) to (*f*) contains the traditional "political" civil liberties and has achieved little impact beyond its purely declaratory value). Because of the similarity of s. 1(*a*) and (*b*) to the language of the Fifth and Fourteenth Amendments to the United States Constitution there has been, in argument at least, frequent resort to American authority. In general the Supreme Court of Canada has been wary of using American judicial experience to interpret the provisions of the Canadian Bill of Rights, in part because the unique role of the Fourteenth Amendment and its relationship to the first eight amendments to the American Constitution have no parallel in Canada, and in part because the American Constitution itself stands on a different footing than a piece of federal legislation (albeit one of paramount force) in a parliamentary system of government. Rejection of the American approach can be seen in *Curr* and *Lavell, supra,* and *Smythe v. R.,* [1971] S.C.R. 680, 16 C.R.N.S. 147, 3 C.C.C. (2d) 366, 19 D.L.R. (3d) 480, 71 D.T.C. 5252. In *Curr* the Court did leave the door open (if there were manageable standards) for future use of the American concept of the due process clause as a means of controlling substantive federal legislation, but it is not open very wide.

There has been some concern that the judicial elevation of the Canadian Bill of Rights to the position of being a statute which can effectively sterilize other federal legislation, has abrogated the doctrine of parliamentary supremacy. In the words of Abbot J., dissenting, in *Drybones,* [1970] S.C.R. 282 at 299 it "necessarily implies a wide delegation of the legislative authority of parliament to the courts".

It may perhaps be stated somewhat differently that the Canadian Bill of Rights provides a prescriptive standard against which all federal legislation past and future must be measured, unless Parliament chooses to avail itself of the exception in s. 2 of the Bill and declare otherwise. Resort has been had to the so called "*non obstante* clause" only once (in the War Measures Act, R.S.C. 1970, c. W-2, s. 6(5)), but its very existence in what is still, after all, only a federal statute capable of being repealed, is at least some evidence that legislative supremacy in Canada has not as yet been imperilled.

There is an extensive literature on the Canadian Bill of Rights. See for example:

McWhinney, A Bill of Rights and Fundamental Law: Illusion and Reality (1958), 5 McGill L.J. 36

Laskin, Canada's Bill of Rights: A Dilemma for the Courts? (1962) 11 Int. & Comp. Law Q. 519

Schmeiser, Disadvantages of an Entrenched Canadian Bill of Rights (1968), 33 Sask. L. Rev. 249

Tarnopolsky, The Canadian Bill of Rights from Diefenbaker to Drybones (1971), 17 McGill L.J. 437.

Hogg, The Canadian Bill of Rights—Equality Before the Law (1974), 52 Can. Bar Rev. 263

Sanders, The Bill of Rights and Indian Status (1972), 7 U.B.C.L. Rev. 81

Leigh, The Indian Act, the Supremacy of Parliament and the Equal Protection of the Laws (1970), 16 McGill L.J. 389

Smith, Regina v. Drybones and Equality Before the Law (1971), 49 Can. Bar Rev. 163

THE QUEEN v. DRYBONES

In the Supreme Court of Canada. [1970] S.C.R. 282, 10 C.R.N.S. 334, 71 W.W.R. 161, 9 D.L.R. (3d) 473, [1970] 3 C.C.C. 355.

Appeal from a judgment of the Court of Appeal for the Northwest Territories, 61 W.W.R. 370, [1968] 2 C.C.C. 69, 64 D.L.R. (2d) 260, affirming the acquittal of the respondent on a charge of being unlawfully intoxicated off a reserve.

CARTWRIGHT C.J.C. (*dissenting*): . . . There is no doubt that on the facts, the respondent was guilty of a breach of s. 94(*b*) of the *Indian Act* and the question to be decided is whether that provision is rendered inoperative by the terms of the *Canadian Bill of Rights*, Statutes of Canada 8-9 Eliz. II, c. 44, hereinafter referred to as the *Bill*.

In approaching this question I will assume the correctness of the view that s. 94(*b*) infringes the right of the respondent to equality before the law declared by clause (*b*) of s. 1 of the *Bill*, in that because he is an Indian it renders him guilty of a punishable offence by reason of conduct which would not have been punishable if indulged in by any person who was not an Indian . . .

In *Robertson and Rosetanni v. The Queen* [[1963] S.C.R. 651, [1964] 1 C.C.C. 1, 41 D.L.R. (2d) 485] I had to deal with a similar question as in my view *The Lord's Day Act* did infringe the freedom of religion. [In [1963] S.C.R. 651] at pages 661 and 662 I used the following words:

> It remains to consider the reasons for judgment of Davey J.A. in *Regina v. Gonzales* (1962) 37 C.R. 56, 37 W.W.R. 257, 132 C.C.C. 237, 32 D.L.R. (2d) 290. At [(1962) 37 C.R. 56 at p. 58] the learned Justice of Appeal says:
>
> In so far as existing legislation does not offend against any of the matters specifically mentioned in clauses (*a*) to (*g*) of s. 2, but is said to otherwise infringe upon some of the human rights and fundamental freedoms declared in s. 1, in my opinion the section does not repeal such legislation either expressly or by implication. On the contrary, it expressly recognizes the continued existence of such legislation, but provides that it shall be construed and applied so as not to derogate from those rights and freedoms. By that it seems merely to provide a canon or rule of interpretation for such legislation. The very language of s. 2, "be so construed and applied as not to abrogate" assumes that the prior Act may be sensibly construed and applied in a way that will avoid derogating from the rights and freedoms declared in s. 1. If the prior legislation cannot be so construed and applied sensibly, then the effect of s. 2 is exhausted, and the prior legislation must prevail according to its plain meaning.
>
> With the greatest respect I find myself unable to agree with this view. The imperative words of s. 2 of the *Canadian Bill of Rights*, quoted above, appear to me to require the courts to refuse to apply any law, coming within the legislative authority of Parliament, which infringes freedom of religion unless it is expressly declared by an Act of Parliament that the law which does so infringe shall operate notwithstanding the *Canadian Bill of Rights*. As already pointed out s. 5(2), quoted above, makes it plain that the *Canadian Bill of Rights* is to apply to all laws of Canada already in existence at the time it came into force as well as to those thereafter enacted. In my opinion where there is irreconcilable conflict between another Act of Parliament and the *Canadian Bill of Rights* the latter must prevail.
>
> Whether the imposition, under penal sanctions, of a certain standard of religious conduct on the whole population is desirable is, of course, a question for Parliament to decide. But in enacting the *Canadian Bill of Rights* Parliament has thrown upon the courts the responsibility of deciding, in each case in which the question arises, whether such an imposition infringes the freedom of religion in Canada. In the case at bar I have reached the conclusion that s. 4 of the *Lord's Day Act* does infringe the freedom of religion declared and preserved in the *Canadian Bill of Rights* and must therefore be treated as inoperative.

After a most anxious reconstruction of the whole question, in the light of the able arguments addressed to us by counsel, I have reached the conclusion that the view expressed by Davey J.A., as he then was, in the words quoted above is the better one.

The question is whether or not it is the intention of Parliament to confer the power and impose the responsibility upon the courts of declaring inoperative any provision in a Statute of Canada although expressed in clear and unequivocal terms, the meaning of which after calling in aid every rule of construction including that prescribed by s. 2 of the *Bill* is perfectly plain, if in the view of the court it infringes any of the rights or freedoms declared by s. 1 of the *Bill*.

In approaching this question it must not be forgotten that the responsibility mentioned above, if imposed at all, is imposed upon every justice of the peace, magistrate and judge of any court in the country who is called upon to apply a Statute of Canada or any order, rule or regulation made thereunder.

If it were intended that the question should be answered in the affirmative there would, in my opinion, have been added after the word "declared" in the seventh line of the opening paragraph of s. 2 of the *Bill* some such words as the following "and if any law of Canada cannot be so construed and applied it shall be regarded as inoperative or *pro tanto* repealed".

What now appears to me to have been the error in my reasoning in the passage from *Robertson and Rosetanni v. The Queen* quoted above is found in the statement that the *Bill* requires the courts to refuse to apply any law of Canada which is successfully impugned as infringing one of the declared rights or freedoms whereas on the contrary, as Davey J.A. had pointed out, the *Bill* directs the courts to apply such a law not to refuse to apply it.

RITCHIE J.: This is an appeal brought with leave of this Court from a judgment of the Court of Appeal for the Northwest Territories 61 W.W.R. 370, [1968] 2 C.C.C. 69, 64 D.L.R. (2d) 260, dismissing an appeal by the Crown from a judgment of Mr. Justice W. G. Morrow of the Territorial Court of the Northwest Territories by which he had acquitted Joseph Drybones of being "unlawfully intoxicated off a reserve" contrary to s. 94(*b*) of the *Indian Act,* R.S.C. 1952, c. 149, after having heard an appeal by way of trial *de novo* from a judgment of Magistrate Anderson-Thompson who had convicted the respondent of this offence and sentenced him to be fined $10 and costs and in default to spend three days in custody. The full charge against Drybones was that he,

> On or about the 8th of April, 1967 at Yellowknife in the Northwest Territories, being an Indian, was unlawfully intoxicated off a reserve, contrary to s. 94(*b*) of the Indian Act.

The respondent is an Indian and he was indeed intoxicated on the evening of April 8, 1967, on the premises of the Old Stope Hotel in Yellowknife in the Northwest Territories where there is no "reserve" within the meaning of the *Indian Act.*

When he was first arraigned before Magistrate Anderson-Thompson, Drybones, who spoke no English, pleaded guilty to this offence, but on appeal to the Territorial Court, Mr. Justice Morrow found that there was some serious doubt as to whether he fully appreciated his plea in the lower court and he was allowed to withdraw that plea whereafter the appeal proceeded as a trial *de novo* with a plea of not guilty . . .

The important question raised by this appeal has its origin in the fact that in the Northwest Territories it is not an offence for anyone except an Indian to be intoxicated otherwise than in a public place. The Liquor Ordinance which is of general application in the Territories, (R.O.N.W.T. 1957, c. 60, s. 19(1) provides that:

> No person shall be in an intoxicated condition in a public place . . .

but unlike s. 94 of the *Indian Act*, there is no provision for a minimum fine and the maximum term of imprisonment is only 30 days as opposed to 3 months under the *Indian Act*.

The result is that an Indian who is intoxicated in his own home "off a reserve" is guilty of an offence and subject to a minimum fine of not less than $10 or a term of imprisonment not exceeding 3 months or both, whereas all other citizens in the Territories may, if they see fit, become intoxicated otherwise than in a public place without committing any offence at all. And even if any such other citizen is convicted of being intoxicated in a public place, the only penalty provided by the Ordinances is "a fine not exceeding $50 or . . . imprisonment for a term not exceeding 30 days or . . . both fine and imprisonment."

The argument which was successfully advanced by the respondent before Mr. Justice Morrow and before the Court of Appeal was that because of this legislation, Indians in the Northwest Territories, by reason of their race, are denied "equality before the law" with their fellow Canadians, and that s. 94(*b*) of the *Indian Act* therefore authorizes the abrogation, abridgement or infringement of one of the human rights and fundamental freedoms recognized and declared as existing in Canada without discrimination by reason of race, pursuant to the provisions of the *Canadian Bill of Rights*, Statutes of Canada 8-9 Eliz. II, c. 44 (hereinafter sometimes referred to as "The Bill of Rights" or "The Bill") which provides, *inter alia*:

1. It is hereby recognized and declared that in Canada there have existed and shall continue to exist without discrimination by reason of race, national origin, colour, religion or sex, the following human rights and fundamental freedoms, namely.

* * *

(*b*) the right of the individual to equality before the law and the protection of the law:

* * *

2. Every law of Canada shall, unless it is expressly declared by an Act of the Parliament of Canada that it shall operate notwithstanding the Canadian Bill of Rights, be so construed and applied as not to abrogate, abridge or infringe, or to authorize the abrogation, abridgement or infringement of any of the rights or freedoms herein recognized and declared

* * *

5. (2) The expression of 'law of Canada' in Part I means an Act of the Parliament of Canada enacted before or after the coming into force of this Act, any order, rule or regulation thereunder, and any law in force in Canada or in any part of Canada at the commencement of this Act that is subject to be repealed, abolished or altered by the Parliament of Canada.

The Court of Appeal agreed with Mr. Justice Morrow that s. 94(*b*) of the *Indian Act* is rendered inoperative by reason of this legislation and the Notice to appeal to this Court is limited to the single ground.

That the Court of Appeal in the Northwest Territories in upholding the decision of the Territorial Court of the Northwest Territories erred in acquitting the respondent of "an offence contrary to s. 94(*b*) of the Indian Act, R.S.C. 1952 Ch. 149 on the ground that s. 94 of the Indian Act is rendered inoperative by reason of the Canadian Bill of Rights, Stat. Can. 1960 Ch. 44."

It was contended on behalf of the appellant that the reasoning and conclusion of the courts below make the question of whether s. 94 has been rendered inoperative by the *Bill of Rights* dependent upon whether or not the law of any province or territory makes it an offence to be intoxicated otherwise than in a public place and that its operation could therefore not only vary from place to place in Canada but also from time to time, depending upon amendments which might be made to the provincial or territorial legislation. I can, however, find no room for the application of this argument in the present case as the ordinance in question is a law of Canada within the meaning of s. 5(2) of the *Bill of Rights* (see *Northwest Territories Act*, R.S.C. 1952, c. 195, s. 17), and it is a law of general application in the territories, whereas the *Indian Act* is, of course, also a law of Canada although it has special application to Indians alone.

The question of whether s. 94 of the *Indian Act* is rendered inoperative by reason of the provisions of the *Bill of Rights* on the ground that it abrogates, abridges or infringes the right of Canadians of the Indian race to "equality before the law" was considered by the Court of Appeal of British Columbia in *Regina v. Gonzales* (1962), 37 W.W.R. 257, 37 C.R. 56, 132 C.C.C. 237, 32 D.L.R. (2d) 290, where Tysoe J.A., speaking for the majority of the Court, concluded that:

> Sec. 94(a) of the *Indian Act* does not abrogate or infringe the right of the appellant to 'equality before the law' as I understand it. Sec. 2 of the *Canadian Bill of Rights* does not therefore affect it.

In reaching the same conclusion, Davey J.A., (as he then was) who wrote separate reasons for judgment from the other two members of the Court, took the view that s. 1 of the *Bill of Rights* should be treated as merely providing a canon of construction for the interpretation of legislation existing at the time when the statute was enacted. The learned judge said:

> In so far as existing legislation does not offend against any of the matters specifically mentioned in clauses (a) to (g) of sec. 2, but is said to otherwise infringe upon some of the human rights and fundamental freedoms declared in sec. 1, in my opinion the section does not repeal such legislation either expressly or by implication. On the contrary, it expressly recognizes the continued existence of such legislation, but provides that it shall be construed and applied so as not to derogate from those rights and freedoms. By that it seems merely to provide a canon or rule of interpretation for such legislation. The very language of sec. 2 '. . . be so construed and applied as not to abrogate . . .' assumes that the prior Act may be sensibly construed and applied in a way that will avoid derogating from the rights and freedoms declared in sec. 1. If the prior legislation cannot be so construed and applied sensibly, then the effect of sec. 2 is exhausted, and the prior legislation must prevail according to its plain meaning.
>
> The application of the rule of construction to existing legislation may require a change in the judicial interpretation of some statutes where the language permits and thus change the law.

The difficulty with sec. 94(a) of the *Indian Act* is that it admits of no construction or application that would avoid conflict with sec. 1(b) of the *Canadian Bill of Rights* as appellant's counsel interprets it. Since the effect of the *Canadian Bill of Rights* is not to repeal such legislation, it is the duty of the courts to apply sec. 94(a) in the only way its plain language permits, and that the learned magistrate did when he convicted.

This proposition appears to me to strike at the very foundations of the *Bill of Rights* and to convert it from its apparent character as a statutory declaration of the fundamental human rights and freedoms which it recognizes, into being little more than a rule for the construction of federal statutes, but as this approach has found favour with some eminent legal commentators, it seems to me to be important that priority should be given to a consideration of it. . . .

I am, however, with respect, of the opinion that Mr. Justice Davey's reasoning is untenable on another ground. The result of that reasoning is to conclude that any law of Canada which can only be "construed and applied sensibly" so that it offends against the *Bill of Rights,* is to operate notwithstanding the provisions of that Bill. I am unable to reconcile this interpretation with the opening words of s. 2 where it is provided that:

> Every law of Canada shall, *unless it is expressly declared by an Act of the Parliament of Canada that it shall operate notwithstanding the Canadian Bill of Rights,* be so construed and applied as not to abrogate . . .

(The italics are my own.)

If Mr. Justice Davey's reasoning were correct and the *Bill of Rights* were to be construed as meaning that all laws of Canada which clearly offend the Bill were to operate notwithstanding its provisions, then the words which I have italicized in s. 2 would be superfluous unless it be suggested that Parliament intended to reserve unto itself the right to exclude from the effect of the *Bill of Rights* only such statutes as are unclear in their meaning.

It seems to me that a more realistic meaning must be given to the words in question and they afford, in my view, the clearest indication that s. 2 is intended to mean and does mean that if a law of Canada cannot be "sensibly construed and applied" so that it does not abrogate, abridge or infringe one of the rights and freedoms recognized and declared by the Bill, then such law is inoperative "unless it is expressly declared by an Act of the Parliament of Canada that it shall operate notwithstanding the *Canadian Bill of Rights*".

I think a declaration by the courts that a section or portion of a section of a statute is inoperative is to be distinguished from the repeal of such a section and is to be confined to the particular circumstances of the case in which the declaration is made. The situation appears to me to be somewhat analogous to a case where valid provincial legislation in an otherwise unoccupied field ceases to be operative by reason of conflicting federal legislation.

I think it is desirable at this stage to deal with the submission made on behalf of the appellant to the effect that the rights and freedoms recognized and declared by the *Bill of Rights* must have reference to *and be circumscribed by* the laws of Canada as they existed on the 10th of August, 1960, when the Bill was passed, which laws included s. 94 of the *Indian Act.* This submission is based in large measure on the following paragraph from the reasons for judgment of this Court in *Robertson and Rosetanni v. The Queen, supra*, where it was said:

> It is to be noted at the outset that the *Canadian Bill of Rights* is not concerned with 'human rights and fundamental freedoms' in any abstract sense but rather with such rights and freedoms as existed in Canada immediately before the statute was enacted (see also s. 5(1)). It is therefore the 'religious freedom' then existing in this country that is safeguarded by the provisions of s. 2 . . .

In considering this contention, it became necessary to examine the decided cases in order to determine what was the accepted meaning of "freedom of religion" as it existed in Canada immediately before the *Bill of Rights* was enacted and the last-quoted excerpt from the reasons for judgment must, in my view, be read in this sense. This appears to me to be confirmed by the succeeding paragraph of these reasons where it is said:

> It is accordingly of first importance to understand the concept of religious freedom which was recognized in this country before the enactment of the *Bill of Rights* and after the enactment of the *Lord's Day Act* in its present form.

If it had been accepted that the right to "freedom of religion" as declared in the *Bill of Rights* was circumscribed by the provisions of the Canadian statutes in force at the date of its enactment, there would have been no need, in determining the validity of the *Lord's Day Act* to consider the authorities in order to examine the situation in light of the concept of religious freedom which was recognized in Canada at the time of the enactment of the *Bill of Rights*. It would have been enough to say that "freedom of religion" as used in the Bill must mean freedom of religion subject to the provisions of the *Lord's Day Act*. This construction would, however, have run contrary to the provisions of s. 5(2) of the Bill which makes it applicable to every "Act of the Parliament of Canada enacted before or after the coming into force of this Act."

In any event, it was not necessary to decide this question in *Robertson and Rosetanni* because it was found that the impugned provisions of the *Lord's Day Act* and the *Bill of Rights* were not in conflict, and I accordingly do not consider that case to be any authority for the suggestion that the *Bill of Rights* is to be treated as being subject to federal legislation existing at the time of its enactment, and more particularly I do not consider that the provisions of s. 1(*b*) of the *Bill of Rights* are to be treated as being in any way limited or affected by the terms of s. 94(*b*) of the *Indian Act*.

The right which is here at issue is "the right of the individual to equality before the law and the protection of the law". Mr. Justice Tysoe, who wrote the reasons for judgment on behalf of the majority of the Court of Appeal of British Columbia in the *Gonzales* case, *supra*, expressed the opinion that as these words occur in the *Bill of Rights* they mean

A right of every person to *whom a particular law relates or extends*, no matter what may be a person's race, national origin, colour, religion or sex, to stand on an equal footing with every other person to whom a particular law relates, or extends and a right to the protection of the law.

(The italics are Mr. Justice Tysoe's)

Like the members of the courts below, I cannot agree with this interpretation pursuant to which it seems to me that the most glaring discriminatory legislation against a racial group would have to be construed as recognizing the right of each of its individual members "to equality before the law", so long as all the other members are being discriminated against in the same way.

I think that the word "law" as used in s. 1(b) of the *Bill of Rights* is to be construed as meaning "the law of Canada" as defined in s. 5(2) (i.e. Acts of the Parliament of Canada and any orders, rules or regulations thereunder) and without attempting any exhaustive definition of "equality before the law" I think that s. 1(b) means at least that no individual or group of individuals is to be treated more harshly than another under the law, and I am therefore of opinion that an individual is denied equality before the law if it is made an offence punishable at law, on account of his race, for him to do something which his fellow Canadians are free to do without having committed any offence or having been made subject to any penalty.

It is only necessary for the purpose of deciding this case for me to say that in my opinion s. 94(b) of the *Indian Act* is a law of Canada which creates such an offence and that it can only be construed in such manner that its application would operate so as to abrogate, abridge or infringe one of the rights declared and recognized by the *Bill of Rights*. For the reasons which I have indicated, I am therefore of opinion that s. 94 (b) is inoperative.

For the purpose of determining the issue raised by this appeal it is unnecessary to express any opinion respecting the operation of any other section of the *Indian Act*.

For all the above reasons I would dismiss this appeal.

Since writing the above I have had the advantage of reading the reasons for judgment prepared by the Chief Justice and by Mr. Justice Pigeon which, when read together, appear to me to lead to the conclusion that, even on the assumption that the application of the provisions of prior federal legislation has the effect of denying equality before the law, and thus discriminating against, a sector of the population "by reason of race", they must nevertheless be given full effect notwithstanding the provisions of the *Bill of Rights*. In view of this conclusion, I find it necessary to restate the position which I take in the matter.

I am in full agreement with the Chief Justice that the question here raised was not decided in the case of *Robertson and Rosetanni v. Her Majesty the Queen, supra,* and that this is the first occasion on which it has become necessary for this Court to decide it.

In my view under the provisions of s. 1 of the *Bill of Rights* "the right of the individual to equality before the law" "without discrimination by reason of race" is recognized as a right which exists in Canada, and by ss. 2 and 5 of that Bill it is provided that every law of Canada enacted before or after the coming into force of the Bill, unless Parliament makes an express declaration to the contrary, is to be "so construed and applied as not to abrogate, abridge or infringe or to authorize the abrogation, abridgement or infringement" of any of the rights so recognized and declared.

It may well be that the implementation of the *Canadian Bill of Rights* by the courts can give rise to great difficulties, but in my view full effect must be given to the terms of s. 2 thereof.

The present case discloses laws of Canada which abrogate, abridge and infringe the right of an individual Indian to equality before the law and in my opinion if those laws are to be applied in accordance with the express language used by Parliament in s. 2 of the *Bill of Rights*, then s. 94(*b*) of the *Indian Act* must be declared to be inoperative.

It appears to me to be desirable to make it plain that these reasons for judgment are limited to a situation in which, under the laws of Canada, it is made an offence punishable at law on account of race, for a person to do something which all Canadians who are not members of that race may do with impunity; in my opinion the same considerations do not by any means apply to all the provisions of the *Indian Act*.

ABBOTT J. (*dissenting*): . . . The interpretation of the *Bill of Rights*, adopted by the courts below, necessarily implies a wide delegation of the legislative authority of Parliament to the courts. The power to make such a delegation cannot be questioned but, in my view, it would require the plainest words to impute to Parliament an intention to extend to the courts, such an invitation to engage in judicial legislation. I cannot find that intention expressed in s. 2 of the *Bill*. On the contrary, I share the opinion expressed by the Chief Justice, by my brother Pigeon and by Davey J.A., as he then was, in the *Gonzales* case that, with respect to existing legislation, the section provides merely a canon or rule of interpretation for such legislation.

I would dispose of the appeal as proposed by my brother Pigeon.

HALL J.: I agree with the reasons of my brother Ritchie and wish only to add some observations regarding the decision in *Regina v. Gonzales* (1962), 37 W.W.R. 257, 37 C.R. 56, 132 C.C.C. 237, 32 D.L.R. (2d) 290.

The concept that the Canadian Bill of Rights is operative in the face of a law of Canada only when that law does not give equality to all persons within the class to whom that particular law extends or relates, as it was expressed by Tysoe J.A. at p. 264:

> Coming now to sec. 1(*b*) of the *Canadian Bill of Rights*. The meaning of the word "equality" is well known. In my opinion, the word "before" in the expression "equality before the law," in the sense in which that expression is used in sec. 1(*b*) means "in the presence of." It seems to me this is the key to the correct interpretation of the expression and makes it clear that "equality before the law" has nothing to do with the application of the law equally to everyone and equal laws for everyone in the sense for which appellant's counsel contends, namely, the same laws for all persons, but to the position occupied by persons to whom a law relates or extends. They shall be entitled to have the law as it exists applied

equally and without fear or favour to all persons to whom it relates or extends.

is analogous to the position taken by the Supreme Court of the United States in *Plessy v. Ferguson* (1896), 163 U.S. 537 and which was wholly rejected by the same Court in its historic desegregation judgment *Brown v. Board of Education* (1953), 347 U.S. 483.

In *Plessy v. Ferguson*, the Court had held that under the "separate but equal" doctrine equality of treatment is accorded when the races are provided substantially equal facilities even though these facilities be separate. In *Brown v. Board of Education*, the Court held the "separate but equal" doctrine to be totally invalid.

The social situations in *Brown v. Board of Education* and in the instant case are, of course, very different, but the basic philosophic concept is the same. The Canadian Bill of Rights is not fulfilled if it merely equates Indians with Indians in terms of equality before the law, but can have validity and meaning only when subject to the single exception set out in s. 2 it is seen to repudiate discrimination in every law of Canada by reason of race, national origin, colour, religion or sex in respect of the human rights and fundamental freedoms set out in s. 1 in whatever way that discrimination may manifest itself not only as between Indian and Indian but as between all Canadians whether Indian or non-Indian.

PIGEON J. (*dissenting*): . . . In the instant case, the question whether all existing legislation should be considered as in accordance with the non-discrimination principle cannot fail to come immediately to mind seeing that it arises directly out of head 24 of s. 91 of the *B.N.A. Act* whereby Parliament has exclusive legislative authority over "Indians, and Lands reserved for the Indians" . . .

If one of the effects of the *Canadian Bill of Rights* is to render inoperative all legal provisions whereby Indians as such are not dealt with in the same way as the general public, the conclusion is inescapable that Parliament, by the enactment of the *Bill* has not only fundamentally altered the status of the Indians in that indirect fashion but has also made any future use of federal legislative authority over them subject to the requirement of expressly declaring every time "that the law shall operate notwithstanding the *Canadian Bill of Rights*". I find it very difficult to believe that Parliament so intended when enacting the *Bill*. If a virtual suppression of federal legislation over Indians as such was meant, one would have expected this important change to be made explicitly not surreptitiously so to speak.

In s. 2, the crucial words are that every law of Canada shall, subject to the exception just noted, "be so construed and applied as not to abrogate, abridge or infringe" any of the rights and freedoms recognized and declared in the *Bill*. The question is whether those words enact something more than a rule of construction. Of themselves, it seems to me that they do not. Certainly the word "construed" implies nothing else. Does the word "applied" express a different intention? I do not think so and, even if this may appear a trite saying, I must point out that what respondent asks the Court to do and what the Courts below have effectively done is not to apply the statute, the Indian Act, but to decline to apply it.

The strongest argument against viewing s. 2 as a canon of construction is undoubtedly that the exception "unless it is expressly declared by an Act of the Parliament of Canada that it shall operate notwithstanding the *Canadian Bill of Rights*" is thereby deprived of any practical meaning. It cannot be denied that the operation of a rule of construction is not normally subject to such a qualification. On the contrary, the principle is that it has no effect against the clearly expressed will of Parliament in whatever form it is put.

On the other hand, in seeking to give effect to some words in s. 2 that cannot for obvious reasons be applicable to any existing law, one must always bear in mind the very starting point of the *Bill*, namely that the rights and freedoms therein recognized are declared as existing, not as being introduced or expanded. If in s. 1 the Act means what it says and recognizes and declares *existing* rights and freedoms only, nothing more than proper construction of existing laws in accordance with the *Bill* is required to accomplish the intended result. There can never be any necessity for declaring any of them inoperative as coming in conflict with the rights and freedoms defined in the *Bill* seeing that these are declared as existing in them. Thus, it appears to me that s. 2 cannot be construed as suggested by respondent without coming in conflict with s. 1.

If, with respect to existing legislation, we had to choose between reading s. 1 as written and failing to adopt a construction of s. 2 that gives some meaningful effect to the exception, it seems to me that the choice should be in favour of giving paramount effect to s. 1. It is the provision establishing the principle on which the whole Act rests.

Another compelling reason is the presumption against implicit alteration of the law, Parliament must not be presumed to have intended to depart from the existing law any further than expressly stated . . .

Appeal dismissed.

[If the *Drybones* case had taken place in the province of Alberta, where there was provincial legislation identical in terms to the Liquor Ordinance of the Northwest Territories, would the result have been the same?]

A.-G. CAN. v. LAVELL; ISAAC v. BEDARD

In the Supreme Court of Canada. (1973), 23 C.R.N.S. 197, 11 R.F.L. 333, 38 D.L.R. (3d) 481.

APPEALS from decisions of the Federal Court of Appeal, [1971] F.C. 347, [1972] 1 O.R. 396n, 14 Cr. L.Q. 236, 22 D.L.R. (3d) 188, and the Supreme Court of Ontario, declaring provisions of the Indian Acts inoperative because of *The Canadian Bill of Rights*.

RITCHIE J.: I have had the advantage of reading the reasons for judgment prepared for delivery by my brother Laskin.

These appeals, which were heard together, are from two judgments holding that the provisions of s. 12(1)(*b*) of the *Indian Act*, R.S.C. 1970, c. I-6, are rendered inoperative by s. 1(*b*) of the *Canadian Bill of Rights*, R.S.C. 1970, App. III, as denying equality before the law to the two respondents.

Both respondents were registered Indians and "band" members within the meaning of s. 11(b) of the *Indian Act* when they elected to marry non-Indians and thereby relinquished their status as Indians in conformity with the said s. 12(1)(b) which reads as follows:

"12(1)   The following persons are not entitled to be registered, namely, . . .

"(b)   a woman who married a person who is not an Indian, unless that woman is subsequently the wife or widow of a person described in section 11."

It is contended on behalf of both respondents that s. 12(1)(b) of the Act should be held to be inoperative as discriminating between Indian men and women and as being in conflict with the provisions of the *Canadian Bill of Rights* and particularly s. 1 thereof which provides:

"1.   It is hereby recognized and declared that in Canada there have existed and shall continue to exist without discrimination by reason of race, national origin, colour, religion or sex, the following human rights and fundamental freedoms, namely, . . .

"(b)   the right of the individual to equality before the law and the protection of the law; . . ."

There cannot, in my view, be any doubt that whatever may have been achieved by the *Bill of Rights*, it is not effective to amend or in any way alter the terms of the *British North America Act* (1867), and it is clear from the third recital in the preamble that the Bill was intended to "reflect the respect of Parliament for its constitutional authority", so that wherever any question arises as to the effect of any of the provisions of the Bill, it is to be resolved within the framework of the *B.N.A. Act*.

It follows, in my view, that the effect of the *Bill of Rights* on the Indian Act can only be considered in light of the provisions of s. 91(24) of the *B.N.A. Act* whereby the subject of "Indians, and Lands reserved for the Indians" is assigned exclusively to the legislative authority of the Parliament of Canada.

It is true that under s. 88 of the *Indian Act* laws of general application in any province are made applicable to and in respect of Indians in the province *except to the extent that such laws make provision for any matter for which provision is made by or under the Indian Act.* But the incorporation of these laws as a part of the Act in no way signifies a relinquishment of Parliament's exclusive legislative authority over Indians, and in any event, the property and civil rights of members of Indian bands living on reserves, which is what we are here concerned with, are matters for which express provision is made by the *Indian Act* and which can only apply to Indians as distinct from other Canadians.

In my opinion the exclusive legislative authority vested in Parliament under s. 91(24) could not have been effectively exercised without enacting laws establishing the qualifications required to entitle persons to status as Indians and to the use and benefit of Crown "Lands reserved for the Indians". The legislation enacted to this end was, in my view, necessary for the implementation of the authority so vested in Parliament under the constitution.

To suggest that the provisions of the *Bill of Rights* have the effect of making the whole *Indian Act* inoperative as discriminatory is to assert that the Bill has rendered Parliament powerless to exercise the authority entrusted to it under the constitution of enacting legislation which treats Indians living on reserves differently from other Canadians in relation to their property and civil rights. The proposition that such a wide effect is to be given to the *Bill of Rights* was expressly reserved by the majority of this Court in the case of *Regina v. Drybones*, [1970] S.C.R. 282 at 298, 10 C.R.N.S. 334, 71 W.W.R. 161, [1970] 3 C.C.C. 355, 9 D.L.R. (3d) 473, to which reference will hereafter be made, and I do not think that it can be sustained.

What is at issue here is whether the *Bill of Rights* is to be construed as rendering inoperative one of the conditions imposed by Parliament for the use and occupation of Crown lands reserved for Indians. These conditions were imposed as a necessary part of the structure created by Parliament for the internal administration of the life of Indians on reserves and their entitlement to the use and benefit of Crown lands situate thereon; they were thus imposed in discharge of Parliament's constitutional function under s. 91(24) and in my view can only be changed by plain statutory language expressly enacted for the purpose. It does not appear to me that Parliament can be taken to have made or intended to make such a change by the use of broad general language directed at the statutory proclamation of the fundamental rights and freedoms enjoyed by all Canadians, and I am therefore of opinion that the Bill of Rights had no such effect.

The responsibility of the Parliament of Canada in relation to the internal administration of the life of Indians on reserves is succinctly stated by Rand J. in *St. Ann's Island Shooting & Fishing Club Ltd. v. The King*, [1950] S.C.R. 211 at 219, [1950] 2 D.L.R. 225, where he was dealing with the effect of s. 51 of the *Indian Act*, R.S.C. 1906, c. 81, in relation to the "surrender" of lands on Indian reserves and said:

> The language of the statute embodies the accepted view that these aborigenes are, in effect, wards of the State, whose care and welfare are a political trust of the highest obligation . . .

The contention that the *Bill of Rights* is to be construed as overriding all of the special legislation imposed by Parliament under the *Indian Act* is, in my view, fully answered by Pigeon J. in his dissenting opinion in the Drybones case . . .

That it is membership in the band which entitles an Indian to the use and benefit of lands on the reserve is made plain by the provisions of ss. 2 and 18 of the *Indian Act* . . .

In considering the meaning to be given to s. 1(b) of the *Bill of Rights*, regard must of course be had to what was said by Laskin J., speaking in this regard for the whole of the Court in *Curr v. The Queen*, [1972] S.C.R. 889 at 896-97, 18 C.R.N.S. 281, 7 C.C.C. (2d) 181, 26 D.L.R. (3d) 603, where he interpreted s. 1(a) and (b) of the Bill in the following passage:

> In considering the reach of s. 1(a) and s. 1(b), and, indeed, of s. 1 as a whole, I would observe, first, that the section is given its controlling force over federal law by its referential incorporation into s. 2; and second, that I do not read it as making the existence of any of the forms

of prohibited discrimination a *sine qua non* of its operation. Rather, the prohibited discrimination is an additional lever to which federal legislation must respond. Putting the matter another way, federal legislation which does not offend s. 1 in respect of any of the prohibited kinds of discrimination may nonetheless be offensive to s. 1 if it is violative of what is specified in any of the clauses (*a*) to (*f*) of s. 1. It is, *à fortiori*, offensive if there is discrimination by reason of race so as to deny equality before the law. That is what this Court decided in *Regina v. Drybones* and I need say no more on this point.

It is, therefore, not an answer to reliance by the appellant on s. 1(*a*) and s. 1(*b*) of the *Canadian Bill of Rights* that s. 223 does not discriminate against any person by reason of race, national origin, colour, religion or sex. The absence of such discrimination still leaves open the question whether s. 223 can be construed and applied without abrogating, abridging or infringing the rights of the individual listed in s. 1(*a*) and s. 1(*b*).

My understanding of this passage is that the effect of s. 1 of the *Bill of Rights* is to guarantee to all Canadians the rights specified in cls. (*a*) to (*f*) of that section, irrespective of race, national origin, colour or sex. This interpretation appears to me to be borne out by the French version which reads:

"1. Il est par les présentes reconnu et déclaré que les droits de l'homme et les libertés fondamentales ci-après énoncés ont existé et continueront à exister pour tout individu au Canada quels que soient sa race, son origine nationale, sa couleur, sa religion ou son sexe: . . ."

It was stressed on behalf of the respondents that the provisions of s. 12(1) (*b*) of the *Indian Act* constituted "discrimination by reason of sex" and that the section could be declared inoperative on this ground alone even if such discrimination did not result in the infringement of any of the rights and freedoms specifically guaranteed by s. 1 of the Bill.

I can find no support for such a contention in the *Curr* case in which, in any event, no question of any kind of discrimination was either directly or indirectly involved. My own understanding of the passage which I have quoted from that case was that it recognized the fact that the primary concern evidenced by the first two sections of the *Bill of Rights* is to ensure that the rights and freedoms thereby recognized and declared shall continue to exist for all Canadians, and it follows, in my view, that those sections cannot be invoked unless one of the enumerated rights and freedoms has been denied to an individual Canadian or group of Canadians. Section 2 of the *Bill of Rights* provides for the manner in which the rights and freedoms which are recognized and declared by s. 1 are to be enforced, and the effect of this section is that every law of Canada shall "be so construed and applied as not to abrogate, abridge or infringe or to authorize the abrogation, abridgment or infringement of any of the rights or freedoms herein recognized and declared" (i.e., by s. 1). There is no language anywhere in the *Bill of Rights* stipulating that the laws of Canada are to be construed without discrimination unless that discrimination involves the denial of one of the guaranteed rights and freedoms, but when, as in the case of *Regina v. Drybones*, denial of one of the enumerated rights is occasioned by reason of discrimination, then, as Laskin J. has said, the discrimination affords an "additional lever to which federal legislation must respond."

The opening words of s. 2 of the *Bill of Rights* are, in my view, determinative of the test to be applied in deciding whether the section here impugned is to be declared inoperative. The words to which I refer are:

> 2. Every law of Canada shall, unless it is expressly declared by an Act of the Parliament of Canada that it shall operate notwithstanding the *Canadian Bill of Rights*, be so construed and applied as not to abrogate, abridge or infringe or to authorize the abrogation, abridgment or infringement of any of the rights or freedoms herein recognized and declared . . .

In the course of the reasons for judgment rendered on behalf of the majority of this Court in *Regina v. Drybones*, supra, this language was interpreted in the following passage at p. 294:

> It seems to me that a more realistic meaning must be given to the words in question and they afford, in my view, the clearest indication that s. 2 is intended to mean and does mean that if a law of Canada cannot be "sensibly construed and applied" so that it does not abrogate, abridge or infringe one of the rights and freedoms recognized and declared by the Bill, then such law is inoperative "unless it is expressly declared by an Act of the Parliament of Canada that it shall operate notwithstanding the *Canadian Bill of Rights*".

Accordingly, in my opinion, the question to be determined in these appeals is confined to deciding whether the Parliament of Canada, in defining the prerequisites of Indian status so as not to include women of Indian birth who have chosen to marry non-Indians, enacted a law which cannot be sensibly construed and applied without abrogating, abridging or infringing the rights of such women to equality before the law.

In my view the meaning to be given to the language employed in the *Bill of Rights* is the meaning which it bore in Canada at the time when the Bill was enacted, and it follows that the phrase "equality before the law" is to be construed in light of the law existing in Canada at that time.

In considering the meaning to be attached to "equality before the law" as those words occur in s. 1(*b*) of the Bill, I think it important to point out that in my opinion this phrase is not effective to invoke the egalitarian concept exemplified by the Fourteenth Amendment of the United States Constitution as interpreted by the courts of that country: see *Smythe v. The Queen*, [1971] S.C.R. 680 at 683 and 686, 16 C.R.N.S. 147, 71 D.T.C. 5252, 3 C.C.C. (2d) 366, 19 D.L.R. (3d) 480, per Fauteux C.J.C. I think rather that having regard to the language employed in the second paragraph of the preamble to the *Bill of Rights*, the phrase "equality before the law" as used in s. 1 is to be read in its context as a part of "the rule of law" to which overriding authority is accorded by the terms of that paragraph.

In this connection I refer to Stephens, Commentaries on the Laws of England, 21st ed. (1950), where it is said in vol. 3, at p. 337:

> Now the great constitutional lawyer Dicey writing in 1885 was so deeply impressed by the absence of arbitrary governments present and past, that he coined the phrase "the rule of law" to express the regime under which Englishmen lived; and he tried to give precision to it in the following words which have exercised a profound influence on all subsequent thought and conduct.

That the "rule of law" which forms a fundamental principle of the constitution has three meanings or may be regarded from three different points of view . . .

The second meaning proposed by Dicey is the one with which we are here concerned and it was stated in the following terms:

It means again equality before the law or the equal subjection of all classes to the ordinary law of the land administered by the ordinary courts; the "rule of law" in this sense excludes the idea of any exemption of officials or others from the duty of obedience to the law which governs other citizens or from the jurisdiction of the ordinary courts.

"Equality before the law" in this sense is frequently invoked to demonstrate that the same law applies to the highest official of government as to any other ordinary citizen and in this regard Professor F. R. Scott in delivering the Plaunt Memorial Lectures on Civil Liberties and Canadian Federalism in 1959 speaking of the case of *Roncarelli v. Duplessis*, [1959] S.C.R. 121, 16 D.L.R. (2d) 689, had occasion to say:

. . . it is always a triumph for the law to show that it is applied equally to all without fear or favour. This is what we mean when we say that all are equal before the law.

The relevance of these quotations to the present circumstances is that "equality before the law" as recognized by Dicey as a segment of the rule of law, carries the meaning of equal subjection of all classes to the ordinary law of the land *as administered by the ordinary courts*, and in my opinion the phrase "equality before the law" as employed in s. 1(*b*) of the *Bill of Rights* is to be treated as meaning equality in the administration or application of the law by the law enforcement authorities and the ordinary courts of the land. This construction is, in my view, supported by the provisions of cls. (*a*) *to* (*g*) of s. 2 of the Bill which clearly indicate to me that it was equality in the administration and enforcement of the law with which Parliament was concerned when it guaranteed the continued existence of "equality before the law".

Turning to the *Indian Act* itself, it should first be observed that by far the greater part of the Act is concerned with the internal regulation of the lives of Indians on reserves and that the exceptional provisions dealing with the conduct of Indians off reserves and their contacts with other Canadian citizens fall into an entirely different category.

It was, of course, necessary for Parliament, in the exercise of s. 91(24) authority, to first define what Indian meant, and in this regard s. 2(1) of the Act provides that:

"Indian" means a person who pursuant to this Act is registered as an Indian or is entitled to be registered as an Indian.

It is therefore clear that registration is a necessary prerequisite to Indian status . . .

It is thus apparent that the marital status of Indian women who marry non-Indians has been the same for at least one hundred years and that their loss of band status on marriage to a member of another band and acquisition of status in that band, for which provision is made under s. 14 of the Indian Act, has been in effect for the same period . . .

A careful reading of the Act discloses that s. 95 (formerly R.S.C. 1952, c. 149, s. 94) is the only provision therein made which creates an offence for any behaviour of an Indian *off* a reserve, and it will be plain that there is a wide difference between legislation such as s. 12(1)(*b*) governing the civil rights of designated persons living on Indian reserves to the use and benefit of Crown lands, and criminal legislation such as s. 95 which creates an offence punishable at law for Indians to act in a certain fashion when *off* a reserve. The former legislation is enacted as a part of the plan devised by Parliament under s. 91(24) for the regulation of the internal domestic life of Indians on reserves. The latter is criminal legislation exclusively concerned with behaviour of Indians *off* a reserve.

Having regard to the express reservations contained in these passages, I have difficulty in understanding how that case can be construed as having decided that any sections of the *Indian Act* except s. 94(*b*) are rendered inoperative by the *Bill of Rights*.

The *Drybones* case can, in my opinion, have no application to the present appeals as it was in no way concerned with the internal regulation of the lives of Indians *on* reserves or their right to the use and benefit of Crown lands therein, but rather deals exclusively with the effect of the *Bill of Rights* on a section of the *Indian Act* creating a crime with attendant penalties for the conduct by Indians *off* a reserve in an area where non-Indians, who were also governed by federal law, were not subject to any such restriction.

The fundamental distinction between the present case and that of *Drybones*, however, appears to me to be that the impugned section in the latter case could not be enforced without denying equality of treatment in the administration and enforcement of the law before the ordinary courts of the land to a racial group, whereas no such inequality of treatment between Indian men and women flows as a necessary result of the application of s. 12(1)(*b*) of the *Indian Act*.

To summarize the above, I am of opinion:

1. That the *Bill of Rights* is not effective to render inoperative legislation, such as s. 12(1)(*b*) of the *Indian Act*, passed by the Parliament of Canada in discharge of its constitutional function under s. 91(24) of the *B.N.A. Act*, to specify how and by whom Crown lands reserved for Indians are to be used.

2. That the *Bill of Rights* does not require federal legislation to be declared inoperative unless it offends against one of the rights specifically guaranteed by s. 1, but where legislation is found to be discriminatory, this affords an added reason for rendering it ineffective.

3. That equality before the law under the *Bill of Rights* means equality of treatment in the enforcement and application of the laws of Canada before the law enforcement authorities and the ordinary courts of the land, and no such inequality is necessarily entailed in the construction and application of s. 12(1)(*b*) . . .

PIGEON J.: I agree in the result with Ritchie J. I certainly cannot disagree with the view I did express in *Regina v. Drybones*, [1970] S.C.R. 282 at 304, 10 C.R.N.S. 334, 71 W.W.R. 161, [1970] 3 C.C.C. 355, 9 D.L.R. (3d) 473, that the enactment of the *Canadian Bill of*

Rights, R.S.C. 1970, App. III, was not intended to effect a virtual suppression of federal legislation over Indians. My difficulty is Laskin J.'s strongly reasoned opinion that, unless we are to depart from what was said by the majority in *Drybones,* these appeals should be dismissed because, if discrimination by reason of race makes certain statutory provisions inoperative, the same result must follow as to statutory provisions which exhibit discrimination by reason of sex. In the end, it appears to me that, in the circumstances, I need not reach a firm conclusion on that point. Assuming the situation is such as Laskin J. says, it cannot be improper for me to adhere to what was my dissenting view, when a majority of those who did not agree with it in respect of a particular section of the *Indian Act,* R.S.C. 1970, c. I-6, now adopt it for the main body of this important statute.

I would observe that this result does not conflict with any of our decisions subsequent to *Drybones.* In no case was the *Canadian Bill of Rights* given an invalidating effect over prior legislation.

LASKIN J. (*dissenting*) : . . . In my opinion, unless we are to depart from what was said in *Drybones,* both appeals now before us must be dismissed. I have no disposition to reject what was decided in *Drybones;* and on the central issue of prohibited discrimination as catalogued in s. 1 of the *Canadian Bill of Rights,* it is, in my opinion, impossible to distinguish *Drybones* from the two cases in appeal. If as in *Drybones,* discrimination by reason of race makes certain statutory provisions inoperative, the same result must follow as to statutory provisions which exhibit discrimination by reason of sex . . .

The contentions of the appellants in both cases in appeal, stripped of their detail, amount to a submission that the *Canadian Bill of Rights* does not apply to Indians on a reserve, nor to Indians in their relations to one another whether or not on a reserve. This submission does not deny that the effect of s. 12(1)(b) of the *Indian Act* is to prescribe substantive discrimination by reason of sex, a differentiation in the treatment of Indian men and Indian women when they marry non-Indians, this differentiation being exhibited in the loss by the women of their status as Indians under the Act. It does, however, involve the assertion that the particular discrimination upon which the two appeals are focused is not offensive to the relevant provisions of the *Canadian Bill of Rights;* and it also involves the assertion that the *Drybones* case is distinguishable or, if not, that it has been overcome by the re-enactment of the *Indian Act* in the Revised Statutes of Canada, 1970, including the then s. 94 (now s. 95) which was in issue in that case. I regard this last-mentioned assertion, which is posited on the fact that the *Canadian Bill of Rights* was not so re-enacted, as simply an oblique appeal for the overruling of the *Drybones* case.

The *Drybones* case decided two things. It decided first — and this decision was a necessary basis for the second point in it — that the *Canadian Bill of Rights* was more than a mere interpretation statute whose terms would yield to a contrary intention; it had paramount force when a federal enactment conflicted with its terms, and it was the incompatible federal enactment which had to give way. This was the issue upon which the then Chief Justice of this Court, Cartwright C.J.C., and Abbott and Pigeon JJ., dissented. Pigeon J. fortified his view on this main point by additional observations, bringing into consideration, inter alia, s. 91(24) of the *British North America Act, 1867*. The second thing decided by *Drybones* was that the accused in that case, an Indian under the *Indian Act*, was denied equality before the law, under s. 1(*b*) of the *Canadian Bill of Rights*, when it was made a punishable offence for him, on account of his race, to do something which his fellow Canadians were free to do without being liable to punishment for an offence. Ritchie J., who delivered the majority opinion of the Court, reiterated this basis of decision by concluding his reasons as follows [[1970] S.C.R. 282 at 298]:

> It appears to me to be desirable to make it plain that these reasons for judgment are limited to a situation in which, under the laws of Canada, it is made an offence punishable at law on account of race for a person to do something which all Canadians who are not members of that race may do with impunity.

It would be unsupportable in principle to view the *Drybones* case as turning on the fact that the challenged s. 94 of the *Indian Act* created an offence visited by punishment. The gist of the judgment lay in the legal disability imposed upon a person by reason of his race when other persons were under no similar restraint. If for the words "on account of race" there are substituted the words "on account of sex" the result must surely be the same where a federal enactment imposes disabilities or prescribes disqualifications for members of the female sex which are not imposed upon members of the male sex in the same circumstances.

It is said, however, that although this may be so as between males and females in general, it does not follow where the distinction on the basis of sex is limited as here to members of the Indian race. This, it is said further, does not offend the guarantee of "equality before the law" upon which the *Drybones* case proceeded. I wish to deal with these two points in turn and to review, in connection with the first point, the legal consequences for an Indian woman under the *Indian Act* when she marries a non-Indian.

It appears to me that the contention that a differentiation on the basis of sex is not offensive to the *Canadian Bill of Rights* where that differentiation operates only among Indians under the *Indian Act* is one that compounds racial inequality even beyond the point that the *Drybones* case found unacceptable. In any event, taking the *Indian Act* as it stands, as a law of Canada whose various provisions fall to be assessed under the *Canadian Bill of Rights*, I am unable to appreciate upon what basis the command of the *Canadian · Bill of Rights*, that laws of Canada shall operate without discrimination by reason of sex, can be ignored in the operation of the *Indian Act*.

The *Indian Act* defines an Indian as a person who is registered as an Indian pursuant to the Act or is entitled to be so registered. It is registration or registrability upon a band list or upon a general list that is the key to the scheme and application of the Act . . .

Registration or registrability entitles an Indian as a member of a band (and that was the status of both Mrs. Lavell and Mrs. Bedard prior to their respective marriages) to the use and benefit of the reserve set aside for the band . . .

Section 12(1)(b) effects a statutory excommunication of Indian women from this society but not of Indian men. Indeed, as was pointed out by counsel for the Native Council of Canada, the effect of ss. 11 and 12(1)(b) is to excommunicate the children of a union of an Indian woman with a non-Indian. There is also the invidious distinction, invidious at least in the light of the *Canadian Bill of Rights*, that the *Indian Act* creates between brothers and sisters who are Indians and who respectively marry non-Indians. . . .

It was urged, in reliance in part on history, that the discrimination embodied in the *Indian Act* under s. 12(1)(b) is based upon a reasonable classification of Indians as a race, that the *Indian Act* reflects this classification and that the paramount purpose of the Act to preserve and protect the members of the race is promoted by the statutory preference for Indian men. Reference was made in this connection to various judgments of the Supreme Court of the United States to illustrate the adoption by that Court of reasonable classifications to square with the due process clause of the Fifth Amendment and with due process and equal protection under the Fourteenth Amendment. Those cases have at best a marginal relevance because the *Canadian Bill of Rights* itself enumerates prohibited classifications which the judiciary is bound to respect; and, moreover, I doubt whether discrimination on account of sex, where as here it has no biological or physiological rationale, could be sustained as a reasonable classification even if the direction against it was not as explicit as it is in the *Canadian Bill of Rights*.

I do not think it is possible to leap over the telling words of s. 1, "without discrimination by reason of race, national origin, colour, religion or sex", in order to explain away any such discrimination by invoking the words "equality before the law" in cl. (b) and attempting to make them alone the touchstone of reasonable classification. That was not done in the *Drybones* case, and this Court made it clear in *Curr v. The Queen*, [1972] S.C.R. 889, 18 C.R.N.S. 281, 7 C.C.C. (2d) 181, 26 D.L.R. (3d) 603, that federal legislation, which might be compatible with the command of "equality before the law" taken alone, may nonetheless be inoperative if it manifests any of the prohibited forms of discrimination. In short, the prescribed discriminations in s. 1 have a force either independent of the subsequently enumerated cls. (a) to (f) or, if they are found in any federal legislation, they offend those clauses because each must be read as if the prohibited forms of discrimination were recited therein as a part thereof.

This seems to me an obvious construction of s. 1 of the *Canadian Bill of Rights*. When that provision states that the enumerated human rights and fundamental freedoms shall continue to exist "without discrimination by reason of race, national origin, colour, religion or sex" it is expressly adding these words to cls. (a) to (f). Section 1 (b) must read therefore as "the right of the individual to equality before the law and the protection of the law without discrimination by reason of race, national origin, colour, religion or sex". It is worth repeating that this is what emerges from the *Drybones* case and what is found in the *Curr* case.

There is no clear historical basis for the position taken by the appellants, certainly not in relation to Indians in Canada as a whole, and this was in effect conceded during the hearing in this Court. In any event, history cannot avail against the clear words of ss. 1 and 2 of the *Canadian Bill of Rights*. It is s. 2 that gives this enactment its effective voice, because without it s. 1 would remain a purely declaratory provision. Section 2 brings the terms of s. 1 into its orbit, and its reference to "every law of Canada" is a reference, as set out in s. 5(2), to any Act of the Parliament of Canada enacted before or after the effective date of the *Canadian Bill of Rights*. Pre-existing Canadian legislation as well as subsequent Canadian legislation is expressly made subject to the commands of the *Canadian Bill of Rights*, and those commands, where they are as clear as the one which is relevant here, cannot be diluted by appeals to history. Ritchie J. in his reasons in the *Drybones* case touched on this very point when he rejected the contention that the terms of s. 1 of the *Canadian Bill of Rights* must be circumscribed by the provisions of Canadian statutes in force at the date of the enactment of the *Canadian Bill of Rights*: see [1970] S.C.R. 282 at 295-96. I subscribe fully to the rejection of that contention. Clarity here is emphasized by looking at the French version of the *Canadian Bill of Rights* which speaks in s. 1 of the enumerated human rights and fundamental freedoms "pour tout individu au Canada quels que soient sa race, son origine nationale, sa couleur, sa religion ou son sexe".

In my opinion, the appellants' contentions gain no additional force because the *Indian Act*, including the challenged s. 12 (1) (b) thereof, is a fruit of the exercise of Parliament's exclusive legislative power in relation to "Indians, and Lands reserved for the Indians" under s. 91(24) of the *British North America Act*, 1867. Discriminatory treatment on the basis of race or colour or sex does not inhere in that grant of legislative power. The fact that its exercise may be attended by forms of discrimination prohibited by the *Canadian Bill of Rights* is no more a justification for a breach of the *Canadian Bill of Rights* than there would be in the case of the exercise of any other head of federal legislative power involving provisions offensive to the *Canadian Bill of Rights*. The majority opinion in the *Drybones* case dispels any attempt to reply on the grant of legislative power as a ground for escaping from the force of the *Canadian Bill of Rights*. The latter does not differentiate among the various heads of legislative power; it embraces all exercises under whatever head or heads they arise. Section 3 which directs the Minister of Justice to scrutinize every Bill to ascertain whether any of its provisions are inconsistent with ss. 1 and 2 is simply an affirmation of this fact which is evident enough from ss. 1 and 2.

There was an intimation during the argument of these appeals that the *Canadian Bill of Rights* is properly invoked only to resolve a clash under its terms between two federal statutes, and the *Drybones* case was relied on in that connection. It is a spurious contention, if seriously advanced, because the *Canadian Bill of Rights* is itself the indicator to which any Canadian statute or any provision thereof must yield unless Parliament has declared that the statute or the particular provision is to operate notwithstanding the *Canadian Bill of Rights*. A statute may in itself be offensive to the *Canadian Bill of Rights*, or it may be by relation to another statute that it is so offensive.

I would dismiss both appeals with costs.

ABBOTT J. (dissenting): The facts which are not in dispute are set out in the reasons of Ritchie and Laskin JJ. which I have had the advantage of reading. I am in agreement with the reasons of Laskin J. and wish to add only a few observations.

In my view the *Canadian Bill of Rights* has substantially affected the doctrine of the supremacy of Parliament. Like any other statute it can of course be repealed or amended, or a particular law declared to be applicable notwithstanding the provisions of the Bill. In form the supremacy of Parliament is maintained but in practice I think that it has been substantially curtailed. In my opinion that result is undesirable, but that is a matter for consideration by Parliament not the courts.

Appeals allowed.

CURR v. THE QUEEN

In the Supreme Court of Canada. [1972] S.C.R. 889, 18 C.R.N.S. 281, 7 C.C.C. (2d) 181, 26 D.L.R. (3d) 603.

APPEAL from a judgment of the Court of Appeal for Ontario, [1971] 3 O.R. 167, 4 C.C.C. (2d) 24, affirming a judgment of Fraser J.

FAUTEUX C.J.C.: This is an appeal by leave from a judgment of the Court of Appeal for Ontario [*supra*] dismissing without recorded reasons an appeal from the decision of Fraser J. who answered affirmatively the following question stated by the Trial Judge:

> Did I err in law in holding that section 223 of the Criminal Code and section 224A(3) of the Criminal Code are rendered inoperative by virtue of a conflict with the Canadian Bill of Rights?

Having had the advantage of reading the reasons prepared by my brothers Ritchie and Laskin, I agree that the appeal should be disposed of as they propose. In view of the all embracing scope of the *Canadian Bill of Rights* [R.S.C. 1970, App. III] and the relatively recent character of this important statute, I would prefer, while I appreciate the learned consideration give to the matter by my brother Laskin, to confine my opinion to the facts of this case, adopt the simpler approach taken by my brother Ritchie and rest my opinion on the reasons he gave which, in my respectful view, are sufficient for the decision of this particular case.

LASKIN J.: The *Canadian Bill of Rights*, 1960 (Can.), c. 44 is invoked in this case to sterilize certain provisions of the *Criminal Code*, viz., ss. 223 and 224A(3), as enacted by s. 16 of the *Criminal Law Amendment Act*, 1968-69 (Can.), c. 38, That it may have a sterilizing effect upon federal legislation was decided by this Court in *Regina v. Dry-*

bones, [1970] S.C.R. 282, 10 C.R.N.S. 334, 71 W.W.R. 161, [1970] 3 C.C.C. 355, 9 D.L.R. (3d) 473. Whether that must be the result here in no way depends upon what was decided in *Regina v. Drybones.*

The appellant was charged under s. 223(2) with failing or refusing without reasonable excuse, to comply with a demand by a peace officer under s. 223 (1) for a breath sample to enable an analysis to be made to determine the proportion of alcohol in his blood. The provincial judge before whom the charge was tried concluded that the Crown had proved its case against the appellant beyond a reasonable doubt. Nonetheless, he dismissed the charge on the ground that s. 223 was inoperative because of the *Canadian Bill of Rights.* Thereafter, he acceded to a Crown request to state a case in which the following question was submitted for determination:

> Did I err in law in holding that section 223 of the Criminal Code and section 224A(3) of the Criminal Code are rendered inoperative by virtue of a conflict with the Canadian Bill of Rights?

Fraser J., after extensive reasons, answered this question in the affirmative, and an appeal from his judgment was dismissed without written reasons. Leave to appeal to this Court was granted by an order of October 6, 1971.

In view of the course of the argument, I deem it prudent to put at the forefront of these reasons two rather obvious propositions; first, the *Canadian Bill of Rights* did not freeze the federal statute book as of its effective date, which was August 10, 1960; and, second, federal law enacted after the date of the *Canadian Bill of Rights* as well as pre-existing federal law may be found to run foul of the prescriptions of the *Canadian Bill of Rights.*

Sections 223 and 224A(3) of the *Criminal Code* are connected with s. 222, as enacted at the same time, and I reproduce all these provisions preliminary to a consideration of the effect of the *Canadian Bill of Rights* upon ss. 223 and 224A(3). They read as follows:

> 222. Every one who, while his ability to drive a motor vehicle is impaired by alcohol or a drug, drives a motor vehicle or has the care or control of a motor vehicle, whether it is in motion or not, is guilty of an ... offence. ....

> 223. (1) Where a peace officer on reasonable and probable grounds believes that a person is committing, or at any time within the preceding two hours has committed, an offence under section 222, he may, by demand made to that person forthwith or as soon as practicable, require him to provide then or as soon thereafter as is practicable a sample of his breath suitable to enable an analysis to be made in order to determine the proportion, if any, of alcohol in his blood, and to accompany the peace officer for the purpose of enabling such a sample to be taken.

> (2) Every one who, without reasonable excuse, fails or refuses to comply with a demand made to him by a peace officer under subsection (1) is guilty of an offence punishable on summary conviction and is liable to a fine of not less than fifty dollars and not more than one thousand dollars or to imprisonment for not more than six months, or both.

> 224A. (3) In any proceedings under section 222, evidence that the accused, without reasonable excuse, failed or refused to comply with a

demand made to him by a peace officer under subsection (1) of section 223 is admissible and the court may draw an inference therefrom adverse to the accused.

The contention of the appellant is that ss. 223 and 224A(3) are in collision with s. 1(a)(b) and s. 2(d)(e)(f) of the *Canadian Bill of Rights* . . .

The operative effect of s. 224A(3) in the light of the *Canadian Bill of Rights* depends, therefore, on the operative effect of s. 223; and if this last-mentioned provision is in any way in conflict with the *Canadian Bill of Rights*, that conflict must be found, if at all, in s. 1(a) or in s. 1(b) or in s. 2(d) thereof.

In considering the reach of s. 1(a) and s. 1(b), and, indeed, of s. 1 as a whole, I would observe, first, that the section is given its controlling force over federal law by its referential incorporation into s. 2; and, second, that I do not read it as making the existence of any of the forms of prohibited discrimination a *sine qua non* of its operation. Rather, the prohibited discrimination is an additional lever to which federal legislation must respond. Putting the matter another way, federal legislation which does not offend s. 1 in respect of any of the prohibited kinds of discrimination may nonetheless be offensive to s. 1 if it is violative of what is specified in any of the clauses (a) to (f) of s. 1. It is, *à fortiori*, offensive if there is discrimination by reason of race so as to deny equality before the law. That is what this Court decided in *Regina v. Drybones* and I need say no more on this point.

It is, therefore, not an answer to reliance by the appellant on s. 1(a) and s. 1(b) of the *Canadian Bill of Rights* that s. 223 does not discriminate against any person by reason of race, national origin, colour, religion or sex. The absence of such discrimination still leaves open the question whether s. 223 can be construed and applied without abrogating, abridging or infringing the rights of the individual listed in s. 1(a) and s. 1(b). What the appellant pointed to in s. 1(a) was the guarantee of "due process of law", and his contention under s. 1(b) was that s. 223 denied him "the protection of the law". I shall deal with these submissions in turn.

The phrase "due process of law" has its context in the words of s. 1(a) that precede it. In the present case, the connection stressed was with "the right of the individual to . . . security of the person". It is obvious that to read "due process of law" as meaning simply that there must be some legal authority to qualify or impair security of the person would be to see it as declaratory only. On this view, it should not matter whether the legal authority is found in enacted law or in unenacted or decisional law. Counsel for the appellant does not, of course, stop here. He contended for a qualitative test of legislation to meet the standard of due process of law and urged that the Court find that s. 223 fell below it. This was, however, a bare submission, not reinforced by any proposed yardstick.

What it amounted to was an invitation to this Court to monitor the substantive content of legislation by reference to s. 1(a). The invitation is to take the phrase "except by due process of law" beyond its antecedents in English legal history, and to view it in terms that have had sanction in the United States in the consideration there of those parts of the Fifth and Fourteenth Amendments to the American Constitution that forbid the federal and state authorities respectively to deprive any person of life, liberty or property without due process of law.

The English antecedents, specifically 28 Edw. III, c. 3 of 1355 ("no man of what state or condition he be, shall be put out of his lands or tenements nor taken, nor disinherited, nor put to death without he be brought to answer by due process of law") as backed up by the earlier Magna Carta, c. 29, reissue of 1225 (famous for the phrase "per legem terrae"), point to procedural considerations although it has been contended that they go farther: see *McIlwain*: Due Process of Law in Magna Carta (1914) 14 Col. L. Rev. 27. It is evident from s. 2 of the *Canadian Bill of Rights* that its specification of particular procedural protections is without limitation of any others that may have a source in s. 1.

In so far as s. 223, and especially s. 223(1), may be regarded as a procedural aid to the enforcement of the substantive offence created by s. 222, I do not find it obnoxious to s. 1(a) of the *Canadian Bill of Rights*. I am unable to appreciate what more can be read into s. 1(a) from a procedural standpoint than is already comprehended by s. 2(e) ("a fair hearing in accordance with the principles of fundamental justice") and by s. 2(f) ("a fair and public hearing by an independent and impartial tribunal"). I need not consider here whether the express concern of s. 2(f) with criminal charges indicates that s. 2(e) must refer to non-criminal proceedings. I would not read these two provisions as pointing to different standards of procedural fairness in their respective applications (if that be the case) to non-criminal and criminal proceedings, save as those standards spring from the nature of the proceeding.

There is no occasion here to look at s. 223 in terms of the revulsion and shock of conscience which influenced the Supreme Court of the United States in *Rochin v. California* (1952), 342 U.S. 165 to hold that the due process clause of the Fourteenth Amendment was there violated. It was a case of forcing upon a suspect the use of an emetic to obtain morphine capsules which he had swallowed. In my opinion, the policy reflected in s. 222 could properly, at the instance of Parliament, be supported by the prescriptions of s. 223 without there being any denial to an accused of a false hearing, that is, of due or just process.

Counsel for the respondent conceded in argument that s. 1(a) could have application to pre-trial matters affecting a person who is or is about to be charged with an offence. He submitted, however, that in the present case self-crimination was the only possible ground of objection under s. 1(a) and, since it was covered expressly in s. 2(d), there was no reason to consider it separately and independently under s. 1(a). The force of this submission depends on a view of the scope of s. 2(d) on which counsel for the appellant and counsel for the Crown are in disagreement; and, accordingly, I defer consideration of the scope of the protection against self-crimination, so far as it may be comprehended under s. 1(a) as well as under s. 2(d), until I give my reasons on the appellant's submissions with respect to s. 2(d)

In so far as s. 223 may be regarded, in the light of s. 223(2), as having specific substantive effect in itself, I am likewise of the opinion that s. 1(a) of the *Canadian Bill of Rights* does not make it inoperative. Assuming that "except by due process of law" provides a means of controlling substantive federal legislation—a point that did not directly arise in *Regina v. Drybones*—compelling reasons ought to be advanced to justify the Court in this case to employ a statutory (as contrasted with a constitutional) jurisdiction to deny operative effect to a substantive measure duly enacted by a Parliament constitutionally competent to do so, and exercising its powers in accordance with the tenets of responsible government, which underlie the discharge of legislative authority under the *British North America Act*. Those reasons must relate to objective and manageable standards by which a Court should be guided if scope is to be found in s. 1(a) due process to silence otherwise competent federal legislation. Neither reasons nor underlying standards were offered here. For myself, I am not prepared in this case to surmise what they might be.

American judicial experience with the Fifth and Fourteenth Amendments, in respect of substantive due process, does not provide any ground upon which this Court might stand for the purpose of resorting to due process in s. 1(a) as a means of controlling such federal laws as s. 223 of the *Criminal Code*. If there is any analogy at all to be drawn between the *Canadian Bill of Rights* and the American Constitution, it is to be found with respect to the first eight amendments to that Constitution, which inhibit federal action, and not with respect to the Fourteenth, which is referable to the states.

A recurring issue in American judicial experience during this century has been the extent to which the Fourteenth Amendment (consisting in its first section of a citizens' privileges and immunities clause and an equal protection clause as well as of a due process clause) protects against state action which involves invasions of what is specified in the first eight amendments. There is no such issue of interaction involved under the *Canadian Bill of Rights* . . .

The immediate issue is, however, the wider one of the extent to which the Fifth Amendment due process clause has been used as a brake on federal law-making, apart from matters of procedural regularity or procedural fairness. Here too there has been a checkered history, involving such questions as unreasonable discrimination, the degree of immunity of private business from public regulation, and the limits of permissible interference with freedom of contract. It appears that so-called economic due process has been abandoned (see *West Coast Hotel Co. v. Parrish* (1937) 300 U.S. 379) in the realization that a Court enters the bog of legislative policy-making in assuming to enshrine any particular theory, as for example, untrammelled liberty of contract, which has not been plainly expressed in the Constitution.

This commends itself to me with respect to due process in the *Canadian Bill of Rights*. Parliament has spoken clearly on certain types of discrimination; it has used familiar, albeit general, words in its legislative guarantees of freedom of religion, speech, assembly, association and the press; and it has been even more specific in what it has enumerated in s. 2, although even here there are difficulties of interpretation. The very large words of s. 1(*a*), tempered by a phrase ("except by due process of law") whose original English meaning has been overlaid by American constitutional imperatives, signal extreme caution to me when asked to apply them in negation of substantive legislation validly enacted by a Parliament in which the major role is played by elected representatives of the people. Certainly, in the present case, a holding that the enactment of s. 223 has infringed the appellant's right to the security of his person without due process of law must be grounded on more than a substitution of a personal judgment for that of Parliament. There is nothing in the record, by way of evidence or admissible extrinsic material, upon which such a holding could be supported. I am, moreover, of the opinion that it is within the scope of judicial notice to recognize that Parliament has acted in a matter that is of great social concern, that is the human and economic cost of highway accidents arising from drunk driving, in enacting s. 223 and related provisions of the *Criminal Code*. Even where this Court is asked to pass on the constitutional validity of legislation, it knows that it must resist making the wisdom of impugned legislation the test of its constitutionality. *A fortiori* is this so where it is measuring legislation by a statutory standard, the result of which may make federal enactments inoperative.

The submission under s. 1(*b*) that s. 223 was a denial of the "protection of the law" amounted at bottom to a contention that the pre-s. 223 state of the law, which was more favourable to a potential accused person, could not be changed to his disadvantage without offending s. 1(*b*). I find no merit in this position, based as it is on the "frozen statute book" theory. It was not argued that the appellant was denied "equality before the law" under s. 1(*b*), and hence it is unnecessary to consider whether s. 1(*b*) must be read as wholly conjunctive so as to make the declaration of the protection of the law a reinforcement of the requirement of equality before the law. This Court has pointed out in *Regina v. Drybones*, [1970] S.C.R. 282 at 297 that "law" in s. 1(*b*) refers to federal law, as defined in s. 5(2) of the *Canadian Bill of Rights*.

This brings me to the final submission of the appellant, that under s. 2(*d*), which was the one argued at greatest length.

Four points are taken by counsel for the appellant in reliance upon s. 2(*d*). First, he submits that a peace officer acting under s. 223(1) is covered by the phrase "other authority" in s. 2(*d*). Second, it is his contention that the unqualified words "to give evidence" in s. 2(*d*) (that is, unqualified by any express limitation to testimony at a hearing) are broad enough and (having regard to the purpose of the *Bill of Rights* as expressed in its preamble and in s. 1) should be construed to cover the results of compelled physical tests as well as compelled oral utterance. Third, it is urged that s. 2(*d*) extends to persons who may be but are not yet parties or witnesses, and the contrast is made with s. 2(*g*) which does speak, *inter alia*, of a party or witness before a court, commission, board or other tribunal in connection with the provision of an interpreter. Fourth, the allegation is that pre-trial compulsion at the instance of a peace officer to submit to a test that may yield incriminating results is a denial of protection against self-crimination within s. 2(d).

[The learned judge discusses the issues raised by s. 2(d) and holds that the appellant's submissions on that section and on the privilege against self-crimination fail. Accordingly he dismisses the appeal.]

MARTLAND J.: I would dismiss this appeal. I agree with the reasons given by my brother Laskin. I also agree with the reasons of my brother Ritchie, but, in so doing, I do not adopt, as final, any specific definition of the phrase "due process of law", as used in s. 1(a) of the *Canadian Bill of Rights*.

RITCHIE J.: I have had the advantage of reading the reasons for judgment prepared for delivery by my brother Laskin and I agree that the appeal should be disposed of in the manner proposed by him . . .

In concluding that the impugned sections of the *Criminal Code* did not offend against the "due process" provisions of s. 1(a) of the *Bill of Rights*, my brother Laskin has made an extensive and instructive review of the meaning of "due process of law", in the course of which he makes reference to the origins of the phrase and its application in decisions of the Supreme Court of the United States of America. While I agree that ss. 223 and 224A do not offend against s. 1(a) of the *Bill of Rights*, I prefer to base this conclusion on my understanding that the meaning to be given to the language employed in the *Bill of Rights* is the meaning which it bore in Canada at the time when the Bill was enacted and it follows that, in my opinion, the phrase "due process of law" as used in s. 1(a) is to be construed as meaning "according to the legal processes recognized by Parliament and the courts in Canada".

I think, as I have said, that the real issue in this case is whether or not the provisions of ss. 223 and 224A(3) in so far as they provide that an individual may be compelled to give a sample of his breath which can later be used against him at his trial, amount to enforced "self crimination" and thus abridge the individual's right to "protection against self crimination" which is recognized by s. 2(d) of the *Bill of Rights*.

In accordance with the view which I have already expressed as to the meaning which I think should be attached to the language of the *Bill of Rights*, I would prefer to base my opinion on the meaning of the words "protection against self crimination" as they occur in s. 2(d) on the cases decided in this Court and more particularly on the cases of *The Attorney General for Quebec v. Begin* [1955] S.C.R. 593, 21 C.R. 217, 112 C.C.C. 209, [1955] 5 D.L.R. 394, and *Validity of Section 94(2) of The Vehicles Act*, 1957 (Sask.), [1958] S.C.R. 608, 121 C.C.C. 321, 15 D.L.R. (2d) 225.

In the course of his reasons for judgment in the latter case, the present Chief Justice, relying on the case of *Begin*, had this to say:

Indeed the confession rule requiring a warning exclusively concerns *self incriminating statements* of the accused, and aims at the exclusion

of those which are untrue. As its subject matter or purpose, the confession rule does not embrace the *incriminating conditions* of the body,
features, fingerprints, clothing or behaviour of the accused, that persons,
other than himself, observe or detect and ultimately report as witnesses
in judicial proceedings.

I think, therefore, that the words "protection against self crimination" as they occur in s. 2(d) of the *Bill of Rights* are to be taken as
meaning protection against "self incriminating statements" and not as
embracing "incriminating conditions of the body" such as the alcoholic content of the breath or blood.

I do not find it necessary to go further afield in order to interpret
this phrase as it occurs in the *Canadian Bill of Rights*.

As I have said, I would dispose of this appeal in the manner proposed by my brother Laskin.

Appeal dismissed.

[On the development of s. 2 guarantees see *R. v. Appleby*, [1972] S.C.R.
303, 16 C.R.N.S. 35, [1971] 4 W.W.R. 601, 3 C.C.C. (2d) 354, 21 D.L.R. (3d) 325,
and *Lowry v. The Queen*, [1974] S.C.R. 195, 19 C.R.N.S. 315, [1972] 5 W.W.R.
229, 6 C.C.C. (2d) 531, 26 D.L.R. (3d) 224. See also *Duke v. The Queen*, [1972]
S.C.R. 917, 18 C.R.N.S. 302, 7 C.C.C. (2d) 474, 28 D.L.R. (3d) 129, which ought
to be considered in light of *Reference Re Criminal Law Amendment Act
1968-69*, [1970] S.C.R. 777, 74 W.W.R. 167, 12 C.R.N.S. 28, [1970] 3 C.C.C. 320,
10 D.L.R. (3d) 699.]

THE QUEEN v. BURNSHINE

In the Supreme Court of Canada. [1974] 4 W.W.R. 49, 2 N.R. 53,
25 C.R.N.S. 270, 15 C.C.C. (2d) 505, 44 D.L.R. (3d) 584.

Appeal by the Crown from the decision of the Court of Appeal for
British Columbia, [1974] 3 W.W.R. 228, 22 C.R.N.S. 271, 13 C.C.C.
(2d) 137, 39 D.L.R. (3d) 161, allowing the accused's appeal from the
sentence of three months definite and two years less a day indeterminate imposed following an appeal by the Crown by way of trial
de novo on a charge of causing a disturbance.

MARTLAND J.: This appeal is brought, with leave, from part of a
judgment of the Court of Appeal for British Columbia which, by a
majority of two to one, held that s. 150 of the *Prisons and Reformatories Act*, R.S.C. 1970, c. P-21, hereinafter referred to as "the
Act", was inoperative because it abrogates, abridges, or infringes or
authorizes the abrogation, abridgment or infringement of the right
of the respondent to equality before the law and its protection as provided in s. 1(b) of the *Canadian Bill of Rights*, R.S.C. 1970, App. III,
hereinafter referred to as "the *Bill of Rights*".

The respondent had been convicted of an offence under the
Criminal Code, R.S.C. 1970, c. C-34, s. 171 [am. 1972, c. 13, s. 11], for
which he was subject to a fine of not more than $500 or to imprison-
ment for six months or both. Following a pre-sentence report, the
respondent was sentenced to a term of three months definite and two
years less one day indeterminate. The authority for the imposition of
this sentence was s. 150 of the Act . . .

The power of the court, under what was then s. 151 of the Act [the *Prisons and Reformatories Act*, R.S.C. 1952, c. 217] to impose sentences of definite and indeterminate terms which, in the aggregate, extend beyond the maximum term fixed by the penal statute, was confirmed by this Court in *Turcotte v. The Queen*, [1970] S.C.R. 843, 11 C.R.N.S. 301, 73 W.W.R. 334, [1970] 5 C.C.C. 245, 12 D.L.R. (3d) 466. Section 151 was substantially the same as the present s. 150. The difference was that s. 151 applied only to males "apparently over the age of sixteen years and under the age of twenty-three years".

The same decision was made in relation to s. 46 of the Act in *Anderson v. The Queen*, which was heard and decided at the same time as the *Turcotte* case . . .

At the outset it should be noted that there can be no contention that s. 150 of the Act involves any discrimination by reason of race, national origin, colour, religion or sex. This fact does not, however, in itself, determine the issue because, as was stated by Laskin J. (as he then was) in *Curr v. The Queen*, [1972] S.C.R. 889 at 896, 18 C.R.N.S. 281, 7 C.C.C. (2d) 181, 26 D.L.R. (3d) 603, the existence of any of the forms of prohibited discrimination is not a sine qua non of the operation of s. 1 of the Bill of Rights. The question has to be determined as to whether the provisions of s. 150 infringe on the respondent's declared right to equality before the law and the protection of the law.

The respondent contends that he has been denied that right because s. 150 permits the court in British Columbia to impose upon him a punishment greater than that which could have been imposed.

(a) By a court in the other provinces of Canada, save Ontario;

(b) Upon a person not within the age group defined in s. 150, in any of the provinces of Canada, including British Columbia, other than Ontario.

This submission, in substance, is that s. 2 of the *Bill of Rights* becomes operative in respect of any statute enacted by the Parliament of Canada which is made applicable to a particular area in Canada, as distinct from the whole of Canada, or which particularly affects a defined group of persons in Canada, as distinct from all other persons in Canada . . .

It is quite clear that, in 1960, when the *Bill of Rights* was enacted, the concept of "equality before the law" did not and could not include the right of each individual to insist that no statute could be enacted which did not have application to everyone and in all areas of Canada. Such a right would have involved a substantial impairment of the sovereignty of Parliament in the exercise of its legislative powers under s. 91 of the *B.N.A. Act* and could only have been created by constitutional amendment, or by statute. In my opinion the wording of the *Bill of Rights* did not do this, because, as has already been noted, by its express wording it declared and continued existing rights and freedoms. It was those existing rights and freedoms which were not to be infringed by any federal statute. Section 2 did not create new rights. Its purpose was to prevent infringement of existing rights.

It did particularize, in paras. (a) to (g), certain rights which were a part of the rights declared in s. 1, but the right claimed by the respondent does not fall within any of those seven paragraphs . . .

The legislative purpose of s. 150 was not to impose harsher punishment upon offenders in British Columbia in a particular age group than upon others. The purpose of the indeterminate sentence was to seek to reform and benefit persons within that younger age group. It was made applicable in British Columbia because that province was equipped with the necessary institutions and staff for that purpose.

In my opinion, it is not the function of this Court, under the *Bill of Rights*, to prevent the operation of a federal enactment, designed for this purpose, on the ground that it applies only to one class of persons, or to a particular area.

The words used by Laskin J. in a slightly different context, in *Curr v. The Queen*, [1972] S.C.R. 889 at 899, 18 C.R.N.S. 281, 7 C.C.C. (2d) 181, 26 D.L.R. (3d) 603, may have application here. He was considering the extent to which this Court might, under s. 1(a) of the *Bill of Rights*, the "due process of law" provision, have power to control substantive federal legislation. He said, on the assumption that such power might exist:

> . . . compelling reasons ought to be advanced to justify the Court in this case to employ a statutory (as contrasted with a constitutional) jurisdiction to deny operative effect to a substantive measure duly enacted by a Parliament constitutionally competent to do so, and exercising its powers in accordance with the tenets of responsible government, which underlie the discharge of legislative authority under the *British North America Act*.

In my opinion, in order to succeed in the present case, it would be necessary for the respondent, at least, to satisfy this Court that, in enacting s. 150, Parliament was not seeking to achieve a valid federal objective. This was not established or sought to be established.

In the result, in my opinion, s. 150 of the Act does not infringe the right of the respondent to equality before the law under s. 1(b) of the *Bill of Rights*. I would allow the appeal and set aside that portion of the judgment of the Court of Appeal which declares s. 150 of the Act to be inoperative.

RITCHIE J.: I would allow this appeal for the reasons stated by my brother Martland.

As is pointed out in those reasons and in the case of *Turcotte v. The Queen; Anderson v. The Queen*, [1970] S.C.R. 843, 11 C.R.N.S. 301, 73 W.W.R. 334, [1970] 5 C.C.C. 245, 12 D.L.R. (3d) 466, the purpose of s. 150 of the *Prisons and Reformatories Act*, R.S.C. 1970, c. P-21, is the reformation and training of young offenders and it appears to me to run contrary to the intent of the *Canadian Bill of Rights*, R.S.C. 1970, App. III, that the provisions of s. 1(b) of that statute which guarantee the right of the individual to equality before the law, should be so construed as to frustrate the very purpose of the impugned legislation on the ground that it only applies to offenders who are young and who have been convicted in a jurisdiction where institutions have been established for its fulfilment.

Unlike the legislation which was under consideration in the case of *Regina v. Drybones*, [1970] S.C.R. 282, 10 C.R.N.S. 334, 71 W.W.R. 161, [1970] 3 C.C.C. 355, 9 D.L.R. (3d) 473, s. 150 of the *Prisons and Reformatories Act* does not provide that one group of individuals is to be treated more harshly than another under the law; it is, on the contrary, in my opinion, designed for the benefit of the individuals concerned so that they may be afforded the opportunity to play a useful and profitable role in society and to avoid the risk of maturing into hardened criminals.

PIGEON J.: I agree with Martland J. subject to the views I have expressed in *A. G. Can. v. Lavell*; *Isaac v. Bedard* (1973), 23 C.R.N.S. 197, 11 R.F.L. 333, 38 D.L.R. (3d) 481 (Can.), so far as they happen to be different from those he has expressed.

LASKIN J. (dissenting): The question in this appeal by the Crown, brought to this Court by its leave, is a double-edged one. It is, first, whether s. 150 of the *Prisons and Reformatories Act*, R.S.C. 1970, c. P-21, is inoperative in the face of s. 1(b) of the *Canadian Bill of Rights*, R.S.C. 1970, App. III; and, second, whether s. 150 is open to a construction that would make it compatible with s. 1(b) aforesaid and thus obviate any need to reach the issue of inoperability. It is a singular feature of this appeal that although counsel for the appellant and counsel for the respondent have joined issue on the first aspect of the case they are at one, on the basis of an alternative argument of each, in supporting a compatible construction. Why this is so will be readily apparent from a short recital of the facts and from a reference to the judgment of this Court in *Turcotte v. The Queen*; *Anderson v. The Queen*, [1970] S.C.R. 843, 11 C.R.N.S. 301, 73 W.W.R. 334, [1970] 5 C.C.C. 245, 12 D.L.R. (3d) 466.

This appeal has its origin in a charge against the respondent, then 17 years of age, of a summary conviction offence for which the maximum punishment prescribed by the *Criminal Code*, R.S.C. 1970, c. C-34, is six months' imprisonment. Although acquitted at first instance, a conviction was entered against the accused after appeal and trial de novo before a County Court Judge. Following a pre-sentence report, the accused was sentenced to a term of three months definite and two years less one day indeterminate pursuant to s. 150 of the *Prisons and Reformatories Act* ...

The present difference between the two sections [s. 150 of the British Columbia Prisons and Reformatories Act and s. 44 of the Ontario Act], apart from the territorial limitation of each, lies in the application of the British Columbia provision to "any person apparently under the age of twenty-two years" (previously it was "any male person apparently over the age of sixteen years and under the age of twenty-three years") and in the application of the Ontario provision to "any male person" (previously it was "any person"). It was because the *Canadian Bill of Rights* might have as great an effect, if any at all, upon s. 44 as upon s. 150 that the Attorney General of Ontario sought and was given leave to intervene in the appeal to this Court. I may say here that although the Attorney General of

Canada intervened in the case before the British Columbia Court of Appeal and supported the efficacy of s. 150, he was not represented in this Court . . .

It is a plain fact that the decisions in *Turcotte* and *Anderson*, *supra*, were made without any consideration of the effect of the *Canadian Bill of Rights* because the Bill was not raised or argued as having any bearing upon the proper construction and application of the now ss. 150 and 44 of the *Prisons and Reformatories Act* . . .

Whatever may be the end result of the invocation and consideration of the *Canadian Bill of Rights* in relation to a piece of federal legislation, undeniably it brings a new dimension to construction. The process of construction must be related to prescriptions and standards under the *Canadian Bill of Rights* which, apart from the statute might or might not be seen as relevant matters, and, even if seen as relevant, would lack the definition that they have as statutory directives. It cannot, therefore, be said that the majority in the *Turcotte* and *Anderson* cases, *supra*, would inevitably have reached the same result if the *Canadian Bill of Rights* had been put into the scale; and similarly with the minority in those cases, because it is as possible that the Bill would have been seen as merely a reinforcement of their conclusion as that it would have carried them to the result reached in the present case by Branca and Nemetz JJ.A.

It is important to appreciate that the *Canadian Bill of Rights* does not invariably command a declaration of inoperability of any federal legislation affected by its terms. That may be the result, under the principle enunciated in the *Drybones* case, *supra*, if a construction and application compatible with the *Canadian Bill of Rights* cannot reasonably be found. The primary injunction of the Bill, however, is to determine whether a challenged measure is open to a compatible construction that would enable it to remain an effective enactment. If the process of construction in the light of the Bill yields this result, it is unnecessary and, indeed, it would be an abuse of judicial power to sterilize the federal measure.

I turn, in the light of these considerations, to the issue left open in the *Turcotte* case, namely, the effect of the *Canadian Bill of Rights* upon the construction and application of s. 150 . . .

As a matter of legislative power only, there can be no doubt about Parliament's right to give its criminal or other enactments special applications, whether in terms of locality of operation or otherwise. This has been recognized from the earliest years of this Court's existence: see, for example, *Fredericton v. The Queen* (1880), 3 S.C.R. 505, 2 Cart. 27. Through the *Canadian Bill of Rights*, Parliament has introduced constraints which, according to their scope, limit the extent to which its valid legislation may be qualified or given special application. The constraints, where they apply, are, of course, as subject to removal by Parliament as they were to introduction; but, to paraphrase what Abbott J. said in his reasons in *A. G. Can. v. Lavell*; *Isaac v. Bedard* (1973), 23 C.R.N.S. 197, 11 R.F.L. 333, 38 D.L.R. (3d) 481 (Can.), Parliament's choice of policy, when acting within its legislative powers, was for it alone, albeit that the courts became charged with duties of construction and application not theretofore before them . . .

In addressing itself to these issues the British Columbia Court of Appeal necessarily had to look to the *Criminal Code*, under which the accused was charged and which prescribed the punishment for his offence, as the reference point for judging whether s. 150 offended the *Canadian Bill of Rights*. Admittedly, the relevant *Criminal Code* provisions are themselves unexceptionable in that respect. In my opinion, the majority of the Court rightly concluded that insofar as s. 150 provided for the imposition of a greater punishment of the accused in British Columbia than elsewhere in Canada (save Ontario) for the same offence, it denied to him as an individual equality before the law.

The inequality resides in the greater disability to which the respondent here has been exposed than would be the case if the trial of his offence had been held in any other part of Canada, save Ontario. It is said, however, that the purpose of s. 150 (as of s. 44) was to provide, through a combination of determinate and indeterminate sentences, for rehabilitative and correctional service that would assist a prisoner to an easier if not speedier reintegration into society. What this submission involves is the contention that this purpose, for British Columbia prisoners in a certain age group and for Ontario male prisoners, establishes a permissible classification within the framework of the individual's right to equality before the law.

The question raised by this submission is whether the purpose alleged necessarily requires a construction of s. 150 that would entitle a convicting magistrate, notwithstanding the *Canadian Bill of Rights*, to impose a combined sentence beyond the limits fixed by the *Criminal Code*. Certainly, s. 150 does not clearly oust the punishment limits fixed by the *Criminal Code*. If it did, it would be necessary to consider whether the policy alleged to be at its base is consistent with the *Canadian Bill of Rights* when that policy embraces any federal offence punishable by at least three months' imprisonment. I do not think I need enter upon such a consideration because in a doubtful case, like the present one, it is preferable to support a construction that would clearly be compatible with the *Canadian Bill of Rights* than to embark upon an inquiry that could entail an examination of the reality of the policy and whether that policy can in any event be squared with s. 1(*b*) of the *Canadian Bill of Rights* when it prevails only in British Columbia in the terms in which it is expressed in s. 150.

I would adopt in respect of issues that are said to collide with the *Canadian Bill of Rights* the same approach that prevails where constitutional collision is suggested, namely, a preference for a construction that would avoid such a collision.

In my opinion, a construction of s. 150 in the light of the *Canadian Bill of Rights* that would enable a court in British Columbia to impose the maximum term of imprisonment fixed for the offence under the *Criminal Code* and in addition an indeterminate term of up to two years less one day appears on its face to be alien to the very purpose which is said to animate it. It seems to me to be very much more consonant with the suggested purpose, considered in the light of the *Canadian Bill of Rights*, that the combined fixed and indeterminate sentences be limited in their totality by the maximum term of imprisonment prescribed by the *Criminal Code* or other federal enactment creating an offence and prescribing its punishment. In this way, there is an umbrella of equality of permitted length of punishment and within that limit a scope for relaxing its stringency to accommodate a rehabilitative and correctional purpose. On this view, which commends itself to me, the age factor under s. 150 does not amount to a punitive element in that provision but rather rebounds to the advantage of an accused who is within the age group. It becomes unnecessary therefore to consider *A. G. B.C. v. Smith*, [1967] S.C.R. 702, 2 C.R.N.S. 277, 61 W.W.R. 236, [1969] 1 C.C.C. 244, 65 D.L.R. (2d) 82, and I note only that the *Canadian Bill of Rights* was not urged in that case which turned on purely constitutional grounds.

This view also leaves s. 150 as an operative provision, consistent both with the *Criminal Code* and with the *Canadian Bill of Rights*. In the result, I would dismiss the appeal but would vary the order of the British Columbia Court of Appeal by deleting the concluding paragraph declaring s. 150 to be inoperative, and substituting for it a declaration that s. 150, construed and applied under ss. 1(*b*) and 2 of the *Canadian Bill of Rights*, does not authorize the imposition of determinate and indeterminate sentences exceeding in their totality that fixed in this case by the *Criminal Code*.

Appeal allowed.

[S. 9(1) of the *Juvenile Delinquents Act*, R.S.C. 1970, c. J-3 provides that a child apparently or actually over the age of 14 years may be transferred to the ordinary courts for trial if "the good of the child and the interest of the community demand it." Is this a denial of equality before the law?

See *Re R. and M.* (1973), 2 O.R. (2d) 86, 23 C.R.N.S. 313 (*sub nom. M. v. R.*).

On s. 1(b) of the *Bill of Rights*, see also *Smythe v. R.*, [1971] S.C.R. 680, 16 C.R.N.S. 147, 3 C.C.C. (2d) 366, 19 D.L.R. (3d) 480, 71 D.T.C. 5252.]

HOGAN v. THE QUEEN

In the Supreme Court of Canada. (1974), 26 C.R.N.S. 207, 2 N.R. 343, 9 N.S.R. (2d) 145, 18 C.C.C. (2d) 65, 48 D.L.R. (3d) 427.

Appeal from conviction reported at (1972), 5 N.S.R. 73, for control of a motor vehicle while having an alcohol content of over 80 milligrams in 100 millilitres of blood.

RITCHIE J.: This is an appeal brought with leave of this Court, from a judgment of the Appeal Division of the Supreme Court of Nova Scotia (1972), 5 N.S.R. (2d) 73, which affirmed the judgment of Anderson Co. Ct. J., rendered after a trial de novo whereby he had affirmed the appellant's conviction entered in the Provincial Magistrate's Court before M. D. Haley, a judge of that Court, on an information charging that he "did unlawfully have the control of a motor vehicle having consumed alcohol in such a quantity that the proportion thereof in his blood exceeded 80 milligrams of alcohol in 100 millilitres of blood, contrary to s. 236 of the *Criminal Code* . . . [The learned judge deals with ss. 235 and 237 of the *Criminal Code* and then with the transcript of some of the evidence in the case.]

The result of the breathalyzer test was a finding of 230 milligrams of alcohol per 100 millilitres of blood and in the course of his cross-examination the appellant agreed that he had been drinking rum and could have had "a good pint".

It was contended on behalf of the appellant that the evidence of the result of the chemical analysis of his breath taken by Constable MacDonald, who was a qualified technician, was inadmissible because it was obtained in violation of s. 2(c)(ii) of the *Canadian Bill of Rights*, R.S.C. 1970, App. III, which provides, in part, that:

> "2. . . . no law of Canada shall be construed or applied so as to . . .
>
> "(c) deprive a person who has been arrested or detained . . .
>
> "(ii) of the right to retain and instruct counsel without delay."

Counsel for the appellant relied on the case of *Brownridge v. The Queen*, [1972] S.C.R. 926, 18 C.R.N.S. 308, 7 C.C.C. (2d) 417, 28 D.L.R. (3d) 1, in support of his contention that the evidence of the result of the breathalyzer test should have been excluded.

In the *Brownridge* case it was held that the denial of the right to retain and instruct counsel without delay to an accused person who was under arrest, afforded that person "reasonable excuse" for refusing to comply with the demand made pursuant to the *Criminal Code*, 1953-54 (Can.), c. 51, s. 223(2) [re-en. 1968-69 (Can.), c. 38, s. 16] (now R.S.C. 1970, c. C-34, s. 235(2)). In considering whether the *Brownridge* case can be said to govern the circumstances disclosed in the present case, it is to be remembered that Brownridge had refused to comply with a demand made under the purported authority of *Code* s. 235(1), and the only question to be determined was whether his having been denied the right to retain and instruct counsel constituted a "reasonable excuse" for such refusal. Laskin J. (as he then was) said in that case, in [1972] S.C.R. 926 at 954:

> This is not a case where the infringement of the *Canadian Bill of Rights* renders a federal enactment inoperative. *Regina v. Drybones* [[1970] S.C.R. 282, 10 C.R.N.S. 334, 71 W.W.R. 161, [1970] 3 C.C.C. 355, 9 D.L.R. (3d) 473] was a case where the particular federal enactment could have no operation at all in the face of the *Canadian Bill of Rights*. The present case does not present such a blunt face; its facts show that s. 223 can operate with due obedience to the *Canadian Bill of Rights*. Hence, all that is required is that in the invocation of or exercise of the powers under s. 223, allowance be made for the exercise of the over-riding right given by s. 2(c)(ii) of the *Canadian Bill of Rights*.
>
> In my view, the result of the failure of the police officer who demanded the breath sample to make that allowance vitiated the conviction in this case. This follows not on any theory that violation of the *Canadian Bill of Rights* carries this consequence in every criminal case, but

because the violation in this case was the very basis upon which the accused was charged with an offence under s. 223(2). In short, the refusal of the accused to give the breath sample until he had an opportunity to consult a lawyer, a position that he was entitled to take on the facts herein and on the application of s. 2(c)(ii) of the *Canadian Bill of Rights* to those facts, was the foundation of the charge and conviction for refusing to give a breath sample when so requested.

In the *Brownridge* case it was the denial of his right to "retain and instruct counsel without delay" which caused the accused to refuse to comply with the demand to provide a sample of his breath for analysis, whereas in the present case the appellant complied with the demand, albeit reluctantly, and there is no causal connection between the denial of the right to counsel and the obtaining of the certificate of the breathalyzer test which led to his conviction.

In my opinion the excerpts from the evidence which I have reproduced above clearly indicate that the initial demand to provide a sample of the breath for analysis was legally made by the constable on the highway in accordance with *Code* s. 235(1) at a time when the appellant was neither "arrested" nor "detained" and he appears to me to have complied with that demand without hesitation at least to the extent of agreeing "to accompany the peace officer for the purpose of enabling such a sample to be taken." There was no request for counsel at this stage, and it was only after he had reached the police station and was sitting waiting for the test that he heard the voice of the lawyer whom he had retained through the agency of his girlfriend and requested to see him in order to find out whether he had to take the test or not. It was then that Constable MacDonald told him that he "didn't have any right to see anyone until after the test and if I refused the test I would be charged with refusal of the breathalyzer." The appellant then took the test.

I have had the advantage of reading the reasons for judgment prepared for delivery by the present Chief Justice and I agree with him that the fact that the appellant could have refused the breathalyzer test unless he first consulted counsel does not mean that the breath test evidence was procured by illegal means or trickery and I agree with him also that the common-law rule of admissibility of illegally or improperly obtained evidence rests primarily on the relevancy of that evidence subject only to the discretion of the trial judge to exclude it on the ground of unfairness as that word was interpreted in this Court in *Regina v. Wray*, [1971] S.C.R. 272, 11 C.R.N.S. 235, [1970] 4 C.C.C. 1, 11 D.L.R. (3d) 673.

The result of the breathalyzer test in the present case was not only relevant, it was in fact of itself the only evidence upon which the appellant could have been convicted of the offence of which he was charged and it therefore constitutes proof of "the main issue before the court". Even if this evidence had been improperly or illegally obtained, there were therefore no grounds for excluding it at common law . . .

Laskin C.J.C., however, characterizes the *Canadian Bill of Rights* as a "quasi constitutional instrument" by which I take him to mean that its provisions are to be construed and applied as if they were constitutional provisions, and in so doing he would adopt as a matter of policy for Canada, apart from and at variance with the common-law position, the rule of absolute exclusion of all evidence obtained under circumstances where one of the provisions of the *Canadian Bill of Rights* has been violated. This approach stems from an acceptance of the reasoning of the Supreme Court of the United States in such cases as *Mapp v. Ohio* (1961), 166 N.E. 2d 387, 367 U.S. 643, where that rule was accepted in relation to evidence obtained after the violation of a right guaranteed by the American Constitution. These American cases, however, turn on the interpretation of a constitution basically different from our own and particularly on the effect to be given to the "due process of law" provision of the 14th Amendment of that Constitution for which I am unable to find any counterpart in the *B.N.A. Act*, 1867, which is the source of the legislative authority of the Parliament of Canada and is characterized in the *B.N.A. Act* (No. 2) 1949, c. 22, as "the Constitution of Canada".

The case of *Regina v. Drybones, supra*, is authority for the proposition that any law of Canada which abrogates, abridges or infringes any of the rights guaranteed by the *Canadian Bill of Rights* should be declared inoperative and to this extent it accorded a degree of paramountcy to the provisions of that statute, but whatever view may be taken of the constitutional impact of the *Bill of Rights*, and with all respect for those who may have a different opinion, I cannot agree that, wherever there has been a breach of one of the provisions of that Bill, it justifies the adoption of the rule of "absolute exclusion" on the American model which is in derogation of the common-law rule long accepted in this country.

I am, on the other hand, in agreement with the reasoning expressed by Lord Hodson in *King v. The Queen*, [1969] 1 A.C. 304, [1968] 2 All E.R. 610 . . .

PIGEON J.: I agree with Ritchie J. that this appeal should be dismissed on the basis that, even if the *Canadian Bill of Rights*, R.S.C. 1970, App. III, is given the same effect as a constitutional instrument, this does not mean that a rule of absolute exclusion, which is in derogation of the common-law rule, should govern the admissibility of evidence obtained wherever there has been a breach of one of the provisions continued in that Bill.

LASKIN J. (dissenting): The issue in this appeal may be formulated as follows. What is the effect of a denial by a police officer of a right to counsel under s. 2(c)(ii) of the *Canadian Bill of Rights*, 1960 (Can.), c. 44, now R.S.C. 1970, App. III, upon the admissibility of subsequently obtained breathalyzer evidence by which the appellant accused may be convicted of an offence under the *Criminal Code*, R.S.C. 1970, c. C-34, s. 236? Under s. 2(c)(ii) of the *Bill of Rights*, no law of Canada shall be construed or applied so as to deprive a person, who has been arrested or detained, of the right to retain and instruct counsel without delay. The offence under Code s. 236 is driving or having care or control of a motor vehicle while having a reading of alcohol in the blood exceeding .08.

In *Brownridge v. The Queen*, [1972] S.C.R. 926, 18 C.R.N.S. 308, 7 C.C.C. (2d) 417, 28 D.L.R. (3d) 1, this Court decided that an arrested person who refused to submit to a breath test when he was denied an opportunity to consult counsel before taking the test could not be found guilty of an offence under what is now *Code* s. 235(2). That provision, so far as material, makes it an offence for a person without reasonable excuse to fail or refuse to comply with a demand by a peace officer under *Code* s. 235(1) to take a breath test. The case now in appeal to this Court involves an accused who, similarly, was denied an opportunity to consult counsel before submitting to a demand that he take a breath test but who, unlike Brownridge, did not continue to insist that he must first consult his counsel. He yielded to the demand and took the test. His conviction under *Code* s. 236 was founded upon the evidence of the breathalyzer technician obtained in accordance with *Code* s. 237. It was conceded that without this evidence, obtained following denial of the accused's request to see his counsel (who was then in the police station to attend upon the accused), the conviction cannot stand.

It is common both to *Brownridge* and to the present case that access to counsel was not for the purpose nor would it have had the effect of delaying the taking of the breath sample beyond the two-hour period specified in *Code* s. 237(1)(c)(ii) . . .

In the present case, the issue goes a little deeper, and the question is not the lawfulness of a resistance to the continuing demand but whether, failing resistance, an accused who has wrongfully been denied counsel before taking the test may successfully contest the admissibility of the breathalyzer evidence which, taken under the special provisions for its use prescribed by *Code* s. 237, is tendered in support of a charge under *Code* s. 236.

In my opinion, the accused appellant is entitled to succeed in this contention. I do not find it necessary to gloss the word "demand" in *Code* s. 237(1)(c) and (f) to mean "lawful demand", consonant with the *Canadian Bill of Rights* in order to qualify the breathalyzer evidence as receivable, with all the statutory advantages for its reception provided by *Code* s. 237. Strictly speaking, if the demand is made in conformity with *Code* s. 235(1) this satisfies *Code* s. 237(1)(c) and (f). The more relevant consideration is the relationship between the *Canadian Bill of Rights* and the resort to special statutory methods of proof where there is previous denial to an accused of a related guarantee of the *Canadian Bill of Rights*. In this connection, I point out that there was in the present case no incompatibility between recognition of the particular guarantee of access to counsel and resort to the special mode of proof; and it was clearly the right of the accused to have access to counsel before the authorities proceeded to administer the breathalyzer test.

The question that arises, therefore, is whether the vindication of this right should depend only on the fortitude or resoluteness of an accused so as to give rise to a *Brownridge* situation, or whether there is not also an available sanction of a ruling of inadmissibility where the police authorities are able to overcome an accused's resistance to a breathalyzer test without prior access to counsel. Nothing short of this would give reasonable assurance of respect of an individual's right to counsel by police authorities whose duty to enforce the law goes hand in hand with a duty to obey it.

There is no suggestion here of any physical force in the ultimate submission of the accused without having had his right to counsel recognized, but I do not think that any distinction should be drawn in the establishment of principle according to whether an accused yields through fear or a feeling of helplessness or as a result of polite or firm importuning or aggressive badgering. I should note also that there was no contention of waiver by the accused of his right to counsel, assuming that would be an answer to an alleged breach of any of his rights as an individual under the *Canadian Bill of Rights*.

The present case does not involve this Court in any reassessment of the principles underlying the admissibility of illegally obtained evidence as they developed at common law. We have a statutory policy to administer, one which this Court has properly recognized as giving primacy to the guarantees of the *Canadian Bill of Rights* by way of a positive suppressive effect upon the operation and application of federal legislation: *Regina v. Drybones*, [1970] S.C.R. 282, 10 C.R.N.S. 334, 71 W.W.R. 161, [1970] 3 C.C.C. 355, 9 D.L.R. (3d) 473. The result may be as in *Drybones*, to render federal legislation inoperative or, as in *Brownridge*, federal legislation may become inapplicable in the particular situation while otherwise remaining operative. The sanction in the present case would be to preclude use against a person of a special form of proof when it is obtained following a deliberate violation or a right of that person under the *Canadian Bill of Rights*. If, as the Bill enjoins, s. 237 of the *Criminal Code* is not to be applied so as to deprive a detained person of access to counsel, I do not see how its provisions can be utilized against a detained person in any case where that person's right of access to counsel has been denied in the course of that utilization. Moreover, it cannot matter that resort to *Code* s. 237 is the only way in which proof can be made of the main element of the offence defined in *Code* s. 236.

Counsel for the Crown in this appeal put forward the decision of the Nova Scotia Supreme Court, sitting en banc, in *Regina v. Steeves*, 49 M.P.R. 227, 42 C.R. 234, [1964] 1 C.C.C. 266, 42 D.L.R. (2d) 335, and the decision of this Court in *O'Connor v. The Queen*, [1966] S.C.R. 619, 48 C.R. 270, [1966] 4 C.C.C. 342, 57 D.L.R. (2d) 123, in support of the conviction of the appellant. Both of these cases antedated *Drybones* . . .

Although it appears to me to be enough to rest my decision in this appeal on the operative view of the *Canadian Bill of Rights* taken in *Drybones*, I feel constrained to elaborate on the considerations which move me to allow this appeal. I do this because otherwise a comparison will inevitably be drawn between the policy underlying the admissibility of relevant evidence, no matter how obtained (unless it falls within the involuntary confession category) and the contrary policy which I would enforce here, and an explanation should be offered for preferring the latter. I approach my elaboration by noting that the present case does not fall easily into the class of cases where evidence is illegally obtained in the sense that illegal means or acts are the vehicles through which the impugned evidence is procured, as for example, by illegal search or seizure or by trespass or by force; nor does it fall easily within that class of cases where tricks or false-hoods are used to get evidence against an accused person . . .

The choice of policy here is to favour the social interest in the repression of crime despite the unlawful invasion of individual inter-ests and despite the fact that the invasion is by public officers charged with law enforcement. Short of legislative direction, it might have been expected that the common law would seek to balance the com-peting interests by weighing the social interest in the particular case against the gravity or character of the invasion, leaving it to the discretion of the trial judge whether the balance should be struck in favour of reception or exclusion of particular evidence. I have already indicated that the discretion has been narrowed, and, I would add, to an extent that underlines a wide preference for admissibility . . .

Opposed to the dominant common-law position is that at which the Supreme Court of the United States has arrived in enforcing the guarantees of the Fourth Amendment of the Constitution, applicable to the central authorities, against unreasonable searches and seizures, and, through it, those of the Fourteenth Amendment enjoining the States not to "deprive any person of life, liberty or property without due process of law". In general, a rule of exclusion of illegally obtained evidence, tendered to show the guilt of an accused, is enforced both in federal and state prosecutions: see *Weeks v. U.S.* (1914), 232 U.S. 383; *Mapp v. Ohio* (191), 166 NE 2d 387, 367 U.S. 643.

The American exclusionary rule, in enforcement of constitutional guarantees, is as much a judicial creation as was the common law of admissibility. It is not dictated by the Constitution, but its rationale appears to be that the constitutional guarantees cannot be adequately served if their vindication is left to civil actions in tort or criminal prosecutions, and that a check rein on illegal police activity which invades constitutional rights can best be held by excluding evidence obtained through such invasions. Whether this has resulted or can result in securing or improving respect for constitutional guarantees is not an easy question to answer, although attempts are being made to do so through empirical studies: see Spiotto, Search and Seizure: An Empirical Study of the Exclusionary Rule and Its Alternative (1973), 2 Jo. Leg. S. 243.

It may be said that the exclusion of relevant evidence is no way to control illegal police practices and that such exclusion merely allows a wrongdoer to escape conviction. Yet where constitutional guarantees are concerned, the more pertinent consideration is whether those guarantees, as fundamentals of the particular society, should be at the mercy of law enforcement officers and a blind eye turned to their invasion because it is more important to secure a conviction. The contention that it is the duty of the courts to get at the truth has in it too much of the philosophy of the end justifying the means; it would equally challenge the present law as to confessions and other out-of-court statements by an accused. In the United States, its Supreme Court, after weighing over many years whether other methods than exclusion of evidence should be invoked to deter illegal searches and seizures in state as well as in federal prosecutions, concluded that the constitutional guarantees could best be upheld by a rule of exclusion.

The Canadian Bill of Rights is a half-way house between a purely common-law regime and a constitutional one; it may aptly be described as a quasi-constitutional instrument. It does not embody any sanctions for the enforcement of its terms, but it must be the function of the courts to provide them in the light of the judicial view of the impact of that enactment. The *Drybones* case, *supra*, has established what the impact is, and I have no reason to depart from the position there taken. In the light of that position, it is to me entirely consistent, and appropriate, that the prosecution in the present case should not be permitted to invoke the special evidentiary provisions of s. 237 of the Criminal Code when they have been resorted to after denial of access to counsel in violation of s. 2(c)(ii) of the Canadian Bill of Rights. There being no doubt as to such denial and violation, the courts must apply a sanction. We would not be justified in simply ignoring the breach of a declared fundamental right or in letting it go merely with words of reprobation. Moreover, so far as denial of access to counsel is concerned, I see no practical alternative to a rule of exclusion if any serious view at all is to be taken, as I think it should be, of this breach of the Canadian Bill of Rights.

My conclusion does not, of course, preclude proof otherwise than by resort to Code s. 237, and such proof might well have been available to the Crown in respect of a charge of impaired driving under Code s. 234, had such a charge been laid in addition to or in lieu of a charge under Code s. 236.

I would, therefore, allow this appeal, set aside the judgments below and quash the conviction.

SPENCE J.:   I have had the opportunity to read the reasons for judgment written by my brother Laskin. I agree with his conclusion and with the reasons for that conclusion. I am also of the opinion that the appeal could also be allowed upon the basis that the word "demand" in s. 237(1)(c) and (f) of the *Criminal Code*, R.S.C. 1970, c. C-34, must be interpreted to mean a lawful demand and that a demand which was made in open defiance of the provisions of the Canadian Bill of Rights, R.S.C. 1970, App. III, could not be a lawful demand. Therefore, the certificate of the result of the test obtained after such unlawful demand is not one made admissible by the provisions of Code s. 237.

I, therefore, would allow the appeal.

Appeal dismissed.

[In *Brownridge v. The Queen*, [1972] S.C.R. 926, 18 C.R.N.S. 308, 7 C.C.C. (2d) 417, 28 D.L.R. (3d) 1, Ritchie J. writing the majority opinion held:

The refusal of the police constable to permit the appellant to speak to his lawyer, in the circumstances of this case, deprived him of the right to retain and instruct counsel without delay, and constituted a reasonable excuse for his refusal to comply with the demand of the police constable that he take a breath test. Having regard to the provisions of the *Bill of Rights*, s. 223(2) of the *Criminal Code* is required to be construed and applied in this sense, so that, unless it is apparent that an accused person is not asserting his right to counsel *bona fide*, but is asserting such right for the purpose of delay or for some other improper reason, the denial of that right affords a "reasonable excuse" for failing to provide a sample of his breath as required by the section.

Laskin J. in a concurring opinion stated *inter alia*:

I agree with this ruling of the trial Judge because I regard the phrase "without reasonable excuse" as adding a defence or a bar to successful prosecution which would not be available without those words, but not as encompassing defences or bars that would exist without them. For example, a right of diplomatic immunity from the domestic criminal law would exist regardless of the absence of the words "without reasonable excuse"; and similarly, in my view, if s. 2(c)(ii) of the *Canadian Bill of Rights* sets up a bar, it is one which is independent of the presence of the words in question. It would be strange, indeed, if the effect of the immunity above mentioned or of the *Canadian Bill of Rights* was vitiated by repeal of the words "without reasonable excuse". . . .

In my view, the result of the failure of the police officer who demanded the breath sample to make that allowance vitiated the conviction in this case. This follows not on any theory that violation of the *Canadian Bill of Rights* carries this consequence in every criminal case, but because the violation in this case was the very basis upon which the accused was charged with an offence under s. 223(2). In short, the refusal of the accused to give the breath sample until he had an opportunity to consult a lawyer, a position that he was entitled to take on the facts herein and on the application of s. 2(c)(ii) of the *Canadian Bill of Rights* to those facts, was the foundation of the charge and conviction for refusing to give a breath sample when so requested.

Fauteux C.J.C., Martland and Spence JJ. agreed with Ritchie J. Hall J. agreed with Laskin J. Abbot, Judson and Pigeon JJ. dissented.]

A.-G. CAN. v. CANARD

In the Supreme Court of Canada. [1975] 3 W.W.R. 1.

Appeal from a judgment of the Manitoba Court of Appeal, [1972] 5 W.W.R. 678, 30 D.L.R. (3d) 9, affirming a judgment of Matas J. [1972] 4 W.W.R. 618 holding that ss. 42 to 44 of the Indian Act, which vest the administration of estates of deceased Indians in the responsible Minister, infringe the Bill of Rights.

BEETZ J.: The respondent is the widow of the late Alexander Canard, an Indian of the Fort Alexander Indian Reserve No. 3 in the Province of Manitoba. Alexander Canard was killed in a traffic accident on July 6th, 1969. He died intestate.

On December 1st, 1969, appellant William Barber Rees, the superintendent in charge of the Clandeboye Fisher River Indian District, in the Province of Manitoba, was appointed to be administrator of Alexander Canard's estate by the Minister of Indian Affairs and Northern Development pursuant to ss. 42 and 43 of the *Indian Act*, R.S.C. 1952, c. 149 (now R.S.C. 1970, c. 1-6). In that capacity, on March 1st, 1970, he commenced an action in the Manitoba Court of Queen's Bench, claiming damages from three defendants in respect of the accident resulting in the death of Alexander Canard.

On March 18th, 1970, pursuant to an applicant made by the respondent, Letters of Administration were issued to her by the Surrogate Court of the Eastern Judicial District of Manitoba. The Minister of Indian Affairs and Northern Development had not given to that Court his consent to the exercise of testamentary jurisdiction under s. 44 of the *Indian Act* in relation to the estate of the late Alexander Canard. In her capacity as administratrix of the estate of her late husband, the respondent also commenced an action in the Court of Queen's Bench on July 6th, 1970, against the same three defendants and against a fourth one.

The respondent then commenced against the appellants the action which gave rise to the present appeal and which puts before us the issue we have to decide: which of the two administrators, if any, is the lawful one?

The respondent claims a judgment declaring that:

(a) Certain sections of the Indian Act dealing, among other matters, with the administration of the property of Indians who die intestate do not govern the administration of the estate of Alexander Canard because s. 4(3) of the Act provides that these sections do not apply to or in respect of any Indian who does not ordinarily reside on a reserve or on lands belonging to Her Majesty in right of Canada or a province; or

(b) Alternatively, if the Indian Act does apply, its ss. 42, 43 and 44 relating to descent of property and the administration of estates of Indians are *ultra vires* of the Parliament of Canada and contrary to the principles of the Canadian Bill of Rights [R.S.C. 1970, App. III] and the appointment of appellant Rees made under these sections is contrary to natural justice and is null and void . . .

The first question to be decided is whether the late Alexander Canard who, at the time of his death, resided on a farm at St. Andrews, did not ordinarily reside on the Fort Alexander Indian Reserve. If he did not, the provisions of the *Indian Act* relating to descent of property, wills, appeals, distribution of property on intestacy (ss. 42 to 50 of the Act) and to some other matters, would not, under s. 4(3) of the Act, govern the administration of his estate . . .

[The learned Judge held that the deceased was ordinarily resident on the reserve].

The next point is whether ss. 41 to 44 of the *Indian Act*, apart from the question of the effect upon them of the *Canadian Bill of Rights*, are *ultra vires* of the Parliament of Canada. This point has not been pressed before us but it appears to have been fully argued before the Court of Appeal which dealt with it in some detail. The respondent and the intervenants refer to it in their factums. The respondent's factum submits that "matters testamentary are property and civil rights" and that "the administration of the estate is therefore a disposition of property and civil rights" . . .

We are not called upon to decide the constitutional validity of ss. 42 *et seq.* in all their substantive and jurisdictional ramifications. Yet, for the purposes of this case, I find myself in agreement with the general proposition that testamentary matters and causes with respect to deceased Indians come within the class of subjects of "Indians and Lands reserved for the Indians" and that Parliament can constitutionally oust the jurisdiction of provincial courts in these as well as in other federal matters and vest it in a federal agency, subject perhaps to an obvious qualification: while Parliament has the power to establish courts for the administration of the laws of Canada, it does not necessarily follow that it can clothe a Minister, or any official or board of a non judicial nature with all the functions of a superior court; the powers of Parliament are limited by the wording of s. 101 of the *British North America Act*, 1867, as well as by the federal and fundamental nature of the Constitution which implies an inherent and entrenched jurisdiction in the courts to adjudicate in constitutional matters . . .

The third question to be decided is whether the impugned sections of the *Indian Act*, (ss. 42, 43 and 44) are in conflict with the *Canadian Bill of Rights*.

The Court of Appeal held that 43 of the *Indian Act* is "inoperative to the extent that, in violation of the *Bill of Rights* guaranteeing the right to equality before the law without discrimination by reason of race, it denies Mrs. Canard administration of the estate of her late husband".

It will have been noted that the Court of Appeal rendered its judgment after *R. v. Drybones*, [1970] S.C.R. 282, 10 C.R.N.S. 334, 71 W.W.R. 161, 9 D.L.R. (3d) 473, [1970] 3 C.C.C. 355, but before the decision of this Court in *A.G. Can. v. Lavell; Isaac v. Bédard* (1973) 11 R.F.L. 333, 23 C.R.N.S. 197, 38 D.L.R. (3d) 481. In both these cases as in the present one, the impact of the *Canadian Bill of Rights* upon certain provisions of the *Indian Act* had to be assessed. More particularly, the complex notion that every individual has the right to equality before the law and the protection of the law without discrimination by reason of race or sex had to be explored in its relationship with Indian status.

Status has been defined in various ways. The *Shorter Oxford Dictionary* describes it as "the legal standing or position of a person as determined by his membership of some class of persons legally enjoying certain rights or subject to certain limitations".

Narrower legal definitions of status have been proposed such as that of R.H. Graveson, in *Status in the Common Law*, 1953, p. 2:

> a special condition of a continuous and institutional nature, differing from the legal position of the normal person, which is conferred by law and not purely by the act of the parties, whenever a person occupies a position of which the creation, continuance or relinquishment and the incidents are a matter of sufficient social or public concern.

The legislative history of the western world has recognized a great diversity of status among which those of married women, infants, aliens, villeins, nobles, slaves, outlaws, merchants, illegitimate children, lunatics, bankrupts, clerics, etc. Flowing from status are special rights, duties, privileges or incapacities which are the consequences of status and which are sometimes called its incidents. While, conceivably, status can be considered apart from its incidents, it may be difficult to do so in many instances lest a particular status be emptied of any significant content.

The principle of equality before the law is generally hostile to the very nature of status and it is no easy task to reconcile the two in Canada when the one is enshrined in a quasi-constitutional statute and the other forms part of the fundamental law of the land. This the courts have attempted to do in *Drybones* and *Lavell*.

I take the following principles to be settled by the decision of this Court in *R. v. Drybones* [*supra*]:

(1) The *Canadian Bill of Rights* is more than a canon of interpretation, the terms of which would give way to any contrary legislative intent. It renders inoperative any law of Canada that cannot be construed and applied so that it does not abrogate, abridge or infringe one of the rights and freedoms recognized by the Bill, unless it is expressly declared by an Act of the Parliament of Canada that it shall operate notwithstanding the Bill, and it confers upon the courts the responsibility to declare any such law inoperative.

(2) Equality before the law without discrimination by reason of race, national origin, colour, religion or sex does not simply mean equality with every other person within the class to whom a particular law relates: such a meaning would render possible all forms of prohibited discrimination so long as the other members of a class were also being discriminated against in the same way.

(3) An Indian is being denied equality before the law contrary to the *Canadian Bill of Rights* if it is made an offence punishable at law, on account of his race, for him to do something which his fellow Canadians are free to do without committing any offence or being made subject to any penalty.

These principles were reaffirmed in this Court by 8 judges out of 9 in the *Lavell* case. (Pigeon J. took the position that he could not disagree with the view he had expressed in *Drybones*).

Considering the division of opinion in *Lavell*, it is admittedly difficult, if it is possible, to formulate the *ratio decidendi* of the case. Still, in the light of the opinion of Ritchie J. whose conclusions are those of the majority, I understand *Lavell* to have primarily decided that Parliament must not be deemed to have subjected to the *Canadian Bill of Rights* the authority vested upon it under s. 91.24 of the *British North America Act*, 1867, exclusively to make laws for "Indians and Lands reserved for the Indians", in so far as this authority, being of a special nature, could not be effectively exercised without the necessarily implied power to define who is and who is not an Indian and how Indian status is acquired or lost. In so defining Indian status, Parliament could, without producing conflict with the *Canadian Bill of Rights,* establish between various sorts of inter-marriages, such distinctions as could reasonably be regarded to be inspired by a legitimate legislative purpose in the light for instance of long and uninterrupted history.

Laskin J. (as he then was), whose opinion was concurred in by three other judges, took the view that the *Canadian Bill of Rights* "does not differentiate among the various heads of legislative power" and that "it embraces all exercises under whatever head or heads they arise".

The *British North America Act*, 1867, under the authority of which the *Canadian Bill of Rights* was enacted, by using the word "Indians" in s. 91.24, creates a racial classification and refers to a racial group for whom it contemplates the possibility of a special treatment. It does not define the expression "Indian". This Parliament can do within constitutional limits by using criteria suited to this purpose but among which it would not appear unreasonable to count marriage and filiation and, unavoidably, intermarriages, in the light of either Indian customs and values which, apparently were not proven in *Lavell*, or of legislative history of which the court could and did take cognizance.

Of course, it is possible to legislate in several ways with respect to Indians without impinging upon the principle of equality and other principles incorporated in the *Canadian Bill of Rights*, and this is a point which has also been made by Laskin J. in *Lavell* where he wrote that "discriminatory treatment on the basis of race or colour or sex does not inhere in that grant of legislative power". Nevertheless, it is not easy so to legislative irrespective or race or sex when it is race which has to be defined and, assuming it were possible if one were to start afresh, it may be next to practically impossible so to do for an already existing group which has been sociologically and legislatively defined since before Confederation. The alternative would appear to have been the abolition of the present Indian status or of any Indian status. A very real issue also in *Lavell* was not only whether a fundamental change in Indian status could be done for one or two individuals, on an *ad hoc* basis and without risk of social disruption but whether, as a matter of principle, it should be done on a possibly large scale, in one stroke, (since the courts are without much power to insure transitory stages for any reform that they be called to bring about), regardless of local wishes, desires or preparation. What was decided in *Lavell* finally was that some exclusive rights or privileges such as registration or registrability and the use and benefit of the reserves can be made incidents of Indian status without conflict with the *Canadian Bill of Rights*. But it is to be noted that these incidents are intimately connected with Indian status. They are not remote or indirect incidents. Registration is the administrative instrumentality whereby Indian status is acknowledged and the right to the exclusive use of the reserve is a necessarily incidental consequence of the idea that certain lands are "reserved" for the Indians.

The issue in *Lavell* is commonly taken to be that of discrimination by reason of sex and, admittedly, it was an essential part of it. However, it was not simply a matter of discriminating between men and women, but of distinguishing between married men and married women, Indian married men and Indian married women, and an Indian male married to a non-Indian woman, and an Indian female married to a non-Indian male. Whether or not it compounded the discrimination, as Laskin J. put it, it certainly did not simplify the problem. But, through and above the question of sex and marriage, what was really at stake was the present Indian status and some of its unseverable incidents.

By contrast, it is not evident that the litigious question in *Drybones* had to do with Indian status or even with the incidents of Indian status. *Drybones*, in the light of *Lavell*, may be rationalized in more than one way: for instance either the attaching of a particular consequence to Indian status could not be characerized as a provision in pith and substance relating to Indians and lands reserved for the Indians but as the use of other federal powers such as the power to enact penal laws for the promotion of temperance and the prevention of drunkenness which would not stand on the same footing *vis-à-vis* the *Canadian Bill of Rights* as the power to make laws for Indians and lands reserved for the Indians; or, assuming a particular consequence of Indian status could be said to pertain to "Indian" legislation, it would not be beyond the reach of the *Canadian Bill of Rights,* if it was so remote or indirect an incident as not to be indispensable to the effective exercise of the federal power under s. 91.24 of the *British North America Act*, 1867. In any event, it was made clear in *Drybones* that Parliament could not, without conflict with the *Canadian Bill of Rights*, purport to attach just any consequence to Indian status.

The present case differs from both *Drybones* and *Lavell*. What is in issue is neither the definition of Indian status nor, directly at least, the attachment of some incapacity to Indian status, such as testamentary incapacity.

In bestowing upon a Minister rather than upon a provincial surrogate court the power to appoint an administrator to the estate of a deceased Indian, the *Indian Act* evidently creates for Indian estates a forum which differs from the forum which would be competent in other testamentary causes. But in my view, the establishment of a special forum does not of itself entail a form of undue discrimination. If it were otherwise, Parliament, by enacting the *Canadian Bill of*

Rights, would have purported to bind itself not to exercise *at all*, except in accordance with the manner and form prescribed by the *Canadian Bill of Rights*, a power which it solely possesses under the Constitution, namely the power to create a forum for the administration of its laws and more particularly a forum for the administration of testamentary matters and causes with respect to deceased Indians. Such a consequence would be tantamount to an amendment of the *British North America Act*, 1867. It would also be contrary to the decision of this Court in *Lavell* with this difference: that *Lavell* dealt with a matter of substantive law whereas the respondent in this case complains that she is being denied access to a provincial court and that the determination of some of her rights depends upon the Minister. Furthermore, the power bestowed upon the Minister by the Indian Act to appoint administrators of Indian estates, given its nature and history, is a power perfectly capable of being exercised by him in a judicial or quasi-judicial manner, under judicial control, in accordance with the due process of law and with standards applicable to other Canadians as well as with all the requirements of the *Canadian Bill of Rights*.

I see nothing in ss. 42 and 43 of the *Indian Act* which prevents the Minister from exercising in this manner the surrogate power devolved upon him. To be more specific, there is nothing in ss. 42 and 43 of the *Indian Act*, the way I read them, which prevents the Minister on account of the respondent's race from authorizing her to administer the estate of her late husband, and nothing which deprives the respondent from the capacity to receive such authorization. The Act empowers the Minister to appoint anyone, including the respondent. In other words, if the respondent has been the victim of racial discrimination, such discrimination was administrative in nature; it does not flow from the *Indian Act*. The *Indian Act* in this respect is capable of being construed and applied so as to provide for Indians a treatment similar to that reserved for their fellow Canadians. Accordingly, it is not in conflict with the *Canadian Bill of Rights* and no part of it ought to be declared inoperative for the purpose of this case.

Although under the *Indian Act* the respondent was capable of being appointed administratrix of her late husband's estate by the Minister, the fact remains that she was not. The outstanding question is whether the Act has been applied in accordance with the principle of equality before the law.

The sections of the federal statute we are concerned with relate to the administration of a private estate a matter which, were it not for the fact that this estate is that of a deceased Indian, would normally fall under provincial jurisdiction. Accordingly, in a case such as the present one, in order to determine whether the principle of equality before the law has been complied with in the administration of federal law (or, in other words, whether an Indian is not deprived of a right generally recognized to other Canadians), some reference to the standards of provincial laws and practices may be unavoidable as there is no other basis for comparison except perhaps the ordinances of the Yukon and the Northwest territories, which, under the *Canadian Bill of Rights*, are laws of Canada. It could be argued that a reference to such a variety of standards might entail complications and variations in the administration of the *Indian Act* across Canada and, indeed, I do not wish to suggest that Parliament, in legislating on testamentary matters and causes with respect to Indians, or the Minister, in administering the *Indian Act*, are bound to follow all provincial enactments and practices over which they have no control in any event: this they might not be able to do, they might not find desirable to do and, in my view, they are not required to do in order to comply with the *Canadian Bill of Rights*. But there may well emerge from the variety of provincial laws on these matters a body of general rules common to all or to many provinces, which for want of other criteria and as a sort of *jus gentium* is susceptible to provide general minimum standards to which reference can be made for the purpose of deciding how the principle of equality can be safe-guarded. . . .

PIGEON J.: I agree in the result with Beetz J. I also concur in his reasons for holding that the late Alexander Canard was, at his death, ordinarily resident on a reserve.

On the constitutional question, I adhere to the view that the very object of s. 91(24) of the *British North America Act* in so far as it relates to Indians, is to enable the Parliament of Canada to make legislation applicable only to Indians as such, and I fail to see any reason why provisions with respect to the administration of the estate of deceased Indians would be excluded from the scope of such authority.

Concerning the contention that such provisions were made in-operative by the *Canadian Bill of Rights*, I would refer to the para-graph from my reasons in *Drybones* quoted by Ritchie J. in *Lavell* (1973), 23 C.R.N.S. 197 at 207-208. Also, it appears to me that the provisions of the *Indian Act* vesting in the Minister jurisdiction for the appointment of administrators, cannot be considered as an infringe-ment of the principle of equality before the law, for much the same reasons as provisions creating a special jurisdiction respecting juvenile delinquents and authorizing discretionary transfers to the ordinary courts cannot be looked upon as violations of that same rule. In this connection, I would refer to the recent judgment of Houlden J. in *Re R. and M.*, (1973), 2 O.R. (2d) 86, 23 C.R.N.S. 313 (sub nom. *M. v. R.*). This conclusion is entirely consistent with the judgment of this Court in *Smythe v. R.*, [1971] S.C.R. 680, 16 C.R.N.S. 147, 3 C.C.C. (2d) 366, 19 D.L.R. (3d) 480, 71 D.T.C. 5252, holding that provisions for stiffer penalties depending on the method of prosecution do not infringe equality before the law although the choice of the method depends on executive discretion. . . .

RITCHIE J.: The *Bill of Rights* was designed to eradicate any dis-criminatory laws passed by the Parliament of Canada and to guaran-tee the rights and freedoms therein specified to all Canadian citizens, but these guarantees are expressly declared in the preamble to the Bill to be enacted so as to "reflect the respect of Parliament for its constitution", and s. 91(24) of that document clearly vests in the Parliament of Canada the authority to pass laws concerning Indians which are different from the laws which the provincial legislatures may enact concerning the citizens of the various provinces.

If the provisions of the *Indian Act* and the regulations made thereunder are to be declared inoperative as offending against the guarantee provided by s. 1(b) of the *Bill of Rights* wherever they have the effect of treating Indians differently from other Canadians, then it seems to me to follow that eventually all such differences will be eradicated and Indians will in all respects be treated in the same way as their fellow citizens under the law. I cannot believe that the special Indian status so clearly recognized in the *British North America Act* is to be whittled away without express legislation being passed by the Parliament of Canada to that effect.

This is not a case like that of *R. v. Drybones*, [*supra*] where there was found to be inequality before the law because of the interaction of two federal statutes, nor is it like the case of *A.-G. Can. v. Lavell* [*supra*] where it was alleged that the *Indian Act* by its own provisions created inequality by reason of sex. It appears to me that in the present context there can only be a conflict between the *Bill of Rights* and the *Indian Act* if the *Indian Act*, standing alone or read in conjunction with other federal legislation, can be said to result in a denial to Indians of the equality before the law guaranteed by s. 1(b) of the *Bill*.

I have had the advantage of reading the reasons for judgment of my brother Beetz and I agree with him that the power to appoint an administrator of the estate of a person who has died intestate is not one which must necessarily be assigned to a court and that there is nothing unconstitutional in Parliament excluding the authority of provincial courts over this subject and bestowing it upon a Minister. I think it of interest also to note that while the provisions respecting the appointment of such an administrator vary from province to province, the ultimate discretion as to such appointment rests with the provincial courts, and although the widow occupies a preferred position in applying for administration of the estate of her deceased husband, it is clear that she is not entitled, *as a matter of right* to administer the estate of her late husband, and that, depending on the circumstances, the court may, in its discretion, appoint some other person (e.g. the *Surrogate Courts Act* of Manitoba, R.S.M. 1970, c. C290, s. 31).

For these reasons, as well as for those advanced by Mr. Justice Pigeon, I would dispose of this appeal in the manner proposed by my brother Beetz.

MARTLAND J.: . . . In my opinion there are legitimate reasons of policy for the enactment of such provisions in relation to the estate assets of deceased Indians ordinarily resident on reserves.

I cannot find in these provisions discrimination against the respondent by reason of race. They relate exclusively to the administration of the estates of deceased Indians, in certain circumstances, and apply generally to such estates. There is no federal legislation relating to the administration of estates of non-Indians in the provinces, and, constitutionally, such legislation could not be enacted. This is not a case in which federal legislation dealing with a subject matter within s. 91 of the *British North America Act* has permitted certain acts or conduct by non-Indians and prohibited Indians from doing the same thing. The provisions of the *Indian Act*, including s. 43, deal only with the legal rights of Indians.

For these reasons, as well as those delivered by my brother Ritchie and by my brother Pigeon, I would allow this appeal and dispose of the matter in the manner proposed by my brother Beetz.

LASKIN C.J.C. (dissenting) : I have had the advantage of reading the reasons prepared by my brother Beetz and the concurring reasons of my brother Pigeon, holding that the Manitoba courts were wrong in concluding that s. 43 of the *Indian Act*, R.S.C. 1952, c. 149, now R.S.C. 1970, c. I-6, was inoperative in the present case because of incompatibility with s. 1(b) of the *Canadian Bill of Rights*. I accept the narrative of facts in the reasons of Beetz J. but I cannot accept his conclusion that s. 1(b) of the *Canadian Bill of Rights* is without effect . . .

The only point for serious consideration in this appeal is whether any of the prescriptions of the *Canadian Bill of Rights* are offended by certain provisions of the *Indian Act* or by the administration of those provisions through regulations promulgated under the *Indian Act*. The Manitoba Court of Appeal took the position that s. 43 of the *Indian Act* disqualified an Indian, whether male or female, from being an administrator or administratrix of his or her deceased spouse's estate and that this created an inequality before the law by reason of race in violation of s. 1(b) of the *Canadian Bill of Rights*. Dickson J.A., as he then was, speaking for the Manitoba Court of Appeal, formulated the conclusion as follows [[1972] 5 W.W.R. 678 at 691-692] :

> In the present case we have a situation in which the Parliament of Canada has said in effect "because you are an Indian you shall not administer the estate of your late husband". Parliament has thereby in a law of Canada placed a legal road block in the way of one particular racial group, placing that racial group in a position of inequality before the law. The inequality does not arise through conflict between a federal statute with a provincial statute. It arises through conflict between the *Bill of Rights* and a federal statute. The Bill of Rights has capacity to render inoperative, racially discriminatory legislation, whether or not there be provincial legislation touching the subject matter . . .
>
> The right of Mrs. Canard to equality before the law of Canada does not depend upon which province she happens to live in. She enjoys that right as a citizen of Canada. If a law of Canada infringes that right on racial grounds, the *Bill of Rights* is available to remedy the injustice.

There is no doubt that this statement of principle carries the operation of s. 1(b) of the *Canadian Bill of Rights* beyond the law as considered in *R. v. Drybones*, [1970] S.C.R. 282 and beyond the law as expounded even in the minority judgment in *A.-G. Can. v. Lavell* (1973), 23 C.R.N.S. 197. In each of those two cases, this Court took the position that the *Canadian Bill of Rights* would have an operative effect if the conflict with any of its provisions arose under federal law in the sense' that there was a discordance either between two federal statutes or between provisions of the same federal statute such as to exhibit that one of the statutes or one of the provisions was *vis-à-vis* the other in conflict with a prescription of the *Canadian Bill of Rights*. The effect of the judgment of Dickson J.A. is to measure the operation of a federal statute, or any provision thereof, by the guarantees (if I may so term them) of the *Canadian Bill of Rights* alone, and thus to treat those guarantees as requiring not only comparative conformity to their terms but conformity by a challenged statute alone.

I do not find this to be other than a proper appreciation of what the *Canadian Bill of Rights* says. This Court in *Curr v. The Queen*, [1972] S.C.R. 889, 18 C.R.N.S. 281, 7 C.C.C. (2d) 181, 26 D.L.R. (3d) 603, explored the issues in that case under the same appreciation. The fact that the Court has not hitherto found it necessary to give effect to the *Canadian Bill of Rights* in relation to a particular statute measured in its own terms against the prescriptions of s. 1(b) of the *Canadian Bill of Rights* is not a ground for refusing to do so in a case which calls for consideration of such an issue. This is what the Supreme Court of the United States has been doing over the years in testing state and federal legislation under the American Bill of Rights. This Court has done exactly this in relation to other provisions of the *Canadian Bill of Rights*, as, for example, in *Brownridge v. The Queen*, [1972] S.C.R. 926, 18 C.R.N.S. 308, 7 C.C.C. (2d) 417, 28 D.L.R. (3d) 1, in relation to s. 2(c)(ii) (the right of a person who has been arrested or detained to retain and instruct counsel without delay), and in *Lowry v. The Queen*, [1974] S.C.R. 195, 19 C.R.N.S. 315, [1972] 5 W.W.R. 229, 6 C.C.C. (2d) 531, 26 D.L.R. (3d) 224, in relation to s. 2(e) (the right to a fair hearing in accordance with the principles of fundamental justice for the determination of rights and obligations), a provision which, as Martland J. speaking for the Court rightly said [[1974] S.C.R. 195 at 201], relates back to those rights guaranteed by s. 1. The proposition advanced by Dickson J.A. is with due recognition of the fact that the Parliament of Canada may take any of its legislation out of the scope of the *Canadian Bill of Rights* by appropriate enactment.

What is involved in this approach, patent on the face of the *Canadian Bill of Rights*, is the premise of our legal system that no legal permission is needed to do anything or act in any manner not prohibited by law, whether statute law or common law. Hence, if a federal enactment were to operate prohibitively against a specified class of persons by reason, for example, of colour or religion, saying nothing about other classes, the question of its operability under the

Canadian Bill of Rights would arise notwithstanding that there was no federal legislation expressly sanctioning for those other classes what was prohibited for a specified class. In short, the question would be whether, having regard to the purpose of the statute, it had accorded equality before the law (to take s. 1(b) of the *Canadian Bill of Rights* as illustrative) to the affected class. It is easy to give examples; for instance, a provision in federal railway legislation prohibiting Indians alone from travelling in first class accommodation; or a provision in federal communications legislation prohibiting members of Jehovah's Witnesses from participating in religious programmes on radio or television; or a provision in federal banking legislation prohibiting persons of Asian descent from being bank directors. None of these illustrations are intended pejoratively, but they do raise the issue that arises here, namely, that it appears to be forbidden to Indians to become administrators of estates of Indian intestates, where no other class is singled out for disqualification.

It is said, however, that because questions of administration of estates are, generally, in the provincial domain, a consideration of the disqualification of Indians under the *Indian Act* would mean testing the operation of the *Canadian Bill of Rights* by reference to provincial legislation and that this is outside the scope of the *Canadian Bill of Rights* which applies only to federal law. In my opinion, this is to obtrude an irrelevant factor into the matter at issue. If provincial legislation respecting the administration of estates exhibited any conflict with the prescriptions of the *Canadian Bill of Rights*, that would be obviously no ground for challenging its operability as provincial legislation. Correlatively, I seen no reason to refer to provincial legislation to test the operability of federal legislation under the *Canadian Bill of Rights*. The question whether any of the prescriptions of the *Canadian Bill of Rights* are offended by federal legislation depends on what that legislation provides and on the reach of the *Canadian Bill of Rights* itself.

It is thus not a telling factor for me that the respondent Mrs. Canard was appointed administratrix of her late husband's estate by letters of administration issued out of a Surrogate Court in Manitoba . . .

On the face of the *Indian Act* as amplified by the Regulations thereunder, and certainly as fortified by the invariable practice of the Department of Indian Affairs, Indians are disqualified from obtaining letters of administration of the estate of an Indian intestate, even in the case where the intestate is a spouse, and a *fortiori* where the intestate may have a lesser relationship to a would-be Indian applicant. The contention is, however, and here the judgment of Ritchie J. in the *Lavell* case is invoked, that federal legislative authority in relation to Indians is itself an expression of a classification that removes the *Indian Act* and allied legislation from any taint under the *Canadian Bill of Rights*. We are told that the reason why the *Drybones* case stands apart is because there other federal legislation had established a position of inequality by reason of race that operated against

Indians alone, and that that is not this case, nor was it the case in *Lavell*.

If anything, the *Drybones* case is quite consistent with the approach I would take here. The fact that the Court had before it a liquor ordinance of the Territories which made it an offence for any person to be intoxicated in a public place and that s. 94(b) of the *Indian Act* made it an offence for an Indian to be intoxicated off a *Reserve*, meant only that whereas all others in the Territories were not subject to liability and penalty for intoxication in other than a public place an Indian was so subject. I cannot believe that the *Drybones* case would have been decided differently if s. 94(b) of the *Indian Act* stood alone, thus making Indians alone subject to liability and penalty for being intoxicated off a Reserve but there was no prohibition against anyone else. The Territories liquor ordinance merely circumscribed the offence and the issue of inequality resided in the want of any prohibition outside of that circumscription affecting others than Indians.

Of course, it is much easier for the courts to apply the *Canadian Bill of Rights* to a federal legislative measure if Parliament itself provides the touchstone of comparison in other federal legislation. Yet, it may equally provide it by what it has done and failed to do in the very measure that is under challenge. The Court's function in such a case is different only in degree but not in kind.

In my opinion, to the extent that there is any majority opinion in the *Lavell* case (having regard to the separate concurring reasons of Pigeon J. since the Court was otherwise evenly split), it resides in the view that the *Indian Act* is a self-contained code which if it exhibits any dissonance with the *Canadian Bill of Rights* is justified by the very fact that Indians have been designated as a special class for which Parliament may legislate. I did not accept that view in *Lavell* and I do not accept it now, because I do not regard the mere grant of legislative power as itself authorizing Parliament to offend against its generally stated protections in the *Canadian Bill of Rights*. If Parliament deems it necessary to treat its grant of legislative power under s. 91(24) of the *British North America Act* in terms that would be offensive to the *Canadian Bill of Rights*, it is open to Parliament to do so, but s. 91(24) is not, in my opinion, an invitation to the courts to do what Parliament has not chosen to do. It seems to me patent that no grant of federal legislative power, as a mere vehicle for legislation, should be viewed as necessarily carrying with it a built-in exclusion of the mandates of the *Canadian Bill of Rights*.

Lavell was, apart from the foregoing, an even more obvious case than *Drybones* for the application of the *Canadian Bill of Rights*, because the inequality in that case, on the ground of sex, was built into the *Indian Act* itself. The present case on its facts is at least as susceptible as was *Drybones* to the purging effect of the *Canadian Bill of Rights*, and I can add nothing more in this respect to what was said more tersely but just as effectively by Dickson J.A.

I would dismiss the appeal with costs but I would vary the judgment of the Manitoba Court of Appeal by avoiding any declaration that s. 43 of the *Indian Act* is inoperative and by declaring instead that s. 43 must be applied consistently with s. 1(b) of the *Canadian Bill of Rights* and that s. 11 of the Indian Estates Regulations is inoperative in so far as it excludes Indians from eligibility to be administrators of the estates of deceased Indians.

The Attorney General of Canada undertook, if he was successful here, to pay the costs of the appellant in this Court on a party and party basis and to forgo costs in the courts below. In view of the result I reach, the appellant does not need this indulgence.

Appeal allowed.

APPENDICES

British North America Acts, 1867-1965

The Canadian Bill of Rights, 1960

APPENDIX I

British North America Acts, 1867-1965

30 & 31 Victoria, c. 3.

(Consolidated with amendments to 1965)

An Act for the Union of Canada, Nova Scotia, and New Brunswick, and the Government thereof; and for Purposes connected therewith.

(29th March, 1867.)

WHEREAS the Provinces of Canada, Nova Scotia and New Brunswick have expressed their Desire to be federally united into One Dominion under the Crown of the United Kingdom of Great Britain and Ireland, with a Constitution similar in Principle to that of the United Kingdom:

And whereas such a Union would conduce to the Welfare of the Provinces and promote the Interests of the British Empire:

And whereas on the Establishment of the Union by Authority of Parliament it is expedient, not only that the Constitution of the Legislative Authority in the Dominion be provided for, but also that the Nature of the Executive Government therein be declared:

And whereas it is expedient that Provision be made for the eventual Admission into the Union of other Parts of British North America: (1)

I.—PRELIMINARY.

1. This Act may be cited as The British North America Act, 1867. Short title.

2. Repealed. (2)

II.—UNION.

3. It shall be lawful for the Queen, by and with the Advice of Her Majesty's Most Honourable Privy Council, to declare by Proclamation that, on and after a Day therein Declaration of Union.

---

(1) The enacting clause was repealed by the *Statute Law Revision Act, 1893,* 56-57 Vict., c. 14 (U.K.). It read as follows:

Be it therefore enacted and declared by the Queen's Most Excellent Majesty, by and with the Advice and Consent of the Lords Spiritual and Temporal, and Commons, in this present Parliament assembled, and by the Authority of the same, as follows:

appointed, not being more than Six Months after the passing of this Act, the Provinces of Canada, Nova Scotia, and New Brunswick shall form and be One Dominion under the Name of Canada; and on and after that Day those Three Provinces shall form and be One Dominion under that Name accordingly. (3)

Construction of subsequent Provisions of Act.

4. Unless it is otherwise expressed or implied, the Name Canada shall be taken to mean Canada as constituted under this Act. (4)

Four Provinces.

5. Canada shall be divided into Four Provinces, named Ontario, Quebec, Nova Scotia, and New Brunswick. (5)

---

(2) Section 2, repealed by the *Statute Law Revision Act, 1893,* 56-57 Vict., c. 14 (U.K.), read as follows:

Application of Provisions referring to the Queen.

2. The Provisions of this Act referring to Her Majesty the Queen extend also to the Heirs and Successors of Her Majesty, Kings and Queens of the United Kingdom of Great Britain and Ireland.

(3) The first day of July, 1867, was fixed by proclamation dated May 22, 1867.

(4) Partially repealed by the *Statute Law Revision Act, 1893,* 56-57 Vict., c. 14 (U.K.). As originally enacted the section read as follows:

> **4.** The subsequent Provisions of this Act shall, unless it is otherwise expressed or implied, commence and have effect on and after the Union, that is to say, on and after the Day appointed for the Union taking effect in the Queen's Proclamation; and in the same Provisions, unless it is otherwise expressed or implied, the Name Canada shall be taken to mean Canada as constituted under this Act.

(5) Canada now consists of ten provinces (Ontario, Quebec, Nova Scotia, New Brunswick, Manitoba, British Columbia, Prince Edward Island, Alberta, Saskatchewan and Newfoundland) and two territories (the Yukon Territory and the Northwest Territories).

The first territories added to the Union were Rupert's Land and the North-Western Territory, (subsequently designated the Northwest Territories), which were admitted pursuant to section 146 of the *British North America Act, 1867* and the *Rupert's Land Act, 1868,* 31-32 Vict., c. 105 (U.K.), by Order in Council of June 23, 1870, effective July 15, 1870. Prior to the admission of these territories the Parliament of Canada enacted the *Act for the temporary Government of Rupert's Land and the North-Western Territory when united with Canada* (32-33 Vict., c. 3), and the *Manitoba Act* (33 Vict., c. 3), which provided for the formation of the Province of Manitoba.

British Columbia was admitted into the Union pursuant to section 146 of the *British North America Act, 1867,* by Order in Council of May 16, 1871, effective July 20, 1871.

Prince Edward Island was admitted pursuant to section 146 of the *British North America Act, 1867,* by Order in Council of June 26, 1873, effective July 1, 1873.

On June 29, 1871, the United Kingdom Parliament enacted the *British North America Act, 1871* (34-35 Vict., c. 28) authorizing the creation of additional provinces out of territories not included in any province. Pursuant to this statute, the Parliament of Canada enacted *The Alberta Act,* (July 20, 1905, 4-5 Edw. VII, c. 3) and *The Saskatchewan Act,* (July 20, 1905, 4-5 Edw. VII, c. 42), providing for the creation of the provinces of Alberta and Saskatchewan respectively. Both these Acts came into force on Sept. 1, 1905.

Meanwhile, all remaining British possessions and territories in North America and the islands adjacent thereto, except the colony of Newfoundland and its

6. The Parts of the Province of Canada (as it exists at the passing of this Act) which formerly constituted respectively the Provinces of Upper Canada and Lower Canada shall be deemed to be severed, and shall form Two separate Provinces. The Part which formerly constituted the Province of Upper Canada shall constitute the Province of Ontario; and the Part which formerly constituted the Province of Lower Canada shall constitute the Province of Quebec. Provinces of Ontario and Quebec.

7. The Provinces of Nova Scotia and New Brunswick shall have the same Limits as at the passing of this Act. Provinces of Nova Scotia and New Brunswick.

8. In the general Census of the Population of Canada which is hereby required to be taken in the Year One thousand eight hundred and seventy-one, and in every Tenth Year thereafter, the respective Populations of the Four Provinces shall be distinguished. Decennial Census.

III.—EXECUTIVE POWER.

9. The Executive Government and Authority of and over Canada is hereby declared to continue and be vested in the Queen. Declaration of Executive Power in the Queen.

10. The Provisions of this Act referring to the Governor General extend and apply to the Governor General for the Time being of Canada, or other the Chief Executive Officer or Administrator for the Time being carrying on the Government of Canada on behalf and in the Name of the Queen, by whatever Title he is designated. Application of Provisions referring to Governor General.

11. There shall be a Council to aid and advise in the Government of Canada, to be styled the Queen's Privy Council for Canada; and the Persons who are to be Members of that Council shall be from Time to Time chosen and summoned by the Governor General and sworn in as Privy Councillors, and Members thereof may be from Time to Time removed by the Governor General. Constitution of Privy Council for Canada.

---

dependencies, were admitted into the Canadian Confederation by Order in Council dated July 31, 1880.

The Parliament of Canada added portions of the Northwest Territories to the adjoining provinces in 1912 by *The Ontario Boundaries Extension Act*, 2 Geo. V, c. 40, *The Quebec Boundaries Extension Act, 1912*, 2 Geo. V, c. 45, and *The Manitoba Boundaries Extension Act, 1912*, 2 Geo. V, c. 32, and further additions were made to Manitoba by *The Manitoba Boundaries Extension Act, 1930*, 20-21 Geo. V, c. 28.

The Yukon Territory was created out of the Northwest Territories in 1898 by *The Yukon Territory Act*, 61 Vict., c. 6, (Canada).

Newfoundland was added on March 31, 1949, by the *British North America Act, 1949*, (U.K.), 12-13 Geo. VI, c. 22, which ratified the Terms of Union between Canada and Newfoundland.

All Powers under Acts to be exercised by Governor General with Advice of Privy Council, or alone.

12. All Powers, Authorities, and Functions which under any Act of the Parliament of Great Britain, or of the Parliament of the United Kingdom of Great Britain and Ireland, or of the Legislature of Upper Canada, Lower Canada, Canada, Nova Scotia, or New Brunswick, are at the Union vested in or exerciseable by the respective Governors or Lieutenant Governors of those Provinces, with the Advice, or with the Advice and Consent, of the respective Executive Councils thereof, or in conjunction with those Councils, or with any Number of Members thereof, or by those Governors or Lieutenant Governors individually, shall, as far as the same continue in existence and capable of being exercised after the Union in relation to the Government of Canada, be vested in and exerciseable by the Governor General, with the Advice or with the Advice and Consent of or in conjunction with the Queen's Privy Council for Canada, or any Member thereof, or by the Governor General individually, as the Case requires, subject nevertheless (except with respect to such as exist under Acts of the Parliament of Great Britain or of the Parliament of the United Kingdom of Great Britain and Ireland) to be abolished or altered by the Parliament of Canada. (6)

Application of Provisions referring to Governor General in Council.

13. The Provisions of this Act referring to the Governor General in Council shall be construed as referring to the Governor General acting by and with the Advice of the Queen's Privy Council for Canada.

Power to Her Majesty to authorize Governor General to appoint Deputies.

14. It shall be lawful for the Queen, if Her Majesty thinks fit, to authorize the Governor General from Time to Time to appoint any Person or any Persons jointly or severally to be his Deputy or Deputies within any Part or Parts of Canada, and in that Capacity to exercise during the Pleasure of the Governor General such of the Powers, Authorities, and Functions of the Governor General as the Governor General deems it necessary or expedient to assign to him or them, subject to any Limitations or Directions expressed or given by the Queen; but the Appointment of such a Deputy or Deputies shall not affect the Exercise by the Governor General himself of any Power, Authority or Function.

Command of armed Forces to continue to be vested in the Queen.

15. The Command-in-Chief of the Land and Naval Militia, and of all Naval and Military Forces, of and in Canada, is hereby declared to continue and be vested in the Queen.

16. Until the Queen otherwise directs, the Seat of Government of Canada shall be Ottawa. *Seat of Government of Canada.*

IV.—Legislative Power.

17. There shall be One Parliament for Canada, consisting of the Queen, an Upper House styled the Senate, and the House of Commons. *Constitution of Parliament of Canada.*

18. The privileges, immunities, and powers to be held, enjoyed, and exercised by the Senate and by the House of Commons, and by the Members thereof respectively, shall be such as are from time to time defined by Act of the Parliament of Canada, but so that any Act of the Parliament of Canada defining such privileges, immunities, and powers shall not confer any privileges, immunities, or powers exceeding those at the passing of such Act held, enjoyed, and exercised by the Commons House of Parliament of the United Kingdom of Great Britain and Ireland, and by the Members thereof. (7) *Privileges, etc., of Houses.*

19. The Parliament of Canada shall be called together not later than Six Months after the Union. (8) *First Session of the Parliament of Canada.*

20. There shall be a Session of the Parliament of Canada once at least in every Year, so that Twelve Months shall not intervene between the last Sitting of the Parliament in one Session and its first Sitting in the next Session. (9) *Yearly Session of the Parliament of Canada.*

The Senate.

21. The Senate shall, subject to the Provisions of this Act, consist of One Hundred and Two Members, who shall be styled Senators. (10) *Number of Senators.*

---

(6) See the notes to section 129, *infra.*

(7) Repealed and re-enacted by the *Parliament of Canada Act, 1875,* 38-39 Vict., c. 38 (U.K.). The original section read as follows:

> 18. The Privileges Immunities, and Powers to be held, enjoyed, and exercised by the Senate and by the House of Commons and by the Members thereof respectively shall be such as are from Time to Time defined by Act of the Parliament of Canada, but so that the same shall never exceed those at the passing of this Act held, enjoyed, and exercised by the Commons House of Parliament of the United Kingdom of Great Britain and Ireland and by the Members thereof.

(8) Spent. The first session of the first Parliament began on November 6, 1867.

(9) The term of the twelfth Parliament was extended by the *British North America Act, 1916,* 6-7 Geo. V, c. 19 (U.K.), which Act was repealed by the *Statute Law Revision Act, 1927,* 17-18 Geo. V, c. 42 (U.K.).

(10) As amended by the *British North America Act, 1915,* 5-6 Geo. V, c. 45 (U.K.), and modified by the *British North America Act, 1949,* 12-13 Geo. VI, c. 22 (U.K.).

Representation
of Provinces
in Senate.

22. In relation to the Constitution of the Senate Canada shall be deemed to consist of Four Divisions:—

1. Ontario;

2. Quebec;

3. The Maritime Provinces, Nova Scotia and New Brunswick, and Prince Edward Island;

4. The Western Provinces of Manitoba, British Columbia, Saskatchewan, and Alberta;

which Four Divisions shall (subject to the Provisions of this Act) be equally represented in the Senate as follows: Ontario by twenty-four senators; Quebec by twenty-four senators; the Maritime Provinces and Prince Edward Island by twenty-four senators, ten thereof representing Nova Scotia, ten thereof representing New Brunswick, and four thereof representing Prince Edward Island; the Western Provinces by twenty-four senators, six thereof representing Manitoba, six thereof representing British Columbia, six thereof representing Saskatchewan, and six thereof representing Alberta; Newfoundland shall be entitled to be represented in the Senate by six members.

In the Case of Quebec each of the Twenty-four Senators representing that Province shall be appointed for One of the Twenty-four Electoral Divisions of Lower Canada specified in Schedule A. to Chapter One of the Consolidated statutes of Canada. (11)

The original section read as follows:

> 21. The Senate shall, subject to the Provisions of this Act, consist of Seventy-two Members, who shall be styled Senators.

The *Manitoba Act* added two for Manitoba; the Order in Council admitting British Columbia added three; upon admission of Prince Edward Island four more were provided by section 147 of the *British North America Act, 1867; The Alberta Act* and *The Saskatchewan Act* each added four. The Senate was reconstituted at 96 by the *British North America Act, 1915,* and six more Senators were added upon union with Newfoundland.

(11) As amended by the *British North America Act, 1915,* and the *British North America Act, 1949,* 12-13 Geo. VI, c. 22 (U.K.). The original section read as follows:

Representation
of Provinces
in Senate.

> 22. In relation to the Constitution of the Senate, Canada shall be deemed to consist of Three Divisions:
> 1. Ontario;
> 2. Quebec;
> 3. The Maritime Provinces, Nova Scotia and New Brunswick;
>
> which Three Divisions shall (subject to the Provisions of this Act) be equally represented in the Senate as follows: Ontario by Twenty-four Senators; Quebec by Twenty-four Senators; and the Maritime Provinces by Twenty-four Senators, Twelve thereof representing Nova Scotia, and Twelve thereof representing New Brunswick.
>
> In the Case of Quebec each of the Twenty-four Senators representing that Province shall be appointed for One of the Twenty-four Electoral Divisions of Lower Canada specified in Schedule A. to Chapter One of the Consolidated Statutes of Canada.

23. The Qualification of a Senator shall be as follows: Qualifications of Senator.

(1) He shall be of the full age of Thirty Years:

(2) He shall be either a natural-born Subject of the Queen, or a Subject of the Queen naturalized by an Act of the Parliament of Great Britain, or of the Parliament of the United Kingdom of Great Britain and Ireland, or of the Legislature of One of the Provinces of Upper Canada, Lower Canada, Canada, Nova Scotia, or New Brunswick, before the Union, or of the Parliament of Canada, after the Union:

(3) He shall be legally or equitably seised as of Freehold for his own Use and Benefit of Lands or Tenements held in Free and Common Socage, or seised or possessed for his own Use and Benefit of Lands or Tenements held in Franc-alleu or in Roture, within the Province for which he is appointed, of the Value of Four thousand Dollars, over and above all Rents, Dues, Debts, Charges, Mortgages, and Incumbrances due or payable out of or charged on or affecting the same:

(4) His Real and Personal Property shall be together worth Four thousand Dollars over and above his Debts and Liabilities:

(5) He shall be resident in the Province for which he is appointed:

(6) In the Case of Quebec he shall have his Real Property Qualification in the Electoral Division for which he is appointed, or shall be resident in that Division.

24. The Governor General shall from Time to Time, in the Queen's Name, by Instrument under the Great Seal of Canada, summon qualified Persons to the Senate; and, subject to the Provisions of this Act, every Person so summoned shall become and be a Member of the Senate and a Senator. Summons of Senator.

25. Repealed. (12)

---

(12) Repealed by the *Statute Law Revision Act, 1893*, 56-57 Vict., c. 14 (U.K.). The section read as follows:

Summons of First Body of Senators.   **25.** Such Persons shall be first summoned to the Senate as the Queen by Warrant under Her Majesty's Royal Sign Manual thinks fit to approve, and their Names shall be inserted in the Queen's Proclamation of Union.

Addition of Senators in certain cases.

26. If at any Time on the Recommendation of the Governor General the Queen thinks fit to direct that Four or Eight Members be added to the Senate, the Governor General may by Summons to Four or Eight qualified Persons (as the Case may be), representing equally the Four Divisions of Canada, add to the Senate accordingly. (13)

Reduction of Senate to normal Number.

27. In case of such Addition being at any Time made, the Governor General shall not summon any Person to the Senate, except upon a further like Direction by the Queen on the like Recommendation, to represent one of the Four Divisions until such Division is represented by Twenty-four Senators and no more. (14)

Maximum Number of Senators.

28. The Number of Senators shall not at any Time exceed One Hundred and ten. (15)

Tenure of Place in Senate.

29. (1) Subject to subsection (2), a Senator shall, subject to the provisions of this Act, hold his place in the Senate for life.

Retirement upon attaining age of seventy-five years.

(2) A Senator who is summoned to the Senate after the coming into force of this subsection shall, subject to this Act, hold his place in the Senate until he attains the age of seventy-five years. (15A)

Resignation of Place in Senate.

30. A Senator may by Writing under his Hand addressed to the Governor General resign his Place in the Senate, and thereupon the same shall be vacant.

Disqualification of Senators.

31. The Place of a Senator shall become vacant in any of the following Cases:

(1) If for Two consecutive Sessions of the Parliament he fails to give his Attendance in the Senate:

---

(13) As amended by the *British North America Act, 1915*, 5-6 Geo. V, c. 45 (U.K.). The original section read as follows:

Addition of Senators in certain cases. 26. If at any Time on the Recommendation of the Governor General the Queen thinks fit to direct that Three or Six Members be added to the Senate, the Governor General may by Summons to Three or Six qualified Persons (as the Case may be), representing equally the Three Divisions of Canada, add to the Senate accordingly.

(14) As amended by the *British North America Act, 1915*, 5-6 Geo. V, c. 45 (U.K.). The original section read as follows:

Reduction of Senate to normal Number. 27. In case of such Addition being at any Time made the Governor General shall not summon any Person to the Senate, except on a further like Direction by the Queen on the like Recommendation, until each of the Three Divisions of Canada is represented by Twenty-four Senators and no more.

(15) As amended by the *British North America Act, 1915*, 5-6 Geo. V, c. 45 (U.K.). The original section read as follows:

Maximum Number of Senators. 28. The Number of Senators shall not at any Time exceed Seventy-eight.

(15A) As enacted by the *British North America Act, 1965*, R.S.C. 1965, c. 4, ss. 1, 2. The section, as originally enacted, read as follows:

Tenure of Place in Senate. 29. A Senator shall, subject to the Provisions of this Act, hold his place in the Senate for life.

(2) If he takes an Oath or makes a Declaration or Acknowledgment of Allegiance, Obedience, or Adherence to a Foreign Power, or does an Act whereby he becomes a Subject or Citizen, or entitled to the Rights or Privileges of a Subject or Citizen, of a Foreign Power:

(3) If he is adjudged Bankrupt or Insolvent, or applies for the Benefit of any Law relating to Insolvent Debtors, or becomes a public Defaulter:

(4) If he is attainted of Treason or convicted of Felony or of any infamous Crime:

(5) If he ceases to be qualified in respect of Property or of Residence; provided, that a Senator shall not be deemed to have ceased to be qualified in respect of Residence by reason only of his residing at the Seat of the Government of Canada while holding an Office under that Government requiring his Presence there.

32. When a Vacancy happens in the Senate by Resignation, Death, or otherwise, the Governor General shall by Summons to a fit and qualified Person fill the Vacancy. *Summons on Vacancy in Senate.*

33. If any Question arises respecting the Qualification of a Senator or a Vacancy in the Senate the same shall be heard and determined by the Senate. *Questions as to Qualifications and Vacancies in Senate.*

34. The Governor General may from Time to Time, by Instrument under the Great Seal of Canada, appoint a Senator to be Speaker of the Senate, and may remove him and appoint another in his Stead. (16) *Appointment of Speaker of Senate.*

35. Until the Parliament of Canada otherwise provides, the Presence of at least Fifteen Senators, including the Speaker, shall be necessary to constitute a Meeting of the Senate for the Exercise of its Powers. *Quorum of Senate.*

36. Questions arising in the Senate shall be decided by a Majority of Voices, and the Speaker shall in all Cases have a Vote, and when the Voices are equal the Decision shall be deemed to be in the Negative. *Voting in Senate.*

The House of Commons.

37. The House of Commons shall, subject to the Provisions of this Act, consist of Two Hundred and sixty-five Members of whom Eighty-five shall be elected for Ontario, *Constitution of House of Commons in Canada.*

(16) **Provision for exercising the functions of Speaker during his absence is** made by the *Speaker of the Senate Act,* R.S.C. 1970, c. S-14. Doubts as to the power of Parliament to enact such an Act were removed by the *Canadian Speaker (Appointment of Deputy) Act, 1895,* 59 Vict., c. 3, (U.K.).

Seventy-five for Quebec, Twelve for Nova Scotia, Ten for New Brunswick, Fourteen for Manitoba, Twenty-two for British Columbia, Four for Prince Edward Island, Seventeen for Alberta, Seventeen for Saskatchewan, Seven for Newfoundland, One for the Yukon Territory and One for the Northwest Territories. (17)

Summoning of House of Commons.

38. The Governor General shall from Time to Time, in the Queen's Name, by Instrument under the Great Seal of Canada, summon and call together the House of Commons.

Senators not to sit in House of Commons.

39. A Senator shall not be capable of being elected or of sitting or voting as a Member of the House of Commons.

Electoral districts of the Four Provinces.

40. Until the Parliament of Canada otherwise provides, Ontario, Quebec, Nova Scotia, and New Brunswick shall, for the Purposes of the Election of Members to serve in the House of Commons, be divided into Electoral Districts as follows:

1.—ONTARIO.

Ontario shall be divided into the Counties, Ridings of Counties, Cities, Parts of Cities, and Towns enumerated in the First Schedule to this Act, each whereof shall be an Electoral District, each such District as numbered in that Schedule being entitled to return One Member.

2.—QUEBEC.

Quebec shall be divided into Sixty-five Electoral Districts, composed of the Sixty-five Electoral Divisions into which Lower Canada is at the passing of this Act divided under Chapter Two of the Consolidated Statutes of Canada, Chapter Seventy-five of the Consolidated Statutes for Lower Canada, and the Act of the Province of Canada of the Twenty-third Year of the Queen, Chapter One, or any other Act amending the same in force at the Union, so that each such Electoral Division shall be for the Purposes of this Act an Electoral District entitled to return One Member.

---

(17) Spent. The allocation is now governed by the *Electoral Boundaries Readjustment Act,* R.S.C. 1970, c. E-2, as amended.

3.—NOVA SCOTIA.

Each of the Eighteen Counties of Nova Scotia shall be an Electoral District. The County of Halifax shall be entitled to return Two Members, and each of the other Counties One Member.

4.—NEW BRUNSWICK.

Each of the Fourteen Counties into which New Brunswick is divided, including the City and County of St. John, shall be an Electoral District. The City of St. John shall also be a separate Electoral District. Each of those Fifteen Electoral Districts shall be entitled to return One Member. (18)

41. Until the Parliament of Canada otherwise provides, all Laws in force in the several Provinces at the Union relative to the following Matters or any of them, namely, —the Qualifications and Disqualifications of Persons to be elected or to sit or vote as Members of the House of Assembly or Legislative Assembly in the several Provinces, the Voters at Elections of such Members, the Oaths to be taken by Voters, the Returning Officers, their Powers and Duties, the Proceedings at Elections, the Periods during which Elections may be continued, the Trial of controverted Elections, and Proceedings incident thereto, the vacating of Seats of Members, and the Execution of new Writs in case of Seats vacated otherwise than by Dissolution,—shall respectively apply to Elections of Members to serve in the House of Commons for the same several Provinces. *Continuance of existing Election Laws until Parliament of Canada otherwise provides.*

Provided that, until the Parliament of Canada otherwise provides, at any Election for a Member of the House of Commons for the District of Algoma, in addition to Persons qualified by the Law of the Province of Canada to vote, every Male British Subject, aged Twenty-one Years or upwards, being a Householder, shall have a Vote. (19)

---

(18) Spent. The electoral districts are now to be fixed pursuant to the *Electoral Boundaries Readjustment Act,* R.S.C. 1970, c. E-2, as amended.

(19) **Spent.** Elections are now provided for by the *Canada Elections Act,* R.S.C. 1970, c. 14 (1st Supp.); controverted elections by the *Dominion Controverted Elections Act,* R.S.C. 1970, c. C-28; qualification and disqualifications of members of the *House of Commons Act,* R.S.C. 1970, c. H-9 and the *Senate and House of Commons Act,* R.S.C. 1970, c. S-8.

42. Repealed. (20)

43. Repealed. (21)

As to Election of Speaker of House of Commons.

44. The House of Commons on its first assembling after a General Election shall proceed with all practicable Speed to elect One of its Members to be Speaker.

As to filling up Vacancy in Office of Speaker.

45. In case of a Vacancy happening in the Office of Speaker by Death, Resignation, or otherwise, the House of Commons shall with all practicable Speed proceed to elect another of its Members to be Speaker.

Speaker to preside.

46. The Speaker shall preside at all Meetings of the House of Commons.

Provision in case of Absence of Speaker.

47. Until the Parliament of Canada otherwise provides, in case of the Absence for any Reason of the Speaker from the Chair of the House of Commons for a Period of Forty-eight consecutive Hours, the House may elect another of its Members to act as Speaker, and the Member so elected shall during the Continuance of such Absence of the Speaker have and execute all the Powers, Privileges, and Duties of Speaker. (22)

Quorum of House of Commons.

48. The Presence of at least Twenty Members of the House of Commons shall be necessary to constitute a Meeting of the House for the Exercise of its Powers, and for that Purpose the Speaker shall be reckoned as a Member.

---

(20) Repealed by the *Statute Law Revision Act, 1893*, 56-57 Vict., c. 14 (U.K.). The section read as follows:

Writs for First Election.

42. For the First Election of Members to serve in the House of Commons the Governor General shall cause Writs to be issued by such Person, in such Form, and addressed to such Returning Officers as he thinks fit.

The Person issuing Writs under this Section shall have the like Powers as are possessed at the Union by the Officers charged with the issuing of Writs for the Election of Members to serve in the respective House of Assembly or Legislative Assembly of the Province of Canada, Nova Scotia, or New Brunswick; and the Returning Officers to whom Writs are directed under this Section shall have the like Powers as are possessed at the Union by the Officers charged with the returning of Writs for the Election of Members to serve in the same respective House of Assembly or Legislative Assembly.

(21) Repealed by the *Statute Law Revision Act, 1893*, 56-57 Vict., c. 14 (U.K.). The section read as follows:

As to Casual Vacancies.

43. In case a Vacancy in the Representation in the House of Commons of any Electoral District happens before the Meeting of the Parliament, or after the Meeting of the Parliament before Provision is made by the Parliament in this Behalf, the Provisions of the last foregoing Section of this Act shall extend and apply to the issuing and returning of a Writ in respect of such vacant District.

(22) Provision for exercising the functions of Speaker during his absence is now made by the *Speaker of the House of Commons Act, R.S.C.* 1970, c. S-13.

49. Questions arising in the House of Commons shall be decided by a Majority of Voices other than that of the Speaker, and when the Voices are equal, but not otherwise, the Speaker shall have a Vote.

50. Every House of Commons shall continue for Five Years from the Day of the Return of the Writs for choosing the House (subject to be sooner dissolved by the Governor General), and no longer.

51. (1) Subject as hereinafter provided, the number of members of the House of Commons shall be two hundred and sixty-three and the representation of the provinces therein shall forthwith upon the coming into force of this section and thereafter on the completion of each decennial census be readjusted by such authority, in such manner, and from such time as the Parliament of Canada from time to time provides, subject and according to the following rules:

1. There shall be assigned to each of the provinces a number of members computed by dividing the total population of the provinces by two hundred and sixty-one and by dividing the population of each province by the quotient so obtained, disregarding, except as hereinafter in this section provided, the remainder, if any, after the said process of division.

2. If the total number of members assigned to all the provinces pursuant to rule one is less than two hundred and sixty-one, additional members shall be assigned to the provinces (one to a province) having remainders in the computation under rule one commencing with the province having the largest remainder and continuing with the other provinces in the order of the magnitude of their respective remainders until the total number of members assigned is two hundred and sixty-one.

3. Notwithstanding anything in this section, if upon completion of a computation under rules one and two, the number of members to be assigned to a province is less than the number of senators representing the said province, rules one and two shall cease to apply in respect of the said province, and there shall be assigned to the said province a number of members equal to the said number of senators.

4. In the event that rules one and two cease to apply in respect of a province then, for the purposes of com-

puting the number of members to be assigned to the provinces in respect of which rules one and two continue to apply, the total population of the provinces shall be reduced by the number of the population of the province in respect of which rules one and two have ceased to apply and the number two hundred and sixty-one shall be reduced by the number of members assigned to such province pursuant to rule three.

5. On any such readjustment the number of members for any province shall not be reduced by more than fifteen per cent below the representation to which such province was entitled under rules one to four of this subsection at the last preceding readjustment of the representation of that province, and there shall be no reduction in the representation of any province as a result of which that province would have a smaller number of members than any other province that according to the results of the then last decennial census did not have a larger population; but for the purposes of any subsequent readjustment of representation under this section any increase in the number of members of the House of Commons resulting from the application of this rule shall not be included in the divisor mentioned in rules one to four of this subsection.

6. Such readjustment shall not take effect until the termination of the then existing Parliament.

Yukon Territory and other part not comprised within a province. (2) The Yukon Territory as constituted by chapter forty-one of the statutes of Canada, 1901, shall be entitled to one member, and such other part of Canada not comprised within a province as may from time to time be defined by the Parliament of Canada shall be entitled to one member. (23)

---

(23) As enacted by the *British North America Act, 1952*, R.S.C. 1952, c. 304, which came into force on June 18, 1952. The section, as originally enacted, read as follows:

Decennial Re-adjustment of Representation. 51. On the Completion of the Census in the Year One Thousand eight hundred and seventy-one, and of each subsequent decennial Census, the Representation of the Four Provinces shall be re-adjusted by such Authority, in such Manner, and from such Time, as the Parliament of Canada from Time to Time provides, subject and according to the following Rules:

(1) Quebec shall have the fixed Number of Sixty-five Members:

(2) There shall be assigned to each of the other Provinces such a Number of Members as will bear the same Proportion to the Number of its Population (ascertained at such Census) as the Number Sixty-five bears to the Number of the Population of Quebec (so ascertained):

(3) In the Computation of the Number of Members for a Province a fractional Part not exceeding One Half of the whole Number requisite for entitling the Province to a Member shall be disre-

garded; but a fractional Part exceeding One **Half of that** Number shall be equivalent to the whole Number:

(4) On any such Re-adjustment the Number of Members for a Province shall not be reduced unless the Proportion which the Number of the Population of the Province bore to the Number of the aggregate Population of Canada at the then last preceding Re-adjustment of the Number of Members for the Province is ascertained at the then latest Census to be diminished by One Twentieth Part or upwards:

(5) Such Re-adjustment shall not take effect until the Termination of the then existing Parliament.

The section was amended by the *Statute Law Revision Act, 1893*, 56-57 Vict., c. 14 (U.K) by repealing the words from "of the census" to "seventy-one and" and the word "subsequent".

By the *British North America Act, 1943*, 6-7 Geo. VI, c. 30 (U.K.) redistribution of seats following the 1941 census was postponed until the first session of Parliament after the war. The section was re-enacted by the *British North America Act, 1946*, 9-10 Geo. VI, c. 63 (U.K.) to read as follows:

51. (1) The number of members of the House of Commons shall be two hundred and fifty-five and the representation of the provinces therein shall forthwith upon the coming into force of this section and thereafter on the completion of each decennial census be readjusted by such authority, in such manner, and from such time as the Parliament of Canada from time to time provides, subject and according to the following rules:—

(1) Subject as hereinafter provided, there shall be assigned to each of the provinces a number of members computed by dividing the total population of the provinces by two hundred and fifty-four and by dividing the population of each province by the quotient so obtained, disregarding, except as hereinafter in this section provided, the remainder, if any, after the said process of division.

(2) If the total number of members assigned to all the provinces pursuant to rule one is less than two hundred and fifty-four, additional members shall be assigned to the provinces (one to a province) having remainders in the computation under rule one commencing with the province having the largest remainder and continuing with the other provinces in the order of the magnitude of their respective remainders until the total number of members assigned is two hundred and fifty-four.

(3) Notwithstanding anything in this section, if upon completion of a computation under rules one and two, the number of members to be assigned to a province is less than the number of senators representing the said province, rules one and two shall cease to apply in respect of the said province, and there shall be assigned to the said province a number of members equal to the said number of senators.

(4) In the event that rules one and two cease to apply in respect of a province then, for the purpose of computing the number of members to be assigned to the provinces in respect of which rules one and two continue to apply, the total population of the provinces shall be reduced by the number of the population of the province in respect of which rules one and two have ceased to apply and the number two hundred and fifty-four shall be reduced by the number of members assigned to such province pursuant to rule three.

(5) Such readjustment shall not take effect until the termination of the then existing Parliament.

(2) The Yukon Territory as constituted by Chapter forty-one of the Statutes of Canada, 1901, together with any Part of Canada not comprised within a province which may from time to time be included therein by the Parliament of Canada for the purposes of representation in Parliament, shall be entitled to one member.

Constitution of House of Commons.

51A. Notwithstanding anything in this Act a province shall always be entitled to a number of members in the House of Commons not less than the number of senators representing such province. (24)

Increase of Number of House of Commons.

52. The Number of Members of the House of Commons may be from Time to Time increased by the Parliament of Canada, provided the proportionate Representation of the Provinces prescribed by this Act is not thereby disturbed.

Money Votes; Royal Assent.

Appropriation and Tax Bills.

53. Bills for appropriating any Part of the Public Revenue, or for imposing any Tax or Impost, shall originate in the House of Commons.

Recommendation of Money Votes.

54. It shall not be lawful for the House of Commons to adopt or pass any Vote, Resolution, Address, or Bill for the Appropriation of any Part of the Public Revenue, or of any Tax or Impost, to any Purpose that has not been first recommended to that House by Message of the Governor General in the Session in which such Vote, Resolution, Address, or Bill is proposed.

Royal Assent to Bills, etc.

55. Where a Bill passed by the Houses of the Parliament is presented to the Governor General for the Queen's Assent, he shall declare, according to his Discretion, but subject to the Provisions of this Act and to Her Majesty's Instructions, either that he assents thereto in the Queen's Name, or that he withholds the Queen's Assent, or that he reserves the Bill for the Signification of the Queen's Pleasure.

Disallowance by Order in Council of Act assented to by Governor General.

56. Where the Governor General assents to a Bill in the Queen's Name, he shall by the first convenient Opportunity send an authentic Copy of the Act to one of Her Majesty's Principal Secretaries of State, and if the Queen in Council within Two Years after Receipt thereof by the Secretary of State thinks fit to disallow the Act, such Disallowance (with a Certificate of the Secretary of State of the Day on which the Act was received by him) being signified by the Governor General, by Speech or Message to each of the Houses of the Parliament or by Proclamation, shall annul the Act from and after the Day of such Signification.

---

(24) As enacted by the *British North America Act, 1915*, 5-6 Geo. V, c. **45** (U.K.).

57. A Bill reserved for the Signification of the Queen's ^{Signification} Pleasure shall not have any Force unless and until, within Two Years from the Day on which it was presented to the Governor General for the Queen's Assent, the Governor General signifies, by Speech or Message to each of the Houses of the Parliament or by Proclamation, that it has received the Assent of the Queen in Council.

Signification of Queen's Pleasure on Bill reserved.

An Entry of every such Speech, Message, or Proclamation shall be made in the Journal of each House, and a Duplicate thereof duly attested shall be delivered to the proper Officer to be kept among the Records of Canada.

V.—PROVINCIAL CONSTITUTIONS.

Executive Power.

58. For each Province there shall be an Officer, styled the Lieutenant Governor, appointed by the Governor General in Council by Instrument under the Great Seal of Canada.

Appointment of Lieutenant Governors of Provinces.

59. A Lieutenant Governor shall hold Office during the Pleasure of the Governor General; but any Lieutenant Governor appointed after the Commencement of the First Session of the Parliament of Canada shall not be removeable within Five Years from his Appointment, except for Cause assigned, which shall be communicated to him in Writing within One Month after the Order for his Removal is made, and shall be communicated by Message to the Senate and to the House of Commons within One Week thereafter if the Parliament is then sitting, and if not then within One Week after the Commencement of the next Session of the Parliament.

Tenure of Office of Lieutenant Governor.

60. The Salaries of the Lieutenant Governors shall be fixed and provided by the Parliament of Canada. (25)

Salaries of Lieutenant Governors.

61. Every Lieutenant Governor shall, before assuming the Duties of his Office, make and subscribe before the Governor General or some Person authorized by him Oaths of Allegiance and Office similar to those taken by the Governor General.

Oaths, etc., of Lieutenant Governor.

62. The Provisions of this Act referring to the Lieutenant Governor extend and apply to the Lieutenant Governor for the Time being of each Province, or other the

Application of provisions referring to Lieutenant Governor.

---

(25) Provided for by the *Salaries Act*, R.S.C. 1970, c. S-2, as amended R.S.C. 1970, c. 14 (2nd Supp.).

Chief Executive Officer or Administrator for the Time being carrying on the Government of the Province, by whatever Title he is designated.

Appointment of Executive Officers for Ontario and Quebec.

63. The Executive Council of Ontario and of Quebec shall be composed of such Persons as the Lieutenant Governor from Time to Time thinks fit, and in the first instance of the following Officers, namely,—the Attorney General, the Secretary and Registrar of the Province, the Treasurer of the Province, the Commissioner of Crown Lands, and the Commissioner of Agriculture and Public Works, with in Quebec the Speaker of the Legislative Council and the Solicitor General. (26)

Executive Government of Nova Scotia and New Brunswick.

64. The Constitution of the Executive Authority in each of the Provinces of Nova Scotia and New Brunswick shall, subject to the Provisions of this Act, continue as it exists at the Union until altered under the Authority of this Act. (26A)

Powers to be exercised by Lieutenant Governor of Ontario or Quebec with Advice, or alone.

65. All Powers, Authorities, and Functions which under any Act of the Parliament of Great Britain, or of the Parliament of the United Kingdom of Great Britain and Ireland, or of the Legislature of Upper Canada, Lower Canada, or Canada, were or are before or at the Union vested in or exerciseable by the respective Governors or Lieutenant Governors of those Provinces, with the Advice or with the Advice and Consent of the respective Executive Councils thereof, or in conjunction with those Councils, or with any Number of Members thereof, or by those Governors or Lieutenant Governors individually, shall, as far as the same are capable of being exercised after the Union in relation to the Government of Ontario and Quebec respectively, be vested in and shall or may be exercised by the Lieutenant Governor of Ontario and Quebec respectively, with the Advice or with the Advice and Consent of or in conjunction with the respective Executive Councils, or any Members thereof, or by the Lieutenant Governor individually, as the Case requires, subject nevertheless (except with respect to such as exist under Acts of the Parliament of Great Britain, or of the Parliament of the

---

(26) Now provided for in Ontario by the *Executive Council Act*, R.S.O. 1970, c. 153, as amended 1971 (2nd Sess.), c. 14, 1972, c. 1, and in Quebec by the *Executive Power Act*, R.S.Q. 1964, c. 9, as amended.

(26A) A similar provision was included in each of the instruments admitting British Columbia, Prince Edward Island, and Newfoundland. The Executive Authorities for Manitoba, Alberta and Saskatchewan were established by the statutes creating those provinces. See the footnotes to section 5, *supra*.

United Kingdom of Great Britain and Ireland,) to be abolished or altered by the respective Legislatures of Ontario and Quebec. (27)

66. The Provisions of this Act referring to the Lieuten- *Application of Provisions* ant Governor in Council shall be construed as referring to *referring to* the Lieutenant Governor of the Province acting by and *Lieutenant Governor in* with the Advice of the Executive Council thereof. *Council.*

67. The Governor General in Council may from Time to *Administration in Absence, etc.,* Time appoint an Administrator to execute the Office and *of Lieutenant* Functions of Lieutenant Governor during his Absence, *Governor.* Illness, or other Inability.

68. Unless and until the Executive Government of any *Seats of* Province otherwise directs with respect to that Province, *Provincial Governments.* the Seats of Government of the Provinces shall be as follows, namely,—of Ontario, the City of Toronto; of Quebec, the City of Quebec; of Nova Scotia, the City of Halifax; and of New Brunswick, the City of Fredericton.

Legislative Power.

1.—ONTARIO.

69. There shall be a Legislature for Ontario consisting *Legislature for Ontario.* of the Lieutenant Governor and of One House, styled the Legislative Assembly of Ontario.

70. The Legislative Assembly of Ontario shall be com- *Electoral districts.* posed of Eighty-two Members, to be elected to represent the Eighty-two Electoral Districts set forth in the First Schedule to this Act. (28)

2.—QUEBEC.

71. There shall be a Legislature for Quebec consisting *Legislature for Quebec.* of the Lieutenant Governor and of Two Houses, styled the Legislative Council of Quebec and the Legislative Assembly of Quebec.

72. The Legislative Council of Quebec shall be composed *Constitution of Legislative* of Twenty-four Members, to be appointed by the Lieutenant *Council.* Governor, in the Queen's Name, by Instrument under the Great Seal of Quebec, One being appointed to represent

---

(27) See the notes to section 129, *infra.*

(28) Spent. Now covered by the *Representation Act*, R.S.O. 1970, c. 413, which provides that the Assembly shall consist of 117 members, representing the electoral districts set forth in the Schedule to that Act.

each of the Twenty-four Electoral Divisions of Lower Canada in this Act referred to, and each holding Office for the Term of his Life, unless the Legislature of Quebec otherwise provides under the Provisions of this Act. (29)

Qualification of Legislative Councillors.

73. The Qualifications of the Legislative Councillors of Quebec shall be the same as those of the Senators for Quebec. (30)

Resignation, Disqualification, etc.

74. The Place of a Legislative Councillor of Quebec shall become vacant in the Cases, *mutatis mutandis,* in which the Place of Senator becomes vacant.

Vacancies.

75. When a Vacancy happens in the Legislative Council of Quebec by Resignation, Death, or otherwise, the Lieutenant Governor, in the Queen's Name, by Instrument under the Great Seal of Quebec, shall appoint a fit and qualified Person to fill the Vacancy.

Questions as to Vacancies, etc.

76. If any Question arises respecting the Qualification of a Legislative Councillor of Quebec, or a Vacancy in the Legislative Council of Quebec, the same shall be heard and determined by the Legislative Council.

Speaker of Legislative Council.

77. The Lieutenant Governor may from Time to Time, by Instrument under the Great Seal of Quebec, appoint a Member of the Legislative Council of Quebec to be Speaker thereof, and may remove him and appoint another in his Stead. (31)

Quorum of Legislative Council.

78. Until the Legislature of Quebec otherwise provides, the Presence of at least Ten Members of the Legislative Council, including the Speaker, shall be necessary to constitute a Meeting for the Exercise of its Powers.

Voting in Legislative Council.

79. Questions arising in the Legislative Council of Quebec shall be decided by a Majority of Voices, and the Speaker shall in all Cases have a Vote, and when the Voices are equal the Decision shall be deemed to be in the Negative.

---

(29), (30), (31) All the provisions (i.e., sections 72-79 inclusive and the relevant portions of section 71) respecting the Legislative Council of Quebec are spent. That body was abolished by 1968 (Que.), c. 9.

80. The Legislative Assembly of Quebec shall be com- posed of Sixty-five Members, to be elected to represent the Sixty-five Electoral Divisions or Districts of Lower Canada in this Act referred to, subject to Alteration thereof by the Legislature of Quebec: Provided that it shall not be lawful to present to the Lieutenant Governor of Quebec for Assent any Bill for altering the Limits of any of the Electoral Divisions or Districts mentioned in the Second Schedule to this Act, unless the Second and Third Readings of such Bill have been passed in the Legislative Assembly with the Concurrence of the Majority of the Members representing all those Electoral Divisions or Districts, and the Assent shall not be given to such Bill unless an Address has been presented by the Legislative Assembly to the Lieutenant Governor stating that it has been so passed. (32)

3.—ONTARIO AND QUEBEC.

81. Repealed. (33)

82. The Lieutenant Governor of Ontario and of Quebec shall from Time to Time, in the Queen's Name, by Instrument under the Great Seal of the Province, summon and call together the Legislative Assembly of the Province.

83. Until the Legislature of Ontario or of Quebec otherwise provides, a Person accepting or holding in Ontario or in Quebec any Office, Commission, or Employment, permanent or temporary, at the Nomination of the Lieutenant Governor, to which an annual Salary, or any Fee, Allowance, Emolument, or Profit of any Kind or Amount whatever from the Province is attached, shall not be eligible as a Member of the Legislative Assembly of the respective Province, nor shall he sit or vote as such; but nothing in this Section shall make ineligible any Person being a Member of the Executive Council of the respective Province, or holding any of the following Offices, that is to say, the Offices of Attorney General, Secretary and Registrar of the Province, Treasurer of the Province, Commissioner of Crown

---

(32) Altered by the *Legislature Act,* R.S.Q. 1964, c. 6 as amended and the *Territorial Division Act,* R.S.Q. 1945, as amended; there are now 95 members representing the districts set out in the *Territorial Division Act.*

(33) Repealed by the *Statute Law Revision Act, 1893,* 56-57 Vict., c. 14 **(U.K.).** The section read as follows:

First Session   81. The Legislatures of Ontario and Quebec respectively shall be of Legislatures. called together not later than Six Months after the Union.

Lands, and Commissioner of Agriculture and Public Works, and in Quebec Solicitor General, or shall disqualify him to sit or vote in the House for which he is elected, provided he is elected while holding such Office. (34)

Continuance of existing Election Laws.

84. Until the Legislatures of Ontario and Quebec respectively otherwise provide, all Laws which at the Union are in force in those Provinces respectively, relative to the following Matters, or any of them, namely,—the Qualifications and Disqualifications of Persons to be elected or to sit or vote as Members of the Assembly of Canada, the Qualifications or Disqualifications of Voters, the Oaths to be taken by Voters, the Returning Officers, their Powers and Duties, the Proceedings at Elections, the Periods during which such Elections may be continued, and the Trial of controverted Elections and the Proceedings incident thereto, the vacating of the Seats of Members and the issuing and execution of new Writs in case of Seats vacated otherwise than by Dissolution,—shall respectively apply to Elections of Members to serve in the respective Legislative Assemblies of Ontario and Quebec.

Provided that, until the Legislature of Ontario otherwise provides, at any Election for a Member of the Legislative Assembly of Ontario for the District of Algoma, in addition to Persons qualified by the Law of the Province of Canada to vote, every male British Subject, aged Twenty-one Years or upwards, being a Householder, shall have a vote. (35)

Duration of Legislative Assemblies.

85. Every Legislative Assembly of Ontario and every Legislative Assembly of Quebec shall continue for Four Years from the Day of the Return of the Writs for choosing the same (subject nevertheless to either the Legislative Assembly of Ontario or the Legislative Assembly of Quebec being sooner dissolved by the Lieutenant Governor of the Province), and no longer. (36)

---

(34) Probably spent. The subject-matter of this section is now covered in Ontario by the *Legislative Assembly Act*, R.S.O. 1970, c. 240, and in Quebec by the *Legislature Act*, R.S.Q. 1964, c. 6.

(35) Probably spent. The subject-matter of this section is now covered in Ontario by the *Election Act*, R.S.O. 1970, c. 142, the *Controverted Elections Act*, R.S.O. 1970, c. 84 and the *Legislative Assembly Act*, R.S.O. 1970, c. 240, and in Quebec by the *Elections Act*, R.S.Q. 1964, c. 7, the *Controverted Elections Act*, R.S.Q. 1948, c. 8, and the *Legislature Act*, R.S.Q. 1964, c. 6.

(36) The maximum duration of the Legislative Assembly for Ontario and Quebec has been changed to five years by the *Legislative Assembly Act*, R.S.O. 1970, c. 240, and the *Legislature Act*, R.S.Q. 1964, c. 6, respectively.

86. There shall be a Session of the Legislature of Yearly Session of Legislature. Ontario and of that of Quebec once at least in every Year, so that Twelve Months shall not intervene between the last Sitting of the Legislature in each Province in one Session and its first Sitting in the next Session.

87. The following Provisions of this Act respecting the Speaker, House of Commons of Canada shall extend and apply to Quorum, etc. the Legislative Assemblies of Ontario and Quebec, that is to say,—the Provisions relating to the Election of a Speaker originally and on Vacancies, the Duties of the Speaker, the Absence of the Speaker, the Quorum, and the Mode of voting, as if those Provisions were here re-enacted and made applicable in Terms to each such Legislative Assembly.

4.—NOVA SCOTIA AND NEW BRUNSWICK.

88. The Constitution of the Legislature of each of the Constitutions of Legislatures of Provinces of Nova Scotia and New Brunswick shall, subject Nova Scotia and to the Provisions of this Act, continue as it exists at the New Brunswick Union until altered under the Authority of this Act. (37)

89. Repealed. (38)

6.—THE FOUR PROVINCES.

90. The following Provisions of this Act respecting the Application to Legislatures of Parliament of Canada, namely,—the Provisions relating Provisions to Appropriation and Tax Bills, the Recommendation of respecting Money Votes, Money Votes, the Assent to Bills, the Disallowance of Acts, etc. and the Signification of Pleasure on Bills reserved,—shall extend and apply to the Legislatures of the several Provinces as if those Provisions were here re-enacted and made applicable in Terms to the respective Provinces and the Legislatures thereof, with the Substitution of the Lieutenant Governor of the Province for the Governor

---

(37) Partially repealed by the *Statute Law Revision Act, 1893*, 56-57 Vict., c. 14 (U.K.) which deleted the following concluding words of the original enactment:

> and the House of Assembly of New Brunswick existing at the passing of this Act shall, unless sooner dissolved, continue for the Period for which it was elected.

A similar provision was included in each of the instruments admitting British Columbia, Prince Edward Island, and Newfoundland. The Legislatures of Manitoba, Alberta and Saskatchewan were established by the statutes creating those provinces. See the footnotes to section 5, *supra*.

(38) Repealed by the *Statute Law Revision Act, 1893*, 56-57 Vict., c. 14 (U.K.). The section read as follows:

General, of the Governor General for the Queen and for a Secretary of State, of One Year for Two Years, and of the Province for Canada.

VI.—DISTRIBUTION OF LEGISLATIVE POWERS.

Powers of the Parliament.

Legislative Authority of Parliament of Canada.

91. It shall be lawful for the Queen, by and with the Advice and Consent of the Senate and House of Commons, to make Laws for the Peace, Order, and good Government of Canada, in relation to all Matters not coming within the Classes of Subjects by this Act assigned exclusively to the Legislatures of the Provinces; and for greater Certainty, but not so as to restrict the Generality of the foregoing Terms of this Section, it is hereby declared that (notwithstanding anything in this Act) the exclusive Legislative Authority of the Parliament of Canada extends to all Matters coming within the Classes of Subjects next herein-after enumerated; that is to say,—

1. The amendment from time to time of the Constitution of Canada, except as regards matters coming within the classes of subjects by this Act assigned exclusively to the Legislatures of the provinces, or as regards rights or privileges by this or any other Constitutional Act granted or secured to the Legislature or the Government of a province, or to any class of persons with respect to schools or as regards the use of the English or the French language or as regards the requirements that there shall be a session of the Parliament of Canada at least once each year, and that no House of Commons shall continue for more than five years from the day of the return of the Writs for choosing the House: provided, however, that a House of Commons may in time of real or apprehended war, invasion or insurrection be continued by the Parliament of Canada if such continuation is not opposed by the votes of more than one-third of the members of such House. (39)

5.—ONTARIO, QUEBEC, AND NOVA SCOTIA.

First Elections.

89. Each of the Lieutenant Governors of Ontario, Quebec and Nova Scotia shall cause Writs to be issued for the First Election of Members of the Legislative Assembly thereof in such Form and by such Person as he thinks fit, and at such Time and addressed to such Returning Officer as the Governor General directs, and so that the First Election of Member of Assembly for any Electoral District or any Subdivision thereof shall be held at the same Time and at the same Places as the Election for a Member to serve in the House of Commons of Canada for that Electoral District.

(39) Added by the *British North America (No. 2) Act, 1949*, 13 Geo. VI, c. 81 **(U.K.).**

1A. The Public Debt and Property. (40)

2. The Regulation of Trade and Commerce.

2A. Unemployment insurance. (41)

3. The raising of Money by any Mode or System of Taxation.

4. The borrowing of Money on the Public Credit.

5. Postal Service.

6. The Census and Statistics.

7. Militia, Military and Naval Service, and Defence.

8. The fixing of and providing for the Salaries and Allowances of Civil and other Officers of the Government of Canada.

9. Beacons, Buoys, Lighthouses, and Sable Island.

10. Navigation and Shipping.

11. Quarantine and the Establishment and Maintenance of Marine Hospitals.

12. Sea Coast and Inland Fisheries.

13. Ferries between a Province and any British or Foreign Country or between Two Provinces.

14. Currency and Coinage.

15. Banking, Incorporation of Banks, and the Issue of Paper Money.

16. Savings Banks.

17. Weights and Measures

18. Bills of Exchange and Promissory Notes.

19. Interest.

20. Legal Tender.

21. Bankruptcy and Insolvency.

22. Patents of Invention and Discovery.

23. Copyrights.

24. Indians, and Lands reserved for the Indians.

25. Naturalization and Aliens.

26. Marriage and Divorce.

27. The Criminal Law, except the Constitution of Courts of Criminal Jurisdiction, but including the Procedure in Criminal Matters.

28. The Establishment, Maintenance, and Management of Penitentiaries.

---

(40) Re-numbered by the *British North America (No. 2) Act, 1949.*

(41) Added by the *British North America Act, 1940,* 3-4 Geo. VI, c. 36 (U.K.).

29. Such Classes of Subjects as are expressly excepted
in the Enumeration of the Classes of Subjects by
this Act assigned exclusively to the Legislatures of
the Provinces.

And any Matter coming within any of the Classes of
Subjects enumerated in this Section shall not be deemed
to come within the Class of Matters of a local or private
Nature comprised in the Enumeration of the Classes of
Subjects by this Act assigned exclusively to the Legis-
latures of the Provinces. (42)

---

(42) Legislative authority has been conferred on Parliament by other Acts as
follows:

1. The *British North America Act, 1871*, 34-35 Vict., c. 28 (U.K.).

Parliament of Canada may establish new Provinces and provide for the constitution etc., thereof. 2. The Parliament of Canada may from time to time establish new Provinces in any territories forming for the time being part of the Dominion of Canada, but not included in any Province thereof, and may, at the time of such establishment, make provision for the constitution and administration of any such Province, and for the passing of laws for the peace, order, and good government of such Province, and for its representation in the said Parliament.

Alteration of limits of Provinces. 3. The Parliament of Canada may from time to time, with the consent of the Legislature of any Province of the said Dominion, increase, diminish, or otherwise alter the limits of such Province, upon such terms and conditions as may be agreed to by the said Legislature, and may, with the like consent, make provision respecting the effect and operation of any such increase or diminution or alteration of territory in relation to any Province affected thereby.

Parliament of Canada may legislate for any territory not included in a Province. 4. The Parliament of Canada may from time to time make provision for the administration, peace, order, and good government of any territory not for the time being included in any Province.

Confirmation of Acts of Parliament of Canada, 32 & 33 Vict. (Canadian) cap. 3. 33 Vict., (Canadian) cap. 3. 5. The following Acts passed by the said Parliament of Canada, and intituled respectively,—"An Act for the temporary government of Rupert's Land and the North Western Territory when united with Canada"; and "An Act to amend and continue the Act thirty-two and thirty-three Victoria, chapter three, and to establish and provide for the government of "the Province of Manitoba," shall be and be deemed to have been valid and effectual for all purposes whatsoever from the date at which they respectively received the assent, in the Queen's name, of the Governor General of the said Dominion of Canada."

Limitation of powers of Parliament of Canada to legislate for an established Province. 6. Except as provided by the third section of this Act, it shall not be competent for the Parliament of Canada to alter the provisions of the last-mentioned Act of the said Parliament in so far as it relates to the Province of Manitoba, or of any other Act hereafter establishing new Provinces in the said Dominion, subject always to the right of the Legislature of the Province of Manitoba to alter from time to time the provisions of any law respecting the qualification of electors and members of the Legislative Assembly, and to make laws respecting elections in the said Province.

The *Rupert's Land Act, 1868,* 31-32 Vict., c. 105 (U.K.) (repealed by the *Statute
Law Revision Act, 1893,* 56-57 Vict., c. 14 (U.K.)) had previously conferred similar
authority in relation to Rupert's Land and the North-Western Territory upon
admission of those areas.

2. The *British North America Act, 1886,* 49-50 Vict., c. 35, (U.K.).

Provision by Parliament of Canada for representation of territories. 1. The Parliament of Canada may from time to time make provision for the representation in the Senate and House of Commons of Canada, or in either of them, of any territories which for the time being form part of the Dominion of Canada, but are not included in any province thereof.

Exclusive Powers of Provincial Legislatures.

92. In each Province the Legislature may exclusively make Laws in relation to Matters coming within the Classes of Subject next herein-after enumerated; that is to say,— Subjects of exclusive Provincial Legislation.

1. The Amendment from Time to Time, notwithstanding anything in this Act, of the Constitution of the Province, except as regards the Office of Lieutenant Governor.

2. Direct Taxation within the Province in order to the raising of a Revenue for Provincial Purposes.

3. The borrowing of Money on the sole Credit of the Province.

4. The Establishment and Tenure of Provincial Offices and the Appointment and Payment of Provincial Officers.

5. The Management and Sale of the Public Lands belonging to the Province and of the Timber and Wood thereon.

6. The Establishment, Maintenance, and Management of Public and Reformatory Prisons in and for the Province.

7. The Establishment, Maintenance, and Management of Hospitals, Asylums, Charities, and Eleemosynary Institutions in and for the Province, other than Marine Hospitals.

8. Municipal Institutions in the Province.

9. Shop, Saloon, Tavern, Auctioneer, and other Licences in order to the raising of a Revenue for Provincial, Local, or Municipal Purposes.

10. Local Works and Undertakings other than such as are of the following Classes:—

    (a) Lines of Steam or other Ships, Railways, Canals, Telegraphs, and other Works and Under-

---

3. The *Statute of Westminster, 1931,* 22 Geo. V. c. 4, (U.K.).

Power of Parliament of a Dominion to legislate extra-territorially. 3. It is hereby declared and enacted that the Parliament of a Dominion has full power to make laws having extra-territorial operation.

takings connecting the Province with any other or others of the Provinces, or extending beyond the Limits of the Province;

(*b*) Lines of Steam Ships between the Province and any British or Foreign Country;

(*c*) Such Works as, although wholly situate within the Province, are before or after their Execution declared by the Parliament of Canada to be for the general Advantage of Canada or for the Advantage of Two or more of the Provinces.

11. The Incorporation of Companies with Provincial Objects.

12. The Solemnization of Marriage in the Province.

13. Property and Civil Rights in the Province.

14. The Administration of Justice in the Province, including the Constitution, Maintenance, and Organization of Provincial Courts, both of Civil and of Criminal Jurisdiction, and including Procedure in Civil Matters in those Courts.

15. The Imposition of Punishment by Fine, Penalty, or Imprisonment for enforcing any Law of the Province made in relation to any Matter coming within any of the Classes of Subjects enumerated in this Section.

16. Generally all Matters of a merely local or private Nature in the Province.

Education.

Legislation respecting Education.

93. In and for each Province the Legislature may exclusively make Laws in relation to Education, subject and according to the following Provisions:—

(1) Nothing in any such Law shall prejudicially affect any Right or Privilege with respect to Denominational Schools which any Class of Persons have by Law in the Province at the Union:

(2) All the Powers, Privileges, and Duties at the Union by Law conferred and imposed in Upper Canada on the Separate Schools and School Trustees of the Queen's Roman Catholic Subjects shall be and the

same are hereby extended to the Dissentient Schools of the Queen's Protestant and Roman Catholic Subjects in Quebec:

(3) Where in any Province a System of Separate or Dissentient Schools exists by Law at the Union or is thereafter established by the Legislature of the Province, an Appeal shall lie to the Governor General in Council from any Act or Decision of any Provincial Authority affecting any Right or Privilege of the Protestant or Roman Catholic Minority of the Queen's Subjects in relation to Education:

(4) In case any such Provincial Law as from Time to Time seems to the Governor General in Council requisite for the due Execution of the Provisions of this Section is not made, or in case any Decision of the Governor General in Council on any Appeal under this Section is not duly executed by the proper Provincial Authority in that Behalf, then and in every such Case, and as far only as the Circumstances of each Case require, the Parliament of Canada may make remedial Laws for the due Execution of the Provisions of this Section and of any Decision of the Governor General in Council under this Section. (43)

---

(43) Altered for Manitoba by section 22 of the *Manitoba Act, 33* Vict., c. 3 (Canada), (confirmed by the *British North America Act, 1871*), which reads as follows:

Legislation touching schools subject to certain provisions.

22. In and for the Province, the said Legislature may exclusively make Laws in relation to Education, subject and according to the following provisions:—

(1) Nothing in any such Law shall prejudicially affect any right or privilege with respect to Denominational Schools which any class of persons have by Law or practice in the Province at the Union:

(2) An appeal shall lie to the Governor General in Council from any Act or decision of the Legislature of the Province, or of any Provincial Authority, affecting any right or privilege, of the Protestant or Roman Catholic minority of the Queen's subjects in relation to Education:

Power reserved to Parliament.

(3) In case any such Provincial Law, as from time to time seems to the Governor General in Council requisite for the due execution of the provisions of this section, is not made, or in case any decision of the Governor General in Council on any appeal under this section is not duly executed by the proper Provincial Authority in that behalf, then, and in every such case, and as far only as the circumstances of each case require, the Parliament of Canada may make remedial Laws for the due execution of the provisions of this section, and of any decision of the Governor General in Council under this section.

Altered for Alberta by section 17 of *The Alberta Act,* 4-5 Edw. VII, c. 3 which reads as follows:

Education.

17. Section 93 of The British North America Act, 1867, shall apply to the said province, with the substitution for paragraph (1) of the said section 93 of the following paragraph:—

Uniformity of Laws in Ontario, Nova Scotia and New Brunswick.

Legislation for
Uniformity of
Laws in Three
Provinces.

94. Notwithstanding anything in this Act, the Parliament of Canada may make Provision for the Uniformity of all or any of the Laws relative to Property and Civil

(1) Nothing in any such law shall prejudicially affect any right or privilege with respect to separate schools which any class of persons have at the date of the passing of this Act, under the terms of chapters 29 and 30 of the Ordinances of the Northwest Territories, passed in the year 1901, or with respect to religious instruction in any public or separate school as provided for in the said ordinances.

2. In the appropriation by the Legislature or distribution by the Government of the province of any moneys for the support of schools organized and carried on in accordance with the said chapter 29 or any Act passed in amendment thereof, or in substitution therefor, there shall be no discrimination against schools of any class described in the said chapter 29.

3. Where the expression "by law" is employed in paragraph 3 of the said section 93, it shall be held to mean the law as set out in the said chapters 29 and 30, and where the expression "at the Union" is employed, in the said paragraph 3, it shall be held to mean the date at which this Act comes into force."

Altered for Saskatchewan by section 17 of *The Saskatchewan* Act, 4-5 Edw. VII, c. 42, which reads as follows:

Education.

17. Section 93 of the British North America Act, 1867, shall apply to the said province, with the substitution for paragraph (1) of the said section 93, of the following paragraph:—

(1) Nothing in any such law shall prejudicially affect any right or privilege with respect to separate schools which any class of persons have at the date of the passing of this Act, under the terms of chapters 29 and 30 of the Ordinances of the Northwest Territories, passed in the year 1901, or with respect to religious instruction in any public or separate school as provided for in the said ordinances.

2. In the appropriation by the Legislature or distribution by the Government of the province of any moneys for the support of schools organized and carried on in accordance with the said chapter 29, or any Act passed in amendment thereof or in substitution therefor, there shall be no discrimination against schools of any class described in the said chapter 29.

3. Where the expression "by law" is employed in paragraph (3) of the said section 93, it shall be held to mean the law as set out in the said chapters 29 and 30; and where the expression "at the Union" is employed in the said paragraph (3), it shall be held to mean the date at which this Act comes into force.

Altered by Term 17 of the Terms of Union of Newfoundland with Canada (confirmed by the *British North America Act, 1949*, 12-13 Geo. VI, c. 22 (U.K.)), which reads as follows:

17. In lieu of section ninety-three of the British North America Act, 1867, the following term shall apply in respect of the Province of Newfoundland:

In and for the Province of Newfoundland the Legislature shall have exclusive authority to make laws in relation to education, but the Legislature will not have authority to make laws prejudicially affecting any right or privilege with respect to denominational schools, common (amalgamated) schools, or denominational colleges, that any class or classes of persons have by law in Newfoundland at the date of Union, and out of public funds of the Province of Newfoundland, provided for education,

(a) all such schools shall receive their share of such funds in accordance with scales determined on a non-discriminatory basis from time to time by the Legislature for all schools then being conducted under authority of the Legislature; and

(b) all such colleges shall receive their share of any grant from time to time voted for all colleges then being conducted under authority of the Legislature, such grant being distributed on a non-discriminatory basis.

Rights in Ontario, Nova Scotia, and New Brunswick, and of the Procedure of all or any of the Courts in Those Three Provinces, and from and after the passing of any Act in that Behalf the Power of the Parliament of Canada to make Laws in relation to any Matter comprised in any such Act shall, notwithstanding anything in this Act, be unrestricted; but any Act of the Parliament of Canada making Provision for such Uniformity shall not have effect in any Province unless and until it is adopted and enacted as Law by the Legislature thereof.

Old Age Pensions.

94A. The Parliament of Canada may make laws in relation to old age pensions and supplementary benefits, including survivors' and disability benefits irrespective of age, but no such law shall affect the operation of any law present or future of a provincial legislature in relation to any such matter. (44) *Legislation respecting old age pensions and supplementary benefits.*

Agriculture and Immigration.

95. In each Province the Legislature may make Laws in relation to Agriculture in the Province, and to Immigration into the Province; and it is hereby declared that the Parliament of Canada may from Time to Time make Laws in relation to Agriculture in all or any of the Provinces, and to Immigration into all or any of the Provinces; and any Law of the Legislature of a Province relative to Agriculture or to Immigration shall have effect in and for the Province as long and as far only as it is not repugnant to any Act of the Parliament of Canada. *Concurrent Powers of Legislation respecting Agriculture, etc.*

VIII.—JUDICATURE.

96. The Governor General shall appoint the Judges of the Superior, District, and County Courts in each Province, except those of the Courts of Probate in Nova Scotia and New Brunswick. *Appointment of Judges.*

97. Until the laws relative to Property and Civil Rights in Ontario, Nova Scotia, and New Brunswick, and the Procedure of the Courts in those Provinces, are made uniform, the Judges of the Courts of those Provinces appointed by the Governor General shall be selected from the respective Bars of those Provinces. *Selection of Judges in Ontario, etc.*

---

(44) Added by the *British North America Act, 1964,* 12-13, Eliz. II, c. 73 (U.K.). Originally enacted by the *British North America Act, 1951,* 14-15 Geo. VI, c. 32 (U.K.), as follows:

> "**94A.** It is hereby declared that the Parliament of Canada may from time to time make laws in relation to old age pensions in Canada, but no law made by the Parliament of Canada in relation to old age pensions shall affect the operation of any law present or future of a Provincial Legislature in relation to old age pensions."

Selection of Judges in Quebec.

98. The Judges of the Courts of Quebec shall be selected from the Bar of that Province.

Tenure of office of Judges.

99. (1) Subject to subsection two of this section, the Judges of the Superior Courts shall hold office during good behaviour, but shall be removable by the Governor General on Address of the Senate and House of Commons.

Termination at age 75.

(2) A Judge of a Superior Court, whether appointed before or after the coming into force of this section, shall cease to hold office upon attaining the age of seventy-five years, or upon the coming into force of this section if at that time he has already attained that age. (44A)

Salaries etc., of Judges.

100. The Salaries, Allowances, and Pensions of the Judges of the Superior, District, and County Courts (except the Courts of Probate in Nova Scotia and New Brunswick), and of the Admiralty Courts in Cases where the Judges thereof are for the Time being paid by Salary, shall be fixed and provided by the Parliament of Canada. (45)

General Court of Appeal, etc.

101. The Parliament of Canada may, notwithstanding anything in this Act, from Time to Time provide for the Constitution, Maintenance, and Organization of a General Court of Appeal for Canada, and for the Establishment of any additional Courts for the better Administration of the Laws of Canada. (46)

VIII.—REVENUES; DEBTS; ASSETS; TAXATION.

Creation of Consolidated Revenue Fund.

102. All Duties and Revenues over which the respective Legislatures of Canada, Nova Scotia, and New Brunswick before and at the Union had and have Power of Appropriation, except such Portions thereof as are by this Act reserved to the respective Legislatures of the Provinces, or are raised by them in accordance with the special Powers conferred on them by this Act, shall form One Consolidated Revenue Fund, to be appropriated for the Public Service of Canada in the Manner and subject to the Charges in this Act provided.

(44A) Repealed and re-enacted by the *British North America Act, 1960,* 9 Eliz. II, c. 2 (U.K.), which came into force on the 1st day of March, 1961. The original section read as follows:

Tenure of office of Judges of Superior Courts.

99. The Judges of the Superior Courts shall hold Office during good Behaviour, but shall be removable by the Governor General on Address of the Senate and House of Commons.

(45) Now provided for in the *Judges Act,* R.S.C. 1970, c. J-1, as amended by R.S.C. 1970, c. 16 (2nd Supp.).

(46) See the *Supreme Court Act,* R.S.C. 1970, c. S-19, and the *Federal Court Act,* R.S.C. 1970, c. 10 (2nd Supp.).

103. The Consolidated Revenue Fund of Canada shall Expenses of be permanently charged with the Costs, Charges, and Expenses incident to the Collection, Management, and Receipt thereof, and the same shall form the First Charge thereon, subject to be reviewed and audited in such Manner as shall be ordered by the Governor General in Council until the Parliament otherwise provides.

104. The annual Interest of the Public Debts of the Interest of several Provinces of Canada, Nova Scotia, and New Bruns- Public Debts. wick at the Union shall form the Second Charge on the Consolidated Revenue Fund of Canada.

105. Unless altered by the Parliament of Canada, the Salary of Salary of the Governor General shall be Ten thousand General. Pounds Sterling Money of the United Kingdom of Great Britain and Ireland, payable out of the Consolidated Revenue Fund of Canada, and the same shall form the Third Charge thereon. (47)

106. Subject to the several Payments by this Act Appropriation charged on the Consolidated Revenue Fund of Canada, Time. the same shall be appropriated by the Parliament of Canada for the Public Service.

107. All Stocks, Cash, Banker's Balances, and Securities Transfer of for Money belonging to each Province at the Time of the Stocks, etc. Union, except as in this Act mentioned, shall be the Property of Canada, and shall be taken in Reduction of the Amount of the respective Debts of the Provinces at the Union.

108. The Public Works and Property of each Province, Transfer of enumerated in the Third Schedule to this Act, shall be Schedule. the Property of Canada.

109. All Lands, Mines, Minerals, and Royalties be- Property in longing to the several Provinces of Canada, Nova Scotia, etc. and New Brunswick at the Union, and all Sums then due or payable for such Lands, Mines, Minerals, or Royalties, shall belong to the several Provinces of Ontario, Quebec, Nova Scotia, and New Brunswick in which the same are situate or arise, subject to any Trusts existing in respect thereof, and to any Interest other than that of the Province in the same. (48)

---

(47) Now covered by the *Governor General's Act*, R.S.C. 1970, c. G-14.

(48) The four western provinces were placed in the same position as the original provinces by the *British North America Act, 1930*, 21 Geo. V, c. 26 (U.K.).

Assets connected with Provincial Debts.

110. All Assets connected with such Portions of the Public Debt of each Province as are assumed by that Province shall belong to that Province.

Canada to be liable for Provincial Debts.

111. Canada shall be liable for the Debts and Liabilities of each Province existing at the Union.

Debts of Ontario and Quebec.

112. Ontario and Quebec conjointly shall be liable to Canada for the Amount (if any) by which the Debt of the Province of Canada exceeds at the Union Sixty-two million five hundred thousand Dollars, and shall be charged with Interest at the Rate of Five per Centum per Annum thereon.

Assets of Ontario and Quebec.

113. The Assets enumerated in the Fourth Schedule to this Act belonging at the Union to the Province of Canada shall be the Property of Ontario and Quebec conjointly.

Debt of Nova Scotia.

114. Nova Scotia shall be liable to Canada for the Amount (if any) by which its Public Debt exceeds at the Union Eight million Dollars, and shall be charged with Interest at the Rate of Five per Centum per Annum thereon. (49)

Debt of New Brunswick.

115. New Brunswick shall be liable to Canada for the Amount (if any) by which its Public Debt exceeds at the Union Seven million Dollars, and shall be charged with Interest at the Rate of Five per Centum per Annum thereon.

Payment of interest to Nova Scotia and New Brunswick.

116. In case the Public Debts of Nova Scotia and New Brunswick do not at the Union amount to Eight million and Seven million Dollars respectively, they shall respectively receive by half-yearly Payments in advance from the Government of Canada Interest at Five per Centum per Annum on the Difference between the actual Amounts of their respective Debts and such stipulated Amounts.

Provincial Public Property.

117. The several Provinces shall retain all their respective Public Property not otherwise disposed of in this Act, subject to the Right of Canada to assume any Lands or Public Property required for Fortifications or for the Defence of the Country.

---

(49) The obligations imposed by this section, sections 115 and 116, and similar obligations under the instruments creating or admitting other provinces, have been carried into legislation of the Parliament of Canada and are now to be found in the *Provincial Subsidies Act*, R.S.C. 1970, c. P-26.

118. Repealed. (50)

(50) Repealed by the *Statute Law Revision Act, 1950,* 14 Geo. VI, c. 6 (U.K.).
As originally enacted, the section read as follows:

Grants to
Provinces.

118. The following Sums shall be paid yearly by Canada to the several Provinces for the Support of their Governments and Legislatures:

	Dollars
Ontario	Eighty thousand.
Quebec	Seventy thousand.
Nova Scotia	Sixty thousand.
New Brunswick	Fifty thousand.

Two hundred and sixty thousand; and an annual Grant in aid of each Province shall be made, equal to Eighty Cents per Head of the Population as ascertained by the Census of One thousand eight hundred and sixty-one, and in the Case of Nova Scotia and New Brunswick, by each subsequent Decennial Census until the Population of each of those two Provinces amounts to Four hundred thousand Souls, at which Rate such Grant shall thereafter remain. Such Grants shall be in full Settlement of all future Demands on Canada, and shall be paid half-yearly in advance to each Province; but the Government of Canada shall deduct from such Grants, as against any Province, all Sums chargeable as Interest on the Public Debt of that Province in excess of the several Amounts stipulated in this Act.

The section was made obsolete by the *British North America Act, 1907,* 7 Edw. VII, c. 11 (U.K.) which provided:

Payments
to be made
by Canada to
provinces.

1. (1) The following grants shall be made yearly by Canada to every province, which at the commencement of this Act is a province of the Dominion, for its local purposes and the support of its Government and Legislature:—

(a) A fixed grant—

where the population of the province is under one hundred and fifty thousand, of one hundred thousand dollars;

where the population of the province is one hundred and fifty thousand, but does not exceed two hundred thousand, of one hundred and fifty thousand dollars;

where the population of the province is two hundred thousand, but does not exceed four hundred thousand, of one hundred and eighty thousand dollars;

where the population of the province is four hundred thousand, but does not exceed eight hundred thousand, of one hundred and ninety thousand dollars;

where the population of the province is eight hundred thousand, but does not exceed one million five hundred thousand, of two hundred and twenty thousand dollars;

where the population of the province exceeds one million five hundred thousand, of two hundred and forty thousand dollars; and

(b) Subject to the special provisions of this Act as to the provinces of British Columbia and Prince Edward Island, a grant at the rate of eighty cents per head of the population of the province up to the number of two million five hundred thousand, and at the rate of sixty cents per head of so much of the population as exceeds that number.

(2) An additional grant of one hundred thousand dollars shall be made yearly to the province of British Columbia for a period of ten years from the commencement of this Act.

(3) The population of a province shall be ascertained from time to time in the case of the provinces of Manitoba, Saskatchewan, and Alberta respectively by the last quinquennial census or statutory estimate of population made under the Acts establishing those provinces or any other Act of the Parliament of Canada making provision for the purpose, and in the case of any other province by the last decennial census for the time being.

(4) The grants payable under this Act shall be paid half-yearly in advance to each province.

(5) The grants payable under this Act shall be substituted for the grants or subsidies (in this Act referred to as existing grants) payable for the like purposes at the commencement of this Act to the several provinces of the Dominion under the provisions of section

30-31 Vict., c. 3.

one hundred and eighteen of the British North America Act 1867, or of any Order in Council establishing a province, or of any Act of the Parliament of Canada containing directions for the payment of

Further Grant
to New
Brunswick.
119. New Brunswick shall receive by half-yearly Payments in advance from Canada for the Period of Ten Years from the Union an additional Allowance of Sixty-three thousand Dollars per Annum; but as long as the Public Debt of that Province remains under Seven million Dollars, a Deduction equal to the Interest at Five per Centum per Annum on such Deficiency shall be made from that Allowance of Sixty-three thousand Dollars. (51)

Form of
Payments.
120. All Payments to be made under this Act, or in discharge of Liabilities created under any Act of the Provinces of Canada, Nova Scotia, and New Brunswick respectively, and assumed by Canada, shall, until the Parliament of Canada otherwise directs, be made in such Form and Manner as may from Time to Time be ordered by the Governor General in Council.

Canadian
Manufactures,
etc.
121. All Articles of the Growth, Produce, or Manufacture of any one of the Provinces shall, from and after the Union, be admitted free into each of the other Provinces.

Continuance of
Customs and
Excise Laws.
122. The Customs and Excise Laws of each Province shall, subject to the Provisions of this Act, continue in force until altered by the Parliament of Canada. (52)

Exportation and
Importation as
between Two
Provinces.
123. Where Customs Duties are, at the Union, leviable on any Goods, Wares, or Merchandises in any Two Provinces, those Goods, Wares, and Merchandises may, from and after the Union, be imported from one of those Provinces

---

any such grant or subsidy, and those provisions shall cease to have effect.

(6) The Government of Canada shall have the same power of deducting sums charged against a province on account of the interest on public debt in the case of the grant payable under this Act to the province as they have in the case of the existing grant.

(7) Nothing in this Act shall affect the obligation of the Government of Canada to pay to any province any grant which is payable to that province, other than the existing grant for which the grant under this Act is substituted.

(8) In the case of the provinces of British Columbia and Prince Edward Island, the amount paid on account of the grant payable per head of the population to the provinces under this Act shall not at any time be less than the amount of the corresponding grant payable at the commencement of this Act, and if it is found on any decennial census that the population of the province has decreased since the last decennial census, the amount paid on account of the grant shall not be decreased below the amount then payable, notwithstanding the decrease of the population.

See the *Provincial Subsidies Act*, R.S.C. 1970, c. P-26, *The Maritime Provinces Additional Subsidies Act*, 1942-43 (Can.), c. 14, and the Terms of Union of Newfoundland with Canada, appended to the *British North America Act, 1949*, and also to *An Act to approve the Terms of Union of Newfoundland with Canada*, 1949 (Can.), c. 1.

(51) Spent.

(52) Spent. Now covered by the *Customs Act*, R.S.C. 1970, c. C-40, the *Customs Tariff*, R.S.C. 1970, c. C-41, the *Excise Act*, R.S.C. 1970, c. E-12 and the *Excise Tax Act*, R.S.C. 1970, c. E-13.

into the other of them on Proof of Payment of the Customs Duty leviable thereon in the Province of Exportation, and on Payment of such further Amount (if any) of Customs Duty as is leviable thereon in the Province of Importation. (53)

124. Nothing in this Act shall affect the Right of New Brunswick to levy the Lumber Dues provided in Chapter Fifteen of Title Three of the Revised Statutes of New Brunswick, or in any Act amending that Act before or after the Union, and not increasing the Amount of such Dues; but the Lumber of any of the Provinces other than New Brunswick **shall** not be subject to such Dues. (54)

Lumber Dues in New Brunswick

125. No Lands or Property belonging to Canada or any Province shall be liable to Taxation.

Exemption of Public Lands, etc.

126. Such Portions of the Duties and Revenues over which the respective Legislatures of Canada, Nova Scotia, and New Brunswick had before the Union Power of Appropriation as are by this Act reserved to the respective Governments or Legislatures of the Provinces, and all Duties and Revenues raised by them in accordance with the special Powers conferred upon them by this Act, shall in each Province form One Consolidated Revenue Fund to be appropriated for the Public Service of the Province.

Provincial Consolidated Revenue Fund.

IX.—MISCELLANEOUS PROVISIONS.

General.

127. Repealed. (55)

128. Every Member of the Senate or House of Commons of Canada shall before taking his Seat therein take and subscribe before the Governor General or some Person authorized by him, and every Member of a Legislative Council or Legislative Assembly of any Province shall before taking his Seat therein take and subscribe before the Lieutenant Governor of the Province or some Person authorized by him, the Oath of Allegiance contained in the Fifth Schedule to this Act; and every Member of the Senate of Canada and every Member of the Legislative Council of Quebec shall also, before taking his Seat therein, take and subscribe before the Governor General, or some

Oath of Allegiance, etc.

---

(53) Spent.

(54) These dues were repealed in 1873 by c. 16 (N.B.). And see *An Act respecting the Export Duties imposed on Lumber, etc.*, 1873 (Can.), c. 41 and the *Provincial Subsidies Act*, R.S.C. 1970, c. P-26, s. 2.

Person authorized by him, the Declaration of Qualification contained in the same Schedule.

Continuance of existing Laws, Courts, Officers, etc. **129.** Except as otherwise provided by this Act, all Laws in force in Canada, Nova Scotia, or New Brunswick at the Union, and all Courts of Civil and Criminal Jurisdiction, and all legal Commissions, Powers, and Authorities, and all Officers, Judicial, Administrative, and Ministerial, existing therein at the Union, shall continue in Ontario, Quebec, Nova Scotia, and New Brunswick respectively, as if the Union had not been made; subject nevertheless (except with respect to such as are enacted by or exist under Acts of the Parliament of Great Britain or of the Parliament of the United Kingdom of Great Britain and Ireland,) to be repealed, abolished, or altered by the Parliament of Canada, or by the Legislature of the respective Province, according to the Authority of the Parliament or of that Legislature under this Act. (56)

Transfer of Officers to Canada. **130.** Until the Parliament of Canada otherwise provides, all Officers of the several Provinces having Duties to discharge in relation to Matters other than those coming within the Classes of Subjects by this Act assigned exclusively to the Legislatures of the Provinces shall be Officers of Canada, and shall continue to discharge the Duties of their respective Offices under the same Liabilities, Responsibilities, and Penalties as if the Union had not been made. (57)

Appointment of new Officers. **131.** Until the Parliament of Canada otherwise provides, the Governor General in Council may from Time to Time appoint such Officers as the Governor General in Council deems necessary or proper for the effectual Execution of this Act.

Treaty Obligations. **132.** The Parliament and Government of Canada shall have all Powers necessary or proper for performing the

---

(55) Repealed by the *Statute Law Revision Act, 1893*, 56-57 Vict., c. 14 (U.K.). The section read as follows:

As to Legislative Councillors of Provinces becoming senators. 127. If any Person being at the passing of this Act a Member of the Legislative Council of Canada, Nova Scotia, or New Brunswick to whom a Place in the Senate is offered, does not within Thirty Days thereafter, by Writing under his Hand addressed to the Governor General of the Province of Canada or to the Lieutenant Governor of Nova Scotia or New Brunswick (as the Case may be), accept the same, he shall be deemed to have declined the same; and any Person who, being at the passing of this Act a Member of the Legislative Council of Nova Scotia or New Brunswick, accepts a Place in the Senate, shall thereby vacate his Seat in such Legislative Council.

(56) The restriction against altering or repealing laws enacted by or existing under statutes of the United Kingdom was removed by the *Statute of Westminster, 1931*, 22 Geo. V, c. 4 (U.K.).

(57) Spent.

Obligations of Canada or of any Province thereof, as Part of the British Empire, towards Foreign Countries, arising under Treaties between the Empire and such Foreign Countries.

133. Either the English or the French Language may be used by any Person in the Debates of the Houses of the Parliament of Canada and of the Houses of the Legislature of Quebec; and both those Languages shall be used in the respective Records and Journals of those Houses; and either of those Languages may be used by any Person or in any Pleading or Process in or issuing from any Court of Canada established under this Act, and in or from all or any of the Courts of Quebec. *Use of English and French Languages*

The Acts of the Parliament of Canada and of the Legislature of Quebec shall be printed and published in both those Languages.

Ontario and Quebec.

134. Until the Legislature of Ontario or of Quebec otherwise provides, the Lieutenant Governors of Ontario and Quebec may each appoint under the Great Seal of the Province the following Officers, to hold Office during Pleasure, that is to say,—the Attorney General, the Secretary and Registrar of the Province, the Treasurer of the Province, the Commissioner of Crown Lands, and the Commissioner of Agriculture and Public Works, and in the Case of Quebec the Solicitor General, and may, by Order of the Lieutenant Governor in Council, from Time to Time prescribe the Duties of those Officers, and of the several Departments over which they shall preside or to which they shall belong, and of the Officers and Clerks thereof, and may also appoint other and additional Officers to hold Office during Pleasure, and may from Time to Time prescribe the Duties of those Officers, and of the several Departments over which they shall preside or to which they shall belong, and of the Officers and Clerks thereof. (58) *Appointment of Executive Officers for Ontario and Quebec.*

135. Until the Legislature of Ontario or Quebec otherwise provides, all Rights, Powers, Duties, Functions, Responsibilities, or Authorities at the passing of this Act vested in or imposed on the Attorney General, Solicitor General, Secretary and Registrar of the Province of Canada, Minister of Finance, Commissioner of Crown Lands, Commissioner of Public Works, and Minister of Agriculture *Powers, Duties, etc. of Executive Officers.*

(58) Spent. Now covered in Ontario by the *Executive Council Act*, R.S.O. 1970, c. 153 as amended and in Quebec by the *Executive Power Act*, R.S.Q. 1964, c. 9 as amended.

and Receiver General, by any Law, Statute, or Ordinance of Upper Canada, Lower Canada, or Canada, and not repugnant to this Act, shall be vested in or imposed on any Officer to be appointed by the Lieutenant Governor for the Discharge of the same or any of them; and the Commissioner of Agriculture and Public Works shall perform the Duties and Functions of the Office of Minister of Agriculture at the passing of this Act imposed by the Law of the Province of Canada, as well as those of the Commissioner of Public Works. (59)

Great Seals.   **136.** Until altered by the Lieutenant Governor in Council, the Great Seals of Ontario and Quebec respectively shall be the same, or of the same Design, as those used in the Provinces of Upper Canada and Lower Canada respectively before their Union as the Province of Canada.

Construction of temporary Acts.   **137.** The words "and from thence to the End of the then next ensuing Session of the Legislature," or Words to the same Effect, used in any temporary Act of the Province of Canada not expired before the Union, shall be construed to extend and apply to the next Session of the Parliament of Canada if the Subject Matter of the Act is within the Powers of the same as defined by this Act, or to the next Sessions of the Legislatures of Ontario and Quebec respectively if the Subject Matter of the Act is within the Powers of the same as defined by this Act.

As to Errors in Names.   **138.** From and after the Union the Use of the Words "Upper Canada" instead of "Ontario," or "Lower Canada" instead of "Quebec," in any Deed, Writ, Process, Pleading, Document, Matter, or Thing, shall not invalidate the same.

As to issue of Proclamations before Union, to commence after Union.   **139.** Any Proclamation under the Great Seal of the Province of Canada issued before the Union to take effect at a Time which is subsequent to the Union, whether relating to that Province, or to Upper Canada, or to Lower Canada, and the several Matters and Things therein proclaimed, shall be and continue of like Force and Effect as if the Union had not been made. (60)

As to issue of Proclamations after Union.   **140.** Any Proclamation which is authorized by any Act of the Legislature of the Province of Canada to be issued under the Great Seal of the Province of Canada, whether relating to that Province, or to Upper Canada, or to Lower

---

(59) Probably spent.
(60) Probably spent.

Canada, and which is not issued before the Union, may be issued by the Lieutenant Governor of Ontario or of Quebec, as its Subject Matter requires, under the Great Seal thereof; and from and after the Issue of such Proclamation the same and the several Matters and Things therein proclaimed shall be and continue of the like Force and Effect in Ontario or Quebec as if the Union had not been made. (61)

141. The Penitentiary of the Province of Canada shall, until the Parliament of Canada otherwise provides, be and continue the Penitentiary of Ontario and of Quebec. (62)

Penitentiary.

142. The Division and Adjustment of the Debts, Credits, Liabilities, Properties, and Assets of Upper Canada and Lower Canada shall be referred to the Arbitrament of Three Arbitrators, One chosen by the Government of Ontario, One by the Government of Quebec, and One by the Government of Canada; and the Selection of the Arbitrators shall not be made until the Parliament of Canada and the Legislatures of Ontario and Quebec have met; and the Arbitrator chosen by the Government of Canada shall not be a Resident either in Ontario or in Quebec. (63)

Arbitration respecting Debts, etc.

143. The Governor General in Council may from Time to Time order that such and so many of the Records, Books, and Documents of the Province of Canada as he thinks fit shall be appropriated and delivered either to Ontario or to Quebec, and the same shall thenceforth be the Property of that Province; and any Copy thereof or Extract therefrom, duly certified by the Officer having charge of the Original thereof, shall be admitted as Evidence. (64)

Division of Records.

144. The Lieutenant Governor of Quebec may from Time to Time, by Proclamation under the Great Seal of the Province, to take effect from a Day to be appointed therein, constitute Townships in those Parts of the Province of Quebec in which Townships are not then already constituted, and fix the Metes and Bounds thereof.

Constitution of Townships in Quebec.

---

(61) Probably spent.

(62) Spent. Penitentiaries are now provided for by the *Penitentiary Act,* R.S.C. 1970, c. P-6.

(63) Spent. See pages (xi) and (xii) of the Public Accounts, 1902-03.

(64) Probably spent. Two orders were made under this section on the 24th of January, 1868.

145. Repealed. (65)

XI.—ADMISSION OF OTHER COLONIES

Power to admit
Newfoundland,
etc., into
the Union.

146. It shall be lawful for the Queen, by and with the Advice of Her Majesty's Most Honourable Privy Council, on Addresses from the Houses of the Parliament of Canada, and from the Houses of the respective Legislatures of the Colonies or Provinces of Newfoundland, Prince Edward Island, and British Columbia, to admit those Colonies or Provinces, or any of them, into the Union, and on Address from the Houses of the Parliament of Canada to admit Rupert's Land and the North-western Territory, or either of them, into the Union, on such Terms and Conditions in each Case as are in the Addresses expressed and as the Queen thinks fit to approve, subject to the Provisions of this Act; and the Provisions of any Order in Council in that Behalf shall have effect as if they had been enacted by the Parliament of the United Kingdom of Great Britain and Ireland. (66)

As to Represen-
tation of
Newfoundland
and Prince
Edward Island
in Senate.

147. In case of the Admission of Newfoundland and Prince Edward Island, or either of them, each shall be entitled to a Representation in the Senate of Canada of Four Members, and (notwithstanding anything in this Act) in case of the Admission of Newfoundland the normal Number of Senators shall be Seventy-six and their maximum Number shall be Eighty-two; but Prince Edward Island when admitted shall be deemed to be comprised in the Third of the Three Divisions into which Canada is, in relation to the Constitution of the Senate, divided by this Act, and accordingly, after the Admission of Prince Edward Island, whether Newfoundland is admitted or not, the Representation of Nova Scotia and New Bruns-

---

(65) Repealed by the *Statute Law Revision Act, 1893,* 56-57 Vict., c. 14, (U.K.). The section reads as follows:

X.—INTERCOLONIAL RAILWAY.

Duty of
Government
and Parliament
of Canada to
make Railway
herein
described.

145. Inasmuch as the Provinces of Canada, Nova Scotia, and New Brunswick have joined in a Declaration that the Construction of the Intercolonial Railway is essential to the Consolidation of the Union of British North America, and to the Assent thereto of Nova Scotia and New Brunswick, and have consequently agreed that Provision should be made for its immediate Construction by the Government of Canada: Therefore, in order to give effect to that Agreement, it shall be the Duty of the Government and Parliament of Canada to provide for the Commencement, within Six Months after the Union, of a Railway connecting the River St. Lawrence with the City of Halifax in Nova Scotia, and for the Construction thereof without Intermission, and the Completion thereof with all practicable Speed.

(66) All territories mentioned in this section are now part of Canada. See the notes to section 5, *supra*.

wick in the Senate shall, as Vacancies occur, be reduced from Twelve to Ten Members respectively, and the Representation of each of those Provinces shall not be increased at any Time beyond Ten, except under the Provisions of this Act for the Appointment of Three or Six additional Senators under the Direction of the Queen.

SCHEDULES

THE THIRD SCHEDULE.

Provincial Public Works and Property to be the Property of Canada.

1. Canals, with Lands and Water Power connected therewith.
2. Public Harbours.
3. Lighthouses and Piers, and Sable Island.
4. Steamboats, Dredges, and public Vessels.
5. Rivers and Lake Improvements.
6. Railways and Railway Stocks, Mortgages, and other Debts due by Railway Companies.
7. Military Roads.
8. Custom Houses, Post Offices, and all other Public Buildings, except such as the Government of Canada appropriate for the Use of the Provincial Legislature and Governments.
9. Property transferred by the Imperial Government, and known as Ordnance Property.
10. Armouries, Drill Sheds, Military Clothing, and Munitions of War, and Lands set apart for general Public Purposes.

THE FOURTH SCHEDULE.

Assets to be the Property of Ontario and Quebec conjointly.

Upper Canada Building Fund.
Lunatic Asylums.
Normal School.

Court Houses,
   in
Aylmer,   Lower Canada
Montreal,
Kamouraska.

Law Society, Upper Canada.
Montreal Turnpike Trust.
University Permanent Fund.
Royal Institution.
Consolidated Municipal Loan Fund, Upper Canada.
Consolidated Municipal Loan Fund, Lower Canada.
Agricultural Society, Upper Canada.
Lower Canada Legislative Grant.
Quebec Fire Loan.
Temiscouata Advance Account.
Quebec Turnpike Trust.
Education—East.
Building and Jury Fund, Lower Canada.
Municipalities Fund.
Lower Canada Superior Education Income Fund.

THE CANADIAN BILL OF RIGHTS
1960 (Can.)

CHAPTER 44

An Act for the Recognition
and Protection of Human Rights
and Fundamental Freedoms.

[Assented to 10th August, 1960.]

The Parliament of Canada, affirming that the Canadian Nation is founded upon principles that acknowledge the supremacy of God, the dignity and worth of the human person and the position of the family in a society of free men and free institutions;

Affirming also that men and institutions remain free only when freedom is founded upon respect for moral and spiritual values and the rule of law;

And being desirous of enshrining these principles and the human rights and fundamental freedoms derived from them, in a Bill of Rights which shall reflect the respect of Parliament for its constitutional authority and which shall ensure the protection of these rights and freedoms in Canada:

THEREFORE Her Majesty, by and with the advice and consent of the Senate and House of Commons of Canada, enacts as follows:

PART I

BILL OF RIGHTS

1. It is hereby recognized and declared that in Canada there have existed and shall continue to exist without discrimination by reason of race, national origin, colour, religion or sex, the following human rights and fundamental freedoms, namely,

- (a) the right of the individual to life, liberty, security of the person and enjoyment of property, and the right not to be deprived thereof except by due process of law;
- (b) the right of the individual to equality before the law and the protection of the law;
- (c) freedom of religion;
- (d) freedom of speech;
- (e) freedom of assembly and association; and
- (f) freedom of the press.

2. Every law of Canada shall, unless it is expressly declared by an Act of the Parliament of Canada that it shall operate notwithstanding the Canadian Bill of Rights, be so construed and applied as not to abrogate, abridge or infringe or to authorize the abrogation, abridgment or infringement of any of the rights

or freedoms herein recognized and declared, and in particular, no law of Canada shall be construed or applied so as to

(a) authorize or effect the arbitrary detention, imprisonment or exile of any person;

(b) impose or authorize the imposition of cruel and unusual treatment or punishment;

(c) deprive a person who has been arrested or detained
    (i) of the right to be informed promptly of the reason for his arrest or detention,
    (ii) of the right to retain and instruct counsel without delay, or
    (iii) of the remedy by way of *habeas corpus* for the determination of the validity of his detention and for his release if the detention is not lawful;

(d) authorize a court, tribunal, commission, board or other authority to compel a person to give evidence if he is denied counsel, protection against self crimination or other constitutional safeguards;

(e) deprive a person of the right to a fair hearing in accordance with the principles of fundamental justice for the determination of his rights and obligations;

(f) deprive a person charged with a criminal offence of the right to be presumed innocent until proved guilty according to law in a fair and public hearing by an independent and impartial tribunal, or of the right to reasonable bail without just cause; or

(g) deprive a person of the right to the assistance of an interpreter in any proceedings in which he is involved or in which he is a party or a witness, before a court, commission, board or other tribunal, if he does not understand or speak the language in which such proceedings are conducted.

3. The Minister of Justice shall, in accordance with such regulations as may be prescribed by the Governor in Council, examine every proposed regulation submitted in draft form to the Clerk of the Privy Council pursuant to the *Regulations Act* and every Bill introduced in or presented to the House of Commons, in order to ascertain whether any of the provisions thereof are inconsistent with the purposes and provisions of this Part and he shall report any such inconsistency to the House of Commons at the first convenient opportunity.

4. The provisions of this Part shall be known as the *Canadian Bill of Rights*.

PART II

5. (1) Nothing in Part I shall be construed to abrogate or abridge any human right or fundamental freedom not enumerated therein that may have existed in Canada at the commencement of this Act.

(2) The expression "law of Canada" in Part I means an Act of the Parliament of Canada enacted before or after the coming into force of this Act, any order, rule or regulation thereunder, and any law in force in Canada or in any part of Canada at the commencement of this Act that is subject to be repealed, abolished or altered by the Parliament of Canada.

(3) The provisions of Part I shall be construed as extending only to matters coming within the legislative authority of the Parliament of Canada.

6. Section 6 of the *War Measures Act* is repealed and the following substituted therefor:
"6. (1) Sections 3, 4, and 5 shall come into force only upon the issue of a proclamation of the Governor in Council declaring that war, invasion or insurrection, real or apprehended, exists.

(2) A proclamation declaring that war, invasion or insurrection, real or apprehended, exists shall be laid before Parliament forthwith after its issue, or, if Parliament is then not sitting, within the first fifteen days next thereafter that Parliament is sitting.

(3) Where a proclamation has been laid before Parliament pursuant to subsection (2), a notice of motion in either House signed by ten members thereof and made in accordance with the rules of that House within ten days of the day the proclamation was laid before Parliament, praying that the proclamation be revoked, shall be debated in that House at the first convenient opportunity within the four sitting days next after the day the motion in that House was made.

(4) If both Houses of Parliament resolve that the proclamation be revoked, it shall cease to have effect, and sections 3, 4 and 5 shall cease to be in force until those sections are again brought into force by a further proclamation but without prejudice to the previous operation of those sections or anything duly done or suffered thereunder or any offence committed or any penalty or forfeiture or punishment incurred.

(5) Any act or thing done or authorized or any order or regulation made under the authority of this Act, shall be deemed not to be an abrogation, abridgement or infringement of any right or freedom recognized by the *Canadian Bill of Rights*."

TABLE OF CASES

[A page number in bold face indicates a case that is reproduced in full or in some material part. The other page numbers indicate cases that are abstracted or referred to in connection with a problem or as illustrative of the text.]

947

SUPPLEMENTARY TABLE OF CASES
Revised Fourth Edition

INDEX

969